Lab Safety

Safety symbol	What it means	What to do in the event of an accident
Eye protection	Wear safety goggles anytime there is the slightest chance that your eyes could be harmed.	If anything gets into your eyes, notify your teacher immediately and flush your eyes with running water for 15 minutes.
Clothing protection	Wear your apron whenever you are working with chemicals or whenever you are instructed to do so.	If you spill a corrosive chemical onto your clothing, rinse it off immediately by using a faucet or the safety shower and remove the affected clothing while calling to your teacher.
Hand safety	Wear appropriate protective gloves when working with an open flame, chemicals, or plants. Your teacher will provide the type of gloves necessary for a given activity. Wash your hands with soap and hot water at the end of every lab.	If any chemical gets on your hands, rinse it off immediately with water for at least 5 minutes while calling to your teacher. Report any burn of the hands to your teacher no matter how minor it seems.
Safety with Gases	Do not inhale any gas or vapor unless directed to do so by your teacher. Handle materials that emit vapors or gases in a well-ventilated area.	Notify your teacher immediately if you have inhaled a gas or vapor, or if your eyes, nose, or throat become irritated.
Hygienic Care	Keep you hands away from your face, hair, and mouth while you are working on any activity. Wash your hands thoroughly before you leave the lab or when you finish any activity. Remove contaminated clothing immediately.	Notify your teacher immediately if you spill corrosive substances on your skin or clothing no matter how minor it seems. Use the safety shower or faucet to rinse. Remove affected clothing while you are under the shower and call to your teacher.
Sharp/pointed object safety	Use knives and other sharp objects with extreme care. Place objects on a suitable work surface for cutting.	Notify your teacher immediately in the event of a cut or puncture no matter how minor it seems.
Animal care and safety	Handle animals only as your teacher directs. Treat animals carefully and respectfully. Wash your hands thoroughly after handling any animal.	Notify your teacher immediately if you injure yourself or any live specimen no matter how minor the injury seems.
Glassware Safety	Inspect glassware before use; do not use chipped or cracked glassware.	Notify your teacher immediately if a piece of glassware or a light bulb breaks.
Electrical safety	Do not place electrical cords where they could trip someone or cause equipment to fall. Do not use equipment with damaged cords. Do not use electrical equipment near water or when your clothing or hands are wet. Make sure that electrical equipment is in the "off" position before plugging it in. Turn off and unplug electrical equipment when you have finished using it.	Notify your teacher immediately if you notice any abnormal or potentially dangerous equipment. In the event of an electric shock, notify your teacher no matter how minor it seems.
Chemical safety	Wear safety goggles, an apron, and gloves whenever working with chemicals.	If a chemical spills onto your skin, rinse it off immediately by using the faucet or safety shower for at least 5 minutes while calling to your teacher.
Proper waste disposal	Dispose of contaminated materials in special containers only as directed by your teacher. Dispose of sharp objects in the appropriate sharps container as directed by your teacher. Clean and sanitize all work surfaces and personal protective equipment after each lab period.	Notify your teacher immediately if a piece of glassware or a light bulb breaks. Dispose of broken glass in the appropriate container as directed by your teacher. Notify your teacher immediately if you spill a chemical or culture of microorganisms. Follow your teacher's instructions for clean up.
Heating safety	Wear safety goggles when using a heating device or flame. Wear heat-resistant gloves when instructed to do so. When heating materials in a test tube, angle the test tube away from yourself and others.	Notify your teacher immediately in the event of a burn or fire no matter how minor it seems.
Plant safety	Do not eat any part of a plant or plant seed. When in nature, do not pick any wild plants unless your teacher instructs you to do so. Wash your hands thoroughly after handling any part of a plant.	Notify your teacher immediately if any potentially dangerous plant material comes into contact with your skin or if any plant matter is inhaled or ingested no matter how minor the event seems.

Commonly Used Word Parts

Word Parts

Word part	Definition	Example
amphi-	both	amphibian: a type of vertebrate that lives both on land and in water
ante-	before	anterior: front of an organism
anti-	against	antibiotic: substance, such as penicillin, capable of killing bacteria
arche-	ancient	Archaeopteryx: an ancient, fossilized bird
arthro-	joint	arthritis: a painful disease affecting the joints
bio-	life	biology: the study of life
chloro-	green	chlorophyll: green pigment in plants; needed for photosynthesis
chondro-	cartilage	Chondrichthyes: fish whose skeletons are made of cartilage
cyte-	cell	cytology: the study of cells
derm-	skin	dermatology: the study of the skin
ecto-	outer, outside	ectoderm: the outer tissue layer in many organisms
endo-	inner, inside	endoderm: the inner tissue layer in many organisms
gastro-	stomach	gastritis: inflammation of the stomach or stomach lining
gen-	produce	generate: to make, produce, or bring into being
hemi-	half	hemisphere: half of a sphere
hetero-	different	heterogeneous: made of unrelated or various parts
homeo-	the same	homeostasis: maintaining steady internal conditions
hydro-	water	hydroponics: growing plants in water instead of soil
hyper-	above, over	hypertension: blood pressure that is higher than normal
hypo-	below, under	hypothermic: body temperature that is below normal
inter-	between, among	interpersonal: relationships between or among people
intra-	within	intracellular: inside a cell
-logy	study of	biology: the study of life
macro-	large	macromolecule: large molecule, such as DNA or a protein
mega-	large	megaspore: a large spore produced by some ferns and flowering pants
meta-	change	metamorphosis: change in form
micro-	small	microscope: a tool for looking at very small objects
morph-	form	morphology: the study of the form of an organism
neo-	new	neonatal: newborn
para-	near, on	parasite: organism that lives on and feeds on another organism
peri-	around	pericardium: the membrane around the heart
photo-	light	phototropism: bending of plants toward light
-phyte-	plant	epiphyte: plant that lives on another plant, as in the branches of trees
poly-	many	polypeptide: many amino acids joined together to make a protein
pre-	before	prediction: a forecast of events before they take place
semi-	partially	semitransparent: allowing some, but not all, light to pass through
sub-	under	submarine: a boat that travels underwater
syn-	with	synapse: a place where two or more nerves come together
trans-	across	transcontinental: going across a continent

HOLT NEW YORK BIOLOGY

The Living Environment

CONTENTS IN BRIEF

TEACHER'S EDITION

Student Edition Contents In Brief

Teacher's Edition Walk-Through

Contents in Brief.................................T1
Program Overview..............................T2
Digital and Print Resources...............T4
Reading and Comprehension...........T6
Why It Matters....................................T7
Lab: Hands-On Learning...................T8
Technology Solutions......................T10
Differentiating Instruction..............T11
Meeting Individual Needs................T12
Pacing Guide...................................T14
Correlation to the New York
  Living Environment Standards.......T16
Safety in Your Laboratory................T24

Unit 1 Introduction
Chapter 1 Biology and You...........................4
Chapter 2 Applications of Biology...............26
Chapter 3 Chemistry of Life.........................48

Unit 2 Ecology
Chapter 4 Ecosystems..................................76
Chapter 5 Populations and
             Communities............................100
Chapter 6 The Environment.......................122

Unit 3 Cells
Chapter 7 Cell Structure
Chapter 8 Cells and Their
             Environment.............................172
Chapter 9 Photosynthesis and
             Cellular Respiration.................194
Chapter 10 Cell Growth and Division.....220

Unit 4 Heredity
Chapter 11 Meiosis and Sexual
             Reproduction..........................244
Chapter 12 Mendel and Heredity...........264
Chapter 13 DNA, RNA, and Proteins.......290

Chapter 14 Genes in Action.....................316
Chapter 15 Gene Technologies and
             Human Applications..............342

Unit 5 Evolution
Chapter 16 Evolutionary Theory..............372
Chapter 17 Population Genetics and
             Speciation...............................396
Chapter 18 Classification..........................420
Chapter 19 History of Life on Earth.........444

Unit 6 Humans
Chapter 20 Homeostasis and Human
             Body Systems.........................468
Chapter 21 Homeostasis and
             Human Disease......................496
Chapter 22 The Body's Defenses.............522
Chapter 23 Reproduction and
             Development..........................546

Appendix..570
English and Spanish Glossary.....................600
Index..632

HOLT, RINEHART AND WINSTON

A Harcourt Education Company

Orlando • **Austin** • New York • San Diego • London

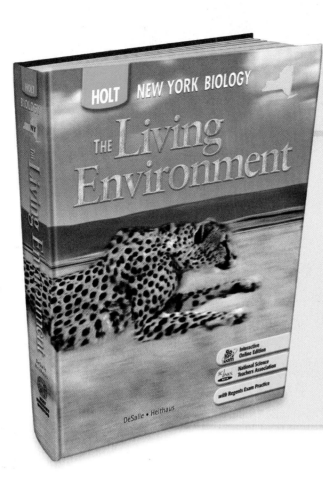

In Pursuit of Life

Holt Biology: The Living Environment is a comprehensive one-year course for high school students. Designed for flexible use, this program focuses on mastery of core biology concepts, while addressing the pedagogical issues that challenge teachers and students today.

The Holt Biology Advantage

Holt Biology is an easy-to-navigate resource organized around four coherent strands.

Holt Biology provides unparalleled reading and comprehension tools. Reading Toolbox activities that open the chapter help students understand the meanings of scientific terms, develop language skills, and practice note-taking strategies. Key terms and academic vocabulary terms are defined at point-of-use, removing the speed-bump of unfamiliar words.

❯ KEY IDEAS

Each section begins with Key Idea questions that help students focus on the main concepts in the chapter. Key Ideas are called out in the text and assessed in the section and chapter reviews. Reading Checks throughout the chapter further reinforce what students have read and allow students to check their own comprehension.

Why It Matters

Provide relevance for students who want to know why learning biology matters in their everyday lives. Why It Matters statements at the beginning of each chapter and section, as well as visually engaging Why It Matters features, help you capture student interest.

Inquiry**Lab**

An extensive lab program provides many opportunities for hands-on instruction to reinforce student understanding. Students will practice real-world laboratory skills needed for college and beyond.

What Makes *Holt Biology: The Living Environment* Special

- *Holt Biology: The Living Environment* has 23 chapters to align with the **Living Environment** curriculum, including two chapters by New York biology teachers.

- New York **Living Environment Standards** are printed on the page at the beginning of every chapter and section.

- At the end of every chapter, **Regents Practice** lets students assess their understanding of the material in the style of the Regents Exam.

- A **Regents Review Guide with Practice Exams** is an ideal way to prepare for the Regents Exam. Teachers have an **Answer Key with Test Doctor** that helps you diagnose how to re-teach where needed.

- We've added past Regents Exam questions to our **ExamView Version 5 Assessment Suite,** available on your **Teacher's One-Stop Planner.** This also contains editable worksheets.

- **Student One Stop** includes the textbook and other valuable student resources on one easy-to-use CD-ROM.

- **Interactive Online Edition** makes it easy to find all the resources for this course online.

- **Live Ink® Online Reading Help** makes the text more accessible for struggling readers.

- **Lab Generator** is a best-in-class product that helps manage all your laboratory needs, allowing you to search, edit, and add your own labs.

- **Lab Materials QuickList** can help you plan and order supplies for an entire teaching year of labs at once.

- **Virtual Investigations** contains more than twenty simulations that make science concepts accessible and engaging.

- **Holt Online Assessment** provides easily accessible formative online assessment.

- **MindPoint® Quiz Show** can even help you make assessment fun.

Resources for the Teacher

Holt Biology: The Living Environment provides you with a wealth of technology tools that combine functionality with content, allowing you to customize, organize, and adapt to your students' changing needs.

Digital Resources

- Holt Calendar Planner
- One-Stop Planner® with editable worksheets
- Lab Generator
- Lab Materials QuickList

- PowerPoint® Resources
- Visual Concepts
- Virtual Investigations
- Transparencies on CD and One-Stop Planner®

PLAN → **PRESENT**

Print Resources

- *Teacher's Edition* Planning Guide
- Strategies for English Language Learners
- *Science Skills Workshop Reading in the Content Area*
- *Professional Reference for Teachers*

- Teaching Transparencies
- Concept Mapping Transparencies
- Chapter Resource File blackline masters

Resources for the Student

If you prefer the familiarity of print resources, or if you're not able to make full use of our digital resources, we also provide a wide variety of traditional print materials for both students and teachers.

Digital Resources

- Interactive Online Edition with Live Ink® and MP3 audio
- Student One Stop with Interactive Reader, Study Guide, and more
- Guided Reading Audio CD program (also in Spanish)
- Visual Concepts

- Virtual Investigations
- Interactive Tutor
- Interactive Concept Maps
- NSTA's SciLinks®
- New Scientist Online®

STUDY → **HANDS-ON**

Print Resources

- *Interactive Reader*
- *Study Guide* (also in Spanish)
- *Note-taking Workbook*
- *Science Skills Workshop: Reading in the Content Area*
- Spanish Resources
- Reading Toolbox

- *Forensics and Applied Science Experiments Workbook* Student Edition
- Inquiry Lab Datasheets
- Quick Lab Datasheets
- Chapter Lab Datasheets
- Supplemental Labs (in Chapter Resource Files only)

- Biology Lab Generator
- Lab Videos DVD
- Virtual Investigations
- Holt PuzzlePro®

HANDS-ON

- *Laboratory Manager's Professional Reference*
- Chapter Resource File Lab Data Sheets (leveled)
- *Forensics and Applied Science Experiments Workbook* Teacher's Edition

- MindPoint® Quiz Show
- ExamView® Version 5 Assessment Suite with Regents Exam Questions
- Holt Online Assessment
- Support for "clicker" response systems

ASSESS

- Regents Review Guide Answer Key and Transparencies
- ExamView® Version 5 Assessment Suite worksheets
- Chapter Resource File Assessments (leveled)
- Spanish Assessments

- Interactive Online Edition with eActivities
- Student One Stop with Study Guide and more
- Interactive Concept Maps

REVIEW

- Directed Reading Worksheets
- Active Reading Worksheets
- Critical Thinking Worksheets
- Science Skills Worksheets
- Special Needs Activities and Modified Tests

- Holt Online Assessment
- Online Section Reviews
- Online Chapter Reviews
- Online Standardized Test Prep Practice

ASSESS

- Pretests
- Section Quizzes
- Chapter Tests A, B, and Special Needs
- Regents Review Guide with Practice Exams

Unparalleled Reading Support

Learning biology requires that students absorb a multitude of facts and vocabulary. Providing tools to students that help them organize concepts and understand terms is essential to a well-rounded biology program.

READING TOOLBOX These reading tools can help you learn the material in this chapter. For more information on how to use these and other tools, see **Appendix: Reading and Study Skills.**

Using Words

Word Parts Knowing the meanings of word parts can help you figure out the meanings of unknown words.

Your Turn Use the table to answer the following questions.

1. The root *-ptera* means "wing." What familiar machine is named for its spiral wing?
2. *Helicobacter* is a genus of bacteria. What shape is a bacterium of this genus?
3. In your own words, write a definition for *bacteriophage*.

Word Parts

Part	Type	Meaning
bacterio	root	involving bacteria
helic	root	spiral
-ase	suffix	enzyme
phage	root	to eat or destroy

Using Language

Describing Time Certain words and phrases can help you understand when something happened and how long it took. These words and phrases are called *specific time markers*. Specific time markers include words and phrases such as *first, next, 1 hour, yesterday, the twentieth century,* and *30 years later.*

Your Turn Read the sentences below and write down the specific time markers.

1. Early in the morning, before the sun rises, Emilio gets up to take his dogs for a walk.
2. Before a cell can divide, it must first make a copy of its DNA.

Using FoldNotes

Three-Panel Flip Chart A three-panel flip chart is useful when you want to organize notes about three topics. It can help you organize the characteristics of the topics side by side.

Your Turn Make a three-panel flip chart to organize your notes about DNA structure and replication.

1. Fold a piece of paper in half from the top to the bottom.
2. Fold the paper in three sections from side to side. Unfold the paper so that you can see the three sections.
3. From the top of the paper, cut along the vertical fold lines to the fold in the middle of the paper. You will now have three flaps.
4. Label the flaps of the three-panel flip chart "Identifying the Genetic Material," "The Structure of DNA," and "The Replication of DNA."
5. Under each flap, write your notes about the appropriate topic.

Reading Toolbox Each chapter begins with a set of reading tools. Students learn the meanings of word parts and learn skills such as how to read diagrams and how to take notes effectively. These activities are reinforced at point-of-use and assessed in the Chapter Review.

Academic Vocabulary Brief definitions at point-of-use help students with nontechnical terms that may be unfamiliar.

Key Ideas Essential learning objectives appear on the opening page of each section. Students find the answers as they read under the blue headings that correspond to each Key Idea.

Reading Checks Check students comprehension with Reading Check questions that appear throughout the text. Caption questions provide an opportunity to open up class discussion.

Key Terms Scientific vocabulary is highlighted in context and defined in the margin for quick reference. Less essential scientific terms are italicized and defined in the Glossary.

Section 1

The Structure of DNA

Key Ideas	Key Terms	Why It Matters
❯ What is genetic material composed of? ❯ What experiments helped identify the role of DNA? ❯ What is the shape of a DNA molecule? ❯ How is information organized in a DNA molecule? ❯ What scientific investigations led to the discovery of DNA's structure?	gene DNA nucleotide purine pyrimidine	DNA is the "blueprint" from which all living things are made, so understanding DNA is key to understanding life.

Unless you have an identical twin, you—like the sisters in **Figure 1**—share some, but not all, characteristics with family members.

DNA: The Genetic Material

In the 1800s, Gregor Mendel showed that traits are passed from parents to offspring. Many years later, scientists have discovered how these traits are passed on. The instructions for inherited traits are called **genes.** Before the 1950s, however, scientists did not know what genes were made of. We now know that genes are made of small segments of deoxyribonucleic acid, or **DNA.** ❯ DNA is the primary material that causes recognizable, inheritable characteristics in related groups of organisms.

DNA is a relatively simple molecule, composed of only four different subunits. For this reason, many early scientists did not consider DNA to be complex enough to be genetic material. A few key experiments led to the discovery that DNA is, in fact, genetic material.

❯ **Reading Check** *What are genes composed of? (See Appendix for answers to Reading Checks.)*

The Living Environment
Standard 4
2.1c Hereditary information is contained in genes, located in the chromosomes of each cell. An inherited trait of an individual can be determined by one or by many genes, and a single gene can influence more than one trait. A human cell contains many thousands of different genes in its nucleus.

2.1f In all organisms, the coded instructions for specifying the characteristics of the organism are carried in DNA, a large molecule formed from subunits arranged in a sequence with bases of four kinds (represented by A, G, C, and T). The chemical and structural properties of DNA are the basis for how the genetic information that underlies heredity is both encoded in genes (as a string of molecular bases) and replicated by means of a template.

2.1h Genes are segments of DNA molecules. Any alteration of the DNA sequence is a mutation. Usually, an altered gene will be passed on to every cell that develops from it.

gene a segment of DNA that is located in a chromosome and that codes for a specific hereditary trait

DNA deoxyribonucleic acid, the material that contains the information that determines inherited characteristics

Figure 1 These sisters share many traits but also have differences. ❯ What role do genes play in passing traits from parents to offspring?

Capturing Student Interest

Do your students struggle to relate the study of biology to their own lives? *Holt Biology: The Living Environment* helps them understand **Why It Matters.**

Why It Matters Visually stunning articles that read like a magazine draw students into *Real-World* biology, *Biotechnology,* and quirky *Weird Science.*

The **Why It Matters** strand continues through the opening page of the chapter and of each section, helping students connect lesson content with their own lives.

Why It Matters

Cells are the basic unit of life. By studying cells, biologists can better understand life's processes.

Online Projects Students have access to **NSTA's SciLinks®**, a library of approved Web links. As a teacher, you also have access to **New Scientist Online®**, the world's most popular weekly science digest.

Scientific Inquiry and Hands-On Learning

Holt Biology: The Living Environment provides many opportunities to gain lab experiences, ranging from ten-minute activities with minimal equipment to full-scale labs with a discovery focus.

InquiryLab

⏱ 15 min

Is It Alive?

Sometimes, it is difficult to tell living things from nonliving things. To be considered alive, something must have *all* of the characteristics of life.

Tree bark
Coffee grounds
Popcorn

Procedure

❶ With your group, discuss some characteristics you could look for with a hand lens to tell whether something is living or nonliving.

❷ Use a **hand lens** to examine an **assortment of objects** given to you by your teacher.

❸ Make a table that has three columns. In the first column, describe each of the objects. In the second column, state whether each object is living or nonliving.

❹ In the third column, write down the characteristics of life that you observed in each object.

Analysis

1. **Identify** characteristics of life that are difficult to see during a brief observation like this one.

2. **Identify** an object or m[...] necessarily among you[...] that undergoes growth [...] has never been alive.

> **Inquiry Labs** Each chapter starts with an **Inquiry Lab**—a brief activity to get students asking the right questions about the chapter topic.

Hands-On
QuickLab

⏱ 15 min

Vein Valves

By applying pressure to your arm, you can locate the valves in the veins of your arm.

Procedure

❶ Have a classmate make a fist and extend his or her arm, with the hand palm up and slightly below elbow level. Use a finger to locate a prominent vein on the inside of the forearm.

❷ Gently place a second finger along the vein about 5 cm from the first finger (toward the elbow). Release the second finger, but not the first. The vein should refill partway. Use a **pen** to mark this point, which indicates the location of a valve. You may have to try

Analysis

1. **Identify** the direction that blood flows in the vein you chose.

2. **Propose** why the subject must make a fist and hold his or her arm slightly down.

3. **Infer** what effect standing in one place for long periods of time might have on the veins in the legs.

Data
QuickLab

⏱ 15 min

The Eradication of Polio

The graph shows the global incidence of polio, and the percent of the population covered by polio vaccines.

Analysis

1. **Determine** how many cases of polio were reported globally in 1980. In 2000?

2. **Determine** what percent of the population was covered by protective polio vaccine in 1980. In 2000?

3. **Describe** the relationship between the number of polio cases and the coverage by preventative vaccine.

4. **Name** the two-year period over which the greatest drop in cases occurred. Explain this decrease.

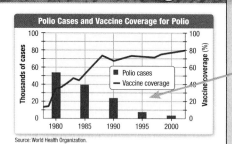

Polio Cases and Vaccine Coverage for Polio

■ Polio cases
— Vaccine coverage

Source: World Health Organization.

5. **CRITICAL THINKING** **Inferring Conclusions** What might cause a sudden yearly increase in the number of polio cases?

> **Quick Labs** Brief activities underscore a point with few demands on time or materials. **Hands-On Quick Labs** pull students in with simple, hands-on equipment. **Data Quick Labs** teach students to analyze data like scientists do.

Inquiry

Chapter 7 Lab

4.1.2f, 4.1.2i

🕐 45 min

Objectives

▶ Identify the structures that you can see in plant cells.

▶ Investigate factors that influence the movement of cell contents.

Materials

- compound light microscope
- safety goggles
- disposable gloves
- lab apron
- elodea sprig
- forceps
- microscope slides and coverslips
- lamp, incandescent
- dropper bottle of Lugol's iodine solution

Safety

Plant Cell Observation

When you look at cells under a microscope, you often can observe cytoplasmic streaming, or movement of cell contents. This effect occurs only in living cells. In this lab, you will investigate factors that influence cytoplasmic streaming.

Preparation

1. **SCIENTIFIC METHODS State the Problem** How do heat and an iodine solution influence cytoplasmic streaming?

2. **SCIENTIFIC METHODS Form a Hypothesis** Form testable hypotheses that explain how heat and iodine influence cytoplasmic streaming.

Procedure

1. ◇ ◇ ✦ Put on safety goggles, gloves, and a lab apron.

2. ◇ CAUTION: **Handle glass slides and coverslips with care.** Using forceps, remove a small leaf near the top of an elodea sprig. Place the whole leaf in a drop of water on a slide, and add a coverslip.

3. ◇ Observe the leaf under low power. Switch to high power. Iden- ... you can.

Chapter Labs A full-scale lab appears in each chapter. **Skills Practice Labs** focus on experimental skills and methodology. **Inquiry Labs** promote the use of scientific methods, guiding students to design their own experiments.

Chapter Resource Files contain supplemental full scale labs and Quick Labs for each chapter.

Holt Lab Generator The **Holt Lab Generator** is a big resource in a little package. All of Holt's biology lab resources are at your fingertips, and are correlated to the New York Living Environment standards. Search the extensive lab database using a topical keyword or a learning standard. Keep textbooks *out* of the lab by printing datasheets that include procedural steps for Student Edition labs.

The **Holt Lab Generator** allows you to edit and save customized versions of Holt labs. You can even download your favorite labs from the Web and save them. The built in **Lab Materials QuickList** makes ordering supplies for a single lab or a year-long course a snap.

Lab Generator CD-ROM

Biology

Class _____ Date _____

MODELING

...ng Cells: Surface Area to Volume

...s to how large a cell can grow? Everything that enters and exits a ...through the cell membrane. As the size of a cell increases, its surface ...es, but so does its volume. Consider how people enter a crowded ...a large stadium. Everyone funnels through a few gates. In a larger stadium, ...s people longer to move in and out. Similarly, in a larger cell, it takes mate-rials longer to reach their destination inside the cell. This means that it is more difficult for a large cell to have its needs met through the cell membrane. In this lab, you will examine surface area-to-volume ratios on a small scale, using model cells. You will use the collected data to draw conclusions about why this ratio might limit the size of a cell.

OBJECTIVES

Prepare and **compare** various cell models.

Calculate surface area and surface area-to-volume ratios.

Use your data to form conclusions about size limitations on cells.

MATERIALS

- calculator (optional)
- cell model patterns (3)
- funnel
- graduated cylinder, large
- metric ruler
- paper, heavy
- safety goggles
- sand
- scissors
- tape

◇ ◇

Procedure

1. Put on your safety goggles. Trace and cut out three cell models. Your teacher will provide you with the patterns or dimensions for each model. Fold the models to form three-dimensional shapes, as in **Figure 1**. Use tape to keep each model together.

2. Use the ruler to measure the length, width, and height dimensions of each model. Record the dimensions in **Table 1**.

3. Calculate the total surface area for each model. To do this, find the area of each side (length × width), then multiply that number by 6. Enter the data in **Table 1**.

FIGURE 1 CELL MODEL

Holt Biology · 43 · Cell Structure

Virtual Investigations Students manipulate variables and change experimental outcomes on the **Virtual Investigations.** Demonstrate cause and effect in more than 20 virtual labs that simulate real data in real experiments.

Biology Video Labs on DVD Prepare your students for Chapter Labs or replace hands-on labs with the **Biology Video Labs on DVD.** Each Chapter Lab in *Holt Biology* is clearly demonstrated by students like yours.

Key Technology

There are many digital components of *Holt Biology: The Living Environment,* but three in particular will become part of your daily work.

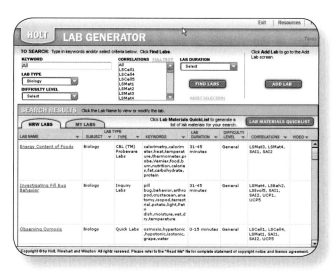

TEACHER'S ONE-STOP PLANNER®

An indispensable collection of resources, all in one place.

- Printable and editable worksheets, lab sheets, assessments, and more.

- Digital images from the textbook.

- Pre-built and editable **PowerPoint®** presentations, complete with embedded animations and illustrations.

- Teacher productivity software, including **ExamView® Version 5 Assessment Suite, Holt Calendar Planner®,** and **Puzzle Pro.**

- A link to download New York-specific resources.

HOLT LAB GENERATOR

Our entire Biology lab database on one CD.

- Contains every lab from **Quick Labs** to **Inquiry Labs,** all searchable by criteria you choose, including ability level (basic, general, advanced), and New York Standards.

- Every lab is editable to suit your needs.

- The database is expandable, so you can add labs you've received from your colleagues or found on the Web.

- **Lab Materials QuickList,** allows you to create an adaptable order sheet, suited to the size of your classes and the number of workgroups, complete with part numbers.

INTERACTIVE ONLINE EDITION

Newly redesigned, **http://my.hrw.com** lets you and your students communicate online.

- Loaded with interactive **eActivities,** it is much more than an online textbook.

- Students have access to ancillary resources with one click, and teachers have their own access to additional resources.

- **ExamView® Version 5 Assessment Suite** and **Holt Online Assessment** let you create custom assignments, control how they are delivered to students, and analyze their progress quickly and easily before you leave the lesson.

Differentiating Instruction

Today's classroom is comprised of students with widely different abilities and learning styles. That's why *Holt Biology: The Living Environment* provides you with resources targeted to meet special needs and to challenge advanced learners.

Differentiated Instruction

Basic Learners

Body Systems Have students research a human body system: digestive, respiratory, circulatory, excretory, nervous, or skeletal. Ask them to find the corresponding system in plants. Students should create a poster comparing the two systems. **LS** **Visual/ Verbal**

Differentiated Instruction

Advanced Learners

Behavior of Cell Colonies Ask students to research *Volvox* or another colonial organism on the Internet. Ask them to find out what scientific research has been done with the organism. They should review at least four sites and record the information they gather. Have them look for discrepancies in the information among the sites and record the source for each. Have students give oral reports to the class. **LS** **Logical/ Verbal**

TEACHER'S EDITION

The wrap-around margin provides tips and strategies for differentiated instruction, always in the same easy-to-find place on the page, and referenced again in the **Chapter Planner** for each chapter.

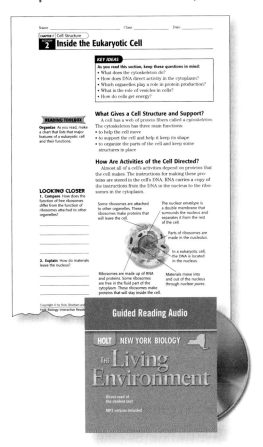

TEACHER'S ONE-STOP PLANNER®

Worksheets and lab data sheets are available in three versions — Basic, General, and Advanced — so all your students can be doing the same lesson, but at their own levels.

SUPPORT FOR ENGLISH-LANGUAGE LEARNERS

With everything from the Student Edition in Spanish audio in Spanish, assessment bank questions translated into Spanish, and even a multilingual dictionary with key terms translated into twelve languages, support for English-language learners is vast.

VISUAL CONCEPTS

Animations and videos online and on CD.

LIVE INK® ONLINE READING HELP technology in the *Interactive Online Edition*, or listen to an audio direct read of each section on their MP3 player or computer.

For more help for today's heterogeneous classroom, turn the page.

Meeting Individual Needs

Students have a wide range of abilities and learning exceptionalities. These pages show you how Holt Biology provides resources and strategies to help you tailor your instruction to engage every student in your classroom.

Learning exceptionality	Resources and strategies	
Struggling Readers Students who have dyslexia, dysgraphia or students reading below grade level.	• Differentiated Instruction labeled Struggling Readers • Reading Toolbox pages with skill building activities • Reading Toolbox activities throughout text • Interactive Reader with reinforcement activities	• Visual Concepts with animation and audio • Directed Reading Worksheets • Active Reading Worksheets • Modified Lab Datasheets, labeled as Level A • Modified Chapter Tests, labeled as Level A • Regents Review Guide with Practice Exams
English Learners Students learning English	• Differentiated Instruction labeled English Learners • English and Spanish Glossary at the back of the book • Multilingual Glossary with twelve languages • Study Guide • Interactive Reader with reinforcement activities	• Visual Concepts with animation and audio • Note-taking Workbook • Directed Reading Worksheets • Active Reading Worksheets • Modified Lab Datasheets, labeled as Level A • Modified Chapter Tests, labeled as Level A • Regents Review Guide with Practice Exams
Special Education Students Students experiencing difficulty completing tasks that have multiple steps, difficulty concentrating, and students functioning below grade level because of mental retardation, autism, or brain injury	• Differentiated Instruction labeled Special Education Students • Special Needs Activities and Modified Tests • Interactive Reader with reinforcement activities	• Visual Concepts with animation and audio • Study Guide • Note-taking Workbook • Directed Reading Worksheets • Active Reading Worksheets • Modified Lab Datasheets, labeled as Level A
Basic Learners Students having difficulty understanding abstract or complex concepts and slow learners.	• Differentiated Instruction labeled Basic Learners • Special Needs Activities and Modified Tests • Interactive Reader with reinforcement activities • Visual Concepts with animation and audio	• Study Guide • Note-taking Workbook • Directed Reading Worksheets • Active Reading Worksheets • Modified Lab Datasheets, labeled as Level A • Regents Review Guide with Practice Exams
Advanced Learners Students who are performing above grade level and demonstrate aptitude in cross-curricular assignments	• Differentiated Instruction labeled Advanced Learners • Math Skills and Science Skills activities • Why It Matters activities that relate content to other disciplines in a relevant way	• Activities that involve multiple tasks, a strong degree of independence, and student initiative • Science Skills Worksheets • Critical Thinking Worksheets • Concept Mapping Worksheets • Advanced Lab Datasheets, labeled as Level C

General Strategies The following strategies can help you modify instruction to help students who struggle with common classroom difficulties.

A student experiencing difficulty with . . .	May benefit if you . . .	
Beginning assignments	• Assign work in small amounts • Have the student use cooperative or paired learning • Provide varied and interesting activities	• Allow choice in assignments or projects • Reinforce participation • Seat the student closer to you
Following directions	• Gain the student's attention before giving directions • Break up the task into small steps • Give written directions rather than oral directions • Use short, simple phrases • Stand near the student when you are giving directions	• Have the student repeat directions to you • Prepare the student for changes in activity • Give visual cues by posting general routines • Reinforce improvement in or approximation of following directions
Keeping track of assignments	• Have the student use folders for assignments • Have the student use assignment notebooks	• Have the student keep a checklist of assignments and highlight assignments when they are turned in
Reading the textbook	• Provide outlines of the textbook content • Reduce the length of required reading • Allow extra time for reading • Have the students read aloud in small groups	• Have the student use peer or mentor readers • Have the student use books on tape or CD • Discuss the content of the textbook in class after reading
Staying on task	• Reduce distracting elements in the classroom • Provide a task-completion checklist • Seat the student near you	• Provide alternative ways to complete assignments, such as oral projects taped with a buddy
Behavioral or social skills	• Model the appropriate behaviors • Establish class rules, and reiterate them often • Reinforce positive behavior • Assign a mentor as a positive role model to the student • Contract with the student for expected behaviors • Reinforce the desired behaviors or any steps toward improvement	• Separate the student from any peer who stimulates the inappropriate behavior • Provide a "cooling off" period before talking with the student • Address academic/instructional problems that may contribute to disruptive behaviors • Include parents in the problem-solving process through conferences, home visits, and frequent communication
Attendance	• Recognize and reinforce attendance by giving incentives or verbal praise • Emphasize the importance of attendance by letting the student know that he or she was missed when he or she was absent	• Encourage the student's desire to be in school by planning activities that are likely to be enjoyable, giving the student a preferred responsibility to be performed in class, and involving the student in extracurricular activities • Schedule problem-solving meeting with parents, faculty, or both
Test-taking skills	• Prepare the student for testing by teaching ways to study in pairs, such as using flashcards, practice tests, and study guides, and by promoting adequate sleep, nourishment, and exercise • During testing, allow the student to respond orally on tape or to respond using a computer; to use	notes; to take breaks; to take the test in another location; to work without time constraints; or to take the test in several short sessions • Decrease visual distraction by improving the visual design of the test through use of larger type, spacing, consistent layout, and shorter sentences

The Living Environment
Regents Correlations

The Living Environment Core Curriculum	Code	Page Correlation
STANDARD 1 Students will use mathematical analysis, scientific inquiry, and engineering design, as appropriate, to pose questions, seek answers, and develop solutions.		
KEY IDEA 1 The central purpose of scientific inquiry is to develop explanations of natural phenomena in a continuing and creative process.		
Performance Indicator 1.1 Elaborate on basic scientific and personal explanations of natural phenomena, and develop extended visual models and mathematical formulations to represent one's thinking.		
Scientific explanations are built by combining evidence that can be observed with what people already know about the world.	**1.1a**	7, 12, 29–30, 378–379
Learning about the historical development of scientific concepts or about individuals who have contributed to scientific knowledge provides a better understanding of scientific inquiry and the relationship between science and society.	**1.1b**	9
Science provides knowledge, but values are also essential to making effective and ethical decisions about the application of scientific knowledge.	**1.1c**	8, 37, 348, 354
Performance Indicator 1.2 Hone ideas through reasoning, library research, and discussion with others, including experts.		
Inquiry involves asking questions and locating, interpreting, and processing information from a variety of sources.	**1.2a**	5, 10, 11–12, 165, 373
Inquiry involves making judgments about the reliability of the source and relevance of information.	**1.2b**	11
Performance Indicator 1.3 Work toward reconciling competing explanations; clarify points of agreement and disagreement.		
Scientific explanations are accepted when they are consistent with experimental and observational evidence and when they lead to accurate predictions.	**1.3a**	12, 13
All scientific explanations are tentative and subject to change or improvement. Each new bit of evidence can create more questions than it answers. This leads to increasingly better understanding of how things work in the living world.	**1.3b**	7, 13, 433
Performance Indicator 1.4 Coordinate explanations at different levels of scale, points of focus, and degrees of complexity and specificity, and recognize the need for such alternative representations of the natural world.		
Well-accepted theories are ones that are supported by different kinds of scientific investigations often involving the contributions of individuals from different disciplines.	**1.4a**	13, 378–379

KEY IDEA 2 Beyond the use of reasoning and consensus, scientific inquiry involves the testing of proposed explanations involving the use of conventional techniques and procedures and usually requires considerable ingenuity.

	Code	Page Correlation
Performance Indicator 2.1 Devise ways of making observations to test proposed explanations.	2.1	9, 11, 68–69, 140–141, 188–189
Performance Indicator 2.2 Refine research ideas through library investigations, including electronic information retrieval and reviews of the literature, and through peer feedback obtained from review and discussion.		
Development of a research plan involves researching background information and understanding the major concepts in the area being investigated. Recommendations for methodologies, use of technologies, proper equipment, and safety precautions should also be included.	2.2a	15, 16, 513
Performance Indicator 2.3 Develop and present proposals including formal hypotheses to test explanations; i.e., predict what should be observed under specific conditions if the explanation is true.		
Hypotheses are predictions based upon both research and observation.	2.3a	10
Hypotheses are widely used in science for determining what data to collect and as a guide for interpreting the data.	2.3b	10
Development of a research plan for testing a hypothesis requires planning to avoid bias (e.g., repeated trials, large sample size, and objective data-collection techniques).	2.3c	11, 140–141, 188–189, 285
Performance Indicator 2.4 Carry out a research plan for testing explanations, including selecting and developing techniques, acquiring and building apparatus, and recording observations as necessary.	2.4	15, 68–69, 94–95, 140–141, 188–189, 285

KEY IDEA 3 The observations made while testing proposed explanations, when analyzed using conventional and invented methods, provide new insights into natural phenomena.

	Code	Page Correlation
Performance Indicator 3.1 Use various methods of representing and organizing observations (e.g., diagrams, tables, charts, graphs, equations, matrices) and insightfully interpret the organized data.		
Interpretation of data leads to development of additional hypotheses, the formulation of generalizations, or explanations of natural phenomena.	3.1a	12, 94–95
Performance Indicator 3.2 Apply statistical analysis techniques when appropriate to test if chance alone explains the results.	3.2	265, 278–279, 415
Performance Indicator 3.3 Assess correspondence between the predicted result contained in the hypothesis and actual result, and reach a conclusion as to whether the explanation on which the prediction was based is supported.	3.3	12, 95, 285
Performance Indicator 3.4 Based on the results of the test and through public discussion, revise the explanation and contemplate additional research.		

REGENTS CORRELATIONS

The Living Environment Core Curriculum	Code	Page Correlation
Hypotheses are valuable, even if they turn out not to be true, because they may lead to further investigation.	**3.4a**	10
Claims should be questioned if the data are based on samples that are very small, biased, or inadequately controlled or if the conclusions are based on the faulty, incomplete, or misleading use of numbers.	**3.4b**	9, 12
Claims should be questioned if fact and opinion are intermingled, if adequate evidence is not cited, or if the conclusions do not follow logically from the evidence given.	**3.4c**	7, 9, 12
Performance Indicator 3.5 Develop a written report for public scrutiny that describes the proposed explanation, including a literature review, the research carried out, its result, and suggestions for further research.		
One assumption of science is that other individuals could arrive at the same explanation if they had access to similar evidence. Scientists make the results of their investigations public; they should describe the investigations in ways that enable others to repeat the investigations.	**3.5a**	13
Scientists use peer review to evaluate the results of scientific investigations and the explanations proposed by other scientists. They analyze the experimental procedures, examine the evidence, identify faulty reasoning, point out statements that go beyond the evidence, and suggest alternative explanations for the same observations.	**3.5b**	8, 12

STANDARD 4 Students will understand and apply scientific concepts, principles, and theories pertaining to the physical setting and living environment and recognize the historical development of ideas in science.

KEY IDEA 1 Living things are both similar to and different from each other and from nonliving things.

	Code	Page Correlation
Performance Indicator 1.1 Explain how diversity of populations within ecosystems relates to the stability of ecosystems.		
Populations can be categorized by the function they serve. Food webs identify the relationships among producers, consumers, and decomposers carrying out either autotropic or heterotropic nutrition.	**1.1a**	86–87
An ecosystem is shaped by the nonliving environment as well as its interacting species. The world contains a wide diversity of physical conditions, which creates a variety of environments.	**1.1b**	80, 82–84
In all environments, organisms compete for vital resources. The linked and changing interactions of populations and the environment compose the total ecosystem.	**1.1c**	106, 113, 115
The interdependence of organisms in an established ecosystem often results in approximate stability over hundreds and thousands of years. For example, as one population increases, it is held in check by one or more environmental factors or another species.	**1.1d**	105–106, 115

The Living Environment Core Curriculum	Code	Page Correlation
Ecosystems, like many other complex systems, tend to show cyclic changes around a state of approximate equilibrium.	**1.1e**	81
Every population is linked, directly or indirectly, with many others in an ecosystem. Disruptions in the numbers and types of species and environmental changes can upset ecosystem stability.	**1.1f**	79, 87, 115, 132–133
Performance Indicator 1.2 Describe and explain the structures and functions of the human body at different organizational levels (e.g., systems, tissues, cells, organelles.		
Important levels of organization for structure and function include organelles, cells, tissues, organs, organ systems, and whole organisms.	**1.2a**	164–165, 476–483
Humans are complex organisms. They require multiple systems for digestion, respiration, reproduction, circulation, excretion, movement, coordination, and immunity. The systems interact to perform the life functions.	**1.2b**	469, 471–475, 481, 525, 529
The components of the human body, from organ systems to cell organelles, interact to maintain a balanced internal environment. To successfully accomplish this, organisms possess a diversity of control mechanisms that detect deviations and make corrective actions.	**1.2c**	175, 223, 469, 471–475, 478–488
If there is a disruption in any human system, there may be a corresponding imbalance in homeostasis.	**1.2d**	473, 487, 499
The organs and systems of the body help to provide all the cells with their basic needs. The cells of the body are of different kinds and are grouped in ways that enhance how they function together.	**1.2e**	164–166, 333, 472, 487
Cells have particular structures that perform specific jobs. These structures perform the actual work of the cell. Just as systems are coordinated and work together, cell parts must also be coordinated and work together.	**1.2f**	154–155, 156–161, 165, 167, 202–203
Each cell is covered by a membrane that performs a number of important functions for the cell. These include: separation from its outside environment, controlling which molecules enter and leave the cell, and recognition of chemical signals. The processes of diffusion and active transport are important in the movement of materials in and out of cells.	**1.2g**	154–155, 173, 175–177, 178–183, 185–186, 188–189
Many organic and inorganic substances dissolved in cells allow necessary chemical reactions to take place in order to maintain life. Large organic food molecules such as proteins and starches must initially be broken down (digested to amino acids and simple sugars respectively), in order to enter cells. Once nutrients enter a cell, the cell will use them as building blocks in the synthesis of compounds necessary for life.	**1.2h**	59–63, 68–69, 197–201

The Living Environment Core Curriculum	Code	Page Correlation
Inside the cell a variety of specialized structures, formed from many different molecules, carry out the transport of materials (cytoplasm), extraction of energy from nutrients (mitochondria), protein building (ribosomes), waste disposal (cell membrane), storage (vacuole), and information storage (nucleus).	**1.2i**	154–155, 157–161, 167, 183, 201, 202–203, 211, 305
Receptor molecules play an important role in the interactions between cells. Two primary agents of cellular communication are hormones and chemicals produced by nerve cells. If nerve or hormone signals are blocked, cellular communication is disrupted and the organism's stability is affected.	**1.2j**	177, 184–186
Performance Indicator 1.3 Explain how a one-celled organism is able to function despite lacking the levels of organization present in more complex organisms.		
The structures present in some single-celled organisms act in a manner similar to the tissues and systems found in multicellular organisms, thus enabling them to perform all of the life processes needed to maintain homeostasis.	**1.3a**	472
KEY IDEA 2 Organisms inherit genetic information in a variety of ways that result in continuity of structure and function between parents and offspring.		
Performance Indicator 2.1 Explain how the structure and replication of genetic material result in offspring that resemble their parents.		
Genes are inherited, but their expression can be modified by interactions with the environment.	**2.1a**	284, 310, 326–327
Every organism requires a set of coded instructions for specifying its traits. For offspring to resemble their parents, there must be a reliable way to transfer information from one generation to the next. Heredity is the passage of these instructions from one generation to another.	**2.1b**	272–275, 301, 304
Hereditary information is contained in genes, located in the chromosomes of each cell. An inherited trait of an individual can be determined by one or by many genes, and a single gene can influence more than one trait. A human cell contains many thousands of different genes in its nucleus.	**2.1c**	248–249, 272–275, 280–281, 282–284, 273, 293
In asexually reproducing organisms, all the genes come from a single parent. Asexually produced offspring are normally genetically identical to the parent.	**2.1d**	247, 475, 498
In sexually reproducing organisms, the new individual receives half of the genetic information from its mother (via the egg) and half from its father (via the sperm). Sexually produced offspring often resemble, but are not identical to, either of their parents.	**2.1e**	248–249, 250–254, 256–257
In all organisms, the coded instructions for specifying the characteristics of the organism are carried in DNA, a large molecule formed from subunits arranged in a sequence with bases of four kinds (represented by A, G, C, and T). The chemical and structural properties of DNA are the basis for how the genetic information that underlies heredity is both encoded in genes (as a string of molecular "bases") and replicated by means of a template.	**2.1f**	154, 273, 291, 293–304, 304, 307, 343

The Living Environment Core Curriculum	Code	Page Correlation
Cells store and use coded information. The genetic information stored in DNA is used to direct the synthesis of the thousands of proteins that each cell requires.	2.1g	304–310, 329
Genes are segments of DNA molecules. Any alteration of the DNA sequence is a mutation. Usually, an altered gene will be passed on to every cell that develops from it.	2.1h	293, 319, 322–323, 403
The work of the cell is carried out by the many different types of molecules it assembles, mostly proteins. Protein molecules are long, usually folded chains made from 20 different kinds of amino acids in a specific sequence. This sequence influences the shape of the protein. The shape of the protein, in turn, determines its function.	2.1i	304, 307, 329, 336–337
Offspring resemble their parents because they inherit similar genes that code for the production of proteins that form similar structures and perform similar functions.	2.1j	272, 274, 281
The many body cells in an individual can be very different from one another, even though they are all descended from a single cell and thus have essentially identical genetic instructions. This is because different parts of these instructions are used in different types of cells, and are influenced by the cells' environment and past history.	2.1k	166, 325–327, 333
Performance Indicator 2.2 Explain how technology of genetic engineering allows humans to alter genetic makeup of organisms.		
For thousands of years new varieties of cultivated plants and domestic animals have resulted from selective breeding for particular traits.	2.2a	267, 350, 377
In recent years new varieties of farm plants and animals have been engineered by manipulating their genetic instructions to produce new characteristics.	2.2b	33, 350–351
Different enzymes can be used to cut, copy, and move segments of DNA. Characteristics produced by the segments of DNA may be expressed when these segments are inserted into new organisms, such as bacteria.	2.2c	350–351, 355, 358–360
Inserting, deleting, or substituting DNA segments can alter genes. An altered gene may be passed on to every cell that develops from it.	2.2d	319–321, 351
Knowledge of genetics is making possible new fields of health care; for example, finding genes which may have mutations that can cause disease will aid in the development of preventive measures to fight disease. Substances, such as hormones and enzymes, from genetically engineered organisms may reduce the cost and side effects of replacing missing body chemicals.	2.2e	31, 346–347, 350–353, 407, 512
KEY IDEA 3 Individual organisms and species change over time.		
Performance Indicator 3.1 Explain the mechanisms and patterns of evolution.		
The basic theory of biological evolution states that the Earth's present-day species developed from earlier, distinctly different species.	3.1a	375–381, 386–387

The Living Environment Core Curriculum	Code	Page Correlation
New inheritable characteristics can result from new combinations of existing genes or from mutations of genes in reproductive cells.	**3.1b**	322–324, 332, 388, 400–403, 405–406
Mutation and the sorting and recombining of genes during meiosis and fertilization result in a great variety of possible gene combinations.	**3.1c**	254, 322–323, 403, 406
Mutations occur as random chance events. Gene mutations can also be caused by such agents as radiation and chemicals. When they occur in sex cells, the mutations can be passed on to offspring; if they occur in other cells, they can be passed on to other body cells only.	**3.1d**	320–323, 403
Natural selection and its evolutionary consequences provide a scientific explanation for the fossil record of ancient life-forms, as well as for the molecular and structural similarities observed among the diverse species of living organisms.	**3.1e**	380–384, 386–387, 390–391
Species evolve over time. Evolution is the consequence of the interactions of (1) the potential for a species to increase its numbers, (2) the genetic variability of offspring due to mutation and recombination of genes, (3) a finite supply of the resources required for life, and (4) the ensuing selection by the environment of those offspring better able to survive and leave offspring.	**3.1f**	380–384, 386–389, 397, 401–403, 405–408, 415
Some characteristics give individuals an advantage over others in surviving and reproducing, and the advantaged offspring, in turn, are more likely than others to survive and reproduce. The proportion of individuals that have advantageous characteristics will increase.	**3.1g**	380–381, 386–387, 408
The variation of organisms within a species increases the likelihood that at least some members of the species will survive under changed environmental conditions.	**3.1h**	380–381
Behaviors have evolved through natural selection. The broad patterns of behavior exhibited by organisms are those that have resulted in greater reproductive success.	**3.1i**	408
Billions of years ago, life on Earth is thought by many scientists to have begun as simple, single-celled organisms. About a billion years ago, increasingly complex multicellular organisms began to evolve.	**3.1j**	154, 454–457
Evolution does not necessitate long-term progress in some set direction. Evolutionary changes appear to be like the growth of a bush: Some branches survive from the beginning with little or no change, many die out altogether, and others branch repeatedly, sometimes giving rise to more complex organisms.	**3.1k**	387
Extinction of a species occurs when the environment changes and the adaptive characteristics of a species are insufficient to allow its survival. Fossils indicate that many organisms that lived long ago are extinct. Extinction of species is common; most of the species that have lived on Earth no longer exist.	**3.1l**	382, 389, 414, 452, 457, 459

The Living Environment Core Curriculum	Code	Page Correlation
KEY IDEA 4 The continuity of life is sustained through reproduction and development.		
Performance Indicator 4.1 Explain how organisms, including humans, reproduce their own kind.		
Reproduction and development are necessary for the continuation of any species.	**4.1a**	19, 257, 407
Some organisms reproduce asexually with all the genetic information coming from one parent. Other organisms reproduce sexually with half the genetic information typically contributed by each parent. Cloning is the production of identical genetic copies.	**4.1b**	247–248, 256–257, 352
The processes of meiosis and fertilization are key to sexual reproduction in a wide variety of organisms. The process of meiosis results in the production of eggs and sperm which each contain half of the genetic information. During fertilization, gametes unite to form a zygote, which contains the complete genetic information for the offspring.	**4.1c**	250–254, 256–259, 547, 558
The zygote may divide by mitosis and differentiate to form the specialized cells, tissues, and organs of multicellular organisms.	**4.1d**	558–560
Human reproduction and development are influenced by factors such as gene expression, hormones, and the environment. The reproductive cycle in both males and females is regulated by hormones such as testosterone, estrogen, and progesterone.	**4.1e**	449–556
The structures and functions of the human female reproductive system, as in almost all other mammals, are designed to produce gametes in ovaries, allow for internal fertilization, support the internal development of the embryo and fetus in the uterus, and provide essential materials through the placenta, and nutrition through milk for the newborn.	**4.1f**	552–560
The structures and functions of the human male reproductive system, as in other mammals, are designed to produce gametes in testes and make possible the delivery of these gametes for fertilization.	**4.1g**	550–551
In humans, the embryonic development of essential organs occurs in early stages of pregnancy. The embryo may encounter risks from faults in its genes and from its mother's exposure to environmental factors such as inadequate diet, use of alcohol/drugs/tobacco, other toxins, or infections throughout her pregnancy.	**4.1h**	127, 559–560
KEY IDEA 5 Organisms maintain a dynamic equilibrium that sustains life.		
Performance Indicator 5.1 Explain the basic biochemical processes in living organisms and their importance in maintaining dynamic equilibrium.		
The energy for life comes primarily from the Sun. Photosynthesis provides a vital connection between the Sun and the energy needs of living systems.	**5.1a**	86, 197–198, 205

The Living Environment Core Curriculum	Code	Page Correlation
Plant cells and some one-celled organisms contain chloroplasts, the site of photosynthesis. The process of photosynthesis uses solar energy to combine the inorganic molecules carbon dioxide and water into energy-rich organic compounds (e.g., glucose) and release oxygen to the environment.	5.1b	160, 199, 202–207
In all organisms, organic compounds can be used to assemble other molecules such as proteins, DNA, starch, and fats. The chemical energy stored in bonds can be used as a source of energy for life processes.	5.1c	65, 67, 197
In all organisms, the energy stored in organic molecules may be released during cellular respiration. This energy is temporarily stored in ATP molecules. In many organisms, the process of cellular respiration is concluded in mitochondria, in which ATP is produced more efficiently, oxygen is used, and carbon dioxide and water are released as wastes.	5.1d	160–161, 197–201, 208–213, 215
The energy from ATP is used by the organism to obtain, transform, and transport materials, and to eliminate wastes.	5.1e	68–69, 182, 200
Biochemical processes, both breakdown and synthesis, are made possible by a large set of biological catalysts called enzymes. Enzymes can affect the rates of chemical change. The rate at which enzymes work can be influenced by internal environmental factors such as pH and temperature.	5.1f	66, 207
Enzymes and other molecules, such as hormones, receptor molecules, and antibodies, have specific shapes that influence both how they function and how they interact with other molecules.	5.1g	66, 186, 530
Performance Indicator 5.2 Explain disease as a failure of homeostasis.		
Homeostasis in an organism is constantly threatened. Failure to respond effectively can result in disease or death.	5.2a	473, 481, 499–501, 510–515
Viruses, bacteria, fungi, and other parasites may infect plants and animals and interfere with normal life functions.	5.2b	500, 502–508, 562–564
The immune system protects against antigens associated with pathogenic organisms or foreign substances and some cancer cells.	5.2c	526–528, 529–532
Some white blood cells engulf invaders. Others produce antibodies that attack them or mark them for killing. Some specialized white blood cells will remain, able to fight off subsequent invaders of the same kind.	5.2d	527, 529–532
Vaccinations use weakened microbes (or parts of them) to stimulate the immune system to react. This reaction prepares the body to fight subsequent invasions by the same microbes.	5.2e	31, 346, 532–533
Some viral diseases, such as AIDS, damage the immune system, leaving the body unable to deal with multiple infectious agents and cancerous cells.	5.2f	539, 561–533
Some allergic reactions are caused by the body's immune responses to usually harmless environmental substances. Sometimes the immune system may attack some of the body's own cells or transplanted organs.	5.2g	534–536

The Living Environment Core Curriculum	Code	Page Correlation
Disease may also be caused by inheritance, toxic substances, poor nutrition, organ malfunction, and some personal behavior. Some effects show up right away; others may not show up for many years.	5.2h	127, 497, 499–501, 510–515
Gene mutations in a cell can result in uncontrolled cell division, called cancer. Exposure of cells to certain chemicals and radiation increases mutations and thus increases the chance of cancer.	5.2i	127, 228, 235, 323
Biological research generates knowledge used to design ways of diagnosing, preventing, treating, controlling, or curing diseases of plants and animals.	5.2j	29–35, 346–347, 500, 516–517
Performance Indicator 5.3 Relate processes at the system level to the cellular level in order to explain dynamic equilibrium in multicelled organisms.		
Dynamic equilibrium results from detection of and response to stimuli. Organisms detect and respond to change in a variety of ways both at the cellular level and at the organismal level.	5.3a	19, 158–160, 175, 469, 471–475, 481
Feedback mechanisms have evolved that maintain homeostasis. Examples include the changes in heart rate or respiratory rate in response to increased activity in muscle cells, the maintenance of blood sugar levels by insulin from the pancreas, and the changes in openings in the leaves of plants by guard cells to regulate water loss and gas exchange.	5.3b	469, 484–488, 490–491
KEY IDEA 6 Plants and animals depend on each other and their physical environment.		
Performance Indicator 6.1 Explain factors that limit growth of individuals and populations.		
Energy flows through ecosystems in one direction, typically from the Sun, through photosynthetic organisms including green plants and algae, to herbivores to carnivores and decomposers.	6.1a	86–89
The atoms and molecules on the Earth cycle among the living and nonliving components of the biosphere. For example, carbon dioxide and water molecules used in photosynthesis to form energy-rich organic compounds are returned to the environment when the energy in these compounds is eventually released by cells. Continual input of energy from sunlight keeps the process going. This concept may be illustrated with an energy pyramid.	6.1b	77, 86–93
The chemical elements, such as carbon, hydrogen, nitrogen, and oxygen, that make up the molecules of living things pass through food webs and are combined and recombined in different ways. At each link in a food web, some energy is stored in newly made structures but much is dissipated into the environment as heat.	6.1c	87–89, 91–93, 199
The number of organisms any habitat can support (carrying capacity) is limited by the available energy, water, oxygen, and minerals, and by the ability of ecosystems to recycle the residue of dead organisms through the activities of bacteria and fungi.	6.1d	80, 105–106

The Living Environment Core Curriculum	Code	Page Correlation
In any particular environment, the growth and survival of organisms depend on the physical conditions including light intensity, temperature range, mineral availability, soil/rock type, and relative acidity (pH).	**6.1e**	80, 106
Living organisms have the capacity to produce populations of unlimited size, but environments and resources are finite. This has profound effects on the interactions among organisms.	**6.1f**	101, 104–106, 116
Relationships between organisms may be negative, neutral, or positive. Some organisms may interact with one another in several ways. They may be in a producer/consumer, predator/prey, or parasite/host relationship; or one organism may cause disease in, scavenge, or decompose another.	**6.1g**	86–87, 109–111, 113–114
Performance Indicator 6.2 Explain the importance of preserving diversity of species and habitats.		
As a result of evolutionary processes, there is a diversity of organisms and roles in ecosystems. This diversity of species increases the chance that at least some will survive in the face of large environmental changes. Biodiversity increases the stability of the ecosystem.	**6.2a**	80, 109, 115, 132, 454–459
Biodiversity also ensures the availability of a rich variety of genetic material that may lead to future agricultural or medical discoveries with significant value to humankind. As diversity is lost, potential sources of these materials may be lost with it.	**6.2b**	132
Performance Indicator 6.3 Explain how the living and nonliving environments change over time and respond to disturbances.		
The interrelationships and interdependencies of organisms affect the development of stable ecosystems.	**6.3a**	81, 115, 132
Through ecological succession, all ecosystems progress through a sequence of changes during which one ecological community modifies the environment, making it more suitable for another community. These long-term gradual changes result in the community reaching a point of stability that can last for hundreds or thousands of years.	**6.3b**	81, 113
A stable ecosystem can be altered, either rapidly or slowly, through the activities of organisms (including humans), or through climatic changes or natural disasters. The altered ecosystem can usually recover through gradual changes back to a point of longterm stability.	**6.3c**	81, 125
KEY IDEA 7 Human decisions and activities have had a profound impact on the physical and living environment.		
Performance Indicator 7.1 Describe the range of interrelationships of humans with the living and nonliving environment.		
The Earth has finite resources; increasing human consumption of resources places stress on the natural processes that renew some resources and deplete those resources that cannot be renewed.	**7.1a**	107, 125–126, 128–133

The Living Environment Core Curriculum	Code	Page Correlation
Natural ecosystems provide an array of basic processes that affect humans. Those processes include but are not limited to: maintenance of the quality of the atmosphere, generation of soils, control of the water cycle, removal of wastes, energy flow, and recycling of nutrients. Humans are changing many of these basic processes and the changes may be detrimental.	**7.1b**	90–93, 125–127, 129–130, 131
Human beings are part of the Earth's ecosystems. Human activities can, deliberately or inadvertently, alter the equilibrium in ecosystems. Humans modify ecosystems as a result of population growth, consumption, and technology. Human destruction of habitats through direct harvesting, pollution, atmospheric changes, and other factors is threatening current global stability, and if not addressed, ecosystems may be irreversibly affected.	**7.1c**	125, 127, 128–133
Performance Indicator 7.2 Explain the impact of technological development and growth in the human population on the living and nonliving environment.		
Human activities that degrade ecosystems result in a loss of diversity of the living and nonliving environment. For example, the influence of humans on other organisms occurs through land use and pollution. Land use decreases the space and resources available to other species, and pollution changes the chemical composition of air, soil, and water.	**7.2a**	127, 128–133
When humans alter ecosystems either by adding or removing specific organisms, serious consequences may result. For example, planting large expanses of one crop reduces the biodiversity of the area.	**7.2b**	127, 132–133, 140–141
Industrialization brings an increased demand for and use of energy and other resources including fossil and nuclear fuels. This usage can have positive and negative effects on humans and ecosystems.	**7.2c**	126, 128–129
Performance Indicator 7.3 Explain how individual choices and societal actions can contibute to improving the environment.		
Societies must decide on proposals which involve the introduction of new technologies. Individuals need to make decisions which will assess risks, costs, benefits, and trade-offs.	**7.3a**	37, 135, 136, 138
The decisions of one generation both provide and limit the range of possibilities open to the next generation.	**7.3b**	134, 138

Safety in Your Laboratory

Risk Assessment

MAKING YOUR LABORATORY A SAFE PLACE TO WORK AND LEARN

Concern for safety must begin before any activity in the classroom and before students enter the lab. A careful review of the facilities should be a basic part of preparation for each school term. You should investigate the physical environment, identify any safety risks, and inspect your work areas for compliance with safety regulations.

The review of the lab should be thorough, and all safety issues must be addressed immediately. Keep a file of your review, and add to the list each year. This will allow you to continue to raise the standard of safety in your lab and classroom.

Many classroom experiments, demonstrations, and other activities are classics that have been used for years. This familiarity may lead to a comfort that can obscure inherent safety concerns. Review all experiments, demonstrations, and activities for safety concerns before presenting them to the class. Identify and eliminate potential safety hazards.

1. Identify the Risks

Before introducing any activity, demonstration, or experiment to the class, analyze it and consider what could possibly go wrong. Carefully review the list of materials to make sure they are safe. Inspect the equipment in your lab or classroom to make sure it is in good working order. Read the procedures to make sure they are safe. Record any hazards or concerns you identify.

2. Evaluate the Risks

Minimize the risks you identified in the last step without sacrificing learning. Remember that no activity you perform in the lab or classroom is worth risking injury. Thus, extremely hazardous activities, or those that violate your school's policies, must be eliminated. For activities that present smaller risks, analyze each risk carefully to determine its likelihood. If the pedagogical value of the activity does not outweigh the risks, the activity must be eliminated.

3. Select Controls to Address Risks

Even low-risk activities require controls to eliminate or minimize the risks. Make sure that in devising controls you do not substitute an equally or more hazardous alternative. Some control methods include the following:

- Explicit verbal and written warnings may be added or posted.

- Equipment may be rebuilt or relocated, parts may be replaced, or equipment be replaced entirely by safer alternatives.

- Risky procedures may be eliminated.

- Activities may be changed from student activities to teacher demonstrations.

4. Implement and Review Selected Controls

Controls do not help if they are forgotten or not enforced. The implementation and review of controls should be as systematic and thorough as the initial analysis of safety concerns in the lab and laboratory activities.

SAFETY WITH ANIMALS

It is recommended that teachers follow the NABT Position Statement "The Use of Animals in Biology Education" issued by the National Association of Biology Teachers (available at www.nabt.org).

SAFETY IN HANDLING PRESERVED MATERIALS

The following practices are recommended when handling or dissecting any preserved specimen:

1. NEVER dissect road-kills or nonpreserved slaughterhouse materials.

2. Wear protective gloves and splash-proof safety goggles at all times when handling preserving fluids and preserved specimens and during dissection.

3. Wear lab aprons. Use of an old shirt or smock under the lab apron is recommended.

4. Conduct dissection activities in a well-ventilated area.

5. Do not allow preservation or body-cavity fluids to contact skin. Fixatives do not distinguish between living or dead tissues. Biological supply firms use formalin-based fixatives of varying concentrations to initially fix zoological and botanical specimens. WARD'S Natural Science Establishment provides specimens that are freezedried and rehydrated in a 10% isopropyl alcohol solution. In these specimens, no other hazardous chemical is present. Many suppliers provide fixed botanical materials in 50% glycerin.

REDUCTION OF FREE FORMALDEHYDE

Currently, federal regulations mandate a permissible exposure level of 0.75 ppm for formaldehyde. Contact your supplier for an MSDS that details the amount of formaldehyde present as well as gas-emitting characteristics for individual specimens. Prewash specimens (in a loosely covered container) in running tap water for 1–4 hours to dilute the fixative. Formaldehyde may also be chemically bound (thereby reducing danger) by immersing washed specimens in a 0.5–1.0% potassium bisulfate solution overnight or by placing them in 1% phenoxyethanol holding solutions.

SAFETY WITH MICROBES

Pathogenic (disease-causing) microorganisms are not appropriate investigational tools in the high school laboratory and should never be used.

SAFETY WITH CHEMICALS

Label student reagent containers with the substance's name and hazard class(es) (flammable, reactive, etc.). Dispose of hazardous waste chemicals according to federal, state, and local regulations. Refer to the Material Safety Data Sheet for recommended disposal procedures.

Remove all sources of flames, sparks, and heat from the laboratory when any flammable material is being used.

MATERIAL SAFETY DATA SHEETS

The purpose of a Material Safety Data Sheet (MSDS) is to provide readily accessible information on chemical substances commonly used in the science laboratory or in industry.

The MSDS should be kept on file and referred to BEFORE handling ANY chemical. The MSDS can also be used to instruct students on chemical hazards, to evaluate spill and disposal procedures, and to warn of incompatibility with other chemicals or mixtures.

STORING CHEMICALS

Never store chemicals alphabetically, as this greatly increases the risk of promoting a violent reaction.

Storage Suggestions

1. Always lock the storeroom and all its cabinets when not in use.
2. Students should not be allowed in the storeroom and preparation area.
3. Avoid storing chemicals on the floor of the storeroom.
4. Do not store chemicals above eye level or on the top shelf in the storeroom.
5. Be sure shelf assemblies are firmly secured to the walls.
6. Provide anti-roll lips on all shelves.
7. Shelving should be constructed out of wood. Metal cabinets and shelves are easily corroded.
8. Avoid metal, adjustable shelf supports and clips. They can corrode, causing shelves to collapse.
9. Acids, flammables, poisons, and oxidizers should each be stored in their own locking storage cabinet.

PERSONAL PROTECTIVE EQUIPMENT

Chemical goggles (Meeting ANSI Standard Z87.1)
These should be worn with any chemical or chemical solution other than water, when heating substances, using any mechanical device, or observing physical processes that could eject an object.

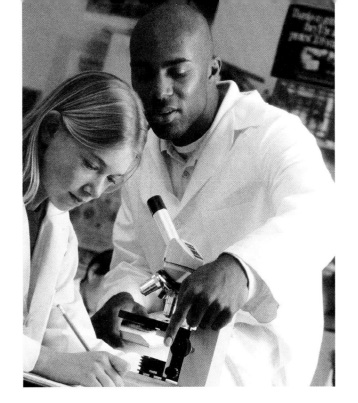

Face shield (Meeting ANSI Standard Z87.1)
Use in combination with eye goggles when working with corrosives.

Contact lenses The wearing of contact lenses for cosmetic reasons should be prohibited in the laboratory. If a student must wear contact lenses prescribed by a physician, that student should be instructed to wear eye-cup safety goggles meeting ANSI Standard Z87.1 (similar to swimmer's cup goggles.)

Eye-wash station The device must be capable of delivering a copious, gentle flow of water to both eyes for at least 15 minutes. Portable liquid supply devices are not satisfactory and should not be used. A plumbed-in fixture or a perforated spray head on the end of a hose attached to a plumbed-in outlet is suitable if it is designed for use as an eye-wash fountain and meets ANSI Standard Z358.1. It must be within a 30-second walking distance from any spot in the room.

Safety shower (Meeting ANSI Standard Z358.1)
Location should be within a 30-second walking distance from any spot in the room. Students should be instructed in the use of the safety shower in the event of a fire or chemical splash on their body that cannot simply be washed off.

Gloves Polyethylene, neoprene rubber, or disposable plastic may be used. Nitrile or butyl rubber gloves are recommended when handling corrosives.

Apron Rubber-coated cloth or vinyl (nylon-coated) halter is recommended.

Some Safety Risks and Preventive Controls

The following list describes several possible safety hazards and controls that can be implemented to resolve them. This list is not complete, but it can be used as a starting point to identify hazards in your laboratory.

Identified risk	Preventive control
Facilities and Equipment	
Lab tables are in disrepair, room is poorly lighted and ventilated, faucets and electrical outlets do not work or are difficult to use because of their location.	Work surfaces should be level and stable. There should be adequate lighting and ventilation. Water supplies, drains, and electrical outlets should be in good working order. Any equipment in a dangerous location should not be used; it should be relocated or rendered inoperable.
Wiring, plumbing, and air circulation systems do not work or do not meet current specifications.	Specifications should be kept on file. Conduct a periodic review of all equipment, and document compliance. Damaged fixtures must be labeled as such and must be repaired as soon as possible.
Eyewash fountains and safety showers are present, but no one knows anything about their specifications.	Ensure that eyewash fountains and safety showers meet the requirements of the ANSI standard (Z358.1).
Eyewash fountains are checked and cleaned once at the beginning of each school year. No records are kept of routine checks and maintenance on the safety showers and eyewash fountains.	Flush eyewash fountains for 5 minutes every month to remove any bacteria or other organisms from pipes. Test safety showers (measure flow in gallons per min) and eyewash fountains every 6 months and keep records of the test results.
Labs are conducted in multipurpose rooms, and equipment from other courses remains accessible.	Only the items necessary for a given activity should be available to students. All equipment should be locked away when not in use.
Students are permitted to enter or work in the lab without teacher supervision.	Lock all laboratory rooms whenever a teacher is not present. Supervising teachers must be trained in lab safety and emergency procedures.
Safety equipment and emergency procedures	
Fire and other emergency drills are infrequent, and no records or measurements are made of the results of the drills.	Always carry out critical reviews of fire or other emergency drills. Be sure that plans include alternate routes. Don't wait until an emergency to find the flaws in your plans.
Emergency evacuation plans do not include instructions for securing the lab in the event of an evacuation during a lab activity.	Plan actions in case of emergency: establish what devices should be turned off, which escape route to use, and where to meet outside the building.
Fire extinguishers are in out-of-the-way locations, not on the escape route.	Place fire extinguishers near escape routes so that they will be of use during an emergency.
Fire extinguishers are not maintained. Teachers are not trained to use them.	Document regular maintenance of fire extinguishers. Train supervisory personnel in the proper use of extinguishers. Instruct students not to use an extinguisher but to call for a teacher.

Identified risk	Preventive control
Teachers in labs and neighboring classrooms are not trained in CPR or first aid.	Teachers should receive training from the local chapter of the the American Red Cross. Certifications should be kept current with frequent refresher courses.
Teachers are not aware of their legal responsibilities in case of an injury or accident.	Review your faculty handbook for your responsibilities regarding safety in the classroom and laboratory. Contact the legal counsel for your school district to find out the extent of their support and any rules, regulations, or procedures you must follow.
Emergency procedures are not posted. Emergency numbers are kept only at the switchboard or main office. Instructions are given verbally only at the beginning of the year.	Emergency procedures should be posted at all exits and near all safety equipment. Emergency numbers should be posted at all phones, and a script should be provided for the caller to use. Emergency procedures must be reviewed periodically, and students should be reminded of them at the beginning of each activity.
Spills are handled on a case-by-case basis and are cleaned up with whatever materials happen to be on hand.	Have the appropriate equipment and materials available for cleaning up; replace them before expiration dates. Make sure students know to alert you to spilled chemicals, blood, and broken glass.

Work habits and environment

Identified risk	Preventive control
Safety wear is only used for activities involving chemicals or hot plates.	Aprons and goggles should be worn in the lab at all times. Long hair, loose clothing, and loose jewelry should be secured.
There is no dress code established for the laboratory; students are allowed to wear sandals or open-toed shoes.	Open-toed shoes should never be worn in the laboratory. Do not allow any footwear in the lab that does not cover feet completely.
Students are required to wear safety gear but teachers and visitors are not.	Always wear safety gear in the lab. Keep extra equipment on hand for visitors.
Safety is emphasized at the beginning of the term but is not mentioned later in the year.	Safety must be the first priority in all lab work. Students should be warned of risks and instructed in emergency procedures for each activity.
There is no assessment of students' knowledge and attitudes regarding safety.	Conduct frequent safety quizzes. Only students with perfect scores should be allowed to work in the lab.
You work alone during your preparation period to organize the day's labs.	Never work alone in a science laboratory or a storage area.
Safety inspections are conducted irregularly and are not documented. Teachers and administrators are unaware of what documentation will be necessary in case of a lawsuit.	Safety reviews should be frequent and regular. All reviews should be documented, and improvements must be implemented immediately. Contact legal counsel for your district to make sure your procedures will protect you in case of a lawsuit.

Purchasing, storing, and using chemicals

Identified risk	Preventive control
The storeroom is too crowded, so you decide to keep some equipment on the lab benches.	Do not store reagents or equipment on lab benches. Keep shelves organized. Never place reactive chemicals (in bottles, beakers, flasks, wash bottles, etc.) near the edges of a lab bench.
You prepare solutions from concentrated stock to save money.	Reduce risks by ordering diluted instead of concentrated substances.

Identified risk	Preventive control
You purchase plenty of chemicals to be sure that you won't run out or to save money. You don't generally read labels on chemicals when preparing solutions for a lab, because you already know about a chemical.	Purchase chemicals in class-size quantities. Do not purchase or have on hand more than one year's supply of each chemical. Read each label to be sure it states the hazards and describes the precautions and first aid procedures (when appropriate) that apply to the contents in case someone else has to deal with that chemical in an emergency.
You never read the Material Safety Data Sheets (MSDSs) that come with your chemicals.	Always read the Material Safety Data Sheet (MSDS) for a chemical before using it. Follow the precautions described in the MSDS. File and organize MSDSs for all chemicals where they can be found easily in case of an emergency.
The main stockroom contains chemicals that haven't been used for years.	Do not leave bottles of chemicals unused on the shelves of the lab for more than one week or unused in the main stockroom for more than one year. Dispose of or use up any leftover chemicals.
No extra precautions are taken when flammable liquids are dispensed from their containers.	When transferring flammable liquids from bulk containers, ground the container; before transferring flammable liquids to a smaller metal container, ground both containers.
Students are told to put their broken glass and solid chemical wastes in the trash can.	Have separate containers for trash, for broken glass, and for different categories of hazardous chemical wastes.
You store chemicals alphabetically instead of by hazard class. Chemicals are stored without consideration of possible emergencies (fire, earthquake, flood, etc.), which could compound the hazard.	Use MSDSs to determine which chemicals are incompatible. Store chemicals, by the hazard class indicated on the MSDS. Store chemicals that are incompatible with common fire-fighting media like water (such as alkali metals) or carbon dioxide (such as alkali and alkaline-earth metals) under conditions that eliminate the possibility of a reaction with water or carbon dioxide if it is necessary to fight a fire in the storage area.
Corrosives are kept above eye level, out of reach from any unauthorized person.	Always store corrosive chemicals on shelves below eye level. Remember, fumes from many corrosives can destroy metal cabinets and shelving.
Chemicals are kept on the stockroom floor on the days that they will be used so that they are easy to find.	Never store chemicals or other materials on floors or in the aisles of the laboratory or storeroom, even for a few minutes.

HOLT NEW YORK BIOLOGY

THE Living Environment

DeSalle • Heithaus

HOLT, RINEHART AND WINSTON

A Harcourt Education Company

Orlando • Austin • New York • San Diego • London

Authors

Robert DeSalle, Ph.D.

is a curator in the Division of Invertebrate Zoology at the American Museum of Natural History in New York City. He is an adjunct professor at Columbia University and City University of New York, and is a Distinguished Research Professor at New York University. His current research focuses on molecular evolution in various organisms, including pathogenic bacteria and insects. He coauthored *Welcome to the Genome: A User's Guide to the Genetic Past, Present, and Future* (Wiley) and *The Science of Jurassic Park and the Lost World* (HarperCollins), and he edited *Epidemic! The World of Infectious Diseases* (W. W. Norton), which are all aimed at nontechnical readers.

Michael R. Heithaus, Ph.D.

is an assistant professor of biological sciences at Florida International University and a former host of National Geographic's *Crittercam* television program. He currently works with the National Geographic Channel to develop programming and educational materials and to give talks to students. His current research centers on predator-prey interactions among marine vertebrates. Mike's research in animal behavior has taken him all over the world to deploy Crittercam on a host of marine and terrestrial animal species, including dolphins, sharks, seals, sea turtles, whales, lions, hyenas, and, most recently, penguins.

Contributing Authors

Linda K. Gaul, Ph.D.
is an epidemiologist at the Texas Department of State Health Services. She conducts surveillance and epidemiological investigations related to infectious diseases. She has taught both biology and epidemiology at the college level.

Shubha Govind, Ph.D.
is a professor of biology at City College, New York. Her current research focuses on the function of proteins as cellular signaling molecules in the immune response and in animal development.

Ann Lumsden, Ph.D.
is a professor of biological science at Florida State University, where she is the coordinator of biology classes for nonmajors. She is a former president of the National Association of Biology Teachers.

Ellen Mandel
is the assistant principal and supervisor for Science at a New York City public high school. She is also a New York Biology Mentor, and an active science administrator in many state organizations.

Alan Seidman
is a teacher of biology, chemistry, and current topics in science at Margaretville Central School in Margaretville, New York. He is also a Fellow of the Science Teachers Association of New York State.

Erika Zavaleta, Ph.D.
is an assistant professor in the environmental-studies department of the University of California, Santa Cruz. Her current research centers on how changes in levels of biodiversity affect society.

New York Teacher Advisory Panel

Marilou Bebak
Science Department Chair;
Biology Teacher; New York State
Regional Biology Mentor
Nardin Academy High School
Buffalo, New York

Stephen M. Berman
Assistant Principal
Bayside High School
Bayside, New York

James M. Buckley, Jr.
Science Instructor
Edwards-Knox Central School
Russell, New York

Linda Rachele Burke, Ph.D.
Teacher
John Jay High School
Cross River, New York

David M. Casamento
Director of Science
North Babylon Union Free
School District
North Babylon, New York

Claudia Waruch Masters
Science Department Chair
Spring Valley High School
Spring Valley, New York

Anthony J. Orapello
Living Environment Teacher
Amsterdam High School
Amsterdam, New York

Robert Raftery
Science Department Chair
Roosevelt High School
Yonkers, New York

Beth Shapiro
Living Environment and Forensic
Science Teacher
Comsewogue High School
Port Jefferson Station, New York

William A. Siebert
Biology Teacher
Arlington High School
Lagrangeville, New York

Joyce G. Valenti
Living Environment Teacher
Windham-Ashland-Central School
Windham, New York

Reading/ESL Consultant

Robin Scarcella, Ph.D.
Director, Academic English and English
as a Second Language Program
University of California, Irvine
Irvine, California

Laboratory Development

Michael A. DiSpezio, MA
Curriculum Specialist and On-Air Host
JASON Project
Cape Cod, Massachusetts

Laboratory Testing

Science Kit, LLC
Tonawanda, New York

Academic Reviewers

Renato J. Aguilera, Ph.D.
Professor of Biology and Director of the
Graduate Program in Biology
The University of Texas at El Paso
Department of Biological Sciences
El Paso, Texas

Michael D. Aldridge, MSN, RN, CCRN, CNS
Assistant Professor of Science
The University of Texas at Austin
School of Nursing
Family Nursing
Austin, Texas

David M. Armstrong, Ph.D.
Professor of Biology
University of Colorado at Boulder
Department of Ecology and
Evolutionary Biology
Boulder, Colorado

Nigel S. Atkinson, Ph.D.
Associate Professor of Neurobiology
The University of Texas at Austin
Department of Neurobiology
Austin, Texas

Lisa M. Baird, Ph.D.
Professor of Biology
University of San Diego
San Diego, California

Sanjoy Chakraborty, Ph.D.
Assistant Professor
New York City College of Technology
Department of Biology
Brooklyn, New York

Tandra R. Chakraborty, Ph.D.
Assistant Professor
Adelphi University
Biology Department
Garden City, New York

James F. Curran, Ph.D.
Professor of Biology
Wake Forest University
Winston-Salem, North Carolina

Gregory Demas, Ph.D.
Assistant Professor
Indiana University
Department of Biology and Center for
the Integrative Study of Animal Behavior
Bloomington, Indiana

William E. Dunscombe
Associate Professor of Biology
Union County College
Biology Department
Cranford, New Jersey

Jordan C. Foster, MD, MS
Assistant Clinical Professor of Medicine
Columbia College of Physicians &
Surgeons
Department of Emergency Medicine
New York, New York

Daniel Garza, MD
Assistant Professor
Stanford University School of Medicine
Orthopaedic Surgery
Palo Alto, California

Herbert Grossman, Ph.D.
Associate Professor of Botany and
Biology
Department of Environmental Sciences
Pennsylvania State University
University Park, Pennsylvania

William B. Guggino, Ph.D.
Professor of Physiology and Director
Johns Hopkins University
School of Medicine
Baltimore, Maryland

Elena L. Keeling, Ph.D.
Assistant Professor of Science
California Polytechnic State University
Biological Sciences
San Luis Obispo, California

Martin K. Nickels, Ph.D.
Professor Emeritus of Anthropology
Illinois State University
Anthropology Program
Normal, Illinois

Eva Oberdörster, Ph.D.
Lecturer
Southern Methodist University
Department of Biology
Dallas, Texas

L. Jeanne Perry, Ph.D.
Director, Protein Expression Technology
Center, Institute for Genomics and
Proteomics, *Associate Adjunct Professor*
University of California, Los Angeles
Department of Molecular, Cell, and
Developmental Biology
Los Angeles, California

Rachael A. Przybyla, MD, FACOG
Associate Medical Director
Texas Medicaid and Healthcare
Partnership
Austin, Texas

Martin G. Ramirez, Ph.D.
Associate Professor and Chair
Loyola Marymount University
Los Angeles, California

Daniel Rozen, Ph.D.
Post-doctoral Fellow
Emory University
Department of Biology
Atlanta, Georgia

Miles R. Silman, Ph.D.
Associate Professor of Biology
Wake Forest University
Biology Department
Winston-Salem, North Carolina

Richard Storey, Ph.D.
Professor of Biology
University of Montana, Western
Dillon, Montana

Sean Veney, Ph.D.
Assistant Professor
Kent State University
Biological Sciences
Kent, Ohio

Teacher Reviewers

Robert S. Akeson
Biology Teacher
Boston Latin School
Boston, Massachusetts

Janet B. Barnett
Biology Teacher
Columbus North High School
Columbus, Indiana

Bob Baronak
Biology Teacher
Donegal High School
Mount Joy, Pennsylvania

Ellen Feuerman Cohen
Science Department Chair
Marjory Stoneman Douglas High School
Parkland, Florida

Jacqueline B. Curley
Teacher
Academy of Science
Loudoun County Public Schools
Sterling, Virginia

Martha M. Day, Ed.D.
Science Department Chairperson
Whites Creek High School
Nashville, Tennessee

Alan Eagy
Biology Teacher
The Dalles Wahtonka High School
The Dalles, Oregon

Benjamin D. Ebersole
Biology and Chemistry Teacher
Donegal High School
Mount Joy, Pennsylvania

Yolanda Michelle Harman
Biology Teacher; Science Chairperson
Northern Garrett High School
Accident, Maryland

Jason Hook
7th Grade Science Teacher
Kealing Middle School
Austin, Texas

Nancy Kossover
Biology Teacher
Leadership High School – Hayward
Hayward, California

Andrew M. Larson
Biology Teacher
Columbus North High School
Columbus, Indiana

Tammie Niffenegger
Science Chair and Teacher
Port Washington High School
Port Washington, Wisconsin

Amy K. Ragan
Biology Teacher
Cedar Park High School
Austin, Texas

Tami Reardon
Biology Teacher
Columbus North High School
Columbus, Indiana

Dale Simon
Biology Teacher
Central High School
Camp Point, Illinois

Bert Wartski
Biology and AP Biology Teacher
Chapel Hill High School
Chapel Hill, North Carolina

Tyson Yager
Biology Teacher
Wichita High School East
Wichita, Kansas

Kathy A. Yorks
Anatomy and Physiology Teacher
Central Mountain High School
Mill Hall, Pennsylvania

Patricia Arnett Zeck, MA
Biology Teacher and Science Department
Facilitator
Northwestern High School
Kokomo, Indiana

Contents in Brief

Safety in the Laboratory xx
How to Use Your Textbook xxiv

Unit 1 Introduction 2
Chapter 1 Biology and You 4
Chapter 2 Applications of Biology 26
Chapter 3 Chemistry of Life 48

Unit 2 Ecology 74
Chapter 4 Ecosystems 76
Chapter 5 Populations and Communities 100
Chapter 6 The Environment 122

Unit 3 Cells 146
Chapter 7 Cell Structure 148
Chapter 8 Cells and Their Environment 172
Chapter 9 Photosynthesis and Cellular
           Respiration 194
Chapter 10 Cell Growth and Division 220

Unit 4 Heredity 242
Chapter 11 Meiosis and Sexual Reproduction 244
Chapter 12 Mendel and Heredity 264
Chapter 13 DNA, RNA, and Proteins 290
Chapter 14 Genes in Action 316
Chapter 15 Gene Technologies and
            Human Applications 342

Unit 5 Evolution 370
Chapter 16 Evolutionary Theory 372
Chapter 17 Population Genetics
            and Speciation 396
Chapter 18 Classification 420
Chapter 19 History of Life on Earth 444

Unit 6 Humans 466
Chapter 20 Homeostasis and Human
            Body Systems 468
Chapter 21 Homeostasis and Human Disease 496
Chapter 22 The Body's Defenses 522
Chapter 23 Reproduction and Development 546

Appendix 570
Reading Toolbox 572
Skills Appendix 578
Reference 590
Answers to Reading Checks 594
Glossary 599
Index 630

Contents

Safety in the Laboratory .... **xx**

How to Use You Textbooks .... **xxiv**

UNIT 1 Introduction   2

Chapter 1 Biology and You **4**

Section 1 The Nature of Science **7**

Section 2 Scientific Methods **10**

Section 3 Tools and Techniques **14**

Section 4 What is Biology? **17**

Regents Exam Practice **23**

Why It Matters Biology in the Wild 18

Labs Make a Prediction 5

Evaluate a Scientific Claim 9

The pH of Common Substances 11

Practice Staining Techniques 15

SI Units 20

Chapter 2 Applications of Biology **26**

Section 1 Health in the 21st Century **29**

Section 2 Biology, Technology, and Society **33**

Section 3 Biology and the Environment **38**

Regents Exam Practice **45**

Why It Matters Bio Bots 41

Labs Artificial Shark Skin 27

Model a Low-Tech Solution 31

Biomimetic Engineering 34

Microbe Growth 42

Chapter 3 Chemistry of Life **48**

Section 1 Matter and Substances **51**

Section 2 Water and Solutions **55**

Section 3 Carbon Compounds **59**

Section 4 Energy and Metabolism **64**

Regents Exam Practice **71**

Why It Matters Water Wonders 58

Labs Yeast Activity 49

Atom Models 53

Telltale Cabbage 57

Brown Paper Test 61

Enzymes in Detergents 68

Chapter 4 Ecosystems 76

Section 1 What Is an Ecosystem? 79
Section 2 Energy Flow in Ecosytems 86
Section 3 Cycling of Matter 90
Regents Exam Practice 97

Why It Matters Maintained by Fire 85

Labs Water Cycle 77
Biodiversity Evaluation 80
The Carbon Cycle 93
Ecosystem Change 94

Math Skills Energy Pyramid 88

Chapter 5 Populations and Communities 100

Section 1 Populations 103
Section 2 Interactions in Communities 109
Section 3 Shaping Communities 112
Regents Exam Practice 119

Why It Matters Growth in Asia 108

Labs Population Size 101
Population Growth 105
The Effects of Herbivores on a Plant Species 110
Changes in a Realized Niche 113
Yeast Population Growth 116

Chapter 6 The Environment 122

Section 1 An Interconnected Planet 125
Section 2 Environmental Issues 128
Section 3 Environmental Solutions 134
Regents Exam Practice 143

Why It Matters Cars of the Future 139

Labs The Greenhouse Effect 123
Contaminated Water 127
Soil Erosion 131
Recycled Paper 135
Effects of Acid Rain on Seeds 140

Chapter 7 Cell Structure 148

Section 1 Introduction to Cells 151
Section 2 Inside the Eukaryotic Cell 156
Section 3 From Cell to Organism 162
Regents Exam Practice 169

Why It Matters Cell Shape 152

Labs Is It Alive? 149
Cell Parts Model 160
Colonies on the Move 165
Plant Cell Observation 167

Math Skills Ratio of Surface Area and Volume 153

Chapter 8 Cells and Their Environment 172

Section 1 Cell Membrane 175
Section 2 Cell Transport 178
Section 3 Cell Communication 184
Regents Exam Practice 191

Why It Matters Heady Effects 187

Labs Salty Cells 173
Osmosis 181
Sensitive Plants 185
Cell Size and Diffusion 188

Chapter 9 Photosynthesis and Cellular Respiration 194

Section 1 Energy in Living Systems 197
Section 2 Photosynthesis 202
Section 3 Cellular Respiration 208
Regents Exam Practice 217

Why It Matters Life in a Biosphere 214

Labs Stored Energy 195
Product of Photosynthesis 198
Photosynthetic Rate 205
Cellular Respiration 215

Chapter 10 Cell Growth and Division 220

Section 1 Cell Reproduction 223
Section 2 Mitosis 228
Section 3 Regulation 233
Regents Exam Practice 239

Why It Matters Replacement Parts 227

Labs Whitefish Cells 221
Chromosome Package 224
Number of Cells Resulting from Mitosis 229
UV and Sunblock 234
Mitosis in Plant Cells 236

Chapter 11 Meiosis and Sexual Reproduction 244

Section 1 Reproduction 247
Section 2 Meiosis 250
Section 3 Multicellular Life Cycles 256
Regents Exam Practice 261

Why It Matters Girls, Girls, Girls 255

Labs Pollen Up-Close 245
Crossing-Over Model 253
Chromosome Combinations 257
Meiosis Model 259

Chapter 12 Mendel and Heredity 264

Section 1 Origins of Hereditary Science 267
Section 2 Mendel's Theory 272
Section 3 Modeling Mendel's Laws 276
Section 4 Beyond Mendelian Heredity 282
Regents Exam Practice 287

Why It Matters Amazing Mutants 271

Labs What Are the Chances? 265
Mendel's Ratios 270
Dominant and Recessive Traits 273
Testcross 277
Probabilities 278
Pedigree Analysis 281
Plant Genetics 285

Math Skills Probability of Two Independant Events 279

Chapter 13 DNA, RNA, and Proteins 290

Section 1 The Structure of DNA 293
Section 2 Replication of DNA 300
Section 3 RNA and Gene Expression 304
Regents Exam Practice 313

Labs Code Combinations 291
DNA's Structure 297
DNA Replication Rate 303
Genetic Code of Keratin 310
DNA Extraction from Wheat Germ 311

Chapter 14 Genes in Action 316

Section 1 Mutation and Genetic Change 319
Section 2 Regulating Gene Expression 325
Section 3 Genome Interactions 330
Regents Exam Practice 339

Why It Matters Forensic Genealogy 335

Labs Where Is the Protein? 317
Make a Model of Mutations 321
A Model of Introns and Exons 328
Protein Detection 336

Chapter 15 Gene Technologies and Human Applications 342

Section 1 The Human Genome 345
Section 2 Gene Technologies in Our Lives 350
Section 3 Gene Technologies in Detail 355
Regents Exam Practice 367

Why It Matters Cleanup Microbes 349

Labs Code Comparison 343
Forensic DNA Fingerprints 347
Gel Electrophoresis Model 356
DNA Fingerprint Analysis 364

Chapter 16 Evolutionary Theory 372

Section 1 Developing a Theory 375
Section 2 Applying Darwin's Ideas 380
Section 3 Beyond Darwinian Theory 386
Regents Exam Practice 393

Why It Matters Breeding 377

Labs Scientific Inference 373
Two Kinds of Growth 378
Selection Model 387
Natural Selection Simulation 390

Chapter 17 Population Genetics and Speciation 396

Section 1 Genetic Variation 399
Section 2 Genetic Change 404
Section 3 Speciation 411
Regents Exam Practice 417

Why It Matters Wild Laboratories 410

Labs Normal Variation 397
Alleles: The Next Generation 403
Genetic Risk Assessment 407
Genetic Drift 415

Math Skills Histograms and Distributions 401
Hardy-Weinberg Equation 405

Chapter 18 Classification 420

Section 1 The Importance of Classification 423
Section 2 Modern Systematics 427
Section 3 Kingdoms and Domains 433
Regents Exam Practice 441

Why It Matters New Species 432

Labs What's Your System? 421
Cladogram Construction 430
Field Guides 435
Dichotomous Keys 438

Chapter 19 History of Life on Earth 444

Section 1 How Did Life Begin? 447
Section 2 The Age of Earth 450
Section 3 Evolution of Life 454
Regents Exam Practice 463

Why It Matters Nearing the End 459

Labs Logical Order 445
Radioactive Decay 452
Timeline of Earth 457
Model of Rock Strata 461

Chapter 20   Homeostasis and Human Body Systems 468

Section 1 Homeostasis 471
Section 2 Human Body Systems 476
Section 3 Feedback Mechanisms 484
Regents Exam Practice 493

Why It Matters Diabetes 489

Labs Blood Pressure and Homeostasis 469
Investigation of Homeostasis 475
Filtration Rate in the Kidney 481
Blood pH Homeostasis 487
Epinephrine and Heart Rate 490

Chapter 21   Homeostasis and Human Diseases 496

Section 1 Disease 499
Section 2 Infectious Disease 502
Section 3 Noninfectious Disease 510
Regents Exam Practice 519

Why It Matters Protist Plague 509

Labs Cigarette Smoke and Disease 497
Emergence of Bird Flu 504
The Nutrition Facts Label 514
Tobacco Mosaic Virus 516

Chapter 22   The Body's Defenses 522

     Section 1 Protecting Against Disease 525
     Section 2 Eliminating Invaders 529
     Section 3 Immune System Disfunctions 534
     Regents Exam Practice 543

        Why It Matters Allergies & Culture 536

        Labs Barrier Breaking 523
             Antigen Binding 528
             The Eradication of Polio 533
             Constricted Airways 535
             Disease Transmission Model 540

Chapter 23   Reproduction and Development 546

     Section 1 The Male Reproductive System 549
     Section 2 The Female Reproductive System 552
     Section 3 Human Development 557
     Section 4 Sexually Transmitted Infections 561
     Regents Exam Practice 567

        Why It Matters Seeing Double 564

        Labs A Closer Look at Gametes 547
             Hormone Secretions 556
             An Amniotic Shock Absorber 559
             STI Rates 562
             Sonography 565

Appendix 570
Glossary 599
Index 630

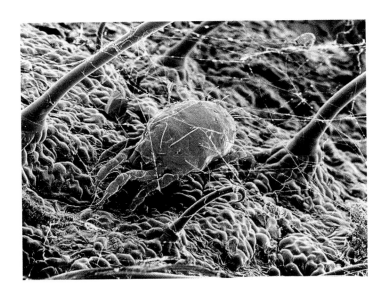

Why It Matters

Have you ever wondered why you should care about learning biology? These short articles show how science relates to your everyday life and to what you might do in the future.

Real World

Biology in the Wild	18
Maintained by Fire	85
Growth in Asia	108
Breeding	377
Wild Laboratories	410
New Species	432
Diabetes	489
Protist Plague	509
Allergies & Culture	536
Seeing Double	564

Biotechnology

Bio Bots	41
Life in a Biosphere	214
Forensic Genealogy	335
Cleanup Microbes	349

Weird Science

Water Wonders	58
Cars of the Future	139
Cell Shape	152
Heady Effects	187
Replacement Parts	227
Girls, Girls, Girls	255
Amazing Mutants	271
Nearing the End	458

READING TOOLBOX

The tools we show you in the Reading Toolbox can be used throughout to help you remember what you read and to mentally organize the concepts. Find the ones that work best for you.

Analogies	266, 344, 470
Cause and Effect	222
Classification	498
Comparisons	246
Comparison Table	50, 318
Describing Space	196
Describing Time	292, 446
Everyday Words in Science	6, 50, 398
Finding Examples	174, 318
Four-Corner Fold	174
General Statements	398
Hypothesis, or Theory?	6, 124, 374
Idea Wheel	6
Key Term Fold	196, 246, 374, 498
Layered Book	78
Mnemonics	422, 524
Outlining	398, 470
Pattern Puzzles	196, 222, 344, 524
Phylogenetic Tree	422
Predictions	28, 102
Prefixes	318
Process Chart	150, 446
Punnet Squares	266
Pyramid	548
Quantifiers	50
Recognizing Main Ideas	548
Similes	150
Summarizing Ideas	374
Three-Panel Flip Chart	28, 292
Two-Column Notes	246, 498
Venn Diagrams	102, 124
Word Families	78, 548
Word Origins	102, 422, 470
Word Parts	28, 124, 150, 174, 222, 292, 344, 446, 524
Word Problems	78

Interactive Art

Many illustrations in the textbook are more easily understood by watching them move and react to you in an online animation. These will be marked by the Interact Online logo and a keyword to use.

Common SI Units 14

Ionic Bonding in Salt 53

Enzyme Action 67

Water Cycle 90

Exponential Growth 104

Water Pollution 130

Making and Exporting Proteins 159

Facilitated Diffusion 179

Sodium-Potassium Pump 182

Photosynthesis and Cellular Respiration 199

Electron Transport Chains of Photosynthesis 204

Calvin Cycle 206

Glycolysis 209

Electron Transport Chain 211

Stages of Mitosis 230

Stages of Meiosis I 250

Three Steps of Mendel's First Experiment 269

Hershey-Chase Experiment 295

DNA Replication 301

Transcription 306

Translation 308

Kinds of Mutations 320

Chain Termination Sequencing 359

Recombinant Cloning 360

The Theory of Evolution by Natural Selection 381

Population Size and Genetic Drift 406

Tree of Life 436

Endosymbiotic Theory 456

Respiratory and Circulatory Systems 482

Inflammation 526

Facilitated Diffusion

Keyword: HX8CENF6

❶ A molecule outside the cell binds to a carrier protein on the cell membrane.

❷ The carrier protein changes shape, which releases the molecule inside the cell.

Outside of cell

Carrier protein

Inside of cell

Outside of cell

Inside of cell

Quick Labs

These short labs are designed to be done quickly during any class period with easy-to-find materials.

Inquiry

Make a Prediction 5
Artificial Shark Skin 27
Yeast Activity 49
Water Cycle 77
Population Size 101
The Greenhouse Effect 123
Is It Alive? 149
Salty Cells 173
Stored Energy 195
Whitefish Cells 221
Pollen Up Close 245
What Are the Chances? 265
Code Combinations 291
Where Is the Protein? 317
Code Comparison 343
Scientific Inference 373
Normal Variation 397
What's Your System? 421
Logical Order 445
Blood Pressure and
  Homeostasis 469
Cigarette Smoke and
  Disease 497
Barrier Breaking 523
A Closer Look at Gametes 547

Hands-On

The pH of Common
  Substances 11
Practice Staining Techniques 15
Model a Low-Tech Solution 31
Biomimetic Engineering 34
Atom Models 53
Telltale Cabbage 57
Brown Paper Test 61
Biodiversity Evaluation 80
The Carbon Cycle 93
Contaminated Water 127
Soil Erosion 131
Recycled Paper 135
Cell Parts Model 160
Colonies on the Move 165
Osmosis 181
Sensitive Plants 185
Product of Photosynthesis 198
Chromosome Package 224
UV and Sunblock 234
Crossing-Over Model 253
DNA's Structure 297
Make a Model of Mutations 321
A Model of Introns
  and Exons 328

Gel Electrophoresis Model 356
Two Kinds of Growth 378
Selection Model 387
Alleles: The Next Generation ... 403
Field Guides 435
Radioactive Decay 452
Timeline of Earth 457
Investigation of Homeostasis .. 475
Blood pH Homeostasis 487
Antigen Binding 528
Constricted Airways 535
An Amniotic Shock Absorber 559

Chapter Labs

Each chapter includes an in-depth, hands-on lab that lets you see how science is really done. You'll learn the scientific method in practice, as well as fundamental experimental skills.

Data

Evaluate a Scientific Claim 9
Population Growth 105
The Effects of Herbivores
    on a Plant Species 110
Changes in a Realized Niche ... 113
Photosynthetic Rate 205
Number of Cells Resulting
    from Mitosis 229
Chromosome Combinations 257
Mendel's Ratios 270
Dominant and Recessive
    Traits 273
Testcross 277
Probabilities 278
Pedigree Analysis 281
DNA Replication Rate 303
Genetic Code of Keratin 310
Forensic DNA Fingerprints 347
Genetic Risk Assessment 407
Cladogram Construction 430
Filtration Rate in the Kidney 481
Emergence of Bird Flu 504
The Nutrition Facts Label 514
The Eradication of Polio 533
Hormone Secretions 556
STI Rates 562

Skills Practice

SI Units 20
Microbe Growth 42
Yeast Population Growth 116
Cellular Respiration 215
Mitosis in Plant Cells 236
Meiosis Model 259
DNA Extraction from
    Wheat Germ 311
Protein Detection 336
DNA Fingerprint Analysis 364
Natural Selection Simulation 390
Dichotomous Keys 438
Model of Rock Strata 461
Tobacco Mosaic virus 516
Disease Transmission Model ... 540

Inquiry

Enzymes in Detergents 68
Ecosystem Change 94
Effects of Acid Rain
    on Seeds 140
Plant Cell Observation 167
Cell Size and Diffusion 188
Plant Genetics 285
Genetic Drift 415
Epinephrine and Heart Rate 490
Sonography 565

Lab Safety

In the laboratory or in the field, you can engage in hands-on explorations, test your scientific hypotheses, and build practical lab skills. However, while you are working, it is your responsibility to protect yourself and your classmates by conducting yourself in a safe manner. You will avoid accidents by following directions, handling materials carefully, and taking your work seriously. Read the following safety guidelines before working in the lab or field. Make sure that you understand all safety guidelines before entering the lab or field.

Before You Begin

- **Read the entire activity before entering the lab.** Be familiar with the instructions before beginning an activity. Do not start an activity until you have asked your teacher to explain any parts of the activity that you do not understand.

- **Student-designed procedures or inquiry activities must be approved by your teacher before you attempt the procedures or activities.**

- **Wear the right clothing for lab work.** Before beginning work, tie back long hair, roll up loose sleeves, and put on any required personal protective equipment as directed by your teacher. Remove all jewelry, and confine all clothing that could knock things over, catch on fire, contact electrical connections, or absorb chemical solutions. Wear pants rather than shorts or skirts. Protect your feet from chemical spills and falling objects. Do not wear open-toed shoes, sandals, or canvas shoes in the lab. In addition, chemical fumes may react with and ruin some jewelry, such as pearl jewelry. Do not apply cosmetics in the lab. Some hair care products and nail polish are highly flammable.

- **Do not wear contact lenses in the lab.** Even though you will be wearing safety goggles, chemicals could get between contact lenses and your eyes and could cause irreparable eye damage. If your doctor requires that you wear contact lenses instead of glasses, then you should wear eye-cup safety goggles—similar to goggles worn for underwater swimming—in the lab. Ask your doctor or your teacher how to use eye-cup safety goggles to protect your eyes.

- **Know the location of all safety and emergency equipment used in the lab.** Know proper fire-drill procedures and the location of all fire exits. Ask your teacher where the nearest eyewash stations, safety blankets, safety shower, fire extinguisher, first-aid kit, and chemical spill kit are located. Be sure that you know how to operate the equipment safely.

While You Are Working

- **Always wear a lab apron and safety goggles.** Wear these items while in the lab, even if you are not working on an activity. Labs contain chemicals that can damage your clothing, skin, and eyes. Aprons and goggles also protect against many physical hazards. If your safety goggles cloud up or are uncomfortable, ask your teacher for help. Lengthening the strap slightly, washing the goggles with soap and warm water, or using an anti-fog spray may help the problem.

- **NEVER work alone in the lab.** Work in the lab only when supervised by your teacher.

- **NEVER leave equipment unattended while it is in operation.**

- **Perform only activities specifically assigned by your teacher.** Do not attempt any procedure without your teacher's direction. Use only materials and equipment listed in the activity or authorized by your teacher. Steps in a procedure should be performed only as described in the activity or as approved by your teacher.

- **Keep your work area neat and uncluttered.** Have only books and other materials that are needed to conduct the activity in the lab. Keep backpacks, purses, and other items in your desk, your locker, or other designated storage areas.

- **Always heed safety symbols and cautions listed in activities, listed on handouts, posted in the room, provided on equipment or chemical labels (whether provided by the manufacturer or added later), and given verbally by your teacher.** Be aware of the potential hazards of the required materials and procedures, and follow all precautions indicated.

- **Be alert, and walk with care in the lab.** Be aware of others near you and your equipment, and be aware of what they are doing.

- **Do not take food, drinks, chewing gum, or tobacco products into the lab.** Do not store or eat food in the lab. Either finish these items or discard them before coming into the lab or beginning work in the field.

- **NEVER taste chemicals or allow them to contact your skin.** Keep your hands away from your face and mouth, even if you are wearing gloves. Only smell vapors as instructed by your teacher and only in the manner indicated.

- **Exercise caution when working with electrical equipment.** Do not use electrical equipment with frayed or twisted wires. Check that insulation on wiring is intact. Be sure that your hands are dry before using electrical equipment. Do not let electrical cords dangle from work stations. Dangling cords can catch on apparatus on tables, can cause you to trip, and can cause an electric shock. The area under and around electrical equipment should be dry; cords should not lie in puddles of spilled liquid, under sink spigots, or in sinks themselves.

- **Use extreme caution when working with hot plates and other heating devices.** Keep your head, hands, hair, and clothing away from the flame or heating area. Never leave a heating device unattended when it is in use. Metal, ceramic, and glass items do not necessarily look hot when they are hot. Allow all items to cool before storing them.

- **Guard against complacency.** Remember that it is human nature to become careless when doing routine things. As you become familiar with apparatus and procedures, remain alert and pay attention.

- **Do not fool around in the lab.** Take your lab work seriously, and behave appropriately in the lab. Lab equipment and apparatus are not toys; never use lab time or equipment for anything other than the intended purpose. Be considerate and be aware of the safety of your classmates as well as your safety at all times.

Emergency Procedures

- **Follow standard fire-safety procedures.** If your clothing catches on fire, do not run; WALK to the safety shower, stand under it, and turn it on. While doing so, call to your teacher.

- **Report any accident, incident, or hazard—no matter how trivial—to your teacher immediately.** Any incident involving bleeding, burns, fainting, nausea, dizziness, chemical exposure, or ingestion should also be reported immediately to the school nurse or to a physician. If you have a close call, tell your teacher so that you and your teacher can find a way to prevent it from happening again.

- **Report all spills to your teacher immediately.** Call your teacher rather than trying to clean a spill yourself. Your teacher will tell you whether it is safe for you to clean up the spill; if it is not safe, your teacher will know how to clean up the spill.

- **If you spill a chemical on your skin, wash the chemical off in the sink and call your teacher.** If you spill a solid chemical onto your clothing, using an appropriate container, brush it off carefully without scattering it onto somebody else and call your teacher. If you spill corrosive substances on your skin or clothing, use the safety shower or a faucet to rinse. Remove affected clothing while you are under the shower, and call to your teacher. (It may be temporarily embarrassing to remove clothing in front of your classmates, but failure to thoroughly rinse a chemical off your skin could result in permanent damage.)

- **If you get a chemical in your eyes, walk immediately to the eyewash station, turn it on, and lower your head so that your eyes are in the running water.** Hold your eyelids open with your thumbs and fingers, and roll your eyeballs around. You have to flush your eyes continuously for at least 15 minutes. Call your teacher while you are flushing your eyes.

When You Are Finished

- **Clean your work area at the conclusion of each lab period as directed by your teacher.** Broken glass, chemicals, and other waste products should be disposed of in separate, special containers. Dispose of waste materials as directed by your teacher. Put away all material and equipment according to your teacher's instructions. Report any damaged or missing equipment or materials to your teacher.

- **Even if you wore gloves, wash your hands with soap and hot water after each lab period.** To avoid contamination, wash your hands at the conclusion of each lab period and before you leave the lab.

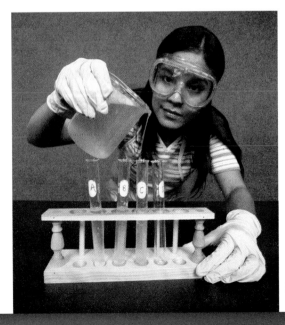

Safety Symbols

Before you begin working on an activity, familiarize yourself with the following safety symbols, which are used throughout your textbook, and the guidelines that you should follow when you see these symbols.

 ## Eye Protection

- **Wear approved safety goggles as directed.** Safety goggles should be worn in the lab at all times, especially when you are working with a chemical or solution, a heat source, or a mechanical device.

- **If chemicals get into your eyes, flush your eyes immediately.** Go to an eyewash station immediately, and flush your eyes (including under the eyelids) with running water for at least 15 minutes. Use your thumb and fingers to hold your eyelids open, and roll your eyeballs around. While doing so, call your teacher or ask another student to notify your teacher.

- **Do not wear contact lenses in the lab.** Chemicals can be drawn up under a contact lens and into the eye. If you must wear contacts prescribed by a physician, tell your teacher. In this case, you must also wear approved eye-cup safety goggles.

- **Do not look directly at the sun or any intense light source or laser.** Do not reflect direct sunlight to illuminate a microscope. Such action concentrates light rays to an intensity that can severely burn your retinas and cause blindness.

 ## Clothing Protection

- **Wear an apron or lab coat at all times in the lab to prevent chemicals or chemical solutions from contacting skin or clothes.**

- **Tie back long hair, secure loose clothing, and remove loose jewelry so that they do not knock over equipment or come into contact with hazardous materials or electrical connections.**

- **Do not wear open-toed shoes, sandals, or canvas shoes in the lab.** Splashed chemicals directly contact skin or quickly soak through canvas. Hard shoes will not allow chemicals to soak through as quickly, and they provide more protection against dropped or falling objects.

 ## Hand Safety

- **Wear appropriate protective gloves when working with a heat source, chemicals, solutions, or wild or unknown plants.** Your teacher will provide the type of gloves necessary for a given activity.

 ## Sharp-Object Safety

- **Use extreme care when handling all sharp and pointed instruments, such as scalpels, sharp probes, and knives.**

- **Do not cut an object while holding the object in your hand.** Cut objects on a suitable work surface. Always cut in a direction away from your body.

- **Do not use double-edged razor blades in the lab.**

 ## Glassware Safety

- **Inspect glassware before use; do not use chipped or cracked glassware.** Use heat-resistant glassware for heating materials or storing hot liquids, and use appropriate tongs or a heat-resistant mitt to handle this equipment.

- **Notify your teacher immediately if a piece of glassware or a light bulb breaks.** Do not attempt to clean up broken glass or remove broken bulbs unless your teacher directs you to do so.

 ## Chemical Safety

- **Always wear safety goggles, gloves, and a lab apron or coat to protect your eyes and skin when you are working with any chemical or chemical solution.**

- **Do not taste, touch, or smell any chemicals or bring them close to your eyes unless specifically instructed to do so by your teacher.**

- **Know where the emergency lab shower and eyewash stations are and how to use them.** If you get a chemical on your skin or clothing, wash it off while calling to your teacher.

- **Handle chemicals or chemical solutions with care.** Check the labels on bottles, and observe safety procedures. Label beakers, flasks, test tubes, or other temporary storage vessels containing chemicals.

- **For all chemicals, take only what you need.** Do not return unused chemicals or solutions to their original containers.

- **NEVER take any chemicals out of the lab.**

- **Do not mix any chemicals unless specifically instructed to do so by your teacher.** Check the labels to make sure that you picked up the correct chemicals before you mix the chemicals. Otherwise harmless chemicals can be poisonous or explosive if combined.

- **Report all spills to your teacher immediately.** Clean up spills promptly as directed by your teacher.

 ## Electrical Safety

- **Do not use equipment with frayed electrical cords or loose plugs.** Do not attempt to remove a plug tine if it breaks off in the socket. Notify your teacher, and stay away from the outlet.

- **Fasten electrical cords to work surfaces by using tape.** Doing so will prevent tripping and will ensure that equipment will not fall or be pulled off the table.

- **Do not use electrical equipment near water or when your clothing or hands are wet.**

- **Hold the plug housing when you plug in or unplug equipment.** Do not touch the metal prongs of the plug, and do not pull on the cord.

 ## Heating Safety

- **Avoid using open flames.** If possible, work only with hot plates that have an on/off switch and an indicator light. Turn off hot plates and open flames when they are not in use.

- **Never leave a hot plate unattended while it is turned on or while it is cooling off.**

- **Know the location of lab fire extinguishers and fire-safety blankets.**

- **Use tongs or appropriate insulated holders when handling heated objects.** Heated objects often do not appear to be hot. Do not pick up an object with your hand if the object could be warm.

- **Keep flammable substances away from heat, flames, and other ignition sources.**

- **Allow all equipment to cool before storing it.**

 ## Animal Care and Safety

- **Handle animals only as directed by your teacher.** Mishandling or abusing animals will not be tolerated.

- **Always get your teacher's permission before bringing any animal (including pets) into the school building.**

- **Do not approach or touch any wild animals.** When working outdoors, be aware of poisonous or dangerous animals in the area.

- **Dispose of specimens only as instructed by your teacher.**

 ## Plant Safety

- **Do not ingest any plant part used in the laboratory (especially commercially sold seeds).** Do not touch any sap or plant juice directly. Always wear gloves.

- **Wear disposable polyethylene gloves when handling any wild plant.**

- **Wash hands thoroughly after handling any plant or plant part (particularly seeds).** Avoid touching your face and eyes.

- **Do not pick wildflowers or other plants unless instructed to do so by your teacher.**

 ## Hygienic Care

- **Keep your hands away from your face, hair, and mouth while you are working on any activity.**

- **Wash your hands thoroughly before you leave the lab or when you finish any activity.**

- **Remove contaminated clothing immediately.** If you spill corrosive substances on your skin or clothing, use the safety shower or a faucet to rinse. Remove affected clothing while you are under the shower, and call to your teacher. (It may be temporarily embarrassing to remove clothing in front of your classmates, but failure to thoroughly rinse a chemical off your skin could result in permanent damage.)

- **Use the proper technique demonstrated by your teacher when you are handling bacteria or other microorganisms.** Treat all microorganisms as if they are pathogens. Do not open Petri dishes to observe or count bacterial colonies.

 ## Proper Waste Disposal

- **Clean and sanitize all work surfaces and personal protective equipment after each lab period as directed by your teacher.**

- **Dispose of contaminated materials (biological or chemical) in special containers only as directed by your teacher.** Never put these materials into a regular waste container or down the drain.

- **Dispose of sharp objects (such as broken glass) in the appropriate sharps or broken glass container as directed by your teacher.**

How to Use Your Textbook

You might notice that there are many unique elements in this textbook. By reading the next four pages, you will learn how these elements will help you to both understand biology and to be successful on the Living Environment Regents Exam. You may be tempted to skip this guide to your textbook, but you should read it. This textbook is an important tool in your exploration of science. Like any tool, the more you know about how to use this textbook, the better your results will be.

Step into Science

The beginning of each chapter is designed to get you involved with science. You will immediately see that science matters!

Chapter Outline You can get a quick overview of the chapter by looking at the chapter's outline. In the outline, the section titles and the topics within that section are listed.

Inquiry Lab This lab gives you a chance to get some hands-on experience right away. It is designed to help you start thinking about what you will learn in the chapter.

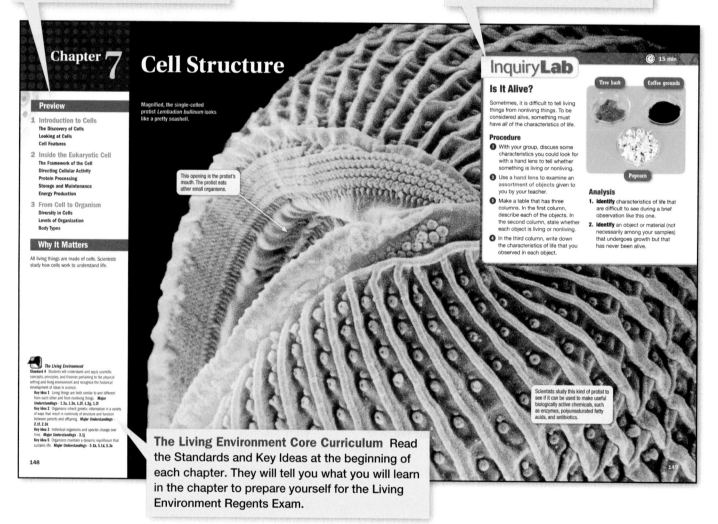

The Living Environment Core Curriculum Read the Standards and Key Ideas at the beginning of each chapter. They will tell you what you will learn in the chapter to prepare yourself for the Living Environment Regents Exam.

Read for Meaning

At the beginning of each chapter you will find tools that will help you grasp the meaning of what you read. Each section also introduces what is important in that section and why.

The **Key Ideas** ask the important questions that you will be able to answer after learning about the science in each section.

The **Key Terms** are science words that you may not be familiar with but that are important to understanding the section. Pay special attention when you see them highlighted in the pages that follow.

Each **Reading Toolbox** contains a variety of learning tools that will help you better understand the content of the chapter.

The **Why It Matters** gives at least one reason that you might be interested in the subject of the section. In some cases, this topic is covered in more detail with an article.

At the beginning of each section are the **Living Environment** major understandings covered in that section.

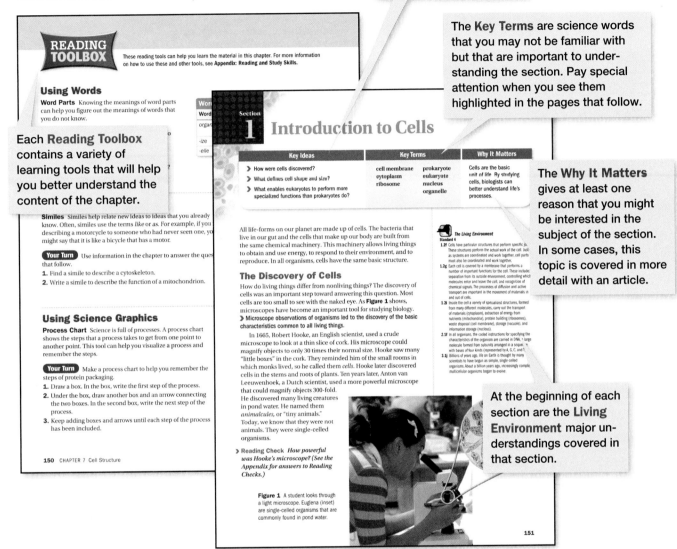

Keep an Eye on Headings

Notice that the headings in this textbook are different sizes and different colors. The headings help you organize your reading and form a simple outline, as shown below.

Green: Section titles

Blue: Key-idea heading

Black: ❯ Key-idea statements

The paragraphs under each blue heading contains a sentence that answers a **Key Idea** question from the section opener. These Key Ideas are indicated with a blue pointer and are printed in bold type.

Science Is Doing

You will get many opportunities throughout this textbook to actually do science. After all, doing is what science is about.

Quick Labs help you get real hands-on experience doing science. Notice the Living Environment standards covered by each Quick Lab.

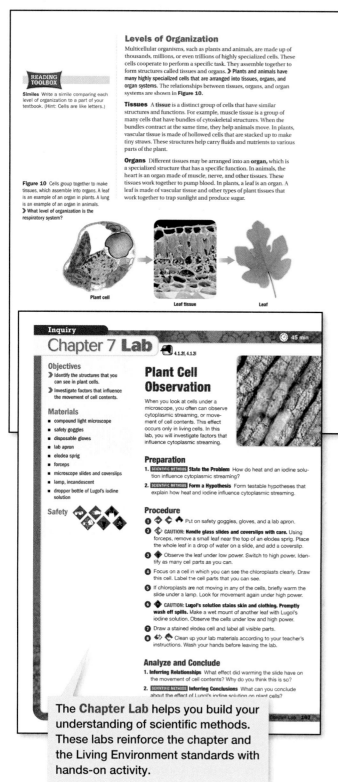

SciLinks lets you use the Internet to link to interesting topics and activities related to the section.

The **Chapter Lab** helps you build your understanding of scientific methods. These labs reinforce the chapter and the Living Environment standards with hands-on activity.

Throughout the book, **interact online** markers on figures indicate that an animated, interactive version of the diagram is available online.

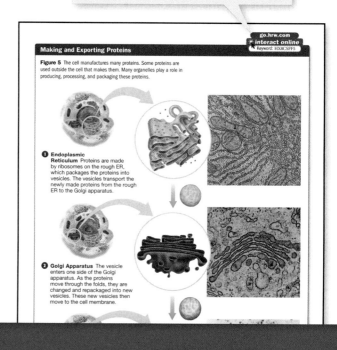

Review What You Have Learned

You can't review too much when learning science. To help you review, a **Section Review** appears at the end of every section, and a **Chapter Summary** appears at the end of every chapter. Following that are **Living Environment Regents Exam Practice** questions that will help you review for the Living Environment Regents Exam.

> **Regents Exam Practice** has questions from previous Living Environment Regents Exams. These questions not only help you to develop a better understanding of the chapter content, but they will get you ready to take the Living Environment Regents Exam.

> Just a few clicks away, each **Super Summary** gives you even more ways to review and study for tests using a computer and the Internet.

Chapter 7 Summary

go.hrw.com
SUPER SUMMARY
Keyword: HX8CSFS

Key Ideas

1 Introduction to Cells
> Microscope observations of organisms led to the discovery of the basic characteristics common to all living things.
> A cell's shape reflects the cell's function. Cell size is limited by a cell's surface area-to-volume ratio.
> Because of their complex organization, eukaryotic cells can carry out more specialized functions than prokaryotic cells can.

2 Inside the Eukaryotic Cell
> The cytoskeleton helps the cell move, keep its shape, and organize its parts.
> DNA instructions are copied as RNA messages, which leave the nucleus. In the cytoplasm, ribosomes use the RNA messages to assemble proteins.
> The endoplasmic reticulum and the Golgi apparatus are organelles that prepare proteins for extracellular export.
> Vesicles help maintain homeostasis by storing and releasing various substances as the cell needs them.
> The energy for cellular functions is produced by chemical reactions that occur in the mitochondria and chloroplasts.

3 From Cell to Organism
> The different organelles and features of cells enable organisms to function in unique ways in different environments.
> Plants and animals have many highly specialized cells that are arranged into tissues, organs, and organ systems.
> A multicellular organism is composed of many individual

Key Terms

cell membrane (154)
cytoplasm (154)
ribosome (154)
prokaryote (154)
eukaryote (155)
nucleus (155)
organelle (155)

vesicle (158)
endoplasmic reticulum (158)
Golgi apparatus (158)
vacuole (160)
chloroplast (161)
mitochondrion (161)

flagellum (162)
tissue (164)
organ (164)
organ system (165)
colonial organism (165)

> Be sure to read the **Key Ideas** to see how they all fit together. If you need to recall any of the **Key Terms,** the page number on which they appear is given.

Chapter 7 The Living Environment Regents Exam Practice

PART A: Answer all questions in this part.

Directions: For each statement or question, write on your separate answer sheet the number of the word or expression that best completes the statement or answers the question.

1 The diagram below represents levels of organization in living things. Which term would best represent X?

Organism
Organ system
Organ
X
Cell

(1) human
(2) tissue
(3) stomach
(4) organelle

2 Which statement best compares a multicellular organism to a single-celled organism?
(1) A multicellular organism has organ systems that interact to carry out life functions, while a single-celled organism carries out life functions without using organ systems.
(2) A single-celled organism carries out fewer life functions than each cell of a multicellular organism.
(3) A multicellular organism always obtains energy through a process that is different from that used by a single-celled organism.
(4) The cell of a single-celled organism is always much larger than an individual cell of a multicellular organism.

3 The levels of organization for structure and function in the human body from least complex to most complex are
(1) systems → organs → tissues → cells
(2) cells → organs → tissues → systems
(3) tissues → systems → cells → organs
(4) cells → tissues → organs → systems

4 The largest amount of DNA in a plant cell is contained in
(1) a nucleus
(2) a chromosome
(3) a protein molecule
(4) an enzyme molecule

5 The diagram below illustrates the movement of materials involved in a process that is vital for the energy needs of organisms. The process illustrated occurs within

Oxygen
Water
Carbon dioxide
Glucose

(1) chloroplasts
(2) mitochondria
(3) ribosomes
(4) vacuoles

6 In a cell, information that controls the production of proteins must pass from the nucleus to the
(1) cell membrane.
(2) chloroplasts.
(3) mitochondria.
(4) ribosomes.

13 Describe how *two* of the cell structures listed below interact to help maintain a balanced internal environment in a cell:
mitochondrion
ribosome
cell membrane
nucleus
vacuole

Regents Exam Practice **169**

Practice **171**

Be Resourceful—Use the Web!

More Resources

There are plenty of resources online for you. When you see a SciLinks code in the book, just go to **scilinks.org** and type the code in for information and activities on a topic. When you see **Super Summary** or **Interact Online** in the book, go to **go.hrw.com** snd type in the keyword for study helps and interactive art.

Your Online Textbook

If your teacher gives you a special password to log onto the **Holt Online Learning** site, you will find your complete textbook on the Web. In addition, you will find some great learning tools and interactive materials. You can now access your textbook anywhere and anytime via the Internet.

Take a Test Drive

How well can you use this book now? Take Chapter 1 out for a spin and see how you do. Log onto **go.hrw.com** and enter the keyword **HX8 TEST DRIVE** for a short list of questions that will test your ability to navigate this book.

UNIT 1 Introduction

1 Biology and You

2 Applications of Biology

3 Chemistry of Life

 The Living Environment

Standard 1: Students will use mathematical analysis, scientific inquiry, and engineering design, as appropriate, to pose questions, seek answers, and develop solutions.

Key Idea 1 The central purpose of scientific inquiry is to develop explanations of natural phenomena in a continuing and creative process.

Key Idea 2 Beyond the use of reasoning and consensus, scientific inquiry involves the testing of proposed explanations involving the use of conventional techniques and procedures and usually requiring considerable ingenuity.

Key Idea 3 The observations made while testing proposed explanations, when analyzed using conventional and invented methods, provide new insights into natural phenomena.

Standard 4 Students will understand and apply scientific concepts, principles, and theories pertaining to the physical setting and living environment and recognize the historical development of ideas in science.

Key Idea 1 Living things are both similar to and different from each other and from nonliving things.

Key Idea 2 Organisms inherit genetic information in a variety of ways that result in continuity of structure and function between parents and offspring.

Key Idea 4 The continuity of life is sustained through reproduction and development.

Key Idea 5 Organisms maintain a dynamic equilibrium that sustains life.

Key Idea 7 Human decisions and activities have had a profound impact on the physical and living environment.

Researcher with Nassau grouper

Giant panda cub with caretaker at Wolong Nature Reserve in China

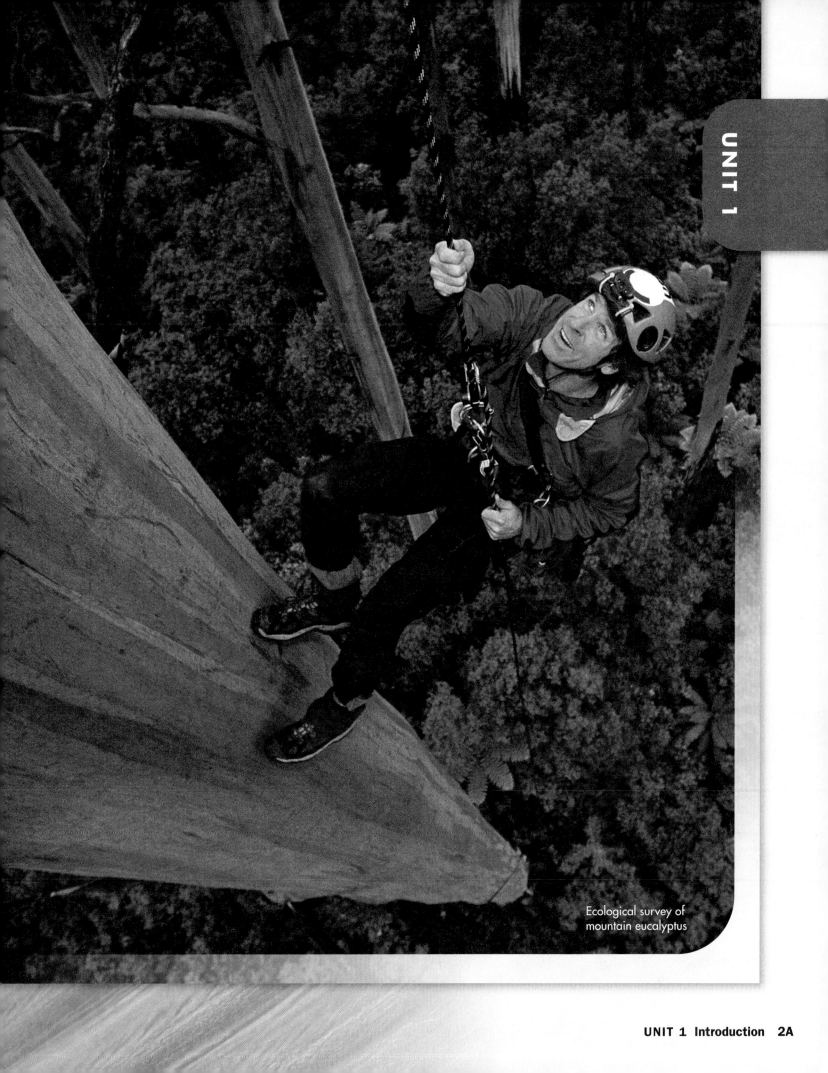

Ecological survey of
mountain eucalyptus

Milestones in Biology

1489

Leonardo da Vinci applies architectural techniques to anatomical drawing. His detailed drawings of the human skull revolutionize scientific illustration.

Statue of Leonardo da Vinci in Italy

1811

At 12 years old, Mary Anning, a British fossil collector, discovers the first complete fossil skeleton of an ichthyosaur. Other scientists use her discoveries to support the theory that fossils are evidence of extinct species.

1898

Marie Curie, a scientist born in Poland, demonstrates that isotopes of certain elements, such as radium and polonium, are the source of radioactive energy in radioactive rocks.

Marie Curie in her laboratory

1910

Alex Carrel publishes a paper reporting his success in using cold storage to preserve blood vessels for long periods of time before transplanting them. His work, related to developing organ-transplant processes, earns him the Nobel Prize in physiology or medicine in 1912.

1918–1919

An influenza epidemic kills between 20 million and 40 million people worldwide. In less than a year, about 675,000 Americans die of the disease, 10 times the number of Americans who died in World War I.

George Washington Carver

1927

George Washington Carver, American inventor and botanist, patents a process for making paints from soybean extracts.

1971

Louis Leaky sponsors Biruté Mary Galdikas to study the orangutans of Borneo. In 1975, Galdikas begins publishing articles about her observations of orangutan behavior. Many articles and lectures follow. Her work helps educate the public about the need to preserve wild habitats.

1996

David Ho is recognized as *Time* magazine's Man of the Year for his pioneering work developing "cocktails" of medicines that fight HIV.

David Ho

Mason wasp with prey

BIOLOGY CAREER

Forensic Scientist
Wayne Moorehead

Wayne Moorehead is a forensic scientist. Forensic scientists use scientific processes to investigate legal matters. Moorehead works with the Trace Evidence and Fire Division of the Orange County Sheriff–Coroner Crime Laboratory in California. He specializes in forensic microscopy, trace evidence, and the analysis of explosives, fire debris, and unusual evidence. Moorehead enjoys his work, especially using critical thinking to answer questions about crimes.

Moorehead traces his interest in forensic science back to his childhood, when he enjoyed using a chemistry set and microscope and reading forensic science books. He still collects books in his field.

Moorehead enjoys using forensic science in criminal investigations but considers his greatest accomplishment to be teaching forensic science to high school students, college students, professors, and the public.

Yellow crinoid and reef fish on a coral reef

Biology and You

		Standards	**Teach Key Ideas**

CHAPTER OPENER, pp. 4–5   15 min.

The Living Environment

SECTION 1 The Nature of Science, pp. 7–9   45 min.

1.1.1b, 1.2.1, 1.3.4b, 1.3.4c, 1.3.5b

> Scientific Thought
> Universal Laws
> Science and Ethics
> Why Study Science?

SECTION 2 Scientific Methods, pp. 10–13   30 min.

1.1.1a, 1.1.2a, 1.1.2b, 1.1.3a, 1.2.3a, 1.2.3b, 1.3.1a, 1.3.4a, 1.3.5a

> Beginning a Scientific Investigation
> Scientific Experiments
> Scientific Theories

Bellringer Transparency
Transparencies A3 Scientific Processes • Concept Map of Scientific Processes
Visual Concepts Scientific Method • Hypothesis • Controlled Experiment and Variable • Independent and Dependent Variables • Comparing Theories and Laws

SECTION 3 Tools and Techniques, pp. 14–16   30 min.

> Measurement Systems
> Lab Techniques
> Safety

Bellringer Transparency
Transparencies A6 SI Base Units • A7 Some SI Prefixes • A8 SI Units
Visual Concepts Types of Microscopes • Parts of a Microscope • Magnification and Resolution

SECTION 4 What is Biology?, pp. 17–21   25 min.

4.4.1a, 4.5.3a

> The Study of Life
> Characteristics of Living Things

Bellringer Transparency
Transparencies A1 The Seven Properties of Life
Visual Concepts Biology • Unifying Themes of Biology • Heredity • Evolution

See also PowerPoint® Resources

Chapter Review and Assessment Resources

SE Super Summary, p. 22
SE Regents Exam Practice, p. 23
   Regents Review Guide
   Review Resources
   Chapter Tests A and B
   Holt Online Assessment
   Regents Question Banks on Teacher's One-Stop Planner

CHAPTER
Fast Track   *Thorough instruction will require the times shown.*

Basic Learners

TE Textbook Overview, p. 7
TE Dependent and Independent Variables, p. 11
TE Bias Has Many Meanings, p. 12
TE Types of Microscopes, p. 15
   Directed Reading Worksheets*
   Active Reading Worksheets*
   Lab Manuals, Level A*
   Study Guide*■
   Note-taking Workbook*
   Special Needs Activities and Modified Tests*

Advanced Learners

TE Ethics and Funding, p. 8
TE The pH Scale, p. 11
   Critical Thinking Worksheets*
   Concept Mapping Worksheets*
   Science Skills Worksheets*
   Lab Datasheets, Level C*

Why It Matters	Hands-On	Skills Development	Assessment
Build student motivation with resources about high-interest applications.	**SE Inquiry Lab** Make a Prediction, p. 5 *■	**TE Reading Toolbox** Assessing Prior Knowledge, p. 4 **SE Reading Toolbox**, p. 6	
	SE Quick Lab Evaluate a Scientific Claim, p. 9 *■ 📁 **Inquiry Lab** Storing Heat*	**SE Reading Toolbox** Everyday Words in Science, p. 9 **TE Reading Toolbox** Everyday Words in Science, p. 9	**SE Section Review** **TE Formative Assessment** Spanish Assessment *■ 📁 Section Quiz ■
TE Demonstration Making Predictions, p. 10 **TE Statistical Tools**, p. 12 **TE Scientists and Detectives**, p. 13	**SE Quick Lab** The pH of Common Substances, p. 11 *■	**TE Reading Toolbox** Hypothesis or Theory?, p. 12 **SE Reading Toolbox** Hypothesis or Theory?, p. 12	**SE Section Review** **TE Formative Assessment** Spanish Assessment *■ 📁 Section Quiz ■
TE Demonstration Measuring, p. 14	**SE Quick Lab** Practice Staining Techniques, p. 15 *■ **SE Skills Practice Lab** SI Units, p. 20 *■	**SE Reading Toolbox** Idea Wheel, p. 16 **TE Reading Toolbox** Idea Wheel, p. 16	**SE Section Review** **TE Formative Assessment** Spanish Assessment *■ 📁 Section Quiz ■
TE Demonstration Alive or Not?, p. 17 **TE Career Development**, p. 18 **SE Biology in the World**, p. 18	📁 **Quick Lab** Comparing Living and Nonliving Things*	**TE Reading Toolbox** Visual Literacy, p. 18	**SE Section Review** **TE Formative Assessment** Spanish Assessment *■ 📁 Section Quiz ■

See also Lab Generator

See also Holt Online Assessment Resources

Resources for Differentiated Instruction

English Learners

TE Vocabulary, p. 8
TE Measurements, Units, and Quantities, p. 14
📁 Directed Reading Worksheets*
📁 Active Reading Worksheets*
📁 Lab Manuals, Level A*
📓 Study Guide *■
📓 Note-taking Workbook*
📓 Multilingual Glossary

Struggling Readers

TE Textbook Overview, p. 7
TE Vocabulary, p. 8
TE Bias Has Many Meanings, p. 12
📁 Directed Reading Worksheets*
📁 Active Reading Worksheets*
📁 Lab Manuals, Level A*
📓 Study Guide*
📓 Note-taking Workbook*
📓 Special Needs Activities and Modified Tests*

Special Education Students

📁 Directed Reading Worksheets*
📁 Active Reading Worksheets*
📁 Lab Manuals, Level A*
📓 Study Guide *■
📓 Note-taking Workbook*
📓 Special Needs Activities and Modified Tests*

Alternative Assessment

📁 Science Skills Worksheets*
📁 Section Quizzes *■
📓 Chapter Tests A, B, and C *■

Chapter 1

Chapter 1

Biology and You

Overview

The purpose of this chapter is to present the nature of scientific thought and scientific methods. SI measurement and lab safety are presented in the context of the tools and techniques that scientists use in scientific research. The chapter closes with a discussion of the basic properties of life.

READING TOOLBOX

Assessing Prior Knowledge Students should understand the following concepts:
• science in daily life
• metric measurement

Visual Literacy Tell students that young puffins are fed fish by their parents several times a day. Adult puffins dive into the ocean water to catch fish. While underwater, they use their wings to swim. Puffins have specialized beaks that enable them to catch and carry many fish for each visit to the nest. They spend the winter in the open ocean far from land. Ask students what characteristics a young puffin would need to leave its nest. (Sample answers are strong wings, waterproof feathers, and fishing skills.)

Preview

1 The Nature of Science
Scientific Thought
Universal Laws
Science and Ethics
Why Study Science?

2 Scientific Methods
Beginning a Scientific Investigation
Scientific Experiments
Scientific Theories

3 Tools and Techniques
Measurement Systems
Lab Techniques
Safety

4 What Is Biology?
The Study of Life
Characteristics of Living Things

Why It Matters

Biology, the study of life, directly applies to your health, life, and future in ways as simple as making daily food choices or as complex as deciding which career to pursue.

 The Living Environment

Standard 1 Students will use mathematical analysis, scientific inquiry, and engineering design, as appropriate, to pose questions, seek answers, and develop solutions.
   Key Idea 1 The central purpose of scientific inquiry is to develop explanations of natural phenomena in a continuing and creative process. *Major Understandings* - 1.1a, 1.1b, 1.2a, 1.2b, 1.3a
   Key Idea 2 Beyond the use of reasoning and consensus, scientific inquiry involves the testing of proposed explanations involving the use of conventional techniques and procedures and usually requiring considerable ingenuity. *Major Understandings* - 2.2a, 2.3a, 2.3b
   Key Idea 3 The observations made while testing proposed explanations, when analyzed using conventional and invented methods, provide new insights into natural phenomena. *Major Understandings* - 3.1a, 3.4a, 3.4b, 3.4c, 3.5a, 3.5b
Standard 4 Students will understand and apply scientific concepts, principles, and theories pertaining to the physical setting and living environment and recognize the historical development of ideas in science.
   Key Idea 4 The continuity of life is sustained through reproduction and development. *Major Understandings* - 4.1a
   Key Idea 5 Organisms maintain a dynamic equilibrium that sustains life. *Major Understandings* - 5.3a

Biologists are curious about living things. This biologist was curious enough about seabirds to climb to the top of this high cliff.

This scientist is taking measurements of a puffin chick to estimate its age. This information will help the scientist predict when the chick will leave its burrow and head out to sea.

One mystery that biologists have yet to solve about puffins is how the chicks, who leave their burrow when they are only 50 days old, are able to return to the same spot many years later to have their own chicks.

Chapter Correlations   *The Living Environment*

Standard 1

1.1a Scientific explanations are built by combining evidence that can be observed with what people already know about the world.

1.1b Learning about the historical development of scientific concepts or about individuals who have contributed to scientific knowledge provides a better understanding of scientific inquiry and the relationship between science and society.

1.2.1 Devise ways of making observations to test proposed explanations.

1.2a Inquiry involves asking questions and locating, interpreting, and processing information from a variety of sources.

1.2b Inquiry involves making judgments about the reliability of the source and relevance of information.

1.2.4 Carry out a research plan for testing explanations, including selecting and developing techniques, acquiring and building apparatus, and recording observations as necessary.

1.3a Scientific explanations are accepted when they are consistent with experimental and observational evidence and when they lead to accurate predictions.

2.2a Development of a research plan involves researching background information and understanding the major concepts in the area being investigated. Recommendations for methodologies, use of technologies, proper equipment, and safety precautions should also be included.

2.3a Hypotheses are predictions based upon both research and observation.

2.3b Hypotheses are widely used in science for determining what data to collect and as a guide for interpreting the data.

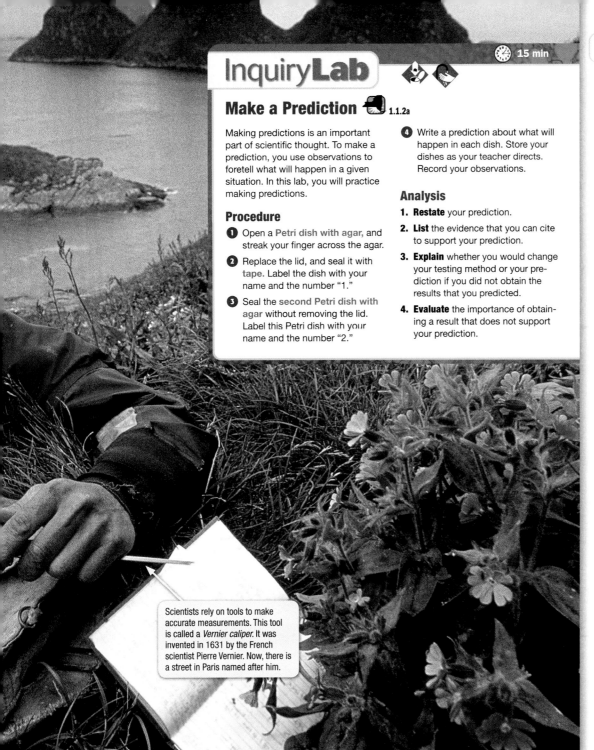

InquiryLab

⏱ 15 min

Make a Prediction 🔬 1.1.2a

Making predictions is an important part of scientific thought. To make a prediction, you use observations to foretell what will happen in a given situation. In this lab, you will practice making predictions.

Procedure

❶ Open a **Petri dish with agar,** and streak your finger across the agar.

❷ Replace the lid, and seal it with **tape.** Label the dish with your name and the number "1."

❸ Seal the **second Petri dish with agar** without removing the lid. Label this Petri dish with your name and the number "2."

❹ Write a prediction about what will happen in each dish. Store your dishes as your teacher directs. Record your observations.

Analysis

1. **Restate** your prediction.

2. **List** the evidence that you can cite to support your prediction.

3. **Explain** whether you would change your testing method or your prediction if you did not obtain the results that you predicted.

4. **Evaluate** the importance of obtaining a result that does not support your prediction.

Scientists rely on tools to make accurate measurements. This tool is called a *Vernier caliper.* It was invented in 1631 by the French scientist Pierre Vernier. Now, there is a street in Paris named after him.

InquiryLab

Teacher's Notes Agar plates can be purchased from science supply companies, or you can prepare your own. Be sure that there is a nutrient and energy source in the agar solution. Luria Broth (LB) is commonly used as a rich nutrient source. Dish 2 should be taped closed to avoid contamination.

Materials

• LB agar plates (2)
• permanent marker

Answers to Analysis

1. Students may predict that bacteria will grow on the agar plate they touched.

2. Students may have previous knowledge that bacteria are found on human skin.

3. You would change your prediction unless there was a flaw with the testing method.

4. Any result of a scientific experiment is important because the observer learns something whether the result supports or contradicts the prediction.

3.1a Interpretation of data leads to development of additional hypotheses, the formulation of generalizations, or explanations of natural phenomena.

3.4a Hypotheses are valuable, even if they turn out not to be true, because they may lead to further investigation.

3.4b Claims should be questioned if the data are based on samples that are very small, biased, or inadequately controlled or if the conclusions are based on the faulty, incomplete, or misleading use of numbers.

3.4c Claims should be questioned if fact and opinion are intermingled, if adequate evidence is not cited, or if the conclusions do not follow logically from the evidence given.

3.5a One assumption of science is that other individuals could arrive at the same explanation if they had access to similar evidence. Scientists make the results of their investigations public; they should describe the investigations in ways that enable others to repeat the investigations.

3.5b Scientists use peer review to evaluate the results of scientific investigations and the explanations proposed by other scientists. They analyze the experimental procedures, examine the evidence, identify faulty reasoning, point out statements that go beyond the evidence, and suggest alternative explanations for the same observations.

Standard 4
4.1a Reproduction and development are necessary for the continuation of any species.

5.3a Dynamic equilibrium results from detection of and response to stimuli. Organisms detect and respond to change in a variety of ways both at the cellular level and at the organismal level.

Using Words

See table below.

Using Language

1. A hypothesis is a testable prediction. A theory is a general explanation for a broad range of data.
2. Accept any hypothesis that can be tested. Sample answer: The chicken crossed the road because there was food on the other side.

Using Graphic Organizers

See graphic below.

These reading tools can help you learn the material in this chapter. For more information on how to use these and other tools, see **Appendix: Reading and Study Skills**.

Using Words

Everyday Words in Science Many words that we use every day have special meanings in science. For example, "matter" in everyday use is an issue or problem. In science, matter is the substance of which all things are made.

Your Turn Make a table like the one shown here.

1. Before you read, write in your own words the everyday meaning of the terms in the table.
2. As you read, fill in the science meaning for the terms in the table.

Everyday Words in Science		
Word	Everyday Meaning	Science Meaning
theory		
reproduction		
control		
conclude		

Using Language

Hypothesis or Theory? In everyday language, there is little difference between a *hypothesis* and a *theory*. But in science, the meanings of these words are more distinct. A *hypothesis* is a specific, testable prediction for a limited set of conditions. A *theory* is a general explanation for a broad range of data. A theory can include hypotheses that have been tested and can also be used to generate new hypotheses. The strongest scientific theories explain the broadest range of data and incorporate many well-tested hypotheses.

Your Turn Use what you have learned about the difference between a hypothesis and a theory to answer the following questions.

1. What is the difference between a hypothesis and a theory?
2. Propose a testable hypothesis to explain why the chicken crossed the road.

Using Graphic Organizers

Idea Wheel An idea wheel is an effective type of visual organization. Ideas in science can be divided up into topics around a central, or main, idea.

Your Turn Create an idea wheel like the one shown here to help you organize your notes about tools and techniques used in science.

1. Draw a circle. Draw a larger circle around the first circle.
2. Divide the ring between the circles into sections by drawing lines from the center circle to the outer circle.
3. Write the main idea *Tools and Techniques* in the smaller circle.
4. Label each section of the ring with a topic that falls under the main idea.
5. In each section of the ring, include notes about each topic.

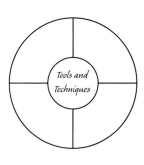

Word	Everyday Meaning	Science Meaning
theory	a guess	ideas supported by a large body of evidence
reproduction	a likeness or copy	the process of producing offspring
control	be in charge of	standard for comparison in an experiment
conclude	to finish or end	to infer on the basis of evidence

Key Ideas	Key Terms	Why It Matters
❯ How can someone practice scientific thought? ❯ What are universal laws in science? ❯ How do ethics apply to science? ❯ Why should someone who is not planning to become a scientist study science?	skepticism	Thinking like a scientist helps you solve problems and think critically about the world around you.

The goal of science is to help us understand the natural world and improve people's lives. Thinking like a scientist can help you solve problems and think critically about your world.

Scientific Thought

❯ Scientific thought involves making observations, using evidence to draw conclusions, being skeptical about ideas, and being open to change when new discoveries are made.

Questioning Ideas Scientists carefully observe the world. They then ask questions about what they observe. Often, the questions that they ask lead to even more questions. This process is the cornerstone of scientific thought. Scientific thought also requires **skepticism**—a questioning and often doubtful attitude. Scientists question everything. They require evidence, not opinions, to support ideas. Many great discoveries have been made when scientists doubted conventional wisdom. For example, people once thought that stress caused stomach ulcers. However, a group of researchers found the bacteria *Helicobacter pylori* in the stomachs of people with ulcers. Studies confirmed that the bacteria, shown in **Figure 1,** caused ulcers.

Discovery and Change As scientists challenge old claims and make new discoveries, they change the way that people view the world. Many scientific discoveries lead to new technologies and medical treatments. For example, discovering that bacteria cause stomach ulcers led to prescribing antibiotics for patients with ulcers. Through the ongoing cycle of challenge and discovery, scientific knowledge grows.

The Living Environment
Standard 1
1.1b Learning about the historical development of scientific concepts or about individuals who have contributed to scientific knowledge provides a better understanding of scientific inquiry and the relationship between science and society.
2.1 Devise ways of making observations to test proposed explanations.
3.4b Claims should be questioned if the data are based on samples that are very small, biased, or inadequately controlled or if the conclusions are based on the faulty, incomplete, or misleading use of numbers.
3.4c Claims should be questioned if fact and opinion are intermingled, if adequate evidence is not cited, or if the conclusions do not follow logically from the evidence given.
3.5b Scientists use peer review to evaluate the results of scientific investigations and the explanations proposed by other scientists. They analyze the experimental procedures, examine the evidence, identify faulty reasoning, point out statements that go beyond the evidence, and suggest alternative explanations for the same observations.

skepticism a habit of mind in which a person questions the validity of accepted ideas

Helicobacter pylori **bacterium**

Figure 1 Doctors once thought that stress caused stomach ulcers. However, in 1982, scientists discovered that *Helicobacter pylori* bacteria were the actual cause.

❯ Focus

This section discusses the characteristics of scientific thinking and the role of ethics and universal laws in science.

🔔 Bellringer

Use the Bellringer transparency to prepare students for this section.

❯ Teach

Demonstration

Asking Questions Show students a photo that people claim is Bigfoot or the Loch Ness Monster. (These images are easily found on the Internet.) Discuss what students know about the photo. Remind students that scientists use evidence that is reproducible and verifiable to give credibility to their arguments. Then, have small groups of students work together to describe how they would evaluate the existence of the organism in the picture. Have groups share their ideas with the class. **LS Logical**

Differentiated Instruction

Basic Learners/Struggling Readers

Textbook Overview Tell students that the text headings generally provide a skeleton for outlining the chapter. Key Ideas are highlighted in bold and new terms are defined in context and in the margin. Give students five minutes to leaf through the chapter, and then ask: "Where do you find the Key Terms for a section?" (on the first page of the section, on the summary page for the chapter, and in the margins of the section) "Where do you find the answers to the Key Ideas questions for each section?" (They are shown in bold in the text.) Ask students to locate the answers to the reading checks. (They can be found at the back of the book.) **LS Verbal**

Section Correlations

1.1.1b	1.3.4c
1.2.1	1.3.5b
1.3.4b	

Teaching Key Ideas

Science Ethics Tell students that many scientific organizations establish guidelines for ethical behavior. For example, the American Association for the Advancement of Science (AAAS) publishes several books and articles on the issue. Many university science departments also have their own ethical guidelines. Ask students what key issues they would include in a set of ethical guidelines for their science class. **LS Interpersonal**

Teaching Key Ideas

Research Gone Awry Ask students to relay any story in the media that is an example of a breach of scientific ethics. The scenario can be real or fictional. Have the student tell the class what part of the guidelines were compromised and why. (Most stories center on economic pressures, i.e. drug development and clinical trials.) Discuss the importance of ethical behavior and how it protects the public. **LS Verbal**

Figure 2 All objects in the universe, from birds to stars, are affected by gravity. Birds must overcome gravity to fly. Stars are formed when gravity pulls a mass of gases together.

ACADEMIC VOCABULARY

aspect the way in which an idea or situation is viewed

www.scilinks.org
Topic: Scientific
Discoveries
Code: HX81356

Universal Laws

> Science is governed by truths that are valid everywhere in the universe. These truths are called *universal laws*. Though branches of science address different aspects of the natural world, universal laws such as the law of gravity, the law of conservation of energy, and the laws of planetary motion apply to all branches of science and to every person. A biologist studying the flight of the bird in **Figure 2** is studying how animals have adapted to overcome the force of gravity. A biologist studying the habits of nocturnal animals is studying the way that animal behavior has adapted to take advantage of the regular pattern of day and night caused by Earth's rotation on its axis.

Science and Ethics

Ethics are a system of moral principles and values. > Because scientific experimentation and discovery can have serious ethical implications, scientific investigations require ethical behavior. Scientists performing investigations must report only accurate data and be willing to allow their peers to review their work. All scientists rely on the work of other scientists. If the data or claims of one scientist are misleading or false, many other scientists may waste time and resources conducting investigations that are based on that unethical work.

Many other people also rely on scientists to be ethical. For example, if a scientist falsely claims to have discovered a cure for diabetes, people with diabetes may change how they manage their condition to take advantage of the discovery. Because the findings are false, the people relying on the discovery could be in danger.

Scientists must also obey laws and behave ethically with people involved in scientific investigations. Ethical scientists adhere to strict guidelines to ensure that no one involved in medical experiments is coerced, exploited, or involuntarily exposed to a known danger.

> **Reading Check** *Why is it important that scientific investigations be done ethically? (See the Appendix for answers to Reading Checks.)*

Differentiated Instruction

Advanced Learners/GATE

Ethics and Funding To help students understand the financial pressures that often create ethics violations, have students research a biotech companies in the local area. Students should create a profile for a company that interests them. The profile should includes: area of research, sources of funding, and regulatory control. If the company is publicly traded, have students research its stock price over the last ten years and how stock price is influenced by discoveries. **LS Verbal/Logical**

English Learners/Struggling Readers

Vocabulary Have students begin a vocabulary notebook or vocabulary flash cards. Tell them to include the Key Terms and any other terms that are unfamiliar in each section. Have them use their own words to write definitions for the terms. Suggest that they also include diagrams and pictures when helpful. Allow time for students to share the information in their notebooks or flashcards with a partner who can make suggestions for improvement. **LS Verbal**

QuickLab

⏱ 15 min

Evaluate a Scientific Claim 1.2.1, 1.3.4c

As a consumer, you need to make wise decisions. Often, your buying choices depend on evaluating claims made by the manufacturer. Are the claims accurate? What can you really expect from the products?

Analysis

1. **CRITICAL THINKING** **Evaluating Conclusions** Suppose that two television commercials claim that their own product is the fastest-acting acne medicine. Design a strategy that could be used to compare the brands. How would you compare their effectiveness?

2. **CRITICAL THINKING** **Determining the Validity of a Claim** New automobiles are sold with a window sticker displaying the expected miles per gallon. Are these manufacturers' estimates realistic and repeatable by consumers? How would you find out?

Why Study Science?

Scientific thinking is not just for scientists. The same critical-thinking process that scientists use is a tool that you can use in your everyday life. ❯ **An understanding of science can help you take better care of your health, be a wiser consumer, and become a better-informed citizen.** For example, you may read an article claiming that riding a bike for 30 minutes a week can lower your blood pressure. How will you know if the claim is accurate? You can investigate the claim by using scientific thought. Ask questions about the claim, be skeptical about what you read, and be ready for discovery and change.

You can also use science to improve the world around you. You may see a problem in your town, such as a struggling recycling program or a dangerous crosswalk. You can investigate these problems with skepticism and creativity to discover helpful solutions. By applying scientific thinking to these problems, you can help yourself and your community.

READING TOOLBOX

Everyday Words in Science In your own words, write the everyday meaning for the word *law*. How does the everyday meanning compare to the science meaning of *law*?

Section 1 Review

❯ KEY IDEAS

1. **Describe** the processes involved in practicing good scientific thought.
2. **Identify** two universal laws.
3. **Explain** how ethics apply to science.
4. **Relate** how science has already helped you in your everyday life.

CRITICAL THINKING

5. **Making Inferences** Most animals have solid bones. However, most birds have bones with hollow spaces. Explain how this feature of birds is related to one of the universal laws.
6. **Evaluating Claims** Two brands of yeast claim to produce a fast-rising dough. Design a strategy that could be used to compare the brands. What would you measure?

WRITING FOR SCIENCE

7. **Persuasive Writing** Write a letter to a younger brother or sister explaining the importance of studying science. Give at least three reasons to support your explanation.

QuickLab

Teacher's Notes Consider providing appropriate print ads for students to review before they do this lab.

Answers to Analysis

1. Students should offer a logical method to compare the products that includes controlled conditions for making a comparison.
2. Students should research the test conditions used by car manufacturers. Their procedures should then offer a logical way to test the listed gas mileage of a car.

READING TOOLBOX

Everyday Words in Science **law** a rule that, when broken, results in a specific punishment; **law** a statement that never varies under certain conditions

❯ Close

Formative Assessment

Which of the following would not be considered unethical?

A. adjusting data to show a trend (Incorrect. Adjusting data to meet predetermined results is unethical behavior.)

B. increasing the number of experimental trials (Correct! More trials provide more data, which leads to greater confidence in the conclusions.)

C. limiting access to a discovery (Incorrect. Ethical science behavior involves making all data available for peer review.)

D. using the data of other scientists as your own (Incorrect. Plagiarism is certainly unethical behavior.)

Answers to Section Review

1. Scientific thought involves making observations, using evidence to draw conclusions, being skeptical about ideas, and being open to change when new discoveries are made.
2. the law of gravity, the law of conservation of energy, or the laws of planetary motion
3. Because scientific experimentation and discovery can have serious ethical implications, scientific investigations require ethical behavior.
4. Sample answer: Science is behind the technologies that students use to get to school and to keep themselves healthy.
5. Birds have hollow bones making them lighter. Having less mass makes flying easier, because the birds can more easily overcome the force of gravity.
6. Strategies should include measuring how fast the dough rises.
7. The sample letter should include some of the following ideas: The same critical thinking that scientists use is a tool that should be used in everyday life. An understanding of science can help you take better care of your health, become a wiser consumer, and become a better-informed citizen.

Scientific Methods

Key Ideas	Key Terms	Why It Matters
❯ How do scientific investigations begin? ❯ What are two methods that scientists can use to test hypotheses? ❯ What is the difference between a theory and a hypothesis?	observation hypothesis experiment control group theory	Scientific thinking can help you understand and analyze information that you come across in your daily life.

The Living Environment

Standard 1

1.1a Scientific explanations are built by combining evidence that can be observed with what people already know about the world.

1.2a Inquiry involves asking questions and locating, interpreting, and processing information from a variety of sources.

1.2b Inquiry involves making judgments about the reliability of the source and relevance of information.

1.3a Scientific explanations are accepted when they are consistent with experimental and observational evidence and when they lead to accurate predictions.

2.3a Hypotheses are predictions based upon both research and observation.

2.3b Hypotheses are widely used in science for determining what data to collect and as a guide for interpreting the data.

3.1a Interpretation of data leads to development of additional hypotheses, the formulation of generalizations, or explanations of natural phenomena.

3.4a Hypotheses are valuable, even if they turn out not to be true, because they may lead to further investigation.

3.5a One assumption of science is that other individuals could arrive at the same explanation if they had access to similar evidence. Scientists make the results of their investigations public; they should describe the investigations in ways that enable others to repeat the investigations.

All scientists have a certain way of investigating the world. Studying an actual scientific investigation is an exciting way to learn how science is done. Our story begins with a population of Canada geese.

Beginning a Scientific Investigation

For many years, the number of Canada geese around Chicago, shown in **Figure 3,** had been rising rapidly. Scientist Charles Paine of the Max McGraw Wildlife Foundation was studying this population growth when he noticed that the number of geese was no longer increasing. Why was the population boom over?

Making Observations ❯ Most scientific investigations begin with observations that lead to questions. **Observation** is the act of noting or perceiving objects or events by using the senses. Scientists must use both direct and indirect observation to study the world around them. Many things, like the Canada geese, can be seen. This means they can be directly observed. Other things, like the force of gravity, cannot be seen. Gravity is observed indirectly by observing the effects of gravity on objects that can be directly observed.

Formulating a Hypothesis To find out what was happening to the population of Canada geese, Paine needed to form a hypothesis. A **hypothesis** is a possible explanation that can be tested by observation or experimentation. Hypotheses are not guesses. Possible hypotheses to explain Paine's observations included these:

• The geese were being killed by predators.

• Many of the geese had become infertile.

• The geese were migrating out of the area.

Figure 3 Chicago's Canada goose population had risen rapidly for several years. After making observations, Charles Paine discovered that the population was now increasing by only about 1% per year.

MISCONCEPTION **ALERT**

Hypotheses Students often equate a hypothesis with a guess. Emphasize that a hypothesis must have some foundation in scientific fact and that it often stems both from observations and from prior knowledge. A hypothesis is an explanation that can be tested through specific and reproducible observations. Hypotheses are an initial part of formulating strategies for studying a problem. Scientists continually modify their hypotheses to accommodate new data.

QuickLab

🕐 15 min

The pH of Common Substances

You can use pH indicator paper to determine the pH of various solutions. The pH indicator paper changes color when it is exposed to a solution. The change in color indicates how acidic or basic the solution is.

Procedure

① Make a data table with three columns. Add these headings: "Solution," "Predicted pH," and "Measured pH." Make a row for **five solutions** to be tested.

② Predict the pH (acid or base) of each solution, and record your predictions in your data table.

③ **Test** each solution with **pH paper,** and record the results in the appropriate row in your data table.

Analysis

1. **Summarize** your findings in two sentences.

2. **Compare** your results with those of the rest of the class. Explain any differences.

3. **List** the scientific methods that you followed in doing this activity.

4. **CRITICAL THINKING** **Analyzing Results** Were the predictions that you made correct? Explain any differences between your predictions and your results.

Scientific Experiments

An **experiment** is a procedure that is carried out under controlled conditions to test a hypothesis. ❯ Scientists conduct controlled experiments or perform studies in order to test a hypothesis.

Controlled Experiments A controlled experiment is a procedure that tests one factor at a time and that uses a control group and an experimental group. A **control group** serves as a standard of comparison because the group receives no experimental treatment. Experimental groups are identical to the control group except for one factor, or *variable.* The single factor that scientists change in an experiment is called the *independent variable.* Factors that may change in response to the independent variable are called *dependent variables.* Scientists analyze changes to the dependent variables to understand how the independent variable affects the system that they are studying.

Study Without Experimentation There are often cases in which experiments are not possible or not ethical. For example, researchers are trying to find out if the bacteria that cause dental plaque also contribute to heart disease. It is not ethical to ask a group of people not to brush their teeth for years in order to find out if they will develop heart disease. Instead, researchers look for connections in data gathered from patients who have heart disease. However, many factors can contribute to heart disease. Researchers try to reduce the number of variables that may affect their data. For example, smoking leads to heart disease. If a person who has heart disease smokes and has dental plaque, determining which factor caused the patient's heart disease is impossible.

> **observation** the process of obtaining information by using the senses
>
> **hypothesis** a testable idea or explanation that leads to scientific investigation
>
> **experiment** a procedure that is carried out under controlled conditions to discover, demonstrate, or test a fact, theory, or general truth
>
> **control group** in an experiment, a group that serves as a standard of comparison with another group to which the control group is identical except for one factor

SCI LINKS.
www.scilinks.org
Topic: Scientific Investigations
Code: HX81358

❯ Teach, *continued*

QuickLab

Teacher's Notes Put the "mystery" solutions in containers labeled *1, 2, 3, 4,* and *5.* Use dilute solutions.

Safety Caution Students should avoid getting the liquids on their hands. Students should wash their hands after the lab. All the solutions can safely be put into school drainage systems.

Materials
- containers (5)
- 4:1 solution of apple juice and water, labeled as *1*
- 4:1 solution of orange juice and water, labeled as *2*
- 4:1 solution of ammonia and water, labeled as *3*
- 4:1 solution of dish detergent and water, labeled as *4*
- distilled water labeled as *5*
- wide range pH paper

Answers to Analysis

1. Solutions 1 and 2 are acidic, 3 and 4 are basic. Solution 5 is neutral.
2. Explanations might include human error, differences in color interpretation, and contamination of the solutions.
3. predicting, experimenting, recording data, drawing conclusions
4. Explanations might include different students' perceptions of the substances.

Differentiated Instruction

Advanced Learners/GATE

The pH Scale Have students find out what the numbers in the pH scale represent. (The numbers are a measure of the relative hydrogen ion concentration of a solution. As a solution becomes more acidic, the hydronium ion concentration increases while the hydroxide ion concentration decreases. As a solution becomes more basic, the hydronium ion concentration decreases as the hydroxide ion concentration increases.) **LS** **Verbal**

Basic Learners

Dependent and Independent Variables To help students understand the cause and effect relationships between variables, ask them to determine the independent variables in the following examples. 1. An experiment to determine how length of day affects plant growth. (length of daylight) 2. An experiment to determine how temperature affects bacterial growth. (temperature) 3. An experiment to determine how a drug's dosage affects heart rate. (drug dosage) 4. An experiment to determine how drug dosage affects recovery rate for an infection. (drug dosage)

Teaching Key Ideas

The Scientific Process Have students perform the following activity and identify the stage of the scientific method at each step. (1) have students record the number of times they breathe in one minute; (observing) (2) have them suggest how exercise might affect this number; (forming a hypothesis) (3) ask students to note the number of breaths they think they will take in one minute after they have jogged in place for one minute; (making predictions) (4) instruct students to carry out the exercise and then immediately record the number of breaths they take; (verifying predictions) (5) ask students to suggest a connection between exercise and their rate of breathing; (drawing conclusions) Then, ask students if the experiment was quantitative or qualitative. (quantitative) **LS Logical**

READING TOOLBOX

Hypothesis or Theory? Hypotheses: many of the geese are infertile; the geese are being killed by predators; the geese are migrating out of the area; the eggs were being eaten by predators. The last hypothesis was supported by evidence. **LS Verbal**

Answers to Caption Questions

Figure 4: Coyotes probably control the goose population by eating the eggs.

> **theory** a system of ideas that explains many related observations and is supported by a large body of evidence acquired through scientific investigation

READING TOOLBOX

Hypothesis or Theory? List the hypotheses that were proposed to explain the decrease in Canada geese in Chicago. Identify which hypothesis was supported by evidence.

Analyzing Results To test his hypothesis, Paine put radio collars on the adult Canada geese. He tracked the geese and learned that very few of the adult geese were being killed by predators. The results of an experiment may support a hypothesis or prove that a hypothesis is not true. After Paine analyzed his results, he had to change his hypothesis. Paine now hypothesized that the eggs, not the adult geese, were being eaten by predators. He discussed his ideas with his colleague Stan Gehrt, who was studying predators in the Chicago area. Gehrt had recently discovered an amazing fact: Chicago was home to about 2,000 coyotes! Gehrt had observed that coyotes, such as the one in **Figure 4,** sometimes ate the eggs of Canada geese.

Drawing Conclusions and Verifying Results Scientists draw conclusions that explain the results of their experiments. Working together, Paine and Gehrt concluded that urban coyotes were controlling the Canada goose population by eating the eggs. How could Paine and Gehrt verify their conclusions? Scientists verify their conclusions by conducting experiments and studies many times. They also check to see if other scientists have found similar results. In this case, urban coyotes have been found in many large cities. Paine and Gehrt could try to find out if these coyotes also eat goose eggs.

Considering Bias Scientists are human and have particular points of view, or biases. Scientists work hard to prevent bias from affecting their work, but bias can still influence an experiment. Also, a conflict of interest could affect a scientific study. For example, an investigation funded by a company may be biased in favor of that company's products or services. For this reason, you should view all scientific claims in their context and question them. Remember that skepticism is an important part of scientific thought, even when considering research done by qualified scientists.

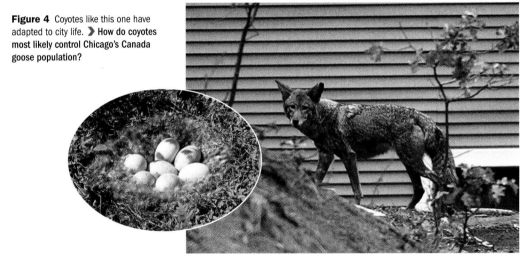

Figure 4 Coyotes like this one have adapted to city life. ❯ **How do coyotes most likely control Chicago's Canada goose population?**

Why It Matters

Statistical Tools Ask students to describe how to analyze data. Emphasize that scientists use mathematical and statistical tools (mean, median, and mode) to describe and compare data. It is possible to compare both quantitative and qualitative data using mathematics and statistics. Arguments provided by scientists would be much weaker if it were not for the integration of math.

Differentiated Instruction

Basic Learners/Struggling Readers

Bias Has Many Meanings Help students understand that the word *bias* has several definitions and can be used as a noun, adjective, verb, and adverb. Ask students to use a dictionary to look up the word *bias* and to write sentences using each of the meanings of the word. Scientific bias results from introducing error into a study by consciously or unconsciously favoring an outcome. Ask students how the methods of science attempt to reduce the effects of bias. (Use of a control group provides a standard for comparison, use of multiple trials reduces the risk of error, peer review of discoveries provides objective oversight.) **LS Verbal**

Scientific Theories

When related hypotheses are well supported and explain a great amount of data, these hypotheses may be put together to form a theory. ❯ The main difference between a theory and a hypothesis is that a hypothesis is a specific, testable prediction for a limited set of conditions and a theory is a general explanation for a broad range of data. Some examples of scientific theories include the quantum theory, the cell theory, and the theory of evolution. As you study science, remember that the word *theory* is used very differently by scientists and by the general public. People may say, "It's just a theory," suggesting that an idea is untested, but scientists view a theory as a highly tested, generally accepted principle that explains a vast number of observations and experimental data.

Constructing a Theory **Figure 5** summarizes the steps in the development of a theory. Constructing a theory often involves considering contrasting ideas and conflicting hypotheses. Argument, disagreement, and unresolved questions are a healthy part of scientific research. Scientists routinely evaluate and critique one another's work. Once a scientist completes an investigation, he or she often writes a report for publication in a scientific journal. Before publication, the research report is reviewed by other scientists. These reviewers ensure that the investigation was carried out with the appropriate controls, methods, and data analysis. The reviewers also check that the conclusions reached by the author are justified by the data obtained. Publishing an investigation allows other scientists to use the information to form their hypotheses. They can also repeat the investigations and confirm the validity of the conclusions.

If the results of an experiment can be reproduced many times, the scientific research may help develop a new theory. However, the possibility always remains that future evidence will cause a scientific theory to be revised or even rejected. Challenging old theories is how scientific understanding grows.

❯ **Reading Check** *How does the scientific use of the word* **theory** *differ from how it is used by the general public?*

Figure 5 Scientists build theories from questions, predictions, hypotheses, and experimental results. ❯ **How can an experiment lead to a theory?**

Section 2 Review

❯KEY IDEAS

1. **Summarize** the processes that scientists often use when beginning scientific investigations.
2. **Describe** two ways that scientists test hypotheses.
3. **Explain** the difference between a hypothesis and a theory.

CRITICAL THINKING

4. **Analyzing Methods** Provide one example of a case in which an experiment would not be possible and one example in which an experiment would not be ethical.
5. **Forming Hypotheses** A friend notices that her dog is getting thinner even though she has not changed how much she feeds him. Propose three testable hypotheses to explain the dog's weight loss.

METHODS OF SCIENCE

6. **Designing an Experiment** Suppose that Paine had hypothesized that the Canada geese in Chicago were not reproducing at a normal rate. What experiment could he use to test whether the geese in Chicago were less fertile than geese elsewhere?

Section **3**

❯ Focus

This section introduces the tools and techniques scientists use, including measurement systems, common lab practices, and laboratory safety procedures.

🔔 Bellringer

Use the Bellringer transparency to prepare students for this section.

❯ Teach

Demonstration

Measuring Have each student use the span of his or her outstretched hand from the tip of the little finger to the tip of the thumb to measure the length of a long object such as a table or chalkboard. Students should report their measurements in *hands*. Tell them to estimate any "partial hands" in finger widths. Then, have students compare their measurements. (Measurements will vary.) Ask students why the measurements differ. (The sizes of their hands differ.) Discuss with students why using a standard system of measurement in science is important. **LS Kinesthetic**

go.hrw.com
✳ interact online

Students can interact with SI relationships by going to go.hrw.com and typing in the keyword HX8BIOF6.

Answers to Caption Questions

Figure 6: There are 1,000 pennies in $10.

Section Correlations
1.2.2a
1.2.4

Key Ideas

Key Ideas	Key Terms	Why It Matters
❯ Why do scientists use SI units for measurement? ❯ What are some tools and techniques that scientists use in the laboratory? ❯ What can you do to stay safe during an investigation?	SI	Understanding the tools and techniques that scientists use can help you work safely and effectively in the lab.

The Living Environment
Standard 1
2.2a Development of a research plan involves researching background information and understanding the major concepts in the area being investigated. Recommendations for methodologies, use of technologies, proper equipment, and safety precautions should also be included.
2.4 Carry out a research plan for testing explanations, including selecting and developing techniques, acquiring and building apparatus, and recording observations as necessary.

Scientists use various units of measurements, tools, and lab techniques to help them make observations and gather and record data.

Measurement Systems

Measurements taken by scientists are expressed in the International System of Units (**SI**), which is the official name of the metric system. ❯**The International System of Units is used by all scientists because scientists need to share a common measurement system. SI is also preferred by scientists because it is scaled in multiples of 10, which makes the system easy to use.** Like the U.S. monetary system, SI is a decimal system, so all relationships between SI units are based on powers of 10. Most SI units have a prefix that indicates the relationship of that unit to a base unit. For example, the SI base unit for length is the meter. The prefix *kilo-* means 1,000. Thus, a kilometer is equal to 1,000 meters. **Figure 6** shows other common SI units.

❯ **Reading Check** *How are prefixes used in names of SI units?*

go.hrw.com
✳ interact online
Keyword: HX8BIOF6

Figure 6 How many dimes are in a dollar? The question is easy to answer because our monetary system, like SI, is built on powers of 10. ❯ How many pennies are there in $10?

 0.01
 0.1
 1
 10

Common SI Units

Prefix	Factor	Volume	Length	Mass
kilo-	1,000	1 kiloliter = 1,000 L	1 kilometer = 1,000 m	1 kilogram = 1,000 g
—	1	1 liter (L)	1 meter (m)	1 gram (g)
centi-	0.01	1 centiliter = 0.01 L	1 centimeter = 0.01 m	1 centigram = 0.01 g
milli-	0.001	1 milliliter = 0.001 L	1 millimeter = 0.001 m	1 milligram = 0.001 g

Key Resources

 Transparencies
A6 SI Base Units
A7 Some SI Prefixes
A8 SI Units

Visual Concepts
Types of Microscopes
Parts of a Microscope
Magnification and Resolution

Differentiated Instruction

English Learners

Measurements, Units, and Quantities Help students understand the difference between measurements, units, and quantities. Have a tape measurer, a measuring cup, and balance to use as props in discussing quantities. Then, proceed to describe the relationships. Five centimeters is a measurement. Centimeter is a unit. Length is a quantity. Ask students to determine the quantity and unit from the following measurements: 50 mL (volume, milliliter), 4.0 mg (mass, microgram), 53 cm³ (volume, cubic centimeters), 25 km² (area, square kilometers). **LS Verbal**

QuickLab

⏱ 15 min

Practice Staining Techniques

The parts (organelles) of a typical cell are mostly transparent. In a technique called *staining*, color is added to cell parts to help identify and distinguish them.

Procedure

1. Use forceps to remove a thin layer of onion skin, and place it in the center of a glass slide. Add a drop of water, and place a coverslip over the specimen.

2. Examine the onion skin with a light microscope. Draw what you see.

3. Place a drop of iodine stain along one edge of the coverslip. Touch a piece of paper towel to the opposite edge to draw the water. When the skin is stained, examine it with the microscope.

Analysis

1. **Describe** how the stain affected the onion skin.

2. **CRITICAL THINKING** **Analyzing Information** What is the advantage of using the paper to draw the stain across the field of view?

Lab Techniques

❯ In the lab, scientists always keep detailed and accurate notes and perform precise measurements. Many scientists also use specialized tools, such as microscopes, and specialized procedures, such as sterile technique.

Microscopy Many organisms, such as bacteria, are too small to see with the unaided eye. Microscopes help magnify these organisms. Two common kinds of microscopes are light microscopes and electron microscopes. In a light microscope, light passes through one or more lenses to produce an enlarged image of an object. An electron microscope forms an image of an object by using a beam of electrons to magnify extremely small objects.

Sterile Technique Scientists who study cells need to be able to grow cells in a controlled setting. Because bacteria live everywhere on Earth, scientists must use sterile technique when growing cells. Sterile technique is a method of keeping unwanted microorganisms out of a lab to minimize the risk of contamination. The tools of sterile technique include an autoclave for sterilizing equipment, sterilized dishes and pipets, a laminar-flow hood, and latex gloves.

Collecting Data Remotely As electronic technology has advanced, more tools have become available for scientists to use. Remote tracking devices to attach to released animals, data collected from satellites, and technology based on the global positioning system (GPS) have enabled scientists to conduct investigations that would have been impossible just a few decades ago.

❯ **Reading Check** *When might sterile technique be used in a lab?*

SI the International System of Units, which is the measurement system that is accepted by scientists worldwide

ACADEMIC VOCABULARY

technique a way of doing something

SC*i*LINKS®
www.scilinks.org
Topic: History of Standard Units
Code: HX80747

Differentiated Instruction

Basic Learners

Teaching Key Ideas

Safety Contract Ask students and their parents to read, sign and date a safety contract that states they understand the safety precautions discussed in the text. Have the students return the signed copy, and keep it in a safe place.

 Intrapersonal

READING TOOLBOX

Idea Wheel Details for each heading follow:

Measurement
• SI as the accepted system
• prefixes determine relative quantity

Microscopy
• view extremely small objects

Sterile technique
• prevents contamination that could distort experimental results

Remote data collection
• based on GPS technology

Close

Formative Assessment

Which of the following is a unit of volume?

A. centimeter (Incorrect. A centimeter is a unit of length.)

B. milliliter (Correct!)

C. gram (Incorrect. A gram is a unit of mass.)

D. kilometer (Incorrect. A kilometer is a unit of length.)

Figure 7 Using proper safety equipment is necessary during every scientific investigation. For example, this scientist must use a special suit to protect his skin from the extreme heat coming from this volcano vent.

READING TOOLBOX

Idea Wheel Complete the idea wheel that you started at the beginning of the chapter. Fill in the outer sections of the wheel with details about the tools and techniques used in science.

Safety

As you can see in **Figure 7,** studying science is exciting, but it can also be dangerous. ❯ Scientists must use caution when working in the lab or doing field research to avoid dangers such as chemical burns, exposure to radiation, exposure to infectious disease, animal bites, or poisonous plants. Here are some guidelines for working safely in the lab:

• Listen carefully to your teacher, and follow all instructions.
• Read your lab procedure carefully before beginning the lab.
• Do not take any shortcuts in your lab procedure.
• Always wear your safety goggles and any other needed safety equipment when working in the lab.
• Measure chemicals precisely.
• Never taste or smell any materials or chemicals that you use in a lab unless your teacher instructs you to do so.
• Do not use any damaged or defective equipment.
• Keep your lab area clean and free from clutter.
• When you place something onto the lab bench, make sure that the object sits securely on the bench and will not fall or tip over.
• Pay attention to where you are walking.
• If you are working outside, be aware of your surroundings. Avoid poisonous plants and animals that live in the area. Wear sunscreen and a hat that shades your neck and ears.

Accidents If an accident does occur, remain calm. Make sure that you are safe and that no one else is in danger. Then, inform your teacher right away. Follow all of the instructions that your teacher gives you. Know the location and proper operation of all lab safety equipment before it is needed. A review of lab safety equipment before labs begin can save valuable time if an accident happens in your lab. For more information about lab safety and how to respond to accidents in the lab, read *Lab Safety* at the front of this book.

❯ **Reading Check** *List at least five actions that you can take in the laboratory to ensure your safety.*

Section 3 Review

❯ KEY IDEAS

1. **Explain** why scientists use SI units for measurement.
2. **Describe** two kinds of microscopes.
3. **Summarize** the steps that you should take if an accident occurs in the lab.

CRITICAL THINKING

4. **Inferring Conclusions** In general, measurement systems that are based on powers of 10 are the easiest for people to use. Infer why these systems are easiest to use.
5. **Analyzing Information** Why is reading the lab procedure before starting an experiment considered an important part of lab safety?

MATH SKILLS

6. **Performing Conversions** A scientist pours 3.48 milliliters (mL) of hydrochloric acid into a beaker. How many liters of hydrochloric acid did the scientist pour into the beaker?

Answers to Section Review

1. Scientists use SI measurements so that they all use a common system. Also, it is the easiest system to use because SI is scaled in multiples of 10.

2. In a light microscope, light passes through one or more lenses to produce an enlarged image of a specimen. An electron microscope also forms an image of a specimen but uses a beam of electrons rather than light.

3. If an accident does occur, remain calm. Make sure that you are safe and that no one else is in danger. Then, inform your teacher right away. Follow all the instructions that your teacher gives you.

4. Sample answer: Our system of math is built in base ten so it is very easy to multiply and divide by factors of ten.

5. By reading the procedure, the experimenter becomes familiar and comfortable with the steps of the lab, and reduces the chance of accidentally making a mistake that could cause harm.

6. 0.00348 L

Section 4 What Is Biology?

Key Ideas	Key Terms		Why It Matters
❯ What are some of the branches of biology? ❯ What are seven characteristics that all living things share?	biology cell homeostasis metabolism	reproduction heredity evolution	All living things on Earth are tied together by common traits and rely on one another for their common survival.

The giant sequoia shown in **Figure 8** is very different from the man standing below it. But both organisms have much in common. Studying living organisms is what the science of biology is all about.

The Study of Life

Biology is the study of life. Life is extremely diverse. It would be impossible for one person to become an expert in all aspects of biology, so scientists specialize. There are many branches of biology. ❯ Biology includes biochemistry, ecology, cell biology, genetics, evolutionary theory, microbiology, botany, zoology, and physiology. Biochemistry is the study of the chemistry of life. Ecology is the study of how organisms interact with each other and with their environment. The study of life on the cellular level is called cell biology. Genetics is the study of how organisms pass traits to their offspring. Evolutionary theory is the study of changes in types of organisms over time. The study of microscopic organisms is called microbiology. The study of plants is called botany. Zoology is the study of animals. Physiology is the study of the human body. As you read, you will learn about each of these fields. You will also have the opportunity to practice techniques that are used in careers in each of these fields.

 The Living Environment
Standard 4
4.1a Reproduction and development are necessary for the continuation of any species.
5.3a Dynamic equilibrium results from detection of and response to stimuli. Organisms detect and respond to change in a variety of ways both at the cellular level and at the organismal level.

biology the scientific study of living organisms and their interactions with the environment

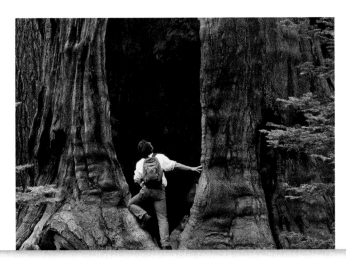

Figure 8 Both the man and the sequoia tree that he is standing on are living organisms.
❯ Which branches of biology would study both humans and trees?

Key Resources

 Transparencies
A1 The Seven Properties of Life

Visual Concepts
Biology
Unifying Themes of Biology
Heredity
Evolution

❯ Focus

This section describes those characteristics that are shared by all living things.

Bellringer

Use the Bellringer transparency to prepare students for this section.

❯ Teach

Demonstration

Alive or Not? Show students a variety of objects and ask them to state whether each is *alive, not alive was alive*, or *never was alive*. Objects you might use include a live plant, a dead leaf, a piece of natural cork, fire, a rock, a bottle of water, a synthetic sponge, and a natural sponge. Challenge students to defend the characteristics they used to determine their answers.
LS Logical

Answers to Caption Questions
Figure 8: Biochemistry, ecology, cell biology, genetics, and evolutionary theory are branches of biology that would study both humans and trees.

Section Correlations
4.4.1a
4.5.3a

Teacher's Notes Field biologists study living things and their relationship to their environment and they work to understand how humans affect organisms. Many use sophisticated technology, such as remote-sensing satellite imagery. They may spend much of their time on a computer analyzing data when they are not working in the field. By studying organisms in their natural habitat, biologists can hopefully gather enough information about various species to protect them from extinction. **LS** Verbal

READING TOOLBOX

Visual Literacy Help students identify the activities each scientist in the picture might be doing. Discuss how the activities relate to the job of the biologist. Ask students whether they would like to work in the conditions shown.

Answer to Research

Many field biologists work in government agencies as wildlife biologists, entomologists, range managers, pollution control experts, toxicologists, soil scientists, and naturalists. Others do consulting work, teach, and write for technical journals.

Properties of Life

All living organisms share certain properties. **>** The seven properties of life are cellular organization, homeostasis, metabolism, responsiveness, reproduction, heredity, and growth. Life is characterized by the presence of all seven properties at some stage in an organism's life.

Cellular Organization A cell is the smallest unit capable of all life functions. A **cell** is a highly organized, tiny structure that is enclosed in a thin covering called a *membrane*. The basic structure of cells is the same in all organisms.

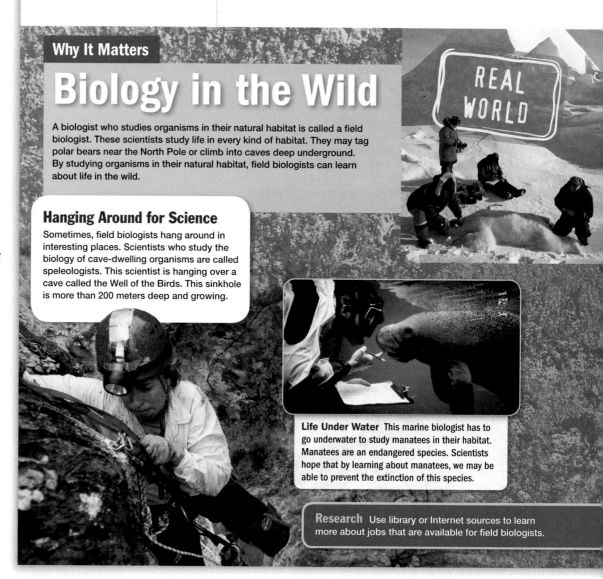

Why It Matters

Biology in the Wild

REAL WORLD

A biologist who studies organisms in their natural habitat is called a field biologist. These scientists study life in every kind of habitat. They may tag polar bears near the North Pole or climb into caves deep underground. By studying organisms in their natural habitat, field biologists can learn about life in the wild.

Hanging Around for Science
Sometimes, field biologists hang around in interesting places. Scientists who study the biology of cave-dwelling organisms are called speleologists. This scientist is hanging over a cave called the Well of the Birds. This sinkhole is more than 200 meters deep and growing.

Life Under Water This marine biologist has to go underwater to study manatees in their habitat. Manatees are an endangered species. Scientists hope that by learning about manatees, we may be able to prevent the extinction of this species.

Research Use library or Internet sources to learn more about jobs that are available for field biologists.

Why It Matters

Career Development Interviews with scientists often describe that their interests in science came from a supportive teacher or inspirational speaker. Bring in outside speakers when possible to expose students to people who work in science. Make career development a part of your monthly schedule and students will thank you for it! Make it a point to have speakers discuss the value of teams and working together to achieve stated goals. **LS** Interpersonal

Homeostasis All living organisms must maintain a stable internal environment in order to function properly. The maintenance of stable internal conditions in spite of changes in the external environment is called **homeostasis.**

Metabolism Living things carry out many chemical reactions in order to obtain energy. **Metabolism** is the sum of all of the chemical reactions carried out in an organism. Almost all of the energy used by living things originally comes from sunlight. Plants, algae, and some bacteria capture this energy and use it to make molecules. These molecules serve as the source of energy, or food, for other organisms.

Responsiveness In addition to maintaining a stable internal environment, living organisms also respond to their external environment. Plants bend toward sunlight. Birds fluff their feathers to insulate their bodies during cold weather. Students, shown in **Figure 9,** also respond to their environment.

Reproduction Most living things can reproduce. **Reproduction** is the process by which organisms make more of their own kind from one generation to the next. Because no organism lives forever, reproduction is an essential part of life.

Heredity When an organism reproduces, it passes on its own traits to its offspring in a process known as **heredity.** Heredity is the reason that children tend to look like their parents. Inherited characteristics change over generations. This process is called **evolution.**

Growth All living organisms grow . Some one-celled organisms only grow briefly, during the time that they are reproducing. Other living things, like the giant sequoia, grow for thousands of years and reach an enormous size. As organisms grow, many change. This process is called *development.* Frogs begin as eggs, develop into tadpoles, and eventually develop into frogs. Development differs from evolution because development refers to change in a single individual during that individual's life.

> **Reading Check** *How is heredity related to evolution?*

Figure 9 These students are responding to the rain by using raincoats. **>** Can you think of a way that you have responded to your environment today?

---

cell In biology, the smallest unit that can perform all life processes

homeostasis the maintenance of a constant internal state in a changing environment

metabolism the sum of all chemical processes that occur in an organism

reproduction the process of producing offspring

heredity the passing of genetic traits from parent to offspring

evolution the development of new types of organisms from preexisting types of organisms over time

---

Teaching Key Ideas

Homeostasis Ask students how humans maintain a constant body temperature. (Sample answers are sweating, shivering, wearing clothing, and physical activity. If students suggest having body fat, tell them that fat does not insulate humans.) To illustrate the maintenance of a human's body temperature, ask a volunteer to have his or her body temperature monitored before and immediately after vigorous exercise. Human body temperature fluctuates based on activity. **LS** Verbal

Answer to Caption Question
Figure 9: Students' answers will vary based on their daily activities.

>Close

Formative Assessment
Which of the following is not a property of an individual organism?
A. evolution (Correct. Individual organisms do not evolve. Species do.)
B. metabolism (Incorrect. Organisms must convert molecules into energy.)
C. heredity (Incorrect. Organisms express the combination of their parent's genetic composition.)
D. homeostasis (Incorrect. Organisms must maintain a stable internal environment.)

Section 4 Review

> KEY IDEAS
1. **Explain** what biology is.
2. **Describe** nine fields that are part of the science of biology.
3. **Name** the basic unit of life.
4. **Discuss** the seven properties all living organisms share.
5. **Define** homeostasis.

CRITICAL THINKING
6. **Recognizing Verifiable Facts** If you find an object that seems alive, how might you determine if the object is indeed an organism?
7. **Elaborating** Give an example of one way that you are interdependent on another type of organism.
8. **Analyzing Information** Relate five of the characteristics of life to an organism familiar to you.

ALTERNATIVE ASSESSMENT
9. **Interview a Biologist** Choose a field of biology that interests you. Locate a biologist working in that field, and conduct an interview by phone or e-mail. Ask the biologist how he or she became interested in his or her field and what the scientist's work is like. Report your findings to the class.

Answers to Section Review
1. Biology is the study of living things.
2. Biology includes biochemistry, ecology, cell biology, genetics, evolutionary theory, microbiology, botany, zoology, and physiology.
3. the cell
4. cellular organization, reproduction and heredity, metabolism, homeostasis, growth, and responsiveness
5. Homeostasis is the ability to maintain a stable internal environment in spite of changes in the external environment.
6. Students might test for the characteristics of living organisms.
7. Students may mention that they depend on other organisms for food.
8. Students may relate the characteristics of life to a pet such as a dog, saying that the dog is composed of cells, is able to reproduce with other dogs, requires food, can pass on its genes to its offspring, and depends on other organisms to survive.
9. Interviews will vary depending on whom students interview.

Lab

Time Required

One 45-minute lab period

Ratings

EASY ——————————→ HARD

Teacher Prep   🧪
Concept Level   🧪
Student Setup   🧪🧪
Clean Up   🧪

Safety Caution

Remind students to wear heat-protective gloves when handling the heat lamp. Do not use the heat lamp near water.

Tips and Tricks

Before the lab begins, review the use of the balance and graduated cylinders. Have half the students do the first part of the lab while the other half does the second part. Switch after 15–25 minutes. You may wish to have students record their cumulative data in a data table on the board. Have students calculate the mean of each range of measurement. Dispose of solutions, broken glass, and sand in the designated containers.

Chapter 1 Lab

Objectives

> Express measurements in SI units.
> Read a thermometer.
> Measure liquid volume by using a graduated cylinder.
> Measure mass by using a balance.
> Determine the density (mass-to-volume ratio) of two liquids.

Materials

- graduated cylinder, 100 mL
- sand, light colored, 75 mL
- cups, plastic (2)
- sand, dark colored, 75 mL
- thermometers, Celsius, alcohol filled (2)
- gloves, heat resistant
- ring stand or lamp support
- light source
- stopwatch or clock
- balance
- corn oil, 25 mL
- water, 25 mL
- cup, clear plastic
- graph paper

Safety

SI Units

Most scientists use SI units for all of the measurements that they take. In this lab, you will practice making measurements in SI units.

Procedure

Measure Sand Temperature

1. In your lab report, prepare a data table similar to the table below.

2. Using a graduated cylinder, measure 75 mL of light-colored sand, and pour it into one of the small plastic cups. Repeat this procedure with the dark-colored sand and another plastic cup.

3. Level the sand by placing the cup on your desk and sliding the cup back and forth. Insert one thermometer into each cup. Relevel the sand if necessary.

4. Using a ring stand or lamp support, position the lamp approximately 9 cm from the top of the sand, as shown in the figure. Make sure that the lamp is evenly positioned between the two cups.

5. Before turning on the lamp, record in your data table the initial temperature of each cup of sand.

6. ⚠ CAUTION: Wear heat-resistant gloves when handling the lamp. The lamp will become very hot and may burn you. Note the time or start the stopwatch when you turn on the lamp. The lamp will become hot and warm the sand. Check the temperature of the sand in each container at 1-minute intervals for 10 minutes. In your data table, record the temperature of the sand after each minute.

Sand Temperature	Temperature (degrees C)	
Time (min)	Dark-colored sand	Light-colored sand
Start		
1		
2		
3		
4		
5		

Compare the Density of Oil and Water

7 In your lab report, prepare a data table similar to the Density of Two Liquids table.

8 Label one clean plastic cup "Oil," and label another "Water." Using a balance, measure the mass of each plastic cup, and record the value in your data table.

9 ⬧ Put on an apron. Using a clean graduated cylinder, measure 25 mL of corn oil, and pour it into the plastic cup labeled "Oil." Using a balance, measure the mass of the plastic cup containing the corn oil, and record the mass in your data table.

10 Repeat step 9 with water and the plastic cup labeled "Water."

11 To find the mass of the oil, subtract the mass of the empty cup from the mass of the cup and the oil together.

12 To find the density of the oil, divide the mass of the oil by the volume of the oil, as shown in the equation below.

$$\text{Density of oil} = \frac{\text{mass of oil}}{\text{volume of oil}} = \underline{\hspace{1cm}} \text{ g/mL}$$

13 Repeat steps 11 and 12 to find the mass and density of water.

14 Combine the oil and water in the clear cup, and record your observations in your lab report.

15 ⬧ ⬧ Clean up your materials according to your teacher's instructions. Wash your hands before leaving the lab.

Density of Two Liquids	
a. Mass of empty oil cup	g
b. Mass of empty water cup	g
c. Mass of cup and oil	g
d. Mass of cup and water	g
e. Volume of oil	25 ml
f. Volume of water	25 ml
Calculating Actual Mass	
Oil Item c − Item a =	g
Water Item d − Item b =	g
g. Density of oil	g/ml
h. Density of water	g/ml

Analyze and Conclude

1. Graphing Data Use graph paper or a graphing calculator to graph the data that you collected in the first part of the lab. Plot time on the x-axis and temperature on the y-axis.

2. SCIENTIFIC METHODS **Interpreting Data** Based on your graph, what is the relationship between color and heat absorption?

3. Inferring Conclusions How might the color of the clothes that you wear affect how warm you are on a sunny day?

4. SCIENTIFIC METHODS **Making Systematic Observations** In the second part of the lab, what did you observe when you combined the oil and water? Relate your observation to the densities that you calculated.

5. SCIENTIFIC METHODS **Using Evidence to Make Explanations** What could you infer about the value for the density of ice if you observe it floating in water?

Extensions

6. Understanding Relationships How would your calculated density values be affected if you misread the volume measurement on the graduated cylinder?

7. Experimental Design Pumice is a volcanic rock that has a density less than 1.00 g/cm³. How would you prove this density if you did not have a balance to weigh the pumice? (Hint: The density of water is 1.00 g/cm³.)

Answers to Analyze and Conclude

1. Students' graphs should show that temperature rises with time.

2. The dark sand absorbs more heat than the light sand does.

3. Wearing light-colored clothing will keep students cooler than wearing dark-colored clothing because light-colored material does not absorb as much heat as dark-colored material does.

4. The oil floated on the water. Therefore, oil is less dense than water.

5. Ice is less dense than water.

Answers to Extensions

6. If the recorded values were too high, then the calculated density would be too low. If the recorded values were too low, then the calculated density would be too high.

7. You could show that the density of pumice was less than that of water by floating some pumice on water.

Key Resources

 Holt Lab Generator

 Lab Datasheet (Levels A, B, C)

 Holt Science Biology Video Labs

 Virtual Investigations

SUPER SUMMARY

Have students connect the major concepts in this chapter through an interactive Super Summary. Visit **go.hrw.com** and type in the key-word **HX8BIOS** to access the Super Summary for this chapter.

Reteaching Key Ideas

Observing and Questioning Have students study the photo of the coyote in this chapter. List questions they have about coyotes in urban environments. Have students identify questions that could be answered through scientific investigation. **LS** Logical

Scientific Investigation Have students design an experiment to test the hypothesis that the skin of an apple protects the apple from drying out. **LS** Logical

Metric Measurement Have students convert 6 kilometers into meters (6,000 m) and then centimeters (600,000 cm). Next, have students convert 6 miles into feet (there are 5,280 feet in 1 mile, so 6 mi = 31,680 ft) and then into inches (380,160 in). Ask students why scientists use the metric system. **LS** Logical

Characteristics of Life Point out a living thing and a nonliving thing in the classroom. Have students draw a graphic organizer to compare and contrast the two using the characteristics of living things discussed in the chapter. **LS** Visual

Key Ideas	Key Terms

1 The Nature of Science

> Scientific thought involves making observations, using evidence to draw conclusions, being skeptical about ideas, and being open to change when new discoveries are made.

> Science is governed by truths that are valid everywhere in the universe. These truths are called *universal laws*.

> Scientific investigations require ethical behavior.

> An understanding of science can help you take better care of your health, be a wiser consumer, and become a better-informed citizen.

skepticism (4)

2 Scientific Methods

> Most scientific investigations begin with observations that lead to questions.

> Scientists can conduct controlled experiments and qualitative studies in order to test a hypothesis.

> The main difference between a theory and a hypothesis is that a hypothesis is a specific, testable prediction for a limited set of conditions and a theory is a general explanation for a broad range of data.

observation (10)
hypothesis (10)
experiment (11)
control group (11)
theory (13)

3 Tools and Techniques

> The International System of Units (SI) is used by all scientists because scientists need to share a common measurement system. SI is scaled in multiples of 10, which makes the system easy to use.

> In the lab, scientists always keep detailed and accurate notes and perform precise measurements. Many scientists also use specialized tools, such as microscopes, and specialized procedures, such as sterile technique.

> Scientists must use caution when working in the lab or doing field research to avoid dangers such as chemical burns, exposure to radiation, exposure to infectious disease, animal bites, or poisonous plants.

SI (14)

4 What Is Biology?

> Biology includes biochemistry, ecology, cell biology, genetics, evolutionary theory, microbiology, botany, zoology, and physiology.

> The seven properties of life are cellular organization, homeostasis, metabolism, responsiveness, reproduction, heredity, and growth.

biology (17)
cell (18)
homeostasis (19)
metabolism (19)
reproduction (19)
heredity (19)
evolution (19)

Regents Exam Practice

PART A: Answer all questions in this part.

Directions: For each statement or question, write on your separate answer sheet the number of the word or expression that best completes the statement or answers the question.

1 Researchers performing a well-designed experiment should base their conclusions on
(1) the hypothesis of the experiment
(2) data from repeated trials of the experiment
(3) a small sample size to insure a reliable outcome of the experiment
(4) results predicted before performing the experiment

2 Which statement best describes a scientific theory?
(1) It is a collection of data designed to provide support for a prediction.
(2) It is an educated guess that can be tested by experimentation.
(3) It is a scientific fact that no longer requires any evidence to support it.
(4) It is a general statement that is supported by many scientific observations.

3 The analysis of data gathered during a particular experiment is necessary in order to
(1) formulate a hypothesis for that experiment.
(2) develop a research plan for that experiment.
(3) design a control for that experiment.
(4) draw a valid conclusion for that experiment.

4 A scientist is planning to carry out an experiment on the effect of heat on the function of a certain enzyme. Which would not be an appropriate first step?
(1) doing research in a library
(2) having discussions with other scientists
(3) completing a data table of expected results
(4) using what is already known about the enzyme

5 Why do scientists consider any hypothesis valuable?
(1) A hypothesis requires no further investigation.
(2) A hypothesis may lead to further investigation even if it is disproved by the experiment.
(3) A hypothesis requires no further investigation if it is proved by the experiment.
(4) A hypothesis can be used to explain a conclusion even if it is disproved by the experiment.

6 In Texas, researchers gave a cholesterol-reducing drug to 2,335 people and an inactive substitute (placebo) to 2,081. Most of the volunteers were men who had normal cholesterol levels and no history of heart disease. After 5 years, 97 people getting the placebo had suffered heart attacks compared to only 57 people who had received the actual drug. The researchers are recommending that to help prevent heart attacks, all people (even those without high cholesterol) take these cholesterol-reducing drugs. In addition to the information above, what is another piece of information that the researchers must have before support for the recommendation can be justified?
(1) Were the eating habits of the two groups similar?
(2) How does a heart attack affect cholesterol levels?
(3) Did the heart attacks result in deaths?
(4) What chemical is in the placebo?

7 A biologist reported success in breeding a tiger with a lion, producing healthy offspring. Other biologists will accept this report as fact only if
(1) research shows that other animals can be crossbred
(2) the offspring are given a scientific name
(3) the biologist included a control in the experiment
(4) other researchers can replicate the experiment

8 Though scientists study the world from differing perspectives, what must all scientists take into account?
(1) universal laws
(2) animal behavior
(3) temperature differences
(4) the importance of biology

1. (2) The choice about results is incorrect as a conclusion should be based on results obtained during the current experiment. The choice about hypothesis is incorrect as conclusions are based on the data obtained and whether they support or reject the hypothesis. The choice about sample size is not true. *(#01, June 2005 Regents Exam)*

2. (4) A scientific theory is a statement that is supported by evidence from many scientific investigations. It is not merely a guess or a prediction. A scientific theory may change as new evidence is discovered. *(#03, August 2005 Regents Exam)*

3. (4) Formulating a hypothesis, developing an research plan, and designing a control for the experiment are all stages that need to be completed before the experiment can begin. *(#01, January 2004 Regents Exam)*

4. (3) Doing research in a library, having discussions with other scientists, and using what is already known about the enzyme will all help the scientist develop a hypothesis and design the experiment. Completing a data table of expected results could result in a bias toward an expected outcome. *(#01, August 2004 Regents Exam)*

5. (2) A hypothesis cannot be used to explain a conclusion if it is disproved by the experiment. However, whether they are true or not, hypotheses can lead to investigations that may further scientific knowledge. *(#02, June 2003 Regents Exam)*

6. (1) A placebo contains harmless substances that are designed to have no effect. In this case, the drug appeared to be more effective than the placebo in preventing heart attacks. However, the eating habits of the two groups, which may have been contributed to heart disease, must be known before the researchers can conclude that the cholesterol-reducing drug prevented the heart attacks and should be given to all people. *(#26, January 2003 Regents Exam)*

Regents Exam Practice Correlations

1.1.2a	14	1.3.4a	5
1.1.2b	12	1.3.4c	11
1.1.4a	2	1.3.5a	7
1.2.3c	1, 4, 9	1.3.5b	6
1.3.1a	3, 15, 16		

7. **(4)** Even if the original experiment included a control, scientists should try to replicate the results before accepting them. These results should not be accepted just because other animals can be crossbred, or because the researchers assigned a scientific name to the offspring. *(#01, January 2003 Regents Exam)*

8. **(1)** Animal behavior, temperature differences, and the importance of biology may not be pertinent for all scientists' work. But universal laws of science hold true in all situations.

9. **(4)** The student would improve the validity of the results by repeating the experiment. Once more results were gathered, the hypothesis might have to be revised. If all results were similar to the original results, the student could conclude that light is not necessary for germination. *(#04, August 2003 Regents Exam)*

10. **(2)** The volume of a liquid in a graduated cylinder is measured at the bottom of the meniscus. *(#37, January 2004 Regents Exam)*

PART B

11. **(3)** The choices about sample size and duplicating results are incorrect as these two factors validate experiments. An unsupported hypothesis does not mean the experiment is invalid, but it can lead to a rejection or revision of the hypothesis. *(#32, June 2006 Regents Exam)*

12. **(3)** The most reliable sources are current articles based on scientific research that have been published in a scientific journal. News broadcasts or magazines may misinterpret information, or leave out important information. News articles from many years past may not represent the most current understanding of a subject. *(#33, August 2005 Regents Exam)*

13. **(3)** For research on a new treatment, scientists may not know if the treatment will be effective or cause side effects. Scientists should always share results with others.

---

9 A student hypothesized that lettuce seeds would not sprout (germinate) unless they were exposed to darkness. The student planted 10 lettuce seeds under a layer of soil and scattered 10 lettuce seeds on top of the soil. The data collected are shown in the table below.

Data Table

Seed Treatment	Number of Seeds Germinated
Planted under soil	9
Scattered on top of soil	8

One way to improve the validity of these results would be to

(1) conclude that darkness is necessary for lettuce seed germination
(2) conclude that light is necessary for lettuce seed germination
(3) revise the hypothesis
(4) repeat the experiment

10 The diagram below shows a portion of a graduated cylinder. What is the volume of the liquid in this cylinder?

(1) 22 mL
(2) 24 mL
(3) 25 mL
(4) 26 mL

PART B

11 A science researcher is reviewing another scientist's experiment and conclusion. The reviewer would most likely consider the experiment invalid if
(1) the sample size produced a great deal of data
(2) other individuals are able to duplicate the results
(3) it contains conclusions not explained by the evidence given
(4) the hypothesis was not supported by the data obtained

12 Which source would provide the most reliable information for use in a research project investigating the effects of antibiotics on disease-causing bacteria?
(1) the local news section of a newspaper from 1993
(2) a news program on national television about antigens produced by various plants
(3) a current professional science journal article on the control of pathogens
(4) an article in a weekly news magazine about reproduction in pathogens

13 A scientist is investigating a new treatment for a disease that affects thousands of people. Many people with this disease volunteer to be part of the study. Which of the following is an ethical concern that the scientist must address before conducting the study?
(1) The scientist must ensure that the treatment will be effective.
(2) The scientist must ensure that the study's results will not be shared with other scientists.
(3) The scientist must inform the volunteers about the potential dangers of participating in the study.
(4) The scientist must demonstrate that the treatment will not cause any side effects.

PART C

14 The diagram below illustrates the result of growing a garlic bulb in a cup of distilled water over five days.

Design an experiment consisting of a control and three different experimental groups to test the prediction, "Garlic grows better as the salt concentration of the solution in which it is grown increases." In your answer, be sure to:
- describe the control to be used in the experiment
- describe the difference between the three experimental groups
- state *one* type of measurement that should be made to determine if the prediction is accurate
- describe *one* example of experimental results that would support the prediction

PART D

Base your answers to the questions on the information below and on your knowledge of biology.

A student squeezes and releases a clothespin as often as possible for 2 minutes and then takes his pulse for 20 seconds. After a 2-minute rest, he repeats the procedure. This pattern is repeated one more time. The student's 20-second pulse counts were 23, 26, and 21.

15 Complete the "Pulse/Min" column in the data table below for all three trials as well as the average pulse rate per minute.

Pulse Rate After Activity

Trial	20-Second Pulse Counts	Pulse/Min
1	23	
2	26	
3	21	
Average		

16 What additional data should the student have collected in order to determine the effect of squeezing a clothespin on his pulse rate?

PART C

14. Allow a maximum of 4 credits for designing an experiment to test the prediction "Garlic grows better as the salt concentration of the solution in which it is grown increases," allocated as follows: Allow 1 credit for describing the control as a garlic bulb grown in (distilled) water.; Allow 1 credit for describing the difference between the three experimental groups. Acceptable responses include, but are not limited to: Each experimental group would have a different concentration of salt solution.; Allow 1 credit for stating one type of measurement that should be made to determine if the prediction is accurate. Acceptable responses include, but are not limited to: the length of the leaf in each group; the length of the roots in each group; the number of roots in each group; Allow 1 credit for describing one example of experimental results that would support the prediction. Acceptable responses include, but are not limited to: There is an increase in the length of the leaves as the salt concentration increases.; There is an increase in the length of the roots as the salt concentration increases.; More salt results in more roots. *(#57, June 2005 Regents Exam)*

PART D

15. Allow 1 credit for correctly completing the data table:

Pulse Rate After Activity

Trial	20-Second Pulse Counts	Pulse/Min
1	23	**69**
2	26	**78**
3	21	**63**
Average		**70**

(#67, June 2006 Regents Exam)

16. Allow 1 credit for indicating that the student would need the resting pulse rate for comparison. *(#68, June 2006 Regents Exam)*

Applications of Biology

CHAPTER OPENER, pp. 26–27 · 15 min.

SECTION 1 Health in the 21st Century,
  pp. 29–32 · 90 min.
》 Meeting the Challenge
》 Disease in a Changing World
》 Biology and Human Potential

SECTION 2 Biology, Technology, and
  Society, pp. 33–37 · 60 min.
》 Biotechnology Around Us
》 Applications of Biological Research
》 Biology, Forensics, and Public Safety
》 The Ethics of Biotechnology

SECTION 3 Biology and the Environment,
  pp. 38–43 · 30 min.
》 A Lost World
》 Technology In Environmental Science
》 Citizen Scientists

Standards	Teach Key Ideas
The Living Environment	
1.1.1a, 4.2.2e, 4.5.2e, 4.5.2j	**Bellringer Transparency** **Transparencies** F6 Important Bacterial Diseases • J37 The Immune Response **Visual Concepts** Pathogen • Vaccine
1.1.1c, 4.2.2b, 4.5.2j, 4.7.3a	**Bellringer Transparency** **Transparencies** A29 How Telescopes Work • C34 Genetic Engineering • C35 Genetically Engineered Medicine • C38 Making a Genetically Engineered Vaccine **Visual Concepts** Genetic Engineering • Using Plasmids to Produce Insulin • Genetically Engineered Vaccines • DNA Fingerprint • Making a DNA Fingerprint
	Bellringer Transparency **Transparencies** E27 Earth's Major Biomes **Visual Concepts** Species • Biodiversity • Conservation • Recycling

See also PowerPoint® Resources

Chapter Review and Assessment Resources

SE Super Summary, p. 44
SE Regents Exam Practice, p. 45
Regents Review Guide
Review Resources
Chapter Tests A and B
go.hrw.com Holt Online Assessment
Regents Question Banks on Teacher's One-Stop Planner

CHAPTER

Fast Track
It is best to cover all of the material in this chapter because it supports science process and technology curriculum objectives.

Basic Learners
TE Vaccination Model, p. 31
TE Word Parts, p. 34
TE Lost World Species, p. 38
Directed Reading Worksheets*
Active Reading Worksheets*
Lab Manuals, Level A*
Study Guide* ■
Note-taking Workbook*
Special Needs Activities and Modified Tests*

Advanced Learners
TE Be the Expert, p. 35
TE DNA Evidence, p. 36
Critical Thinking Worksheets*
Concept Mapping Worksheets*
Science Skills Worksheets*
Lab Datasheets, Level C*

Why It Matters	Hands-On	Skills Development	Assessment
Build student motivation with resources about high-interest applications.	**SE Inquiry Lab** Artificial Shark Skin, p. 27*■	**TE Reading Toolbox** Assessing Prior Knowledge, p. 26 **SE Reading Toolbox,** p. 28	
	SE Quick Lab Model a Low-Tech Solution, p. 31*■ **SE Skills Practice Lab** Microbe Growth, p. 42*■	**SE Reading Toolbox** Predictions, p. 31 **TE Reading Toolbox** Predictions, p. 31	**SE Section Review** **TE Formative Assessment** Spanish Assessment*■ 📁 Section Quiz■
TE Synthetic Hormones, p. 34	**SE Quick Lab** Biomimetic Engineering, p. 34*■ 📁 **Quick Lab** Using Bacteria to Make Food*	**SE Reading Toolbox** Word Parts, p. 35 **TE Reading Toolbox** Word Parts, p. 35	**SE Section Review** **TE Formative Assessment** Spanish Assessment*■ 📁 Section Quiz■
TE Rainforest Medicines, p. 38 **SE Bio Bots,** p. 41	📁 **Inquiry Lab** Collecting Data Through a Survey*	**SE Reading Toolbox** Three-Panel Flip Chart, p. 39 **TE Reading Toolbox** Three-Panel Flip Chart, p. 39 **TE Reading Toolbox** Visual Literacy, p. 41	**SE Section Review** **TE Formative Assessment** Spanish Assessment*■ 📁 Section Quiz■

See also Lab Generator

See also Holt Online Assessment Resources

Resources for Differentiated Instruction

English Learners

TE New Terms, p. 30
TE Word Origins, p. 39
📁 Directed Reading Worksheets*
📁 Active Reading Worksheets*
📁 Lab Manuals, Level A*
📖 Study Guide*■
📖 Note-taking Workbook*
📖 Multilingual Glossary

Struggling Readers

TE New Terms, p. 30
TE Sequencing Events, p. 31
TE Vaccination Model, p. 31
📁 Directed Reading Worksheets*
📁 Active Reading Worksheets*
📁 Lab Manuals, Level A*
📖 Study Guide*
📖 Note-taking Workbook*
📖 Special Needs Activities and Modified Tests*

Special Education Students

TE Biological Research, p. 35
TE Modeling GIS, p. 39
📁 Directed Reading Worksheets*
📁 Active Reading Worksheets*
📁 Lab Manuals, Level A*
📖 Study Guide*■
📖 Note-taking Workbook*
📖 Special Needs Activities and Modified Tests*

Alternative Assessment

TE Understanding Ethics, p. 36
📁 Science Skills Worksheets*
📁 Section Quizzes*■
📖 Chapter Tests A, B, and C*■

Overview

This chapter describes how research connects biology to our everyday lives. This chapter illustrates how knowledge helps us better understand ourselves and the world around us.

Assessing Prior Knowledge Students should understand the following concepts:
• characteristics of life
• nature of scientific thinking

Visual Literacy Ask students what characteristics of living things can be attributed to a robot. (Sample answers: ability to move, ability to communicate, require energy, and the ability to process information) What characteristics of living things are not exhibited by a robot? (Sample answers: ability to reproduce, ability to grow and develop)

Biology is on the verge of creating tools that can target specific cells and deliver therapy. This technique would minimize damage to surrounding cells while maximizing therapeutic efficiency. **LS Visual**

Preview

1 Health in the 21st Century
Meeting the Challenge
Disease in a Changing World
Biology and Human Potential

2 Biology, Technology, and Society
Biotechnology Around Us
Applications of Biological Research
Biology, Forensics, and Public Safety
The Ethics of Biotechnology

3 Biology and the Environment
A Lost World
Technology in Environmental Science
Citizen Scientists

Why It Matters

Biological research affects many aspects of our lives. Many of the products we use, the food we eat, and the medicine we take have been improved through applications of biology.

The Living Environment

Standard 1 Students will use mathematical analysis, scientific inquiry, and engineering design, as appropriate, to pose questions, seek answers, and develop solutions.
Key Idea 1 The central purpose of scientific inquiry is to develop explanations of natural phenomena in a continuing and creative process. *Major Understandings* - 1.1a, 1.1c
Standard 4 Students will understand and apply scientific concepts, principles, and theories pertaining to the physical setting and living environment and recognize the historical development of ideas in science.
Key Idea 2 Organisms inherit genetic information in a variety of ways that result in continuity of structure and function between parents and offspring. *Major Understandings* - 2.2e, 2.2b
Key Idea 5 Organisms maintain a dynamic equilibrium that sustains life. *Major Understandings* - 5.2e, 5.2j
Key Idea 7 Human decisions and activities have had a profound impact on the physical and living environment. *Major Understandings* - 7.3a

Applications of Biology

A robotic instrument in your blood vessels—is this possible? Not yet, but someday doctors may be able to use tiny robots to fix problems inside your body.

This tiny instrument has captured a disease-ridden cell and is destroying it. Though this technology does not exist yet, it may be developed in the near future.

Chapter Correlations   The Living Environment

Standard 1

1.1a Scientific explanations are built by combining evidence that can be observed with what people already know about the world.

1.1c Science provides knowledge, but values are also essential to making effective and ethical decisions about the application of scientific knowledge.

Standard 4

2.2e Knowledge of genetics is making possible new fields of health care; for example, finding genes which may have mutations that can cause disease will aid in the development of preventive measures to fight disease. Substances, such as hormones and enzymes, from genetically engineered organisms may reduce the cost and side effects of replacing missing body chemicals.

2.2b In recent years new varieties of farm plants and animals have been engineered by manipulating their genetic instructions to produce new characteristics.

5.2e Vaccinations use weakened microbes (or parts of them) to stimulate the immune system to react. This reaction prepares the body to fight subsequent invasions by the same microbes.

5.2j Biological research generates knowledge used to design ways of diagnosing, preventing, treating, controlling, or curing diseases of plants and animals.

7.3a Societies must decide on proposals which involve the introduction of new technologies. Individuals need to make decisions which will assess risks, costs, benefits, and trade-offs.

When biologists and engineers work together to solve problems that affect our lives, amazing inventions can result.

InquiryLab

⏱ 15 min

Artificial Shark Skin

Shark skin contains small channels that offer paths that water easily flows through around a shark's body. With reduced water resistance, the animal moves more quickly—a quality that competitive swimmers desire.

Procedure

1. Examine a **prepared slide of shark skin** under low power on a **microscope.**

2. Switch to higher magnification. Move through the entire depth of the field. Vary the fine focus in order to examine the full depth of the specimen.

3. Select several overlapping scales. Sketch their pattern.

4. Observe a **swatch of Fastskin® fabric** used in the manufacture of competitive swimsuits. Compare this fabric to the shark skin.

Analysis

1. **Propose** how the arrangement of scales produces channels in the shark skin.

2. **Describe** how the Fastskin® fabric resembles the shark skin.

3. **Explain** how the Fastskin® might give an advantage to swimmers.

Using Words

1. life measurement
2. having to do with genes
3. all parts of something to do with life
4. all parts of something to do with genes

Using Language

1. The newly gathered evidence suggests that the bird is not actually extinct.
2. Humans will travel to Mars, assuming that resources become available.

Using FoldNotes

The three-panel flip chart aids the organization of students' thoughts around a single idea. Many flip charts can be made throughout a chapter depending on the number of ideas the student needs to organize. Students can modify the flip chart to have as few as two and as many as six panels, depending on the complexity of the topic. **LS Verbal**

These reading tools can help you learn the material in this chapter. For more information on how to use these and other tools, see **Appendix: Reading and Study Skills.**

Using Words

Word Parts You can tell a lot about a word by taking it apart and examining its prefix, root, and suffix.

Your Turn Use the table to hypothesize the meanings of the following words.

1. *biometrics*
2. *genetics*
3. *biome*
4. *genome*

Word Parts		
Part	**Type**	**Meaning**
bio-	prefix	life
metric	root	measurement
-ic	suffix	having to do with
-ome	suffix	all parts of something
gen	root	born; to become; to produce

Using Language

Predictions A prediction is a statement about what might happen in the future. You can identify predictions in the material you read by locating terms such as *might*, *impossible*, and *likely*.

Your Turn Read the following sentences, and write the author's prediction.

1. Scientists agree that the birdcall heard on the tape is likely a bird thought to be extinct.
2. With enough funding and effort, humans might travel to Mars one day.

Using FoldNotes

Three-Panel Flip Chart A three-panel flip chart is useful when you want to compare the characteristics of three topics. The three-panel flip chart can help you organize the characteristics of the three topics side by side under the flaps. Similarities and differences between the three topics can then be easily identified.

Your Turn Create a flip chart that compares areas of biological research such as epidemiology, genetics, and environmental science.

1. Fold a piece of paper in half from the top to the bottom.
2. Fold the paper in thirds from side to side. Then, unfold the paper so that you can see the three sections.
3. From the top of the paper, cut along each of the vertical fold lines to the fold in the middle of the paper. You now have three flaps.

Health in the 21st Century

Key Ideas	Key Terms	Why It Matters
❯ How are biologists working to eliminate major diseases that affect human populations? ❯ How has our understanding of the biological nature of disease changed over time? ❯ How might medical advances improve and extend human lives?	epidemiology vaccination genetics genome	Studying how diseases spread and developing ways to prevent and treat diseases can help reduce human suffering.

Biological research in the 20th century led to incredible advances in the prevention and treatment of disease. Yet, despite this progress, we still have more to learn and understand about how diseases affect humans. One of the great challenges of biology is to apply our understanding of the natural world to these issues.

Meeting the Challenge

❯ **Biologists combine research and data from many different fields of science to help reduce the spread of disease.** For example, biologist Rita Colwell has applied biological research, data from the ocean, and chemistry to reduce the number of outbreaks of cholera. Cholera is a disease that is caused by ingesting food or water that contains the cholera bacterium. This bacterium is a *pathogen,* that is, an agent that causes disease. Normally, a person must ingest millions of cholera bacteria to contract the disease. However, Colwell and her students found that tiny animals called *copepods* give the bacteria an advantage. The bacteria cluster around the mouthparts and egg casings of female copepods, which are shown in **Figure 1.** The copepods benefit from this behavior because the bacteria help burst the copepods' egg casings and release the copepod eggs. Then, the bacteria feed on the broken egg casings. Copepods feed on plankton—microscopic plant and animal life—in ocean water. When the amount of plankton in the water increases, the number of copepods (and, thus, bacteria) in the water increases and a cholera outbreak could occur.

❯ **Reading Check** *Why is the cholera bacterium a pathogen? (See the Appendix for answers to Reading Checks.)*

 The Living Environment

Standard 1

1.1a Scientific explanations are built by combining evidence that can be observed with what people already know about the world.

Standard 4

2.2e Knowledge of genetics is making possible new fields of health care; for example, finding genes which may have mutations that can cause disease will aid in the development of preventive measures to fight disease. Substances, such as hormones and enzymes, from genetically engineered organisms may reduce the cost and side effects of replacing missing body chemicals.

5.2e Vaccinations use weakened microbes (or parts of them) to stimulate the immune system to react. This reaction prepares the body to fight subsequent invasions by the same microbes.

5.2j Biological research generates knowledge used to design ways of diagnosing, preventing, treating, controlling, or curing diseases of plants and animals.

www.scilinks.org
Topic: Disease Prevention
Code: HX80414

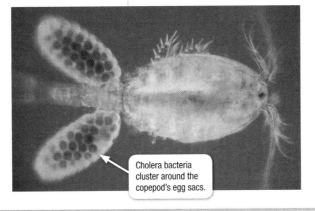

Cholera bacteria cluster around the copepod's egg sacs.

Figure 1 This micrograph illustrates two egg sacs (left, dark yellow) that are attached to a copepod (right, light yellow). The cholera bacteria is spread in part when the egg sacs rupture.

Key Resources

 Transparencies
F6 Important Bacterial Diseases
J37 The Immune Response

Visual Concepts
Pathogen
Vaccine

❯ Focus

This section explains the role biology played in improving human health during the last one hundred years and explores where research is leading us in the future.

🔊 Bellringer

Use the Bellringer transparency to prepare students for this section.

❯ Teach

Teaching Key Ideas

Parasites Ask students for other examples of parasites that can make humans extremely ill. (Some examples are malaria virus *Plasmodia* carried by *Anopheles* mosquitoes; *Rikettesia* which causes Rocky Mountain Spotted Fever, carried by ticks in the eastern United States and Lyme disease, carried by deer ticks.)
LS Visual

Section Correlations	
1.1.1a	4.5.2e
4.2.2e	4.5.2j

Teaching Key Ideas

Integrating the Sciences The cholera example shows how science is an integrated field of study. Researchers must understand the organism, its environment and biochemistry, and the geography of the area. Emphasize that educated citizens integrate many fields of study including geography, computer science, and mathematics. Challenge students to research other discoveries that illustrate the integration of the sciences. (For example, any cellular research requires an in-depth knowledge of chemistry. Prosthesis research requires an understanding of physics.) **LS Verbal**

Teaching Key Ideas

Scientific Models Explain that the use of models to make predictions is an important aspect of science. Just like an automobile engineer builds a small version of the car they are designing to see how it will be affected by environmental factors, biologists build models to predict how a bacteria will spread in an environment. Often, the scientific models include complex mathematical relationships between variables in the environment and how they affect the organism under research.

Figure 2 Colwell analyzed satellite data of the ocean to predict cholera outbreaks. In this image, warm colors such as red represent warmer water temperatures.

Figure 3 Today, many people use saris to filter water. This low-tech solution has greatly reduced the frequency of cholera outbreaks.

Solving the Riddle After Colwell established a link between cholera and copepods, she focused on some interesting data. Cholera outbreaks occurred regularly in water that tested negative for cholera bacteria. As a result, researchers assumed that the bacteria were not present in the water. However, Colwell was convinced that the bacteria existed in a form that could not be detected by the tests.

Colwell developed a more sensitive test that relied on the chemical properties of the bacteria's cell wall. She used this new test to detect cholera bacteria in water that had previously tested negative for the bacteria. This research suggested that cholera bacteria exist in a dormant state in cold water and that they become active when water temperature increases.

Using Models Colwell was able to predict cholera outbreaks with much greater accuracy because she now understood the role of water temperature in the cholera life cycle. She used satellite data, shown in **Figure 2,** to study the characteristics of ocean water and to predict cholera outbreaks. These predictions allowed health workers to anticipate cholera outbreaks and save lives. Even so, warm water is only one of many factors that play a role in cholera outbreaks.

A Low-Tech Solution Although researchers could predict cholera outbreaks, it was still difficult to prevent the spread of the disease. So Colwell focused on a low-tech solution to reduce the spread of cholera. Cholera bacteria attach to copepods that are much larger by comparison. The researchers demonstrated that the copepods could be filtered from water by using a folded piece of cotton cloth, such as a *sari*. A sari is a traditional garment worn by Indian woman and is shown in **Figure 3.** In some areas, these simple filters have reduced cases of cholera by almost 50%. Colwell's work is just one example of how biological research can make a huge difference in people's lives.

❯ Reading Check *Relate water temperature to cholera outbreaks.*

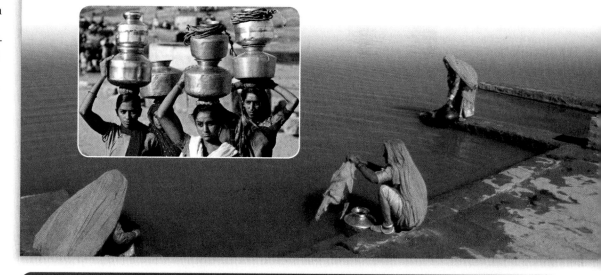

Differentiated Instruction

Struggling Readers/English Learners

New Terms Key vocabulary is highlighted for students. However, you will need to help students with unfamiliar terms in this section by writing them on the board and working with students to construct definitions. Accept drawings and simple memory aids in addition to verbal definitions. Have students copy this information to index cards, or in their notebooks for use while reading. Have them classify each by its part of speech. (Most will be nouns, but not all.) The list should include the following words: *cholera, gastrointestinal, bacterium, pathogen, copepod, plankton, dormant, sari, immune system, expression, assistive technology.* Encourage students to add their own words to the list as needed and to use this strategy throughout the year to help them with the reading. **LS Verbal**

🕐 15 min

QuickLab

Model a Low-Tech Solution

Procedure

❶ Put on **gloves**. Use an **eyedropper** to put a copepod from a **copepod culture** onto a **well slide**. Examine the specimen under a **microscope**. Record your observations.

❷ Stretch a **piece of dark cotton cloth** over the mouth of a **beaker**. Secure the fabric with a **rubber band.**

❸ Pour the copepod culture onto the fabric. Examine a sample of the strained liquid under the microscope, and record your observations. Return any strained copepods and the culture solution to the culture jar.

❹ Repeat steps 2 and 3, but replace the cloth with a **funnel** lined with **filter paper.**

Analysis

1. **Compare** the pore size of the cotton cloth with that of the filter paper.

2. **Determine** which filter(s) strains out the copepods.

3. **CRITICAL THINKING** **Inferring Relationships** From your observation, is the filter with the smallest pore size the most practical to use for obtaining drinking water? Explain.

Disease in a Changing World

Rita Colwell's work is an example of **epidemiology**—the study of how diseases spread. ❭ **As scientists learn more about the nature of disease, our ability to prevent and treat diseases has improved.**

Disease "Conquered" by Biology In 1979, scientists announced that they had destroyed the smallpox virus. Smallpox is a disease that causes terrible scarring and even death. Vaccination, a technique first developed during the 1800s, played an important role in getting rid of smallpox. A **vaccination** is a medical procedure that allows a person to resist infection by a disease. During this procedure, genetic information from a dead or weakened pathogen is introduced into the body. As a result, the body's immune system "learns" to fight the pathogen. Today, the development of vaccinations and global health programs have nearly succeeded in getting rid of many other diseases.

New Insights into Disease Discoveries in the field of genetics have produced many new tools to study and treat diseases that are caused by abnormalities in a person's genes. **Genetics** is the science of heredity and the study of how traits are passed on to offspring. Genetics research will benefit greatly from discoveries made by the Human Genome Project. In 2003, the project finished sequencing the entire human genome. A **genome** is the complete set of genetic information for an organism. Now, researchers can begin to study single genes in order to understand their role in genetic diseases.

❭ **Reading Check** *How do vaccination programs prevent diseases?*

READING TOOLBOX

Predictions Scientists use observations to make predictions. Make a list of the predictions in this section and the hypotheses that they address.

---

epidemiology (EP uh DEE mee AHL uh jee) the study of the distribution of diseases in populations and the study of factors that influence the occurrence and spread of disease

vaccination (VAK suh NAY shuhn) the administration of treated microorganisms into humans or animals to induce an immune response

genetics (juh NET iks) the science of heredity and of the mechanisms by which traits are passed from parents to offspring

genome (JEE NOHM) the complete genetic material contained in an individual or species

---

Teaching Key Ideas

Life Expectancy Have students research the life expectancy of people in countries like the United States and England over the past 100 years. Compare those values with life expectancies of people living in countries such as Bangledesh and Somolia. What diseases are most prevalent in developing countries such as these and how do they compare with diseases in developed countries? (Students will find greater life expectancies in economically stable countries. They will also note major differences in the most prevalent diseases. Lifestyle diseases such as diabetes are more prevalent in the U.S. and England.) **LS Verbal**

> Close

Formative Assessment

Monitoring the spread of flu each winter would be an example of ___.

A. geography (Incorrect. Geography would play a role in the data analysis, but it is not the study of the spread of disease.)

B. immunity (Incorrect. Immunity is the body's response to a previously introduced pathogen.)

C. epidemiology (Correct! Monitoring flu outbreaks is an example of epidemiology.)

D. copepod biology (Incorrect. Copepods are a factor in the spread of cholera.)

Figure 4 Advances in battlefield medicine include remote surgery. The doctor on the left is performing a surgery from a remote site. The surgery is aided by nurses, such as those on the right.

Biology and Human Potential

The length of human lives in developed countries has nearly doubled in the past century. **> As our understanding of medicine, biology, and science in general increases, humans will live longer and healthier lives.**

Assistive Technologies People who have injuries, diseases, or disabilities can use assistive technology products to help them accomplish everyday tasks. These products include bionic limbs and computer interfaces, and can help a person speak, see, or hear. They can also help a person coordinate his or her movements.

Battlefield Medicine Battlefield medicine is a new field of medicine which includes remote surgery, as shown in **Figure 4.** This field also includes new products designed for use in battle. For example, heavy blood loss is a common cause of death in war zones. Researchers have developed a bandage that can stop the flow of blood from serious wounds in a short period of time, before massive blood loss occurs. This device might eventually be used in hospitals to treat patients with gunshot wounds and other injuries.

ACADEMIC VOCABULARY
device a piece of equipment made for a specific use

> **Reading Check** *Give an example of an assistive technology.*

Section 1 Review

> KEY IDEAS

1. **Describe** ways in which biologists are "meeting the challenge" to reduce the spread of diseases.
2. **Describe** how our understanding of the nature of disease has changed over time.
3. **Explain** how advances in biology have improved human potential.

CRITICAL THINKING

4. **Forming Hypotheses** Rita Colwell's success in tracking cholera outbreaks was due to her open-minded approach to the available data. What were her assumptions, and how did they differ from assumptions of other scientists? Explain your answer.
5. **Expressing an Opinion** What is the future of battlefield medicine? Explain your answer.

WRITING FOR SCIENCE

6. **Writing an Essay** Write an essay that explains your thoughts on why humans would be able to live longer, healthier lives as our understanding of biology increases. Include examples of technologies that would enable humans to live longer lives.

Answers to Section Review

1. Students' answers may include as an example the work of Rita Colwell because she applied biological research oceanographic data, and chemistry to discover methods for reducing outbreaks of cholera.

2. We better understand how diseases are transmitted and treated. In addition, we have learned how to prevent diseases through breakthroughs such as vaccination and the eradication of pathogens.

3. The ability to conquer diseases and feed the world's population increases life expectancies.

4. Colwell knew that the bacteria had to be in the water even though it had tested negative. Her work involved the development of a more sensitive test that relied on chemical properties.

5. Students may mention that the extreme conditions of the battlefield call for new medical solutions. Many of the medical discoveries that increase the survival rates of the wounded might aid patients outside war zones.

6. Answers will vary but may include how addressing disease, illness, and aging, and research into debilitating injuries or illnesses will extend and improve the quality of life.

Biology, Technology, and Society

Key Ideas	Key Terms	Why It Matters
❯ What is one way that genetic engineering affects our lives? ❯ How has biotechnology provided new tools for scientists to understand biological processes? ❯ How are biological factors used to verify an individual's identity and to ensure public safety? ❯ What ethical issues are raised by the use of biotechnology?	genetic engineering biometrics	Understanding the potential applications of biotechnology will help you make ethical decisions about its use.

What do hook-and-loop fasteners, a database of fingerprints, and a pet fish that glows in the dark have in common? They are all examples of how biological research affects society.

Biotechnology Around Us

Biotechnology affects many aspects of our lives, including our food sources. Genetic engineering is one of the most common examples of biotechnology. **Genetic engineering** is a technology in which the genetic material of a living cell is changed. ❯ **In agriculture, genetic engineering is used to create crops that yield more product or are resistant to pests.** For example, **Figure 5** shows a genetically modified type of corn called Bt corn. Bt corn has been altered to contain a gene from a naturally occurring soil bacterium called *Bacillus thuringiensis.* This gene allows the corn to make a toxin that kills a crop pest called the European corn borer. The use of Bt corn has raised crop yields and lowered the amount of pesticides that farmers use to control European corn borers.

 The Living Environment

Standard 1

1.1c Science provides knowledge, but values are also essential to making effective and ethical decisions about the application of scientific knowledge.

Standard 4

2.2b In recent years new varieties of farm plants and animals have been engineered by manipulating their genetic instructions to produce new characteristics.

5.2j Biological research generates knowledge used to design ways of diagnosing, preventing, treating, controlling, or curing diseases of plants and animals.

7.3a Societies must decide on proposals which involve the introduction of new technologies. Individuals need to make decisions which will assess risks, costs, benefits, and trade-offs.

genetic engineering (juh NET ik EN juh NIR ing) a technology in which the genome of a living cell is modified for medical or industrial use

Figure 5 The use of Bt corn reduces the amount of pesticides that farmers use to control pests. However, its use is controversial.

Key Resources

 Transparencies

L9 How a Refracting Telescope Works
C34 Genetic Engineering
C35 Genetically Engineered Medicine
C38 Making a Genetically Engineered Vaccine

 Visual Concepts
Genetic Engineering
Using Plasmids to Produce Insulin
Genetically Engineered Vaccines
DNA Fingerprint
Making a DNA Fingerprint

 ❯Focus

This section introduces biotechnology—the relationship between biology and technology and its application in our every day lives. It also raises ethical issues on the appropriate use of these new technologies.

🔊 Bellringer

Use the Bellringer transparency to prepare students for this section.

❯Teach

Teaching Key Ideas

Technological Drawbacks The controversy over Bt corn concerns evidence that the pollen from this strain of corn is toxic to Monarch butterfly larvae. Thus, an agricultural breakthrough has the potential to destroy wildlife. Ask students to name some technological advances that concern them or someone they know. (Responses may include: genetically engineered foods that could cause illness or mutations, cloning of organisms, genetic screenings for diseases, stem-cell research, cosmetic surgery, food additives, and drug development.) Start a discussion about the importance of understanding these technologies before forming opinions. Talk to students about finding unbiased sources of information to learn more about technological advances that concern them. **LS Interpersonal**

Section Correlations	
1.1.1c	4.5.2j
4.2.2b	4.7.3a

QuickLab

Teacher's Notes Make sure that your water basin is at least twice as deep as the cup is wide. Tape the spoon to the outside of the cup. Duct tape works well. When constructing the model make sure there is an air-tight seal between the straw and balloon.

Materials
- balloon, large
- basin
- duct tape
- soda straws, plastic (6)
- spoon, metal
- water

Safety Caution Make sure that the balloons have been stretched out before you attempt to blow them up through the straw "pipe."

Answers to Analysis
1. When the model bladder is inflated, the cup rises to the surface. When air escapes, the model bladder sinks.
2. As the volume of the inflated bag increases, the buoyancy increases. As the volume of the inflated bag decreases, the buoyancy decreases.
3. The cup is the hull of the submarine. The metal spoon is the equipment and personnel. The balloon is the ballast tanks that fill with air when the submarine rises and with water when it dives.

Hands-On

QuickLab

Biomimetic Engineering

Bony fishes have a swim bladder that controls their buoyancy. This structure fills with gas to make the fish more buoyant. To become less buoyant, gas is released from the bladder. Engineers modeled submarines after this principle. In this lab, you will model a swim bladder and relate its structure and function to that of a submarine.

Procedure
❶ Fill a **basin** about two-thirds full with **water**. Use **tape** to secure a **metal spoon** to a **cup**. Put the cup in the water (the cup should sink).

❷ Link **three straws** together to form a long tube. Tape the straw "pipe" inside the mouth of a **large balloon**.

❸ Secure the balloon in the cup, and put the cup in the water. Blow into the straws to add air to the balloon.

Analysis
1. **Describe** what happens when you blow air into the model bladder and when you let air escape.
2. **Assess** how the volume of the inflated balloon affects the overall buoyancy of the model.
3. **CRITICAL THINKING** **Relating Concepts** What structures of the swim bladder relate to the parts of a submarine?

ACADEMIC VOCABULARY

process a set of steps, events, or changes

Figure 6 Nanotechnology often takes the form of tiny robotic items that look like animals. This robot was formed from a computer microchip.

Applications of Biological Research

Biotechnology is also used to produce medicines, to perform scientific research, and to develop new materials. ❯ **Tools such as genetic engineering, nanotechnology, and computer models have expanded the potential applications of biological research.**

Biotechnology and Scientific Research Scientists often use genetic engineering tools to study biological processes. For example, Nigel Atkinson is a biologist who studies the effects of alcohol and other compounds on fruit flies. To do this, he uses genetically modified fruit flies to determine if certain genes help the flies form resistance to the effects of alcohol. This research may help other scientists develop new methods of treating alcoholism in humans.

Scientists also take advantage of gene technology to make vaccines and medical products such as insulin. Insulin is a hormone that controls the metabolism of sugar as well as carbohydrates, fats, and proteins from the diet. Some people who have diabetes must take regular doses of insulin because their bodies cannot produce enough of the hormone. Before genetic engineering, insulin was obtained from pigs and cows. Now, it is made from bacteria that are changed so that they contain the human gene that produces insulin.

Nanotechnology Biological research has also gained from advances in nanotechnology. One application of this technology is shown in **Figure 6.** Nanotechnology is the science of creating products by changing individual atoms or molecules. For example, the release of a drug can be controlled by putting the drug compound inside a shell of atoms. Nanotechnology can also help repair damaged body tissue. For example, researchers are developing a very small, biodegradable template that may help damaged brain cells grow back after an injury.

Why It Matters

Synthetic Hormones
Scientists today produce dozens of products by employing biotechnology. For example, human growth hormone can be synthetically produced to treat people with growth hormone deficiencies. Before biotechnology, it took the pituitary glands from fifty cadavers to produce one dose. Tissue plasminogen activator, which dissolves blood clots in heart attack victims, is produced through biotechnology, too.

Differentiated Instruction

Basic Learners

Word Parts Have students research the meaning of the prefix *nano-*. (one billionth, or 10^{-9}) Ask them how the prefix relates to the definition given. (Nanotechnology is the science of creating products that are at the sizes of atoms and molecules. Sizes of atoms are expressed in nanometers, 1×10^{-9}.) Ask students for definitions of *nanosecond* and *nanogram*. (1×10^{-9} second and 1×10^{-9} gram) **LS** **Verbal**

Biomolecular Materials Some cells and organisms have amazing ways of putting together organic compounds, or *biomolecules*. These methods inspire scientists to develop new, synthetic, biomolecular materials. For example, new types of ceramics are based on the process that clams use to form their own shells. Scientists are trying to create a stronger glue by studying how bacteria stick to rocks in fast-moving streams. Artificial spider silk is being used to make a new lightweight, strong fabric.

Biomimetics New products are also based on larger-scale biological structures and processes. *Biomimetics* (BIE oh muh ME tiks) is the application of biological processes and systems to solve design and engineering problems. Hook-and-loop fasteners, originally made by the company Velcro®, are one of the most familiar biomimetic products. These fasteners were modeled after prickly burrs that attach to animal fur or clothing. Another example is the submarine, which was modeled after the swimbladder of bony fishes. Studies of animal eyes have helped astronomers design new telescopes such as the lobster-eye telescope, which collects and focuses X-rays. Other amazing products are being developed every day!

Adapting Tools and Methods Tools and methods that are developed for one purpose are often adapted for other uses. For example, computerized axial tomography (CAT) scanning technology was originally developed to help doctors make detailed three-dimensional images of internal organs. Biologists can now use CAT scans to create models of fossils and of living organisms. **Figure 7** shows one of these kinds of models. Now, scientists can study specimens without dissecting them.

❯ **Reading Check** *How is the lobster-eye telescope unique from other types of telescopes?*

Word Parts Using your knowledge of word parts, write a definition in your own words for *nanotechnology*, *biotechnology*, and *biomolecules*.

Figure 7 Digital scanning technology combines CAT scans and digital imaging to create three-dimensional models of organisms.

This image is a digital scan of a mouse's skeleton.

This digital scan shows a three-dimensional representation of the mouse.

Using Words Students should show evidence of breaking down the following words into their prefixes and roots.

nano on the order of 10^{-9}

technology newly developed materials or techniques that give additional capacity to the user

nanotechnology materials or techniques on the order of one billionth that give additional capacity to the user

bio- of or relating to life

molecular on the scale of molecules, structures composed of atoms

biomolecular life at a molecular scale

biotechnology newly developed materials or techniques relating to living things

Teaching Key Ideas

Biomimetics Ask students for other biomimetics examples. Here are some clues: How has a bird's ability to fly influenced engineering? (airplane design) How has a bat's ability to communicate influenced communication? (sonar) How has the shape of a maple seed influenced engineering? (helicopter design)
LS Logical

Differentiated Instruction

Advanced Learners/GATE

Be the Expert Assign students to groups of three. Assign one student as the biotechnology expert, another the biomolecular materials expert, and the third student as the biomimetics expert. Have the students conduct research and make a timeline for major developments in each of their fields. Have the groups present their timelines to the class. **LS** Interpersonal

Special Education Students

Biological Research List the different applications of biological research on the board or chart paper: biotechnology, nanotechnology, biomolecules, biomimetics, and adapted tools. Have students list examples from the text or your discussions of each application on large self-sticking notes. Then, have students place their notes under the appropriate heading. Review each list with the class and reclassify examples as needed.

Teaching Key Ideas

DNA Fingerprinting Restriction Fragment Length Polymorphism, or RFLP, analysis is the method by which a DNA fingerprint is made. Special enzymes, called restriction enzymes are mixed with a person's DNA. These enzymes cut DNA along specific sequences. Because everyone's DNA is different, restriction enzymes will cut at different places, leaving a unique combination of DNA fragments. The pattern of these fragments produces the "fingerprint" of a person's DNA. Just as everyone's fingerprints have loops, whirls, and swirls, people also have a specific set of DNA fragments.

Biology, Forensics, and Public Safety

Biological research is also used in criminal investigations and to make sure that the public is safe. ❯ **Because biological factors such as fingerprints, iris patterns, and genetic material are unique, they can be used to identify individuals.** The use of biological traits to determine a person's identity is called **biometrics.**

biometrics (BIE oh ME triks) the statistical analysis of biological data; the measurement and analysis of unique physical or behavioral characteristics to verify the identity of a person

Two Types of Fingerprinting Fingerprints are one of the most common forms of evidence used in criminal investigations. For example, the FBI fingerprint database is the largest database of its kind in the world. A fingerprint scanner is shown in **Figure 8.** Another method of identification is called *DNA fingerprinting*. A DNA fingerprint has nothing to do with a person's actual finger but rather is a unique pattern of DNA that represents the total of a person's genetic material. Evidence such as hair or skin cells that are left behind at a crime scene can be identified by using DNA fingerprinting.

Other Forms of Biometric Identification Improved computer processing power has led to the development of many new biometric technologies. For example, **Figure 8** shows examples of different iris patterns. Iris scans are very fast and reliable, and are as unique as a fingerprint. These scans can also detect changes in a person's iris. Other software programs can tell the difference between human faces, or can analyze brain waves and speech patterns.

❯ **Reading Check** *What is DNA fingerprinting, and how is it used to identify someone?*

Figure 8 Iris scans (left) show ridges, strings of tissue, and tiny pits in the iris. These features make every person's iris unique. The fingerprint scan (right) is also used to identify people.

Iris scans

Fingerprint technology

Differentiated Instruction

Alternative Assessment

Understanding Ethics Ask the class why they should be concerned about ethical practices in biotechnology. Then, ask each student to submit anonymously a short paragraph on an application that could have ethical implications. Their paragraphs should identify the application, describe possible benefits and drawbacks, and the steps that would aid an informed opinion on the ethics related to the application. Provide a closed shoebox to hold the paragraphs. Give general feedback to the class after reviewing the submissions.

Advanced Learners/GATE

DNA Evidence Biotechnology has aided the justice system convicting criminals and setting the innocent free. Have students research the use of biotechnology in the criminal justice system. Students should seek information on both pros and cons of biotechnology use. **LS** Verbal

Preventing Bioterrorism Biologists and other scientists are working to develop new ways to detect and prevent the use of biological agents by terrorists. After the events of September 11, 2001, people have become more concerned about the possibility of a bioterrorist attack. Drills such as the one shown in **Figure 9** help people prepare for such an event. Handheld probes have been developed that can quickly detect common biological agents. Other research focuses on making vaccines and new antibiotic treatments for victims of anthrax or other biological weapons.

The Ethics of Biotechnology

Although biotechnology has great potential to improve our lives, its use also raises many ethical concerns. ❯Advances in biotechnology raise ethical concerns that must be addressed, both by individuals and by society.

Manipulating DNA People have many concerns about genetic engineering. Some people worry that putting genetically engineered organisms into an ecosystem could harm the environment. Others worry that eating food that is made from genetically modified organisms might be harmful to their health. Some people object to the idea of changing an organism's DNA, or to techniques such as cloning, or to the use of human stem cells in research. Others feel that limiting the kinds of scientific research that might save lives and cure diseases is unethical.

Personal Security Putting biometric identification methods to use also raises ethical issues. Many people feel that databases of personal, biological information represents an invasion of privacy. The concern is that governments or other organizations could use this information improperly.

❯ **Reading Check** *What are some ethical concerns faced by society that relate to genetically modified organisms?*

Figure 9 Bioterrorism drills such as this one can help populations prepare for bioterrorist attacks.

SCI
LINKS.
www.scilinks.org
Topic: Biological
Weapons
Code: HX81692

Teaching Key Ideas

Debate Hold a class debate on biometric identification versus personal freedoms. The following are some questions teams that could debate: How does a country manage public safety in a global economy? When do security measures compromise the rights of citizens? How have these questions influenced politics within the United States? **LS** Logical

> **Close**

Formative Assessment

Advances in biotechnology have resulted in all of the following, except the ____.
A. development of synthetic hormones that help regulate sugar metabolism (Incorrect. Insulin, for example, has been synthesized.)
B. development of iris scanning to establish identity (Incorrect. This technology is available and is more accurate than fingerprinting.)
C. cloning of animals (Incorrect. Animals have been cloned.)
D. cloning of humans. (Correct! This issue raises too many ethical concerns for individuals and society as a whole.)

Section 2 Review

❯**KEY IDEA**

1. **Describe** briefly how genetic engineering has improved agricultural crops.
2. **Explain** how biotechnology research has affected modern life.
3. **Describe** the biological features that are considered to be unique to an individual's identity.

4. **State** an example of an ethical issue that is brought up by advances in biotechnology.

CRITICAL THINKING

5. **Applying Information** Explain how crime investigators use biometrics to determine who is and who is not the perpetrator of a crime.
6. **Applying Information** Why should both individuals and society address ethical concerns? Explain your reasoning.

ALTERNATIVE ASSESSMENT

7. **Product Design** Biomimetics is described as "the abstraction of good design from nature." What does *biomimetics* mean? Describe an example of the type of product that would exemplify the abstraction of good design from nature. Be specific in your example.

Answers to Section Review

1. Genetic engineering is used to create crops that are more productive or that are resistant to pests.
2. Sample answer: The design of new tools used by scientists in genetic engineering, nanotechnology, and computer modeling, by the creation of new ways to produce medicines and materials, and new techniqes in scientific research.
3. Biological features such as fingerprints, iris patterns, and DNA are considered unique.
4. ethical concerns such as the invasion of privacy; reduction of personal freedoms; potential adverse health effects from new foods, drugs, or treatments; use of living cells and organisms for research

5. Biological factors such as fingerprints, iris patterns, and genetic materials are unique to individuals. Therefore, they can be used to determine an individual's identity.
6. To be scientifically literate, individuals should be aware of ethical questions or standards for research. Society has to decide whether the benefits of research outweigh the potential harm.
7. Biomimetics is the application of biological processes and systems to solve design and engineering problems. Hook-and-loop fasteners are an outcome of studying seeds that have tiny hooks that attach to animal fur. This adaptation allows the seeds to be dispersed.

Biology and the Environment

Key Ideas

❯ How does biological research help protect the environment?

❯ How do new technologies help us study the environment?

❯ How do biologists rely on the contributions of community members to develop solutions for environmental problems?

Key Terms

ecology
environmental science

Why It Matters

Studying the environment will help us make wise choices about the conservation and protection of natural resources.

The study of the interactions of living organisms with one another and with their environment is called **ecology.** The study of ecology and the environment, or **environmental science,** is one of the most important applications of biology.

A Lost World

In February 2006, an international team of biologists announced an amazing discovery. In a mountainous region of western New Guinea, the researchers discovered a "lost world" that appeared untouched by humans. During just two weeks of fieldwork, the team discovered more than 40 species of plants and animals. **Figure 10** shows a few of the species that were discovered by the team.

The discovery of the lost world stresses the fact that parts of the world still exist that we know little about. Therefore, the need to study and protect these areas is very important. ❯ **Biological research helps us understand, value, and protect the environment. We learn how to protect the environment by learning more about what affects it.** The environment provides natural resources such as water, food, and energy sources that are vital to human societies and to all organisms. Biologists are working to protect areas such as the lost world in New Guinea and to find ways that Earth's resources can continue to meet the needs of growing human populations.

Figure 10 These photographs show the habitat of New Guinea and examples of two species that were recently discovered there.

This biologist is tracking the fish's behavior.

The mola is the largest bony fish in the world.

Figure 11 Biologists use satellite tagging to help protect the mola. ❯ What information can you learn about a fish by tracking its location?

Technology in Environmental Science

Biologists are using many new technologies to study the environment. ❯ Tools such as satellite tagging, geographic information systems (GISs), and genetics are used to study and protect the environment.

Satellite Tagging The scientist in **Figure 11** is part of a research team that is tracking the movements of molas, some of the largest fish in the world. In this study, molas are tagged with a transmitter that sends data about the fish's movements to a satellite. The data will help the team understand the mola's behavior, such as its role in ocean food webs. By keeping track of individual fish, the team also hopes to find out if the molas are overfished. Satellite tagging is used in many other kinds of wildlife studies, such as to track polar bears and sea turtles. This technology gives scientists the information they need to plan conservation strategies.

Geographic Information Systems Satellite data can be used in computer modeling programs called *geographic information systems* (GIS). A GIS is a powerful tool in environmental research because it allows biologists to compare different kinds of data. For example, mola researchers could use a GIS to map the relationship between ocean temperature, the location of food sources, and the movement of the mola. A GIS also allows researchers to have access to data from many different studies so that they can work together.

Genetic Tools Scientists use genetics in many ways to study and protect the environment. For example, many species of endangered wildlife are killed for their body parts. Wildlife agents are using DNA fingerprinting to identify the remains of endangered animals and to identify the people who killed the animals. Biologists are also collecting DNA samples from endangered animals so that they can still be studied if the animals become extinct. In the future, DNA samples could possibly be used to clone extinct animals.

❯ **Reading Check** *How does a GIS allow scientists to work together?*

READING TOOLBOX

Three-panel Flip Chart Construct a three-panel flip chart to compare satellite tagging, GIS technology, and genetic tools in the study of environmental science.

ecology (ee KAHL uh jee) the study of the interactions of living organisms with one another and with their environment

environmental science (en VIE ruhn MENT'l) the study of the air, water, and land surrounding an organism or a community, which ranges from a small area to Earth's entire biosphere

Answer to Caption Question
Figure 11: By tracking a fish, its behavior can be learned, including what it eats, where it lives, and what its habits are.

READING TOOLBOX

Three-Panel Flip Chart Satellite tagging allows scientists to follow the paths of individual organisms. This information tells scientists about the location of potential food sources, energy budgets, and group dynamics.

GIS technologies allow scientists to analyze sets of geographic data to find relationships. For example, scientists can plot an individual's path against specific geographic characteristics, such as mountains, valleys, or rivers. If botanical surveys have been conducted, scientists can plot the animal's path against the types of resources present in an area.

Genetic tools allow scientists to catalog genetic samples from animals around the world. Studies could lead to information on common ancestry or immunity against certain diseases based on genetic disposition.

Formative Assessment

The "lost world" discovery is important to science because ____.

A. there's a new place to shoot reality TV shows (Incorrect. Visitors who are not scientists would likely need special clearance.)

B. there's a new area for people to live (Incorrect. The area is very remote and not suitable for large numbers of new inhabitants.)

C. new species enhance our understanding of data collected from all over the world (Correct! Discoveries of unknown species increase the knowledge base.)

D. it provides more funding for GIS research (Incorrect. Discoveries do not generate funds by themselves.)

Figure 12 The Raptor Rehabilitation Center is one of the most exciting projects that the students of the SWCC take part in. At the center, students help care for injured and orphaned birds of prey such as eagles, hawks, and owls.

ACADEMIC
VOCABULARY

contribution a part given toward a whole

SCI**LINKS**®
www.scilinks.org
Topic: Environmental
    Decision Making
Code: HX80525

Citizen Scientists

❯ **Biologists rely on the contributions of individuals and communities to help develop solutions for environmental problems.** These "citizen scientists" make valuable <u>contributions</u> to biological research and environmental conservation.

Environmental Clubs Many high schools have clubs that involve students in environmental research and conservation. For example, **Figure 12** shows members of the Southwestern High School Conservation Club (SWCC) in Somerset, Kentucky. SWCC's mission is to help other students understand the natural world through hands-on activities. This project is just one example of how biology students can become involved in environmental science.

Getting Involved If your school does not have an environmental club, find a teacher who can help you start one. Begin by working with other students to create a list of local environmental issues. Then, discuss some ways that your science class can learn more about these issues. You never know where environmental research can lead you, so keep an open mind and get involved!

❯ **Reading Check** *What is the mission of the SWCC?*

Section 3 Review

❯ KEY IDEA

1. **Evaluate** how the study of biology protects the environment.
2. **State** some tools that are used to protect the environment.
3. **Explain** why biologists rely on citizens to develop solutions to environmental problems.

CRITICAL THINKING

4. **Forming Reasoned Opinions** Why should biologists work on solutions that both protect fragile areas and support human needs? Explain your answer.
5. **Analyzing Methods** How can information gained from GIS technology aid environmental research? Explain your answer.

ALTERNATIVE ASSESSMENT

6. **New Species Table** Conduct Internet research on the "lost world" recently discovered by scientists in New Guinea. Make a table that includes at least five new species. Name each organism, and describe its characteristics. Why is the discovery of new species important in biology?

Answers to Section Review

1. Biological research helps us understand, value, and protect the environment.

2. Tools such as satellite tagging, GIS, and DNA collections are used to study and protect the environment.

3. Citizen scientists are considered valuable to scientific researchers because they are able to contribute information from wider areas than one biologist can cover. For example, many universities conduct bird studies and ask citizens to record bird sightings. This information becomes part of larger database so that documented migratory patterns, nesting habits, and other changes may be studied.

4. Fragile areas contain natural resources that support human needs. For example, fragile areas are pollution free and may contain unique forms of life that can provide clues or materials in the treatment of diseases.

5. GIS is able to collect data from multiple areas through satellite tagging. Using various forms of analysis, scientists can better predict trends and changes in an environment.

6. Answers are acceptable as long as they include five species that were discovered in the lost world. Examples include: the golden-mantled tree kangaroo, smoky honeyeater bird, golden-fronted bowerbird, giant echidna, or Berlepsch's six-wired bird of paradise. The discovery of new species is important to biology because it adds to the overall body of knowledge of living things.

Bio Bots

A robot that can play miniature golf? The boundary between living things and mechanical devices is not as clear as it used to be. These boundaries are being tested at every level, from biochemistry to intelligent behavior. Many fields of science and technology have been brought together to develop *bionics* (combinations of biological organisms and electronic devices) and *artificial intelligence* (computers that can learn and make decisions).

BIOTECHNOLOGY

Bugs in the Machine

Insects are particularly popular subjects for bionic and artificial-intelligence work. One reason is because insects are easy to study in terms of both anatomy and behavior. Another reason is that many insects have "swarm" behaviors, which means that group behaviors emerge from the independent decisions of individuals. Scientists are using computer software to study and model these kinds of behaviors, and this software is being used in applications that range from environmental management to computer games.

Bug Bots A wide variety of "bug bots" have been developed. Some bug bots can be remotely controlled by insects, such as this roach.

Bionics Robotic limbs, such as this model of a human hand, almost eliminate the need for more traditional prosthetic limbs.

Quick Project Ask 10 people to define what being "alive" and being "intelligent" mean. (Do not tell them your reason for asking until after you record their answers.) Make a graphic organizer that compares the responses, and then write your own response.

Teacher's Notes The term *artificial intelligence* was first coined in 1955 in a study carried out during the summer of 1956 at Dartmouth College in Hanover, New Hampshire. Today's artificial intelligence ranges from washing machines whose settings automatically adjust based on the types of clothes present to face recognition systems and e-mail filters. Artificial intelligence is closing the gap between "alive" and "intelligent."

READING TOOLBOX

Visual Literacy Describe the characteristics of the robots on this page that correspond to characteristics of living organisms. How do you know that they are not alive? (They neither reproduce nor develop.) Is there a difference between being alive and being intelligent? (Answers will vary.) Explain.

Answer to Quick Project

Use students' work as the starting point to discuss the public's perception of intelligence.

Time Required

30 to 45 minutes are needed for the initial setup and review of safety procedures associated with sterile technique. The second day follow-up session requires 15 to 30 minutes depending on who sets up the boiling-water bath. If you manage this step, day 2 will take less time. Each successive day of observation requires about 5 to 10 minutes. Be sure to schedule time for hand-washing, which is essential after each part of the experiment.

Ratings

EASY ——————→ HARD

Teacher Prep   🧪🧪🧪🧪
Student Setup   🧪🧪
Concept Level   🧪🧪🧪
Cleanup   🧪🧪🧪🧪

Safety Cautions

- Review safety procedures associated with sterile technique and the growth of microbes in the classroom.
- Remind students that they may not open the sealed tubes. The stoppers must remain in place throughout the activity.
- All students must be supplied with safety goggles and laboratory gloves for use during all parts of this investigation.
- All students must thoroughly wash their hands and wipe the desk surfaces when they are finished with each part of this investigation. Remind them to keep their hands out of their mouths. There is to be no eating during this investigation.

Objectives

▷ Observe the effect of sterile and nonsterile conditions on the growth of microbes.

▷ Make daily observations, and organize data.

▷ Hypothesize about the conditions under which microbes grow.

Materials

- lab apron, safety goggles, and disposable gloves
- test tubes, sterile (4)
- pencil, wax
- test-tube rack
- broth, nutrient
- rubber stoppers, sterile (4)
- water, sterilized
- test-tube holder
- gloves, heat-resistant
- water bath, boiling

Safety

Microbe Growth

To prepare for field research, Rita Colwell, a biologist, read that cholera, like other infectious diseases, was caused by a particular microbe. Thus, a person would need to be exposed to the disease-causing microbe to become infected with cholera. Colwell developed a low-tech method of sterilization, in which living organisms are removed, to prevent disease.

There are millions of different microbes. Not all of them cause disease, but many can interfere with scientific experiments. How do scientists keep laboratories free of such organisms? Sterile techniques, though common today, were not always common in the laboratory. Scientists such as Francesco Redi, Lazzaro Spallanzani, and Louis Pasteur demonstrated the importance of sterilization in preventing the growth of the microbes. In this lab, you will explore conditions under which microbes grow, and you will ask questions about the variables that might affect the microbes' growth.

Procedure

Prepare the Lab Materials

❶ Work with a partner. Review all safety procedures, including sterile techniques and safe handling of microbe cultures, with your teacher.

❷ ✦ ◈ ◖ Put on a lab apron, safety goggles, and disposable gloves.

❸ ◈ CAUTION: Handle glass test tubes carefully. Obtain four sterilized test tubes and a test-tube rack. Use a wax pencil to label the tubes "A" through "D," and place the tubes in the test-tube rack.

Observations of Microbe Growth		Day 1	Day 2	Day 3	Day 4	Day 5	Day 6	Day 7
	Tube Contents							
Tube A	sterile broth							
Tube B	broth exposed to air							
Tube C	exposed broth, then sterilized							
Tube D	sterilized water, exposed to air							

- Review safety rules associated with the use of boiling water. If the use of a boiling water bath is inappropriate or impractical do this step as a demonstration.

Tips and Tricks

You can obtain sterile nutrient solution locally by using commercial chicken broth, available at any grocery store. Make sure to sterilize the test tubes and stoppers before adding the broth. Alternatively, dehydrated broth may be used. Follow the rehydration instructions included with the product. Any stopper or lid can be used for the test (e.g., a screw-top lid), provided that an air-tight seal is established and maintained. For example, screw-top lids can only be used

with corresponding test tubes. Remember that once the container is opened, the sterility is compromised. You can boil broth that is exposed to air, which will destroy most of the microbes that might have infected it. To insure sterility, use an autoclave or pressure cooker.

Culture Disposal The cultures must be disposed of in a safe manner as outlined by local and school safety protocol. Often this protocol involves sterilization of the used glassware in an autoclave.

④ Fill tubes A, B, and C halfway with sterile nutrient broth solution.

⑤ Insert a sterile rubber stopper into the mouth of tube A. For now, leave the other broth-filled tubes unsealed.

⑥ Fill tube D halfway with sterilized water and add the tube to the test-tube rack.

⑦ Make a table for your observations of microbe growth. Observe the appearance of the broth in all four test tubes, and record your observations in the column labeled "Day 1."

⑧ Once you have recorded your observations, place the test-tube rack in an area where it will not be disturbed for 24 hours.

Make Observations on Day Two

⑨ Put on a lab apron, safety goggles, and disposable gloves.

⑩ Observe the appearance of the solution in each of the four test tubes. Record your observations in the column labeled "Day 2."

⑪ ◆ CAUTION: **Review the safety procedures associated with boiling water baths.** Put on heat-resistant gloves. With your teacher's guidance, use a test-tube holder to move tube C into a boiling water bath. Keep the test tube in the bath for 10 min.

⑫ Remove tube C from the boiling water bath, allow the tube to cool, and return it to the test-tube rack.

⑬ Insert a sterile rubber stopper into the mouth of tubes B, C, and D.

⑭ Place the rack with all four sealed test tubes in an area where it will not be disturbed for several days.

Make Continued Observations

⑮ Each day for the next 5 days, put on safety goggles and gloves. Carefully examine the contents of each tube. (Note: Make sure that the stopper remains in place, sealing the tube's opening.)

⑯ Write down your observations of the broth. Note any changes in the clarity of the solution. Also, look for changes in the appearance of the broth surface.

⑰ ◆ ◆ Clean up your materials according to your teacher's instructions. Wash your hands before leaving the lab.

Analyze and Conclude

1. **Summarizing Data** Did you observe any changes in the appearance of the tube contents over time? Describe your results for each of the four test tubes.

2. **Using Evidence to Make Explanations** If any of the tubes remained unchanged, explain why they did not support microbe growth.

3. **SCIENTIFIC METHODS Formulating Scientific Questions** Why was keeping all of the tubes sealed throughout the experiment essential?

www.scilinks.org
Topic: Microbes
Code: HX80956

Extensions

4. **Further Inquiry** Does temperature affect microbe growth? How could you find out? Based on this investigation, design an experiment that would uncover any relationship between microbe growth and temperature. Share your experimental design with your teacher. With your teacher's permission, perform the investigation.

Answers to Analyze and Conclude

1. Yes, the solution in tube B turned cloudy and the surface had a mat of growing microbes. The solution in the other tubes should be clear.

2. In tube A, no airborne microbes were introduced to the solution. In tube C, boiling killed airborne microbes in the broth. In tube D, there were no nutrients to support microbe growth.

3. Sealing the tubes prevented contamination by and the release of any microbes that might have been cultured in the tubes.

Answers to Extensions

4. Answers will vary but should reflect a step-by-step procedure focusing on how microbes grow in various temperatures.

Key Resources

 Holt Lab Generator

 Lab Datasheet (Levels A, B, C)

 Holt Science Biology Video Labs

 Virtual Investigations

Chapter 2

Chapter 2 Summary

go.hrw.com
SUPER SUMMARY
Keyword: HX8APBS

SUPER SUMMARY

Have students connect the major concepts in this chapter through an interactive Super Summary. Visit **go.hrw.com** and type in the key word **HX8APBS** to access the Super Summary for this chapter.

Reteaching Key Ideas

Healthcare Advances Have students describe the advancements in healthcare in the 20ᵗʰ century and how those advancements were spurred by biology. **LS** Logical

Biotechnology Have students describe five applications of biotechnology to their every day lives. **LS** Logical

Environmental Issues Have students identify local environmental concerns that could be addressed by a local community group. Help students organize an action plan that will involve local leaders and politicians in addressing local environmental concerns. **LS** Interpersonal

Key Ideas	Key Terms

1 Health in the 21st Century

> Biologists combine research and data from many different fields to help reduce the spread of disease.

> As scientists learn more about the nature of disease, our ability to prevent and treat diseases has improved.

> As our understanding of medicine, biology, and science in general increases, humans will live longer and healthier lives.

epidemiology (31)
vaccination (31)
genetics (31)
genome (31)

2 Biology, Technology, and Society

> Genetic engineering is used to create crops that yield more product or are resistant to pests.

> Tools such as genetic engineering, nanotechnology, and computer models have expanded the potential applications of biological research.

> Because biological factors such as fingerprints, iris patterns, and genetic material are unique, they can be used to determine an individual's identity.

> Advances in biotechnology raise ethical concerns that must be addressed by individuals and by society.

genetic engineering (33)
biometrics (36)

3 Biology and the Environment

> Biological research helps us understand, value, and protect the environment. We learn how to protect the environment by learning more about what affects it.

> Tools such as satellite tagging, geographic information systems, and genetics are used to study and protect the environment.

> Biologists rely on the contributions of individuals and communities to help develop solutions for environmental problems.

ecology (38)
environmental science (38)

PART A: Answer all questions in this part.

Directions: For each statement or question, write on your separate answer sheet the number of the word or expression that best completes the statement or answers the question.

1 Which statement best describes a scientific theory?
 (1) It is a collection of data designed to provide support for a prediction.
 (2) It is an educated guess that can be tested by experimentation.
 (3) It is a scientific fact that no longer requires any evidence to support it.
 (4) It is a general statement that is supported by many scientific observations.

2 A student observes that an organism is green. A valid conclusion that can be drawn from this observation is that
 (1) the organism must be a plant
 (2) the organism cannot be single celled
 (3) the organism must be an animal
 (4) not enough information is given to determine whether the organism is a plant or an animal

3 The graph below represents data obtained from an experiment on starch digestion. Which statement best describes point A and point B on the graph?

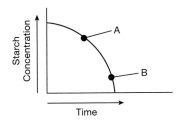

 (1) The concentration of sugars is greater at point A than it is at point B.
 (2) The concentration of sugars is greater at point B than it is at point A.
 (3) The starch concentration is the same at point A as it is at point B.
 (4) The starch concentration is greater at point B than it is at point A.

PART B

Base your answers to question 4 and 5 on the graph below and on your knowledge of biology.

Incidence of Three Human Diseases in Four Different Years

4 Which statement provides the best possible reason for the decrease in number of cases of bacterial pneumonia from 1940 to 1970?
 (1) As a result of genetic engineering, humans became immune to the bacteria.
 (2) Antibiotics were made available for the treatment of bacterial infections.
 (3) The bacteria did not respond to medical treatments.
 (4) As a result of sexual reproduction, the bacteria evolved into a harmless form.

5 The greatest difference between the incidence of measles and the incidence of bacterial pneumonia occurred in
 (1) 1940　　　　(3) 1960
 (2) 1950　　　　(4) 1970

6 Which source would provide the most reliable information for use in a research project investigating the effects of antibiotics on disease-causing bacteria?
 (1) the local news section of a newspaper from 1993
 (2) a news program on national television about antigens produced by various plants
 (3) a current professional science journal article on the control of pathogens
 (4) an article in a weekly news magazine about reproduction in pathogens

PART A

1. **(1)** Epidemiology specializes in studying how diseases spread. Biology is the very general study of all living organisms. The study of genetics focuses specifically on the patterns of heredity between generations of organisms. The Human Genome Project focuses on the complete sequencing of the DNA in the human genome.

2. **(4)** Plants and some animals are green. Some single-celled organisms are also green. More information is needed to classify the organism. *(#01, June 2003 Regents Exam)*

3. **(2)** Because starch breaks down into sugars, the concentration of sugars would increase over time as more starch was digested. *(#05, August 2003 Regents Exam)*

PART B

4. **(2)** Bacterial pneumonia decreased, due to medical treatments with antibiotics. Genetic engineering was not available during this time. Bacteria reproduce asexually. *(#37, August 2005 Regents Exam)*

5. **(3)** The biggest height difference occurs between the bars above 1960 that represent these two diseases. *(#35, August 2005 Regents Exam)*

6. **(3)** Some products are biodegradable, and biotechnology refers to general technologies related to biological principles. Nanotechnology specifically refers to products on a nanoscale.

Regents Exam Practice Correlations

1.1.1a	16	1.3.4c	2
1.2.2a	7	4.5.2j	4
1.3.1a	3, 5, 9, 15		

7. (4) The diaphragm and fine adjustment could be adjusted to focus the image without damaging the microscope or slide. By changing the objective, you'd be moving back to low power. Adjusting the coarse adjustment could damage the microscope or slide. Adjusting the ocular or nosepiece would not change the focus. *(#39, August 2003 Regents Exam)*

8. (2) Skin cells have only recently been able to be used as biometric evidence. Fingerprints have been recorded and catalogued for decades as biometric evidence. Hair follicles have only recently been used as biometric evidence. DNA fragments are useful, but not a common form of biometric evidence.

9. (2) The dotlike structures are present, albeit in smaller numbers, in cells that are no longer dividing. Therefore, their presence in a cell does not imply that the cell is dividing. The dotlike structures are not present in some cells, and therefore cannot affect cell division of all cells. One cannot deduce that the structures can cure genetic disorders. They may however increase the rate of mitosis in human cells. *(#39, January 2004 Regents Exam)*

10. (4)
11. (2)
12. (4)
13. (2)
14. (4)

---

7 A slide of human blood cells was observed in focus under the low-power objective of a compound light microscope that had clean lenses. When the microscope was switched to high power, the image was dark and fuzzy. Which parts of the microscope should be used to correct this situation?

(1) nosepiece and coarse adjustment
(2) diaphragm and ocular
(3) objective and fine adjustment
(4) diaphragm and fine adjustment

8 A science researcher is reviewing another scientist's experiment and conclusion. The reviewer would most likely consider the experiment invalid if

(1) the sample size produced a great deal of data
(2) other individuals are able to duplicate the results
(3) it contains conclusions not explained by the evidence given
(4) the hypothesis was not supported by the data obtained

9 Recently, scientists noted that stained chromosomes from rapidly dividing cells, such as human cancer cells, contain numerous dark, dotlike structures. Chromosomes from older human cells that have stopped dividing have very few, if any, dotlike structures. The best generalization regarding these dotlike structures is that they

(1) will always be present in cells that are dividing.
(2) may increase the rate of mitosis in human cells.
(3) definitely affect the rate of division in all cells.
(4) can cure all genetic disorders.

10 Cholera bacteria cluster

(1) around the plankton where the copepods feed in the ocean water.
(2) throughout the shells of both the male and female copepods.
(3) only around the mouthparts of both male and female copepods.
(4) around the mouthparts and egg casings of female copepods.

---

11 What area of biology applications does genetic engineering represent?

(1) bioscience
(2) biotechnology
(3) bioengineering
(4) bioagriculture

Base your answer to questions 12 through 14 on the graph below and on your knowledge of biology. The graph depicts the global distribution of paralytic polio since 1994.

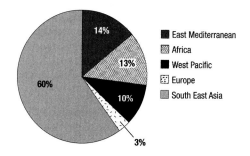

Paralytic Polio

Source: Centers for Disease Control and Prevention, 1994.

12 Where were the greatest number of paralytic polio cases in the world?

(1) Africa
(2) Europe
(3) West Pacific
(4) Southeast Asia

13 Where were the least number of paralytic polio cases in the world?

(1) Africa
(2) Europe
(3) West Pacific
(4) Southeast Asia

14 If the number of paralytic polio cases in Europe was 1,950, what would be the number of cases in the East Mediterranean?

(1) 164   (3) 455
(2) 437   (4) 273

Number of Colonies of Bacteria Present at Various pH Levels

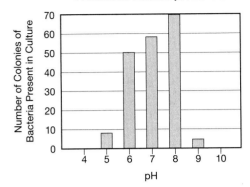

15 Which statement is supported by data from this graph?

(1) All species of bacteria can grow well at pH 7.

(2) This type of bacterium would grow well at pH 7.5.

(3) This type of bacterium would grow well at pH 2.

(4) Other types of bacteria can grow well at pH 4.

PART C

Base your answers to question 16 on the information below.

Where is the Beef? Out Being Irradiated

E. coli bacteria in food cause an estimated 73,000 cases of infection leading to some deaths in the United States each year. Until recently, the only way to guarantee meat free of E. coli was to heat it to 160°F, which kills E. coli. The rare hamburgers preferred by many people are not heated to this temperature, and just a few E. coli may cause severe illness.

Recently, ground beef has been decontaminated by irradiation using electron beam technology. The packaged ground beef is scanned by an electron beam that disrupts the genetic structure of the pathogens. This kills them or leaves them unable to reproduce.

This process is considered safe and has been endorsed by various governmental groups in this country as well as the World Health Organization. Irradiation is effective in preserving only certain foods, such as herbs, wheat flour, fresh fruits, vegetables, and some meats. Although some methods of irradiation can change the taste of some foods, this is not an effect of electron beam technology on ground beef.

Opponents of irradiating food are concerned that the process may result in the formation of chemicals that may be harmful or result in a loss of vitamins. Supporters claim that irradiation is safe and should be considered as just another technique for preservation of food.

16 Explain how irradiation helps preserve meat.

15. **(2)** The graph indicates that this type of bacterium would grow well at pH 7.5. The graph does not provide data to support the other conclusions. *(#38, June 2003 Regents Exam)*

PART C

16. Allow 1 credit for explaining how irradiation helps preserve meat. Acceptable responses include, but are not limited to: Irradiation kills the bacteria that cause the meat to spoil.; disrupts the structure of bacteria that cause the meat to spoil *(#57, January 2006 Regents Exam)*

Chemistry of Life

	Standards	Teach Key Ideas

CHAPTER OPENER, pp. 48–49 **15 min.**

The Living Environment

SECTION 1 Matter and Substances, pp. 51–54 **45 min.**

〉 Atoms
〉 Chemical Bonds
〉 Polarity

Bellringer Transparency

Visual Concepts Matter • Atom • Element Compound • Covalent Bonding • Molecule Hydrogen Bonding • Ionic Bonding • Ion • Comparing Polar and Nonpolar Bonds

---

SECTION 2 Water and Solutions, pp. 55–57 **45 min.**

〉 Properties of Water
〉 Solutions

Bellringer Transparency

Visual Concepts Comparing Cohesion and Adhesion • Solutes, Solvents, and Solutions • Acids • Bases pH

SECTION 3 Carbon Compounds, pp. 59–63 **45 min.**

〉 Building Blocks of Cells
〉 Carbohydrates
〉 Lipids
〉 Proteins
〉 Nucleic Acids

4.1.2h

Bellringer Transparency

Transparencies A27 Saturated and Unsaturated Fatty Acids • A28 Structure of Nucleic Acids

Visual Concepts Carbohydrates • Monosaccharides • Disaccharides • Types of Lipids • Fats, Fatty Acids • Proteins • Amino Acid • Nucleic Acid • Nucleotide DNA Overview • Ribonucleic Acid (RNA) • Comparing ADP and ATP

SECTION 4 Energy and Metabolism, pp. 64–69 **90 min.**

〉 Changing Matter
〉 Chemical Reactions
〉 Biological Reactions

1.2.4, 4.1.2.h, 4.5.1c, 4.5.1.e, 4.5.1f, 4.5.1g

Bellringer Transparency

Transparencies A16 Energy and Chemical Reactions • A17 Activation Energy With and Without Enzymes A25 Enzyme Activity

Visual Concepts Biology • Energy • Activation Energy and Chemical Reactions • Enzyme • Factors Affecting Reaction Rates

See also PowerPoint® Resources

Chapter Review and Assessment Resources

SE Super Summary, p. 70
SE Regents Exam Practice, p. 71
Regents Review Guide
Review Resources
Chapter Tests A and B
Holt Online Assessment
Regents Question Banks on Teacher's One-Stop Planner

CHAPTER
Fast Track

This chapter contains necessary prerequisite content for the study of cells. The Quick Labs in Sections 1, 2, and 3 can be eliminated.

Basic Learners

TE Electron Sharing Model, p. 52
TE Ionic Bonding by the Numbers, p. 53
TE Relating Diagrams, p. 56
TE Comparing Carbon Compounds, p. 62
Directed Reading Worksheets*
Active Reading Worksheets*
Lab Manuals, Level A*
Study Guide* ■
Note-taking Workbook*
Special Needs Activities and Modified Tests*

Advanced Learners

TE Artifical Sweeteners, p. 60
Critical Thinking Worksheets*
Concept Mapping Worksheets*
Science Skills Worksheets*
Lab Datasheets, Level C*

Why It Matters	Hands-On	Skills Development	Assessment
Build student motivation with resources about high-interest applications.	SE **Inquiry Lab** Yeast Activity, p. 49*■	TE **Reading Toolbox** Assessing Prior Knowledge, p. 48 SE **Reading Toolbox,** p. 50	
	SE **Quick Lab** Atom Models, p. 53*■	TE **Reading Toolbox** Visual Literacy, p. 52 SE **Reading Toolbox** Comparison Table, p. 52 TE **Reading Toolbox** Comparison Table, p. 52 TE **Reading Toolbox** Visual Literacy, p. 54	SE **Section Review** TE **Formative Assessment** Spanish Assessment*■ 📁 **Section Quiz**■
TE **Demonstration** Oil and Water, p. 55 TE **Demonstration** Acids and Bases, p. 56 SE **Water Wonders,** p. 58	SE **Quick Lab** Telltale Cabbage, p. 57*■	TE **Reading Toolbox** Everyday Words in Science, p. 56 SE **Reading Toolbox** Everyday Words in Science, p. 57	SE **Section Review** TE **Formative Assessment** Spanish Assessment*■ 📁 **Section Quiz**■
TE **Demonstration** Carbon, p. 59 TE **Demonstration** Oil and Water Don't Mix, p. 59	SE **Quick Lab** Brown Paper Test, p. 61*■ 📁 **Exploration Lab** Identifying Food Nutrients*	TE **Reading Toolbox** Everyday Words in Science, p. 60 SE **Reading Toolbox** Quantifiers, p. 62 TE **Reading Toolbox** Quantifiers, p. 62 TE **Reading Toolbox** Visual Literacy, p. 62	SE **Section Review** TE **Formative Assessment** Spanish Assessment*■ 📁 **Section Quiz**■
TE **Carbonic Acid,** p. 65 TE **Onions and Enzymes,** p. 66 TE **Demonstration** Pineapple Enzymes, p. 67	SE **Inquiry Lab** Enzymes in Detergents, p. 68*■ 📁 **Skills Practice Lab** Observing the Effect of Temperature on Enzyme Activity*	TE **Reading Toolbox** Visual Literacy, p. 18	SE **Section Review** TE **Formative Assessment** Spanish Assessment*■ 📁 **Section Quiz**■

See also Lab Generator

See also Holt Online Assessment Resources

Resources for Differentiated Instruction

English Learners
📁 Directed Reading Worksheets*
📁 Active Reading Worksheets*
📁 Lab Manuals, Level A*
📓 Study Guide*■
📓 Note-taking Workbook*
📓 Multilingual Glossary
💿 Interactive Tutor

Struggling Readers
TE Electron Sharing Model, p. 52
TE Ionic Bonding by the Numbers, p. 53
TE Reading Symbols, p. 56
TE Summarizing, p. 61
📁 Directed Reading Worksheets*
📁 Active Reading Worksheets*
📁 Lab Manuals, Level A*
📓 Study Guide*

Special Education Students
TE Reaction Conditions, p. 65
TE Text Text
📁 Directed Reading Worksheets*
📁 Active Reading Worksheets*
📁 Lab Manuals, Level A*
📓 Study Guide*■
📓 Note-taking Workbook*
📓 Special Needs Activities and Modified Tests*

Alternative Assessment
📁 Science Skills Worksheets*
📁 Section Quizzes*■
📓 Chapter Tests A, B, and C*■

Chapter 3

Chemistry of Life

Overview

This chapter introduces the basic chemistry students need to understand biochemical systems. Much of the body is composed of organic compounds, and students learn the fundamentals of chemical bonding and the characteristics of the important classes of biomolecules (proteins, lipids, carbohydrates, and nucleic acids). These compounds are involved in many metabolic reactions that help organisms maintain homeostasis.

Assessing Prior Knowledge Students should understand the following concepts:
- states of matter
- characteristics of solutions
- forms of energy

Visual Literacy Ask students what is required to produce heat from the fire. (wood) Ask students to name the type of reaction that occurs when wood burns. (combustion) Tell students that this combustion reaction requires oxygen from the air. Ask them to predict the most likely products of the reaction. (carbon dioxide and water) Ask students what fuel enables humans to generate heat. (food) Ask what gas we inhale that our bodies need. (oxygen) What gas is released when we exhale? (carbon dioxide)

Preview

1 Matter and Substances
Atoms
Chemical Bonds
Polarity

2 Water and Solutions
Properties of Water
Solutions

3 Carbon Compounds
Building Blocks of Cells
Carbohydrates
Lipids
Proteins
Nucleic Acids

4 Energy and Metabolism
Changing Matter
Chemical Reactions
Biological Reactions

Why It Matters

The chemicals that make up living things are more complex than those in nonliving things. Learning the chemical basis of biology can help you understand how processes occur and how living things respond to their environment.

 The Living Environment
Standard 4 Students will understand and apply scientific concepts, principles, and theories pertaining to the physical setting and living environment and recognize the historical development of ideas in science.
Key Idea 1 Living things are both similar to and different from each other and from nonliving things. ***Major Understandings - 1.2h***
Key Idea 5 Organisms maintain a dynamic equilibrium that sustains life. ***Major Understandings - 5.1c, 5.1f, 5.1g***

What do people and igloos have in common? Both are made from matter that has a very precise structure.

> Igloos are built from blocks of compressed snow. Snow is nonliving matter made up of simple water molecules.

> The fire inside the igloo gives off heat energy in a chemical reaction. Living things also produce heat in chemical reactions to stay alive.

Chapter Correlations 📖 The Living Environment

Standard 1

1.2h Many organic and inorganic substances dissolved in cells allow necessary chemical reactions to take place in order to maintain life. Large organic food molecules such as proteins and starches must initially be broken down (digested to amino acids and simple sugars respectively), in order to enter cells. Once nutrients enter a cell, the cell will use them as building blocks in the synthesis of compounds necessary for life.

5.1c In all organisms, organic compounds can be used to assemble other molecules such as proteins, DNA, starch, and fats. The chemical energy stored in bonds can be used as a source of energy for life processes.

5.1f Biochemical processes, both breakdown and synthesis, are made possible by a large set of biological catalysts called enzymes. Enzymes can affect the rates of chemical change. The rate at which enzymes work can be influenced by internal environmental factors such as pH and temperature.

5.1g Enzymes and other molecules, such as hormones, receptor molecules, and antibodies, have specific shapes that influence both how they function and how they interact with other molecules.

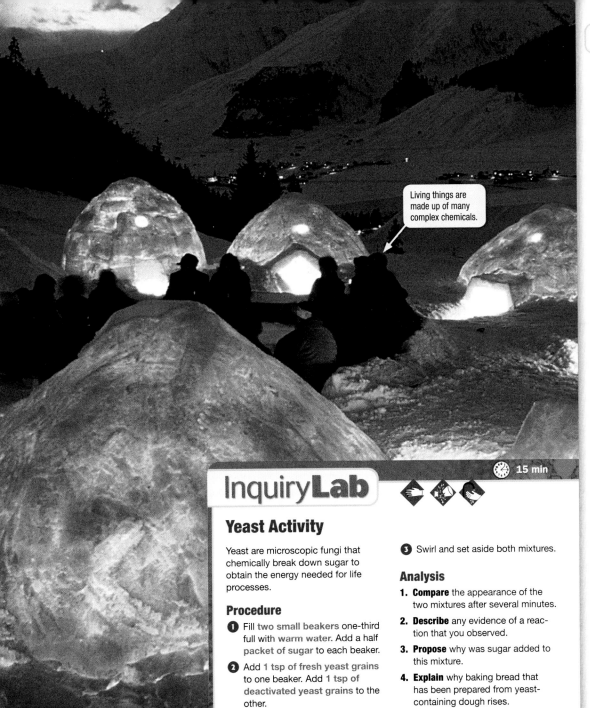

Living things are made up of many complex chemicals.

Teacher's Notes Make sure that you use fresh baker's yeast for a vigorous, gas-generating reaction. Warm water will also accelerate the reaction, producing a visible froth within minutes. Deactivated yeast is dead yeast. Mix the materials in a small beverage container, then slip a balloon over the opening of the container. The carbon dioxide that is produced will inflate the balloon.

Materials
- beakers, 100 mL (2)
- packets of sugar
- fresh baker's yeast
- deactivated yeast grains

Answers to Analysis
1. The mixture with the fresh yeast took on a frothy appearance. The other mixture did not appear to change.
2. Bubbles were evidence that a gas-producing reaction was occurring.
3. Sugar was one of the reactants in this chemical reaction. It was broken down into products that included carbon dioxide gas.
4. The yeast in the dough created tiny bubbles of carbon dioxide. As the yeast converts more starch to CO_2 and sugar, larger pockets of CO_2 are formed causing the dough to rise.

InquiryLab

⏱ 15 min

Yeast Activity

Yeast are microscopic fungi that chemically break down sugar to obtain the energy needed for life processes.

Procedure
1. Fill **two small beakers** one-third full with **warm water**. Add a half **packet of sugar** to each beaker.
2. Add **1 tsp of fresh yeast grains** to one beaker. Add 1 tsp of **deactivated yeast grains** to the other.
3. Swirl and set aside both mixtures.

Analysis
1. **Compare** the appearance of the two mixtures after several minutes.
2. **Describe** any evidence of a reaction that you observed.
3. **Propose** why was sugar added to this mixture.
4. **Explain** why baking bread that has been prepared from yeast-containing dough rises.

Using Words

1. Answers will vary. Have the students return to complete the last column of the table after they have completed the lesson.

Word	Everyday meaning	Scientific meaning
compound	something consisting of several parts	a substance made from two or more different elements
solution	mixture with water; answer to a problem	a homogeneous mixture with a solute and solvent
energy	enthusiasm, excitement	the capacity to do work

Using Language

1. April, March, February, January
2. younger

Using Graphic Organizers

See table below.

These reading tools can help you learn the material in this chapter. For more information on how to use these and other tools, see **Appendix: Reading and Study Skills.**

Using Words

Everyday Words in Science Many words that we use every day have special meanings in science. For example, *matter* in everyday use is "an issue or problem." In science, matter means "anything that has mass and takes up space."

Everyday Words in Science		
Word	**Everyday meaning**	**Scientific meaning**
compound		
solution		
energy		

Your Turn Make a table like the one shown here.
1. Before you read, write in your own words the everyday meaning of the terms in the table.
2. As you read, fill in the scientific meaning for the terms in the table.

Using Language

Quantifiers Quantifiers are words that describe how much, how large, and how often. Quantifiers can also describe the order in which things occur. Words that describe an order include *first, second, third, fourth, primary, secondary, tertiary,* and *quaternary.*

Your Turn Use what you have learned about quantifiers to answer the following questions.
1. Place the following months in order of fourth, third, second, and first: January, March, April, February.
2. Would a student attending primary school be younger or older than a student attending secondary school?

Taking Notes

Comparison Table A comparison table is useful for comparing characteristics of topics in science. All topics in a table are described in terms of the same characteristics. This approach helps you compare several topics at one time.

	Carbohydrates	*Lipids*
Structure		
Function		
Energy Content		

Your Turn Make a comparison table to compare carbohydrates and lipids.
1. Draw a table like the one shown here.
2. In the top row, write the topics *Carbohydrates* and *Lipids*.
3. In the left column, write the general characteristics *Structure, Function,* and *Energy Content.* As you read the chapter, fill in the characteristics for each topic in the appropriate cells.

	Carbohydrates	**Lipids**
Structure	• contain carbon, hydrogen, and oxygen	• contain carbon, hydrogen, and oxygen
Function	• source of energy • structural support • cellular ID • breaks down quickly during metabolism, limited storage capacity	• source of energy and energy storage • controls movement of water
Energy Content	• less energy per gram than lipids	• stores more energy per gram than carbohydrates

Matter and Substances

Key Ideas	Key Terms	Why It Matters
› What makes up matter? › Why do atoms form bonds? › What are some important interactions between substances in living things?	atom element valence electron compound molecule ion	All living things are made of matter, so understanding the structure and behavior of matter can help you understand how your body works.

Every living and nonliving thing is made of matter. Matter is anything that has mass and takes up space. To understand how living things work and interact, you must first understand the structure of matter.

Atoms

What does all matter have in common? It is made of very small particles called atoms. An **atom** is the smallest unit of matter that cannot be broken down by chemical means. › **All matter is made up of atoms. An atom has a positively charged core surrounded by a negatively charged region.**

Atomic Structure Atoms are made of three types of particles. *Protons* have a positive charge, *electrons* have a negative charge, and *neutrons* have no charge. Atoms have no overall charge because each atom has as many electrons as protons. Protons and neutrons have about the same mass and make up the core, or nucleus, of an atom. Electrons have very little mass and move around the nucleus in a region called the *electron cloud*, which is much larger than the nucleus.

Elements An **element** is a substance made up of atoms that have the same number of protons. For example, each atom of the element carbon has six protons, as **Figure 1** shows. Atoms of an element may have different numbers of neutrons. These atoms are called *isotopes* of elements.

› **Reading Check** *What is a proton? (See the Appendix for answers to Reading Checks.)*

atom the smallest unit of an element that maintains the chemical properties of that element

element a substance that cannot be separated or broken down into simpler substances by chemical means

Nucleus

Electron energy levels

Figure 1 The graphite in pencil lead is made of atoms of the element carbon.
› **If an uncharged carbon atom (inset) has six protons in its nucleus, how many electrons does it have?**

Key Resources

Visual Concepts
Matter
Atom
Element
Compound
Covalent Bonding
Molecule
Hydrogen Bonding
Ionic Bonding
Ion
Comparing Polar and Nonpolar Bonds

This section introduces students to atoms, the fundamental units of matter. Students learn that atoms can bond to form compounds.

Bellringer

Use the Bellringer transparency to prepare students for this section.

› **Teach**

Teaching Key Ideas

Atomic Particles Students will know about protons, electrons, and neutrons from previous science classes. Show students a periodic table, which includes all of the elements. Tell them that an element's identity is based on its atomic number, which is the number of protons in an atom of that element. If the number of protons in an atom were to change, then the atom would become a different element. The chemical reactions covered in this chapter involve electrons. A change in the number of electrons does not change an atom's identity.

Answers to Caption Questions
Figure 1: six electrons

READING TOOLBOX

Visual Literacy Have students look at the models in **Figure 2.** Tell them that atoms, molecules, and compounds are represented in different ways. Each representation best conveys an idea. Ask what each model shows and how they differ. (The electron cloud model shows an interior view of water. The space-filling model shows an exterior view, which emphasizes the 3-dimensional geometry of water.) Students will see other representations in **Figures 9** and **10.** **Visual**

READING TOOLBOX

Comparison Table The answer is shown in a linear way, to fit in the margin.
Covalent Bonding
Electron pairs are shared.
Molecules are produced.
Bond is the attraction for shared electrons.
Ionic Bonding
Elections are transferred.
Ions are produced.
Bond is the attraction between ions of opposite charge. **LS Verbal**

Figure 2 A water molecule consists of an oxygen atom covalently bonded to two hydrogen atoms. The electron cloud model (left) shows the interaction between the atoms of the molecule. The space-filling model (right) shows the three-dimensional structure of a molecule.

READING TOOLBOX

Comparison Table Make a comparison table that compares covalent bonding and ionic bonding.

valence electron an electron that is found in the outermost shell of an atom and that determines the atom's chemical properties

compound a substance made up of atoms of two or more different elements joined by chemical bonds

molecule a group of atoms that are held together by chemical forces

ion an atom, radical, or molecule that has gained or lost one or more electrons and has a negative or positive charge

Electron cloud model

Space-filling model

Chemical Bonds

The electron cloud of an atom may have levels. The innermost level can hold only two electrons. Levels farther from the nucleus can usually hold eight electrons. Electrons in the outermost level, or shell, are called **valence electrons.** Atoms tend to combine with each other such that eight electrons will be in the valence shell.

When atoms combine, a force called a *chemical bond* holds them together. ❯ Chemical bonds form between groups of atoms because most atoms become stable when they have eight electrons in the valence shell. However, the smallest atoms, such as hydrogen, are stable when they have only two valence electrons. When atoms of different elements bond, a compound forms. A **compound** is a substance made of the bonded atoms of two or more different elements.

Covalent Bonding One way that atoms bond is by sharing valence electrons to form a *covalent bond.* A **molecule** is a group of atoms held together by covalent bonds. Not all substances that have covalent bonds are compounds. The oxygen in the air you breathe consists of molecules made of two oxygen atoms sharing electrons in a covalent bond. To represent an oxygen molecule, write "O_2," not "O." A carbon dioxide molecule has two oxygen atoms bonded to a single carbon atom, so its formula is CO_2.

Water: A Covalent Compound As **Figure 2** shows, a water molecule, H_2O, forms when an oxygen atom combines with two hydrogen atoms. The atoms form chemical bonds by sharing electrons in a way that gives oxygen eight valence electrons, making it stable. The hydrogen atoms become stable because sharing gives each two valence electrons.

❯ **Reading Check** *What is a chemical bond?*

Differentiated Instruction

Basic Learners/Struggling Readers

Electron Sharing Model The concepts of valence electrons and electron sharing are easier to understand if you use Lewis Dot structures to illustrate valence electrons. Draw the Lewis structure for an oxygen atom and two hydrogen atoms. Describe how a hydrogen atom needs one electron to have a filled energy level and how an oxygen atom needs two electrons to fill its outer energy level. Covalent bonds in water satisfies this condition.
H• H• •Ö• **LS Visual**

QuickLab

🕐 **15 min**

Atom Models

Scientists use models to represent their understanding of things that they cannot directly observe.

Procedure

❶ Using assorted materials provided by your teacher, work in groups to make model atoms for hydrogen, carbon, oxygen, sodium, and chlorine.

❷ Model the covalent bonds in a water molecule.

❸ Model an ionic bond in sodium chloride.

Analysis

1. **Model** the covalent bonds in a carbon dioxide molecule, CO_2. How many electrons are shared?

2. **CRITICAL THINKING** **Critiquing Models** Exchange models with another group. What is accurate and useful about those models? What could be improved? Write down your comments for the other group.

Ionic Bonding Atoms can achieve a stable valence level in another way—by losing or gaining electrons. This results in a positive or negative charge. An **ion** is an atom or group of atoms that has an electric charge because it has gained or lost electrons. The attractive force between oppositely charged ions is an *ionic bond.*

Table Salt: An Ionic Compound One familiar example of an ionic compound is table salt, NaCl, shown in **Figure 3.** A sodium atom has one valence electron, while a chlorine atom has seven. ❶ Sodium readily gives up its electron, while chlorine readily accepts an electron. ❷ The sodium atom is now a sodium ion, Na$^+$. The chlorine atom is now a chloride ion, Cl$^-$. ❸ The positively charged sodium ion and negatively charged chloride ion attract each other and form sodium chloride, NaCl. ❹ The attractive forces between several sodium ions and chloride ions form a crystal of table salt.

Figure 3 Salt crystals in sodium chloride, NaCl, are formed by the interaction between sodium ions, Na$^+$, and chloride ions, Cl$^-$. ❯ How many electrons are in the valence shell of a chloride ion?

go.hrw.com
✳ **interact online**
Keyword: HX8BCMF3

Ionic Bonding in Salt

❶ A Na atom loses an electron to a Cl atom.

❷ Each atom becomes a stable, charged ion.

❸ The attraction of the oppositely charged ions forms an ionic bond.

❹ Several ions interact to form a salt crystal.

Teacher's Notes You'll want to review the electron structures for hydrogen, carbon, oxygen, sodium, and chlorine before students begin the lab. To avoid frustration, tell students about electron sharing in double bonds (for carbon dioxide). Using Lewis Dot structures is suggested.

Materials

- gum drops, toothpicks, colored marshmallows, raisins, cotton candy, paper plates, pipe cleaners

Answers to Analysis

1. In carbon dioxide, a carbon atom shares two electrons with an oxygen atom. Carbon also shares its other two valence electrons with the other oxygen atom. Eight electrons are shared (four electrons from carbon and two from each oxygen atom).

2. When critiquing other models, students should note that protons and neutrons should be approximately the same size and that electrons are smaller. Protons and neutrons should be packed together tightly, while electrons surround this nucleus.

Answers to Caption Questions
Figure 3: eight

go.hrw.com
✳ **interact online**

Students can interact online with "Ionic Bonding in Salt" by going to go.hrw.com and typing in the keyword HX8BCMF3.

Differentiated Instruction

Basic Learners/Struggling Readers

Ionic Bonding by the Numbers Use Lewis Dot models to represent the process shown in **Figure 3.** Show students mathematically how atoms take on a charge. Sodium atoms have 11 protons and 11 electrons. The loss of an electron means that the particle now has 11 protons, 10 electrons, and a resulting positive charge results. Ask students to tell you why the chloride ion has a negative charge. (It has 17 protons and 18 electrons.) **LS Logical/Visual**

MISCONCEPTION ALERT

Atomic Size Students often do not realize that atoms consist mostly of empty space. If the nucleus of an atom were the size of a typical marble, the first electron level would be about 0.8 km (0.5 miles) away from the nucleus. **LS Visual**

Figure 4 Water dissolves ionic compounds. When sodium chloride, NaCl, is dissolved in water, sodium ions, Na⁺, and chloride ions, Cl⁻, become surrounded by water molecules, H₂O.

SCI**LINKS**.
www.scilinks.org
Topic: Hydrogen Bonding
Code: HX80777

Polarity

In some covalent bonds, the shared electrons are attracted more strongly to one atom than to the other. As a result, one end, or pole, of the molecule has a partial negative charge, while the opposite end has a partial positive charge. Molecules with partial charges on opposite ends are said to be *polar*. The water molecule is polar.

Solubility The partially charged ends of polar molecules attract opposite charges. Because of this behavior, water can dissolve polar molecules, such as sugar, and ionic compounds, such as the salt in **Figure 4.** Nonpolar substances, such as oil, grease, and wax, do not dissolve well in water. Instead, they remain together in clumps or a separate layer. The reason is that water molecules are more attracted to each other than to the nonpolar molecules.

Hydrogen Bonds When bonded to an oxygen, nitrogen, or fluorine atom, a hydrogen atom has a partial charge nearly as great as a proton's charge. It attracts the negative pole of other nearby molecules. This attraction, called a *hydrogen bond*, is stronger than attractions between other molecules, but not as strong as a covalent bond. ❯ Hydrogen bonding plays an important role in many of the molecules that make up living things. For example, the two strands of a DNA molecule are held together by hydrogen bonds between the bases.

❯ **Reading Check** *Why does salt dissolve in water?*

Section 1 Review

❯KEY IDEAS

1. **Identify** the parts of atoms and their locations.

2. **Name** two ways that atoms can combine to become more stable in compounds.

3. **Explain** how charges cause salt and sugar to dissolve in water.

CRITICAL THINKING

4. **Analyzing Information** Scientists use the isotope carbon-14 in radiocarbon dating. How many protons, neutrons, and electrons are in a carbon-14 atom?

5. **Recognizing Differences** Explain the difference between polar and nonpolar molecules. Give an example of a polar molecule, and describe its structure.

USING SCIENCE GRAPHICS

6. **Periodic Table** Elements on the periodic table are arranged in groups based on how many electrons their atoms have in the valence shell. Using the periodic table in the Appendix, propose why the noble gases in Group 18 rarely form chemical bonds.

Key Ideas	Key Terms	Why It Matters
❯ What makes water a unique substance? ❯ How does the presence of substances dissolved in water affect the properties of water?	cohesion base adhesion pH solution buffer acid	The processes of life take place in water. Without water's unique properties, life as we know it could not exist.

Humans can survive for a few weeks without food but only a few days without water. In fact, all life on Earth depends on this simple substance.

Properties of Water

Water has many unique properties that make it an important substance for life. ❯ **Most of the unique properties of water result because water molecules form hydrogen bonds with each other.**

- **Ice floats.** When water freezes, hydrogen bonds lock water molecules into a crystal structure that has empty spaces. This structure makes water less dense as a solid than as a liquid, so ice floats. Floating ice prevents rivers, lakes, and oceans from freezing solid, so life can exist in the water under the ice.

- **Water absorbs and retains heat.** Hydrogen bonds are constantly breaking and forming between water molecules. Because of this, water can absorb a large amount of heat without changing temperature. It is also why water takes a long time to cool. Large bodies of water can help keep temperatures on Earth from changing too fast. This property of water can also help organisms maintain a constant internal temperature.

- **Water molecules stick to each other.** Hydrogen bonds hold water molecules together in much the same way holding hands keeps a crowd of people together. Thus small drops, such as the dewdrops on the flower in **Figure 5,** are pulled into a ball shape. **Cohesion** is the attraction of particles of the same substance. Water is a liquid at ordinary temperatures because such forces keep it from evaporating easily.

- **Water molecules stick to other polar substances.** Attraction between particles of different substances is called **adhesion.** As **Figure 5** shows, a combination of adhesion and cohesion causes water to move upward through the stem of a plant from the roots to the leaves.

cohesion the force that holds molecules of a single material together

adhesion the attractive force between two bodies of different substances that are in contact with each other

Inside of stem

Figure 5 Cohesion and adhesion contribute to the upward movement of water from the roots of plants.

Key Resources

◎ **Visual Concepts**
Comparing Cohesion and Adhesion
Solutes, Solvents, and Solutions
Acids
Bases
pH

Teaching Key Ideas

Water Density Fill a drinking glass with water and add ice cubes. Ask students why the ice floats. (Ice is less dense than liquid water. The molecules align in the solid to form a network structure.) On the board, draw a network arrangement for ice, and the close-packed arrangement of molecules in liquid water. **LS** Visual

Everyday Words in Science *Basic* commonly refers to something fundamental or primary. Sample answers: My brother is in *basic* training. Many soaps and cleaning products are *basic* materials.

Answers to Caption Questions

Figure 7: An antacid is a basic compound that reacts with acids to form a salt and water.

Demonstration

Acids and Bases Use pH paper or and phenolphthalein solution dilute solutions of vinegar and sodium hydroxide to show the neutralization process. Prepare the vinegar solution using 25 mL vinegar and 25 mL of water. Prepare the sodium hydroxide using 0.4 g NaOH in 100 mL of water. Test each solution, and note the color and pH of each. Add NaOH in 10 mL increments to the vinegar solution. Test the pH after each addition. Use the indicator to show when the solution reaches the neutral point. Then, add another 10 mL of base so students can see the solution is now basic. **LS** Visual

Figure 6 A hydronium ion, H_3O^+, and a hydroxide ion, OH^-, form when a hydrogen ion, H^+, separates from a water molecule and bonds to another. This reaction can also re-form two water molecules from a hydronium ion and a hydroxide ion.

H_2O Water molecule + H_2O Water molecule ⇌ H_3O^+ Hydronium ion + OH^- Hydroxide ion

solution a homogeneous mixture throughout which two or more substances are uniformly dispersed

acid any compound that increases the number of hydronium ions when dissolved in water

base any compound that increases the number of hydroxide ions when dissolved in water

pH a value that is used to express the acidity or alkalinity (basicity) of a system

buffer a solution made from a weak acid and its conjugate base that neutralizes small amounts of acids or bases added to it

Solutions

A **solution** is a mixture in which ions or molecules of one or more substances are evenly distributed in another substance. Many substances are transported throughout living things as solutions of water. Dissolved substances can move more easily within and between cells. Water dissolves many ionic and polar substances but does not dissolve nonpolar substances.

Acids and Bases Some water molecules break apart to form ions, as **Figure 6** shows. In pure water, hydronium ions and hydroxide ions are present in equal numbers. **>** In solutions, some substances change the balance of these ions. **Acids** are compounds that form extra hydronium ions when dissolved in water. Your stomach uses a solution of hydrochloric acid, HCl, to digest food.

In contrast, **bases** are compounds that form extra hydroxide ions when dissolved in water. Many bases contain hydroxide ions. An example is sodium hydroxide, NaOH, which is used to remove clogs from drains. Other bases react with water molecules. For example, ammonia, NH_3, reacts with a water molecule, H_2O, to form an ammonium ion, NH_4^+, and a hydroxide ion, OH^-.

When acids and bases are mixed, the extra hydronium and hydroxide ions react to form water. Depending on the amounts of extra ions, the solution will be either less acidic, less basic, or neutral.

Figure 7 The pH scale is based on the concentration of hydronium ions in a solution. **>** How does an antacid relieve acid indigestion?

Lemon Vinegar   Milk   Antacid Hand soap Household amomonia

pH 0 1 2 3 4 5 6 7 8 9 10 11 12 13 14

More acidic Neutral More basic

Differentiated Instruction

Struggling Readers

Reading Symbols Have students look at **Figure 6.** To help students focus on important subtleties ask: What makes a molecule different from an ion? (Ions are charged.) How does water differ from a hydronium ion? (Water has two hydrogen atoms and no charge. The hydronium ion has three hydrogen atoms and a positive charge.) Why are there two water molecules but only one of each of the ions? (Two water molecules are needed to produce one of each ion.) Which ion imparts acidic properties? (H_3O^+ or H^+) **LS** Verbal

Basic Learners

Relating Diagrams Refer students to **Figures 6** and **7,** and ask the following: Which ion in **Figure 6** predominates in the solutions on the left side of **Figure 7?** (H_3O^+) What do the different colors represent on the scale in **Figure 7?** (indicator changes at each pH) What is the mathematical relationship between the numbers on the scale? (As the numbers increase, the H_3O^+ concentration decreases by a factor of 10 times.) **LS** Visual

QuickLab

⏱ 15 min

Telltale Cabbage

Red cabbage contains a natural indicator that can be used to identify how acidic or basic a solution is.

Procedure

1 Cut up a cabbage leaf into very tiny clippings by using scissors.

2 Put on safety goggles. Place the clippings in a beaker of warm water. Swirl the mixture. Wait several minutes until the water changes color.

3 Add several drops of lemon juice. Note any changes in appearance.

4 Add about 1/4 tsp of baking soda. Note any changes in appearance. Continue adding small amounts of baking soda, and observe additional color changes.

Analysis

1. **Describe** what happened when the leaf clippings were placed in warm water.

2. **Describe** what happened when lemon juice (an acid) was added to the indicator solution.

3. **Describe** what happened when the baking soda was added to the acidic solution.

4. **CRITICAL THINKING** **Inferring Relationships** From your observations, what probably happened when the baking soda was added to the acidic solution?

pH and Buffers pH is a measure of how acidic or basic a solution is. The pH scale is shown in **Figure 7.** Each one-point increase in pH represents a 10-fold decrease in hydronium ion concentration. So, the H_3O^+ concentration in a solution of pH 2 is 10 times as great as it is in a solution of pH 3. Pure water has a pH of 7. Acidic solutions have a pH below 7, and basic solutions have a pH above 7.

▶ The pH of the solutions in living things must be stable. The pH of human blood is about 7.4. If the pH goes down to 7.0 or up to 7.8, an individual will die within minutes. For a stable pH to be maintained, the solutions in living things contain buffers. A **buffer** is a substance that reacts to prevent pH changes in a solution. An important buffer in living things is the bicarbonate ion, HCO_3^-.

READING TOOLBOX

Everyday Words in Science Write a sentence that uses the everyday meaning of the word *basic*. Then, write a sentence that uses the scientific meaning of the word *basic*.

Section 2 Review

▶ KEY IDEAS

1. **Identify** four unique properties of water that make life on Earth possible.

2. **Differentiate** between acids and bases.

3. **Explain** the role of buffers in maintaining homeostasis.

CRITICAL THINKING

4. **Recognizing Relationships** Cells contain mostly water. If cells contained mostly oil, how would an organism's ability to maintain homeostasis be affected?

5. **Applying Information** The active ingredient in aspirin is acetylsalicylic acid. Why would doctors recommend buffered aspirin, especially for people with a sensitive stomach?

MATH SKILLS

6. **Exponents** The pH of solution A is 2. The pH of solution B is 4. Which solution has the greater concentration of hydronium ions? The concentration of that solution is how many times the concentration of the other solution?

QuickLab

Teacher's Notes To speed up the extraction, use smaller clippings and hotter water. Remove the clippings and allow the solution to cool before giving it to students.

Materials
- baking soda
- beaker, 250 mL
- cabbage leaves
- lemon juice
- safety goggles
- scissors
- water

Answers to Analysis
1. The purple substance was released into the warm water.
2. The color of the solution changed from purple to pink.
3. The color changed back to purple, then to blue–green.
4. The baking soda reacted with the lemon juice caused the indicator to once again change colors.

▶ Close

Formative Assessment

Which of the following examples illustrates cohesion?

A. Water molecules adhere to the polar molecules of another substance. (Incorrect. This is an example of adhesion.)

B. Water freezes and the ice floats on water. (Incorrect. Floating is related to density.)

C. Water takes a longer time to heat and cool compared to the air above it. (Incorrect. Heat retention relates to specific gravity.)

D. Water drops on the surface of a car pull together into a ball shape. (Correct!)

Answers to Section Review

1. Water's density enables life to exist under a layer of ice in freezing temperatures because ice floats. Water's capacity to absorb and retain heat helps moderate temperatures near large bodies of water. Water's cohesive properties reduce its evaporation rate. Water's adhesion properties enable it to overcome the force of gravity and travel upward (helpful to plants).

2. Compounds that increase the concentration of hydronium ions in a solution are acids. Compounds that reduce the concentration of hydronium ions in a solution are bases.

3. Living things must maintain a stable pH. A buffer reacts with acids and bases to help keep pH stable in living things.

4. An organism's internal temperature would likely change more abruptly and drastically in response to environmental temperature changes.

5. The buffer reduces the acidity of the aspirin, which makes aspirin less irritating to the stomach.

6. Each consecutive value on the pH scale represents a factor of 10. The lower the pH, the more acidic, and therefore the higher the concentration of hydronium ions. Therefore the concentration of hydronium ions in solution A is 100 times the concentration of the hydronium ions in solution B.

Why It Matters

Why It Matters

Water Wonders

A water spider can live underwater by capturing air bubbles at the surface. Most of the life cycle of this "bubble breather" occurs below the water surface. All organisms depend on water. Water has many unique properties that make life on Earth possible.

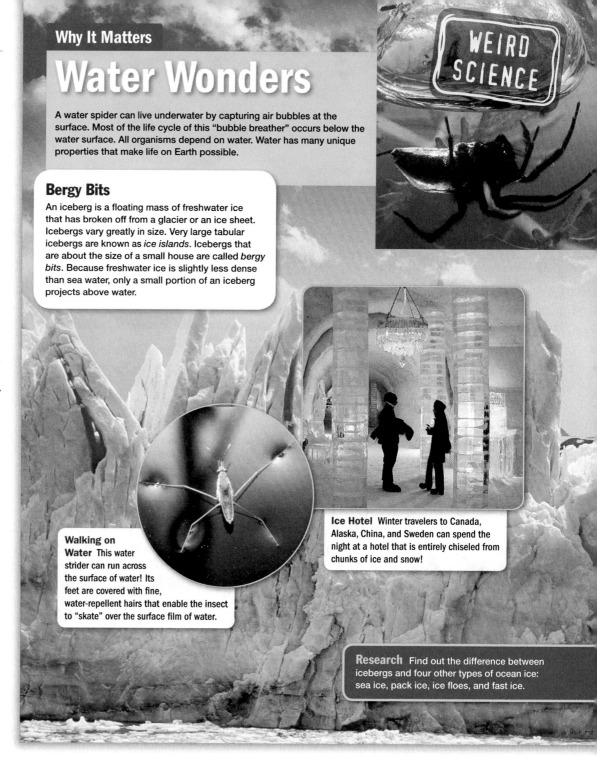

WEIRD SCIENCE

Bergy Bits

An iceberg is a floating mass of freshwater ice that has broken off from a glacier or an ice sheet. Icebergs vary greatly in size. Very large tabular icebergs are known as *ice islands*. Icebergs that are about the size of a small house are called *bergy bits*. Because freshwater ice is slightly less dense than sea water, only a small portion of an iceberg projects above water.

Ice Hotel Winter travelers to Canada, Alaska, China, and Sweden can spend the night at a hotel that is entirely chiseled from chunks of ice and snow!

Walking on Water This water strider can run across the surface of water! Its feet are covered with fine, water-repellent hairs that enable the insect to "skate" over the surface film of water.

Research Find out the difference between icebergs and four other types of ocean ice: sea ice, pack ice, ice floes, and fast ice.

Key Ideas

> What are chemicals of life made from?
> What is the role of carbohydrates in cells?
> What do lipids do?
> What determines the functions of proteins?
> What do nucleic acids do?

Key Terms

carbohydrate	nucleotide
lipid	DNA
protein	RNA
amino acid	ATP
nucleic acid	

Why It Matters

Your body works by using the same four types of molecules that bacteria and plants do.

Suppose that you are building a house. You need wood for framing and metal for nails, screws, and electrical wiring. You also need concrete for the foundation, glass for windows, and drywall siding. This complex structure is made of a few basic materials that must be assembled in a highly organized way. The same is true of the molecules that make up living things.

Building Blocks of Cells

The parts of a cell are made up of large, complex molecules, often called *biomolecules.* > **Large, complex biomolecules are built from a few smaller, simpler, repeating units arranged in an extremely precise way.** These simple units are like the toy blocks in **Figure 8,** which connect to build the large sculpture. Not all of the blocks are exactly the same, but they all connect with other blocks in a few different ways.

Carbon Compounds The basic units of most biomolecules contain atoms of carbon. Carbon atoms have four valence electrons, so they can form covalent bonds with as many as four other atoms. Carbon atoms can bond with each other to form chains or rings. The carbon atoms in these chains and rings can also connect with atoms of other elements to form the basic units of most biomolecules.

> **Reading Check** *What element is the basis of biomolecules?*

The Living Environment
Standard 4
1.2h Many organic and inorganic substances dissolved in cells allow necessary chemical reactions to take place in order to maintain life. Large organic food molecules such as proteins and starches must initially be broken down (digested to amino acids and simple sugars respectively), in order to enter cells. Once nutrients enter a cell, the cell will use them as building blocks in the synthesis of compounds necessary for life.

Figure 8 Large, complex structures can be built from a few basic units arranged in a precise way. > Describe two shapes that you could make from these five blocks.

Key Resources

Transparencies
A27 Saturated and Unsaturated Fatty Acids
A28 Structure of Nucleic Acids

Visual Concepts
Carbohydrates
Monosaccharides
Disaccharides
Types of Lipids
Fats, Fatty Acids
Proteins
Amino Acid
Nucleic Acid
Nucleotide
DNA Overview
Ribonucleic Acid (RNA)
Comparing ADP and ATP

> Focus

This section introduces students to the kinds of organic compounds that are found in living organisms that are essential for biological processes.

Bellringer

Use the Bellringer transparency to prepare students for this section.

> Teach

Demonstration

Carbon Draw the structural formula for methane (CH_4) on the board. Then, draw the structural formula for butane (C_4H_8), so students can see what is meant by the term *carbon chain.* Emphasize that this simple chain can get much longer and branch to form complex structures, such as ATP. **LS Visual**

Answers to Caption Questions

Figure 8: Answers will vary.

Section Correlations
4.1.2h

Teaching Key Ideas

Chemical Representations Point out that biomolecules can be shown in different ways. When students look at **Figure 9,** they should notice that the condensed formula and structural formula are both correct ways to represent glucose. The hexagon shapes in **Figure 10** are still another representation, though not quite as accurate. Ask students how the three models vary and why they are all useful. (Structural formulas show a 2-dimensional representation and the bonding patterns. Condensed formulas show the number of atoms for each element in the compound. Stylized representations provide a simple way to display more complex structures.) **LS** **Visual**

READING TOOLBOX

Everyday Words in Science Ask students to define *sugar*. Most students will probably refer to the white crystalline substance they use to sweeten foods. Tell them that sugar also the common name for carbohydrates. When they say *sugar*, what do they really mean sucrose, or any one of a number of different compounds such as fructose, glucose, or maltose? **LS** **Verbal**

Answers to Caption Questions
Figure 10: lactose

CH₂OH

Figure 9 The sugar glucose, $C_6H_{12}O_6$, is made from carbon, hydrogen, and oxygen atoms. Sugars are the building blocks of carbohydrates.

---

carbohydrate a class of molecules that includes sugars, starches, and fiber; contains carbon, hydrogen, and oxygen

lipid a fat molecule or a molecule that has similar properties, including waxes and steroids

ACADEMIC VOCABULARY

vary to make a minor or partial change in

Carbohydrates

You may have heard about carbohydrates in foods such as grains, fruits, and vegetables. **Carbohydrates** are molecules made of sugars. A sugar contains carbon, hydrogen, and oxygen in a ratio of 1:2:1. **Figure 9** shows the ring structure of glucose, a common sugar found in grape juice. Glucose is a *monosaccharide,* or "single sugar."

Two sugars can be linked to make a *disaccharide.* Examples of disaccharides are sucrose (table sugar) and lactose (found in milk). Many sugars can be linked together to make a *polysaccharide.* Starch consists of hundreds of glucose units bonded together. Glycogen (found in animals) consists of many branched chains of glucose.

Monosaccharides and disaccharides are considered simple carbohydrates. Polysaccharides are considered complex carbohydrates. **Figure 10** shows an example of each carbohydrate. **>** Cells use carbohydrates for sources of energy, structural materials, and cellular identification.

Energy Supply Carbohydrates are a major source of energy for many organisms, including humans. Plants store the sun's energy for future use by making glucose and converting it to starch. Organisms release chemical energy for cell activities by breaking down glucose.

Structural Support *Chitin* and *cellulose* are two complex carbohydrates that provide support. The shells of crabs, lobsters, and insects are made of chitin. Chitin is also found in the cell walls of mushrooms and molds. The cell walls of plants are made of cellulose. Bundles of cellulose are stiff enough to hold plants upright.

Cell Recognition Cells may have short, branched chains of varying sugar units on their outer surface. In a complex organism, cells recognize neighboring cells by these carbohydrates. Carbohydrates on the outside of invading cells allow the body to recognize them as not being part of the body so that they can be destroyed.

> Reading Check *What is the basic unit of a carbohydrate?*

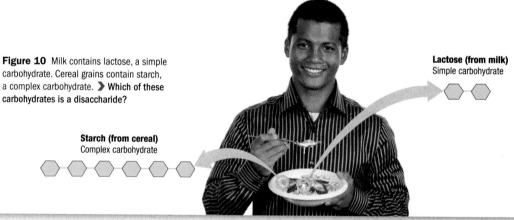

Figure 10 Milk contains lactose, a simple carbohydrate. Cereal grains contain starch, a complex carbohydrate. **>** Which of these carbohydrates is a disaccharide?

Starch (from cereal)
Complex carbohydrate

Lactose (from milk)
Simple carbohydrate

MISCONCEPTION ALERT

Carbohydrates Due to trendy diets, some people think foods with "carbs" are different than those containing carbohydrates. Tell students that vegetables like broccoli, carrots, and spinach contain carbohydrates just like "high carb" potatoes and bread.

Differentiated Instruction

Advanced Learners/GATE

Artificial Sweeteners Have students research artificial sweeteners and how they are used to create foods that taste sweet but have fewer calories than foods with sucrose. Have the students explore the structure of these compounds and explain how they provide the taste without the calories. Ask students to find out how the taste buds are stimulated. **LS** **Logical**

Lipids

Lipids are another class of biomolecules, which includes fats, phospholipids, steroids, and waxes. Lipids consist of chains of carbon atoms bonded to each other and to hydrogen atoms. This structure makes lipids repel water. ❯The main functions of lipids include storing energy and controlling water movement. Lipids also include steroid hormones, used as signaling molecules, and some pigments, which absorb light.

Energy Stores The main purpose of fats is to store energy. Fats can store energy even more efficiently than carbohydrates. Many animals, such as the dormouse in **Figure 11,** can survive without a steady diet because of fat storage. When food is plentiful, the animal converts the excess food into fats for long-term energy storage. When food is scarce, the animal can break down the fat molecules to release energy for life processes. Plant oils are stored in seeds to provide energy to start the growth of a new plant.

Water Barriers The cell's boundary is made of phospholipids. One end of this molecule is attracted by water molecules. The other end, which is made of long carbon chains, is not. You will learn more about the behavior of these molecules when you study the structure of cell membranes.

The stems and leaves of many plants are covered with a thin layer of wax, another type of lipid. This wax helps prevent the evaporation of water from the cells at the surface of a plant. Waxy feathers can also help keep ducks and other aquatic birds dry. One type of wax molecule found on bird feathers is shown in **Figure 11.**

Hands-On
QuickLab

⏱ 15 min

Brown Paper Test

You can test substances for fats by using ordinary brown paper. Oils are fats that are liquid at room temperature. This test also works for oils.

Procedure

❶ Place a drop of water in one area of your brown paper. Place a drop of oil in another area. Rub a spot of butter into a third area.

❷ Fan the paper to evaporate any of these substances. Hold the stained paper to the light. What do you see?

❸ Now, test other substances provided by your teacher.

Analysis

1. **Compare** how the butter, oil, and water affected the paper.

2. **Describe** how each of the other substances that you tested affected the paper. Which ones contained lipids?

Dormouse

Fat molecule

Duck feather

Wax molecule

Figure 11 Many fat molecules have three long chains of carbons. Waxes may be composed of chains of about 24 to 34 carbon atoms.

❯Teach, continued

QuickLab

Teacher's Notes Fats and oils belong to a group of substances called lipids. Fats are solids at room temperature. Oils are liquids at room temperature. Saturated fats have backbones comprised of single carbon-carbon bonds. Unsaturated oils have double bonds between carbon atoms within the fatty acid carbon chain. Ask students what saturated means in *saturated fat.* (All bonds other than the C–C backbone are saturated with hydrogen.)

Materials

• brown paper
• samples of water, oils, and butter
• food samples, such as cookies, pretzels, potato chips, muffins, cake, ketchup, mustard, salad dressings, candy, and chocolate

Answers to Analysis

1. The places where paper contacted fats and oils were translucent. The place where water was dropped appeared translucent at first but then returned to its opaque appearance after the water evaporated.

2. Substances that contain high quantities of lipids should turn the paper translucent.

Demonstration

Oil and Water Don't Mix Show the insoluble nature of fats and oils by mixing some samples with water. To show the hydrophobic qualities of waxes, drip some wax from a burning candle into a container of water. Students will need to recall these properties when they study the cell membrane. **LS** Visual

Differentiated Instruction

Struggling Readers

Summarizing Have students read Section 3 silently. After a designated time, assign students to cooperative pairs. Have one student summarize what he or she read while the other student listens. The listener should point out inaccuracies and mention concepts that the other left out. Both students should work together during the final clarification process, referring to the text as needed. **LS** Interpersonal

READING TOOLBOX

Quantifiers **primary** order of amino acids in the chain; **secondary** the bending and twisting of the chain; **tertiary** the overall shape of a single folded protein; **quaternary** the overall shape of a folded multi-subunit protein complex

Teaching Key Ideas

Enzymes Enzymes are proteins that affect the rate of chemical reactions in the body. Enzymes are a very important part of the metabolic process because they assist in vital processes such as digestion. Enzymes work by speeding up reactions by providing an alternate reaction pathway at a lower E_a.

READING TOOLBOX

Visual Literacy Have students look at the generalized formula for an amino acid in **Figure 12.** Ask students if it makes sense that hooves, horns, hair, and muscles can all have the same building blocks. (Though it may seem odd, all of these body parts contain proteins. Use the analogy in **Figure 8** to make the point that combinations of the same building blocks, amino acids coupled with the primary, secondary, tertiary, and quaternary structure of the protein results in different properties.)

READING TOOLBOX

Quantifiers Describe the levels of protein structure, and identify the quantifier used to describe each level.

protein an organic compound that is made of one or more chains of amino acids and that is a principal component of all cells

amino acid a compound of a class of simple organic compounds that contain a carboxyl and an amino group and that combine to form proteins

SCLINKS.
www.scilinks.org
Topic: Proteins
Code: HX81241

Proteins

Proteins are the workhorse molecules of all living things. There are many types of proteins that perform many types of functions. **> Proteins are chains of amino acids that twist and fold into certain shapes that determine what the proteins do.** Some proteins provide structure and support. Others enable movement. Some proteins aid in communication or transportation. Others help carry out important chemical reactions.

Amino Acids A **protein** is a molecule (usually a large one) made up of **amino acids,** the building blocks link to form proteins. **Figure 12** shows the basic structure of an amino acid. Every amino acid has an amino group (-NH₂), a carboxyl group (-COOH), and a variable side group. The carboxyl group of one unit can link to the amino group of another. This link is a *peptide bond.*

The side group gives an amino acid its unique properties. Twenty different amino acids are found in proteins. In order to build proteins, the body requires a supply of the correct amino acids. The body can make many amino acids from other substances, but a few amino acids must be included in the diet. To get these amino acids, your body breaks apart the proteins in the foods you eat.

Levels of Structure For each type of protein, amino acids are arranged in a specific order. This order is the protein's primary structure. The various side groups interact to bend and twist the chain. Portions of the chain may form coils and folds. These patterns are known as the protein's secondary structure.

Some small proteins consist of only one chain, but most proteins consist of two or more chains. The tertiary structure of proteins is the overall shape of a single chain of amino acids. The quaternary structure is the overall shape that results from combining the chains to form the protein. This shape suits the function of each protein.

> **Reading Check** *What is a protein's primary structure?*

Figure 12 Proteins are chains of amino acids linked by peptide bonds. An amino acid (top) has a side group (blue). Various combinations of amino acids result in specific types of proteins, such as the proteins that make up the muscles, hair, horns, and hooves of this highland cow.

A *peptide bond* (orange) forms between the carboxyl group (yellow) of one amino acid and the amino group (red) of another.

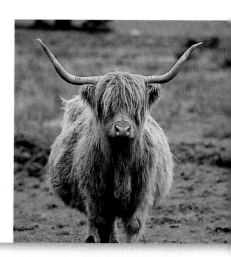

Differentiated Instruction

Basic Learners

Comparing Carbon Compounds Have students make a table that lists information about carbon compounds. Along the top, have them write *Carbohydrates, Lipids, Proteins,* and *Nucleic acids.* Along the sides, have them write *Characteristics* and *Examples.* As they review this section, have students add information to their tables. **LS Logical**

DNA

Base

Phosphate group

P

Sugar

Nucleotide

ATP
(Adenosine triphosphate)

Base (adenine)

Phosphate groups

P P P

Sugar (ribose)

Figure 13 DNA is made of two strands of multiple nucleotides (inset) linked by hydrogen bonds. ATP is also a nucleotide and is made up of a sugar, a base, and three phosphate groups. ❯ **What is the function of ATP?**

Nucleic Acids

All of your cells contain nucleic acids. A **nucleic acid** is a long chain of nucleotide units. A **nucleotide** is a molecule made up of three parts: a sugar, a base, and a phosphate group. Nucleotides of deoxyribonucleic acid, or **DNA,** contain the sugar deoxyribose. Nucleotides of ribonucleic acid, or **RNA,** contain the sugar ribose.

Hereditary Information DNA molecules act as "instructions" for the processes of an organism's life. These instructions, called the *genetic code,* depend on the order of bases in the nucleotides of the DNA molecule. DNA consists of two strands of nucleotides that spiral around each other, as **Figure 13** shows. The bases in one strand of nucleotides form hydrogen bonds with the bases on the other to hold the DNA molecule together and protect the code. RNA also interacts with DNA to help decode the information. ❯ **Nucleic acids store and transmit hereditary information.**

Energy Carriers Some single nucleotides have other important roles. Cells need a steady supply of adenosine triphosphate, or **ATP,** to function. ATP, shown in **Figure 13,** is a nucleotide that has three phosphate groups. Energy is released in the reaction that breaks off the third phosphate group. Other single nucleotides transfer electrons or hydrogen atoms for other life processes.

nucleic acid an organic compound, either RNA or DNA, whose molecules are made up of one or two chains of nucleotides and carry genetic information

nucleotide an organic compound that consists of a sugar, a phosphate, and a nitrogenous base

DNA deoxyribonucleic acid, the material that contains the information that determines inherited characteristics

RNA ribonucleic acid, a natural polymer that is present in all living cells and that plays a role in protein synthesis

ATP adenosine triphosphate, an organic molecule that acts as the main energy source for cell processes

Section 3 Review

❯ **KEY IDEAS**

1. **Discuss** how one type of atom (carbon) can be the basis of so many types of biomolecules.
2. **List** three major functions of carbohydrates.
3. **Describe** two functions of lipids.
4. **Explain** how two different proteins will have two different shapes.
5. **Summarize** the role of nucleic acids in a cell.

CRITICAL THINKING

6. **Applying Information** Before a long race, runners often "carbo load." In other words, they eat substantial quantities of carbohydrates. How might this practice help their performance?

METHODS OF SCIENCE

7. **Identifying Unknown** Analysis of an unknown substance shows that that the substance contains carbon, hydrogen, and oxygen and is soluble in oil, but not in water. Which of the four types of biomolecules could this substance be?

Teaching Key Ideas

It's Exothermic! Explain that the reaction of ATP to form ADP results in the release of energy that can be used by cells. Ask students how cells keep a steady supply of ATP. (The breakdown of ATP is a reversible reaction. ADP can once again become ATP through another reaction that adds a phosphate group.)

Answers to Caption Questions

Figure 13: ATP supplies energy to cells.

❯ Close

Formative Assessment

Which class of carbon compounds is used as long-term energy storage in the human body?

A. lipids (Correct! Lipids, or fats, are used to store energy and can be broken down for use when food is scarce.)

B. proteins (Incorrect. Proteins can provide some immediate energy.)

C. nucleic acids (Incorrect. Nucleic acids are used to encode information and also are a part of ATP, which supplies immediate energy.)

D. carbohydrates (Incorrect. Carbohydrates can supply short-term energy and can form other structures.)

Answers to Section Review

1. Carbon atoms can bond to four other atoms, including other carbon atoms. Carbon that bond to each other can form long-chain molecules with complex shapes. Small, simple building blocks are put together in a coordinated fashion to produce large complex biomolecules.

2. Carbohydrates are sources of energy, structural materials, and structures for cellular identification.

3. storing energy and controlling water movement

4. Proteins are a class of compounds, not a specific compound. Proteins vary depending on their amino acid sequences. Different amino acid sequences result in proteins that will likely have different shapes.

5. Nucleic acids store and transmit hereditary information.

6. Carbohydrates breakdown quickly in reactions that release energy.

7. It would be a lipid-based substance. Carbohydrates and lipids contain carbon, hydrogen, and oxygen. Carbohydrates dissolve in water, but lipids do not.

Energy and Metabolism

Key Ideas	Key Terms	Why It Matters
❯ Where do living things get energy? ❯ How do chemical reactions occur? ❯ Why are enzymes important to living things?	energy enzyme reactant substrate product active site activation energy	All living things need energy to survive. You get that energy by breaking complex molecules from food you eat into simpler, stabler molecules.

 The Living Environment
Standard 4
5.1c In all organisms, organic compounds can be used to assemble other molecules such as proteins, DNA, starch, and fats. The chemical energy stored in bonds can be used as a source of energy for life processes.
5.1f Biochemical processes, both breakdown and synthesis, are made possible by a large set of biological catalysts called enzymes. Enzymes can affect the rates of chemical change. The rate at which enzymes work can be influenced by internal environmental factors such as pH and temperature.
5.1g Enzymes and other molecules, such as hormones, receptor molecules, and antibodies, have specific shapes that influence both how they function and how they interact with other molecules.

Figure 14 This athlete uses energy to move the basketball. ❯ **What form of energy is used to move the basketball?**

Changes constantly occur in living things. In fact, you could say that a key feature of life is change. The ability to move or change matter is called **energy.** Energy exists in many forms—including light, heat, chemical energy, mechanical energy, and electrical energy—and can be converted from one form to another. The athlete in **Figure 14** is using mechanical energy to move the basketball.

Changing Matter

Living things are made of matter, which consists of a substance with a form. A physical change occurs when only the form or shape of the matter changes. The substances that make up the matter do not change into different substances. When you pour sugar into iced tea and stir, the sugar crystals disappear. The sweet taste shows that the sugar is still there but has changed form.

A chemical change occurs when a substance changes into a different substance. In a chemical change, the identity of the matter changes. When wood burns, the carbohydrates in the wood fibers combine with oxygen, O_2, in the air. The wood fibers change to different substances: carbon dioxide, CO_2, and water vapor, H_2O.

Conservation of Mass Matter is neither created nor destroyed in any change. The same mass is present before and after the wood burns and the sugar dissolves. This observation is called the *law of conservation of mass.*

Conservation of Energy Every change in matter requires a change in energy. Energy may change from one form to another, but the total amount of energy does not change. This observation is called the *law of conservation of energy.* In some changes, energy is taken in from the surroundings. In others, energy is released into the surroundings. The total amount of *usable* energy decreases because some energy is given off to the surroundings as heat. ❯ **Living things use different chemical reactions to get the energy needed for life processes.**

❯ **Reading Check** *What is a chemical change?*

Chemical Reactions

Changing a substance requires a chemical reaction. During this process, bonds between atoms are broken, and new ones are formed. A **reactant** is a substance that is changed in a chemical reaction. A **product** is a new substance that is formed. Scientists summarize reactions by writing equations in the following form:

$$Reactants \longrightarrow Products$$

The arrow means "changes to" or "forms." For example, carbon dioxide and water can react to form carbonic acid, H_2CO_3, in your blood. The following equation represents this reaction:

$$CO_2 + H_2O \rightleftharpoons H_2CO_3$$

The double arrow indicates that the products can reform reactants. In this example, carbonic acid changes back to carbon dioxide and water in your lungs.

Activation Energy Chemical reactions can occur only under the right conditions. To form new bonds, particles must get close enough to share electron clouds. However, even though the particles move constantly, as they get close, their negatively charged electron clouds tend to push them apart. To react, the particles must collide fast enough to have kinetic energy to overcome the repulsion between them. The **activation energy** of the reaction is the minimum kinetic energy that colliding particles need to start a chemical reaction.

Alignment Even if enough energy is available, the product still may not form. When the reactant particles collide, the correct atoms must be brought close together in the proper <u>orientation</u>, as **Figure 15** shows. Otherwise, the product will not form. ❯ Chemical reactions can occur only when the activation energy is available and the correct atoms are aligned. In living things, chemical reactions occur between large, complex biomolecules. Life can only exist if these molecules collide in the correct orientation.

❯ **Reading Check** *What causes particles to repel other particles?*

energy the capacity to do work

reactant a substance or molecule that participates in a chemical reaction

product a substance that forms in a chemical reaction

activation energy the minimum amount of energy required to start a chemical reaction

ACADEMIC VOCABULARY

orientation the relative position or direction of something

Reaction Conditions			
Reactants	**Conditions**	**Result**	**Products**
	not enough energy	no reaction	none
	enough energy; wrong orientation	no reaction	none
	enough energy; proper orientation	reaction	

Figure 15 Chemical reactions can occur only under the right conditions. The correct atoms of reactants must be aligned, and they must collide with enough energy.
❯ What term describes the minimum amount of energy needed for a reaction to occur?

Teaching Key Ideas

Enzyme Names Enzymes are often named by incorporating the name of an enzyme's substrate with the function that the enzyme performs and then placing the suffix *–ase* at the end. For example, a dehydrogenase is an enzyme that removes hydrogen atoms from a substrate. Adding the suffix *–ase* to the name of the substrate without adding the functional name usually means that the enzyme breaks the substrate down into products. For example, sucrase breaks sucrose down to glucose and fructose. Ask students to suggest the function of the enzymes lactase and lipase. (Lactase breaks lactose down to glucose and galactose. Lipase breaks lipids down to glycerol and fatty acids.) Have the students research the names and functions of other enzymes.

Teaching Key Ideas

Enzymes Make It Happen Refer students to the photograph at the beginning of the chapter. Burning fuel generates a lot of heat. Because the body functions over a limited temperature range, burning fuel in the body has to occur at much lower temperatures. Help students understand that enzymes make it possible for these reactions to occur because the activation energy is lower for enzyme-catalyzed reactions.

---

enzyme a molecule, either protein or RNA, that acts as a catalyst in biochemical reactions

active site on an enzyme, the site that attaches to a substrate

substrate the reactant in reactions catalyzed by enzymes

SC*I*LINKS.
www.scilinks.org
Topic: Enzymes
Code: HX80531

Figure 16 Enzymes decrease the amount of energy needed to start a chemical reaction without changing the amount of energy contained in either the reactants or the products.

Biological Reactions

Living things carry out many chemical reactions that help maintain a stable internal environment. Many of these reactions require large activation energies. Often, the reactants are large biomolecules that must collide in a very specific orientation. Many of these reactions would not occur without the help of enzymes.

Enzymes An **enzyme** is a molecule that increases the speed of biochemical reactions. Enzymes hold molecules close together and in the correct orientation. This way, the molecules do not have to depend on random collisions to react. An enzyme lowers the activation energy of a reaction, as **Figure 16** shows. ❯ **By assisting in necessary biochemical reactions, enzymes help organisms maintain homeostasis.** Without enzymes, chemical reactions would not occur quickly and easily enough for life to go on.

Enzyme Activity Enzymes fit with reactants like a lock fits a key. As **Figure 17** shows, each enzyme has an **active site,** the region where the reaction takes place. The shape of the active site determines which reactants, or **substrates,** will bind to it. Each different enzyme acts only on specific substrates.

Step ❶ Two substrates bind to an enzyme's active site. The substrates fit in a specific position and location, like a key in a lock.

Step ❷ Binding of the substrates causes the enzyme's shape to change slightly. The substrates fit more tightly in the enzyme's active site. The change in shape causes some bonds in the substrates to break and new bonds to form.

Step ❸ The chemical reaction is complete when the product, a new substance, is formed. The unchanged enzyme releases the product, and can then be reused for another reaction.

Conditions Many enzymes are proteins. Changes in temperature and pH can change a protein's shape. If an enzyme changes shape, it won't work well. Most enzymes need a certain range of temperatures and pH.

Effect of Enzyme on Activation Energy

Energy absorbed / Energy released

Reactants

Activation energy without an enzyme

Activation energy with an enzyme

Products

Reaction progress

Why It Matters

Onions and Enzymes Onions contain sulfur compounds called *amino acid sulfoxides*. When an onion is cut, peeled, or crushed, enzymes called *allinases* are released from the tissue of the onion. These enzymes convert the amino acid sulfoxides into sulfenic acids, which forms a gas. When the gas reacts with water on the surface of the eye, sulfuric acid forms. The acid stings and triggers tear production in the eyes.

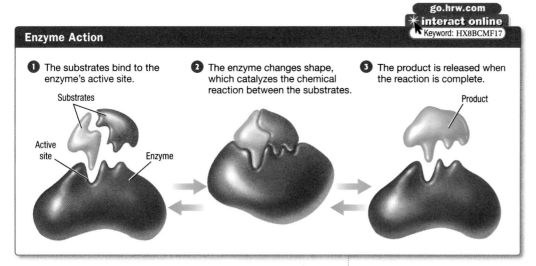

Enzyme Action

❶ The substrates bind to the enzyme's active site.

Substrates

Active site

Enzyme

❷ The enzyme changes shape, which catalyzes the chemical reaction between the substrates.

❸ The product is released when the reaction is complete.

Product

Students can interact with the characteristics of "Enzyme Action" by going to go.hrw.com and typing in the keyword HX8BCMF17.

Metabolism Your cells get most of the energy needed for metabolism from the food you eat. When food is digested, it is broken into small molecules that can enter the blood, which delivers them to cells. Here, chemical reactions release energy by breaking down these food molecules so that cells can use it. The release of energy from food molecules involves many steps and many enzymes.

Consider the breakdown of sugar to release energy. You can use a match to supply enough activation energy to set fire to cellulose, a polysaccharide, when you burn wood. However, the match flame is hot, and the reaction of glucose with oxygen gets even hotter because it is so fast. Living things also "burn" sugars, but they use enzymes to do so. The enzymes reduce the activation energy so much that only a little energy is needed to start the reaction. Then, a series of enzymes carries out the reaction in a slower, step-by-step manner so that the energy can be captured in the form of ATP molecules. In this process, very little heat is produced.

❯ **Reading Check** *Why is the shape of an enzyme important?*

Figure 17 Enzymes catalyze specific reactions between specific reactants.
❯ **How would a change in the shape of the active site affect the enzyme's activity?**

Demonstration

Pineapple Enzymes If fresh pineapple is added to a gelatin mixture, the protein will not gel. Prior to class, prepare gelatin in three separate cups. Cut 1 contains gelatin only. Cup 2 contains gelatin with fresh pineapple placed on the surface. Cup 3 contains gelatin with canned pineapple placed on the surface. Tell students that pineapple contains *bromelin*, an enzyme that breaks down gelatin. Ask students to explain the results. (The heating process in canned pineapple destroys bromelin. Gelatin stays gelled when canned pineapple is used.)

Answers to Caption Questions
Figure 17: The substrate would not fit the enzyme, so it would no longer be effective.

❯ **Close**

Formative Assessment

1. The role of enzymes in chemical reactions is to ___.
A. increase activation energy (Incorrect. Enzymes reduce activation energy requirements.)
B. eliminate proteins (Incorrect. Enzymes are proteins.)
C. reduce the number of reactants (Incorrect. Enzymes do not affect the number of reactants.)
D. speed up the rate of reaction (Correct. Enzymes speed up the rate of a reaction.)

Section 4 Review

❯ **KEY IDEAS**
1. **Explain** the importance of chemical reactions in living things.
2. **Describe** two conditions necessary for a chemical reaction to occur.
3. **Relate** enzymes and homeostasis.

CRITICAL THINKING
4. **Applying Information** Explain the difference between usable energy and the total amount of energy. How is this difference accounted for in living organisms?
5. **Recognizing Relationships** Your body breaks down starch into glucose molecules. In this reaction, which substance is the reactant, and which is the product?

WRITING FOR SCIENCE
6. **Predicting Outcomes** Research the enzyme carbonic anhydrase. Explain its role in maintaining homeostasis in the human body. How might a molecule that interferes with the action of carbonic anhydrase affect your body?

Answers to Section Review

1. Chemical reactions provide the energy and structural components needed for life processes.
2. Reactants need sufficient activation energy for a reaction to occur. The reactants must also be aligned properly during collisions to form products.
3. Enzymes enable biochemical reactions to occur at the temperature ranges and pH ranges needed for homeostasis.
4. Usable energy is what enables the organism to function. Usable energy always decreases within an organism because some of the total energy is given off to the surroundings as heat. The total

amount of energy in a system never changes during the transfer of energy from one form to another.

5. Starch is the reactant, and glucose is the product.
6. Carbonic anhydrase catalyzes the production of carbonic acid from carbon dioxide and water. When carbonic acid in the blood is carried to the lung's alveoli, it reacts to form carbon dioxide and water. Carbon dioxide is then released from the body during exhalation. A molecule that interferes with the action of carbonic anhydrase would result in the accumulation of CO_2 in the blood, which can become toxic to the body.

Time Required

One 45-minute lab period for Day 1; 30 minutes for Day 2; and 15 minutes for Day 3

Ratings

EASY ———————→ HARD

Teacher Prep	🔬🔬
Student Setup	🔬🔬🔬
Concept Level	🔬🔬🔬
Cleanup	🔬🔬

Safety Caution

Make sure students wear safety goggles and a lab apron. Caution students to avoid burns by working carefully when heating and pouring boiling water.

Tips and Tricks

Review the Role of Enzymes Before starting the lab, ask students why enzymes are added to detergents. (to help break down proteins and other substances from foods that may stain clothing) Ask students why detergent enzymes are stable during the hot water cycle. (The enzymes found in commercial laundry soap have been engineered to withstand high temperatures.)

Gelatin Preparation The rate of hydrolysis is slower in instant gelatin, which contains sugar, than in sugar-free gelatin.

Detergent Samples Each students should bring in a 1-cup sample of their home laundry detergent. Each sample should be labeled with the following: the name or brand, and the

Lab Correlations

1.2.4 Carry out a research plan for testing explanations, including selecting and developing techniques, acquiring and building apparatus, and recording observations as necessary.

4.1.2h Many organic and inorganic substances dissolved in cells allow necessary chemical reactions to take place in order to maintain life. Large organic food molecules such as proteins and starches must initially be broken down (digested to amino acids and simple sugars respectively), in order to enter cells. Once nutrients enter a cell, the cell will use them as building blocks in the synthesis of compounds necessary for life.

4.5.1e The energy from ATP is used by the organism to obtain, transform, and transport materials, and to eliminate wastes.

Chapter 3 Lab

 1.2.4, 4.1.2h, 4.5.1e

Objectives

▶ Recognize the function of enzymes in laundry detergents.

▶ Relate temperature and pH to the activity of enzymes.

Materials

- lab apron, safety goggles, and disposable gloves
- balance
- graduated cylinder
- stirring rod, glass
- beaker, 150 mL
- gelatin, instant, regular (18 g) or sugar-free (1.8 g)
- NaHCO₃ (0.1 g)
- tongs or a hot mitt
- boiling water, 50 mL
- thermometer
- pH paper
- test tubes (6)
- test-tube rack
- pipet with bulb
- plastic wrap
- tape
- beakers, 50 mL (6)
- distilled water, 50 mL
- detergent, laundry, powdered, five brands (1 g of each)
- wax pencil
- metric ruler

Safety

Enzymes in Detergents

Some laundry detergents contain enzymes, substances that speed up chemical reactions. A protease is an enzyme that helps break down proteins. In this lab, you will investigate the effectiveness of laundry detergents that contain enzymes. To do so, you will use a protein mixture to simulate food stains.

Preparation

1. **SCIENTIFIC METHODS** **State the Problem** How can you determine if a detergent contains proteases?

2. **SCIENTIFIC METHODS** **Form a Hypothesis** Form a testable hypothesis that explains how a protein mixture might be affected by a detergent that contains protease.

Procedure

Make a Protein Substrate

1 🔺 🧤 🥽 Put on a lab apron, safety goggles, and gloves.

2 🔶 🔶 🔥 **CAUTION: Use tongs or a hot mitt to handle heated glassware.** Put 18 g of regular gelatin in a 150 mL beaker. Slowly add 50 mL of boiling water to the beaker, and stir the mixture with a stirring rod. Test and record the pH of this solution.

active ingredients listed on the container. Collect all of the samples and distribute 3–5 tablespoons of five different samples to each lab group for testing. Check that each group gets one sample of a non-enzyme detergent to use as a control.

Experimental Control Students should have a control test tube with 15 drops (1 mL) of water (no detergent) added to the gelatin surface. Require students to present a written procedure for their experiment and a list of all safety precautions before allowing them to gather materials for the lab. When students add the detergent solutions to the gelatin, the mixture will foam. During this reaction, carbon dioxide gas is released. The addition of baking soda (NaHCO₃) to the gelatin raises the pH of the

gelatin from 4 to 8, which is the optimum pH for protease activation in the detergent samples.

Marking the Tubes Have students use a wax pencil to mark the test tubes at the uppermost level of the cooled gelatin in each tube. They will use this mark to measure the hydrolysis of the gelatin each day. Label the test tubes 1 through 6.

Preparing the Detergent Solution To prepare a 10 percent solution of laundry detergent, students should dissolve 1 g of detergent in 9 mL of distilled water. Have students record the pH for each numbered detergent sample. Students can measure protein hydrolysis after 24 hours by using a wax pencil to draw a second line at the top of the gelatin layer and then measuring the distance (in mm) between the first line and the second line. This measurement indicates

❸ ◈ Very slowly add 0.1 g of NaHCO₃, baking soda, to the hot gelatin while stirring. Note any reaction. Test and record the pH of this solution.

❹ Place six test tubes in a test-tube rack. Pour 5 mL of the gelatin-NaHCO₃ mixture into each tube. Use a pipet to remove any bubbles from the surface of the mixture in each tube. Cover the tubes tightly with plastic wrap and tape. Cool the tubes, and store them at room temperature until you begin your experiment.

❺ ◈ ◈ Clean up your lab materials according to your teacher's instructions. Wash your hands before you leave the lab.

Design an Experiment

❻ Design an experiment that tests your hypothesis and that uses the materials listed for this lab. Predict what will happen during your experiment if your hypothesis is supported.

❼ Write a procedure for your experiment. Identify the variables that you will control, the experimental variables, and the responding variables. Construct any tables you will need to record your data. Make a list of all safety precautions you will take. Have your teacher approve your procedure before you begin the experiment.

Conduct Your Experiment

❽ ◆ ◈ ◈ Put on a lab apron, safety goggles, and gloves.

❾ ◈ ◈ Make a 10% solution of each laundry detergent by dissolving 1 g of detergent in 9 mL of distilled water.

❿ Carry out your experiment. Observe the test tubes after 24 h. Record your data in a data table.

⓫ ◈ ◈ Clean up your lab materials according to your teacher's instructions. Wash your hands before you leave the lab.

Analyze and Conclude

1. **SCIENTIFIC METHODS** **Analyzing Methods** Suggest a reason for adding NaHCO₃ to the gelatin solution.

2. **SCIENTIFIC METHODS** **Summarizing Data** Make a bar graph of your data. Plot the amount of gelatin that has broken down (change in the depth of the gelatin) on the *y*-axis. Plot detergent on the *x*-axis.

3. **SCIENTIFIC METHODS** **Inferring Conclusions** What conclusions did your group infer from the results? Explain.

4. **Designing an Experiment** How can you test the effect of pH and temperature on action of enzymes in detergents?

5. **Further Inquiry** Write a new question about enzymes in detergents that could be explored in another investigation.

SCILINKS.

www.scilinks.org
Topic: Enzymes
Code: HX80531

Extensions

6. **Relating Concepts** What other active ingredients are present in laundry detergents, and how do they help clean clothes?

7. **Applying Information** What other household products contain enzymes, and what types of enzymes do they contain?

Sample Procedure

1. Prepare a 10 percent solution of each of five different detergents. (mark the one known to be nonenzyme)

2. Test the pH of each detergent solution with pH paper. Record the pH for each sample in a data table similar to the one below.

3. Add about 15 drops (1 mL) of the first detergent solution to the gelatin surface of the first test tube. Repeat for each of the other samples. Reseal the test tubes and place them in a test-tube rack for observation.

4. Add 15 drops of water to the gelatin surface of the sixth test tube.

5. Put the tubes aside for 24 hours at room temperature.

6. Draw another wax-pencil line at the top of the gelatin layer. Measure the distance in mm between the first line and the second line. Record the data in a data table.

Sample Data

Detergent	pH	Amount of Protein Broken Down
1	8	7 mm
2	8	0 mm
3	8	9 mm
4	8	0 mm
5	8	6 mm

Answers to Extensions

6. Answers will vary. Ingredients that breakdown the components of specific stains, such as blood, urine, and grass pigments.

7. Answers will vary. For example, digestive supplements for dairy products contain lactase. Contact-lens cleaning solutions contain enzymes to break down the protein build-up on lenses.

the amount of protein hydrolysis in the gelatin by enzymes in the detergent. The level of the gelatin layer in the tube with the nonenzyme detergent should not change. This indicates that the detergent alone does not cause the protein hydrolysis reaction.

Answers to Analyze and Conclude

1. Baking soda increases the pH of the gelatin from 4 to 8, the optimum pH for enzyme activity in this reaction.

2. Graphs will vary.

3. Answers will vary. For example, enzymes are most effective at optimum temperature and pH.

4. Answers will vary. For example run the procedure again placing the tubes in a refrigerator or oven (250°F).

5. Answers will vary. For example: Are enzymes in detergent stable in the presence of bleach?

Key Resources

 Holt Lab Generator

Lab Datasheet (Levels A, B, C)

 Holt Science Biology Video Labs

 Virtual Investigations

Reteaching Key Ideas

Interpreting Food Labels/Math Skills Have students bring to class several Nutrition Facts labels from food containers and determine the following using the information on the labels:

1. Calories per gram

$$\left(\frac{\text{Calories per serving}}{\text{serving size}} \right)$$

2. percentage of fat

$$\left(\frac{\text{mass of fat per serving}}{\text{total mass of serving}} \right) \times 100$$

3. percentage of carbohydrate

$$\left(\frac{\text{mass of carbohydrate per serving}}{\text{total mass of serving}} \right) \times 100$$

4. percentage of sugar

$$\left(\frac{\text{mass of sugar per serving}}{\text{total mass of serving}} \right) \times 100$$

5. percentage of protein

$$\left(\frac{\text{mass of protein per serving}}{\text{total mass of serving}} \right) \times 100$$

Have students compare the nutritional contents of the labels they've analyzed. Summarize the class data to determine which foods have the most fat, carbohydrate, and protein per serving. **LS** Visual/ Logical

Key Ideas	Key Terms

1 Matter and Substances

> All matter is made up of atoms. An atom has a positively charged nucleus surrounded by a negatively charged electron cloud.

> Chemical bonds form between groups of atoms because most atoms become more stable when they have eight electrons in the valence shell.

> Polar attractions and hydrogen bonds are forces that play an important role in many of the molecules that make up living things.

Key Terms:
atom (51)
element (51)
valence electron (52)
compound (52)
molecule (52)
ion (53)

2 Water and Solutions

> The hydrogen bonding between water molecules explains many of the unique properties that make water an important substance for life.

> Acids and bases change the concentration of hydronium ions in aqueous solutions. The pH of solutions in living things must be stable.

Key Terms:
cohesion (55)
adhesion (55)
solution (56)
acid (56)
base (56)
pH (57)
buffer (57)

3 Carbon Compounds

> Large, complex biomolecules are built from a few smaller, simpler, repeating units arranged in an extremely precise way.

> Cells use carbohydrates for sources of energy, structural materials, and cellular identification.

> The main functions of lipids include storing energy and controlling water movement.

> Proteins are chains of amino acids that twist and fold into shapes that determine what the protein does.

> Nucleic acids store and transmit hereditary information.

Key Terms:
carbohydrate (60)
lipid (61)
protein (62)
amino acid (62)
nucleic acid (63)
nucleotide (63)
DNA (63)
RNA (63)
ATP (63)

4 Energy and Metabolism

> Living things use different chemical reactions to get the energy needed for life processes.

> An activation energy is needed to start a chemical reaction. The reactants must also be aligned to form the product.

> By assisting in necessary biochemical reactions, enzymes help organisms maintain homeostasis.

Key Terms:
energy (64)
reactant (65)
product (65)
activation energy (65)
enzyme (66)
active site (66)
substrate (66)

PART A: Answer all questions in this part.

Directions: For each statement or question, write on your separate answer sheet the number of the word or expression that best completes the statement or answers the question.

1 The diagram below represents a series of reactions that can occur in an organism. This diagram best illustrates the relationship between

Original molecules

Final molecule

Biological catalyst

(1)   enzymes and synthesis
(2)   amino acids and glucose
(3)   antigens and immunity
(4)   ribosomes and sugars

2 Which statement concerning proteins is not correct?

(1)   Proteins are long, usually folded, chains.
(2)   The shape of a protein molecule determines its function.
(3)   Proteins can be broken down and used for energy.
(4)   Proteins are bonded together, resulting in simple sugars.

3 Which row in the chart below contains correct information concerning synthesis?

Row	Building Blocks	Substance Synthesized Using the Building Blocks
(1)	glucose molecules	DNA
(2)	simple sugars	protein
(3)	amino acids	enzyme
(4)	molecular bases	starch

4 The graph below shows the effect of temperature on the relative rate of action of enzyme X on a protein. Which change would not affect the relative rate of action of enzyme X?

(1)   the addition of cold water when the reaction is at 50°C
(2)   an increase in temperature from 70°C to 80°C
(3)   the removal of the protein when the reaction is at 30°C
(4)   a decrease in temperature from 40°C to 10°C

5 What substance could be represented by the letter X in the diagram below?

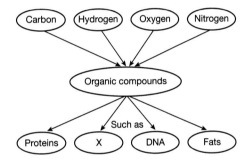

(1)   carbohydrates   (3)   carbon dioxide
(2)   ozone   (4)   water

6 Which condition is necessary for enzymes and hormones to function properly in the human body?

(1)   These chemicals must have a specific shape.
(2)   These chemicals must be able to replicate.
(3)   Body temperature must be above 40°C.
(4)   Body pH must be above 10.

PART A

1. **(1)** Amino acids form proteins, and thus are not involved in making sugars. Antigens and immunity are not represented in the diagram. Ribosomes and sugars are not represented, either. However, the diagram shows an enzyme joining two subunits together during synthesis. *(#20, June 2005 Regents Exam)*

2. **(4)** Proteins do not make up sugars. *(#12, June 2006 Regents Exam)*

3. **(3)** Glucose molecules are not found in DNA; simple sugars are not found in proteins, and molecular bases do not make up starch molecules, but enzymes are typically proteins made of amino acids. *(#04, August 2006 Regents Exam)*

4. **(2)** It is apparent from the graph that the reaction works best at 50°C. Therefore the addition of cold water when the reaction is at 50°C would affect the rate of reaction, as would the removal of the enzyme (a protein) when the reaction is at 30°C. Likewise, decreasing the temperature from 40°C to 10°C would affect the rate of the reaction. *(#21, January 2005 Regents Exam)*

5. **(1)** Ozone, carbon dioxide, and water are not organic molecules. Carbohydrates are organic molecules. *(#26, January 2004 Regents Exam)*

6. **(1)** Most enzymes and hormones (both proteins) do not replicate, do not function above 40°C, and do not work at a pH above 10. Their shapes affects their functionality, though. *(#28, August 2006 Regents Exam)*

Regents Exam Practice Correlations

1.3.1a 9	4.5.1c 5
4.1.2h 3, 11	4.5.1f 1, 4, 7, 8, 10, 12, 13
4.2.1i 2	4.5.1g 6, 14

7. (4) Structure A is large, and therefore likely to be an undigested molecule. Structures B and C appear to be the enzymes that are digesting the structure A molecules. Structures D and E are small and are most likely the breakdown products of structure A. (*#18, June 2004 Regents Exam*)

PART B

8. (2) The graph that identifies the following is the best graph: an increase in activity with temperature increase, an optimum temperature of activity (peak of graph), and a decline in activity as the temperature continues to increase. (*#35, August 2004 Regents Exam*)

9. (3) A choice of less than one gram is associated with temperatures below 10°C. A choice of 1 to 4 grams is associated with a temperature range of 10°C to 20°C. A choice specifying more than 9 grams is associated with temperatures greater than 37°C. (*#49, June 2005 Regents Exam*)

10. Allow 1 credit for explaining why no starch was digested. Acceptable responses include, but are not limited to: The enzyme in stomach fluid will not digest starch.; The enzyme in stomach fluid is specific for protein digestion. (*#50, June 2005 Regents Exam*)

---

7 The diagram below represents a beaker containing a solution of various molecules involved in digestion.

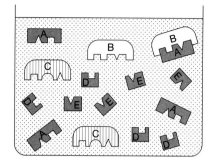

Which structures represent products of digestion?

(1) A and D   (3) B and E
(2) B and C   (4) D and E

PART B

8 Enzymes have an optimum temperature at which they work best. Temperatures above and below this optimum will decrease enzyme activity. Which graph best illustrates the effect of temperature on enzyme activity?

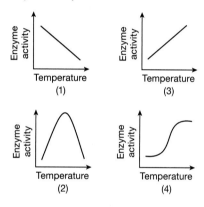

Base your answers to questions 9 and 10 on the information and data table below and on your knowledge of biology.

The effect of temperature on the action of pepsin, a protein-digesting enzyme present in stomach fluid, was tested. In this investigation, 20 milliliters of stomach fluid and 10 grams of protein were placed in each of five test tubes. The tubes were then kept at different temperatures. After 24 hours, the contents of each tube were tested to determine the amount of protein that had been digested. The results are shown in the table below.

Protein Digestion at Different Temperatures

Tube #	Temperature (°C)	Amount of Protein Digested (grams)
1	5	0.5
2	10	1.0
3	20	4.0
4	37	9.5
5	85	0.0

9 If a sixth test tube identical to the other tubes was kept at a temperature of 30°C for 24 hours, the amount of protein digested would most likely be

(1) less than 1.0 gram
(2) between 1.0 and 4.0 grams
(3) between 4.0 and 9.0 grams
(4) more than 9.0 grams

10 This investigation was repeated using 10 grams of starch instead of protein in each test tube. The contents of each tube were tested to determine the amount of starch that had been digested. The test results showed that no starch digestion occurred. Explain why no starch digestion occurred.

---

11 Which words best complete the lettered blanks in the two sentences below?

Organic compounds, such as proteins and starches, are too A to diffuse into cells. Proteins are digested into B and starches are digested into C.

(1) A—large, B—simple sugars, C—amino acids
(2) A—small, B—simple sugars, C—amino acids
(3) A—large, B—amino acids, C—simple sugars
(4) A—small, B—amino acids, C—simple sugars

Base your answers to questions 12 and 13 on the graph and on your knowledge of biology.

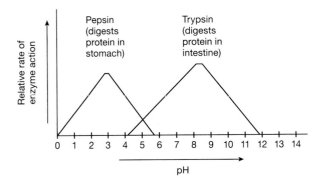

12 Pepsin works best in which type of environment?

(1) acidic, only
(2) basic, only
(3) neutral
(4) sometimes acidic, sometimes basic

13 Neither enzyme works at a pH of

(1) 1
(2) 5
(3) 3
(4) 13

PART C

Base your answer to the question on the statement below and on your knowledge of biology.

Some internal environmental factors may interfere with the ability of an enzyme to function efficiently.

14 Explain why changing the shape of an enzyme could affect the ability of the enzyme to function.

11. **(3)** Proteins and starches are too large to diffuse into cells. Proteins are composed of amino acids; starches are composed of simple sugars. (*#38, January 2003 Regents Exam*)

12. **(1)** The rate of pepsin activity is highest at pH 3, which is a very acidic pH. (*#40, January 2004 Regents Exam*)

13. **(4)** Activity of both pepsin and trypsin is absent at pH 13. (*#41, January 2004 Regents Exam*)

PART C

14. Allow 1 credit for explaining why changing the shape of an enzyme could affect the ability of the enzyme to function. Acceptable responses include, but are not limited to: If the shape changes, it will not fit with the same substrate.; The enzyme no longer fits with the molecules with which it interacted before.; Shape determines function. (*#61, June 2006 Regents Exam*)

UNIT 2 Ecology

4 Ecosystems

5 Populations and Communities

6 The Environment

 The Living Environment

Standard 4 Students will understand and apply scientific concepts, principles, and theories pertaining to the physical setting and living environment and recognize the historical development of ideas in science.

Key Idea 1 Living things are both similar to and different from each other and from nonliving things.

Key Idea 5 Organisms maintain a dynamic equilibrium that sustains life.

Key Idea 6 Plants and animals depend on each other and their physical environment.

Key Idea 7 Human decisions and activities have had a profound impact on the physical and living environment.

Atlantic puffins

Plastic bottles for recycling

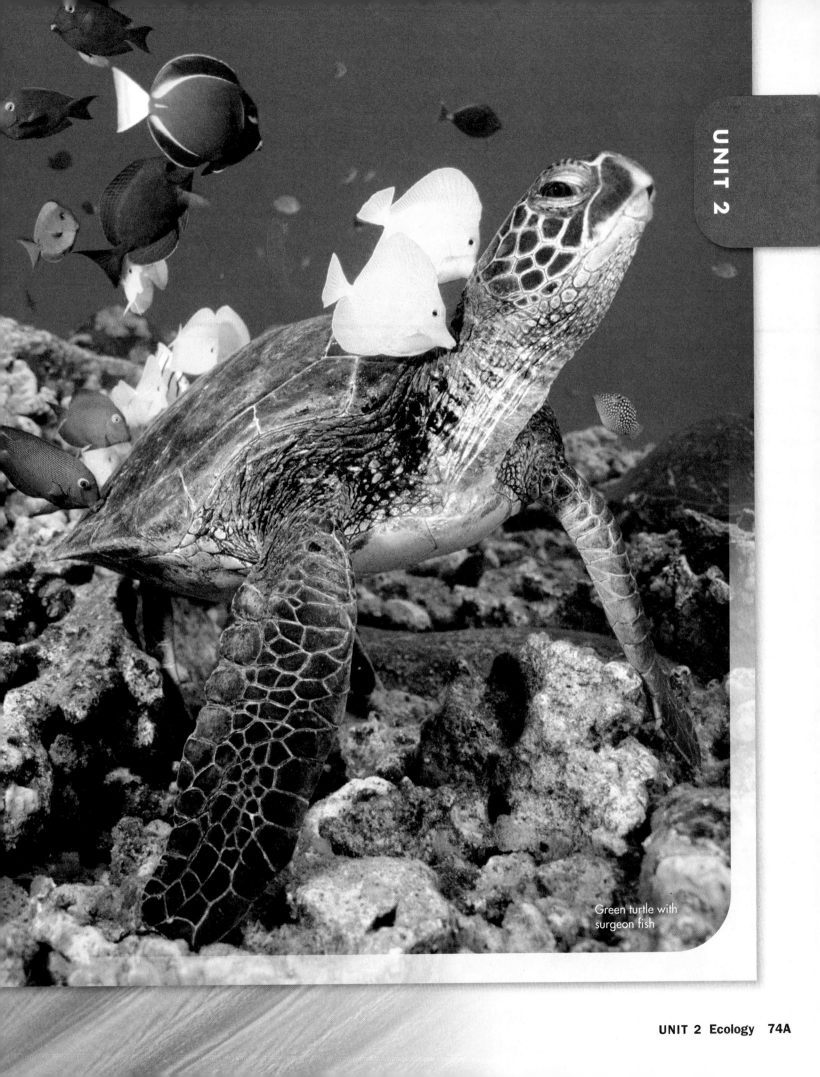

Green turtle with surgeon fish

The Changing Environment

AROUND 250

Mayan farmers build terraces to control the flow of water to crops. The irrigated terraces greatly increase crop yields and enable farmers to make use of farmland on steep hillsides.

1791

A canal for Washington D.C. is designed to connect the James and Tiber Creeks. The canal drains wet areas of the city and provides a new commercial transportation route.

Washington, D.C., capital of the United States

1890

John Muir and others successfully persuade Congress to create Yosemite National Park, the first national park in the world.

Half Dome, Yosemite National Park

1936

The captive thylacine, or Tasmanian tiger, dies in a zoo in Hobart, Tazmania. Sightings in the wild continue but are rare. The population dwindles because of predation by humans and dogs. The thylacine is declared extinct in 1986.

1962

Rachel Carson's book, *Silent Spring,* which describes the careless use of pesticides and their damage to the environment, is published.

Rachel Carson

1986

In the Ukraine, an accident at the Chernobyl nuclear power plant releases large amounts of nuclear radiation. The area around the power plant becomes one of the most highly radioactive places on Earth. A cloud of radioactive fallout travels as far as the eastern United States.

1990

Three large tuna companies announce that they will sell only tuna that is caught using nets that do not trap dolphins. This change is attributed to a successful consumer boycott of tuna caught using conventional nets that can trap and drown dolphins.

1999

Hybrid cars, which run on gas and electricity, hit the mass market in the United States.

Prototype Daihatsu UFE II hybrid

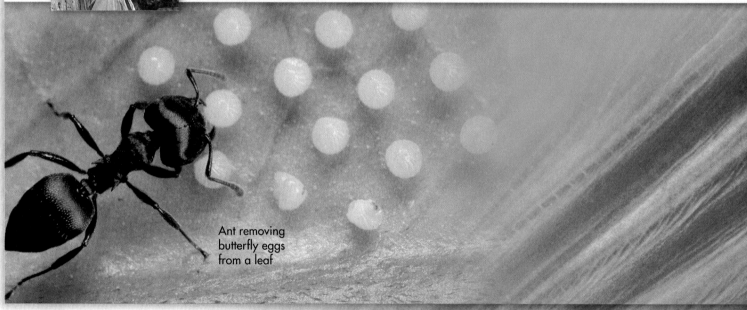

Ant removing butterfly eggs from a leaf

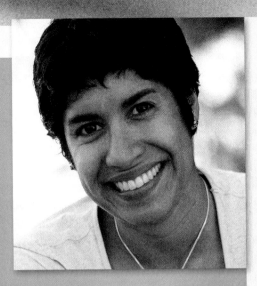

BIOLOGY CAREER

Ecologist
Erika Zavaleta

Erika Zavaleta is an assistant professor in the Environmental Studies department of the University of California, Santa Cruz. Her current research focuses on changes in levels of biodiversity in biological communities and ecosystems that result from environmental challenges and changes.

A high school science teacher, Dr. Roberts, inspired Zavaleta to become a scientist. Roberts used scientific nonfiction and an inquiry-based approach to inspire her students. Zavaleta still loves to read and engage scientific problems with a creative and open mind.

Zavaleta considers her greatest accomplishment in science to be bridging scientific disciplines to explore changes from many angles. These changes include climate change, the invasive species, the ecological and socioeconomic implications of losing biodiversity, and woodland restoration.

Apart from science, Zavaleta enjoys traveling, reading, and outdoor activities such as surfing, bodyboarding, bicycling, hiking, and backpacking.

Hamster and grasshopper predator-prey relationship

Ecosystems

		Standards	**Teach Key Ideas**

CHAPTER OPENER, pp. 76–77 `15 min.`

The Living Environment

SECTION 1 What Is an Ecosystem?,
pp. 79–85 `45 min.`

> Ecosystems
> Succession
> Major Biological Communities
> Terrestrial Biomes
> Aquatic Ecosystems

Standards: 4.1.1b, 4.1.1e, 4.6.1e, 4.6.3b, 4.6.3c

Teach Key Ideas:
- **Bellringer Transparency**
- **Transparencies** E25 Ecological Succession at Glacier Bay
- **Visual Concepts** Levels of Ecology • Habitat • Community • Ecosystem • Comparing Biotic and Abiotic Factors • Pioneer Species • Ecological Succession

---

SECTION 2 Energy Flow in Ecosystems,
pp. 86–89 `45 min.`

> Trophic Levels
> Loss of Energy

Standards: 1.2.4, 1.3.1a, 4.1.1a, 4.5.1.a, 4.6.1a, 4.6.1b, 4.6.1c, 4.6.1e

Teach Key Ideas:
- **Bellringer Transparency**
- **Transparencies** E4 Trophic Levels • E5 Food Chain in an Antarctic Ecosystem • E6 Food Web in an Antarctic System • E8 Energy Transfer Through Trophic Levels • E11 Energy Efficiency in Food Consumption
- **Visual Concepts** Comparing Consumers and Producers • Food Chains and Food Webs • Types of Consumers • Food Chains and Energy Transfer • Energy Pyramid • Biomass

---

SECTION 3 Cycling of Matter, pp. 90–93 `45 min.`

> Water Cycle
> Carbon and Oxygen Cycles
> Phosphorus Cycle
> Nitrogen Cycle

Standards: 4.6.1b, 4.6.1c, 4.7.1b

Teach Key Ideas:
- **Bellringer Transparency**
- **Transparencies** E12 Water Cycle • E13 Carbon Cycle • E14 Nitrogen Cycle
- **Visual Concepts** Biogeochemical Cycle • Water Cycle • Groundwater • Water Table • Carbon Cycle • The Nitrogen Cycle • Nitrogen Fixation

See also PowerPoint® Resources

Chapter Review and Assessment Resources

SE Super Summary, p. 96
SE Regents Exam Practice, p. 97
Regents Review Guide
Review Resources
Chapter Tests A and B
Holt Online Assessment
Regents Question Banks on Teacher's One-Stop Planner

CHAPTER
Fast Track *Instructional time for this chapter can be reduced by eliminating the activities.*

Basic Learners

TE Succession Timeline, p. 81
TE Biome Postcards, p. 82
TE Increases in Atmospheric CO$_2$, p. 91
Directed Reading Worksheets*
Active Reading Worksheets*
Lab Manuals, Level A*
Study Guide* ■
Note-taking Workbook*
Special Needs Activities and Modified Tests*

Advanced Learners

TE Factors Affecting Rainfall, p. 83
TE Sustainable Agriculture, p. 92
Critical Thinking Worksheets*
Concept Mapping Worksheets*
Science Skills Worksheets*
Lab Datasheets, Level C*

Key

SE Student Edition

TE Teacher's Edition

Chapter Resource File

Workbook

Transparency

CD or CD-ROM

* Datasheet or blackline master available

■ Also available in Spanish

All resources listed below are also available on the Teacher's One-Stop Planner.

Why It Matters	Hands-On	Skills Development	Assessment
Build student motivation with resources about high-interest applications.	SE **Inquiry Lab** Water Cycle, p. 77 * ■	TE **Reading Toolbox** Assessing Prior Knowledge, p. 76 SE **Reading Toolbox** p. 78	
TE **Pioneer Species,** p. 81 TE **Latitude and Longitude,** p. 83 SE **Maintained by Fire,** p. 85	SE **Quick Lab** Evaluation Biodiversity, p. 80 * ■	TE **Reading Toolbox** Visual Literacy, p. 82 SE **Reading Toolbox** Word Families, p. 84 TE **Reading Toolbox** Word Families, p. 84 TE **Reading Toolbox** Visual Literacy, p. 85	SE **Section Review** TE **Formative Assessment** Spanish Assessment * ■ **Section Quiz** ■
TE **Demonstration** Field Food Web, p. 86	SE **Inquiry Lab** Ecosystem Change, p. 94 * ■ **Skills Practice Lab** Mapping Biotic Factors in the Environment *	SE **Math Skills** Energy Pyramid, p. 88 TE **Math Skills** Energy in Trophic Levels, p. 88 SE **Reading Toolbox** Word Problem, p. 89 TE **Reading Toolbox** Word Problem, p. 89	SE **Section Review** TE **Formative Assessment** Spanish Assessment * ■ **Section Quiz** ■
TE **Crop Rotation,** p. 92 TE **Demonstration** Nitrogen–Fixing Plants, p. 92	SE **Quick Lab** The Carbon Cycle, p. 93 * ■ **Skills Practice Lab** Assessing Abiotic Factors in the Environment *	SE **Reading Toolbox** Word Families, p. 91 TE **Reading Toolbox** Word Families, p. 91	SE **Section Review** TE **Formative Assessment** Spanish Assessment * ■ **Section Quiz** ■

See also Lab Generator

See also Holt Online Assessment Resources

Resources for Differentiated Instruction

English Learners

TE Biotic and Abiotic Factors, p. 80

Directed Reading Worksheets *

Active Reading Worksheets *

Lab Manuals, Level A *

Study Guide * ■

Note-taking Workbook *

Multilingual Glossary

Interactive Tutor

Struggling Readers

TE Summarize the Water Cycle, p. 91

Directed Reading Worksheets *

Active Reading Worksheets *

Lab Manuals, Level A *

Study Guide *

Note-taking Workbook *

Special Needs Activities and Modified Tests *

Interactive Tutor

Special Education Students

Directed Reading Worksheets *

Active Reading Worksheets *

Lab Manuals, Level A *

Study Guide * ■

Note-taking Workbook *

Special Needs Activities and Modified Tests *

Alternative Assessment

TE Flow of Energy, p. 88

Science Skills Worksheets *

Section Quizzes * ■

Chapter Tests A, B, and C * ■

Chapter 4 Ecosystems

Overview

The purpose of this chapter is to explain the interactions between organisms and their environment in an ecosystem. The biodiversity of an ecosystem depends on the biotic and abiotic factors of the ecosystem. In all ecosystems, energy flows through food chains. Materials, such as water, carbon, phosphorus and nitrogen, cycle through an ecosystem.

READING TOOLBOX

Assessing Prior Knowledge Students should understand the following concepts:
• atoms and molecules
• cellular nature of life

Visual Literacy Ask students why water quality is important for the survival of both species in this illustration. (The spider gets its food from the water, and the water is where the fish lives and get the things it needs to survive.) What materials would these and the organisms that live in this water other need? (Possible answers: oxygen, sunlight, food) Ask students why water quality is important to humans, even though we don't live in the water. (Humans cannot live without a sufficient supply of clean water.)

Preview

1 What Is an Ecosystem?
Ecosystems
Succession
Major Biological Communities
Terrestrial Biomes
Aquatic Ecosystems

2 Energy Flow in Ecosystems
Trophic Levels
Loss of Energy

3 Cycling of Matter
Water Cycle
Carbon and Oxygen Cycles
Nitrogen Cycle
Phosphorus Cycle

Why It Matters

An ecosystem is a community of organisms that interact with one another and their physical environment. Humans are part of ecosystems and are dependent on healthy ecosystems. However, humans can disrupt ecosystems, and the disruption may harm the organisms of the ecosystems and humans themselves.

The Living Environment
Standard 4 Students will understand and apply scientific concepts, principles, and theories pertaining to the physical setting and living environment and recognize the historical development of ideas in science.
Key Idea 1 Living things are both similar to and different from each other and from nonliving things. *Major Understandings* – 1.1a, 1.1b, 1.1e
Key Idea 5 Organisms maintain a dynamic equilibrium that sustains life. *Major Understandings* – 5.1a
Key Idea 6 Plants and animals depend on each other and their physical environment. *Major Understandings* – 6.1a, 6.1b, 6.1c, 6.1e, 6.3b, 6.3c
Key Idea 7 Human decisions and activities have had a profound impact on the physical and living environment. *Major Understandings* – 7.1b

Organisms in ecosystems interact with each other. This small fish has an unusual predator—a spider. This fishing spider from French Guiana waits at the surface of the water for its prey.

Some species of fishing spiders can walk on the water's surface, aided by fine hairs on the legs which trap air and act as buoys.

Chapter Correlations   *The Living Environment*

Standard 4

1.1a Populations can be categorized by the function they serve. Food webs identify the relationships among producers, consumers, and decomposers carrying out either autotropic or heterotrophic nutrition.

1.1b An ecosystem is shaped by the nonliving environment as well as its interacting species. The world contains a wide diversity of physical conditions, which creates a variety of environments.

1.1e Ecosystems, like many other complex systems, tend to show cyclic changes around a state of approximate equilibrium.

5.1a The energy for life comes primarily from the Sun. Photosynthesis provides a vital connection between the Sun and the energy needs of living systems.

6.1a Energy flows through ecosystems in one direction, typically from the Sun, through photosynthetic organisms including green plants and algae, to herbivores to carnivores and decomposers.

6.1b Carbon dioxide and water molecules used in photosynthesis to form energy-rich organic compounds are returned to the environment when the energy in these compounds is eventually released by cells. Continual input of energy from sunlight keeps the process going. This concept may be illustrated with an energy pyramid.

6.1c The chemical elements, such as carbon, hydrogen, nitrogen, and oxygen, that make up the molecules of living things pass through food webs and are combined and recombined in different ways. At each link in a food web, some energy is stored in newly made structures but much is dissipated into the environment as heat.

6.1e In any particular environment, the growth and survival of organisms depend on the physical conditions including light intensity, temperature range, mineral availability, soil/rock type, and relative acidity (pH).

Like most spiders, the fishing spider has eight eyes.

The unlucky prey is nearly as large as its predator.

InquiryLab

🕐 15 min

Water Cycle 4.6.1b

The cycling of water in an ecosystem is necessary for the organisms that are part of the ecosystem. In this activity, you will model the water cycle.

Procedure

1. Place a **small, dark-colored bowl** inside a **large, sealable, plastic freezer bag.** Position the bag so that the opening is at the top.

2. Fill the bowl halfway with **water**. Place three drops of **red food coloring** in the water. Seal the bag.

3. Place the bowl and bag under a strong and warm light source, such as a **lamp** or direct sunlight.

4. Leave the bag in the light for one hour. Observe the bag at regular intervals.

Analysis

1. **Describe** how your model mimics the behavior of water in the environment

2. **Predict** how organisms such as plants would be affected if water did not cycle through the environment.

6.3b Through ecological succession, all ecosystems progress through a sequence of changes during which one ecological community modifies the environment, making it more suitable for another community. These long-term gradual changes result in the community reaching a point of stability that can last for hundreds or thousands of years.

6.3c A stable ecosystem can be altered, either rapidly or slowly, through the activities of organisms (including humans), or through climatic changes or natural disasters. The altered ecosystem can usually recover through gradual changes back to a point of longterm stability.

7.1b Natural ecosystems provide an array of basic processes that affect humans. Those processes include but are not limited to: maintenance of the quality of the atmosphere, generation of soils, control of the water cycle, removal of wastes, energy flow, and recycling of nutrients. Humans are changing many of these basic processes and the changes may be detrimental.

READING TOOLBOX

Using Words

1. In the carbon cycle, carbon moves in a circular process through living things and the environment. In the water cycle, water moves in a circular process through living things and the environment. In the phosphorus cycle, phosphorus moves through living things and the environment.

2. The three cycles differ in the kinds of matter that are cycled and the paths they take. Phosphorus does not have a gaseous form.

Using Language

1. 10% × 2000 kcal = 200 kcal

Using FoldNotes

Create a sample FoldNote and display it for students before they make their own. Suggest using FoldNotes for each of the four cycles of matter.

READING TOOLBOX

These reading tools can help you learn the material in this chapter. For more information on how to use these and other tools, see **Appendix: Reading and Study Skills.**

Using Words

Word Families Word families include words that can be combined to create a meaning that differs from the meaning of each word in the combination. The names of natural cycles of Earth are formed from word families that you will find in this chapter.

Your Turn Use the information in the table to answer the following questions.

1. What do you think happens in the carbon, water, and phosphorus cycles?
2. How do the three cycles differ?

Word Parts		
Word part	**Type**	**Meaning**
carbon	noun	an element common to all living things
water	noun	a liquid necessary for life
phosphorus	noun	a chemically reactive, nonmetallic element
cycle	noun	a circular process

Using Language

Word Problems Read word problems several times before trying to solve them. After you understand what the problems are asking, write down all of the relevant information on a piece of paper. Then, use the mathematical processes that apply to the situation.

Your Turn Solve the following word problem about energy.

1. When a snake a eats a mouse, only about 10% of the energy stored in the mouse's body is stored in the snake. If the body of a mouse contains 2000 kcal of energy, how much energy is stored in the snake?

Using FoldNotes

Layered Book A layered book is a useful tool for taking notes as you read a chapter. The four flaps of the layered book can summarize information into four categories. Write details of each category on the appropriate flap to create a summary of the chapter.

Your Turn Create a layered book FoldNote.

1. Lay one sheet of paper on top of another sheet. Slide the top sheet up so that 2 cm of the bottom sheet is showing.
2. Holding the two sheets together, fold down the top of the two sheets so that you see four 2 cm tabs along the bottom.
3. Using a stapler, staple the top of the FoldNote.
4. On each tab, write the category of the information that will appear on that layer.

Key Ideas	Key Terms	Why It Matters
❯ What are the parts of an ecosystem? ❯ How does an ecosystem respond to change? ❯ What two key factors of climate determine a biome? ❯ What are the three major groups of terrestrial biomes? ❯ What are the four kinds of aquatic ecosystems?	community ecosystem habitat biodiversity succession climate biome	Ecosystems are important units of the natural world. Humans are part of ecosystems and depend on ecosystems for food and many products. Without healthy ecosystems, humans would be in trouble!

When you walk through a forest, you see many different organisms. There are trees, birds, ants, mushrooms, and much more. You may not see many of these organisms interact. But all organisms, including humans, that live together are interdependent.

Ecosystems

A species never lives alone. A group of various species that live in the same place and interact with one another is called a **community.** The group, along with the living and nonliving environment, make up an **ecosystem.** ❯ An ecosystem includes a community of organisms and their physical environment.

Community of Organisms A community of organisms is a web of relationships. One relationship is that of a predator eating its prey. For example, some fish eat spiders, as **Figure 1** shows. Some species help each other. For example, some bacteria fix nitrogen into a form that plants can use to grow. Relationships between organisms are examples of biotic factors that affect an ecosystem. *Biotic* describes living factors in an ecosystem. Biotic factors also include once-living things, such as dead organisms and the waste of organisms.

 The Living Environment
Standard 4

1.1b An ecosystem is shaped by the nonliving environment as well as its interacting species. The world contains a wide diversity of physical conditions, which creates a variety of environments.

1.1e Ecosystems, like many other complex systems, tend to show cyclic changes around a state of approximate equilibrium.

6.1e In any particular environment, the growth and survival of organisms depend on the physical conditions including light intensity, temperature range, mineral availability, soil/rock type, and relative acidity (pH).

6.3b Through ecological succession, all ecosystems progress through a sequence of changes during which one ecological community modifies the environment, making it more suitable for another community. These long-term gradual changes result in the community reaching a point of stability that can last for hundreds or thousands of years.

6.3c A stable ecosystem can be altered, either rapidly or slowly, through the activities of organisms (including humans), or through climatic changes or natural disasters. The altered ecosystem can usually recover through gradual changes back to a point of longterm stability.

community a group of various species that live in the same habitat and interact with each other

ecosystem a community of organisms and their abiotic environment

Figure 1 In this relationship, the fish is the predator, and the spider is the prey. ❯ Give another example of a relationship between two species in a community.

Key Resources

 Transparencies
E25 Ecological Succession at Glacier Bay

 Visual Concepts
Levels of Ecology
Habitat
Community
Ecosystem
Comparing Biotic and Abiotic Factors
Biodiversity
Pioneer Species
Ecological Succession
Climate
Biomes, Climate, and Species

Biomes on Land
Tropical Rain Forest
Desert
Savanna
Temperate Deciduous Forest
Temperate Grassland
Taiga
Tundra
Freshwater Biomes
Intertidal Zone
Neritic Zone
Oceanic Zone
Benthic Zone

❯ Focus

This section identifies some biotic and abiotic factors of an ecosystem and describes how those factors change over time in a process called succession. It also describes the seven major terrestrial biomes and discusses aquatic communities.

🔊 Bellringer

Use the Bellringer transparency to prepare students for this section.

❯ Teach

Demonstration

Species Count If possible, take students on a walk-around tour of your school. Point out different species of plants and animals that you observe. Have students count the number of species identified on the campus. When finished, mention that biologists sampling a tropical rain forest in Ecuador obtained samples suggesting that there are as many as 24,000 different insect species per acre. **LS** Visual

Answers to Caption Questions
Figure 1: trees provide shade to humans and other animals.

Section Correlations	
4.1.1b	4.6.3b
4.1.1e	4.6.3c
4.6.1e	

QuickLab

Teacher's Notes Have each student use an area of equal dimensions, at least 50 m × 50 m to make the task more manageable and to allow comparisons between different ecosystems. Encourage students to take their time; they will observe much more if they do.

Answers to Analysis

1. Answers will vary.
2. Answers will vary. Example: 3 robins/29 total organisms = 0.103 = 10%
3. Answers will vary. Example: Mosquitos are an important food source for the frog population.
4. Sample answer: In general, the abiotic factors in an ecosystem provide organisms (biotic factors) with a physical place to live, energy, nutrients, and water. The organisms alter and recycle some of these abiotic factors, changing the landscape in the process.

Hands-On

QuickLab

Biodiversity Evaluation 4.1.1b, 4.6.1.d

By making simple observations, you can draw some conclusions about biodiversity in an ecosystem.

30 min

Procedure

CAUTION: Follow your teacher's instructions about handling organisms. Prepare a list of biotic and abiotic factors to observe around your home or in a nearby park, and record your observations.

Analysis

1. **Identify** the habitat and community that you observed.
2. **Calculate** the number of individual organisms and the number of different species that you saw.
3. **Rank** the importance of biotic factors within the ecosystem that you observed.
4. **Infer** what the relationships are between biotic factors and abiotic factors in the observed ecosystem.

> **habitat** a place where an organism usually lives
>
> **biodiversity** the variety of organisms in a given area, the genetic variation within a population, the variety of species in a community, or the variety of communities in an ecosystem
>
> **succession** the replacement of one type of community by another at a single location over a period of time

Physical Factors The physical or nonliving factors of an environment are called *abiotic factors*. Examples of abiotic factors are oxygen, water, rocks, sand, sunlight, temperature, and climate. These physical factors shape organisms. For example, plants and animals in deserts are small because deserts do not have enough water to support large organisms. Water supply also affects the amount and variety of species that an ecosystem can support. A crop of corn will have a higher yield in a wetter habitat than in a drier habitat. A **habitat** is the place where an organism lives.

Biodiversity Suppose you counted the various species in a pine forest. Then, you counted the number of species in a tropical rain forest. Do you think the number of species in each ecosystem would be the same? No, a tropical rain forest has many more species than a pine forest does. The variety of organisms in a given area is called **biodiversity.**

Physical factors can have a big influence on biodiversity. In places that have very high or very low temperatures, biodiversity is often lower. Limited water and food also cause lower biodiversity. The biodiversity of habitats and ecosystems varies greatly. The vast expanse of the open ocean has very low biodiversity. In contrast, rain forests and coral reefs have very high biodiversity. When ecosystems have high biodiversity, they are often more able to resist damage. Damage to ecosystems can be caused by severe weather events or human activities. Systems with low biodiversity can be severely damaged easily. When biodiversity decreases in any ecosystem, that ecosystem is not as healthy as it could be.

> **Reading Check** *List three examples of physical parts of an ecosystem. (See the Appendix for answers to Reading Checks.)*

MISCONCEPTION ///ALERT

Ecosystems Students may think that an ecosystem must be an area that is delineated by specific boundaries, like the walls of an aquarium or the edge of a pond. Point out that the limits of an ecosystem are defined by the observer. Thus, an ecosystem could be in a jar of pond water, or it could be the entire pond itself.

Differentiated Instruction

English Learners

Biotic and Abiotic Factors Point to a classroom aquarium or show a picture of an aquarium with a variety of organisms. Ask student to list all the organisms they see. When they finish, have them list all the factors that affect the survival of the organisms in the aquarium. (Sample answer: water, food, temperature range, light, pH, and oxygen) **LS Visual**

Succession

When we observe at an ecosystem, it may look like an unchanging feature of the landscape. However, all ecosystems change. As an ecosystem changes, the kinds of species that the ecosystem supports change. The replacement of one kind of community by another at a single place over a period of time is called **succession.**

Change in an Ecosystem When a volcano forms a new island or a fire burns the vegetation of an area, new opportunities are made for organisms. The first organisms to appear in a newly made habitat are called *pioneer species*. Pioneer species are often small, fast-growing plants that reproduce quickly. They change the habitat in such a way that other species can live in the ecosystem. For example, pioneer plants will break down volcanic rock on a new island to help form soil. Other new plant species can then grow in the soil. Often, the new species will replace the pioneer species. For example, grasses and weeds may cover a new volcanic island at first. Shrubs and trees often outcompete and replace the grass. Then, the grassland turns into a forest. **Figure 2** shows an example of succession in response to the receding of a glacier.

Equilibrium If a major change strikes a community, many of the organisms may be wiped out. But the ecosystem reacts to the change. ❯ An ecosystem responds to change in such a way that the ecosystem is restored to equilibrium. When a tree falls down in a rain forest, for example, the newly vacant patch proceeds through succession until the patch returns to its original state. Sometimes, the ecosystem will find an equilibrium in which different species dominate after a change. In the grasslands of Africa, for example, weather conditions can lead to succession. When there is a lot of rain in the grasslands, one species of grass dominates the savanna. But when conditions are drier, a drought-resistant species of grass will dominate.

❯ **Reading Check** *Why are pioneer species helpful to other species?*

Figure 2 At Glacier Bay in Alaska, a receding glacier makes succession possible.

Pioneer species quickly modify the land recently exposed after a glacier has receded.

Alders, grasses, and shrubs take over from the pioneer plants and help form more soil.

As the amount of soil increases, spruce and hemlock trees become plentiful.

Teaching Key Ideas

Primary Succession Have students examine the photos in **Figure 2.** Ask them what other events might lead to primary succession. (Sample answers: landslides and volcanic eruptions.) Tell students that primary succession can be a very slow process. Scientists estimate that the primary succession from sand dunes to the beech-maple forest along the shores of Lake Michigan took about 1,000 years. In contrast, secondary succession may take less than 100 years. Ask students why hemlock and spruce trees don't grow in an area before grasses and shrubs. (Grasses and shrubs often help form soil that makes it possible for the seeds of trees to survive.) **LS** Logical

Why It Matters

Pioneer Species Bring to class a rock covered with lichens or mosses. Ask students why these organisms are known as "pioneer species." (Like pioneer settlers, they are the first to inhabit a new area.) Point out that lichens can extract nutrients from the bare rock. **LS** Visual

Differentiated Instruction

Basic Learners

Succession Timeline Have each student draw an illustrated timeline representing the succession that occurs after a forest fire has burned all of the vegetation in an area. (Starting at time zero, the land should be barren, followed by the appearance of grasses and weeds, then small bushes, and finally trees.) **LS** Visual

Teaching Key Ideas

Characteristics of Biomes Show students photographs of the five major biomes found in the lower 48 states and Alaska: desert, temperate grassland, temperate forest (both deciduous and evergreen), tundra, and taiga. Ask students what they can deduce about the physical and biological characteristics of these biomes from examining the photos. **LS Visual**

READING TOOLBOX

Visual Literacy Have students refer to **Figure 3.** Emphasize that a biome is a category and not a place and that the boundaries of biomes are not as well defined as they are shown in this figure. **LS Visual**

Answers to Caption Questions

Figure 3: Sample answer: I live in the temperate forest biome.

Major Biological Communities

Polar ice
Tundra
Taiga
Mountain zones
Temperate forest
Tropical forest
Temperate grassland
Savanna
Desert or semidesert

60°N
30°N
Equator
30°S

Tropical biome: rain forest

Figure 3 Biomes cover most of Earth's land surface. Because mountainous areas do not belong to any one biome, they are given their own designation. Polar ice covers Greenland and Antarctica, which is not shown in the map. **> Identify the biome that you live in.**

ACADEMIC VOCABULARY

range a scale or series between limits

climate the average weather conditions in an area over a long period of time

biome a large region characterized by a specific type of climate and certain types of plant and animal communities

Major Biological Communities

If you drive across the United States, you notice a change in the kinds of plants and animals. The kinds of species that live in a particular place are determined partly by climate. **Climate** is the average weather conditions in an area over a long period of time. At places near the North Pole, you may see polar bears. Polar bears have thick, white fur and insulating fat that keep them warm on the frozen tundra. The same adaptations that help polar bears in the tundra would hurt polar bears in a tropical forest. Polar bears must live in a biome to which they are adapted. A **biome** is a large region characterized by a specific kind of climate and certain kinds of plant and animal communities.

> **Two key factors of climate that determine biomes are temperature and precipitation.** Most organisms are adapted to live within a particular range of temperatures and cannot survive at temperatures too far above or below that range. Precipitation also determines the kinds of species that are found in a biome. In biomes where precipitation is low, for example, the vegetation is made up mostly of plants that need little water, such as cactuses.

Terrestrial Biomes

There are many different biomes on land. > **Earth's major terrestrial biomes can be grouped by latitude into tropical, temperate biomes, and high-latitude.** As **Figure 3** shows, tropical biomes are generally near the equator. For the most part, temperate biomes are between 30° and 60° latitude. High-latitude biomes are at latitudes 60° and higher. Latitude affects the amount of solar energy that a biome receives and thus affects a biome's temperature range.

Differentiated Instruction

English Learners

Peer Group Research Pair English learners with English-proficient students. Have each pair create a table and graph showing their monthly estimates for average temperature and rainfall in their locale. Then have students research the same information on the Internet. Have them graph the researched data and compare their two graphs. Students should provide explanations for differences that they notice. This activity can be used to help reinforce the importance of accurate measurements. **LS Verbal, Interpersonal**

Basic Learners/Struggling Readers

Biome Postcards Have students use index cards to create postcards to send to the class from a biome they have visited. Students should include a description of the biome, its climate, the kinds of animals and plants that live there, and the location of the biome exists. On the postcard, students can draw a picture that represents the characteristics of the biome or cut pictures from discarded magazines. **LS Verbal**

Temperate biome: temperate grasslands

Polar biome: taiga

Tropical Biomes Because they are located at low latitudes near the equator, all tropical biomes are warm. However, each tropical biome receives a different amount of rain. *Tropical rain forests* receive large amounts of rain and are warm all year. They have the greatest biodiversity of any land biome. At least half of Earth's species of land organisms live in tropical rain forests. *Savannas* are tropical grasslands. They get less rain than tropical rain forests do. Savannas also have long dry seasons and shorter wet seasons. The most well-known savannas are in eastern Africa, where zebras, giraffes, lions, and elephants roam the grasslands. *Tropical deserts* get very little rain. Because the deserts have less water, they have fewer plants and animals than other biomes do.

Temperate Biomes Biomes at mid-latitudes have a wide range of temperatures throughout the year. *Temperate grasslands* have moderate precipitation and cooler temperatures than savannas do. Temperate grasslands are often highly productive when used for agriculture. Herds of grazing animals, like bison, used to live on the temperate grasslands of North America. *Temperate forests* grow in mild climates that receive plenty of rain. Trees of the temperate deciduous forests shed their leaves in the fall because of the cold winters. Trees of temperate evergreen forests do not lose their leaves or needles during the winter. Temperate forests are home to deer, bears, beavers, and raccoons. Like tropical deserts, *temperate deserts* receive little precipitation. However, unlike tropical deserts, temperate deserts have a wide temperature range throughout the year.

High-Latitude Biomes Biomes at high latitudes have cold temperatures. Coniferous forests in cold, wet climates are called *taiga*. Winters are long and cold. Most of the precipitation falls in the summer. Moose, wolves, and bears live in the taiga. The *tundra* gets very little rain, so plants are short. Much of the water in the soil is not available because the water is frozen for most of the year. Foxes, lemmings, owls, and caribous live in the tundra.

❯ **Reading Check** *In what latitudes are savannas found?*

SCI**LINKS**.
www.scilinks.org
Topic: Biomes
Code: HX80158

READING TOOLBOX

Word Families **aquatic** growing or living in water; **ecosystem** the complex of a community of organisms and its environment functioning as an ecological unit **aquatic ecosystem** a community of organisms living in a water environment

>Close

Formative Assessment

Which biome is a transitional area between tropical rain forest and desert?

A. taiga (Incorrect. A taiga is a high latitude biome having a cold, wet climate.)

B. savanna (Correct! The savanna is a tropical grassland, receiving less rainfall than the rain forest, but more than the desert.)

C. temperate forest (Incorrect. A temperate forest is a temperate biome with a wide range of temperatures and is much cooler than tropical biomes.)

D. tundra (Incorrect. A tundra is a high-latitude biome with very little rain and short vegetation.)

Figure 4 A bayou, such as this one in Louisiana, is an example of a wetland. The coral reef is an example of a marine ecosystem.

READING TOOLBOX

Word Families Use a dictionary to find the meanings of the words *aquatic* and *ecosystem*. Then, use the definitions to write your own definition of *aquatic ecosystem*.

SciLINKS.
www.scilinks.org
Topic: Estuaries
Code: HX80536

Aquatic Ecosystems

The diverse regions in the world's bodies of water are not usually called *biomes*. They are often called *aquatic ecosystems*. **>Aquatic ecosystems are organized into freshwater ecosystems, wetlands, estuaries, and marine ecosystems.**

Freshwater ecosystems are located in bodies of fresh water, such as lakes, ponds, and rivers. These ecosystems have a variety of plants, fish, arthropods, mollusks, and other invertebrates.

Wetlands provide a link between the land and fully aquatic habitats. Water-loving plants dominate wetlands. This ecosystem supports many species of birds, fishes, and plants, as shown in **Figure 4.** Wetlands are important because they moderate flooding and clean the water that flows through them.

An *estuary* is an area where fresh water from a river mixes with salt water from an ocean. Estuaries are productive ecosystems because they constantly receive fresh nutrients from the river and the ocean.

Marine ecosystems are found in the salty waters of the oceans. Kelp forests, seagrass communities, and coral reefs are found near land. The open ocean, far from land, has plankton and large predators, such as dolphins, whales, and sharks.

> Reading Check *Which aquatic ecosystems have salt water?*

Section 1 Review

>KEY IDEAS

1. **Describe** the difference between an ecosystem and a community.
2. **Explain** how an ecosystem responds to change.
3. **Identify** the three major groups of terrestrial biomes.
4. **Describe** the four types of aquatic ecosystems.
5. **Identify** two factors of climate that determine a biome.

CRITICAL THINKING

6. **Relating Concepts** If two areas on separate continents have similar climates, do they have similar communities? Explain your answer.

WRITING FOR SCIENCE

7. **Essay** Identify a biome in which the plants are short and require little water and the animals are small. Then, write a one page description of this biome.

Answers to Section Review

1. A community is a group of different species that live in the same habitat and interact with each other. An ecosystem is the community of organisms and their abiotic environment.

2. An ecosystem responds to change in a way that restores the ecosystem to equilibrium.

3. The three major groups of terrestrial biomes are tropical biomes, temperate biomes, and high-latitude biomes.

4. Freshwater ecosystems have organisms that live in bodies of fresh water. Wetland ecosystems are dominated by water-loving plants. Estuaries have organisms that live where fresh water and salt water mix. Marine ecosystems live in the salty water of the oceans.

5. Two factors of climate that determine a biome are temperature and precipitation.

6. Sample answer: Two areas on separate continents with similar climates would have similar communities because the climate of an area affects the type of organisms that can live in an area.

7. Students should describe a tropical desert, a temperate desert, or a tundra.

Maintained by Fire

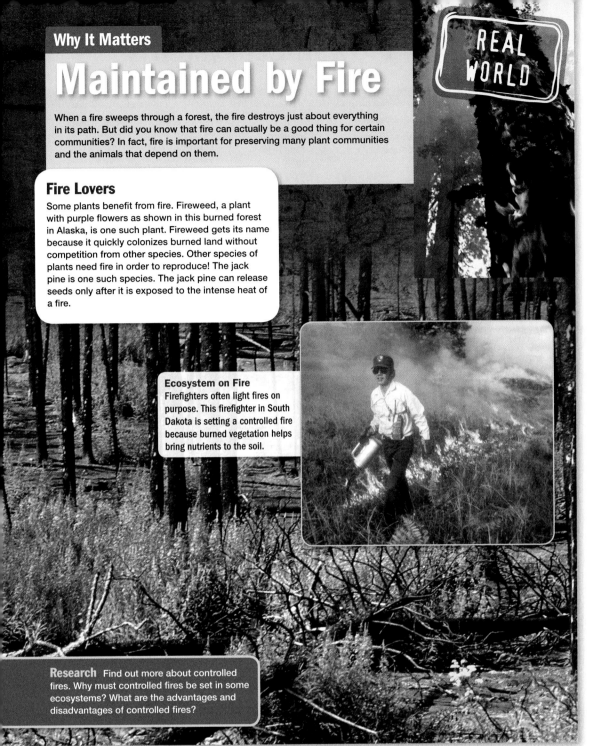

REAL WORLD

When a fire sweeps through a forest, the fire destroys just about everything in its path. But did you know that fire can actually be a good thing for certain communities? In fact, fire is important for preserving many plant communities and the animals that depend on them.

Fire Lovers

Some plants benefit from fire. Fireweed, a plant with purple flowers as shown in this burned forest in Alaska, is one such plant. Fireweed gets its name because it quickly colonizes burned land without competition from other species. Other species of plants need fire in order to reproduce! The jack pine is one such species. The jack pine can release seeds only after it is exposed to the intense heat of a fire.

Ecosystem on Fire
Firefighters often light fires on purpose. This firefighter in South Dakota is setting a controlled fire because burned vegetation helps bring nutrients to the soil.

Research Find out more about controlled fires. Why must controlled fires be set in some ecosystems? What are the advantages and disadvantages of controlled fires?

Answer to Research
Exposure to fire is necessary for some plant species to reproduce. Advantages: low cost, highly effective, and advantageous for many plant and animal communities. Disadvantages: killing desirable trees and vegetation, burning out of control, and threatening or destroying wildlife.

Section **2**
Energy Flow in Ecosystems

Key Ideas	Key Terms	Why It Matters
❯ How does energy flow through an ecosystem? ❯ What happens to energy as it is transferred between trophic levels in a community?	producer consumer decomposer trophic level energy pyramid	The way in which energy flows through an ecosystem is critical to the ecosystem's productivity and ability to support its species. By understanding this flow of energy, we can learn how to develop food more efficiently.

The Living Environment
Standard 4
1.1a Populations can be categorized by the function they serve. Food webs identify the relationships among producers, consumers, and decomposers carrying out either autotropic or heterotropic nutrition.
5.1a The energy for life comes primarily from the Sun. Photosynthesis provides a vital connection between the Sun and the energy needs of living systems.
6.1a Energy flows through ecosystems in one direction, typically from the Sun, through photosynthetic organisms including green plants and algae, to herbivores to carnivores and decomposers.
6.1b Carbon dioxide and water molecules used in photosynthesis to form energy-rich organic compounds are returned to the environment when the energy in these compounds is eventually released by cells. Continual input of energy from sunlight keeps the process going. This concept may be illustrated with an energy pyramid.
6.1c At each link in a food web, some energy is stored in newly made structures but much is dissipated into the environment as heat.

www.scilinks.org
Topic: Food Webs
Code: HX80600

Figure 5 Each step in the transfer of energy through an ecosystem is called a *trophic level.*

Everything that organisms do requires energy. Running, breathing, and even sleeping require energy. Every species must somehow get food for energy. A zebra grazes on savanna grass. A lion chases down the zebra and eats it. The lion eventually dies and is eaten by scavengers. The rest of the carcass is decomposed by bacteria and other microbes. At each step in this process, energy flows through the ecosystem.

Trophic Levels

An organism eating another organism is the most obvious interaction in a community. This interaction transfers energy through an ecosystem. The way in which energy flows through an ecosystem determines how many species and individuals live in the ecosystem.

The primary source of energy for an ecosystem is the sun. Photosynthetic organisms, such as plants and algae, change light energy from the sun into energy that they can use to grow. These photosynthetic organisms are **producers,** the basic food source for an ecosystem. **Consumers** are organisms that eat other organisms instead of producing their own food. **Decomposers,** such as bacteria and fungi, are organisms that break down the remains of animals. ❯ In an ecosystem, energy flows from the sun to producers to consumers to decomposers. Each step in the transfer of energy through an ecosystem is called a **trophic level. Figure 5** shows the trophic levels through which energy passes to a blue jay.

❯ **Reading Check** *Where do consumers get their energy?*

The sun is the primary energy source.

Producers use energy from the sun to produce their own food.

Some consumers eat producers to get energy.

Some consumers eat other consumers.

Food Chains In ecosystems, energy flows from one trophic level to the next, forming a *food chain*. The first trophic level of ecosystems is made up of producers. Plants, algae, and some bacteria use the energy in sunlight to build energy-rich carbohydrates. The second trophic level of a food chain is made up of *herbivores,* which eat producers. Cows are an example of an herbivore. The third trophic level includes animals that eat herbivores. Any animal that eats another animal is a *carnivore*. Some carnivores are on the third trophic level because they eat herbivores. For example, small birds eat caterpillars, which feed on plant leaves. Other carnivores are on the fourth trophic level or an even higher trophic level because they eat other carnivores. For example, hawks eat small birds. *Omnivores,* such as bears, are animals that are both herbivores and carnivores.

Food Web In most ecosystems, energy does not follow a simple food chain. Energy flow is much more complicated. Ecosystems almost always have many more species than a single food chain has. In addition, most organisms eat more than one kind of food. For example, hawks eat fish, small birds, and rabbits. Rabbits are food not only for hawks but also for wolves, mountain lions, and many other carnivores. This complicated, interconnected group of food chains, such as the group in **Figure 6,** is called a *food web*.

---

producer a photosynthetic or chemosynthetic autotroph that serves as the basic food source in an ecosystem

consumer an organism that eats other organisms or organic matter instead of producing its own nutrients or obtaining nutrients from inorganic sources

decomposer an organism that feeds by breaking down organic matter from dead organisms

trophic level one of the steps in a food chain or food pyramid

---

Figure 6 A food web shows a more complete picture of the feeding relationships in an ecosystem. The arrows show the direction in which energy travels. ❱ **In the diagram, identify the animals that receive energy from the rabbit.**

Teaching Key Ideas

Food Webs and Biodiversity Organize students into groups of four. Obtain large sheets of butcher paper. Have one student in each group write the name of an organism anywhere on the sheet, followed by one of these letters: *P* (producer), *C* (carnivore), *H* (herbivore), *O* (omnivore), and *D* (decomposer). Each student writes the name of another organism randomly on the sheet and draws an arrow from this organism to anything that eats it and an arrow to this organism from organisms it would eat. Continue until the web gets very messy.

Ask each group to hold up their paper, and have the class "vote" on which food web shows the greatest biodiversity. Discuss what would happen to the "winning" food web if just one organism became extinct. (In most cases there would be no effect if there was a lot of biodiversity, but if the extinct organism was the only producer, it could have a profound effect.) **LS** Visual

Answers to Caption Questions

Figure 6: The mountain lion, coyote, and predatory bird receive energy from the rabbit when they eat the rabbit.

Teaching Key Ideas

Energy Changes Remind students that the first law of thermodynamics states that energy cannot be created or destroyed but only changed in form. Have students give examples of energy changes from one form into another. (Sample answers: electricity to heat and light in a light bulb; chemical energy changed to electrical energy in a battery) The second law of thermodynamics states that energy change between forms is never 100 percent efficient. Ask students to think of an example that shows the inefficiency of energy conversions. (Sample answer: In an automobile engine, gasoline and chemical energy is changed to kinetic energy to turn the wheels; however, much of the energy is converted to heat, which is unavailable to power the automobile.) **LS** Logical

Math Skills

Energy in Trophic Levels Tell students that if an average of 1,500 kcal of light energy per day falls on a square meter of land surface covered by plants, only about 15–30 kcal become incorporated into chemical compounds through photosynthesis. Ask how much of this energy could end up in a person who eats these plants. (1.5–3.0 kcal) How much of this energy could end up in a person who eats a steak from a steer that ate the plants? (0.15–0.30 kcal) **LS** Logical

Figure 7 This girl is eating producers, which form the base of an energy pyramid.

Loss of Energy

When a zebra eats 20 lb of grass, the zebra does not gain 20 lb. A lot of the energy that was stored in the grass is lost. Where did the energy go? ❯ Energy is stored at each link in a food web. But some energy that is used dissipates as heat into the environment and is not recycled.

The Ten Percent Rule When a zebra eats grass, some of the energy in the grass is stored in the zebra. The energy may be stored as fat or as tissue. However, most of the energy does not stay in the zebra. As the zebra uses energy from the grass to run and grow, the energy is changed into heat energy. Then, the heat energy is dispersed into the environment. Thus, the zebra does not keep 90% of the energy that it gets from the grass. Only about 10% of the energy in the grass becomes part of the zebra's body. This amount of stored energy is all that is available to organisms at the next trophic level that consume the zebra. For example, a 100 kg lion needs 1,000 kg of zebras. And combined, the zebras need 10,000 kg of plants!

By understanding energy flow between trophic levels, we can learn how to feed more people. If people eat big fish that are in the third trophic level, it takes 1,000 kg of producers to build 1 kg of human. If people eat cows that are in the second trophic level, 100 kg of producers are needed for 1 kg of human. If people, such as the girl in **Figure 7,** eat producers—such as vegetables, fruits, and grains—only 10 kg of producers are needed to produce 1 kg of human.

❯ **Reading Check** *When energy is transferred from one trophic level to another, where does 90% of the energy go?*

Math Skills ❯ Energy Pyramid

This energy pyramid shows the trophic levels in a marine ecosystem. You can use the pyramid to help you understand how energy is transferred from one trophic level to another.

The base of a pyramid is the producer, which contains the most energy. Phytoplankton is the base of this pyramid. As energy is transferred from one trophic level to the next trophic level, 90% of the energy is lost. Only 10% of the energy is available to the next trophic level.

If the phytoplankton level has 10,000 units of energy, the amount of energy stored in the copepod level can be calculated as follows:

10,000 units of energy × 10% = 1,000 units of energy

The amount of energy stored in the herring level can be calculated as follows:

1,000 units of energy × 10% = 100 units of energy

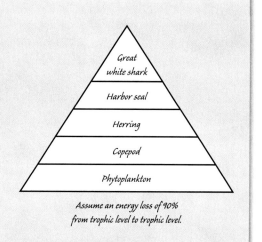

Assume an energy loss of 90% from trophic level to trophic level.

Differentiated Instruction

Alternative Assessment

Flow of Energy Have students draw a graphic organizer that summarizes the flow of energy from producers to herbivores, omnivores, carnivores, and decomposers. A sample graphic organizer is shown. **LS** Visual

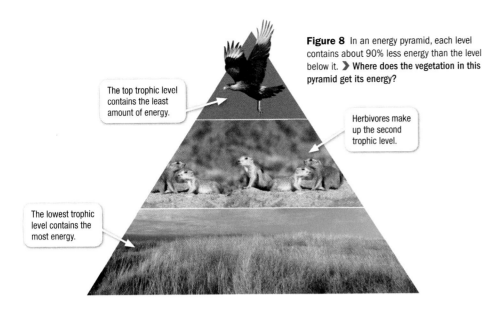

Figure 8 In an energy pyramid, each level contains about 90% less energy than the level below it. ❯ Where does the vegetation in this pyramid get its energy?

The top trophic level contains the least amount of energy.

Herbivores make up the second trophic level.

The lowest trophic level contains the most energy.

Answers to Caption Questions
Figure 8: The vegetation gets its energy from the sun.

READING TOOLBOX

Word Problem 35,000 units × 10% = 3,500 units

❯Close

Formative Assessment
Which of the following is an example of consumers outnumbering the producers they are feeding upon?
A. a 10-acre grassy field with grasshoppers (Incorrect. There are more producers than grasshoppers.)
B. carnivores feeding upon several herbivores (Incorrect. Both carnivores and herbivores are consumers.)
C. several omnivores feeding on hundreds of wild berry plants (Incorrect. The omnivores are consumers, but they do not outnumber the plants.)
D. a tree with thousands of insects feeding on it. (Correct! The insect population easily outnumbers the single tree producer.)

Energy Pyramid A triangular diagram that shows an ecosystem's loss of energy, which results as energy passes through the ecosystem's food chain, is called an **energy pyramid.** An energy pyramid is shown in **Figure 8.** Each layer in the energy pyramid represents one trophic level. Producers form the pyramid's base, which is the lowest trophic level. The lowest level has the most energy in the pyramid. Herbivores have less energy and make up the second level. Carnivores that feed on herbivores make up the higher level. The energy stored by the organisms at each trophic level is about one-tenth the energy stored by the organisms in the level below. So, the diagram takes the shape of a pyramid.

Big predators, such as lions, are rare compared to herbivores. Big predators are rare because a lot more energy is required to support a single predator than a single herbivore. Many ecosystems do not have enough energy to support a large population of predators.

energy pyramid a triangular diagram that shows an ecosystem's loss of energy, which results as energy passes through the ecosystem's food chain

READING TOOLBOX

Word Problem If the prairie dog level in a food pyramid contains 35,000 units of energy, how much of that energy can be stored in the eagle level of the food pyramid?

Section 2 Review

❯KEY IDEAS
1. **Describe** how energy flows in an ecosystem.
2. **Explain** why only 10% of energy is transferred from one trophic level to the next.
3. **Describe** the difference between a herbivore, a carnivore, and an omnivore.

CRITICAL THINKING
4. **Justifying Conclusions** What limits the length of food chains in an ecosystem?
5. **Evaluating an Argument** Explain why scientists believe that most animals would become extinct if all plants died.
6. **Analyzing Data** Which trophic level contains more energy: a trophic level of herbivores or a trophic level of carnivores? Why?

USING SCIENCE GRAPHICS
7. **Creating Diagrams** Draw a diagram of a food web that has four trophic levels and at least one species that is an omnivore. Be sure to label producers, consumers, omnivores, and top predators. Label each trophic level.

Answers to Section Review
1. Energy flows from the sun to producers to consumers to decomposers in an ecosystem.
2. Only 10 percent of energy is transferred from one energy level to the next because energy is converted to heat energy and is lost to the environment.
3. A herbivore is an animal that eats producers. A carnivore is an animal that eats other animals. An omnivore is an animal that eats both producers and other animals.
4. Because energy is used and lost to the environment at each trophic level, an ecosystem needs a large number of producers to provide enough energy for organisms at the top trophic level.
5. Plants are the producers in most ecosystems. Animals obtain energy either by eating plants directly or by eating other animals that eat plants. Without plants, animals would not have food.
6. The trophic level of herbivores contain more energy, because herbivores are lower on the energy pyramid than carnivores.
7. Diagrams may vary. Students should use specific examples of organisms for each level.

Section 3

Cycling of Matter

Key Ideas	Key Terms	Why It Matters
❯ What is the water cycle? ❯ Why are plants and animals important for carbon and oxygen in an ecosystem? ❯ Why must nitrogen cycle through an ecosystem? ❯ Why must phosphorus cycle through an ecosystem?	carbon cycle respiration nitrogen cycle phosphorus cycle	Water, carbon, phosphorus, and nitrogen are critical resources for organisms, including humans. Natural cycles of these resources are important to ecosystems, but humans can disrupt these cycles.

❯ Focus

This section explains how important materials necessary for survival, such as water, carbon, phosphorus, and nitrogen, circle through natural systems, constantly re-supplying organisms. It also describes the important role that bacteria play in the recycling of many materials.

 Bellringer

Use the Bellringer transparency to prepare students for this section.

❯ Teach

Teaching Key Ideas

Energy Have students look at **Figure 9** and notice the two arrows labeled *Evaporation* and the one arrow labeled *Transpiration*. Ask what is needed for evaporation or transpiration to occur. (an input of energy) Next, ask how could this energy be harvested? (Water runoff from precipitation may eventually enter a river and run through turbines, spinning them and converting the energy of the water into electrical energy.) **LS** Logical

go.hrw.com
✳ interact online

Students can interact with a model for the water cycle by going to go.hrw.com and typing in the keyword HX8ECOF9.

Section Correlations
4.6.1b
4.6.1c
4.7.1b

 The Living Environment
Standard 4
6.1b The atoms and molecules on the Earth cycle among the living and nonliving components of the biosphere. For example, carbon dioxide and water molecules used in photosynthesis to form energy-rich organic compounds are returned to the environment when the energy in these compounds is eventually released by cells. Continual input of energy from sunlight keeps the process going. This concept may be illustrated with an energy pyramid.
6.1c The chemical elements, such as carbon, hydrogen, nitrogen, and oxygen, that make up the molecules of living things pass through food webs and are combined and recombined in different ways. At each link in a food web, some energy is stored in newly made structures but much is dissipated into the environment as heat.
7.1b Natural ecosystems provide an array of basic processes that affect humans. Those processes include but are not limited to: maintenance of the quality of the atmosphere, generation of soils, control of the water cycle, removal of wastes, energy flow, and recycling of nutrients. Humans are changing many of these basic processes and the changes may be detrimental.

go.hrw.com
✳ interact online
Keyword: HX8ECOF9

Figure 9 Water cycles through ecosystems by the processes of transpiration, evaporation, condensation, precipitation and percolation.

Water, carbon, oxygen, nitrogen, and phosphorus are five of the most important substances for life. An ecosystem must be able to cycle these kinds of matter in order to support life.

Water Cycle

Life could not exist without the *water cycle.* ❯ The water cycle continuously moves water between the atmosphere, the land, and the oceans. As **Figure 9** shows, water vapor *condenses* and falls to Earth's surface as *precipitation*. Some of this water *percolates* into the soil and becomes groundwater. Other water runs across the surface of Earth into rivers, lakes, and oceans. Then, the water is heated by the sun and reenters the atmosphere by *evaporation*. Water also evaporates from trees and plants in a process called *transpiration*.

Key Resources

 Transparencies
E12 Water Cycle
E13 Carbon Cycle
E14 Nitrogen Cycle

Visual Concepts
Biogeochemical Cycle
Water Cycle
Groundwater
Water Table
Carbon Cycle
The Nitrogen Cycle
Nitrogen Fixation
Ammonification
Nitrification
Denitrification

Carbon dioxide CO_2 in atmosphere

Photosynthesis

Cellular respiration

Combustion

Dissolved CO_2 in water

Death and decomposition

Marine plankton remains

Fossil fuels

Limestone

Figure 10 In the carbon cycle, carbon moves from organisms to the atmosphere, to the soil, and to other living things.
❯ How is the carbon in fossil fuels released into the atmosphere?

SCI LINKS.
www.scilinks.org
Topic: Carbon Cycle
Code: HX80216

Carbon and Oxygen Cycles

Carbon and oxygen are critical for life on Earth, and their cycles are tied closely together. The **carbon cycle** is the continuous movement of carbon from the nonliving environment into living things and back. The carbon cycle is shown in **Figure 10.**

❯ Animals, plants, and other photosynthesizing organisms play an important role in cycling carbon and oxygen through an ecosystem. Plants use the carbon dioxide, CO_2, in air to build organic molecules during the process of photosynthesis. During photosynthesis, oxygen is released into the surroundings. Many organisms, such as animals, use this oxygen to help break down organic molecules, which releases energy and CO_2. Then, plants can use the CO_2 in photosynthesis. The process of exchanging oxygen and CO_2 between organisms and their surroundings is called **respiration.**

Carbon is also released into the atmosphere in the process of combustion. *Combustion* is the burning of a substance. All living things are made of carbon. When living things or once-living things are burned, they release carbon into the atmosphere. For example, the burning of trees releases carbon into the atmosphere as CO_2. Fossil fuels are formed from the remains of dead plants and animals. Thus, the burning of fossil fuels releases CO_2 into the atmosphere. Humans burn fossil fuels to generate electricity and to power vehicles. Examples of fossil fuels that humans burn are oil and coal.

❯ **Reading Check** *How does respiration play a role in cycling carbon and oxygen through an ecosystem?*

carbon cycle the movement of carbon from the nonliving environment into living things and back

respiration the exchange of oxygen and carbon dioxide between living cells and their environment

READING TOOLBOX

Word Families Explain how the carbon cycle and the oxygen cycle are similar. Explain how they are different.

Teaching Key Ideas

Nitrogen Gas Have students study **Figure 11.** Point out the difference between nitrogen fixation (nitrogen combines with hydrogen to form ammonia) and nitrification (ammonia is converted to nitrates). Tell students that lightning also changes nitrogen gas to ammonia, but such atmospheric action amounts to less than 10 percent of that carried out by organisms through nitrogen fixation. Finally, have students recognize that denitrification returns nitrates to the atmosphere as nitrogen gas. **LS Logical**

Demonstration

Nitrogen-Fixing Plants Tell students that beans are leguminous plants, the roots of which have nodules containing nitrogen-fixing bacteria. Then explain that other nitrogen-fixing plants include clover, peas, alfalfa, lupines, and locust trees. If any of these plants are available nearby, see if you can find examples to show the class any nodules that may be present. **LS Visual**

nitrogen cycle the cycling of nitrogen between organisms, soil, water, and the atmosphere

phosphorus cycle the cyclic movement of phosphorus in different chemical forms from the environment to organisms and then back to the environment

ACADEMIC VOCABULARY

convert to change from one form to another

Figure 11 Bacteria carry out many of the important steps in the nitrogen cycle, including the conversion of atmospheric nitrogen into a usable form, such as ammonia.

Nitrogen Cycle

All organisms, including you, need nitrogen. ❯ **Nitrogen must be cycled through an ecosystem so that the nitrogen is available for organisms to make proteins.** The **nitrogen cycle** is the process in which nitrogen circulates among the air, soil, water, and organisms in an ecosystem. The nitrogen cycle is shown in **Figure 11.**

The atmosphere is about 78% nitrogen gas, N_2. But most organisms cannot use nitrogen gas. It must be changed into a different form. A few bacteria have enzymes that can break down N_2. These bacteria supply the nitrogen that all other organisms need. The bacteria split N_2 and then bind nitrogen atoms to hydrogen to form ammonia, NH_3. The process of combining nitrogen with hydrogen to form ammonia is called *nitrogen fixation.* Nitrogen may be fixed by lightning. But more nitrogen is fixed by bacteria. Nitrogen-fixing bacteria live in the soil and on the roots of some plants. Nitrogen is also fixed when humans burn fuels in vehicles and industrial plants.

Plants get nitrogen by assimilation. *Assimilation* is the process in which plants absorb nitrogen. When an animal eats a plant, nitrogen compounds become part of the animal's body. During *ammonification,* nitrogen from animal waste or decaying bodies is returned to the soil by bacteria. Ammonia is then converted to nitrite and then nitrate by the process of *nitrification.* Finally, in *denitrification,* nitrate is changed to nitrogen gas, N_2, which returns to the atmosphere.

❯ **Reading Check** *Explain the role of bacteria in the nitrogen cycle.*

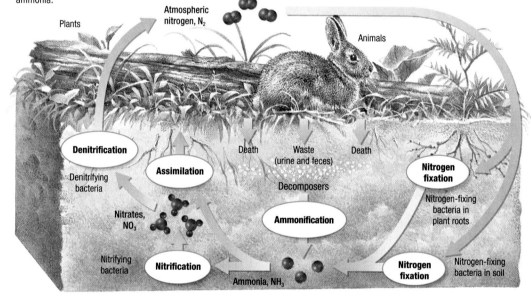

Why It Matters

Crop Rotation Tell students that farmers often rotate a nonleguminous crop, such as corn, with a leguminous one, such as alfalfa. The alfalfa will fix nitrogen and release some of it into the soil. If a crop of alfalfa is plowed back into the soil, it may add as much as 350 kg (770 lb) of nitrogen per hectare (2.5 acres) of soil. This mass of nitrogen is enough to grow a crop of nonleguminous plants without the need for additional fertilizer. **LS Verbal**

Differentiated Instruction

Advanced Learners

Sustainable Agriculture Organic farming is a form of sustainable agriculture that does not use inorganic fertilizers or pesticides. Have students find out how "organic" is used in marketing products. Ask students to find out if organic farming methods lead to bigger profits for farmers. Have them explain their answers in the form of a report, supporting their opinions with information that they have gathered through research. **LS Logical**

QuickLab

⏱ 15 min

The Carbon Cycle 4.6.1.c

You are part of the carbon cycle. Every time that you exhale, you release CO_2 into the atmosphere. But the CO_2 does not stay as CO_2 for very long.

Procedure

1 Pour **100 mL of water** into a **250 mL beaker.** Add **several drops of bromthymol blue** to the water. Add enough drops to make the solution dark blue.

2 ⚠ **CAUTION: Be sure not to inhale or ingest the solution.** Exhale through a **straw** into the solution until the CO_2 in your breath turns the solution yellow.

3 Pour the yellow solution into a **large test tube** that contains a **sprig of Elodea.**

4 Use a **stopper** to seal the test tube. Then, place the test tube in a sunny location.

5 Observe the solution in the test tube after 15 min.

Analysis

1. **CRITICAL THINKING** **Inferring Conclusions** What do you think happened to the carbon dioxide that you exhaled into the solution?

2. **CRITICAL THINKING** **Analyzing Methods** How do plants, such as the *Elodea,* affect the carbon cycle?

QuickLab

Teacher's Notes *Elodea* can be purchased at aquarium shops.

Materials
- beaker, 250 mL
- bromthymol blue indicator
- Elodea sprig
- eyedropper
- rubber stopper (to fit test tube)
- soda straw
- test tube
- water

Answers to Analysis

1. The elodea used the carbon dioxide during photosynthesis.
2. Plants use atmospheric carbon dioxide during photosynthesis and release carbon dioxide into the atmosphere during cellular respiration.

❯Close

Formative Assessment

Plants obtain nitrogen in a process called _____.
A. denitrification (Incorrect. In this process, nitrates are converted to a nitrogen gas.)
B. nitrogen fixation (Incorrect. In this process, nitrogen combines with hydrogen to form ammonia.)
C. nitrification (Incorrect. In this process, ammonia is converted to nitrite and then nitrate)
D. assimilation (Correct! In this process, plants absorb and incorporate nitrogen into organic compounds.)

Phosphorus Cycle

❯ Like water, carbon, oxygen, and nitrogen, phosphorus must be cycled in order for an ecosystem to support life. The **phosphorus cycle** is the movement of phosphorus in different chemical forms from the surroundings to organisms and then back to the surroundings. Phosphorus is often found in soil and rock as calcium phosphate, which dissolves in water to form phosphate. The roots of plants absorb phosphate. Humans and animals that eat the plants reuse the organic phosphorus. When the humans and animals die, phosphorus is returned to the soil.

❯ **Reading Check** *How is phosphorus passed from soil to plants?*

Section 3 Review

❯**KEY IDEAS**

1. **Explain** how carbon and oxygen are cycled through an ecosystem.
2. **Describe** why nitrogen must cycle through an ecosystem.
3. **Explain** why it is important that phosphorus be cycled through an ecosystem.

4. **Summarize** the steps of the water cycle.

CRITICAL THINKING

5. **Making Connections** Explain why the oxygen and carbon cycles are tied so closely together.
6. **Predicting Outcomes** Describe what would happen if matter could not cycle through ecosystems.
7. **Analyzing Processes** Defend the argument that nutrients can cycle but energy cannot.

METHODS OF SCIENCE

8. **Designing an Experiment** Design an experiment in which you would determine whether nitrogen-fixing bacteria really help plants grow faster.

Answers to Section Review

1. During photosynthesis, plants use carbon dioxide and release oxygen. Organisms use the oxygen during respiration. Carbon is also released during combustion and when bodies of dead organisms decay.
2. Nitrogen must be cycled through an ecosystem so that the nitrogen is available for organisms to make proteins.
3. Phosphorus must be cycled in order for an ecosystem to support life.
4. Water vapor condenses and falls as precipitation. Some percolates into the soil and becomes groundwater. Other water runs into rivers, lakes, and oceans. The water reenters the atmosphere by evaporation and transpiration.

5. During photosynthesis and respiration, carbon and oxygen cycle between living things and the environment.
6. Nutrients would eventually be used up and living things would die.
7. There is currently no mechanism to efficiently recycle energy lost as heat into the surroundings. This is the reason why energy is lost at each trophic level.
8. Grow the same plants in soil with and without nitrogen-fixing bacteria.

Lab

Time Required

20 minutes on day 1 for setup; 10 minutes each day thereafter over a period of three weeks

Ratings

EASY —————→ HARD

Teacher Prep 🧪
Concept Level 🧪🧪
Student Setup 🧪🧪
Cleanup 🧪

Safety Cautions

Warn students to take care when handling insects and other small animals, which are easily harmed. Some are capable of biting when disturbed.

Tips and Tricks

Have students bring clear plastic 2- or 3-L bottles from home. Create a separate terrarium that students can use as a control. Soil can be collected from around the school, brought from home, or purchased from a garden center. You may be able to find earthworms and crickets in the local environment or at bait shops. Remind students that the ecosystems are dependent on humans for care. They should not be permitted to overheat or become too cold. Water should be replenished as needed.

Objectives
➤ Construct an ecosystem model.
➤ Observe interactions of organisms in an ecosystem model.
➤ Compare an ecosystem model with a natural ecosystem.

Materials
- goggles, gloves, and lab apron
- coarse sand or pea gravel
- terrarium or glass jar, large, with a lid
- soil
- grass seeds, a pinch of
- clover seeds, a pinch of
- water, 150 mL
- rolled oats
- mealworms (beetle larvae)
- mung bean seeds
- earthworms
- isopods (pill bugs)
- crickets

Safety

Ecosystem Change

Organisms in an ecosystem interact with one another and with their environment. Feeding is one interaction that occurs among the organisms in an ecosystem. A food web describes the feeding relationships among the organisms in an ecosystem. In this lab, you will use a terrarium or a jar to model a closed ecosystem. A *closed ecosystem* is a system that allows energy to enter but that is closed to the transfer of matter.

Preparation

1. **SCIENTIFIC METHODS** **State the Problem** How might the different organisms interact in an ecosystem model?

2. **SCIENTIFIC METHODS** **Form a Hypothesis** Form a testable hypothesis about how the number of individuals of each species in an ecosystem model will change over time.

Procedure

Build an Ecosystem in a Jar

❶ ⚠ **CAUTION: Glassware is fragile. Notify your teacher promptly of any broken glass or cuts. Do not clean up broken glass or spills that contain broken glass unless your teacher tells you to do so.** Place 5 cm of sand or pea gravel in the bottom of a large, clean, glass jar that has a lid. Cover the gravel with 5 cm of soil.

❷ Sprinkle the seeds of two or three kinds of small plants, such as grasses and clovers, onto the surface of the soil. Add about 150 mL of water. Put the lid on the jar loosely, and place the jar in indirect sunlight. Let the jar remain undisturbed for one week.

❸ ⚠ **CAUTION: Handle animals carefully.** Do not allow animals to escape from containers. After one week, place a handful of rolled oats into the jar. Place the mealworms in the oats. Then, place the other animals into the jar, and replace the lid. Place the lid on the jar loosely so that air can enter the jar.

Answer to Form a Hypothesis

Sample answer: The continuous exposure of the ecosystem to bright light will cause an increase in the number of organisms in the ecosystem.

Sample Experiment Design

1. Place the ecosystem near an artificial light that is left on continuously.
2. Continue to add food and moisture to the system as needed. Using a mister, add four squirts of water per square decimeter of soil surface every other day.
3. Record population data every other day for two weeks.

Design an Experiment

4 Work with the members of your lab group to design an experiment that will test the hypothesis that you recorded previously. Design your experiment to use the ecosystem model that you built.

5 Write a procedure for your experiment. Make a list of all of the safety precautions that you will take. Have your teacher approve your procedure and safety precautions before you begin the experiment.

6 Set up your group's experiment. Conduct your experiment for at least 14 days.

Cleanup and Disposal

7 ◈ Dispose of solutions, broken glass, and other materials in the designated waste containers. Do not put lab materials in the trash unless your teacher tells you to do so.

8 ◈ Clean up your lab materials according to your teacher's instructions. Wash your hands before you leave the lab.

Analyze and Conclude

1. Summarizing Results Make graphs showing how the number of individuals of each species in your ecosystem changed over time. Be sure to count both plants and animals. Plot time on the *x*-axis and the number of organisms on the *y*-axis.

2. SCIENTIFIC METHODS Analyzing Data Compare your results with your hypothesis. Explain any differences.

3. Inferring Conclusions Construct a food web for the ecosystem that you observed.

4. SCIENTIFIC METHODS Recognizing Relationships Does your ecosystem model resemble a natural ecosystem? Explain your answer.

5. Analyzing Methods How can you build an ecosystem model that better represents a natural ecosystem?

6. Critiquing Models Was your ecosystem model truly a closed ecosystem? List your model's strengths and weaknesses as a closed ecosystem.

7. Analyzing Data List the biotic and abiotic factors in your ecosystem model.

www.scilinks.org
Topic: Ecosystems
Code: HK80466

Extensions

8. Further Inquiry Write a new question to explore with another investigation using an ecosystem model.

9. Making Comparisons Use the library or Internet to learn about Biosphere 2. What problems did the Biosphere 2 crew encounter during the 1991–1993 project?

Answers to Analyze and Conclude

1. Students should make one graph for each species or use different colors to indicate each species.
2. Answers will vary.
3. Answer will vary. All plants are producers; earthworms feed on dead plant material; crickets feed on plants; mealworms (beetle larvae) feed on plants; isopods eat wood.
4. Yes and no. Both contain organisms at several trophic levels, have biotic and abiotic factors, and depend on the sun for energy. The model ecosystem is less diverse, younger, and has more definite boundaries than a natural ecosystem.
5. Answers will vary.
6. No. Strengths: Organisms in the model did not leave the ecosystem; outside organisms could not enter. Weaknesses: Water and air had to be added to maintain a healthy ecosystem.
7. Sample answer: The biotic factors were the animals and plants. The abiotic factors were water, soil, glass jar, air, and sunlight.

Answers to Extensions

8. Answers will vary. Sample answer: What are the effects of temperature on organisms in an ecosystem?
9. Biosphere 2 is a 204,000 m³ glass-and-steel structure containing seven artificial ecosystems near Tucson, Arizona. The structure has been used for research on the biosphere. Problems included significant drops in oxygen levels. Most vertebrate species and insect pollinators died.

Key Resources

 Holt Lab Generator

 Lab Datasheet (Levels A, B, C)

 Holt Science Biology Video Labs

 Virtual Investigations

SUPER SUMMARY

Have students connect the major concepts in this chapter through an interactive Super Summary. Visit **go.hrw.com** and type in keyword **HX8ECOS** to access the Super Summary for this chapter.

Reteaching Key Ideas

Succession Show students a picture of a forest ecosystem. Have them describe the events that would take place after a fire there. **LS** Visual

Food Webs and Energy Pyramids Have students construct a food web and energy pyramid for a particular area. Ask students to identify producers, consumers, decomposers, herbivores, carnivores, and omnivores. **LS** Visual

A World Without Fungi or Bacteria Ask students to write a short essay describing what the world would be like without fungi or bacteria. **LS** Verbal

Key Ideas	Key Terms
1 What Is an Ecosystem? ❯ An ecosystem is a community of organisms and their abiotic environment. ❯ An ecosystem responds to change in such a way that the ecosystem is restored to equilibrium. ❯ Two key factors of climate that determine biomes are temperature and precipitation. ❯ Earth's major terrestrial biomes can be grouped by latitude into tropical, temperate biomes, and high-latitude. ❯ Aquatic ecosystems are organized into freshwater ecosystems, wetlands, estuaries, and marine ecosystems.	**community** (79) **ecosystem** (79) **habitat** (80) **biodiversity** (80) **succession** (81) **climate** (82) **biome** (82)
2 Energy Flow in Ecosystems ❯ In an ecosystem, energy flows from the sun to producers to consumers to decomposers. ❯ Energy is stored at each link in a food web, but some energy that is used dissipates as heat into the environment and is not recycled.	**producer** (86) **consumer** (86) **decomposer** (86) **trophic level** (86) **energy pyramid** (89)
3 Cycling of Matter ❯ The water cycle is the continuous movement of water between the atmosphere, the land, and the oceans. ❯ Animals, plants, and other photosynthesizing organisms play an important role in cycling carbon and oxygen through an ecosystem. ❯ Nitrogen must be cycled through an ecosystem so that the nitrogen is available for organisms to make proteins. ❯ Like water, carbon, oxygen, and nitrogen, phosphorus must be cycled in order for an ecosystem to support life.	**carbon cycle** (91) **respiration** (91) **nitrogen cycle** (92) **phosphorus cycle** (93)

PART A: Answer all questions in this part.

Directions: For each statement or question, write on your separate answer sheet the number of the word or expression that best completes the statement or answers the question.

1 Many years ago, a volcanic eruption killed many plants and animals on an island. Today the island looks much as it did before the eruption. Which statement is the best possible explanation for this?

(1) Altered ecosystems regain stability through the evolution of new plant species.

(2) Destroyed environments can recover as a result of the process of ecological succession.

(3) Geographic barriers prevent the migration of animals to island habitats.

(4) Destroyed ecosystems always return to their original state.

2 A fire burns an oak forest down to bare ground. Over the next 150 years, if the climate remains constant, this area will most likely

(1) remain bare ground

(2) return to an oak forest

(3) become a rain forest

(4) become a wetland

3 What impact do the amounts of available energy, water, and oxygen have on an ecosystem?

(1) They act as limiting factors.

(2) They are used as nutrients.

(3) They recycle the residue of dead organisms.

(4) They control environmental temperature.

4 As succession proceeds from a shrub community to a forest community, the shrub community modifies its environment, eventually making it

(1) more favorable for itself and less favorable for the forest community

(2) more favorable for itself and more favorable for the forest community

(3) less favorable for itself and more favorable for the forest community

(4) less favorable for itself and less favorable for the forest community

5 Nutritional relationships between organisms are shown in the diagram below.

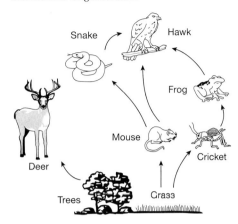

The mouse population would most likely decrease if there were

(1) an increase in the frog and tree populations

(2) a decrease in the snake and hawk populations

(3) an increase in the number of decomposers in the area

(4) a decrease in the amount of available sunlight

6 In the diagram below, what does X most likely represent?

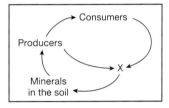

(1) autotrophs

(2) herbivores

(3) decomposers

(4) carnivores

Regents Exam Practice Correlations

4.1.1a 6	**4.6.1e** 13	
4.6.1a 5, 8, 9, 10, 12	**4.6.3b** 1, 2, 4	
4.6.1d 3, 11	**4.7.1c** 7	

PART A

1. **(2)** The choices about stability and barriers do not show how the island returned to its original state. Disturbed ecosystems may not always return to their original state as succession proceeds. (*#24, June 2006 Regents Exam*)

2. **(2)** Secondary succession would eventually lead to re-vegetation of the area, and thus the choice about bare ground is incorrect. It is unlikely that the area would become that different from the original forest so choices about becoming a rain forest or wetland are incorrect. (*#27, January 2006 Regents Exam*)

3. **(1)** Although nutrients are used to make energy, the choice about nutrients is not true as energy is not considered a nutrient. Energy, water , and oxygen are not decomposers and so they do not recycle. Although water can impact surrounding temperature, energy and oxygen do not affect temperature. (*#23, June 2006 Regents Exam*)

4. **(3)** Choices that indicate that the area becomes more favorable for the early shrub community and less favorable for the more mature forest community are incorrect. (*#23, August 2006 Regents Exam*)

5. **(4)** Decreasing the number of mice predators, such as snakes and hawks, would not decrease the number of mice. On the contrary, mice might increase. An increase in frogs would decrease the demand for mice by shared predators. An increase in trees would benefit the mice as well. Also, increasing decomposers would not negatively affect the mice population. (*#25, January 2006 Regents Exam*)

6. **(3)** The choice autotrophs is incorrect as producers are already in the diagram. Herbivores are also represented as the consumers feeding on the producers. The choice carnivores is incorrect as producers would not have an arrow leading to them. However, decomposers get energy from all organisms and release minerals back into the soil. (*#01, January 2006 Regents Exam*)

7. (2) Humans do not contain or give rise to ecosystems, as shown in incorrect choices. Humans are a part of Earth's ecosystems. *(#29, June 2005 Regents Exam)*

PART B

8. (4) Group A are producers, group B are herbivores, and group C are consumers. *(#42, June 2006 Regents Exam)*

9. (1) Lupine must be in the beginning of the food chain as the larvae feed on this plant. Wasps must be at the end of the food chain as wasps feed on the larvae. *(#41, June 2006 Regents Exam)*

10. (2) The larvae are not autotrophs that comprise group A, they are not carnivores as in group C, and they are not decomposers like group D. *(#40, June 2006 Regents Exam)*

11. (1) The choice describing energy is incorrect because autotrophs generally get their energy from the sun. The choice describing soil fertility is incorrect because bacterial and fungal recyclers increase soil fertility. The choice about mutations is not true. *(#14, August 2006 Regents Exam)*

7 Which diagram best illustrates the relationship between humans (H) and ecosystems (E)?

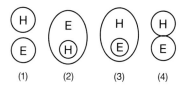

(1)   (2)   (3)   (4)

PART B

Base your answers to questions 8 through 10 on the passage below which describes an ecosystem in New York State and on your knowledge of biology.

The Pine Bush ecosystem near Albany, New York, is one of the last known habitats of the nearly extinct Karner Blue butterfly. The butterfly's larvae feed on the wild green plant, lupine. The larvae are in turn consumed by predatory wasps. The four groups below represent other organisms living in this ecosystem.

Group A	Group B	Group C	Group D
algae mosses ferns pine trees oak trees	rabbits tent caterpillars moths	hawks moles hognosed snakes toads	soil bacteria molds mushsrooms

8 Which group contains decomposers?

(1) A   (3) C
(2) B   (4) D

9 Which food chain best represents information in the passage?

(1) lupine → Karner Blue larvae → wasps
(2) wasps → Karner Blue larvae → lupine
(3) Karner Blue larvae → lupine → wasps
(4) lupine → wasps → Karner Blue larvae

10 The Karner Blue larvae belong in which group?

(1) A   (3) C
(2) B   (4) D

11 What would most likely happen if most of the bacteria and fungi were removed from an ecosystem?

(1) Nutrients resulting from decomposition would be reduced.
(2) Energy provided for autotrophic nutrition would be reduced.
(3) The rate of mutations in plants would increase.
(4) Soil fertility would increase.

12 Which level of the energy pyramid below would contain the plant species of a salt marsh?

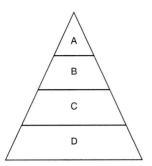

(1) A
(2) B
(3) C
(4) D

13 The graph below shows the effect of moisture on the number of trees per acre of five three species. Which observation best represents information shown in the graph?

(1) All five species grow in the same habitat.
(2) The American elm grows in the widest range of moisture conditions.
(3) Red oaks can grow in wetter conditions than black willows.
(4) Sugar maples can grow anywhere black oaks can grow.

12. (4) "A" and "B" refer to consumers, whereas "C" represents herbivores. Only "D" contains producers (plants, in this case). (*#55, August 2006 Regents Exam*)

13. (2) The trees do not share the same exact habitat as some trees prefer moist conditions and some prefer dry conditions. Red oaks grow in dryer, not wetter, conditions than black oaks according to the graph. Sugar maples would not necessarily grow anywhere black oaks do; black oaks predominate in dryer habitats based on the graph. (*#31, June 2006 Regents Exam*)

Populations and Communities

	Standards	Teach Key Ideas
CHAPTER OPENER, pp. 100–101 · 15 min.	🦅 *The Living Environment*	
SECTION 1 Populations, pp. 103–108 · 60 min. ❯ What Is a Population? ❯ Population Growth ❯ Factors That Affect Population Size ❯ Human Population	4.1.1c, 4.1.1d, 4.6.1d, 4.6.1e, 4.6.1f	**Bellringer Transparency** **Transparencies** D32 Exponential Growth • D33 Logistic Growth **Visual Concepts** Population • Characteristics of Populations • Exponential Growth • Limiting Factors and Carrying Capacity • Comparing Density-Dependent and Density-Independent Factors • Logistic Model
SECTION 2 Interactions in Communities, pp. 109–111 · 60 min. ❯ Predator-Prey Interactions ❯ Other Interactions	4.6.1g, 4.6.2a	**Bellringer Transparency** **Visual Concepts** Coevolution • Predation • Plant Protection Mechanisms • Symbiosis
SECTION 3 Shaping Communities, pp. 112–117 · 60 min. ❯ Carving a Niche ❯ Competing for Resources ❯ Ecosystem Resiliency	4.1.1c, 4.1.1d, 4.1.1f, 4.6.2a, 4.6.3a	**Bellringer Transparency** **Transparencies** E22 Warbler Foraging Zones • E21 Effects of Competition on Two Species of Barnacles **Visual Concepts** Competition • Niche • Biodiversity

See also PowerPoint® Resources

Chapter Review and Assessment Resources

SE Super Summary, p. 118
SE Regents Exam Practice, p. 119
📄 Regents Review Guide
📄 Review Resources
📄 Chapter Tests A and B
💻 Holt Online Assessment
⊙ Regents Question Banks on Teacher's One-Stop Planner

CHAPTER
***Fast*Track**
Thorough instruction will require the times shown.

Basic Learners

TE Population Sampling, p. 104
TE Competition, p. 113
📄 Directed Reading Worksheets*
📄 Active Reading Worksheets*
📄 Lab Manuals, Level A*
📖 Study Guide* ■
📖 Note-taking Workbook*
📖 Special Needs Activities and Modified Tests*

Advanced Learners

TE Local Population Growth, p. 105
TE Toxic Plants, p. 110
📄 Critical Thinking Worksheets*
📄 Concept Mapping Worksheets*
📄 Science Skills Worksheets*
📄 Lab Datasheets, Level C*

Why It Matters	Hands-On	Skills Development	Assessment
Build student motivation with resources about high-interest applications.	**SE Inquiry Lab** Population Size, p. 101* ■	**TE Reading Toolbox** Assessing Prior Knowledge, p. 100 **SE Reading Toolbox,** p. 102	
TE Demonstration Population Density, p. 103 **SE Growth in Asia,** p. 108	**SE Quick Lab** Population Growth, p. 105* ■ **SE Skills Practice Lab** Yeast Population Growth, p. 116* ■	**TE Math Skills** Experimental Growth, p. 104 **TE Science Skills** Logistic Growth, p. 105 **SE Reading Toolbox** Word Origins, p. 106 **TE Reading Toolbox** Word Origins, p. 106 **TE Reading Toolbox** Visual Literacy, p. 108	**SE Section Review** **TE Formative Assessment** Spanish Assessment* ■ **Section Quiz** ■
TE Demonstration Species Interactions, p. 109	**SE Quick Lab** The Effects of Herbivores on a Plant Species, p. 110* ■ **Skills Practice Lab** Examining Owl Pellets*	**SE Reading Toolbox** Venn Diagram, p. 110 **TE Reading Toolbox** Venn Diagram, p. 110	**SE Section Review** **TE Formative Assessment** Spanish Assessment* ■ **Section Quiz** ■
TE Demonstration Species Competition, p. 114	**SE Quick Lab** Changes in a Realized Niche, p. 113* ■ **Exploration Lab** Life in a Pine Cone*	**SE Reading Toolbox** Predictions, p. 115 **TE Reading Toolbox** Predictions, p. 115	**SE Section Review** **TE Formative Assessment** Spanish Assessment* ■ **Section Quiz** ■

See also Lab Generator

See also Holt Online Assessment Resources

Resources for Differentiated Instruction

English Learners
TE Word Parts, p. 104
TE Biotic and Abiotic Factors, p. 106
Directed Reading Worksheets*
Active Reading Worksheets*
Lab Manuals, Level A*
Study Guide* ■
Note-taking Workbook*
Multilingual Glossary
Interactive Tutor

Struggling Readers
TE Word Parts, p. 104
TE Biotic and Abiotic Factors, p. 106
Directed Reading Worksheets*
Active Reading Worksheets*
Lab Manuals, Level A*
Study Guide*
Note-taking Workbook*
Special Needs Activities and Modified Tests*
Interactive Tutor

Special Education Students
TE Competition Story, p. 114
Directed Reading Worksheets*
Active Reading Worksheets*
Lab Manuals, Level A*
Study Guide* ■
Note-taking Workbook*
Special Needs Activities and Modified Tests*

Alternative Assessment
TE Habitats and Niches, p. 113
Science Skills Worksheets*
Section Quizzes* ■
Chapter Tests A, B, and C* ■

Populations and Communities

Overview

The purpose of this chapter is to explain the concept of biological communities, populations of different species living together. Organisms interact in communities through predator-prey relationships, parasitism, mutualism, and commensalism. Competition among species and other factors influence the stability of an ecosystem.

READING TOOLBOX

Assessing Prior Knowledge Students should understand the following concepts:
• biodiversity
• components of an ecosystem

Visual Literacy Have students review the picture of the marine iguana and sally lightfoot crab. Explain that these two organisms are involved in a close relationship. Ask if students can think of other close relationships between species that might exist on the island. (Sample answer: parasites on the iguana or other animals)

Preview

1 Populations
What Is a Population?
Population Growth
Factors That Affect Population Size
Human Population

2 Interactions in Communities
Predator-Prey Interactions
Other Interactions

3 Shaping Communities
Carving a Niche
Competing for Resources
Ecosystem Resiliency

Why It Matters

How many species are in an area, how their populations grow, and how they interact with other species, including humans, are major factors that shape ecosystems and the environment's resources.

The Living Environment
Standard 4 Students will understand and apply scientific concepts, principles, and theories pertaining to the physical setting and living environment and recognize the historical development of ideas in science.
Key Idea 1 Living things are both similar to and different from each other and from nonliving things. **Major Understandings – 1.1c, 1.1d, 1.1f**
Key Idea 6 Plants and animals depend on each other and their physical environment. **Major Understandings – 6.1d, 6.1e, 6.1f, 6.1g, 6.2a, 6.3a**

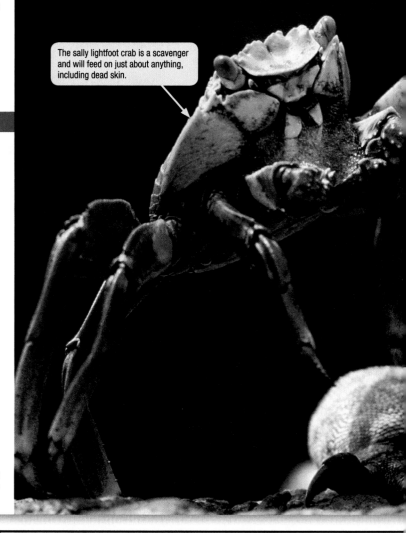

This crab and iguana have a relationship in which both benefit. The crab eats the iguana's dead skin. The iguana gets the irritating, dead, flaky skin removed, and the crab gets a meal.

The sally lightfoot crab is a scavenger and will feed on just about anything, including dead skin.

Chapter Correlations   The Living Environment

Standard 4

1.1c In all environments, organisms compete for vital resources. The linked and changing interactions of populations and the environment compose the total ecosystem.

1.1d The interdependence of organisms in an established ecosystem often results in approximate stability over hundreds and thousands of years. For example, as one population increases, it is held in check by one or more environmental factors or another species.

1.1f Every population is linked, directly or indirectly, with many others in an ecosystem. Disruptions in the numbers and types of species and environmental changes can upset ecosystem stability.

6.1d The number of organisms any habitat can support (carrying capacity) is limited by the available energy, water, oxygen, and minerals, and by the ability of ecosystems to recycle the residue of dead organisms through the activities of bacteria and fungi.

6.1e In any particular environment, the growth and survival of organisms depend on the physical conditions including light intensity, temperature range, mineral availability, soil/rock type, and relative acidity (pH).

6.1f Living organisms have the capacity to produce populations of unlimited size, but environments and resources are finite. This has profound effects on the interactions among organisms.

The marine iguana and the sally lightfoot crab live on the Galápagos Islands in the Pacific Ocean.

The marine iguana is the only true saltwater lizard. It is an excellent swimmer and feeds on marine algae.

InquiryLab

⏱ 30 min

Population Size 4.6.1f

In this activity, you will model the change in size of a population.

Procedure

1 Using **110 g of dry beans,** count out five beans to represent the starting population of a species.

2 Assume that each year, 20% of the beans have two offspring. Also, assume that 20% of the beans die each year.

3 Calculate the number of beans to add or subtract for 1 year.

4 Add to or remove beans from your population as appropriate. Record the new population size.

5 Continue modeling your population changes over the course of 10 years. Record the population size for each year.

Analysis

1. Calculate the final population size after 10 years.

2. Graph your data. Describe the changes in your population.

6.1g Relationships between organisms may be negative, neutral, or positive. Some organisms may interact with one another in several ways. They may be in a producer/consumer, predator/prey, or parasite/host relationship; or one organism may cause disease in, scavenge, or decompose another.

6.2a As a result of evolutionary processes, there is a diversity of organisms and roles in ecosystems. This diversity of species increases the chance that at least some will survive in the face of large environmental changes. Biodiversity increases the stability of the ecosystem.

6.3a The interrelationships and interdependencies of organisms affect the development of stable ecosystems.

Using Words

1. Sample answer: An organism's role is what it does and how it uses its habitat. It could be said that its role is the "home" the organism builds for itself in its habitat such as a nest.
2. A tick lives beside or on the dog and feeds off it.

Using Language

1. Condition: the deer population reaching 600 individuals
   Prediction: Most of the vegetation will be eaten and the number of deer will decrease.
2. Condition: removal of the otters
   Prediction: All the sea urchins will eat all the kelp.

Using Graphic Organizers

See the sample Venn diagram below.

 READING TOOLBOX

These reading tools can help you learn the material in this chapter. For more information on how to use these and other tools, see **Appendix: Reading and Study Skills.**

Using Words

Word Origins Many common English words derive from Greek or Latin words. Learning the meanings of some Greek or Latin words can help you understand the meaning of many modern English words.

Your Turn Answer the following questions.
1. Why might an organism's role be called its *niche?*
2. Why might a tick on a dog be considered a parasite?

Word Origins		
Word	Origin	Meaning
niche-	Latin (nidus)	nest
para-	Greek	beside
-site	Greek	food

Using Language

Predictions Some predictions are conditional: Something might happen, but only if something else happens first. For example, if the temperature drops below freezing, snow might fall. The prediction is that snow might fall tonight. But snow might fall under one condition. First, the temperature has to drop below freezing.

Your Turn In the following sentences, identify the condition and the prediction.
1. After the deer population reaches 600 individuals on the island, the deer will eat most of the vegetation, and the number of deer will decrease.
2. If the otters are removed from the ecosystem, the sea urchins will eat all of the kelp.

Using Graphic Organizers

Venn Diagram A Venn diagram is a useful tool for comparing two or three topics in science. A Venn diagram shows which characteristics are shared by the topics and which characteristics are unique to each topic.

Your Turn Create a Venn diagram that compares the characteristics of communities, ecosystems, and populations.
1. Draw a diagram like the one shown here. Draw one circle for each topic. Make sure that each circle partially overlaps the other circles.
2. In each circle, write a topic that you want to compare with the topics in the other circles.
3. In the areas of the diagram where circles overlap, write the characteristics that the topics in the overlapping circles share.
4. In the areas of the diagram where circles do not overlap, write the characteristics that are unique to the topic of the particular circle.

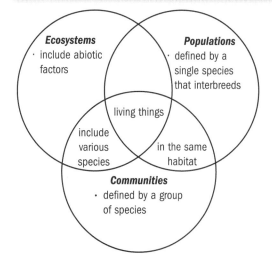

Key Ideas

> Why is it important to study populations?

> What is the difference between exponential growth and logistic growth?

> What factors affect population size?

> How have science and technology affected human population growth?

Key Terms

population
carrying capacity

Why It Matters

Understanding how populations grow and shrink is critical to managing agricultural pests and diseases and also for knowing how to protect ecosystems.

In the 1850s, about two dozen rabbits from Europe were introduced into Australia. The rabbits had plenty of vegetation to eat, no competition, and no predators. Their numbers increased rapidly. By the 1950s, there were 600 million rabbits! The rabbits ate so much vegetation that the numbers of native plants and animals declined and crops were damaged.

What Is a Population?

As Australia learned, understanding populations is important for protecting ecosystems. A **population** is made up of a group of organisms of the same species that live together in one place at one time and interbreed. **Figure 1** shows members of a zebra population. As new zebras are born, the population size increases. As other zebras fall prey to predators, the population decreases. Hundreds of miles away, there may be another zebra population that lives together and interbreeds.

Populations can be small or large. Some populations stay at nearly the same number for years at a time. Some populations die out from lack of resources. Other populations grow rapidly, such as the rabbit population in Australia. The rapid growth of the rabbit population caused problems with Australia's ecosystems, other species, and farmland. > Understanding population growth is important because populations of different species interact and affect one another, including human populations.

> **Reading Check** *What distinguishes one zebra population from another zebra population? (See Appendix for answers to Reading Checks.)*

Figure 1 This zebra population lives in Kenya near Mount Kilimanjaro.

 The Living Environment

Standard 4

1.1c In all environments, organisms compete for vital resources. The linked and changing interactions of populations and the environment compose the total ecosystem.

1.1d The interdependence of organisms in an established ecosystem often results in approximate stability over hundreds and thousands of years. For example, as one population increases, it is held in check by one or more environmental factors or another species.

6.1d The number of organisms any habitat can support (carrying capacity) is limited by the available energy, water, oxygen, and minerals, and by the ability of ecosystems to recycle the residue of dead organisms through the activities of bacteria and fungi.

6.1e In any particular environment, the growth and survival of organisms depend on the physical conditions including light intensity, temperature range, mineral availability, soil/rock type, and relative acidity (pH).

6.1f Living organisms have the capacity to produce populations of unlimited size, but environments and resources are finite. This has profound effects on the interactions among organisms.

population a group of organisms of the same species that live in a specific geographical area and interbreed

Key Resources

 Transparencies
D32 Exponential Growth Curve
D33 Logistic Growth Curve

Visual Concepts
Population
Characteristics of Populations
Exponential Growth
Limiting Factors and Carrying Capacity
Comparing Density-Dependent and Density-Independent Factors
Logistic Model

> Focus

This section explains populations, their characteristics, and how different populations grow.

Bellringer

Use the Bellringer transparency to prepare students for this section.

> Teach

Demonstration

Population Density Have students calculate the population density of their own state. Explain that population density is the number of individuals in a given area. Ask students what information they need to get started. (the size of the population and the size of the geographical area in question) Supply the information, and have students make the calculations. Ask why the calculated population density might be misleading. (Certain areas, such as mountaintops, deserts, or lakes, might be uninhabitable, making the population density seem less than it really is in many places in the state.)

LS Logical

Section Correlations	
4.1.1c	4.6.1e
4.1.1d	4.6.1f
4.6.1d	

go.hrw.com
✴ **interact online**

Students can interact with "Exponential Growth" by going to go.hrw.com and typing in the keyword HX8COMF2.

Teaching Key Ideas

Population Growth Rate Explain that for a population in which the birthrate and death rate are the same, population growth is 0. For populations where the birthrate is greater than the death rate, the growth rate is positive; for those in which the death rate exceeds the birthrate, population growth is negative. Ask students if the population growth in the United States is 0, positive, or negative. (positive) **LS** **Logical**

Math Skills

Exponential Growth How does the use of *exponential* to describe the graph in **Figure 2** relate to what students know about exponents in math? (They represent "fast" multiplication.) Ask students why an exponential growth curve would have a "J" shape. (Growth begins slowly, then increases quickly, which is similar to raising a number to a higher power, e.g., 10^1 is 10, and 10^{10} is 10,000,000,000.) **LS** **Logical**

Exponential Growth

Figure 2 Exponential growth is characterized by a J-shaped curve. Rabbits and bacteria are two examples of populations that can grow exponentially.

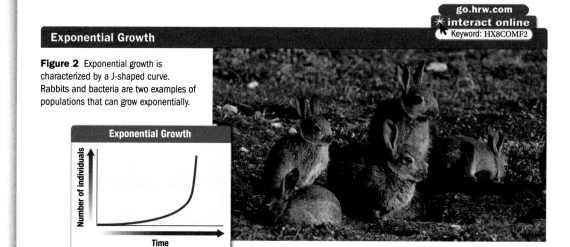

carrying capacity the largest population that an environment can support at any given time

www.scilinks.org
Topic: Population
Growth Factors
Code: HX81187

Population Growth

One of the most basic questions ecologists ask is "How do populations grow and shrink?" To help answer this question, biologists make population models. A population model attempts to show key growth characteristics of a real population.

Whether a population grows or shrinks depends on births, deaths, immigration, and emigration. *Immigration* is the movement of individuals into a population. *Emigration* is the movement of individuals out of a population. So, a simple population model describes the rate of population growth as the difference between birthrate, death rate, immigration, and emigration. Plotting population changes against time on a graph creates a model in the form of a curve. Two major models of population growth are *exponential growth* and *logistic growth*.

Exponential Growth One important part of a population model is the growth rate. When more individuals are born than die, a population grows. In exponential growth, there are always more births than deaths. As time goes by, more and more individuals enter the population. ❯ *Exponential growth occurs when numbers increase by a certain factor in each successive time period.* This type of increase causes the J-shaped curve of exponential growth seen in **Figure 2.**

In exponential growth, population size grows slowly when it is small. But as the population gets larger, growth speeds up. Bacteria are an example of a population that can grow exponentially. Populations of bacteria grow very fast. A single bacterial cell that divides every 30 minutes will have produced more than 1 million bacteria in 10 hours. Some populations, such as the rabbits shown in **Figure 2,** may grow exponentially for a while. If they continued to grow exponentially forever, the world would fill up with rabbits!

❯ **Reading Check** *What are the characteristics of a population that grows exponentially?*

Differentiated Instruction

English Learners/Struggling Readers

Word Parts Help students remember the meanings of the four italicized terms on this page by doing a word-part analysis. *Immigration* is movement *into* population (**i** and **i**). *Emigration* is movement *out* of the population. When students think of *exponential* growth, they should recall a string of *exponential* numbers. When they think of *logistic* growth, the **S**-shaped growth curve should come to mind (**s** and **s**). **LS** **Verbal**

Basic Learners

Population Sampling Divide the class into small groups. Ask each group to estimate the number of blades of grass in a local athletic field. Since it is impossible to count the blades of grass, ask each group to outline a method of estimating the number of blades of grass. (Some groups may suggest a method of population sampling.) Ask students how animal populations could be sampled. (Sample answer: trapping, tagging and releasing) What is the value of tagging? (The same animals won't be counted twice.) **LS** **Logical**

QuickLab

4.6.1f

🕐 30 min

Population Growth

You can learn a lot about a population by plotting its changes on a graph. In this activity, you will plot the growth of a deer population.

Procedure

❶ On a graph, plot the data from the table.

❷ Title the graph. Then, label the x-axis and the y-axis.

Analysis

1. **Identify** the dependent and independent variables.

2. **Describe** the growth curve. Does the population increase logistically or exponentially?

3. **Identify** the point at which the population is growing fastest.

4. **CRITICAL THINKING** **Analyzing Results** Are you able to determine the carrying capacity from this graph? If so, label it on the graph. What is its value?

Year	Number of individuals
1930	30
1935	50
1940	98
1945	175
1950	250
1955	273
1960	201
1965	159
1970	185
1975	205
1980	194
1985	203

Logistic Growth Populations do not grow unchecked forever. Factors such as availability of food, predators, and disease limit the growth of a population. Eventually, population growth slows and may stabilize.

An ecosystem can support only so many organisms. The largest population that an environment can support at any given time is called the **carrying capacity.** *Density-dependent factors* are variables affected by the number of organisms present in a given area. An example of a density-dependent factor is the availability of nesting sites. As the number of adult birds increases, there are no longer enough nesting sites for the entire population. So, many birds will not have young, and growth of the population is limited. *Density-independent factors* are variables that affect a population regardless of the population density. Examples of density-independent factors are weather, floods, and fires.

The logistic model takes into account the declining resources available to populations. ❯*Logistic growth is population growth that starts with a minimum number of individuals and reaches a maximum depending on the carrying capacity of the habitat.* When a population is small, the growth rate is fast because there are plenty of resources. As the population approaches the carrying capacity, resources become scarce. Competition for food, shelter, and mates increases between individuals of a population. As a result, the rate of growth slows. The population eventually stops growing when the death rate equals the birthrate. On a graph, logistic growth is characterized by an S-shaped curve, as **Figure 3** shows. Populations of most organisms, such as the macaws shown in **Figure 3,** show a logistic growth pattern.

Figure 3 Logistic growth is characterized by an S-shaped curve.

Teaching Key Ideas

Population Density Pose the following question to students: If you heard of an area inhabited by only seven birds, would you consider the area to be crowded? (Sample answer: It would depend on the size of the area.) Ask students if they think the penguins shown in the figure appear crowded. (Most students will probably answer that the penguins are crowded *by human standards.*) Tell students that penguins spend much of their time feeding in the ocean. Point out that the *number* of organisms in a population may not be as important for survival as the *density* of the organisms in the population. Ask what factors would limit the size of the penguin population. (available food, predators, climate, disease, parasites)

 Logical

READING TOOLBOX

Word Origins
biotic relating to living
abiotic relating to nonliving
bio- life

Answers to Caption Questions
Figure 4: Another abiotic factor that might affect the population size of penguins is the presence of water in the ocean where the penguins fish.

ACADEMIC VOCABULARY

affect to act upon

READING TOOLBOX

Word Origins Write down the definitions of the words *biotic* and *abiotic*. Then, write down what you think that *bio-* means. Use a dictionary to check your answer.

Figure 4 Climate is an abiotic factor that affects the population size of these emperor penguins in Antarctica. ❯ Name another abiotic factor that may affect the population size of these penguins.

Factors That Affect Population Size

Most populations increase or decrease. Some change with the seasons. Others have good years and bad years. Many factors cause populations to grow and shrink. ❯ Water, food, predators, and human activity are a few of many factors that affect the size of a population.

Abiotic Factors Nonliving factors that <u>affect</u> population size are called *abiotic factors.* Weather and climate are the most important abiotic factors. For example, the population size of the penguins shown in **Figure 4** is affected by the climate of Antarctica. Unusually low temperatures can reduce the number of young penguins that survive. The amount of water available can also influence populations. Kangaroo populations in Australia grew when farmers gave water to their livestock that was also available for kangaroos to drink.

Biotic Factors A factor that is related to the activities of living things is called a *biotic factor.* Food, such as grass or other animals, is a biotic factor. When there is plenty of food, populations tend to grow. When food is scarce, populations decline. Predators are another kind of biotic factor. When populations of Canadian lynx grow, they eat a lot of snowshoe hares. The population of hares is then reduced. Diseases and parasites, when they infect many individuals, can also cause populations to decline. Biotic factors are often density dependent because they can have a stronger influence when crowding exists. As the density of a population increases, the effects of starvation, predators, and disease often also increase.

Humans affect populations of many species. Most of the time, humans cause populations to drop by disrupting habitats, introducing diseases, or introducing nonnative species. But some organisms do better around humans. Elk thrive near some Canadian towns because wolves will not come close to humans.

❯ **Reading Check** *Describe the difference between biotic and abiotic factors.*

Differentiated Instruction

Struggling Readers/English Learners
Biotic and Abiotic Factors Have students look up the meaning of the root word *bio* (of living things) and the prefix *a-* (not). Then ask them to write their own definitions of *biotic* and *abiotic* and to give examples of biotic and abiotic factors that affect populations. **Logical**

Human Population

Today, the world population is more than 6 billion people and is increasing. ❯ Better sanitation and hygiene, disease control, and agricultural technology are a few ways that science and technology have decreased the death rate of the human population. As more humans live on the planet, more resources will be needed to support them. As demand for resources increases, more pressure will be put on Earth's ecosystems.

Historic Growth For most of human history, there have been fewer than 10 million people. Once agriculture was developed, the population began to grow, but relatively slowly. Two thousand years ago, there were only 300 million people. Around the time of the Industrial Revolution, the human population started to accelerate rapidly. **Figure 5** shows the human population accelerating exponentially starting in the late 1700s. Now, there are more than 6 billion people, and some scientists think that the population will grow to 9 billion in 50 years. How many people Earth can support depends in part on science and technology.

Science and Technology Science and technology are major reasons why the human population is growing so rapidly. Advances in agricultural technology have allowed efficient production of crops and other foods. More food supports more people. As a result, the human population has begun to grow faster. Medical advances have also allowed the human population to increase. Vaccines have lowered the death rate. More children are surviving to adulthood. Other medical advances have allowed adults to live longer lives.

❯ **Reaching Check** *How have advances in technology allowed the human population to grow faster?*

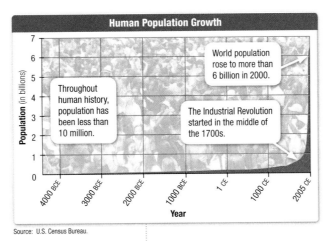

Source: U.S. Census Bureau.

Figure 5 During the last 200 years, the human population has grown exponentially.

Teaching Key Ideas

Human Population Growth Tell students that rapid human population growth is a relatively recent phenomenon. Advances in health care, agriculture, commerce, and technology accelerated population growth. From 1750 to 1900, the population doubled from 800 million to 1.6 billion. From 1900 to 1965, it doubled again to 3.2 billion. In 2002, the estimated global population was about 6.24 billion.

❯ Close

Formative Assessment

The movement of individuals into a population is called _____.

A. emigration (Incorrect. Emigration refers to individuals moving out of a population.)

B. exponential growth (Incorrect. This term refers to population numbers increasing by a certain factor in each successive period.)

C. logistic growth (Incorrect. Logistic growth refers to a population reaching its maximum number.)

D. immigration (Correct! Immigration refers to individuals moving into a population.)

Section 1 Review

❯ KEY IDEAS

1. **Explain** the importance of studying populations.
2. **Compare** exponential growth with logistic growth.
3. **Identify** an abiotic factor that affects populations.
4. **Explain** how science and technology have affected human population growth.

CRITICAL THINKING

5. **Relating Concepts** A small species of mouse lives in a desert in Arizona. What factors do you think influence the size of this mouse population?

6. **Predicting Outcomes** Identify a biotic factor that could affect the size of the human population. Predict the effect of this biotic factor.

USING SCIENCE GRAPHICS

7. **Making Graphs** Draw a graph with a growth curve for a population that starts at 10 individuals and experiences exponential growth. Draw a second graph with a growth curve for a population that starts with 10 individuals and undergoes logistic growth. The second graph should have a carrying capacity of 100 individuals.

Answers to Section Review

1. It is important to study populations because populations of different species, including human populations, interact and affect each other.

2. With exponential growth, numbers increase by a certain factor in each successive period. With logistic growth, a population starts with a minimum number of individuals and reaches a maximum number, depending on the carrying capacity of the habitat.

3. Accept any of the following: availability of water, weather, climate, or air quality.

4. Science and technology have provided better sanitation, disease control, and agricultural advances that have decreased the death rate of the human population resulting in population growth.

5. Accept any of the following: predators, food supply, water supply, and disease resistance.

6. Sample answer: Disease is a biotic factor that could affect the size of the human population. For example, the bubonic plague killed millions of people in the 14th century.

7. Students should have two graphs. Both should have the *x*- and *y*-axis labeled. One graph should show the *J*-curve of exponential growth; the other graph should show the *S*-curve of logistic growth.

Teacher's Notes In 2002, the world's population increased by 74 million people. That is about 200,000 people per day—enough to fill two large sports stadiums. Asia has held more than half the world's population since before 1950, and that is expected to continue through 2050. In 2002, the country with the largest population was China. Its population was greater than most of the world's regions, including Eastern Europe, sub-Saharan Africa, Latin America and the Caribbean, and the Near East and North Africa. However, over the next 50 years, China is expected to lose population. The population of India, the second most populous country, is expected to surpass the population of China around 2037.

READING TOOLBOX

Visual Literacy Have students review the captions on this page. Ask them how recycling and population growth are related and why recycling is so important. (As populations increase, demand for products will increase, resulting in greater demand for resources. Recycling helps conserve resources.)

Answer to Research
Strategies include financial incentives, mandatory population control, socioeconomic development, family-planning counseling, and education.

Growth in Asia

REAL WORLD

The world population is more than 6 billion and growing by about 9,000 people per hour. Most of the growth is coming from Asia. Because Asia's current population is already so large, one child per couple in Asia adds more to the world population than two children per couple in other areas of the world. As the world population continues to grow, pressure will increase on availability of food, energy, livable space, and landfill space.

A Recycling Society
As landfills quickly approach full capacity, the Japanese government has become a world leader in waste-recycling measures. Japan recycles refrigerators, washing machines, televisions, and even air conditioners. By 2015, Japan plans to recycle 95% of discarded cars. In the United States, 60% to 70% of waste is sent to landfills. In Japan, only 16% of waste is sent to landfills!

World Population Growth by Region, 1750–2050

Legend:
- Asia
- Africa
- Latin America
- Europe
- Northern America
- Oceania

World population (in billions) vs. Year (1750–2050, projected)

Source: National Geographic

Old to New These workers in Tokyo, Japan, are dismantling computers and sorting the parts for recycling.

Crowed City With 6,380 people per square kilometer, Hong Kong, China, shown here, is one of the most densely populated regions of the world.

Research Identify four strategies used by various countries to slow the rate of population growth.

Interactions in Communities

Key Ideas	Key Terms	Why It Matters
➤ How do predator-prey interactions influence both predators and prey? ➤ What are two other types of interaction in a community?	predation coevolution parasitism symbiosis mutualism commensalism	Interactions between organisms are the basis of communities and are shaped by evolution.

Interactions in communities can take many forms. Predators and prey are locked in a struggle for survival. Organisms with the same needs compete for food. Parasites and hosts try to get ahead of one another. Some organisms even depend on one another for survival.

Predator-Prey Interactions

One of the most common interactions in communities is that between predators and their prey. **Predation** is the act of one organism killing another for food. As **Figure 6** shows, predators try to get a meal, and prey do their best not to become one! We often think of predators as big animals, such as lions chasing zebras or sharks eating fish. Predators come in all sizes. Even microscopic organisms can be predators. In fact, most animals are both predators and prey. Only a few species, such as killer whales, are not hunted by any other animals.

Many interactions between species are the result of a long evolutionary history. Evolutionary changes in one species can result in changes in another species. ➤ **Species that involve predator-prey or parasite-host relationships often develop adaptations in response to one another.** For example, predators evolve to be more cunning to catch their prey. In response, prey evolve to be faster runners to escape more easily. Back-and-forth evolutionary adjustment between two species that interact is called **coevolution.**

The Living Environment
Standard 4

6.1g Relationships between organisms may be negative, neutral, or positive. Some organisms may interact with one another in several ways. They may be in a producer/consumer, predator/prey, or parasite/host relationship; or one organism may cause disease in, scavenge, or decompose another.

6.2a As a result of evolutionary processes, there is a diversity of organisms and roles in ecosystems. This diversity of species increases the chance that at least some will survive in the face of large environmental changes. Biodiversity increases the stability of the ecosystem.

predation an interaction between two organisms in which one organism, the predator, kills and feeds on the other organism, the prey

coevolution the evolution of two or more species that is due to mutual influence

Figure 6 This lion is hoping to have the zebra for lunch.

Key Resources

⊙ **Visual Concepts**
Coevolution
Predation
Plant Protection Mechanisms
Symbiosis

➤ Focus

This section describes how predator-prey interactions affect both predators and prey. It also describes several symbiotic relationships.

🎧 Bellringer

Use the Bellringer transparency to prepare students for this section.

➤ Teach

Demonstration

Species Interactions On the board, prepare a four-column chart with these headings: *Animal pair, Both benefit, One benefits/one suffers, and One benefits/one not affected.* Show students pictures of two animals interacting, or describe various interactions. Write the names of the interacting animals in the first column of the chart. Ask students to identify the type of interaction for each animal pair by placing a checkmark in the appropriate column of the chart. **LS Logical**

Section Correlations

4.6.1g
4.6.2a

QuickLab

Teacher's Notes There are several species of *Gilia.* Most species live in semi-desert conditions. The plants are related to the common garden plant phlox.

Answers to Analysis

1. The grazed plant would most likely produce more seeds.
2. Grazing leads to dense regrowth and the production of more flower heads.
3. The production of more flower heads may allow this plant to spread in its environment and out compete other plants.
4. If new stems were not produced in response to grazing, the grazed plants would produce few, if any, seeds and become rare or extinct.

READING TOOLBOX

Venn Diagram

See the sample Venn diagram below.

Teaching Key Ideas

Tapeworms Show pictures of tapeworms and their adaptations for parasitism: hooks on the head to attach to the intestinal wall, permeable body that readily absorbs nutrients, and body segments specialized for reproduction.

Data

QuickLab

The Effects of Herbivores on a Plant Species 4.6.1g

Background

Some plant species, such as *Gilia*, respond to grazing by growing new stems. Consider the three images of *Gilia* to the right. Then, answer the statements below.

Analysis

1. **Identify** the plant that is likely to produce more seeds.
2. **Explain** how grazing affects this plant species.
3. **Evaluate** the significance to its environment of the plant's regrowth pattern.
4. **Hypothesize** how this plant species might be affected if individual plants did not produce new stems in response to grazing.

⏱ 15 min

Ungrazed plant   **Grazed plant**   **Regrowth after grazing**

READING TOOLBOX

Venn Diagram Make a Venn diagram to help you compare the similarities and differences between predators, parasites, and herbivores.

parasitism a relationship between two species in which one species, the parasite, benefits from the other species, the host, which is harmed

symbiosis (SIM bie OH sis) a relationship in which two different organisms live in close association with each other

mutualism a relationship between two species in which both species benefit

commensalism a relationship between two organisms in which one organism benefits and the other is unaffected

Parasitism In **parasitism,** one organism feeds on another organism called a *host*. The host is almost always larger than the parasite and is usually harmed but not killed. Parasites often live on or in their host. Therefore, the parasite depends on its host not only for food but for a place to live as well. For example, tapeworms live in the digestive system of their hosts. Fleas that live on the skin of their host are another example.

Hosts try to keep parasites from infecting them. Hosts can defend themselves with their immune systems or behaviors such as scratching. In response, parasites may evolve ways to overcome the host's defenses.

Herbivory Herbivores are animals that eat plants. Unlike predators, herbivores do not often kill the plants. But plants do try to defend themselves. Some plants have thorns or spines that cause pain for herbivores that try to eat them. Other plants have chemical compounds inside them that taste bad. Some chemical compounds can make an herbivore sick or kill the herbivore.

Some herbivores have evolved ways to overcome plant defenses. For example, monarch butterfly caterpillars feed on milkweed, which is a plant that is toxic to many herbivores. Not only can the caterpillars survive eating the toxic milkweed but the plant toxins then make the monarch butterfly inedible to bird predators.

❯ **Reading Check** *Identify one way in which herbivores and plants coevolve.*

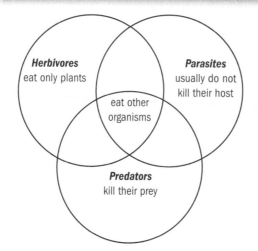

Herbivores eat only plants

Parasites usually do not kill their host

eat other organisms

Predators kill their prey

Differentiated Instruction

Advanced Learners/GATE

Toxic Plants Using reference materials or the Internet, have students make a chart of houseplants that are toxic to humans or pets. Included in the chart should be names, pictures or drawings the plants, descriptions of how each plant affects humans or pets, and ways to treat the reactions caused by plant ingestion or contact. **LS** Verbal

Cleaner fish eat parasites from the eel's mouth.

Orchids receive more sunlight when attached to trees.

Other Interactions

Not all interactions between organisms result in a winner and a loser. **Symbiosis** is a relationship in which two species live in close association with each other. In some forms of symbiosis, a species may benefit from the relationship. ❯ **Mutualism and commensalism are two kinds of symbiotic relationships in which at least one species benefits.**

Mutualism A relationship between two species in which both species benefit is called **mutualism.** Some shrimp and fishes on coral reefs clean the bodies of large fish and turtles. The cleaners even venture into the mouths of big predators that could easily swallow them, as **Figure 7** shows. Why don't the cleaners become an easy meal? The reason is that the big fish is having parasites removed by the cleaner. Because the cleaner gets a meal, both species win.

Commensalism In **commensalism,** two species have a relationship in which one species benefits and the other is neither harmed nor helped. **Figure 7** shows an example of commensalism between orchids and trees. In thick, tropical forests, little sunlight reaches the forest floor. Orchids need sunlight to survive. To reach the sunlight, orchids get a boost from the forest trees. Orchids will attach themselves and grow on the trunks of the trees. In this way, the orchids move up off the dark forest floor and closer to the sunny canopy.

❯ **Reading Check** *Compare mutualism and commensalism.*

Figure 7 This yellow-edged moray eel is getting its mouth cleaned by a humpback cleaner shrimp. Orchids avoid the dark forest floor by attaching themselves to the trunks of trees. ❯ **Name another symbiotic relationship.**

www.scilinks.org
Topic: Symbiosis
Code: HX81486

Section 2 Review

❯ KEY IDEAS

1. **Explain** how predator-prey interactions influence both predators and prey.
2. **Define** symbiosis.
3. **Describe** two types of relationships in a community.

CRITICAL THINKING

4. **Analyzing Results** The cookie-cutter shark feeds by taking a bite of flesh out of whales and large fish. The shark does not kill the larger fish it feeds on. Is the shark a predator or a parasite? Why?
5. **Relating Concepts** In commensalism, would both species coevolve?

WRITING FOR SCIENCE

6. **Essay** In a report, explain what might happen to an ecosystem if one species in a mutualistic relationship disappeared. What would happen if a new predator were introduced to prey with which it has not coevolved?

Answers to Section Review

1. Species involved in predator-prey relationships often develop adaptations in response to one another.
2. Symbiosis is a relationship in which two different organisms live in close association with one another.
3. Two symbiotic relationships are mutualism, a relationship in which both species benefit, and commensalism, a relationship in which only one of the species benefits although the other is unharmed. Students might also describe predator-prey, parasite-host, or herbivory relationships.
4. The shark would be better described as a parasite because it does not kill the whale or other large fish it feeds on.

5. In commensalism, one species is not affected by the relationship and that species will not coevolve with the other species.
6. Reports should indicate that the loss of one species in a mutualistic relationship would negatively affect the other species; the species may even die out. Introduced predators may have an advantage over prey that have not coevolved with them. The predator may be so successful at hunting that all the prey are killed. The prey may have the advantage, and the predator may be unable to catch enough prey to survive.

Shaping Communities

Focus

This section explains how a species' niche affects other organisms. It focuses on competition and how it affects populations comprising a community.

 Bellringer

Use the Bellringer transparency to prepare students for this section.

Teach

Teaching Key Ideas

Aspects of a Niche Tell students that a niche is very complex and includes all the ways an organism affects and is affected by its environment. Draw students' attention to **Figure 8.** Explain that this photo shows only a small portion of the beaver's niche, for example, that it uses trees to build its home. Ask students to lists other aspects of the beaver's niche. (Sample answer: Beavers live in ponds, cut down trees to build dams, live in lodges they build, and eat plants and dead fish.)
LS Logical

Answers to Caption Questions

Figure 8: Sample answer: The cutting down of trees by the beavers destroys the nesting habitats for birds.

Key Ideas

> How does a species' niche affect other organisms?

> How does competition for resources affect species in a community?

> What factors influence the resiliency of an ecosystem?

Key Terms

niche
fundamental niche
realized niche
competitive exclusion
keystone species

Why It Matters

The interactions among organisms in communities shape the ecosystem and the organisms that live there.

The Living Environment
Standard 4

1.1c In all environments, organisms compete for vital resources. The linked and changing interactions of populations and the environment compose the total ecosystem.

1.1d The interdependence of organisms in an established ecosystem often results in approximate stability over hundreds and thousands of years. For example, as one population increases, it is held in check by one or more environmental factors or another species.

1.1f Every population is linked, directly or indirectly, with many others in an ecosystem. Disruptions in the numbers and types of species and environmental changes can upset ecosystem stability.

6.2a As a result of evolutionary processes, there is a diversity of organisms and roles in ecosystems. This diversity of species increases the chance that at least some will survive in the face of large environmental changes. Biodiversity increases the stability of the ecosystem.

6.3a The interrelationships and interdependencies of organisms affect the development of stable ecosystems.

No organism can live everywhere. Each organism has its own set of conditions where it can live and where it does best. Some plants, such as cactuses, can survive in deserts, but other plants need a lot of water. The desert plants cannot live in areas that have a lot of water because other plants outcompete them.

Carving a Niche

Think of your favorite plant or animal. How does it use the physical environment? How does it interact with other species? The unique position occupied by a species, both in terms of its physical use of its habitat and its function in an ecological community, is called a **niche.** A niche is not the same as a habitat. A *habitat* is the place where an organism lives. **A niche includes the role that the organism plays in the community. This role affects the other organisms in the community.** For example, the beaver shown in **Figure 8** cuts down trees with its sharp teeth. The beaver then uses the trees to make dams that divert, or redirect, water flow in rivers and streams. These actions directly affect the trees by killing the trees. These actions also affect organisms that depend on the trees for shelter or food. However, some plants would benefit: fewer trees would allow the plants access to more sunlight. Diverting water flow in a stream could be beneficial to some forms of aquatic life. For others, a dam in a stream could prevent them from traveling upstream to mating grounds. The beaver's role affects many other organisms. If you took the beaver out of this ecosystem, the community would be very different.

> **Reading Check** *How is a niche different from a habitat?*

Figure 8 Beavers build dams from trees and tree branches that they cut with their sharp, powerful teeth. **How might these dams affect other organisms in the community?**

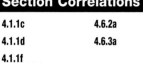
Section Correlations

4.1.1c	4.6.2a
4.1.1d	4.6.3a
4.1.1f	

 Key Resources

Transparencies
E22 Warbler Foraging Zones
E21 Effects of Competition on Two Species of Barnacles

Visual Concepts
Competition
Niche
Biodiversity

#

⏱ 15 min

Changes in a Realized Niche

4.1.1c, 4.6.3b

This graph shows the location where species A feeds and the size of its preferred prey. The darkest shade in the center of the graph indicates the prey size and feeding location most frequently selected by species A.

Analysis

1. **State** the range of lengths of prey on which species A prefers to feed.

2. **Identify** the maximum height above ground at which species A feeds.

3. **Describe** what the palest shade at the edge of the contour lines represents.

4. **CRITICAL THINKING** **Predicting Outcomes** Species B is introduced into species A's ecosystem. Species B has the same feeding preferences but hunts at a different time of day. How might this affect species A?

Prey Length and Location for Species A

Height above ground (m) vs Prey length (mm)

5. **CRITICAL THINKING** **Interpreting Graphics** Species C is now introduced into species A's feeding range. Species C feeds at the same time of day as species A but prefers prey that are between 10 and 13 mm long. How might this change affect species A?

Competing for Resources

The entire range of conditions where an organism or species could survive is called its **fundamental niche.** Many species share parts of their fundamental niche with other species. Sometimes, species compete for limited resources. Because of this competition, a species almost never inhabits its entire fundamental niche. ❯ **Competition for resources between species shapes a species' fundamental niche.** The actual niche that a species occupies in a community is called its **realized niche.**

Sometimes, competition results in fights between rivals. Hyenas and lions will even steal food from one another. The stealing of food is called *kleptoparasitism.* Many competitive interactions do not involve direct contests. But when one individual takes a resource, the resource is no longer available for another individual. Many plants compete fiercely for access to light. Some do so by growing quickly to get above other plants. Other plants can tolerate periods of shade and grow slowly. As the slow-growing plants become larger, they eventually shade out other plants.

Competition has several possible outcomes. Sometimes, one species wins, and the other loses. The loser is eliminated from the habitat. Other times, competitors can survive together in the same habitat. They are able to survive together because they divide the resources.

❯ **Reading Check** *Why do organisms rarely occupy their entire fundamental niche?*

niche the unique position occupied by a species, both in terms of its physical use of its habitat and its function within an ecological community

fundamental niche the largest ecological niche where an organism or species can live without competition

realized niche the range of resources that a species uses, the conditions that the species can tolerate, and the functional roles that the species plays as a result of competition in the species' fundamental niche

SCiLINKS
www.scilinks.org
Topic: Habitats and Niches
Code: HX80707

QuickLab

Teacher's Notes Explain to students that this type of graph is a convenient way to represent three variables: height above the ground, prey length, and frequency of selection of a combination of prey length and feeding height.

Answers to Analysis

1. Species A will feed on prey that ranges in length from about 1.2 mm up to about 13.4 mm. Most of the selected prey are approximately 3.2 to 4.5 mm.

2. Maximum feeding height is nearly 11 m.

3. The lightest shade represents the combination of feeding height and prey length least frequently selected but still exploited by Species A.

4. Even though it is feeding at a different time of day, species B might reduce the prey available to species A, since it has the same feeding preference.

5. Species C would reduce species A's realized niche by competing with species A for large prey. Since species A prefers smaller prey, however, competition from species C would be minimal.

Differentiated Instruction

Alternative Assessment

Habitats and Niches An analogy may help students understand the difference between habitat and niche. Point out that their homes and the places they frequent make up their habitats. Their activities in their habitats—patterns of living—are their niches. Ask students to write a description of their habitats and their niches. **LS** **Verbal**

Basic Learners

Competition Ask students to write a paragraph explaining why competition is usually most intense between closely related organisms. (Closely related organisms are likely to be very similar and therefore are likely to use resources in similar ways.) **LS** **Logical**

Demonstration

Species Competition Show the class photographs of a starling and a bluebird. Explain that starlings were first introduced into Central Park in New York City in 1890. Today starlings are found throughout the continental United States. In many areas they have out-competed bluebirds for nesting sites, causing a drastic decline in bluebirds. Make plans available for students to build their own bluebird houses. Select an area to post them. Emphasize the importance of monitoring the houses to keep out non-native competitors, such as starlings.
LS Kinesthetic

Teaching Key ideas

Predation and Diversity Tell students that the removal of a predator can actually reduce the diversity of an ecosystem. An example occurred in England when a viral epidemic wiped out the rabbit population. The grasses, once controlled by rabbits, grew out of control, and the many species of wildflowers that once thrived there disappeared.

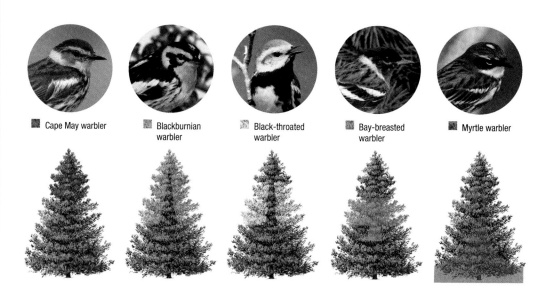

Cape May warbler   Blackburnian warbler   Black-throated warbler   Bay-breasted warbler   Myrtle warbler

Figure 9 Each of these five warbler species feeds on insects in a different portion of the same tree, as indicated by the five colors shown in the figure.

competitive exclusion the exclusion of one species by another due to competition

keystone species a species that is critical to the functioning of the ecosystem in which it lives because it affects the survival and abundance of many other species in its community

ACADEMIC
VOCABULARY
potential possible

Competitive Exclusion No two species that are too similar can coexist. Why? If species are too similar in their needs, one will be slightly better at getting the resources on which they both depend. The more successful species will dominate the resources. The less successful species will either die off or have to move to another ecosystem. Eventually, the better competitor will be the only one left. One species eliminating another through competition is called **competitive exclusion.**

Competitive exclusion is seen in many places. When there are no predators around, mussels take over all of the space on rocks in the surf zone. The mussels eliminate barnacles from the surf-zone rocks that are part of the mussels' fundamental niche. Introduced species can also competitively exclude native species. When introduced species multiply quickly, they can use up all of the available resources. When resources are used up, other species that depend on the resources may become extinct.

Dividing Resources Sometimes, competitors eat the same kinds of food and are found in the same places. How do these species live together? Some competitors divide resources by feeding in slightly different ways or slightly different places. The five warblers shown in **Figure 9** are all potential competitors. All five species feed on insects in the same spruce trees at the same time. But they divide the habitat so that they do not compete. Each species feeds in a different part of the tree. Every one of the warbler species would feed everywhere in the tree if it had the tree to itself. Therefore, all the warbler species have the same fundamental niche. But when they are all present in the tree, they each have a smaller realized niche.

> **Reading Check** *How might two different species divide resources?*

MISCONCEPTION ALERT

Environment and Competition Students may have a misconception that the same species of a competing pair will always eliminate the other species. Tell students that altering the environment can reverse the outcome. Thomas Park at the University of Chicago conducted competition experiments on two species of flour beetles (*Tribolium*). The temperature and humidity at which the beetles were raised determined which species was the superior competitor.

Differentiated Instruction

Special Education Students
Competition Story To help visually impaired students understand competition, have them choose an organism to study. They should identify at least one organism that competes for resources with the organism they selected. They should use library or Internet resources to gather information about the two organisms. With the information they gather, have students write a story about an interaction between the organisms, focusing on how this interaction affects the organisms' resource use and realized niche. **LS Verbal**

Ecosystem Resiliency

Ecosystems can be destroyed or damaged by severe weather, humans, or introduced species. Some factors can help keep an ecosystem stable. ❯ **Interactions between organisms and the number of species in an ecosystem add to the resiliency of an ecosystem.**

Predation and Competition Predation can reduce the effects of competition among species. Many aquatic species compete for space in the intertidal zone along the Pacific coast. Mussels are fierce competitors that can take over that space. All other species are excluded. However, sea stars eat mussels. When sea stars eat the mussels, a variety of species can live in the intertidal zone.

Predators can influence more than their prey. Sea otters, as shown in **Figure 10,** eat sea urchins. Sea urchins eat kelp. When sea otters are present, lush kelp forests grow along the west coast of North America. These kelp forests provide habitat for many fishes and aquatic animals. When sea otters disappeared because of overhunting, the sea urchins ate all of the kelp. All of the species that depended on the kelp also disappeared. Sea otters are an example of a keystone species. A **keystone species** is a species that is critical to an ecosystem because the species affects the survival and number of many other species in its community.

Biodiversity and Resiliency One community has 50 species. Another community has 100 species. If a severe drought affected both communities equally, the community with 100 species would be more likely to recover quickly. The reason is that higher biodiversity often helps make an ecosystem more resilient. Predation helps increase biodiversity. The sea stars prevented the mussels from excluding other species. In response, the inter tidal zone had a higher biodiversity.

❯ **Reading Check** *List two factors that contribute to the resiliency of an ecosystem.*

Figure 10 Sea otters off the coast of California are a threatened species. The decrease in their population has affected the stability of the ecosystem. ❯ **Why is the sea otter considered a keystone species?**

READING TOOLBOX

Predictions Using the term *keystone species*, write a sentence with a prediction based on a condition.

READING TOOLBOX

Predictions Sample answer: If a keystone species is eliminated from an ecosystem, many other species may not survive.

❯ Close

Formative Assessment

One competing species eliminating another through competition is called _____.
- **A.** a keystone species (Incorrect. A keystone species affects the survival of many other species in the ecosystem.)
- **B.** a niche (Incorrect. A niche is the role an organism plays in the community.)
- **C.** competitive exclusion (Correct! One species eliminating another through competition is called competitive exclusion.)
- **D.** kleptoparasitism (Incorrect. This term refers to one species stealing food from another.)

Answers to Caption Questions

Figure 10: The sea otters are a keystone species because their presence in an ecosystem affects the survival of other species in the ecosystem.

Section 3 Review

❯ **KEY IDEAS**
1. **Explain** why an organism's role is important for a community.
2. **Describe** one example of how competition for resources affects species in a community.
3. **Explain** how predation can help make an ecosystem resilient.
4. **Compare** niche and habitat.

CRITICAL THINKING
5. **Inferring Conclusions** Two predators feed on small antelope. One predator weighs 100 kg, and the other weighs 35 kg. Explain what might happen if the two predators share the same area.
6. **Evaluating Results** Wolves are reintroduced into a park. As a result, the vegetation changes. Explain how the changes to the vegetation happened.

ALTERNATIVE ASSESSMENT
7. **Essay** Search the Internet to find out about the niche of wolves in their community. Determine if they are a keystone species. Then, write a one-page essay describing their role in their ecosystem.

Answers to Section Review
1. An organism's role affects other organisms in the community.
2. Competition for resources between species shapes other species' fundamental niches.
3. Predation helps increase diversity; higher diversity often makes an ecosystem more resilient.
4. A niche is an organism's function in a community. A habitat is where an organism lives.
5. One possibility is that one predator will be eliminated. Another possibility is that the competitors will survive together by dividing their resources.

6. The wolves feed on herbivores, such as deer. When the wolves were reintroduced to the park, the herbivore population decreased, and the vegetation that the herbivores ate grew without being eaten.
7. Students should find that wolves are a keystone species. For example, when wolves are present in ecosystems that support elk, the elk browse in different areas, and the structure of the vegetation changes. This results in increases in bird populations that rely on the plants that elk normally would have eliminated from the ecosystem by their grazing.

Lab

Time Required
20–30 minutes each day for 5 consecutive days

Ratings

EASY ——————— HARD

Teacher Prep   🧪
Student Setup   🧪🧪
Concept Level   🧪🧪🧪
Cleanup   🧪

Safety Cautions
Caution students to treat all microorganisms as potential pathogens. Remind students to keep their hands away from their faces as they handle the yeast cultures. Remind students to wash their hands after this lab.

Tips and Tricks
Yeast Preparation Prepare the yeast population by dissolving 1.0 g of yeast and 1.0 g of sugar in 40 mL of warm water. Remove 1 mL of the solution and dilute with 9 mL of water. Mix well and again remove 1 mL of the solution and dilute with 9 mL of water.

    If using dried yeast or freeze-dried yeast, the yeast should be prepared a week in advance. Fresh yeast may be prepared up to 4 hours before the investigation. Keep the yeast in a warm, dark area for the duration of the investigation.

Chapter 5 Lab

 4.6.1.f

Objectives
➤ Observe the growth and decline of a population of yeast cells.
➤ Determine the carrying capacity of a yeast culture.

Materials
- lab apron, safety goggles, and gloves
- yeast cell culture
- test tube (2)
- pipets, 1 mL (2)
- methylene blue solution, 1%
- microscope slide, ruled
- coverslip
- microscope, compound

Safety

Yeast Population Growth

You have learned that a population will keep growing until limiting factors slow or stop this growth. In this lab, you will observe the changes in a population of yeast cells. The cells will grow in a container and have limited food over several days.

Procedure

Collecting Data

① ⬥ **CAUTION: Do not touch or taste any chemicals. Know the location of the emergency shower and eyewash station and how to use them. Methylene blue will stain your skin and clothing.** Transfer 1 mL of yeast culture to a test tube. Add two drops of methylene blue to the test tube. The methylene blue will remain blue in dead cells but will turn colorless in living cells.

② Make a wet mount by placing 0.1 mL, or about one drop, of the yeast culture and methylene blue mixture on a ruled microscope slide. Cover the slide with a coverslip.

③ Observe the wet mount under low power of a compound microscope. Notice the squares on the slide. Then, switch to high power. (Note: Adjust the light so that you can clearly see both stained and unstained cells.) Move the slide so that the top left-hand corner of one square is in the center of your field of view. This area will be area 1, as shown in the diagram.

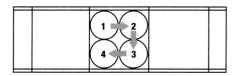

④ Make two data tables like the one shown. One table will contain your observations of living cells. The other table will contain your observations of dead cells.

Number of cells							
Time (h)	1	2	3	4	5	6	Average
0							
24							
48							
72							
96							

Methylene Blue Preparation Use gloves when preparing methylene blue and avoid creating dust while working. Make 1.0 percent solution by dissolving 1.0 g of methylene blue in 100 mL of distilled water.

Slide Measurements Ruled microscope slides can be purchased or can be made: make a transparency copy of a piece of graph paper and then cut the transparency into coverslip-size pieces.

Disposal Solutions of yeast and of methylene blue can be rinsed down the drain. Wash thoroughly and air-dry all glassware.

Methylene blue stains the dead yeast cells.

5 Count the live (unstained) cells and the dead (stained) cells in the four corners of a square by using the pattern shown in the diagram in step 3. Record the number of live cells and dead cells that you counted in the entire square.

6 Repeat step 5 until you have counted all six squares on the slide.

7   Clean up your lab materials according to your teacher's instructions. Wash your hands before leaving the lab.

Compiling Data

8 Refer to your first data table. Find the total number of live cells in the six squares. Divide this total by 6 to find the average number of live cells per square. Record this number in your data table. Repeat this procedure for the dead cells.

9 Repeat steps 1 through 5 each day for four more days.

Analyze and Conclude

1. Evaluating Methods Explain why several areas were counted and averaged each day.

2. Analyzing Data Graph the changes in the numbers of live yeast cells and dead yeast cells over time. Plot the number of cells in 1 mL of yeast culture on the *y*-axis and the time (in hours) on the *x*-axis.

3. Evaluating Results Describe the general population changes that you observed in the yeast cultures over time.

4. SCIENTIFIC METHODS **Inferring Conclusions** Did the yeast population appear to reach a certain carrying capacity? What limiting factors probably caused the yeast population to decline?

SC*i*LINKS.

www.scilinks.org
Topic: Characteristics
of Populations
Code: HX80260

Extensions

5. Designing an Investigation Write a question about population growth that could be explored in another investigation. Design an investigation that could help answer that question.

Answers to Analyze and Conclude

1. An average was taken to allow for variation within a population.

2. Sample data graph:

3. Sample answer: Initially the yeast population increased, but then it began to decline.

4. Yes, the yeast population appeared to reach a carrying capacity. A lack of food and lack of space could have limited the yeast cells. The yeast cells could also have been limited because their own wastes were poisoning them.

Answers to Extensions

5. Sample answer: Would the carrying capacity of the yeast's environment expand if the size of the environment increased? Check student investigations to make sure they identify variables and controls.

Key Resources

 Holt Lab Generator

Lab Datasheet (Levels A, B, C)

Holt Science Biology Video Labs

Virtual Investigations

go.hrw.com
SUPER SUMMARY
Keyword: HX8COMS

SUPER SUMMARY

Have students connect the major concepts in this chapter through an interactive Super Summary. Visit **go.hrw.com** and type in the keyword **HX8COMS** to access the Super Summary for this chapter.

Reteaching Key Ideas

Human Population Ask students to list the biotic and abiotic factors that affect human population size.

Species Interactions Have students make a chart of the different types of species interactions—predation, parasitism, mutualism, and commensalism. Tell them to use the four interactions as headings. Then have them place plus and minus signs in the row below each interaction to indicate whether each of the two organisms is helped or harmed by the interaction. For example, mutualisms would have + / + because both organisms are helped.

Environmental Concerns Have the class organize and implement a school-wide project that addresses one of the environmental concerns explored in this chapter.

Key Ideas

1 Populations

> Understanding population growth is important because populations of different species interact and affect one another, including human populations.

> Exponential growth occurs when numbers increase by a certain factor in each successive time period. Logistic growth is population growth that starts with a minimum number of individuals and reaches a maximum depending on the carrying capacity of the habitat.

> Water, food, predators, and human activity are a few of many factors that affect the size of a population.

> Better sanitation and hygiene, disease control, and agricultural technology are a few ways that science and technology have decreased the death rate of the human population.

2 Interactions in Communities

> Species that involve predator-prey or parasite-host relationships often develop adaptations in response to one another.

> Mutualism and commensalism are two types of symbiotic relationships in which one or both of the species benefit.

3 Shaping Communities

> A niche includes the role that the organism plays in the community. This role affects the other organisms in the community.

> Competition for resources between species shapes a species' fundamental niche.

> Interactions between organisms and the number of species in an ecosystem add to the stability of an ecosystem.

Key Terms

population (103)
carrying capacity (105)

predation (109)
coevolution (109)
parasitism (110)
symbiosis (111)
mutualism (111)
commensalism (111)

niche (112)
fundamental niche (113)
realized niche (113)
competitive exclusion (114)
keystone species (115)

Regents Exam Practice

PART A: Answer all questions in this part.

Directions: For each statement or question, write on your separate answer sheet the number of the word or expression that best completes the statement or answers the question.

1 When habitats are destroyed, there are usually fewer niches for animals and plants. This action would most likely not lead to a change in the amount of
(1) biodiversity
(2) competition
(3) interaction between species
(4) solar radiation reaching the area

2 The growth of a population is shown in the graph below. Which letter indicates the carrying capacity of the environment for this population?

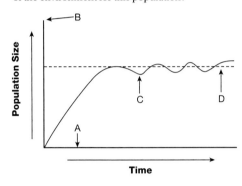

(1) A
(2) B
(3) C
(4) D

3 The removal of nearly all the predators from an ecosystem would most likely result in
(1) an increase in the number of carnivore species
(2) a decrease in new predators migrating into the ecosystem
(3) a decrease in the size of decomposers
(4) an increase in the number of herbivores

4 Ten breeding pairs of rabbits are introduced onto an island with no natural predators and a good supply of water and food. What will most likely happen to the rabbit population?
(1) It will remain relatively constant due to equal birth and death rates.
(2) It will die out due to an increase in the mutation rate.
(3) It will increase until it exceeds carrying capacity.
(4) It will decrease and then increase indefinitely.

5 The graph below shows how the human population has grown over the last several thousand years. Which statement is a valid inference that can be made if the human population continues to grow at a rate similar to the rate shown between 1000 A.D. and 2000 A.D.?

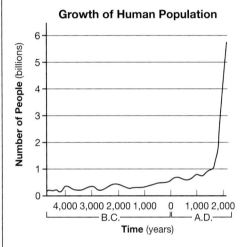

(1) Future ecosystems will be stressed and many animal habitats may be destroyed.
(2) Global warming will decrease as a result of a lower demand for fossil fuels.
(3) One hundred years after all resources are used up, the human population will level off.
(4) All environmental problems can be solved without a reduction in the growth rate of the human population.

PART A

1. **(4)** Niche availability would not affect solar radiation, but solar radiation may affect niche availability. Niche availability would affect species interactions and the diversity of species. (*#26, June 2006 Regents Exam*)

2. **(4)** Choice A is the x axis, choice B is the y axis, and choice C is a population size that is fluctuating near the carrying capacity (D). (*#25, June 2006 Regents Exam*)

3. **(4)** The choice about carnivores is wrong because carnivores are predators. Removing predators would not necessarily decrease the number of migrating predators. The choice about decomposers is incorrect as they feed on all the trophic levels. (*#30, June 2006 Regents Exam*)

4. **(3)** It is incorrect that mutation rates will increase. It is also incorrect that a population can grow indefinitely. It is unlikely that population growth will remain constant when the rabbits reach their carrying capacity on the island. A breeding rabbit population with no predators is likely to increase until other regulating factors begin to limit population growth. (*#22, January 2006 Regents Exam*)

5. **(1)** The choice about global warming is incorrect as there should be a greater demand for fossil fuels. The choices about environmental problems and the leveling of population growth are incorrect. (*#33, June 2006 Regents Exam*)

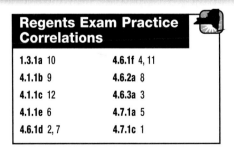

Regents Exam Practice Correlations

1.3.1a	10	4.6.1f	4, 11
4.1.1b	9	4.6.2a	8
4.1.1c	12	4.6.3a	3
4.1.1e	6	4.7.1a	5
4.6.1d	2, 7	4.7.1c	1

6. (2) Choices that indicate a general increase in the number of mosquitoes over time do not show a state of equilibrium. In addition, the choice that shows a fluctuating population that eventually crashes is not in equilibrium either. (*#27, August 2006 Regents Exam*)

7. (1) The part of the curve labeled "X" represents the carrying capacity of the habitat, that is, the maximum number of organisms the habitat can support. Flies may still reproduce at "X", but the death rates may cancel out birth rates. Lifespan is not measured by "X" on the graph. This graph does not indicate how the population is adapting or evolving. (*#25, June 2005 Regents Exam*)

8. (4) The choice about the amount of energy at each height of the tree is incorrect as it does not explain the advantage of a unique niche for each bird. The choice about abiotic resources is incorrect as the tree provides feeding (biotic) resources. The choice about predators is not necessarily true. (*#28, June 2005 Regents Exam*)

9. (1) The choice about competition is incorrect as this would make it harder for two species to coexist. The choices about reproduction are incorrect as they are two different species and thus unable to interbreed. (*#02, January 2006 Regents Exam*)

---

6 Which graph illustrates changes that indicate a state of dynamic equilibrium in a mosquito population?

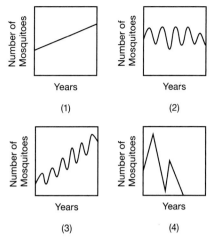

(1)   (2)

(3)   (4)

7 Which statement best describes the fruit fly population in the part of the curve labeled X in the graph shown below?

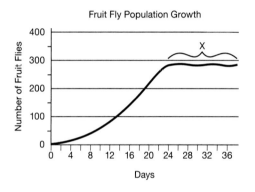

Fruit Fly Population Growth

(1) The fruit fly population has reached the number of organisms the habitat can support.
(2) The fruit fly population can no longer mate and produce fertile offspring.
(3) The fruit fly population has an average life span of 36 days.
(4) The fruit fly population is no longer able to adapt to the changing environmental conditions.

---

8 The ecological niches of three bird species are shown in the diagram below. What is the advantage of each bird species having a different niche?

Cape May warblers feed in the upper area of the tree.

Bay-breasted warblers feed in the middle of the tree.

Yellow-rumped warblers feed in the lower part of the tree.

(1) As the birds feed higher in the tree, available energy increases.
(2) More abiotic resources are available for each bird.
(3) Predators are less likely to feed on birds in a variety of locations.
(4) There is less competition for food.

9 Two closely related species of birds live in the same tree. Species A feeds on ants and termites, while species B feeds on caterpillars. The two species coexist successfully because

(1) each occupies a different niche
(2) they interbreed
(3) they use different methods of reproduction
(4) birds compete for food

PART B

Base your answers to questions 10 and 11 on the information and graph below and on your knowledge of biology.

A population of paramecia (single-celled aquatic organisms) was grown in a 200-mL beaker of water containing some smaller single-celled organisms. Population growth of the organisms for 28 hours is shown in the graph below.

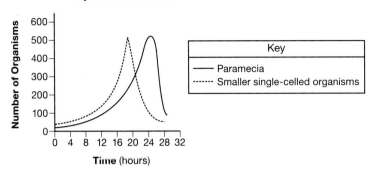

10 Which factor most likely accounts for the change in the paramecium population from 8 to 20 hours?

(1) an increase in the nitrogen content of water

(2) an increase in wastes produced

(3) an increase in available food

(4) an increase in water pH

11 One likely explanation for the change in the paramecium population from 26 hours to 28 hours is that the

(1) carrying capacity of the beaker was exceeded

(2) rate of reproduction increased

(3) time allowed for growth was not sufficient

(4) oxygen level was too high

PART C

Base your answers to question 12 on the information below and on your knowledge of biology.

A student uses a covered aquarium to study the interactions of biotic and abiotic factors in an ecosystem. The aquarium contains sand, various water plants, algae, small fish, snails, and decomposers. The water contains dissolved oxygen and carbon dioxide, as well as tiny amounts of minerals and salts.

12 Explain how oxygen is cycled between organisms in this ecosystem.

PART B

10. (3) The choices about nitrogen content and pH of the water are inaccurate based on the information given. The choice about an increase in wastes would lead to a declining population, rather than an increasing populations shown in the diagram. *(#39, August 2006 Regents Exam)*

11. (1) The choice about increasing reproductive rates is incorrect because the population is declining. The choices about time and oxygen are untrue. Reaching carrying capacity can slow down growth, though. *(#40, August 2006 Regents Exam)*

PART C

12. Allow a maximum of 2 credits, 1 credit for each part of the cycle explaining how oxygen is cycled between organisms in this ecosystem. Acceptable 2-credit responses include, but are not limited to: It is given off by plants and used by animals (plants and/or decomposers).; Oxygen is given off as a result of photosynthesis and used for respiration. *(#59, June 2005 Regents Exam)*

The Environment

CHAPTER OPENER, pp. 122–123 — 15 min.

SECTION 1 An Interconnected Planet, pp. 125–127 — 45 min.
> Humans and the Environment
> Resources
> The Environment and Health

SECTION 2 Environmental Issues, pp. 128–133 — 90 min.
> Air Pollution
> Global Warning
> Water Pollution
> Soil Damage
> Ecosystem Disruption

SECTION 3 Environmental Solutions, pp. 134–139 — 90 min.
> Conservation and Restoration
> Reducing Resource Use
> Environmental Awareness
> Planning for the Future

Standards

The Living Environment

4.7.1a, 4.7.1b, 4.7.1c, 4.7.2a, 4.7.2b

4.6.2b, 4.7.1c, 4.7.2a, 4.7.2b, 4.7.2c

4.7.3a, 4.7.3b

Teach Key Ideas

Bellringer Transparency
Transparencies E34 World Population Growth Patterns
Visual Concepts Human Population

Bellringer Transparency
Transparencies E29 The Greenhouse Effect • E31 Atmospheric Temperature and Carbon Dioxide Levels • E32 Change in Global Temperature • E33 Biological Magnification of DDT
Visual Concepts Acid Precipitation • Ozone and Ecosystems • Greenhouse Effect • Global Warning • Biological Magnification of Toxins

Bellringer Transparency
Visual Concepts Recycling • Conservation

See also PowerPoint® Resources

Chapter Review and Assessment Resources

SE Super Summary, p. 142
SE Regents Exam Practice, p. 143
Regents Review Guide
Review Resources
Chapter Tests A and B
Holt Online Assessment
Regents Question Banks on Teacher's One-Stop Planner

CHAPTER
Fast Track
Thorough instruction will require the times shown.

Basic Learners
TE Mapping Endangered Organisms, p. 132
TE Research and Solutions, p. 136
TE Project, p. 137
Directed Reading Worksheets*
Active Reading Worksheets*
Lab Manuals, Level A*
Study Guide* ■
Note-taking Workbook*
Special Needs Activities and Modified Tests*

Advanced Learners
TE Ozone and Marine Ecosystems, p. 129
TE Groundwater Contamination, p. 130
Critical Thinking Worksheets*
Concept Mapping Worksheets*
Science Skills Worksheets*
Lab Datasheets, Level C*

Why It Matters	Hands-On	Skills Development	Assessment
Build student motivation with resources about high-interest applications.	**SE Inquiry Lab** The Greenhouse Effect, p. 123*■	**TE Reading Toolbox** Assessing Prior Knowledge, p. 122 **SE Reading Toolbox,** p. 124	
TE Sustainability, p. 126	**SE Quick Lab** Contaminated Water, p. 127*■	**SE Reading Toolbox** Word Parts, p. 127 **TE Reading Toolbox** Word Parts, p. 127	**SE Section Review** **TE Formative Assessment** Spanish Assessment*■ 🗁 **Section Quiz** ■
TE Demonstration Environmental Issues, p. 128 **TE Long-Term Effects of Acid Rain,** p. 128 **TE Consequences of Global Warming,** p. 129 **TE Freshwater Ecosystem,** p. 131 **TE Rain-forest Nutrients,** p. 132	**SE Quick Lab** Soil Erosion, p. 131*■ **SE Inquiry Lab** Effects of Acid Rain on Seeds, p. 140*■ 🗁 **Exploration Lab** Effects of Acid Precipitation* 🗁 **Inquiry Lab** How Pollutants Affect a Lake*	**SE Reading Toolbox** Hypothesis or Theory, p. 131 **TE Reading Toolbox** Hypothesis or Theory, p. 131	**SE Section Review** **TE Formative Assessment** Spanish Assessment*■ 🗁 **Section Quiz** ■
TE Demonstration Catalytic Converters, p. 134 **SE Cars of the Future,** p. 139	**SE Quick Lab** Recycled Paper, p. 135*■	**SE Reading Toolbox** Venn Diagram, p. 137 **TE Reading Toolbox** Venn Diagram, p. 137	**SE Section Review** **TE Formative Assessment** Spanish Assessment*■ 🗁 **Section Quiz** ■

See also Lab Generator

See also Holt Online Assessment Resources

Resources for Differentiated Instruction

English Learners

TE Visual Literacy, p. 130
TE Identifying Environmental Damage, p. 131
TE Mapping Endangered Organisms, p. 132
🗁 Directed Reading Worksheets*
🗁 Active Reading Worksheets*
🗁 Lab Manuals, Level A*
📓 Study Guide* ■
📓 Note-taking Workbook*
📓 Multilingual Glossary
💿 Interactive Tutor

Struggling Readers

TE Educating the Public, p. 137
🗁 Directed Reading Worksheets*
🗁 Active Reading Worksheets*
🗁 Lab Manuals, Level A*
📓 Study Guide*
📓 Note-taking Workbook*
📓 Special Needs Activities and Modified Tests*
💿 Interactive Tutor

Special Education Students

TE Renewable or Nonrenewable, p. 126
TE Identifying Environmental Damage, p. 126
🗁 Directed Reading Worksheets*
🗁 Active Reading Worksheets*
🗁 Lab Manuals, Level A*
📓 Study Guide* ■
📓 Note-taking Workbook*
📓 Special Needs Activities and Modified Tests*

Alternative Assessment

TE Making a Commitment, p. 135
🗁 Science Skills Worksheets*
🗁 Section Quizzes* ■
📓 Chapter Tests A, B, and C* ■

Overview

The purpose of this chapter is to explain how human activities affect the quality of Earth's environment—specifically how chemical pollution, loss of natural resources, and human population growth affect the environment. The chapter also discusses worldwide efforts that are being undertaken to reduce pollution, as well as steps that students can take to improve or preserve their environment.

READING TOOLBOX

Assessing Prior Knowledge Students should understand the following concepts:
- needs of organisms
- relationship between organisms and the environment

Visual Literacy Direct students' attention to the features of Neversink Pit. Ask how human activities might change these features. (Pollution or rocks falling as a result of human activities might cause the ferns to die.) Tell students that thoughtful planning and dedicated efforts can help protect and preserve the environment.
LS Visual

Chapter 6 — The Environment

Preview

1 An Interconnected Planet
   Humans and the Environment
   Resources
   The Environment and Health

2 Environmental Issues
   Air Pollution
   Global Warming
   Water Pollution
   Soil Damage
   Ecosystem Disruption

3 Environmental Solutions
   Conservation and Restoration
   Reducing Resource Use
   Technology
   Environmental Awareness
   Planning for the Future

Why It Matters

The environment provides the basic support system for all life on Earth, including humans. By taking care of the environment, we take care of ourselves and all other life on Earth.

 The Living Environment
Standard 4 Students will understand and apply scientific concepts, principles, and theories pertaining to the physical setting and living environment and recognize the historical development of ideas in science.
   Key Idea 6 Plants and animals depend on each other and their physical environment. *Major Understandings* - 6.2b
   Key Idea 7 Human decisions and activities have had a profound impact on the physical and living environment. *Major Understandings* - 7.1a, 7.1b, 7.1c, 7.2a, 7.2b. 7.2c, 7.3a, 7.3b

The Neversink Pit in Alabama has recently been bought by local cavers who plan to preserve its ecosystem.

Neversink is an open air pit that is 162 ft deep.

A rare species of fern lives in the Neversink Pit.

Chapter Correlations   *The Living Environment*

Standard 4

6.2b Biodiversity also ensures the availability of a rich variety of genetic material that may lead to future agricultural or medical discoveries with significant value to humankind. As diversity is lost, potential sources of these materials may be lost with it.

7.1a The Earth has finite resources; increasing human consumption of resources places stress on the natural processes that renew some resources and deplete those resources that cannot be renewed.

7.1b Natural ecosystems provide an array of basic processes that affect humans. Those processes include but are not limited to: maintenance of the quality of the atmosphere, generation of soils, control of the water cycle, removal of wastes, energy flow, and recycling of nutrients. Humans are changing many of these basic processes and the changes may be detrimental.

7.1c Human beings are part of the Earth's ecosystems. Human activities can, deliberately or inadvertently, alter the equilibrium in ecosystems. Humans modify ecosystems as a result of population growth, consumption, and technology.

7.2a Human activities that degrade ecosystems result in a loss of diversity of the living and nonliving environment.

7.2b When humans alter ecosystems either by adding or removing specific organisms, serious consequences may result.

7.2c Industrialization brings an increased demand for and use of energy and other resources including fossil and nuclear fuels. This usage can have positive and negative effects on humans and ecosystems.

7.3a Societies must decide on proposals which involve the introduction of new technologies. Individuals need to make decisions which will assess risks, costs, benefits, and trade-offs.

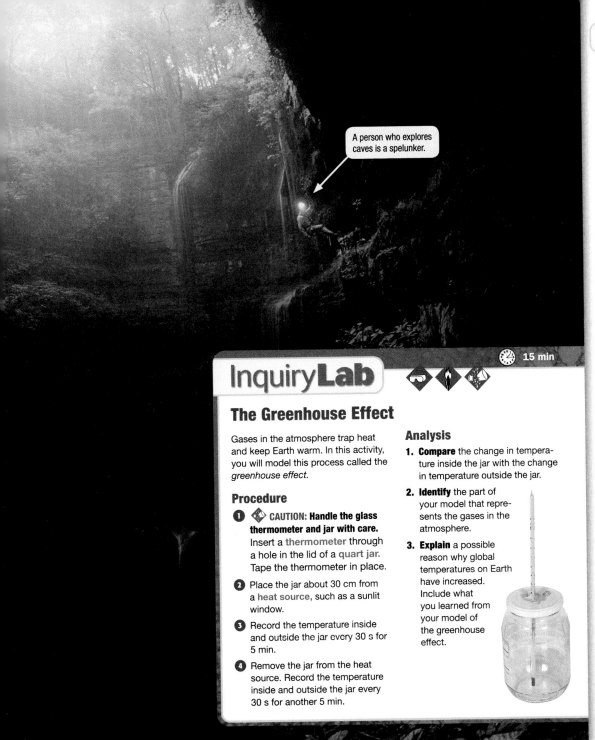

A person who explores caves is a spelunker.

InquiryLab

Teacher's Notes: Precut holes in jar lids. If an MBL/CBL system is not available, have students record the temperature manually every minute for 15 minutes. Use lamps as a heat source if direct sunlight is not available.

Materials
- glass jar with lid
- thermometer
- tape
- heat source

Safety Caution
Have students review safety rules before beginning this exercise.

Answers to Analysis
1. The temperature inside the jar became warmer than the air outside the jar.
2. The glass of the jar represents the gases in the atmosphere.
3. Like the glass jar, certain gases in the atmosphere trap heat. Global temperatures on Earth have increased because the amount of heat-trapping gases in the atmosphere has increased.

Key Resources

Interactive Tutor

InquiryLab

🕑 **15 min**

The Greenhouse Effect

Gases in the atmosphere trap heat and keep Earth warm. In this activity, you will model this process called the *greenhouse effect*.

Procedure

❶ ⚠ **CAUTION: Handle the glass thermometer and jar with care.** Insert a **thermometer** through a hole in the lid of a **quart jar.** Tape the thermometer in place.

❷ Place the jar about 30 cm from a **heat source,** such as a sunlit window.

❸ Record the temperature inside and outside the jar every 30 s for 5 min.

❹ Remove the jar from the heat source. Record the temperature inside and outside the jar every 30 s for another 5 min.

Analysis

1. **Compare** the change in temperature inside the jar with the change in temperature outside the jar.

2. **Identify** the part of your model that represents the gases in the atmosphere.

3. **Explain** a possible reason why global temperatures on Earth have increased. Include what you learned from your model of the greenhouse effect.

7.3b The decisions of one generation both provide and limit the range of possibilities open to the next generation.

READING TOOLBOX

Using Words

1. the variety of living things
2. not populated by trees

Using Language

1. The greenhouse effect is a theory. Scientific tests provide data that shows that certain atmospheric gases, such as carbon dioxide, can trap heat. Tests also show that the amount of carbon dioxide in Earth's atmosphere is increasing.
2. Accept all reasonable answers.

Using Graphic Organizers

The diagram at bottom of the page is one possible way to complete the Venn diagram:

Using Words

Word Parts You can tell a lot about a word by taking it apart and examining its prefix, root, and suffix.

Your Turn Use the information in the table to define the following words.
1. biodiversity
2. deforestation

Word Parts		
Word Part	Type	Meaning
bio-	prefix	life
versi	root	various
de-	prefix	remove
-ation	suffix	a state of being

Using Language

Hypothesis or Theory? To scientists, a theory is a well-supported scientific explanation that makes useful predictions. The main difference between a theory and a hypothesis is that a hypothesis has not been tested, and a theory has been tested repeatedly and seems to correctly explain all the available data.

Your Turn Use information from the chapter to answer the following questions.
1. Is the greenhouse effect a hypothesis or theory? Explain.
2. Write your own hypothesis that explains the increase in global temperatures.

Using Graphic Organizers

Venn Diagrams A Venn diagram is a useful tool for comparing two or three topics in science. A Venn diagram shows which characteristics the topics share and which characteristics are unique to each topic.

Your Turn Create a Venn diagram that describes the characteristics of renewable and nonrenewable resources.
1. Draw a diagram like the one shown here. Draw one circle for each topic. Make sure that each circle partially overlaps the other circles.
2. In each circle, write a topic that you want to compare with the topics in the other circles.
3. In the areas of the diagram where circles overlap, write the characteristics that the topics in the overlapping circles share.
4. In the areas of the diagram where circles do not overlap, write the characteristics that are unique to the topic of the particular circle.

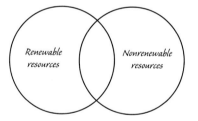

Renewable resources can be replaced at the same rate at which they are consumed — *used to take care of a need* — *Nonrenewable resources* form at a rate that is much slower than the rate at which they are consumed

An Interconnected Planet

Key Ideas	Key Terms	Why It Matters
❯ How are humans and the environment connected? ❯ What is the difference between renewable resources and nonrenewable resources? ❯ How can the state of the environment affect a person's health and quality of life?	fossil fuel	The environment provides the resources that we need to live. When the environment is damaged, our resources are damaged.

We depend on the environment for food, water, air, shelter, fuel, and many other resources. However, human actions can affect the quality and availability of these important resources. The study of the impact of humans on the environment is called *environmental science.*

Humans and the Environment

10,000 years ago, there were only about 5 million people on Earth. The development of dependable food supplies, sanitation, and medical care have allowed the population to grow to more than 6 billion. The population will likely exceed 10 billion before it stabilizes. All 10 billion of these people will need a place to live. Humans now live in almost every kind of ecosystem on Earth. **Figure 1** shows one type of ecosystem in which humans live. As human population increases, the impact of humans on the environment increases. ❯ **Humans are a part of the environment and can affect the resilience of the environment.** The more that the human population grows, the more resources from the environment we will need to survive. Today's humans consume more resources than their ancestors did. The environment does not have an infinite amount of resources with which to meet human's demand.

Earth is an interconnected planet: we depend on the environment, and the environment is affected by our actions. Learning about this connectedness helps us care for the environment and ensures that the environment will continue to support us and other species on Earth.

❯ **Reading check** *How is Earth an interconnected planet? (See the Appendix for answers to Reading Checks.)*

 The Living Environment
Standard 4
7.1a The Earth has finite resources; increasing human consumption of resources places stress on the natural processes that renew some resources and deplete those resources that cannot be renewed.

7.1b Natural ecosystems provide an array of basic processes that affect humans. Those processes include but are not limited to: maintenance of the quality of the atmosphere, generation of soils, control of the water cycle, removal of wastes, energy flow, and recycling of nutrients. Humans are changing many of these basic processes and the changes may be detrimental.

7.1c Human beings are part of the Earth's ecosystems. Human activities can, deliberately or inadvertently, alter the equilibrium in ecosystems. Humans modify ecosystems as a result of population growth, consumption, and technology.

7.2a Human activities that degrade ecosystems result in a loss of diversity of the living and nonliving environment.

7.2b When humans alter ecosystems either by adding or removing specific organisms, serious consequences may result.

Figure 1 This housing development lies in the marshlands along Myrtle Beach, South Carolina. **Can you describe another ecosystem that humans live in?**

Key Resources

 Transparencies
E34 World Population Growth Patterns

Visual Concepts
Human Population

❯ Focus

This section describes how humans and the environment are connected, and explains the difference between renewable and nonrenewable resources.

🔔 Bellringer

Use the Bellringer transparency to prepare students for this section.

❯ Teach

Demonstration

Negative Environmental Impacts So much has been written and said about the negative impact of humans on the environment that students may be "turned off" when the issue is raised. To stimulate their interest, show them a picture that reveals the magnitude of the problem. For example, show a picture of the Fresh Kills landfill in New York State, and emphasize the enormity of the problem at this site. It covers nearly 20 km² (7.7 mi²), and it receives about 15 million kg (34 million lbs) of garbage every day. **LS Visual**

Answers to Caption Questions

Figure 1: Sample answer: grassland prairies of the Midwest, United States

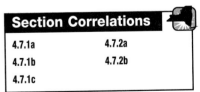
Section Correlations

4.7.1a	4.7.2a
4.7.1b	4.7.2b
4.7.1c	

Teaching Key Ideas

Fossil Fuels Ask students to think of ways they directly use fossil fuels, for example, to provide home heat, to power cars, or to cook food. Then, help them recognize that other energy sources, such as electricity, may originate with fossil fuels. Ask students how their daily life would change if fossil fuels were no longer available. **LS Interpersonal**

Why It Matters

Sustainability The idea of sustainability is key to preventing the loss of natural resources. When a resource is used sustainably, it is consumed only as fast as it is naturally replenished, and therefore it remains abundant. Some resources, such as fossil fuels, groundwater, and topsoil, are replenished only over thousands or millions of years. The creation of these resources proceeds far too slowly to keep up with today's rapid rate of consumption. Living resources, such as trees, are easier to use sustainably because they replace themselves more quickly.

Answers to Caption Questions

Figure 2: Sample answer: Examples of a renewable resource are the fruits and vegetables we eat. Examples of nonrenewable resources are minerals, such as gold or aluminum.

ACADEMIC VOCABULARY

resource anything that can be used to take care of a need

SC*L*INKS.
www.scilinks.org
Topic: Renewable and nonrenewable resources
Code: HX81290

fossil fuel a nonrenewable energy resource formed from the remains of organisms that lived long ago; examples include oil, coal, and natural gas

Figure 2 Windmills produce renewable wind energy, while the oil rig extracts a nonrenewable energy resource. ❯ **Can you think of another example for each renewable and nonrenewable resource?**

Resources

What would your day be like if you didn't have water to drink or electricity to provide lighting and heat? Water and fuel that generates electricity are two of Earth's many <u>resources</u>. Earth's resources are described as renewable or nonrenewable, as shown in **Figure 2**.

Renewable Resources Fresh water, solar energy, and fish are examples of renewable resources. ❯ *Renewable resources* are natural resources that can be replaced at the same rate at which they are consumed. A renewable resource's supply is either so large or so constantly renewed that it will never be used up. However, a resource can be renewable but still be used up if it is used faster than it can be renewed. For example, trees are renewable. But, some forests are being cut down faster than new forests can grow to replace them.

Nonrenewable Resources Many resources that we depend on, such as minerals, coal and oil, are nonrenewable resources. ❯ *Nonrenewable resources* are resources that form at a rate that is much slower than the rate at which they are consumed. Most of our energy today comes from fossil fuels. **Fossil fuels** are nonrenewable energy resources that formed from the remains of organisms that lived long ago. Examples of fossil fuels are coal, oil, and natural gas. Coal, oil, and natural gas are nonrenewable resources because it takes millions of years for them to form. They form from the remains of organisms that were buried by sediment millions of years ago. As sediment accumulated over the remains, heat and pressure increased. Over time, the heat and pressure caused chemical changes that changed the remains into oil and natural gas. We use fossil fuels at a rate that is faster than the rate at which they form. So, when these resources are gone, millions of years will pass before more have formed.

❯ **Reading check** *Explain why natural gas is a nonrenewable resource.*

Renewable Resources
• wind energy
• solar energy
• fresh water
• trees

Nonrenewable Resources
• oil
• coal
• natural gas

Differentiated Instruction

Special Education Students

Renewable or Nonrenewable Show developmentally delayed students objects or pictures of objects. Have them name each object and tell you whether it's made from renewable or nonrenewable resources. **LS Visual**

QuickLab

⏱ 15 min

Contaminated Water 4.7.1c, 4.7.1b

In this activity, you will learn how contaminated water can spread an infectious disease.

Procedure

1. ☠ **CAUTION: Do not taste or touch the fluids used in this lab.** Obtain one test tube of fluid from your teacher. Some test tubes contain pure water. One test tube contains water that has been "contaminated".

2. Pour half your fluid into the test tube of a classmate. Your classmate will then pour an equal amount back into your test tube. Exchange water with three classmates in this way.

3. Your teacher will now put a small amount of a **test chemical** into your test tube. If your water turns cloudy, you have been "contaminated."

Analysis

1. **CRITICAL THINKING** **Analyzing Conclusions** Who had the test tube that started the "infection?"

2. **Identify** a disease that could be spread in water.

The Environment and Health

Our health and quality of life are affected by the state of the environment. ❯ **Pollution and habitat destruction destroy the resources we need to live, such as the air we breathe, the water we drink, and the food we eat.** Air pollution can cause headaches, sore throats, nausea, and upper respiratory infections. Air pollution has also been connected to lung cancer and heart disease. Some chemical pollutants in drinking water can lead to birth defects and cancer. Many infectious diseases, such as cholera, are spread by water polluted by sewage. Habitat destruction can also affect our safety. The root networks of trees help hold soil in place. Cutting down trees increases the number of landslides and floods, which can cause deaths and injuries.

READING TOOLBOX

Word Parts Look up the suffix *-tion* in the dictionary. Also, look up the words *pollute* and *destroy* in a dictionary. Then, write your own definition for *pollution* and *destruction*.

Section 1 Review

❯ KEY IDEAS

1. **Explain** how human population affects the environment.
2. **Describe** the difference between renewable resources and nonrenewable resources.
3. **State** a nonrenewable resource that you used today.
4. **State** three ways that environmental problems may affect human health.

CRITICAL THINKING

5. **Inferring relationships** Events such as floods and landslides are commonly called *natural disasters*. Explain how both natural events and human actions might have contributed to a natural disaster that you have learned about.
6. **Analyzing data** Consider a 1,000-year-old forest and a 30-year-old tree farm. How do differences between these resources affect how renewable the resources are?

WRITING FOR SCIENCE

7. **Evaluating viewpoints** A classmate argues that pollution is a necessary evil to produce food, jobs, and a high standard of living. Write a one-page paper describing your opinion of your classmates argument. Support your opinion with facts.

QuickLab

Teacher's Notes Prepare a test tube with water for each student. Dissolve 1 g of salt in half of the test tubes. The saltwater tubes represent an infectious disease. Do not label the tubes. After students do the water exchange, add 5 mL of aqueous silver nitrate to each test tube. Samples with salt (infectious disease) will become cloudy when silver nitrate is added.

Materials
- salt
- silver nitrate, aqueous
- test tube with clear liquid

Answers to Analysis
1. Answers will vary.
2. cholera

READING TOOLBOX

Word Parts pollution—the act of making dirty; destruction—the act of breaking down **LS** **Verbal**

❯ Close

Formative Assessment

Which term describes a resource that is replenished at a rate that is lower than the rate at which it is used?

A. renewable (Incorrect. The resource would have to be replenished at a higher rate to be renewable.)

B. nonrenewable (Correct! The resource is being depleted.)

C. in equilibrium (Incorrect. The rates would have to be equal for this condition.)

D. infinite (Incorrect. The resource is being depleted, so its supply is not infinite.)

Answers to Section Review

1. The human population affects the environment by using resources, causing pollution, and destroying habitats.

2. A renewable resource can be replaced at the same rate at which the resource is consumed. A nonrenewable resource forms at a rate that is much slower than the rate at which the resource is consumed.

3. Sample answer: Oil is a nonrenewable resource that I used when I rode in a car.

4. Air pollution can cause headaches and respiratory infections. Polluted water can lead to birth defects, cancer, and infectious disease. Deforestation can increase the number of landslides that can cause death and injury.

5. The flooding of the Gulf Coast in 2006 was a natural disaster made worse by the overdevelopment in lowland areas and flood plains.

6. The trees in the tree farm are more renewable because they can be replaced every 30 years. Trees in the forest could be harvested only once every 1,000 years. The forest also has habitats for many other organisms, which would be damaged by its harvest, whereas the tree farm exists specifically to be harvested periodically.

7. Accept all reasonable responses. Make sure students state facts from this section or other sources to support their opinions.

❯ Focus

This section identifies the causes and effects of pollution, acid rain, climate change, erosion, and ecosystem disruption.

🌐 Bellringer

Use the Bellringer transparency to prepare students for this section.

❯ Teach

Demonstration

Environmental Issues Show the class pictures of changes caused by environmental issues such as air and water pollution, erosion, and habitat disruption. Ask students what they think has happened in each picture and why. Then have students list the three environmental issues they think are most important. Compile a class list. After students read this section, return to the list and ask if they would like to make any changes or additions. **LS** **Visual**

Key Ideas

❯ What are the effects of air pollution?

❯ How might burning fossil fuels lead to climate change?

❯ What are some sources of water pollution?

❯ Why is soil erosion a problem?

❯ How does ecosystem disruption affect humans?

Key Terms

acid rain
global warming
greenhouse effect
erosion
deforestation
biodiversity
extinction

Why It Matters

In the course of meeting their basic needs, humans can unintentionally damage the global environment.

The Living Environment
Standard 4

6.2b Biodiversity also ensures the availability of a rich variety of genetic material that may lead to future agricultural or medical discoveries with significant value to humankind. As diversity is lost, potential sources of these materials may be lost with it.

7.1c Human destruction of habitats through direct harvesting, pollution, atmospheric changes, and other factors is threatening current global stability, and if not addressed, ecosystems may be irreversibly affected.

7.2a Human activities that degrade ecosystems result in a loss of diversity of the living and nonliving environment. For example, the influence of humans on other organisms occurs through land use and pollution. Land use decreases the space and resources available to other species, and pollution changes the chemical composition of air, soil, and water.

7.2b When humans alter ecosystems either by adding or removing specific organisms, serious consequences may result. For example, planting large expanses of one crop reduces the biodiversity of the area.

7.2c Industrialization brings an increased demand for and use of energy and other resources including fossil and nuclear fuels. This usage can have positive and negative effects on humans and ecosystems.

Human activities can affect every ecosystem on Earth. Understanding these effects and the problems that they can cause is the first step to successfully solving them.

Air Pollution

Have you ever breathed air that smelled bad or made your lungs burn? The bikers in **Figure 3** have. Natural processes, such as volcanic activity, can affect air quality. However, most air pollution is caused by human activities. Industries, power plants, and vehicles must burn fossil fuels for energy. The burning of fossil fuels releases the pollutants carbon dioxide (CO_2), sulfur dioxide (SO_2), and nitrogen oxides (NO_2 and NO_3) into the air. ❯ **Air pollution causes respiratory problems for people, results in acid rain, damages the ozone layer, and may affect global temperature.**

Acid rain is precipitation that has an unusually high concentration of sulfuric or nitric acids, which is caused by pollution. Acid rain damages forests and lakes. The ozone layer protects life on Earth from the sun's damaging ultraviolet (UV) rays. The ozone layer has been damaged by *chlorofluorocarbons (CFCs)*. CFCs are human-made chemicals that are used as coolants in refrigerators and air conditioners and as propellants in spray cans. Global temperature may be affected by air pollutants. **Global warming** is the gradual increase in the average global temperature.

Figure 3 Workers leaving the steel mill in Baotou, China, wear masks to avoid breathing in the pollution.

Section Correlations

4.6.2b	4.7.2b
4.7.1c	4.7.2c
4.7.2a	

Key Resources

Transparencies
E29 The Greenhouse Effect
E31 Atmospheric Temperature and Carbon Dioxide Levels
E32 Change in Global Temperature
E33 Biological Magnification of DDT

Visual Concepts
Acid Precipitation
Ozone and Ecosystems
Greenhouse Effect
Global Warming
Biological Magnification of Toxins

Why It Matters

Long-Term Effects of Acid Rain Explain that the United States, Canada, and many European nations have reduced sulfur emissions in recent years, but that the lakes and forests damaged by acid rain have not recovered as quickly as hoped. Ask students why they think acid rain has long-term effects. (One reason is that acid rain alters soil chemistry, an effect that may take many decades to reverse.) **LS** **Logical**

① Solar radiation passes through the atmosphere and warms Earth's surface.

② Some heat radiates away from Earth into the atmosphere. Some heat escapes into space.

③ Greenhouse gases also absorb some of the sun's energy and radiate it back toward Earth's surface.

Global Warming

What does it feel like to climb into a car on a hot, sunny day? The inside of the car is hot because the sun's energy passes through the glass windows. The inside of the car absorbs the solar energy and changes it to heat energy. The heat energy cannot easily pass back through the glass windows. Therefore, the heat is trapped and makes the inside of the car hot. The atmosphere traps heat and warms the Earth in a similar way. The **greenhouse effect** is the warming of the surface and lower atmosphere of Earth that happens when greenhouse gases in the air absorb and reradiate heat. Examples of greenhouse gases are CO_2 and water vapor. **Figure 4** shows how this process works.

The greenhouse effect is necessary to keep Earth's temperatures stable. However, Earth's global temperatures have been rising steadily for many decades. Most scientists think that this increase in temperatures is caused by an increase in CO_2. ❯ Burning fossil fuels increases the amount of CO_2 in the atmosphere. Increases in atmospheric CO_2 may be responsible for an increase in global temperatures.

Effects of Global Warming A continued increase in global temperatures has the potential to cause a number of serious environmental problems. For example, ice sheets over Antarctica and Greenland have already started to melt. If these ice sheets continue to melt, they could raise sea levels around the world. Coastal ecosystems would be destroyed. People who live along a coast could lose their homes. Global weather patterns would also be affected. For example, warmer oceans make hurricanes and typhoons more intense and could make such storms more common. Droughts could become more frequent, causing damage to crops. The equilibrium in ecosystems could be altered. Migration patterns of some birds have already changed.

❯ **Reading check** *How might the burning of fossil fuels affect climate?*

CO₂ and Global Temperature Trends, 1960–2005

Source: Scripps Institute of Oceanography and National Oceanic & Atmospheric Administration.

Figure 4 The greenhouse effect is a natural process that keeps Earth warm.
❯ How does the increase in CO_2 relate to global warming?

acid rain precipitation that has a pH below normal and has an unusually high concentration of sulfuric or nitric acids, often as a result of chemical pollution of the air from sources such as automobile exhausts and the burning of fossil fuels

global warming a gradual increase in the average global temperature

greenhouse effect the warming of the surface and lower atmosphere of Earth that occurs when carbon dioxide, water vapor and other gases in the air absorb and reradiate infrared radiation

Why It Matters

Consequences of Global Warming
Ask students how they think the following global changes would affect their community: acid rain, ozone depletion, and global warming. (Accept all answers that are supported with logical reasoning.) **LS** Logical

Answers to Caption Questions
Figure 4: As CO_2 concentrations have increased over the years, so has the global temperature.

Differentiated Instruction

Advanced Learners/GATE

Ozone and Marine Ecosystems Scientists estimate that every 1% drop in upper atmosphere ozone concentration will lead to a 6% rise in skin cancer. Also, certain marine algae (the producers in marine ecosystems) are very sensitive to UV levels. Have students research the possible effects on marine ecosystems of reductions in algal populations. Encourage students to present their findings in a visual display, such as with a graphic organizer or with presentation software. **LS** Visual

Teaching Key Ideas

Agricultural Pollution Ask students what they think is the primary source of water pollution. They may be surprised to learn that agriculture, not industry, has the greatest impact on water quality. Explain that the runoff of silt, pesticides, and fertilizers from farmland is difficult to control because it comes from so many sources rather than a single point, such as a pipe or a smokestack. **LS** Logical

go.hrw.com
✳ interact online

Students can interact with **Figure 5** by going to go.hrw.com and typing in the keyword HX8ENVF5.

Answers to Caption Questions

Figure 5: Sample answer: Three sources of water pollution that might occur in my neighborhood are petroleum storage tank leaks, road salt runoff, and industrial waste.

SCI**LINKS.**
www.scilinks.org
Topic: Chemical
Pollution
Code: HX80272

Figure 5 Pollutants on Earth's surface run off the land and into ground water and other water systems. **>** List the sources of water pollution that might occur in your neighborhood.

go.hrw.com
✳ interact online
Keyword: HX8ENVF5

Water Pollution

Every person needs 20–70 L (5–18 gal) of clean water each day to meet his or her drinking, washing, and sanitation needs. Unfortunately, many sources of water are polluted. **Figure 5** shows major sources of water pollution. **>** Water pollution can come from fertilizers and pesticides used in agriculture, livestock farms, industrial waste, oil runoff from roads, septic tanks, and unlined landfills. Pollution enters groundwater when polluted surface water percolates down through the soil. Oil on roads can be washed into the ground by rain. Pesticides, fertilizers, and livestock waste seep into the ground in a similar way. Landfills and leaking underground septic tanks are also major sources of groundwater pollution.

When pollutants run off land and into rivers, both aquatic habitats and public water sources may be contaminated. For example, the pesticide, DDT, harmed many species, such as the bald eagle. The bald eagle was in danger of becoming extinct until the U.S. restricted the use of DDT in 1972. Pollution can also affect ecosystems. Fertilizers from farms, lawns, and golf courses can run off into a body of water, which increases the amount of nutrients in the water. An increase in some nutrients in a body of water can lead to an excessive growth of algae called a "bloom." Algal blooms can deplete the dissolved oxygen in a body of water. Fish and other organisms then suffocate in the oxygen-depleted water.

> Reading check *List three sources of water pollution.*

Industrial waste

Urban pollutants

Wastewater plant

Runoff

Pesticides

Hazardous waste
injection well

Lawn fertilizer

City

Road
salt

Private well

Landfill

Petroleum
storage tank

Water
table

Septic
system

Municipal
well

Percolation

Aquifer

Differentiated Instruction

Advanced Learners/GATE

Groundwater Contamination Ask students to suggest how chemicals might pollute ground water in urban areas. Explain that underground storage tanks, which hold liquid fuels and industrial chemicals, often leak. In the United States, about one quarter million underground tanks at service stations are thought to be leaking. Have students investigate the methods and costs entailed in disposal of groundwater contaminated with gas or oil and report their findings to the class. **LS** Verbal

English Learners

Visual Literacy Using **Figure 5,** have students identify an example for each of the pollutant types shown. (Sample answers for urban pollution: CO_2 from cars; wastewater from baths, showers, washing machines, dishwashers, and toilets. For runoff: salt, fertilizers, pesticides, and oil.) **LS** Verbal

QuickLab

⏱ 30 min

Soil Erosion 4.7.1b, 4.7.2a

In this lab you will investigate factors that affect erosion.

Procedure

1. Fill **three trays**: one with **sod**, one with **topsoil**, and one with a type of **mulch**.

2. Place each tray at an angle on a "hill" of stacked **textbooks**. Place the same type of **large bowl** at the bottom of each tray to catch the runoff.

3. Pour **2 L of water** slowly and evenly on each tray to simulate heavy rainfall.

4. Use a **scale** to weigh the runoff of soil and water that collected in each bowl.

Analysis

1. **Determine** which tray had the most soil erosion and water runoff. Which tray had the least? Why?

2. **CRITICAL THINKING** **Inferring Conclusions** What does this lab demonstrate about soil erosion?

Soil Damage

Fertile soil allows agriculture to supply the world with food. The United States is one of the most productive farming countries, largely because of its fertile soils. Fertile soil forms from rock that is broken down by weathering. Nutrients that make soil fertile come from the weathered rock as well as from bacteria, fungi and the remains of plants and animals. The processes that form just a few centimeters of fertile soil can take thousands of years. Without fertile soil, we cannot grow crops to feed ourselves or the livestock we depend on.

Soil Erosion The greatest threat to soil is soil erosion. **Erosion** is a process in which the materials of Earth's surface are worn away and transported from one place to another by wind, gravity, or water. ❯ Soil erosion destroys fertile soil that we need in order to produce food. Roots from plants and trees help hold soil together and protect it from erosion. When vegetation is removed, soil is left vulnerable to erosion. Many farming methods can lead to soil erosion. Plowing loosens the topsoil and removes plants that hold the soil in place. The topsoil can then be washed away by wind or rain.

Soil Conservation Sustainable agricultural practices can help conserve fertile soil. For example, *terracing* changes a steep field into a series of flat steps that stop gravity from eroding the soil. Planting a *cover crop,* such as soybeans, restores nutrients to the soil. *Crop rotation,* or planting a different crop every year, slows down the depletion of nutrients in the soil. In *contour plowing,* rows are plowed in curves along hills instead of in straight lines. The rows then act as a series of dams, which prevent water from eroding the soil.

❯ **Reading check** *How does erosion damage soil?*

> **erosion** a process in which the materials of Earth's surface are loosened, dissolved, or worn away and transported from one place to another by a natural agent, such as wind, water, ice, or gravity

READING TOOLBOX

Hypothesis or Theory? A lake in your state has had hundreds of dead fish wash up on shore. Write your own hypothesis that might explain why so many fish in the lake died.

Why It Matters

Freshwater Ecosystems Nitrogen fertilizers and plant and animal wastes can seriously disrupt a freshwater ecosystem. Large amounts of nitrates and phosphates can stimulate explosive algal growth. Then, only the topmost algal layer receives enough light for photosynthesis, while lower layers die and are decomposed by bacteria. These bacteria use up large mounts of dissolved oxygen, slowly suffocating fish and other lake organisms.

Teaching Key Ideas

Rain-forest Deforestation Direct students' attention to the photo on this page. Ask them to identify ecosystem changes that would result now that the forest has been slashed and burned. (soil erosion, temperature increase in area, pollution of water due to soil erosion, decrease in the number of species in the area) **LS Visual**

Why It Matters

Rain-forest Nutrients Explain that rain-forest nutrients are found mostly in living plants and fungi rather than in the soil. When a rain forest is cut down, most of the nutrients are lost when the living organisms are removed. As a result, it takes a very long time for plants to grow back. Ask student to suggest ways that rain-forest farmers might generate income from the forest without cutting down trees. (Many products that come from rain forests can be a source of income. Foods such as nuts, fruits, spices, and coffee; rubber; and medicines are just a few.) **LS Logical**

Answers to Caption Questions

Figure 6: When a forest is cut down, organisms lose their habitat. They cannot find food, shelter, or nesting areas and therefore die.

---

deforestation the process of clearing forests

biodiversity the variety of organisms in a given area, the genetic variation within a population, the variety of species in a community, or the variety of communities in an ecosystem

extinction the death of every member of a species

ACADEMIC VOCABULARY

sustain to maintain or keep in existence

Figure 6 This forest in Brazil was slashed and burned to provide land for cattle and crops. ❯ How does deforestation decrease biodiversity?

Ecosystem Disruption

We share Earth with about 5 million to 15 million species. We depend on many of these species for fulfillment of our basic needs. We get food, clothing, medicines, and building material from many plants and animals. Yet as the human population has grown and affected every ecosystem, this wondrous diversity of life has suffered.

❯ **Ecosystem disruptions can result in loss of biodiversity, food supplies, potential cures for diseases, and the balance of ecosystems that supports all life on Earth.** We cannot avoid disrupting ecosystems as we try to meet the needs of a growing human population. But we can learn about how our actions affect the environment so that we can create ways to conserve it.

Habitat Destruction Over the last 50 years, about half of the world's tropical rain forests have been cut down or burned. The forests have been cleared for timber, pastureland, or farmland, as shown in **Figure 6.** This process of clearing forests is called **deforestation.** Many more thousands of square miles of forest will be destroyed this year. Some of the people who cut down the trees are poor farmers trying to make a living. The problem with deforestation is that as the rain forests and other habitats disappear, so do their inhabitants. In today's world, habitat destruction and damage cause more extinction and loss of biodiversity than any other human activities do.

Loss of Biodiversity Ecosystem disruption decreases the number of Earth's species. Biodiversity affects the stability of ecosystems and the sustainability of populations. **Biodiversity** is the variety of organisms in a given area. Every species plays an important role in the cycling of energy and nutrients in an ecosystem. Each species either depends on or is depended on by at least one other species. When a species disappears, a strand in a food web disappears. If a keystone species disappears, other species may also disappear. The species that disappears may be one that humans depend on.

There are many ways in which humans benefit from a variety of life forms on Earth. Humans have used a variety of organisms on Earth for food, clothing, shelter, and medicine. At least one-fourth of the medicines prescribed in the world are derived from plants. Fewer species of plants could mean fewer remedies for illnesses.

MISCONCEPTION ALERT

Species Preservation Students may think that setting aside a habitat as a park or reserve is the best way to preserve a species. Clarify that "locking away" large tracts of land may not be practical in developing countries that depend on the land for subsistence. The use of extractive reserves preserves habitats while allowing the sustainable harvest of products such as fruits, seeds, and rubber. This allows for a sustainable income and keeping the habitat intact for all species.

Differentiated Instruction

Basic Learners/English Learners

Mapping Endangered Organisms Have students work in groups to identify endangered organisms from several different countries. Provide a large world map and removable tape, and ask them to post small pictures (either hand-drawn or cut from discarded nature magazines) or printouts (from Web sites) of the organisms close to the country or countries they inhabit. Encourage English learners to focus on organisms that live in their native countries. **LS Verbal/Visual**

Figure 7 The zebra mussel (left) is an invasive species that has disrupted the ecosystems of the Great Lakes region. The red panda (right) is an endangered species because its habitat, located in China and Myanmar, is being disrupted. **❯** Name another example of an invasive species. Name three other endangered species.

Invasive Species Humans have disrupted ecosystems by intentionally and unintentionally introducing nonnative species. One example of an invasive species is the zebra mussel, shown in **Figure 7.** In the 1980s, the zebra mussel was unintentionally introduced to the Great Lakes by ships traveling from the Black and Caspian Seas. The zebra mussel disrupted the Great Lakes ecosystem, causing some species to struggle while others flourished. Zebra mussels have also had a negative impact on humans. Zebra mussels clog the pipes of water treatment facilities which costs the public millions of dollars a year.

Extinction Many species are on the edge of extinction. **Extinction** is the death of every member of a species. One species that is at risk of extinction is the red panda. A red panda is shown in **Figure 7.** When a species becomes extinct, we lose forever the knowledge and benefits that we might have gained from the species. For example, two anticancer drugs have been developed from the rosy periwinkle, a flower in Madagascar that is threatened by deforestation. If this flower becomes extinct, a possible source of new drugs is gone.

❯ Reading Check *How has the introduction of the zebra mussel into the Great Lakes affected humans?*

Teaching Key Ideas

Rate of Extinction Inform students that about 1.6 million species have been described and named. Estimates of the total number of species on Earth range from 5 million to 100 million. Tell students to assume that there are 10 million species on Earth. Ask how many species would remain if 20 percent of them became extinct in the next 50 years (8 million) and in the following 50 years. (6.4 million)
LS Logical

❯ Close

Formative Assessment

Which substances are the primary causes of acid rain?

A. chlorofluorocarbons mixing with water (Incorrect. These chemicals damage the ozone layer.)
B. SO_2, NO_2, and NO_3 mixing with water (Correct! Acid rain is precipitation with an unusually high concentration of these acids.)
C. increase in the amount of atmospheric CO_2 (Incorrect. Increases in CO_2 may be responsible for global warming.)
D. fertilizers and pesticides (Incorrect. These materials pollute groundwater.)

Answers to Caption Questions

Figure 7: Sample answer: Rabbits in Australia are an example of an invasive species. The leopard, bighorn sheep, and Florida panther are examples of endangered species.

Section 2 Review

❯ KEY IDEAS
1. **Identify** the affects of air pollution.
2. **Explain** how the burning of fossil fuels, such as oil, might lead to climate change.
3. **Identify** five sources of water pollution.
4. **Explain** why soil erosion is a problem.
5. **List** four ways ecosystem disruption affects humans.

CRITICAL THINKING
6. **Evaluating Viewpoints** A classmate asserts that extinction is not a problem because everything goes extinct eventually. Explain how extinction can be both a natural process and a current problem for society.

USING SCIENCE GRAPHICS
7. **Predicting Patterns** Using the chart, "CO_2 and Global Temperature Trends, 1960–2005," predict temperature and CO_2 levels for the year 2020. Describe how the temperature you predict would affect humans.

Answers to Section Review
1. Air pollution can cause respiratory problems in people, acid rain, damage to the ozone layer, and changes to global climate.
2. The burning of fossil fuels releases CO_2 into the atmosphere. Increases in atmospheric CO_2 may increase global temperatures.
3. industrial waste, lawn fertilizer runoff, leaking landfills, wastewater plants, and livestock farms
4. When topsoil erodes, the remaining soil doesn't have the nutrients plants need to grow.
5. loss of food supplies, loss of shelter and clothing materials, loss of potential cures for diseases, and clogging pipes of water treatment facilities

6. Although extinctions are a natural process, human actions, such as habitat destruction and damage, can increase the rate of extinction.
7. In 2020 the CO_2 concentrations may be up to 400 parts per million, and the temperature may be 0.4°C warmer. Ice sheets may melt further, raising sea levels around the world. Warmer temperatures may lead to more droughts in some areas of the world, resulting in fewer crops and less food. Warmer temperatures may also lead to an increase in the number and intensity of typhoons and hurricanes, which cause death and destruction.

Section **3**
Environmental Solutions

Focus

This section describes strategies for reducing pollution and solving environmental problems.

🔔 Bellringer

Use the Bellringer transparency to prepare students for this section.

Teach

Demonstration

Catalytic Converters Display a catalytic converter or a diagram of one. Explain that a few grams of platinum, palladium or rhodium are embedded in the converter. They act as catalysts in reactions that break down emissions, which would otherwise pass through the car's exhaust system and into the atmosphere. **LS** Visual

Teaching Key Ideas

Environmental Impact Ask students whether an organism exists that does not have an impact on its environment in any way? (No. All organisms use substances from their environment and produce wastes.) **LS** Logical

Answers to Caption Questions
Figure 8: Answers depend on local preserves and restoration projects.

Section Correlations
4.7.3a
4.7.3b

Key Ideas

> How do conservation and restoration solve environmental issues?

> What are three ways that people can reduce the use of environmental resources?

> How can research and technology affect the environment?

> How do education and advocacy play a part in preserving the environment?

> Why is it important for societies to consider environmental impact when planning for the future?

Key Terms
recycling
ecotourism

Why It Matters
Everyone can play an important role in sustaining a healthy environment for all of us.

📺 The Living Environment
Standard 4
7.3a Societies must decide on proposals which involve the introduction of new technologies. Individuals need to make decisions which will assess risks, costs, benefits, and trade-offs.
7.3b The decisions of one generation both provide and limit the range of possibilities open to the next generation.

Protecting the environment is critical to human well-being. With new technologies and the effort of individuals and governments, many environmental problems can be solved.

Conservation and Restoration

Two major techniques for dealing with environmental problems are conservation and restoration. **> Conservation involves protecting existing natural habitats. *Restoration* involves cleaning up and restoring damaged habitats.** The best way to deal with environmental problems is to prevent them from happening. Conserving habitats prevents environmental issues that arise from ecosystem disruption. For example, parks and reserves protect a large area in which many species live.

Restoration reverses damage to ecosystems. Boston Harbor, shown in **Figure 8,** is one restoration success story. Since the colonial period, the city dumped sewage directly into the harbor. The buildup of waste caused outbreaks of disease. Beaches were closed. Most of the marine life disappeared and as a result, the shellfish industry shut down. To solve the problem, the city built a sewage-treatment complex. Since then, the harbor waters have cleared up. Plants and fish have returned, and beaches have been reopened.

> **Reading check** *What is the difference between restoration and conservation?*

Figure 8 Once considered one of the most polluted harbors in the world, Boston Harbor has been cleaned up as part of a restoration project.
> Name a restoration project or natural preserve in your state.

Key Resources

💿 **Visual Concepts**
Recycling
Conservation

QuickLab

Recycled Paper 4.7.3a

In this activity, you will learn how to recycle paper.

⏱ 30 min

Procedure

1. Tear **two sheets of used paper** into small pieces.

2. Put the pieces in a **blender** with **1 L of water**. Cover and blend until the mixture is soupy.

3. Fill a square **pan** with **2–3 cm of water**. Place a **wire screen** in the pan.

4. Pour 250 mL of the paper mixture onto the screen and spread the mixture evenly.

5. Lift the screen and paper mixture out of the water.

6. Place the screen inside a section of **newspaper**. Close the newspaper and turn it over so that the screen is on top of the mixture.

7. Cover the newspaper with a **flat board** and press on the board to squeeze out the water.

8. Open the newspaper and let your paper dry overnight.

Analysis

1. **Evaluate** whether the paper you made is as strong as the paper that it was made from.

2. **CRITICAL THINKING** **Analyzing Methods** How might you improve your technique to produce stronger paper?

Reduce Resource Use

The impact of humanity on the environment depends on how many resources we use. We can decrease our impact by using fewer resources. ❯ We can reduce our use of resources, such as water and fossil fuels for energy. We can reuse goods rather than disposing of them. Furthermore, we can recycle waste to help protect the environment.

Reduce One of the best ways that you can help solve environmental problems is by reducing the amount of energy that you use and the amount of waste that you produce. You can use ceramic plates instead of a disposable paper plate. Low-flow toilets and shower heads can decrease the amount of water used.

Reuse The reuse of goods saves both money and resources. Many things are thrown away and wasted though they are still useful. Plastic bags and utensils can be used several times, rather than only once before disposal.

Recycle The process of reusing things instead of taking more resources from the environment is called **recycling.** Recycling existing products generally costs less than making new ones from raw materials does. For example, recycling aluminum uses about 95 percent less energy than mining and processing the aluminum from Earth does. Recycling also prevents pollution. For example, recycling motor oil keeps toxic substances out of landfills.

❯ **Reading Check** *What are three ways that you can reduce your use of resources?*

ACADEMIC VOCABULARY

impact the effect of one thing on another

recycling the process of recovering valuable or useful materials from waste or scrap

---

Teacher's Notes Remove any glue, tape, or other materials that might be attached to the paper. Soak the paper for at least 30 minutes before students begin the lab.

Materials
- blender, small appliance
- paper (2 sheets)
- water
- wire screen
- flat wood board
- square pan
- newspaper
- beaker, 250 mL

Answers to Analysis
1. The recycled paper is easier to tear than regular paper.
2. Students may suggest using less water or squeezing more water out of the mixture.

Teaching Key Ideas

Conservation Actions Have students brainstorm actions they can take on a daily basis to reduce, reuse, and recycle. (Use less water when bathing; build a compost pile; use reusable plates, cups, and napkins; carpool or ride a bus or a bicycle whenever possible instead of a car; and dry clothes on a line.) **LS Intrapersonal**

Differentiated Instruction

Alternative Assessment

Making a Commitment Have students identify ways they can help the environment. Then have each student carefully consider and select four actions he or she is not already doing and carry out these actions for two weeks. At the end of the period, ask students to write an appraisal of their efforts, addressing how consistently they performed their actions, why some actions were easier than others, and any unexpected benefits or impediments. **LS Intrapersonal**

Teaching Key Ideas

Pollution in History Tell students that large-scale pollution problems are not just recent events. Explain that sediment samples from the beds of lakes in Sweden show that lead concentrations were above natural levels 2,600 years ago. Ice cores removed from Greenland's icecap also have higher lead levels, which started about the same time. The cause most likely was early metal smelting operations in what is now Spain.

SCI **LINKS**.

www.scilinks.org
Topic: Environment
Code: HX80524

Technology

Advances in technology have lead to the production of cars and the development of industry. Both of these processes have contributed to the problem of pollution. But, technology brings not only problems but also environmental solutions. ❯ **Research and technology can help protect our environment by providing cleaner energy sources, better ways to deal with waste, and improved methods for cleaning up pollution.**

Solar panels, shown in **Figure 9,** hybrid cars, and scrubbers are examples of advances in technology. Hybrid cars use a combination of electricity and gasoline as their source of energy. Hybrid cars designed to be fuel-efficient, burn less gasoline and release less pollution into the atmosphere than the average car. Scrubbers are devices that reduce harmful sulfur emissions from industrial smoke-stacks. Scrubbers have decreased emissions of sulfur dioxide, carbon monoxide, and soot by more than 30%!

Researching Solutions Researchers must determine the cause of an environmental problem before they can provide a solution to it. Researching such problems requires the use of scientific methods. Scientists make observations and collect data. After analyzing the data, a scientist may propose a solution to the environmental problem that was studied. Proposals should take into account the costs, risks, and benefits of implementing the solution. Mario Molina is a scientist who researched the effects of CFCs on the ozone layer of the atmosphere. He determined that CFCs damage the ozone layer, which protects us from the sun's harmful ultra-violet radiation. His research convince the nations of the world to limit the use of CFCs.

Research by students can also help solve environmental problems. **Figure 9** shows students trying to find out why the dwarf wedge mussel is disappearing from rivers.

❯ **Reading Check** *How can fuel-efficient hybrid cars help solve environmental problems?*

Figure 9 Students at Keene High School in New Hampshire do field research on dwarf wedge mussels (left). Solar panels in California generate energy without producing pollution (right).

Differentiated Instruction

Basic Learners

Research and Solutions Have groups of students research one of the following issues in their home city, region, or state: (1) characteristics of the groundwater, including its locations; (2) sources and types of pollutants reaching the groundwater; (3) quality and quantity issues in the groundwater; (4) solutions to improving groundwater (5) possible future threats to groundwater quality and/or quantity. Have each group prepare an oral presentation on their topic and present it to the class. **LS Verbal**

Environmental Awareness

Addressing environmental issues requires cooperation among conservation groups, individuals, and governments. Education and advocacy help more individuals take an active role in this process.

❯ Education makes people more aware of environmental issues. Education also shows people how they can help address such issues. Expressing support, or *advocating*, for efforts to protect the environment can help get more people involved in these efforts.

Advocacy Many environmental problems have been solved because of the efforts of those who advocate for a solution. Conservation groups make efforts to educate people, protect land, and influence laws through advocacy. Some organizations work on an international level. Others work on local environmental problems. Some groups help farmers, ranchers, and other landowners ensure the long-term conservation of their land.

Individuals and the media also play an important role in raising awareness of environmental issues. With her 1962 book *Silent Spring*, biologist Rachel Carson made millions of people aware of the dangers of pesticides. Her efforts contributed to the restriction on the use of the dangerous pesticide DDT.

Education Educating the public about the environment helps gain public support for solving environmental issues. Environmental education can enrich people's experience of their world and empower them to care for it. Ecotourism is one way to educate the public about the environment. **Ecotourism** is a form of tourism that supports conservation of the environment. **Figure 10** shows ecotourists in Costa Rica. Ecotourists may learn about the particular environmental problems of an area. Often, an ecotourist is given an opportunity to help solve environmental problems as part of his or her tour.

❯ **Reading check** *How can advocacy and education help solve environmental problems?*

Figure 10 From a skybridge, ecotourists learn about the unique ecosystems at Monteverde Biological Cloud Forest Preserve in Costa Rica, without disturbing wildlife.

READING TOOLBOX

Venn Diagram Make a Venn diagram to help you compare the similarities and differences between advocacy and education relating to environmental science.

ecotourism a form of tourism that supports the conservation and sustainable development of ecologically unique areas

Teaching Key Ideas

Ecotourism Explain to students that a person need not travel to exotic places to participate in ecotourism. A visit to many local, state, and national parks and preserves provides opportunities to learn about and help solve environmental problems. Ask students to tell about any ecotourism opportunities they are familiar with. **LS Intrapersonal**

READING TOOLBOX

Venn Diagram left circle: Advocacy influences laws, helps others to protect the environment, and gets others involved; right circle: Education teaches how environmental problems affect people and how to prevent environmental problems; overlapping circle: Both promote awareness of environmental problems.
LS Verbal/Visual

Differentiated Instruction

Struggling Readers

Educating the Public Ask students to design educational flyers titled "Energy Conservation: What's Your Contribution?" to distribute to classes in the school. The flyers should include examples and ideas of what students and their families can do to conserve energy and to reduce pollution and waste in their community. The ideas and examples should make students and teachers aware of things they can do at school and at home. **LS Kinesthetic**

Basic Learners

Students Project Have the class organize and implement a schoolwide project that addresses one of the environmental concerns discussed in this chapter. **LS Interpersonal**

> **Close**

Formative Assessment

Limiting development in rural coastal areas is _____.

A. conservation (Correct! Preserving a natural habitat is conservation.)

B. restoration (Incorrect. Restoration is restoring the enviroment to its predevelopment state.)

C. recycling (Incorrect. Recycling is resource reuse.)

D. reduction (Incorrect. This term is not related to habitat preservation.)

Answers to Caption Questions

Figure 11: Answers depend on local conservation or restoration projects.

Figure 11 The Fresh Kills landfill (left) occupies 2,200 acres on Staten Island. To the right is the plan for the Fresh Kills of tomorrow. ❯ **In what ways does your community plan to conserve or restore the environment?**

www.scilinks.org
Topic: Solving
Environmental
Problems
Code: HX81424

Planning for the Future

What will our planet look like in 50 years? Will it still supply the basic needs and quality of life that we enjoy today, or will we lack the resources we need? ❯ **Careful planning for the future can help us avoid damaging the environment and can help us solve the environmental issues that we face.** If we want a safe, healthy, bright future, we need to actively aim for it. **Figure 11** shows how Staten Island is planning for the future by turning a landfill into a park.

Society can plan by noting the effects of certain activities, such as development and resource use. For example, if a builder wants to develop an area that is near an aquifer's recharge zone, the local government may evaluate the effects of development on the aquifer. After analyzing risks, costs, and benefits to the community, the government may choose to enforce limitations on the development. When governments plan for the future, they can protect resources for the community for years to come.

❯ **Reading check** *Why do we need to evaluate effects of development before following through with the development?*

Section 3 Review

❯ **KEY IDEAS**

1. **Explain** how conservation might help an endangered species.

2. **Describe** three ways you can reduce the use of environmental resources.

3. **Describe** how research and technology affect the environment.

4. **Explain** how education on the resources that we use can help preserve the environment?

5. **Describe** how planning can prevent damage to the environment.

CRITICAL THINKING

6. **Analyzing Methods** To join a global agreement to fight climate change, the United States must reduce CO_2 levels by 10%. What would be the positive and negative effects on society of such a reduction in CO_2.

METHODS OF SCIENCE

7. **Predicting Outcomes** A land manager proposes planting shrubs to help restore land damaged by erosion. Describe a study or experiment that you could carry out to evaluate whether this proposal will work.

Answers to Section Review

1. Conserving a species' habitat protects the resources that species needs to survive.

2. Reduce the amount of energy used, use ceramic plates instead of disposable ones, and use low-flow shower heads and toilets

3. Research and technology can help provide cleaner energy resources, better ways to deal with waste, and improved methods for cleaning pollution.

4. Knowing where resources come from helps people understand that some resources are limited and should be conserved.

5. Planning where homes will be built can help prevent damaging effects to the area's aquifer.

6. The positive effects of reducing CO_2 levels are cleaner air and possibly reducing global warming. Negative effects might include the need for new, costly technology, such as more efficient scrubbers or vehicles that are more fuel efficient.

7. Use soil, sand, and other materials to make two identical models of the land area being studied. Plant one hill with vegetation. Place the models outdoors, and allow rain to fall on them. Compare the results.

Cars of the Future

For many Americans, a car is a necessity. People rely on cars to get to work, to school, and to run errands. However, most cars are the main contributor of pollutants, such as CO_2, in the atmosphere. To help reduce the amount of pollutants released into the atmosphere, scientists have been developing cars that use nonpolluting forms of energy.

WEIRD SCIENCE

Different Forms of Energy

Scientists have developed many cars of the future that are more fuel efficient than other cars of today or that use nonpolluting forms of energy. The hybrid, a type of car that is becoming popular in the United States, uses electricity as well as gasoline. Some cars of the future run on only solar power! Solar-car races, as shown in the image above right, inspire advancements in car technology through friendly competitions. The FIA Alternative Energies Cup in Japan has solar cars compete in an eight-hour endurance race. Scientists have also developed cars that can run on ethanol and hydrogen. Some day, you may be riding in one of these cars.

Research Many technical universities have teams that compete in solar car races. Conduct Internet research and investigate some of the more successful teams. Create a Web site or poster supporting one of the teams you learn about.

Obvio!—Gas or Ethanol This fuel-efficient Brazilian minicar can run on either gas or ethanol. Ethanol produces less pollution than gas and is renewable. Ethanol is formed from biomass, such as corn or potatoes.

Toyota Fine-N Fuel Cell Hybrid (FCHV) The FCHV doesn't burn fossil fuels. It gets its energy from a fuel cell that produces chemical energy by combining oxygen and hydrogen. The best thing about the fuel cell is that it doesn't produce any pollution. The only byproduct of the fuel cell is water!

Teacher's Notes Motor vehicles add millions of tons of pollutants to the atmosphere each year. Some of these pollutants are toxins that are known to cause cancer. The pollutants also contribute to the problems of acid rain and global warming. Although pollution control methods have drastically reduced the amount of pollutants emitted by motor vehicles in the last 20 years, the number of miles driven during that same period has doubled. The result is even higher levels of atmospheric pollutants in many parts of the United States.

Most hybrid cars on the road today are gasoline-electric hybrids. These cars produce a lot less pollution than gasoline-powered cars. Some hybrids also can get more than 50 miles per gallon of gasoline on the highway compared to around 20 miles per gallon for gasoline-powered cars.

READING TOOLBOX

Visual Literacy Ask students to study the Obvio and name other features that may save fuel. (small size and small engine) Tell students that ethanol can be made from many agricultural products and food wastes. Ethanol vehicles exhibit the same power, acceleration, and cruise speed as conventional vehicles. Ethanol is not toxic at levels likely to be inhaled as a motor fule and is much less flammable than gasoline. **LS Visual**

Answer to Research
Students can find information about solar car races by using an Internet search engine. Tell students to be sure to include information on their poster or Web site about their team's car and how it was developed.

Lab

Time Required

Day 1: 45 minutes
Day 2: 55 minutes
Days 3–10: 15 minutes,
every other day

Ratings

EASY ——————→ HARD

Teacher Prep   🧪🧪🧪
Concept Level   🧪🧪🧪
Student Setup   🧪🧪
Cleanup   🧪🧪

Safety Cautions

Prepare solutions under a ventilated hood. Wear goggles, impermeable gloves, and a lab apron.

Tips and Tricks

Prepare 600 mL of mold inhibitor for 25 students (one part concentrated bleach to four parts water). Prepare solutions of different pH as follows: Use distilled water to dilute 5 mL of 1.0 M sulfuric acid (H_2SO_4) to 1 L to prepare a 0.01 M H_2SO_4 solution with a pH of 2. Dilute 50 mL of the 0.01 M H_2SO_4 solution to 1 L to make a solution with a pH of 3. Repeat this procedure using 5 mL and 0.5 mL of the 0.01 M H_2SO_4 solution to make pH 4 and pH 5 solutions, respectively. Verify the pH of each solution. Allow two days between the start of the experiment and the first observation.

Objectives

▶ Simulate an environmental condition in the laboratory.

▶ Measure the difference between treated and untreated seedlings.

▶ Analzye the effects of acidic conditions on plants.

Materials

- goggles, gloves, and lab apron
- seeds (50)
- beaker (250 mL)
- mold inhibitor (20 mL)
- water, distilled
- paper towels
- solutions of various pH
- pencil, wax (or marker)
- bags, plastic, resealable
- metric ruler
- graph paper

Safety

Effects of Acid Rain		
Solution	Date	Observations

Effects of Acid Rain on Seeds

Living things, such as salamander embryos, can be damaged by acid rain at certain times during their lives. In this lab, you will design an experiment to investigate the effects of acidic solutions on seeds. To do this, you will germinate seeds under various experimental conditions that you determine.

Preparation

1. **SCIENTIFIC METHODS** **State the Problem** How does acid rain affect plants?

2. **SCIENTIFIC METHODS** **Form a Hypothesis** Form a testable hypothesis that explains how a germinating plant might be affected by acid rain. Record your hypothesis.

Procedure

Design an Experiment

❶ Design an experiment that tests your hypothesis and that uses the materials listed for this lab. Predict what will happen during your experiment if your hypothesis is supported.

❷ Write a procedure for your experiment. Identify the variables that you will control, the experimental variables, and the responding variables. Construct any tables that you will need to record your data. Make a list of all of the safety precautions that you will take. Have your teacher approve your procedure before you begin.

Conduct Your Experiment

❸ Put on safety goggles, gloves, and a lab apron.

❹ **CAUTION: The mold inhibitor contains household bleach, which is a toxic chemical and a base.** Place your seeds in a 250 mL beaker, and slowly add enough mold inhibitor to cover the seeds. Soak the seeds for 10 minutes, and then pour the mold inhibitor into the proper waste container. Gently rinse the seeds with distilled water, and place them on clean paper towels.

❺ **CAUTION: Solutions that have a pH below 7.0 are acids.** Carry out your experiment for 7–10 days. Make observations every 1–2 days, and note any changes. Record your observations each day in a data table, similar to the one shown.

❻ Clean up your lab materials according to your teacher's instructions. Wash your hands before leaving the lab.

Lab Correlations

1.2.3c Development of a research plan for testing a hypothesis requires planning to avoid bias (e.g., repeated trials, large sample size, and objective data-collection techniques).

1.2.4 Carry out a research plan for testing explanations, including selecting and developing techniques, acquiring and building apparatus, and recording observations as necessary.

4.7.2b When humans alter ecosystems either by adding or removing specific organisms, serious consequences may result.

Answer to Form a Hypothesis

As the pH of the acid rain decreases, plant growth will decrease.

Sample Data

Seedling Growth* (mm)

Day	pH 3	pH 4	pH 5	Control
1	0	0	0	0
3	12	15	21	25
5	24	27	37	43
7	32	35	50	58

*Lengths recorded are to the nearest millimeter.

Analyze and Conclude

1. **Summarizing Results** Describe any changes in the look of your seeds during the experiment. Discuss seed type, average seed size, number of germinated seeds, and changes in seedling length.

2. **Analyzing Results** Were there any differences between the solutions? Explain.

3. **Analyzing Methods** What was the control group in your experiment?

4. **Analyzing Data** Make graphs of your group's data. Plot seedling growth (in millimeters) on the *y*-axis. Plot number of days on the *x*-axis.

5. **SCIENTIFIC METHODS Interpreting Data** How do acidic conditions appear to affect seeds?

6. **Predicting Outcomes** How might acid rain affect the plants in an ecosystem?

7. **SCIENTIFIC METHODS Critiquing Procedures** How could your experiment be improved?

8. **SCIENTIFIC METHODS Formulating Scientific Questions** Write a new question about the effect of acid rain that could be explored with another investigation.

SC*LINKS*.
www.scilinks.org
Topic: Acid Rain
Code: HX80008

Extensions

9. **Inferring Relationships**
Research to identify the parts of the United States that are most affected by acid rain. Explain why acid rain affects these areas more than it affects other areas.

10. **Analyzing Methods** Describe how factories have changed to reduce the amount of acid rain.

Answers to Procedure

Students should devise their own procedure for this experiment using lab materials. The following is a sample procedure.

1. Label plastic bags *pH 3, pH 4, pH 5,* and *control.*

2. Moisten three layers of paper towels with each solution.

3. Arrange 10 seeds that have been treated with mold inhibitor on one half of each set of treated paper towels. Fold the other half over the seeds. Place paper towels and seeds in the proper bag and seal the bag.

4. Record the number of seeds germinated and the length of each seedling. Note any other changes in the seedlings.

5. After each observation, re-wet the paper towels with the same solution as noted on each bag. Return the seeds to the bag.

Answers to Analyze and Conclude

1. Answers will vary.

2. The solutions each had a different pH.

3. The seeds germinated in distilled water were the control.

4. See the sample data.

5. In general, very acidic conditions inhibit seedling growth.

6. Acidic rain might inhibit plant growth or kill plants.

7. Students may suggest increasing the sample size in each group.

8. Sample answer: What are the effects of acidic solutions on mature plants?

Answers to Extensions

9. Upstate New York and other eastern states, the Pacific Northwest, and several Midwestern states are most affected. These areas have heavy industries, many of which produce gases that make up acid rain.

10. Industries have installed devices that remove sulfur and nitrogen compounds from industrial emissions before they reach the atmosphere.

SUPER SUMMARY

Have students connect the major concepts in this chapter through an interactive Super Summary. Visit **go.hrw.com** and type in keyword **HX8ENVS**.

Reteaching Key Ideas

Ecosystem Interdependence Ask students to write a short essay on ecosystem interdependence and to hypothesize how damage to one ecosystem can affect other ecosystems. **LS** Verbal

Ecological Consequences Have students prepare an outline for a movie script about an actual ecological disaster. Students should include the actual consequences of the disaster. **LS** Verbal

Environmental Issues Display Have the class create a display titled "Human Impact on the Environment" to inform the rest of the school about the severity of the environmental issues raised in this chapter. The display should cover a range of issues, provide specific information, and show possible solutions and ways individuals can make a difference. Make arrangements to place the display where it will be viewed by the entire student body. **LS** Visual

Key Ideas	Key Terms

1 An Interconnected Planet

> Humans are a part of the environment and can affect the resilience of the environment.

> Renewable resources are natural resources that can be replaced at the same rate at which they are consumed.

> Nonrenewable resources are resources that form at a rate that is much slower than the rate at which they are consumed.

> Pollution and habitat destruction destroy the resources we need to live, such as the air we breathe, the water we drink, and the food we eat.

fossil fuel (126)

2 Environmental Issues

> Air pollution causes respiratory problems for people, results in acid rain, damages the ozone layer, and affects global temperature.

> Burning fossil fuels increases the amount of CO_2 in the atmosphere. Increases in atmospheric CO_2 may be responsible for an increase in global temperatures.

> Water pollution can come from fertilizers and pesticides used in agriculture and from livestock farms, industrial waste, oil runoff from roads, septic tanks, and unlined landfills.

> Soil erosion destroys fertile soil that we need in order to produce food.

> Ecosystem disruptions can result in loss of biodiversity, food supplies, potential cures for diseases, and the balance of ecosystems that supports all life on Earth.

acid rain (128)
global warming (128)
greenhouse effect (129)
erosion (131)
deforestation (132)
biodiversity (132)
extinction (133)

3 Environmental Solutions

> Conservation involves protecting existing natural habitats. Restoration involves cleaning up and restoring damaged habitats.

> We can reduce our use of natural resources, such as water and fossil fuels for energy. We can reuse goods rather than disposing of them. Furthermore, we can recycle waste to help protect the environment.

> Research and technology can help protect our environment by providing cleaner energy sources, better ways to deal with waste, and improved methods for cleaning up pollution.

> Education makes people more aware of environmental issues and of ways that they can help. Expressing support, or *advocating*, for efforts to protect the environment can help get more people involved.

> Careful planning for the future can help us avoid damaging the environment and solve environmental issues that we currently face.

recycling (135)
ecotourism (137)

Regents Exam Practice

PART A: Answer all questions in this part.

Directions: For each statement or question, write on your separate answer sheet the number of the word or expression that best completes the statement or answers the question.

1 Which human activity would have the most positive effect on the environment of an area?
(1) using fire to eliminate most plants in the area
(2) clearing the area to eliminate weed species
(3) protecting native flowers and grasses in the area
(4) introducing a foreign plant species to the area

2 A forest is cut down and is replaced by a cornfield. A negative consequence of this practice is
(1) an increase in the carbon dioxide released into the atmosphere
(2) an increase in the size of predators
(3) a decrease in biodiversity
(4) a decrease in the amount of soil that is washed away during rainstorms

3 A change in the acidity of mountain lakes would most likely be a result of
(1) ecological succession of the area at the top of the mountain
(2) the introduction of new species into the lakes
(3) air pollution from smoke stacks miles away
(4) planting grasses and shrubs around the lakes

4 Continued depletion of the ozone layer will most likely result in
(1) an increase in skin cancer among humans
(2) a decrease in atmospheric pollutants
(3) an increase in marine ecosystem stability
(4) a decrease in climatic changes

5 Which human activity would have the least negative impact on the quality of the environment?
(1) adding animal wastes to rivers
(2) cutting down tropical rain forests for plywood
(3) using species-specific sex attractants to trap and kill insect pests
(4) releasing chemicals into the groundwater

6 Which long-term change could directly cause the other three?
(1) pollution of air and water
(2) increasing human population
(3) scarcity of suitable animal habitats
(4) depletion of resources

7 Water from nearby rivers or lakes is usually used to cool down the reactors in nuclear power plants. The release of this heated water back into the river or lake would most likely result in
(1) an increase in the sewage content in the water
(2) a change in the biodiversity in the water
(3) a change in the number of mutations in plants growing near the water
(4) a decrease in the amount of sunlight necessary for photosynthesis in the water

8 Some organizations are buying up sections of forest land. Once purchased, these sections of forest will never be cut down. The main reason for protecting these sections of forest is to
(1) cause the extinction of undesirable animal species.
(2) prevent these trees from reproducing too fast.
(3) maintain the diversity of the living environment.
(4) provide more land for agricultural purposes.

9 The rapid destruction of tropical rain forests may be harmful because
(1) removing trees will prevent scientists from studying ecological succession.
(2) genetic material that may be useful for future medical discoveries will be lost.
(3) energy cycling in the environment will stop.
(4) the removal of trees will limit the construction of factories that will pollute the environment.

10 Which of the following is a result of ecosystem disruption?
(1) acid rain
(2) global warming
(3) greenhouse effect
(4) loss of biodiversity

Regents Exam Practice Correlations

4.6.2b 9	**4.7.2a** 12, 13
4.7.1b 4, 15	**4.7.2b** 1, 2
4.7.1c 3, 5, 6, 7, 8, 11, 14	

PART A

1. **(3)** Choices that discuss using fire in a non-specific way, clearing native plants, and introducing non-native plants to an area will not benefit the environment. Rather, these events are likely to have a negative impact on habitats. *(#22, June 2006 Regents Exam)*

2. **(3)** The choice about cornfields is incorrect as only bare soil would wash away during intense rain. The choice about increasing predators is not true. Replacing a forest with corn fields will not significantly increase carbon dioxide levels. *(#30, January 2006 Regents Exam)*

3. **(3)** Planting grasses and shrubs would not create acid lakes. Introducing new species would not acidify lakes, either. Succession is not known to be associated with acidifying lakes, unlike air pollution. *(#29, January 2006 Regents Exam)*

4. **(1)** A decrease in atmospheric ozone would not necessarily decrease climatic changes and atmospheric pollutants, or increase marine ecosystem stability. It would, however, intensify the amount of ultraviolet radiation reaching earth's surface. *(#28, January 2006 Regents Exam)*

5. **(3)** Adding wastes or chemicals to water can be harmful to the environment. Cutting down tropical rainforests can also damage habitats. Trapping insect pests that are already in excess is usually not a danger to the environment. *(#30, August 2006 Regents Exam)*

6. **(2)** An increasing human population can lead to the replacement of habitats, depletion of resources for use by other organisms, and pollution of air and water. *(#27, August 2005 Regents Exam)*

7. **(2)** The choice about sewage is incorrect as sewage is a product of human, household, and industrial wastes. The choice about mutation is incorrect as this should affect organisms in the water. The choice about sunlight is untrue. However, nuclear waste could affect the biodiversity of organisms in the water. *(#24, June 2005 Regents Exam)*

8. (3) Conservation efforts such as keeping sections of a forest as they are, aim to maintain the diversity of the forest environment. Such efforts should not result in the extinction of undesirable animal species, or prevent trees from reproducing "too fast". *(#24, January 2005 Regents Exam)*

9. (2) The removal of trees would not prevent scientists from studying succession. Energy cycling may be slowed down by destruction of rainforests, but it would not stop. Nor would the removal of trees curtail the construction of factories. The loss of tropical rain forests causes the destruction and extinction of many types of plants, insects, and animals, which makes them unavailable for scientific study. *(#25, January 2005 Regents Exam)*

10. (4) Acid rain, global warming, and the greenhouse effect can all contribute to ecosystem disruption, but only loss of bio-diversity is likely to be a result of ecosystem disruption.

PART B

11. (2) The questions states that the inorganic compounds are harmless so it is unlikely that the modified bacteria will interfere with the environment. Removing a few pollutants is not a negative effect, but rather, it is the positive effect. If bacteria are human derived, they will probably not cause human disease and they are unlikely to produce more pollutants. However, they may out-compete native bacteria. *(#25, August 2006 Regents Exam)*

PART C

12. Allow a maximum of 3 credits for discussing the use of pesticides to control the mosquito population, allocated as follows: Allow 1 credit for stating one advantage of killing all of the mosquitoes. Acceptable responses include, but are not limited to: Killing all the mosquitoes will end the West Nile virus infections of people.; People will get fewer mosquito bites.; Allow 1 credit for stating one disadvantage of killing all of the mosquitoes. Acceptable responses

include, but are not limited to: Killing all the mosquitoes will reduce the food supply for bats and birds.; Fish that rely on mosquito larvae for food will have less food.; Allow 1 credit for stating one danger to humans of spraying pesticides into the air. Acceptable responses include, but are not limited to: Pesticides can enter food and water supplies (causing illness).; People may breathe in the pesticide. *(#60, January 2006 Regents Exam)*

13. Allow a maximum of 3 credits for describing a cause and an effect of deforestation and a way to lessen this effect, allocated as follows: Allow 1 credit for stating one reason deforestation is occurring. Acceptable responses include, but are not limited to: There is a great

PART B

11 Bacteria that are removed from the human intestine are genetically engineered to feed on organic pollutants in the environment and convert them into harmless inorganic compounds. Which row in the table below best represents the most likely negative and positive effects of this technology on the ecosystem?

Row	Negative Effect	Positive Effect
(1)	Inorganic compounds interfere with cycles in the environment.	Human bacteria are added to the environment.
(2)	Engineered bacteria may out-compete native bacteria.	The organic pollutants are removed.
(3)	Only some of the pollutants are removed.	Bacteria will make more organic pollutants.
(4)	The bacteria will cause diseases in humans.	The inorganic compounds are buried in the soil.

(1) 1
(2) 2
(3) 3
(4) 4

12 Which statement describes what most likely happened to the dodo bird within 100 years of the arrival of humans on Mauritius?
(1) Dodo birds developed the ability to fly in order to escape predation and their population increased.
(2) The dodo bird population increased after the birds learned to build their nests in trees.
(3) Human exploitation and introduced species significantly reduced dodo bird populations.
(4) The dodo bird population became smaller because they preyed upon the introduced species.

PART C

13 Mosquitoes are eaten by many birds and bats. In the New York City area, mosquitoes have been found to transmit West Nile Virus to some people who have been bitten by a mosquito carrying this virus. As a result, New York City health officials have sprayed pesticides into the air in order to kill as many mosquitoes as possible.

Discuss the use of pesticides to control the mosquito population. In your answer be sure to:
- state *one* advantage of killing all of the mosquitoes
- state *one* disadvantage of killing all of the mosquitoes
- state *one* danger to humans of spraying pesticides in the air

demand for lumber for building new homes and other structures.; Forested areas are being cut down to allow for grazing areas for animals.; Allow 1 credit for stating one environmental problem that results from widespread deforestation. Acceptable responses include, but are not limited to: Habitats are lost.; When many trees are cut down, the carbon dioxide they would normally use remains in the atmosphere (and may intensify the process of global warming).; Deforestation promotes erosion.; Allow 1 credit for stating one way to lessen the effects of deforestation other than planting trees. Acceptable responses include, but are not limited to: protect present forested areas;

14 Deforestation is viewed as a problem in the world today. Describe a cause and an effect of deforestation and a way to lessen this effect. In your answer, be sure to:

- state *one* reason deforestation is occurring
- state *one* environmental problem that results from widespread deforestation
- state *one* way to lessen the effects of deforestation, other than planting trees

15 Currently, Americans rely heavily on the burning of fossil fuels as sources of energy. As a result of increased demand for energy sources, there is a continuing effort to find alternatives to burning fossil fuels. Discuss fossil fuels and alternative energy sources. In your answer be sure to:

- state one disadvantage of burning fossil fuels for energy
- identify one energy source that is an alternative to using fossil fuels
- state one advantage of using this alternative energy source
- state one disadvantage of using this alternative energy source

16 For over 100 years scientists have monitored the carbon dioxide concentrations in the atmosphere in relation to changes in the atmospheric temperature. The graphs below show the data collected for these two factors.

On a separate piece of paper, discuss the overall relationship between carbon dioxide concentration and changes in atmospheric temperature and the effect of these factors on ecosystems. Your answer must include:

- a statement identifying the overall relationship between the concentration of carbon dioxide and changes in atmospheric temperature
- one way in which humans have contributed to the increase in atmospheric carbon dioxide
- one specific negative effect the continued rise in temperature would be likely to have on an ecosystem
- one example of how humans are trying to reduce the problem of global warming

water is not available worldwide. (*#59, August 2006 Regents Exam*)

15. Allow a maximum of 4 credits for discussing the overall relationship between carbon dioxide concentration and changes in atmospheric temperature and the effect of these factors on ecosystems, allocated as follows: Allow 1 credit for indicating that as CO^2 increases, the atmospheric temperature increases.; Allow 1 credit for stating one way in which humans have contributed to the increase in atmospheric carbon dioxide. Acceptable responses include, but are not limited to: deforestation; combustion; increasing human population. Note: Do not allow credit for pollution unless a specific source of pollution is mentioned.; Allow 1 credit for stating one specific negative effect the continued rise in temperature would be likely to have on an ecosystem. Acceptable responses include, but are not limited to: Increased ocean temperatures will destroy fish.; Polar ice could melt and flood land.; may cause extinction of organisms; may cause change in population numbers; Allow 1 credit for stating one example of how humans are trying to reduce the problem of global warming. Acceptable responses include, but are not limited to: plant more trees; reduce the use of fossil fuels; use alternative energy sources; carpool; recycling (*#58, June 2005 Regents Exam*)

allow succession to take place on deforested land; reduce the amount of CO2 that is released to the atmosphere; recycle paper; cut down fewer trees (*#62, June 2006 Regents Exam*)

14. Allow a maximum of 4 credits for discussing fossil fuels and alternative energy sources, allocated as follows: Allow 1 credit for stating one disadvantage of burning fossil fuels for energy. Acceptable responses include, but are not limited to: They pollute the atmosphere.; They lead to acid rain.; They lead to global warming.; Fossil fuels are a limited resource. Allow 1 credit for identifying one energy source that is an alternative to using fossil fuels. Acceptable responses include, but are not limited to: solar energy; windmills; water power; nuclear fuels. Allow 1 credit for stating one advantage of using the alternative energy source identified. Acceptable responses include, but are not limited to: does not pollute the environment (solar energy); is renewable (water power); Fossil fuels are not burned. (nuclear). Allow 1 credit for stating one disadvantage of using the alternative energy source identified. Acceptable responses include, but are not limited to: Windmills are very noisy.; Dams built for water power destroy habitats.; Nuclear fuels produce dangerous wastes.; high cost of changing technology; Sufficient solar, wind, or

UNIT 3 Cells

7 Cell Structure

8 Cells and Their Environment

9 Photosynthesis and Cellular Respiration

10 Cell Growth and Division

 The Living Environment

Standard 4 Students will understand and apply scientific concepts, principles, and theories pertaining to the physical setting and living environment and recognize the historical development of ideas in science.

Key Idea 1 Living things are both similar to and different from each other and from nonliving things.

Key Idea 2 Organisms inherit genetic information in a variety of ways that result in continuity of structure and function between parents and offspring.

Key Idea 3 Individual organisms and species change over time.

Key Idea 5 Organisms maintain a dynamic equilibrium that sustains life.

Key Idea 6 Plants and animals depend on each other and their physical environment.

Macrophage (purple) attack on a cancer cell (yellow)

Sex chromosomes of a human male: Y (left) and X (right)

Human motor
neuron

DISCOVERIES IN SCIENCE

Cell Biology

1665

Robert Hooke builds a microscope to look at tiny objects. He discovers cells after observing a thin piece of cork under a microscope. He also finds cells in plants and fungi.

Hooke's microscope

1772

British clergyman and chemist, Joseph Priestly, presents his paper, *On Different Kinds of Air,* in which he describes his discovery of oxygen and other previously-unknown gases found in air. He also demonstrates that oxygen is produced by plants.

1839

Theodor Schwann shows that all animal tissue is made of cells. With plant biologist, Matthias Schleiden, Schwann identifies cell components, such as membranes and a nucleus common, to many eukaryotic cells.

1855

Rudolf Virchow publishes a theory stating that all cells come from another cells. He explains, "Where a cell exists, there must have been a preexisting cell."

Animal cells

1945

Keith R. Porter, Albert Claude, and Ernest F. Fullam publish the first electromicrograph of a cell. Small organelles, such as the endoplasmic reticulum and the Golgi apparatus, are visible for the first time.

LATE 1950s

Canadian scientists Ernest McCulloch and James Till begin research on stem cells in rodents. Bone marrow stem cells can produce several types of blood cells.

Bone marrow stem cell

1971

Lynn Margulis proposes the endosymbiotic theory of the origins of cell organelles. This theory states that chloroplasts and mitochondria in eukaryotes evolved from prokaryotes.

Lynn Margulis

2004

Richard Axel, and Linda Buck earn the Noble Prize in Medicine or Physiology for their discovery of how olfactory cells detect odors and how the brain processes information to provide a sense of smell.

Microtubules (green) and chromosomes (blue) in a dividing cell

BIOLOGY CAREER

Cell Biologist
Shubha Govind

Shubha Govind is a professor of biology at City College, City University of New York. Govind considers her most important scientific contribution to be developing a model system for using genetic tools to study the molecular basis of host-parasite interaction in fruit flies. She is studying how blood cells of fruit flies are formed and how they guard against infections when flies are attacked by parasites. She is also studying how parasites have evolved to overcome the immune reactions of the fly.

Govind grew up in India, and her family traveled a lot. As she traveled, she was impressed with the diversity of flora and fauna in different parts of the country. By the time she reached middle school, she knew that she wanted to be a biologist.

Apart from science, Govind enjoys reading, listening to music and spending time with family and friends.

Freeze fracture of cell

Cell Structure

	Standards	Teach Key Ideas

CHAPTER OPENER, pp. 148–149 `15 min.`

The Living Environment

SECTION 1 Introduction to Cells, pp. 151–155 `45 min.`

› **The Discovery of Cells**
› **Looking at Cells**
› **Cell Features**

Standards: 4.1.2f, 4.1.2g, 4.1.2i, 4.2.1f, 4.3.1j

Teach Key Ideas:

Bellringer Transparency

Transparencies A10 Metric Units of Length and Equivalents • A4 Objects Size and Magnifying Power of Microscopes • A5 Compound Light Microscope • B2 Relationship Between Surface Area and Volume • B8 Structure of Lipid Bilayer • B9 Organelles

Visual Concepts Types of Microscopes • Magnification and Resolution • Parts of a Light Microscope • Cell Theory • Cell Membrane • Cytoplasm • Ribosomes • Internal Organization of a Cell • Parts of a Prokaryotic Cell • Parts of a Cell Wall

---

SECTION 2 Inside the Eukaryotic Cell, pp. 156–161 `60 min.`

› **The Framework of the Cell**
› **Directing Cellular Activity**
› **Protein Processing**
› **Storage and Maintenance**
› **Energy Production**

Standards: 4.1.2f, 4.1.2i, 4.5.1b, 4.5.1d, 4.5.3a

Teach Key Ideas:

Bellringer Transparency

Transparencies B13 Processing of Proteins • B12 Mitochondrion

Visual Concepts Cytoskeleton • Nucleus of a Cell • Endoplasmic Reticulum (ER) and Ribosomes • Golgi Apparatus • Mitochondrion • Chloroplasts • Vacuoles

---

SECTION 3 From Cell to Organism, pp. 162–166 `90 min.`

› **Diversity in Cells**
› **Levels of Organization**
› **Body Types**

Standards: 4.1.2a, 4.1.2e, 4.2.1k

Teach Key Ideas:

Bellringer Transparency

Transparencies B4 Animal Cells

Visual Concepts Structure of Cilia and Flagella • Comparing Prokaryotes and Eukaryotes • Parts of an Animal Cell • Comparing Plant and Animal Cells • Parts of a Plant Cell

See also PowerPoint® Resources

Chapter Review and Assessment Resources

SE Super Summary, p. 168
SE Regents Exam Practice, p. 169
Regents Review Guide
Review Resources
Chapter Tests A and B
Holt Online Assessment
Regents Question Banks on Teacher's One-Stop Planner

CHAPTER
Fast Track
Thorough instruction will require the times shown.

Basic Learners

TE Magnification, p. 152
TE What Am I?, p. 158
TE 3-D Representations, p. 159
TE Body Systems, p. 164
Directed Reading Worksheets*
Active Reading Worksheets*
Lab Manuals, Level A*
Study Guide* ■
Note-taking Workbook*
Special Needs Activities and Modified Tests*

Advanced Learners

TE Specimen Size, p. 153
TE Mitochondria, p. 160
TE Behavior of Cell Colonies, p. 165
Critical Thinking Worksheets*
Concept Mapping Worksheets*
Science Skills Worksheets*
Lab Datasheets, Level C*

Why It Matters	Hands-On	Skills Development	Assessment
Build student motivation with resources about high-interest applications.	SE **Inquiry Lab** Is It Alive?, p. 149*■	TE **Reading Toolbox** Assessing Prior Knowledge, p. 148 SE **Reading Toolbox,** p. 150	
TE **Bacteria in Yogurt,** p. 151 SE **Cell Shape,** p. 152 TE **Prokaryote Diversity,** p. 154	📁 **Quick Lab** Modeling Cells: Surface Area to Volume* 📁 **Skills Practice Lab** Using a Microscope*	TE **Reading Toolbox** Visual Literacy, p. 152 TE **Math Skills** Surface Area–to-Volume Ratio, p. 153 SE **Reading Toolbox** Word Parts, p. 155 TE **Reading Toolbox** Word Parts, p. 155	SE **Section Review** TE **Formative Assessment** Spanish Assessment*■ 📁 **Section Quiz**■
TE **Amoeboid Movement,** p. 156 TE **Demonstration** Observing Cell Structure, p. 157 TE **Lysosmal Malfunction,** p. 158 TE **Filtering Out Toxins,** p. 158 TE **History Connection,** p. 159	SE **Quick Lab** Model Cell Parts, p. 160*■	SE **Reading Toolbox** Process Chart, p. 158 TE **Reading Toolbox** Process Chart, p. 158	SE **Section Review** TE **Formative Assessment** Spanish Assessment*■ 📁 **Section Quiz**■
TE **Diversity,** p. 162 TE **Endosymbiosis,** p. 163 TE **Career Development,** p. 164 TE **Cryogenics,** p. 165	SE **Quick Lab** Colonies On the Move, p. 165*■ SE **Skills Practice Lab** Plant Cell Observation, p. 167*■	TE **Reading Toolbox** Fold Notes, p. 162 SE **Reading Toolbox** Similes, p. 164 TE **Reading Toolbox** Similes, p. 164	SE **Section Review** TE **Formative Assessment** Spanish Assessment*■ 📁 **Section Quiz**■

See also Lab Generator

See also Holt Online Assessment Resources

Resources for Differentiated Instruction

English Learners

TE Paired Reading, p. 157
TE Reading Organizer, p. 163
📁 Directed Reading Worksheets*
📁 Active Reading Worksheets*
📁 Lab Manuals, Level A*
📖 Study Guide*■
📖 Note-taking Workbook*
📖 Multilingual Glossary
💿 Interactive Tutor

Struggling Readers

TE TE Paired Reading, p. 157
📁 Directed Reading Worksheets*
📁 Active Reading Worksheets*
📁 Lab Manuals, Level A*
📖 Study Guide*
📖 Note-taking Workbook*
📖 Special Needs Activities and Modified Tests*
💿 Interactive Tutor

Special Education Students

TE Cell Model, p. 154
📁 Directed Reading Worksheets*
📁 Active Reading Worksheets*
📁 Lab Manuals, Level A*
📖 Study Guide*■
📖 Note-taking Workbook*■
📖 Special Needs Activities and Modified Tests*

Alternative Assessment

TE Fold Notes, p. 157
📁 Science Skills Worksheets*
📁 Section Quizzes*■
📖 Chapter Tests A, B, and C*■

Chapter 7

Chapter 7 Cell Structure

Overview

The purpose of this chapter is to describe the relationships between structure and function at the cellular and sub-cellular levels of an organism. The structural features of cells and the differences between prokaryotes and eukaryotes are described. A study of cell organelles confirms that proper functioning of all cell structures is needed to maintain homeostasis.

READING TOOLBOX

Assessing Prior Knowledge Students should understand the following concepts:
- the function of ATP
- microscope use and slide preparation
- micro measurements
- surface area and volume

Visual Literacy Ask students to study the picture of *Lembadion bullinum*. What features does this organism have that would indicate that it is living? (It has a mouth.) Explain that this organism is a predatory protist— a type of single-celled organism. It preys on smaller single-celled organisms that exist in its environment. Its large mouth allows it to engulf its prey. When the prey is larger, populations of *Lembadion bullinum* are composed of larger individuals. Have interested students research this organism.

Preview

1 Introduction to Cells
The Discovery of Cells
Looking at Cells
Cell Features

2 Inside the Eukaryotic Cell
The Framework of the Cell
Directing Cellular Activity
Protein Processing
Storage and Maintenance
Energy Production

3 From Cell to Organism
Diversity in Cells
Levels of Organization
Body Types

Why It Matters

All living things are made of cells. Scientists study how cells work to understand life.

 The Living Environment
Standard 4 Students will understand and apply scientific concepts, principles, and theories pertaining to the physical setting and living environment and recognize the historical development of ideas in science.
Key Idea 1 Living things are both similar to and different from each other and from nonliving things. *Major Understandings* - 1.2a, 1.2e, 1.2f, 1.2g, 1.2i
Key Idea 2 Organisms inherit genetic information in a variety of ways that result in continuity of structure and function between parents and offspring. *Major Understandings* - 2.1f, 2.1k
Key Idea 3 Individual organisms and species change over time. *Major Understandings* - 3.1j
Key Idea 5 Organisms maintain a dynamic equilibrium that sustains life. *Major Understandings* - 5.1b, 5.1d, 5.3a

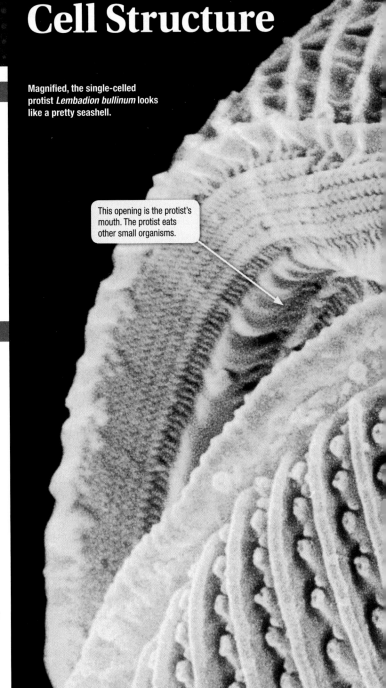
Magnified, the single-celled protist *Lembadion bullinum* looks like a pretty seashell.

This opening is the protist's mouth. The protist eats other small organisms.

Chapter Correlations   The Living Environment

Standard 4

1.2a Important levels of organization for structure and function include organelles, cells, tissues, organs, organ systems, and whole organisms.

1.2e The organs and systems of the body help to provide all the cells with their basic needs. The cells of the body are of different kinds and are grouped in ways that enhance how they function together.

1.2f Cells have particular structures that perform specific jobs. These structures perform the actual work of the cell. Just as systems are coordinated and work together, cell parts must also be coordinated and work together.

1.2g Each cell is covered by a membrane that performs a number of important functions for the cell. These include: separation from its outside environment, controlling which molecules enter and leave the cell, and recognition of chemical signals. The processes of diffusion and active transport are important in the movement of materials in and out of cells.

1.2i Inside the cell a variety of specialized structures, formed from many different molecules, carry out the transport of materials (cytoplasm), extraction of energy from nutrients (mitochondria), protein building (ribosomes), waste disposal (cell membrane), storage (vacuole), and information storage (nucleus).

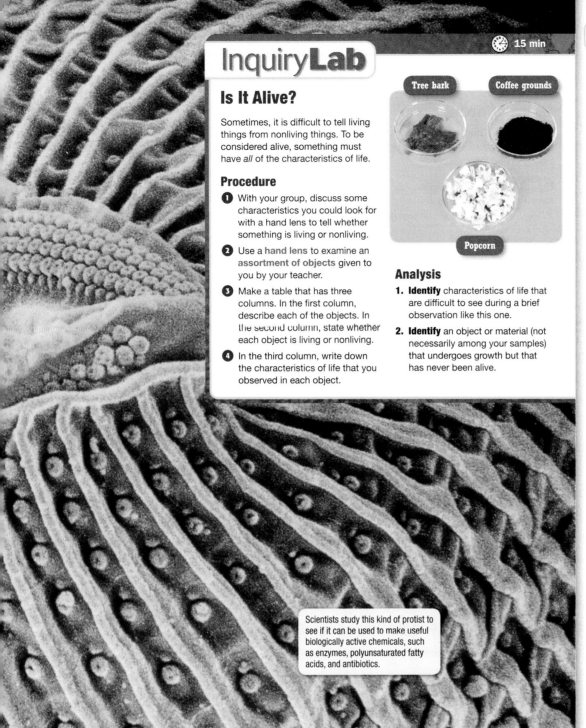

InquiryLab

⏱ 15 min

Is It Alive?

Sometimes, it is difficult to tell living things from nonliving things. To be considered alive, something must have *all* of the characteristics of life.

Procedure

1. With your group, discuss some characteristics you could look for with a hand lens to tell whether something is living or nonliving.

2. Use a **hand lens** to examine an **assortment of objects** given to you by your teacher.

3. Make a table that has three columns. In the first column, describe each of the objects. In the second column, state whether each object is living or nonliving.

4. In the third column, write down the characteristics of life that you observed in each object.

Tree bark

Coffee grounds

Popcorn

Analysis

1. **Identify** characteristics of life that are difficult to see during a brief observation like this one.

2. **Identify** an object or material (not necessarily among your samples) that undergoes growth but that has never been alive.

Scientists study this kind of protist to see if it can be used to make useful biologically active chemicals, such as enzymes, polyunsaturated fatty acids, and antibiotics.

InquiryLab

Teacher's Notes Provide students with a variety of objects, both living and nonliving. Objects might include plants, seeds, a goldfish, mineral crystals, and so on.

Materials
• assorted objects
• hand lens

Answers to Procedure

Students' tables should accurately describe objects and materials. If students conclude that an object (such as a plant or a goldfish) is living, students should have noted that the object displays (or potentially displays) all of the characteristics of life (Living things are composed of cells, maintain homeostasis, take in and use energy, grow and develop, respond to the environment, reproduce and pass traits to offspring, and evolve over generations.)

Answers to Analysis

1. Students should be guided to realize that it is difficult to see most characteristics of life in a cursory examination. Students may acknowledge that they infer that certain things, such as a goldfish or a plant, are living based on experience. Students may realize that with more powerful magnification than a hands lens, the cellular structure of living things can be seen. And under certain conditions and in a relatively short term, homeostasis, metabolism, response to the environment, and even reproduction might be observed. Evolution is not likely to be observable in real time.

2. Sample answer: mineral crystals, clouds

2.1f In all organisms, the coded instructions for specifying the characteristics of the organism are carried in DNA, a large molecule formed from subunits arranged in a sequence with bases of four kinds (represented by A, G, C, and T). The chemical and structural properties of DNA are the basis for how the genetic information that underlies heredity is both encoded in genes (as a string of molecular "bases") and replicated by means of a template.

2.1k The many body cells in an individual can be very different from one another, even though they are all descended from a single cell and thus have essentially identical genetic instructions. This is because different parts of these instructions are used in different types of cells, and are influenced by the cells' environment and past history.

3.1j Billions of years ago, life on Earth is thought by many scientists to have begun as simple, single-celled organisms. About a billion years ago, increasingly complex multicellular organisms began to evolve.

5.1b Plant cells and some one-celled organisms contain chloroplasts, the site of photosynthesis…

5.1d In all organisms, the energy stored in organic molecules may be released during cellular respiration. This energy is temporarily stored in ATP molecules. In many organisms, the process of cellular respiration is concluded in mitochondria, in which ATP is produced more efficiently, oxygen is used, and carbon dioxide and water are released as wastes.

5.3a Dynamic equilibrium results from detection of and response to stimuli. Organisms detect and respond to change in a variety of ways both at the cellular level and at the organismal level.

Using Words

1. to make a group of parts work together
2. An organelle functions like a small organ, or is one of the working parts of an organ.

Using Language

1. The *cytoskeleton* supports the cell, much like your bones make up the skeleton that supports your body.
2. A mitochondria is like an electric plant that turns the energy of coal into electricity, a more easily used form of energy.

Using Science Graphics

Proteins are produced at the rough endoplasmic reticulum (ER).

↓

ER membrane pinches off forming a vesicle around the protein.

↓

Vesicles move to the Golgi apparatus.

↓

Vesicle membrane fuses with the Golgi membrane.

↓

Enzymes modify the proteins as they move through the Golgi apparatus.

↓

Finished proteins are enclosed in new vesicles that bud from the surface of the Golgi apparatus.

↓

Vesicles move to the cell membrane.

↓

Vesicle membrane fuses with the cell membrane and releases the protein outside the cell.

 READING TOOLBOX

These reading tools can help you learn the material in this chapter. For more information on how to use these and other tools, see **Appendix: Reading and Study Skills.**

Using Words

Word Parts Knowing the meanings of word parts can help you figure out the meanings of words that you do not know.

Your Turn Use the information in the table to answer the questions that follow.

1. Use the table to write your own definition for *organize*.
2. What do you think an organelle does in a cell?

Word Parts		
Word part	Type	Meaning
organ	root	a group of parts that work together
-ize	suffix	to make or become
-elle	suffix	small part

Using Language

Similes Similes help relate new ideas to ideas that you already know. Often, similes use the terms *like* or *as*. For example, if you were describing a motorcycle to someone who had never seen one, you might say that it is like a bicycle that has a motor.

Your Turn Use information in the chapter to answer the questions that follow.

1. Find a simile to describe a cytoskeleton.
2. Write a simile to describe the function of a mitochondrion.

Using Science Graphics

Process Chart Science is full of processes. A process chart shows the steps that a process takes to get from one point to another point. This tool can help you visualize a process and remember the steps.

Your Turn Make a process chart to help you remember the steps of protein packaging.

1. Draw a box. In the box, write the first step of the process.
2. Under the box, draw another box and an arrow connecting the two boxes. In the second box, write the next step of the process.
3. Keep adding boxes and arrows until each step of the process has been included.

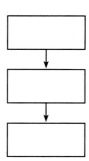

Introduction to Cells

Key Ideas	Key Terms	Why It Matters
❯ How were cells discovered? ❯ What defines cell shape and size? ❯ What enables eukaryotes to perform more specialized functions than prokaryotes do?	cell membrane prokaryote cytoplasm eukaryote ribosome nucleus organelle	Cells are the basic unit of life. By studying cells, biologists can better understand life's processes.

All life-forms on our planet are made up of cells. The bacteria that live in our gut and the cells that make up our body are built from the same chemical machinery. This machinery allows living things to obtain and use energy, to respond to their environment, and to reproduce. In all organisms, cells have the same basic structure.

The Discovery of Cells

How do living things differ from nonliving things? The discovery of cells was an important step toward answering this question. Most cells are too small to see with the naked eye. As **Figure 1** shows, microscopes have become an important tool for studying biology. ❯ **Microscope observations of organisms led to the discovery of the basic characteristics common to all living things.**

In 1665, Robert Hooke, an English scientist, used a crude microscope to look at a thin slice of cork. His microscope could magnify objects to only 30 times their normal size. Hooke saw many "little boxes" in the cork. They reminded him of the small rooms in which monks lived, so he called them *cells*. Hooke later discovered cells in the stems and roots of plants. Ten years later, Anton van Leeuwenhoek, a Dutch scientist, used a more powerful microscope that could magnify objects 300-fold.
He discovered many living creatures in pond water. He named them *animalcules,* or "tiny animals." Today, we know that they were not animals. They were single-celled organisms.

❯ **Reading Check** *How powerful was Hooke's microscope? (See the Appendix for answers to Reading Checks.)*

Figure 1 A student looks through a light microscope. Euglena (inset) are single-celled organisms that are commonly found in pond water.

 The Living Environment
Standard 4
1.2f Cells have particular structures that perform specific jobs. These structures perform the actual work of the cell. Just as systems are coordinated and work together, cell parts must also be coordinated and work together.
1.2g Each cell is covered by a membrane that performs a number of important functions for the cell. These include: separation from its outside environment, controlling which molecules enter and leave the cell, and recognition of chemical signals. The processes of diffusion and active transport are important in the movement of materials in and out of cells.
1.2i Inside the cell a variety of specialized structures, formed from many different molecules, carry out the transport of materials (cytoplasm), extraction of energy from nutrients (mitochondria), protein building (ribosomes), waste disposal (cell membrane), storage (vacuole), and information storage (nucleus).
2.1f In all organisms, the coded instructions for specifying the characteristics of the organism are carried in DNA, a large molecule formed from subunits arranged in a sequence with bases of four kinds (represented by A, G, C, and T).
3.1j Billions of years ago, life on Earth is thought by many scientists to have begun as simple, single-celled organisms. About a billion years ago, increasingly complex multicellular organisms began to evolve.

❯ Focus

This section introduces students to the discovery of the cell and the development of the cell theory. Cell features are presented. The similarities and differences of prokaryotic and eukaryotic cells are discussed.

◉ Bellringer

Use the Bellringer transparency to prepare students for this section.

❯ Teach

Teaching Key Ideas

Overview of Cells Display micrographs of various cells. Have students make deductive statements about the cells they observe. Why are there so many varieties of cells? (Cells with different structures have different functions.)
LS Visual/Verbal

Why It Matters

Bacteria in Yogurt Smear yogurt with live cultures on a microscope slide. Mix a drop of water into the yogurt and add a coverslip. Allow students to examine the slide under high power using a compound light microscope. They should see *Lactobacillus*. Ask them to compare the size and shape of these cells with prepared slides of human and plant tissue cells and the *Euglena* shown in **Figure 1**. (Euglena are approx. 25μm in length.) **LS Kinesthetic**

Section Correlations	
4.1.2f	4.2.1f
4.1.2g	4.3.1j
4.1.2i	

Key Resources

🗄 **Transparencies**
A10 Metric Units of Length and Equivalents
A4 Object Size and Magnifying Power of Microscopes
A5 Compound Light Microscope
B2 Relationship Between Surface Area and Volume
B8 Structure of Lipid Bilayer
B9 Organelles

◉ **Visual Concepts**
Types of Microscopes
Magnification and Resolution
Parts of a Light Microscope
Cell Theory
Cell Membrane
Cytoplasm
Ribosomes
Internal Organization of a Cell
Parts of a Prokaryotic Cell
Parts of a Cell Wall

Why It Matters

Cell Shape A study of micrographs of cell structures shows that common shapes of true bacterial cells include cocci (circular) bacilli (rod-shaped) and spirilli (squiggly). Human epithelial cells (cells lining the interior and exterior surfaces of the body) are also classified by shape: squamous (flattened), cuboidal (cube-shaped), or columnar (taller than wide). The cells are classified as *simple* if they are arranged in a single layer, or *stratified* if they are arranged in several layers. Specialized cells routinely have a unique shape, such as an axon or dendrite, or additional structures, such as multiple nuclei in a skeletal muscle cell or cilia on cells lining the respiratory system.

READING TOOLBOX

Visual Literacy Help students classify the cells shown in the photographs by shape.
• plant cell – columnar or cuboidal
• skin cells – flat; scale-like

Answer to Quick Project

The largest eukaryotic cell in the world is about the size of a baseball! By volume, the largest single cell is the yolk of an ostrich egg.

Cell Theory It took more than 150 years for scientists to fully appreciate the discoveries of Hooke and Leeuwenhoek. By the 1830s, microscopes were powerful enough to resolve structures only 1 μm apart. In 1838, Matthias Schleiden, a German botanist, concluded that cells make up every part of a plant. A year later, Theodor Schwann, a German zoologist, discovered that animals are also made up of cells. In 1858, Rudolph Virchow, a German physician, proposed that cells come only from the division of existing cells. The observations of Schleiden, Schwann, and Virchow form the *cell theory*:

• All living things are made up of one or more cells.

• Cells are the basic units of structure and function in organisms.

• All cells arise from existing cells.

The cell theory has withstood the rigorous examination of cells by scientists equipped with today's high-powered microscopes. As new tools and techniques are invented, scientists will learn more about the characteristics of cells.

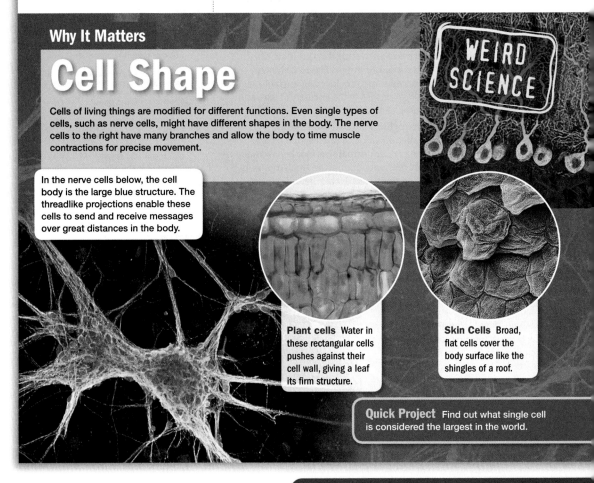

Why It Matters

Cell Shape

WEIRD SCIENCE

Cells of living things are modified for different functions. Even single types of cells, such as nerve cells, might have different shapes in the body. The nerve cells to the right have many branches and allow the body to time muscle contractions for precise movement.

In the nerve cells below, the cell body is the large blue structure. The threadlike projections enable these cells to send and receive messages over great distances in the body.

Plant cells Water in these rectangular cells pushes against their cell wall, giving a leaf its firm structure.

Skin Cells Broad, flat cells cover the body surface like the shingles of a roof.

Quick Project Find out what single cell is considered the largest in the world.

Differentiated Instruction

Basic Learners

Magnification Remind students that microscopes magnify objects, making them appear larger than their actual size. Pair students, and ask each pair to calculate the diameter of a Lincoln penny if it were magnified 270 times. Have students report their answers in meters and using a comparison to another object. (A Lincoln penny is 2 cm wide. Magnified 270 times, it would appear 5.4 m wide, about as wide as a large room.) **LS Logical**

Math Skills — Ratio of Surface Area and Volume

A ratio compares two numbers by dividing one number by the other number. A ratio can be expressed in three ways:

$$x \text{ to } y \qquad \frac{x}{y} \qquad x:y$$

You can improve your understanding of a cell's surface area-to-volume ratio by practicing with cubes of various sizes. What is the surface area-to-volume ratio of a cube that has a side length (l) of 4 mm?

❶ Find the surface area of the cube. A cube has six square faces. The surface area of one face is $l \times l$, or l^2.
- *total surface area of cube* = $6 \times l^2$
- *total surface area of cube* = $6 \times (4 \text{ mm})^2 = 96 \text{ mm}^2$

❷ Find the volume of the cube.
- *volume of cube* = l^3
- *volume of cube* = $(4 \text{ mm})^3 = 64 \text{ mm}^3$

Surface Area and Volume

Side length	Surface area	Volume	Surface area-to-volume
1 mm	6 mm²	1 mm³	6:1
2 mm	24 mm²	8 mm³	3:1
4 mm	96 mm²	64 mm³	3:2

❸ Divide the total surface area by volume:
- *surface area-to-volume ratio* = $\dfrac{total\ surface\ area}{volume}$

Reduce both numbers by their greatest common factor:
- *surface area-to-volume ratio* = $\dfrac{(96 \div 32)}{(64 \div 32)} = \dfrac{3}{2}$

Looking at Cells

Cells vary greatly in size and in shape. ❯ **A cell's shape reflects the cell's function.** Cells may be branched, flat, round, or rectangular. Some cells have irregular shapes, while other cells constantly change shapes. These differences enable different cells to perform highly specific functions in the body. There are at least 200 types of cells. The human body is made up of about 100 trillion cells, most of which range from 5 to 20 μm in diameter. Why are cells so small?

Cell Size All substances that enter or leave a cell must pass through the surface of the cell. As a cell gets larger, it takes up more nutrients and releases more wastes. These substances must move farther to reach their destination in a larger cell. ❯ **Cell size is limited by a cell's surface area-to-volume ratio.**

Scientists can estimate a cell's ability to exchange materials by calculating the cell's surface area-to-volume ratio. Cells with greater surface area-to-volume ratios can exchange substances more efficiently. When cells that are the same shape as one another are compared, the smaller cells have greater surface area-to-volume ratios than larger cells do.

Cell Shape Larger cells often have shapes that increase the surface area available for exchange. A cell may grow large in one or two dimensions but remain small in others. For example, some skin cells are broad and flat. Some nerve cells are highly extended and can be more than 10,000 times as long as they are thick. In both of these types of cells, the surface area-to-volume ratio is larger than it would be if the cells were spheres.

❯ **Reading Check** *How does a cell's size affect the cell's function?*

ACADEMIC VOCABULARY

dimension a measurement in a particular direction

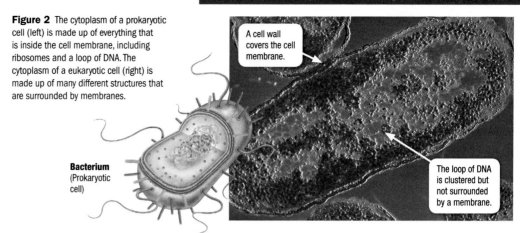

Teaching Key Ideas

Interpreting Graphics Draw students' attention to **Figure 2**. Tell students that any color shown in electron micrographs is usually digitally applied; that is, the colors are "painted" by computers. These colors are artificial; the cell is not colored as is shown in the micrograph. Ask students why colorized electron micrographs might be useful. (to highlight or point out structures) Ask students which structures are shown in **Figure 2**. (cell wall and DNA) What other structures are in the cytoplasm of this cell that is not visible in the micrograph? (ribosomes)

LS **Visual**

Features of Prokaryotic and Eukaryotic Cells

Figure 2 The cytoplasm of a prokaryotic cell (left) is made up of everything that is inside the cell membrane, including ribosomes and a loop of DNA. The cytoplasm of a eukaryotic cell (right) is made up of many different structures that are surrounded by membranes.

A cell wall covers the cell membrane.

The loop of DNA is clustered but not surrounded by a membrane.

Bacterium (Prokaryotic cell)

www.scilinks.org
Topic: Cell Features
Code: HX80238

cell membrane a phospholipid layer that covers a cell's surface and acts as a barrier between the inside of a cell and the cell's environment

cytoplasm (SIET oh PLAZ uhm) the region of the cell within the membrane

ribosome (RIE buh SOHM) a cell organelle where protein synthesis occurs

prokaryote a single-celled organism that does not have a nucleus or membrane-bound organelles

eukaryote an organism made up of cells that have a nucleus and membrane-bound organelles

nucleus in a eukaryotic cell, a membrane-bound organelle that contains the cell's DNA

organelle one of the small bodies that are found in the cytoplasm of a cell and that are specialized to perform a specific function

Cell Features

All cells—from bacteria to those in a berry, bug, or bunny—share common structural features. All cells have a cell membrane, cytoplasm, ribosomes, and DNA. The **cell membrane** is the cell's outer boundary. It acts as a barrier between the outside environment and the inside of the cell. The *cytosol,* the fluid inside the cell, is full of dissolved particles. The **cytoplasm** includes this fluid and almost all of the structures that are suspended in the fluid. Many ribosomes are found in the cytoplasm. A **ribosome** is a cellular structure on which proteins are made. All cells also have DNA, the genetic material. DNA provides instructions for making proteins, regulates cellular activities, and enables cells to reproduce.

Features of Prokaryotic Cells The bacterium shown in **Figure 2** is an example of a **prokaryote,** an organism that is a single prokaryotic cell. A prokaryotic cell is quite simple in its organization. The genetic material is a single loop of DNA, which looks like a tangled string and usually lies near the center of the cell. Ribosomes and enzymes share the cytoplasm with the DNA.

Prokaryotic cells have a cell wall that surrounds the cell membrane and that provides structure and support. Some prokaryotic cell walls are surrounded by a *capsule,* a structure that enables prokaryotes to cling to surfaces, including teeth, skin, and food.

Scientists think that the first prokaryotes may have lived 2.5 billion years ago or more. For millions of years, prokaryotes were the only organisms on Earth. They were very simple and small (1 to 2 µm in diameter). Like their ancestors, modern prokaryotes are also very small (1 to 15 µm), and they live in a wide range of habitats. Prokaryotes make up a very large and diverse group of cells.

> **Reading Check** *What is a ribosome?*

Why It Matters

Prokaryote Diversity Modern prokaryotes include archaea (archaebacteria) and bacteria (eubacteria). They can be found in nearly any environment on Earth, including volcanic vents at the bottom of the ocean and ice in Arctic and Antarctic regions. Some archaeae seem to thrive in harsh conditions. These types of organisms are referred to as *extremophiles.*

Many bacteria live in or on the bodies of other organisms, including humans. They can cause bacterial infection, but in most cases the organisms are harmless or even beneficial to the host.

Differentiated Instruction

Special Education Students

Cell Model Have students use food to make a model of a eukaryotic cell. Students should use their understanding of the organelle structures to choose appropriate foods to represent them. Gelatin (cytoplasm) could be poured into a large, clear cellophane bag (cell membrane). Organelles can be represented by kidney beans (mitochondria), poppy seeds (ribosomes), sections of lasagna noodles (ER and Golgi apparatus), peppercorns (lysosomes), spaghetti noodles (cytoskeleton), and an orange (nucleus). **LS** **Kinesthetic**

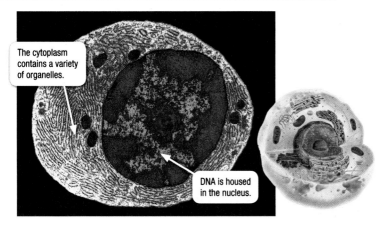

The cytoplasm contains a variety of organelles.

DNA is housed in the nucleus.

Animal cell
(Eukaryotic cell)

Eukaryotic Cells All multicellular plants and animals are composed of eukaryotic cells. Stress that the eukaryotic cell can exist independently, not just as a component of a larger organism. Have students research single-celled eukaryotic organisms, such as yeast or a single-celled protist. Have them compare the single-celled eukaryotes with eukaryotic cells that are *part* of a multicellular plant or animal. Students should include drawings and record their findings on a fact sheet. **LS Verbal/Visual**

Features of Eukaryotic Cells A **eukaryote** is an organism that is made up of one or more eukaryotic cells. Some eukaryotes live as single cells. Others are multicellular organisms. In fact, all multicellular organisms are made up of eukaryotic cells. **❯ Because of their complex organization, eukaryotic cells can carry out more specialized functions than prokaryotic cells can.**

Primitive eukaryotic cells first appeared about 1.5 billion years ago. As shown in the animal cell in **Figure 2,** a eukaryotic cell contains compartments that are separated by membranes. The cell's DNA is housed in an internal compartment called the **nucleus.**

In addition to having a membrane, cytoplasm, ribosomes, and a nucleus, all eukaryotic cells have membrane-bound organelles. An **organelle** is a structure that carries out specific activities inside the cell. The animal cell in **Figure 2** shows many of the organelles found in eukaryotic cells. Each organelle performs distinct functions. Many organelles are surrounded by a membrane. Some of the membranes are connected by channels that help move substances within the cell.

READING TOOLBOX

Word Parts The root *kary* means "kernel," which describes the nucleus. *Eu-* means "true," so a eukaryotic cell has a true nucleus. If *pro-* means "before," what does prokaryotic mean?

Word Origins *Prokaryotic* means "existing before the development of the nucleus."

❯ Close

Formative Assessment

Cells of unknown origin are examined and found to contain DNA, proteins, and enzymes. A cell wall is present along with a cluster of stringy material in the cytoplasm. No other components are visible. The cells are most likely _____.

A. sperm cells (Incorrect. Sperm cells have very distinct tails.)

B. skin cells (Incorrect. Animal cells do not have cell walls.)

C. prokaryotic cells (Correct. Prokaryotes contain ribosomes which produce protein, and enzymes in their cytoplasm. The DNA is a single circular molecule that is often located near the center of the cell.)

D. eukaryotic cells (Incorrect. Eukaryotes have distinct nuclei.)

Section 1 Review

❯ KEY IDEAS

1. **List** the three parts of the cell theory.

2. **Describe** the importance of a cell's surface area–to-volume ratio.

3. **Compare** the structure of a eukaryotic cell with that of a prokaryotic cell.

CRITICAL THINKING

4. **Explaining Relationships** The development of the cell theory is directly related to advances in microscope technology. Why are these two developments related?

5. **Making Comparisons** How do the membrane-bound organelles of a eukaryotic cell act in a manner similar to the organs in a multicellular organism?

METHODS OF SCIENCE

6. **Extraterrestrial Cells** You are a scientist with NASA. Some samples of extraterrestrial material containing living things have arrived on your spaceship. Your first job is to determine if the samples contain prokaryotic or eukaryotic cells. How will you proceed?

Answers to Section Review

1. All living things are made of one or more cells. Cells are the basic units of structure and function in organisms. All cells arise from existing cells.

2. If the SA–to-V ratio of a cell is too small, substances cannot penetrate or leave the cell quickly enough to meet its needs.

3. Prokaryotic cells lack organelles; eukaryotic cells have organelles, which enable them to carry out unique, specialized functions in organized ways.

4. As microscopes became more powerful, scientists were able to observe the structure and function of cells. These observations led to the development of the cell theory.

5. The membrane-bound organelles of a eukaryotic cell are like separate organs in a multicellular organism in that they differ in structure and function and are adapted for specific and different jobs.

6. Using a microscope, determine if the live material has single-celled organisms, or if the cells form tissues or organs. Focus on one cell and use criteria of size, presence of nucleus, and organelles to distinguish prokaryotes from eukaryotes.

Inside the Eukaryotic Cell

Section 2

› Focus

This section presents the structure and function of eukaryotic cell organelles and cytoskeleton. Protein processing and energy production are also explained.

Bellringer

Use the Bellringer transparency to prepare students for this section.

› Teach

Why It Matters

Amoeboid Movement Have students make wet mounts of live amoebas. Amoeboid movement is a dramatic example of actin-based cell movement. Although students will not be able to see the actin fibers, they will be able to observe the granular cytoplasm streaming into the projection as it begins to form. Explain to students that some of their own white blood cells exhibit such movement to catch and ingest foreign invaders, such as bacteria.

LS Visual

Answers to Caption Questions

Figure 3: Microfilaments, microtubules, and intermediate fibers

---

Key Ideas

› What does the cytoskeleton do?

› How does DNA direct activity in the cytoplasm?

› What organelles participate in protein production?

› What is the role of vesicles in cells?

› How do cells get energy?

Key Terms

vesicle
endoplasmic reticulum
Golgi apparatus
vacuole
chloroplast
mitochondrion

Why It Matters

Knowing how cells work helps you understand how your body functions and what goes wrong when you get sick.

The Living Environment
Standard 4

1.2f Cells have particular structures that perform specific jobs. These structures perform the actual work of the cell. Just as systems are coordinated and work together, cell parts must also be coordinated and work together.

1.2i Inside the cell a variety of specialized structures, formed from many different molecules, carry out the transport of materials (cytoplasm), extraction of energy from nutrients (mitochondria), protein building (ribosomes), waste disposal (cell membrane), storage (vacuole), and information storage (nucleus).

5.1b Plant cells and some one-celled organisms contain chloroplasts, the site of photosynthesis.

5.1d In all organisms, the energy stored in organic molecules may be released during cellular respiration. This energy is temporarily stored in ATP molecules. In many organisms, the process of cellular respiration is concluded in mitochondria, in which ATP is produced more efficiently, oxygen is used, and carbon dioxide and water are released as wastes.

5.3a Dynamic equilibrium results from detection of and response to stimuli. Organisms detect and respond to change in a variety of ways both at the cellular level and at the organismal level.

Figure 3 The cytoskeleton's network of protein fibers anchors cell organelles and other components of the cytoplasm. › **What are the three types of cytoskeleton fibers?**

The cytoplasm of a eukaryotic cell is packed with all sorts of structures and molecules. Molecules can be concentrated in certain parts of the cell because of the membranes that divide the cytoplasm into compartments. This organization enables each organelle to perform highly sophisticated and specialized functions.

The Framework of the Cell

The *cytoskeleton* is a web of protein fibers, shown in **Figure 3,** found in eukaryotic cells. The cytoskeleton supports the cell in much the same way that bones support your body. › **The cytoskeleton helps the cell move, keep its shape, and organize its parts.** There are three kinds of cytoskeleton fibers.

Microfilaments are long, thin fibers that are made of the protein actin. Some are attached to the cell membrane. They contract to pull the membrane in some places and expand to push it out in others. *Microtubules* are thick, hollow fibers that are made of the protein tubulin. Information molecules move through these tubes to various parts of the cell. *Intermediate fibers* are moderately thick and mainly anchor organelles and enzymes to certain parts of the cell.

Nucleus

Ribosomes

Cytoskeleton fibers

Organelles

Section Correlations

4.1.2f	4.5.1d
4.1.2i	4.5.3a
4.5.1b	

Key Resources

 Transparencies
B13 Processing of Proteins
B12 Mitochondrion

 Visual Concepts
Cytoskeleton
Nucleus of a Cell
Endoplasmic Reticulum (ER) and Ribosomes
Golgi Apparatus
Mitochondrion
Chloroplasts
Vacuoles

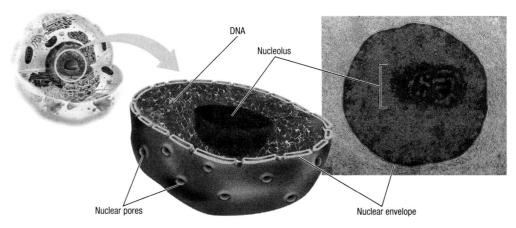

DNA

Nucleolus

Nuclear pores

Nuclear envelope

Figure 4 The nucleus stores the cell's DNA. The nuclear envelope is a double membrane that surrounds the nucleus of a cell. Ribosomes are made in the nucleolus. ❯ **How do molecules move from the nucleus to the cytoplasm?**

Directing Cellular Activity

Almost all cellular activity depends on the proteins that the cell makes. The instructions for making proteins are stored in the DNA. In a eukaryotic cell, the DNA is packed into the nucleus. This location separates the DNA from the activity in the cytoplasm and helps protect the information from getting lost or destroyed. ❯ **DNA instructions are copied as RNA messages, which leave the nucleus. In the cytoplasm, ribosomes use the RNA messages to** assemble **proteins.**

Nucleus As **Figure 4** shows, the nucleus is surrounded by a double membrane called the *nuclear envelope*. The nuclear envelope has many nuclear pores. Nuclear pores are small channels that allow certain molecules to move into and out of the nucleus. Even though the inside of the nucleus appears to be quite jumbled, the DNA is very organized. Within the nucleus is a prominent structure called the *nucleolus*. The nucleolus is the region where ribosome parts are made. These "preassembled" parts of ribosomes pass through the nuclear pores into the cytoplasm. Outside the nucleus, the parts are assembled to form a complete ribosome.

Ribosomes Each ribosome is made of RNA and many proteins. Some ribosomes in a eukaryotic cell are suspended in the cytosol, as they are in prokaryotic cells. These "free" ribosomes make proteins that remain inside the cell, such as proteins that build new organelles or enzymes to speed chemical reactions. Other ribosomes are attached to the membrane of another organelle. These "bound" ribosomes make proteins that are exported from the cell. Some of these proteins are important in cell communication. Bound ribosomes also make proteins that must be kept separate from the rest of the cytoplasm. Ribosomes can switch between being bound or free depending on the kind of protein that the cell needs to make.

❯ **Reading Check** *What kind of protein do "free" ribosomes make?*

ACADEMIC VOCABULARY

assemble to fit together parts or pieces; to build

Filtering Out Toxins Enzymes found in the abundant smooth ER of the liver help detoxify drugs and environmental pollutants. Detoxification usually involves a series of chemical reactions within the smooth ER of the liver that make the drug more water soluble, so it can be excreted in the urine. The ingestion of many drugs, including barbiturates and alcohol, trigger an increase in the amount of smooth ER and accompanying enzymes in liver cells. Have students research this detoxifying function of the smooth ER. **LS Verbal**

Process Chart Have students refer to the Reading Tool Box activity at the beginning of the chapter to create a process chart explaining the protein sequence. **LS Logical/Visual**

---

vesicle a small cavity or sac that contains materials in a eukaryotic cell

endoplasmic reticulum (EN doh PLAZ mik ri TIK yuh luhm) a system of membranes that is found in a cell's cytoplasm and that assists in the production, processing, and transport of proteins and in the production of lipids

Golgi apparatus (GOHL jee) a cell organelle that helps make and package materials to be transported out of the cell

---

SCI LINKS.
www.scilinks.org
Topic: Proteins
Code: HX81241

Process Chart Make a process chart that shows how the cell digests food particles.

Protein Processing

The proteins produced by cells have many uses. The proteins that are sent outside the cell must be kept separate from the rest of the cytoplasm. To achieve this separation, the cell packages the proteins in vesicles. A **vesicle** is a small, often spherical-shaped sac that is formed by a membrane.

In a eukaryotic cell, two structures are mainly responsible for modifying, packaging, and transporting proteins for use outside the cell. **› The endoplasmic reticulum and the Golgi apparatus are organelles that prepare proteins for extracellular export.**

Endoplasmic Reticulum The **endoplasmic reticulum** (ER) is a system of internal membranes that moves proteins and other substances through the cell. The membrane of the ER is connected to the outer membrane of the nuclear envelope.

Rough ER Ribosomes are attached to some parts of the surface of the ER. This *rough ER* has a bumpy appearance when viewed with an electron microscope, as shown in **Figure 5.** ❶ As proteins are made, they cross the ER membrane, entering the ER. Then, the ER membrane pinches off to form a vesicle around the proteins.

Smooth ER The rest of the ER, called *smooth ER*, has no attached ribosomes. Thus it appears smooth when viewed with an electron microscope. Enzymes of the smooth ER performs various functions, such as making lipids and breaking down toxic substances.

Golgi Apparatus The **Golgi apparatus** is a set of flattened, membrane-bound sacs. Cell products enter one side of the Golgi apparatus, which modifies, sorts, and packages them for distribution.

Repackaging Vesicles that contain newly made proteins move through the cytoplasm from the ER to the Golgi apparatus. ❷ The vesicle membrane fuses with the Golgi membrane. Inside the Golgi apparatus, enzymes modify the proteins as they move through the organelle. On the other side, the finished proteins are enclosed in new vesicles that bud from the surface of the Golgi apparatus.

Exporting Many of these vesicles then migrate to the cell membrane. ❸ As the vesicle membrane fuses with the cell membrane, the completed proteins are released to the outside the cell.

Storage and Maintenance

Vesicles have many functions in the cell. Some transport materials within the cell. Others have important storage roles. **› Vesicles help maintain homeostasis by storing and releasing various substances as the cell needs them.**

Lysosome A lysosome is a vesicle that contains specific enzymes that break down large molecules. These enzymes can digest food particles to provide nutrients for the cell. They also help recycle materials in the cell by digesting old, damaged, or unused organelles. Lysosomes work by fusing with other vesicles. Lysosomes, made by the Golgi apparatus, prevent the enzymes from destroying the cell.

Lysosomal Malfunctions Tay-Sachs disease is caused by the deficiency of a lysosomal enzyme that digests lipids. As a result, cells in the brain fill with lipids, eventually causing death. Pompe's disease results when a lysosomal enzyme that breaks down glycogen is absent. Glycogen is the energy storage compound for the body, so it's abundant in muscle. Without the enzyme to break down glycogen, the lysosomes in the heart and skeletal muscle quickly accumulate large amounts of glycogen. These muscles are progressively weakened, especially the heart.

Basic Learners

What Am I? Have each student choose one cell part or organelle and write a "What Am I?" essay. The essay should be written in the first person and should describe the structure and function of that cell part. Encourage students to be creative in their writing styles. Have students read their essays aloud in class. The class should guess the structure or organelle described in the essay. **LS Verbal/Interpersonal**

Making and Exporting Proteins

Figure 5 The cell manufactures many proteins. Some proteins are used outside the cell that makes them. Many organelles play a role in producing, processing, and packaging these proteins.

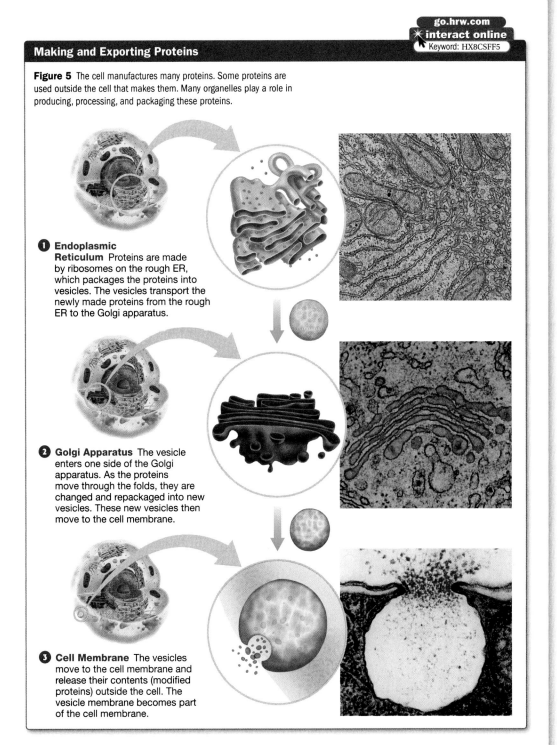

❶ Endoplasmic Reticulum Proteins are made by ribosomes on the rough ER, which packages the proteins into vesicles. The vesicles transport the newly made proteins from the rough ER to the Golgi apparatus.

❷ Golgi Apparatus The vesicle enters one side of the Golgi apparatus. As the proteins move through the folds, they are changed and repackaged into new vesicles. These new vesicles then move to the cell membrane.

❸ Cell Membrane The vesicles move to the cell membrane and release their contents (modified proteins) outside the cell. The vesicle membrane becomes part of the cell membrane.

Teaching Key Ideas

Visual Literacy Ask students to interpret **Figure 6.** Confirm their understanding of the increasing level of detail at each step of the graphic sequence. Help students relate the 3-dimensional drawings to the 2-dimensional photos. Ask students to identify the organelles involved in the process and the locations in the cell where the process is occurring. (Organelles shown are ribosomes, rough ER, Golgi apparatus, vesicles, and cell membrane. The process starts with the ribosomes on the rough ER, proceeds to the Golgi apparatus, and ends with the release of modified proteins at the cell membrane.) **LS Visual**

Differentiated Instruction

Basic Learners

3-D Representations Divide the class into three cooperative groups. Assign each group one step of the protein process presented on this page. Ask each group to create a 3-dimensional model on poster board for their portion of the process. Have each group brainstorm ideas for materials that can be used to represent the organelles (twine, small round beads, etc.). Give general size and scale guidelines so that the three panels can be displayed together to create a unified model of the protein process. **LS Intrapersonal/ Kinesthetic**

Why It Matters

History Connection In 1945, Belgian-American cytologist Albert Claude discovered the endoplasmic reticulum and the detailed structure of mitochondria. Along with Christian de Duve and George E. Palade, Claude was awarded the Nobel Prize in Medicine in 1974 for discoveries of the structural and functional organization of the cell.

QuickLab

Modeling Cell Parts

Teacher's Notes This activity is designed to increase students' understanding the cell's structure and the relationship among some of its parts. Students should imagine the model to be a plant cell.

Materials

- plastic bags with leakproof seals
  - large 1-gallon-size (1)
  - sandwich size (2)
  - jewelry size (2)
- blue food color
- green food color
- adhesive tape, transparent

Answers to Analysis

1. The blue water-filled bag is the central vacuole. The smaller green water-filled bags are chloroplasts. The outer bag represents the cell membrane/wall.
2. The central vacuole pushes against the cell contents (cytosol and chloroplasts) and the cell wall to give the cell its shape.
3. If water is removed from the central bag, there would be less pressure against the outer bag and it would become limp.

Teaching Key Ideas

Chloroplasts Ask students how energy from the sun gets into the food we eat? (sun transfers energy to plants; plants use energy to make food; animals eat plants and obtain energy; we eat animals and plants to obtain this energy) **LS Logical**

Answers to Caption Questions

Figure 6: Photosynthesis occurs in the chloroplast.

QuickLab

⏱ 10 min

Cell Parts Model 4.1.2f, 4.1.2i

No space is wasted inside a cell. Packed into the cell are all parts essential to its survival.

Procedure

1 Fill a **sealable plastic sandwich bag** halfway with **tap water**. Add several drops of **blue food dye**. Before you seal the bag, push out any remaining air.

2 Roll this water-filled bag into a cylindrical shape. Use two long strips of **tape** to secure this shape.

3 Fill **two small plastic jewelry bags** with water. Before sealing the bags, add several drops of **green food coloring** to each bag.

4 Place the water-filled sandwich bag and the two small jewelry bags into a **gallon-size plastic bag**.

5 Fill this outer bag two-thirds full with water. Push out any remaining air, and seal the bag.

Analysis

1. **State** what each plastic bag in this model represented.

2. **Describe** how the "central vacuole" affects the contents of your cell model.

3. **CRITICAL THINKING** **Predicting Outcomes** Explain how removing water from the model's central bag might affect the tension and shape of the outer plastic bag.

Central Vacuole Many plant cells contain a large, membrane-bound compartment called the central **vacuole.** This large vacuole stores water, ions, nutrients, and wastes. It can also store toxins or pigments. When water fills the central vacuole, as shown in **Figure 6,** it makes the cell rigid, allowing the plant to stand upright. When the vacuole loses water, the cell shrinks, and the plant wilts.

Other Vacuoles Some protists have contractile vacuoles, which pump excess water out of the cell. This process controls the concentration of salts and other molecules and helps the cell maintain homeostasis. Another type of vacuole forms when the cell membrane surrounds food particles outside the cell and pinches off to form a vesicle inside the cell. When the food vacuole later fuses with a lysosome, the enzymes that digest the stored food are released.

Figure 6 A plant cell may have a large central vacuole and several chloroplasts. When filled, the central vacuole pushes the other organelles against the membrane. **❯ In which organelle does photosynthesis occur?**

Nucleus

Central vacuole

Chloroplast

Stored sugar

Plant cell

Energy Production

Cells need a constant source of energy. **❯ The energy for cellular functions is produced by chemical reactions that occur in the mitochondria and chloroplasts.** Nearly all eukaryotic cells contain mitochondria. Chloroplasts are found in plants and some plant-like protists, such as seaweed, but not in animal cells. In both organelles, chemical reactions produce adenosine triphosphate (ATP), the form of energy that fuels almost all cell processes.

Inner membrane   Outer membrane

Figure 7 A mitochondrion uses the energy in organic molecules to make ATP for the cell. The mitochondrion has two membranes. ❯ **Where in the mitochondrion is ATP produced?**

Chloroplasts A **chloroplast** is an organelle that uses light energy to make sugar from carbon dioxide and water. As **Figure 6** shows, plant cells may have several chloroplasts. Each chloroplast is surrounded by a pair of membranes. Inside the inner membrane are many stacks of flattened sacs. The ATP-producing chemical reactions take place on the membranes of these sacs.

Mitochondria A **mitochondrion** is an organelle that uses energy from organic compounds to make ATP. Although some ATP is made in the cytosol, most of a cell's ATP is made inside mitochondria. Cells that have a high energy requirement, such as muscle cells, may contain hundreds or thousands of mitochondria. As **Figure 7** shows, a mitochondrion has a smooth outer membrane. It also has a greatly folded inner membrane, which divides the organelle into two compartments. Many ATP-producing enzymes are located on the inner membrane.

❯ **Reading Check** *In what kinds of cells are mitochondria found?*

vacuole (VAK yoo OHL) a fluid-filled vesicle found in the cytoplasm of plant cells or protozoans

chloroplast an organelle found in plant and algae cells where photosynthesis occurs

mitochondrion (MIET oh KAHN dree uhn) in eukaryotic cells, the cell organelle that is surrounded by two membranes and that is the site of cellular respiration

Section 2 Review

❯ KEY IDEAS

1. **Compare** the functions of the three types of cytoskeletal fibers.
2. **Describe** the nucleus.
3. **Trace** a protein's path through the cell, from assembly to export.
4. **Contrast** vesicles and vacuoles.
5. **Compare** the role of mitochondria and chloroplasts.

CRITICAL THINKING

6. **Constructing Explanations** Is it accurate to say that organelles are floating freely in the cytosol? Why or why not?
7. **Real World** Research Tay-Sachs disease, and explain what goes wrong in diseased cells.

ALTERNATIVE ASSESSMENT

8. **Analogy** Compare the organelles of a eukaryotic cell to the parts of a city. For example, the lysosome could be a recycling center.

Key Ideas	Key Terms	Why It Matters
> What makes cells and organisms different? > How are cells organized in a complex multicellular organism? > What makes an organism truly multicellular?	flagellum organ system tissue colonial organ organism	Diverse organisms have unique cells and cellular organization.

The Living Environment
Standard 4

1.2a Important levels of organization for structure and function include organelles, cells, tissues, organs, organ systems, and whole organisms.

1.2e The organs and systems of the body help to provide all the cells with their basic needs. The cells of the body are of different kinds and are grouped in ways that enhance how they function together.

2.1k The many body cells in an individual can be very different from one another, even though they are all descended from a single cell and thus have essentially identical genetic instructions. This is because different parts of these instructions are used in different types of cells, and are influenced by the cells' environment and past history.

flagellum a long, hairlike structure that grows out of a cell and enables the cell to move

Figure 8 The bacterium *Escherichia coli* is a rod-shaped prokaryote that has both pili and flagella. **> What do flagella enable prokaryotic cells to do?**

More than 50 million types of organisms live on Earth. Each organism is made up of different types of cells. Differences in cells enable organisms to adapt to their natural environments.

Diversity in Cells

Prokaryotes are always unicellular and limited in size. Eukaryotes are often larger and can be either unicellular or multicellular. Prokaryotic cells lack a nucleus and membrane-bound organelles, which are found in eukaryotic cells. Within both types, cells can have a variety of shapes and structures. Recall that a cell's shape reflects its function. **> The different organelles and features of cells enable organisms to function in unique ways in different environments.**

Diversity in Prokaryotes Prokaryotes can vary in shape, the way that they obtain and use energy, the makeup of their cell walls, and their ability to move. Many prokaryotes have **flagella**—long, threadlike structures that rotate to quickly move an organism through its environment. Many prokaryotes have pili. Pili are short, thick outgrowths that allow prokaryotes to attach to surfaces or to other cells. These features are shown in **Figure 8.**

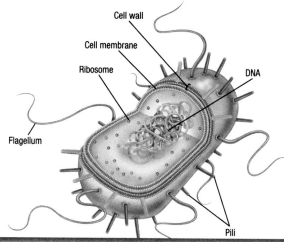

Cell wall

Cell membrane

Ribosome

DNA

Flagellum

Pili

Diversity in Eukaryotic Cells Animal and plant cells are two types of eukaryotic cells, as **Figure 9** shows. Both have many of the same organelles, but plant cells also have chloroplasts, a large central vacuole, and a cell wall that surrounds the cell membrane.

Like prokaryotic cells, eukaryotic cells vary in structure according to their function. Also, some organelles are more prominent in some cell types. By varying in their internal makeup, cells can become specialized for certain functions. For example, muscle cells, which use large amounts of energy, have many mitochondria.

> **Reading Check** *What are flagella?*

Eukaryotic Cells

Figure 9 Most eukaryotic cells contain all of the organelles shown here. Depending on their function, cells may have different shapes and different amounts of certain organelles. > What are three features that plant cells have, but animal cells lack?

Animal cell

Mitochondrion
Nucleus
Nucleolus
Cytoskeleton fibers
Ribosomes
Cell membrane
Vesicle
Golgi apparatus
Smooth ER
Rough ER

Plant cell

Vesicle
Chloroplast
Golgi apparatus
Cell membrane
Cell wall
Central vacuole
Mitochondrion
Smooth ER
Nucleolus
Nucleus
Cytoskeleton fibers
Rough ER
Ribosome

> **Teach**, *continued*

Teaching Key Ideas

Visual Literacy Explain that **Figure 11** shows only a few of the microtubules and microfilaments in a cell. In reality, these structures form the dense network, or cytoskeleton, of the cell. Ask students to compare the structures in each cell. What structures found in the plant cell are not in the animal cell? (chloroplasts, central vacuole and cell wall) Ask students to name human cells that have specialized structures to carry out their functions. (Sample answers: Muscle cells have increased numbers of mitochondria for increased ATP production. Sperm cells have tails for mobility.)
LS **Visual**

Answers to Caption Questions
Figure 9: Cell wall, central vacuole, and chloroplasts

Differentiated Instruction

English Learners
Reading Organizer After students have read about prokaryotes and eukaryotes, ask them design a chart that identifies and describes all of the differences between the two cell types. Encourage ELL students to work with native English speakers. **LS** **Logical**

Why It Matters

Endosymbiosis This theory holds that prokaryotes lived in association with other cells but lost their ability to reproduce independently and became organelles of today's eukaryotes. Scientists think that chloroplasts evolved from endosymbiotic photosynthetic bacteria and mitochondria evolved from endosymbiotic aerobic bacteria. This theory is supported by the fact that both chloroplasts and mitochondria have their own DNA and can be inactivated with antibiotics that affect prokaryotes but not eukaryotes.

Similes Cells in a multicellular organism are like letters on a written page. Cells form tissues like a group of letters forms a word. Groups of words create a sentence like tissues combine to form organs.

Teaching Key Ideas

Respiratory Systems Help students understand the gas exchange process for plants and animals. The leaf tissue shown in **Figure 12** contains cells that take in carbon dioxide and give off oxygen in the light. For humans, the alveolar cells of the lung are the sites of oxygen/carbon dioxide exchange. The lungs are connected to the bronchi and trachea which allow gases to enter and leave the lungs. **LS Visual**

Answers to Caption Questions

Figure 10: The respiratory system is an organ system.

READING TOOLBOX

Similes Write a simile comparing each level of organization to a part of your textbook. (Hint: Cells are like letters.)

Figure 10 Cells group together to make tissues, which assemble into organs. A leaf is an example of an organ in plants. A lung is an example of an organ in animals.
❯ What level of organization is the respiratory system?

Levels of Organization

Multicellular organisms, such as plants and animals, are made up of thousands, millions, or even trillions of highly specialized cells. These cells cooperate to perform a specific task. They assemble together to form structures called tissues and organs. ❯ Plants and animals have many highly specialized cells that are arranged into tissues, organs, and organ systems. The relationships between tissues, organs, and organ systems are shown in **Figure 10.**

Tissues A **tissue** is a distinct group of cells that have similar structures and functions. For example, muscle tissue is a group of many cells that have bundles of cytoskeletal structures. When the bundles contract at the same time, they help animals move. In plants, vascular tissue is made of hollowed cells that are stacked up to make tiny straws. These structures help carry fluids and nutrients to various parts of the plant.

Organs Different tissues may be arranged into an **organ,** which is a specialized structure that has a specific function. In animals, the heart is an organ made of muscle, nerve, and other tissues. These tissues work together to pump blood. In plants, a leaf is an organ. A leaf is made of vascular tissue and other types of plant tissues that work together to trap sunlight and produce sugar.

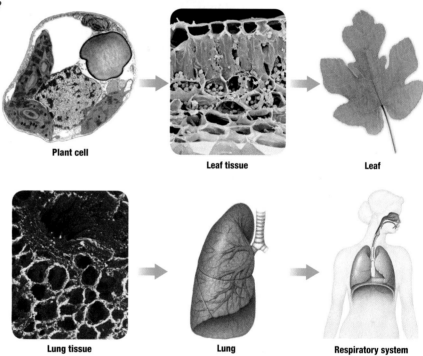

Plant cell → **Leaf tissue** → **Leaf**

Lung tissue → **Lung** → **Respiratory system**

Why It Matters

Career Development *Cytotechnologists* stain, mount, and study cells to detect malignancies or other abnormal conditions. Invite a *cytotechnologist* from a local hospital to talk to your class. Ask him or her to discuss recommended high school courses, working conditions, employment opportunities, and salary ranges.

A *cytotechnologist* must be able to obtain precise results and work under stress during emergency situations. An undergraduate degree in *cytotechnology* or medical technology is usually needed for entry level positions.

Differentiated Instruction

Basic Learners

Body Systems Have students research a human body system: digestive, respiratory, circulatory, excretory, nervous, or skeletal. Ask them to find the corresponding system in plants. Students should create a poster comparing the two systems. **LS Visual/ Verbal**

QuickLab

Colonies on the Move

1.1.2a, 4.1.2f

Volvox is a green colonial alga. A single colony may contain over 500 cells and is visible to the unaided eye.

⏱ 10 min

Procedure

1. With the unaided eye, examine a container of Volvox colonies. What do you see?

2. Use a dropper to transfer some of the colonies to a well slide.

3. Examine the colonies using a light microscope.

Analysis

1. **Draw** the shape and structure of Volvox.

2. **Describe** the motion of a Volvox colony.

3. **CRITICAL THINKING** **Inferring Relationships** From your observations, do you think that the movements of the colony members are coordinated? Explain.

Organ System Various organs that carry out a major body function make up an **organ system.** One example of an organ system is the circulatory system, which is made up of the heart, the blood vessels, and blood. In plants, the shoot system consists of stems, leaves, and the vascular tissue that connects them.

Body Types

Sometimes, the entire body of an organism is made up of a single cell. This cell must carry out all of the organism's activities, including growing, using energy, responding to the environment, and reproducing. More than half of the biomass on Earth is composed of unicellular organisms.

While single cells cannot grow larger than a certain size, multicellular organisms can be large. ❯ A multicellular organism is composed of many individual, permanently associated cells that coordinate their activities. Distinct types of cells have specialized functions that help the organism survive. Individual cells cannot survive alone and are dependent on the other cells of the organism.

Cell Groups Some unicellular organisms can thrive independently, but others live in groups. Cells that live as a connected group but depend on each other for survival are considered **colonial organisms.** For example, the cell walls of some bacteria adhere to one another after dividing. These formations are not considered multicellular, because the cells can survive when separated.

Another type of cell grouping occurs in certain types of slime molds. These organisms spend most of their lives as single-celled amoebas. When starved, the individual cells form a large mass, which produces spores.

tissue a group of similar cells that perform a common function

organ a collection of tissues that carry out a specialized function of the body

organ system a group of organs that work together to perform body functions

colonial organism a collection of genetically identical cells that are permanently associated but in which little or no integration of cell activities occurs

SC**LINKS.**
www.scilinks.org
Topic: Organ Systems
Code: HX81075

Differentiated Instruction

Advanced Learners

Behavior of Cell Colonies Ask students to research *Volvox* or another colonial organism on the Internet. Ask them to find out what scientific research has been done with the organism. They should review at least four sites and record the information they gather. Have them look for discrepancies in the information among the sites and record the source for each. Have students give oral reports to the class.
LS Logical/ Verbal

Why It Matters

Cryogenics Donated blood is frozen in a special process called cryopreservation. Similar methods are used to preserve human eggs, embryos, and blood from the umbilical cord, a rich source of immune-system cells. The cells are frozen very quickly, which prevents the formation of large ice crystals that would damage the cells.

❯**Teach,** *continued*

QuickLab

Teacher's Notes *Volvox* is a green algae that exists as a spherical colony. Individual alga are connected to each other by thin strands of cytoplasm. Each alga has two whip-like flagella that aid in movement of the colony. Each alga also has a red eye spot that is sensitive to light. The colony will move in water to find a spot for the maximum absorption of sunlight.

Materials

- *Volvox* colonies
- medicine dropper
- microscope slide with well
- low-powered compound microscope

Answer to Procedure

Volvox will appear as little green dots in the sample.

Answers to Analysis

1. Drawings should be spherical shapes and may contain smaller spheres inside the larger one.
2. A *Volvox* colony moves with a spinning motion.
3. Movement of the colony appears to be coordinated as the colony moves toward light.

› Close

Formative Assessment

Eukaryotic cells vary in structure according to their function. An example of a characteristic of a eukaryotic cell that relates closely to the cell's function is _____.

A. a bacterial cell wall providing support for the cell (Incorrect. A bacterium is a prokaryote.)

B. the trachea aiding in the exchange of gases in the lungs (Incorrect. The trachea is part of an organ system.)

C. muscle cells having an elongated shape (Correct. The cells combine to form fiber bundles, which provide strength to the muscle.)

D. plant cells containing a nucleus (Incorrect. Most eukaryotic cells contain a nucleus, so it is not a special feature.)

Answers to Caption Questions

Figure 11: Prokaryotes are never multicellular.

Protist

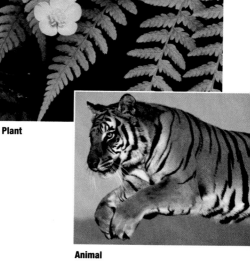

Plant

Fungus

Animal

Figure 11 The giant kelp is a multicellular protist. Mushrooms are multicellular fungi. All plants and animals are multicellular organisms. **› Can prokaryotes be multicellular?**

Multicellularity True multicellularity occurs only in eukaryotes, such as the organisms shown in **Figure 11.** Some protists, most fungi, and all plants and animals have a multicellular body. The cells of a multicellular body perform highly specific functions. Some cells protect the organism from predators or disease. Others may help with movement, reproduction, or feeding.

Most multicellular organisms begin as a single cell. For example, as a chicken develops from an egg, new cells form by cell division. These cells then grow and undergo differentiation, the process by which cells develop specialized forms and functions. The specialized cells are arranged into tissues, organs, and organ systems, making up the entire organism.

› Reading Check *What is differentiation?*

Section 3 Review

› KEY IDEAS

1. **Relate** the structure of a cell to the cell's function.
2. **Describe** the four levels of organization that make up an organism.
3. **Explain** what makes a group of cells a truly multicellular organism.

CRITICAL THINKING

4. **Comparing** Describe how the circulatory system in animals is similar to the vascular system in plants.
5. **Making Inferences** How would the formation of bacterial colonies be affected if bacterial cells did not contain pili?

WRITING FOR SCIENCE

6. **Cell Group Therapy** Write a short play set in a therapy group that contains cells belonging to a unicellular colony and cells belonging to a multicellular organism. Have the cells discuss issues such as communication and individuality.

Answers to Section Review

1. The structure of the cell is determined by its shape, the organelles within the cell, and the features on its surface. The function of a cell determines its structure.

2. Cells of similar structure make up tissues. Tissues are arranged to form organs. Organs work together to form organ systems.

3. The specialized cells of a multicellular organism are interdependent and cannot survive individually when separated from the rest of the organism.

4. Both systems move water, nutrients, and dissolved gases to cells in every part of each organism.

5. Without pili, the formation of bacterial colonies might not be possible.

6. The cells of a colony would be self-sufficient, with little or no communication with other cells. They would all look the same and perform the same functions. The cells of a multicellular organism would look different and have unique features and perform highly specialized functions. The cells would be communicating constantly. If an individual cell separated from the organism, it would probably die.

Chapter 7 Lab

4.1.2f, 4.1.2i

⏱ 45 min

Lab

Objectives

▶ Identify the structures that you can see in plant cells.

▶ Investigate factors that influence the movement of cell contents.

Materials

- compound light microscope
- safety goggles
- disposable gloves
- lab apron
- elodea sprig
- forceps
- microscope slides and coverslips
- lamp, incandescent
- dropper bottle of Lugol's iodine solution

Safety

Plant Cell Observation

When you look at cells under a microscope, you often can observe cytoplasmic streaming, or movement of cell contents. This effect occurs only in living cells. In this lab, you will investigate factors that influence cytoplasmic streaming.

Preparation

1. **SCIENTIFIC METHODS** **State the Problem** How do heat and an iodine solution influence cytoplasmic streaming?

2. **SCIENTIFIC METHODS** **Form a Hypothesis** Form testable hypotheses that explain how heat and iodine influence cytoplasmic streaming.

Procedure

① ◇ ◈ ↑ Put on safety goggles, gloves, and a lab apron.

② ◈ **CAUTION: Handle glass slides and coverslips with care.** Using forceps, remove a small leaf near the top of an elodea sprig. Place the whole leaf in a drop of water on a slide, and add a coverslip.

③ ◆ Observe the leaf under low power. Switch to high power. Identify as many cell parts as you can.

④ Focus on a cell in which you can see the chloroplasts clearly. Draw this cell. Label the cell parts that you can see.

⑤ If chloroplasts are not moving in any of the cells, briefly warm the slide under a lamp. Look for movement again under high power.

⑥ ◆ **CAUTION: Lugol's solution stains skin and clothing. Promptly wash off spills.** Make a wet mount of another leaf with Lugol's iodine solution. Observe the cells under low and high power.

⑦ Draw a stained elodea cell and label all visible parts.

⑧ ◇ ◈ Clean up your lab materials according to your teacher's instructions. Wash your hands before leaving the lab.

Analyze and Conclude

1. **Inferring Relationships** What effect did warming the slide have on the movement of cell contents? Why do you think this is so?

2. **SCIENTIFIC METHODS** **Inferring Conclusions** What can you conclude about the effect of Lugol's iodine solution on plant cells?

Answers to Procedure

Drawings will vary. For the stained cells, make sure students label the cell wall, cell membrane, chloroplasts, central vacuole, nucleus, and any other visible cell structures.

Answers to Analyze and Conclude

1. Warming the slide caused the cell contents to move more. Possible reasons for this may vary.

2. The chloroplasts stop moving, so Lugol's solution must kill the cell.

Time Required

One 45-minute lab period

Ratings

⚗ ⚗⚗ ⚗⚗⚗ ⚗⚗⚗⚗
EASY ———————→ HARD

Teacher Prep ⚗⚗⚗
Concept Level ⚗⚗
Student Set-Up ⚗⚗
Clean Up ⚗⚗

Safety Cautions

Review all safety symbols and caution statements before beginning the lab. Students must wear safety goggles when working with Lugol's iodine solution because iodine can cause severe eye damage.

Tips and Tricks

Set up labeled containers for the disposal of broken glass and materials stained with Lugol's solution. Place enough materials for one class on a supply table. Allow students to take off their safety goggles when looking through the microscope. Have students use a scale of 1 µm = 1 cm when drawing cells. Help students take measurements of cell size.

Disposal Combine all wastes containing Lugol's solution. To this mixture add a few drops of a strong acid, such as 1.0 M sulfuric acid (H_2SO_4), to make the mixture slightly acidic. Then slowly add 0.1 m sodium thiosulfate ($Na_2S_2O_3$) while stirring until the mixture loses its yellowish-orange color. Pour the resulting mixture down the drain.

Lab Correlations

4.1.2f Cells have particular structures that perform specific jobs. . .

4.1.2i Inside the cell a variety of specialized structures, formed from many different molecules, carry out the transport of materials (cytoplasm), extraction of energy from nutrients (mitochondria). . .

Key Resources

 Holt Lab Generator

 Lab Datasheet (Levels A, B, C)

 Holt Science Biology Video Labs

 Virtual Investigations

go.hrw.com
SUPER SUMMARY
Keyword: HX8CSFS

SUPER SUMMARY

Have students connect the major concepts in this chapter through an interactive Super Summary. Visit **go.hrw.com** and type in the keyword **HX8CSFS** to access the Super Summary for this chapter.

Reteaching Key Ideas

Organelles Pass out copies of electron micrographs of cells. Ask each student to choose three cell organelles, and color them with different colors. Students should name the organelles and describe what each does within the cell. **LS** Verbal/Visual

Prokaryotes and Eukaryotes Divide the class into two cooperative groups. Group A represents a prokaryotic cell and group B represents a eukaryotic cell. Have each group take turns describing a characteristic of their cell or something that their cell is able to do. Write the responses on the board. Give the other group an opportunity to challenge the responses. **LS** Interpersonal/Verbal

---

Key Ideas	Key Terms

1 Introduction to Cells

> Microscope observations of organisms led to the discovery of the basic characteristics common to all living things.

> A cell's shape reflects the cell's function. Cell size is limited by a cell's surface area-to-volume ratio.

> Because of their complex organization, eukaryotic cells can carry out more specialized functions than prokaryotic cells can.

Key Terms:
cell membrane (154)
cytoplasm (154)
ribosome (154)
prokaryote (154)
eukaryote (155)
nucleus (155)
organelle (155)

2 Inside the Eukaryotic Cell

> The cytoskeleton helps the cell move, keep its shape, and organize its parts.

> DNA instructions are copied as RNA messages, which leave the nucleus. In the cytoplasm, ribosomes use the RNA messages to assemble proteins.

> The endoplasmic reticulum and the Golgi apparatus are organelles that prepare proteins for extracellular export.

> Vesicles help maintain homeostasis by storing and releasing various substances as the cell needs them.

> The energy for cellular functions is produced by chemical reactions that occur in the mitochondria and chloroplasts.

Key Terms:
vesicle (158)
endoplasmic reticulum (158)
Golgi apparatus (158)
vacuole (160)
chloroplast (161)
mitochondrion (161)

3 From Cell to Organism

> The different organelles and features of cells enable organisms to function in unique ways in different environments.

> Plants and animals have many highly specialized cells that are arranged into tissues, organs, and organ systems.

> A multicellular organism is composed of many individual, permanently associated cells that coordinate their activities.

Key Terms:
flagellum (162)
tissue (164)
organ (164)
organ system (165)
colonial organism (165)

PART A: Answer all questions in this part.

Directions: For each statement or question, write on your separate answer sheet the number of the word or expression that best completes the statement or answers the question.

1 The diagram below represents levels of organization in living things. Which term would best represent X?

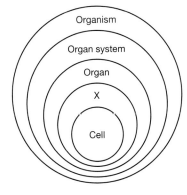

(1) human
(2) tissue
(3) stomach
(4) organelle

2 Which statement best compares a multicellular organism to a single-celled organism?

(1) A multicellular organism has organ systems that interact to carry out life functions, while a single-celled organism carries out life functions without using organ systems.
(2) A single-celled organism carries out fewer life functions than each cell of a multicellular organism.
(3) A multicellular organism always obtains energy through a process that is different from that used by a single-celled organism.
(4) The cell of a single-celled organism is always much larger than an individual cell of a multicellular organism.

3 The levels of organization for structure and function in the human body from least complex to most complex are

(1) systems → organs → tissues → cells
(2) cells → organs → tissues → systems
(3) tissues → systems → cells → organs
(4) cells → tissues → organs → systems

4 The largest amount of DNA in a plant cell is contained in

(1) a nucleus
(2) a chromosome
(3) a protein molecule
(4) an enzyme molecule

5 The diagram below illustrates the movement of materials involved in a process that is vital for the energy needs of organisms. The process illustrated occurs within

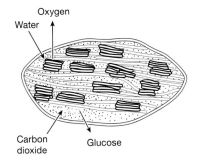

(1) chloroplasts
(2) mitochondria
(3) ribosomes
(4) vacuoles

6 In a cell, information that controls the production of proteins must pass from the nucleus to the

(1) cell membrane.
(2) chloroplasts.
(3) mitochondria.
(4) ribosomes.

Regents Exam Practice Correlations

1.1.3a 14	**4.2.1c** 4
4.1.2a 1, 3	**4.2.1g** 7
4.1.2f 8, 10, 12, 13	**4.5.1b** 5
4.1.2i 6	**4.5.1d** 11
4.1.3a 2	

PART A

1. **(2)** The terms "human" and "stomach" are not levels of organization. Organelles are smaller units of organization than cells, and thus cannot be found above cells. Tissues, however, are more complex than cells but less complex than organs. *(#01, June 2006 Regents Exam)*

2. **(1)** Single-celled organisms carry out the same number and kind of basic life functions and processes that multicellular organisms do, but groups of cells making up tissues and organs in multicellular organisms are often specialized to carry out a specific function. The choice about the size of cells is not true. *(#06, August 2006 Regents Exam)*

3. **(4)** Cells are the least complex of the structures in the human body, so only choices that begin with "cells" are possible answers. Tissues are less complex than organs, so the answer must have tissues listed before organs. *(#01, August 2006 Regents Exam)*

4. **(1)** DNA is not found in a protein or an enzyme molecule. DNA is not contained inside, but rather is found along, a chromosome. Furthermore, the largest amount of DNA would have to be found as the sum of all the chromosomes inside the nucleus. *(#07, June 2005 Regents Exam)*

5. **(1)** Water and carbon dioxide move into a chloroplast and undergo photosynthesis to produce oxygen and sugars, which move out. Oxygen and sugars move into mitochondria and are converted to energy, water, and carbon dioxide. Ribosomes assemble proteins. Water or wastes move into vacuoles for storage within the cell. *(#21, August 2005 Regents Exam)*

6. **(4)** Ribosomes are the sites of protein synthesis in the cell. Therefore information that controls the production of proteins would need to pass from the nucleus to the ribosomes. *(#06, June 2004 Regents Exam)*

7. (4) The genetic information in DNA directs the synthesis of proteins. Glucose, a carbohydrate, is produced in the chloroplasts during photosynthesis. Fats are often obtained through food. Minerals must be obtained from food. *(#06, August 2005 Regents Exam)*

8. (4) Mitochondria produce the ATP that supplies the energy needed for the muscle cells to contract. Therefore, a muscle cell that contains many mitochondria probably has a greater demand for energy than a muscle cell with less mitochondria. *(#06, August 2004 Regents Exam)*

9. (1) When considering this question, the word differ is important. Because both eukaryotic and prokaryotic cells may have cell walls 4 is incorrect. Eukaryotic cells contain ribosomes, organelles, and a nucleus which make 2 and 3 incorrect, and 1 the correct choice.

10. (1) Nerve cells communicate with skeletal muscle cells to allow you to lift objects or perform other movements. Nerves communicate with smooth muscles to help with food digestion. Cells send chemical signals to coordinate functions within organelles. Enzymes carry out protein synthesis. *(#02, August 2003 Regents Exam)*

PART B

11. (3) Mitochondria produce energy for cell processes, so cells with fewer mitochondria would require less energy. *(#42, June 2003 Regents Exam)*

12. (4) Structure X is the nucleus; its DNA would be involved in protein synthesis. Lysosomes store digestive enzymes. Chloroplasts perform photosynthesis. Bacteria and viruses can develop into pathogens. *(#38, August 2005 Regents Exam)*

7 The diagram below represents a portion of an organic molecule. This molecule controls cellular activity by directing the synthesis of

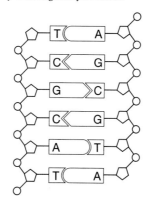

(1) carbohydrates
(2) minerals
(3) fats
(4) proteins

8 Muscle cells in athletes often have more mitochondria than muscle cells in nonathletes. Based on this observation, it can be inferred that the muscle cells in athletes

(1) have a smaller demand for cell proteins than the muscle cells of nonathletes
(2) reproduce less frequently than the muscle cells of nonathletes
(3) have nuclei containing more DNA than nuclei in the muscle cells of nonathletes
(4) have a greater demand for energy than the muscle cells of nonathletes

9 The largest amount of DNA in a plant cell is contained in
(1) a nucleus
(2) a chromosome
(3) a protein molecule
(4) an enzyme molecule

10 Two types of human cells are shown in the diagram below. Cell A causes the cells at B to contract. This activity would be most useful for

Nerve cell   Muscle cells that attach to the skeleton

A   B

(1) lifting a book from a bookshelf
(2) coordinating the functions of organelles
(3) digesting food in the small intestine
(4) carrying out the process of protein synthesis

PART B

11 Studies of fat cells and thyroid cells show that fat cells have fewer mitochondria than thyroid cells. A biologist would most likely infer that fat tissue
(1) does not require energy
(2) has energy requirements equal to those of thyroid tissue
(3) requires less energy than thyroid tissue
(4) requires more energy than thyroid tissue

Base your answer to question 12 on the diagram below of a cell associated with coordination and on your knowledge of biology.

12 Structure X would be involved in the
(1) storage of digestive enzymes
(2) absorption of energy from the Sun
(3) development of pathogens
(4) synthesis of proteins

13 Describe how *two* of the cell structures listed below interact to help maintain a balanced internal environment in a cell:

    mitochondrion
    ribosome
    cell membrane
    nucleus
    vacuole

In your answer be sure to:

- select *two* of these structures, write their names, and state one function of each
- describe how each structure you selected contributes to the functioning of the other

Base your answer to question 14 on the passage below and on your knowledge of biology.

    ... Some of the most common and deadly bacteria do their mischief by forming a sticky scum called biofilm. Individually, the microbes are easy to control, but when they organize themselves into biofilms they can become deadly, said Dr. Barbara Iglewski of the University of Rochester. ...

    Biofilms are actually intricately organized colonies of billions of microbes, all working in a coordinated way to defend against attack and to pump out a toxin that can be deadly.

    Once they are organized, the bacteria are highly resistant to antibiotics and even strong detergents often cannot wash them away or kill them.

    Iglewski and colleagues from Montana State University and the University of Iowa report in *Science* that they discovered how the microbes in the colonies communicate and found that once this conversation is interrupted, the deadly bugs can be easily washed away.

    Using *Pseudomonas aeruginosa*, a common bacteria that is a major infection hazard in hospitals and among cystic fibrosis patients, the researchers isolated a gene that the bacteria uses to make a communications molecule. The molecule helps the microbes organize themselves into a biofilm — a complex structure that includes tubes to carry in nutrients and carry out wastes, including deadly toxins.

    In their study, the researchers showed that if the gene that makes the communications molecule was blocked, the *Pseudomonas aeruginosa* could form only wimpy [weak], unorganized colonies that could be washed away with just a soap that has no effect on a healthy colony. ...

Adapted from: Paul Recer, "Researchers find new means to disrupt attack by microbes," *The Daily Gazette*, April 26, 1998.

14 What is one characteristic of a biofilm?

(1) presence of tubes to transport materials into annd out of the colony
(2) presence of a nervous system for communication within the colony
(3) ease with which colonies can be broken down by detergents
(4) lack of resistance of the bacterial colony to antibiotics

13. Allow a maximum of 4 credits for describing how two cell structures interact to help maintain a balanced internal environment in a cell, allocated as follows: Allow a maximum of 2 credits, 1 credit for each correct function of the two structures selected. Acceptable responses include, but are not limited to: mitochondrion: release of energy from nutrients; ribosome: protein synthesis; cell membrane: regulates movement of materials into and out of the cell; nucleus: regulates cell functions or carries the genetic code; vacuole: storage. Allow a maximum of 2 credits, 1 credit for describing how each of the two structures selected contributes to the functioning of the other. Acceptable responses include, but are not limited to: The nucleus contains the code for the enzymes that function in the mitochondrion. The mitochondrion provides energy that is needed by the nucleus. *(#58, August 2006 Regents Exam)*

14. (1) Biofilms do not possess a nervous system. Biofilms are resistant to antibiotics and to breakdown by detergents. *(#31, June 2004 Regents Exam)*

Cells and Their Environment

		Standards	Teach Key Ideas

CHAPTER OPENER, pp. 172–173 `15 min.`

The Living Environment

SECTION 1 Cell Membrane, pp. 175–177 `45 min.`

> Homeostasis
> Lipid Bilayer
> Membrane Proteins

Standards: 4.1.2c, 4.1.2g, 4.5.3a

Teach Key Ideas:
- Bellringer Transparency
- Transparencies B10 Membrane Proteins
- Visual Concepts Phospholipid • Lipid Bilayer • Parts of the Cell Membrane

---

SECTION 2 Cell Transport, pp. 178–183 `90 min.`

> Passive Transport
> Osmosis
> Active Transport

Standards: 4.1.2g, 4.1.2i, 4.5.1e

Teach Key Ideas:
- Bellringer Transparency
- Transparencies B19 Ion Channels • B18 Facilitated Diffusion • B16 Osmosis • B17 Hypertonic, Hypotonic and Isotonic Solutions • B21 Sodium-Potassium Pump • B22 Endocytosis and Exocytosis
- Visual Concepts Concentration Gradient • Equilibrium • Diffusion in a Liquid • Osmosis • Comparing Hypertonic, Isotonic, and Hypotonic Conditions • Diffusion Through Ion Channels • Passive Transport: Facilitated Diffusion • Comparing Active and Passive Transport • Active Transport • Sodium-Potassium Pump • Endocytosis • Exocytosis

---

SECTION 3 Cell Communication, pp. 184–189 `45 min.`

> Sending Signals
> Receiving Signals
> Responding to Signals

Standards: 4.1.2g, 4.1.2j, 4.5.1g

Teach Key Ideas:
- Bellringer Transparency
- Transparencies B20 Changes in Permeability

See also PowerPoint® Resources

Chapter Review and Assessment Resources

- **SE** Super Summary, p. 190
- **SE** Regents Exam Practice, p. 191
- Regents Review Guide
- Review Resources
- Chapter Tests A and B
- Holt Online Assessment
- Regents Question Banks on Teacher's One-Stop Planner

CHAPTER
Fast Track *Thorough instruction will require the times shown.*

Basic Learners
- **TE** Organizing Concepts, p. 176
- **TE** Demonstrating Osmosis, p. 180
- Directed Reading Worksheets*
- Active Reading Worksheets*
- Lab Manuals, Level A*
- Study Guide* ■
- Note-taking Workbook*
- Special Needs Activities and Modified Tests*

Advanced Learners
- **TE** Developing Metaphors, p. 185
- Critical Thinking Worksheets*
- Concept Mapping Worksheets*
- Science Skills Worksheets*
- Lab Datasheets, Level C*

Why It Matters
Build student motivation with resources about high-interest applications.

Hands-On

Skills Development

Assessment

Why It Matters	Hands-On	Skills Development	Assessment
	SE Inquiry Lab Salty Cells, p. 173* ■	**TE Reading Toolbox** Assessing Prior Knowledge, p. 172 **SE Reading Toolbox,** p. 174	
TE Demonstration Selectively Permeable Membrane, p. 176		**SE Reading Toolbox** Four-Corner Fold, p. 177	**SE Section Review** **TE Formative Assessment** Spanish Assessment* ■ 📁 **Section Quiz** ■
TE Salt Pollution, p. 181 **TE Demonstration** Cell Membrane Analogy, p. 182	**SE Quick Lab** Osmosis, p. 181* ■ **SE Inquiry Lab** Cell Size and Diffusion, p. 188* ■ 📁 **Quick Lab** Demonstrating Diffusion* 📁 **Skills Practice Lab** Observing Osmosis in Eggs*	**SE Reading Toolbox** Word Parts, p. 180 **TE Reading Toolbox** Word Parts, p. 180	**SE Section Review** **TE Formative Assessment** Spanish Assessment* ■ 📁 **Section Quiz** ■
SE Heady Effects p. 187 **TE Demonstration** Sending Signals, p. 184	**SE Quick Lab** Sensitive Plants, p. 185* ■	**SE Reading Toolbox** Finding Examples, p. 186 **TE Reading Toolbox** Finding Examples, p. 186 **TE Reading Toolbox** Visual Literacy, p. 187	**SE Section Review** **TE Formative Assessment** Spanish Assessment* ■ 📁 **Section Quiz** ■

See also Lab Generator

See also Holt Online Assessment Resources

Resources for Differentiated Instruction

English Learners
TE Analogies, p. 175
TE What's the Difference?, p. 180
TE Relating Text and Visuals, p. 182
TE Understanding Terms, p. 184
📁 Directed Reading Worksheets*
📁 Active Reading Worksheets*
📁 Lab Manuals, Level A*
📓 Study Guide* ■
📓 Note-taking Workbook*
📓 Multilingual Glossary
💿 Interactive Tutor

Struggling Readers
TE Organizing Concepts, p. 176
TE What's the Difference?, p. 180
TE Relating Text and Visuals, p. 182
📁 Directed Reading Worksheets*
📁 Active Reading Worksheets*
📁 Lab Manuals, Level A*
📓 Study Guide*
📓 Note-taking Workbook*
📓 Special Needs Activities and Modified Tests*
💿 Interactive Tutor

Special Education Students
TE A Model for Diffusion, p. 179
📁 Directed Reading Worksheets*
📁 Active Reading Worksheets*
📁 Lab Manuals, Level A*
📓 Study Guide* ■
📓 Note-taking Workbook*
📓 Special Needs Activities and Modified Tests*

Alternative Assessment
TE Making Drawings, p. 179
📁 Science Skills Worksheets*
📁 Section Quizzes* ■
📓 Chapter Tests A, B, and C* ■

Chapter 8

Chapter 8

Cells and Their Environment

Preview

1 Cell Membrane
Homeostasis
Lipid Bilayer
Membrane Proteins

2 Cell Transport
Passive Transport
Osmosis
Active Transport

3 Cell Communication
Sending Signals
Receiving Signals
Responding to Signals

Overview

The purpose of this chapter is to describe the structure of the cell membrane and its role in homeostasis. Substances are moved in and out of cells through cell transport mechanisms, such as diffusion, osmosis, pumps, and vesicles. Cells communicate and coordinate activity by sending chemical signals that carry information to other cells.

Assessing Prior Knowledge Students should understand the following concepts:
• cellular nature of life
• basic biochemistry

Visual Literacy Ask students to point out the basic cell parts in the image, such as the cell membrane, nucleus, and cytoplasm. Have them describe their functions to foreshadow the diagrams they will see in the lessons. **LS Visual**

Why It Matters

Cells interact with their environment to exchange nutrients and wastes and to coordinate activities over long distances.

Did you know that cells drink? This blood capillary cell wraps its cell membrane around the surrounding fluid and takes in a big gulp.

The lumen (blue) is the hollow part of a capillary.

A row of vesicles forms in the upper cell membrane (purple) and moves toward the bottom of the capillary. These vesicles help transport serum.

The Living Environment
Standard 4 Students will understand and apply scientific concepts, principles, and theories pertaining to the physical setting and living environment and recognize the historical development of ideas in science.
Key Idea 1 Living things are both similar to and different from each other and from nonliving things. *Major Understandings* - 1.2c, 1.2g, 1.2i, 1.2j
Key Idea 5 Organisms maintain a dynamic equilibrium that sustains life *Major Understandings* **5.1e, 5.1g, 5.3a**

Chapter Correlations   *The Living Environment*

Standard 4

1.2c The components of the human body, from organ systems to cell organelles, interact to maintain a balanced internal environment. To successfully accomplish this, organisms possess a diversity of control mechanisms that detect deviations and make corrective actions.

1.2g Each cell is covered by a membrane that performs a number of important functions for the cell. These include: separation from its outside environment, controlling which molecules enter and leave the cell, and recognition of chemical signals. The processes of diffusion and active transport are important in the movement of materials in and out of cells.

1.2i Inside the cell a variety of specialized structures, formed from many different molecules, carry out the transport of materials (cytoplasm), extraction of energy from nutrients (mitochondria), protein building (ribosomes), waste disposal (cell membrane), storage (vacuole), and information storage (nucleus).

1.2j Receptor molecules play an important role in the interactions between cells. Two primary agents of cellular communication are hormones and chemicals produced by nerve cells. If nerve or hormone signals are blocked, cellular communication is disrupted and the organism's stability is affected.

5.1e The energy from ATP is used by the organism to obtain, transform, and transport materials, and to eliminate wastes.

5.1g Enzymes and other molecules, such as hormones, receptor molecules, and antibodies, have specific shapes that influence both how they function and how they interact with other molecules.

5.3a Dynamic equilibrium results from detection of and response to stimuli. Organisms detect and respond to change in a variety of ways both at the cellular level and at the organismal level.

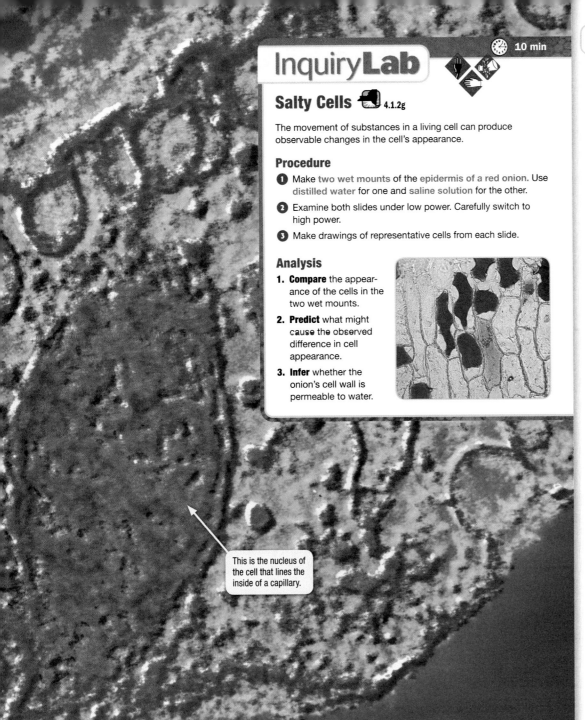

InquiryLab

⏱ 10 min

Salty Cells 🧅 4.1.2g

The movement of substances in a living cell can produce observable changes in the cell's appearance.

Procedure

1 Make two wet mounts of the epidermis of a red onion. Use distilled water for one and saline solution for the other.

2 Examine both slides under low power. Carefully switch to high power.

3 Make drawings of representative cells from each slide.

Analysis

1. **Compare** the appearance of the cells in the two wet mounts.

2. **Predict** what might cause the observed difference in cell appearance.

3. **Infer** whether the onion's cell wall is permeable to water.

This is the nucleus of the cell that lines the inside of a capillary.

InquiryLab

Teacher's Notes Use at least a 5% saline solution.

Materials
- cover slip (2)
- distilled water
- compound microscope
- microscope slide (2)
- red onion
- saline solution
- dropper
- knife

Answers to Analysis

1. The cells that were placed in the saline solution appeared to have shriveled contents that pulled away from the cell wall. The other cells seemed to be full of cytoplasm.

2. Water leaving the saline immersed cell would cause the cell contents to shrivel. Water that enters the cells immersed in water would cause the cytoplasm to swell.

3. Yes. If water can move from the inside of the cell to the cell's outer surroundings, the cell wall must be water permeable.

Key Resources

💿 Interactive Tutor

READING TOOLBOX

Using Words

Accept reasonable answers.
1. A *phospholipid* is a fat containing phosphorus.
2. *Exocytosis* refers to a process that occurs outside the cell.

Using Language

1. bacteria and fungal spores
2. for example, such as, like, including

Using Fold Notes

You may want to review students' Fold Notes to see if they have followed the directions accurately. Conduct a short class discussion on the similarities and differences so students can check their own work.

These reading tools can help you learn the material in this chapter. For more information on how to use these and other tools, see **Appendix: Reading and Study Skills**.

Using Words

Word Parts You can tell a lot about a word by taking it apart and examining its prefix and root.

Your Turn Use the information in the table to predict the meaning of the following words:
1. *phospholipid*
2. *exocytosis*

Word Parts		
Word part	Type	Meaning
phospho-	prefix	containing phosphorus
lipid	root	a fat
exo-	prefix	outside
cyto	root	cell

Using Language

Finding Examples Concrete examples often help clarify new information. Certain words and phrases can help you recognize examples. These words include *for example, such as, like,* and *including.*

Your Turn Use what you have learned about examples to answer the following questions.
1. Find the examples in the following sentence: Some cells also use exocytosis to remove infecting microbes, such as bacteria or fungal spores.
2. Find the examples in the introductory paragraph above.

Using FoldNotes

Four-Corner Fold A four-corner fold is useful when you want to compare the characteristics of four topics. The four-corner fold can organize the characteristics of the four topics side by side under the flaps. Similarities and differences between the four topics can then be easily identified.

Your Turn Make a four-corner fold to help you learn about four topics in this chapter.
1. Fold a sheet of paper in half from top to bottom. Then, unfold the paper.
2. Fold the top and bottom of the paper to the crease in the center.
3. Fold the paper in half from side to side. Then, unfold the paper.
4. Using scissors, cut the top flap creases made in step 3 to form four flaps.

Cell Membrane

Key Ideas	Key Terms	Why It Matters
❯ How does the cell membrane help a cell maintain homeostasis? ❯ How does the cell membrane restrict the exchange of substances? ❯ What are some functions of membrane proteins?	phospholipid lipid bilayer	A simple defect in a cell membrane protein can make a life-or-death difference. In people who have cystic fibrosis, the cell membrane is does not work properly.

Every cell is surrounded by a cell membrane. The cell membrane protects the cell and helps move substances and messages in and out of the cell. By regulating transport, the membrane helps the cell maintain constancy and order.

Homeostasis

All living things respond to their environments. For example, we sweat when we are hot and shiver when we are cold. These reactions help our bodies maintain homeostasis. Recall that homeostasis is the maintenance of stable internal conditions in a changing environment. Individual cells, as well as organisms, must maintain homeostasis in order to live. ❯ **One way that a cell maintains homeostasis is by controlling the movement of substances across the cell membrane.**

Like the swimmer and the jellyfish in **Figure 1,** cells are suspended in a fluid environment. Even the cell membrane is fluid. It is made up of a "sea" of lipids in which proteins float. By allowing some materials but not others to enter the cell, the cell membrane acts as a gatekeeper. In addition, it provides structural support to the cytoplasm, recognizes foreign material, and communicates with other cells. These functions also contribute to maintaining homeostasis.

❯ **Reading Check** *What are some roles of the cell membrane? (See the Appendix for answers to Reading Checks.)*

 The Living Environment
Standard 4

1.2c The components of the human body, from organ systems to cell organelles, interact to maintain a balanced internal environment. To successfully accomplish this, organisms possess a diversity of control mechanisms that detect deviations and make corrective actions.

1.2g Each cell is covered by a membrane that performs a number of important functions for the cell. These include: separation from its outside environment, controlling which molecules enter and leave the cell, and recognition of chemical signals. The processes of diffusion and active transport are important in the movement of materials in and out of cells.

5.3a Dynamic equilibrium results from detection of and response to stimuli. Organisms detect and respond to change in a variety of ways both at the cellular level and at the organismal level.

www.scilinks.org
Topic: Homeostasis
Code: HX80753

Cells in this jellyfish exchange substances with the water.

The skin of the swimmer forms a watertight seal.

Figure 1 The cells of the jellyfish exchange materials more freely with the sea water than do the cells of the swimmer.

Differentiated Instruction

English Learners

Analogies Have students think of analogies for the role of the cell membrane. For example, the membrane could be compared to checkpoints at a nation's border. At checkpoints, shipments are stopped and inspected, and admitted to enhance the nation's economy. Ask how customs inspections are like the cell membrane. (Incoming molecules are also inspected at the cell membrane, and admitted to enhance the functioning of the cell. The cell would shut down if the cell membrane were not permeable.) **LS Logical**

Key Resources

🗒 **Transparencies**
B10 Membrane Proteins

💿 **Visual Concepts**
Phospholipid
Lipid Bilayer
Parts of the Cell Membrane

❯ Focus

This section describes how the structure of the cell membrane helps maintain homeostasis, and restricts the exchange of substances. The functions of membrane proteins also are discussed.

💿 Bellringer

Use the Bellringer transparency to prepare students for this section.

❯ Teach

Teaching Key Ideas

Maintaining Homeostasis Remind students that snakes and lizards are ectothermic. Have students suggest ways a lizard maintains homeostasis, such as moving to sun or shade and hibernation. Ask students to imagine their "normal body covering" as a T-shirt and shorts. Have them hypothesize how their own activities might change if they were ectothermic and what special precautions they would need to take to maintain a constant body temperature. **LS Interpersonal**

Section Correlations

4.1.2c
4.1.2g
4.5.3a

Selectively Permeable Membrane Choose 3 to 5 different brands of plastic bags. Mix some cornstarch and water in each bag and close tightly. Place each bag into a larger, clear container of water with iodine mixed in. Remind students that iodine is an indicator for starch. With students, determine which bags represent a permeable membrane (starch water and iodine water is purple), a selectively permeable membrane (starch water is purple and iodine water is orange, or starch water is white and iodine water is purple), or a nonpermeable membrane (starch water is white and iodine water is orange). **LS Visual/ Logical**

phospholipid (FAHS foh LIP id) a lipid that contains phosphorus and that is a structural component in cell membranes

lipid bilayer (LIP id BIE LAY uhr) the basic structure of a biological membrane, composed of two layers of phospholipids

Lipid Bilayer

The cell membrane is made of a "sea" of phospholipids. As **Figure 2** shows, a **phospholipid** is a specialized lipid made of a phosphate "head" and two fatty acid "tails." The phosphate head is polar and is attracted to water. In contrast, the fatty acid tails are nonpolar and are repelled by water.

Structure Because there is water inside and outside the cell, the phospholipids form a double layer called the **lipid bilayer.** The nonpolar tails, repelled by water, make up the interior of the lipid bilayer. The polar heads are attracted to the water, so they point toward the surfaces of the lipid bilayer. One layer of polar heads faces the cytoplasm, while the other layer is in contact with the cell's immediate surroundings.

Barrier Only certain substances can pass through the lipid bilayer. ❯ The phospholipids form a barrier through which only small, nonpolar substances can pass. Ions and most polar molecules are repelled by the nonpolar interior of the lipid bilayer.

Membrane Proteins

Various proteins can be found in the cell membrane. Some proteins face inside the cell, and some face outside. Other proteins may stretch across the lipid bilayer and face both inside and outside.

Proteins in Lipids What holds these proteins in the membrane? Recall that proteins are made of amino acids. Some amino acids are polar, and others are nonpolar. Nonpolar portions of a protein are attracted to the interior of the lipid bilayer but are repelled by water on either side of the membrane. In contrast, polar parts of the protein are attracted to the water on both sides of the lipid bilayer. These opposing attractions help hold the protein in the membrane.

❯ **Reading Check** *Why can't ions pass through the lipid bilayer?*

Figure 2 The membrane that surrounds the cell is made of a lipid bilayer, a double layer of phospholipids.

The lipid bilayer is the foundation of the cell membrane.

The arrangement of phospholipids in the lipid bilayer makes the cell membrane selectively permeable.

A phospholipid's "head" is polar, and its two fatty acid "tails" are nonpolar.

Differentiated Instruction

Basic Learners/Struggling Readers

Organizing Concepts Have students fill in the concept map shown using the following terms: *cell surface markers, receptor proteins, enzymes,* and *transport proteins.* To help students remember the terms, ask them to come up with an icon and descriptor for each. Examples are shown. **LS Visual**

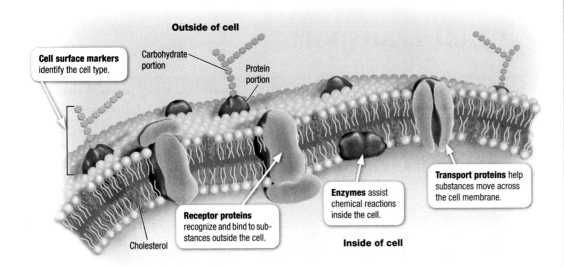

Outside of cell

Cell surface markers identify the cell type.

Carbohydrate portion

Protein portion

Receptor proteins recognize and bind to substances outside the cell.

Enzymes assist chemical reactions inside the cell.

Transport proteins help substances move across the cell membrane.

Cholesterol

Inside of cell

Types of Proteins As **Figure 3** shows, membranes contain different types of proteins. ❭ **Proteins in the cell membrane include cell-surface markers, receptor proteins, enzymes, and transport proteins.**

• **Cell-Surface Markers** Like a name tag, a chain of sugars acts as a marker to identify each type of cell. Liver cells have a different chain of sugars from heart cells. These sugars (carbohydrates) are attached to the cell surface by proteins called *glycoproteins*. Glycoproteins help cells work together.

• **Receptor Proteins** Receptor proteins enable a cell to sense its surroundings by binding to certain substances outside the cell. When this happens, it causes changes inside the cell.

• **Enzymes** Many proteins in the cell membrane help with important biochemical reactions inside the cell.

• **Transport Proteins** Many substances that the cell needs cannot pass through the lipid bilayer. Transport proteins aid the movement of these substances into and out of the cell.

Figure 3 The cell membrane contains various proteins that have specialized functions.

READING TOOLBOX

Four-Corner Fold Make a four-corner fold to compare four types of proteins found in the cell membrane.

Section 1 Review

❭ **KEY IDEAS**

1. **Relate** the functions of the cell membrane to homeostasis.
2. **Describe** the types of substances that can pass through the lipid bilayer of the cell membrane.
3. **Outline** four functions of proteins within the cell membrane.

CRITICAL THINKING

4. **Applying Logic** What would happen if the cell membrane were fully permeable to all substances in the cell's environment?
5. **Predicting Outcomes** What would happen if the cell were exposed to a drug that disabled the transport proteins in the cell membrane?

ALTERNATIVE ASSESSMENT

6. **Making Models** Create a model of the lipid bilayer, including its associated proteins. Your model may be made of clay or household items. Present your model to the class. Indicate the role of each type of protein in maintaining homeostasis.

Section **2** # Cell Transport

Key Ideas	Key Terms	Why It Matters
❯ What determines the direction in which passive transport occurs? ❯ Why is osmosis important? ❯ How do substances move against their concentration gradients?	equilibrium osmosis concentration sodium- gradient potassium diffusion pump carrier protein	The cell's membrane is a little like a country's border. Both barriers regulate who or what enters and who or what leaves.

❯ Focus

This section describes how substances move across cell membranes either directly or through channels. Passive transport, osmosis, and active transport are discussed.

 Bellringer

Use the Bellringer transparency to prepare students for this section.

Teaching Key Ideas

Create Operational Definitions Ask students to define the terms *passive, active,* and *transport* in their own words. Then ask them to imagine sitting in a boat that is moving downstream with the current. Then, imagine using a small motor to move the same boat upstream against the current. Ask students to determine which action shows passive transport and which shows active transport. Help them realize that active transport requires an input of energy and goes against the natural flow like the motor moving the boat upstream. **LS Verbal**

Answers to Caption Questions
Figure 4: crowded areas
Figure 6: outside of cell membrane

 The Living Environment
Standard 4
1.2g Each cell is covered by a membrane that performs a number of important functions for the cell. These include: separation from its outside environment, controlling which molecules enter and leave the cell, and recognition of chemical signals. The processes of diffusion and active transport are important in the movement of materials in and out of cells.
1.2i Inside the cell a variety of specialized structures, formed from many different molecules, carry out the transport of materials (cytoplasm), extraction of energy from nutrients (mitochondria), protein building (ribosomes), waste disposal (cell membrane), storage (vacuole), and information storage (nucleus).
5.1e The energy from ATP is used by the organism to obtain, transform, and transport materials, and to eliminate wastes.

Figure 4 If people acted like molecules, they would fill up the space in this room evenly over time. ❯ What area of this room has a high concentration of people?

The cell must move substances of varying size, electrical charge, and composition into and out of the cell. Substances may enter and leave the cell in a variety of ways. Sometimes the cell must use energy to move a substance across the cell membrane. In *active transport,* the cells is required to use energy to move a substance. In *passive transport,* the cell does not use energy.

Passive Transport

In a solution, randomly moving molecules tend to fill up a space. When the space is filled evenly, a state called **equilibrium** is reached. The amount of a particular substance in a given volume is called the *concentration* of the substance. When one area has a higher concentration than another area does, as **Figure 4** shows, a **concentration gradient** exists. Substances move from an area of higher concentration to an area of lower concentration. This movement down the concentration gradient is called **diffusion.**

The cell membrane separates the cytoplasm from the fluid outside the cell. Some substances enter and leave the cell by diffusing across the cell membrane. The direction of movement depends on the concentration gradient and does not require energy. ❯ **In passive transport, substances cross the cell membrane down their concentration gradient.** Some substances diffuse through the lipid bilayer. Others diffuse through transport proteins.

Section Correlations

4.1.2g
4.1.2i
4.5.1e

Key Resources

 Transparencies
B19 Ion Channels
B18 Facilitated Diffusion
B16 Osmosis
B17 Hypertonic, Hypotonic, and Isotonic Solutions
B21 Sodium-Potassium Pump
B22 Endocytosis and Exocytosis

 Visual Concepts
Concentration Gradient
Equilibrium
Diffusion in a Liquid
Osmosis
Comparing Hypertonic, Isotonic, and Hypotonic Conditions
Diffusion Through Ion Channels
Passive Transport: Facilitated Diffusion
Comparing Active and Passive Transport
Active Transport
Sodium-Potassium Pump
Endocytosis
Exocytosis

Simple Diffusion Small, nonpolar molecules can pass directly through the lipid bilayer. This type of movement is called *simple diffusion*. As **Figure 5** shows, oxygen diffuses into the cell through the lipid bilayer. The concentration of oxygen is higher outside the cell than it is inside. Thus, oxygen moves down its concentration gradient into the cell. In contrast, the concentration of carbon dioxide is often higher inside the cell than it is outside. So, carbon dioxide diffuses out of the cell. Natural steroid hormones, which are nonpolar and fat soluble, can also diffuse across the lipid bilayer.

Facilitated Diffusion Many ions and polar molecules that are important for cell function do not diffuse easily through the nonpolar lipid bilayer. During *facilitated diffusion,* transport proteins help these substances diffuse through the cell membrane. Two types of transport proteins are channel proteins and carrier proteins.

Channel Proteins Ions, sugars, and amino acids can diffuse through the cell membrane through channel proteins. These proteins, sometimes called *pores,* serve as tunnels through the lipid bilayer. Each channel allows the diffusion of specific substances that have the right size and charge. For example, only sodium ions can pass through the sodium ion channel shown in **Figure 5.**

Carrier Proteins Carrier proteins transport substances that fit within their binding site, as **Figure 6** shows. A carrier protein binds to a specific substance on one side of the cell membrane. This binding causes the protein to change shape. As the protein's shape changes, the substance is moved across the membrane and is released on the other side.

❯ **Reading Check** *Why does oxygen diffuse into the cell?*

Figure 5 Nonpolar molecules, such as O_2, diffuse through the lipid bilayer. Channel proteins allow certain ions, such as Na^+, to diffuse through the cell membrane. Cl^- ions cannot pass through the sodium ion channel.

equilibrium a state that exists when the concentration of a substance is the same throughout a space

concentration gradient a difference in the concentration of a substance across a distance

diffusion the movement of particles from regions of higher density to regions of lower density

carrier protein a protein that transports substances across a cell membrane

Facilitated Diffusion

go.hrw.com
✳ **interact online**
Keyword: HX8CENF6

❶ A molecule outside the cell binds to a carrier protein on the cell membrane.

❷ The carrier protein changes shape, which releases the molecule inside the cell.

Outside of cell

Carrier protein

Inside of cell

Outside of cell

Inside of cell

Figure 6 Carrier proteins allow the diffusion of specific molecules by binding the molecules on one side of the cell membrane and releasing them on the other side.
❯ Which side of this membrane has a higher concentration of molecules?

Teaching Key Ideas

Transport Proteins Contrast transport proteins for students. As you describe how a channel protein functions, use a puzzle or toddler's "matching shape" toy—objects can pass only through holes of the same shape. Contrast this with a carrier protein by using a piece of flexible tubing or the top of a small sock and moving the same objects through it. Have students notice how the protein (tubing) changes shape to move the object through.

go.hrw.com
✳ **interact online**

Students can interact with "Facilitated Diffusion" by going to go.hrw.com and typing in the keyword HX8CENF6.

Differentiated Instruction

Alternative Assessment

Making Drawings Have students make their own drawings of the processes of simple diffusion, facilitated diffusion, osmosis, and active transport. Ask students to include brief captions in their own words that describe what is happening in each process. **LS Visual**

Special Education Students

A Model for Diffusion This simple demonstration helps developmentally delayed students see the concrete results of diffusion. Have students fill a beaker about three-fourths full of water. Let the beaker stand until the water is still. Add one drop of food coloring to the surface of the water. Students will observe that the drop spreads out until the water is uniformly colored. This may take several minutes. Ask students what happened to the drop of food coloring. (It moved throughout the water, from where it was more concentrated to where it is less concentrated.) **LS Visual**

Teaching Key Ideas

Sore Throat Remedy Explain the role of osmosis when gargling with a saltwater solution to soothe a sore throat. Swollen throat tissue, which contains water, causes some of the pain. Throat tissue has a higher concentration of water than the surrounding saltwater environment. As a result, water moves by osmosis from the throat tissue into the saltwater solution. The loss of water reduces the swelling and relieves some of the pain.

Teaching Key Ideas

Applications of Osmosis Put the following questions on the board or overhead transparency.

1. Why are green leafy vegetables sprinkled with water at the supermarket? (prevents wilting due to water loss)
2. Why is salt sometimes used to preserve foods? (Microorganisms present on the foods shrink and die in the hypertonic solution.)

READING TOOLBOX

Word Parts *Hypotonic* means "lower concentration." Give students other examples of words using these prefixes and elicit operational definitions. Examples are: hyperactive, hypersensitive, hyperventilate, hypodermis, hypoglycemic, hypothermia.

Hypertonic Solution The fluid outside is more concentrated. As water moves out of the cell, the cell shrinks.

Hypotonic Solution The fluid outside is less concentrated. As water moves into the cell, the cell swells.

Isotonic Solution Water moves into and out of the cell at the same rate. The cell stays the same size.

Figure 7 Red blood cells change shape due to the movement of water. The direction of water movement depends on the difference between the concentration of the solution outside the cell and the concentration of the cytosol.

READING TOOLBOX

Word Parts The prefix *hyper-* means "higher than," and *hypertonic* means "higher concentration." If *hypo-* means "lower than," what does *hypotonic* mean?

osmosis the diffusion of water or another solvent from a more dilute solution (of a solute) to a more concentrated solution (of the solute) through a membrane that is permeable to the solvent

Osmosis

Water can diffuse across a selectively permeable membrane in a process called **osmosis.** Osmosis is a type of passive transport that is very important to keeping cells functional. ❯ **Osmosis allows cells to maintain water balance as their environment changes.**

When ions and polar substances dissolve in water, they attract and bind some water molecules. The remaining water molecules are free to move around. If a concentration gradient exists across a membrane for solutes, a concentration gradient also exists across the membrane for free water molecules. Osmosis occurs as free water molecules move down their concentration gradient into the solution that has the lower concentration of free water molecules.

Water Channels Polar water molecules do not diffuse directly through the bilayer. But the cell membrane contains channel proteins that only water molecules can pass through. Thus, osmosis in cells is a form of facilitated diffusion. In humans, water channels help in the regulation of body temperature, in digestion, in reproduction, and in water conservation in the kidneys.

Predicting Water Movement The direction of water movement in a cell depends on the concentration of the cell's environment. **Figure 7** shows a red blood cell in solutions of three concentrations.

1. Water moves out. If the solution is *hypertonic,* or has a higher solute concentration than the cytoplasm does, water moves out of the cell. The cell loses water and shrinks.

2. Water moves in. If the solution is *hypotonic,* or has a lower solute concentration than the cytoplasm does, water moves into the cell. The cell gains water and expands in size.

3. No net change in water movement occurs, or equilibrium is reached. If the solution is *isotonic,* or has the same solute concentration that the cytoplasm does, water diffuses into and out of the cell at equal rates. The cell stays the same size.

Differentiated Instruction

Struggling Readers/English Learners

What's the Difference? *Hypotonic, isotonic,* and *hypertonic* are terms that indicate the relative concentrations of solute in two systems. Ask students to think of memory aids for these terms. For example, a cell in a hypertonic environment shrinks (*hyper*—shrinking). A cell in a hypotonic environment swells (*hypo*—swells like a hippo). **LS Verbal**

Basic Learners

Demonstrating Osmosis Cut three potato slices about 1 cm thick. Place one slice in distilled water, one in tap water, and one in a saltwater solution (15 g salt in 250 mL tap water). Leave them overnight. Explain that distilled water is a hypotonic environment; tap water is an isotonic environment; and salt water is a hypertonic environment. Have students predict what will happen to the potato slices. Compare the resulting size of the potato slices with the blood cells in **Figure 7**. **LS Visual**

QuickLab

MULTI-DAY ⏱ 15 min

Osmosis 4.1.2g

You will observe the movement of water into or out of a grape under various conditions.

Procedure

❶ Make a data table with four columns and three rows.

❷ Fill one jar with a sugar solution. Fill a second jar with grape juice. Fill a third jar with tap water. Label each jar with the name of the solution that it contains.

❸ Use a balance to find the mass of each of three grapes. Place one grape in each jar, and put the lids on the jars.

❹ Predict whether the mass of each grape will increase or decrease over time. Explain your predictions.

❺ After 24 h, remove each grape from its jar, and dry the grape gently with a paper towel. Using the balance, find each grape's mass again. Record your results.

Analysis

1. **Identify** the solutions in which osmosis occurred.

2. **CRITICAL THINKING** **Evaluating Conclusions** How did you determine whether osmosis occurred in each of the three solutions?

3. **CRITICAL THINKING** **Evaluating Hypotheses** Did the mass of each grape change as you had predicted? Why or why not?

Effects of Osmosis If left unchecked, the swelling caused by a hypotonic solution could cause a cell to burst. The rigid cell walls of plants and fungi prevent the cells of these organisms from expanding too much. In fact, many plants are healthiest in a hypotonic environment, as **Figure 8** shows. Some unicellular eukaryotes have *contractile vacuoles,* which collect excess water inside the cell and force the water out of the cell. Animal cells have neither cell walls nor contractile vacuoles. However, many animal cells can avoid swelling caused by osmosis by actively removing solutes from the cytoplasm. The removal of dissolved solutes from a cell increases the concentration of free water molecules inside the cell.

Figure 8 Plant cells are healthiest in a hypotonic environment. When its cells swell, the plant stands rigid. In an isotonic environment, a plant wilts. ❯ **What would happen if you added water to the plant on the right?**

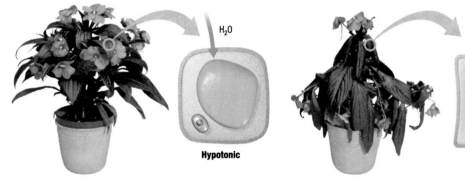

Hypotonic

Isotonic

QuickLab

Teacher's Notes Review the use of a balance to find the mass of objects. Make a saturated sugar solution by stirring sugar into sugar to water one teaspoon at a time until no more sugar dissolves.

Materials
• balance
• grape juice
• grapes (3)
• jars or similar containers (3)
• sugar
• water
• paper towel

Answers to Analysis

1. The tap water is a hypotonic solution because the grape swelled. The sugar solution is a hypertonic solution because it caused the grape to shrink. Depending on the sugar content of the grape juice, the juice may be isotonic (the grape neither swelled nor shrunk) or hypertonic (the grape swelled).

2. The evidence for osmosis is an increase or a decrease in the mass of the grapes.

3. Students who had a clear understanding of osmosis before the experiment probably will not change their thinking.

Why It Matters

Salt Pollution Tell students that in some areas, salt is sprinkled over icy roads to melt the ice. Plants growing along the roadside are often seriously damaged or killed. The damaged plants look similar to those that have been through a very hot, dry summer. A higher-than-normal salt concentration in the environment causes plant cells to lose water through osmosis. Without sufficient water, the plants die.

Cell Membrane Analogy Bring an air pump and an inflatable ball to class. Ask a student to inflate the ball with the pump. Relate this activity to a cell membrane pump. (The air pump uses the energy supplied by the student to move air against a pressure gradient.) Tell students that membrane pumps use energy supplied by the cell to move substances against their concentration gradient. **LS** **Logical/Visual**

Answers to Caption Questions
Figure 9: outside the cell

sodium-potassium pump a carrier protein that uses ATP to actively transport sodium ions out of a cell and potassium ions into the cell

Figure 9 The sodium-potassium pump actively transports both Na⁺ and K⁺ ions across the cell membrane. ❯ **In this figure, is the concentration of sodium ions higher inside the cell or outside the cell?**

Active Transport

Sometimes, cells must transport substances against their concentration gradients. This movement is called *active transport* because the cell must use energy to move these substances. ❯ Active transport requires energy to move substances against their concentration gradients. Most often, the energy needed for active transport is supplied directly or indirectly by ATP.

Pumps Many active transport processes use carrier proteins to move substances. In facilitated diffusion, the carrier proteins do not require energy. In active transport, the carrier proteins do require energy to "pump" substances against their concentration gradient.

One of the most important carrier proteins in animal cells is the **sodium-potassium pump,** shown in **Figure 9.** Sodium ions inside the cell bind to the carrier protein. A phosphate group from ATP transfers energy to the protein. The protein changes shape and releases the sodium ions outside the cell membrane. Outside the cell, potassium ions bind to the pump. As a result, the phosphate group is released from the pump. The pump returns to its original shape and releases the potassium ions inside the cell membrane. For every three sodium ions taken out, two potassium ions are brought inside.

This pump prevents sodium ions from building up in the cell. Osmosis results when sodium ion levels are high. The cell could swell or even burst if too much water enters. The concentration gradients of sodium ions and potassium ions also help transport other substances, such as glucose, across the cell membrane.

Sodium-Potassium Pump

❶ Three sodium ions bind to the pump. A phosphate from ATP also binds, which transfers energy.

❷ The pump changes shape, releasing the three sodium ions on the other side of the membrane.

❸ Two potassium ions bind to the pump and are tranported across the cell membrane.

❹ The phosphate group is released. The pump returns to its original shape, releasing the two potassium ions.

Outside of cell
Sodium ion, Na+
Potassium ion, K+
ATP
P + ADP
Phosphate group
Inside of cell

Differentiated Instruction

English Learners/Struggling Readers

Relating Text and Visuals Interpreting **Figure 9** can be difficult for students with reading and language difficulties. Review each step slowly. Put a visual key on the board for all of the names, codes, and symbols shown in the figure. Ask students to describe what happens to each component in the drawing (ATP, ADP, Na⁺, K⁺, and P) from steps 1 to 4. Be sure that they realize that *P* and *potassium* are not the same. **LS** **Visual**

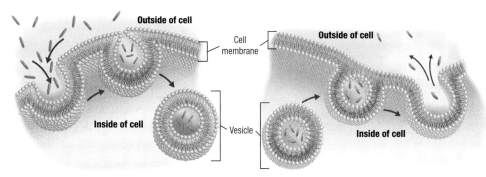

Endocytosis   Exocytosis

Outside of cell

Cell
membrane

Inside of cell

Outside of cell

Vesicle

Inside of cell

Vesicles Many substances, such as proteins and polysaccharides, are too large to be transported by carrier proteins. Instead, they cross the cell membrane in vesicles. Recall that vesicles are membrane-bound sacs. The vesicle membrane is a lipid bilayer, like the cell membrane. Therefore, vesicles can bud off from the membrane, fuse with it, or fuse with other vesicles.

The movement of a large substance into a cell by means of a vesicle is called *endocytosis*. During endocytosis, shown in **Figure 10**, the cell membrane forms a pouch around the substance. The pouch then closes up and pinches off from the membrane to form a vesicle inside the cell. Vesicles that form by endocytosis may fuse with lysosomes or other organelles.

The movement of material out of a cell by means of a vesicle is called *exocytosis*. During exocytosis, shown in **Figure 10**, vesicles inside the cell fuse with the cell membrane. From the cell membrane, the contents of the vesicle are <u>released</u> to the outside of the cell. Cells use exocytosis to export proteins modified by the Golgi apparatus. Some protists release their waste products through this process. Some cells also use exocytosis to remove bacteria or other microbes.

❯ **Reading Check** *What is the structure of the vesicle membrane?*

Figure 10 A cell moves large substances or large amounts of materials in vesicles. Vesicles can fuse with the cell membrane to take in and release substances.

ACADEMIC VOCABULARY

release to set free

Teaching Key Ideas

Contrasting Processes Direct students to look at **Figure 10.** Two opposite processes are shown. Ask students to cite evidence from the diagram that the processes are opposite. To many students, the diagrams will look the same unless you help them see the differences.
LS Visual

Teaching Key Ideas

Phagocytosis Remind students how amoebas take in food and release wastes through phagocytosis. Compare this process of taking in fragments of organic matter or entire cells and releasing wastes with endocytosis and exocytosis.

❯**Close**

Formative Assessment

The direction of water movement in cells depends on _____.
A. which carrier proteins are in the cell membrane (Incorrect. Carrier proteins transport materials other than water.)
B. whether the surrounding solution is hypertonic, hypotonic, or isotonic (Correct! The concentration of water in the environment determines whether it moves in or out of the cell.)
C. the actions of the sodium-potassium pump (Incorrect. This pump moves sodium and potassium against the concentration gradient.)
D. whether vesicles are present (Incorrect. Vesicles help cells take in fragments of organic matter or entire cells.)

Section
2 **Review**

❯ **KEY IDEAS**

1. **Compare** the functions of channel proteins and carrier proteins in facilitated diffusion.
2. **Explain** why the presence of dissolved particles on one side of a membrane results in diffusion of water across the membrane.

3. **List** two ways that a cell can move a substance against its concentration gradient.

CRITICAL THINKING

4. **Applying Logic** Based on have learned about homeostasis and osmosis, why should humans avoid drinking sea water?
5. **Predicting Outcomes** If a cell were unable to make ATP, how would the cell membrane's transport processes be affected?

METHODS OF SCIENCE

6. **Designing an Experiment** What data would a biologist need to collect to determine whether a specific molecule is transported into cells by diffusion, by facilitated diffusion, or by active transport?

Answers to Section Review

1. Channel proteins act as tunnels through the lipid bilayer for ions, sugars, and amino acids—substances that have the right size and charge. Carrier proteins bind to substances with the right shape, moving these substances to the other side of the cell membrane.

2. Dissolved particles reduce the number of water molecules that can move freely on that side. Water then moves by osmosis from the side where the free water molecule concentration is higher to the side where the concentration is lower.

3. pumps and vesicles

4. Sea water has a higher concentration of salt than that in the fluids surrounding human cells. Drinking sea water increases the concentration of salt in the body's fluids, which causes water to leave the cells by osmosis.

5. Active transport processes would stop, because they use the energy in ATP. Passive transport processes would continue until the concentration gradients disappeared.

6. size of molecule, polarity of molecule, whether the molecule can accumulate inside a cell despite higher concentration inside than outside, and whether the cell uses up more energy in the presence of the molecule than in its absence

Section 3

Cell Communication

Key Ideas	Key Terms	Why It Matters
❯ How do cells use signal molecules? ❯ How do cells receive signals? ❯ How do cells respond to signaling?	signal receptor protein second messenger	Cells developed sophisticated methods of communication long before humans developed the Internet, cell phones, or even regular conversation.

The Living Environment
Standard 4

1.2g Each cell is covered by a membrane that performs a number of important functions for the cell. These include: separation from its outside environment, controlling which molecules enter and leave the cell, and recognition of chemical signals. The processes of diffusion and active transport are important in the movement of materials in and out of cells.

1.2j Receptor molecules play an important role in the interactions between cells. Two primary agents of cellular communication are hormones and chemicals produced by nerve cells. If nerve or hormone signals are blocked, cellular communication is disrupted and the organism's stability is affected.

5.1g Enzymes and other molecules, such as hormones, receptor molecules, and antibodies, have specific shapes that influence both how they function and how they interact with other molecules.

Figure 11 This young man dials a phone number, which sends a signal to a target. ❯ **Is this target general or specific?**

We communicate in many ways to share information. In **Figure 11,** one person is surfing the Internet, another is talking on her cell phone, and two are having a face-to-face conversation. All of these are forms of communication. To coordinate activities, information must be shared. Cells in multicellular organisms depend on the activities of other cells to survive. Even unicellular organisms need to communicate—for example, to find a mate.

Sending Signals

You use different methods to communicate in different ways. You may whisper a secret to a trusted friend, or you may shout a warning to several people nearby. You may phone a friend who is far away, or you may put an ad in the newspaper for everyone to see.

Cells also use various methods of communication. These methods vary depending on whether the target is specific or general. They also depend on whether the target is nearby or far away. ❯ **Cells communicate and coordinate activity by sending chemical signals that carry information to other cells.** A *signaling cell* produces a **signal,** often a molecule, that is detected by the *target cell*. Typically, target cells have specific proteins that recognize and respond to the signal.

Targets Neighboring cells can communicate through direct contact between their membranes. Short-distance signals may act locally, a few cells away from the originating cell. Long-distance signals are carried by hormones and nerve cells. Hormones are signal molecules that are made in one part of the body. Hormones are distributed widely in the bloodstream throughout the body, but they affect only specific cells. Nerve cells also signal information to distant locations in the body, but their signals are not widely distributed.

Environmental Signals While most signal molecules originate within the body, some signals come from outside. For example, light has a great effect on the action of hormones in plants. The length of the day determines when some plants flower.

❯ **Reading Check** *Compare the targets of signaling hormones and nerve cells.*

QuickLab

🕐 10 min

Sensitive Plants 4.1.2j

The sensitive plant *(Mimosa pudica)* reacts to touch. This reaction results from rapid cell-to-cell communication.

Procedure

❶ Observe and sketch the extended leaves on the *Mimosa* plant branch.

❷ Touch the tip of the end leaf on this branch. Observe the plant's reaction.

❸ Make a sketch showing the branch's new appearance.

Analysis

1. Identify what stimulus produced the plant's response.

2. Describe the plant's response.

3. Explain whether the reaction behavior was communicated beyond the leaf that was touched.

4. CRITICAL THINKING Making Inferences Plants can respond to touch, although they lack a nervous system. Propose a mechanism for the response you observed.

Receiving Signals

A target cell is bombarded by hundreds of signals. But it recognizes and responds only to the few signals that are important for its function. This response to some signals, but not to others, is made possible by **receptor proteins,** such as the ones in the cell's membrane.

Binding Specificity A receptor protein binds specific substances, such as signal molecules. The outer part of the protein is folded into a unique shape, called the *binding site.* ❯ A receptor protein binds only to signals that match the specific shape of its binding site. As **Figure 12** shows, only signal molecules that have the "right" shape can fit into the receptor protein. Signal molecules that have the "wrong" shape have no effect on that particular receptor protein. A cell may also have receptor proteins that bind to molecules in its environment. Some cells may have receptor proteins that can detect and respond to light. Receptor proteins enable a cell to detect its environment.

Effect Once it binds the signal molecule, the receptor protein changes its shape in the membrane. This change in shape relays information into the cytoplasm of the target cell.

signal anything that serves to direct, guide, or warn

receptor protein a protein that binds specific signal molecules, which causes the cell to respond

SCI LINKS.
www.scilinks.org
Topic: Receptor Proteins
Code: HX81274

Receptor binding site

Receptor protein

Figure 12 The binding site of this receptor protein has a specific shape to which only one type of signal molecule can bind. ❯ **Which of these molecules would bind with the receptor?**

Finding Examples Ion channels are the examples of transport proteins on this page.

❯ **Close**

Formative Assessment

Which of the following changes shape immediately after a receptor protein binds with a signal molecule?

A. receptor protein (Correct! The binding of a signal molecule results in a change in the receptor protein's shape.)

B. signal molecule (Incorrect. The signal molecule does not change shape after binding.)

C. transport proteins (Incorrect. Transport proteins may change as a result of the change in the receptor protein's shape, but the change in the receptor protein's shape occurs immediately after the receptor protein binds with the signal molecule.)

D. second messenger (Incorrect. After binding, the change in the receptor protein's shape results in the activation of an intermediary protein, which activates an enzyme, which then forms a second messenger.)

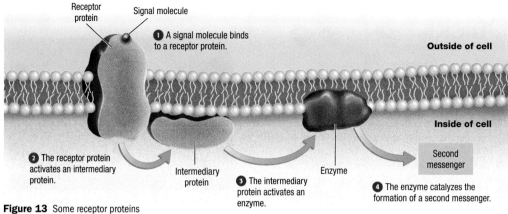

❶ A signal molecule binds to a receptor protein.

Receptor protein   Signal molecule

Outside of cell

Inside of cell

❷ The receptor protein activates an intermediary protein.

Intermediary protein

❸ The intermediary protein activates an enzyme.

Enzyme

Second messenger

❹ The enzyme catalyzes the formation of a second messenger.

Figure 13 Some receptor proteins trigger the production of second messengers.

Finding Examples Search the text on this page to find an example of the function of a transport protein.

second messenger a molecule that is generated when a specific substance attaches to a receptor on the outside of a cell membrane, which produces a change in cellular function

Responding to Signals

When a signal molecule binds to a receptor protein, the protein changes shape, which triggers changes in the cell membrane. ❯ **The cell may respond to a signal by changing its membrane permeability, by activating enzymes, or by forming a second messenger.**

- **Permeability Change** Transport proteins may open or close in response to a signal. For example, a nerve impulse may result when ion channels in nerve cells open after receiving a signal.

- **Enzyme Activation** Some receptor proteins activate enzymes in the cell membrane. Some receptors are enzymes themselves and are activated by the binding of a signal molecule. Enzymes trigger chemical reactions in the cell.

- **Second Messenger** Binding of a signal molecule outside the cell may cause a second messenger to form, as **Figure 13** shows. The **second messenger** acts as a signal molecule within the cell and causes changes in the cytoplasm and nucleus.

❯ **Reading Check** *How does membrane permeability change?*

Section 3 Review

❯ **KEY IDEAS**

1. **Identify** one function of signal molecules in a multicellular organism.

2. **Describe** the relationship between receptor proteins and signal molecules.

3. **List** three ways that a receptor protein may respond when a signal molecule binds to it.

CRITICAL THINKING

4. **Applying Logic** Why do you think that there are many forms of communication between body cells?

5. **Applying Logic** Why is specificity between a receptor protein and a signal molecule important?

WRITING FOR SCIENCE

6. **Finding Information** Use library or Internet resources to research a human disease that results from problems in the transport of molecules across the cell membrane. Describe the disease's symptoms and treatments. Summarize your findings in a written report.

Answers to Section Review

1. to carry information to other cells of the body

2. Receptor proteins bind to the signal molecules with a very specific complementary shape.

3. Receptor proteins can activate enzymes, cause a change in membrane permeability, or cause the formation of a second messenger that will have an effect in another part of the cell.

4. Many different forms of communication might be due to the many different types of body cells and the need for specific messages over long distances.

5. Specificity helps ensure that only that particular signal molecule is received by a particular cell and responded to.

6. Answers will vary. Cystic fibrosis is caused by a mutation that results in a faulty transport protein that no longer allows chloride ions in and out of the cell, or is missing altogether. Students might also research pigmentation defects that result from abnormal transport of melanin granules, cancer due to defective transport of growth factor receptors, or other diseases.

Heady Effects

Many people start their day with a hot cup of coffee. Coffee contains a chemical stimulant, caffeine, that produces a feeling of heightened alertness.

WEIRD SCIENCE

Caffeine

The shape of the caffeine molecule is similar to the shape of a signal molecule that your body produces naturally. Receptor proteins respond to this signal in a chain of events that increases heart rate, blood flow, and the amount of sugar in the bloodstream.

Wacky Webs Most spider webs look like the one on the left. This web was created by a common garden spider, *Araneus diadematus*. The web on the right was created by the same spider after it was fed caffeine-dosed flies.

Quick Project Find out the average caffeine content in milligrams (mg) of coffee, tea, cola drinks, energy drinks, chocolate milk, dark chocolate, and milk chocolate.

Why It Matters

Teacher's Notes Caffeine—one of a group of chemicals called xanthines—is found not only in coffee, but also in tea, many soft drinks (not just colas), chocolate, and over-the-counter as a stimulant. While heightened alertness may come with a normal dose—the amount found in one to three cups of coffee—more than that can produce nervousness, insomnia, and tremors. Student athletes who use large amounts of caffeine may exhibit irritability, hypertension, seizures, or other symptoms. While the effects of caffeine on athletic performance are not significant, the NCAA limits the amount of caffeine in a urine specimen to 15 micrograms per mL, or the amount in about five to six cups of coffee.

READING TOOLBOX

Visual Literacy Have students review the photographs of the web before and after the spider was fed the caffeine-dosed flies. Help them hypothesize how the responses that caffeine evokes results in a skewed web. **LS Verbal**

Answers to Research
(average values)
Coffee (8 oz, brewed) 135 mg
Tea (8 oz, brewed) 50 mg
Sport drink (i.e. Gatorade®) 0 mg
Cola drink (12 oz) 45 mg
Chocolate milk (8 oz) 5 mg
Dark chocolate (1.5 oz) 31 mg
Milk chocolate (1.5 oz) 10 mg

Time Required
One 45-minute lab period

Safety Cautions
Phenolphthalein solutions are flammable, and the vapors can explode when mixed with air. Make sure that there are no flames or sources of ignition, such as sparks, when you are using the phenolphthalein solution.

Tips and Tricks
Agar Preparation Prepare phenolphthalein agar by adding drops of 0.1 M sodium hydroxide solution (prepared by using 4 g NaOH diluted to 1 L) to turn the agar red. Pour the mixture into a flat pan to a depth of slightly more than 3 cm. After the agar hardens, cut it into 3 × 3 × 6 cm rectangles.

Make sure that students rinse their knives between each cutting to prevent vinegar on the previous cube from contaminating the next cube.

Disposal Wrap the phenolphthalein agar in newspaper, and then place the newspaper in the garbage. Dilute the vinegar with water, and then pour the vinegar down the sink.

Lab Correlations
1.2.4 Carry out a research plan for testing explanations, including selecting and developing techniques, acquiring and building apparatus, and recording observations as necessary.

4.1.2g Each cell is covered by a membrane that performs a number of important functions for the cell. These include: separation from its outside environment, controlling which molecules enter and leave the cell, and recognition of chemical signals. The processes of diffusion and active transport are important in the movement of materials in and out of cells.

Chapter 8 Lab 1.2.4, 4.1.2g

Objectives
> Relate a cell's size to its surface area–to-volume ratio.
> Predict how the surface area–to-volume ratio of a cell will affect the diffusion of substances into the cell.

Materials
- safety goggles
- lab apron
- disposable gloves
- block of phenolphthalein agar (3 cm × 3 cm × 6 cm)
- knife, plastic
- ruler, metric
- beaker, 250 mL
- vinegar, 150 mL
- spoon, plastic
- paper towel

Safety

Cell Size and Diffusion

Substances enter and leave a cell in several ways, including by diffusion. Substances that a cell needs must come from outside the cell to the cell's center. How easily a cell can exchange substances depends on the ratio of its surface area to its volume (surface area ÷ volume). Surface area is a measure of the exposed outer surface of an object. Volume is the amount of space that an object takes up.

In this lab, you will design an experiment to investigate how a cell's size affects the diffusion of substances into the cell. To do so, you will make cell models using agar that contains phenolphthalein. Phenolphthalein is an indicator that changes color in the presence of an acidic solution.

Preparation
1. SCIENTIFIC METHODS **State the Problem** How does a cell's size affect the delivery of substances via diffusion to the center of the cell?
2. SCIENTIFIC METHODS **Form a Hypothesis** Form a testable hypothesis that explains how a cell's size affects the rate of diffusion of substances from outside the cell.

Procedure
Design an Experiment
❶ Design an experiment that tests your hypothesis and that uses the materials listed for this lab. Predict what will happen during your experiment if your hypothesis is correct.

Answer to Preparation
2. Sample answer: The larger the cell, the longer it takes for substances to diffuse into the cell's center.

Answers to Procedure
Sample Procedure
1. Trim the agar block with a knife to make three cubes with side lengths of 1 cm, 2 cm, and 3 cm. Calculate the surface area, volume, and surface area–to-volume ratio for each cube.
2. Place the three cubes in the beaker, and cover them with vinegar. Using the plastic spoon, turn the cubes frequently.
3. After 10 minutes, use the spoon to remove the agar cubes. Blot the cubes dry using a paper towel.
4. Cut each cube in half. Measure the distance (in mm) the vinegar diffused.
5. Calculate the rate of diffusion (mm/min).

2 Write a procedure for your experiment. Identify the variables that you will control, the experimental variables, and the responding variables. Construct any tables that you will need to record your data. Make a list of all safety precautions that you will take. Have your teacher approve your procedure before you begin.

Diffusion in Cubes		
Size (cm)	Ratio	Distance (mm)

Conduct Your Experiment

3 ◇ ◇ ◆ Put on safety goggles, gloves, and a lab apron.

4 ◆ ◆ ◇ Carry out your experiment. Record your observations in your data table.

5 ◇ ◆ Follow your teacher's instructions for cleaning up your lab materials. Wash your hands before leaving the lab.

Analyze and Conclude

1. **Interpreting Observations** Describe any changes in the appearance of the agar cubes. Explain why these changes occurred.

2. **Summarizing Results** Make a graph labeled "Diffusion distance (mm)" on the vertical axis and "Surface area–to-volume ratio" on the horizontal axis. Plot your group's data on the graph.

3. **SCIENTIFIC METHODS** **Analyzing Results** Using the graph you made in item 2, make a statement relating the surface area–to-volume ratio and the distance that the substance diffuses.

4. **Summarizing Results** Make a second graph using your group's data. Label the vertical axis "Rate of diffusion (mm/min)" (distance that vinegar moved ÷ time). Label the horizontal axis "Surface area–to-volume ratio." Plot your group's data on the graph.

5. **Analyzing Results** Referring to the graph that you made in item 4, write a statement that relates the surface area–to-volume ratio and the rate at which the substance diffuses.

6. **SCIENTIFIC METHODS** **Evaluating Methods** In what ways do your agar models simplify or fail to simulate the features of cells?

7. **Calculating** Calculate the surface area and the volume of a cube that has a side length of 5 cm. Calculate the surface area and volume of a cube that has a side length of 10 cm. Determine the surface area–to-volume ratio of each cube. Which cube has the greater surface area–to-volume ratio?

8. **SCIENTIFIC METHODS** **Evaluating Conclusions** How does the size of a cell affect the rate at which substances diffuse into the cell?

9. **Further Inquiry** Write a new question about cell size and diffusion that could be explored in another investigation.

SCI LINKS
www.scilinks.org
Topic: Diffusion
Code: HX80406

Extensions

10. How does cell transport in prokaryotic cells differ from cell transport in eukaryotic cells?

11. Which of the following can diffuse across the cell membrane without the help of a transport protein: water, carbohydrates, lipids, or proteins?

Answers to Analyze and Conclude

1. Cubes appear light pink near their surfaces because the phenolphthalein changed color in response to the acid in the vinegar.

2. The line plotted on the graph should be horizontal.

3. The diffusion distance is the same regardless of the surface area–to-volume ratio.

4. The line plotted on the graph should be horizontal.

5. The rate of diffusion is constant regardless of the surface area–to-volume ratio.

6. Agar models ignore the selective permeability of cell membranes, the role of membrane proteins in facilitated diffusion and active transport, and other mechanisms of cell transport.

7. For a cube with a side length of 5 cm: surface area = 150 cm², volume = 125 cm³; surface-to-volume ratio = 6:5. For a cube with side length of 10 cm: surface area = 600 cm²; volume = 1,000 cm³; surface-area-to-volume ratio = 3:5. The small cube has the greater surface-area-to-volume ratio.

8. The size of the cell does not affect the rate of diffusion.

9. Sample answer: How does cell size affect the amount of a substance that diffuses into it?

Answers to Extensions

10. The transport of materials across the cell membrane is essentially the same in prokaryotes and eukaryotes, except that prokaryotes do not exhibit endocytosis or exocytosis.

11. water and lipids

Key Resources

 Holt Lab Generator

 Lab Datasheet (Levels A, B, C)

 Holt Science Biology Video Labs

 Virtual Investigations

SUPER SUMMARY

Have students connect the major concepts in this chapter through an interactive Super Summary. Visit **go.hrw.com** and type in the key word **HX8CENS** to access the Super Summary for this chapter.

Reteaching Key Ideas

Identifying Structure and Function
Ask students to make a drawing of a cell membrane, including the lipid bilayer and the types of proteins in the membrane. Have them use captions to describe the functions of the cell membrane. **LS Visual**
Demonstrating Transport Divide students into four groups, and assign each group the task of demonstrating simple diffusion, facilitated diffusion, osmosis, or active transport. For example, part of a skit might have one student grasping another's arm to show binding. **LS Kinesthetic**
Constructing a Graphic Organizer
Ask students to construct a graphic organizer that shows the cause and effect relationships that are involved in cell communication. **LS Visual**

Key Ideas	Key Terms

1 Cell Membrane

> One way that a cell maintains homeostasis is by controlling the movement of substances across the cell membrane.

> The lipid bilayer is selectively permeable to small, nonpolar substances.

> Proteins in the cell membrane include cell-surface markers, receptor proteins, enzymes, and transport proteins.

phospholipid (176)
lipid bilayer (176)

2 Cell Transport

> In passive transport, substances cross the cell membrane down their concentration gradient.

> Osmosis allows cells to maintain water balance as their environment changes.

> Active transport requires energy to move substances against their concentration gradients.

equilibrium (178)
concentration gradient (178)
diffusion (178)
carrier protein (178)
osmosis (180)
sodium-potassium pump (182)

3 Cell Communication

> Cells communicate and coordinate activity by sending chemical signals that carry information to other cells.

> A receptor protein binds only to the signals that match the specific shape of its binding site.

> The cell may respond to a signal by changing its membrane permeability, by activating enzymes, or by forming a second messenger.

signal (184)
receptor protein (185)
second messenger (186)

PART A: Answer all questions in this part.

Directions: For each statement or question, write on your separate answer sheet the number of the word or expression that best completes the statement or answers the question.

1 Which row in the chart below best describes the active transport of molecule X through a cell membrane?

Row	Movement of Molecule X	ATP
(1)	high concentration → low concentration	used
(2)	high concentration → low concentration	not used
(3)	low concentration → high concentration	used
(4)	low concentration → high concentration	not used

(1) 1   (3) 3

(2) 2   (4) 4

2 Molecule X moves across a cell membrane by diffusion. Which row in the chart above best indicates the relationship between the relative concentrations of molecule X and the use of ATP for diffusion?

(1) 1   (3) 3

(2) 2   (4) 4

3 Which letter indicates a cell structure that directly controls the movement of molecules into and out of the cell?

(1) A   (3) C

(2) B   (4) D

4 Cellular communication is illustrated in the diagram below.

Key

● Signal 1
▲ Signal 2

Information can be sent from

(1) cell A to cell B because cell B is able to recognize signal 1

(2) cell A to cell B because cell A is able to recognize signal 2

(3) cell B to cell A because cell A is able to recognize signal 1

(4) cell B to cell A because cell B is able to recognize signal 2

5 Which substances are found on cell surfaces and respond to nerve and hormone signals?

(1) starches and simple sugars

(2) subunits of DNA

(3) vitamins and minerals

(4) receptor molecules

6 After a hormone enters the bloodstream, it is transported throughout the body, but the hormone affects only certain cells. The reason only certain cells are affected is that the membranes of these cells have specific

(1) receptors   (3) antibodies

(2) tissues   (4) carbohydrates

Regents Exam Practice Correlations

4.1.2g 1, 2, 3, 7, 9, 10, 13, 14, 15

4.1.2j 4, 5, 6, 11, 12

4.5.1e 8

PART A

1. (3) Substances diffuse from regions of high concentration regions of low concentration, so only choices that indicate low to high movement indicate active transport. Diffusion does not require energy, but active transport does require the use of ATP. *(#03, June 2006 Regents Exam)*

2. (2) Substances only diffuse from regions of high concentration to regions of low concentration, so only choices that indicate high to low movement are possible answers. Diffusion does not require energy, so the answer should not indicate the use of ATP. *(#05, August 2006 Regents Exam)*

3. (2) The cell membrane controls the movement of materials into and out of the cell. The large vacuole within the cell stores materials. Chloroplasts perform photosynthesis within the cell. The nucleus contains the genetic information for the cell. *(#03, June 2003 Regents Exam)*

4. (3) Receptors have a specific shape to fit a specific signal molecule. Cell B can only recognize signal molecules from cell A (signal 2) and cell A can only recognize signal molecules from cell B (signal 1). *(#34, June 2006 Regents Exam)*

5. (4) Receptor molecules can respond to nerve and hormone signals. Subunits of DNA can be copied by RNA molecules. Starches and simple sugars are processed by enzymes. Vitamins and minerals are delivered to cells through the bloodstream. *(#01, August 2005 Regents Exam)*

6. (1) Cells do not contain special tissues, carbohydrates, or antibodies that recognize specific hormones. Cells do have specific protein receptors that bind signal molecules. *(#03, January 2006 Regents Exam)*

7. (3) The concentration of K+ and Mg++ ions inside the cell is much greater than their concentration outside the cell. The ions have been pumped into the cell against their concentration gradients, and the process that causes this is active transport. *(#03, January 2005 Regents Exam)*

8. (1) ATP is needed to move molecules out of a cell against a concentration gradient. Therefore, ATP is being used by cell A. Cell B is using diffusion to move molecules down a concentration gradient. *(#11, January 2003 Regents Exam)*

PART B

9. (1) The diagram illustrates the process of communication between two neurons. *(#35, June 2004 Regents Exam)*

10. (4) Nerve cell X is releasing neurotransmitter molecules (substance A), and in order for nerve cell Y to receive the communication it has receptor molecules for substance A. *(#36, June 2004 Regents Exam)*

11. (2) The shape of molecule two best complements substance A. Therefore it will bond with substance A and prevent substance A from interacting with the receptors on nerve cell Y. *(#37, June 2004 Regents Exam)*

12. Allow 1 credit for describing one possible effect of LSD on the action of acetylcholine. Acceptable responses include, but are not limited to: Cell communication would be disrupted.; The work of acetylcholine would occur continuously.; Nerve signals would not be turned off. *(#44, January 2006 Regents Exam)*

---

7 The graph below shows the relative concentrations of different ions inside and outside of an animal cell.

Which process is directly responsible for the net movement of K+ and Mg++ into the animal cell?

(1) electrophoresis   (3) active transport
(2) diffusion   (4) circulation

8 In the diagram below, the dark dots indicate small molecules. These molecules are moving out of the cells, as indicated by the arrows. The number of dots inside and outside of the two cells represents the relative concentrations of the molecules inside and outside of the cells.

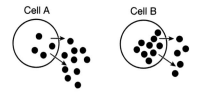

ATP is being used to move the molecules out of the cell by

(1) cell A, only
(2) cell B, only
(3) both cell A and cell B
(4) neither cell A nor cell B

Base your answers to questions 9 through 11 on the diagram below and on your knowledge of biology.

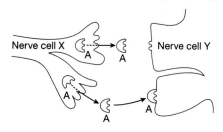

9 The process represented in the diagram best illustrates

(1) cellular communication
(2) muscle contraction
(3) extraction of energy from nutrients
(4) waste disposal

10 Which statement best describes the diagram?

(1) Nerve cell X is releasing receptor molecules.
(2) Nerve cell Y is signaling nerve cell X.
(3) Nerve cell X is attaching to nerve cell Y.
(4) Nerve cell Y contains receptor molecules for substance A.

11 A drug is developed that, due to its molecular shape, blocks the action of substance A. Which shape would the drug molecule most likely resemble?

    (1)   (2)   (3)   (4)

12 Acetylcholine is a chemical secreted at the ends of nerve cells. This chemical helps to send nerve signals across synapses (spaces between nerve cells). After the signal passes across a synapse, an enzyme breaks down the acetylcholine. LSD is a drug that blocks the action of this enzyme. Describe one possible effect of LSD on the action of acetylcholine.

PART D

13 The diagram below represents a container of water and two different kinds of molecules, A and B, separated into two chambers by a membrane through which only water and molecule A can pass.

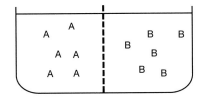

On a seperate piece of paper, copy the diagram of the container below. On your diagram, indicate the distribution of molecules A and B after the net movement of these molecules stops.

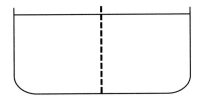

Base your answers to questions 14 and 15 on the information below and on your knowledge of biology.

Students prepared four models of cells by using dialysis tubing containing the same blue solution. Each of the model cells originally weighed 10 grams. They then placed each model cell in a beaker containing a different concentration of water. After 24 hours, they recorded the mass of the model cells as shown in the data table below.

Concentration of Water

Surrounding the Model Cell	Mass of Model Cell
100%	12 grams
90%	11 grams
80%	10 grams
70%	9 grams

14 Why did the model cell that was placed in 100% water increase in mass?

15 What was the concentration of water in the original blue solution? State evidence in support of your answer.

13. Allow a maximum of 2 credits, 1 for indicating that there will be three molecules of A in each chamber and 1 for indicating that there will be six molecules of B in the right chamber.

(#66, January 2006 Regents Exam)

14. Allow 1 credit for explaining that the model cell that was placed in 100% water increased in mass because water diffused into the model cell. *(#72, January 2006 Regents Exam)*

15. Allow 1 credit for stating that the concentration of water in the original blue solution was 80% and for stating evidence in support of this answer. Acceptable responses include, but are not limited to: 80%, because the model cell did not increase in mass; 80%, because the model cell did not change; According to the table, when the mass of the model cell is 10 grams, the concentration of water outside the model cell is 80%. This would be the same as the concentration of water inside the model cell. *(#73, January 2006 Regents Exam)*

Cellular Respiration and Photosynthesis

	Standards	Teach Key Ideas

CHAPTER OPENER, pp. 194–195 — 15 min.

The Living Environment

SECTION 1 Energy in Living Systems, pp. 197–201 — 45 min.

> Chemical Energy
> Metabolism and the Carbon Cycle
> Transferring Energy

Standards: 4.1.2h, 4.5.1a, 4.5.1c, 4.5.1e, 4.6.1c

Teach Key Ideas:

- **Bellringer Transparency**
- **Transparencies** B32 ATP Releases Energy • B34 Breakdown of Starch • B35 Photosynthesis-Cellular Respiration Cycle
- **Visual Concepts** Comparing Autotrophs and Heterotrophs • Comparing ADP and ATP • Linking Photosynthesis and Respiration

---

SECTION 2 Photosynthesis, pp. 202–207 — 90 min.

> Harvesting Light Energy
> Two Electron Transport Chains
> Producing Sugar
> Factors that Affect Photosynthesis

Standards: 4.1.2f, 4.1.2i, 4.5.1b, 4.5.1f

Teach Key Ideas:

- **Bellringer Transparency**
- **Transparencies** B52 Photosynthesis • B25 Absorption Spectra of Photosynthesis Pigments • B24 Chloroplasts • B30 Summary of Processes in Light Reactions • B31 Calvin Cycle
- **Visual Concepts** Photosynthesis • Spectrum of Light and Plant Pigments • Chlorophyll a and b • Carotenoid • Parts of a Chloroplast • Electron Transport Chain • Energy Yield in Aerobic Respiration • Calvin Cycle • Environmental Influences on Photosynthesis

---

SECTION 3 Cellular Respiration, pp. 208–213 — 90 min.

> Glycolysis
> Aerobic Respiration
> Fermentation

Standards: 4.1.2i, 4.5.1d

Teach Key Ideas:

- **Bellringer Transparency**
- **Transparencies** B53 Cellular Respiration • B37 Glycolysis • B39 Krebs Cycle • B54 Electron Transport Chain of Aerobic Respiration
- **Visual Concepts** Cellular Respiration • Glycolysis • NAD and NADH • Krebs Cycle • FAD and $FADH_2$ • Fermentation

See also PowerPoint® Resources

Chapter Review and Assessment Resources

SE Super Summary, p. 216
SE Regents Exam Practice, p. 217
Regents Review Guide
Review Resources
Chapter Tests A and B
Holt Online Assessment
Regents Question Banks on Teacher's One-Stop Planner

CHAPTER
Fast Track
Thorough instruction will require the times shown.

Basic Learners

TE Comprehension Strategy, p. 198
TE ATP Structure, p. 200
TE Stages of Photosynthesis, p. 204
TE NADPH, p. 205
TE Role Playing, p. 206
TE Relating Processes, p. 208
TE Glycolysis, p. 209
TE Electron Transport Chain, p. 211
Directed Reading Worksheets*
Active Reading Worksheets*
Lab Manuals, Level A*
Study Guide* ∎

Advanced Learners

TE Carotenoids, p. 203
Critical Thinking Worksheets*
Concept Mapping Worksheets*
Science Skills Worksheets*
Lab Datasheets, Level C*

Key

SE Student Edition	🗀 Chapter Resource File
TE Teacher's Edition	🗐 Workbook
	🖨 Transparency

💿 CD or CD-ROM
* Datasheet or blackline master available

■ Also available in Spanish

All resources listed below are also available on the Teacher's One-Stop Planner.

Why It Matters	Hands-On	Skills Development	Assessment
Build student motivation with resources about high-interest applications.	**SE Inquiry Lab** Stored Energy, p. 195* ■	**TE Reading Toolbox** Assessing Prior Knowledge, p. 194 **SE Reading Toolbox,** p. 196	
TE Demonstration Forms of Energy, p. 197 **TE Food Energy,** p. 199	**SE Quick Lab** Product of Photosynthesis, p. 198* ■ 🗀 **Exploration Lab** Plant and Animal Interrelationships*	**TE Math Skills** Balancing Equations, p. 199 **SE Reading Toolbox** Key-Term Fold, p. 200 **TE Reading Toolbox** Key-Term Fold, p. 200	**SE Section Review** **TE Formative Assessment** Spanish Assessment* ■ 🗀 **Section Quiz** ■
TE Demonstration Products of Photosynthesis, p. 202 **TE Demonstration** The Thylakoid Model, p. 203 **TE Increasing Levels of Carbon Dioxide,** p. 206	**SE Quick Lab** Photosynthetic Rate, p. 205* ■	**TE Science Skills** Spectroscopy, p. 203 **SE Reading Toolbox** Describing Space, p. 205 **TE Reading Toolbox** Describing Space, p. 205	**SE Section Review** **TE Formative Assessment** Spanish Assessment* ■ 🗀 **Section Quiz** ■
TE Life Without Oxygen, p. 209 **TE Cyanide,** p. 212 **SE Life in a Biosphere,** p. 214	**SE Skills Practice Lab** Cellular Respiration, p. 215* ■ 🗀 **Inquiry Lab** Conditions That Favor Cellular Respiration*	**SE Reading Toolbox** Pattern Puzzles, p. 211 **TE Reading Toolbox** Pattern Puzzles, p. 211 **TE Math Skills** ATP Molecules, p. 211	**SE Section Review** **TE Formative Assessment** Spanish Assessment* ■ 🗀 **Section Quiz** ■

See also Lab Generator

See also Holt Online Assessment Resources

Resources for Differentiated Instruction

English Learners

TE Autotrophs and Heterotrophs, p. 198
TE Fermentation, p. 212
🗀 Directed Reading Worksheets*
🗀 Active Reading Worksheets*
🗀 Lab Manuals, Level A*
🗐 Study Guide* ■
🗐 Note-taking Workbook*
🗐 Multilingual Glossary
💿 Interactive Tutor

Struggling Readers

TE Comprehension Strategy, p. 198
TE Electron Transport Chain, p. 211
🗀 Directed Reading Worksheets*
🗀 Active Reading Worksheets*
🗀 Lab Manuals, Level A*
🗐 Study Guide*
🗐 Note-taking Workbook*
🗐 Special Needs Activities and Modified Tests*
💿 Interactive Tutor

Special Education Students

TE ATP Structure, p. 200
TE NADPH, p. 205
🗀 Directed Reading Worksheets*
🗀 Active Reading Worksheets*
🗀 Lab Manuals, Level A*
🗐 Study Guide* ■
🗐 Note-taking Workbook*
🗐 Special Needs Activities and Modified Tests*

Alternative Assessment

TE Calvin Cycle, p. 206
🗀 Science Skills Worksheets*
🗀 Section Quizzes* ■
🗐 Chapter Tests A, B, and C* ■

Chapter 9

Chapter 9

Photosynthesis and Cellular Respiration

Overview

The purpose of this chapter is to examine how energy is made available to cells to power metabolism. Students will learn how energy is captured and stored during photosynthesis in autotrophs, and how that energy becomes usable to both autotrophs and heterotrophs through cellular respiration.

READING TOOLBOX

Assessing Prior Knowledge Students should understand the following concepts:
• the roles of autotrophs and heterotrophs in the food chain
• transformation of energy and matter

Visual Literacy Ask students to describe how energy is being obtained by the organisms in the photo. (The plant leaf obtains energy from the sun; the caterpillar obtains energy by eating the leaf.) Which organism uses photosynthesis to obtain energy? (the plant)

Preview

1 Energy in Living Systems
Chemical Energy
Metabolism and the Carbon Cycle
Transferring Energy

2 Photosynthesis
Harvesting Light Energy
Two Electron Transport Chains
Producing Sugar
Factors that Affect Photosynthesis

3 Cellular Respiration
Glycolysis
Aerobic Respiration
Fermentation

Why It Matters

Everything you do—from moving, to breathing, to thinking—requires energy. The energy your body uses is mostly derived from the processes of photosynthesis and cellular respiration.

 The Living Environment
Standard 4 Students will understand and apply scientific concepts, principles, and theories pertaining to the physical setting and living environment and recognize the historical development of ideas in science.
Key Idea 1 Living things are both similar to and different from each other and from nonliving things. **Major Understandings** - 1.2f, 1.2h, 1.2i
Key Idea 5 Organisms maintain a dynamic equilibrium that sustains life. **Major Understandings** - 5.1a, 5.1b, 5.1c, 5.1d, 5.1e, 5.1f
Key Idea 6 Plants and animals depend on each other and their physical environment **Major Understandings** - 6.1c

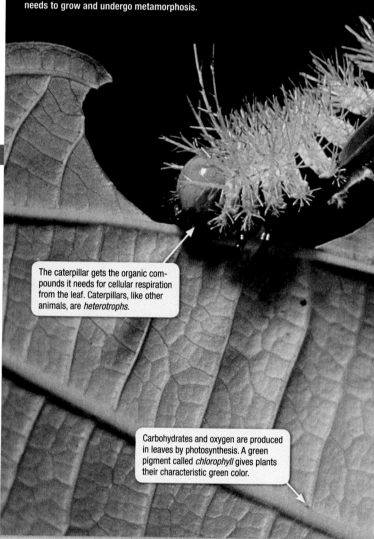

A saturniid caterpillar feeds on a leaf. The leaf provides the energy the caterpillar needs to grow and undergo metamorphosis.

The caterpillar gets the organic compounds it needs for cellular respiration from the leaf. Caterpillars, like other animals, are *heterotrophs*.

Carbohydrates and oxygen are produced in leaves by photosynthesis. A green pigment called *chlorophyll* gives plants their characteristic green color.

Chapter Correlations   *The Living Environment*

Standard 4

1.2f Cells have particular structures that perform specific jobs. These structures perform the actual work of the cell. Just as systems are coordinated and work together, cell parts must also be coordinated and work together.

1.2h Many organic and inorganic substances dissolved in cells allow necessary chemical reactions to take place in order to maintain life.

1.2i Inside the cell a variety of specialized structures, formed from many different molecules, carry out the transport of materials (cytoplasm), extraction of energy from nutrients (mitochondria), protein building (ribosomes), waste disposal (cell membrane), storage (vacuole), and information storage (nucleus).

5.1a The energy for life comes primarily from the Sun. Photosynthesis provides a vital connection between the Sun and the energy needs of living systems.

5.1b Plant cells and some one-celled organisms contain chloroplasts, the site of photosynthesis. The process of photosynthesis uses solar energy to combine the inorganic molecules carbon dioxide and water into energy rich organic compounds (e.g., glucose) and release oxygen to the environment.

5.1c In all organisms, organic compounds can be used to assemble other molecules such as proteins, DNA, starch, and fats. The chemical energy stored in bonds can be used as a source of energy for life processes.

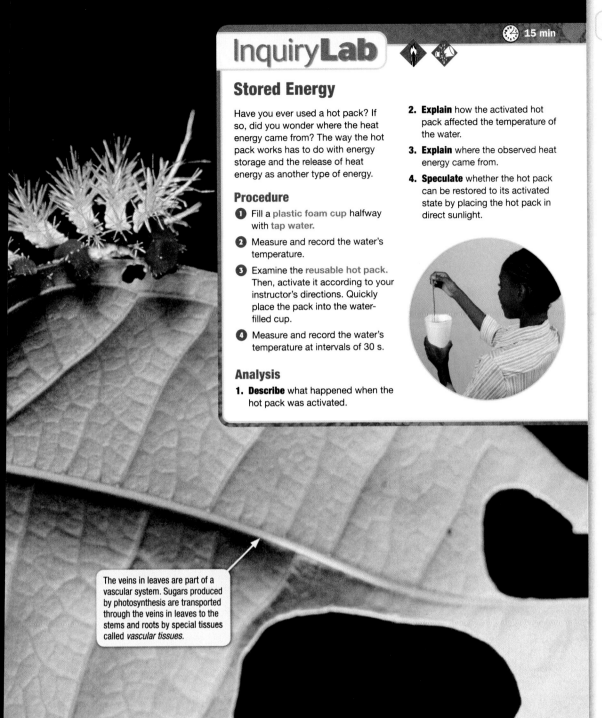

InquiryLab

🕐 15 min

Stored Energy

Have you ever used a hot pack? If so, did you wonder where the heat energy came from? The way the hot pack works has to do with energy storage and the release of heat energy as another type of energy.

Procedure

1. Fill a plastic foam cup halfway with tap water.
2. Measure and record the water's temperature.
3. Examine the reusable hot pack. Then, activate it according to your instructor's directions. Quickly place the pack into the water-filled cup.
4. Measure and record the water's temperature at intervals of 30 s.

Analysis

1. **Describe** what happened when the hot pack was activated.
2. **Explain** how the activated hot pack affected the temperature of the water.
3. **Explain** where the observed heat energy came from.
4. **Speculate** whether the hot pack can be restored to its activated state by placing the hot pack in direct sunlight.

> The veins in leaves are part of a vascular system. Sugars produced by photosynthesis are transported through the veins in leaves to the stems and roots by special tissues called *vascular tissues.*

InquiryLab

Teacher's Notes Remind students that the energy transfer they observe can be traced back to the sun. To "restore" the pack with energy, it must be placed in a boiling water solution or microwave oven. Read the directions to insure that you are following the correct procedure. The boiling water was heated by either an electric or fossil fuel–dependent device. Students should trace both electricity generation and the formation of fossil fuels to their initial solar source.

Materials
- hot pack
- plastic foam cup
- thermometer

Safety: Remind students that glassware is easily broken. Caution students to be careful when handling the activated hot pack.

Answers to Analysis
1. The liquid crystallized.
2. The water temperature increased.
3. The heat energy was stored in the initial liquid state of the chemical. When it changed to a crystal, this heat was released.
4. No, it can't. You need a more concentrated energy source to restore the pack.

Key Resources

🔘 Interactive Tutor

5.1d In all organisms, the energy stored in organic molecules may be released during cellular respiration. This energy is temporarily stored in ATP molecules. In many organisms, the process of cellular respiration is concluded in mitochondria, in which ATP is produced more efficiently, oxygen is used, and carbon dioxide and water are released as wastes.

5.1e The energy from ATP is used by the organism to obtain, transform, and transport materials, and to eliminate wastes.

5.1f Biochemical processes, both breakdown and synthesis, are made possible by a large set of biological catalysts called enzymes. Enzymes can affect the rates of chemical change. The rate at which enzymes work can be influenced by internal environmental factors such as pH and temperature.

6.1c The chemical elements, such as carbon, hydrogen, nitrogen, and oxygen, that make up the molecules of living things pass through food webs and are combined and recombined in different ways. At each link in a food web, some energy is stored in newly made structures but much is dissipated into the environment as heat.

Using Words

Check students' Key-Term Folds to see that they correctly followed the directions.

Using Language

1. in chloroplasts
2. in cell mitochondria

Using Graphic Organizers

The steps in the correct order are as follows:

> breakdown of glucose
> production of NADH
> production of pyruvate

READING TOOLBOX

These reading tools can help you learn the material in this chapter. For more information on how to use these and other tools, see **Appendix: Reading and Study Skills.**

Using Words

Key-Term Fold A key-term fold is useful for studying definitions of key terms in a chapter. Each tab can contain a key term on one side and its definition on the other side.

Your Turn Make a key-term fold for the terms in this chapter.
1. Fold a sheet of lined notebook paper in half from left to right.
2. Using scissors, cut along every third line from the right edge of the paper to the center fold to make tabs.

Using Language

Describing Space As you read the chapter, look for language clues that answer the question, "Where does this process take place?" Words such as *inside, outside,* and *between* can help you learn where these processes happen. Knowing where these processes take place can help you better understand them.

Your Turn Describe as precisely as you can where the following processes happen.
1. photosynthesis
2. cellular respiration

Using Graphic Organizers

Pattern Puzzles You can use pattern puzzles to help you remember information. Exchanging puzzles with a classmate can help you study.

Your Turn Make pattern puzzles for the steps of glycolysis.
1. Write down the steps of the process. On a sheet of notebook paper, write down one step per line. Do not number the steps.
2. Cut the sheet of paper into strips with only one step per strip of paper. Shuffle the paper strips so that they are out of sequence.
3. Place the strips in the correct sequence. Confirm the order of the steps of the process by checking your text or class notes.

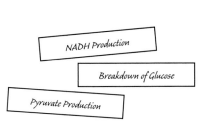
NADH Production
Breakdown of Glucose
Pyruvate Production

Energy in Living Systems

Key Ideas	Key Terms	Why It Matters
❯ What type of energy is used in cells, and what is the ultimate source of this energy? ❯ How is an organism's metabolism related to the carbon cycle? ❯ How is energy released in a cell?	photosynthesis cellular respiration ATP ATP synthase electron transport chain	Plants convert sunlight into chemical energy. This chemical energy can be used for biological processes in nearly all living things.

❯ **Focus**

This section is a broad overview of energy flow in natural systems. It also serves as an introduction to the process that converts food into ATP.

Imagine an abandoned house that is falling apart. The house, like almost everything else in the universe, breaks down over time. Restoring order to the house would require an input of energy, such as the energy needed to apply a fresh coat of paint. Living things also need energy in order to stay in good repair, or maintain their *homeostasis*. Remember that homeostasis is the process of maintaining internal order and balance even when the environment changes. Every organism must maintain homeostasis as long as it lives. Therefore, organisms require a constant source of energy.

Chemical Energy

❯ Organisms use and store energy in the chemical bonds of organic compounds. Almost all of the energy in organic compounds comes from the sun. Solar energy enters living systems when plants, algae, and certain prokaryotes use sunlight to make organic compounds from carbon dioxide and water through the process of **photosynthesis.** Organisms that are able to perform photosynthesis, such as the wheat plants shown in **Figure 1**, are *autotrophs*. Autotrophs make organic compounds that serve as food for them and for almost all of the other organisms on Earth.

Most autotrophs have a supply of food as long as sunlight is available. But how do other organisms get food molecules? To survive, organisms that cannot make their own food must absorb food molecules made by autotrophs, eat autotrophs, or eat organisms that consume autotrophs. Food molecules that are made or consumed by an organism are the fuel for its cells. Cells use these molecules to release the energy stored in the molecules' bonds. The energy is used to carry out life processes.

❯ **Reading Check** *Why do organisms need a constant supply of energy? (See the Appendix for answers to Reading Checks.)*

 The Living Environment
Standard 4
1.2h Many organic and inorganic substances dissolved in cells allow necessary chemical reactions to take place in order to maintain life.
5.1a The energy for life comes primarily from the Sun. Photosynthesis provides a vital connection between the Sun and the energy needs of living systems.
5.1c In all organisms, organic compounds can be used to assemble other molecules such as proteins, DNA, starch, and fats. The chemical energy stored in bonds can be used as a source of energy for life processes.
5.1e The energy from ATP is used by the organism to obtain, transform, and transport materials, and to eliminate wastes.
6.1c The chemical elements, such as carbon, hydrogen, nitrogen, and oxygen, that make up the molecules of living things pass through food webs and are combined and recombined in different ways. At each link in a food web, some energy is stored in newly made structures but much is dissipated into the environment as heat.

photosynthesis the process by which plants, algae, and some bacteria use sunlight, carbon dioxide, and water to produce carbohydrates and oxygen

Figure 1 Food crops such as wheat supply humans and other animals with the chemical energy needed to carry out life processes.

❯ **Teach**

Demonstration

Forms of Energy Ask students to look around the classroom and identify as many forms of energy being used as they can. (Answers will vary, but students should identify some forms of heat, light, chemical energy, mechanical energy, and electrical energy.) **LS Visual**

Teaching Key Ideas

Sandwich Energy Have students trace the energy in a ham and cheese sandwich back to the sun. (Ham → pig → grains → sun; cheese → milk → cow → grass → sun; bread → wheat → sun).

Key Resources

📺 **Transparencies**
B32 ATP Releases Energy
B34 Breakdown of Starch
B35 Photosynthesis–Cellular Respiration Cycle

💿 **Visual Concepts**
Comparing Autotrophs and Heterotrophs
Comparing ADP and ATP
Linking Photosynthesis and Respiration

Section Correlations	
4.1.2h	4.5.1e
4.5.1a	4.6.1c
4.5.1c	

QuickLab

Teacher's Notes Elodea can be found at some pet stores and most stores that sell aquarium fish. A 0.25 percent solution of baking soda can be made by dissolving 0.25 g of baking soda in 100 mL of water. Students may need to practice placing the test tube over the inverted funnel. First, fill the test tube with the solution. Place your thumb over the opening tightly so no air can get in. Submerge your thumb and the mouth of the test tube under water. Once the mouth of the test tube is underwater, you can release your thumb and maneuver the test tube over the stem of the funnel. Be sure you have the elodea in place under the funnel before you begin.

Safety Cautions Remind students that glassware is easily broken. Remind students to not eat any part of a plant used in the lab and to wash their hands thoroughly after handling any part of a plant.

Materials
- 0.25% baking-soda-and-water solution, 500 mL
- beaker, 600 mL
- elodea sprigs, 20-cm long (2–3)
- glass funnel
- test tube
- protective gloves

Answers to Analysis
1. The level of the solution in the test tube went down as gas (oxygen) displaced the liquid.
2. The snail would use some of the oxygen generated by the plant.

Hands-On
QuickLab

Product of Photosynthesis 4.5.1d

Plants use photosynthesis to produce food. One product of photosynthesis is oxygen. In this activity, you will observe the process of photosynthesis in elodea.

Procedure

1 Add 450 mL of baking-soda-and-water solution to a beaker.

2 Put two or three sprigs of elodea into the beaker. The baking soda will provide the elodea with the carbon dioxide it needs for photosynthesis.

3 Place the wide end of a glass funnel over the elodea. The elodea and the funnel should be completely submerged in the solution.

4 Fill a test tube with the remaining solution. Place your thumb over the end of the test tube. Turn the test tube upside down, taking care that no air enters. Hold the opening of the test tube under the solution, and place the test tube over the small end of the funnel.

5 Place the beaker setup in a well-lit area near a lamp or in direct sunlight, and leave it overnight.

Analysis

1. **Describe** what happened to the solution in the test tube.

2. **CRITICAL THINKING** **Predicting Patterns** Explain what may happen if an animal, such as a snail, were put into the beaker with the elodea sprig.

> **cellular respiration** the process by which cells produce energy from carbohydrates
>
> **ATP** adenosine triphosphate, an organic molecule that acts as the main energy source for cell processes; composed of a nitrogenous base, a sugar, and three phosphate groups

Metabolism and the Carbon Cycle

❯ Metabolism involves either using energy to build organic molecules or breaking down organic molecules in which energy is stored. Organic molecules contain carbon. Therefore, an organism's metabolism is part of Earth's carbon cycle. The carbon cycle not only makes carbon compounds continuously available in an ecosystem but also delivers chemical energy to organisms living within that ecosystem.

Photosynthesis Energy enters an ecosystem when organisms use sunlight during photosynthesis to convert stable carbon dioxide molecules into glucose, a less stable carbon compound. In plant cells and algae, photosynthesis takes place in chloroplasts. **Figure 2** summarizes the process by which energy from the sun is converted to chemical energy in chloroplasts.

Cellular Respiration Organisms extract energy stored in glucose molecules. Through the process of **cellular respiration,** cells make the carbon in glucose into stable carbon dioxide molecules and produce energy. Thus, stable and less stable compounds alternate during the carbon cycle and provide a continuous supply of energy for life processes in an ecosystem.

The breakdown of glucose during cellular respiration is summarized in **Figure 2**. The inputs are a glucose molecule and six oxygen molecules. The final products are six carbon dioxide molecules and six water molecules. Energy is also released and used to make **ATP** (adenosine triphosphate), an organic molecule that is the main energy source for cell processes.

❯ **Reading Check** *How is solar energy related to the carbon cycle?*

Differentiated Instruction

English Learners

Autotrophs and Heterotrophs Have students use a dictionary to define the root words of *autotroph* and *heterotroph.* (*auto* means "self;" *hetero* means "other;" *troph* means "nutrition or feeding;" an *autotroph* is literally "self-feeding," and a *heterotroph* is literally "other-feeding") **LS** **Verbal**

Basic Learners/Struggling Readers

Comprehension Strategy To help students comprehend the text on this page, use **Figure 2**. As they read each sentence under the headings *Photosynthesis* and *Cellular Respiration*, have them find the part of Figure 2 that the text is describing. For example, the sun shining on the watermelon and the arrow showing the reaction of CO_2 and H_2O to form glucose is described by the first sentence under *Photosynthesis*. **LS** **Verbal/Visual**

Students can interact with the cycle for "Photosynthesis and Cellular Respiration" by going to go.hrw.com and typing in the keyword HX8PHRF2.

Figure 2 Photosynthesis and cellular respiration are major steps in the carbon cycle. ❯ **Compare the end results of photosynthesis and cellular respiration.**

ATP produced in cellular respiration provides energy for life processes.

ATP

Solar energy is converted to chemical energy during photosynthesis.

Light energy

$CO_2 + H_2O$

Chloroplast

$C_6H_{12}O_6 + O_2$

Mitochondrion

Chloroplasts contain pigments that absorb light to provide energy for photosynthesis.

Cellular respiration takes place in mitochondria.

Teaching Key Ideas

Understanding the Flow of Carbon in the Carbon Cycle Review **Figure 2** with students and ask them to summarize how carbon flows in cellular respiration and photosynthesis. (Carbon is taken in as carbon dioxide by plants in photosynthesis and converted to glucose. Glucose is broken down in mitochondria, producing carbon dioxide and energy.) **LS** Visual

Math Skills

Balancing Equations Write the equation $CO_2 + H_2O \rightarrow C_6H_{12}O_6 + O_2$ on the board and explain that it is the equation for photosynthesis that produces glucose. Ask the students to balance the equation. ($6CO_2 + 6H_2O \rightarrow C_6H_{12}O_6 + 6O_2$) Ask them why equations need to be balanced. (Reactions satisfy the Law of Conservation of Mass. A balanced equation symbolizes mass conservation.) **LS** Logical

Answers to Caption Questions

Figure 2: Both processes convert carbon compounds into different carbon compounds. Photosynthesis works to store energy in a carbon compound, and cellular respiration works to release energy from a carbon compound.

Why It Matters

Food Energy Sometimes food is literally burned for energy. For years, grain has been fermented to make ethanol, an alcohol that can be added to gasoline to boost power and reduce pollution. New research is producing fuels based entirely on renewable sources. These fuels can be made from grains, such as corn and wheat, or even from trees and grasses. Biodiesel is a diesel-like fuel made from vegetable oil.

MISCONCEPTION ///ALERT\\\

Plant Respiration Many students believe that plants undergo photosynthesis while other organisms undergo respiration. Point out that the reason plants undergo photosynthesis is to produce organic compounds that the plants can then use in respiration. Remind students that plant cells contain both chloroplasts and mitochondria. The mitochondria use the organic compounds to make ATP, which powers cellular activities.

Key-Term Fold **photosynthesis** plants use light energy and CO_2 to make glucose

cellular respiration organisms break down glucose to make ATP

ATP energy "currency" for the cell

ATP synthase catalyzes synthesis of ATP

electron transport chain molecules that pump H^+ out of the mitochondrion

READING TOOLBOX

Key-Term Fold On the back of your key-term fold, write a definition in your own words for each key term in this section.

ACADEMIC VOCABULARY

process a set of steps, events, or changes

Figure 3 The energy of falling water can turn a water wheel, which provides energy to do work. In ATP synthase, the movement of hydrogen ions provides energy to convert ADP to ATP.

Transferring Energy

In chemical reactions, energy can be absorbed and released during the breaking and forming of bonds. For example, when a log burns, the energy stored in wood molecules is released in a burst of heat and light. **> In cells, chemical energy is gradually released in a series of chemical reactions that are assisted by enzymes.** Recall that enzymes are proteins that act as catalysts in biochemical reactions.

ATP When cells break down food molecules, some of the energy in the molecules is released as heat. Cells use much of the remaining energy to make ATP. When glucose is broken down during cellular respiration, energy is stored temporarily in molecules of ATP. ATP can be used to power chemical reactions, such as those that build molecules. Paper money is portable and can be earned in one place and spent in another. Like money, ATP is a portable form of energy "currency" inside cells. ATP can be "earned," or made, in one place and "spent," or used, in another place. For example, ATP can be used to contract a muscle cell, to actively transport protein, or to help make more ATP.

ATP is a nucleotide made up of a chain of three phosphate groups. This chain is unstable because the phosphate groups are negatively charged and thus repel each other. When the bond of the third phosphate group is broken, energy is released. This produces adenosine diphosphate, or ADP. The equation below summarizes the <u>process</u>.

$$ATP \longrightarrow ADP + P + energy$$

The reaction in which ATP is converted to ADP requires a small input of energy. But much more energy is released than is used during the reaction.

> Reading Check *How is ATP used inside a cell?*

ATP Energy Because ATP supplies most of the energy that drives metabolism, ATP is sometimes called an energy-rich compound, and the bonds between its phosphate groups are sometimes called "high-energy" bonds. These terms are misleading because they imply that ATP contains an unusually large amount of energy. ATP serves as the cell's energy currency. The bonds between phosphate groups are unstable and therefore break easily. When they break, energy is released that can be used to drive metabolic processes.

Basic Learners/Special Education Students

ATP Structure Have students build a three-dimensional model of ATP (adenosine triphosphate). Students should use everyday materials and include the three phosphate groups, the sugar, and the base. Visually-impaired students can use well-designed models to learn the structure and role of ATP in respiration. Make sure students understand which part of the nucleotide is removed to release energy for cellular reactions. (the last phosphate group)
LS **Visual/Kinesthetic**

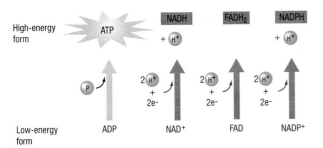

High-energy form

Low-energy form

Figure 4 Electron carriers store energy by bonding with hydrogen, just as ATP stores energy by bonding a third phosphate group. ❯ Where is the electron transport chain found in animal cells?

Teaching Key Ideas

Recycling ATP ATP and ADP cycle constantly in the cell. Reusing the molecules is convenient because it does not require the cell to keep making all new molecules. In addition, the ADP molecule contains a small amount of energy that can be used for some functions by the cell without converting it to ATP. Most cell functions still require ATP, though.

❯ Close

Formative Assessment

Which of the following organisms is most likely an autotroph?

A. a sponge (Incorrect. The habitat of a sponge is such that it is not likely to be a photosynthetic organism.)

B. a Venus flytrap (Correct! Although a Venus flytrap traps insects for some nutrients, it still obtains energy from the sun.)

C. a worm (Incorrect. A worm is a heterotroph.)

D. a mushroom (Incorrect. A mushroom does not obtain energy through photosynthesis.)

ATP Synthase In many cells, **ATP synthase,** an enzyme that catalyzes the synthesis of ATP, recycles ADP by bonding a third phosphate group to the molecule. As **Figure 3** shows, ATP synthase acts as both an enzyme and a carrier protein for hydrogen (H^+) ions. The flow of H^+ ions through ATP synthase powers the production of ATP. You can think of the H^+ ions moving through ATP synthase to produce ATP as falling water turning a water wheel to produce power. As H^+ ions flow, ATP synthase catalyzes a reaction in which a phosphate group is added to a molecule of ADP to make ATP.

Hydrogen Ion Pumps Recall how diffusion across cell membranes works. Particles of a substance diffuse through a membrane from a region of higher concentration to a region of lower concentration. The inner mitochondrial membrane allows H^+ ions to diffuse through only ATP synthase. When glucose is broken down during cellular respiration, NAD^+ (nicotinamide adenine dinucleotide) accepts electrons and hydrogen ions, which changes NAD^+ to NADH. As **Figure 4** shows, NADH enters an **electron transport chain,** a series of molecules in the inner membrane of a mitochondrion. The electron transport chain allows electrons to drop in energy as they are passed along and uses the energy released to pump H^+ ions out of a mitochondrion's inner compartment. This action increases the concentration of H^+ ions in the outer compartment. The ions then diffuse back into the inner compartment through ATP synthase.

ATP synthase an enzyme that catalyzes the synthesis of ATP

electron transport chain a series of molecules, found in the inner membranes of mitochondria and chloroplasts, through which electrons pass in a process that causes protons to build up on one side of the membrane

SC*i*LINKS.
www.scilinks.org
Topic: ATP
Code: HX80123

Review

❯ KEY IDEAS

1. **Identify** the primary source of energy that flows through most living systems.
2. **Explain** how an organism's metabolism is related to Earth's carbon cycle.
3. **Describe** how energy is released from ATP.

CRITICAL THINKING

4. **Analyzing Patterns** Explain how life involves a continuous flow of energy.
5. **Inferring Relationships** How can the energy in the food that a fox eats be traced back to the sun?
6. **Summarizing Information** What is the difference between cellular respiration and the process by which energy is released from a burning log?

WRITING FOR SCIENCE

7. **Career Connection** Research the educational background that a person needs to become an enzymologist. List the courses required, and describe additional degrees or training that are recommended for this career. Write a report on your findings.

Photosynthesis

Key Ideas	Key Terms	Why It Matters
› What is the role of pigments in photosynthesis? › What are the roles of the electron transport chains? › How do plants make sugars and store extra unused energy? › What are three environmental factors that affect photosynthesis?	thylakoid pigment chlorophyll Calvin cycle	Nearly all of the energy for life processes comes from the sun and is stored in organic molecules during the process of photosynthesis.

› Focus

This section describes the major events of the three stages of photosynthesis. These include the capture of energy (stage 1), the conversion of light energy to chemical energy (stage 2), and the formation of organic compounds using stored chemical energy (stage 3).

🔔 Bellringer

Use the Bellringer transparency to prepare students for this section.

› Teach

Demonstration

Products of Photosynthesis Use a scalpel to make thin cross sections of a potato. Use a projection microscope to show the potato section, or have students examine the potato under a compound microscope. Ask them to look for starch granules, which should appear as large, translucent structures inside the potato cells. Adding iodine stain will make the starch granules more visible. Explain that much of the mass of the organic compounds plants make during photosynthesis is stored as starch. **LS** Visual

Answers to Caption Questions

Figure 5: inside chloroplasts

The Living Environment
Standard 4

1.2f Cells have particular structures that perform specific jobs. These structures perform the actual work of the cell. Just as systems are coordinated and work together, cell parts must also be coordinated and work together.

1.2i Inside the cell a variety of specialized structures, formed from many different molecules, carry out the transport of materials (cytoplasm), extraction of energy from nutrients (mitochondria), protein building (ribosomes), waste disposal (cell membrane), storage (vacuole), and information storage (nucleus).

5.1b Plant cells and some one-celled organisms contain chloroplasts, the site of photosynthesis. The process of photosynthesis uses solar energy to combine the inorganic molecules carbon dioxide and water into energy rich organic compounds (e.g., glucose) and release oxygen to the environment.

5.1f Biochemical processes, both breakdown and synthesis, are made possible by a large set of biological catalysts called enzymes. Enzymes can affect the rates of chemical change. The rate at which enzymes work can be influenced by internal environmental factors such as pH and temperature.

Figure 5 Pigments, as well as other molecules that participate in photosynthesis, are embedded in thylakoids. › Where are thylakoids located?

Plants, algae, and certain prokaryotes capture about 1% of the energy in the sunlight that reaches Earth and convert it to chemical energy through photosynthesis. Photosynthesis is the process that provides energy for almost all life.

Harvesting Light Energy

The cells of many photosynthetic organisms have chloroplasts, organelles that convert light energy into chemical energy. Study the diagram of a chloroplast in **Figure 5.**

A chloroplast has an outer membrane and an inner membrane. Molecules diffuse easily through the outer membrane. The inner membrane is much more selective about what substances enter and leave. Both membranes allow light to pass through.

The space inside the inner membrane is the stroma. Within the stroma is a membrane called the *thylakoid membrane*. This membrane is folded in a way that produces flat, disc-like sacs called **thylakoids.** These sacs, which contain molecules that absorb light energy for photosynthesis, are arranged in stacks. The first stage of photosynthesis begins when light waves hit these stacks.

› **Reading Check** *Describe the structure of a chloroplast.*

Leaf   Plant cell   Outer membrane   Inner membrane   Chloroplast

Section Correlations	
4.1.2f	4.5.1b
4.1.2i	4.5.1f

Key Resources

Transparencies
B52 Photosynthesis
B25 Absorption Spectra of Photosynthesis Pigments
B24 Chloroplasts
B30 Summary of Processes in Light Reactions
B31 Calvin Cycle

Visual Concepts
Photosynthesis
Spectrum of light and Plant Pigments
Chlorophyll a and b
Carotenoid
Parts of a Chloroplast
Electron Transport Chain
Energy Yield in Aerobic Respiration
Calvin Cycle
Environmental Influences on Photosynthesis

Electromagnetic Radiation Light is a form of electromagnetic radiation, energy that can travel through empty space in the form of waves. Radio waves, X-rays, and microwaves are also forms of electromagnetic radiation. The difference between these forms of radiation is that they have different wavelengths. Each wavelength corresponds to a certain amount of energy. The wavelength is the distance between consecutive wave peaks. Sunlight contains all of the wavelengths of visible light. You see these wavelengths as different colors.

Pigments What makes the human eye sensitive to light? Cells in the back of the eye contain pigments. A **pigment** is a substance that absorbs certain wavelengths (colors) of light and reflects all of the others. ❯ In plants, light energy is harvested by pigments that are located in the thylakoid membrane of chloroplasts. **Chlorophyll** is a green pigment in chloroplasts that absorbs light energy to start photosynthesis. It absorbs mostly blue and red light and reflects green and yellow light, which makes plants appear green. Plants have two types of chlorophyll: chlorophyll *a* and chlorophyll *b*. Plants also have pigments called *carotenoids*. Carotenoids absorb blue and green light, and they reflect yellow, orange, and red light. When chlorophyll fades away in the fall, the colors of carotenoids are exposed. Carotenoids aid photosynthesis by allowing plants to absorb additional light energy. **Figure 6** shows the wavelengths of light that are absorbed by chlorophyll *a*, chlorophyll *b*, and carotenoids—the pigments found in thylakoid membranes.

Electron Carriers When light hits a thylakoid, energy is absorbed by many pigment molecules. They all funnel the energy to a special chlorophyll molecule in a region called the *reaction center,* where the energy causes the electrons to become "excited" and to move to a higher energy level. These electrons are transferred quickly to other nearby molecules and then to an electron carrier.

Absorption Spectra of Photosynthetic Pigments

Chlorophyll b
Carotenoid
Chlorophyll a

Figure 6 This graph show the colors of light that three different pigments absorb. Where a curve peaks, much of the light at that wavelength is absorbed. Where a curve dips, much of the light at that wavelength is reflected or transmitted.

thylakoid (THIE luh KOYD) a membrane system found within chloroplasts that contains the components for photosynthesis

pigment a substance that gives another substance or a mixture its color

chlorophyll (KLAWR uh FIL) a green pigment that is present in most plant and algae cells and some bacteria, that gives plants their characteristic green color, and that absorbs light to provide energy for photosynthesis

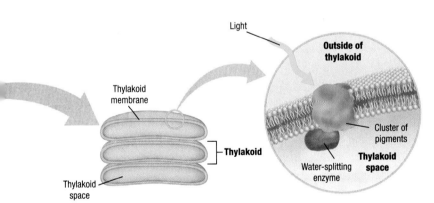

Teaching Key Ideas

Electron Transport Chain Guide students through the electron transport chains of photosynthesis shown in **Figure 7** by asking the following questions: "What is the source of the excited electrons?" (chlorophyll molecules) "What is the source of some of the replacement electrons?" (split water molecules) "What type of transport occurs when hydrogen ions are pumped into the thylakoid?" (active transport) "What type of transport occurs when hydrogen ions move out of the thylakoid?" (passive transport) "What kind of membrane protein is involved?" (carrier protein) Have students record the questions and answers in their notebooks. **LS** Visual

Answers to Caption Questions

Figure 7: The concentration of H⁺ ions is greater inside the thylakoid than outside the thylakoid (ions move down the concentration gradient).

Figure 7 Photosynthesis converts light energy to chemical energy. This figure shows key molecules involved in the capture of light, electron transport, and synthesis of ATP and NADPH. ❯ What causes H⁺ ions to move through the carrier protein that produces ATP?

Two Electron Transport Chains

Electrons from the electron carrier are used to produce new molecules, including ATP, that temporarily store chemical energy. The carrier transfers the electrons to the first of two electron transport chains in the thylakoid membrane. Trace the path taken by the electrons in the electron transport chains shown in **Figure 7.** ❯ During photosynthesis, one electron transport chain provides energy to make ATP, while the other provides energy to make NADPH. Both chains use energy from electrons excited by light.

Producing ATP In mitochondria, electron transport chains pump H⁺ ions through a membrane, which produces a concentration gradient. This process also happens in chloroplasts.

Step ❶ Water Splitting The excited electrons that leave chlorophyll molecules must be replaced by other electrons. Plants get these replacement electrons from water molecules, H_2O. During photosynthesis, an enzyme splits water molecules inside the thylakoid. When water molecules are split, chlorophyll molecules take the electrons from the hydrogen atoms, H, which leaves H⁺ ions. The remaining oxygen atoms, O, from the split water molecules combine to form oxygen gas, O_2. This oxygen gas is not used for any later steps of photosynthesis, so it is released into the atmosphere.

Electron Transport Chains of Photosynthesis

MISCONCEPTION ALERT

Why Plants Look Green Many people think that plants are green because plants use green light during photosynthesis. In fact, plants use very little green light, and instead use mainly red and blue light. Tell students that plants look green because they contain chlorophyll, which reflects green and yellow light while absorbing red and blue light.

Differentiated Instruction

Basic Learners

Stages of Photosynthesis Help students remember the three stages of photosynthesis by having them make flash cards with a structure or process on one side and a description of its role on the other side. Topics should include the names of the pigment molecules, thylakoids, electron transport chains, ATP, and NADPH. **LS** Visual

QuickLab

🕐 **15 min**

Photosynthetic Rate 4.5.1a

Changes in a plant's surroundings influence photosynthetic rate. The two graphs illustrate how photosynthetic rate responds to changes in light intensity and temperature. Use the graphs to answer the following questions.

Analysis

1. **Describe** how increasing light intensity affects the rate of photosynthesis.

2. **Explain** whether continuing to increase light intensity will increase the rate of photosynthesis.

3. **Describe** how increasing temperature affects the rate of photosynthesis.

Environmental Influences on Photosynthesis

(a) Light intensity

(b) Temperature

4. **CRITICAL THINKING** **Inferring Relationships** Explain how a global temperature increase could affect plants.

Step 2 **Hydrogen Ion Pump** A protein acts as a membrane pump. Excited electrons transfer some of their energy to pump H⁺ ions into the thylakoid. This process creates a concentration gradient across the thylakoid membrane.

Step 3 **ATP Synthase** The energy from the diffusion of H⁺ ions through the carrier protein is used to make ATP. These carrier proteins are unusual because they function both as an ion channel and as the enzyme ATP synthase. As hydrogen ions pass through the channel portion of the protein, ATP synthase catalyzes a reaction in which a phosphate group is added to a molecule of ADP. The result of the reaction is ATP, which is used to power the final stage of photosynthesis.

Producing NADPH While one electron transport chain provides energy used to make ATP, a second electron transport chain receives excited electrons from a chlorophyll molecule and uses them to make NADPH. The second electron transport chain is to the right of the second cluster of pigment molecules in **Figure 7.**

Step 4 **Reenergizing** In this second chain, light excites electrons in the chlorophyll molecule. The excited electrons are passed on to the second chain. They are replaced by the de-energized electrons from the first transport chain.

Step 5 **Making NADPH** Excited electrons combine with H⁺ ions and an electron acceptor called NADP⁺ to form NADPH. NADPH is an electron carrier that provides the high-energy electrons needed to store energy in organic molecules. Both NADPH and the ATP made during the first stage of photosynthesis will be used to provide the energy to carry out the final stage of photosynthesis.

❯ **Reading Check** *Summarize how ATP and NADPH are formed during photosynthesis.*

READING TOOLBOX

Describing Space Use spatial language to describe production of ATP and NADPH during photosynthesis.

QuickLab

Teacher's Notes Discuss strategies for measuring the photosynthetic rate. Suppose the rate was inferred by measuring the amount of generated oxygen. Tell students that at very low light levels, the oxygen level does not increase, because any generated gas is absorbed by the cell for respiration. At higher levels, the generated oxygen is much greater than the needs of the cells and therefore its accumulation can be used to infer rate.

Answers to Analysis

1. At first, the rate steadily increases. Then, the rate slows. It soon levels off, remaining at peak value.

2. It won't. At a certain point, increasing intensity has no effect on the rate.

3. The rate steadily increases, peaks, then steadily decreases.

4. Plant growth might increase initially, but increased temperatures might also kill unadapted plants.

READING TOOLBOX

Describing Space Steps in ATP production are as follows: Water splitting occurs *within the thylakoid.* Hydrogen ions are pumped *into the thylakoid* by a protein that acts as a membrane pump. ATP synthase, *in a channel protein,* catalyzes the reaction to make ATP from ADP.

Steps in NADPH production are as follows: Light reenergizes electrons in *chlorophyll.* Excited electrons, hydrogen ions, and NADP⁺ react in the *thylakoid.*

Differentiated Instruction

Basic Learners/Special Education Students

NADPH Have students make a model of NADPH from clay or some other moldable material. Make the H in the model so that it can be taken on and off and demonstrate how the molecule accepts and donates electrons as it changes between the two. Visually-impaired students can use the best models to follow the process of NADPH production. **LS** **Visual/Kinesthetic**

Teaching Key Ideas

The Calvin Cycle Have students count the total number of carbon atoms present at each step in the summary of the Calvin cycle in **Figure 8.** Ask students the following questions: "How are ATP and NADPH important to the Calvin cycle?" (They supply energy used to form new compounds.) "How many carbon dioxide molecules are needed?" (3) "How many 3-carbon sugars are made?" (6) "How many of these sugars are actually used to make organic compounds that the plant uses for energy?" (1) Emphasize that most of the 3-carbon sugars are "recycled" and used to make the starting 5-carbon compound that begins the cycle again. **LS Visual**

Why It Matters

Increasing Levels of Carbon Dioxide In general, higher carbon dioxide levels mean that more biomass, or plant tissue, is made during photosynthesis. This increase in biomass may help to counter the effects of rising carbon dioxide levels caused by burning fossil fuels. Other effects appear to be a reduction of nutrients in plant tissues, which may impact the heterotrophs that feed on plants.

go.hrw.com
✳ interact online

Students can interact with the "Calvin Cycle" by going to go.hrw.com and typing in the keyword HX8PHRF8.

Calvin cycle a biochemical pathway of photosynthesis in which carbon dioxide is converted into glucose using ATP and NADPH

ACADEMIC VOCABULARY

method a way of doing something

Figure 8 The Calvin cycle is the most common method of carbon dioxide fixation. **▶ What is formed when the three six-carbon molecules split during step 2 of the Calvin cycle?**

Producing Sugar

The first two stages of photosynthesis depend directly on light because light energy is used to make ATP and NADPH. **▶ In the final stage of photosynthesis, ATP and NADPH are used to produce energy-storing sugar molecules from the carbon in carbon dioxide.** The use of carbon dioxide to make organic compounds is called *carbon dioxide fixation,* or *carbon fixation.* The reactions that fix carbon dioxide are light-independent reactions, sometimes called *dark reactions.* Among photosynthetic organisms, there are several ways in which carbon dioxide is fixed. The most common <u>method</u> of carbon dioxide fixation is the **Calvin cycle,** which is described in the following steps:

Step ❶ Carbon Fixation In carbon dioxide fixation, an enzyme adds a molecule of carbon dioxide, CO_2, to a five-carbon compound. This process occurs three times to yield three six-carbon molecules.

Step ❷ Absorbing Energy Each six-carbon compound splits into two three-carbon compounds. Phosphate groups from ATP and electrons from NADPH are added to the three-carbon compounds to form three-carbon sugars.

Step ❸ Making Sugar One of the resulting three-carbon sugars leaves the cycle and is used to make organic compounds—including glucose, sucrose, and starch—in which energy is stored for later use by the organism.

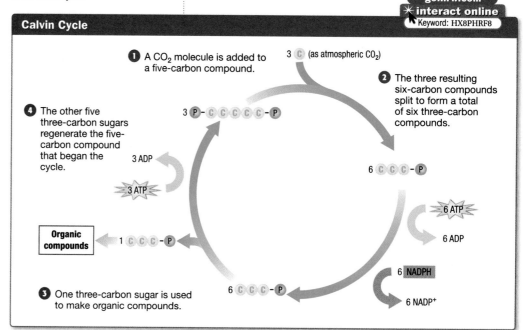

go.hrw.com
✳ interact online
Keyword: HX8PHRF8

Calvin Cycle

❶ A CO_2 molecule is added to a five-carbon compound.

3 Ⓒ (as atmospheric CO_2)

❷ The three resulting six-carbon compounds split to form a total of six three-carbon compounds.

❹ The other five three-carbon sugars regenerate the five-carbon compound that began the cycle.

3 Ⓟ-ⒸⒸⒸⒸⒸ-Ⓟ

3 ADP

3 ATP

6 ⒸⒸⒸ-Ⓟ

6 ATP

6 ADP

6 NADPH

6 NADP⁺

Organic compounds

1 ⒸⒸⒸ-Ⓟ

6 ⒸⒸⒸ-Ⓟ

❸ One three-carbon sugar is used to make organic compounds.

Differentiated Instruction

Basic Learners

Role Playing Form six groups of students for a peer learning activity. Assign one of the following factors to each group: water, chlorophyll, light, carbon dioxide, NADPH, and ATP. Have each group decide on the role their factor plays in photosynthesis. After a designated time, select a person in each group to describe the role to the rest of the class. Encourage students to be creative. **LS Interpersonal**

Alternative Assessment

Calvin Cycle Have students describe the events of the Calvin Cycle from the perspective of one of the carbon atoms in a CO_2 molecule. Students should include the main steps of the process and what happens to "them" as a carbon atom in each step.

Figure 9 Some plants, such as a cactus (left), grow in extremely sunny, dry environments. Others, such as the bromeliad (right), are able to grow in shady areas.

Step ④ Recycling The remaining five three-carbon sugars are rearranged. Using energy from ATP, enzymes reform three molecules of the initial five-carbon compound. This process completes the cycle. The reformed compounds are used to begin the cycle again.

Factors that Affect Photosynthesis

❯ **Light intensity, carbon dioxide concentration, and temperature are three environmental factors that affect photosynthesis.** The most obvious of these factors is light. **Figure 9** shows plants that are adapted to different levels of light. In general, the rate of photosynthesis increases as light intensity increases until all of the pigments in a chloroplast are being used. At this saturation point, the rate of photosynthesis levels off because the pigments cannot absorb more light.

The concentration of carbon dioxide affects the rate of photosynthesis in a way similar to light. Once a certain concentration of carbon dioxide is present, photosynthesis cannot proceed any faster.

Photosynthesis is most efficient in a certain range of temperatures. Like all metabolic processes, photosynthesis involves many enzyme-assisted chemical reactions. Unfavorable temperatures may inactivate certain enzymes so that reactions cannot take place.

❯ **Reading Check** *How does temperature affect photosynthesis?*

Section 2 Review

❯ **KEY IDEAS**

1. **Summarize** how autotrophs capture the energy in sunlight.
2. **Compare** the roles of water molecules and H⁺ ions in electron transport chains.
3. **Describe** the role of the Calvin cycle in photosynthesis.
4. **Name** the three main environmental factors that affect the rate of photosynthesis in plants.

CRITICAL THINKING

5. **Organizing Information** Make a table in which you identify the role of each of the following in photosynthesis: light, water, pigments, ATP, NADPH, and carbon dioxide.

METHODS OF SCIENCE

6. **Inferring Relationships** How do you think photosynthesis will be affected if the sun's rays are blocked by clouds or by smoke from a large fire? How might the levels of atmospheric carbon dioxide and oxygen be affected? What experiments could scientists conduct in the laboratory to test your predictions?

Section **3**

Focus

This section describes how organic compounds are processed to form ATP, the energy currency of all cells. Students will learn the basic events of glycolysis and cellular respiration, as well as alternate energy pathways that take place in the absence of oxygen.

 Bellringer

Use the Bellringer transparency to prepare students for this section.

Teach

Teaching Key Ideas

Fermentation Ask students what they know about fermentation. Students may speak of rotting, foul smells, or alcohol production. Explain that fermentation is a way that cells are able to make ATP in the absence of oxygen. Fermentation can cause foul odors. It also helps produce cheese, yogurt, bread, and wine. **LS** Verbal

Answers to Caption Questions

Figure 10: photosynthesis
Figure 11: glucose

Key Ideas

> How does glycolysis produce ATP?
> How is ATP produced in aerobic respiration?
> Why is fermentation important?

Key Terms

glycolysis
anaerobic
aerobic
Krebs cycle
fermentation

Why It Matters

Cellular respiration is the process used by humans and most other organisms to release the energy stored in the food they consume.

The Living Environment
Standard 4
1.2i Inside the cell a variety of specialized structures, formed from many different molecules, carry out the transport of materials (cytoplasm), extraction of energy from nutrients (mitochondria), protein building (ribosomes), waste disposal (cell membrane), storage (vacuole), and information storage (nucleus).
5.1d In all organisms, the energy stored in organic molecules may be released during cellular respiration. This energy is temporarily stored in ATP molecules. In many organisms, the process of cellular respiration is concluded in mitochondria, in which ATP is produced more efficiently, oxygen is used, and carbon dioxide and water are released as wastes.

Where do the students shown in **Figure 10** get energy? Most of the foods we eat contain energy. Much of the energy in a hamburger, for example, is stored in proteins, carbohydrates, and fats. But before you can use that energy, it must be released and transferred to ATP. Like cells of most organisms, your cells transfer the energy in organic compounds, especially the glucose made during photosynthesis, to ATP through cellular respiration, which begins with glycolysis.

Glycolysis

The primary fuel for cellular respiration is glucose, which is formed when carbohydrates, such as starch and sucrose, are broken down. If too few carbohydrates are available to meet an organism's energy needs, other molecules, such as fats, can be broken down to make ATP. In fact, one gram of fat releases more energy than two grams of carbohydrates do. Proteins and nucleic acids can also be used to make ATP, but they are usually used for building important cell parts.

Figure 10 These students get their energy by eating carbohydrates, fats, proteins, and other organic molecules. > What is the origin of the energy-containing organic molecules in these students' food?

Overset p. 208 (bottom)

Comparing Aerobic and Anaerobic Respiration

Section Correlations

4.1.2i
4.5.1d

Key Resources

Transparencies
B53 Cellular Respiration
B37 Glycolysis
B39 Krebs Cycle
B54 Electron Transport Chain of Aerobic Respiration

 Visual Concepts
Cellular Respiration
Glycolysis
NAD^+ and NADH
Krebs Cycle
FAD and $FADH_2$
Fermentation

Differentiated Instruction

Basic Learners

Relating Processes Ask students to answer the following questions in their notebooks: How are the products of photosynthesis and cellular respiration related? (The products of photosynthesis are the starting materials for cellular respiration.) What kinds of organisms undergo cellular respiration? (All organisms, including photosynthetic organisms, undergo cellular respiration.) **LS** Logical

Glycolysis

Glucose

2 ATP   2 ADP

2 P

2 NAD⁺ 2 NADH + 2H⁺

4 ADP

4 ATP

2 pyruvates

1 Two ATP molecules are used to break glucose into two smaller units. A phosphate group is added to the 6-carbon compound.

2 Each 3-carbon compound reacts with a phosphate group. Hydrogen atoms are transferred to NAD⁺, producing NADH.

3 Each 3-carbon sugar is converted to a 3-carbon molecule of pyruvate. Four ATP molecules are produced.

Steps of Glycolysis In the first stage of cellular respiration, glucose is broken down in the cytoplasm by glycolysis. In **glycolysis,** enzymes break down one six-carbon molecule of glucose into two three-carbon pyruvate molecules, as **Figure 11** shows. Most of the energy that was stored in the glucose molecule is stored in the pyruvate.

Step ❶ Breaking Down Glucose In the first stage of glycolysis, two ATP molecules are used to break glucose into two smaller units. This stage has four steps with four different enzymes. A phosphate group from ATP is added to the six-carbon compound. This makes the molecule reactive so that an enzyme can break it into two three-carbon sugars, each with a phosphate group. ATP is produced in the next two stages.

Step ❷ NADH Production In the second stage, each three-carbon compound reacts with another phosphate group (not from ATP). As the two three-carbon sugars react further, hydrogen atoms, including their electrons, are transferred to two molecules of NAD⁺, which produces two molecules of the electron carrier NADH. NADH is used later in other cell processes, where it is recycled to NAD⁺.

Step ❸ Pyruvate Production In a series of four reactions, each three-carbon sugar is converted into a three-carbon molecule of pyruvate. This process produces four ATP molecules. ❯ Thus, the breaking of a sugar molecule by glycolysis results in a net gain of two ATP molecules.

Glycolysis is the only source of energy for some prokaryotes. This process is **anaerobic,** so it takes place without oxygen. Other organisms use oxygen to release even more energy from a glucose molecule. Metabolic processes that require oxygen are **aerobic.** In aerobic respiration, the pyruvate product of glycolysis undergoes another series of reactions to produce more ATP molecules.

❯ **Reading Check** *What are the three products of glycolysis?*

Figure 11 Glycolysis uses two ATP molecules but produces four ATP molecules. The process results in a net gain of ATP. ❯ What is the starting material in glycolysis?

glycolysis (glie KAHL i sis) the anaerobic breakdown of glucose to pyruvate, which makes a small amount of energy available to cells in the form of ATP

anaerobic (AN uhr OH bik) describes a process that does not require oxygen

aerobic (er OH bik) describes a process that requires oxygen

SC*L*INKS.

www.scilinks.org
Topic: Cellular Respiration
Code: HX80244

Students can interact with the stages of "Glycolysis" by going to go.hrw.com and typing in the keyword HX9PHRF11.

Teaching Key Ideas

Metabolic Pathways Review the term *metabolism* with students. (Metabolism describes the sum of all chemical reactions within an organism.) Tell students that glycolysis is an example of a metabolic pathway. In glycolysis, the energy stored in glucose is gradually released in a series of enzyme-assisted chemical reactions. **LS Verbal**

Why It Matters

Life Without Oxygen Early life probably used glycolysis to make ATP long before oxygen was present in Earth's atmosphere. According to fossil records, prokaryotes were present on Earth 3.5 billion years ago, but oxygen was not abundant in the atmosphere until around 2.5 billion years ago. Because glycolysis is an anaerobic metabolic pathway that occurs in all cells, glycolysis most likely occurred in early cells.

Differentiated Instruction

Basic Learners

Glycolysis Have students examine **Figure 11,** and ask them to identify the starting material in glycolysis. (glucose) Work with students to summarize the events that take place in each step. Explain that as glucose is broken down during glycolysis, some of the energy contained in glucose is transferred to the products of glycolysis. Ask students to identify these products. (pyruvate, ATP, and NADH) Explain that pyruvate is the ion of the organic molecule pyruvic acid. **LS Visual**

Teaching Key Ideas

Coenzymes A coenzyme is an organic chemical that is necessary for the action of many enzymes. Ask students why it is important for glucose to be partially broken down to pyruvate. (The formation of pyruvate releases some energy.) Tell students that when pyruvate enters a mitochondrion and is broken down to a 2-carbon acetyl group, coenzyme A attaches to the acetyl group, forming acetyl-CoA. Coenzyme A enables the acetyl group to enter the Krebs cycle.

Teaching Key Ideas

The Krebs Cycle Guide students through the steps of **Figure 12.** Have students count the number of carbon atoms present at each step during the Krebs cycle. Ask them where the Krebs cycle occurs. (in mitochondria) Remind students that for every molecule of glucose that is broken down, two pyruvate ions are produced. Thus the Krebs cycle occurs for each pyruvate. Also tell them that a specific enzyme is involved in each step. Emphasize the role of the Krebs cycle as a precursor of the electron transport chain. **LS** Visual

Krebs cycle a series of biochemical reactions that convert pyruvate into carbon dioxide and water

---

Krebs Cycle

Figure 12 The Krebs cycle is the stage of aerobic respiration in which carbon dioxide is released and electron carriers are produced.

❶ Pyruvate, the end product of glycolysis, releases a carbon dioxide molecule, CO_2. The resulting two-carbon compound enters the Krebs cycle and combines with a four-carbon compound.

❷ CO_2 is released from the six-carbon compound, which leaves a five-carbon compound. Then, a second CO_2 is released, which leaves a four-carbon compound.

❸ The resulting four-carbon compound is rearranged in several steps to form a different four-carbon compound. This four-carbon compound combines with a new two-carbon unit from pyruvate.

YIELD:
1 ATP
3 NADH
1 $FADH_2$

Aerobic Respiration

Organisms such as humans can use oxygen to produce ATP efficiently through aerobic respiration. Pyruvate is broken down in the **Krebs cycle,** a series of reactions that produce electron carriers. The electron carriers enter an electron transport chain, which powers ATP synthase. Up to 34 ATP molecules can be produced from one glucose molecule in aerobic respiration.

Krebs Cycle The first stage of aerobic respiration, the Krebs cycle, is named for Hans Krebs, a German biochemist. He was awarded the Nobel Prize in 1953 for discovering it. As **Figure 12** shows, the Krebs cycle begins with pyruvate, which is produced during glycolysis. Pyruvate releases a carbon dioxide molecule to form a two-carbon compound. An enzyme attaches this two-carbon compound to a four-carbon compound and forms a six-carbon compound.

The six-carbon compound releases one carbon dioxide molecule and then another. Energy is released each time, which forms an electron carrier, NADH. The remaining four-carbon compound is converted to the four-carbon compound that began the cycle. This conversion takes place in a series of steps that produce ATP, then $FADH_2$, and another NADH. The four-carbon compound combines with a new two-carbon unit from pyruvate to continue the cycle.

Products of the Krebs Cycle Each time the carbon-carbon bonds are rearranged or broken, energy is released. **❯ The total yield of energy-storing products from one time through the Krebs cycle is one ATP, three NADH, and one FADH$_2$.** Electron carriers transfer energy through the electron transport chain, which ultimately powers ATP synthase.

Electron Transport Chain The second stage of aerobic respiration takes place in the inner membranes of mitochondria. Recall that electrons pass through a series of molecules called an *electron transport chain*, as **Figure 13** shows. ❶ The electrons that are carried by NADH and FADH$_2$ pass through this chain. Energy is transferred into each molecule through which the electrons pass. Some of the molecules are hydrogen ion pumps. ❷ Energy from the electrons is used to actively transport hydrogen ions, H$^+$, out of the inner mitochondrial compartment. As H$^+$ ions accumulate in the outer compartment, a concentration gradient across the inner membrane is created.

ATP Production The enzyme ATP synthase is also present on the inner membranes of mitochondria. ❸ Hydrogen ions diffuse through a channel in this enzyme. This movement provides energy, which is used to produce several ATP molecules from ADP.

The Role of Oxygen At the end of the electron transport chain, the electrons have given up most of their energy. ❹ An oxygen atom combines with these electrons and two H$^+$ ions to form two water molecules, H$_2$O. If oxygen is not present, the electron transport chain stops. The electron carriers cannot be recycled, so the Krebs cycle also stops. Without oxygen, a cell can produce ATP only by glycolysis.

❯ Reading Check *Why is glycolysis important to the Krebs cycle?*

Pattern Puzzles Make a pattern puzzle to help you remember the steps in aerobic respiration.

Figure 13 Along the inner mitochondrial membrane, an electron transport chain produces a hydrogen ion gradient. The diffusion of hydrogen ions provides energy for the production of ATP by ATP synthase.

Electron Transport Chain

go.hrw.com
✳ **interact online**
🖰 Keyword: HX8PHRF13

Pattern Puzzles Puzzle parts should include the following: electrons carried by NADH and FADH$_2$; hydrogen ions pumped from the inner to outer mitochondrial compartment; hydrogen ions diffuse through ATP synthase channel; oxygen, electrons, and hydrogen ions react to form water; Krebs cycle begins with pyruvate and produces 1 ATP, 3NADH, and 1FADH$_2$

Teaching Key Ideas

Electron Transport Ask students how the electron transport chains of photosynthesis and cellular respiration are similar. (In both processes, electrons are passed along an electron transport chain and are picked up by an electron acceptor. The energy of these electrons is used to produce a hydrogen ion concentration gradient, which provides the energy needed to make ATP.)

Math Skills

ATP Molecules The human body uses about 1 million molecules of ATP per cell per second. There are more than 100 trillion cells in the human body. That's about 1×10^{20}, or 100,000,000,000,000,000,000 ATP molecules used in your body each second.

go.hrw.com
✳ **interact online**

🖰 Students can interact with the "Electron Transport Chain" by going to go.hrw.com and typing in the keyword HX8PHRF13.

Differentiated Instruction

Basic Learners/Struggling Readers

Electron Transport Chain Have students follow the path of electrons, shown by the red arrows, through the electron transport chain in **Figure 13.** Point out that the energy of these electrons is used to pump hydrogen ions out of the inner compartment. Ask students to identify this type of transport. (active transport) These ions then diffuse back into the inner compartment through the specialized carrier protein, ATP synthase, providing enough energy to make ATP. Ask students to identify this type of transport. (passive transport) Ask students why the folds of the mitochondria are important. (They increase the surface area of the membranes, which allows more ATP to be made.) Ask students to identify the role of oxygen in the electron transport chain. (Oxygen is the final electron acceptor, and water is produced when the spent electrons, hydrogen ions, and oxygen combine.) **LS Visual**

Teaching Key Ideas

Effects of Exercise Invite one of the physical education teachers or coaches from your school to discuss the physiological effects of exercise on the body. Be certain that the speaker discusses oxygen debt, muscle fatigue, the role of myoglobin in muscles, and the role of lactate in muscle soreness.
LS Intrapersonal

Why It Matters

Cyanide Students may be familiar with the poison cyanide. Tell students that cyanide is a fast-acting poison that blocks the action of the electron transport chain. It exists as hydrogen cyanide gas or cyanide salts used in gold and other metal extractions, electroplating, and metal cleaning. Cyanide enters the body by absorption through the lungs, skin, or gastrointestinal tract. It is highly toxic, and symptoms appear soon after exposure. Ingesting as little as 3 grams of cyanide can soon be fatal.

Answers to Caption Questions

Figure 14: Possible answer: Lactic acid fermentation produces lactate, while alcoholic fermentation produces carbon dioxide and ethanol.
Figure 15: The electron transport chain that occurs during aerobic respiration

---

ACADEMIC VOCABULARY

transfer to carry or remove something from one thing to another

fermentation the breakdown of carbohydrates by enzymes, bacteria, yeasts, or mold in the absence of oxygen

---

Fermentation

Many prokaryotes live entirely on the energy released in glycolysis. Recall that glycolysis produces two ATP molecules and one molecule of the electron carrier NADH. The NADH must be able to <u>transfer</u> its electrons to an acceptor so that NAD^+ is continuously available. Under anaerobic conditions, the electron transport chain, if present, does not work. Organisms must have another way to recycle NAD^+. So, electrons carried by NADH are transferred to pyruvate, which is produced during glycolysis. This process in which carbohydrates are broken down in the absence of oxygen, called **fermentation,** recycles the NAD^+ that is needed to continue making ATP through glycolysis.
> **Fermentation enables glycolysis to continue supplying a cell with ATP in anaerobic conditions.** Two types of fermentation are lactic acid fermentation and alcoholic fermentation.

Lactic Acid Fermentation Recall that the end products of glycolysis are three-carbon pyruvate molecules. In some organisms, pyruvate accepts electrons and hydrogen from NADH. Pyruvate is converted to lactic acid in a process called *lactic acid fermentation,* as **Figure 14** shows. Lactic acid fermentation also occurs in the muscles of animals, including humans. During vigorous exercise, muscle cells must operate without enough oxygen. So, glycolysis becomes the only source of ATP as long as the glucose supply lasts. For glycolysis to continue, NAD^+ is recycled by lactic acid fermentation.

Alcoholic Fermentation In other organisms, an enzyme removes carbon dioxide from the three-carbon pyruvate to form a two-carbon molecule. Then, a second enzyme adds electrons and hydrogen from NADH to the molecule to form ethanol (ethyl alcohol) in a process called *alcoholic fermentation.* In this process, NAD^+ is recycled and glycolysis can continue to produce ATP.

> **Reading Check** *Explain how fermentation recycles NAD^+.*

Figure 14 When oxygen is not present, cells recycle NAD^+ through fermentation. > Compare lactic acid fermentation with alcoholic fermentation.

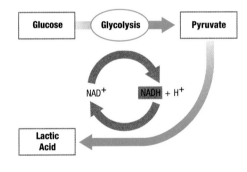

Lactic acid fermentation
In lactic acid fermentation, pyruvate is converted to lactic acid.

Alcoholic fermentation
In alcoholic fermentation, pyruvate is broken down to ethanol, releasing carbon dioxide.

Glucose

Glycolysis → (Net) 2 ATP

Pyruvate

Without O_2 — Anaerobic processes

With O_2 — Aerobic respiration

Fermentation

Lactate

Ethanol and CO_2

Krebs cycle → 2 ATP

Electron transport chain → (Up to) 34 ATP

Figure 15 Most ATP is produced during aerobic respiration. ❯ Which cellular respiration process produces ATP molecules most efficiently?

Efficiency of Cellular Respiration The total amount of ATP that a cell harvests from each glucose molecule depends on the presence or absence of oxygen. **Figure 15** compares the amount of ATP produced in both cases.

In the first stage of cellular respiration, glucose is broken down to pyruvate during glycolysis. Glycolysis is an anaerobic process, and it results in a net gain of two ATP molecules.

In the second stage of cellular respiration, pyruvate either passes through the Krebs cycle or undergoes fermentation. When oxygen is not present, fermentation occurs. The NAD^+ that is recycled during fermentation allows glycolysis to continue producing ATP.

Cells release energy most efficiently when oxygen is present because they make most of their ATP during aerobic respiration. For each molecule of glucose that is broken down, as many as two ATP molecules are made during the Krebs cycle. The Krebs cycle feeds NADH and $FADH_2$ to the electron transport chain. The electron transport chain can produce up to 34 ATP molecules.

Section 3 Review

❯ **KEY IDEAS**

1. **List** the products of glycolysis, and explain the role of each of these products in both aerobic respiration and anaerobic respiration.
2. **Summarize** the roles of the Krebs cycle and the electron transport chain during aerobic respiration.
3. **Describe** the role of fermentation in the second stage of cellular respiration.

CRITICAL THINKING

4. **Inferring Conclusions** Excess glucose in your blood is stored in your liver as glycogen. How might your body sense when to convert glucose to glycogen and glycogen back to glucose again?

ALTERNATIVE ASSESSMENT

5. **Analyzing Methods** Research ways that fermentation is used in food preparation. Find out what kinds of microorganisms are used in cultured dairy products, such as yogurt, sour cream, and some cheeses. Research the role of alcoholic fermentation by yeast in bread making. Prepare an oral report to summarize your findings.

Why It Matters

Life in a Biosphere

BIOTECHNOLOGY

The Biosphere 2 research facility has seven ecosystems that mirror those on Earth, including a desert, a savannah, a saltwater ocean that contains a millions gallons of water, an Amazonian rain forest, a mangrove marsh, an area of intensive agriculture, and a habitat for humans. The giant, self-contained system of Biosphere 2 is a miniature version of the flows and balances that occur on Earth. But in Biosphere 2, they are occurring at a much faster pace.

A World Under Glass

Located on 3.15 acres in southern Arizona, this miniature, airtight world is sealed on the bottom by a stainless steel liner and on the top by a steel and glass structure. The seven ecosystems were built from scratch with soils, water, and plant and animal life from around the world. Biosphere 2 has more than 1,000 sensors that monitor the vital statistics of this living laboratory by measuring temperature, humidity, oxygen, carbon dioxide, and other qualities of the air and soil.

Biospherians Eight researchers, known as *biospherians*, lived entirely within the facility. They controlled the technical systems and gathered results for more than 60 research projects, including studies of carbon dioxide and oxygen cycles, soil composition, coral reef health, agricultural pest management, and waste and water recycling.

Quick Project Biosphere 2 research is being used to help develop environmental technologies for use in space. Find out details about the Mars on Earth Project and its connection to Biosphere 2.

Biosphere 2 The research facility opened in 1991 as an ecological experiment designed for research, education, and the development of environmental technologies.

Objectives

➢ Demonstrate how carbon dioxide affects bromothymol blue when added to the indicator solution.

➢ Describe the effect of temperature on carbon dioxide production by yeast.

Materials

- safety goggles
- disposable gloves
- lab apron
- plastic cups, clear (4)
- room temperature water
- bromothymol blue
- drinking straw, plastic
- warm water
- ice water
- baker's yeast
- ¼ teaspoon
- hand lens
- sugar

Safety

Cellular Respiration

In cellular respiration, sugar is broken down and energy is released. This energy is harnessed and used to produce ATP. In addition to releasing energy, respiration generates reaction byproducts such as carbon dioxide gas. Carbon dioxide readily dissolves in water to produce a mild acid. This change to an acid can be confirmed through the use of an acid-base indicator, such as bromothymol blue. In this activity, you will use bromothymol blue to confirm respiration, and you will explore how temperature may affect this metabolic process.

Procedure

1. ◈ ◈ ◆ Put on safety goggles, gloves, and a lab apron. Fill a clean plastic cup halfway with room temperature water. Add several drops of bromothymol blue to the water. Swirl to mix the solution. ◆ **CAUTION: Bromothymol blue is a skin and eye irritant.**

2. Insert a clean straw into the solution. Gently blow a steady stream of air through the straw. Note any changes in the solution's appearance. **CAUTION: Be careful not to accidentally drink the solution while blowing into the straw.**

3. Label three plastic cups, "A," "B" and "C."

4. Fill cup A with ice water, fill cup B with room temperature water, and fill cup C with warm water. Add several drops of bromothymol blue solution to each cup to ensure a uniform appearance.

5. Add ¼ teaspoon of baker's yeast to each cup. Swirl the cups, and observe the appearance of the solutions every 30 s. After 5 min, examine the surface of each solution with a hand lens.

6. ◈ ◆ Clean up your lab materials according to your teacher's instructions. Wash your hands before leaving the lab.

Analyze and Conclude

1. **Drawing Conclusions** What happened to the indicator as exhaled air bubbled through the solution? What caused this change?

2. **SCIENTIFIC METHODS Evaluating Results** Did the yeast produce a similar color change? Explain your answer.

3. **SCIENTIFIC METHODS Evaluating Results** Did temperature affect the yeast's production of carbon dioxide? Explain your answer.

4. **SCIENTIFIC METHODS Summarizing Results** What did you observe on the surface of the solutions?

5. **Predicting Outcomes** Will adding sugar to the yeast solution affect the respiration rate? Make a guess. Then, design a method for inquiry that would test the effects of various sugar concentrations on yeast metabolism.

Time Required

One 45-minute class period

Ratings

⚗	⚗⚗	⚗⚗⚗	⚗⚗⚗⚗
EASY			HARD

Teacher Prep ⚗⚗⚗

Student Setup ⚗⚗

Concept Level ⚗⚗⚗

Cleanup ⚗⚗

Safety Cautions

Tell students that bromothymol blue is a skin and eye irritant. It can stain skin and clothing. Remind students to be careful not to accidentally drink the solution while blowing into the straw. Make sure students wear safety goggles to protect their eyes from splashes-especially when blowing into the indicator-stained solution. The water used when activating yeast should be warm, not hot.

Tips and Tricks

Make sure that all yeast used in this activity is fresh. Use fast-rising yeast for quicker results. Remind students that the grains contained within the yeast packet are not individual yeast cells. They are freeze-dried clumps of many cells that when activated regain an observable metabolic function.

Bromothymol blue (bromthymol blue), can be obtained locally from pet and tropical fish stores.

Answers to Analysis and Conclusions

1. The indicator changed from blue to yellow. The carbon dioxide in exhaled air reacted in water forming a mild acid. This acid caused a color change in the indicator solution.

2. Yes. As yeast cells respired, they generated carbon dioxide gas. This gas produced a mild acid that caused the indicator to change color.

3. Yes. Yeast in the warmest water produced the quickest change in indicator appearance. Yeast in the ice water produced a very minimal change in the indicator's appearance.

4. The surface of the warm water and room-temperature water had tiny bubbles. These bubbles most likely contained carbon dioxide that was generated by the respiring yeast.

5. Answers will vary. Students may guess that adding sugar to the solution will cause the respiration rate to increase. With approval of the experimental design, offer students the supplies and tools they need to carry out their proposed experiments. Testing sugar concentrations on yeast metabolism can be performed during a lab period.

Lab Correlations

4.5.1d In all organisms, the energy stored in organic molecules may be released during cellular respiration... oxygen is used, and carbon dioxide and water are released as wastes.

Key Resources

◉ Holt Lab Generator

📋 Lab Datasheet (Levels A, B, C)

💿 Holt Science Biology Video Labs

◉ Virtual Investigations

◉ HB Dissection Labs

SUPER SUMMARY

Have students connect the major concepts in this chapter through an interactive Super Summary. Visit **go.hrw.com** and type in the keyword **HX8PHRS** to access the Super Summary for this chapter.

Reteaching Key Ideas

Pick the Right Pathway Assign students to work with a partner. Have each pair evaluate the following scenario. "Suppose you are an organism that can respire aerobically and anaerobically. Which pathway provides the better advantage and why?" (If oxygen is available, aerobic respiration would be the preferred pathway because more ATP is produced.)

Role Play and the Krebs Cycle Have students work in pairs to write a description of the Krebs cycle from the perspective of a sportscaster giving a play-by-play description.

Key Ideas	Key Terms

1 Energy in Living Systems

❯ Organisms use and store energy in the chemical bonds of organic compounds.

❯ Metabolism involves either using energy to build organic molecules or breaking down organic molecules in which energy is stored. Organic molecules contain carbon. Therefore, an organism's metabolism is part of Earth's carbon cycle.

❯ In cells, chemical energy is gradually released in a series of chemical reactions that are assisted by enzymes.

photosynthesis (197)
cellular respiration (198)
ATP (198)
ATP synthase (201)
electron transport chain (201)

2 Photosynthesis

❯ In plants, light energy is harvested by pigments located in the thylakoid membrane of chloroplasts.

❯ During photosynthesis, one electron transport chain provides energy used to make ATP, while the other provides energy to make NADPH.

❯ In the final stage of photosynthesis, chemical energy is stored by being used to produce sugar molecules from the carbon in the gas carbon dioxide.

❯ Light intensity, carbon dioxide concentration, and temperature are three environmental factors that affect photosynthesis.

thylakoid (202)
pigment (203)
chlorophyll (203)
Calvin cycle (206)

3 Cellular Respiration

❯ The breaking of a sugar molecule by glycolysis results in a net gain of two ATP molecules.

❯ The total yield of energy-storing products from one time through the Krebs cycle is one ATP, three NADH, and one $FADH_2$. Electron carriers transfer energy through the electron transport chain, which ultimately powers ATP synthase.

❯ Fermentation enables glycolysis to continue supplying a cell with ATP in anaerobic conditions.

glycolysis (209)
anaerobic (209)
aerobic (209)
Krebs cycle (210)
fermentation (212)

PART A: Answer all questions in this part.

Directions: For each statement or question, write on your separate answer sheet the number of the word or expression that best completes the statement or answers the question.

1 Plants in areas with short growing seasons have more chloroplasts in their cells than plants in areas with longer growing seasons. Compared to plants in areas with longer growing seasons, plants in areas with shorter growing seasons most likely

(1) make and store food more quickly.

(2) have a higher rate of protein metabolism.

(3) grow taller.

(4) have a different method of respiration.

2 Most of the starch stored in the cells of a potato is composed of molecules that originally entered these cells as

(1) enzymes   (3) amino acids

(2) simple sugars   (4) minerals

3 The dissolved carbon dioxide in a lake is used directly by

(1) autotrophs   (3) fungi

(2) parasites   (4) decomposers

4 When organisms break the bonds of organic compounds, the organisms can

(1) use the smaller molecules to plug the gaps in the cell membrane to slow diffusion.

(2) use the energy obtained to digest molecules produced by respiration that uses oxygen.

(3) obtain energy or reassemble the resulting materials to form different compounds.

(4) excrete smaller amounts of solid waste materials during vigorous exercise.

5 Which statement best describes cellular respiration?

(1) It occurs in animal cells but not in plant cells.

(2) It converts energy in food into a more usable form.

(3) It uses carbon dioxide and produces oxygen.

(4) It stores energy in food molecules.

6 The production of energy-rich ATP molecules is the direct result of

(1) recycling light energy to be used in the process of photosynthesis

(2) releasing the stored energy of organic compounds by the process of respiration

(3) breaking down starch by the process of digestion

(4) copying coded information during the process of protein synthesis

7 The green aquatic plant represented in the diagram below was exposed to light for several hours. Which gas would most likely be found in the greatest amount in the bubbles?

(1) oxygen

(2) nitrogen

(3) ozone

(4) carbon dioxide

8 Which process is directly used by autotrophs to store energy in glucose?

(1) diffusion

(2) photosynthesis

(3) respiration

(4) active transport

9 In heterotrophs, energy for the life processes comes from the chemical energy stored in the bonds of

(1) water molecules

(2) oxygen molecules

(3) organic compounds

(4) inorganic compounds

Regents Exam Practice Correlations

1.2.3a 11		**4.5.1c** 4, 9	
4.1.1a 3		**4.5.1d** 5, 6, 10, 15	
4.1.1d 13		**4.5.1e** 14	
4.1.2h 2		**4.5.1f** 16	
4.5.1b 1, 7, 8, 12			

PART A

1. **(1)** Chloroplasts are the organelles that use light energy to make carbohydrates, or food, from carbon dioxide. Therefore a plant with many chloroplasts can make and store food more quickly than a plant with fewer chloroplasts. (*#18, January 2005 Regents Exam*)

2. **(2)** Starch is not made from the joining of enzymes or amino acids. Starch is also not made from the joining of minerals. Simple sugars join to form starch, though. (*#06, June 2006 Regents Exam*)

3. **(1)** Carbon dioxide is used during photosynthesis. Thus, the gas can only be used by producers and not parasites, fungi, or decomposers. (*#20, January 2006 Regents Exam*)

4. **(3)** Breaking the bonds between the molecules in organic compounds causes large amounts of energy to be released. This energy is used to form ATP. The resulting molecules can be used by the body to form different compounds to help maintain health. (*#22, January 2005 Regents Exam*)

5. **(2)** Cellular respiration converts energy in food so that the energy can be used to power cell processes. It occurs in both plants and animals. Cellular respiration uses oxygen and produces carbon dioxide as a waste product. It is the opposite of photosynthesis, which is the process that stores energy in sugar molecules. (*#19, August 2005 Regents Exam*)

6. **(2)** The choices about starch breakdown and protein synthesis are incorrect as these processes do not directly make ATP. Light energy is used to temporarily make ATP for the purpose of making organic compounds. Only respiration directly makes a large amount of ATP. (*#23, June 2005 Regents Exam*)

7. **(1)** Plants do not release nitrogen or ozone. Carbon dioxide is released during plant respiration. However, since the plant was exposed to light and this is a critical part of photosynthesis, the most probable gas released is oxygen. (*#22, June 2005 Regents Exam*)

8. (2) During photosynthesis, carbon dioxide and water react with light energy to produce glucose and oxygen. Respiration breaks down glucose to provide energy to cell processes such as active transport. Diffusion is a passive process that does not use or store energy. *(#26, August 2003 Regents Exam)*

9. (3) Heterotrophs gain energy by processing organic compounds that are found in plant or animal tissue. Inorganic compounds, water, and oxygen are necessary for life, but they do not provide energy to an organism. *(#13, June 2003 Regents Exam)*

10. (3) Light energy can only be captured by photosynthesis, not respiration. Energy is then stored as organic molecules, not inorganic molecules. Organic molecules are used in respiration. *(#27, June 2006 Regents Exam)*

11. (1) The diagram does not show that roots absorb minerals or that plants grow best in the absence of light. The diagram also does not show that plants need light for cell division. *(#39, June 2006 Regents Exam)*

12. Allow 1 credit for identifying one type of organism that carries out process 1. Acceptable responses include, but are not limited to: plants; autotroph; producer; trees *(#52, June 2006 Regents Exam)*

13. Allow 1 credit for identifying process 3. Acceptable responses include, but are not limited to: respiration *(#54, June 2006 Regents Exam)*

14. Allow 1 credit for identifing what letter X represents. Acceptable responses include, but are not limited to: ATP; energy *(#55, June 2006 Regents Exam)*

10 Which set of terms best identifies the letters in the diagram below?

	A	B	C
(1)	photosynthesis	inorganic molecules	decomposition
(2)	respiration	organic molecules	digestion
(3)	photosynthesis	organic molecules	respiration
(4)	respiration	inorganic molecules	photosynthesis

PART B

11 An experimental setup is shown in the diagram below. Which hypothesis would most likely be tested using this setup?

(1) Green water plants release a gas in the presence of light.
(2) Roots of water plants absorb minerals in the absence of light.
(3) Green plants need light for cell division.
(4) Plants grow best in the absence of light.

Base your answers to questions 12 through 14 on the diagram below and on your knowledge of biology. The arrows in the diagram represent biological processes.

12 Identify *one* type of organism that carries out process 1.

13 Identify process 3.

14 Identify what letter *X* represents.

PART C

15 Photosynthesis and respiration are two important processes. Discuss one of these processes and explain its importance to an organism. In your answer, be sure to:
- identify the process being discussed
- identify the organelle where this process occurs
- identify two raw materials necessary for this process
- identify one energy-rich molecule that is produced by this process
- state how organisms use the energy-rich molecule that is produced
- state how a gas produced by this process is recycled in nature

Base your answers to question 16 on the statement below and on your knowledge of biology.

Some internal environmental factors may interfere with the ability of an enzyme to function efficiently.

16 Identify *two* internal environmental factors that directly influence the rate of enzyme action.

PART D

17 State whether you think the following viewpoint can be supported, and justify your answer. "If Earth's early atmosphere had been rich in oxygen, photosynthetic organisms would not have been able to evolve."

PART C

15. Allow of maximum of 5 credits for discussing photosynthesis or respiration, allocated as follows: Allow 1 credit for identifying the organelle where the process occurs. Photosynthesis: chloroplast; Respiration: mitochondrion; Allow 1 credit for identifying two raw materials necessary for the process. Acceptable responses include, but are not limited to: Photosynthesis: CO_2 and H_2O; Respiration: organic molecules and O_2; sugar and oxygen; Allow 1 credit for identifying one energy-rich molecule that is produced by the process. Acceptable responses include, but are not limited to: Photosynthesis: glucose; Respiration: ATP; Allow 1 credit for stating how organisms use the energy-rich molecule that is produced. Acceptable responses include, but are not limited to: Glucose: to produce ATP; to produce starch ATP: to provide energy for metabolism; Allow 1 credit for stating how a gas produced by the process is recycled in nature. Acceptable responses include, but are not limited to: Photosynthesis: The gas is used for respiration.; provides O_2 for respiration; Respiration: provides CO_2 for photosynthesis; The gas is used for photosynthesis. *(#59, January 2006 Regents Exam)*

16. Allow a maximum of 2 credits, 1 credit for each of two internal environmental factors that directly influence the rate of enzyme action. Acceptable responses include, but are not limited to: temperature; pH; concentration of enzyme; substrate *(#60, June 2006 Regents Exam)*

PART D

17. Students should acknowledge that photosynthetic organisms today carry out photosynthesis in the presence of oxygen.

	Standards	**Teach Key Ideas**
CHAPTER OPENER, pp. 220–221 — 15 min.	The Living Environment	
SECTION 1 Cell Reproduction, pp. 223–227 — 30 min. ❯ Why Cells Reproduce ❯ Chromosomes ❯ Preparing for Cell Division	4.1.2c	Bellringer Transparency Transparencies B43 Chromosome Structure Visual Concepts Comparing Cell Division in Prokaryotes and Eukaryotes • Gene • Chromosome
SECTION 2 Mitosis, pp. 228–232 — 90 min. ❯ Eukaryotic Cell Cycle ❯ Stages of Mitosis ❯ Cytokinesis	4.5.2i	Bellringer Transparency Transparencies B47 Stages of Mitosis Visual Concepts Cell Cycle Introduction • Cell Cycle – G1 Phase • Cell Cycle – S Phase • Cell Cycle – G2 Phase • Cell Cycle – M Phase • Control of the Cell Cycle • Snapshot of Mitotic Structures • Mitosis • Comparing Cell Division in Plants and Animals
SECTION 3 Regulation, pp. 233–237 — 30 min. ❯ Controls ❯ Checkpoints ❯ Cancer	4.5.2i	

See also PowerPoint® Resources

Chapter Review and Assessment Resources

SE Super Summary, p. 238
SE Regents Exam Practice, p. 239
Regents Review Guide
Review Resources
Chapter Tests A and B
Holt Online Assessment
Regents Question Banks on Teacher's One-Stop Planner

CHAPTER
Fast Track — *Thorough instruction will require the times shown. You can eliminate the Quick Labs in Sections 1 and 3.*

Basic Learners
TE Relating Terms, p. 225
Directed Reading Worksheets*
Active Reading Worksheets*
Lab Manuals, Level A*
Study Guide* ■
Note-taking Workbook*
Special Needs Activities and Modified Tests*

Advanced Learners
TE How Many Base Pairs?, p. 224
Critical Thinking Worksheets*
Concept Mapping Worksheets*
Science Skills Worksheets*
Lab Datasheets, Level C*

Why It Matters	Hands-On	Skills Development	Assessment
Build student motivation with resources about high-interest applications.	**SE Inquiry Lab** Whitefish Cells, p. 221 *■	**TE Reading Toolbox** Assessing Prior Knowledge, p. 220 **SE Reading Toolbox,** p. 222	
TE What If DNA Was Not Coiled?, p. 224 **SE Replacement Parts,** p. 227	**SE Quick Lab** Chromosome Package, p. 224 *■ **Skills Practice Lab** Preparing a Root Tip Squash*	**SE Reading Toolbox** Word Parts, p. 225 **TE Reading Toolbox** Word Parts, p. 225 **TE Reading Toolbox** Visual Literacy, p. 225 **TE Reading Toolbox** Visual Literacy, p. 227	**SE Section Review** **TE Formative Assessment** Spanish Assessment* ■ **Section Quiz** ■
TE Demonstration Cell Division Rate, p. 228 **TE Demonstration** Recognizing Mitotic Stages, p. 231	**SE Quick Lab** Number of Cells Resulting from Mitosis, p. 229 *■ **SE Skills Practice Lab** Mitosis in Plant Cells, p. 236 *■ **Exploration Lab** Mitosis*	**TE Reading Toolbox** Word Origins, p. 230 **TE Reading Toolbox** Visual Literacy, p. 230 **SE Reading Toolbox** Pattern Puzzle, p. 231	**SE Section Review** **TE Formative Assessment** Spanish Assessment* ■ **Section Quiz** ■
	SE Quick Lab UV and Sunblock, p. 234 *■	**SE Reading Toolbox** Cause and Effect, p. 234 **TE Reading Toolbox** Cause and Effect, p. 234	**SE Section Review** **TE Formative Assessment** Spanish Assessment* ■ **Section Quiz** ■

See also Lab Generator

See also Holt Online Assessment Resources

Resources for Differentiated Instruction

English Learners

TE Mitotic Pattern Puzzle, p. 230
TE Traffic Jam, p. 234
Directed Reading Worksheets*
Active Reading Worksheets*
Lab Manuals, Level A*
Study Guide* ■
Note-taking Workbook*
Multilingual Glossary
Interactive Tutor

Struggling Readers

TE Relating Terms, p. 225
TE Mitotic Pattern Puzzle, p. 230
TE Traffic Jam, p. 234
Directed Reading Worksheets*
Active Reading Worksheets*
Lab Manuals, Level A*
Study Guide*
Note-taking Workbook*
Special Needs Activities and Modified Tests*
Interactive Tutor

Special Education Students

TE Chromosome Structure, p. 225
TE Cell Model, p. 231
Directed Reading Worksheets*
Active Reading Worksheets*
Lab Manuals, Level A*
Study Guide* ■
Note-taking Workbook*
Special Needs Activities and Modified Tests*

Alternative Assessment

TE Cell Cycle, p. 229
TE Pitfalls of Rapid Cell Divison, p. 234
Science Skills Worksheets*
Section Quizzes* ■
Chapter Tests A, B, and C* ■

Chapter 10 Cell Growth and Division

Overview

This chapter describes the significance and process of cell division. Cell division is necessary for the growth, repair, and maintenance of organisms. There are specific stages and checkpoints as a cell matures and prepares to divide. When an error occurs in the genetic code of a cell, these normal checkpoints are not always recognized and uncontrolled cellular division may ensue. This unregulated cellular division is known as cancer. Any cell that divides can potentially develop into a cancer cell.

Assessing Prior Knowledge Students should understand the following concepts:
• differences between eukaryotic and prokaryotic cells
• role of DNA in cellular function

Visual Literacy Ask students to describe any differences between the two *Stenotrophomonas maltophilia* bacteria to the right. (The bacteria at the top is nearly divided, having formed two identical cells from the single original.) Explain to students that even the smallest and simplest of cells must divide to reproduce. **LS Visual**

Preview

1 Cell Reproduction
Why Cells Reproduce
Chromosomes
Preparing for Cell Division

2 Mitosis
Eukaryotic Cell Cycle
Stages of Mitosis
Cytokinesis

3 Regulation
Controls
Checkpoints
Cancer

Why It Matters

The cell is the basic unit of life—common to all living things. The growth and division of cells is essential to the continuity of life.

 The Living Environment
Standard 4 Students will understand and apply scientific concepts, principles, and theories pertaining to the physical setting and living environment and recognize the historical development of ideas in science.
Key Idea 1 Living things are both similar to and different from each other and from nonliving things. *Major Understandings - 1.2c*
Key Idea 5 Organisms maintain a dynamic equilibrium that sustains life. *Major Understandings - 5.2i*

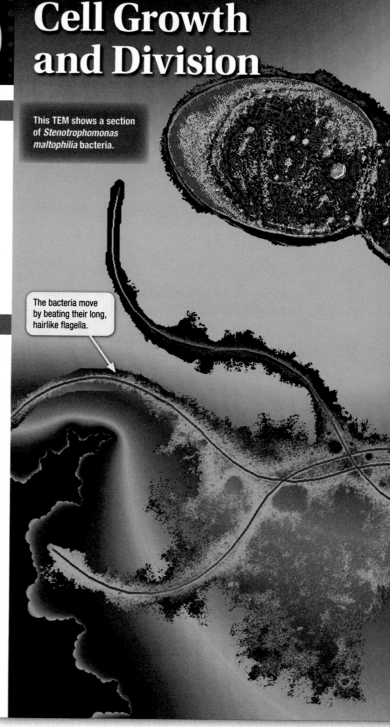

This TEM shows a section of *Stenotrophomonas maltophilia* bacteria.

The bacteria move by beating their long, hairlike flagella.

Chapter Correlations *The Living Environment*

Standard 4

1.2c The components of the human body, from organ systems to cell organelles, interact to maintain a balanced internal environment. To successfully accomplish this, organisms possess a diversity of control mechanisms that detect deviations and make corrective actions.

5.2i Gene mutations in a cell can result in uncontrolled cell division, called cancer. Exposure of cells to certain chemicals and radiation increases mutations and thus increases the chance of cancer.

This cell is dividing to form two identical daughter cells.

This rod-shaped bacterium lives in soil, water, and milk. It causes diseases in plants and can cause opportunistic infections in humans.

InquiryLab

🕐 15 min

Whitefish Cells

As an embryo develops, its cells divide rapidly. Few of these cells remain in a resting state, so when observing them, you will see groups of these cells in various stages of division.

Procedure

❶ Place a slide of whitefish cells on the stage of a microscope. Examine the cells under low power. Do all of the cells look alike? If not, how do they differ? Draw several representative cells.

❷ Carefully switch to high power. Slowly scan the slide, and look for obvious differences between cells. Pay particular attention to the appearance of the nuclei.

❸ Make a sketch of each distinct pattern of cells that you see.

Analysis

1. **Describe** any differences you observed in the nuclei of these cells.

2. **Determine** whether all the cells you observed had a distinct nucleus. Explain.

InquiryLab

Teacher's Note: Whitefish mitosis slides are most often used to demonstrate the stages of division in animal cells. Before the students examine these slides, review the cell features they should be looking for. As a class, identify the characteristics of each stage that can be used to identify it and differentiate it from other stages.

Materials
• prepared whitefish cell slide(s)
• compound microscope

Answers to Analysis

1. Yes, the nucleus varied considerably among the cells. In some, you could observe the chromosomes in various states and positions.

2. No. Only some of the cells had a distinct nucleus surrounded by a nuclear membrane. In the other cells, a distinct nucleus or obvious nuclear membrane was not apparent

Key Resources

💿 Interactive Tutor

Using Words

1. chromosome – a colored body
2. mitosis – a thread-like condition or process

Using Language

1. The cause is the cold, and the effect is to shiver.
2. The cause is the increasing brightness of light, and the effect is the pupil gets smaller.
3. The cause is the cell passing G_2, and the effect is the cell begins to divides.

Using Pattern Puzzles

The correct order follows:
1. Prophase
2. Metaphase
3. Anaphase
4. Telophase

These reading tools can help you learn the material in this chapter. For more information on how to use these and other tools, see **Appendix: Reading and Study Skills.**

Using Words

Word Parts You can tell a lot about a word by taking it apart and examining its prefix and root.

Your Turn Use the information in the table to define the following terms.
1. *chromosome*
2. *mitosis*

Word Parts		
Word part	Type	Meaning
mito-	prefix	thread
chromo-	prefix	color
-osis	suffix	condition or process
-some	root	body

Using Language

Cause and Effect In biological processes, one step leads to another step. When reading, you can often recognize these cause-and-effect relationships by words that indicate a result, such as *so, consequently, if-then,* and *as a result.*

Your Turn Identify the cause and effect in the following sentences.
1. People often shiver as a result of being cold.
2. The light got brighter, so the pupil of the eye got smaller.
3. If the cell passes the G_2 checkpoint, then the cell may begin to divide.

Using Graphic Organizers

Pattern Puzzles You can use pattern puzzles to help you remember sequential information. Exchanging puzzles with a classmate can help you study.

Your Turn Make a pattern puzzle for the stages of mitosis.
1. Write down the steps of the process. On a sheet of notebook paper, write down one step per line. Do not number the steps.
2. Cut the sheet of paper into strips so that each strip of paper has only one step. Shuffle the paper strips so that they are out of sequence.
3. Place the strips in their proper sequence. Confirm the order of the process by checking your text or class notes.

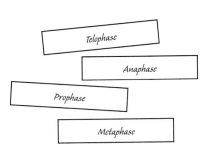

Cell Reproduction

Key Ideas	Key Terms	Why It Matters
❯ Why do cells divide? ❯ How is DNA packaged into the nucleus? ❯ How do cells prepare for division?	gene nucleosome chromosome chromatid chromatin centromere histone	Cells are busy making more cells. The reproduction of cells allows you to grow and heal.

The adult human body produces roughly 2 trillion cells per day. The new cells are exact copies of the cells they replace. This process is called *cell reproduction*. Some cells, such as hair and skin cells, are replaced frequently throughout your life. Other cells, such as brain and nerve cells, are rarely produced after infancy.

Why Cells Reproduce

As the body of a multicellular organism grows larger, its cells do not also grow large. Instead, the body grows by producing more cells. New cells are needed to help tissues and organs grow. Even after organisms reach adulthood, old cells die and new cells take their place. This replacement and renewal is important for keeping the body healthy. New cells also replace damaged cells. As **Figure 1** shows, the body repairs a wound by making more cells.

Cell Size A cell grows larger by building more cell products. To do this, the cell must take in more nutrients, process them, and get rid of wastes. Recall that a cell's ability to exchange substances is limited by its surface area–to–volume ratio. As a cell gets larger, substances must travel farther to reach where they are needed.

Cell Maintenance The work of cells is done by proteins. As a cell gets larger, more proteins are required to maintain its function. Recall that the instructions for making these proteins are copied from the cell's DNA. If the cell gets too large, DNA instructions cannot be copied quickly enough to make the proteins that the cell needs to support itself. Thus, cell size is also limited by the cell's DNA.

Making New Cells Cell division can solve the problems of cell size. Each "daughter" cell has a higher surface area–to–volume ratio than its parent does. Each new cell also gets an entire copy of the cell's DNA. ❯ Because larger cells are more difficult to maintain, cells divide when they grow to a certain size.

The Living Environment
Standard 4
1.2c The components of the human body, from organ systems to cell organelles, interact to maintain a balanced internal environment. To successfully accomplish this, organisms possess a diversity of control mechanisms that detect deviations and make corrective actions.

Figure 1 When these stitches are removed, this cut will be healed. Cell division enables the body to repair a wound.

Key Resources

 Transparencies
B43 Chromosome Structure

 Visual Concepts
Comparing Cell Division in Prokaryotes and Eukaryotes
Gene
Chromosome

QuickLab

Teacher's Notes Prepare the lengths of kite string, as well as the plastic wrap, before class. Make sure students do not unfold the paperclips.

Materials
- kite string, 2 one-meter pieces
- paperclip
- plastic wrap, 2 pieces about 10 cm × 10 cm

Answers to Analysis

1. The string is DNA. The plastic wrap is the nuclear envelope (nucleus), and the paperclip is the protein scaffold.

2. The volume occupied by the string without the paperclip is greater than the volume of the string-wrapped paperclip system.

3. The object that could replace the paperclip could allow for easy winding and way to secure the string at both ends.

Why It Matters

What If DNA Was Not Coiled? If the DNA inside one cell is stretched out, it would be approximately two meters long (78 in.). If all the bases in the human genome were put in a line 1 mm apart, the genome would stretch from Memphis to Los Angeles (1810 miles; 2919 kilometers). **LS** Logical

---

Hands-On
QuickLab

🕐 **15 min**

Chromosome Package

DNA is condensed to reduce the space that it occupies in the cell. In eukaryotic cells, the linear DNA molecule is condensed by being wrapped around a core of proteins.

Procedure

❶ Scrunch a **1 m length of kite string** into a wad. Cover this wad with a piece of **plastic wrap.**

❷ Wind another **1 m length of string** tightly and uniformly around a **paper clip.** Cover this shape with another piece of plastic wrap.

Analysis

1. **Identify** what the string, the plastic wrap, and the paper clip represent in each model.

2. **Compare** the volumes of space that the two models occupy.

3. **CRITICAL THINKING Evaluating Models** Describe an object that would be more effective than a paper clip as a core to wrap the string around. Explain your answer.

---

gene a unit of heredity that consists of a segment of nucleic acid that codes for a functional unit of RNA or protein

chromosome in a eukaryotic cell, one of the structures in the nucleus that are made up of DNA and protein; in a prokaryotic cell, the main ring of DNA

chromatin the substance of which eukaryotic chromosomes are composed

histone a type of protein molecule found in the chromosomes of eukaryotic cells but not prokaryotic cells

nucleosome (NOO klee uh SOHM) a eukaryotic structural unit of chromatin that consists of DNA wound around a core of histone proteins

chromatid one of the two strands of a chromosome that become visible during meiosis or mitosis

centromere the region of the chromosome that holds the two sister chromatids together during mitosis

---

Chromosomes

Recall that a cell's activity is directed by its DNA. The large molecule of DNA is organized into hereditary units called **genes.** A gene is a segment of DNA that codes for RNA and protein. The simplest organisms have thousands of genes. Each cell has a large amount of DNA that must be condensed into a very small volume. DNA is organized and packaged into structures called **chromosomes.**

Prokaryotic Chromosome A prokaryotic cell has a single circular molecule of DNA. This loop of DNA contains thousands of genes. A prokaryotic chromosome is condensed through repeated twisting or winding, like a rubber band twisted upon itself many times.

Eukaryotic Chromosome The challenge of packaging DNA into the eukaryotic nucleus is much greater. Eukaryotic cells contain many more genes arranged on several linear DNA molecules. A human cell contains 46 separate, linear DNA molecules that are packaged into 46 chromosomes. ❯ Eukaryotic DNA into highly condensed chromosome structures with the help of many proteins. The DNA and proteins make up a substance called **chromatin.**

Forms of Chromatin The first level of packaging is done by a class of proteins called **histones.** A group of eight histones come together to form a disc-shaped histone core. As **Figure 2** shows, the long DNA molecule is wound around a series of histone cores in a regular manner. The structure made up of a histone core and the DNA around it is called a **nucleosome.** Under an electron microscope, this level of packaging resembles beads on a string. The string of nucleosomes line up in a spiral to form a cord that is 30 nm in diameter.

Differentiated Instruction

Advanced Learners/GATE

How Many Base Pairs? For a special project have students gather research on the following
- the total number of base pairs present in the human genome
- the length of each nucleotide

They should use this data to calculate the length of the DNA in one cell. **LS** Logical

---

Packaging During Cell Division During most of a cell's life, its chromosomes exist as coiled or uncoiled nucleosomes. As the cell prepares to divide, the chromosomes condense even further. This ensures that the extremely long DNA molecules do not get tangled up during cell division. The 30-nm fiber (the nucleosome cord) forms loops that are attached to a protein scaffold. These looped domains then coil into the final, most highly condensed form of the chromosome. Many dense loops of chromatin form the rod-shaped structures that can be seen in regular light microscopes.

Chromosome Structure A fully condensed, duplicated chromosome is shown in **Figure 2.** Each of the two thick strands, called a **chromatid,** is made of a single, long molecule of DNA. Identical pairs, called *sister chromatids,* are held together at a region called the **centromere.** During cell division, the sister chromatids are separated at the centromere, and one ends up in each daughter cell. This ensures that each new cell has the same genetic information as the parent cell.

❯ **Reading Check** *What is a chromatid? (See the Appendix for answers to Reading Checks.)*

Figure 2 A eukaryotic chromosome consists of DNA tightly coiled around proteins. As a cell prepares to divide, the duplicated chromosomes are condensed. ❯ Why do chromosomes condense during cell division?

Eukaryotic Chromosome Structure

Nucleosome DNA winds around a histone core to make a "bead."

Linker DNA ("string")

Looped Domains As the cell prepares to divide, the 30-nm fiber forms loops attached to a protein scaffold.

DNA

Histones

30-nm Fiber The string of nucleosomes coil to form a cord that is 30 nm in diameter.

Protein scaffold

Centromere

"Beads on a String" When extended, a chromatin fiber resembles beads on a string.

Condensed Chromosome Looped domains fold into a structure that is visible during cell division.

Sister chromatids

Teaching Key Ideas

Is it a Chromosome, Chromatin or Chromatid? Students often become confused when asked to define these three words. Remind them that a *chromosome* is a cellular structure that carries genetic info. Chromosomes may have many forms. *Chromatin* is the substance that makes up chromosomes. Chromatin is DNA wrapped around histones. When chromosomes are duplicated, each copy is called a *chromatid.* When joined, the two chromatids together are considered one chromosome. When separated, each chromatid is considered its own chromosome. **LS Verbal**

Visual Literacy Help students the chromosome structure model shown in **Figure 2.** Ask them where the diagram begins. (at the DNA strand on the left) What is the diagram showing? (The process of tightly winding DNA in preparation for cell division.) What role do histones play in this process? (Histones provide a surface for winding DNA.) What role do nucleosomes play? (They coil the DNA/histone complexes.) What happens when the chromosome condenses? (Coiled nucleosomes loop around a protein scaffold. These loops coil further to create the condensed form.) **LS Visual**

Differentiated Instruction

Basic Learners/Struggling Readers

Relating Terms Give students a copy of **Figure 2** that is not labeled. Ask them to identify the following structures on the figure: centromere, chromatid, chromatin, chromosome, DNA, histone, and nucleosome. Then, ask students to select pairs of the terms and write a sentence that describes their relationship. Tell students to write at least four sentences using term pairs. **LS Verbal/Visual**

Special Education Students

Chromosome Structure To help visually impaired students understand **Figure 2,** create a demonstration model for them. Use the following materials: yarn or lightweight rope with twisted strands for DNA; sewing machine bobbins for histones; a long string of beads wound around a plastic straw could represent the 30-nm fiber; a large spool of sewing thread, twine, or cord could be used for the condensed chromosome. **LS Kinesthetic**

Formative Assessment

As a cell is preparing to divide, the DNA ___.

A. has copied itself twice so that each daughter cell is diploid (Incorrect. DNA replicates only once. The newly formed cell is already diploid as it has one set of the chromosomes from the mother and one from the father.)

B. has replicated and condensed into chromosomes, each consisting of two sister chromatids (Correct. There must be duplicate material in the old cell before it can divide to form two fully-functional new cells.)

C. has caused the cell to double in size before it must divide (Incorrect. Different cells grow to different proportions of the original cell before they are too large to function properly.)

D. forms one long continuous loop composed of individual chromosomes that are linked together (Incorrect. A bacteria has a single, circular chromosome. Eukaryotes have individual rod-shaped chromosomes that behave independently of each other.)

Prokaryotic cell → DNA is copied. → Cell begins to divide. → Cell completely divides. / Two genetically identical cells

Cell dividing

Figure 3 A prokaryotic cell divides by copying its single, circular chromosome and building a cell membrane between the two copies. A new cell wall forms around the membrane, squeezing the cell. Eventually it pinches off into two independent daughter cells.

www.scilinks.org
Topic: Cell Division
Code: HX80236

ACADEMIC VOCABULARY

complex having many parts or functions

Preparing for Cell Division

All new cells are produced by the division of preexisting cells. The process of cell division involves more than cutting a cell into two pieces. Each new cell must have all of the equipment needed to stay alive. ❯**All newly-formed cells require DNA, so before a cell divides, a copy of DNA is made for each daughter cell.** This way, the new cells will function in the same way as the cells that they replace.

Prokaryotes In prokaryotic cells, the circular DNA molecule is attached to the inner cell membrane. As **Figure 3** shows, the cytoplasm is divided when a new cell membrane forms between the two DNA copies. Meanwhile the cell continues to grow until it nearly doubles in size. The cell wall also continues to form around the new cell membrane, pushing inward. The cell is constricted in the middle, like a long balloon being squeezed near the center. Eventually the dividing prokaryote is pinched into two independent daughter cells, each of which has its own circular DNA molecule.

Eukaryotes The reproduction eukaryotic cells is more complex than that of prokaryotic cells. Recall that eukaryotic cells have many organelles. In order to form two living cells, each daughter cell must contain enough of each organelle to carry out its functions. The DNA within the nucleus must also be copied, sorted, and separated.

❯ **Reading Check** *Where does a prokaryotic cell begin to divide?*

Section 1 Review

❯ KEY IDEAS

1. **List** two reasons for cell reproduction in multicellular organisms.
2. **Describe** three levels of structure in the DNA packaging system found within a eukaryotic nucleus.
3. **Explain** why daughter cells are identical to the parent cell.

CRITICAL THINKING

4. **Evaluating Conclusions** If cells constantly double in number each time they divide, why doesn't a multicellular organism continue to grow in size?
5. **Inferring Relationships** Why do chromosomes condense before they divide?

MATH SKILLS

6. **Exponents** Imagine you are observing a cell that divides once every hour for 12 h. Assume that none of the cells die during this period. How many cells would exist after each hour? How many cells would exist after 12 h?

Answers to Section Review

1. New cells are needed for tissue and organ growth. Damaged cells, such as those from a wound, need to be replaced.

2. Nucleosomes, 30-nm fibers, and rod-shaped chromosomes enable complex DNA molecules to become compact to fit within a cell.

3. Before a cell divides, a copy of its DNA is produced. Each daughter cell receives an exact copy so that the cell can continue functioning in the same manner as the original parent cell.

4. All of the cells in each generation do not survive. Some cells are dying while new cells are taking their place.

5. so that the extremely long DNA molecules do not get entangled during cell division

6. After 1 hour, 2 cells. After 2 h, 4 cells. After 3 h, 8. Then 16, 32, 64, 128, 256, 512, 1,024, 2,048. After 12 h, 8,192 cells would exist.

Replacement Parts

WEIRD SCIENCE

If you look closely at the camouflaged green anole lizard at right, you will see that it appears to be growing a new tail. The process by which an organism replaces or restores a lost or amputated body part is called *regeneration*. A series of rapid cell divisions allows certain organisms to regenerate certain lost parts.

Sea Star Comets

To keep sea stars from destroying oyster beds, oyster fishermen used to chop up sea stars and throw the pieces back into the sea. Unfortunately, this practice increased the number of sea stars! Some sea stars can regenerate their entire bodies from just a small piece of arm. Specimens such as the one shown below are sometimes called "comets." The regeneration of these sea stars is possible because they keep their vital organs in their arms.

Tail Regeneration Lizards, such as the gecko at left, are well known for their ability to "release" their tails. Lizards use this ability as a defense mechanism to escape predators. The broken piece of tail twists and wiggles, which diverts the attention of the predator while the lizard escapes. When the tail regenerates, it is made up of cartilage, rather than bone.

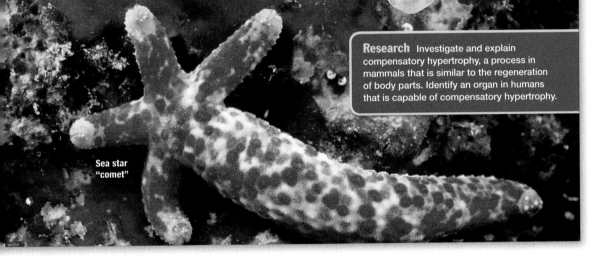

Sea star "comet"

Research Investigate and explain compensatory hypertrophy, a process in mammals that is similar to the regeneration of body parts. Identify an organ in humans that is capable of compensatory hypertrophy.

Section 2

Section 2 Mitosis

Key Ideas	Key Terms		Why It Matters
❯ What are the phases of the eukaryotic cell cycle? ❯ What are the four stages of mitosis? ❯ How does cytokinesis occur?	cell cycle interphase mitosis	cytokinesis spindle centrosome	The events of the cell cycle ensure that new cells will be just like the old cell.

Focus

Students will examine the cell cycle. They will learn that during interphase, cells grow and DNA is replicated. During mitosis each new cell receives the proper assortment of chromosomes. During cytokinesis, the cytoplasm divides and a new cell membrane or cell wall forms.

 Bellringer

Use the Bellringer transparency to prepare students for this section.

Teach

Demonstration

Cell Division Rate Display either a model or a photograph of a human brain. Point out that once the brain is fully formed, most of the nerve cells do not divide again. These cells remain in the G_1 phase of the cell cycle. Then display either a model or a photograph of a human bone. Point out that red blood cells are produced from cells in the marrow of long bones. An average red blood cell lives for about 120 days. Each second, about two million red blood cells are produced by cell division in the bone marrow. Cells in the marrow, unlike those in the brain, continue going through the cell cycle as long as a person lives. **LS Visual**

Answers to Caption Questions
Figure 4: S, G_2, mitosis

Section Correlations

4.5.2i

Key Resources

 Transparencies
B47 Stages of Mitosis

◉ **Visual Concepts**
Cell Cycle Introduction
Cell Cycle – G_1 Phase
Cell Cycle – S Phase
Cell Cycle – G_2 Phase
Cell Cycle – M Phase
Control of the Cell Cycle
Snapshot of Mitotic Structures
Mitosis
Comparing Cell Division in Plants and Animals

The Living Environment
Standard 4
5.2i Gene mutations in a cell can result in uncontrolled cell division, called cancer. Exposure of cells to certain chemicals and radiation increases mutations and thus increases the chance of cancer.

Unlike prokaryotic cells, eukaryotic cells cannot simply be pinched into two new cells. The physical division of one cell into two cells requires many preparations.

Eukaryotic Cell Cycle

The **cell cycle** is a repeating sequence of cellular growth and division during the life of a cell. ❯ **The life of a eukaryotic cell cycles through phases of growth, DNA replication, preparation for cell division, and division of the nucleus and cytoplasm.** The cell cycle is made up of five phases, shown in **Figure 4.** The first three phases together are known as **interphase.** The remaining two phases make up cell division.

Interphase During interphase, the cell is not dividing. It is growing and preparing to divide. Different types of cells spend different amounts of time in interphase. Cells that divide often, such as skin cells, spend less time in interphase. Cells that divide seldom, such as nerve cells, spend most of their time in interphase.

During mitosis, the chromosomes are packaged in their highly condensed form.

During the synthesis phase, the DNA in each chromosome is copied.

Figure 4 The cell cycle consists of five phases. In three of the phases, shown in blue, the cell grows and prepares for division. Cell division, shown in green, occurs in two phases. ❯ **During which phases do cells have duplicated chromosomes?**

QuickLab

⏱ 5 min

Number of Cells Resulting from Mitosis

In the human body, the rate of mitosis is about 25 million (2.5×10^7) cells produced per second. By using this rate, you can calculate the number of cells produced by mitosis in a given amount of time.

Procedure

❶ Calculate the number of cells produced by mitosis in the time given. For example, to find the number of cells produced in 3 min, determine how many seconds are in 3 min (because the rate is given in seconds).

$$\frac{60 \text{ seconds}}{1 \text{ minute}} \times 3 \text{ minutes} = 180 \text{ seconds}$$

❷ Multiply the rate of mitosis by the time (in seconds) given in the problem (180 s).

$$\frac{2.5 \times 10^7 \text{ cells}}{\text{second}} \times 180 \text{ seconds} = 4.5 \times 10^9 \text{ cells}$$

4.5×10^9 cells = 4,500,000,000 cells = 4.5 billion cells

Analysis

1. **Calculate** the number of cells that would be produced in 1 h.

2. **Calculate** the number of cells that would be produced in 1 day.

3. **CRITICAL THINKING** **Predicting Patterns** Identify factors that might increase or decrease the rate of mitosis.

QuickLab

Teacher's Notes Tell students that the factor label method shown will be used in future science courses (chemistry and physics), so learning the technique now will give them an advantage later.

Answers to Analysis

1. 9×10^{10} cells/h
   2.5×10^7 cells/s $\times$ 60 s/min $\times$ 60 min/h $= 9 \times 10^{10}$ cells/h

2. 2.2×10^{12} cells per day
   9×10^{10} cells/h $\times$ 24 h/day $= 2.2 \times 10^{12}$ cells/day

3. Some factors are the following: the type of cell, the availability of nutrients and chemical energy, the temperature and pH of the environment, the density of cells in area, and whether the cell is attached to a substrate **LS** **Logical**

Teaching Key Ideas

Pattern Puzzles Have students read Section 2, and list all the events described during the cell cycle on index cards (one event per card). Draw a large version of **Figure 4** at the front of the room. Call on one student at a time to come to the front of the room, read a card out loud, and then tape the card to the proper stage of the cell cycle. Repeat until all events are shown on the diagram. **LS** **Kinesthetic**

Teaching Key Ideas

Cells Are Busy Remind students that during interphase, a cell is not only growing, it is also producing the proteins and carrying out the functions that are characteristic of that type of cell.

- **G₁** During the *first gap phase* (G₁), a cell grows rapidly as the cell builds more organelles. For most organisms, this phase occupies the major portion of the cell's life. Cells that are not dividing remain in the G₁ phase.

- **S** During the *synthesis phase* (S), a cell's DNA is copied. At the end of the S phase, the cell's nucleus has twice as much DNA as it did in the G₁ phase. Each chromosome now consists of two identical chromatids that are attached at the centromere.

- **G₂** During the *second gap phase* (G₂), the cell continues to grow and prepares to divide. The cell forms some special structures that help the cell divide. Hollow protein fibers called *microtubules* are organized in the cytoplasm during G₂ in preparation for division.

Cell Division Each new cell requires a complete set of organelles, including a nucleus. The process of dividing the nucleus into two daughter nuclei is called **mitosis.** The process of separating the organelles and the cytoplasm is called **cytokinesis.**

- **Mitosis** During mitosis, the nucleus divides to form two nuclei. Each nucleus contains a complete set of the cell's chromosomes. The nuclear membrane breaks down briefly. The two sister chromatids of each chromosome are pulled to the opposite sides of the dividing cell.

- **Cytokinesis** As the nucleus divides, the cytoplasm also begins to divide. Each daughter cell receives about half of the original cell's organelles. During cytokinesis, the two daughter cells are physically separated.

❯ **Reading Check** *What phases are included in interphase?*

> **cell cycle** the life cycle of a cell
>
> **interphase** the period of the cell cycle during which activities such as cell growth and protein synthesis occur without visible signs of cell division
>
> **mitosis** in eukaryotic cells, a process of cell division that forms two new nuclei, each of which has the same number of chromosomes
>
> **cytokinesis** the division of the cytoplasm of a cell

SCI**LINKS**.
www.scilinks.org
Topic: Cell Cycle
Code: HX80235

Differentiated Instruction

Alternative Assessment

Cell Cycle Have students write a description of what is happening inside of each of the cell models shown in **Figure 4.** (G₁: cell is growing and functioning normally; S: DNA is copied, there's twice as much DNA shown than in G₁; G₂: microtubules form in preparation for division; mitosis: sister chromatids are separated and travel to opposite sides of the cell; cytokinesis: nucleus and cytoplasm divide.) **LS** **Visual**

Word Origins To help students with vocabulary, relate the term mitosis to its Greek origin, *mitos*, meaning "thread." Ask students to explain why mitosis would be related to thread. (The hereditary material consists of long, threadlike molecules.) **LS** **Verbal**

go.hrw.com
✳ **interact online**

Students can interact with the "Stages of Mitosis" by going to go.hrw.com and typing in the keyword HX8CRPF5.

Visual Literacy Ask students why the drawings look so different from the photos in **Figure 5**. (The drawings are simplified to show representative activities and structures.) The cell's nucleus is clearly visible in the second photo, where is it in the third photo? (The nuclear membrane dissolved and the contents lines up along the cell's equator.) How do the third and fourth photos differ from the drawings? (The spindle at each pole is more symmetrical than shown in the drawings.) How does the photograph of telophase differ from the drawing? (The photo shows that the daughter cells are not equal in size.) **LS** **Visual**

Answers to Caption Questions
Figure 5: to move the chromatids of each chromosome to opposite poles

spindle a network of microtubules that forms during mitosis and moves chromatids to the poles

centrosome an organelle that contains the centrioles and is the center of dynamic activity in mitosis

Figure 5 During mitosis, the copies (sister chromatids) of each chromosome are separated into two nuclei. ❯ **What is the role of the spindle fibers?**

Stages of Mitosis

Although mitosis is a continuous process, biologists traditionally divide it into four stages, as shown in **Figure 5**. ❯Mitosis is a continuous process that can be observed in four stages: prophase, metaphase, anaphase, and telophase.

Stage ❶ Prophase Within the nucleus, chromosomes begin to condense and become visible under a light microscope. The nuclear membrane breaks down. Outside the nucleus, a special structure called the **spindle** forms. The spindle is made up of several spindle fibers. Each spindle fiber in turn is made up of an individual microtubule—a hollow tube of protein. Microtubules organize into a spindle that runs at a right angle to the cell's equator.

Cells have an organelle called the **centrosome,** which helps assemble the spindle. In animal cells, the centrosome includes a pair of centrioles, shown in **Figure 5**. Each centriole is made up of nine triplets of microtubules arranged as a short, hollow tube. Before mitosis, the cell's centrosome is duplicated. During prophase, the centrosomes move to opposite poles of the cell.

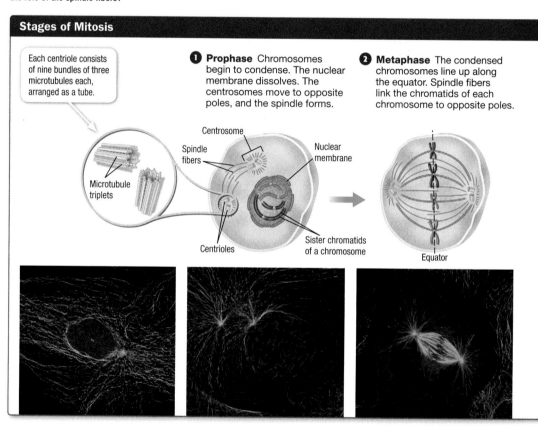

Stages of Mitosis

Each centriole consists of nine bundles of three microtubules each, arranged as a tube.

Microtubule triplets

❶ **Prophase** Chromosomes begin to condense. The nuclear membrane dissolves. The centrosomes move to opposite poles, and the spindle forms.

❷ **Metaphase** The condensed chromosomes line up along the equator. Spindle fibers link the chromatids of each chromosome to opposite poles.

Centrosome
Spindle fibers
Nuclear membrane
Centrioles
Sister chromatids of a chromosome
Equator

Differentiated Instruction

Struggling Readers/English Learners

Mitotic Pattern Puzzle Students will need 12 index cards—three cards per mitotic stage labeled as follows: (A) the stage, (B) a sketch of the events occurring during that stage, and (C) a narrative of the events occurring during that stage. Each student should have A, B, and C cards for each of the four stages. Students should then shuffle their cards and trade them with a partner. Draw the following grid on the board. Each student organizes the "traded" cards to match the grid.

Stage	1	2	3	4
Name				
Drawing				
Description				

LS **Visual, Verbal and Logical**

Stage ② Metaphase During metaphase, the chromosomes are packaged into their most condensed form. The nuclear membrane is fully dissolved, and the condensed chromosomes move to the center of the cell and line up along the cell's equator. Spindle fibers form a link between the poles and the centromere of each chromosome.

Stage ③ Anaphase Once all of the chromosomes are lined up, the spindle fibers shorten. The spindle fibers shorten by breaking down the microtubules bit by bit. Sister chromatids move toward opposite poles as the spindle fibers that are attached continue to shorten. Each pole now has a full set of chromosomes.

Stage ④ Telophase A nuclear envelope forms around the chromosomes at each pole of the cell. Chromosomes, now at opposite poles, uncoil and change back to their original chromatin form. The spindle dissolves. The spindle fibers break down and disappear. Mitosis is complete.

❯ **Reading Check** *What is the spindle composed of?*

READING TOOLBOX

Pattern Puzzles Cut each piece of the pattern puzzle that you made for the stages of mitosis so that each strip describes one of the events that occurs. Shuffle the strips and match the events with the correct stage.

go.hrw.com
✳ interact online
Keyword: HX8CRPF5

③ Anaphase As the spindle fibers shorten, the chromatids are pulled toward opposite poles of the cell.

④ Telophase A new nuclear envelope forms at each pole. The spindle dissolves, and the chromosomes uncoil. Cytokinesis begins.

Two genetically identical cells

Demonstration

Recognizing Mitotic Stages Set up several numbered stations with microscopes that have prepared slides of cells at various stages of mitosis. The stations will not be in the proper sequence of events. Have students view the slides and use the station numbers to record the proper order of events. If microscopes and slides are not available, the various stages can be shown with photographs or drawn on the board, out of order and labeled. **LS Visual, Kinesthetic, Logical**

Teaching Key Ideas

Visual Literacy Lead students through each stage shown in **Figure 5,** focusing on the behavior of chromosomes. Point out that the various stages are not of equal duration. Using movie film as an analogy, help students avoid the misconception that mitosis "jumps" from stage to stage. Although a movie consists of individual frames of film, the images on the film appear to change continuously. Explain that mitosis progresses in a similar fashion. **LS Visual**

Differentiated Instruction

Special Education Students

Cell Model Provide visually-impaired students with yarn to represent chromosomes, nuclear envelopes, and cell membranes; tie tabs to represent centromeres and string to represent spindle fibers. Have them recreate a cell undergoing mitosis on their desktops. **LS Kinesthetic**

Teaching Key Ideas

Mitosis Versus Cytokinesis Students may think that mitosis is the same as cell division. Be sure they understand that mitosis refers strictly to the division of chromosomes, whereas cytokinesis refers to the division of the cytoplasm. Ask students to think of a memory device that will help them keep the terms straight. (Cytokinesis goes with cytoplasm. Both terms have the word part *cyto-*.) Remind students that cell division is just one of the four events that make up the cell cycle.

LS Verbal

> Close

Formative Assessment

Once a new cell forms, the stages of development that follow are____.

A. S, G_2, G_1, Mitosis, Cytokinesis (Incorrect. Synthesis occurs after G_1.)

B. Mitosis, Cytokinesis, G_1, S, G_2 (Incorrect. Mitosis can not occur until the cell has developed and reproduced its DNA.)

C. G_1, S, G_2, Mitosis, Cytokinesis (Correct! The cell grows, replicates DNA, grows, and creates two new cells.)

D. S, G_2, Mitosis, Cytokinesis, G_1 (Incorrect. A cell must mature before it can duplicate its DNA.)

Answers to Section Review

1. G_1 is the growth stage. S is the DNA replication stage. During G_2, the cell grows and prepares for division. During mitosis the nucleus divides. Cytokinesis is the stage in which the cytoplasm divides.

Cell wall — Forming cell plate — Nucleus

Figure 6 During cytokinesis in an animal cell (left), the cell membrane is pinched in half by a belt of protein threads. During cytokinesis in plant cells (right), a cell plate forms down the middle of the dividing cell.

Belt of protein threads

ACADEMIC VOCABULARY

rigid stiff, firm, inflexible

Cytokinesis

As mitosis ends, cytokinesis begins. The cytoplasm is separated, and two cells are formed. **> During cytokinesis, the cell membrane grows into the center of the cell and divides it into two daughter cells of equal size. Each daughter cell has about half of the parent's cytoplasm and organelles.** The end result of mitosis and cytokinesis is two genetically identical cells in place of the original cell.

Separating the Cytoplasm In animal cells and other cells that lack cell walls, the cell is pinched in half by a belt of protein threads, as **Figure 6** shows. In plant cells and other cells that have rigid cell walls, the cytoplasm is divided in a different way. Vesicles holding cell wall material line up across the middle of the cell. These vesicles fuse to form a large, membrane-bound cell wall called the *cell plate*, shown in **Figure 6.** When it is completely formed, the cell plate separates the plant cell into two new plant cells.

Continuing the Cell Cycle After cytokinesis is complete, each cell enters the G_1 stage of interphase. The daughter cells are about equal in size—about half the size of the original cell. The activity of each cell continues because each has its own DNA and organelles. The cell cycle continues for each new cell.

> Reading Check *What is a cell plate?*

Section 2 Review

> KEY IDEAS

1. Describe the five phases of the cell cycle.

2. List in order the four stages of mitosis and the changes that occur during each stage.

3. Compare the products of cytokinesis.

CRITICAL THINKING

4. Evaluating Information Why are individual chromosomes more difficult to see during interphase than they are during mitosis?

5. Predicting Results What would happen if the cell did not have spindle fibers?

6. Making Connections Compare cell division in prokaryotic cells with cell division in eukaryotic cells.

ALTERNATIVE ASSESSMENT

7. Animated Flipbook Make a series of drawings that show the cell cycle of a plant cell. Be sure to include the five phases of the cell cycle and the four stages of mitosis.

2. Prophase – chromosomes condense; nuclear membrane dissolves; centrosomes move to the opposite poles; spindle forms

Metaphase – chromosomes line up on the equator; spindle fibers link chromatids to opposite poles

Anaphase – spindle fibers shorten; chromatids travel to the opposite poles

Telophase – nuclear envelope forms at poles; spindle dissolves; chromosomes uncoil; cytokinesis begins

3. The parent cell became two equally-sized daughter cells, each with half the parent's cytoplasm and organelles.

4. Chromosomes condense right before a cell divides in mitosis. During most of interphase, chromosomes are not condensed and are harder to see with a microscope.

5. Without spindle fibers, the sister chromatids would not separate, and each daughter cell would not receive a complete set of genes.

6. Both cell types undergo growth, DNA replication, and physical separation. For eukaryotic cells, the chromosomes are sorted and separated within the nucleus, so that each daughter cell has all the necessary organelles.

7. Student flipbooks should include five phases of the cell cycle and the four stages of mitosis.

Regulation

Key Ideas

- What are some factors that control cell growth and division?
- How do feedback signals affect the cell cycle?
- How does cancer relate to the cell cycle?

Key Terms

cancer
tumor

Why It Matters

Understanding how to control cell growth could be the key to curing cancer!

Your body grows when more cells are added to the tissues and organs that make up the body. To stay healthy, cells continue to divide as needed to replace or renew tissues. How is the cell cycle regulated?

Controls

Scientists study the cell cycle by observing cells in a culture medium. When a few healthy cells are placed in a dish with plenty of nutrients, they divide rapidly. But when they come in contact with one another or with the edge of the dish, the cells stop dividing.

These observations apply to real life. For example, when you cut your skin or break a bone, your cells start growing and dividing more rapidly to repair the wounds. The cells shown in **Figure 7** will begin dividing to replace the cells cut by the scalpel. As more cells form, the new cells come into contact with each other and close the wound. When the wound is healed, the cells slow down or stop dividing.

Cell division is highly controlled. **Cell growth and division depend on protein signals and other environmental signals.** Many proteins within the cell control the phases of the cell cycle. Signals from surrounding cells or even from other organs can also regulate cell growth and division. Environmental conditions, including the availability of nutrients, also affect the cell cycle.

Reading Check *What are two factors that affect the cell cycle?*

The Living Environment

5.2i Gene mutations in a cell can result in uncontrolled cell division, called cancer. Exposure of cells to certain chemicals and radiation increases mutations and thus increases the chance of cancer.

Figure 7 The cells surrounding this surgical incision will begin dividing more often to fill in the gap. **What signals the cells to stop dividing when the wound is healed?**

QuickLab

Teachers Notes UV sensitive beads are found in science supply catalogues. Make sure there is no UV absorbing film on the glass of the window that you use.

Materials
• UV-sensitive beads (30)
• sun-block, one tablespoon

Answers to Analysis

1. The beads are clear and transparent.
2. No. Household light bulbs do not emit UV radiation.
3. Those without sun-block changed colors. Those with sun-block either did not change color, or their color change was minimal due to exposure from the sides of the dish.
4. Sun-block limits exposure to UV radiation thus reducing the risk of it damaging the DNA in cells.

Cause and Effect

G_1 Checkpoint
Cause: Cell is not healthy, too small, or conditions are unsuitable for division (i.e. lack of nutrients, low or high pH).
G_2 Checkpoint
Cause: Recognizes mistakes that occurred when the DNA was copied or cell is still too small.
Metaphase Checkpoint
Cause: Chromosomes are not properly aligned to spindle fibers.
LS Verbal

Hands-On
QuickLab

 30 min

UV and Sunblock

Prolonged exposure to the sun's UV radiation can damage DNA, disrupting the cell cycle and causing skin cancer.

Procedure

1 In a dimly lit room, expose **UV-sensitive beads** to a bright, incandescent light source. Record any changes that you observe.

2 Thoroughly coat five beads in a thick covering of **sunblock**. Place three beads on one side of a **paper plate**. Place five uncoated beads on the other side.

3 Expose the plate to direct sunlight for a moment. Examine the beads in dim surroundings. Record any changes that you observe.

Analysis

1. **Describe** the appearance of the beads before they were exposed to bright light sources.
2. **Determine** whether exposure to the artificial light source affect their appearance.
3. **Describe** how direct sunlight affected the beads.
4. **CRITICAL THINKING** **Making Inferences** How can using sunblock protect you from getting cancer?

READING TOOLBOX

Cause and Effect At each checkpoint, identify a cause that would result in a delay of the next phase of the cell cycle.

Figure 8 The eukaryotic cell cycle has three checkpoints. Many proteins play a role in controlling the cell cycle.

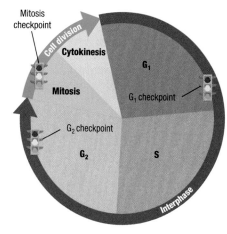

Checkpoints

During the cell cycle, a cell undergoes an inspection process to ensure that the cell is ready for the next phase in the cell cycle. ▶ **Feedback signals at key checkpoints in the cell cycle can delay or trigger the next phase of the cell cycle.** There are three main checkpoints in the cell cycle, as **Figure 8** shows.

G_1 Checkpoint Before the cell copies its DNA, the cell checks its surroundings. If conditions are favorable and the cell is healthy and large enough, the cell enters the synthesis phase. If conditions are not favorable, the cell goes into a resting period. Certain cells, such as some nerve and muscle cells, remain in this resting period for a long time. They do not divide very often.

G_2 Checkpoint Before mitosis begins, the cell checks for any mistakes in the copied DNA. Enzymes correct mistakes that are found. This checkpoint ensures that the DNA of the daughter cells will be identical to the DNA of the original cell. Proteins also double-check that the cell is large enough to divide. If the cell passes the G_2 checkpoint, then the cell may begin to divide. Once past this checkpoint, proteins help to trigger mitosis.

Mitosis Checkpoint During the metaphase stage of mitosis, chromosomes line up at the equator. At this point, the cell checks that the chromosomes are properly attached to the spindle fibers. Without this point, the sister chromatids of one or more chromosomes may not separate properly. This checkpoint ensures that the genetic material is distributed equally between the daughter cells.

▶ **Reading Check** *What happens at the G_2 checkpoint?*

Differentiated Instruction

English Learners/Struggling Readers

Traffic Jam Struggling readers and students learning English may not understand the traffic light analogy shown in **Figure 8.** Model a stop and go process for them, such as crossing a busy street. Engage them in a discussion that makes the point that one can proceed safely only after checking for oncoming traffic.
LS Visual/Kinesthetic

Alternative Assessment

Pitfalls of Rapid Cell Division Cancer therapies target rapidly dividing cells. Hair loss, nausea, anemia, and low white cell count are some of the common side effects of chemotherapy and radiation therapy. Ask students what might be causing these symptoms. (Cell division rates are higher for cells in hair follicles, the stomach, and in bone marrow. As a result, these cells are also targets during treatments causing the unpleasant side effects.)

Cancer

Each year, more than 1 million Americans are diagnosed with cancer. **Cancer** is a group of severe and sometimes fatal diseases that are caused by uncontrolled cell growth. ❱ **Uncontrolled cell growth and division can result in masses of cells that invade and destroy healthy tissues.** Preventing or curing cancer requires an understanding of how a healthy person's cells can become cancerous.

Loss of Control Normally, a cell responds properly to signals and controls. However, damage to a cell's DNA can cause the cell to respond improperly or to stop responding. The cell cycle can no longer be controlled. The defective cell divides and produces more defective cells, such as the cells in **Figure 9.** Eventually, these cells can form a mass called a **tumor.**

Development A *benign tumor* does not spread to other parts of the body and can often be removed by surgery. A *malignant tumor* invades and destroys nearby healthy tissues and organs. Malignant tumors, or cancers, can break loose from their tissue of origin and grow throughout the body. This process is called *metastasis*. Once a cancer has metastasized, it becomes difficult to treat.

Treatment Some cancers can be treated by using drugs that kill the fast-growing cancer cells. Because drugs are chemicals, this method of treatment is called *chemotherapy,* or "chemo" for short. Some cancers can be treated by surgery to remove of the affected organ. In radiation therapy, high-energy rays are focused on an area in order to destroy cancerous cells. Doctors choose the most effective treatment for a particular kind of cancer.

Prevention The best way to prevent cancer is to avoid things that can cause cancer. Ultraviolet radiation in sunlight can damage genes that control the cell cycle. Chemicals in cigarette smoke also affect how cell growth and division is regulated.

❱ **Reading Check** *What causes cells to lose control of the cell cycle?*

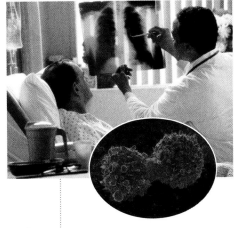

Figure 9 A doctor often can see a lung tumor on an X ray. Tumors are masses of cells (inset) that divide out of control.

cancer a group of diseases characterized by uncontrolled growth and spread of abnormal cells

tumor a growth that arises from normal tissue but that grows abnormally in rate and structure and lacks a function

---

Lab

Time Required

One 45-minute lab period

Ratings

EASY			HARD

Teacher Prep   🔬

Student Setup   🔬

Concept Level   🔬🔬

Cleanup   🔬

Safety Cautions

Have students handle glass slides with care.

Tips and Tricks

Preparing Your Own Slides You can prepare your own slides with the following materials:
- aceto-orcein stain
- cork
- forceps
- glass dish
- onions
- paper towels
- scalpel
- slides and cover slips
- 2 M HCl

Place the onion root tips in water for several days before the lab to initiate root-tip lengthening. About one-half hour before the lab, use a sharp scalpel to cut root tips that are 3 mm long. Pour 2 M HCl into a beaker that is in a fume hood. Place the root tips in the beaker for 10 minutes. Use forceps to transfer the soaked root tips to slides. Add a drop of aceto-orcein stain to each slide. Use a scalpel to mince the tips

Chapter 10 Lab

Objectives

▸ Examine the dividing root-tip cells of an onion.

▸ Identify the phase of mitosis that each cell in an onion root tip is undergoing.

▸ Determine the relative length of time each phase of mitosis takes in onion root-tip cells.

Materials

- compound light microscope
- prepared microscope slide of a longitudinal section of *Allium* (onion) root tip

Safety

Mitosis in Plant Cells

Look at the photograph of a longitudinal section of an onion root tip. In the tips of plant roots and shoots, mitosis is ongoing in growth regions called *meristems*. Mitosis occurs in four phases: prophase, metaphase, anaphase, and telophase. In this lab, you will determine the relative length of time each phase of mitosis takes in onion root-tip cells. To do this, you will count the number of cells undergoing each phase of mitosis in the meristem of an onion root section.

Procedure

Identify the Phases of Mitosis

❶ ◈ ◈ ◈ **CAUTION: Put on safety goggles, gloves, and a lab apron.**

❷ ◈ **CAUTION: Handle glass slides and cover slips with care.** Using low power on your microscope, bring the meristem region on your slide into focus.

❸ Examine the meristem carefully. Choose a sample of about 50 cells. Look for a group of cells that appear to have been actively dividing at the time that the slide was made. The cells will appear to be in rows, so it should be easy to keep track of them. The dark-staining bodies are the chromosomes.

❹ For each of the cells in your sample, identify the stage of mitosis. Make a data table of the relative duration of each phase of mitosis. Record your observations in the data table.

Relative Duration of Each Phase of Mitosis				
Phase of mitosis	Tally marks	Count	Percentage of all cells	Time (min)
Prophase				
Metaphase				
Anaphase				
Telophase				

Calculate the Relative Length of Each Phase

❺ When you have classified each cell in your sample, count the tally marks for each phase and fill in the "Count" column. In which phase of mitosis was the number of cells the greatest? In which phase of mitosis was the number of cells the fewest?

and then cover the specimens with coverslips. Put a paper towel and a cork over the coverslip and press gently but firmly until the tips are flattened. Flattening an improperly prepared root tip can break a glass coverslip. If the tip cannot be flattened, return it to the acid for 10 more minutes and try again.

Mitosis Projection Students often have trouble identifying the phases of mitosis. It is helpful to project a slide or CD-ROM image of root tip mitosis for reference during the lab.

Disposal If you throw the prepared slides of the onion tip away, make sure they are deposited in biohazard/glass safety bin. This type of bin can be purchased from a medical supply house, or you can also use a heavy plastic jug (bleach or orange juice jug).

6 Calculate what percentage of all cells were found in each phase. Divide the number of cells in a phase by the total number of cells in your sample, and multiply by 100%. Enter these figures under the "Percentage" column.

$$\text{Percentage} = \frac{\text{number of cells in phase}}{\text{total number of cells in sample}} \times 100\%$$

7 The percentage of the total number of cells that are found in each phase can be used to estimate how long each phase lasts. For example, if 25% of the cells are in prophase, then prophase takes 25% of the total time that a cell takes to undergo mitosis. Mitosis in onion cells takes about 80 min. Using this information and the percentages you have just determined, calculate the time for each phase and record it in your data table.

$$\text{Duration of phase (in minutes)} = \frac{\text{percentage}}{100} \times 80 \text{ min}$$

8 Make another table to record the data for the entire class. Collect and add the counts for each phase of mitosis for the entire class. Fill in the percentage and time information by using these data.

9 ♦ ◆ Clean up your lab materials according to your teacher's instructions. Wash your hands before leaving the lab.

Analyze and Conclude

1. **Identifying Structures** What color are the chromosomes stained?

2. **Recognizing Relationships** How can you distinguish between early and late anaphase?

3. **SCIENTIFIC METHODS Making Systematic Observations** According to your data table, which phase takes the least amount of time? Which phase of mitosis lasts the longest? Why might this phase require more time than other phases of mitosis do?

4. **SCIENTIFIC METHODS Summarizing Data** How do your data compare with the data of the entire class?

5. **SCIENTIFIC METHODS Critiquing Procedures** In this investigation, you assumed that the percentage of the total time that any given phase takes is equal to the percentage of the total number of cells in that phase at any moment. Why might this not be true for very small samples of cells?

Class Data			
Phase of mitosis	Count	Percentage of all cells	Duration (min)
Prophase			
Metaphase			
Anaphase			
Telophase			

Extensions

6. **Applying Methods** Cancerous tissue is composed of cells undergoing uncontrolled, rapid cell division. How could you develop a procedure to identify cancerous tissue by counting the number of cells undergoing mitosis?

Answers to Extensions

6. Students would have to find out the percentage of cells undergoing mitosis at any given time in a normal tissue sample and compare it with the cancerous tissue sample.

⏱ **60 min**

Answers to Procedure

5. The number of tally marks beside each stage will vary. The greatest number of cells in the sample should be in prophase. The fewest number of cells should be in anaphase, but answers may vary.

6. Answers should reflect the data. Roughly 85 percent of the cells should be in prophase, 8 percent in metaphase, 3 percent in anaphase, and 4 percent in telophase.

7. Answers should reflect the data. Roughly 68 minutes are spent in prophase, 6 minutes in metaphase, 2 minutes in anaphase, and 3 minutes in telophase.

9. Class data and calculations based on class data will vary.

Answers to Analyze and Conclude

1. Chromosomes are often stained pink or purple, depending on the stain used.

2. In early anaphase, the chromosomes are just beginning to pull away from the midline. In late anaphase, the chromosomes are near the poles.

3. Answers may vary, but usually anaphase or telophase takes the least amount of time. Prophase usually takes the longest time. More events occur during this prophase, which is why it is longer.

4. Answers may vary depending on class data.

5. Simply by chance, a small area might have an overrepresentation of one mitotic phase. Larger samples would yield more representative data.

Key Resources

 Holt Lab Generator

 Lab Datasheet (Levels A, B, C)

 Holt Science Biology Video Labs

 Virtual Investigations

go.hrw.com
SUPER SUMMARY
Keyword: HX8CRPS

SUPER SUMMARY

Have students connect the major concepts in this chapter through an interactive Super Summary. Visit **go.hrw.com** and type in the keyword **HX8CRPS** to access the Super Summary for this chapter.

Reteaching Key Ideas

Cell Parts and Reproduction Ask students to differentiate each of the following terms using both definitions and drawings: *chromosomes, chromatids, DNA,* and *genes.* Students should label their sketches. (chromosomes – coiled DNA and associated proteins; chromatids – condensed chromatin; DNA – the chain of nucleic acids containing genetic code; genes – the sequences of DNA that code for specific proteins or RNA.) **LS** **Verbal/Visual**

Parts of the Cell Cycle Assign students to groups and have each group draw a stage in the cell cycle. Each group displays their drawing in a circle that you've drawn to represent the cell cycle. **LS** **Visual**

Key Ideas	Key Terms
1 **Cell Reproduction** ❯ Because larger cells are more difficult to maintain, cells divide when they grow to a certain size. ❯ Many proteins help package eukaryotic DNA into highly condensed chromosome structures. ❯ All newly-formed cells require DNA, so before a cell divides, a copy of its DNA is made for each daughter cell.	gene (224) chromosome (224) chromatin (224) histone (224) nucleosome (224) chromatid (225) centromere (225)
2 **Mitosis** ❯ The life of a eukaryotic cell cycles through phases of growth, DNA replication, preparation for cell division, and division of the nucleus and cytoplasm. ❯ Mitosis is a continuous process that can be observed in four stages: prophase, metaphase, anaphase, and telophase. ❯ During cytokinesis, the cell membrane grows into the center of the cell and divides it into two daughter cells of equal size. Each daughter cell has about half of the parent's cytoplasm and organelles.	cell cycle (228) interphase (228) mitosis (229) cytokinesis (229) spindle (230) centrosome (230)
3 **Regulation** ❯ Cell growth and division depend on protein signals and other environmental signals. ❯ Feedback signals at key checkpoints in the cell cycle can delay or trigger the next phase of the cell cycle. ❯ Uncontrolled cell growth and division results in tumors, which can invade surrounding tissues and cause cancer.	cancer (235) tumor (235)

PART A: Answer all questions in this part.

Directions: For each statement or question, write on your separate answer sheet the number of the word or expression that best completes the statement or answers the question.

1 Hereditary information is stored inside the
   (1) ribosomes, which have chromosomes that contain many genes
   (2) ribosomes, which have genes that contain many chromosomes
   (3) nucleus, which has chromosomes that contain many genes
   (4) nucleus, which has genes that contain many chromosomes

2 Which sequence of terms represents a decrease from the greatest number of structures to the least number of structures present in a cell?
   (1) nucleus → gene → chromosome
   (2) gene → nucleus → chromosome
   (3) gene → chromosome → nucleus
   (4) chromosome → gene → nucleus

3 Which statements best describe the relationship between the terms chromosomes, genes, and nuclei?
   (1) Chromosomes are found on genes. Genes are found in nuclei.
   (2) Chromosomes are found in nuclei. Nuclei are found in genes.
   (3) Genes are found on chromosomes. Chromosomes are found in nuclei.
   (4) Genes are found in nuclei. Nuclei are found in chromosomes.

4 Which of the following is a reason that the size of a cell is limited?
   (1) Larger cells are easier for an organism to produce than smaller cells.
   (2) The cell's ability to exchange substances is limited by its surface area–to-volume ratio.
   (3) The larger the cell becomes, the easier it is for substances to reach where they are needed.
   (4) The size of a cell has no relationship to the cell's function in a multicellular organism.

5 What factors can cause cells to divide in a culture medium?
   (1) protein signals
   (2) lack of nutrients
   (3) contact with other cells
   (4) contact with the edge of the dish

6 What is the importance of feedback signals at key checkpoints within the cell cycle?
   (1) to indicate the end of the cycle
   (2) to indicate the presence of proteins
   (3) to identify the meiosis and mitosis indicators
   (4) to delay or trigger the next phase of the cycle

7 What is a gene?
   (1) a large molecule of chromosomes
   (2) a protein that directs the activity of a cell
   (3) a segment of DNA that codes for RNA and protein
   (4) a segment of RNA that moves from the nucleus to the cytoplasm

8 What might happen if cytokinesis were omitted from the cell cycle?
   (1) The daughter cells would die.
   (2) The cell would lose its mitochondria.
   (3) The daughter cells would not have nuclei.
   (4) The cell would not divide into two daughter cells.

9 Mitosis could not proceed if a mutation interrupted the assembly of the
   (1) cell wall.
   (2) spindle fibers.
   (3) cell membrane.
   (4) nuclear envelope.

PART A

1. **(3)** Hereditary information is found along chromosomes inside the nucleus, and not in ribosomes. Chromosomes are not found in genes, but genes are found along the structure of a chromosome. (*#04, June 2006 Regents Exam*)

2. **(3)** Based on increasing complexity, the sequence gene → chromosome → nucleus, is the only answer choice that is in the correct order. (*#04, January 2005 Regents Exam*)

3. **(3)** Chromosomes are not found on genes, genes are found on chromosomes. Nuclei are not found in genes or chromosomes. (*#04, June 2004 Regents Exam*)

4. **(2)**
5. **(1)**
6. **(4)**
7. **(3)**
8. **(4)**
9. **(2)**

Regents Exam Practice

Correlations	
4.1.2a 2	**4.2.1d** 13
4.1.2b 14	**4.4.1b** 11
4.2.1c 1, 3	**4.4.1d** 10, 12

10. (1) Because anaphase involves chromatids being pulled to opposite poles, the chromosome number is maintained and not doubled. DNA is replicated in prophase and not in anaphase. The chromatids, and not the cells, are split from each other. *(#38, June 2005 Regents Exam)*

11. (1) After mitosis, each daughter cell should end up with the same number and kinds of chromosomes as the parent cell (note that the main image shows the parent cell's chromatids). Therefore the diagrams that show reduced chromosome numbers in the duaghter cells are incorrect. Likewise, diagrams that indicate that the daughter cells end up with differing chromosomes are also incorrect. *(#30, August 2004 Regents Exam)*

10 The diagram below illustrates the process of cell division. What is the significance of anaphase in this process?

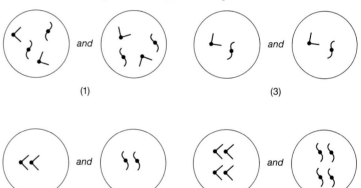

4 chromosomes

Interphase (parent cell)   Prophase   Metaphase   Anaphase   Telophase   Interphase (daughter cells)

(1) Anaphase usually ensures that each daughter cell has the same number of chromosomes as the parent cell.
(2) Anaphase usually ensures that each daughter cell has twice as many chromosomes as the parent cell.
(3) In anaphase, the cell splits in half.
(4) In anaphase, the DNA is being replicated.

The chromosome content of a skin cell that is about to form two new skin cells is represented in the diagram below.

11 Which diagram best represents the chromosomes that would be found in the two new skin cells produced as a result of this process?

and

(1)

and

(3)

and

(2)

and

(4)

PART B

12 Which activity most directly involves the process represented in the diagram below?

(1) a gamete reproducing sexually
(2) a white blood cell engulfing bacteria
(3) a zygote being produced in an ovary
(4) an animal repairing damaged tissue

13 The diagram below represents single-celled organism A dividing by mitosis to form cells B and C. Cells A, B, and C all produced protein X. What can best be inferred from this observation?

(1) Protein X is found in all organisms.
(2) The gene for protein X is found in single celled organisms, only.
(3) Cells A, B, and C ingested food containing the gene to produce protein X.
(4) The gene to produce protein X was passed from cell A to cells B and C.

14 Arrange the following structures from largest to smallest.

a chromosome
a nucleus
a gene

Largest

↓

Smallest

12. (4) The diagram illustrates mitosis, which produces new body cells. Meiosis produces haploid sex cells that have half the number of chromosomes than the original diploid cell. Zygotes are produced through fertilization, which joins two haploid cells to form a diploid cell. As a white blood cell engulfs bacteria, no chromosomes are copied and no new cells are produced. (*#37, August 2003 Regents Exam*)

13. (4) The choice about food is incorrect as genes are not passed by ingestion. The choices about protein X in all organisms and single-celled organisms cannot be inferred from the diagram. (*#35, June 2006 Regents Exam*)

14. Allow 1 credit for indicating that the correct order is:

Largest   **nucleus**
↓   **chromosome**
Smallest   **gene**

(*#53, January 2004 Regents Exam*

UNIT 4 Heredity

11 Meiosis and Sexual Reproduction

12 Mendel and Heredity

13 DNA, RNA, and Proteins

14 Genes in Action

15 Gene Technology and Human Applications

 The Living Environment

Standard 1 Students will use mathematical analysis, scientific inquiry, and engineering design, as appropriate, to pose questions, seek answers, and develop solutions.

Key Idea 3 The observations made while testing proposed explanations, when analyzed using conventional and invented methods, provide new insights into natural phenomena.

Standard 4 Students will understand and apply scientific concepts, principles, and theories pertaining to the physical setting and living environment and recognize the historical development of ideas in science.

Key Idea 1 Living things are both similar to and different from each other and from nonliving things.

Key Idea 2 Organisms inherit genetic information in a variety of ways that result in continuity of structure and function between parents and offspring.

Key Idea 3 Individual organisms and species change over time

Key Idea 4 The continuity of life is sustained through reproduction and development.

Key Idea 5 Organisms maintain a dynamic equilibrium that sustains life.

Fruit fly embryo, marked to show pattern of genes being expressed

Eggs of the red-eyed tree frog stuck to the underside of a leaf

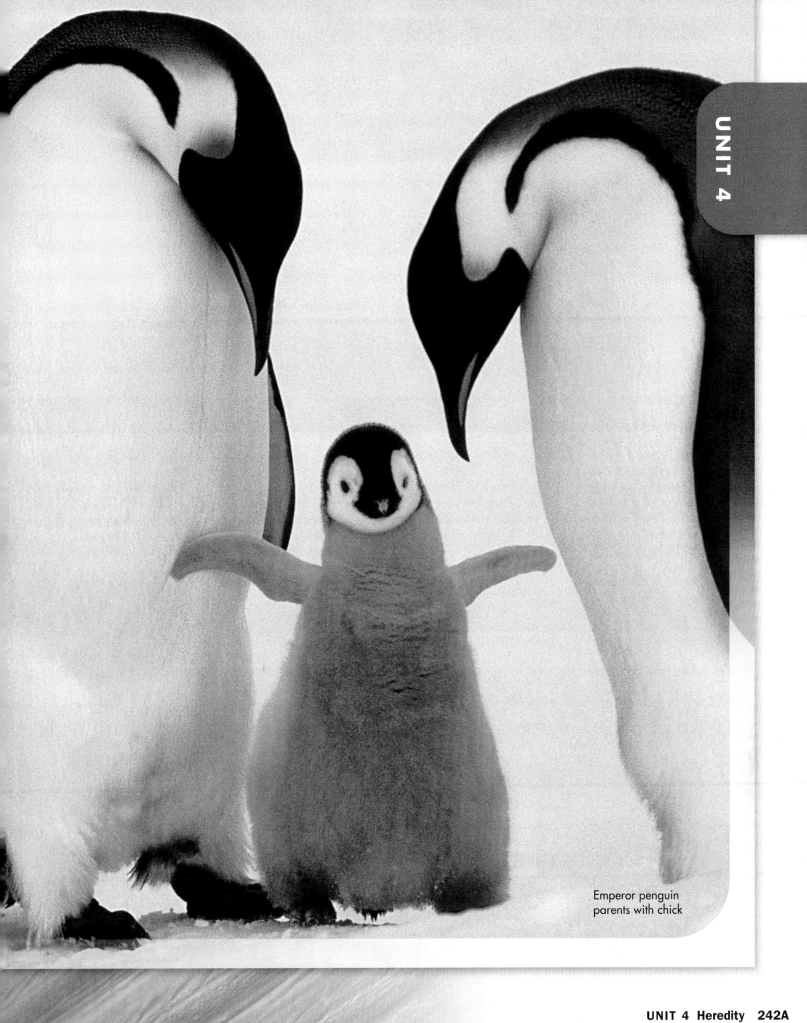

Emperor penguin
parents with chick

Heredity and Genetics

1865

Gregor Mendel publishes the results of his studies of genetic inheritance in pea plants. Although his work is not widely known until much later, Mendel is remembered as the founder of the science of genetics.

Gregor Mendel

1879

After staining cells with Perkins dye and viewing them under a microscope, Walter Fleming identifies chromatin in cells. Soon after, he observes and describes all stages of mitosis, using terms such as *metaphase, anaphase and telophase.*

1905

Nettie Maria Stephens describes how human gender is determined by the X and Y chromosomes.

Nettie Stevens

1909

The Elements of Heredity, by Wilhelm Johannsen, a Danish biologist, is revised and translated into German. In the book, Johannsen develops many of the concepts of modern genetics, particularly phenotype and genotype. This book becomes a founding text of genetics.

1913

Alfred Henry Sturtevant, an undergraduate student at Columbia University, determines the relative location of genes on a fruit fly chromosome. He publishes a genetic map showing the order of genes and their relative distance from each other.

1915

Thomas Hunt publishes the book *Mechanism of Mendelian Heredity,* which explains the phenomenon of sex-linked traits observed in fruit flies.

Drosophila melanogaster (fruit fly)

1989

Francis Collins and Lap-Chee Tsui identify a mutant version of a gene on chromosome 7 that causes cystic fibrosis. Discovery of the gene leads to the development of tests that can determine whether potential parents are carriers of the gene.

2003

The Human Genome Project is completed. Research teams around the world collaborated to identify all genes and decode the sequence of all DNA in human cells.

Genetic sequences on a computer screen

Albino peacock

BIOLOGY CAREER

Genetics Researcher
Rob Desalle

Rob DeSalle is a curator in the Division of Invertebrate Zoology at the American Museum of Natural History in New York City. His current research focuses on molecular evolution in a variety of organisms, including pathogenic bacteria and insects.

DeSalle studies molecular evolution through comparative genomics, which is the study of similarities and differences between the genomes of various species or strains within species. Comparing the genomes of species can help determine how the species are related.

DeSalle also helped found the Conservation Genetics Program at the American Museum of Natural History. This program uses the tools of molecular genetics to help protect wildlife around the world. For example, DeSalle helped develop a genetic test to determine if caviar sold in the United States was illegally harvested from endangered species of sturgeon in the Caspian Sea.

Genetic analysis by gel electrophoresis

11 Meiosis and Sexual Reproduction

	Standards	Teach Key Ideas

CHAPTER OPENER, pp. 244–245 *15 min.*

The Living Environment

SECTION 1 Reproduction, pp. 247–249 *45 min.*

> Asexual Reproduction
> Sexual Reproduction
> Chromosome Number

Standards: 4.2.1c, 4.2.1d, 4.2.1e, 4.4.1b

Teach Key Ideas:
- **Bellringer Transparency**
- **Transparencies** B44 Chromosome Number of Various Organisms
- **Visual Concepts** Sexual Reproduction • Fertilization • Comparing Haploid and Diploid Cells

---

SECTION 2 Meiosis, pp. 250–255 *90 min.*

> Stages of Meiosis
> Comparing Mitosis and Meiosis
> Genetic Variation

Standards: 4.2.1e, 4.3.1c, 4.4.1c

Teach Key Ideas:
- **Bellringer Transparency**
- **Transparencies** B49 Stages of Meiosis • B51 Meiosis in Male and Female Animals
- **Visual Concepts** Tetrads and Crossing-over of Genetic Material • Independent Assortment • Formation of a Sperm • Formation of an Egg Cell • Comparing the Results of Meiosis and Mitosis • Comparing Meiosis and Mitosis

---

SECTION 3 Multicellular Life Cycles, pp. 256–259 *60 min.*

> Diploid Life Cycle
> Haploid Life Cycle
> Alternation of Generations

Standards: 4.2.1e, 4.4.1b, 4.4.1c

Teach Key Ideas:
- **Bellringer Transparency**
- **Transparencies** B48 Diploid Life Cycle • F13 Haploid Life Cycle • G5 Alternation of Generations
- **Visual Concepts** Comparing Haploid and Diploid Cells • Alternation of Generations

See also PowerPoint® Resources

Chapter Review and Assessment Resources

SE Super Summary, p. 260
SE Regents Exam Practice, p. 261
Regents Review Guide
Review Resources
Chapter Tests A and B
Holt Online Assessment
Regents Question Banks on Teacher's One-Stop Planner

CHAPTER FastTrack *Thorough instruction will require the times shown.*

Basic Learners
TE Advantages and Disadvantages, p. 248
TE Crossing-Over, p. 253
Directed Reading Worksheets*
Active Reading Worksheets*
Lab Manuals, Level A*
Study Guide* ■
Note-taking Workbook*
Special Needs Activities and Modified Tests*

Advanced Learners
TE Genetic Variation, p. 253
Critical Thinking Worksheets*
Concept Mapping Worksheets*
Science Skills Worksheets*
Lab Datasheets, Level C*

Why It Matters	Hands-On	Skills Development	Assessment
Build student motivation with resources about high-interest applications.	SE **Inquiry Lab** Pollen Up Close, p. 245* ■	TE **Reading Toolbox** Assessing Prior Knowledge, p. 244 SE **Reading Toolbox,** p. 246	
	📁 **Exploration Lab** Karyotyping* 📁 **Skills Practice Lab** Laboratory Techniques: Staining DNA and RNA*	TE **Math Skills** Asexual Reproduction in Bacteria, p. 248 SE **Reading Toolbox** Key-Term Fold, p. 249 TE **Reading Toolbox** Key-Term Fold, p. 249	SE **Section Review** TE **Formative Assessment** **Spanish Assessment*** ■ 📁 **Section Quiz** ■
TE **Demonstration** Counting Chromosomes, p. 250 TE **Development In Eggs,** p. 252 SE **Girls, Girls, Girls,** p. 255	SE **Quick Lab** Crossing-Over Model, p. 253* ■ SE **Skills Practice Lab** Meiosis Model, p. 259* ■	SE **Reading Toolbox** Comparisons, p. 252 TE **Reading Toolbox** Comparisons, p. 252 TE **Reading Toolbox** Visual Literacy, p. 255	SE **Section Review** TE **Formative Assessment** **Spanish Assessment*** ■ 📁 **Section Quiz** ■
	SE **Quick Lab** Chromosome Combinations, p. 257* ■	SE **Reading Toolbox** Two-Column Notes, p. 258 TE **Reading Toolbox** Two-Column Notes, p. 258	SE **Section Review** TE **Formative Assessment** **Spanish Assessment*** ■ 📁 **Section Quiz** ■
	See also Lab Generator		**See also Holt Online Assessment Resources**

Resources for Differentiated Instruction

English Learners

TE Reading Organizer, p. 257
📁 Directed Reading Worksheets*
📁 Active Reading Worksheets*
📁 Lab Manuals, Level A*
📓 Study Guide* ■
📓 Note-taking Workbook*
📓 Multilingual Glossary
💿 Interactive Tutor

Struggling Readers

TE Counting Chromosomes, p. 251
📁 Directed Reading Worksheets*
📁 Active Reading Worksheets*
📁 Lab Manuals, Level A*
📓 Study Guide*
📓 Note-taking Workbook*
📓 Special Needs Activities and Modified Tests*
💿 Interactive Tutor

Special Education Students

TE Modeling Meiosis, p. 252
📁 Directed Reading Worksheets*
📁 Active Reading Worksheets*
📁 Lab Manuals, Level A*
📓 Study Guide* ■
📓 Note-taking Workbook*
📓 Special Needs Activities and Modified Tests*

Alternative Assessment

TE Modeling Life Cycles, p. 257
📁 Science Skills Worksheets*
📁 Section Quizzes* ■
📓 Chapter Tests A, B, and C* ■

Chapter 11

Chapter 11

Meiosis and Sexual Reproduction

Overview

The purpose of this chapter is to explain the different types of reproduction. In sexual reproduction, genes are rearranged in the process of meiosis, which results in genetic variation in a population. Organisms that reproduce sexually have diploid and haploid stages in their life cycles. Some organisms have a life cycle that alternates between haploid and diploid phases.

READING TOOLBOX

Assessing Prior Knowledge Students should understand the following concepts:
• sexual and asexual reproduction
• cellular structure
• DNA and genes
• mitosis

Visual Literacy Ask students to think of friends or acquaintances who look more like their mothers than their fathers (and vice versa). Ask them to also think about acquaintances who look like a blend of both parents. Have students look at the offspring. Do they look alike? (yes) Are they identical to their parents? (no) Ask students how they know that the babies are different. (Their genes come from both parents, so they cannot be identical to one parent.) **LS Visual**

Preview

1 Reproduction
Asexual Reproduction
Sexual Reproduction
Chromosome Number

2 Meiosis
Stages of Meiosis
Comparing Mitosis and Meiosis
Genetic Variation

3 Multicellular Life Cycles
Diploid Life Cycle
Haploid Life Cycle
Alternation of Generations

Why It Matters

You know that in sexual reproduction, an egg and a sperm combine to form a new organism. But how are eggs and sperm produced? In this chapter, you will learn about a special type of cell division called *meiosis*.

Like many organisms, the daddy long-legs spider reproduces sexually. Meiosis is a process that forms the eggs and sperm that make sexual reproduction possible for the daddy longlegs spiders.

A mother daddy longlegs spider will watch over her newly hatched young for nine days. After nine days, the young shed their skin and leave the web to build their own webs.

The Living Environment
Standard 4 Students will understand and apply scientific concepts, principles, and theories pertaining to the physical setting and living environment and recognize the historical development of ideas in science.
Key Idea 2 Organisms inherit genetic information in a variety of ways that result in continuity of structure and function between parents and offspring. *Major Understandings* - 2.1c, 2.1d, 2.1e
Key Idea 3 Individual organisms and species change over time. *Major Understandings* - 3.1c
Key Idea 4 The continuity of life is sustained through reproduction and development. *Major Understandings* - 4.1b, 4.1c

---

Chapter Correlations   The Living Environment

Standard 4

2.1c Hereditary information is contained in genes, located in the chromosomes of each cell. An inherited trait of an individual can be determined by one or by many genes, and a single gene can influence more than one trait. A human cell contains many thousands of different genes in its nucleus.

2.1d In asexually reproducing organisms, all the genes come from a single parent. Asexually produced offspring are normally genetically identical to the parent.

2.1e In sexually reproducing organisms, the new individual receives half of the genetic information from its mother (via the egg) and half from its father (via the sperm). Sexually produced offspring often resemble, but are not identical to, either of their parents.

3.1c Mutation and the sorting and recombining of genes during meiosis and fertilization result in a great variety of possible gene combinations.

4.1b Some organisms reproduce asexually with all the genetic information coming from one parent. Other organisms reproduce sexually with half the genetic information typically contributed by each parent. Cloning is the production of identical genetic copies.

4.1c The processes of meiosis and fertilization are key to sexual reproduction in a wide variety of organisms. The process of meiosis results in the production of eggs and sperm which each contain half of the genetic information. During fertilization, gametes unite to form a zygote, which contains the complete genetic information for the offspring.

The newly hatched spiders, or *prenymphs*, may all look alike. However, because they formed from sexual reproduction, they are all genetically different.

Teacher's Notes Prior to presenting this activity to students, preview all the prepared slides to ensure that each one offers an assortment of meiotic stages. You may also wish to display a complete male lily flower, so students may better understand the structure they are observing in the prepared cross-section. Explain to students that pollen is a male gamete produced by the process of meiosis. Explain to students that pollen is a male gamete produced by the process of meiosis.

Materials
• compound microscope
• prepared slides of lily anther

Answers to Analysis

1. The anther has several chambers. Each chamber contains pollen grains or the cells from which they will develop.
2. Answers will vary depending upon the slide examined.
3. The dividing cells are observed in clusters of up to four in various stages of division. The pollen grains have a textured coat and contain two distinct nuclei.
4. When the pollen fertilizes the egg, the union contains the chromosome number of the typical organism cell.

InquiryLab

🕐 30 min

Pollen Up Close

Pollen is produced in the male reproductive part of a flower called the *anther*. Pollen develops from cells called *microspores*. The mature pollen grain encloses two nuclei. Each nucleus contains half of the number of chromosomes found in most cells of the mature, flower-producing plant.

Procedure

❶ **CAUTION: Handle glass slides with care.** Place a prepared slide of a lily anther on the microscope stage. Examine the slide under low power.

❷ Identify the large chambers called *pollen sacs*. How many can you find in your cross-sectional view? Are they whole or broken? Make a sketch of what you see.

❸ Depending upon the stage of development, the pollen sacs will contain either clustered cells in various stages of division or mature grains of pollen. You can identify a pollen grain by its two stained nuclei and textured coat. Select several representative cells within the pollen sac. Make a sketch of each cell.

Analysis

1. **Describe** the structure of the lily anther.
2. **Determine** whether the observed pollen sacs contain dividing cells, pollen grains, or both.
3. **Describe** the appearance of the nuclei in either the dividing cells or the pollen grains.
4. **Explain** what advantage is achieved by halving the chromosome number in pollen nuclei.

Using Words

1. Check students' work to make sure that they choose appropriate terms. The Chapter Summary page lists all of the key terms for this chapter.

Using Language

1. Meiosis and mitosis are being compared.
2. The Burmese python is being contrasted to other reptiles.

Taking Notes

1. Left-hand column: Tell students that key idea questions are answered in the bold-faced sentences. Example: An individual formed by asexual reproduction is genetically identical to its parent.
2. Right-hand column: Make sure students write notes in this column that correspond to the key ideas in the left column. Example: Organisms such as prokaryotes, starfish, amoebas, hydras, potatoes, and water fleas can reproduce this way. Tell students they may include drawings and diagrams in the right column.

These reading tools can help you learn the material in this chapter. For more information on how to use these and other tools, see **Appendix: Reading and Study Skills.**

Using Words

Key-Term Fold A key-term fold is a useful tool for studying definitions of key terms in a chapter. Each tab can contain a key term on one side and its definition on the other.

Your Turn Make a key-term fold for the terms of this chapter.
1. Fold a sheet of lined notebook paper in half from left to right.
2. Using scissors, cut along every third line from the right edge of the paper to the center fold to make tabs.

Using Language

Comparisons Comparing is a way of looking for the similarities between different things. Contrasting is a way of looking for the differences. Certain words and phrases can help you determine if things are being compared or contrasted. Comparison words include *and, like, just as,* and *in the same way.* Contrast words include *however, unlike, in contrast,* and *on the other hand.*

Your Turn In the following sentences, find the things that are being compared or contrasted.
1. Like mitosis, meiosis is a process that reproduces new cells.
2. In contrast to many other reptiles, the Burmese python does not reproduce sexually.

Taking Notes

Two-Column Notes Two-column notes can help you summarize the key ideas of a topic, chapter, or process. The left column of the table contains key ideas. The right column contains details and examples of each main idea.

Your Turn As you read the chapter, create two-column notes that summarize the key ideas of this chapter.
1. Write the key ideas in the left-hand column. The key ideas are listed in the section openers. Include one key idea in each row.
2. As you read the section, add detailed notes and examples in the right-hand column. Be sure to put these details and examples in your own words.

Meiosis and Sexual Reproduction	
Key Ideas	Details and Examples

Key Ideas

> In asexual reproduction, how does the offspring compare to the parent?

> In sexual reproduction, how does the offspring compare to the parent?

> Why are chromosomes important to an organism?

Key Terms

gamete
zygote
diploid
haploid
homologous chromosomes

Why It Matters

Living organisms produce offspring. How closely the offspring resemble their parents depends on how the organism reproduces.

Reproduction is the process of producing offspring. Some offspring are produced by two parents, and others are produced by just one parent. Some organisms look exactly like their parents, and others look very similar. Whether an organism is identical or similar to its parent is determined by the way that the organism reproduces.

Asexual Reproduction

In *asexual reproduction*, a single parent passes a complete copy of its genetic information to each of its offspring. **> An individual formed by asexual reproduction is genetically identical to its parent.**

Prokaryotes reproduce asexually by a kind of cell division called *binary fission*. Many unicellular eukaryotes also reproduce asexually. Amoebas reproduce by splitting into two or more individuals of about equal size. Some multicellular eukaryotes, such as starfish, go through fragmentation. *Fragmentation* is a kind of reproduction in which the body breaks into several pieces. Some or all of these fragments regrow missing parts and develop into complete adults.

Other animals, such as the hydra shown in **Figure 1,** go through *budding.* In budding, new individuals split off from existing ones. Some plants, such as potatoes, can form whole new plants from parts of stems. Other plants can reproduce from roots or leaves. Some crustaceans, such as water fleas, reproduce by parthenogenesis. *Parthenogenesis* is a process in which a female makes a viable egg that grows into an adult without being fertilized by a male.

> **Reading Check** *What is fragmentation? (See the Appendix for answers to Reading Checks.)*

The Living Environment
Standard 4

2.1c Hereditary information is contained in genes, located in the chromosomes of each cell. An inherited trait of an individual can be determined by one or by many genes, and a single gene can influence more than one trait. A human cell contains many thousands of different genes in its nucleus.

2.1d In asexually reproducing organisms, all the genes come from a single parent. Asexually produced offspring are normally genetically identical to the parent.

2.1e In sexually reproducing organisms, the new individual receives half of the genetic information from its mother (via the egg) and half from its father (via the sperm). Sexually produced offspring often resemble, but are not identical to, either of their parents.

4.1b Some organisms reproduce asexually with all the genetic information coming from one parent. Other organisms reproduce sexually with half the genetic information typically contributed by each parent. Cloning is the production of identical genetic copies.

Figure 1 This hydra is in the process of reproducing asexually. The smaller hydra budding from the parent is genetically identical to the parent.

Key Resources

 Transparencies
B44 Chromosome Number of Various Organisms

Visual Concepts
Sexual Reproduction
Fertilization
Comparing Haploid and Diploid Cells

Teaching Key Ideas

Hermaphroditism Students may be surprised to learn that in certain species, a single animal can sexually reproduce. For example, in some species of nematodes, the organism produces sperm, which are stored until eggs are produced. Egg production is followed by self-fertilization.

Math Skills

Asexual Reproduction in Bacteria
Bacteria can reproduce asexually. The rate of reproduction (time required for a cell to divide) varies from minutes to hours. Have students use the rate of 15 minutes to calculate the number of bacteria produced from a single bacterium after each hour for 6 hours. (After hour 1, 16 bacteria; after hour 2, 256 bacteria; after hour 3, 4,096 bacteria; after hour 4, 65,536 bacteria; after hour 5, 1,048,576 bacteria; after hour 6, 16,777,216 bacteria) Tell students that at this rate, Earth would quickly be covered with bacteria. Ask students why this doesn't happen. (Ideal growth conditions for bacteria seldom occur in nature for very long.) **LS** **Logical**

Answers to Caption Questions
Figure 2: Germ cells produce gametes.

> **gamete** (GAM eet) a haploid reproductive cell that unites with another haploid reproductive cell to form a zygote
>
> **zygote** (ZIE GOHT) the cell that results from the fusion of gametes
>
> **diploid** a cell that contains two haploid sets of chromosomes
>
> **haploid** describes a cell, nucleus, or organism that has only one set of unpaired chromosomes
>
> **homologous chromosomes** (hoh MAHL uh guhs) chromosomes that have the same sequence of genes, that have the same structure, and that pair during meiosis

SCI*LINKS.*
www.scilinks.org
Topic: Sexual and Asexual Reproduction
Code: HX81386

Figure 2 Two gametes, an egg and a sperm, combine during fertilization to form a zygote. ⟩ **What types of cells produce gametes?**

Sexual Reproduction

Most eukaryotic organisms reproduce sexually. ⟩ In *sexual reproduction*, two parents give genetic material to produce offspring that are genetically different from their parents. Each parent produces a reproductive cell, called a **gamete.** A gamete from one parent fuses with a gamete from the other parent, as **Figure 2** shows. The resulting cell, called a **zygote,** has a combination of genetic material from both parents. This process is called *fertilization.* Because both parents give genetic material, the offspring has traits of both parents but is not exactly like either parent.

Germ Cells and Somatic Cells Recall that the cells of a multi-cellular organism are often specialized for certain functions. Muscle cells, for example, contract and move your body. Cells that are specialized for sexual reproduction are called *germ cells.* Only germ cells can produce gametes. Other body cells are called *somatic cells.* Somatic cells do not participate in sexual reproduction.

Advantages of Sexual Reproduction Asexual reproduction is the simplest, most efficient method of reproduction. Asexual reproduction allows organisms to produce many offspring in a short period of time without using energy to make gametes or to find a mate. But the genetic material of these organisms varies little between individuals, so they may be at a disadvantage in a changing environment. Sexual reproduction, in contrast, produces genetically diverse individuals. A population of diverse organisms is more likely to have some individuals that survive a major environmental change.

Chromosome Number

Genes are located on chromosomes. ⟩ Each chromosome has thousands of genes that play an important role in determining how an organism develops and functions. Each species has a characteristic number of chromosomes. As shown in **Figure 3,** mosquitoes have only 6 chromosomes in each cell. Chimpanzees have 48 chromosomes in each cell. Some ferns have more than 500! An organism must have exactly the right number of chromosomes. If an organism has too many or too few chromosomes, the organism may not develop and function properly.

In humans, each cell has two copies of 23 chromosomes for a total of 46. When fertilization happens, two cells combine to form a zygote, which still has only 46 chromosomes. Why is the number the same? The gametes that form a zygote have only *one* copy of each chromosome, or one set of 23 chromosomes. This reduction of chromosomes in gametes keeps the chromosome number of human somatic cells at a constant 46.

⟩ **Reading Check** *What kind of cells do germ cells produce?*

Differentiated Instruction

Basic Learners

Advantages and Disadvantages Ask students to explain the difference between asexual and sexual reproduction. During discussion, lead students to realize that both types of reproduction have advantages and disadvantages depending on the species involved and the environment it inhabits. Pose the following question:

"If all members of a species were genetically identical, what would happen if a fatal virus spread through the population?" (All members of the species would most likely be wiped out.) **LS** **Logical**

Haploid and Diploid Cells A cell, such as a somatic cell, that has two sets of chromosomes is **diploid**. A cell is **haploid** if it has one set of chromosomes. Gametes are haploid cells. The symbol n is used to represent the number of chromosomes in one set. Human gametes have 23 chromosomes, so $n = 23$. The diploid number in somatic cells is written as $2n$. Human somatic cells have 46 chromosomes ($2n = 46$).

Homologous Chromosomes Each diploid cell has pairs of chromosomes made up of two homologous chromosomes. **Homologous chromosomes** are chromosomes that are similar in size, in shape, and in kinds of genes that they contain. Each chromosome in a homologous pair comes from one of the two parents. In humans, one set of 23 chromosomes comes from the mother, and one set comes from the father. Homologous chromosomes can carry different forms of genes. For example, flower color in peas is determined by a gene on one of its chromosomes. The form of this gene can be white or purple. The cells of each pea plant will have two flower-color genes, one on each of the chromosomes that carry the flower-color gene. Both could be genes for white flower color, or both could be genes for purple flower color. Or one gene could be for white color, and the other could be for purple color.

Autosomes and Sex Chromosomes *Autosomes* are chromosomes with genes that do not determine the sex of an individual. *Sex chromosomes* have genes that determine the sex of an individual. In humans and many other organisms, the two sex chromosomes are referred to as the *X* and *Y chromosomes*. The genes that cause a zygote to develop into a male are located on the Y chromosome. Human males have one X chromosome and one Y chromosome (XY), and human females have two X chromosomes (XX).

Chromosome Number of Various Organisms	
Organism	Number ($2n$) of chromosomes
Penicillium	1–4
Saccharomyces (yeast)	16
Mosquito	6
Housefly	12
Garden pea	14
Corn	20
Fern	480–1,020
Frog	26
Human	46
Orangutan	48
Dog	78

Figure 3
Different species have different numbers of chromosomes.

READING TOOLBOX

Key-Term Fold On the back of your key-term fold, write a definition in your own words for the key terms in this section.

Section 1 Review

> **KEY IDEAS**

1. **Compare** the offspring in asexual reproduction with the parent.
2. **Describe** how the offspring in sexual reproduction compares genetically with its parent.
3. **Compare** the number of sets of chromosomes between a haploid cell and a diploid cell.
4. **Explain** why chromosomes are important for organisms.

CRITICAL THINKING

5. **Inferring Relationships** Why are haploid cells important in sexual reproduction?
6. **Forming Reasoned Opinions** Do you agree or disagree that homologous chromosomes occur in gametes? Explain.

METHODS OF SIENCE

7. **Evaluating Hypotheses** A student states that organisms that reproduce asexually are at a disadvantage in a stable environment. If you agree with this hypothesis, name one or more of its strengths. If you disagree, name one or more of its weaknesses.

Answers to Section Review

1. The offspring is genetically identical to its parent.
2. The offspring is genetically different from its parents.
3. A haploid cell has half the number of sets of chromosomes as a diploid cell.
4. Chromosomes contain the genes needed for the organism to develop and function.
5. Haploid cells provide offspring with half the genetic material from one parent and the other half of their genetic material from the other parent. This makes the offspring different from its parents and its siblings.
6. Students should disagree. Homologous chromosomes are pairs of similar chromosomes. Because gametes are haploid, they contain only one set of chromosomes. Thus, homologous chromosomes are not normally found in gametes.
7. Most students should disagree. In a stable environment, asexual reproduction allows organisms to produce offspring without using energy to produce gametes or to find a mate.

Section
2 Meiosis

› Focus

This section explains the process of meiosis, the difference between meiosis and mitosis, and the three mechanisms of genetic variation that can result from meiosis.

Bellringer

Use the Bellringer transparency to prepare students for this section.

› Teach

Demonstration

Counting Chromosomes On the board, draw a sperm cell near an egg cell. Draw three homologous chromosome pairs in each cell. Tell students that when the sperm fertilizes the egg, the number of chromosomes in the resulting cell, the new individual, will be double the number in either the egg or the sperm cell. Lead students to the conclusion that the number of chromosomes in sperm and egg cells must be halved, or the number of chromosomes in each subsequent generation will continue to double. Tell students that the process by which the chromosome number is halved when reproductive cells are formed is called meiosis. **LS Visual**

Key Ideas	Key Terms	Why It Matters
› What occurs during the stages of meiosis? › How does the function of mitosis differ from the function of meiosis? › What are three mechanisms of genetic variation?	meiosis crossing-over independent assortment	Meiosis allows genetic information from two parents to combine to form offspring that are different from both parents.

The Living Environment
Standard 4
2.1e In sexually reproducing organisms, the new individual receives half of the genetic information from its mother (via the egg) and half from its father (via the sperm). Sexually produced offspring often resemble, but are not identical to, either of their parents.
3.1c Mutation and the sorting and recombining of genes during meiosis and fertilization result in a great variety of possible gene combinations.
4.1c The processes of meiosis and fertilization are key to sexual reproduction in a wide variety of organisms. The process of meiosis results in the production of eggs and sperm which each contain half of the genetic information. During fertilization, gametes unite to form a zygote, which contains the complete genetic information for the offspring.

Most cells that divide and produce new cells form two offspring cells that have the same number of chromosomes as the parent cell. How do haploid gametes form from a diploid germ cell? **Meiosis** is a form of cell division that produces daughter cells with half the number of chromosomes that are in the parent cell.

Stages of Meiosis

Before meiosis begins, the chromosomes in the original cell are copied. Meiosis involves two divisions of the nucleus—meiosis I and meiosis II. › **During meiosis, a diploid cell goes through two divisions to form four haploid cells.** In meiosis I, homologous chromosomes are separated. In meiosis II, the sister chromatids of each homologue are separated. As a result, four haploid cells are formed from the original diploid cell. **Figure 4** illustrates the steps of meiosis.

Stages of Meiosis I

① Prophase I
Chromosomes condense. The nuclear envelope breaks down.

② Metaphase I
Pairs of homologous chromosomes move to the cell's equator.

③ Anaphase I
Homologous chromosomes move to the cell's opposite poles.

④ Telophase I
Chromosomes gather at the poles. The cytoplasm divides.

Spindle

Homologous chromosomes

Section Correlations
4.2.1e
4.3.1c
4.4.1c

Key Resources

 Transparencies
B49 Stages of Meiosis
B51 Meiosis in Male and Female Animals

 Visual Concepts
Meiosis
Tetrads and Crossing-over of Genetic Material
Independent Assortment
Formation of a Sperm
Formation of an Egg Cell
Comparing the Results of Meiosis and Mitosis
Comparing Meiosis and Mitosis

Meiosis I Meiosis begins with a diploid cell that has copied its chromosomes. The first phase is prophase I. ❶ During prophase I, the chromosomes condense, and the nuclear envelope breaks down. Homologous chromosomes pair. Chromatids exchange genetic material in a process called **crossing-over.** ❷ In metaphase I, the spindle moves the pairs of homologous chromosomes to the equator of the cell. The homologous chromosomes remain together. ❸ In anaphase I, the homologous chromosomes separate. The spindle fibers pull the chromosomes of each pair to opposite poles of the cell. But the chromatids do not separate at their centromeres. Each chromosome is still made of two chromatids. The genetic material, however, has recombined. ❹ During telophase I, the cytoplasm divides (cytokinesis), and two new cells are formed. Both cells have one chromosome from each pair of homologous chromosomes.

Meiosis II Meiosis II begins with the two cells formed at the end of telophase I of meiosis I. The chromosomes are not copied between meiosis I and meiosis II. ❺ In prophase II, new spindles form. ❻ During metaphase II, the chromosomes line up along the equators and are attached at their centromeres to spindle fibers. ❼ In anaphase II, the centromeres divide. The chromatids, which are now called *chromosomes,* move to opposite poles of the cell. ❽ During telophase II, a nuclear envelope forms around each set of chromosomes. The spindle breaks down, and the cell goes through cytokinesis. The result of meiosis is four haploid cells.

❯ **Reading Check** *In what phase of meiosis is genetic material exchanged?*

meiosis a process in cell division during which the number of chromosomes decreases to half the original number by two divisions of the nucleus, which results in the production of sex cells (gametes or spores)

crossing-over the exchange of genetic material between homologous chromosomes during meiosis

Figure 4 During meiosis, four haploid cells are produced from a diploid cell.
❯ *What is the difference between anaphase I and anaphase II?*

go.hrw.com
✴ **interact online**
Keyword: HX8MEIF4

Stages of Meiosis II

❺ **Prophase II**
A new spindle forms around the chromosomes.

❻ **Metaphase II**
Chromosomes line up at the equators.

❼ **Anaphase II**
Centromeres divide, and chromatids move to opposite poles.

❽ **Telophase II**
A nuclear envelope forms around each set of chromosomes. The cells divide.

Differentiated Instruction

Struggling Readers

Counting Chromosomes Have students look at the first cell at the left in **Figure 4.** Ask them how many chromosomes are in the cell. Some will answer "four" while others may say "eight." Tell students that as long as chromatids are connected by a centromere they are considered a single chromosome. As soon as the chromatid pairs separate, they are considered two separate chromosomes. The first cell in **Figure 4** has four chromosomes, and the final four cells, on the far right, each have two chromosomes. **LS** Visual

MISCONCEPTION ///ALERT\\\

Which Organisms Use Sexual Reproduction?
Students may think that animals are the only organisms that reproduce sexually. Remind students that many plants, fungi, and algae also reproduce sexually. Point out that a flower, for example, may contain both sperm and egg cells.

Teaching Key Ideas

Meiosis Timeframe In human males, meiosis and sperm production take about 9 weeks. It's a continuous process that begins at puberty. In females, meiosis and egg production begin before birth. The process stops abruptly, however, and does not resume until a female enters puberty. Until a female reaches menopause, one egg each month resumes meiosis and finishes its development. Therefore, the meiosis of a single egg may take up to 50 years to complete!

Teaching Key Ideas

Sequencing Have students list each of the stages of meiosis I and II on an index card. Have students shuffle the cards. With their books closed, students should draw the process described on each card. After the drawings are complete, have students trade illustrated cards with a partner and place those cards in the correct sequence. **LS** Verbal/Visual

go.hrw.com
✴ **interact online**

Students can interact with "Stages of Meiosis" by going to go.hrw.com and typing in the keyword **HX8MEIF4**.

Answers to Caption Questions

Figure 4: In anaphase I, homologous chromosomes move to opposite poles of the cell. In anaphase II, the centromeres divide and the chromatids move to opposite poles.

READING TOOLBOX

Comparisons

1. Both meiosis and mitosis are processes that result in new cells.

2. Meiosis and mitosis both have a metaphase stage.

1. Mitosis produces two diploid cells; in contrast, meiosis produces four haploid cells.

2. Mitosis produces genetically identical cells; in contrast, meiosis results in genetically different cells.

Why It Matters

Development in Eggs Stanford University researchers recently discovered how sperm-egg contact initiates development in sea urchins. Sea urchin sperm contain an enzyme called nitric oxide synthase that becomes active a few seconds before fertilization. The enzyme quickly causes the production of a large amount of nitric oxide gas, which is injected into the egg once the sperm and egg make contact. The injection of this gas triggers the release of calcium inside the egg. As the calcium levels rise, metabolic changes cause the egg to divide and form into an embryo.

Answers to Caption Questions

Figure 5: Centromeres divide during the anaphase of mitosis. Centromeres do not divide in anaphase I of meiosis I.

READING TOOLBOX

Comparisons Write two sentences that compare and two sentences that contrast meiosis and mitosis.

Figure 5 Mitosis produces two diploid daughter cells that are identical to the parent cell. Meiosis produces four haploid cells from a diploid cell. ❯ *What is the difference between anaphase in mitosis and anaphase I in meiosis I?*

Comparing Mitosis and Meiosis

The processes of mitosis and meiosis are similar but meet different needs and have different results. ❯ Mitosis makes new cells that are used during growth, development, repair, and asexual reproduction. Meiosis makes cells that enable an organism to reproduce sexually and happens only in reproductive structures. Mitosis produces two genetically identical diploid cells. In contrast, meiosis produces four genetically different haploid cells. The haploid cells produced by meiosis contain half the genetic information of the parent cell. When two such cells, often an egg cell and a sperm cell, combine, the resulting zygote has the same number of chromosomes as each of the parents' cells.

If you compare meiosis and mitosis, as shown in **Figure 5**, you may think that they are alike. For example, in metaphase of mitosis and metaphase I of meiosis, the chromosomes move to the equator. However, there is a major difference that happens in an earlier stage.

In prophase I of meiosis, every chromosome pairs with its homologue. A pair of homologous chromosomes is called a *tetrad*. As the tetrads form, different homologues exchange parts of their chromatids in the process of crossing-over. The pairing of homologous chromosomes and the crossing-over do not happen in mitosis. Therefore, a main difference between meiosis and mitosis is that in meiosis, genetic information is rearranged. The rearranging of genetic information leads to genetic variation in offspring. Crossing-over is one of several processes that lead to genetic variation.

❯ **Reading Check** *How are cells formed by mitosis different from cells formed by meiosis in relation to number of chromosomes?*

Comparing Mitosis and Meiosis

Mitosis — Prophase, Metaphase, Anaphase, Telophase → 2 identical diploid cells

Meiosis — Prophase I, Metaphase I, Anaphase I, Telophase I, Meiosis II → 4 nonidentical haploid cells

Differentiated Instruction

Special Education Students

Modeling Meiosis Have students work in groups of four. Give each group 32 beads of one color (red, for example) and 32 of a contrasting color (blue, for example). Give each group four 4-inch sections of pipe cleaner to act as centromeres. Have students make two 6-bead red strands. Attach with a pipe cleaner. This represents a chromosome with 2 chromatids. Make two 6-bead blue strands and attach these together. This represents the homologous chromosome. Make two 10-bead blue strands and

attach together, and two 10-bead red strands. Ask what the diploid number is for this cell. (4) Have students show the process of meiosis. Crossing-over can be demonstrated by removing two beads at the ends of non-sister chromatids (having opposite colors) and switching them. When finished, the four gametes should each have one long and one short chromosome with varying crossover patterns. Blind and visually impaired students can use different sizes of beads. **LS Kinesthetic**

QuickLab

⏱ 30 min

Crossing-Over Model

You can use paper strips and pencils to model the process of crossing-over.

Homologous chromosomes

Procedure

❶ Use a colored pencil to write "A" and "B" on two paper strips. These two strips will represent one of the two homologous chromosomes shown.

❷ Use a second colored pencil to write "a" and "b" on two paper strips. These two strips will represent the second homologous chromosome shown.

❸ **CAUTION: Handle scissors with care.** Use your chromosome models, scissors, and tape to demonstrate crossing-over between two chromatids.

Analysis

1. **Determine** what the letters A, B, a, and b represent.

2. **Explain** why the chromosomes that you made are homologous.

3. **Compare** the number of different types of chromatids (combinations of A, B, a, and b) before crossing-over with the number after crossing-over.

4. **CRITICAL THINKING Analyzing Information** How does crossing-over relate to genetic recombination?

Genetic Variation

Genetic variation is advantageous for a population. Genetic variation can help a population survive a major environmental change. For example, in the Arctic, if temperatures drop below average, those polar bears with genes that make thicker fur will survive. Polar bears without the genes for thicker fur may die out. The polar bears with the genes for thicker fur reproduce, and the population grows. Now, suppose that all of the individuals in the population have the same genes, but none of the genes are for thicker fur. What do you think will happen if the temperature drops below average? The entire population of polar bears may die out.

Genetic variation is made possible by sexual reproduction. In sexual reproduction, existing genes are rearranged. Meiosis is the process that makes the rearranging of genes possible. Fusion of haploid cells from two different individuals adds further variation.

❯ Three key contributions to genetic variation are crossing-over, independent assortment, and random fertilization.

Crossing-Over During prophase I, homologous chromosomes line up next to each other. Each homologous chromosome is made of two sister chromatids attached at the centromere. Crossing-over happens when one arm of a chromatid crosses over the arm of the other chromatid, as illustrated in the QuickLab. The chromosomes break at the point of the crossover, and each chromatid re-forms its full length with the piece from the other chromosome. Thus, the sister chromatids of a homologous chromosome no longer have identical genetic information.

❯ **Reading Check** How can crossing-over increase genetic variation?

SCLINKS

www.scilinks.org
Topic: Genetic Variation
Code: HX80658

ACADEMIC VOCABULARY

exist to occur or be present

QuickLab

Teacher's Notes Prepare the paper strips before assigning the lab.

Materials
• colored pencils, different colors (2)
• paper
• scissors
• tape

Answers to Analysis

1. individual genes

2. The chromosomes are of similar size, shape, and genetic content.

3. before crossing-over: AB, AB ab, and ab; after crossing over: answers will vary (for example, AB, Ab, aB, and ab)

4. Crossing-over causes genetic recombination.

Teaching Key Ideas

Crossing-Over Model Have students look at the diagram of the two homologous chromosomes in the Quick Lab. Point out that the two green strands attached together by a centromere are called *sister chromatids*. Ask students how sister chromatids compare genetically. (They are identical.) The green and blue chromatids are known as *non-sister chromatids*. Ask students what would happen to the genetic makeup of a chromosome if crossing-over occurred between sister chromatids. (Because sister chromatids are copies of each other, the genetic makeup would not change.)

LS Visual

Differentiated Instruction

Basic Learners

Crossing-Over Draw two large chromosomes on the board with colored chalk. Each chromosome should have two chromatids and a centromere. Use different colors along the length of each chromatid to represent genes. Ask volunteers to show crossing-over in two different places by erasing and redrawing the chromosomes with the corresponding gene color. Point out that because of the random orientation of chromosomes at metaphase I and because of crossing-over, children resemble their parents but never look exactly like them. **LS Interpersonal**

Advanced Learners/GATE

Genetic Variation Have interested students research genetic variation in a population of their choice and report their findings to the class. **LS Verbal**

Teaching Key Ideas

Distinguishing Between Mitosis and Meiosis Have students make a graphic organizer using **Figure 5** to summarize the difference in chromosomal number between mitosis and meiosis. Ask students to include a brief paragraph that compares the two processes. **LS** **Logical**

> **Close**

Formative Assessment

Which type of cell might only result from mitosis?

A. egg cell (Incorrect. Egg cells result from meiosis.)

B. sperm cell (Incorrect. Sperm cells result from meiosis.)

C. germ cell (Incorrect. Germ cells also result from meiosis.)

D. somatic cell (Correct! Somatic cells are non-sexual cells that could result from mitosis.)

Figure 6 The same cell is shown twice. Because each pair of homologous chromosomes separates independently, four different gametes can result in each case.

Possibility 1

The arrangement of chromosomes in each of these cells is equally probable.

Possibility 2

Metaphase of meiosis I

Metaphase of meiosis II

These gametes show different possible combinations.

independent assortment the random distribution of the pairs of genes on different chromosomes to the gametes

Independent Assortment During metaphase I, homologous pairs of chromosomes line up at the equator of the cell. The two pairs of chromosomes can line up in either of two equally probable ways. This random distribution of homologous chromosomes during meiosis is called **independent assortment.** The four haploid cells formed in possibility 1 in **Figure 6** have entirely different combinations of chromosomes than do the four cells made in possibility 2.

In humans, each gamete receives one chromosome from each of 23 pairs of homologous chromosomes. Each of the 23 pairs of chromosomes separates independently. Thus, 2^{23} (about 8 million) gametes with different gene combinations can be made from one original cell.

Random Fertilization Fertilization is a random process that adds genetic variation. The zygote that forms is made by the random joining of two gametes. Because fertilization of an egg by a sperm is random, the number of possible outcomes is *squared.* In humans, the possibility is $2^{23} \times 2^{23}$, or 64 trillion, different combinations!

Section 2 Review

> KEY IDEAS

1. **Summarize** the different phases of meiosis.
2. **Explain** how the function of meiosis differs from the function of mitosis.
3. **Describe** three mechanisms of genetic variation.

CRITICAL THINKING

4. **Comparing Functions** Compare the processes of crossing-over and independent assortment. How does each contribute to genetic variation?
5. **Inferring Conclusions** Why might sexual reproducers better adapt to a changing environment than asexual reproducers?

ALTERNATIVE ASSESSMENT

6. **Word Problem** If one cell in a dog (2n = 78) undergoes meiosis and another cell undergoes mitosis, how many chromosomes will each resulting cell contain?

Answers to Section Review

1. Students' answers should be consistent with the stages in **Figure 4.**

2. Mitosis produces new cells that are used during growth, development, repair, and asexual reproduction. Meiosis produces cells that enable an organism to reproduce sexually, and it occurs only in reproductive structures.

3. crossing-over, independent assortment, and random fertilization

4. Crossing-over occurs when the arms of two chromatids exchange genetic material. This process leads to genetic variation among the chromosomes. Independent assortment is the random distribution of homologous chromosomes during meiosis. This process leads to further genetic variation in the gametes formed from meiosis.

5. Meiosis leads to the rearranging of genes, which leads to genetic variation throughout a species. Genetic variation ensures individuals throughout a species have different traits. Varied traits give a species an advantage in surviving and producing more offspring. This is the mechanism necessary for evolution to occur.

6. The cells resulting from meiosis will contain 39 chromosomes each. The cells resulting from mitosis will contain 78 chromosomes each.

Girls, Girls, Girls

WEIRD SCIENCE

Did you know that some species, such as the predatory brush cricket to the right, and the lupin aphid below, have only females? These species, with only females, reproduce asexually.

Parthenogenesis

In animals, the process of a female producing an egg that can grow into a new individual without being fertilized by a male is called *parthenogenesis*. The major advantage of parthenogenesis is that every individual can reproduce and the population can grow quickly. The disadvantage is that every individual has the same genes. The animals may not have the genes that produce the traits that are necessary for adaptation. If a species cannot adapt, it could become extinct.

Apomixis Asexual reproduction in plants in which embryos develop in the absence of fertilization by pollen is called *apomixis*. There are more than 300 apomictic plant species, such as dandelions. Apomictic plants still produce seeds, and the offspring are genetically identical to the mother plant.

New Discovery Until recently, scientists believed that all snakes reproduced sexually. However, this Burmese python is parthenogenetic. Scientists discovered that the Burmese python was parthenogenetic only after an isolated female in a zoo had offspring.

Research Some species of mango and of cereals are apomictic. Conduct Internet research, and investigate how these species can benefit humans.

Multicellular Life Cycles

Key Ideas	Key Terms	Why It Matters
❯ What is a diploid life cycle? ❯ What is a haploid life cycle? ❯ What is alternation of generations?	life cycle sperm ovum	Some life cycles are mainly diploid, others are mainly haploid, and still others alternate between haploid and diploid phases.

 The Living Environment
Standard 4
2.1e In sexually reproducing organisms, the new individual receives half of the genetic information from its mother (via the egg) and half from its father (via the sperm). Sexually produced offspring often resemble, but are not identical to, either of their parents.
4.1b Some organisms reproduce asexually with all the genetic information coming from one parent. Other organisms reproduce sexually with half the genetic information typically contributed by each parent. Cloning is the production of identical genetic copies.
4.1c The processes of meiosis and fertilization are key to sexual reproduction in a wide variety of organisms. The process of meiosis results in the production of eggs and sperm which each contain half of the genetic information. During fertilization, gametes unite to form a zygote, which contains the complete genetic information for the offspring.

Figure 7 Humans and most other animals have a life cycle dominated by a diploid individual. ❯ *What are the only haploid cells in a diploid life cycle?*

life cycle all of the events in the growth and development of an organism until the organism reaches sexual maturity

sperm the male gamete (sex cell)

ovum a mature egg cell

All of the events in the growth and development of an organism until the organism reaches sexual maturity are called a **life cycle.** All organisms that reproduce sexually have both diploid stages and haploid stages.

Diploid Life Cycle

Most animals have a diploid life cycle. **Figure 7** illustrates this type of life cycle. Most of the life cycle is spent in the diploid state. All of the cells except the gametes are diploid.

A diploid germ cell in a reproductive organ goes through meiosis and forms gametes. The gametes, the sperm and the egg, join during fertilization. The result is a diploid zygote. This single diploid cell goes through mitosis and eventually gives rise to all of the cells of the adult, which are also diploid. ❯ **In diploid life cycles, meiosis in germ cells of a multicellular diploid organism results in the formation of haploid gametes.**

Diploid Life Cycle

Adult male   Adult female   Baby

Meiosis   Mitosis

Sperm   Egg

Fertilization   Zygote

Key Resources

Transparencies
B48 Diploid Life Cycle
F13 Haploid Life Cycle
G5 Alternation of Generations

Visual Concepts
Comparing Haploid and Diploid Cells
Alternation of Generations

Meiosis and Gamete Formation

Male animals produce gametes called **sperm**. As **Figure 8** illustrates, a diploid germ cell goes through meiosis I. Two cells are formed, each of which goes through meiosis II. The result is four haploid cells. The four cells change in form and develop a tail to form four sperm.

Female animals produce gametes called eggs, or ova (singular, **ovum**). A diploid germ cell begins to divide by meiosis. Meiosis I results in the formation of two haploid cells that have unequal amounts of cytoplasm. One of the cells has nearly all of the cytoplasm. The other cell, called a *polar body*, is very small and has a small amount of cytoplasm. The polar body may divide again, but its offspring cells will not survive. The larger cell goes through meiosis II, and the division of the cell's cytoplasm is again unequal. The larger cell develops into an ovum. The smaller cell, the second polar body, dies. Because of its larger share of cytoplasm, the mature ovum has a rich storehouse of nutrients. These nutrients nourish the young organism that develops if the ovum is fertilized.

❯ **Reading Check** *How many gametes are formed from one female germ cell?*

Figure 8 Meiosis of diploid germ cells results in haploid gametes.

Meiosis in Male and Female Animals

Spermatogenesis

Diploid germ cell

Meiosis I

Meiosis II

Haploid cells

Sperm

Oogenesis

Diploid germ cell

Haploid cell

Haploid polar bodies (All 3 will die.)

Ovum

READING TOOLBOX

Two-Column Notes Advise students to use the text to help them write the steps shown in **Figure 9,** and then to use the figure to organize their notes into two columns.

Teaching Key Ideas

Using Models Remind students that **Figure 9** is another form of a life cycle diagram. The illustration shows a generic model, meaning that it reflects a process for most haploid organisms without being specific to any. Ask the following: "Why is there a line down the middle of each cycle?" (to separate the diploid and haploid stages) "What is misleading about the placement of the line?" (It conveys the idea that each stage is about equal in the organism's life span.)

Close

Formative Assessment

All of the following are haploid cells in the alternation of generations cycle except _____.

A. a gametophyte (Incorrect! A gametophyte is haploid.)

B. a gamete (Incorrect. A gamete is haploid.)

C. a spore (Incorrect. A spore is haploid.)

D. a zygote (Correct! The zygote is a fertilized egg, so it is diploid.)

Figure 9 Some organisms, such as fungi, have haploid cells as a major portion of their life cycles.

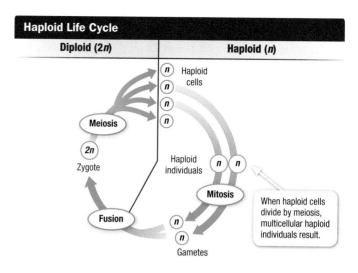

READING TOOLBOX

Two-column notes Use two-column notes to summarize the stages and details of the haploid life cycle.

Haploid Life Cycle

The haploid life cycle, shown in **Figure 9,** happens in most fungi and some protists. Haploid stages make up the major part of this life cycle. The zygote, the only diploid structure, goes through meiosis immediately after it is formed and makes new haploid cells. The haploid cells divide by mitosis and give rise to multicellular haploid individuals. ❯ In haploid life cycles, meiosis in a diploid zygote results in the formation of the first cell of a multicellular haploid individual.

Alternation of Generations

❯ Plants and most multicellular protists have a life cycle that alternates between a haploid phase and a diploid phase called *alternation of generations.* In plants, the multicellular diploid phase in the life cycle is called a *sporophyte*. Spore-forming cells in the sporophyte undergo meiosis and produce spores. A spore forms a multicellular gametophyte. The *gametophyte* is the haploid phase that produces gametes by mitosis. The gametes fuse and give rise to the diploid phase.

Section
3 Review

❯ KEY IDEAS

1. **Summarize** the process in a diploid life cycle.
2. **Describe** what happens in a haploid life cycle.
3. **Describe** what happens to the polar bodies formed during meiosis of a female diploid cell in animal.
4. **Explain** the alternation of generations life cycle.

CRITICAL THINKING

5. **Evaluating Processes** How does the formation of sperm through meiosis of a diploid germ cell differ from the formation of an ovum from a diploid germ cell?
6. **Analyzing Information** What type of cell or structure is the first stage of every sexual life cycle?

WRITING IN SCIENCE

7. **Lesson Plan** Write a lesson plan that you can use to teach a classmate the difference between a haploid and a diploid life cycle. In your own words, write a summary of each. Include diagrams with your explanation.

Answers to Section Review

1. In the diploid life cycle, meiosis in germ cells of a multicellular diploid organism results in the formation of haploid gametes.
2. In haploid life cycles, meiosis in a diploid zygote results in the formation of the first cell of a multicellular haploid individual.
3. The polar bodies have very little cytoplasm and disintegrate.
4. Plants and most multicellular protists have a life cycle that alternates between a haploid phase and a diploid phase.

5. Because meiosis in oogenesis produces cells with unequal amounts of cytoplasm, only one gamete is formed. However, in spermatogenesis, four gametes are produced.
6. A zygote is the first stage in all sexual reproductive life cycles.
7. Students' lesson plans should include a presentation and comparison of haploid and diploid life cycles. Diagrams of the two cycles should be included.

Chapter 11 Lab 4.4.1c

🕐 45 min

Lab

Objectives

▶ Model the stages of meiosis.

▶ Describe the events that occur in each stage of the process of meiosis.

▶ Compare your meiosis model to meiosis stages in a set of prepared slides of lily anther microsporocytes.

Materials

- beads, wooden (40)
- index cards (8)
- marker
- microscope
- microscope slides of lilium anther, 1st and 2nd meiotic division
- scissors
- tape, masking
- yarn

Safety

Meiosis Model

In this laboratory, you will work with a partner to develop a meiosis model. You will also have the opportunity to compare your model to the stages of meiosis found in the sacs of a lily anther.

Procedure

Build a Model

1 Work in a team of two. Review the stages of meiosis I and meiosis II. Note the structures and organization that are characteristic of each stage. Pay particular attention to the appearance and behavior of the chromosomes.

2 Work with your partner to design a model of a cell by using the materials listed for this lab. Select and assign a different material to represent each cell structure and keep this consistent in all models. Have your teacher approve the plan.

3 Label each of eight index cards with a specific stage of meiosis, such as "Prophase II."

4 Using your model plan that you designed in step 2, you or your partner will construct a set of models representing the four stages of meiosis I. The other team member will construct another set of models representing the four stages of meiosis II.

5 Once you have completed your set of models, position the cards in two horizontal rows. The top row illustrates the stages of meiosis I. The bottom row illustrates the stages of meiosis II. Compare and contrast the corresponding stages.

Observe Meiosis

6 ◈ **CAUTION: Handle glass slides with care.** Obtain a set of prepared slides of lily anther microsporocytes that include a variety of meiotic stages.

7 Use your microscope to view each slide. Locate the various stages of meiosis within the anther sacs.

8 Compare what you observe in the prepared slides to the models that you have constructed.

Analyze and Conclude

1. **Analyzing Processes** Identify and label each stage of meiosis as a haploid stage or a diploid stage.

2. **Comparing Functions** How does anaphase I differ from anaphase II?

3. **SCIENTIFIC METHODS** **Critiquing Models** Based upon the observations of real cells, evaluate your model. How would you improve your model?

Time Required

One 45-minute lab period

Ratings

| EASY | | | → HARD |

Teacher Prep 🧪🧪
Student Setup 🧪
Concept Level 🧪🧪
Cleanup 🧪🧪

Safety Caution

Review all safety symbols with students before beginning the lab.

Tips and Tricks

Review the stages of meiosis before beginning the lab. If students have difficulty building their models, ask the following questions to guide them:

1. Which of these materials would make the best cell membrane? (yarn)
2. Which would make the best spindle fibers? (yarn)
3. Which would make the best chromosomes? (pipe cleaners)
4. Which would make the best centromeres? (beads)

Emphasize that each pair of chromatids represents one chromosome. Be sure students show that homologous chromosomes pair during metaphase I of meiosis.

Answers to Analyze and Conclude

1. Refer students to **Figure 4** and **Figure 8** for help identifying the different stages. Within meiosis I and meiosis II but prior to telophase II, the cell is in the diploid state. At the end of telophase II, the haploid state is formed.

2. In anaphase I, chromosomes are pulled to opposite sides of the cell. In anaphase II, chromosomes are separated into chromatids, which are each pulled to opposite sides of the cell.

3. Students may suggest using different materials.

Lab Correlations

4.4.1c The processes of meiosis and fertilization are key to sexual reproduction in a wide variety of organisms. The process of meiosis results in the production of eggs and sperm which each contain half of the genetic information. During fertilization, gametes unite to form a zygote, which contains the complete genetic information for the offspring.

Key Resources

 Holt Lab Generator

 Lab Datasheet (Levels A, B, C)

 Holt Science Biology Video Labs

 Virtual Investigations

Reteaching Key Ideas

Asexual Reproduction Models Have students draw their own interpretations of binary fission, fragmentation, budding, and parthenogenesis. Student drawings should indicate why the offspring is genetically identical to the parent. **LS Visual**

Meiosis Ask students to describe the outcome of a meiotic process where one set of homologous chromosomes does not separate during anaphase I. (Two of the four cells would have an extra pair of chromosomes; the other two cells would have one less pair of chromosomes than is normal.) **LS Verbal**

Organizing Concepts Have students construct a graphic organizer that compares and contrasts the diploid life cycle, haploid life cycle, and alternation of generations. **LS Visual**

Key Ideas	Key Terms

1 Reproduction

> An individual formed by asexual reproduction is genetically identical to its parent.

> In sexual reproduction, two parents give genetic material to produce offspring that are genetically different from their parents.

> Each chromosome has thousands of genes that play an important role in determining how an organism develops and functions.

Key Terms

gamete (248)
zygote (248)
diploid (249)
haploid (249)
homologous chromosomes (249)

2 Meiosis

> During meiosis, a diploid cell goes through two divisions to form four haploid cells.

> Mitosis produces cells that are used during growth, development, repair, and asexual reproduction. Meiosis makes cells that enable an organism to reproduce sexually and it only happens in reproductive structures.

> Three key contributions to genetic variation are crossing-over, independent assortment, and random fertilization.

meiosis (250)
crossing-over (251)
independent assortment (254)

3 Multicellular Life Cycles

> In diploid life cycles, meiosis in germ cells of a multicellular diploid organism results in the formation of haploid gametes.

> In haploid life cycles, meiosis in a diploid zygote results in the formation of the first cell of a multicellular haploid individual.

> Plants and most multicellular protists have a life cycle that alternates between a haploid phase and a diploid phase called *alternation of generations*.

life cycle (256)
sperm (257)
ovum (257)

PART A: Answer all questions in this part.

Directions: For each statement or question, write on your separate answer sheet the number of the word or expression that best completes the statement or answers the question.

1 Offspring that result from meiosis and fertilization each have
(1) twice as many chromosomes as their parents
(2) one-half as many chromosomes as their parents
(3) gene combinations different from those of either parent
(4) gene combinations identical to those of each parent

2 Which diagram best illustrates an event in sexual reproduction that would most directly lead to the formation of a human embryo?

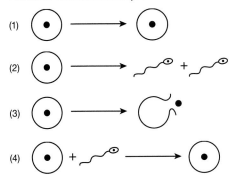

3 Certain bacteria produce a chemical that makes them resistant to penicillin. Since these bacteria reproduce asexually, they usually produce offspring that
(1) can be destroyed by penicillin
(2) mutate into another species
(3) are genetically different from their parents
(4) survive exposure to penicillin

4 Which statement about the gametes represented in the diagram below is correct?

(1) They are produced by females.
(2) They are fertilized in an ovary.
(3) They transport genetic material.
(4) They are produced by mitosis.

5 Which of the following is a difference between a sporophyte and a gametophyte?
(1) A sporophyte is diploid, and a gametophyte is haploid.
(2) A sporophyte is a plant, and a gametophyte is an animal.
(3) A sporophyte is multicellular, and a gametophyte is unicellular.
(4) A sporophyte undergoes only mitosis, and a gametophyte undergoes both mitosis and meiosis.

6 Compared to human cells resulting from mitotic cell division, human cells resulting from meiotic cell division would have
(1) twice as many chromosomes
(2) the same number of chromosomes
(3) one-half the number of chromosomes
(4) one-quarter as many chromosomes

7 In an environment that undergoes frequent change, species that reproduce sexually may have an advantage over species that reproduce asexually because the sexually reproducing species produce
(1) more offspring in each generation
(2) identical offspring
(3) offspring with more variety
(4) new species of offspring in each generation

PART A

1. (3) Offspring resulting from sexual reproduction do not have half or twice the number of chromosomes as their parents. They have the same number of chromosomes, but have unique gene combinations due to genetic recombination. *(#16, June 2006 Regents Exam)*

2. (4) Sexual reproduction involves the joining of a male and female gamete, so all answer choices are incorrect that start with only one gamete. *(#15, June 2006 Regents Exam)*

3. (4) Offspring produced asexually are genetically identical to the parent organism. Therefore, offspring of bacteria that are resistant to penicillin would also be resistant to penicillin. *(#05, January 2003 Regents Exam)*

4. (3) Male gametes (sperm) are produced by meiosis, so the choices about mitosis and females are incorrect. Sperm are produced in the testes, so the choice about ovaries is incorrect. *(#19, January 2006 Regents Exam)*

5. (1)

6. (3) During meiosis, a diploid cell forms four haploid cells, or cells that each have half the number of chromosomes than a body cell does. Two haploid cells are united during fertilization. *(#22, August 2003 Regents Exam)*

7. (3) Sexually reproducing organisms do not necessarily produce more offspring than asexually reproducing organisms. Asexual (and not sexual) organisms generally produce identical offspring. The choice regarding new species is incorrect. *(#11, August 2006 Regents Exam)*

Regents Exam Practice Correlations

4.2.1d 3, 9, 12	**4.3.1h** 7
4.2.1e 4, 16, 18, 19	**4.4.1b** 1
4.3.1c 11, 13, 17	**4.4.1c** 2, 6, 8, 10, 14, 15

8. (4) Choices that indicate that sperm cells have pairs of chromosomes are incorrect. In addition, sperm cells are genetically unique cells, and not identical. *(#10, August 2006 Regents Exam)*

9. (1) The choices about mutations and genetic variation are wrong as asexual reproduction leads to offspring that are genetically identical to the parents. The choice about environmental conditions is not true. *(#16, June 2005 Regents Exam)*

10. (3) Human reproduction is sexual and does not involve cloning. Gametes are produced by meiosis and not mitosis. Human reproduction is internal, and not external. *(#13, June 2005 Regents Exam)*

11. (4) Producing a large number of gametes is not the most important factor for the survival of offspring, and neither is the production of multicellular organisms. Cloning is not part of sexual reproduction. Genetic diversity is a key result for the survival of species, though. *(#12, June 2005 Regents Exam)*

12. (3) Nuclei do not travel to other plants through runners. The offspring of sexual reproduction are not genetically identical to their parents, unlike the offspring of asexual reproduction. The production of runners by strawberry plants is independent of the plants' proximity to other plants. *(#09, January 2005 Regents Exam)*

13. (4) Genes are exchanged between chromosomes during crossing-over, which leads to greater genetic variation within the species. Crossing-over occurs during gamete formation, but it does not stimulate gamete production. *(#15, January 2003 Regents Exam)*

14. (4) Meiosis is not involved in asexual reproduction, mitosis occurs in somatic cells, and only meiosis causes a halving of chromosome numbers. Both mitosis and meiosis are types of DNA replication that occur before cell division. *(#14, January 2005 Regents Exam)*

---

8 Which statement correctly describes the genetic makeup of the sperm cells produced by a human male?
(1) Each cell has pairs of chromosomes and the cells are usually genetically identical.
(2) Each cell has pairs of chromosomes and the cells are usually genetically different.
(3) Each cell has half the normal number of chromosomes and the cells are usually genetically identical.
(4) Each cell has half the normal number of chromosomes and the cells are usually genetically different.

9 Which statement describes asexual reproduction?
(1) Adaptive traits are usually passed from parent to offspring without genetic modification.
(2) Mutations are not passed from generation to generation.
(3) It always enables organisms to survive in changing environmental conditions.
(4) It is responsible for many new variations in offspring.

10 Reproduction in humans usually requires
(1) the process of cloning
(2) mitotic cell division of gametes
(3) gametes with chromosomes that are not paired
(4) the external fertilization of sex cells

11 Meiosis and fertilization are important for the survival of many species because these two processes result in
(1) large numbers of gametes
(2) increasingly complex multicellular organisms
(3) cloning of superior offspring
(4) genetic variability of offspring

12 Strawberries can reproduce by means of runners, which are stems that grow horizontally along the ground. At the region of the runner that touches the ground, a new plant develops. The new plant is genetically identical to the parent because
(1) it was produced sexually.
(2) nuclei traveled to the new plant through the runner to fertilize it.
(3) it was produced asexually.
(4) there were no other strawberry plants in the area to provide fertilization.

---

13 During meiosis, crossing-over (gene exchange between chromosomes) may occur. Crossing-over usually results in
(1) overproduction of gametes
(2) fertilization and development
(3) the formation of identical offspring
(4) variation within the species

14 Which statement is true of both mitosis and meiosis?
(1) Both are involved in asexual reproduction.
(2) Both occur only in reproductive cells.
(3) The number of chromosomes is reduced by half.
(4) DNA replication occurs before the division of the nucleus.

15 Human egg cells are most similar to human sperm cells in their
(1) degree of motility.
(2) amount of stored food.
(3) chromosome number.
(4) shape and size.

16 The arrows in the diagram below illustrate processes in the life of a species that reproduces sexually. Which processes result directly in the formation of cells with half the amount of genetic material that is characteristic of the species?

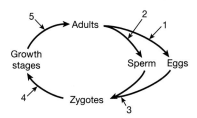

(1) 1 and 2
(2) 2 and 3
(3) 3 and 4
(4) 4 and 5

---

15. (3) Sperm cells are motile, eggs are not. Sperm store a small amount of "food" in the form of ATP, but eggs do not. Sperm are much smaller than eggs. They both have 23 chromosomes, half of the 46 found in somatic cells. *(#21, January 2004 Regents Exam)*

16. (1) The female and male gametes are formed in processes 1 and 2, respectively. Gametes contain half the genetic material of body cells so that when they unite in fertilization, the correct chromosome number is obtained by the developing offspring. *(#09, August 2004 Regents Exam)*

17 The diagram below shows a process that can occur during meiosis. The most likely result of this process is

- (1) a new combination of inheritable traits that can appear in the offspring
- (2) an inability to pass either of these chromosomes on to offspring
- (3) a loss of genetic information that will produce a genetic disorder in the offspring
- (4) an increase in the chromosome number of the organism in which this process occurs

PART B

18 A sperm cell from an organism is represented in the diagram below. Which statement regarding this sperm cell is not correct?

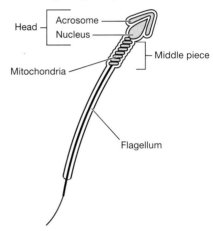

- (1) The acrosome contains half the normal number of chromosomes.
- (2) Energy to move the flagellum originates in the middle piece.
- (3) The head may contain a mutation.
- (4) This cell can unite with another cell resulting in the production of a new organism.

19 Sexually produced offspring often resemble, but are not identical to, either of their parents. Explain why they resemble their parents but are not identical to either parent.

---

17. **(1)** When chromosomes cross over, they exchange alleles and create a new combination of inheritable traits. Genes are not lost or gained during this process. (#15, June 2003 Regents Exam)

PART B

18. **(1)** All choices have true statements except the choice about acrosomes. Acrosomes contain enzymes that allow the sperm to penetrate the egg. (#35, June 2005 Regents Exam)

19. Allow 1 credit for explaining why sexually produced offspring resemble, but are not identical to, either parent. Acceptable responses include, but are not limited to: Offspring receive only half their genes (or DNA or chromosomes or genetic information) from each parent.; They receive some genes from each parent. (#39, June 2005 Regents Exam)

Mendel and Heredity

	Standards	**Teach Key Ideas**

CHAPTER OPENER, pp. 264–265   `15 min.`

🔦 *The Living Environment*

SECTION 1 Origins Of Heredity Science,
            pp. 267–271   `45 min.`

〉 Mendel's Breeding Experiments
〉 Features of Pea Plants
〉 Mendel's First Experiments
〉 Ratios in Mendel's Results

Standards: 4.2.2a

Teach Key Ideas:
- Bellringer Transparency
- Transparencies C1 Three Steps of Mendel's Experiment • C2 Mendel's Crosses and Results
- Visual Concepts Heredity • Mendel's Experiments • Punnett Square with Heterozygous Cross • True Breeding • Parental Generation • First Filial Generation • Second Filial Generation • Mendel's Conclusion

---

SECTION 2 Mendel's Theory, pp. 272–275   `60 min.`

〉 Explaining Mendel's Results
〉 Random Segregation of Alleles
〉 Mendel's Findings in Modern Terms
〉 Mendel's Second Experiments

Standards: 4.2.1b, 4.2.1c, 4.2.1j

Teach Key Ideas:
- Bellringer Transparency
- Transparencies C3 Mendel's Factors
- Visual Concepts Alllele • Comparing Dominant and Recessive Traits • Comparing Homozygous and Heterozygous Genotypes • Genotype • Phenotype • Comparing Genotype and Phenotype • Segregation • Law of Independent Assortment

---

SECTION 3 Modeling Mendel's Laws,
            pp. 276–281   `45 min.`

〉 Using Punnett Squares
〉 Using Probability
〉 Using a Pedigree

Standards: 1.3.2, 4.2.1c

Teach Key Ideas:
- Bellringer Transparency
- Transparencies C4 Probability with Two Coins • C5 Monohybrid Cross of Homozygous Plants • C6 Monohybrid Cross of Heterozygous Plants • C8 Dihybrid Crosses
- Visual Concepts Punnett Square with Homozygous Cross • Testcross • Calculating Probability • Pedigree • Sex Linkage

---

SECTION 4 Beyond Mendelian Heredity,
            pp. 282–284   `60 min.`

〉 Many Genes, Many Alleles
〉 Genes Affected by the Environment
〉 Genes Linked Within Chromosomes

Standards: 4.2.1a, 4.2.1c

Teach Key Ideas:
- Bellringer Transparency
- Transparencies C7 Incomplete Dominance
- Visual Concepts Comparing Single Allele, Multiple Allele, and Polygenic Traits • Comparing Complete, Incomplete, and Co-Dominance • Comparing X-Linked and Sex-Influenced Traits

See also PowerPoint® Resources

Chapter Review and Assessment Resources

SE Super Summary, p. 286
SE Regents Exam Practice, p. 287
📖 Regents Review Guide
📖 Review Resources
📖 Chapter Tests A and B
💻 Holt Online Assessment
💿 Regents Question Banks on Teacher's One-Stop Planner

CHAPTER
Fast Track   *Thorough instruction will require the times shown.*

Basic Learners

TE All Pea Plants Are Not the Same, p. 268
TE Mendel's Steps, p. 269
TE Law of Independent Assortment, p. 274
TE Reading the Signs, p. 279
TE Create a Chart, p. 283
📁 Directed Reading Worksheets*
📁 Active Reading Worksheets*
📁 Lab Manuals, Level A*
📖 Study Guide* ■
📖 Note-taking Workbook*
📖 Special Needs Activities and Modified Tests*

Advanced Learners

TE Organizing Concepts, p. 268
TE Trait Research, p. 273
📁 Critical Thinking Worksheets*
📁 Concept Mapping Worksheets*
📁 Science Skills Worksheets*
📁 Lab Datasheets, Level C*

Why It Matters	Hands-On	Skills Development	Assessment
Build student motivation with resources about high-interest applications.	**SE Inquiry Lab** What Are the Chances?, p. 265* ■	**TE Reading Toolbox** Assessing Prior Knowledge, p. 264 **SE Reading Toolbox**, p. 266	
TE Demonstration Patterns of Heredity, p. 267 **TE Demonstration** Genetic Make-Up, p. 268 **TE Trends in Genetics,** p. 269 **SE Amazing Mutants,** p. 271	**SE Quick Lab** Mendel's Ratios, p. 270* ■	**TE Math Skills** Ratios, p. 269 **SE Reading Toolbox** Word Parts, p. 269 **TE Reading Toolbox** Word Parts, p. 269 **TE Reading Toolbox** Visual Literacy, p. 271	**SE Section Review** **TE Formative Assessment** Spanish Assessment* ■ 📁 **Section Quiz** ■
TE Blood Lines, p. 273 **TE Demonstration** Hairy Knuckles, p. 275	**SE Quick Lab** Dominant and Recessive Traits, p. 273* ■	**SE Reading Toolbox** Word Parts, p. 274 **TE Reading Toolbox** Word Parts, p. 274	**SE Section Review** **TE Formative Assessment** Spanish Assessment* ■ 📁 **Section Quiz** ■
TE Recessive Genes, p. 276 **TE Punnett Who?** p. 277 **TE Probability in Real Life,** p. 278 **TE Pedigreed Dogs,** p. 280	**SE Quick Lab** Test Cross, p. 277* ■ **SE Quick Lab** Prrobabilities p. 278* ■ **SE Quick Lab** Pedigree Analysis, p. 281* ■ 📁 **Quick Lab** Interpreting Information in a Pedigree*	**TE Reading Toolbox** Visual Literacy, p. 276 **TE Reading Toolbox** Analogies, p. 277 **TE Math Skills** Probability of Two Independent Events, p. 279 **TE Reading Toolbox** Visual Literacy, p. 280	**SE Section Review** **TE Formative Assessment** Spanish Assessment* ■ 📁 **Section Quiz** ■
TE Human Inheritance, p. 283	**SE Inquiry Lab** Plant Genetics, p. 285* ■ 📁 **Inquiry Lab** Analyzing Corn Genetics*	**TE Math Skills** Phenotypic Ratios, p. 283 **TE Science Skills** Using Punnett Squares, p. 284	**SE Section Review** **TE Formative Assessment** Spanish Assessment* ■ 📁 **Section Quiz** ■

See also Lab Generator

See also Holt Online Assessment Resources

Resources for Differentiated Instruction

English Learners
TE Law of Independent Assortment, p. 277
TE Create a Chart, p. 283
📁 Directed Reading Worksheets*
📁 Active Reading Worksheets*
📁 Lab Manuals, Level A*
📓 Study Guide* ■
📓 Note-taking Workbook*
📓 Multilingual Glossary
💿 Interactive Tutor

Struggling Readers
TE Vocabulary, p. 280
📁 Directed Reading Worksheets*
📁 Active Reading Worksheets*
📁 Lab Manuals, Level A*
📓 Study Guide*
📓 Note-taking Workbook*
📓 Special Needs Activities and Modified Tests*
💿 Interactive Tutor

Special Education Students
TE Modeling Punnett Squares, p. 278
📁 Directed Reading Worksheets*
📁 Active Reading Worksheets*
📁 Lab Manuals, Level A*
📓 Study Guide* ■
📓 Note-taking Workbook*
📓 Special Needs Activities and Modified Tests*

Alternative Assessment
TE Phenotypic Ratios, p. 277
TE Mathematical Equivalents, p. 278
TE Evaluating Arguments, p. 282
📁 Science Skills Worksheets*
📁 Section Quizzes* ■
📓 Chapter Tests A, B, and C* ■

Chapter 12 Mendel and Heredity

Overview

The purpose of this chapter is to explain how genetic traits are passed from one generation to another. The passing of different genetic traits is fundamental to evolutionary change. The genetic variation that results from various combinations of parental genes is the basis for natural selection.

READING TOOLBOX

Assessing Prior Knowledge Students should understand the following concepts:
• cellular nature of life
• passing of genetic information

Visual Literacy Ask students to list some disadvantages for snakes that lack the genetic information to make red or black skin. (Snakes without red or black skin won't blend well into the background. Prospective mates might not recognize them.) Explain to students that variations in skin color are attractive to some pet owners. However, unusual coloring may limit a snake's survival or it's chances to reproduce.

Preview

1 Origins of Hereditary Science
Mendel's Breeding Experiments
Features of Pea Plants
Mendel's First Experiments
Ratios in Mendel's Results

2 Mendel's Theory
Explaining Mendel's Results
Random Segregation of Alleles
Mendel's Findings in Modern Terms
Mendel's Second Experiments

3 Modeling Mendel's Laws
Using Punnett Squares
Using Probability
Using a Pedigree

4 Beyond Mendelian Heredity
Many Genes, Many Alleles
Genes Affected by the Environment
Genes Linked Within Chromosomes

Why It Matters

Your genetic makeup influences your appearance, your personality, your abilities, and your health. We now know that many human traits, such as talents and diseases, have their origins in genes. As we come to understand how traits are inherited, we can use this information to better our lives.

The Living Environment
Standard 1 Students will use mathematical analysis, scientific inquiry, and engineering design, as appropriate, to pose questions, seek answers, and develop solutions.
Key Idea 3 The observations made while testing proposed explanations, when analyzed using conventional and invented methods, provide new insights into natural phenomena.
Standard 4 Students will understand and apply scientific concepts, principles, and theories pertaining to the physical setting and living environment and recognize the historical development of ideas in science.
Key Idea 2 Organisms inherit genetic information in a variety of ways that result in continuity of structure and function between parents and offspring. *Major Understandings* - 2.1a, 2.1b, 2.1c, 2.1j, 2.2a

The common corn snake (*Elaphe guttata*) is a popular pet. Snake breeders have discovered many variations of colors and patterns in this species.

This color pattern is common in wild corn snakes. It is a combination of black, red, and yellow skin colors.

Chapter Correlations The Living Environment

Standard 1
3.2 Applying statistical analysis techniques when appropriate to test if chance alone explains the results.

Standard 4
2.1a Genes are inherited, but their expression can be modified by interactions with the environment.

2.1b Every organism requires a set of coded instructions for specifying its traits. For offspring to resemble their parents, there must be a reliable way to transfer information from one generation to the next. Heredity is the passage of these instructions from one generation to another.

2.1c Hereditary information is contained in genes, located in the chromosomes of each cell. An inherited trait of an individual can be determined by one or by many genes, and a single gene can influence more than one trait. A human cell contains many thousands of different genes in its nucleus.

2.1j Offspring resemble their parents because they inherit similar genes that code for the production of proteins that form similar structures and perform similar functions.

2.2a For thousands of years new varieties of cultivated plants and domestic animals have resulted from selective breeding for particular traits.

InquiryLab

What Are the Chances? 1.3.2

Do you think you can predict the result of a coin toss? What if you flip the coin many times? In this activity, you will test your predictions.

Procedure

❶ Read steps 2 and 3. Predict the results, and write down your prediction.

❷ Flip a **coin,** and let it land. Record which side is up (heads or tails). Repeat this step 10 times.

❸ Calculate what fraction of the total number of flips resulted in heads. Calculate what fraction of flips resulted in tails.

❹ Read steps 5 and 6. Predict the results, and write down your prediction.

❺ Tally the flip results of the entire class.

❻ Calculate the fraction of heads and the fraction of tails in step 5.

Analysis

1. **Compare** your predictions from steps 1 and 4 with the results in steps 3 and 6.

2. **Compare** your own results in step 3 to those of other individuals in your class. Identify how closely each individual result matches the total class results.

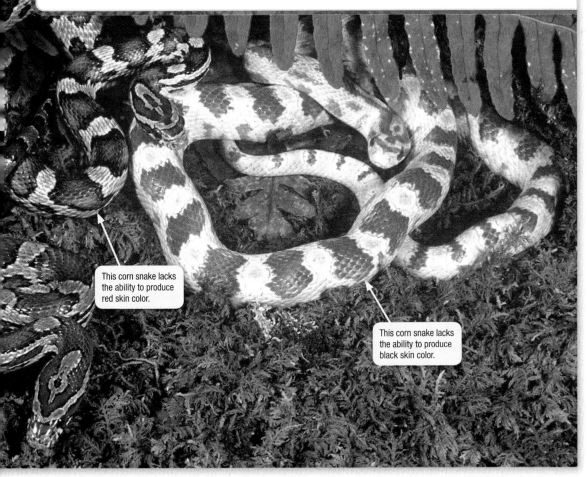

This corn snake lacks the ability to produce red skin color.

This corn snake lacks the ability to produce black skin color.

InquiryLab

Teacher's Notes The important ideas to learn from this lab are as follows. Multiple samples are averaged to find a *normal* or *probable* ratio of conditions. Individual samples (events) can differ greatly from the average, normal, or probable condition. Knowing about the events that generate a set of possible outcomes allows one to predict, imperfectly, the probable ratio of possible outcomes.

Materials
• one coin per student

Answers to Analysis

1. Answers will vary; many students will reasonably predict that $\frac{1}{2}$ of the flips will result in heads and $\frac{1}{2}$ in tails. However, very few students will obtain this exact result for their individual series of flips. The totaled class results will tend to balance the variations and the average probability will be closer to $\frac{1}{2}$ for both heads and tails.

2. Students will likely find greater differences between individual results (and thus wider variations among them) than between an individual's results and the class average.

Key Resources

 Interactive Tutor

Using Words

1. Students should convey the idea that heredity has to do with traits inherited or left behind.
2. Answers will vary, but students should realize that phenotype relates to visible markings.

Using Language

character

Using Science Graphics

1. 2
2. yellow shirt with shorts
3. 9 combinations

These reading tools can help you learn the material in this chapter. For more information on how to use these and other tools, see **Appendix: Reading and Study Skills.**

Using Words

Word Parts Knowing the meanings of word parts can help you figure out the meaning of words that you do not know.

Your Turn Use the table to answer the following.

1. Heritage is something handed down from one's ancestors. What do you think *heredity* is?
2. Use the meaning of the prefix *phen-* and the suffix *-type* to figure out what *phenotype* means.

Word Parts		
Word part	**Type**	**Meaning**
gen-	prefix	born; to become; to produce
her-	prefix	heir; remains; to be left behind
phen-	prefix	to show
-type	suffix	form; mark; kind

Using Language

Analogies An analogy question asks you to analyze the relationship between two words in one pair and to identify a second pair of words that have the same relationship. Colons are used to express the analogy for this type of question. For example, the analogy "up is to down as top is to bottom" is written "up : down :: top : bottom. In this example, the relationship between the words in each pair is the same.

Your Turn Use information in the chapter to complete this analogy.

allele : gene :: trait : _____

(Hint: Finding out how alleles and genes are related will help you figure out which word to use to fill in the blank.)

Using Science Graphics

Punnet Squares A Punnet square is a tool that is used to figure out possible combinations when combining items from a group. For example, if you have a red shirt, a green shirt, and a yellow shirt that you could wear with either blue jeans or shorts, how many combinations could you make?

Your Turn Finish filling in the Punnet square shown here to answer the following questions.

1. How many combinations include a red shirt?
2. What combination of shirt and pants do you find in the bottom right corner of this Punnet square?
3. How many combinations would you have if you added a pair of brown pants to the group?

	Red shirt	Green shirt	Yellow shirt
Blue jeans	Red shirt with blue jeans		
Shorts		Green shirt with shorts	

Origins of Hereditary Science

Key Ideas	Key Terms	Why It Matters
❯ Why was Gregor Mendel important for modern genetics? ❯ Why did Mendel conduct experiments with garden peas? ❯ What were the important steps in Mendel's first experiments? ❯ What were the important results of Mendel's first experiments?	character trait hybrid generation	Our understanding of genetics, including what makes us unique, can be traced back to Mendel's discoveries.

Since they first learned how to breed plants and animals, people have been interested in heredity. In the 1800s, one person figured out some of the first key ideas of genetics. Recall that *genetics* is the science of heredity and the mechanism by which traits are passed from parents to offspring.

Mendel's Breeding Experiments

A monk named Gregor Johann Mendel lived in the 1800s in Austria. Mendel did breeding experiments with the garden pea plant, *Pisum sativum,* shown in **Figure 1.** Farmers had done similar experiments before, but Mendel was the first person to develop rules that accurately predict the patterns of heredity in pea plants. ❯ **Modern genetics is based on Mendel's explanations for the patterns of heredity in garden pea plants.**

As a young man, Mendel studied to be a priest. Later, he went to the University of Vienna. There, he learned how to study science through experimentation and how to use mathematics to explain natural events. Mendel lived the rest of his life in a monastery, where he taught high school and cared for a garden. It was in this garden that he completed his important experiments.

Most of Mendel's experiments involved crossing different types of pea plants. In this case, the word *cross* means "to mate or breed two individuals." Mendel crossed a type of garden pea plant that had purple flowers with a type that had white flowers. All of the offspring from that cross had purple flowers. However, when two of these purple-flowered offspring were crossed, some offspring had white flowers and some had purple flowers.

The white color had reappeared in the second group of offspring! Mendel decided to investigate this strange occurrence. So, he carefully crossed different types of pea plants and recorded the numbers of each type of offspring. He did this experiment many times.

❯ **Reading Check** *How did Mendel experiment with pea plants? (See the Appendix for answers to Reading Checks.)*

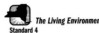

The Living Environment
Standard 4
2.2a For thousands of years new varieties of cultivated plants and domestic animals have resulted from selective breeding for particular traits.

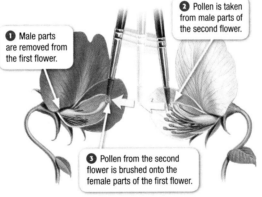

Figure 1 To cross plants that each had flowers of a different color, Mendel controlled the pollen that fertilized each flower.

❶ Male parts are removed from the first flower.

❷ Pollen is taken from male parts of the second flower.

❸ Pollen from the second flower is brushed onto the female parts of the first flower.

Key Resources

Transparencies
C1 Three Steps of Mendel's Experiment
C2 Mendel's Crosses and Results

Visual Concepts
Heredity
Mendel's Experiments
Punnett Square with Heterozygous Cross
True Breeding
Parental Generation
First Filial Generation
Second Filial Generation
Mendel's Conclusion

Teaching Key Ideas

Benefits of Peas Organize the class into small groups. Have each group design newspaper ads that would have attracted someone such as Mendel to purchase peas for research. The ads should mention all of the benefits of *Pisum sativum* that make it useful for genetic research. Ask students to use illustrations in their ads. Encourage students to be creative. They may use butcher paper, computer paper, construction paper, and so on. Post the ads on a bulletin board, and lead a discussion on the benefits of the garden pea for genetic research.
LS Interpersonal

Demonstration

Genetic Make-Up Bring photos of animals with interesting traits. Use these props to emphasize that many genes are involved in giving an animal its overall appearance, and that the genes for most traits have two or more versions. Ask students to guess how many genes animals have in common with each other. For example, chimpanzees and humans share approximately 98 percent of their genetic makeup.
LS Visual

Answers to Caption Questions

Figure 2: The pea plant is a good subject for studying heredity because the plant has contrasting traits, usually self-pollinates, and grows easily.

ACADEMIC VOCABULARY

contrast to show differences when compared.

---

character a recognizable inherited feature or characteristic of an organism

trait a genetically determined characteristic

hybrid the offspring of a cross between parents that have contrasting traits

generation the entire group of offspring produced by a given group of parents

---

Features of Pea Plants

Mendel studied seven features in his pea plants, as **Figure 2** shows. ❯The garden pea plant is a good subject for studying heredity because the plant has contrasting traits, usually self-pollinates, and grows easily.

Contrasting Traits In the study of heredity, physical features that are inherited are called **characters.** Several characters of the garden pea plant exist in two clearly different forms. The plant's flower color is either purple or white—there are no intermediate forms. A **trait** is one of several possible forms of a character. Purple is one of two possible traits for the flower-color character in pea plants. Other contrasting traits of pea plants are shown in **Figure 2.** (For some characters, more than two traits may be possible). Mendel wanted to see what would happen when he crossed individuals that have different traits. In such a cross, the offspring that result are called **hybrids.**

Self-Pollination In garden pea plants, each flower contains both male and female reproductive parts. This arrangement allows the plant to *self-pollinate*, or fertilize itself. Pea plants can also reproduce through *cross-pollination*. This process occurs when pollen from the flower of one plant is carried by insects or by other means to the flower of another plant. To cross-pollinate two pea plants, Mendel had to make sure that the plants could not self-pollinate. So, he removed the male parts (which produce pollen) from some of the flowers. But he did not remove the female parts (which produce eggs, fruit, and seeds). Then, he dusted the female parts of one plant with pollen from another plant.

Easy to Grow The garden pea is a small plant that needs little care and matures quickly. Also, each plant produces many offspring. Thus, many results can be compared for each type of cross. Recall that collecting repeated data is an important scientific method.

❯ **Reading Check** *What is the difference between a trait and a character?*

Figure 2 In the experiments in his garden, Mendel grew and studied many kinds of pea plants. ❯ **Why did Mendel study pea plants?**

Flower color	Seed color	Seed shape	Pod color	Pod Shape	Flower position	Plant height
purple	yellow	round	green	smooth	mid-stem	tall
white	green	wrinkled	yellow	bumpy	end of stem	short

Seven Characters with Contrasting Traits Studied by Mendel

Differentiated Instruction

Basic Learners

All Pea Plants Are Not the Same Review **Figure 2** with students. Be sure they realize that all of the traits shown are options for a single pea plant. Every plant will show some combination of these seven characters. **LS** Visual

Advanced Learners/GATE

Organizing Concepts Have students write and illustrate a chart explaining the meaning of the terms *monohybrid cross, true-breeding, P generation, F₁ generation,* and *F₂ generation.* **LS** Visual

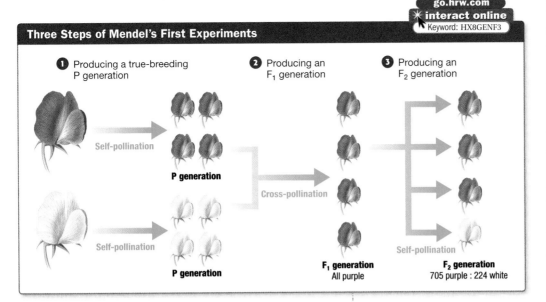

Three Steps of Mendel's First Experiments

go.hrw.com
✳ interact online
Keyword: HX8GENF3

1 Producing a true-breeding P generation

2 Producing an F₁ generation

3 Producing an F₂ generation

Self-pollination

P generation

Self-pollination

P generation

Cross-pollination

Self-pollination

F₁ generation
All purple

F₂ generation
705 purple : 224 white

Mendel's First Experiments

A *monohybrid cross* is a cross that is done to study one pair of contrasting traits. For example, crossing a plant that has purple flowers with a plant that has white flowers is a monohybrid cross. ❯ Mendel's first experiments used monohybrid crosses and were carried out in three steps. The three steps are shown in **Figure 3.** Each step involved a new generation of plants. A **generation** is a group of offspring from a given group of parents.

Step ❶ Mendel allowed plants that had each type of trait to self-pollinate for several generations. This process ensured that each plant always produced offspring of the same type. Such a plant is said to be *true-breeding* for a given trait. For example, every time a true-breeding plant that has purple flowers self-pollinates, its offspring will have purple flowers. Mendel used true-breeding plants as the first generation in his experiments. The first group of parents that are crossed in a breeding experiment are called the *parental generation,* or *P generation.*

Step ❷ Mendel crossed two P generation plants that had contrasting traits, such as purple flowers and white flowers. He called the offspring of the P generation the *first filial generation,* or *F₁ generation.* He recorded the number of F₁ plants that had each trait.

Step ❸ Mendel allowed the F₁ generation to self-pollinate and produce new plants. He called this new generation of offspring the *second filial generation,* or *F₂ generation.* He recorded the number of F₂ plants that had each trait.

❯ **Reading Check** *What is a monohybrid cross?*

Figure 3 In his garden experiments, Mendel carefully selected and grew specific kinds of pea plants. ❯ What is the relationship between each generation in these experiments?

READING TOOLBOX

Word Parts The word *filial* is from the Latin *filialis*, which means "of a son or daughter." Thus, F (filial) generations are all of the generations that follow a P (parental) generation. What do you think *filiation* means?

go.hrw.com
✳ interact online

Students can interact with "The Steps of Mendel's First Experiments" by going to go.hrw.com and typing the keycode HX8GENF3.

Teaching Key Ideas

Monohybrid Crosses Ask students if they can tell by looking at the purple pea flowers in **Figure 3** which ones are true-breeding for the purple trait and which ones are not. Point out that you cannot always tell the genetic makeup of an organism by looking at it. Ask students how a cross helps determine if a plant is true-breeding for a trait.

Math Skills

Ratios Ask students to practice reducing ratios to their simplest forms. Survey the class for some numbers to use. For example, ask how many students own a cat. Have them divide each number (class size and cat owners) by the smallest number (cat owners) and write it as a ratio. If there are 30 students in class and 10 own a cat, the ratio is 30:10. Simplified, $\frac{30}{10} = 3$ and $\frac{10}{10} = 1$, so the ratio is 3:1. **LS Logical**

READING TOOLBOX

Word Parts *Filiation* describes the process of determining the parental relationship. **LS Verbal**

Answers to Caption Questions

Figure 3: The F₂ generation is the offspring of the F₁ generation, and the F₁ generation is the offspring of the P generation.

Differentiated Instruction

Basic Learners

Mendel's Steps Be sure that students realize that only one character (flower color) from **Figure 2** is shown. Ask students to use **Figure 3** as a model to replicate the three steps in Mendel's experiments, substituting another character from **Figure 2.** Have students draw pictures of the phenotypes produced. Remind them that Mendel studied seven characters. **LS Verbal**

Why It Matters

Trends in Genetics Many scientists who study genetics use the fruit fly *Drosophila melanogaster* or the roundworm *Caenorhabditis elegans* in their research. These organisms show a variety of traits, are easy to obtain and breed, have short generation time (less than 2 weeks for fruit flies and less than 3 days for roundworms), and produce a large number of offspring. How long would it take to study three generations of humans? (approximately 75 years)

QuickLab

Teacher's Notes Review how to calculate ratios.

Answers to Procedure

1. seed color, 6,022:2,001; seed shape, 5,474:1,850; pod color, 428:152; pod shape 882:299; flower position, 651:207; plant height, 787:277.

2. seed color, 3.01:1; seed shape, 2.96:1; pod color, 2.82:1; pod shape 2.95:1; flower position, 3.14:1; plant height, 2.84:1.

Answers to Analysis

1. all are 3:1

2. The sample sizes for each character vary.

Close

Formative Assessment

What makes an organism "true-breeding"?

A. It can self-pollinate. (Incorrect. Self-pollination is one way to produce true-breeding organisms (as Mendel did), but many generations must self-pollinate to guarantee that the offspring will share the traits of the parents.)

B. It always produces offspring with similar traits. (Correct!)

C. It always produces offspring with contrasting traits. (Incorrect. To "breed true" is to produce offspring with the same traits as the parents.)

D. It can mate with other organisms that are like it. (Incorrect. Most organisms can mate with other organisms that are like them, but this does not guarantee that the offspring will share the traits of the parents.)

Data

QuickLab

⏱ 10 min

Mendel's Ratios

You can calculate and compare the F_2 generation ratios that Mendel obtained from his first experiments.

Procedure

❶ Copy this partially complete table onto a separate **sheet of paper**. Then, fill in the ratios of F_2 traits.

❷ Simplify the ratios, and round the terms in each ratio to the nearest hundredth digit.

Analysis

1. **Identify** the similarities between the ratios by rounding each term to the nearest whole number.

2. **CRITICAL THINKING** **Analyzing Data** Why weren't all of the ratios exactly the same?

Character	Traits in F_2 generation		Ratio
Flower color	705 purple	224 white	705:224 or 3.15:1.00
Seed color	6,022 yellow	2,001 green	
Seed shape	5,474 round	1,850 wrinkled	
Pod color	428 green	152 yellow	
Pod shape	882 smooth	299 bumpy	
Flower position	651 mid-stem	207 end of stem	
Plant height	787 tall	277 short	

www.scilinks.org
Topic: Gregor Mendel
Code: HX80698

Ratios in Mendel's Results

All of Mendel's F_1 plants expressed the same trait for a given character. The contrasting trait had disappeared! But when the F_1 plants were allowed to self-pollinate, the missing trait reappeared in some of the F_2 plants. Noticing this pattern, Mendel compared the ratio of traits that resulted from each cross.

When F_1 plants that had purple flowers were crossed with one another, 705 of the F_2 offspring had purple flowers and 224 had white flowers. So, the F_2 ratio of purple-flowered plants to white-flowered plants was 705:224, or about 3:1. Mendel's studies of the other characters gave a similar pattern. ❯ For each of the seven characters that Mendel studied, he found a similar 3-to-1 ratio of contrasting traits in the F_2 generation. As you will learn, Mendel tried to explain this pattern.

❯ **Reading Check** *What was the important difference between Mendel's F_1 and F_2 generations?*

Section 1 Review

❯ KEY IDEAS

1. **Identify** Gregor Mendel's contribution to modern genetics.

2. **Describe** why garden pea plants are good subjects for genetic experiments.

3. **Summarize** the three major steps of Mendel's first experiments.

4. **State** the typical ratio of traits in Mendel's first experiments.

CRITICAL THINKING

5. **Using Scientific Methods** Why did Mendel record the results of so many plant crosses?

6. **Predicting Outcomes** Squash plants do not usually self-pollinate. If Mendel had used squash plants, how might his experiments have differed?

WRITING FOR SCIENCE

7. **Technical Writing** Imagine that you are Gregor Mendel and you need to document your first experiments for a science magazine. Write out your procedure for breeding pea plants. Be sure to explain how you controlled variables and assured that data was reliable.

Answers to Section Review

1. Mendel studied and tried to explain the hereditary patterns in garden pea plants. Modern genetics is based on his conclusions.

2. The plant has numerous discernable contrasting traits, usually self-pollinates, and grows easily.

3. (1) start with a true-breeding P generation by; (2) produce an F_1 generation by cross-pollination; (3) produce an F_2 generation by self-pollination

4. 3 to 1

5. Mendel understood that the larger the number of results, the better the data would be statistically.

6. He would have had to pollinate the plants under controlled conditions until he was satisfied that he had a true-breeding P generation. Otherwise he would not have been able to control the ratio of traits in the F_1 and F_2 generations.

7. Check that students provide ample detail for the procedure, describe how they plan to control variables, and show some calculations for the ratios of F_2 traits.

Amazing Mutants

Fruit flies are widely used in genetic research because "mutant" forms provide clues about how genes work. One fly species, *Drosophila melanogaster*, has been studied so much that scientists understand its genes better than those of most other organisms. Still, there are many bizarre mutations yet to be understood.

Popular in the Lab

Fruit flies are popular with scientists because the flies are easy to breed and raise in a laboratory. The flies grow and reproduce quickly and reproduce in large numbers. Also, the flies have been used in important genetic experiments since 1910.

Many Mutations

Most scientists who study fruit flies are interested in genetic variation and mutations. Thousands of "mutant" forms that have unique *alleles* (versions of a gene) have been observed in species of the genus *Drosophila*. Databases on the Internet are used to share information on over 14,000 fruit fly genes. Just a few of the many kinds of fruit fly "mutants" are described here.

Research Find out more about *Drosophila*, such as its life cycle, size, and use in research.

WEIRD SCIENCE

Normal "wild" fruit fly

Fly lacking eye color

Fly with extra pair of eyes— on antennae!

Fly with malformed wings

Fly with legs in place of antennae

Different Colors Differences in color are easy to recognize in a lab. Some fruit fly mutations affect eye color and body patterns. Some of the genes for coloration in flies show simple inheritance patterns, like the patterns that Mendel observed in garden pea plants.

Malformed Body Parts Some genes control the development of body parts. Mutations in such genes often cause body parts to develop improperly, as did the malformed wings shown here. This particular trait is seen only when a fly has a normal allele paired with the malformed-wing allele. A fly that has two such alleles will not survive.

Misplaced Body Parts Imagine growing legs from your head! Some mutations cause legs, antennae, mouthparts, and wings to grow in various places on a fly's body. By studying these oddities, scientists have begun to understand the genes that control the arrangement of body parts in insects and other animals.

> ## Focus

This section covers the logic Mendel used to formulate his theory and explains the laws of segregation and independent assortment.

 Bellringer

Use the Bellringer transparency to prepare students for this section.

> ## Teach

Teaching Key Ideas

Traits of Offspring Ask students if it is possible for an offspring to have traits that differ from both parents. Explain that some hidden traits in parents can combine and appear in the offspring. An example would be tongue rolling or earlobe attachment.
LS Interpersonal

Answers to Caption Questions

Figure 4: Only one allele for seed color is passed on from the parent to each offspring.

Key Ideas	Key Terms	Why It Matters
❯ What patterns of heredity were explained by Mendel's hypotheses? ❯ What is the law of segregation? ❯ How does genotype relate to phenotype? ❯ What is the law of independent assortment?	allele phenotype dominant homozygous recessive heterozygous genotype	Mendel's theory explains why you have some, but not all, of the traits of your parents.

The Living Environment
Standard 4

2.1b Every organism requires a set of coded instructions for specifying its traits. For offspring to resemble their parents, there must be a reliable way to transfer information from one generation to the next. Heredity is the passage of these instructions from one generation to another.

2.1c Hereditary information is contained in genes, located in the chromosomes of each cell. An inherited trait of an individual can be determined by one or by many genes, and a single gene can influence more than one trait. A human cell contains many thousands of different genes in its nucleus.

2.1j Offspring resemble their parents because they inherit similar genes that code for the production of proteins that form similar structures and perform similar functions.

Explaining Mendel's Results

Mendel developed several hypotheses to explain the results of his experiments. His hypotheses were basically correct but have been updated with newer terms and more-complete knowledge. Mendel's hypotheses, collectively called the *Mendelian theory of heredity,* form the foundation of modern genetics. ❯ Mendelian theory explains simple patterns of inheritance. In these patterns, two of several versions of a gene combine and result in one of several possible traits.

Alternate Versions of Genes Before Mendel's experiments, many people thought that the traits of offspring were always a blend of the traits from parents. If this notion were true, a tall plant crossed with a short plant would result in offspring of medium height. But Mendel's results did not support the blending hypothesis. Mendel noticed that his pea plants would express only one of two traits for each character, such as purple or white flower color. Today, scientists know that different traits result from different versions of genes. Each version of a gene is called an **allele.**

❯ **Reading Check** *What is the "blending" hypothesis?*

Figure 4 Each individual has two alleles for a given character. A single gamete carries only one of the two alleles. ❯ In pea plants, how many alleles for seed color does each parent pass on to each offspring?

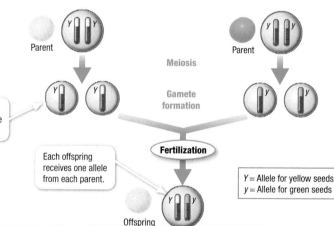

Each gamete receives one allele from the parent.

Each offspring receives one allele from each parent.

Meiosis

Gamete formation

Fertilization

Y = Allele for yellow seeds
y = Allele for green seeds

Section Correlations
4.2.1b
4.2.1c
4.2.1j

Key Resources

 Transparencies
C3 Mendel's Factors

 Visual Concepts
Allele
Comparing Dominant and Recessive Traits
Comparing Homozygous and Heterozygous Genotypes
Genotype
Phenotype
Comparing Genotype and Phenotype
Segregation
Law of Independent Assortment

QuickLab

Dominant and Recessive Traits 4.2.1j

🕐 15 min

Can you find Mendelian patterns in humans? Look for ratios between these contrasting traits.

Procedure

① On a separate sheet of paper, draw a table like the one shown here. For each character, circle the trait that best matches your own trait.

② Tally the class results to determine how many students in your class share each trait.

Analysis

1. **Summarize** the class results for each character.

2. **Calculate** the ratio of dominant traits to recessive traits for each character.

3. **CRITICAL THINKING** **Mathematical Reasoning** Are each of the ratios the same? Why is this unlikely to happen?

Freckles

Dimples

Dominant trait	Recessive trait
freckles	no freckles
no cleft	cleft chin
dimples	no dimples

4. **CRITICAL THINKING** **Analyzing Results** For which traits must a person who has the given trait receive the same allele from both parents? Explain your answer.

One Allele from Each Parent Mendel also noticed that traits can come from either parent. The reason is related to meiosis, as **Figure 4** shows. When gametes form, each pair of alleles is separated. Only one of the pair is passed on to offspring.

Dominant and Recessive Alleles For every pair of traits that Mendel studied, one trait always seemed to "win" over the other. That is, whenever both alleles were present, only one was fully expressed as a trait. The other allele had no effect on the organism's physical form. In this case, the expressed allele is called **dominant.** The allele that is not expressed when the dominant allele is present is called **recessive.** Traits may also be called *dominant* or *recessive*. For example, in pea plants, the yellow-seed trait is dominant, and the green-seed trait is recessive.

Random Segregation of Alleles

Mendel did not understand how chromosomes separate during meiosis, but he learned something important about this process. Because chromosome pairs split up randomly, either one of a pair of homologous chromosomes might end up in any one gamete. As **Figure 4** shows, offspring receive one allele from each parent. But only chance decides which alleles will be passed on through gametes. Mendel showed that segregation is random, and he stated his hypothesis as a law. ❯ In modern terms, the *law of segregation* holds that when an organism produces gametes, each pair of alleles is separated and each gamete has an equal chance of receiving either one of the alleles.

allele (uh LEEL) one of two or more alternative forms of a gene, each leading to a unique trait

dominant (DAHM uh nuhnt) describes an allele that is fully expressed whenever the allele is present in an individual

recessive (ri SES iv) describes an allele that is expressed only when there is no dominant allele present in an individual

ACADEMIC VOCABULARY

random without aim

Why It Matters

Blood Lines The Greek philosopher Aristotle associated inheritance with blood. He thought blood carried hereditary information from the body's various structures to the reproductive organs. Though incorrect, this idea is ingrained in many languages. For example, "blue blood," "blood stock," and "It is in the blood" are English phrases that associate inheritance with blood. Likewise, "Corre en la sangre" means "It runs in the blood," in Spanish; "Bon sang ne peut mentir" means "Good blood cannot lie," in French; and "Es liegt im Blute," means "It lies in the blood," in German.

Word Parts The root of the words *phenomenon* and *phenotype* is *phen-* which means "to make visible." A *phenomenon* is an occurrence, something that can be witnessed, and a *phenotype* is the visible appearance resulting from the genotype.

Teaching Key Ideas

Genotype and Phenotype Have students practice using the important terms in this section by providing several examples. For example, tell them that the gene for plant height has two versions: *T* tall and *t* short. Ask students to identify the two alleles for plant height. (*T* and *t*) Write *Tt*, *tt*, and *TT* on the board and ask students to identify the genotype and phenotype of each set of alleles. (genotypes— *Tt*, *tt*, *TT*; phenotypes: tall, dwarf, and tall) Ask students to identify whether a plant with *TT* alleles is homozygous or heterozygous. (homozygous)

Visual Literacy Ask students to describe how **Figure 5** demonstrates dominance, segregation, genotype, and phenotype.

Answers to Caption Questions

Figure 5: If a plant has the dominant allele in its genotype, the flower's phenotype will be purple flowers.

Word Parts Look up the word *phenomenon* in a dictionary. What is the meaning of the Greek root of this word? How does this meaning apply to the word *phenotype* as used in biology?

genotype (JEE nuh TIEP) a specific combination of alleles in an individual

phenotype (FEE noh TIEP) the detectable trait or traits that result from the genotype of an individual

homozygous (HOH moh ZIE guhs) describes an individual that carries two identical alleles of a gene

heterozygous (HET uhr OH ZIE guhs) describes an individual that carries two different alleles of a gene

Figure 5 Mendel's first experiments demonstrated dominance, segregation, genotype, and phenotype. ❯ What is the relationship between the genotypes and phenotypes in each generation shown here?

Mendel's Findings in Modern Terms

Although Mendel did not use the term allele, he used a code of letters to represent the function of alleles. Today, scientists use such a code along with modern terms, as shown in **Figure 5.** A dominant allele is shown as a capital letter. This letter is usually the first letter of the word for the trait. For example, purple flower color is a dominant trait in pea plants, so the allele is written as *P*. A recessive allele is shown as a lowercase letter. The letter is usually the same as the one used for the dominant allele. So, white flower color is written as *p*.

Genotype and Phenotype Mendel's experiments showed that an offspring's traits do not match one-to-one with the parents' traits. In other words, offspring do not show a trait for every allele that they receive. Instead, combinations of alleles determine traits. The set of alleles that an individual has for a character is called the **genotype.** The trait that results from a set of alleles is the **phenotype.** In other words, ❯ genotype determines phenotype. For example, if the genotype of a pea plant is *pp*, the phenotype is white flowers. If the genotype is *Pp* or *PP*, the phenotype is purple flowers, as shown in **Figure 5.**

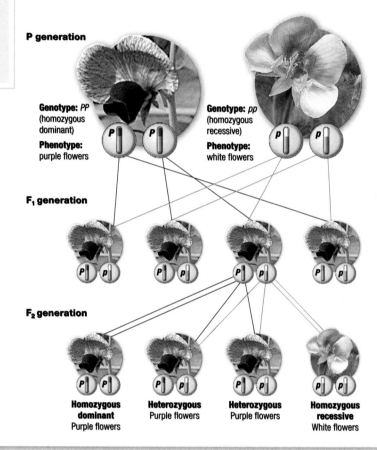

Basic Learners/English Learners

Law of Independent Assortment Have students work in pairs to make a graphic organizer to demonstrate the law of independent assortment. Ask students to illustrate their graphic organizer with at least one example showing the inheritance of two pairs of contrasting traits. Have them write a brief explanation. Ask each group to put their examples on the board or overhead projector. Work with the groups to create the best model. **LS Logical**

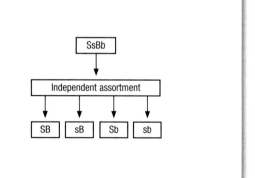

Homozygous and Heterozygous If an individual has two of the same alleles of a certain gene, the individual is **homozygous** for the related character. For example, a plant that has two white-flower alleles (*pp*) is homozygous for flower color. On the other hand, if an individual has two different alleles of a certain gene, the individual is **heterozygous** for the related character. For example, a plant that has one purple-flower allele and one white-flower allele (*Pp*) is heterozygous for flower color. In the heterozygous case, the dominant allele is expressed. This condition explains Mendel's curious results, as **Figure 5** shows.

Mendel's Second Experiments

Mendel not only looked for patterns, he also looked for a lack of patterns. For example, the round-seed trait did not always show up in garden pea plants that had the yellow-seed trait. Mendel made dihybrid crosses to study these results. A *dihybrid cross*, shown in **Figure 6,** involves two characters, such as seed color and seed shape.

Independent Assortment In these crosses, Mendel found that the inheritance of one character did not affect the inheritance of any other. He proposed another law. ❯ In modern terms, the *law of independent assortment* holds that during gamete formation, the alleles of each gene segregate independently. For example, in **Figure 6,** the alleles for seed color (*Y* and *y*) can "mix and match" with the alleles for seed shape (*R* and *r*). So, round seeds may or may not be yellow.

Genes Linked on Chromosomes Mendel's second law seems to say that each gene has nothing to do with other genes. But we now know that many genes are linked to each other as parts of chromosomes. So, genes that are located close together on the same chromosome will rarely separate independently. Thus, genes are said to be *linked* when they are close together on chromosomes. The only genes that follow Mendel's law are those that are far apart.

❯ **Reading Check** *What is a dihybrid cross?*

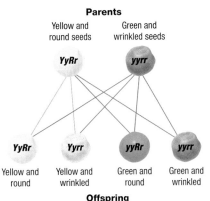

Parents

Yellow and round seeds — **YyRr**
Green and wrinkled seeds — **yyrr**

Offspring

YyRr Yellow and round
Yyrr Yellow and wrinkled
yyRr Green and round
yyrr Green and wrinkled

Figure 6 Mendel used dihybrid crosses in his second experiments. He found that the inheritance of one character, such as seed color, did not affect the inheritance of another character, such as seed shape.
❯ What law did Mendel propose to explain these findings?

SC*LINKS*.
www.scilinks.org
Topic: Mendel's Laws
Code: HX80938

Answers to Caption Questions
Figure 6: the law of independent assortment

Demonstration

Hairy Knuckles Have students determine whether or not they have hair on their fingers near their knuckles. Tell students that the presence of this hair is caused by a dominant allele, *H*. Then, ask them to identify the genotype of a person who does not have hair above his or her knuckles. (*hh*) Have students determine how a parent without hair near the knuckles can produce a child with hair above the knuckles. (The second parent must have the *H* allele.) **LS** **Interpersonal**

❯ **Close**

Formative Assessment

What is a possible genotype of a pea plant with purple flowers?
A. *pp* (Incorrect. *pp* is a genotype that would result in white flowers. Review the ways that dominant and recessive alleles are represented.)
B. *Pp* (Correct! Either *PP* or *Pp* would result in purple flowers.)
C. purple (Incorrect. Purple flower color is the phenotype, not the genotype.)
D. white (Incorrect. White flower color is a phenotype, not a genotype. Review the meanings of these terms.)

Answers to Section Review
1. Mendelian theory explains simple patterns of inheritance in which two of several versions of an allele combine and result in one of several possible traits.
2. The law of segregation holds that when an organism produces gametes, each pair of alleles is separated and each gamete has an equal chance of receiving either one of the alleles.
3. Genotype determines phenotype. For example, the genotype *PP* or *Pp* results in purple flowers, while the genotype *pp* results in white flowers.
4. The law of independent assortment holds that during gamete formation, the alleles of each gene segregate independently.
5. Sample answers: allele, genetics, chromosome, genotype, phenotype
6. No, in Mendelian inheritance, a heterozygous genotype must always yield a dominant phenotype. The term *recessive,* if referring to the phenotype, would require that two recessive alleles be present, in which case the genotype would be homozygous recessive.
7. strength: explains the inheritance patterns that Mendel observed in pea plants; weakness: does not hold true in many cases where genes are linked on chromosomes
8. He performed many dihybrid crosses with various combinations of characters.

❯Focus

This section explains the use of Punnett squares for predicting outcomes, the concept of probability, and the use pedigrees to show the transmission of traits.

🎧Bellringer

Use the Bellringer transparency to prepare students for this section.

❯Teach

Teaching Key Ideas

Selective Breeding Ask students to list some examples of selective breeding in domestic animals or crops. Dogs are good examples. Then ask them to explain how to select for a particular character.
LS Verbal

READING TOOLBOX

Visual Literacy Discuss the use of the Punnett square to predict the outcome of two genetic crosses. Using **Figure 7,** review how the genotype in each square is obtained. Assign several monohybrid crosses for students to practice. **LS** Logical

Answers to Caption Questions
Figure 7: A Punnett square shows the ratio of possible genotypes that could result from a given cross.

Section Correlations

1.3.2
4.2.1c

Key Ideas

❯ How can a Punnett square be used in genetics?

❯ How can mathematical probability be used in genetics?

❯ What information does a pedigree show?

Key Terms

Punnett square
probability
pedigree
genetic disorder

Why It Matters

Mendel's laws can be used to help breed exotic pets, thoroughbred livestock, and productive crops.

The Living Environment
Standard 1
3.2 Apply statistical analysis techniques when appropriate to test if chance alone explains the results.
Standard 4
2.1c Hereditary information is contained in genes, located in the chromosomes of each cell. An inherited trait of an individual can be determined by one or by many genes, and a single gene can influence more than one trait. A human cell contains many thousands of different genes in its nucleus.

Punnett square (PUHN uht SKWER) a graphic used to predict the results of a genetic cross

Why are Mendel's laws so important? Mendel's laws can be used to predict and understand the results of certain kinds of crosses. Farmers, gardeners, animal keepers, and biologists need to make predictions when they try to breed organisms that have desired character. Medical professionals need to know about the inheritance of traits in their patients. Graphical models that can help with these tasks include Punnett squares and pedigrees.

Using Punnett Squares

A **Punnett square** is a model that predicts the likely outcomes of a genetic cross. The model is named for its inventor, Reginald Punnett.
❯ **A Punnett square shows all of the genotypes that could result from a given cross.**

The simplest Punnett square consists of a square divided into four boxes. As **Figure 7** shows, the possible alleles from one parent are written along the top of the square. The possible alleles from the other parent are written along the left side. Each box inside the square holds two letters. The combination of letters in each box represents one possible genotype in the offspring. The letters in each box are a combination of two alleles—one from each parent.

Figure 7 Each of these Punnett squares shows a monohybrid cross involving seed color in peas. ❯ How does a Punnett square predict the outcome of a cross?

YY = homozygous dominant
Yy = heterozygous
yy = homozygous recessive

Homozygous Cross In a cross of homozygous parents that have contrasting traits, 100% of the offspring will be heterozygous and will show the dominant trait.

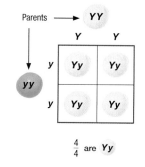

$\frac{4}{4}$ are **Yy**

Heterozygous Cross In a cross of heterozygous parents that have the same traits, the ratio of genotypes will be 1:2:1. The ratio of phenotypes will be 3:1.

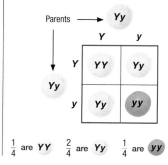

$\frac{1}{4}$ are **YY** $\frac{2}{4}$ are **Yy** $\frac{1}{4}$ are **yy**

Key Resources

🖳 **Transparencies**
C4 Probability with Two Coins
C5 Monohybrid Cross of Homozygous Plants
C6 Monohybrid Cross of Heterozygous Plants
C8 Dihybrid Crosses

💿 **Visual Concepts**
Punnett Square with Homozygous Cross
Testcross
Calculating Probability
Pedigree
Sex Linkage

Why It Matters

Recessive Genes Basenjis are small dogs with pointed ears, short silky hair, and rows of wrinkles on their foreheads. Tell students that the basenjis cannot bark, but they can make yodeling type sounds. Basenjis can mate with barking breeds to produce puppies that bark. Ask students to hypothesize a genetic explanation for why basenjis cannot bark. (The ability to bark is a dominant trait in dogs. Basenjis have two recessive genes for this character.) Ask students to suggest other traits that have been selected for in breeding dogs or cats. **LS** Logical

QuickLab

⏱ 10 min

Testcross

When genotypes are known, Punnett squares can be used to predict phenotypes. But can genotypes be determined if only phenotypes are known?

Suppose a breeder has a rabbit that has a dominant phenotype, such as black fur (as opposed to recessive brown fur). How could the breeder know whether the rabbit is homozygous (*BB*) or heterozygous (*Bb*) for fur color? The breeder could perform a testcross.

A *testcross* is used to test an individual whose phenotype for a characteristic is dominant but whose genotype is not known. This individual is crossed with an individual whose genotype is known to be homozygous recessive. In our example, the breeder would cross the black rabbit (*BB* or *Bb*) with a brown rabbit (*bb*).

Procedure

On a separate sheet of paper, copy the two Punnett squares shown here. Write the appropriate letters in the boxes of each square.

Cross A   **Cross B**

Analysis

1. **Label** what each pair of letters represents in each of the Punnett squares.

2. **Identify** which figure represents a testcross involving a heterozygous parent.

3. **Identify** which figure shows a cross in which all offspring will have black fur.

4. **CRITICAL THINKING** **Applying Models** If half of the offspring in a testcross have brown fur, what is the genotype of the parent that has black fur?

QuickLab

Teacher's Notes Remind struggling students that Cross A follows the same pattern as the homozygous cross on the facing page. Have them refer to this cross as model before trying the testcrosses in this lab.

Answers to Procedure

Cross A, all are *Bb*
Cross B, the two squares on the left are *Bb*, the two on the right are *bb*.

Answers to Analysis

1. *Bb* = heterozygous with black fur; *bb* = homozygous recessive with brown fur
2. Cross B
3. Cross A
4. heterozygous, *Bb*

Teaching Key Ideas

Constructing Punnett Squares Write the following genotypes on the board: (1) *PP*, (2) *Pp*, and (3) *pp*. Pair each student with a partner. Have each pair select two of the three genotypes and use them to construct complete Punnett squares showing the crosses.

READING TOOLBOX

Analogies The symbol *yy* shows a homozygous condition. Thus, *Yy* is analogous to heterozygous.

Analyzing Monohybrid Crosses Two kinds of monohybrid crosses are shown in **Figure 7**. A simple Punnett square can be used to analyze a monohybrid cross. Recall that this cross involves parents who each have a trait that <u>contrasts</u> with the trait of the other parent. The parents may be homozygous or heterozygous.

Monohybrid Homozygous Crosses Consider a cross between a pea plant that is homozygous for yellow seed color (*YY*) and a pea plant that is homozygous for green seed color (*yy*). The first Punnett square in **Figure 7** shows that all of the offspring in this type of cross will be heterozygous (*Yy*) and will express the dominant trait of yellow seed color. Other results are not possible in this case.

Monohybrid Heterozygous Crosses The second Punnett square in **Figure 7** predicts the results of a monohybrid cross between two pea plants that are heterozygous (*Yy*) for seed color. This cross is more complex than a homozygous cross. About one-fourth of the offspring will be *YY*. About two-fourths (or one-half) will be *Yy*. And about one-fourth will be *yy*. Another way to express this prediction is to say that the genotypic ratio will be 1 *YY* : 2 *Yy* : 1 *yy*. Because the *Y* allele is dominant, three-fourths of the offspring will be yellow (*YY* or *Yy*) and one-fourth will be green (*yy*). Thus, the phenotypic ratio will be 3 yellow : 1 green.

❯ **Reading Check** *Explain the boxes inside a Punnett square?*

ACADEMIC VOCABULARY

contrast different when compared

READING TOOLBOX

Analogies Use the information on this page to solve the following analogy.

yy : Yy :: Homozygous : _____

Differentiated Instruction

Alternative Assessment

Phenotypic Ratios After reviewing **Figure 7,** ask students to create a Punnett square showing the cross of a homozygous recessive parent with a heterozygous parent. Have them determine the phenotypic ratios.

	Y	y	
y	Yy	yy	$\frac{2}{4}$ are *Yy*
y	Yy	yy	$\frac{2}{4}$ are *yy*

Why It Matters

Punnett Who? The Punnett square is named after Reginald Punnett, one of the scientists who developed it. Punnett was a student at Cambridge University. Along with William Bateson, Punnett published a paper on the genetics of sweet peas. The square was developed as an elegant way to illustrate their research.

Teacher's Notes Help students get started by demonstrating how to set up and fill in the first Punnett square (ZZ × Zz cross).

Answers to Analysis

1. $\left(\frac{1}{2} \times \frac{1}{2}\right) = \frac{1}{4}$

2. $\left(\frac{1}{4} + \frac{1}{4}\right) = \frac{1}{2}$

3. The cross is ZZ × zz. All of the offspring will be heterozygous (Zz). Thus, the probability is 1.

4. The cross is Zz × zz. None of the offspring will be homozygous dominant (ZZ). Thus, the probability is 0.

Why It Matters

Probability in Real Life No one can predict the future with absolute certainty, but scientists often use mathematics and computer models try to determine the probable outcomes of many events and circumstances. Using data from past events, scientists can develop models that show how patterns from the past may be relevant to patterns occurring now.

Data

QuickLab

⏱ 15 min

Probabilities

Some people are born with extra fingers or toes. This condition, known as *polydactyly*, is rare. However, it is usually the result of a dominant allele.

Procedure

Draw Punnett squares to represent all possible combinations of alleles for each the crosses discussed below. Use Z to represent a dominant allele and z to represent a recessive allele.

Analysis

1. **Calculate** the probability that a cross of two heterozygous (Zz) parents will produce homozygous dominant (ZZ) offspring.

2. **Determine** the probability that a cross of a heterozygous parent (Zz) and a homozygous recessive (zz) parent will produce heterozygous offspring.

3. **Calculate** the probability that a cross of a homozygous dominant parent and a homozygous recessive parent will produce heterozygous offspring.

4. **Determine** the probability that a cross between a heterozygous parent and a homozygous recessive parent will produce homozygous dominant offspring.

▲ Polydactyly (extra fingers or toes) is usually a dominant trait.

ACADEMIC VOCABULARY

occur to take place

probability (PRAHB uh BIL uh tee) the likelihood that a specific event will occur; expressed in mathematical terms

Using Probability

Punnett squares allow direct and simple predictions to be made about the outcomes of genetic crosses, but those predictions are not certain. A Punnett square shows the possible outcomes of a cross, but it can also be used to calculate the probability of each outcome. **Probability** is the likelihood that a specific event will <u>occur</u>.

Calculating Probability Punnett squares are one simple way to demonstrate probability. Probability can be calculated and expressed in many ways. Probability can be expressed in words, as a decimal, as a percentage, or as a fraction. For example, if an event will definitely occur, its probability can be expressed as either 1 out of 1 (in words), 100 % (as a percentage), 1.0 (as a decimal), or $\frac{1}{1}$ (as a fraction). If an event is just as likely to occur as to not occur, its probability can be expressed as either 1 out of 2, 50 %, 0.5, or $\frac{1}{2}$. Probability can be determined by the following formula:

$$\text{probability} = \frac{\text{number of one kind of possible outcome}}{\text{total number of all possible outcomes}}$$

Consider the example of a coin tossed into the air. The total number of possible outcomes is two—heads or tails. Landing on heads is one possible outcome. Thus, the probability that the coin will land on heads is $\frac{1}{2}$. Likewise, the probability that it will land on tails is $\frac{1}{2}$. Of course, the coin will not land on tails exactly half of the time, but it will tend to do so. The average number of total flips that result in tails will tend to be $\frac{1}{2}$.

Differentiated Instruction

Special Education Students

Modeling Punnett Squares To help visually impaired students, work with the Punnett square concept, create the Punnett grid on the desktop using thick tape or clay. Provide objects of two different sizes to represent dominant and recessive alleles. For example, game pieces could be used. Use this model to create a 3-dimensional version of Figure 7. These materials can also be used for the Testcross QuickLab. 🄻🅂 **Kinesthetic**

Alternative Assessment

Mathematical Equivalents Ask students to determine the probability of selecting an ace from a single suit of cards. Then, ask them to express this fraction as a decimal and percentage. ($\frac{1}{13}$, 0.08, 8%) 🄻🅂 **Logical**

Probability of a Specific Allele in a Gamete Recall the law of segregation, which states that each gamete has an equal chance of receiving either one of a pair of alleles. If a pea plant has two alleles for seed color, only one of the two alleles (yellow or green) can end up in a gamete. ❯ **Probability formulas can be used to predict the probabilities that specific alleles will be passed on to offspring.** For a plant that has two alleles for seed color, the total number of possible outcomes is two—green or yellow. The probability that a gamete from this plant will carry the allele for green seed color is $\frac{1}{2}$. The probability that a gamete will carry the allele for yellow seed color is also $\frac{1}{2}$.

Probability in a Heterozygous Cross The possible results of a heterozygous cross are similar to those of flipping two coins at once. Consider the possible results of a cross of two pea plants that are heterozygous for seed shape (Rr). Either parent is equally likely to pass on a gamete that has either an R allele or an r allele. So, the chance of inheriting either allele is $\frac{1}{2}$. Multiplying the probabilities for each gamete shows that the probability that the offspring will have RR alleles is $\frac{1}{4}$. The probability that the offspring will have rr alleles is also $\frac{1}{4}$. The combination Rr has two possible outcomes, so the probability that the offspring will have Rr alleles is $\frac{2}{4}$, or $\frac{1}{2}$.

❯ **Reading Check** *What is the probability that a heterozygous cross will produce homozygous recessive offspring?*

SCI LINKS®
www.scilinks.org
Topic: Probability
Code: HX81217

Math Skills — Probability of Two Independent Events

Because two parents are involved in a genetic cross, both parents must be considered when predicting the probable outcomes. Consider the example of tossing two coins at the same time. The probability that a penny will land on heads is $\frac{1}{2}$, and the probability that a nickel will land on heads is $\frac{1}{2}$. How one coin falls does not affect how the other coin falls.

What is the probability that the nickel and the penny will both land on heads at the same time? To find the probability that a specific combination of two independent events will occur, multiply the probabilities of each event. Thus, the probability that both coins will land on heads is

$$\frac{1}{2} \times \frac{1}{2} = \frac{1}{4}$$

What about the probability that one coin will land on heads while the other coin lands on tails? Because the combination of heads and tails has two possible outcomes, the probabilities of each possible combination are added together:

$$\frac{1}{4} + \frac{1}{4} = \frac{2}{4} = \frac{1}{2}$$

Each coin has the same probability of landing on heads or tails.

The green boxes have the same combination (heads and tails), so these two probabilities can be added together.

Differentiated Instruction

Basic Learners

Reading the Signs Review the reasons why the probabilities are multiplied in the first example (both heads) and added in the second example (one heads, one tails).

Visual Literacy Before teaching students to interpret a pedigree such as that shown in **Figure 8,** introduce the symbols: male (square), female (circle), trait expressed (shaded circle or square), and trait not expressed (circle or square not shaded). Once students are comfortable with the meanings of the symbols, have them interpret the pedigree in **Figure 8.** Tell students the gene for this trait not only results in a deficiency of skin, hair, and eye pigmentation but also causes defects in vision. **LS Visual**

Teaching Key Ideas

Human X-Linked Genes Tell the students that some human genes are not inherited equally by both sexes. An X-linked recessive gene is more likely to be expressed in the phenotype of the son. The son gets one X chromosome, so one recessive gene will show in the phenotype. Daughters get two X chromosomes, so to express a recessive X-linked trait, the daughter must get a recessive gene on each X chromosome. Ask students how a male might inherit an X-linked trait from his mother. (The mother carries the recessive allele on one of her X chromosomes. The son inherits this chromosome from his mother and a Y from his father.) **LS Verbal**

Figure 8 Albinism is a genetic disorder carried by a recessive allele. Because of this disorder, this baby koala's skin and hair cells do not produce pigments, so the baby is mostly white. In the wild, albino animals have little chance of survival.

pedigree (PED i GREE) a diagram that shows the occurrence of a genetic trait in several generations of a family

genetic disorder an inherited disease or disorder that is caused by a mutation in a gene or by a chromosomal defect

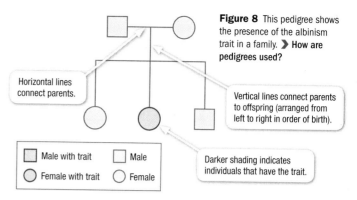

Figure 8 This pedigree shows the presence of the albinism trait in a family. **›** How are pedigrees used?

Horizontal lines connect parents.

Vertical lines connect parents to offspring (arranged from left to right in order of birth).

Darker shading indicates individuals that have the trait.

☐ Male with trait ☐ Male
◯ Female with trait ◯ Female

Using a Pedigree

Mendel observed several generations of pea plants to see patterns in the inheritance of traits. A simple way to model inheritance is to use a pedigree. A **pedigree** is a family history that shows how a trait is inherited over several generations. A healthcare worker may use a pedigree to help a family understand a genetic disorder. A **genetic disorder** is a disease or disorder that can be inherited. If a family has a history of a genetic disorder, the parents may want to know if their children could inherit the disorder. Some parents are carriers. Carriers have alleles for a disorder but do not show symptoms. Carriers can pass the allele for the disorder to their offspring.

Figure 8 shows a pedigree for a family in which albinism is present. A body affected by the genetic disorder albinism is unable to produce the pigment that gives dark color to skin, eyes, and hair. Without this pigment, the body may appear white or pink, as **Figure 9** shows. A recessive allele causes albinism. The pedigree helps show how this trait is inherited. **›** A pedigree can help answer questions about three aspects of inheritance: sex linkage, dominance, and heterozygosity.

Sex-Linked Gene The sex chromosomes, X and Y, carry genes for many characters other than gender. A *sex-linked gene* is located on either an X or a Y chromosome, but most are located on the X chromosome. Because it is much shorter than the X chromosome, the Y chromosome holds fewer genes. Females have two X chromosomes. A recessive allele on one of the X chromosomes will often have a corresponding dominant allele on the other. Thus, the trait for the recessive allele is not expressed in the female. Males, on the other hand, have an X chromosome and the much shorter Y chromosome. Because it has few genes, the shorter Y chromosome may lack an allele that corresponds to a recessive allele on the longer X chromosome. So, the trait for the single recessive allele will be expressed in the male. Traits that are not expressed equally in both sexes are commonly sex-linked traits. Colorblindness is an example of a sex-linked trait that is expressed more in males than in females.

› Reading Check *How can one identify a sex-linked trait?*

Why It Matters

Pedigreed Dogs About 10 percent of Dalmatians are deaf. Because many dogs are inbred—that is, they have closely related parents—some of them are homozygous for certain recessive disorders. Ask students who have purebred dogs to find out if their dog's breed is prone to a genetic disorder. [Some pedigreed dogs that are prone to genetic disorders include Irish setters (blindness), German shepherds (hip dysplasia), and dachshunds (dwarfism).] **LS Verbal**

Differentiated Instruction

Struggling Readers

Vocabulary Ask students to differentiate between *Punnett squares, probabilities,* and *pedigrees.* (*Punnett squares* predict the expected outcome of a cross by considering all possible combinations of gametes in a cross. *Probabilities* predict the mathematical likelihood that a specific event, such as the outcome of a cross, will occur. *Pedigrees* provide a visual representation of how a trait is inherited over several generations.) **LS Verbal**

QuickLab

Pedigree Analysis 4.2.1j

You will practice interpreting a pedigree. The pedigree to the right shows the presence or absence of the albinism trait in several generations of a family.

	Male		Male with trait
○	Female		Female with trait

Generation

Analysis

1. **Determine** whether the albinism trait is dominant or recessive. Explain your reasoning.

2. **Determine** if Female A could be heterozygous for albinism. Do the same for Female B.

3. **CRITICAL THINKING Applying Information** Suppose that Female B is homozygous and produces children with Male C. If Male C is heterozygous, what is the probability that the children will have the albinism trait?

Female A   Female B   Male C

This family's daughter has the albinism trait.

Dominant or Recessive? If a person has a trait that is autosomal and dominant and has even one dominant allele, he or she will show the trait. A dominant allele is needed to pass on the trait. If a person has a recessive trait and only one recessive allele, he or she will not show the trait but may pass it on. So, if a trait appears in a child whose parents lack the trait, it is most likely recessive.

Heterozygous or Homozygous? If a person is either heterozygous or homozygous dominant for an autosomal gene, his or her phenotype will show the dominant trait. If a person is homozygous recessive, his or her phenotype will show the recessive trait. Heterozygous parents can produce a child who is homozygous recessive. Thus, a recessive trait in the child shows that both parents were heterozygous carriers of the recessive allele.

Section 3 Review

KEY IDEAS

1. **Describe** how a Punnett square is used in genetics.

2. **List** ways to express mathematical probability in genetics.

3. **Sketch** a pedigree for an imaginary family of three generations and describe what the pedigree shows.

CRITICAL THINKING

4. **Scientific Methods** How can you determine the genotype of a pea plant that has purple flowers?

5. **Mathematical Reasoning** If you flip two coins at once, will at least one coin land on heads? Explain.

6. **Analyzing Graphics** When analyzing a pedigree, how can you determine if an individual is a carrier (heterozygous) for the trait being studied?

USING SCIENCE GRAPHICS

7. **Pedigree** Some kinds of colorblindness are sex-linked traits carried on the X chromosome. So, males can inherit the trait from mothers that are not colorblind. Draw a pedigree that demonstrates this pattern of inheritance.

QuickLab

Teacher's Notes Encourage students to use "If-then" statements to organize their thoughts and interpret the pedigree. Example: If a gene is expressed by an offspring but not by either parent, then the gene is likely to be inherited recessively.

Answers to Analysis

1. It is recessive, because it sometimes appears in the children of parents who lack the trait, as was the case with Female A.

2. Female A must be homozygous to express the recessive trait. Female B does not have albinism, so she could be heterozygous. (One cannot tell for certain without seeing whether the trait shows up in her descendants.)

3. There is no chance that the children will have the albinism trait.

› Close

Formative Assessment

A Punnett Square is used to show _____, while a pedigree is used to show _____.

A. parents, offspring (Incorrect. Both a Punnett square and a pedigree show parents and offspring. Review the section to understand Punnett squares and pedigrees.)

B. offspring, parents (Incorrect. Both a Punnett square and a pedigree show offspring and parents. Review the section to understand Punnett squares and pedigrees.)

C. genotypes, phenotypes (Correct!)

D. phenotypes, genotypes (Incorrect. A Punnett square is mostly used to show genotypes, while a pedigree is mostly used to show phenotypes.)

Answers to Section Review

1. A Punnett square shows the relative probabilities of all of the possible genotypes that could result from a specified cross for a given character.

2. in words, as a percentage, as a decimal, or as a fraction

3. Look for the following in students' work: three generations; males and females; the presence of traits; and Mendelian inheritance patterns. Students should select one trait to represent in the pedigree, such as freckles or albinism.

4. Sample answer: Perform a test cross with a white-flowered pea plant. If any of the offspring are white, the purple-flowered parent must be heterozygous. If none of the offspring have white flowers, then the purple-flowered parent is probably

homozygous dominant. This result assumes that a large number of offspring have been produced.

5. Sample answer: Not necessarily; the chances are only 1/2 that either coin will land on heads, and each flip is independent of the other.

6. Sample answer: If a trait appears in both the offspring and the parents of an individual that lacks the trait, and the trait is known to be recessive, then that individual is probably a carrier of the recessive allele.

7. Sample answer:

XY	—	XXᶜ
	XᶜY	

Beyond Mendelian Heredity

Section
4

❯ Focus

This section discusses complex patterns of inheritance such as incomplete dominance, codominance, polygenic traits, linked traits, and environmental influences

🔊 Bellringer

Use the Bellringer transparency to prepare students for this section.

❯ Teach

Teaching Key Ideas

Multiple Alleles Ask students to look at the variations in human characters shown in **Figure 9**. Ask them to propose a mechanism for the inheritance of a character such as eye color in humans, which can appear as brown, green, blue, and gray. (There are at least three alleles involved, brown, green and blue. Brown is dominant to green and blue, and green is dominant to blue.)
LS Logical/Verbal

Key Ideas	Key Terms	Why It Matters
❯ Are there exceptions to the simple Mendelian pattern of inheritance? ❯ How do heredity and the environment interact to influence phenotype? ❯ How do linked genes affect chromosome assortment and crossover during meiosis?	polygenic character codominance linked	Some inheritance is more complex than Mendel showed. This complexity helps explain the large variety of human traits.

The Living Environment
Standard 4
2.1a Genes are inherited, but their expression can be modified by interactions with the environment.
2.1c Hereditary information is contained in genes, located in the chromosomes of each cell. An inherited trait of an individual can be determined by one or by many genes, and a single gene can influence more than one trait. A human cell contains many thousands of different genes in its nucleus.

Figure 9 A physical feature—such as height, weight, hair color, and eye color—is often influenced by more than one gene.

Suppose a horse that has red hair mates with a horse that has white hair. The offspring of the horses has both red and white hair on its body. How can this be? Shouldn't the colt's hair be one color or the other? Not always! In fact, most characters are not inherited in the simple patterns identified by Mendel. Although Mendel was correct about the inheritance of the traits that he studied, most patterns of inheritance are more complex than those that Mendel identified.

Many Genes, Many Alleles

If you look at people and animals around you, you will notice a variety of physical features, as **Figure 9** shows. Why do so few of these features have only two types? First, not all genes have only two alleles. Second, not all characters are controlled by one gene. ❯ The Mendelian inheritance pattern is rare in nature; other patterns include polygenic inheritance, incomplete dominance, multiple alleles, and codominance.

Polygenic Inheritance When several genes affect a character, it is called a **polygenic character.** For example, eye color is affected by several genes. One gene controls the relative amount of greenness of the eye, and another gene controls brownness. (The recessive condition in both cases is blue eyes.) Other genes also affect eye color. Sorting out the effects of each gene is difficult. The genes may be on the same or different chromosomes. Other examples of polygenic characters in humans are height and skin color. In fact, most characters are polygenic.

Incomplete Dominance Recall that in Mendel's pea-plant crosses, one allele was completely dominant over the other. In some cases, however, an offspring has a phenotype that is intermediate between the traits of its two parents. This pattern is called *incomplete dominance.*

Section Correlations
4.2.1a
4.2.1c

Key Resources

📦 **Transparencies**
C7 Incomplete Dominance

💿 **Visual Concepts**
Comparing Single Allele, Multiple Allele, and Polygenic Traits

Comparing Complete, Incomplete, and Co-Dominance

Comparing X-Linked and Sex-Influenced Traits

Differentiated Instruction

Alternative Assessment

Evaluating Arguments Evaluate students' ability to analyze, review, and critique scientific explanations by asking them to identify and describe the limitations of Mendel's understanding of inheritance based on his pea plant experiments. Complete this exercise by comparing and contrasting simple patterns of trait inheritance associated with pea plants with more complex patterns of trait inheritance such as polygenic, incomplete dominance, codominance, and multiple alleles. **LS Logical**

Possible alleles

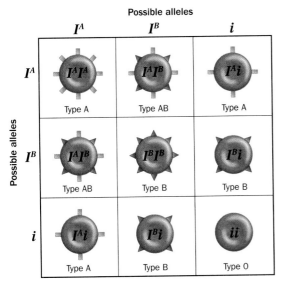

Possible alleles

	I^A	I^B	i
I^A	I^AI^A Type A	I^AI^B Type AB	I^Ai Type A
I^B	I^AI^B Type AB	I^BI^B Type B	I^Bi Type B
i	I^Ai Type A	I^Bi Type B	ii Type O

Blood type molecules

▲ Molecule A

▲ Molecule B

Figure 10 Multiple alleles control the ABO blood groups. Different combinations of three alleles (I^A, I^B, and i) result in four blood phenotypes (A, AB, B, and O). For example, a person who has the alleles I^A and i has type A blood. ❯ **What is another kind of inheritance pattern demonstrated by the ABO blood groups?**

When a snapdragon that has red flowers is crossed with a snapdragon that has white flowers, the offspring have pink flowers. Neither the red allele nor the white allele is completely dominant over the other. The pink flowers simply have less red pigment than the red flowers do.

Multiple Alleles Genes that have three or more possible alleles are said to have *multiple alleles*. For example, multiple alleles exist for hair color in cats. Still, only two alleles for a gene can be present in one individual. The determination of dominance may be complex.

In humans, the ABO blood groups (blood types) are determined by three alleles: I^A, I^B, and i. **Figure 10** shows how various combinations of the three alleles can produce four blood types: A, B, AB, and O. The I^A and I^B alleles cause red blood cells to make certain molecules. The letters A and B refer to the two kinds of molecules. The i allele does not cause either molecule to be made. So, both the I^A and I^B alleles are dominant over i. But I^A and I^B are not dominant over each other. So, a person who has both I^A and I^B alleles has type AB blood. A person who has two i alleles has type O blood.

Codominance For some characters, two traits can appear at the same time. **Codominance** is a condition in which both alleles for the same gene are fully expressed.

The genetics of human blood groups, which was discussed above, is also an example of codominance. A person who has I^AI^B alleles will have type AB blood because neither allele is dominant over the other. Type AB blood cells make both A-type and B-type molecules.

❯ **Reading Check** *How does codominance differ from incomplete dominance?*

polygenic (PAHL uh JEN ik) **character** a character that is influenced by more than one gene

codominance (KOH DAHM uh nuhns) a condition in which both alleles for a gene are fully expressed

ACADEMIC VOCABULARY

various many kinds of

www.scilinks.org
Topic: Mendelian Genetics
Code: HX80940

Answers to Caption Questions
Figure 10: Another inheritance pattern demonstrated by the ABO blood group is codominance.

Teaching Key Ideas

Incomplete Dominance Ask students whether a plant breeder could produce only pink-flowering snapdragons by crossing pink-flowering snapdragons and white-flowering snapdragons. (no) Help students understand that because all pink-flowering snapdragons are heterozygous, mating a pink-flowering snapdragon with a white-flowering one would produce pink-flowering and white-flowering offspring in a ratio of 1:1 **LS Logical**

Math Skills

Phenotypic Ratios Ask students to write the phenotypic ratios for the combinations shown in **Figure 11**. (type A = $\frac{3}{9}$ or $\frac{1}{3}$; type B = $\frac{3}{9}$ or $\frac{1}{3}$; type AB = $\frac{2}{9}$; type O = $\frac{1}{9}$)

Differentiated Instruction

Basic Students/English Learners

Create a Chart Assign pairs of students to create a chart that illustrates three of the following: polygenic inheritance, incomplete dominance, characters controlled by multiple alleles, codominance, and characters influenced by the environment. Students can use drawings or photographs. **LS Interpersonal**

Why It Matters

Human Inheritance Mendel's work with garden-pea plants showed that the characters he studied are controlled by single genes. In humans, single-factor inheritance has been found in about 600 recessively inherited characters, and in such dominant conditions as Huntington's disease. However, many more conditions are determined by polygenic inheritance, which involves several genes. Such conditions include cleft lip and palate, some types of schizophrenia, hypertension, and diabetes.

Figure 11: The character for fur color can be affected by conditions in the environment.

Science Skills

Using Punnett Squares Ask students to use a Punnett square to figure out the following problem. The mother of a blood type O child is type A. List the mother's genotype and the possible genotypes for the father. (The mother is I^Ai; possible genotypes for the father are I^Ai, I^Bi, ii) **LS** **Logical**

> Close

Formative Assessment

A cross between a red-flowered plant and a white-flowered plant results in offspring that have pink flowers. This result is an example of _____.

A. polygenic inheritance (Incorrect. Polygenic inheritance occurs when multiple genes affect one character. In this case, a pattern of blending of traits occurs. Review the exceptions to Mendelian inheritance patterns.)

B. incomplete dominance (Correct! Incomplete dominance occurs when a blend or intermediate form results from a cross of two contrasting traits.)

C. multiple alleles (Incorrect. Multiple alleles tend to produce a wide range of phenotypes. The case of pink flowers is simply a blending of two phenotypes.)

D. codominance (Incorrect. Codominance is when both traits are fully expressed.)

Figure 11 Many Arctic mammals, such as the Arctic fox, develop white fur during the winter and dark fur during the summer. **>** What does this change indicate about the character for fur color in these animals?

linked in genetics, describes two or more genes that tend to be inherited together

Genes Affected by the Environment

Genes are the key to life, but there is more to life than genes. **> Phenotype can be affected by conditions in the environment, such as nutrients and temperature.** For example, temperature affects the fur color of the Arctic fox, shown in **Figure 11.** During summer, genes in the fox's skin cells cause pigments to be made. These pigments make the fox's coat darker. Dark fur color helps the fox blend in with grass or woods. But during cold weather, the genes stop causing pigment to be made. Then, the fox's fur grows white, and the fox can blend in with the winter snow.

In humans, many of the characters that are partly determined by heredity are also affected by the environment. For example, a person's height is partly hereditary. Tall parents tend to produce tall children. But nutrition also affects height. A person who has an unhealthy diet may not grow as tall as he or she could have. Many aspects of human personality and behavior are strongly affected by the environment, but genes also seem to play an important role.

Genes Linked Within Chromosomes

Many traits do not follow Mendel's laws, but Mendel's pea traits did. Why? One reason is that Mendel studied the simplest kinds of heredity: characters determined by one gene that has two alleles. Also, he studied characters that are determined by independent genes.

Recall how meiosis relates to the *law of independent assortment*. If genes are on different chromosomes, the alleles for each gene can be sorted independently. Then, each set of alleles can be recombined in any way. For example, in the pea plants, the two alleles for seed color could be combined in any way with the two alleles for seed shape.

Some genes are close together on the same chromosome. **> During meiosis, genes that are close together on the same chromosome are less likely to be separated than genes that are far apart.** Genes that are close together, as well as the traits that they determine, are said to be **linked.**

> **Reading Check** *What term describes genes that are close together on the same chromosome and that are unlikely to be separated?*

Section 4 Review

> **KEY IDEAS**

1. **List** exceptions to the Mendelian pattern of one character controlled by two alleles.
2. **Describe** the relationship between heredity and the environment.
3. **Relate** gene linkage to chromosome assortment and crossover during meiosis.

CRITICAL THINKING

4. **Evaluating an Argument** A classmate states that Mendel's hypotheses are incorrect because they do not consider intermediate forms of a character. Evaluate this argument.
5. **Justifying Conclusions** A classmate states that a person cannot have type BO blood. Do you agree or disagree? Explain your reasoning.

USING SCIENCE GRAPHICS

6. **Punnett Square** Predict the ratios of each of the ABO blood groups in an average population. Use a Punnett square like the one shown in Figure 11 and explain your results. Assume that the population has equal numbers of I^A, I^B, and i alleles.

Answers to Section Review

1. polygenic inheritance, incomplete dominance, multiple alleles, and codominance

2. Although genotype is the initial determinant of phenotype, phenotype can also be affected by conditions in the environment, such as nutrients and temperature.

3. During meiosis, genes that are close (on the same chromosome) are less likely to be separated (due to crossover) than genes that are far apart. Genes that are on separate chromosomes will have complete independent assortment.

4. Sample answer: Mendel's "laws" apply under specific conditions, as in the pea plants he studied. These laws are of limited use to predict or

model more complex inheritance patterns, such as polygenic inheritance.

5. Sample answer: Type BO blood does not exist because type B is co-dominant (with type A) and type O is always recessive. If a person has I^B and i alleles, he or she would simply have type B blood.

6. Type AB $\frac{2}{9}$ or 22.2%

    Type A $\frac{3}{9} = \frac{1}{3}$ or 33.3%

    Type B $\frac{3}{9} = \frac{1}{3}$ or 33.3%

    Type O $\frac{1}{9}$ or 11.1%

Objectives

▶ Develop a hypothesis to predict the yield of a corn crop.

▶ Design and conduct an experiment to test your hypothesis.

▶ Compare germination and survival rates of three lots of corn seeds.

Materials

- lab apron, disposable gloves
- corn seeds, normal (10 from lot A and 10 from lot B)
- corn seeds, 3:1 mix of normal and albino (10 from lot C)
- plant tray or pots
- soil, potting (3 kg)
- water

Safety

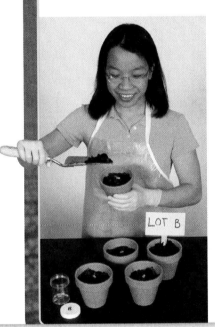

LOT B

Plant Genetics

In plants, albinism is characterized by the failure to produce chlorophyll, a plant pigment necessary for photosynthesis. Because the trait is recessive, parent plants with the normal phenotype may produce offspring (seeds) that carry the alleles for albinism. In this lab, you will investigate a question about albinism alleles in plants.

Preparation

1. **SCIENTIFIC METHODS** **State the Problem** What might happen to a seed that has one or more albinism alleles?

2. **SCIENTIFIC METHODS** **Form a Hypothesis** Form a hypothesis about how albinism affects the success of plants grown from seed.

Procedure

Design an Experiment

❶ Design an experiment that will determine the germination and survival rates of three lots of corn seeds. Write out a procedure for your experiment on a separate sheet of paper. Be sure to include safety procedures, and construct tables to organize your data. Have your teacher approve your plan before you begin.

❷ Predict the outcome of your experiment, and record this prediction.

Conduct Your Experiment

❸ **CAUTION: Wear gloves and a lab apron whenever handling soil, seeds, or plants.**

❹ Follow your written procedure. Make note of any changes.

❺ Record all data in your tables. Also record any other observations.

❻ At the end of the experiment, present your results to the class. Devise a way to collect the class data in a common format.

❼ Clean up your lab materials according to your teacher's instructions. Wash your hands before leaving the lab.

Analyze and Conclude

1. **SCIENTIFIC METHODS** **Evaluating Experimental Design** Did you get clear results? How might you improve your design?

2. **SCIENTIFIC METHODS** **Analyzing Results** Did your results support your hypothesis? Explain your answer.

3. **Analyzing Data** Use the class data to calculate the average germination rate and survival rate for each lot of corn seeds. Describe any patterns that you notice.

Time Required

One 45 minute class period

Ratings

EASY ────────────▶ HARD

Teacher Prep 🧪🧪🧪
Student Setup 🧪🧪🧪
Concept Level 🧪🧪🧪
Cleanup 🧪🧪

Preparation

1. No student answer is expected here, but they might simply copy the question.

2. Sample hypothesis: If seeds have two albinism alleles, then they cannot germinate.

Safety Cautions

Be sure students have read the safety rules for working in the lab.

Tips and Tricks

Corn seeds can be purchased from Ward's. Tell students that lot C is the result of the cross between two corn plants that were heterozygous for the albinism allele. Lots A and B are homozygous dominant and are normal. Ensure that factors such as light, temperature, and water are held constant for all groups to avoid introducing variables other than genotype.

Answers to Procedure

1. Check students' experimental designs at this point. Their plans should include safety procedures and empty data tables.

2. Sample prediction: Albino corn seeds (homozygous recessive) will not grow to adulthood. Heterozygous and homozygous dominant seeds will grow to adulthood normally.

6. Organize an opportunity for brief presentations. Students are presenting results only. Analysis and conclusions should come later.

Answers to Analyze and Conclude

1. Answers will vary depending on the source of the seeds used as lots A, B, and C. Some students may not get clear results if they did not measure carefully or control experimental conditions. All students should suggest improvements to their experimental design.

2. Some students will not get the results they predicted. Students' responses should include terms such as "supporting" or "refuting" a hypothesis, but not "proving" it.

3. Students should note variance among individual data sets. The trend for class data should show that albino corn germinates at about the same rate as non-albino corn, but grows less vigorously and dies early.

Lab Correlations

1.2.4 Carry out a research plan for testing explanations, including selecting and developing techniques, acquiring and building apparatus, and recording observations as necessary.

SUPER SUMMARY

Have students connect the major concepts in this chapter through an interactive Super Summary. Visit **go.hrw.com** and type in the keyword **HX8GENS** to access the Super Summary for this chapter.

Reteaching Key Ideas

Mendel's Steps Ask students to replicate the three steps in Mendel's experiments as illustrated in **Figure 3,** substituting two additional characters from **Figure 2.**
LS Verbal

Segregation of Alleles Students struggling with the random segregation of alleles may benefit from this exercise. Group four students into pairs that stand together. Each pair represents the two alleles of the same gene in each parent. Each student is one allele. Have each pair separate and flip a coin. The winners of each coin-flip join as a new pair. **LS** Kinesthetic

Key Ideas	Key Terms

1 Origins of Hereditary Science

> Modern genetics is based on Mendel's explanations for the patterns of heredity that he studied in garden pea plants.

> The garden pea plant is a good subject for studying heredity because the plant has contrasting traits, usually self-pollinates, and grows easily.

> Mendel's first experiments used monohybrid crosses and were carried out in three steps.

> For each of the seven characters that Mendel studied, he found a similar 3-to-1 ratio of contrasting traits in the F_2 generation.

Key Terms:
character (268)
trait (268)
hybrid (268)
generation (269)

2 Mendel's Theory

> Mendelian theory explains simple patterns of inheritance in which the combination of two alleles results in one of several possible traits.

> In modern terms, the *law of segregation* holds that when an organism produces gametes, each pair of alleles is separated and each gamete has an equal chance of receiving either one of the alleles.

> Genotype determines phenotype.

> In modern terms, the *law of independent assortment* holds that during gamete formation, the alleles of each gene segregate independently.

Key Terms:
allele (272)
dominant (273)
recessive (273)
genotype (274)
phenotype (274)
homozygous (275)
heterozygous (275)

3 Modeling Mendel's Laws

> A Punnett square shows all of the genotypes that could result from a given cross.

> Probability formulas can be used to predict the probabilities that specific alleles will be passed on to offspring.

> A pedigree can help answer questions about three aspects of inheritance: sex linkage, dominance, and heterozygosity.

Key Terms:
Punnett square (276)
probability (278)
pedigree (280)
genetic disorder (280)

4 Beyond Mendelian Heredity

> The Mendelian inheritance is rare in nature; other patterns include polygenic inheritance, incomplete dominance, multiple alleles, and codominance.

> Phenotype can be affected by conditions in the environment, such as nutrients and temperature.

> Genes that are close together on the same chromosome are linked.

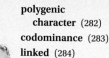

Key Terms:
polygenic character (282)
codominance (283)
linked (284)

PART A: Answer all questions in this part.

Directions: For each statement or question, write on your separate answer sheet the number of the word or expression that best completes the statement or answers the question.

1 Which statement provides accurate information about the technique illustrated below?

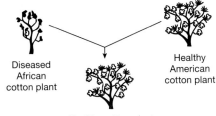

Diseased African cotton plant

Healthy American cotton plant

Healthy cotton plant produced to grow in Africa

(1) This technique results in offspring that are genetically identical to the parents.

(2) New varieties of organisms can be developed by this technique known as selective breeding.

(3) This technique is used by farmers to eliminate mutations in future members of the species.

(4) Since the development of cloning, this technique is no longer used in agriculture.

2 Which statement best explains the fact that some identical twins appear different from one another?

(1) Their DNA is essentially the same and the environment plays little or no role in the expression of their genes.

(2) Their DNA is very different and the environment plays a significant role in the expression of their genes.

(3) Their DNA is very different and the environment plays little or no role in the expression of their genes.

(4) Their DNA is essentially the same and the environment plays a significant role in the expression of their genes.

3 Genes are inherited, but their expressions can be modified by the environment. This statement explains why

(1) some animals have dark fur only when the temperature is within a certain range

(2) offspring produced by means of sexual reproduction look exactly like their parents

(3) identical twins who grow up in different homes have the same characteristics

(4) animals can be cloned, but plants cannot

4 Scientific studies show that identical twins who were separated at birth and raised in different homes may vary in height, weight, and intelligence. The most probable explanation for these differences is that

(1) original genes of each twin increased in number as they developed

(2) one twin received genes only from the mother while the other twin received genes only from the father

(3) environments in which they were raised were different enough to affect the expression of their genes

(4) environments in which they were raised were different enough to change the genetic makeup of both individuals

5 In a particular variety of corn, the kernels turn red when exposed to sunlight. In the absence of sunlight, the kernels remain yellow. Based on this information, it can be concluded that the color of these corn kernels is due to

(1) a different type of DNA that is produced when sunlight is present

(2) a different species of corn that is produced in sunlight

(3) the effect of sunlight on the number of chromosomes inherited

(4) the effect of environment on gene expression

PART A

1. **(2)** Breeding organisms with two unique parents cannot lead to genetically identical offspring. Selective breeding is still in use today. The choice about mutations is untrue. (*#09, January 2006 Regents Exam*)

2. **(4)** The choices about different DNA are not true as identical twins arise from the same egg and sperm cells. If the identical twins appear different, it must arise from environmental factors inside and/or outside the womb. (*#06, January 2006 Regents Exam*)

3. **(1)** The choice describing offspring is incorrect because asexual (not sexual) reproduction involves offspring that are exactly like their parents. The choice describing twins does not show how gene expression is changing because of the environment. The choice about animal and plant cloning is not true. (*#02, August 2006 Regents Exam*)

4. **(3)** Identical twins have identical genes, received from both the mother and father. The environment in which they are raised can affect gene expression. (*#09, June 2003 Regents Exam*)

5. **(4)** In this variety of corn, sunlight can affect the expression of genes that control kernel color. Sunlight does not change the DNA into a different type, or change the number of chromosomes that are inherited. (*#08, August 2003 Regents Exam*)

Regents Exam Practice
Correlations

4.2.1a	3, 4, 5
4.2.1k	2
4.2.2a	1, 6, 10, 11

6. (4) Direct harvesting does not
lead to combining plant traits,
and neither does asexual
reproduction or cloning.
(#06, June 2005 Regents Exam)

7. (2)

8. (4) The table shows a 3:1 ratio
using the following data:
77:23 ≈ 3:1; 74:26 ≈ 3:1.
75:25 ≈ 3:1; 73:27 ≈ 3:1.

9. (1)

---

6 One variety of strawberry is resistant to a damaging fungus, but produces small fruit. Another strawberry variety produces large fruit, but is not resistant to the same fungus. The two desirable qualities may be combined in a new variety of strawberry plant by

(1) cloning
(2) asexual reproduction
(3) direct harvesting
(4) selective breeding

7 Some people are born with an extra finger or toe. People who have this trait have inherited either one or two of the same allele. So, the trait is

(1) recessive.
(2) dominant.
(3) phenotypic.
(4) independent.

Base your answers to the following questions on the table below and on your knowledge of biology.

Experimental group	Dominant trait	Recessive trait
Group 1	77	23
Group 2	74	26
Group 3	75	25
Group 4	73	27

8 What is the approximate average ratio of dominant traits to recessive traits?

(1) 1:0
(2) 2:1
(3) 1:2
(4) 3:1

9 What kind of cross would result in these ratios?

(1) two heterozygous parents
(2) two homozygous recessive parents
(3) two homozygous dominant parents
(4) one heterozygous parent and one homozygous recessive parent

PART B

Base your answer to question 10 on the passage below and on your knowledge of biology.

In Search of a Low-Allergy Peanut

Many people are allergic to substances in the environment. Of the many foods that contain allergens (allergy-inducing substances), peanuts cause some of the most severe reactions. Mildly allergic people may only get hives. Highly allergic people can go into a form of shock. Some people die each year from reactions to peanuts.

A group of scientists is attempting to produce peanuts that lack the allergy-inducing proteins by using traditional selective breeding methods. They are searching for varieties of peanuts that are free of the allergens. By crossing those varieties with popular commercial types, they hope to produce peanuts that will be less likely to cause allergic reactions and still taste good. So far, they have found one variety that has 80 percent less of one of three complex proteins linked to allergic reactions. Removing all three of these allergens may be impossible, but even removing one could help.

Other researchers are attempting to alter the genes that code for the three major allergens in peanuts. All of this research is seen as a possible long-term solution to peanut allergies.

10 Explain how selective breeding is being used to try to produce commercial peanuts that will not cause allergic reactions in people.

Base your answer to question 11 on the passage below and on your knowledge of biology.

Better Rice

The production of new types of food crops will help raise the quantity of food grown by farmers. Research papers released by the National Academy of Sciences announced the development of two new superior varieties of rice—one produced by selective breeding and the other by biotechnology.

One variety of rice, called Nerica (New Rice for Africa), is already helping farmers in Africa. Nerica combines the hardiness and weed resistance of rare African rice varieties with the productivity and faster maturity of common Asian varieties.

Another variety, called Stress-Tolerant Rice, was produced by inserting a pair of bacterial genes into rice plants for the production of trehalose (a sugar). Trehalose helps plants maintain healthy cell membranes, proteins, and enzymes during environmental stress. The resulting plants survive drought, low temperatures, salty soils, and other stresses better than standard rice varieties.

11 Nerica was most likely produced by
  (1) crossing a variety of African rice with a variety of Asian rice
  (2) cloning genes for hardiness and weed resistance from Asian rice
  (3) using Asian rice to compete with rare African varieties
  (4) inserting genes for productivity and faster maturity into Asian rice

PART B

10. Allow 1 credit for explaining how selective breeding is being used to try to produce commercial peanuts that will not cause allergic reactions in people. Acceptable responses include, but are not limited to: Varieties of peanuts that are low in the allergens will be crossed with commercial types.; Varieties of peanuts that are free of the allergens will be crossed with commercial types.; A variety of peanut that has 80% less of one of the allergens will be crossed with commercial types. *(#51, June 2006 Regents Exam)*

11. **(1)** If Nerica is an African variety, then it can't be created using only an Asian rice, as described in one of the choices. Since hardiness and weed resistance are African variety traits, it cannot be cloned only from the Asian variety. Producing new varieties of food crops cannot occur fast enough by competition alone, either.

DNA, RNA, and Proteins

		Standards	**Teach Key Ideas**

CHAPTER OPENER, pp. 290–291   15 min.

The Living Environment

SECTION 1 The Structure of DNA, pp. 293–299   90 min.

❯ DNA: The Genetic Material
❯ Searching for the Genetic Material
❯ The Shape of DNA
❯ The Information in DNA
❯ Discovering DNA's Structure

Standards: 4.2.1c, 4.2.1f, 4.2.1h

Teach Key Ideas:

Bellringer Transparencies

Transparencies C9 Griffith's Discovery of Transformation • C10 The Hershey-Chase Experiment • C11 DNA Double Helix

Visual Concepts Transformation • Hershey and Chase's Experiment • Bacteriophage • DNA Overview • Double Helix • Nucleotide • Structure of a Nucleotide • Comparing Purines and Pyrimidines • Complementary Base Pairing

---

SECTION 2 Replication of DNA, pp. 300–303   60 min.

❯ DNA Replication
❯ Replication Proteins
❯ Prokaryotic and Eukaryotic Replication

Standards: 4.2.1b, 4.2.1f

Teach Key Ideas:

Bellringer Transparencies

Transparencies C12 DNA Replication • C13 Replication Forks

Visual Concepts DNA Replication • Snapshots of Replication • Replication Forks Increase the Speed of Replication

---

SECTION 3 RNA and Gene Expression, pp. 304–310   60 min.

❯ An Overview of Gene Expression
❯ RNA: A Major Player
❯ Transcription: Reading the Gene
❯ The Genetic Code: Three-Letter "Words"
❯ Translation: RNA to Proteins
❯ Complexities of Gene Expression

Standards: 4.1.2i, 4.2.1a, 4.2.1g, 4.2.1i

Teach Key Ideas:

Bellringer Transparencies

Transparencies C15 Transcription • C16 Codons in mRNA • C17 Translation: Assembling Proteins

Visual Concepts Ribonucleic Acid • Comparing DNA and RNA • Gene Expression • Transcription • Promoter• Codons in mRNA • Genetic Code • tRNA and Anticodon • Translation • Snapshot of Translation • Ribosomes

See also PowerPoint® Resources

Chapter Review and Assessment Resources

SE Super Summary, p. 312
SE Regents Exam Practice, p. 313
  Regents Review Guide
  Review Resources
  Chapter Tests A and B
  Holt Online Assessment
  Regents Question Banks on Teacher's One-Stop Planner

CHAPTER
Fast Track
To shorten instruction due to time limitations, eliminate the Skills Practice Lab: DNA Extraction.

Basic Learners

TE Organizing Concepts, p. 294
TE Replication Model, p. 301
TE Recognizing the Code, p. 306
  Directed Reading Worksheets*
  Active Reading Worksheets*
  Lab Manuals, Level A*
  Study Guide* ■
  Note-taking Workbook*
  Special Needs Activities and Modified Tests*

Advanced Learners

TE Genetics in the News, pg. 298
  Critical Thinking Worksheets*
  Concept Mapping Worksheets*
  Science Skills Worksheets*
  Lab Datasheets, Level C*

Why It Matters	Hands-On	Skills Development	Assessment
Build student motivation with resources about high-interest applications.	**SE Inquiry Lab** Code Combinations, p. 291	**TE Reading Toolbox** Assessing Prior Knowledge, p. 290 **SE Reading Toolbox,** p. 292	
TE Why Protein?, p. 293 **TE The Importance of Molecular Shape,** p. 296 **TE Demonstration** The Shape of DNA, p. 296 **TE Crediting Rosalind Franklin,** p. 298	**SE Quick Lab** DNA's Structure, p. 297 **SE Skills Practice Lab** DNA Extraction from Wheat Germ, p. 311 📁 **Exploration Lab** Extracting DNA*	**SE Reading Toolbox** Describing Time, p. 294 **TE Reading Toolbox** Scientific Illustrations, p. 294 **TE Reading Toolbox** Visual Literacy, p. 294 **TE Reading Toolbox** Visual Literacy, p.295 **TE Reading Toolbox** Visual Literacy, p.298	**SE Section Review** **TE Formative Assessment** Spanish Assessment* ■ 📁 **Section Quiz** ■
	SE Quick Lab DNA Replication Rate, p. 303 📁 **Skills Practice Lab** Karyotyping: Genetic Disorders*	**SE Reading Toolbox** Visual Literacy, p. 300 **TE Reading Toolbox** Visual Literacy, p. 301 **SE Reading Toolbox** Word Parts, p. 302 **TE Reading Toolbox** Word Parts, p. 302 **TE Reading Toolbox** Visual Literacy, p. 302	**SE Section Review** **TE Formative Assessment** Spanish Assessment* ■ 📁 **Section Quiz** ■
TE Redundant Condons, p. 307 **TE Antibiotic Function,** p. 308 **TE Polyribosomes,** p. 309	**SE Quick Lab** Genetic Code of Keratin, p. 310	**TE Reading Toolbox** Word Parts, p. 305 **SE Reading Toolbox** Three-Panel Flip Chart, p. 306 **TE Reading Toolbox** Three-Panel Flip Chart, p. 306 **TE Reading Toolbox** Visual Literacy, p. 307 **TE Reading Toolbox** Visual Literacy, p. 308 **TE Reading Toolbox** Visual Literacy, p. 309	**SE Section Review** **TE Formative Assessment** Spanish Assessment* ■ 📁 **Section Quiz** ■
	See also Lab Generator		**See also Holt Online Assessment Resources**

Resources for Differentiated Instruction

English Learners

TE Genes, Proteins, and DNA, p. 305
TE RNA Pairing Rules, p. 306
📁 Directed Reading Worksheets*
📁 Active Reading Worksheets*
📁 Lab Manuals, Level A*
📓 Study Guide* ■
📓 Note-taking Workbook*
📓 Multilingual Glossary
💿 Interactive Tutor

Struggling Readers

TE Deciphering Symbols, p. 295
📁 Directed Reading Worksheets*
📁 Active Reading Worksheets*
📁 Lab Manuals, Level A*
📓 Study Guide*
📓 Note-taking Workbook*
📓 Special Needs Activities and Modified Tests*
💿 Interactive Tutor

Special Education Students

Replication Fork Model, p. 302
📁 Directed Reading Worksheets*
📁 Active Reading Worksheets*
📁 Lab Manuals, Level A*
📓 Study Guide* ■
📓 Note-taking Workbook*
📓 Special Needs Activities and Modified Tests*

Alternative Assessment

TE Replication, p. 305
TE Translation, p. 309
📁 Science Skills Worksheets*
📁 Section Quizzes* ■
📓 Chapter Tests A, B, and C* ■

DNA, RNA, and Proteins

Overview

The purpose of this chapter is to explain the universal nature of DNA and its importance to life on Earth. The research that led to the discovery of DNA is an example of how the accumulation of information gathered from scientific processes adds to the body of information we call science. The nature of the DNA molecule makes it possible for it to replicate itself, but more importantly, it has the code needed to direct the assembly of amino acids into polypeptides. Another nucleic acid, RNA, facilitates this process of gene expression.

READING TOOLBOX

Assessing Prior Knowledge Students should understand the following concepts:
- structural characteristics of basic biomolecules
- cell structure and function

Visual Literacy Ask students to define the term *model* as it applies to this photograph. (It's a description used to help visualize something that cannot be seen.) Ask students why the parts of the model are different sizes. (Some parts are closer, and others are farther away in the part that is coiled) Explain that this photo shows only a fraction of a typical DNA molecule.

Preview

1 The Structure of DNA
DNA: The Genetic Material
Searching for the Genetic Material
The Shape of DNA
The Information in DNA
Discovering DNA's Structure

2 Replication of DNA
DNA Replication
Replication Proteins
Prokaryotic and Eukaryotic Replication

3 RNA and Gene Expression
An Overview of Gene Expression
RNA: A Major Player
Transcription: Reading the Gene
The Genetic Code: Three-Letter "Words"
Translation: RNA to Proteins
Complexities of Gene Expression

Why It Matters

Did you know that DNA is found in the cells of all organisms? A unique set of genes makes one organism different from another, but DNA is the universal molecule found in all genes.

The shape of a DNA molecule is called a *double helix*, which looks a bit like a twisted ladder. The rails and the rungs of the ladder are each composed of different molecules.

Nucleotide bases pair together to form the rungs of the ladder. Hydrogen bonds hold the bases together.

 The Living Environment
Standard 4 Students will understand and apply scientific concepts, principles, and theories pertaining to the physical setting and living environment and recognize the historical development of ideas in science.
Key Idea 1 Living things are both similar to and different from each other and from nonliving things. *Major Understandings - 1.2i*
Key Idea 2 Organisms inherit genetic information in a variety of ways that result in continuity of structure and function between parents and offspring. *Major Understandings – 2.1a, 2.1b, 2.1c, 2.1f, 2.1g, 2.1h, 2.1i*

Chapter Correlations 🔷 The Living Environment

Standard 4

1.2i Inside the cell a variety of specialized structures, formed from many different molecules, carry out the transport of materials (cytoplasm), extraction of energy from nutrients (mitochondria), protein building (ribosomes), waste disposal (cell membrane), storage (vacuole), and information storage (nucleus).

2.1a Genes are inherited, but their expression can be modified by interactions with the environment.

2.1b Every organism requires a set of coded instructions for specifying its traits. For offspring to resemble their parents, there must be a reliable way to transfer information from one generation to the next. Heredity is the passage of these instructions from one generation to another.

2.1c Hereditary information is contained in genes, located in the chromosomes of each cell. An inherited trait of an individual can be determined by one or by many genes, and a single gene can influence more than one trait. A human cell contains many thousands of different genes in its nucleus.

2.1f In all organisms, the coded instructions for specifying the characteristics of the organism are carried in DNA, a large molecule formed from subunits arranged in a sequence with bases of four kinds (represented by A, G, C, and T). The chemical and structural properties of DNA are the basis for how the genetic information that underlies heredity is both encoded in genes (as a string of molecular bases) and replicated by means of a template.

2.1g Cells store and use coded information. The genetic information stored in DNA is used to direct the synthesis of the thousands of proteins that each cell requires.

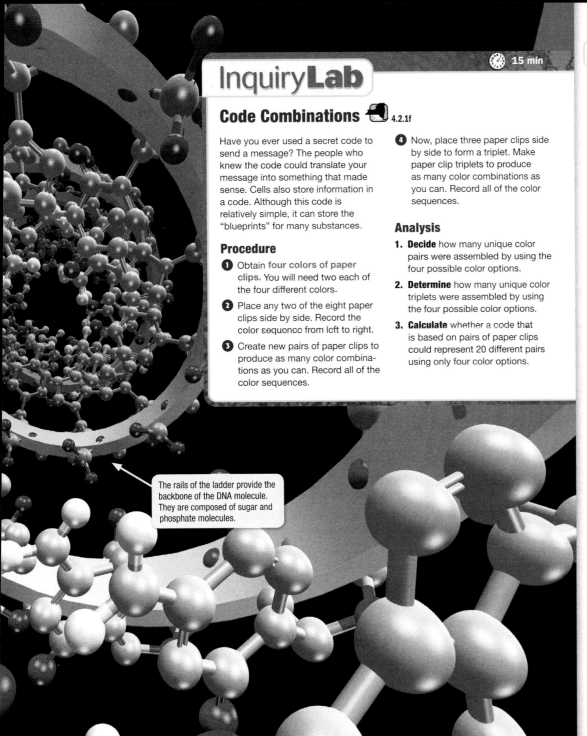

InquiryLab

Code Combinations 🖱 4.2.1f

Have you ever used a secret code to send a message? The people who knew the code could translate your message into something that made sense. Cells also store information in a code. Although this code is relatively simple, it can store the "blueprints" for many substances.

Procedure

❶ Obtain **four colors of paper clips.** You will need two each of the four different colors.

❷ Place any two of the eight paper clips side by side. Record the color sequence from left to right.

❸ Create new pairs of paper clips to produce as many color combinations as you can. Record all of the color sequences.

❹ Now, place three paper clips side by side to form a triplet. Make paper clip triplets to produce as many color combinations as you can. Record all of the color sequences.

Analysis

1. **Decide** how many unique color pairs were assembled by using the four possible color options.

2. **Determine** how many unique color triplets were assembled by using the four possible color options.

3. **Calculate** whether a code that is based on pairs of paper clips could represent 20 different pairs using only four color options.

The rails of the ladder provide the backbone of the DNA molecule. They are composed of sugar and phosphate molecules.

InquiryLab

Teacher's Notes This lab establishes the importance of the triplet code composed of three of the four nitrogen bases to correctly specify all twenty amino acids. Students should record all color sequences; green-red (G-R) is not the same as red-green (R-G).

Materials
• paper clips (8, 2 each of 4 different colors)

Answers to Analysis

1. There are sixteen possible combinations using two-colored clips.

2. There are sixty-four possible combinations using three-colored clips. Some students may not find all these combinations, but they should have more than twenty.

3. A code based on *pairs* of paper clips is not sufficient to represent twenty separate items.

Key Resources

 Interactive Tutor

2.1h Genes are segments of DNA molecules. Any alteration of the DNA sequence is a mutation. Usually, an altered gene will be passed on to every cell that develops from it.

2.1i The work of the cell is carried out by the many different types of molecules it assembles, mostly proteins. Protein molecules are long, usually folded chains made from 20 different kinds of amino acids in a specific sequence. This sequence influences the shape of the protein. The shape of the protein, in turn, determines its function.

Using Words

1. helicopter
2. A bacterium of this genus should be spiral shaped.
3. Answers will vary, but students should convey the idea that a bacteriophage is a virus that infects bacteria.

Using Language

1 before the sun rises
2. first

Using FoldNotes

Check to see that students have accurately followed the directions.

These reading tools can help you learn the material in this chapter. For more information on how to use these and other tools, see **Appendix: Reading and Study Skills.**

Using Words

Word Parts Knowing the meanings of word parts can help you figure out the meanings of unknown words.

Your Turn Use the table to answer the following questions.

1. The root *-ptera* means "wing." What familiar machine is named for its spiral wing?
2. *Helicobacter* is a genus of bacteria. What shape is a bacterium of this genus?
3. In your own words, write a definition for *bacteriophage.*

Word Parts		
Part	Type	Meaning
bacterio	root	involving bacteria
helic	root	spiral
-ase	suffix	enzyme
phage	root	to eat or destroy

Using Language

Describing Time Certain words and phrases can help you understand when something happened and how long it took. These words and phrases are called *specific time markers*. Specific time markers include words and phrases such as *first, next, 1 hour, yesterday, the twentieth century,* and *30 years later.*

Your Turn Read the sentences below and write down the specific time markers.

1. Early in the morning, before the sun rises, Emilio gets up to take his dogs for a walk.
2. Before a cell can divide, it must first make a copy of its DNA.

Using FoldNotes

Three-Panel Flip Chart A three-panel flip chart is useful when you want to organize notes about three topics. It can help you organize the characteristics of the topics side by side.

Your Turn Make a three-panel flip chart to organize your notes about DNA structure and replication.

1. Fold a piece of paper in half from the top to the bottom.
2. Fold the paper in three sections from side to side. Unfold the paper so that you can see the three sections.
3. From the top of the paper, cut along the vertical fold lines to the fold in the middle of the paper. You will now have three flaps.
4. Label the flaps of the three-panel flip chart "Identifying the Genetic Material," "The Structure of DNA," and "The Replication of DNA."
5. Under each flap, write your notes about the appropriate topic.

The Structure of DNA

Key Ideas	Key Terms	Why It Matters
❯ What is genetic material composed of? ❯ What experiments helped identify the role of DNA? ❯ What is the shape of a DNA molecule? ❯ How is information organized in a DNA molecule? ❯ What scientific investigations led to the discovery of DNA's structure?	gene DNA nucleotide purine pyrimidine	DNA is the "blueprint" from which all living things are made, so understanding DNA is key to understanding life.

Unless you have an identical twin, you—like the sisters in **Figure 1**—share some, but not all, characteristics with family members.

DNA: The Genetic Material

In the 1800s, Gregor Mendel showed that traits are passed from parents to offspring. Many years later, scientists have discovered how these traits are passed on. The instructions for inherited traits are called **genes.** Before the 1950s, however, scientists did not know what genes were made of. We now know that genes are made of small segments of deoxyribonucleic acid, or **DNA.** ❯ **DNA is the primary material that causes recognizable, inheritable characteristics in related groups of organisms.**

DNA is a relatively simple molecule, composed of only four different subunits. For this reason, many early scientists did not consider DNA to be complex enough to be genetic material. A few key experiments led to the discovery that DNA is, in fact, genetic material.

❯ **Reading Check** *What are genes composed of? (See Appendix for answers to Reading Checks.)*

Figure 1 These sisters share many traits but also have differences. ❯ **What role do genes play in passing traits from parents to offspring?**

 The Living Environment
Standard 4

2.1c Hereditary information is contained in genes, located in the chromosomes of each cell. An inherited trait of an individual can be determined by one or by many genes, and a single gene can influence more than one trait. A human cell contains many thousands of different genes in its nucleus.

2.1f In all organisms, the coded instructions for specifying the characteristics of the organism are carried in DNA, a large molecule formed from subunits arranged in a sequence with bases of four kinds (represented by A, G, C, and T). The chemical and structural properties of DNA are the basis for how the genetic information that underlies heredity is both encoded in genes (as a string of molecular bases) and replicated by means of a template.

2.1h Genes are segments of DNA molecules. Any alteration of the DNA sequence is a mutation. Usually, an altered gene will be passed on to every cell that develops from it.

gene a segment of DNA that is located in a chromosome and that codes for a specific hereditary trait

DNA deoxyribonucleic acid, the material that contains the information that determines inherited characteristics

Why It Matters

Why Protein? Most scientists thought that genes must be made of protein because protein is more complex than other biological molecules known at the time. Because proteins are made of many different amino acids, they were thought to be the only molecules complex enough to carry information for the huge variety of traits controlled by genes. **LS Logical**

Key Resources

 Transparencies
C9 Griffith's Discovery of Transformation
C10 The Hershey-Chase Experiment
C11 DNA Double Helix

Visual Concepts
Transformation
Hershey and Chase's Experiments
Bacteriophage
DNA Overview
Double Helix
Nucleotide
Structure of a Nucleotide
Comparing Purines and Pyrimidines
Complementary Base Pairing

>Teach, *continued*

READING TOOLBOX

Describing Time Sample answer: *First,* Griffith determines that live *S* bacteria cause mice to die. The *R* bacteria are harmless (mice do not die). *Then,* Griffith mixes live *R* bacteria with dead S bacteria and the mice die. He *then* concludes that a transformation has occurred. **LS** **Visual and Logical**

READING TOOLBOX

Visual Literacy Have students draw Avery's experiment. Have them fold a paper in half vertically. Have them draw an *S* bacterial cell at the top of each column. Label the protein capsule on the *S* bacterium and label the DNA on the interior. Use different colored pencils to represent each of the two enzymes. On the left side, color the protein coat and draw an arrow below to show R bacteria are dead ("x" out) and not transformed. On the right side, color the DNA only. Draw an arrow below to show that R cells are not transformed, but are still alive. **LS** **Visual**

Answers to Caption Questions

Figure 2: The independent variable was the type of bacteria injected into the mouse (S bacteria vs. R bacteria) and the dependent variable was mortality rate (whether or not the mouse would die after injection) in Griffith's experiment.

READING TOOLBOX

Describing Time Use specific time markers and **Figure 2** to describe Griffith's experiment.

Figure 2 Griffith discovered that harmless bacteria could cause disease when they were mixed with killed disease-causing bacteria. ❯ What were the variables in Griffith's experiments?

Searching for the Genetic Material

Once scientists discovered DNA, they began to search for its location. By the 1900s, scientists had determined that genetic material was located in cells, but they did not know exactly where. ❯ **Three major experiments led to the conclusion that DNA is the genetic material in cells. These experiments were performed by Griffith, Avery, Hershey, and Chase.**

Griffith's Discovery of Transformation In 1928, Frederick Griffith was working with two related strains of bacteria. The S strain causes pneumonia and is covered by a capsule of polysaccharides. The R strain has no capsule and does not cause pneumonia. Mice that are infected with the S bacteria get sick and die. Griffith injected mice with heat-killed S bacteria. The bacteria were dead, but the capsule was still present. The mice lived. Griffith concluded that the S bacteria cause disease.

However, when harmless, live R bacteria were mixed with the harmless, heat-killed S bacteria and were injected into mice, the mice died. Griffith had discovered *transformation,* which is a change in genotype that is caused when cells take up foreign genetic material. Griffith's experiments, shown in **Figure 2,** led to the conclusion that genetic material could be transferred between cells. But no one knew that this material was DNA.

Avery's Experiments with Nucleic Acids In the 1940s, Oswald Avery wanted to determine whether the transforming agent in Griffith's experiments was protein, RNA, or DNA. Avery and his colleagues used enzymes to destroy each of these molecules in heat-killed S bacteria. They found that bacteria that were missing protein and RNA were able to transform R cells into S cells. However, bacteria that were missing DNA did not transform R cells. The scientists concluded that DNA is responsible for transformation in bacteria.

In 1952, Alfred Hershey and Martha Chase thought that they could support Avery's conclusions by showing how DNA and proteins cross the cell membrane. Their experiment would determine how DNA affected other cells.

Capsule
Bacterium

❶ S bacteria kill the mouse.

❷ R bacteria do not kill the mouse.

❸ Heat-killed S bacteria do not kill the mouse.

❹ R bacteria and heat-killed S bacteria kill the mouse.

Differentiated Instruction

Basic Learners

Organizing Concepts Have students make posters that give a visual interpretation of Griffith's experiment, showing the heat-killing process, and injections. Check their drawings for accuracy. **LS** **Visual**

Hershey-Chase Experiment

Experiment 1

Bacteriophage

35S-labeled protein

Result
35S radioactivity did not enter bacterial cell.

Conclusion
Protein is not the hereditary material.

Phage proteins

Bacteria

Experiment 2

32P-labeled DNA

Result
32P radioactivity entered bacterial cell.

Conclusion
DNA is the hereditary material.

Phage proteins

Bacteria

1 Bacteriophages were labeled "35S" or "32P" and were used to infect separate batches of bacteria.

2 A blender removed the virus's coat from the surface of the bacterial cells. The mixture was spun in a centrifuge to separate heavier bacteria from the lighter bacteriophages.

3 35S radioactivity did not enter bacterial cells, but 32P radioactivity did enter bacterial cells.

Figure 3 Bacteriophages were used to show that DNA, not protein, is the genetic material in viruses.

Hershey-Chase Experiment Hershey and Chase studied bacteriophages, viruses that infect bacterial cells and cause the cells to produce viruses. Bacteriophages are made up of proteins and DNA, but which of these two molecules is the genetic material in viruses? **Figure 3** illustrates their experiment.

Step 1 First, Hershey and Chase knew that proteins contain some sulfur but no phosphorus and that DNA contains phosphorus but no sulfur. The scientists grew two sets of viruses in environments that were enriched with different radioactive isotopes. One set of viruses had radioactive sulfur (35S) atoms attached to proteins. The other set had radioactive phosphorus (32P) atoms attached to DNA.

Step 2 Second, each set of viruses was allowed to infect separate batches of nonradioactive bacteria. Because radioactive elements release particles that can be detected with machines, they can be tracked in a biological process. Each of the batches was then separated into parts that contained only bacteria or only viruses.

Step 3 The infected bacteria from the 35S batch did not contain radioactive sulfur, so proteins could not have infected the bacteria. However, the infected bacteria from the 32P batch did contain radioactive phosphorus. DNA had infected the bacteria.

Hershey and Chase concluded that only the DNA of viruses is injected into bacterial cells. The injected DNA caused the bacteria to produce viral DNA and proteins. This finding indicated that rather than proteins, DNA is the hereditary material, at least in viruses.

Teaching Key Ideas

Radioactive Tracers Radioactive elements have unstable nuclei that emit particles to become stable. These particles can be detected by instruments, so their presence in a part of a molecule can be traced. Sulfur is found in protein and phosphorous is in DNA, so these radioactive elements were used in this experiment.

READING TOOLBOX

Visual Literacy Draw **Figure 3** on the board. Have five student volunteers to go to the board to color/identify the part of phage that would contain radioactive sulfur, 35S in Experiment 1, and radioactive phosphorous, 32P in Experiment 2. Have students predict where the 35S and 32P would be in Step 2. (*outside* in Experiment 1 and *inside* in Experiment 2.) Have students refer to **Figure 3** and identify the locations for the radioactive sulfur and phosphorus in the test tubes.
LS Visual

Differentiated Instruction

Struggling Readers

Deciphering Symbols Some students will have trouble following the steps of the Hershey-Chase experiment because the isotope symbols pose an additional challenge. Have students substitute common names or colors for the symbols to make the process easier for them to follow while reading.

Teaching Key Ideas

Demonstration

The Shape of DNA Use a model of DNA as students look at **Figure 4.** If possible, show the model untwisted. Call attention to the ladder or staircase shape. Ask what substances make up the sides, or *rails*? (phosphates and deoxyribose sugars) What substances make up the center/steps? (nitrogen bases) What holds the nitrogen bases and the two strands together? (hydrogen bonds)

Now call students' attention to the two side strands of the molecule shown in **Figure 4.** Ask students, "What subunits make up these strands?" (nucleotides) "What parts of each nucleotide are the same?" (sugar and phosphate) "What parts are different?" (nitrogen bases) "How many nitrogen bases are there?" (four) "Are the nitrogen bases the same in appearance; What's different?" (some have one ring, some have two) "How does the arrangement of bases affect the shape of the molecule?" (A double-ringed base is always paired with a single-ringed base.) Conclude the demonstration by twisting the staircase or ladder, to form a double helix. Have students identify this shape. **LS Visual**

SCILINKS.
www.scilinks.org
Topic: DNA
Code: HX80418

Figure 4 Watson and Crick's model of DNA is a double helix that is composed of two nucleotide chains. The chains are twisted around a central axis and are held together by hydrogen bonds.

The Shape of DNA

After the important experiments in the early 1950s, most scientists were convinced that genes were made of DNA, but nothing was known about DNA's structure. The research of many scientists led James Watson and Francis Crick, two young researchers at Cambridge University, to piece together a model of DNA's structure. Knowing the structure of DNA allowed scientists to understand how DNA could serve as genetic material.

A Winding Staircase > A DNA molecule is shaped like a spiral staircase and is composed of two parallel strands of linked subunits. This spiral shape is known as a *double helix,* as **Figure 4** shows. Each strand is made up of linked subunits called nucleotides.

Parts of the Nucleotide Subunits Each **nucleotide** is made up of three parts: a phosphate group, a five-carbon sugar molecule, and a nitrogen-containing base. **Figure 4** shows how these three parts are arranged to form a nucleotide. The phosphate groups and the sugar molecules of nucleotides link together to form a "backbone" for a DNA strand. The five-carbon sugar in DNA is called *deoxyribose,* from which DNA gets its full name, *deoxyribonucleic acid.* The bases of nucleotides pair together to connect the two strands.

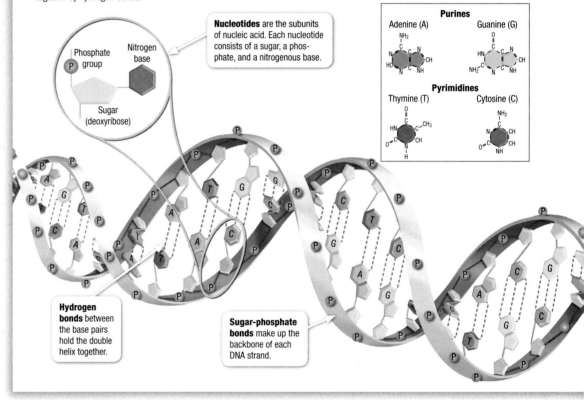

Nucleotides are the subunits of nucleic acid. Each nucleotide consists of a sugar, a phosphate, and a nitrogenous base.

Phosphate group
Nitrogen base
Sugar (deoxyribose)

Purines
Adenine (A)   Guanine (G)

Pyrimidines
Thymine (T)   Cytosine (C)

Hydrogen bonds between the base pairs hold the double helix together.

Sugar-phosphate bonds make up the backbone of each DNA strand.

Why It Matters

The Importance of Molecular Shape When double-ringed bases are paired with single-ringed bases, the steps of the ladder or staircase have a consistent width. Ask students to imagine the stability of a ladder with adjacent steps of varying widths. **LS Visual**

QuickLab

⏱ 15 min

DNA's Structure 4.2.1f

Build a model to help you understand the structure of DNA.

Procedure

❶ Use the following materials to build a model of DNA: plastic straws cut into 3 cm sections, a metric ruler, scissors, pushpins (four different colors), and paper clips. Your model should have at least 12 nucleotides on each strand.

❷ As you design your model, decide how to use the straws, pushpins, and paper clips to represent the three components of a nucleotide and how to link the nucleotides together.

Analysis

1. **Describe** your model by using words or drawings. Are the two strands in your model identical? Explain why or why not.

2. **Explain** how you determined which nucleotides were placed on each strand of DNA in your model.

3. CRITICAL THINKING **Inferring Relationships** How might the structure of DNA be beneficial when a cell copies its DNA before cell division?

The Information in DNA

The structure of DNA is very important in the transfer of genetic information. ❯ **The information in DNA is contained in the order of the bases, while the base-pairing structure allows the information to be copied.**

Nitrogenous Bases In DNA, each nucleotide has the same sugar molecule and phosphate group, but the nucleotide can have one of four nitrogenous bases. The four kinds of bases, shown in **Figure 4,** are *adenine* (A), *guanine* (G), *thymine* (T), and *cytosine* (C). Bases A and G are classified as **purines.** Purines have two rings of carbon and nitrogen atoms per base. Bases T and C are **pyrimidines.** Pyrimidines have one ring of carbon and nitrogen atoms per base.

Base-Pairing Rules A purine on one strand of a DNA molecule is always paired with a pyrimidine on the other strand. More specifically, adenine always pairs with thymine, and guanine always pairs with cytosine. These *base-pairing rules* are dictated by the chemical structure of the bases. The structure and size of the nitrogenous bases allow for only these two pair combinations. The base pairs are held together by weak hydrogen bonds. Adenine forms two hydrogen bonds with thymine, while cytosine forms three hydrogen bonds with guanine. The hydrogen bonds are represented by dashed lines in **Figure 4.** The hydrogen bonds between bases keep the two strands of DNA together.

❯ **Reading Check** *How are base-pairs held together?*

nucleotide (NOO klee oh TIED) in a nucleic acid chain, a subunit that consists of a sugar, a phosphate, and a nitrogenous base

purine (PYOOR EEN) a nitrogenous base that has a double-ring structure; adenine or guanine

pyrimidine (pi RIM uh DEEN) a nitrogenous base that has a single-ring structure; in DNA, either thymine or cytosine

---

QuickLab

Teacher's Notes Let students know that they might need more or less of the colored components depending on the sequence they choose.

Materials
• metric ruler
• paper clips (48)
• plastic straws (8)
• push pins (48, 12 each of a different color)
• scissors

Safety Cautions Caution students to be careful of the sharp tips of the pushpins. Account for all materials at the end of the lab.

Answers to Analysis
1. No, they are complementary. They differ from each other but pair up together.
2. The nucleotides on the first strand were placed randomly. The nucleotides on the second strand were complementary to those on the first strand.
3. The structure contains two complementary strands. Therefore, a dividing cell division would have a copy of the DNA for each daughter cell.

Teaching Key Ideas

DNA's Code Because the sugar-phosphate "backbone" of the DNA molecule is always the same, the parts of the DNA molecule that are different, the nitrogen bases, must contain the genetic code.

Teaching Key Ideas

Representation of DNA The sugar-phosphate backbone of the DNA molecule does not code for a gene, only for the nucleotide bases. Therefore just the letters of the corresponding bases are shown. Have students practice base-pairing by matching letters to any series of base letters you write on the board.

READING TOOLBOX

Visual Literacy Have students look at **Figure 5** and determine which bases seem to pair. (A, *adenine* with T, and G, *guanine* with C, *cytosine*. Have students think of mnemonics to help them remember this order. (G looks like a good fit for C.)

ACADEMIC VOCABULARY

complementary being separate parts that improve or enhance each other

Complementary Sides Figure 5 shows a simpler way to represent base-pairing. Paired bases are said to be complementary because they fit together like puzzle pieces. For example, if the sequence of nitrogen bases on one strand is TATGAGAGT, the sequence of nitrogen bases on the other strand must be ATACTCTCA. The pairing structure ensures that each strand of a DNA molecule contains the same information. However, the information on one strand is in reverse order from that on the other strand.

Discovering DNA's Structure

How were James Watson and Francis Crick able to determine the double-helical structure of DNA? **❯ Watson and Crick used information from experiments by Chargaff, Wilkins, and Franklin to determine the three-dimensional structure of DNA.**

Observing Patterns: Chargaff's Observations In 1949, biochemist Erwin Chargaff made an interesting observation about DNA. His data showed that for each organism that he studied, the amount of adenine always equaled the amount of thymine (A = T). Similarly, the amount of guanine always equaled the amount of cytosine (G = C). **Figure 6** shows some of Chargaff's data. Watson and Crick used this information to determine how nucleotides are paired in DNA.

Using Technology: Photographs of DNA The significance of Chargaff's data became clear when scientists began using X rays to study the structures of molecules. In 1952, Rosalind Franklin, shown in **Figure 6,** and Maurice Wilkins developed high-quality X-ray diffraction images of strands of DNA. These photographs suggested that the DNA molecule resembled a tightly coiled helix and was composed of two or three chains of nucleotides.

Figure 5 The diagram of DNA below the double helix simplifies the base pairing that occurs between DNA strands.

Complementary bases link together in pairs with hydrogen bonds. Adenine (A) always pairs with thymine (T), and cytosine (C) always pairs with guanine (G).

This schematic shows how complementary base pairs join together.

Why It Matters

Crediting Rosalind Franklin Watson and Crick are generally credited with determining the structure of DNA. However, Franklin's X-ray diffraction photograph was crucial to their discovery. Franklin would have received the Nobel Prize, along with Watson, Crick, and Wilkins, had she been alive when it was awarded.

Differentiated Instruction

Advanced Learners/GATE

Genetics in the News Have students research the history of the Nobel Prize. How many prizes have been awarded since 1962 for discoveries related to genetics?

Chargaff's Data

■ A ■ T ■ G ■ C

Number of nitrogen bases

Organism: *E. coli*, Fruit fly, Salmon, Human

Watson & Crick

Franklin

Figure 6 Chargaff's data and Franklin's X-ray diffraction studies were instrumental in the discovery of DNA's structure. Watson and Crick are shown with their tin and wire model of DNA.

Watson and Crick's Model of DNA To determine the three-dimensional structure of DNA, Watson and Crick set out to build a model of DNA. They knew that any model would have to take into account both Chargaff's data and the findings from Franklin's X-ray diffraction studies. In 1953, Watson and Crick used these findings, along with knowledge of chemical bonding, to create a complete three-dimensional model of DNA. By using paper models of the bases, Watson and Crick worked out the pairing structure of purines with pyrimidines. Then, they built a large model of a DNA double helix by using tin, wire, and other materials. Their model showed a "spiral staircase" in which two strands of nucleotides twisted around a central axis. **Figure 6** shows Watson and Crick with their model.

Nine years later, in 1962, the Nobel Prize was awarded to Watson, Crick, and Wilkins for their discovery. Rosalind Franklin died in 1958 and was not named in the award.

❯ **Reading Check** *How was X-ray diffraction used to model the structure of DNA?*

Teaching Key Ideas

Watson and Crick's Model Stress that Watson and Crick built the three-dimensional model shown in **Figure 6.** Their model showed the chemical arrangement of the components of DNA. They published their findings in a historic one-page article in the journal *Nature*, in April of 1953.

❯ **Close**

Formative Assessment

Base-pairing is very important to the structure of DNA, because it allows ____.

A. adenine to bond with guanine (Incorrect. Adenine bonds with thymine.)

B. pyrimidines to bond with each other (Incorrect. Pyrimidines cannot bond with each other.)

C. DNA to be copied (Correct! DNA's information is in the order of the bases.)

D. nucleotides to form (Incorrect. A nucleotide exists independent of base-pairing.)

Section 1 Review

❯ **KEY IDEAS**

1. **Identify** the substance that makes up genetic material.

2. **Name** the experiments that identified the role of DNA.

3. **Draw** the shape of a DNA molecule.

4. **Relate** the structure of DNA to the function of DNA as a carrier of information.

5. **Name** the studies that led to the discovery of DNA's structure.

CRITICAL THINKING

6. **Applying Information** If a DNA strand has the nucleotide sequence of CCGAGATTG, what is the nucleotide sequence of the complementary strand?

7. **Applying Information** What might Hershey and Chase have concluded if they had found ^{35}S instead of ^{32}P in bacterial cells? Explain your answer.

USING SCIENCE GRAPHICS

8. **Evaluating Graphics** Look at the graph of Chargaff's data in **Figure 6.** How do the amounts of adenine compare with the amounts of thymine across species? How do the amounts of cytosine and guanine compare? How did these data lead to the discovery of the base-pairing rules by Chargaff? How was this discovery used to determine DNA's structure?

Answers to Section Review

1. DNA is the primary substance that makes up genetic material.

2. The experiments of Griffith, Avery, Hershey, and Chase led to the conclusion that DNA is the primary carrier of genetic information in cells.

3. Drawings should show a spiral staircase composed of two parallel strands of linked subunits.

4. The information in DNA is contained in the order of bases. The base-pairing structure allows the information to be copied.

5. those of Chargaff, Franklin, and Wilkins

6. GGCTCTAAC.

7. They would have concluded that protein was the carrier of genetic information. Sulfur is found in proteins but not in DNA.

8. The amount of adenine is almost equal to the amount of thymine; the amount of guanine is almost equal to the amount of cytosine. This data revealed that nucleotides pair in a predictable manner.

Key Ideas	Key Terms	Why It Matters
❯ How does DNA replicate, or make a copy of itself? ❯ What are the roles of proteins in DNA replication? ❯ How is DNA replication different in prokaryotes and eukaryotes?	**DNA replication** **DNA helicase** **DNA polymerase**	Understanding how DNA is copied has led to a better understanding of genetic diseases and cancer.

The Living Environment
Standard 4

2.1b Every organism requires a set of coded instructions for specifying its traits. For offspring to resemble their parents, there must be a reliable way to transfer information from one generation to the next. Heredity is the passage of these instructions from one generation to another.

2.1f In all organisms, the coded instructions for specifying the characteristics of the organism are carried in DNA, a large molecule formed from subunits arranged in a sequence with bases of four kinds (represented by A, G, C, and T). The chemical and structural properties of DNA are the basis for how the genetic information that underlies heredity is both encoded in genes (as a string of molecular bases) and replicated by means of a template.

Figure 7 When the two strands of the DNA helix separate, Y-shaped replication forks form.

When cells divide, each new cell contains an exact copy of the original cell's DNA. How is this possible?

DNA Replication

Remember that DNA is made of two strands of complementary base pairs. Adenine always pairs with thymine, and guanine always pairs with cytosine. If the strands of DNA are separated, as shown in **Figure 7,** each strand can serve as a pattern to make a new complementary strand. This separation allows two exact copies of DNA to be made from the original DNA molecule. Copying the DNA before cell division allows each new cell to have DNA identical to the original cell's.

The process of making a copy of DNA is called **DNA replication.** ❯ In DNA replication, the DNA molecule unwinds, and the two sides split. Then, new bases are added to each side until two identical sequences result. DNA replication occurs before a cell divides so that each cell has a complete copy of DNA. The basic steps of DNA replication are described below and are illustrated in **Figure 8** on the next page.

Step ❶ Unwinding and Separating DNA Strands Before DNA replication can begin, the double helix unwinds. The two complementary strands of DNA separate from each other and form Y shapes. These Y-shaped areas are called *replication forks*. **Figure 7** shows two replication forks in a molecule of DNA.

Step ❷ Adding Complementary Bases At the replication fork, new nucleotides are added to each side and new base pairs are formed according to the base-pairing rules. For example, if one of the original strands has thymine, then adenine will be paired with thymine as the new strand forms. Thus, the original two strands serve as a template for two new strands. As more nucleotides are added, two new double helixes begin to form. The process continues until the whole DNA sequence has been copied.

Step ❸ Formation of Two Identical DNA Molecules This process of DNA replication produces two identical DNA molecules. Each double-stranded DNA helix is made of one new strand of DNA and one original strand of DNA. The nucleotide sequences in both of these DNA molecules are identical to each other and to the original DNA molecule.

DNA Replication

① Proteins called *helicases* separate the two original DNA strands.

② Complementary nucleotides are added to each strand by DNA polymerases.

③ Two DNA molecules are formed that are identical to the original DNA molecule.

Figure 8 DNA replication results in two identical DNA strands.

Replication Proteins

❯ **During the replication of DNA, many proteins form a machinelike complex of moving parts.** Each protein has a specific function.

DNA Helicase Proteins called **DNA helicases** unwind the DNA double helix during DNA replication. These proteins wedge themselves between the two strands of the double helix and break the hydrogen bonds between the base pairs. This process causes the helix to unwind and forms a replication fork, as **Figures 7** and **8** show. Additional proteins keep the two strands separated so that replication can occur.

DNA Polymerase Proteins called **DNA polymerases** catalyze the formation of the DNA molecule. At the replication fork, DNA polymerases move along each strand. The polymerases add nucleotides that pair with each base to form two new double helixes. After all of the DNA has been copied, the polymerases are released.

DNA polymerases also have a "proofreading" function. During DNA replication, errors sometimes occur, and the wrong nucleotide is added to the new strand. DNA polymerases cannot add another nucleotide unless the previous nucleotide is correctly paired with its complementary base. If a mismatch occurs, the DNA polymerase can backtrack, remove the incorrect nucleotide, and replace it with the correct one. Proofreading reduces the replication errors to about one per 1 billion nucleotides.

❯ **Reading Check** *Why is proofreading critical during replication?*

DNA replication the process of making a copy of DNA

DNA helicase (HEEL uh KAYS) an enzyme that unwinds the DNA double helix during DNA replication

DNA polymerase (puh LIM uhr AYS) an enzyme that catalyzes the formation of the DNA molecule

---

Students can interact with "DNA Replication" by going to go.hrw.com and typing the keycode HX8DNAF8.

Teaching Key Ideas

Role of Enzymes Before DNA can make copies of itself, it must "unzip," by breaking the hydrogen bonds that hold the nitrogen bases together. Ask students what kinds of molecules can break bonds in a chemical reaction. (enzymes) Then, ask them what kind of molecules assist in the bonding process. (enzymes) Close by reviewing the names of the enzymes involved in both processes. (DNA helicases and DNA polymerases) **LS Verbal**

READING TOOLBOX

Visual Literacy Ask students to describe how the original strand of DNA is distinguished from the new molecule, in Step 3 of **Figure 8.** (They are different colors.) Call attention to the fact that each half of the original DNA molecule serves as a template for the new molecule. This *semi-conservative* model is distinguished from a *conservative* model, in which the parent molecule is *conserved*, and the new molecule is formed from scratch. **LS Visual**

Differentiated Instruction

Basic Learners

Replication Model Use two pieces of red yarn to represent the DNA a chromosome. Use colored paperclips, joined in the center, to represent the nitrogen bases holding the two strands together. Describe the role of DNA helicase as you separate the two strands by unhooking the paperclips. Take two blue pieces of yarn and add paperclips in a sequence that pairs them to each side of the red strands. Join the new strands to each half of the original strand. *One* original molecule is serving as a template for *two* new molecules. **LS Visual**

Word Parts **helicase** an enzyme that acts on a spiral structure; **polymerase** an enzyme that acts on a polymer

Visual Literacy Ask students to interpret **Figure 9**. (From a "circle" of DNA, replication begins at one point, inside the circular piece of DNA and proceeds in opposite directions.) Have students compare the process of replication, on the eukaryotic DNA to the prokaryotic DNA. Ask how both processes are alike. (Both processes proceed in opposite directions.) **LS** **Visual, Kinesthetic**

Answers to Caption Questions
Figure 9: Replication occurs at multiple replication forks so that the single, long strand of DNA is replicated more rapidly.

Word Parts In your own words, write a definition of *helicase* and *polymerase*, the names of the enzymes involved in DNA replication, based on the meanings of each term's word parts.

ACADEMIC
VOCABULARY

distinct separate; not the same

Prokaryotic and Eukaryotic Replication

Both prokaryotes and eukaryotes replicate their DNA to reproduce and grow. Recall that the packaged DNA in a cell is called a *chromosome*. All cells have chromosomes, but eukaryotes and prokaryotes replicate their chromosomes differently. ❯ **In prokaryotic cells, replication starts at a single site. In eukaryotic cells, replication starts at many sites along the chromosome.**

Prokaryotic DNA Replication Prokaryotic cells usually have a single DNA molecule, or chromosome. Prokaryotic chromosomes are a closed loop, may contain protein, and are attached to the inner cell membrane. Replication begins at one place along the DNA loop. Two replication forks begin at that single point, which is known as the origin of replication. Replication occurs in opposite directions until the replication forks meet on the opposite side of the DNA loop and the entire molecule has been copied. **Figure 9** shows prokaryotic DNA replication.

Eukaryotic DNA Replication While prokaryotes have a single chromosome, eukaryotic cells often have several chromosomes. Eukaryotic chromosomes differ from the simple, looped chromosomes found in prokaryotic cells. Eukaryotic chromosomes are linear, and they contain both DNA and protein. Recall that the long molecules of DNA are tightly wound around proteins called *histones* and are packaged into thick chromosome fibers.

By starting replication at many sites along the chromosome, eukaryotic cells can replicate their DNA faster than prokaryotes can. As in prokaryotic replication, two distinct replication forks form at each start site, and replication occurs in opposite directions. This process forms replication "bubbles" along the DNA molecule. The replication bubbles continue to get larger as more of the DNA is copied. As **Figure 9** shows, they eventually meet to form two identical, linear DNA molecules. Because multiple replication forks are working at the same time, an entire human chromosome can be replicated in about eight hours. Then, the cell will be ready to divide.

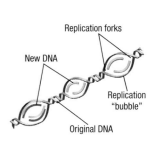

Figure 9 Prokaryotic and eukaryotic DNA have different numbers of replication forks. ❯ Why does replication in eukaryotes involve more replication forks?

Original DNA   New DNA

Replication forks

Prokaryotic DNA

Replication forks

New DNA

Replication "bubble"

Original DNA

Eukaryotic DNA

Differentiated Instruction

Special Education Students
Replication Fork Model To help visually impaired and developmentally delayed students understand the work of replication forks, try the following model. Obtain two perfectly matched, separating, fabric zippers for each student. Tag the second zipper in some way so that visually impaired students can tell the difference between the two zippers. You can use different colors for developmentally delayed students. Give students one zipper and let them manipulate it. Ask them what part of the zipper–DNA model represents helicase? (the zipper mechanism) After they separate the first zipper, give them the second zipper that is already separated into the two strands. Have them create two new zippers by zipping the "replication" strands. Students should have two matching zippers, each made of the parent strand and the replication strand. Ask them what happens if the replication strand is not a complementary match. (The zipper won't close.) **LS** **Visual**

QuickLab

🕐 15 min

DNA Replication Rate

Cancer is a disease caused by cells that divide uncontrollably. Scientists studying drugs that prevent cancer often measure the effectiveness of a drug by its effect on DNA replication. During normal DNA replication, nucleotides are added at a rate of about 50 nucleotides per second in mammals and 500 nucleotides per second in bacteria.

Analysis

1. **Calculate** the time it would take a bacterium to add 4,000 nucleotides to one DNA strand undergoing replication.

2. **Calculate** the time it would take a mammalian cell to add 4,000 nucleotides to one DNA strand undergoing replication.

3. **CRITICAL THINKING** **Predicting Outcomes** How would the total time needed to add the 4,000 nucleotides be affected if a drug that inhibits DNA polymerases were present? Explain your answer.

Size of Eukaryotic DNA The smallest eukaryotic chromosomes are often 10 times the size of a prokaryotic chromosome. If a scientist took all of the DNA in a single human cell and laid the DNA in one line (that is, laid the DNA from all 46 chromosomes end to end), the line would be 2 m long. In contrast, if the scientist laid out the DNA from one bacterial chromosome, the line would be only about 0.25 cm long. In fact, the length of eukaryotic chromosomes is so long that replication of a typical human chromosome would take 33 days if there were only one origin of replication.

Each human chromosome is replicated in about 100 sections that are 100,000 nucleotides long, each section with its own starting point. With multiple replication forks working in concert, an entire human chromosome can be replicated in about 8 hours.

❯ **Reading Check** *How is a "replication bubble" formed?*

www.scilinks.org
Topic: DNA Replication
Code: HX80420

Section 2 Review

❯ KEY IDEAS

1. **Describe** the steps of DNA replication.

2. **Compare** the roles of DNA helicases and DNA polymerases.

3. **Compare** the process of DNA replication in prokaryotes and in eukaryotes.

CRITICAL THINKING

4. **Inferring Relationships** What is the relationship between DNA polymerases and mutations in DNA?

5. **Relating Concepts** Cancer is a disease caused by cells that divide uncontrollably. Scientists are researching drugs that inhibit DNA polymerase as potential anti-cancer drugs. Why would these drugs be useful against cancer?

ALTERNATIVE ASSESSMENT

6. **Replication Model** Conduct research on the shapes of prokaryotic and eukaryotic chromosomes. Draw a model of each type of chromosome. How does the structure of chromosomes in prokaryotic cells and eukaryotic cells affect the DNA replication processes in a cell?

Answers to Section Review

1. The DNA molecule unwinds and separates. Nucleotides are matched to each side, creating two identical sequences and forming two new molecules.

2. DNA helicase breaks the bonds between the nitrogen bases, "unzipping" the molecule; DNA polymerase adds nucleotides in a strand to the original half, and "proofreads" the added nucleotides.

3. Prokaryotic replication starts at a single site. Eukaryotic replication starts at several sites. Both processes proceed in opposite directions.

4. DNA polymerase prevents mutations by eliminating incorrectly-placed nucleotides during replication.

5. Because DNA polymerase joins new nucleotides to make DNA before cell division, its absence may prevent uncontrolled cell division.

6. Eukaryotes have more chromosomes and longer DNA. Thus, replication would take too long if the eukaryotic cell followed the same process as the smaller prokaryotic cell.

QuickLab

Teacher's Notes Remind students that rates are ratios that compare different quantities, such as miles per hour.

Answers to Analysis

1. 8 seconds

2. 80 seconds

3. The total time would increase. A drug that inhibits DNA polymerase action would slow down the total time needed to add nucleotides.

Teaching Key Ideas

Explanation for Differences in Replication Call attention to the fact that multiple replication forks are necessary in eukaryotes because of the amount of DNA that needs to be replicated. There is efficiency in processing several at once. **LS Logical**

❯ Close

Formative Assessment

Why does a eukaryotic cell need a replication process that's different from that for a prokaryotic cell?

A. The prokaryotic DNA is longer and needs several replication sites to increase the rate. (Incorrect. Eukaryotic DNA is longer.)

B. The eukaryotic DNA is longer and needs several replication sites to increase the replication rate. (Correct!)

C. The bacterial DNA is longer and needs several replication sites to increase the rate. (Incorrect! Bacteria are prokaryotes, and have shorter DNA.)

D. Prokaryotes have more chromosomes. (Incorrect. Eukaryotes have more chromosomes and longer DNA.)

RNA and Gene Expression

Section **3**

▶ Focus

This section discusses the role of DNA in directing the formation of proteins. RNA is introduced as the nucleic acid that assembles amino acids to form a protein. Students learn how a three-letter sequence on DNA is transcribed onto mRNA. This three-letter codon dictates the sequence of amino acids on the ribosome using tRNA as a "taxi service" to deliver the specific amino acid specified by a particular codon.

Bellringer

Use the Bellringer transparency to prepare students for this section.

▶ Teach

Teaching Key Ideas

Clarifying Terms Ask students to define the term *gene*. (unit of hereditary information on a section of DNA) Stress that genes contain the code for an amino acid sequence. Ask where amino acid assembly takes place. (ribosomes) Ask why the *entire* DNA molecule is not copied. (there is too much unneeded information) DNA is a large molecule that cannot exit the nucleus. Ask students how this problem is solved for the cell. (Directions are given to a carrier molecule. This molecule is RNA.) **LS** **Verbal**

Key Ideas

> What is the process of gene expression?

> What role does RNA play in gene expression?

> What happens during transcription?

> How do codons determine the sequence of amino acids that results after translation?

> What are the major steps of translation?

> Do traits result from the expression of a single gene?

Key Terms

RNA
gene expression
transcription
translation
codon

Why It Matters

Traits, such as eye color, are determined by proteins that are built according to instructions coded in DNA.

The Living Environment
Standard 4

1.2i Inside the cell a variety of specialized structures, formed from many different molecules, carry out the transport of materials (cytoplasm), extraction of energy from nutrients (mitochondria), protein building (ribosomes), waste disposal (cell membrane), storage (vacuole), and information storage (nucleus).

2.1a Genes are inherited, but their expression can be modified by interactions with the environment.

2.1g Cells store and use coded information. The genetic information stored in DNA is used to direct the synthesis of the thousands of proteins that each cell requires.

2.1l The work of the cell is carried out by the many different types of molecules it assembles, mostly proteins. Protein molecules are long, usually folded chains made from 20 different kinds of amino acids in a specific sequence. This sequence influences the shape of the protein. The shape of the protein, in turn, determines its function.

RNA ribonucleic acid, a natural polymer that is present in all living cells and that plays a role in protein synthesis

gene expression the manifestation of the genetic material of an organism in the form of specific traits

transcription the process of forming a nucleic acid by using another molecule as a template

translation the portion of protein synthesis that takes place at ribosomes and that uses the codons in mRNA molecules to specify the sequence of amino acids in polypeptide chains

---

Proteins perform most of the functions of cells. DNA provides the original "recipe," or information, from which proteins are made in the cell. However, DNA does not directly make proteins. A second type of nucleic acid, ribonucleic acid, or **RNA,** is essential in taking the genetic information from DNA and building proteins.

An Overview of Gene Expression

Gene expression is the manifestation of genes into specific traits. ▶ **Gene expression produces proteins by transcription and translation. This process takes place in two stages, both of which involve RNA. Figure 10** illustrates the parts of the cell that play a role in gene expression.

Transcription: DNA to RNA The first stage of gene expression, which is making RNA from the information in DNA, is called **transcription.** You can think of transcription as copying (transcribing) notes from the board (DNA) to a notebook (RNA).

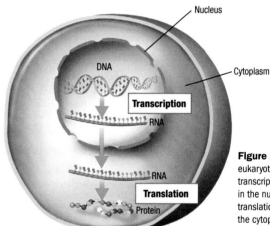

Figure 10 In eukaryotic cells, gene transcription occurs in the nucleus and translation occurs in the cytoplasm.

Section Correlations	
4.1.2i	4.2.1g
4.2.1a	4.2.1i

Key Resources

Transparencies
C15 Transcription
C16 Codons in mRNA
C17 Translation: Assembling Proteins

Visual Concepts
Ribonucleic Acid
Comparing DNA and RNA
Gene Expression
Transcription
Promoter
Codons in mRNA
Genetic Code
tRNA and Anticodon
Translation
Snapshot of Translation
Ribosomes

Translation: RNA to Proteins The second stage of gene expression, called **translation,** uses the information in RNA to make a specific protein. Translation is similar to translating a sentence in one language (RNA, the nucleic acid "language") to another language (protein, the amino acid "language").

RNA: A Major Player

All of the steps in gene expression involve RNA. Several types of RNA are used in transcription and translation. **❯ In cells, three types of RNA complement DNA and translate the genetic code into proteins.** But what exactly is RNA, and how does it compare to DNA?

RNA Versus DNA Like DNA, RNA is a nucleic acid—a molecule made of nucleotide subunits linked together. Like DNA, RNA has four bases and carries information in the same way that DNA does.

RNA differs from DNA in three ways. First, RNA usually is composed of one strand of nucleotides rather than two strands. The structural difference between the two nucleotides is shown in **Figure 11.** Second, RNA nucleotides contain the five-carbon sugar *ribose* rather than the sugar deoxyribose. Ribose contains one more oxygen atom than deoxyribose does. And third, RNA nucleotides have a nitrogenous base called *uracil* (U) instead of the base thymine (T). Although no thymine (T) bases are found in RNA, the other bases (A, G, and C) are identical to the bases found in DNA. In place of thymine, uracil (U) is complementary to adenine (A) whenever RNA pairs with another nucleic acid.

Types of RNA There are several types of RNA. Three main types of RNA play a role in gene expression. These types are messenger RNA, transfer RNA, and ribosomal RNA.

Messenger RNA When DNA is transcribed into RNA, *messenger RNA* (mRNA) is the type of RNA that is produced. mRNA is complementary to the DNA sequence of a gene. The mRNA carries instructions for making a protein from a gene and delivers them to the site of translation.

Transfer RNA During translation, *transfer RNA* (tRNA) "reads" the mRNA sequence. Then, tRNA translates the mRNA sequence into a specific sequence of protein subunits, or amino acids. tRNA molecules have amino acids attached to them, and the tRNA molecules act as decoders by matching the mRNA sequence and placing the amino acids on growing protein chains.

Ribosomal RNA Protein production occurs on cellular structures called *ribosomes*. Ribosomes are made up of about 80 protein molecules (ribosomal proteins) and several large RNA molecules. The RNA that is found in ribosomes is called *ribosomal RNA* (rRNA). A cell's cytoplasm contains thousands of ribosomes. In eukaryotic cells, ribosomes are attached to the endoplasmic reticulum (ER), which transports proteins as the proteins are produced.

❯ Reading Check *What are the structural differences between RNA and DNA?*

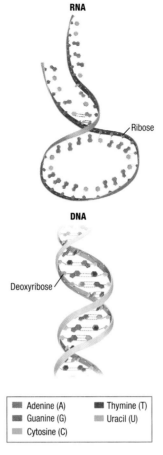

Figure 11 Both RNA (top) and DNA (bottom) are nucleic acids.

Legend:
- Adenine (A)
- Guanine (G)
- Cytosine (C)
- Thymine (T)
- Uracil (U)

READING TOOLBOX

Three-Panel Flip Chart Students' charts should include the following information:

mRNA produced by transcription, complementary to the gene DNA; delivers code for protein synthesis to the ribosome

tRNA reads mRNA during translation at the ribosome; codes for a specific amino acid sequence to create proteins

rRNA a component of the ribosome

Teaching Key Ideas

Transcription Process Tell students that the section of DNA that is transcribed is called the "sense" strand. The sense strand is only one-half of the DNA molecule. RNA polymerase recognizes the "start" site—the promoter region on DNA. RNA polymerase then "reads" the sequence of DNA bases and then "writes" it into mRNA language, linking complementary RNA nucleotides until it reaches a "stop" signal. The rate of transcription is about 60 nucleotides per second.

READING TOOLBOX

Three-Panel Flip Chart Make a three-panel flip chart to help you compare the roles of the three types of RNA used in gene expression.

Transcription

❶ RNA polymerase binds to the gene's promoter.

❷ The two DNA strands unwind and separate.

❸ Complementary RNA nucleotides are added.

RNA polymerase

Promoter site on DNA

RNA

Figure 12 Transcription is the process in which mRNA is made to complement the DNA of a gene.

Transcription: Reading the Gene

❯ During transcription, the information in a specific region of DNA (a gene) is transcribed, or copied, into mRNA. Transcription is carried out by a protein called *RNA polymerase*. The steps of transcription are described below and are shown in **Figure 12.**

Step ❶ Transcription begins when RNA polymerase binds to the specific DNA sequence in the gene that is called the *promoter*. The promoter is the "start" location.

Step ❷ RNA polymerase then unwinds and separates the two strands of the double helix to expose the DNA bases on each strand.

Step ❸ RNA polymerase adds and links complementary RNA bases as it "reads" the gene. RNA polymerase moves along the bases on the DNA strand in much the same way that a train moves along a track. Transcription follows the base-pairing rules for DNA replication except that in RNA, uracil—rather than thymine—pairs with adenine. As RNA polymerase moves down the DNA strand, a single strand of mRNA grows. Behind the moving RNA polymerase, the two strands of DNA close up and re-form the double helix.

The RNA polymerase eventually reaches a "stop" location in the DNA. This stop signal is a sequence of bases that marks the end of each gene in eukaryotes or the end of a set of genes in prokaryotes. The result is a single strand of mRNA.

❯ **Reading Check** *What is the role of a promoter?*

Differentiated Instruction

Basic Learners

Recognizing the Code Draw a figure similar to Step 2 of **Figure 12.** Randomly assign base letters to the right half (sense strand) of DNA. Make sure they are a number that is a multiple of three. Label the promoter region, and the stop location. Have student volunteers come to the board to add letters for RNA nucleotides. The letters added should be connected. Label the newly-transcribed single strand as mRNA. Have students design their own sequences using the model on the board. **LS Visual**

English Learners

RNA Pairing Rules Reinforce that adenine, A, on DNA pairs with uracil, U, instead of thymine, T. RNA never includes thymine. Have students recite base pairings to help reinforce this change. **LS Verbal**

Transcription Versus Replication Like DNA replication, transcription uses DNA as a template for making a new molecule. In transcription, a new molecule of RNA is made from the DNA. However, in DNA replication, a new molecule of DNA is made from the DNA. Also, in DNA replication, both strands of DNA serve as templates. In contrast, during transcription only part of one of the two strands of DNA (a gene) serves as a template for the new RNA.

The Genetic Code: Three-Letter "Words"

A gene can be thought of as a "sentence" of "words" that is first transcribed and then translated into a functional protein. Once a section of a gene is transcribed into mRNA, the words can be carried from the nucleus to ribosomes in the cytoplasm. There, the words are translated to make proteins.

Codons of mRNA Each of the words in mRNA is made up of three adjacent nucleotide bases. Each three-nucleotide sequence is called a **codon**. Each codon is matched to 1 of 20 amino acids or acts as a start or stop signal for the translation stage. **Figure 13** shows this matching system for each of the possible 64 mRNA codons. For example, the codon GCU specifies the amino acid alanine. Notice that each codon specifies only one amino acid but that several amino acids have more than one codon. This system of matching codons and amino acids is called the *genetic code.* ❯ **The genetic code is based on codons that each represent a specific amino acid.**

codon in DNA and mRNA, a three-nucleotide sequence that encodes an amino acid or signifies a start signal or a stop signal

Figure 13 The amino acid coded for by a specific mRNA codon can be determined by following the three steps below. ❯ What amino acid does the codon GAA code for?

Codons in mRNA

1. Find the first base of the mRNA codon in this column of the table.
2. Follow that row to the column that matches the second base of the codon.
3. Move up or down in that box until you match the third base of the codon with this column of the chart.

First base	Second base				Third base
	U	**C**	**A**	**G**	
U	UUU UUC Phenylalanine / UUA UUG Leucine	UCU UCC UCA UCG Serine	UAU UAC Tyrosine / UAA UAG Stop	UGU UGC Cysteine / UGA–Stop / UGG–Tryptophan	U C A G
C	CUU CUC CUA CUG Leucine	CCU CCC CCA CCG Proline	CAU CAC Histidine / CAA CAG Glutamine	CGU CGC CGA CGG Arginine	U C A G
A	AUU AUC Isoleucine / AUA / AUG–Start	ACU ACC ACA ACG Threonine	AAU AAC Asparagine / AAA AAG Lysine	AGU AGC Serine / AGA AGG Arginine	U C A G
G	GUU GUC GUA GUG Valine	GCU GCC GCA GCG Alanine	GAU GAC Aspartic acid / GAA GAG Glutamic acid	GGU GGC GGA GGG Glycine	U C A G

Teaching Key Ideas

Triplet Combination Have students recall the number of amino acids (20), and have them think back to the Inquiry Lab that involved paperclips. Two color combinations could provide only sixteen choices. **LS Logical**

Math Skills

Counting Methods When four bases are joined in three combinations (codons), there are sixty-four possible choices. Represent this as 4^3 (four bases and three combinations). **LS Logical**

READING TOOLBOX

Visual Literacy Familiarize students with codons and the amino acids they specify. Use the transparency, call out the three-letter sequence for several codons, and have students name the amino acid. Next, show the students how to read the chart, if *given* a codon. (Follow cues 1–3.) Ask students whether *all* codons specify an amino acid. (No, there are three stop codons: UAA, UAG, UGU. Therefore, only 61 codons actually code for an amino acid.) **LS Visual**

Answers to Caption Questions
Figure 13: The codon GAA codes for glutamic acid.

Why It Matters

Redundant Codons Call students' attention to several amino acids that have more than one codon. (leucine, serine, glycine, and so on.) In each case, ask which of the three bases in the codon is different. (the last one) Ask what advantage this might have. (A mistake in the *last* letter of the codon would still specify the same amino acid.) Suggest that these amino acids might be more crucial to the growth and survival of an organism. **LS Logical**

Teaching Key Ideas

"Taxi" RNA In the last step of protein synthesis, the language of mRNA codons is translated into the language of proteins (amino acid sequences). Transfer RNA (tRNA) acts as a "taxi service," bringing the specific amino acid to the ribosome for assembly. An anticodon sequence, matching the mRNA codon, makes this specificity possible.

READING TOOLBOX

Visual Literacy Use the codon sequence from **Figure 14** and write this sequence on a long strip(s) of paper. Post these on the board and mark off every three bases. Pass out prepared tRNA paper molecules with a circle on top, and call on individual students to name the amino acid and write its name on the circle. (Use **Figure 13.**) Emphasize the role of the ribosome in serving as a "workbench" that allows two amino acids to become closely positioned, so that peptide bonds can form between them. (Step 2) **LS** Visual

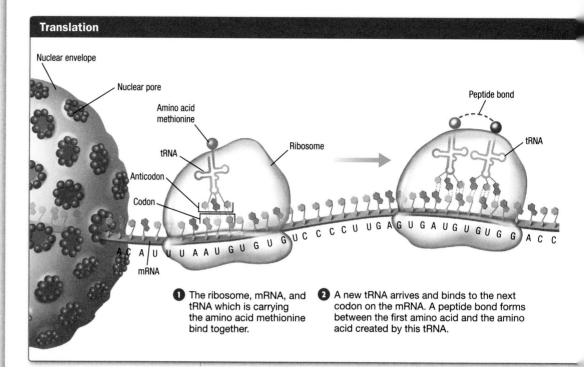

Translation

❶ The ribosome, mRNA, and tRNA which is carrying the amino acid methionine bind together.

❷ A new tRNA arrives and binds to the next codon on the mRNA. A peptide bond forms between the first amino acid and the amino acid created by this tRNA.

Figure 14 During translation, amino acids are assembled from information encoded in mRNA. As the mRNA codons move through the ribosome, tRNAs add specific amino acids to the growing polypeptide chain. This process continues until a stop codon is reached and the newly made protein is released.

Translation: RNA to Proteins

Translation is the process of converting the "language" of RNA (nucleotide sequences) into the "language" of proteins (amino acid sequences). ❯Translation occurs in a sequence of steps, involves three kinds of RNA, and results in a complete *polypeptide.* In the cytoplasm, ribosomes are formed as tRNA, rRNA, and mRNA interact to assemble amino acid sequences that are based on the genetic code. The process of translation is summarized below and in **Figure 14.**

Step ❶ Each tRNA is folded into a compact shape, as **Figure 15** shows. An amino acid is added to one end of each tRNA. The other end of the tRNA has an anticodon. An *anticodon* is a three-nucleotide sequence that is complementary to an mRNA codon. Each tRNA molecule carries the amino acid that corresponds with the tRNA's anticodon. After leaving the nucleus, the mRNA joins with a ribosome and tRNA. The mRNA start codon, AUG, signals the beginning of a protein chain. A tRNA molecule carrying methionine at one end and the anticodon, UAC, at the other end binds to the start codon.

Step ❷ A tRNA molecule that has the correct anticodon and amino acid binds to the second codon on the mRNA. A peptide bond forms between the two amino acids, and the first tRNA is released from the ribosome. The tRNA leaves its amino acid behind.

MISCONCEPTION ALERT

Translation Make sure that students use the mRNA codons, not tRNA anticodons, for translation. Recall that DNA's triplet code is given to the RNA "messenger," mRNA. Its codons dictate the amino acids.

Why It Matters

Antibiotic Function The prokaryotic ribosome is smaller than the eukaryotic ribosome. Its protein and RNA content is also different. These differences allow selective antibiotics, such as tetracycline, to bind to prokaryotic ribosomes. This bonding interferes with protein synthesis, which kills the disease-causing bacteria. Humans can safely take antibiotics because the ribosomes are different and will not be affected by the antibiotic.

Large ribosomal subunit

Small ribosomal subunit

Newly made polypeptide

Stop codon

mRNA

U U U A A U G U G U G U C C C G U U G A G U G U A G A U U G G A C C G C A C A U U U A

❸ The first tRNA detaches and leaves its amino acid. With each new tRNA, the amino acid chain grows.

❹ The process ends when a stop codon is reached.

❺ The amino acid chain is released, and the ribosome complex falls apart.

Step ❸ The ribosome moves one codon down the mRNA. Because the anticodon remains attached to the codon, the tRNA molecule and the mRNA molecule move as a unit, which leaves the next mRNA codon open and ready to receive the next tRNA and its amino acid. The amino acid chain continues to grow as each new amino acid binds to the chain and the previous tRNA is released.

Step ❹ This process is repeated until a stop codon is reached. A *stop codon* is one of three codons: UAG, UAA, or UGA. No tRNAs have anticodons for these stop codons, so protein production stops.

Step ❺ The newly made polypeptide falls off the ribosome. The ribosome complex falls apart. The last tRNA leaves the ribosome, and the ribosome moves away from the mRNA. The ribosome is then free to begin translation again on the same mRNA or on another mRNA.

Repeating Translation Like replication, translation needs to happen quickly and often. As a segment of mRNA moves through a ribosome, another ribosome can form on the AUG codon on the same mRNA segment and can begin a new translation process. Thus, several ribosomes can translate the same mRNA at the same time, which allows many copies of the same protein to be made rapidly from a single mRNA molecule.

❯ **Reading Check** *How do codons and anticodons differ?*

Figure 15 tRNA folds into this shape such that an anticodon is on one end and a binding site for amino acids is on the other end.

Why It Matters

Polyribosomes A single ribosome can make an average-sized polypeptide in less than a minute. However, a single mRNA is often used to make many polypeptides by having several ribosomes trail along the mRNA, one after another, making the same polypeptide. These clusters, seen with the electron microscope, are called *polyribosomes*.

Teacher's Notes Use **Figure 14** to review translation. Make sure students understand the terms codon and anticodon.

Answers to Analysis

1. serine–arginine–glutamic acid–phenylalanine–serine
2. AGA, GCA, CUU, AAA, AGG
3. AGAGCACTTAAAAGG
4. TCTCGTGAATTTTCC

Teaching Key Ideas

It's All There While the genetic code is specific and straightforward, the expression of genes is complex. There are several factors that influence gene expression. Stress that all of the DNA in a particular cell is not expressed. For example, genes coding for the formation of hemoglobin will not be expressed in a skin cell. Genes coding for the formation of a liver enzyme will not be expressed in a neuron. Remind students that *every cell contains all of the DNA for that organism.*

❯ Close

Formative Assessment

RNA polymerase splits DNA as part of the _____ process.

A. translation (Incorrect. There is no splitting of DNA in translation.)

B. transcription (Correct! RNA polymerase splits the strand in the second step of translation.)

C. replication (Incorrect. DNA splitting in replication does not involve RNA enzymes.)

D. base-pairing (Splitting DNA does not involve base-pairing.)

Data

QuickLab

Genetic Code of Keratin 🔖 4.2.1g

Keratin is one of the proteins in hair. The gene for keratin is transcribed and translated by certain skin cells. The sequence below is part of the mRNA molecule that is transcribed from the gene for keratin.

U C U C G U G A A U U U U C C

Analysis

1. **Determine** the sequence of amino acids that will result from the translation of the segment of mRNA above. Use the genetic code in **Figure 13.**

2. **Determine** the anticodon of each tRNA molecule that will bind to this mRNA segment.

3. **CRITICAL THINKING** **Recognizing Patterns** Determine the sequence of nucleotides in the segment of DNA from which this mRNA strand was transcribed.

4. **CRITICAL THINKING** **Recognizing Patterns** Determine the sequence of nucleotides in the segment of DNA that is complementary to the DNA segment that is described in item 3.

Complexities of Gene Expression

❯ The relationship between genes and their effects is complex. Despite the neatness of the genetic code, every gene cannot be simply linked to a single outcome. Some genes are expressed only at certain times or under specific conditions. Some traits result from the expression of multiple genes. Variations, mistakes, feedback, and other complex interactions can occur at each of the steps in replication and expression. The final outcome of gene expression is affected by the environment of the cells, the presence of other cells, and the timing of gene expression.

Overall, knowledge of the basic process of gene expression has allowed scientists to better understand the workings of all organisms. The next chapters delve into the exciting results of applying this knowledge.

Section

3 Review

❯ KEY IDEAS

1. **Describe** gene expression.
2. **Explain** the role of RNA in gene expression.
3. **Summarize** transcription.
4. **Explain** how codons determine the amino acid sequence of a protein.

5. **Describe** the steps of translation.
6. **Identify** a complexity of gene expression.

CRITICAL THINKING

7. **Inferring Relationships** Multiple codons can produce the same amino acid. What is the advantage of this redundancy?

8. **Relating Concepts** What amino acid is coded for by the mRNA codon CCU?

ALTERNATIVE ASSESSMENT

9. **Gene Poster** Research two methods used to sequence the nucleotides in a gene. Compare the two methods. Give examples of how this technology might be used in a clinical setting. Prepare a poster to summarize the two methods that you researched.

Answers to Section Review

1. Proteins are produced through a process that involves the transcription of information in the DNA into an mRNA strand in the nucleus, and then the translation of that information into the amino acid sequence of the protein.

2. Messenger RNA (mRNA) transcribes DNA's code and takes it to ribosomal RNA (rRNA) to direct the assembly of amino acids in the proper sequence, using transfer RNA (tRNA) as a "taxi" service.

3. The information contained in a sequence of DNA (gene) is written into the language of RNA, using RNA nucleotides to produce mRNA.

4. With four bases, three-letter combinations are needed to provide codes for twenty amino acids. Each three-letter combination is called a codon.

5. During translation, mRNA is read by the ribosome, calling for the delivery of specific amino acids by tRNA. Two tRNAs are positioned on the ribosome, allowing the amino acids to form a peptide bond.

6. Some traits require multiple genes to be expressed. Gene expression is also affected by timing and the cell's environment.

7. If an error occurs during translation, the codon may still signal the correct amino acid.

8. proline

9. Shotgun sequencing is used for sequencing longer strands of DNA. The older Sanger method is used for shorter fragments.

Objectives

❯ Extract DNA from wheat germ.

❯ Explain the role of detergents, heat, and alcohol in the extraction of DNA.

Materials

- disposable gloves
- safety goggles
- lab apron
- wheat germ, raw (1 g)
- test tube or beaker (50 mL)
- water, hot tap (55°C, 20 mL)
- salt, table
- soap, liquid dishwashing (1 mL)
- Isopropyl alcohol, cold (15 mL)
- glass rod, 8 cm long
- inoculating loop
- glass slide

Safety

DNA Extraction from Wheat Germ

The extraction and purification of DNA are the first steps in the analysis and manipulation of DNA. Very pure DNA can be easily extracted from cells in a research laboratory, and somewhat less pure DNA can be extracted with some simple techniques easily performed in a classroom.

The first step in extracting DNA from a cell is to lyse, or break open, the cell. Cell walls, cell membranes, and nuclear membranes are broken down by physical smashing, heating, and the addition of detergents. In water, DNA is soluble. When isopropyl alcohol is added, the DNA uncoils and precipitates, leaving behing many other cell components that are not soluble in isopropyl alcohol. The DNA can be then spooled, or wound onto an inoculating loop, and pulled from the solution. In this lab, you will extract the DNA from wheat germ. Wheat germ is simply the ground-up cells of wheat kernels, or seeds.

Procedure

1 Put on safety goggles, lab apron, and gloves.

2 CAUTION: Glassware, such as a test tube, is fragile and can break. Place 1 g of wheat germ into a clean test tube.

3 Add 20 mL hot (55°C) tap water and stir with glass rod for 2 to 3 min.

4 Next, add a pinch of table salt, and mix well.

5 Add a few drops (1 mL) of liquid dishwashing soap. Stir the mixture with the glass rod for 1 min until it is well mixed.

6 CAUTION: Isopropyl alcohol is flammable. Bunsen burners and hot plates should be removed from the lab. Slowly pour 15 mL cold isopropyl alcohol down the side of the tilted tube or beaker. The alcohol should form a top layer over the original solution. Note: Do not pour the alcohol too fast or directly into the wheat germ solution.

7 Tilt the tube upright, and watch the stringy, white material float up into the alcohol layer (this result should occur after 10 to 15 min). This material is the DNA from the wheat germ.

8 Carefully insert the inoculating loop into the white material in the alcohol layer. Gently twist the loop as you wind the DNA around the loop. Remove the loop from the tube, and tap the DNA onto a glass slide.

9 Clean up your lab materials according to your teacher's instructions. Wash your hands before leaving the lab.

Analyze and Conclude

1. **Describing Events** Describe the appearance of the DNA on the slide.

2. **Interpreting Information** Explain the role of detergent, heat, and isopropyl alcohol in the extraction of DNA.

3. SCIENTIFIC METHODS **Comparing Structures** How do the characteristics of your DNA sample relate to the structure of eukaryotic DNA?

4. SCIENTIFIC METHODS **Designing Experiments** Design a DNA extraction experiment in which you explore the effect of changing the variables.

Time Required

One 50-minute class period

Ratings

EASY ──────────→ HARD

Teacher Prep	🧪🧪🧪
Student Setup	🧪🧪🧪
Concept Level	🧪🧪🧪
Cleanup	🧪🧪🧪

Safety Cautions

Students must wear the listed safety equipment to do this lab. Because they will be working with a flammable liquid, all heat sources must be removed from the area. Fumes can easily catch fire.

Tips and Tricks

This lab works best in groups of two to four students.

Set up 55°C hot-water baths for students ahead of time.

Isopropyl alcohol should be kept cold, preferably on ice or in a freezer, prior to use.

Weigh out the wheat germ and detergent for each group of students prior to class to save time.

Hot (50–60°C) water will soften the membrane and denature deoxyribonuclease. This enzyme will cut DNA into small fragments. Seal the test tube with a rubber stopper. When swirling the detergent, use a gentle motion to avoid forming suds. *Cold* ethanol can be substituted for isopropanol with good results. Using a piece of wire, with a hook, allows the DNA to be lifted very slowly from the test tube.

Answers to Analyze and Conclude

1. Students should describe the color as clear or white, and a viscosity that is similar to mucus. The length of the DNA sample may differ; it may be several short strands or a single giant thread. Some students may note its sticky texture and elastic nature.

2. Detergent breaks down and emulsifies the fat and proteins that make up the cell membrane and the nuclear membrane, causing the the DNA to be released into solution. Heat softens the cell and nuclear membranes and inactivates (denatures) some enzymes that cut DNA into small fragments. Alcohol causes the DNA to precipitate out of solution. This allows the DNA to be collected and helps to partially purify the DNA from other cellular components that are soluble in water but not alcohol.

3. The sample sticks to itself, which relates to the double helix structure. It also forms long strings, which relates to the fact that eukaryotic DNA is very long.

4. Answers will vary but should include how the characteristics of the alcohol, detergent, and water temperatures are related to their proposed roles in DNA extraction.

Key Resources

   Holt Lab Generator

Lab Datasheet (Levels A, B, C)

Holt Science Biology Video Labs

 Virtual Investigations

SUPER SUMMARY

Have students connect the major concepts through an interactive Super Summary. Visit **go.hrw.com** and type in the keyword **HX8DNAS** to access the Super Summary for this chapter.

Reteaching Key Ideas

DNA Structure and Base-Pairing
Group students into pairs and give them sets of index cards, with the components of DNA written on separate cards. Each set of cards should include at least sixteen sugars, sixteen phosphates and four of each of the bases. Ask students to arrange the cards in a pattern that shows the structure of DNA. **LS** Visual

Vocabulary Activity To help students with the vocabulary in this chapter, write the following terms on separate index cards: *amino acid, codon, anti-codon, DNA, mRNA, tRNA, rRNA, ribosome, transcription, translation.* Give a set of cards to each group of four students. Ask students to organize the cards and describe the connection between terms. Monitor the groups to check for accuracy. **LS** Verbal/Visual

Key Ideas	Key Terms

1 The Structure of DNA

> DNA is the primary material that causes recognizable, inheritable characteristics in related groups of organisms.

> Three major experiments led to the conclusion that DNA is the genetic material in cells. These experiments were performed by Griffith, Avery, Hershey, and Chase.

> A DNA molecule is shaped like a spiral staircase and is composed of two parallel strands of linked subunits.

> The information in DNA is contained in the order of the bases, while the base-pairing structure allows the information to be copied.

> Watson and Crick used information from experiments by Chargaff, Wilkins, and Franklin to determine the three-dimensional structure of DNA.

Key Terms
gene (293)
DNA (293)
nucleotide (296)
purine (297)
pyrimidine (297)

2 Replication of DNA

> In DNA replication, the DNA molecule unwinds, and the two sides split. Then, new bases are added to each side until two identical sequences result.

> The replication of DNA involves many proteins that form a machinelike complex of moving parts.

> In prokaryotic cells, replication starts at a single site. In eukaryotic cells, replication starts at many sites along the chromosome.

DNA replication (300)
DNA helicase (301)
DNA polymerase (301)

3 RNA and Gene Expression

> Gene expression produces proteins by transcription and translation. This process takes place in two stages, both of which involve RNA.

> In cells, three types of RNA complement DNA and translate the genetic code into proteins.

> During transcription, the information in a gene is transcribed, or copied, into mRNA.

> The genetic code is based on codons that each represent a specific amino acid.

> Translation occurs in a sequence of steps, involves three kinds of RNA, and results in a complete polypeptide.

> Despite the neatness of the genetic code, every gene cannot be simply linked to a single outcome.

RNA (304)
gene expression (304)
transcription (305)
translation (305)
codon (307)

PART A: Answer all questions in this part.

Directions: For each statement or question, write on your separate answer sheet the number of the word or expression that best completes the statement or answers the question.

1 Hereditary traits are transmitted from generation to generation by means of
  (1) specific sequences of bases in DNA in reproductive cells.
  (2) proteins in body cells.
  (3) carbohydrates in body cells.
  (4) specific starches making up DNA in reproductive cells.

2 Which statement best expresses the relationship between the three structures represented below?

Part of a
protein molecule

Cell

Part of a
DNA molecule

  (1) DNA is produced from protein absorbed by the cell.
  (2) Protein is composed of DNA that is produced in the cell.
  (3) DNA controls the production of protein in the cell.
  (4) Cells make DNA by digesting protein.

3 A characteristic of a DNA molecule that is not characteristic of a protein molecule is that the DNA molecule
  (1) can replicate itself.
  (2) can be very large.
  (3) is found in nuclei.
  (4) is composed of subunits.

4 Synthesis of a defective protein may result from an alteration in
  (1) vacuole shape.
  (2) the number of mitochondria.
  (3) a base sequence code.
  (4) cellular fat concentration.

5 The genetic code of a DNA molecule is determined by a specific sequence of
  (1) ATP molecules.
  (2) sugar molecules.
  (3) chemical bonds.
  (4) molecular bases.

6 The sequence of subunits in a protein is most directly dependent on the
  (1) region in the cell where enzymes are produced.
  (2) DNA in the chromosomes in a cell.
  (3) type of cell in which starch is found.
  (4) kinds of materials in the cell membrane.

7 Most of the hereditary information that determines the traits of an organism is located in
  (1) only those cells of an individual produced by meiosis.
  (2) the nuclei of body cells of an individual.
  (3) certain genes in the vacuoles of body cells.
  (4) the numerous ribosomes in certain cells.

8 The instructions for the traits of an organism are coded in the arrangement of
  (1) glucose units in carbohydrate molecules.
  (2) bases in DNA in the nucleus.
  (3) fat molecules in the cell membrane.
  (4) energy-rich bonds in starch molecules.

9 When DNA separates into two strands, the DNA would most likely be directly involved in
  (1) replication.
  (2) fertilization.
  (3) differentiation.
  (4) evolution.

Regents Exam Practice Correlations

4.2.1a 14	4.2.1g 2, 4, 6, 20
4.2.1b 1	4.2.1i 10
4.2.1c 7	4.4.1h 13
4.2.1f 3, 5, 8, 9, 11, 12, 15, 19	

PART A

  1. **(1)** Carbohydrates and proteins do not carry hereditary information, but DNA does. (*#07, June 2006 Regents Exam*)

  2. **(3)** DNA is not made from proteins, nor are proteins made of DNA. Cells can only make DNA from nucleic acid subunits. (*#07, January 2006 Regents Exam*)

  3. **(1)** DNA and protein can be large molecules and found in nuclei, and both are made of subunits. DNA replicates but most proteins do not replicate. (*#04, January 2006 Regents Exam*)

  4. **(3)** Mitochondria and vacuoles are not involved in making proteins. Cellular fat concentration is unrelated to protein production. However, the DNA base sequence directly influences protein synthesis and shape. (*#05, June 2005 Regents Exam*)

  5. **(4)** The genetic code is determined by the specific sequence of bases on a strand of DNA. The sequence made up of three bases together code for a specific amino acid. (*#09, January 2004 Regents Exam*)

  6. **(2)** The specific sequence of three bases in DNA code for specific amino acids. Amino acids are the subunits of protein. (*#07, January 2004 Regents Exam*)

  7. **(2)** Only gametes are produced by meiosis, and heredity information is also found in body cells that are produced by mitosis. Genes are not found in vacuoles. Ribosomes do not contain genes. The majority of the genetic information in a cell is found in the nucleus. (*#08, August 2004 Regents Exam*)

  8. **(2)** DNA carries the instructions for all traits of an organism. Glucose, fat, and starch can provide energy to an organism, but these molecules do not determine an organism's traits. (*#11, June 2003 Regents Exam*)

  9. **(1)** DNA separates into two strands in order to replicate. Separation of strands does not occur during fertilization. Cell differentiation occurs as certain cells replicate. Mutations in genes during replication may eventually lead to evolution. (*#10, June 2003 Regents Exam*)

10. (3) Each amino acid is determined by a specific sequence of three bases. If a mutation occurred that changed the order of bases, the sequence of amino acids would change. The altered DNA would not be destroyed by enzymes or the immune system. The change would not result in the production of starch--a substance that is formed from the sugars produced during photosynthesis. *(#07, January 2003 Regents Exam)*

11. (3) The diagram shows paired bases in a DNA molecule. DNA controls the inheritance of traits. *(#14, August 2003 Regents Exam)*

12. (4) DNA molecules make up the genes that are found on a chromosome, so they are like paragraphs within a chapter. None of the other choices fit neatly into the "book." Amino acids are coded by the bases in a DNA molecule. An egg is composed of many proteins that have been assembled from amino acids. A starch molecule is formed from the sugars produced during photosynthesis. *(#10, August 2003 Regents Exam)*

13. (2) Non-disjunction of chromosome 21 during gamete formation (meiotic cell division) leads to the formation of gametes with three copies of chromosome 21. If an abnormal gamete fuses with a normal gamete during fertilization, the resulting offspring will have Down syndrome (trisomy 21). *(#16, January 2005 Regents Exam)*

14. (4) The pigment is produced in the mammal only if the environment reaches a certain temperature. That implies that the genes are stable, and are expressed season after season. The genes are not destroyed or mutated. *(#07, August 2004 Regents Exam)*

15. (2) Genes are determined by different sequences that are formed by the bases A, T, C, and G in a cell's DNA. Proteins are formed by amino acid sequences that are determined by genes. The size of sugar molecules can determine the amount of energy available for cell function, not the kinds of genes an organism possesses. *(#09, August 2003 Regents Exam)*

16. (3)

17. (3)

18. (3)

---

10 A change in the order of DNA bases that code for a respiratory protein will most likely cause

(1) the production of a starch that has a similar function.

(2) the digestion of the altered gene by enzymes.

(3) a change in the sequence of amino acids determined by the gene.

(4) the release of antibodies by certain cells to correct the error.

11 A portion of a molecule is shown in the diagram below. Which statement best describes the main function of this type of molecule?

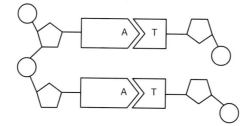

(1) It is a structural part of the cell wall.

(2) It stores energy for metabolic processes.

(3) It determines what traits may be inherited.

(4) It transports materials across the cell membrane.

12 If a set of instructions that determines all of the characteristics of an organism is compared to a book, and a chromosome is compared to a chapter in the book, then what might be compared to a paragraph in the book?

(1) a starch molecule

(2) an egg

(3) an amino acid

(4) a DNA molecule

13 Down syndrome is a genetic disorder caused by the presence of an extra chromosome in the body cells of humans. This extra chromosome occurs in a gamete as a result of

(1) an error in the process of cloning.

(2) an error in meiotic cell division.

(3) a gene mutation.

(4) replication of a single chromosome during mitosis.

14 Some mammals have genes for fur color that produce pigment only when the outside temperature is above a certain level. This pigment production is an example of how the environment of an organism can

(1) destroy certain genes.

(2) cause new mutations to occur.

(3) stop the process of evolution.

(4) influence the expression of certain genes.

15 What determines the kind of genes an organism possesses?

(1) type of amino acids in the cells of the organism

(2) sequence of the subunits A, T, C, and G in the DNA of the organism

(3) size of simple sugar molecules in the organs of the organism

(4) shape of the protein molecules in the organelles of the organism

16 What does the process of transcription produce?

(1) tRNA   (3) mRNA

(2) RNA   (4) DNA

17 During protein synthesis, transfer RNA (tRNA)

(1) produces a new RNA molecule.

(2) acts as a start signal for protein synthesis.

(3) produces protein subunits by translating the codons on mRNA.

(4) delivers the instructions for protein synthesis to the site of translation.

18 Erwin Chargaff's data on nitrogenous bases

(1) suggested that DNA bases are paired.

(2) suggested that DNA is a tightly coiled helix.

(3) suggested that certain bases are found in equal amounts in DNA.

(4) proved that DNA's structure is similar to a twisted ladder.

PART D

Base your answers to questions 19 and 20 on the Universal Genetic Code Chart below and on your knowledge of biology. Some DNA, RNA, and amino acid information from four similar sequences of four plant species is shown in the chart below.

Universal Genetic Code Chart
Messenger RNA Codons and the Amino Acids They Code For

		SECOND BASE				
		U	**C**	**A**	**G**	
FIRST BASE	**U**	UUU UUC } PHE, UUA UUG } LEU	UCU UCC UCA UCG } SER	UAU UAC } TYR, UAA UAG } STOP	UGU UGC } CYS, UGA } STOP, UGG } TRP	U C A G
	C	CUU CUC CUA CUG } LEU	CCU CCC CCA CCG } PRO	CAU CAC } HIS, CAA CAG } GLN	CGU CGC CGA CGG } ARG	U C A G
	A	AUU AUC } ILE, AUA AUG } MET or START	ACU ACC ACA ACG } THR	AAU AAC } ASN, AAA AAG } LYS	AGU AGC } SER, AGA AGG } ARG	U C A G
	G	GUU GUC GUA GUG } VAL	GCU GCC GCA GCG } ALA	GUA GAC } ASP, GAA GAG } GLU	GGU GGC GGA GGG } GLY	U C A G

(right side label: THIRD BASE)

19 Using the information given, identify the missing mRNA base sequence for species B. Record your answer on a separate sheet of paper.

20 Using the Universal Genetic Code Chart, identify the missing amino acid. Record your answer on a separate sheet of paper.

Species A	DNA base sequence	CCG	TGC	ATA	CAG	GTA
	mRNA base sequence	GGC	ACG	UAU	GUC	CAU
	Amino acid sequence	**GLY**	**THR**	**TYR**	**VAL**	**HIS**
Species B	DNA base sequence	TGC	TGC	ATA	CAG	GTA
	mRNA base sequence	___	___	___	___	___
	Amino acid sequence	**THR**	**THR**	**TYR**	**VAL**	**HIS**
Species C	DNA base sequence	CCG	TGC	ATA	CAG	GTT
	mRNA base sequence	GGC	ACG	UAU	GUC	CAA
	Amino acid sequence	___	___	___	___	___
Species D	DNA base sequence	CCT	TGT	ATG	CAC	GTC
	mRNA base sequence	GGA	ACA	UAC	GUG	CAG
	Amino acid sequence	**GLY**	**THR**	**TYR**	**VAL**	**GLN**

PART D

19. Allow 1 credit for filling in the missing mRNA base sequence for species B: ACG ACG UAU GUC CAU (*#63, June 2006 Regents Exam*)

20. Allow 1 credit for filling in the missing amino acid sequence for species C: GLY THR TYR VAL GLN (*#64, June 2006 Regents Exam*)

Genes in Action

CHAPTER OPENER, pp. 316–317   `15 min.`

The Living Environment

SECTION 1 Mutation and Genetic Change,
          pp. 319–324   `45 min.`

⟩ **Mutation: The Basis of Genetic Change**
⟩ **Several Kinds of Mutations**
⟩ **Effects of Genetic Change**
⟩ **Large-Scale Genetic Change**

Standards: 4.2.1h, 4.2.2d, 4.3.1b, 4.3.1c, 4.3.1d, 4.5.2i

Teach Key Ideas:
- 📓 **Bellringer Transparency**
- 📀 **Transparencies** C26 The Major Types of Mutations
- 💿 **Visual Concepts** Mutation • Types of Gene Mutations • Genetic Disorder • Comparing X-Linked and Sex-Influenced Traits • Sickle-Cell Anemia • Hemophilia • Huntington's Disease • Disorders Due to Nondisjunction

---

SECTION 2 Regulating Gene Expression,
          pp. 325–329   `120 min.`

⟩ **Complexities of Gene Expression**
⟩ **Gene Regulation in Prokaryotes**
⟩ **Gene Regulation in Eukaryotes**
⟩ **The Many Roles of Proteins**

Standards: 4.2.1a, 4.2.1g, 4.2.1i, 4.2.1k

Teach Key Ideas:
- 📓 **Bellringer Transparency**
- 💿 **Visual Concepts** Operon • Repression of Transcription in the *lac* Operon • Regulator Gene • Activation of Transcription in the *lac* Operon • Enhancers for Control of Gene Expression • Comparing Introns and Exons

---

SECTION 3 Genome Interactions, pp. 330–337   `90 min.`

⟩ **Genomes and the Diversity of Life**
⟩ **Moving Beyond Chromosomes**
⟩ **Multicellular Development and Aging**

Standards: 4.1.2e, 4.2.1k, 4.3.1b

Teach Key Ideas:
- 📓 **Bellringer Transparency**

See also PowerPoint® Resources

Chapter Review and Assessment Resources

SE Super Summary, p. 338
SE Regents Exam Practice, p. 339
📖 Regents Review Guide
📖 Review Resources
📖 Chapter Tests A and B
🌐 Holt Online Assessment
💿 Regents Question Banks on Teacher's One-Stop Planner

CHAPTER
Fast Track   To shorten instruction due to time limitations, eliminate the Skills Practice Lab.

Basic Learners
TE Chromosomal Mutation Models, p. 321
TE Ultraviolet Radiation and Sunscreen, p. 322
TE Vocabulary Refresher, p. 323
TE Exon Splicing, p. 328
TE Distinguishing Data, p. 331
📄 Directed Reading Worksheets*
📄 Active Reading Worksheets*
📄 Lab Manuals, Level A*
📄 Study Guide* ■
📄 Note-taking Workbook*
📄 Special Needs Activities and Modified Tests*

Advanced Learners
TE Advantage of Sickle Cell, p. 320
TE Down Syndrome, p. 323
TE Nobel Winners in Genetics, p. 327
TE Endosymbiont Theory, p. 331
TE Retroviruses, p. 332
TE The Mitochondrial DNA Question, p. 335
📄 Critical Thinking Worksheets*
📄 Concept Mapping Worksheets*
📄 Science Skills Worksheets*
📄 Lab Datasheets, Level C*

Why It Matters	Hands-On	Skills Development	Assessment
Build student motivation with resources about high-interest applications.	SE **Inquiry Lab** Where Is the Protein, p. 317* ■	TE **Reading Toolbox** Assessing Prior Knowledge, p. 316 SE **Reading Toolbox,** p. 318	
TE **Sickle Cell Disease,** p. 320 TE **Radiation and Cancer,** p. 322	SE **Quick Lab** Make a Model of Mutations, p. 321* ■	SE **Reading Toolbox** Finding Examples, p. 320 TE **Reading Toolbox** Finding Examples, p. 320	SE **Section Review** TE **Formative Assessment** Spanish Assessment* ■ 📁 Section Quiz ■
TE **Demonstration** Using an Analogy, p. 325 TE **Lactose Intolerance,** p. 326 TE **Demonstration** Modeling the Regulation Process, p. 327 TE **Demonstration** Splicing, p. 328	SE **Quick Lab** A Model of Introns and Exons, p. 328* ■ SE **Skills Practice Lab** Protein Detection, p. 336* ■	SE **Reading Toolbox** Sample Comparison Table, p. 326 TE **Reading Toolbox** Sample Comparison Table, p. 326	SE **Section Review** TE **Formative Assessment** Spanish Assessment* ■ 📁 Section Quiz ■
TE **Demonstration** Relative Size of Genomes, p. 331 TE **A Passion for Research,** p. 332 SE **Forensic Genealogy,** p. 335	📁 **Skills Practice Lab** Introduction to Agarose Gel Electrophoresis* ■ 📁 **Exploration Lab** DNA Whodunnit* ■	SE **Reading Toolbox** Prefixes, p. 333 TE **Reading Toolbox** Prefixes, p. 333 TE **Reading Toolbox** Visual Literacy, p. 335	SE **Section Review** TE **Formative Assessment** Spanish Assessment* ■ 📁 Section Quiz ■
	See also Lab Generator		**See also Holt Online Assessment Resources**

Resources for Differentiated Instruction

English Learners
TE Vocabulary, p. 326
TE Exon Splicing, p. 328
📁 Directed Reading Worksheets*
📁 Active Reading Worksheets*
📁 Lab Manuals, Level A*
📓 Study Guide* ■
📓 Note-taking Workbook*
📓 Multilingual Glossary

Struggling Readers
TE Mutation, Mutant, or Mutagen?, p. 319
TE Vocabulary Refresher, p. 323
TE Vocabulary, p. 326
TE Distinguishing Data, p. 331
TE Key-Term Fold, p. 333
📁 Directed Reading Worksheets*
📁 Active Reading Worksheets*
📁 Lab Manuals, Level A*
📓 Study Guide*
📓 Note-taking Workbook*
📓 Special Needs Activities and Modified Tests*

Special Education Students
TE Chromosomal Mutation Models, p. 321
📁 Directed Reading Worksheets*
📁 Active Reading Worksheets*
📁 Lab Manuals, Level A*
📓 Study Guide* ■
📓 Note-taking Workbook*
📓 Special Needs Activities and Modified Tests*

Alternative Assessment
📁 Science Skills Worksheets*
📁 Section Quizzes* ■
📓 Chapter Tests A, B, and C* ■

Chapter 14 Genes in Action

Overview

The purpose of this chapter is to expand on the roles of genes—how they can change, how their expression is regulated, and how they control development and lifespan of the cell. The universality of the genetic code is reiterated by comparing genomes and seeing interactions at the genetic level.

READING TOOLBOX

Assessing Prior Knowledge Students should be familiar with the following concepts:
- heredity
- structure of genes
- gene expression
- triplet code for amino acids

Visual Literacy Ask students whether extra legs provide an adaptive advantage for the frogs in the photo. (Students may think extra legs would be an advantage. However, the extra legs hamper the agility of these frogs. Thus, the frogs pictured are more likely targets for predators.)

Preview

1 Mutation and Genetic Change
Mutation: The Basis of Genetic Change
Several Kinds of Mutations
Effects of Genetic Change
Large-Scale Genetic Change

2 Regulating Gene Expression
Complexities of Gene Expression
Gene Regulation in Prokaryotes
Gene Regulation in Eukaryotes
The Many Roles of Proteins

3 Genome Interactions
Genomes and the Diversity of Life
Moving Beyond Chromosomes
Multicellular Development and Aging

Why It Matters

Knowing the genetic code is not enough to understand how genes work. To understand our own bodies, we must study thousands of genes, proteins, and other molecules that interact as our bodies grow and develop.

The Living Environment
Standard 4 Students will understand and apply scientific concepts, principles, and theories pertaining to the physical setting and living environment and recognize the historical development of ideas in science.
Key Idea 1 Living things are both similar to and different from each other and from nonliving things. *Major Understandings - 1.2e*
Key Idea 2 Organisms inherit genetic information in a variety of ways that result in continuity of structure and function between parents and offspring. *Major Understandings – 2.1a, 2.1g, 2.1h, 2.1i, 2.1k, 2.2d*
Key Idea 3 Individual organisms and species change over time. *Major Understandings – 3.1b, 3.1c, 3.1d*
Key Idea 5 Organisms maintain a dynamic equilibrium that sustains life. *Major Understandings – 5.2i*

Genes in Action

These frogs have extra legs! When many mutated or deformed organisms are found in one area, scientists want to find out why.

Scientists have found several factors that increase the numbers of deformities in frogs. These factors include UV radiation, pesticides, and parasites. Parasites invade the frogs' bodies and may disrupt development.

Chapter Correlations ● The Living Environment

Standard 4

1.2e The organs and systems of the body help to provide all the cells with their basic needs. The cells of the body are of different kinds and are grouped in ways that enhance how they function together.

2.1a Genes are inherited, but their expression can be modified by interactions with the environment.

2.1g Cells store and use coded information. The genetic information stored in DNA is used to direct the synthesis of the thousands of proteins that each cell requires.

2.1h Genes are segments of DNA molecules. Any alteration of the DNA sequence is a mutation. Usually, an altered gene will be passed on to every cell that develops from it.

2.1i The work of the cell is carried out by the many different types of molecules it assembles, mostly proteins. Protein molecules are long, usually folded chains made from 20 different kinds of amino acids in a specific sequence. This sequence influences the shape of the protein. The shape of the protein, in turn, determines its function.

2.1k The many body cells in an individual can be very different from one another, even though they are all descended from a single cell and thus have essentially identical genetic instructions. This is because different parts of these instructions are used in different types of cells, and are influenced by the cells' environment and past history.

2.2d Inserting, deleting, or substituting DNA segments can alter genes. An altered gene may be passed on to every cell that develops from it.

3.1b New inheritable characteristics can result from new combinations of existing genes or from mutations of genes in reproductive cells.

3.1c Mutation and the sorting and recombining of genes during meiosis and fertilization result in a great variety of possible gene combinations.

InquiryLab

🕐 15 min

Where Is the Protein?

Protein test strips are inexpensive and easy-to-use measuring tools. Sold in local pharmacies, these strips are purchased by individuals who must monitor the concentration of protein in their urine. The strips can also be used to confirm the presence of protein in various foods.

Procedure

❶ Work with a partner. Label **five small cups** "A," "B," "C," "D," and "E."

❷ Use a **mortar and pestle** to crush **20 lentil beans.** Place the crushed beans into cup A.

❸ Place **1 g of instant oatmeal** into cup B.

❹ Pour **10 mL of water** into cups A and B. Swirl each cup to mix its contents.

❺ Pour **10 mL of water** into cup C.

❻ Pour **10 mL of milk** into cup D.

❼ Pour **10 mL of fruit juice** into cup E.

❽ Obtain **five protein test strips.** Follow the label instructions to detect and measure the presence of protein in each cup.

Analysis

1. **Identify** the cups in which protein was present.

2. **Identify** the cups that had the most and least amounts of protein.

3. **Identify** the control group in this experiment. Explain its purpose.

Each stage of growth and development is directed by genes. Sometimes, changes in DNA result in changes in cell function. Or sometimes, the cells' environment can switch some genes "off" or "on."

The development of adult animals, such as frogs, is the result of a complex series of stages involving many cells. A frog starts out as an egg, becomes a tadpole, and then becomes an adult. Legs grow in the adult stage.

InquiryLab

Teacher's Notes Using a blender to pulverize the lentils will save time. Protein test strips are also known as urine reagent test strips. They are available locally at most pharmacies. Such strips can be used in other activities as a convenient way to measure pH, ketones, and nitrates. Make sure students rinse the graduated cylinder between steps 6 and 7.

Materials

- small paper or plastic cups (5)
- mortar and pestle
- lentil beans (20)
- instant oatmeal, 1 g
- graduated cylinders, 10 or 25 mL
- water, 30 mL
- milk, 10 mL
- fruit juice, apple, 10 mL
- multiple test sticks or protein test sticks for urine analysis (5)

Answers to Analysis

1. Protein should be detected in cups A, B, and D.

2. Cup A should have the most protein. Cup B should have the least amount of protein.

3. Cup C, water, was the control. It was used to show the effect of a liquid that is unreactive on the strip.

3.1d Mutations occur as random chance events. Gene mutations can also be caused by such agents as radiation and chemicals. When they occur in sex cells, the mutations can be passed on to offspring; if they occur in other cells, they can be passed on to other body cells only.

5.2i Gene mutations in a cell can result in uncontrolled cell division, called cancer. Exposure of cells to certain chemicals and radiation increases mutations and thus increases the chance of cancer.

READING TOOLBOX

Using Words

1. Accept answers that are synonymous with "cannot be changed."
2. Accept answers that suggest a change that allows something to "cross" over into another state.

Using Language

1. Accept reasonable answers. Students will likely offer physical features of themselves, animals, and possibly plants. Traits may include hair color, eye color, height, or flower color.
2. inherit, inheritable, inheritance, inherent, inherence, heritage, or heredity

Using Science Graphics

Sample answer:

	Lactose absent	Lactose present
Similarities	RNA polymerase at promoter	RNA polymerase at promoter
Differences	repressor attached	lactose binds to repressor, releasing it

READING TOOLBOX

These reading tools can help you learn the material in this chapter. For more information on how to use these and other tools, see **Appendix: Reading and Study Skills.**

Using Words

Prefixes A prefix is a word part that is attached to the beginning of a word. Prefixes add to the meaning of words. For example, the prefix *im-* means "not." So, *immovable* means "not able to be moved." This table shows some additional prefixes that you may see in this chapter.

Prefixes	
Prefix	**Meaning**
in- or *im-*	not
mut-	change
trans-	cross
homeo-	the same

Your Turn Use the table to answer the questions that follow.
1. In your own words, define *immutable*.
2. What do you think the word *transmutation* means?

Using Language

Finding Examples When you are reading scientific explanations, finding examples can help you put a concept into practical terms. Thinking of your own examples will help you remember what you read.

Your Turn For each category of items below, brainstorm as many examples as you can think of that could fit into the category.
1. hereditary traits
2. words that include the word part *-her-*.

Using Science Graphics

Comparison Table A comparison table can help you understand what is happening in two similar situations. For example, this graphic shows the effect of lactose on specific genes in some prokaryotic cells. If you compare the two situations shown, you will find similarities and differences.

Your Turn Make a comparison table like the one shown here to compare what happens when lactose is present and when lactose is absent.
1. Draw a table with two columns.
2. Label the first column "Lactose absent."
3. Label the second column "Lactose present."
4. Use the graphic as a reference as you list the structures and events that are similar or different.

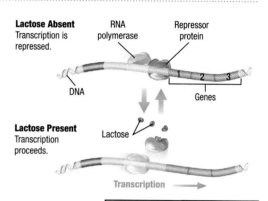

Mutation and Genetic Change

Key Ideas	Key Terms	Why It Matters
❯ What is the origin of genetic differences among organisms? ❯ What kinds of mutations are possible? ❯ What are the possible effects of mutations? ❯ How can genetic change occur on a larger scale?	mutation nondisjunction polyploidy	Understanding mutation is key to understanding the differences among organisms over time.

In general, *mutation* simply means "change," and any organism that has changed from some previous or normal state can be called a *mutant*. So, a frog that has extra legs may be called a *mutant*, although the extra legs may or may not have a genetic cause.

Mutation: The Basis of Genetic Change

In genetics, a **mutation** is a change in the structure or amount of the genetic material of an organism. A genetic *mutant* is an individual whose DNA or chromosomes differ from some previous or normal state. ❯ For the most part, genetic differences among organisms originate as some kind of genetic mutation. Every unique allele of every gene began as a mutation of an existing gene.

Causes of Mutations Mutations occur naturally as accidental changes to DNA or to chromosomes during the cell cycle. Recall that enzymes repair most DNA that is mismatched during replication, but rarely, some DNA is not repaired. Other kinds of mistakes are possible, as you will learn. Also, the rate of mutation can be increased by some environmental factors. Such factors, called *mutagens,* include many forms of radiation and some kinds of chemicals.

Effects of Mutations Because of the way DNA is translated, a mutation can have many possible effects. A small change in DNA may affect just one amino acid in the protein that results from a gene. However, as you will see, other results are possible. A mutation may have no effect, or may harm or help in some way. The effect depends on where and when the mutation occurs. We notice mutations when they cause an unusual trait or disease, such as *sickle cell anemia,* shown in **Figure 1.** However, many mutations may go unnoticed.

❯ **Reading Check** *Where do new alleles come from?*
(See the Appendix for answers to Reading Checks.)

 The Living Environment
Standard 4
2.1h Genes are segments of DNA molecules. Any alteration of the DNA sequence is a mutation. Usually, an altered gene will be passed on to every cell that develops from it.
2.2d Inserting, deleting, or substituting DNA segments can alter genes. An altered gene may be passed on to every cell that develops from it.
3.1b New inheritable characteristics can result from new combinations of existing genes or from mutations of genes in reproductive cells.
3.1c Mutation and the sorting and recombining of genes during meiosis and fertilization result in a great variety of possible gene combinations.
3.1d Mutations occur as random chance events. Gene mutations can also be caused by such agents as radiation and chemicals. When they occur in sex cells, the mutations can be passed on to offspring; if they occur in other cells, they can be passed on to other body cells only.
5.2i Gene mutations in a cell can result in uncontrolled cell division, called cancer. Exposure of cells to certain chemicals and radiation increases mutations and thus increases the chance of cancer.

> **mutation** a change in the structure or amount of the genetic material of an organism

Normal red blood cell

Sickle-shaped cell

Figure 1 One out of 500 African Americans has sickle cell anemia, which is caused by a mutation in the gene that produces hemoglobin. Blood cells with the defective hemoglobin tend to bend, rupture, and get stuck.

Differentiated Instruction

Struggling Readers

Mutation, Mutant, or Mutagen? Students with reading difficulties often do not recognize the subtle differences between words. Review the meanings of *mutation, mutant* and *mutagen.* Ask students to come up with ways that will help them remember the differences. (Accept meaningful answers.) **LS Verbal**

Key Resources

Transparencies
C26 The Major Types of Mutations

Visual Concepts
Mutation
Types of Gene Mutations
Genetic Disorder
Comparing X-Linked and Sex-Influenced Traits
Sickle-Cell Anemia
Hemophilia
Huntington's Disease
Disorders Due to Nondisjunction

Section Correlations	
4.2.1h	4.3.1c
4.2.2d	4.3.1d
4.3.1b	4.5.2i

Finding Examples Possible responses are the following:
- insertion: the cat sat e
- deletion: tec ata te
- nonsense: the cat (stop)

LS Visual

Teaching Key Ideas

Kinds of Mutations Have students look at **Figure 2** and identify the three original, correct amino acids. Next, look at the *silent mutation,* and identify the point mutation. (A for T) Why is this mutation silent? (It still codes for proline.) Next, look at the *missense mutation.* Why is it so named? (T for G results in a different amino acid, Glu.) Conclude with the *frameshift mutation.* Ask what has been inserted. (G) What is the result? (From this point, all the codons change.) **LS** Visual

go.hrw.com
✳ interact online

Students can interact with "Kinds of Mutations" by going to go.hrw.com and typing in the keyword HX8GNXF2.

READING TOOLBOX

Finding Examples Use the phrase "the cat ate" to create examples of mutations. For example, a point mutation could change the letter *c* to *b* and would result in "the bat ate." The new phrase is also a missense mutation. Use the original phrase to make examples of an insertion, a deletion, and a nonsense mutation.

Figure 2 A mutation is a change, insertion, or deletion of one or more nucleotides in a gene. The change may or may not result in a different amino acid sequence within a protein.

Several Kinds of Mutations

DNA and chromosomes are involved in many processes, so there are many kinds of mutations. Most mutations involve a misplacement of a nucleotide in a DNA segment. A mutation may change the results of a gene (when the gene is translated and transcribed), but not all mutations do so. **›** Different kinds of mutations are recognized as either changes in DNA or changes in the results of genes, as shown in **Figure 2.**

Mutations as Changes in DNA During DNA replication, the wrong nucleotide may be paired or placed in a sequence.

Point Mutation A *point* mutation is a change of a single nucleotide in a sequence from one kind of base to another.

Insertion or Deletion Rarely, errors in replication can cause the *insertion* or *deletion* of one or more nucleotides in a sequence.

Mutations as Changes in Results of Genes Changes in a DNA sequence may affect the results of genes in many ways.

Silent Mutation A mutation is *silent* when it has no effect on a gene's function. Point mutations are often silent because the genetic code is redundant (each amino acid has multiple codons).

Missense Mutation A *missense* mutation results when a codon is changed such that the new codon codes for a different amino acid. This kind of mutation is also called a *replacement* mutation.

Frameshift Mutation Recall that the genetic code is "read" in "words" of three letters each (codons). The *reading frame* of a sequence depends on the starting point for reading. An insertion or deletion can shift the reading frame, or cause a *frameshift.* In this case, the remaining sequence may be "read" as different codons.

go.hrw.com
✳ interact online
Keyword: HX8GNXF2

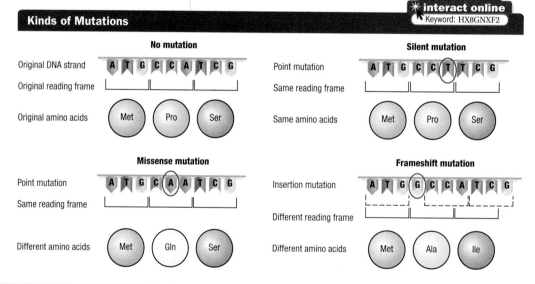

Kinds of Mutations

Why It Matters

Sickle Cell Disease A point mutation in DNA that codes for normal hemoglobin and that results in CAT rather than CTT replaces valine for glutamine. The resulting hemoglobin causes the red blood cell (RBC) to deform to a sickle shape, which causes the effects of this disease. This example illustrates the large-scale effects of a mutation in just one nucleotide base.

Differentiated Instruction

Advanced Learners/GATE

Advantage of Sickle Cell Have students investigate the heterozygous advantage of the sickle cell trait from an evolutionary perspective.
LS Logical

⏱ 15 min

Make a Model of Mutations 🔬 4.2.1h

You have learned about (and may have built models of) DNA replication and gene expression. Now, challenge yourself to build (or add to) a model that demonstrates each type of mutation described in this section.

Analysis

1. **List** each mutation type on **12 separate sheets of paper**. Work with a partner.

2. **Demonstrate** each mutation type by using **assorted materials** (or models that you have built previously).

3. **Draw** the "before" and "after" state for each mutation.

4. **CRITICAL THINKING** **Critiquing Models** Trade your drawings with another group. What is accurate and useful about their model? What could be improved? Write down your comments for the other group.

Nonsense Mutation A *nonsense* mutation results when a codon is changed to a "stop" signal. In this case, the resulting string of amino acids may be cut short, and the protein may fail to function.

More or Fewer Amino Acids If an insertion or deletion is a multiple of 3, the reading frame will be preserved. However, the protein that results may have a few more or less amino acids in it. An insertion or deletion of many codons is likely to disrupt the resulting protein's structure and function.

Chromosomal Mutations ❯ In eukaryotic cells, the process of meiosis creates the chance of mutations at the chromosomal level. Recall that during this process, chromosomes pair up and may undergo *crossover*. Usually, the result is an equal exchange of alleles between homologous chromosomes. But errors in the exchange can cause *chromosomal mutations*, as shown in **Figure 3.**

Deletion A *deletion* occurs when a piece of a chromosome is lost. At the end of meiosis, one of the cells will lack the genes from that missing piece. Such deletions are usually harmful.

Duplication A *duplication* occurs when a piece remains attached to its homologous chromosome after meiosis. One chromosome will then carry both alleles for each of the genes in that piece.

Inversion An *inversion* occurs when a piece reattaches to its original chromosome, but in a reverse direction.

Translocation A *translocation* occurs when a chromosome piece ends up in a completely different, nonhomologous chromosome.

Gene Rearrangement A chromosomal mutation can move an entire gene to a new location. Such a change, called a *gene rearrangement,* is likely to disrupt the gene's function in other ways, as you will learn.

❯ **Reading Check** *Why are point mutations often silent?*

Figure 3 Four kinds of chromosomal mutations can result from errors in crossover during meiosis. ❯ How are the types of chromosomal mutations similar to the types of smaller-scale mutations?

Teaching Key Ideas

Melanoma Melanoma is named for melanin, a brownish-black pigment found under the skin. Use the diagrams in **Figure 4** to discuss melanoma in terms of mutation. Ask what the *mutagen* is that sometimes causes melanoma. (exposure to ultraviolet rays) Ask if melanoma is inherited. (No, it is found in somatic cells.) What does a melanoma look like? (a very dark, irregularly shaped growth) Stress that melanoma is a malignant form of cancer. It is easily detected and can be treated successfully if identified in early stages. Explain that, although most cancers occur in somatic cells and are thus not heritable, the genetic risk of specific cancers can be inherited. For example, a specific allele has been linked to an increased risk of one type of melanoma. **LS Visual**

Answers to Caption Questions

Figure 4: No, only mutations in germ cells can be passed on.

ACADEMIC
VOCABULARY
_____
dramatic vivid or striking

Figure 4 Melanoma is a type of skin cancer caused by mutations in melanocytes, the cells that make skin pigment. Melanoma is an example of a somatic cell cancer. ❯ **Can this kind of cancer be passed on to offspring?**

Effects of Genetic Change

Many genetic changes will cause no change in the appearance or function of organisms. Moreover, many changes in the DNA of cells may not be passed on to other cells by mitosis or meiosis. ❯ **The results of genetic change may be harmful, beneficial, or neutral; most changes are neutral and may not be passed on to offspring.** Mutations that occur in gametes can be passed on to offspring, but mutations in body cells affect only the individual in which they occur.

Heritable or Not Multicellular eukaryotes have two primary cell types: germ cells and somatic cells. *Germ cells* make up gametes, and *somatic cells* make up the rest of the body. Mutations can occur in either type of cell. However, if a mutation occurs in a somatic cell, that genetic change will be lost when the owner of the cell dies. For example, a mutation in a person's lung cell could cause the cell to grow into lung cancer. The mutated genes in the cancer cells will not be transferred to the person's children.

Only a mutation in a germ cell may be passed on to the next generation. However, any such mutation may be silent or have little effect. Only rarely do mutations cause <u>dramatic</u> changes in future generations.

If a mutation occurs in a somatic cell, the change may be silent or it may change the function of the cell. Recall that most tissues are derived from a few parent cells. So, if a mutation occurs in a parent cell, all cells that arise by mitosis from that cell will have copies of the mutation. If the new cells can function at all, each will have the altered structure or function caused by the mutation. If the other parent cells were normal, the resulting tissue may include both normal tissue and mutant tissue.

Melanoma, a cancerous growth of skin cells

Cancerous skin cells (stained yellow) among normal skin cells (stained green)

Why It Matters

Radiation and Cancer In 1986, a nuclear explosion occurred in Chernobyl, Ukraine. The release of radiation has been linked to over 5,000 cases of thyroid cancer in individuals who were children at the time of the incident, and who drank milk from cows that ingested radioactive iodine while grazing. Radiation has been linked to the incidence of cancer as a primary mutagen.

Differentiated Instruction

Basic Learners

Ultraviolet Radiation and Sunscreen Have students investigate the incidence of melanoma in sunbelt states—Florida, Texas, Arizona, and New Mexico. Have them find out the science behind sunscreens. Have students use the information and work in pairs to create consumer awareness posters about the dangers of melanoma and prevention strategies. This information is especially important for teens, who often don't adequately protect themselves from the dangers of prolonged exposure to the sun. **LS Visual, Verbal**

Some Human Genetic Disorders

Disorder	Inheritance pattern	Major physical symptoms	Genetic effect of mutant allele	Number of cases (United States)
Sickle cell anemia	recessive	poor blood circulation; pain; damage to organs such as liver, kidney, lungs, and heart	abnormal hemoglobin in red blood cells	72,000
Tay-Sachs disease	recessive in most cases	deterioration of central nervous system; death in early childhood	defective form of an enzyme in nerve cells	< 100
Cystic fibrosis	recessive	mucus buildup in organs such as lungs, liver, and pancreas; difficulty breathing and digesting; shortened life span	defective form of an enzyme in secretory cells	30,000
Hemophilia A (classical)	recessive, sex-linked	failure of blood to clot; excessive bleeding and bruising when injured	defective form of a protein for blood clotting	18,000
Huntington disease	dominant	gradual deterioration of brain tissue in middle age; shortened life expectancy	abnormal protein in brain cells	30,000

Tumors and Cancers Certain genes control the normal growth, division, and specialization of cells in bodies. Mutations in these genes can cause a normal somatic cell to "lose control" and begin growing and dividing abnormally. The group of cells that grows will become a *tumor*. If the tumor cells begin to invade other parts of the body, they become a form of *cancer*. An example of a somatic cell tumor is shown in **Figure 4.** Note that although cancers result from somatic cell mutations, not all somatic cell mutations cause cancer.

New Alleles You previously learned that for any given gene, many alleles, or variations, may exist. Now, you should see that any new allele must begin as a mutation of an existing allele. Most new alleles are simply the result of silent mutations, so these changes make little difference to the organisms in which they occur. However, sometimes a new allele can cause a change in a gene's function. Depending on the gene, the result may be harmful or beneficial to the organism.

Genetic Disorders Harmful effects produced by inherited mutations (defective alleles) are called *genetic disorders*. Several human genetic disorders are summarized in **Figure 5.** Often, such a disorder results because a mutation has altered the normal function of a gene. However, a person may still have one allele of the original, functioning gene. For this reason, many disorders are recessive—that is, the disorder develops only in a person who is homozygous for the mutated allele. So, two heterozygous people may be healthy, yet have children who develop a genetic disorder. A person who is heterozygous for such an allele is said to be a *carrier* of the disorder.

> **Reading Check** *How are mutations related to cancer?*

Figure 5 Genetic disorders are caused by inherited mutations that disrupt the normal function of a gene. ❯ Why are genetic disorders relatively rare?

sciLINKS.
www.scilinks.org
Topic: Genetic Disorders
Code: HX80652

Answers to Caption Questions
Figure 5: Mutations are relatively rare and any mutation can be carried on recessive alleles.

Teaching Key Ideas
Genetic Disorders Genetic disorders result only from mutations that are inherited and produce defective alleles that disrupt the function of the gene. For all except one of the genetic disorders presented on this page, an individual would need to inherit a recessive allele from *both* parents in order to have the disorder. However, this is not the case with Huntington disease, which is caused by a dominant allele, so either parent can pass on the defective allele. Ask why the Huntington allele remains in the population. (Huntington's symptoms are not detected until later in life—30s and 40s, by which time the allele may have been unknowingly been passed on.)

Differentiated Instruction

Advanced Learners/GATE
Down Syndrome Have students investigate Down syndrome, with an emphasis on the correlation between nondisjunction during oogenesis and the age of the mother. Have them represent this connection in a graphic form. **LS** Verbal

Basic Learners/Struggling Readers
Vocabulary Refresher To understand genetic disorders, students should review the following terms from the chapter on Mendel's work: *allele, heterozygous, homozygous,* and *carrier.* Then, have them describe the inheritance pattern for each disorder listed in **Figure 5.** (recessive disorders—one recessive allele comes from each parent; dominant disorders—offspring needs only one dominant allele for the disorder; recessive sex-linked—recessive alleles are passed on via X or Y chromosomes) **LS** Verbal

> **Teach,** continued

Answers to Caption Questions
Figure 6: missing chromosome (usually fatal), polyploidy

Teaching Key Ideas

Large-Scale Genetic Change In multicellular organisms, offspring (zygtoes) that receive incomplete chromosomes cannot usually develop because essential parts of their "blueprint" are missing. However, offspring that receive additional genes or chromosomes may have various results. Many plant species have enlarged parts due to chromosomal duplications.

Teaching Key Ideas

Nondisjunction Ask students how *nondisjunction,* which causes *trisomy 21,* differs from *polyploidy.* (In nondisjunction, only one pair of chromosomes fails to separate; in polyploidy, there is an extra set of all chromosomes because all chromosomes fail to separate.)

> **Close**

Formative Assessment

Which type of point mutation has no effect on a gene's function?
A. missense (Incorrect. Missense mutations can change the amino acid sequence.)
B. nonsense (Incorrect. The stop codon prevents further translation.)
C. silent (Correct! A changed codon still calls for the same amino acid.)
D. insertion (Incorrect. Insertions could change all codons in the sequence.)

Chromosome 21 pair (normal)

Extra chromosome (trisomy 21)

Figure 6 Most people with Down syndrome have an extra copy of chromosome 21. The extra chromosome can be seen in a karyotype. ❯ What other conditions can result from accidents in chromosome sorting?

nondisjunction (NAHN dis JUHNK shuhn) a failure of homologous chromosomes to separate during meiosis I or the failure of sister chromatids to separate during mitosis or meiosis II

polyploidy (PAH lee PLOY dee) an abnormal condition of having more than two sets of chromosomes

Large-Scale Genetic Change

At another scale, accidents can happen to entire sets of chromosomes. ❯ Very large-scale genetic change can occur by misplacement, recombination, or multiplication of entire chromosomes.

Recombination During Crossover Genetic recombination through sexual reproduction has many important consequences. Recall that during the *crossover* step of meiosis, the alleles from one parent are recombined with the alleles from the other parent. So, meiosis creates new combinations of alleles in offspring. Over time, sexual reproduction and meiotic recombination maintain genetic variety within a population.

Errors in Sorting Chromosomes Each of your chromosomes has thousands of genes. Together, these genes control cell structure and function. So, all 46 chromosomes (23 pairs) are needed for your body to develop and function normally. Human embryos with missing chromosomes rarely survive. Humans with an extra chromosome may survive but do not develop normally.

Nondisjunction Recall that when gametes form by meiosis, each pair of chromosomes separates in the step called *disjunction.* When the pairs fail to separate properly, the error is called **nondisjunction.** For example, nondisjunction of chromosome 21 can lead to a disabling condition called *Down syndrome,* or *trisomy 21,* as shown in **Figure 6.** In this case, one of the parent's gametes received both copies of chromosome 21 instead of one. When that gamete joined with a normal gamete, the child received three copies instead of two.

Polyploidy The largest scale of genetic change can happen if the entire genome is duplicated. Such duplication can occur—rarely—during meiosis, by nondisjunction of *all* chromosomes. The result is a cell with multiple sets of chromosomes, a condition known as **polyploidy.** A polyploid cell has genetic material "to spare." In future offspring, mutations can happen in some genes without losing the functions of the original genes. Thus, polyploidy is another way that organisms can change over time. Polyploidy is common in plants.

> **Reading Check** *How can a child be born with extra chromosomes?*

Section 1 Review

> **KEY IDEAS**
1. **Identify** the primary mechanism for genetic change and differences among organisms.
2. **List** the kinds of mutations.
3. **Relate** the possible kinds of mutations to their effects.
4. **Relate** changes in chromosome number to possible results.

CRITICAL THINKING
5. **Evaluating Significance** Compare DNA mutations with chromosomal mutations in terms of the severity of the results of each.
6. **Justifying Conclusions** You read in a magazine that all mutations are bad. Do you agree? Explain.

USING SCIENCE GRAPHICS
7. **Visualizing** Look at **Figure 2** in this section. Notice that it shows only a single strand of the original DNA sequence and a final amino acid sequence. Sketch the matching DNA and RNA strands for the steps in between. Review the steps of gene expression if needed.

Answers to Section Review
1. mutation
2. DNA mutations: point mutations, and insertions/deletions; chromosomal mutations: deletions, duplications, inversions, translocations, and gene rearrangement
3. Point mutations, insertions, and deletions cause changes in amino acid sequences. Chromosomal mutations involve the addition, deletion, or rearrangement of entire genes.
4. Nondisjunction in animals produces individuals that are not as fit as their counterparts. However, polyploidy can be beneficial by producing offspring with more desirable qualities.
5. DNA mutations are less severe because they may or may not cause a change in one gene. Chromosomal mutations typically affect many genes.
6. No, mutations cause changes that are sometimes beneficial to a species. Mutations have contributed to the variety of life on Earth.
7. Sample answer (with no mutation):

DNA:	TAC	GGT	ACG
mRNA:	AUG	CCA	UCG
amino acid:	met	pro	ser

Regulating Gene Expression

Key Ideas	Key Terms	Why It Matters
❯ Can the process of gene expression be controlled? ❯ What is a common form of gene regulation in prokaryotes? ❯ How does gene regulation in eukaryotes differ from gene regulation in prokaryotes? ❯ Why are proteins so important and versatile?	operon transcription factor intron exon protein domain	Understanding gene regulation may enable us to treat or prevent diseases that were previously unbeatable.

How do butterflies develop from caterpillars? We now know that genes determine traits such as patterns on butterfly wings, as shown in **Figure 7.** And we know that every cell in an individual starts with the same genes. So, in a butterfly's lifetime, every trait of every gene is not always "at work."

Complexities of Gene Expression

Scientists have learned that gene expression (transcription and translation) can be regulated. It is now clear that not all genes are expressed in every cell, nor are many genes expressed all of the time. ❯ **Cells have complex systems that regulate whether or not specific genes are expressed. Expression depends on the cell's needs and environment.**

Through *gene regulation,* a given genetic sequence can be expressed in different ways—in different bodies or tissues, under different conditions, or at different times. Thus, gene regulation accounts for changes during development as well as differences among organisms that have similar genes. One benefit of gene regulation is that cells can use energy and materials efficiently.

Recall that many steps take place in the expression of a gene. Also, other molecules play a role in the processes. Because complex interactions happen at each step, there are many opportunities to regulate gene expression. So, nearly every step in the process of gene expression can be regulated or controlled.

A molecular system that controls the expression of a specific gene is called a *genetic switch.* Like a light switch, a genetic switch can be turned "on" or "off." Often, the switch is triggered by factors or conditions outside the cell. Also, the product of one gene may serve to regulate another gene in the same organism.

❯ **Reading Check** *Are all genes expressed all of the time?*

The Living Environment
Standard 4
2.1a Genes are inherited, but their expression can be modified by interactions with the environment.
2.1g Cells store and use coded information. The genetic information stored in DNA is used to direct the synthesis of the thousands of proteins that each cell requires.
2.1i The work of the cell is carried out by the many different types of molecules it assembles, mostly proteins. Protein molecules are long, usually folded chains made from 20 different kinds of amino acids in a specific sequence. This sequence influences the shape of the protein. The shape of the protein, in turn, determines its function.
2.1k The many body cells in an individual can be very different from one another, even though they are all descended from a single cell and thus have essentially identical genetic instructions. This is because different parts of these instructions are used in different types of cells, and are influenced by the cells' environment and past history.

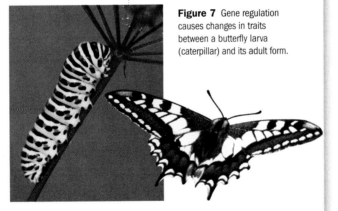
Figure 7 Gene regulation causes changes in traits between a butterfly larva (caterpillar) and its adult form.

Key Resources

 Visual Concepts
Operon
Repression of Transcription in the *lac* Operon
Regulator Gene
Activation of Transcription in the *lac* Operon
Enhancers for Control of Gene Expression
Comparing Introns and Exons

Teaching Key Ideas

The *lac* Operon Ask students to speculate on how the operon got its name. (It controls the "operation" of enzymes that break down lactose.) The *lac* operon is a system found in *E. coli* bacteria that illustrates how the environment controls gene regulation. This system includes a promoter and operator site, a repressor protein, and the section of DNA to be transcribed, three genes that enable the bacterium to use the lactose in its environment. This system limits the expression of these genes only to times when lactose is available, thereby conserving energy and materials.

READING TOOLBOX

Sample Comparison Table

	Prokaryotes	**Eukaryotes**
Similarities	Promoter turns on system	More complex operons are rarely found
Differences	Operons control gene expression	Transcription factors, activators, repressors, enhancers

LS Visual

Figure 8 The *lac* operon controls the genes that code for the proteins that help a bacterium use lactose. The operon "turns on" and expresses the genes only in the presence of lactose. ❯ **How common are operons?**

READING TOOLBOX

Comparison Table Make a comparison table to compare **Figure 8** and **Figure 9.** Which roles do proteins have in the eukaryotic system but not in the prokaryotic system?

Repressor gene codes for repressor protein.

Repressor protein

When lactose is absent, repressor protein binds to operator and operon is "off."

RNA polymerase

Structural genes

Promoter   Operator   1   2   3

DNA   Repressor gene

lac operon

When lactose is present, repressor protein binds to lactose and releases operator. Operon "turns on," and transcription proceeds.

Lactose

Transcription ⟶

Gene Regulation in Prokaryotes

Scientists have studied and compared gene expression in prokaryotes and eukaryotes. Each has very different ways of regulating how genes are expressed. One reason for the differences can be found in the structure of genes in the two kinds of organisms.

❯ The major form of gene regulation in prokaryotes depends upon operons that respond to environmental factors. An **operon** is a gene-regulation system in which adjacent DNA segments control the expression of a group of genes with closely related functions. Operons are common in bacteria but uncommon in eukaryotes.

Interactions with the Environment Recall that bacteria are single cells that must get food directly from the environment. Given a stable environment, a bacterium will need a steady supply of proteins and will tend to keep expressing the same genes in the same way. But if the environment changes, a cascade of changes in gene expression may result. In a way, the environment "flips a switch."

The *lac* Operon Example An example of gene regulation is found in the bacterium *Escherichia coli*. Usually, when you eat or drink a dairy product, the chemical lactose ("milk sugar") is digested by *E. coli* cells living in your gut. These cells can use the lactose for energy or for other needs. But first, the cells must attach to, absorb, and then break down the lactose. These tasks require three different enzymes, each of which is coded for by a different gene.

The system that involves the *lac* genes is called the *lac* operon and is shown in **Figure 8.** This system includes the three genes plus a *promoter* site and an *operator* site. When lactose is available, the system "turns on" and the three genes are transcribed. When lactose is absent, the system "turns off" and transcription is blocked.

Why It Matters

Lactose Intolerance Humans who are lactose intolerant lack enzymes that will break down lactose into monosaccharide sugars for use. People who consume lactose products and are lactose intolerant experience gas, bloating, and diarrhea. Lactase enzymes are available as dietary supplements to remedy this problem.

Differentiated Instruction

Struggling Readers/English Learners

Vocabulary Students will need help with the number of unfamiliar words on these two pages: *activator, enhancer, Eschericia coli (E. coli), lac, lactose, operator, operon, promoter, repressor gene,* and *repressor protein.* Have students create a key-term fold for these words to use while they are reading this section. Give them other reference materials, including the dictionary, to help them write reasonable definitions for each term. **LS** Verbal

Gene Regulation in Eukaryotes

Eukaryotic cells, too, must turn genes on and off in response to signals from their environment. However, ❯ **gene regulation in eukaryotes is more complex and variable than gene regulation in prokaryotes.** To begin with, gene expression in eukaryotes involves more steps and interactions than gene expression in prokaryotes.

As you shall see, regulation can occur before transcription, after transcription, or after translation. Furthermore, in eukaryotes, a nuclear membrane separates these processes. So, each process can be regulated separately.

Eukaryotic gene regulation is unique in other ways. Operons are very rare in eukaryotic cells. Also, groups of genes with related functions may be scattered on different chromosomes and controlled by multiple factors. Finally, much of the DNA in eukaryotes may never be transcribed, and even less is ultimately translated into proteins.

Controlling Transcription Like prokaryotic cells, eukaryotic cells have proteins that regulate transcription. But many more proteins are involved, and the interactions are more complex. Most often, the genetic switch involves the first step of transcription, when RNA polymerase binds to the promoter region. The proteins involved in this kind of genetic switch are called **transcription factors.**

As shown in **Figure 9,** transcription factors interact with RNA polymerases around promoter regions of DNA. A given gene can be influenced by many transcription factors. Some transcription factors act as *activators,* and some act as *repressors.*

One kind of DNA sequence that can be bound by an activator is called an *enhancer.* Enhancers are often located thousands of bases away from the promoter. A loop in the DNA forms as the factors interact at the promoter site. Each factor may also affect other factors.

❯ **Reading Check** *Which parts of gene expression can be regulated?*

Figure 9 Control of transcription is complex in eukaryotes. For example, an activator may bind to an enhancer site and also to RNA polymerase. This action will activate another transcription factor, and finally transcription will begin.
❯ Why is gene regulation more complex in eukaryotes than in prokaryotes?

---

operon (AHP uhr AHN) a unit of adjacent genes that consists of functionally related structural genes and their associated regulatory genes

transcription factor an enzyme that is needed to begin and/or continue genetic transcription

ACADEMIC VOCABULARY

regulate to control, direct, or govern; to adjust

❯ Teach

Demonstration

Modeling the Regulation Process
Cut out shapes from colored paper to represent the components of the *lac* operon. Show the repressor without lactose bound to the operator, and then show it removed from the operator site, because lactose is bound to it. Ask students why transcription is allowed to proceed. (The repressor, when bound to lactose, changes shape, disengaging the operator site to allow transcription.)
LS Visual

Teaching Key Ideas

Eukaryotic Gene Regulation A eukaryote gene has more control elements than a prokaryote gene. Typically there are distal enhancer elements and proximal control elements next to the promoter, which is adjacent to the gene. Other differences are the presence of introns and exons.

Answers to Caption Questions
Figure 9: More steps are involved in gene expression in eukaryotes.

Differentiated Instruction

Advanced Learners/GATE

Nobel Winners in Genetics Have students investigate how double-stranded RNA interferes with eukaryotic transcription, which was studied by 2006 Nobel Prize winners Andrew Fire and Craig Mello. **LS Verbal**

MISCONCEPTION ///ALERT\\\

Gene Expression in Individual Cells Students may think that all genes are expressed in a eukaryotic organism. Clarify that not all genes are expressed in a particular cell. Each cell contains the full complement of DNA, but only a small portion is actually needed for that cell. For example, a gene to make an enzyme needed or produced in a liver cell will never be expressed in a skin cell. The enzyme will be used to aid in digestion, which is not a function of a skin cell. Different conditions signal that genes will be turned on relative to the function of the cell.

QuickLab

⏱ 10 min

QuickLab

Teacher's Notes Make sure that students keep the letters in the order of the original as they cut and separate them. Use the text picture as a guide.

Materials
- masking tape, 20 cm
- pens, 2 different colors

Answers to Analysis
1. exons: the strip that spells "protein;" introns: the remaining strip
2. There would be extra and possibly different amino acids, so a different protein would be synthesized.

Demonstration

Splicing To distinguish between the terms *slice* and *splice*, show how electrical wires are joined together for *splicing*.

A Model of Introns and Exons

You can model introns and exons with masking tape.

Procedure

1. Place a **15 to 20 cm strip of masking tape** on your desk. The tape represents a gene.

2. Use **two colored pens** to write letters on the tape, exactly as shown in the example here. Space the letters to take up the entire length of the tape. The segments in one color represent introns; those in the other color represent exons.

3. Lift the tape. Working from left to right, use **scissors** to cut apart each group of letters of the same color.

appropriately joined

4. Stick the pieces of tape to your desk as you cut them. Make two strips of matching colors, and join the pieces in their original order.

Analysis

1. **Determine** from the resulting two strips which strip represents "introns" and which represents "exons."

2. **CRITICAL THINKING** **Predicting Results** What might happen to the protein if an intron were not removed?

Figure 10 After transcription in eukaryotes, the entire new mRNA segment may not be translated into proteins. Instead, introns are removed, and only exons are translated.

Processing RNA After Transcription It is simplest to think of a gene as a string of nucleotides that code for a protein. However, this simple arrangement is usually found only in prokaryotes. In eukaryotes, many genes contain *noncoding* sequences, or segments of code that will not be translated into amino acids. The noncoding segments are called **introns,** while those portions of the gene that *do* code for amino acids and will be translated are called **exons.**

RNA Splicing Exons and introns are handled in a process called *RNA splicing,* as shown in **Figure 10.** After a eukaryotic gene is transcribed, the introns are removed with the help of certain proteins. The exons that remain are *spliced,* or rejoined together, to form a smaller mRNA molecule. Finally, the spliced mRNA leaves the nucleus and is then translated.

Alternative Splicing The splicing of eukaryotic genes creates additional opportunities for variation over time. Because each exon encodes a different part of a protein, cells can occasionally shuffle exons between genes and thus make new proteins. The thousands of proteins in human cells appear to result from shuffling and recombining a few thousand exons. Some human genes, such as those for hemoglobin, are made up of multiple copies of similar exons.

Processing Proteins After Translation After translation, a chain of amino acids is formed, but the protein may not go directly into action. Further chemical changes may alter the structure and function of the protein. Such changes may affect the protein's shape, stability, or interactions with other molecules.

Final Destination A newly made protein may be needed in a specific location within the cell. The process of getting proteins to their correct destination is called *protein sorting.* Protein sorting occurs in many parts of the cell, such as the Golgi apparatus.

MISCONCEPTION ALERT

Protein Complexity Most proteins range from 150 to 400 amino acids in length. All of the protein synthesis modeling students have done so far does not represent anything close to a real protein. Their models are short segments of a polypeptide.

Differentiated Instruction

Basic Learners/English Learners

Exon Splicing Have pairs of students join at least five colored plastic-coated paper clips and five aluminum paper clips together in any order to represent DNA. Then, have students copy the sequence with a second set of paperclips to represent *transcription.* Have students remove the metal clips as a model for introns being removed. They then join the colored clips together to represent exon *splicing.*
LS Visual / Kinesthetic

Sorting Signals Protein sorting is often directed by *sorting signals*, small parts of a protein that bind to other molecules within the cell. Some signals bind the protein to its final location in the cell. Some signals bind proteins to ribosomes while translation is in progress, and sends them together to the ER for further processing. This variation is another example of the complexity of genes.

The Many Roles of Proteins

Recall that proteins are complex strings of amino acids that do much of the work in cells. The diversity of protein structures relates to the many functions that proteins serve in cells. These functions range from forming the cell's shape to regulating gene expression. Proteins range in size from about 50 amino acids to more than 25,000 amino acids. The average protein is about 250 amino acids.

Protein Structure Because they can form many shapes, proteins can serve many roles. ❯ **The sequence of amino acids in a protein determines its three-dimensional structure and chemical behavior.** In turn, this folding determines the function of the protein, as shown in **Figure 11.** Some parts of a protein that have a specific chemical structure and function are protein **domains.** A protein may have several domains, each with a specific function. In eukaryotes, each domain is usually the result of a specific exon. Finally, large proteins may be made up of several smaller proteins, or *subunits*.

Proteins in Gene Expression Proteins serve important roles in gene expression. For example, several forms of RNA polymerase function to make mRNA, tRNA, and rRNA. Other proteins serve as *regulatory proteins* by binding to genetic switches in specific genes.

Because transcription is more complex in eukaryotes than in prokaryotes, more proteins are involved in the process. Likewise, more enzymes and structural proteins are required for translation in eukaryotes. Even after translation, additional steps may be needed to make a protein fully active in its proper place in a cell.

❯ **Reading Check** *What determines a protein's shape?*

DNA
Active domain
cro proteins

Figure 11 Many of the proteins involved in gene regulation have a shape that fits closely with DNA or RNA molecules. The example shown here is a model of two molecules of bacterial *cro* protein (orange and red) binding to a molecule of DNA (blue and purple). The parts of the protein molecules that are chemically active are called *active domains.*

intron a nucleotide sequence that is part of a gene and that is transcribed from DNA into mRNA but not translated into amino acids

exon one of several nonadjacent nucleotide sequences that are part of one gene and that are transcribed, joined together, and then translated

domain in proteins, a functional unit that a has a distinctive pattern of structural folding

Teaching Key Ideas

Protein Structure The primary structure, or the amino acid sequence, of a protein determines how atoms and functional groups will interact. By pleating and folding a three-dimensional molecule is produced that has a specific region of activity. "Form dictating function" makes proteins the most diverse group of biomolecules.

❯ Close

Formative Assessment

What is the function of the *lac* operon?

A. It makes genes. (Incorrect. It is a system made up of genes and other components.)

B. It makes lactase enzymes. (Incorrect. There are three genes, none of which specifically code for lactase.)

C. It makes a lactose sugar. (Incorrect. Lactose sugar engages the repressor, which is part of the *lac* operon system.)

D. It switches "on" the *lac* genes. (Correct. When the repressor is engaged by lactose, the operator is turned "on.")

❯ **KEY IDEAS**

1. **Generalize** the ways that gene expression can be regulated.

2. **Describe** an example of gene regulation in prokaryotes.

3. **Identify** how gene regulation in eukaryotes is unique.

4. **Relate** protein structure to function in gene expression and regulation.

CRITICAL THINKING

5. **Proposing Mechanisms** Propose one other mechanism, not yet mentioned, for gene regulation in either prokaryotes or eukaryotes.

6. **Using Models** Use letters and words to show how a sequence could be spliced in several ways.

ALTERNATIVE ASSESSMENT

7. **Electronic Research** Use electronic resources to find three-dimensional computer models of proteins. Be sure that the models are based on scientific research. Make a display of several models.

Answers to Section Review

1. interactions of the genetic material and the cellular environment

2. In the presence of an environmental trigger, the *lac* operon switches "on" to start transcription.

3 Regulation can occur before or after transcription, or after translation. Each process can be regulated separately. Operons are rare in eukaryotic cells. Genes with related functions may be separated and controlled by multiple factors. Much of the DNA in eukaryotes is not fully transcribed and translated.

4. The sequence of amino acids determines the three-dimensional configuration that produces an active domain on the protein.

5. Sample answer: The presence of an antibiotic in the environment may inhibit gene expression in prokaryotes.

6. Have students create a display of the color-enhanced models they find.

7. Check that student displays are based on scientific sources and show 3-D models of proteins. If possible, display these in the classroom.

Section 3

Genome Interactions

Key Ideas	Key Terms	Why It Matters
❯ What can we learn by comparing genomes? ❯ Can genetic material be stored and transferred by mechanisms other than chromosomes? ❯ What are the roles of genes in multicellular development?	genome plasmid transposon cell differentiation apoptosis	We can understand how our own bodies work by comparing our genetic systems to those of other organisms.

The Living Environment
Standard 4
1.2e The organs and systems of the body help to provide all the cells with their basic needs. The cells of the body are of different kinds and are grouped in ways that enhance how they function together.
2.1k The many body cells in an individual can be very different from one another, even though they are all descended from a single cell and thus have essentially identical genetic instructions. This is because different parts of these instructions are used in different types of cells, and are influenced by the cells' environment and past history.
3.1b New inheritable characteristics can result from new combinations of existing genes or from mutations of genes in reproductive cells.

Do you share genes with bacteria? In a way, you do. About 10% of human genes are nearly identical to bacterial genes. **Figure 12** shows the similarity between human genes and genes of other organisms.

Genomes and the Diversity of Life

Studying genomes has revolutionized how we look at gene regulation and gene expression. Recall that a **genome** is all of the DNA that an organism or species has within its chromosomes. A genome contains all the genes needed to make more of that organism. Today, the genomes of hundreds of organisms have been extensively studied. ❯ **Comparisons among the genetic systems of many organisms reveal basic biological similarities and relationships.**

Universal Code With few exceptions, the genetic code is the same in all organisms. For example, the codon GUC codes for the amino acid valine in bacteria, in eagles, in plants, and in your own cells. For this reason, the genetic code is often described as being universal. However, some exceptions exist to the universal aspects of the genetic code. For example, some bacteria use a slightly different set of amino acids in making proteins.

Figure 12 This graph shows the ratios of human genes that are nearly identical to genes in each of these species. ❯ What can we learn from such comparisons?

Slime mold 16%

Mouse-ear cress 17%

Nematode 31%

Fruit fly 39%

Genome Sizes Genome size can be measured as an amount of DNA or a number of genes. Either way, genome size is only roughly related to complexity. Genomes in microbes range from 400,000 to millions of base pairs and include from 400 to 9,300 genes. Eukaryote genomes range from 100 million to more than 3 billion base pairs with 6,000 to 100,000 genes. The human genome has about 30,000 genes. Some plants have more than 100,000 genes.

DNA Versus Genes Not all DNA in a cell is part of a gene or even part of a chromosome. Special kinds of DNA include the following:

- **Plasmids in Prokaryotes** Recall that bacterial DNA is usually stored in one long, circular chromosome. However, most bacteria have extra pieces of DNA called **plasmids.** These small, circular DNA segments are replicated independently and can be transferred between cells. So, plasmids are an important source of genetic variation in bacteria.

- **Noncoding DNA in Eukaryotes** Eukaryotes have a great deal of *noncoding* DNA. For example, introns are transcribed but never translated. Also, long stretches of repeating sequences exist that are never transcribed. The function of most noncoding DNA is unclear.

- **DNA in Cell Organelles** Recall that mitochondria and chloroplasts, shown in **Figure 13,** are organelles that have special roles in eukaryotic cells. Chloroplasts enable plants to harvest energy from sunlight. Mitochondria act as the source of energy for cell function. Each of these organelles has its own small genome that is separate from that in the nucleus. These genomes code for proteins and RNAs (rRNA and tRNA) that assist in the function of each organelle.

Endosymbiotic Theory Why do mitochondria and chloroplasts have their own DNA? Scientists suspect that each organelle had its origin in ancient bacterial cells. This idea is known as the *endosymbiotic theory.* For example, chloroplast-like bacteria could have been engulfed, but not killed, by larger cells. Each kind of cell may have benefited from this relationship. Over time, the cells would live together in a close relationship called *symbiosis.*

❯ **Reading Check** *What kinds of organisms have large genomes?*

Figure 13 Chloroplasts and mitochondria have their own DNA. Each organelle's genome is stored and replicated separately from the chromosomes of the cell.

genome (JEE NOHM) the complete genetic material contained in an individual or species

plasmid (PLAZ mid) a genetic structure that can replicate independently of the main chromosome(s) of a cell

Zebra fish 63%
Chicken 67%
Dog 81%
Human (all genes compared to others)

Teaching Key Ideas

Mobile Genes The spotted and streaked colors on Indian corn result from genes that have been *transposed* from one chromosome to the middle of a coding sequence on another chromosome, which changes gene expression at the new location. These "jumping genes" illustrate how the movement of genetic elements in a cell can cause change.

Teaching Key Ideas

Retroviruses These viruses are named because of their ability to commandeer a cell's DNA using their own RNA as a template, thus reversing the process of transcription and changing the cell's genome. Mention that HIV is a retrovirus.

Answers to Caption Questions

Figure 14: MGEs can transfer antibiotic resistance genes between cells.

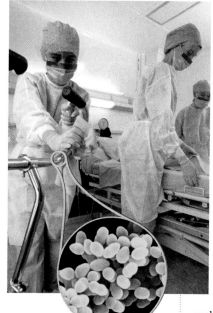

Staphylococcus bacteria

Figure 14 We use antibiotic chemicals in drugs and cleaning products in an attempt to kill bacteria. However, some bacteria have become resistant to most antibiotics. ❯ What is the role of mobile genetic elements in antibiotic resistance?

www.scilinks.org
Topic: Antibiotic
    Resistance
Code: HX80081

Moving Beyond Chromosomes

We now know that cells can interact at the genetic level. And we know that genetic material exists outside of chromosomes. The closer we study genetics, the more complexities we find. ❯ Small bits of genetic material can be stored, moved, and changed by a variety of interactions.

Mobile Genetic Elements Plasmids are just one kind of *mobile genetic element (MGE)*. MGEs are units of DNA or RNA that are sometimes *transposed,* or moved as a functional unit, from one place to another in a genome. Other MGEs are transposons and viruses.

Transposons Sets of genes that are transposed randomly are *jumping genes,* or **transposons.** When a transposon moves to a new place, it may inactivate a nearby gene, much like an operon does. All organisms seem to have transposons in their genomes. Some bacteria have transposons that jump between plasmids and chromosomes.

Viruses In terms of structure and function, transposons are similar to viruses. *Viruses* are very small, nonliving particles that consist of DNA or RNA inside a protein coating. Viruses infect cells by using the cells' own replication processes to make new virus copies. Sometimes, viruses take away copies of the cells' DNA or leave some DNA behind. Thus, viruses can move genetic material between cells. Certain kinds of RNA viruses, called *retroviruses,* produce DNA that becomes part of the host cell's genome.

Genetic Change The discovery of MGEs has helped us further understand genetic change. It has also enabled us to manipulate genetic change for our own purposes, as you will learn. MGEs cause genetic change by bringing together new combinations of genes. Furthermore, MGEs can transfer genetic material between individuals and even between species. For example, the genome of *Escherichia coli* (common gut bacteria) is about 15% similar to that of *Salmonella* (food-borne, illness-causing bacteria). Scientists suspect that the similar genetic sequences are the result of MGEs being passed between the species.

Antibiotic Resistance Like mutations, transpositions may have helpful or harmful effects. And what helps one organism may harm another. An effect that is helpful to bacteria but harmful to humans is the evolution of antibiotic resistance. Antibiotic chemicals are often used to prevent or combat bacterial infections, as shown in **Figure 14.** But if just one bacterial cell has a gene that makes the cell resist the effect of a particular antibiotic, that cell may survive and reproduce. Furthermore, the gene could be passed to other bacteria as part of an MGE. Scientists fear that this process is indeed happening, because increasing numbers and kinds of bacteria are becoming resistant to each of the antibiotics that have been produced.

❯ **Reading Check** *How are transposons and viruses similar?*

Why It Matters

A Passion for Research Barbara McClintock introduced the idea of jumping genes in the 1950s, and her ideas were not accepted for over 30 years. In 1983, at the age of 81, she was awarded the Nobel Prize for her research on transposons. She continued her experiments at Cold Spring Harbor until her death at age 90. Her tenacity in pursuing her beliefs in the face of adversity is an example of a dedicated scientist.

Differentiated Instruction

Advanced Learners/GATE

Retroviruses Have students investigate RNA retroviruses such as HIV and how they use reverse transcriptase to change the genetic makeup of a host cell. **LS Verbal**

Multicellular Development and Aging

You have learned that external or environmental cues can regulate gene expression in cells. In multicellular eukaryotes, gene regulation can also happen because of internal cues. In particular, the development of an embryo involves complex gene regulation. Many cells will develop from one beginning cell. And different kinds of cells will develop to have different functions in different parts of the body. ❯ **Each cell within a developing body will express specific genes. Gene expression depends on the cell's age and location within the body.**

Cell Differentiation In the process of **cell differentiation,** each new cell is modified and specialized as the cells multiply to form a body. Gene regulation plays an important role in this process. *Homeotic* genes are examples of genes that regulate differentiation. Scientists first discovered these genes in fruit flies. Mutations in these genes can cause one body part, such as a leg, to develop in place of another body part, such as an antenna.

As scientists studied many genomes, they found that many kinds of organisms have homeotic genes. And these genes always seem to control similar developmental processes by similar mechanisms. All homeotic genes code for proteins that regulate the expression of other genes. Many homeotic genes contain a similar sequence of 180 bases. This sequence, called a *homeobox,* codes for a DNA-binding domain in the resulting protein.

In general, the genetic regulation of development seems to be similar in all animals. A specific set of homeotic genes, called *hox,* is found in all animals that have a head end and a tail end. Hox genes direct development relative to body position, as shown in **Figure 15.**

❯ **Reading Check** *What is a homeobox?*

---

transposon (trans POH ZAHN) a genetic sequence that is randomly moved, in a functional unit, to new places in a genome

cell differentiation the process by which a cell becomes specialized for a specific structure or function during multicellular development

---

READING TOOLBOX

Prefixes The prefix *homeo-* is used several times on this page. Use the Reading Toolbox page to find the meaning of the prefix *homeo-.* Write a definition for *homeotic* and *homeobox* in your own words.

Fruit fly embryo

Fruit fly adult

Mouse embryo

Mouse adult

Figure 15 *Hox* genes are found in animals from insects to mammals. These genes control the development of body parts relative to the head and tail ends of the body. ❯ **What are some possible results of mutations in these genes?**

Answers to Caption Questions

Figure 16: Some cells need to be removed or replaced for normal development or to repair damage.

> **Close**

Formative Assessment

Which of the following can add new genes to a eukaryotic genome?

A. transposons (Incorrect. These genes are part of the genome; they just move.)

B. homeotic genes (Incorrect. These genes are developmental and already part of the genome.)

C. plasmids (Incorrect. These circular rings of DNA are part of prokaryote genomes.)

D. retroviruses (Correct! When these viruses invade a cell, they use their RNA to create new DNA in the host cell.)

Figure 16 Sunburn is the result of apoptosis—or cell suicide. When skin cells are heavily damaged by over-exposure to the sun, a genetic switch in the cells may signal the cells to stop functioning. > Why is apoptosis important in multicellular organisms?

apoptosis (AP uhp TOH sis) in multicellular organisms, a genetically controlled process that leads to the death of a cell; programmed cell death

Cell Growth and Maintenance Although scientists have long been aware of the *cell cycle*, only recently have they begun to understand how genes regulate the cell cycle and cell growth. In 2001, three scientists received the Nobel Prize for discovering the genetic systems that regulate the cell cycle. The scientists identified two kinds of proteins that regulate the cell cycle: *CDK* and *cyclin*. These proteins are present in all eukaryotes and drive the cell cycle forward. The CDK molecules function like an engine, and the cyclins function like gears. Together, they control the speed of the cell cycle. Cancer results when control of cells has been lost because either the "engine" or the "gears" malfunction.

Cell Death and Aging In multicellular organisms, all cells have arisen from the division of other cells. But most of these cells stop dividing once the organism is mature. In fact, almost all body cells are "programmed" to age and die. At some point, the cell will simply shut down all functioning, gradually shrink, and eventually fall apart. This process of cellular "suicide" is known as **apoptosis.** Apoptosis seems to occur in consistent steps, much like other cellular processes, such as mitosis. Scientists are still studying the genetic systems that may control apoptosis.

Function of Apoptosis Why do some cells need to die? In some cases, the full development of a body part requires the removal of some cells. For example, apoptosis is responsible for the loss of a tadpole's tail as the tadpole becomes an adult. Likewise, human fingers and toes are formed through the loss of in-between tissue in the embryonic limbs. Also, apoptosis is at work when sunburned skin begins to peel off, as shown in **Figure 16.**

Telomeres Aging has many effects on cells. An example is the effect of aging on the ends of chromosomes (called *telomeres*). As cells divide repeatedly, the telomeres lose nucleotides and become shortened. In older cells, this shortening may cause mishandling of the chromosomes during mitosis and thus result in nonfunctioning cells. However, telomere shortening is not the only cause of aging.

> **Reading Check** *What are the roles of proteins in the cell cycle?*

Section 3 Review

> **KEY IDEAS**

1. **Justify** comparing gene expression in various life-forms.

2. **List** mechanisms other than chromosomes by which genetic material may be stored and moved.

3. **Relate** gene expression to multicellular development.

CRITICAL THINKING

4. **Forming Hypotheses** Could any other cell organelles have arisen through endosymbiosis? If so, what findings may support such a hypothesis?

5. **Predicting** What could be the result of a mutation in a hox gene?

6. **Logical Reasoning** Could apoptosis occur in prokaryotes? Explain your answer.

ALTERNATIVE ASSESSMENT

7. **Gallery of Genetic Curiosities** Create a poster, slide show, or other display that exhibits mutants and other interesting examples of genetic complexity. Be sure to provide a caption and a reference source for each of your images.

Answers to Section Review

1. Comparing gene expression provides a clue to basic biological similarities and relationships among organisms.

2. plasmids, transposons, and viruses

3. Genes cause differentiation of parts during development.

4. Other organelles would need to have their own DNA or RNA and protective membranes to live as an endosymbiont.

5. A mutation in a hox gene would result in abnormal body development.

6. No, because apoptosis is a characteristic of multicellular organisms.

7. The investigation could be limited to exploring one mutant in detail. Accept all well-researched and well-presented displays.

Forensic Genealogy

BIOTECHNOLOGY

Genealogy (JEE nee AHL uh jee) is the study of family histories. Forensic genealogy can involve finding lost relatives, identifying bodies, or confirming a claim of parenthood.

Clues in DNA

Because DNA is passed from parents to offspring, scientists can use DNA to find hereditary links between people. Samples of DNA can be analyzed to find similarities and differences. People who are related by birth will share at least some of the DNA of their common ancestors. DNA can be extracted from living cells and from dead cells in hair or bone.

Mother's or Father's DNA

Every cell in a person's body contains DNA from both parents. However, chromosome recombination makes it hard to tell which DNA came from which parent. But two kinds of DNA are unique. One kind is the DNA in a Y chromosome in males. The Y chromosome always comes from the father.

Mitochondrial DNA is also unique. The DNA in the mitochondria of cells is unrelated to the DNA in the nucleus. In humans, the mitochondria in all cells have been copied from the mother's egg cell. So, your mitochondrial DNA is the same as your mother's.

Analyses of these two kinds of DNA have solved crimes and mysteries. In some cases, people have been able to learn their true family history. In other cases, the identity of a dead body has been confirmed (or not) based on DNA comparisons with living or dead relatives.

Who is buried here? This tomb in the Cathedral of Seville, Spain, is supposed to contain the remains of Christopher Columbus. But the history of the remains is disputed, and some people claim that the true remains lie elsewhere. DNA analysis may solve the case.

Whose coffin is this? In 2005, Hurricane Katrina caused disastrous flooding in areas along the coast of the Gulf of Mexico. Many coffins floated out of burial sites. To help find the living or dead relatives of unidentified bodies, scientists could compare DNA samples. For example, mitochondrial DNA will be identical among siblings.

Quick Project Find out the latest findings from DNA analyses of the supposed remains of Christopher Columbus.

Differentiated Instruction

Advanced Learners/GATE

The Mitochondrial DNA Question Have students investigate how mtDNA sampling has been used to compare Neanderthals to modern *Homo sapiens*. **[LS] Verbal**

Teacher's Notes Each cell's approximately 1,700 mitochondria contain an identical loop of DNA containing 37 genes. Mitochondrial DNA, mtDNA, contained in the cytoplasm of the egg, is retained during fertilization, while the mtDNA of the sperm is not, because only the nuclear DNA joins the egg nucleus. As a result, all of the mtDNA in all cells of an individual are that of the mother. Because this DNA is passed only through the mother, it can be used to trace human ancestry.

READING TOOLBOX

Visual Literacy Refer students to the picture of the coffin, and ask them to infer what might remain of a body that was buried for a long time. (bones, teeth, hair) Explain that hair shafts, bone, and teeth contain much more mitochondrial DNA (mtDNA) than nuclear DNA; this is another reason why mitochondrial DNA is used in forensics. **[LS] Visual**

Answer to Quick Project

Both Spain and the Dominican Republic claim to have the authentic remains of Columbus. Students should report whether DNA testing has been used and what results, if any, were reported.

Lab

Time Required
135 min (45 min/day over 3 days)

Ratings

		EASY ——————————→ HARD

Teacher Prep   🧪🧪🧪🧪

Student Setup   🧪🧪🧪

Concept Level   🧪🧪🧪🧪

Cleanup   🧪🧪🧪

Safety Cautions
Review with students all safety procedures related to the use of chemicals and electricity. Electrophoresis requires high voltage electricity; make sure that students use electrical equipment in a safe, dry area of the laboratory. For any dyes, buffers, or samples to be used, consult the labels and packaging for guidelines for handling and disposal.

Tips and Tricks
Timing To finish this lab over two or three class periods, pause at the end of step 5, step 11, and step 14.
- Initial setup and loading of the chamber: 30–45 min
- Running the gel: 0.5–24 h (exact time depends on the applied voltage; higher voltage, faster rate)
- Staining process: 2–24 h
- Rinsing the gels: 5–15 min

Materials If you have not performed electrophoresis before, consider buying a "starter" kit or a PAGE Protein Analysis kit to gain familiarity with the process and materials. To make your own chambers, consult the Chapter Resource File for this chapter.

Lab Correlations

4.2.1i The work of the cell is carried out by the many different types of molecules it assembles, mostly proteins. Protein molecules are long, usually folded chains made from 20 different kinds of amino acids in a specific sequence. This sequence influences the shape of the protein. The shape of the protein, in turn, determines its function.

Objectives
➤ Perform a protein assay to detect the results of gene expression.

➤ Use gel electrophoresis and staining to detect size differences.

➤ Infer the presence of similar genes in different species.

Materials
- lab apron, safety goggles, and disposable gloves
- fish muscle samples (3 to 6 unknowns)
- microtubes, flip-top (3 to 6)
- protein buffer solution with dye
- microtubes, screw-cap (3 to 6)
- water bath
- precast gel for electrophoresis chamber
- micropipettes or tips, sterile, disposable (3 to 6)
- electrophoresis chamber with power supply and wires
- running buffer solution
- protein stain solution
- water, distilled

Safety 🔺 🥽 🧤 ☠️ 🍴 🔥

Protein Detection

Because genes code for proteins, the presence of specific proteins in cells indicates the presence of specific genes. In this lab, you will detect the presence of specific proteins in several species of fishes. You will separate the different proteins by using gel electrophoresis.

Electrophoresis relies on a simple fact of biochemistry: opposite charges attract one another, and like charges repel. So, molecules that have a charge can be pulled around by an electric field. To separate molecules by electrophoresis, the molecules can be pulled through a microscopic "obstacle course" that will slow down larger molecules. If the "course" is "run" for a time, the molecules will be sorted by size.

In *gel electrophoresis*, the "obstacle course" is a slab of jellylike material, simply referred to as a *gel*. Several types of gels can be used to separate samples of DNA, RNA, or proteins. The samples can be stained to see where the parts ended up. Also, *standard* mixtures of known molecules can be run alongside the samples for comparison.

Procedure

Prepare Protein Samples

1 🔺 🥽 🧤 Put on a lab apron, safety goggles, and gloves. Read all procedures, and prepare to collect your data. For each sample of fish muscle, record the type of fish, and assign it a code letter. Then, mark the letter onto one each of two kinds of microtubes.

2 🍴 **CAUTION: Never eat or taste food in the lab.** Obtain a small piece of each fish muscle sample. Place each piece in a fliptop microtube that has the correct code label.

3 ☠️ **CAUTION: Never taste chemicals or allow them to contact your skin.** For each sample, add enough protein buffer solution to cover the sample piece. Cap the tube, then gently flick it to mix the contents. The buffer will cause the proteins from each fish muscle sample to become suspended in the solution.

4 Let the tubes sit at room temperature for 5 min. Then, pour just the liquid from each into the screw-cap tube with the matching label.

5 🔥 **CAUTION: Use extreme caution when working with heating devices.** Heat the samples in the water bath at 95 °C for 5 min. The heat will cause the proteins from each fish muscle sample to denature.

Separate Proteins by Gel Electrophoresis

6 Examine the gel that is precast within its chamber. Note the row of small wells along one edge. These wells are where you will place the samples to be separated. Keep the gel level as you work.

7 Slowly add running buffer solution to the chamber. Add just enough to flood the wells and to cover the gel surface with buffer about 2 mm deep. Be careful not to damage the gel while pouring.

- For fish samples, obtain small amounts of fresh shark, sturgeon, walleye, catfish, perch, trout, or salmon; variety is best.
- For protein separation, it is best to use polyacrylamide (PAGE) gels (15% Tris-HCl) and vertical electrophoresis chambers. An alternative is to use agarose gels (4% low-melt) and horizontal chambers, but these will take longer and will not separate the proteins clearly. Note time and voltage differences for running each type of gel.
- It is safest and easiest to buy gels that are precast in trays that fit your electrophoresis chamber. You can precast your own agarose gels, but raw polyacrylamide is hazardous.
- Always read and follow any specific instructions that come with gel materials and your electrophoresis chamber.

- Use caution when working with high voltages. Each chamber should come with an appropriate high voltage DC source.
- To save time, prepare the protein extracts (steps 2–5) ahead of time and store them on ice.
- The protein buffer solution (also called solubilization buffer) should be appropriate to the kind of gel being used. If using PAGE gels, use SDS buffer. This contains SDS (sodium dodecyl sulfate, a detergent to dissolve and polarize proteins), tris buffer (to adjust pH), glycerol (to weight down the samples in the wells), and bromophenol blue (a dye that can be seen during electrophoresis, to show the "front" of the moving molecules). If using agarose gels, use a TBE (Tris-Borate-EDTA) buffer and add bromophenol blue. Follow any directions that come with the buffer solution.

8 Using a clean micropipette, transfer 10 μL of one sample solution into one well. Be careful not to overflow the well or puncture the gel with the pipette tip. Record the sample's "lane" position.

9 Repeat step 8 for each sample. Make sure to use a clean pipette for each transfer.

10 ◆ **CAUTION: Use caution when working with electrical equipment.** Assemble the electrophoresis chamber and power source as directed by your teacher. With your teacher's approval, connect the power supply to the chamber electrodes. The negative terminal should be connected to the electrode closest to the wells, and the positive terminal should be connected to the opposite electrode.

11 Leave the chamber running but undisturbed for the amount of time specified by your teacher. During this time, the samples and dye should move toward the positive side of the gel.

View the Separated Proteins

12 When the moving front of the dye has migrated across the entire gel, disconnect the electrodes from the power source.

13 ◆ **CAUTION: Dispose of materials as directed by your teacher.** Gently pour off the buffer solution into an appropriate container as directed by your teacher.

14 Slowly pour the protein stain solution over the chamber, and then wait for the amount of time specified by your teacher.

15 Destain the gel by soaking and rinsing it several times in distilled water. Dispose of the rinse water as directed by your teacher. Some of the stain will remain on the proteins in the gel. Draw, photograph, or photocopy the gel for analysis.

15 ◆ ✋ Clean up and dispose of your lab materials according to your teacher's instructions. Wash your hands before leaving the lab.

Analyze and Conclude

1. **SCIENTIFIC METHODS Organizing Data** On your picture of the gel, mark the position of each visible band in each lane of the unknown samples.

2. **SCIENTIFIC METHODS Analyzing Data** Compare the numbers and positions of visible bands among all lanes. Identify which bands of the unknown samples appear to match each other. Identify which of the samples share the most similarities.

SC*L*INKS.
www.scilinks.org
Topic: Gene
Expression
Code: HX80642

Extension

3. **Cladistic Analysis** Use the number of similarities between the samples to construct a cladogram (as explained in an later chapter). First, make a table to analyze each similarity. Then, draw a simple cladogram.

• The water bath should be temperature-controlled; an automatic incubator is best.

• For Step 14, use a Coomassie stain.

Procedure Tips

• In step 11, if using a vertical PAGE system, run at 200 V for 30 min; if using horizontal agarose, run at 100 V for 45 min; if using batteries, you may need several hours. Watch the advancing front of dye to gauge how fast electrophoresis is proceeding.

• In step 13, be sure to remove the gel to a separate tray before adding stain. Never add stain to the electrophoresis chamber.

• In step 14, leave the stain for several hours or overnight.

Troubleshooting

• If the samples run the wrong way when running the gel, the electrodes are reversed.

• To keep one hand steady while using a pipette, hold the wrist with the other hand, and lean the elbow of the other hand on the table. You can sometimes see scientists doing this in photos.

Enhancement To help identify bands in the gels, use standard reagents that contain known substances, to compare to the samples. Standards should be loaded in another lane of the gels and will show the expected location of those substances in your test samples. Look for actin and myosin standards to help locate these proteins in the fish muscle samples. You might also use a molecular-mass or "kaleidoscope" marker.

Answers to Analysis and Conclusions

1. Check that students have accurately depicted and annotated their gels.

2. All of the fish samples should have at least one band that matches (the myosin heavy chain), while some should have a few other bands in common (actin, tropomyosin, or myosin light chains). If size standards were used, some of the samples should have a few bands of smaller size (farther migration in the gel) than others.

Answer to Extension

3. Sample answer: Salmon and trout have the most similar proteins and are thus the most closely related among the fish studied; salmon and shark have the most different proteins and are thus the least related.

Key Resources

 Holt Lab Generator

 Lab Datasheet (Levels A, B, C)

 Holt Science Biology Video Labs

 Virtual Investigations

Reteaching Key Ideas

Genetic Change Have students give examples of the effects of genetic change. Emphasize that those genetic changes that do not interfere with the viability of the organism produce variations that may promote future success. **LS Verbal**

Gene Expression Have students review transcription to identify only exons as mRNA. Then use the example of the *lac* operon to illustrate how the environment controls gene expression. Reinforce that most genes in eukaryotes are not expressed. **LS Verbal**

Interactions With the Genome Ask students to explain why transposons, plasmids and homeoboxes are considered part of the genome. **LS Logical**

Key Ideas

1 **Mutation and Genetic Change**

> For the most part, genetic differences among organisms originate as some kind of mutation.

> Different kinds of mutations are recognized as either changes in DNA or changes in the results of genes. In eukaryotic cells, the process of meiosis creates the chance of mutations at the chromosome level.

> The results of genetic change may be harmful, beneficial, or neutral; most changes are neutral and may not be passed on to offspring.

> Very large-scale genetic change can occur by misplacement, recombination, or multiplication of entire chromosomes.

2 **Regulating Gene Expression**

> Cells have complex systems that regulate whether or not specific genes are expressed, depending on the cell's needs and environment.

> The major form of gene regulation in prokaryotes depends upon operons that respond to environmental factors.

> Gene expression in eukaryotes is more complex and variable than gene expression in prokaryotes.

> The sequence of amino acids in a protein determines its three-dimensional structure and chemical behavior.

3 **Genome Interactions**

> Comparisons among the genetic systems of many organisms reveal basic biological similarities and relationships.

> Small bits of genetic material can be stored, moved, and changed by a variety of interactions.

> Each cell within a developing body will express specific genes, depending on the cell's age and location within the body.

Key Terms

mutation (319)
nondisjunction (324)
polyploidy (324)

operon (326)
transcription factor (327)
intron (328)
exon (328)
domain (329)

genome (370)
plasmid (331)
transposon (332)
cell differentiation (333)
apoptosis (334)

Regents Exam Practice

PART A: Answer all questions in this part.

Directions: For each statement or question, write on your separate answer sheet the number of the word or expression that best completes the statement or answers the question.

1 Mutations that occur in skin or lung cells have little effect on the evolution of a species because mutations in these cells
  (1) usually lead to the death of the organism.
  (2) cannot be passed on to offspring.
  (3) are usually beneficial to the organism.
  (4) lead to more serious mutations in offspring.

2 Which statement indicates that different parts of the genetic information are used in different kinds of cells, even in the same organism?
  (1) The cells produced by a zygote usually have different genes.
  (2) As an embryo develops, various tissues and organs are produced.
  (3) Replicated chromosomes separate during gamete formation.
  (4) Offspring have a combination of genes from both parents.

3 Plants inherit genes that enable them to produce chlorophyll, but this pigment is not produced unless the plants are exposed to light. This is an example of how the environment can
  (1) cause mutations to occur.
  (2) influence the expression of a genetic trait.
  (3) result in the appearance of a new species.
  (4) affect one plant species, but not another.

4 Genes involved in the production of abnormal red blood cells have an abnormal sequence of
  (1) ATP molecules.
  (2) amino acids.
  (3) sugars.
  (4) bases.

5 A mutation occurs in the liver cells of a certain field mouse. Which statement concerning the spread of this mutation through the mouse population is correct?
  (1) It will spread because it is beneficial.
  (2) It will spread because it is a dominant gene.
  (3) It will not spread because it is not in a gamete.
  (4) It will not spread because it is a recessive gene.

6 A sudden change in the DNA of a chromosome can usually be passed on to future generations if the change occurs in a
  (1) skin cell.   (3) sex cell.
  (2) liver cell.   (4) brain cell.

7 The ozone layer of Earth's atmosphere helps to filter ultraviolet radiation. As the ozone layer is depleted, more ultraviolet radiation reaches Earth's surface. This increase in ultraviolet radiation may be harmful because it can directly cause
  (1) photosynthesis to stop in all marine organisms.
  (2) abnormal migration patterns in waterfowl.
  (3) mutations in the DNA of organisms.
  (4) sterility in most species of mammals and birds.

8 How does the karyotype of a person with Down syndrome differ from a normal karyotype?
  (1) It lacks a chromosome.
  (2) It has two sex chromosomes.
  (3) It has twice the number of chromosomes.
  (4) It has an extra copy of a single chromosome.

9 A human liver cell is very different in structure and function from a nerve cell in the same person. This is best explained by the fact that
  (1) different genes function in each type of cell.
  (2) liver cells can reproduce while the nerve cells cannot.
  (3) liver cells contain fewer chromosomes than nerve cells.
  (4) different DNA is present in each type of cell.

Regents Exam Practice Correlations

1.1.1a 19	**4.3.1b** 10
4.2.1a 3, 15, 18	**4.3.1d** 1, 5, 6
4.2.1h 4, 11, 13	**4.4.1d** 12
4.2.1k 2, 9	**4.5.2i** 7
4.2.2e 14	

PART A

1. **(2)** Mutations are often neutral, that is, neither helpful nor harmful. The choice regarding more serious mutations does not explain how evolution is affected, and only mutations in gametes can affect the evolution of future generations. *(#12, August 2006 Regents Exam)*

2. **(2)** The choice describing cells produced by a zygote is incorrect because most cells contain the same genes. The choices describing offspring as a combination of parental genes and replicated chromosomes separating in gamete formation do not show how different genes are activated and expressed in different cells. *(#07, August 2006 Regents Exam)*

3. **(2)** The choices about mutations and species do not show how genes sometimes need to be activated by environmental cues. *(#04, June 2005 Regents Exam)*

4. **(4)** Genes do not contain ATP molecules or amino acids. Genes are made up of sequences of nucleotides. The genetic code is "stored" within the sequence of bases along the length of the gene. An abnormal sequence of bases is likely to give rise to an abnormal protein. *(#10, January 2005 Regents Exam)*

5. **(3)** A mutation can only be passed to offspring if it occurs within a gamete. This mutation occurred in a liver cell, so it will not be passed on. *(#10, August 2005 Regents Exam)*

6. **(3)** Mutations are only passed on to the next generation if the mutation occurs in a sex cell. *(#06, January 2003 Regents Exam)*

7. **(3)** Radiation can cause gene mutations, which sometimes result in cancer. There is little evidence for the other outcomes listed. *(#27, August 2003 Regents Exam)*

8. **(4)**

9. **(1)** The choices describing number of chromosomes and type of DNA are incorrect because most cells contain the same number of chromosomes and type of DNA. The choice describing cell reproduction does not show how different genes are activated and expressed in these different cells. *(#05, June 2006 Regents Exam)*

10. (3) Only mutations in gametes, and not the already formed zygote and body cells, can affect the inheritance of future generations. *(#08, June 2006 Regents Exam)*

11. (1) An alteration in DNA is a mutation. A mutation may be advantageous, and may be passed on to offspring if it occurs in the sex cells. Mutations may be detected using gel electrophoresis, not chromatography. *(#12, June 2003 Regents Exam)*

12. (2) Differentiation, or specialization of the embryonic stem cells in a developing zygote gives rise to tissues and organs. *(#11, August 2004 Regents Exam)*

PART B

13. (1) The change in the base sequence would be the first to occur, and the appearance of the changed characteristic would be the last event to occur in the process of a DNA mutation. *(#38, January 2004 Regents Exam)*

14. (1) Females with the SRY gene have masculine features, and males without the gene appear to be female. Therefore, the production of testosterone must influence male characteristics. Technology has nothing to do with the development of traits in this example. *(#34, August 2005 Regents Exam)*

15. (3) The only difference between the two groups of fruit flies was the temperature. The most logical deduction from the observed results is that environment affects the expression of the genes for the wing traits. *(#08, January 2004 Regents Exam)*

16. (1)

17. (3)

18. Allow 1 credit for explaining why these genetically identical cells can differ in structure and function. Acceptable responses include, but are not limited to: Different parts of genetic information are used in different cells.; Different cells are influenced by their environments in the body. *(#40, June 2005 Regents Exam)*

---

10 Which process can produce new inheritable characteristics within a multicellular species?

(1) cloning of the zygote
(2) mitosis in muscle cells
(3) gene alterations in gametes
(4) differentiation in nerve cells

11 Which statement is true regarding an alteration or change in DNA?

(1) It is always known as a mutation.
(2) It is always advantageous to an individual.
(3) It is always passed on to offspring.
(4) It is always detected by the process of chromatography.

12 Which process can produce new inheritable characteristics within a multicellular species?

(1) cloning of the zygote
(2) mitosis in muscle cells
(3) gene alterations in gametes
(4) differentiation in nerve cells

13 The development of specialized tissues and organs in a multicellular organism directly results from

(1) a change in a base sequence in DNA.
(2) recombination of traits.
(3) the failure of chromosomes to separate.
(4) blocked nerve messages.

PART B

14 A mutation occurs in a cell. Which sequence best represents the correct order of the events involved for this mutation to affect the traits expressed by this cell?

(1) a change in the sequence of DNA bases → joining amino acids in sequence → appearance of characteristic
(2) joining amino acids in sequence → a change in the sequence of DNA bases → appearance of characteristic
(3) appearance of characteristic → joining amino acids in sequence → a change in the sequence of DNA bases
(4) a change in the sequence of DNA bases → appearance of characteristic → joining amino acids in sequence

---

15 The Y-chromosome carries the SRY gene that codes for the production of testosterone in humans. Occasionally a mutation occurs resulting in the SRY gene being lost from the Y-chromosome and added to the X-chromosome, as shown in the diagram below. Based on the diagram, which statement is correct?

(1) The production of testosterone influences the development of male characteristics.
(2) Reproductive technology has had an important influence on human development.
(3) Normal female characteristics develop from a single X-chromosome.
(4) Male characteristics only develop in the absence of X-chromosomes.

16 Fruit flies with the curly-wing trait will develop straight wings if kept at a temperature of 16°C during development and curly wings if kept at 25°C. The best explanation for this change in the shape of wings is that the

(1) genes for curly wings and genes for straight wings are found on different chromosomes.
(2) type of genes present in the fruit fly is dependent on environmental temperature.
(3) environment affects the expression of the genes for this trait.
(4) higher temperature produces a gene mutation.

17 An example of a mobile genetic element is

(1) a transposon.   (3) a cancer cell.
(2) a bacterium.   (4) a hox gene.

18 Programmed cell death is called

(1) aging.   (3) apoptosis.
(2) cyclin.   (4) transposition.

19 The types of human cells shown below are different from one another, even though they all originated from the same fertilized egg and contain the same genetic information. Explain why these genetically identical cells can differ in structure and function.

Skin

Muscle

Nerve

PART C

20 Explain how irradiation could interfere with the process of reproduction in bacteria that survive the irradiation.

PART D

Base your answer to question 21 on the portion of the mRNA codon chart and information below.

| AUU AUC AUA } **ILE** (Isoleucine) AUG } **MET** (Methionine) | ACU ACC ACA ACG } **THR** (Threonine) | AAU AAC } **ASN** (Asparagine) AAA AAG } **LYS** (Lysine) | AGU AGC } **SER** (Serine) AGA AGG } **ARG** (Arginine) |

Series I represents three mRNA codons. Series II includes a mutation of series I.

Series I   AGAUCGAGU

Series II   ACAUCGAGU

21 How would the amino acid sequence produced by the mutant strand (series II) compare to the amino acid sequence produced by series I?

(1) The amino acid sequence would be shorter.

(2) One amino acid in the sequence would change.

(3) The amino acid sequence would remain unchanged.

(4) More than one amino acid in the sequence would change.

19. (2) One codon is different in series II, and it codes for a different amino acid, so only one amino acid in the sequence would change. There are three codons in each series, so the amino acid sequence in series II would not be shorter. (*#73, August 2005 Regents Exam*)

Chapter Planner

15

Gene Technologies and Human Applications

	Standards	Teach Key Ideas
CHAPTER OPENER, pp. 342–343 `15 min.`	**The Living Environment**	
SECTION 1 The Human Genome, pp. 345–349 `90 min.` ❭ Secrets of the Human Genome ❭ Applications of Human Genetics ❭ Ongoing Work	1.1.1c, 4.2.2e, 4.5.2e, 4.5.2j	▣ **Bellringer Transparency** ▣ **Visual Concepts** Vaccine • Genetically Engineered Vaccines • DNA Fingerprint • Making a DNA Fingerprint
SECTION 2 Gene Technologies in Our Lives, pp. 350–354 `45 min.` ❭ Manipulating Genes ❭ Manipulating Bodies and Development ❭ Ethical and Social Issues	1.1.1c, 4.2.2b, 4.2.2c, 4.2.2d, 4.2.2e, 4.4.1b	▣ **Bellringer Transparency** ▣ **Transparencies** C34 Genetic Engineering • C38 Making a Genetically Engineered Vaccine ◉ **Visual Concepts** Genetic Engineering • Cloning
SECTION 3 Gene Technologies in Detail, pp. 355–365 `45 min.` ❭ Basic Tools for Genetic Manipulation ❭ Major Gene Technology Processes ❭ Exploring Genomes	4.2.2c	▣ **Bellringer Transparency** ▣ **Transparencies** C32 Restriction Enzymes Cut DNA • C33 Gel Electrophoresis • C35 Genetically Engineered Medicine ◉ **Visual Concepts** Gel Electrophoresis • Polymerase Chain Reaction • Cloning Vectors and Plasmids • Using Plasmids to Produce Insulin

See also PowerPoint® Resources

Chapter Review and Assessment Resources

SE Super Summary, p. 366
SE Regents Exam Practice, p. 367
▯ Regents Review Guide
▯ Review Resources
▯ Chapter Tests A and B
▤ Holt Online Assessment
◉ Regents Question Banks on Teacher's One-Stop Planner

CHAPTER
FastTrack
To shorten instruction due to time limitations, eliminate the Skills Practice Lab.

Basic Learners

TE Cloned Animals, p. 352
TE Models of Blotting Processes, p. 358
▢ Directed Reading Worksheets*
▢ Active Reading Worksheets*
▢ Lab Manuals, Level A*
▯ Study Guide* ■
▯ Note-taking Workbook*
▯ Special Needs Activities and Modified Tests*

Advanced Learners

TE Cystic Fibrosis, p. 347
TE Genetically Modified Tomatoes, p. 351
TE Computational Biology, p. 361
▢ Critical Thinking Worksheets*
▢ Concept Mapping Worksheets*
▢ Science Skills Worksheets*
▢ Lab Datasheets, Level C*

Why It Matters *Build student motivation with resources about high-interest applications.*	**Hands-On**	**Skills Development**	**Assessment**
	SE **Inquiry Lab** Code Comparison, p. 343∗■	TE **Reading Toolbox** Assessing Prior Knowledge, p. 342 SE **Reading Toolbox**, p. 344	
TE **Demonstration** DNA Fingerprints, p. 345 TE **The Human Genome Project,** p. 345 TE **Genetically Engineered Vaccines,** p. 346 TE **Genetically Engineered Insulin,** p. 347 TE **Future Decision-Makers,** p. 348 SE **Cleanup Microbes,** p. 349	SE **Quick Lab** Forensic DNA Fingerprints, p. 347∗■ SE **Skills Practice Lab** DNA Fingerprint Analysis, p. 364∗■ ⬛ **Exploration Lab** DNA Fingerprinting∗	TE **Math Skills** Unique DNA, p. 345 TE **Reading Toolbox** Using Words, p. 346 SE **Reading Toolbox,** Word Parts, p. 347 TE **Reading Toolbox** Word Parts, p. 347 TE **Reading Toolbox** Visual Literacy, p. 349	SE **Section Review** TE **Formative Assessment** Spanish Assessment∗■ ⬛ **Section Quiz**■
TE **Key Discoveries,** p. 350 TE **Demonstration** Better Produce, p. 350 TE **Flavor Savor™ Tomato,** p. 351 TE **Success of Cloning,** p. 352 TE **Stem Cell Research,** p. 353	⬛ **Skills Practice Lab** Transforming Bacteria with a Firefly Gene∗	SE **Reading Toolbox** Analogies, p. 353 TE **Reading Toolbox** Analogies, p. 353	SE **Section Review** TE **Formative Assessment** Spanish Assessment∗■ ⬛ **Section Quiz**■
TE **Naming Restriction Enzymes,** p. 355 TE **Molecular Scissors,** p. 360 TE **Demonstration** Recombinant DNA, p. 360	SE **Quick Lab** Gel Electrophoresis Model, p. 356∗■	TE **Science Skills** DNA Electric Charge, p. 356 TE **Math Skills** DNA Replication, p. 357 SE **Reading Toolbox** Learning Steps, p. 361 TE **Reading Toolbox** Learning Steps, p. 361	SE **Section Review** TE **Formative Assessment** Spanish Assessment∗■ ⬛ **Section Quiz**■

See also Lab Generator

See also Holt Online Assessment Resources

Resources for Differentiated Instruction

English Learners

TE Identifying DNA Differences, p. 356
TE Sequencing, p. 359
TE Mapping, p. 362
⬛ Directed Reading Worksheets∗
⬛ Active Reading Worksheets∗
⬛ Lab Manuals, Level A∗
⬛ Study Guide∗■
⬛ Note-taking Workbook∗
⬛ Multilingual Glossary
⊙ Interactive Tutor

Struggling Readers

TE Types of Stem Cells, p. 353
TE Outlining, p. 357
⬛ Directed Reading Worksheets∗
⬛ Active Reading Worksheets∗
⬛ Lab Manuals, Level A∗
⬛ Study Guide∗
⬛ Note-taking Workbook∗
⬛ Special Needs Activities and Modified Tests∗
⊙ Interactive Tutor

Special Education Students

TE Identifying Separation Patterns, p. 356
TE Modeling Processes, p. 360
⬛ Directed Reading Worksheets∗
⬛ Active Reading Worksheets∗
⬛ Lab Manuals, Level A∗
⬛ Study Guide∗■
⬛ Note-taking Workbook∗
⬛ Special Needs Activities and Modified Tests∗

Alternative Assessment

TE Implications of Genomics and Gene Technologies, p. 346
⬛ Science Skills Worksheets∗
⬛ Section Quizzes∗■
⬛ Chapter Tests A, B, and C∗■

Gene Technologies and Human Applications

Overview

The purpose of this chapter is to explain modern advancements and applications of genetics, such as the Human Genome Project. The chapter also explains how genes are manipulated and discusses the ethical issues that arise from gene technologies.

READING TOOLBOX

Assessing Prior Knowledge Students should be familiar with the following:
• components of a DNA nucleotide
• genes and gene expression
• somatic and germ cells

Visual Literacy After students look at the picture and read the captions, ask what scientists needed to know to make this pig turn green. (understanding of gene expression, how to insert a gene from one organism into another, understanding of light and fluorescence) Ask why scientists would put a gene like the one for fluorescence into another organism. (to study how genes are expressed)

Preview

1 The Human Genome
Secrets of the Human Genome
Applications of Human Genetics
Ongoing Work

2 Gene Technologies in Our Lives
Manipulating Genes
Manipulating Bodies and Development
Ethical and Social Issues

3 Gene Technologies in Detail
Basic Tools for Genetic Manipulation
Major Gene Technology Processes
Exploring Genomes

Why It Matters

Gene technologies aid the study of basic biology. They have many other applications, such as producing food and treating disease.

The Living Environment
Standard 1 Students will use mathematical analysis, scientific inquiry, and engineering design, as appropriate, to pose questions, seek answers, and develop solutions.
  Key Idea 1 The central purpose of scientific inquiry is to develop explanations of natural phenomena in a continuing and creative process. *Major Understandings* - 1.1c
Standard 4 Students will understand and apply scientific concepts, principles, and theories pertaining to the physical setting and living environment and recognize the historical development of ideas in science.
  Key Idea 2 Organisms inherit genetic information in a variety of ways that result in continuity of structure and function between parents and offspring. *Major Understandings* - 2.2a, 2.2b, 2.2c, 2.2d, 2.2e
  Key Idea 4 The continuity of life is sustained through reproduction and development. *Major Understandings* - 4.1b
  Key Idea 5 Organisms maintain a dynamic equilibrium that sustains life. *Major Understandings* - 5.2e, 5.2j

Why would scientists make a pig that glows green? So they can study how genes work.

> This is a normal pig.

> This pig is greenish and glows under fluorescent light because it has a gene from a jellyfish that has the "glowing" trait.

Chapter Correlations The Living Environment

Standard 1

1.1c Science provides knowledge, but values are also essential to making effective and ethical decisions about the application of scientific knowledge.

Standard 4

2.2b In recent years new varieties of farm plants and animals have been engineered by manipulating their genetic instructions to produce new characteristics.

2.2c Different enzymes can be used to cut, copy, and move segments of DNA. Characteristics produced by the segments of DNA may be expressed when these segments are inserted into new organisms, such as bacteria.

2.2d Inserting, deleting, or substituting DNA segments can alter genes. An altered gene may be passed on to every cell that develops from it.

2.2e Knowledge of genetics is making possible new fields of health care; for example, finding genes which may have mutations that can cause disease will aid in the development of preventive measures to fight disease. Substances, such as hormones and enzymes, from genetically engineered organisms may reduce the cost and side effects of replacing missing body chemicals.

4.1b Cloning is the production of identical genetic copies.

5.2e Vaccinations use weakened microbes (or parts of them) to stimulate the immune system to react. This reaction prepares the body to fight subsequent invasions by the same microbes.

5.2j Biological research generates knowledge used to design ways of diagnosing, preventing, treating, controlling, or curing diseases of plants and animals.

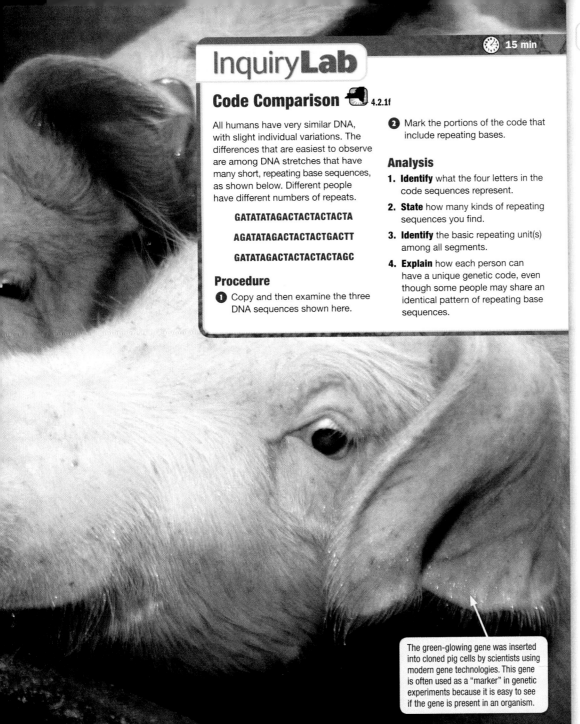

InquiryLab

🕐 15 min

Code Comparison 4.2.1f

All humans have very similar DNA, with slight individual variations. The differences that are easiest to observe are among DNA stretches that have many short, repeating base sequences, as shown below. Different people have different numbers of repeats.

GATATATAGACTACTACTACTA

AGATATAGACTACTACTGACTT

GATATAGACTACTACTACTAGC

Procedure

❶ Copy and then examine the three DNA sequences shown here.

❷ Mark the portions of the code that include repeating bases.

Analysis

1. **Identify** what the four letters in the code sequences represent.

2. **State** how many kinds of repeating sequences you find.

3. **Identify** the basic repeating unit(s) among all segments.

4. **Explain** how each person can have a unique genetic code, even though some people may share an identical pattern of repeating base sequences.

The green-glowing gene was inserted into cloned pig cells by scientists using modern gene technologies. This gene is often used as a "marker" in genetic experiments because it is easy to see if the gene is present in an organism.

InquiryLab

Teacher's Notes Have students revisit this lab when they get to the parts of the chapter on DNA fingerprinting and polymorphisms. Repeating DNA patterns similar to these are called *tandem repeats*; repeats of the same few nucleotides are called *short tandem repeats* (STRs). Since STRs have been identified in similar places in every person's genome, DNA fingerprinting has begun to depend on the analysis of STRs. Students should highlight each repeating sequence on each segment. There are at least two tandem repeats per segment.

Answers to Analysis

1. Each letter represents a DNA nucleotide: adenine, thymine, guanine, and cytosine.
2. At least three.
3. TA, TAC, and ACT
4. It is unlikely that two people will share the same tandem repeats.

Key Resources

◉ Interactive Tutor

Using Words

1. *Electrophoresis* is the use of electricity to carry something.
2. A *microarray* is a very small, orderly arrangement of something.

Using Language

protein or amino acid chain

Using Graphic Organizers

Paper strips might include the following:

- Use a restriction enzyme to cut a gene of interest.
- Use the same enzyme to cut a bacterial plasmid.
- Splice the DNA into the bacterial plasmid using ligase enzyme.
- Reinsert plasmid into bacterial cell.
- Allow bacteria to reproduce. "Harvest" the gene product.

READING TOOLBOX

These reading tools can help you learn the material in this chapter. For more information on how to use these and other tools, see **Appendix: Reading and Study Skills.**

Using Words

Word Parts You can tell a lot about a word by taking it apart and examining its parts, such as the prefix and root.

Your Turn Use the information in the table to define the following terms:

1. *electrophoresis*
2. *microarray*

Word Parts	
Word Part	**Meaning**
electro-	using electricity
phore	to carry
micro-	very small
array	orderly arrangement

Using Language

Analogies Analogies compare words with similar relationships. You can write analogies with words or with colons. For example, the analogy "up is related to down in the same way that top is related to bottom" can be written "up : down :: top : bottom." To answer an analogy problem, you must figure out how the words are related. In this example, up is above down, and top is above bottom.

Your Turn Use information found in prior chapters to complete the following analogy:

transcription : RNA :: translation : ___.

Using Graphic Organizers

Pattern Puzzles You can use pattern puzzles to help you remember sequential information. Exchanging puzzles with a classmate can help you study.

Your Turn Make a pattern puzzle for the steps of a recombinant gene cloning process, as shown in this chapter.

1. Write the steps of the process on a sheet of notebook paper, one step per line. Do not number the steps.
2. Cut the paper so that there is one step per strip of paper.
3. Shuffle the paper strips so that they are out of sequence.
4. Try to place the strips in their proper sequence.
5. Check your sequence by consulting your textbook, class notes, or a classmate.

The Human Genome

Key Ideas	Key Terms	Why It Matters
❯ Why is the Human Genome Project so important? ❯ How do genomics and gene technologies affect our lives? ❯ What questions about the human genome remain to be studied?	genomics microarray DNA fingerprint	Many diseases may someday be cured by genetic technologies.

In 2000, headlines announced that scientists had deciphered the "book of life" by listing almost the entire sequence of bases in human DNA. This major feat was only the beginning of a new era.

Secrets of the Human Genome

The term *genome* refers to all of the genetic material in an organism, population, or species. **Genomics** is the study of entire genomes, especially by using technology to compare genes within and between species. A major part of genomics is to *sequence* genomes, or to identify every DNA base pair that makes up each genome. Only recently has it been possible to sequence the human genome.

The *Human Genome Project* (HGP) was an international cooperative effort to sequence the human genome. More than 20 laboratories in six countries worked together to sequence the 3.2 billion DNA base pairs that make up the human genome. ❯ **The sequencing of the human genome has advanced the study of human biology yet created new questions.**

Surprising Findings The major draft of the human genome sequence was completed and reported in 2003. Scientists were surprised and excited by findings such as these:

- **Humans have few genes.** Scientists expected to find 120,000 genes but found only about 25,000.

- **Most human DNA is noncoding.** Less than 2% of human DNA seems to code for proteins. The rest is either introns or is not yet fully explained.

- **Many human genes are identical to those of other species.** Much of what we learn about mice and flies can be used to understand ourselves.

- **All humans are genetically close.** If the DNA of any two people is compared, 99.9% is identical.

❯ **Reading Check** *How big is the human genome? (See the Appendix for answers to Reading Checks.)*

Figure 1 Despite differences in appearance, the DNA of any two humans is 99.9% similar.

 The Living Environment

Standard 1
1.1c Science provides knowledge, but values are also essential to making effective and ethical decisions about the application of scientific knowledge.

Standard 4
2.2e Knowledge of genetics is making possible new fields of health care; for example, finding genes which may have mutations that can cause disease will aid in the development of preventive measures to fight disease. Substances, such as hormones and enzymes, from genetically engineered organisms may reduce the cost and side effects of replacing missing body chemicals.

5.2e Vaccinations use weakened microbes (or parts of them) to stimulate the immune system to react. This reaction prepares the body to fight subsequent invasions by the same microbes.

5.2j Biological research generates knowledge used to design ways of diagnosing, preventing, treating, controlling, or curing diseases of plants and animals.

> **genomics** (juh NOH miks) the study of entire genomes, especially by using technology to compare genes within and between species

Key Resources

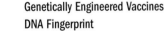

Visual Concepts
Vaccine
Genetically Engineered Vaccines
DNA Fingerprint
Making a DNA Fingerprint

Why It Matters

The Human Genome Project Tell students that the HGP was launched in 1990. Its goal was to determine the entire nucleotide sequence of the human genome. Completion of the initial sequencing was announced in June 2000, and in April 2003 complete sequencing was announced. In May 2006, *Nature* announced complete sequencing of the last chromosome. Despite these announcements, the project will not be finished for years. Areas such as the centromere and telomere regions have highly repetitive sequences that are problematic.

❯ Focus

This section explains how information from the Human Genome Project is being used today. It also discusses its future applications and considerations for gene technology.

🔊 Bellringer

Use the Bellringer transparency to prepare students for this section.

❯ Teach

Demonstration

DNA Fingerprints Have students use an inkpad and white paper to take their own fingerprints. Then, have small groups of students compare their prints. Ask students what they observe about the prints. (Each person's prints are unique.) Explain that just as everyone has different fingerprints, each person also has a unique pattern of DNA sequences, called a DNA fingerprint. **LS Interpersonal**

Math Skills

Unique DNA Given the information from the HGP findings, have students calculate the amount of an individual's DNA that is unique. (3.2 billion bases × 0.01% difference = 3,200,000 bases) **LS Logical**

Section Correlations

1.1.1c	4.5.2e
4.2.2e	4.5.2j

Teaching Key Ideas

Genetic Engineering The term *genetic engineering* may have a negative connotation to some people. Address this issue by asking students why they think that some people have negative ideas about gene technology. (Sample answers: Movies show "mad" scientists making monsters by genetic engineering; uninformed people have made incorrect statements in the press.)
 Interpersonal

READING TOOLBOX

Using Words Ask students to name a vaccine they have received. (Sample answers: polio, hepatitis B, mumps, flu) Explain that a traditional vaccine is made from dead or weakened forms of the organism. Tell students that the word *vaccine* comes from the Latin word *vacca*, which means "cow," because the first vaccine (to treat smallpox) was made from cowpox. **LS Verbal**

Answers to Caption Questions

Figure 2: signs of genetic disorders or cancer

---

microarray (MIE kroh uh RAY) a device that contains a micro-scale, orderly arrangement of biomolecules; used to rapidly test for the presence of a range of similar substances, such as specific DNA sequences

DNA fingerprint a pattern of DNA characteristics that is unique, or nearly so, to an individual organism

---

Figure 2 A microarray contains an assortment of gene sequences, each set in a dot. The colors indicate whether a sample of genetic material has bound to the sequence at that dot. Thus, a pattern of gene expression can be seen. ❯ **What conditions could be detected this way?**

Applications of Human Genetics

Studying the human genome opens new doors to understanding our bodies. In addition, we have new ways to apply this knowledge. *Gene technologies* allow us to find genes, copy them, turn them on or off, and even move them between organisms. ❯ **Genomics and gene technologies have many applications in human healthcare and society.**

A major part of gene technologies is *genetic engineering,* which usually refers to the transfer of genes from one organism to another. For example, the human gene for insulin has been inserted into bacteria. Insulin is lacking in people with some forms of diabetes. So, the engineered bacteria are used to produce insulin to treat diabetes.

Diagnosing and Preventing Disease The first challenge to fighting disease is simply to diagnose, or identify, the problem. Modern gene technologies can help. For example, a **microarray,** shown in **Figure 2,** shows which genes are being actively transcribed in a sample from a cell. Some patterns of gene activity can be recognized as signs of genetic disorders or cancer.

Although most genetic disorders cannot be cured, they may be avoided in the future. For example, a person with a family history of genetic disorders may wish to undergo genetic counseling before becoming a parent. *Genetic counseling* informs people about the risk of genetic problems that could affect them or their offspring.

Many viral diseases are best prevented by vaccination. However, vaccines can be dangerous because they are made from disease-causing agents. Vaccines made through genetic engineering may limit such dangers by being more carefully designed. Various vaccines are now produced through genetic engineering. Some of these vaccines prevent diseases that were not preventable before.

❯ **Reading Check** *When might a person seek genetic counseling?*

Why It Matters

Genetically Engineered Vaccines Inform students that the FDA approved the vaccine for Hepatitis B for human use in 1981. This virus is 100 times more contagious than HIV, infecting over 200,000 people a year in the United States alone. The actual viral DNA is not used to produce the vaccine; instead, surface antigens on the virus' protein coat are the source of the vaccine. The future of recombinant vaccines depends on the cost of research-to-market and the effectiveness of such vaccines, which are less immunogenic than their conventional counterparts.

Differentiated Instruction

Alternative Assessment

Implications of Genomics and Gene Technologies Ask students to choose a topic under the passage Applications of Human Genetics. Have them write a two- to three-paragraph essay that describes the implications of a specific application to society. Essays should give reasons why understanding these implications is important. **LS Verbal/Interpersonal**

QuickLab

⏱ 15 min

Forensic DNA Fingerprints

DNA "fingerprinting" is useful in forensics because it can be performed on a sample of DNA from body tissues such as hair or blood. Samples can be compared to find genetically identical or closely related people. Identical segments of DNA will form identical patterns of bands in the columns of a DNA fingerprint, as shown here.

Analysis

1. **Identify** the number of individuals whose DNA samples are being analyzed in this DNA fingerprint.

2. **CRITICAL THINKING** **Interpreting Graphics** Identify the suspect sample that matches the sample from the crime scene.

3. **CRITICAL THINKING** **Analyzing Methods** Column 6 shows every possible position of a DNA fingerprint band. Propose a purpose for these columns in this method.

1 2 3 4 5 6 7 8 9 10 11 12

1 Control
3 Sample from crime scene
4 Victim
6 Standard size marker
8 Suspect A
9 Suspect B
10 Suspect C
12 Suspect D

Treating Disease

Treating Disease Many genetic disorders occur when a specific protein, such as insulin, is missing or malformed because a gene has been mutated. So, the disorder can often be treated by supplying the needed protein. Many drug companies are now genetically engineering organisms to produce specific proteins for human use.

Another possible treatment for genetic disorders is to insert a functional "replacement" gene into a person's cells by using a genetically engineered virus. This technique is called *gene therapy*. However, gene therapy has had limited success because the human body has many protections against the invasion and genetic change that viruses cause.

The use of genomics to produce drugs is called *pharmacogenomics*. Currently, most drugs are made to combat diseases in a broad way. The drugs are generally effective for many people but not tailored to individuals. Soon, drugs could be custom-made for individuals based on a personal genetic profile. Such a profile could be produced by technologies that rapidly sequence a person's DNA.

Identifying Individuals Each person (other than identical twins) has some parts of the DNA sequence that are unique. So, samples of DNA can be compared to determine if the samples came from the same person or from people related by ancestry. These samples of DNA are cut, sorted, and "tagged" to produce a pattern of banding called a **DNA fingerprint**. DNA fingerprints are now used regularly to confirm the identity of criminals, family members, or dead bodies.

❯ **Reading Check** *Why is insulin used to treat genetic diabetes?*

READING TOOLBOX

Word Parts The prefix *pharma-* means "medicine" or "drug." Use this information to analyze the meaning of the term *pharmacogenomics*.

Why It Matters

Future Decision-Makers Point out that as knowledge about the human genome increases, students will be faced with increasingly complex social, medical, and ethical issues. In order to be informed decision-makers, they will need to know the facts about gene technologies.

>Close

Formative Assessment

Which is *not* an application of gene technologies?

A. producing insulin (Incorrect. The human gene for insulin has been inserted into bacteria.)

B. diagnosing diseases and disorders (Incorrect. Patterns of gene activity can indicate signs of certain disorders or cancer.)

C. eliminating ethical issues (Correct! As a result of gene technologies, many ethical questions arise.)

D. better drugs (Incorrect. Custom-made drugs may be possible by knowing a person's DNA.)

Figure 3 The human genome contains as much information as 180 phone books from different major cities.

SCI*LINKS*.
www.scilinks.org
Topic: Human Genome Project
Code: HX80770

ACADEMIC VOCABULARY

implication something involved or resulting from

Ongoing Work

Making a list of all of the bases in the human genome was only a first step. Understanding this "book of life" will take much more work. First, a huge amount of information is involved, as **Figure 3** shows. Second, although we know how to read the "letters" of this "book," we do not understand most of its meaning. We have compiled a long list of genes, but we do not know what many of the genes actually do. **> Many important questions about the human genome remain to be investigated or decided.** These questions include the following:

• **How do our genes interact?** To understand how genes interact, scientists are looking closely at the processes of gene expression. For example, they study how the protein that results from one gene may regulate the expression of other genes.

• **How unique are we?** Scientists are increasingly comparing our genome to those of other organisms to find out how small differences in genomes result in different species. Genome projects for many other species have been completed or are under way.

• **Can genetics help us live longer?** Gene technologies and genomics are thus leading to increased knowledge of how we could live longer, healthier lives. We are just beginning to find genetic clues about complex conditions such as asthma, obesity, schizophrenia, cancer, and aging. These conditions are affected by complex interactions between many genes as well as our environment. For many disorders, we are not likely to find a single cause, much less a simple cure.

• **How should we deal with ethical issues?** With so much information about human DNA being recorded, many questions arise that cannot be answered by scientific lab work. For example, Who should get the information? Who owns it? Should it be used to make decisions about individuals? Scientists and governments expect these issues to arise. In the United States, a portion of the federal funds for the HGP are dedicated to a special program of the HGP called *Ethical Legal and Social Implications* (ELSI).

> Reading Check *Why is asthma difficult to cure?*

Section 1 Review

> KEY IDEAS

1. **Describe** the major findings of the Human Genome Project.

2. **Identify** some applications of genomics and genetic engineering that benefit humans.

3. **List** remaining questions about the human genome.

CRITICAL THINKING

4. **Proposing Explanations** Propose some possible explanations for the large volume of noncoding DNA in the human genome.

5. **Applying Logic** Scientists say that knowing the sequence of nucleotides in the human genome is only the first step in understanding the genome. What are some possible next steps?

WRITING FOR SCIENCE

6. **Genetics on Trial** When were gene technologies first used as evidence in criminal cases? Research the early history of this field, and summarize your findings in a news-style oral report.

Answers to Section Review

1. Humans have fewer genes than predicted, most human DNA is noncoding, many human genes are identical to those of other species, all humans are genetically similar.

2. Applications of genomics and genetic engineering include diagnosing, preventing, and treating disease; and identifying individuals.

3. How do genes interact? Will we be able to live longer? How are we related to other species? How should we deal with ethical issues?

4. Sample answer: Noncoding intron segments of DNA may be genes once useful to other organisms or needed to control transcription.

5. Sample answer: determining which nucleotides make up genes and how they become expressed

6. The first use of DNA for a criminal case was in the 1980s, by Professor Alec Jeffries of the University of Leicester in England.

Cleanup Microbes

BIOTECHNOLOGY

Using microbes for environmental cleanup is called *bioremediation*. For example, oil-devouring microbes are used to help clean up oil spills. Increasingly, genetically modified organisms (GMOs) are being engineered for use in bioremediation.

Oil Spills

Spills of fuel oil can be devastating to environments because the oil is toxic, floats on water, and soaks into soils. Fortunately, scientists have found that some marine bacteria are capable of using oil as food. Some of the first genetically modified (GM) microbes were derived from such bacteria. In fact, the first organism to be patented was an oil-eating, genetically engineered bacterium

Radioactive Waste

Nuclear waste is another bioremediation challenge with which GM microbes may help. Water near nuclear waste dumps may become polluted with radioactive substances. Again, bacteria naturally exist that can break down most of these substances, but those bacteria cannot survive high levels of radiation. So, scientists have turned to another kind of bacteria that can withstand 3,000 times the normal radiation levels. They hope to engineer a solution by transferring genes between these species.

An impossible job? Cleaning oil and dangerous chemical spills out of sand or soil can be nearly impossible for humans, even with tools. However, this cleanup is simple work for a microbe.

An Enormous Mess Oil spills at sea are dangerous to wildlife, dangerous to the people involved in fighting them, and difficult to contain.

Quick Project Find out the date that the first patent for a GMO was awarded in the United States. Also find out the name of the scientist to whom it was awarded.

Why It Matters

Teacher's Notes While bacteria that can digest oil were used to clean up the *Exxon Valdez* oil spill, those bacteria were not genetically modified. Genetically modified bacteria have the potential to be used for bioremediation purposes, but their use is heavily regulated and controversial because of the possibility that they could "escape" into the environment and cause unforeseen problems.

READING TOOLBOX

Visual Literacy Before students read the text, have them study the pictures. Ask them how an oil spill might harm an ecosystem. (kill organisms living there and disrupt the food web) Then, ask how they would clean up an oil spill. (Accept any reasonable answers.)
LS Logical/Visual

Answer to Quick Project

The question of awarding patents on genetically modified organisms arose when a microbiologist Ananda Chakrabarty filed for a patent on a bacterium capable of digesting the components of crude oil. His patent request was controversial because it would be the first patent on a living organism. The case was eventually brought before the U.S. Supreme Court, which ruled in 1980 that human-engineered organisms are patentable under federal law. The first patent for gene cloning was awarded to Herb Boyer and Stanley Cohen in 1980.

Section **2** # Gene Technologies in Our Lives

> Focus

This section focuses on applications of gene technologies and the ethical and social issues associated with them.

Bellringer

Use the Bellringer transparency to prepare students for this section.

> Teach

Demonstration

Better Produce Provide student groups with different fruits or vegetables. Have them list ways that they would like to improve their item. Tell them to consider not only how it tastes, but also how it is grown, picked, transported, and sold. What properties would make the fruit or vegetable better able to withstand these processes? Then, tell students that genetic engineering has already improved produce. Point out that students most likely have already eaten genetically altered crops because many crops raised in the United States—including more than 80 percent of the soy and 40 percent of the corn—are genetically altered.

LS Logical

Key Ideas	Key Terms	Why It Matters
> For what purposes are genes and proteins manipulated? > How are cloning and stem cell research related? > What ethical issues arise with the uses of gene technologies?	genetic engineering recombinant DNA clone stem cell	Gene technologies have many applications in modern life, but ethical issues exist for each of these applications.

The Living Environment
Standard 1
1.1c Science provides knowledge, but values are also essential to making effective and ethical decisions about the application of scientific knowledge.

Standard 4
2.2b In recent years new varieties of farm plants and animals have been engineered by manipulating their genetic instructions to produce new characteristics.
2.2c Different enzymes can be used to cut, copy, and move segments of DNA. Characteristics produced by the segments of DNA may be expressed when these segments are inserted into new organisms, such as bacteria.
2.2d Inserting, deleting, or substituting DNA segments can alter genes. An altered gene may be passed on to every cell that develops from it.
2.2e Knowledge of genetics is making possible new fields of health care; for example, finding genes which may have mutations that can cause disease will aid in the development of preventive measures to fight disease. Substances, such as hormones and enzymes, from genetically engineered organisms may reduce the cost and side effects of replacing missing body chemicals.
4.1b Cloning is the production of identical genetic copies.

Figure 4 These fish "glow" because scientists have copied a gene from a naturally "glowing" jellyfish and inserted it into the fishes' genomes.

Recall that a gene has a DNA sequence that is translated into the sequence of amino acids in a protein. In a sense, proteins are the "actors" in biology, and genes are the "directors." To understand how genes work, scientists have studied both the instructions in the genes and the actions of the proteins. Meanwhile, some have tried to modify the instructions to change the actions that result.

Manipulating Genes

Gene technologies include a wide range of procedures that analyze, decode, or manipulate genes from organisms. **> Gene technologies are now widely applied to study organisms in new ways, to alter organisms for human use, and to improve human lives.** Gene technologies have rapidly changed over the past two decades, yet the basic applications are not so new. Human beings have been influencing the lives and genes of organisms for thousands of years. The first farmers and herders did so when they selected plants and animals to breed. But today, we have more specific knowledge, molecular tools, and the ability to move genes between organisms.

Genetic Engineering The application of science for specific purposes is often referred to as *engineering*. **Genetic engineering** is the deliberate alteration of the genetic material of an organism. The process often involves inserting copies of a gene from one organism into another. DNA that has been recombined by genetic engineering is called **recombinant DNA.** Organisms with recombinant genes may be called *recombinant, transgenic,* or *genetically modified.* In everyday use, they are often referred to as *genetically modified organisms* (GMOs). An example of a GMO is shown in **Figure 4.**

Many applications of gene technologies have become part of our everyday lives, from food to healthcare. In some ways, we are starting to depend on gene technologies, just as we depend on electricity and telephones. As with other technologies, gene technologies raise new social and ethical issues.

> Reading Check *What is a GMO?*

Section Correlations	
1.1.1c	4.2.2d
4.2.2b	4.2.2e
4.2.2c	4.4.1b

Key Resources

Transparencies
C34 Genetic Engineering
C38 Making a Genetically Engineered Vaccine

Visual Concepts
Genetic Engineering
Cloning

Why It Matters

Key Discoveries Tell students that genetic engineering relies on two important discoveries. In 1952, Joshua Lederberg identified and named the plasmid, a ring of DNA found in some bacteria. In 1970, Hamilton Smith discovered restriction enzymes in bacteria that act as molecular "scissors" to cut pieces of invading viral DNA. Because DNA is universal, the bacteria could be used to cut DNA from any source. In 1972, relying on both of these discoveries, Paul Berg successfully assembled the first recombinant DNA molecule—a plasmid with an external source of DNA that was incorporated into the plasmid genome.

Everyday Applications Genetic engineering was first applied to bacteria, viruses, and plants and is now applied to many life-forms. Today, GMOs are widely used in agriculture, medicine, industry, and basic research. Following are examples of the many uses of GMOs.

- **Food Crops** Most corn and soybean products sold in grocery stores in the United States are made from GMOs. In many cases, the crops have a gene added from the bacterium *Bacillus thuringiensis* (*Bt*). The gene produces an insecticide and thus benefits the crop grower. Many food crops are engineered to be easier to grow or to be more nutritious.

- **Livestock** New breeds of livestock are being engineered to grow faster or to have more muscle or less fat. Some are made to produce milk with specific proteins. Some GMOs are sold as unusual pets.

- **Medical Treatment** As you have learned, many genetic disorders, such as hemophilia and diabetes, result from a missing or abnormal protein. If the normal human gene for needed protein has been identified, the gene can be spliced into bacterial cells. Then, the recombinant bacteria will rapidly produce the human protein in large quantities. People with hemophilia and diabetes are being treated with proteins produced in this way.

- **Basic Research Tools** A variety of GMOs have been made just for laboratory research. Some plants and animals have been engineered with genes from other organisms that "glow." Often, this engineering is done so that researchers can study another, less obvious gene. In this case, the two foreign genes are spliced into the GMO at the same time. The "glow" gene then serves as a "marker" of the presence of the second gene being studied.

Manipulating Cell Interactions Gene technologies involve more than just inserting genes. Cells and bodies are affected by when and where each gene is expressed. So, gene technologies are also used to control the expression of genes or to redirect the products.

The study of how proteins interact within cells is called *proteomics* (PROH tee OHM iks). As you have learned, these interactions are very complex. Gene technologies can be used to manipulate the production of specific proteins at specific times and in specific cells, tissues, organs, or individuals. This manipulation can be done for medical treatment or simply for research.

One way to study the actions of genes in cells is to work with living tissues. To do so, scientists can remove living cells from an organism and grow them in a laboratory as tissue culture, as **Figure 5** shows. Then, the cells can be studied closely and experimentally controlled.

❯ **Reading Check** *What is the* Bt *gene used for?*

> **genetic engineering** a technology in which the genome of a living cell is modified for medical or industrial use
>
> **recombinant DNA** (ree KAHM buh nuhnt) DNA molecules that are artificially created by combining DNA from different sources

Figure 5 Tissue culture is often used to study living cells. ❯ **What can we learn about genes from tissue culture?**

Teaching Key Ideas

Food Crops Food crops, such as corn and soybeans, have been altered genetically to be resistant to glycophosate, a weed killer that is harmless to humans. The weed killer will thus kill weeds but not the engineered crop, so crop yields may increase. Other plants have been altered to be resistant to insects. This application is important because a large percentage of the world's food supply is lost to pests. Pesticides have traditionally been used, but although effective, they have disadvantages. Ask students what some disadvantages of pesticides might be. (Over time the pests become resistant to the pesticide; other organisms might be harmed by the pesticide.) **LS Verbal**

Answers to Caption Questions

Figure 5: We can learn when and where genes are expressed in different cells, and learn how each cells' environment affects gene expression.

Differentiated Instruction

Advanced Learners/GATE

Genetically Modified Tomatoes Have students investigate why the tomato was chosen as the first GM food to be sold, how it was altered, and its advantages. **LS Verbal**

Why It Matters

Flavor Savor™ Tomato Explain to students that not all genetically modified crops have met with marketing success. The Flavor Savor™ tomato was the first genetically modified food approved by the FDA for market in 1994, but it was not very popular. The public was apprehensive about eating a genetically modified plant. The product was also very expensive in order to offset the expense of research and development. In 1997, the tomato was pulled from the marketplace.

Teaching Key Ideas

Multicellular Cloning Explain to students that in mammals the egg cell cytoplasm generally directs the "program" for development, which is normally triggered by fertilization. During SCNT, an unfertilized haploid egg nucleus is replaced by a diploid, somatic cell nucleus. Environmental conditions are then controlled to trigger development of an embryo.

Teaching Key Ideas

Cloning and Age Make sure students note the difference in the muzzle of the donor of the somatic cell and the surrogate mother in **Figure 6.** Ask what the muzzle of Dolly would look like. (white like the donor) Point out that as Dolly grew older, her chromosomes began showing signs of premature aging. Ask students to speculate on Dolly's "chromosomal" age at birth. (Her chromosomes were the age of the donor!) **LS Logical**

clone an organism, cell, or piece of genetic material that is genetically identical to one that was preexisting; to make a genetic duplicate

stem cell a cell that can divide repeatedly and can differentiate into specialized cell types

SCI**LINKS**.

www.scilinks.org
Topic: Cloning
Code: HX80303

Manipulating Bodies and Development

Biologists still have much to learn about the development of multi-cellular organisms. To do so, they must study cells in the process of multiplying and differentiating into the many types of cells found in a body. **》Cloning and stem cell techniques are used in research on animal development and have potential for treating certain diseases.**

Cloning A **clone** is an organism or piece of genetic material that is genetically identical to one that was preexisting. Making a clone in a lab is called *cloning,* but the process does occur in nature. Organisms clone themselves whenever they reproduce asexually. Single-celled organisms clone themselves by simple division. Multicellular organisms may clone themselves by budding off parts, as some plants and fungi do, or by self-fertilization, as many plants and some animals do.

Very few large animals can clone themselves. Also, animals have complex processes of fertilization and embryo development. So, scientists are still experimenting with cloning animals. The first such experiments made clones from eggs or embryos. Then, a clone was made from an adult mammal, as **Figure 6** shows. The clone was made using a process called *somatic-cell nuclear transfer* (SCNT). In this process, the nucleus of an egg cell is replaced with the nucleus of an adult cell. Then, the egg begins to develop into an embryo.

Problems with Cloning Although scientists have successfully cloned many kinds of animals, only a few of the cloned offspring have survived for long. In some cases, the fetuses have grown beyond normal size. Many have failed to develop normally with age. Because of such problems and because of ethical issues, efforts to clone humans are illegal in most countries.

Genomic Imprinting Some problems with cloning may be related to the ways that eggs and sperm normally develop. Chemicals in the reproductive system turn "on" or "off" certain genes in the developing gametes. These genes later affect development from embryo to adult. Such an effect, called *genomic imprinting,* is altered when animals are cloned in a lab. So, different genes may be activated early on, and the remaining development may be altered.

Figure 6 Dolly, a cloned sheep, was born in 1997. Dolly was the first successful clone produced from the nucleus of an adult somatic cell.

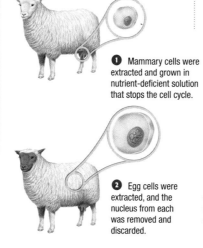

❶ Mammary cells were extracted and grown in nutrient-deficient solution that stops the cell cycle.

❷ Egg cells were extracted, and the nucleus from each was removed and discarded.

❸ A mammary cell was placed next to an "empty" egg cell.

❹ An electric shock opened up the cell membranes so that the cells fused.

❺ Cell division was triggered, and an embryo began to develop.

❻ The developing embryo was later implanted into a surrogate mother.

Why It Matters

Success of Cloning Point out to students that the success rate of SCNT is very low. There were 246 failures before cloning Dolly. Not only does embryonic development depend on genomic imprinting, there are many other factors that come into play after implantation into the uterus. These points should be underscored so that students recognize that the possibility of human cloning is very remote.

Differentiated Instruction

Basic Learners

Cloned Animals Have students research which have been cloned, when, and where. Ask students to present their findings in the form of a poster, with photos if possible. **LS Verbal**

① An adult stem cell can be removed from a specific tissue, such as bone marrow.

② The cell can be grown in tissue culture to produce more cells of a specific tissue type.

③ The cells can be re-implanted into a patient whose tissues are lacking or damaged.

Figure 7 Adult stem cells can be removed and used to grow more cells of specific tissue types. This kind of therapy can replace tissue that is damaged or deficient due to disease or other medical treatment. **❯ How do adult stem cells differ from embryonic stem cells?**

Using Stem Cells

A **stem cell** is a cell that can continuously divide and differentiate into various tissues. Some stem cells have more potential to differentiate than others. *Totipotent* cells can give rise to any cell or tissue type, *pluripotent* cells can give rise to all types except germ cells, and *multipotent* cells can give rise to just a few other cell types. The state of the cell depends on the stage of development of the body and the tissue of which the cell is part.

Adults' bodies have some multipotent cells, such as bone marrow cells, that give rise to various blood cells. These cells can be removed, frozen or cultured, and used for medical treatments, as **Figure 7** shows. The cells of new embryos have more potential uses. These cells are totipotent at first and pluripotent during development.

Issues with Stem Cell Research

The first major source of human embryos for stem cell research was fertility clinics. Such clinics help people have children, often by uniting people's gametes and culturing embryos in a lab. Many extra embryos are stored in a frozen state in clinics. In some cases, the parents have given scientists permission to use the embryos for research. But such uses of human embryos pose ethical problems. In the United States, there have been strong debates about the use of federal funds for this kind of research.

Stem Cells from SCNT

A newer source of embryonic stem cells is through cloning using SCNT. Some people believe that using this kind of stem cell for medical research and treatment should be ethically acceptable. One reason is that an embryo made through SCNT does not have true parents. Another reason is that the cells of the embryo are separated early in its development, so there is no chance of the embryo developing further.

❯ **Reading Check** *What are the two main types of stem cells?*

Teaching Key Ideas

Embryonic and Adult Stem Cells Ask students which stem cell has more potential: an adult bone marrow cell or a cell from a very young embryo. (embryo cell) Why? (Embryonic stem cells can give rise to all kinds of cells; adult bone marrow stem cells can give rise only to various blood cells.) Ask why adult stem cells are being used even though they have less potential. (lack of availability of embryos, ethical considerations) **LS Logical**

READING TOOLBOX

Analogies First, have students review the definitions of *pluripotent* and *multipotent*. Then, ask them which term applies to embryonic stem cells and which term to adult stem cells. Finally, ask students to write the analogy. (multipotent: adult stem cells :: pluripotent: embryonic stem cells) **LS Verbal**

Answers to Caption Questions
Figure 7: Adult stem cells have less potential to differentiate; they are multipotent, whereas embryonic stem cells are either totipotent or pluripotent.

Differentiated Instruction

Struggling Readers

Types of Stem Cells Have students make a three-column chart with these column headings: *Cell Type, Definition, Where Found.* Have them fill in the chart with information about totipotent cells, pluripotent cells, and multipotent cells. **LS Verbal**

Why It Matters

Stem Cell Research Tell students that the use of embryonic stem cells in research remains controversial, partly because it is a complex and rapidly advancing field. Meanwhile, laws regarding such research differ between different states in the U.S. and between the U.S. and other countries. Debate in the U.S. has centered on limiting the practices of laboratories that receive any form of federal funding. Research in this area has continued with funding from private, state, and foreign sources. **LS Verbal**

> Close

Formative Assessment

The process of changing the DNA of an organism is called _____.

A. proteomics (Incorrect. Proteomics is the study of how proteins interact within cells.)

B. genomic imprinting (Incorrect. Genomic imprinting is an effect on the genes of a developing embryo.)

C. genetic engineering (Correct! Genetic engineering is deliberately changing the genetic material of an organism.)

D. recombinant DNA (Incorrect. Recombinant DNA is a result of changing DNA.)

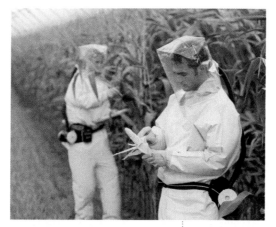

Figure 8 This corn has been genetically modified to carry the *Bt* gene, which causes the corn plant to produce an insect-killing chemical. As with any use of pesticides, this practice presents risks. An additional danger is that the gene may be transferred to other plants.

ACADEMIC VOCABULARY

ethical conforming to moral standards

Ethical and Social Issues

Ethical issues involve differing values and perspectives. For example, the use of GMOs is prohibited or tightly controlled by laws in some countries. In others, GMOs are widely used, and GM foods are sold with few restrictions. **> Ethical issues can be raised for every use of gene technologies.**

Safety One danger of GMOs is that they can "escape" and have unforeseen effects. For example, the *Bt* toxin gene from GM corn crops, such as those in **Figure 8,** has been transferred to other plants. In addition, the toxic corn pollen seems to be harming populations of the monarch butterfly. Ecologists worry that we do not know enough to safely manipulate genes on a large scale.

Human Rights Being able to predict disease before it happens is a major achievement of modern medicine. Today, the DNA of individuals can be tested to find the risk of genetic disorders. But what should we do with this information? Many decisions could be influenced by such genetic information, such as whom to marry or what to eat. Who should have this information? Who should make these decisions? How can future probabilities be weighed against current human needs and rights? There are no easy answers to these ethical questions, but the questions need to be considered carefully.

Property Laws Gene technologies have also created new issues for old laws, especially those related to intellectual property and patents. Intellectual property (IP) is the ownership of the ideas or plans that a person creates. A patent is a specific set of rights that allows an inventor to control and profit from the uses of his or her idea. In the 1980s, the first patent for a GMO was awarded to a scientist who had engineered an oil-eating bacterium. Before this event, living organisms were considered a part of nature and, as such, were not patentable. Now, specific DNA sequences can be patented.

> Reading Check *What issues does the use of genetic testing raise?*

Section 2 Review

> KEY IDEAS

1. **Identify** applications of manipulating genes and proteins.
2. **Relate** stem cell research to the potential use of cloning.
3. **Describe** a specific ethical issue related to a gene technology.

CRITICAL THINKING

4. **Inferring Relationships** How can manipulating gene expression help advance the study of proteomics?
5. **Evaluating Risks** Given the difficulties that researchers have had with raising cloned animals, do you think it is safe to grow tissues or organs from cloned embryonic stem cells for the purpose of transplanting? Explain.

ALTERNATIVE ASSESSMENT

6. **Debate** Suppose that genetic analysis could predict a person's ability in sports, math, or music. Should genetic screening be used to determine the course selections and team assignments of every student in school? Prepare and conduct a formal debate on the subject.

Answers to Section Review

1. genetic engineering to produce new crops, livestock and medical treatments, and as a research tool to study the roles of proteins

2. Cloning can produce organisms that are genetically identical to preexisting individuals; stem cells can be used to grow new tissues.

3 Sample answer: GM crops may have unforeseen, harmful effects on the environment.

4. Manipulating gene expression changes protein production. Therefore, researchers can determine the proteins that specific genes code for.

5. Sample answer: No, because there may be abnormalities in the organs of cloned animals that would make them unsuitable for transplantation, as well as posing a risk to the recipient. Accept all reasonable answers.

6. Sample arguments: pros: Students might be more successful in courses for which they had an aptitude; cons: students would limit their exposure to other areas, which might make them less "well-rounded."

Gene Technologies in Detail

Key Ideas	Key Terms		Why It Matters
❯ What are the basic tools of genetic manipulation? ❯ How are these tools used in the major processes of modern gene technologies? ❯ How do scientists study entire genomes?	restriction enzyme DNA polymorphisms electrophoresis polymerase chain reaction (PCR)	DNA sequencing bioinformatics genome mapping genetic library	Humans now have the ability to identify and manipulate genes in many organisms.

How do you find a needle in a haystack? This phrase is often used to speak of a nearly impossible task. But if the haystack is a genome and the needle is a gene, the task is now possible!

Basic Tools for Genetic Manipulation

Molecular biologists spent many years developing tools and methods to manipulate genetic material. The methods continue to be used and adapted for a wide range of applications, but the basic tools are similar. ❯ **The basic tools of DNA manipulation rely on the chemical nature of genetic material and are adapted from natural processes discovered in cells.** These tools include restriction enzymes, polymorphisms, gel electrophoresis, denaturation, and hybridization. For example, the first GMOs were made by using plasmids and enzymes that are naturally present in some bacterial cells.

Restriction Enzymes Among the first tools used to manipulate DNA were enzymes that are made by bacteria as a defense. The enzymes serve to slice up any invading DNA sequences or genes from other organisms. These **restriction enzymes** recognize a specific sequence of DNA, called a *restriction site*. The enzymes will cut DNA strands at all such sites, as **Figure 9** shows.

These enzymes are useful in two ways. First, different enzymes recognize different sequences, so the enzymes can be used to cut up a DNA sample in specific ways. Second, the cuts of most restriction enzymes create sticky ends. A *sticky end* has a few bases on one strand that are unpaired but complementary to unpaired bases on other sticky ends. So, sticky ends will easily bind to one another.

❯ **Reading Check** *Which basic genetic tools were used to make the first GMOs?*

Figure 9 Restriction enzymes recognize and cut DNA at specific sequences. Usually, complementary ("sticky") ends are created. ❯ **In what ways are restriction enzymes useful?**

The Living Environment
Standard 4
2.2c Different enzymes can be used to cut, copy, and move segments of DNA. Characteristics produced by the segments of DNA may be expressed when these segments are inserted into new organisms, such as bacteria.

restriction enzyme an enzyme that cuts double-stranded DNA into fragments by recognizing specific nucleotide sequences and cutting the DNA at those sequences

DNA — Restriction enzyme

G A A T T C
C T T A A G

Sticky end
G
C T T A A

A A T T C
G

Sticky end

Why It Matters

Naming Restriction Enzymes Tell students that each specific type of restriction enzyme is named for the species of bacteria from which it was isolated. For example *EcoRI*, the restriction enzyme shown in the student book, comes from *E. coli*. The first three letters come from genus and species; the fourth letter, *R*, represents the strain, and the Roman numerals represent the order of discovery. Point out that there are thousands of types of restriction enzymes, and each recognizes a different DNA sequence.

Key Resources

 Transparencies
C32 Restriction Enzymes Cut DNA
C33 Gel Electrophoresis
C35 Genetically Engineered Medicine

Visual Concepts
Gel Electrophoresis
Polymerase Chain Reaction
Cloning Vectors and Plasmids
Using Plasmids to Produce Insulin

❯ **Focus**

This section identifies basic tools used for genetic manipulation and explains the processes of modern gene technologies.

🔊 **Bellringer**
Use the Bellringer transparency to prepare students for this section.

❯ **Teach**

Teaching Key Ideas
Restriction Enzymes Point out that restriction enzymes work by identifying a specific sequence of nucleotide bases that are palindromes— words, phrases, numbers, or other sequences of units that read the same in either direction. Write the palindrome "Madam I'm Adam" on the board. Point out that when read from right to left and adjusting the spacing and punctuation, the letters state the same message as when read from left to right. Have students look at **Figure 9** and notice that the bases on the upper strand are read in reverse of the sequence on the lower strand. **LS** Visual

Answers to Caption Questions
Figure 9: They can be used to find specific sites on DNA or to cut it so that pieces can be spliced together.

Section Correlations

4.2.2c

Teacher's Notes Use beads of three different sizes and colors. The large beads should be big enough so that the smallest beads can flow through the spaces between them.

Materials
• beads, 3 sizes
• beaker, 500 mL
• jar, 1 qt or larger

Answers to Analysis

1. The smallest beads flowed faster.
2. In gel electrophoresis, small bits of DNA are pulled (by electrical force instead of gravity) through a matrix of other molecules.
3. They were slowed less by the larger beads (the matrix).

Science Skills

DNA Electric Charge Tell students that the phosphate functional group of a nucleotide has a negative charge, making the overall charge on a DNA molecule negative. When an electric current is applied to a gel containing DNA fragments, the DNA moves through the gel in response to its attraction to the positive electrode. **LS** Logical

Answers to Caption Questions

Figure 10: The semisolid property of the gel slows down large molecules as they are pulled through it by an electric field.

Hands-On
QuickLab

⏱ 15 min

Gel Electrophoresis Model

You can use beads to model how DNA fragments are separated in a gel during electrophoresis.

Procedure

1. Fill a **large jar** with the largest of **three sets of beads** (each set should be a different size and different color). The filled jar represents a gel.

2. Mix the smaller sets of beads in a **500 mL beaker**, and then pour them slowly on top of the "gel." The smaller beads represent DNA fragments.

3. Observe the flow of the beads through the "gel." Lightly agitate the jar if the beads do not flow easily.

Analysis

1. **Identify** which beads flowed through faster.

2. **Relate** this model to how electrophoresis works.

3. **CRITICAL THINKING** **Using Models** Why did the beads identified in item 1 pass through the "gel" more quickly?

ACADEMIC VOCABULARY

slight very small or barely detectable

Figure 10 Gel electrophoresis separates samples of molecules, such as DNA or proteins, into bands that are ordered by size. ❯ What is the role of the gel?

Polymorphisms Differences between the DNA sequences of individuals are called **DNA polymorphisms.** These differences may be slight but can be compared and analyzed for several purposes, as you will learn. Differences of just one nucleotide are called *single nucleotide polymorphisms* (SNPs). SNPs result from point mutations and are usually unique to individuals or populations. At a broader level, each species has a unique pattern of restriction sites. When different DNA samples are cut with the same restriction enzyme, the segments that result will have different lengths. These differences are called *restriction fragment length polymorphisms* (RFLPs).

Gel Electrophoresis DNA carries an electric charge, so an electric current can be used to push or pull DNA fragments. This process is called **electrophoresis.** Often, the DNA fragments are forced though a *gel*, a semisolid that allows molecules to move slowly through it. When a current is applied, shorter fragments will move faster through the gel than longer fragments will. The result is a lane of fragments sorted by size, as shown in **Figure 10.** If the fragments separate clearly, each lane is called a *ladder*. If the fragments have overlapping sizes and do not separate clearly, each lane is called a *smear*.

There are many types of electrophoresis. Different kinds of gels are used to sort different sizes of DNA fragments, and other methods are used to sort RNA or proteins. Newer methods use tiny tubes of gel to sort tiny samples that can then be "read" by a machine and analyzed by a computer.

❯ **Reading Check** *What property of a gel does gel electrophoresis depend upon?*

Differentiated Instruction

English Learners

Identifying DNA Differences Have students make drawings to illustrate SNPs and RFLPs. Tell them to label their drawing with these terms: *SNP, RFLP, nucleotide, DNA segment.* **LS** Visual

Special Education Students

Identifying Separation Patterns Have students work in mixed groups. Provide a sheet of paper with strips marked with DNA bases that include GAATTC restriction sites at irregular intervals. Have students cut the strips and tape them into one long segment. Using scissors, have the students cut at the restriction sites. Have students position the segments from largest to smallest in a line to represent how the segments would sort by size during electrophoresis. **LS** Kinesthetic

---

Denaturation Recall that DNA in cells is usually double stranded, twisted, and often associated with proteins. Some conditions, such as heat or strong chemicals, can cause DNA to denature, or untwist and split into single strands. Scientists can easily denature and renature DNA and use the single strands for further manipulations.

Hybridization When single-stranded segments of DNA or RNA are mixed together under the right conditions, complementary segments will bind together, or hybridize. Genetic tools that take advantage of this natural process include the following:

- **Primers** *Primers* are short, single strands of DNA that will hybridize with a specific sequence. For this use, the sequence is one that will be recognized by an enzyme, such as DNA polymerase. Thus, primers can be used to initiate replication of single strands of DNA.

- **Probes** When DNA samples are sorted in a gel, probes are used to "tag" and find specific sequences. Probes are much like primers but carry radioactive or fluorescent materials that can be detected.

- **cDNA** Complementary DNA (cDNA) is DNA that has been made to match mRNA from cells. Recall that this mRNA is the result of transcription and has exons removed. So, making cDNA is a shortcut to getting just the expressed DNA of complete genes.

Major Gene Technology Processes

❯ **The major methods for working with genes use some combination of the basic tools and mechanisms of cellular machinery.** These methods include PCR, blotting, DNA sequencing, and gene recombination.

Polymerase Chain Reaction (PCR) The **polymerase chain reaction (PCR)** process is widely used to clone DNA sequences for further study or manipulation. PCR imitates the normal process of DNA replication in cells. So, using PCR is as simple as combining the right components in a test tube and then controlling the temperature, as **Figure 11** shows. The process is called a *chain reaction* because it is repeated over and over.

DNA polymorphisms (PAHL ee MAWR FIZ uhmz) variations in DNA sequences; used as a basis for comparing genomes

electrophoresis (ee LEK troh fuh REE sis) the process by which electrically charged particles suspended in a liquid move through the liquid because of the influence of an electric field

polymerase chain reaction (puh LIM uhr ays) a technique that is used to make many copies of selected segments of DNA (abbreviation, PCR)

Figure 11 PCR rapidly produces many copies of a DNA sample. The process can make 1 billion copies of a DNA sample within a few hours!

Polymerase Chain Reaction (PCR)

❶ Add DNA polymerase, nucleotides, and primers. Heat to separate strands.

❷ Cool to allow primers to bind to original strands.

Primers

❸ DNA polymerase will add nucleotides to complete the strands.

❹ Heat and cool again to repeat the process.

Teaching Key Ideas

Southern Blot Process Refer students to **Figure 12,** and ask what the Roman numerals represent. (DNA from different individuals) Ask how the fragments in step 2 were generated. (restriction digest followed by gel electrophoresis) Point out that these fragments are of different sizes, with the smallest fragments closest to the positive pole. Ask why there are fewer bands in step 4 than in step 2. (Only those segments of interest were supplied with radioactive probes to match.) How does this process relate to an RFLP? (RFLPs are what create the differences in fragment size between different individuals.) **LS Visual**

Answers to Caption Questions

Figure 12: restriction enzymes, gel electrophoresis, and hybridization (probes)

SCI*LINKS*.
www.scilinks.org
Topic: Gene
      Technologies
Code: HX80539

Figure 12 In this example, a DNA sample is analyzed by using the Southern blot process. **>** Which basic genetic tools are used as part of this process?

Blotting Processes and Applications Several gene technologies use a combination of restriction enzymes, gel electrophoresis, and hybridization with probes. The goal is to find or compare sequences of DNA or RNA. Many include a blotting step in which sorted segments are preserved by transferring from the gel to another surface or grid (such as a sheet of special paper). Then, probes are used to reveal the location of specific sequences.

Southern Blot The Southern blot process, shown in **Figure 12,** is used specifically for DNA, and especially for DNA fingerprints. The process may vary by using either different restriction enzymes on one DNA sample or different DNA samples with the same enzyme.

Fingerprints and Bar Codes DNA polymorphisms can be used to identify individuals or species. When restriction fragments are sorted through a Southern blot process, each person's DNA will have a unique pattern of banding called a *DNA fingerprint*. Similarly, a *DNA bar code* can be made to help identify species.

Northern Blot The Northern blot process differs from Southern blot in that the sample fragments are mRNA instead of DNA. Recall that mRNA in cells comes from genes being transcribed. So, Northern blot can be used to tell which genes in a cell are "turned on" (being expressed) or to tell the size of the expressed parts of a gene (after exons are removed).

Microarrays A *microarray* is a device that enables thousands of tiny Northern blots to be done at once. Microarrays can be used to show patterns of gene expression. For example, a cancer cell will have certain genes turned on or off. The pattern of gene activity seen in a microarray can help identify specific kinds of cancer.

> Reading Check *What does "blotting" refer to?*

Southern Blot Process

1 The Southern blot process begins with a sample of DNA. The DNA is cut into fragments using restriction enzymes. A unique enzyme may be used to create several batches of sample DNA.

2 The DNA fragments are sorted by gel electrophoresis. One lane in the gel is used for each batch. Then, a chemical splits all fragments into single-stranded form.

3 The DNA strands are transferred (blotted) onto a piece of nylon paper. A solution containing probes is applied to the nylon paper. The probes bind to specific sites on the single strands.

4 The exposure of photographic or X-ray film to the nylon paper reveals the location of those sample strands that hybridized with the probe. Each person's DNA will make a unique pattern.

Differentiated Instruction

Basic Learners

Models of Blotting Processes Have students research and prepare models to explain any of the blotting processes explained in the text. **LS Visual**

Chain Termination Sequencing

go.hrw.com
interact online
Keyword: HX8GTCF13

1 Copy The unknown DNA sequence is copied, denatured, and incubated with specific genetic molecules.

2 Terminate New copies of the original sequence begin to form, but some are terminated randomly by tagged nucelotides.

3 Sort The resulting strands are denatured and sorted in a gel. The color-coded bands in the gel will match the orginal sequence.

"Template" sequence strand of original

Original, unknown DNA sequence

Copies of "template" sequence

"Free" DNA nucleotides

DNA polymerase

Primers

Color-tagged "terminator" nucleotides

Short, known part of sequence

A
T
G
A
C

Teaching Key Ideas

DNA Sequencing Ask students what chain termination sequencing is used for. (sequencing DNA, including the human genome) How is the process like DNA fingerprinting? (Gel electrophoresis is used to separate fragments.) How does it differ from DNA fingerprinting? (Each band on the gel contains pieces that have been tagged to identify only one specific nucleotide base.) How are the bands analyzed? (They are read from the bottom of the gel to the top; since the same piece of DNA was used to generate all of the bands, each band represents the position of one of the bases of the original sequence.) **LS Visual, Logical**

Answers to Caption Questions

Figure 13: This method is now widely used to rapidly sequence genomes.

go.hrw.com
interact online

Students can interact with "Chain Termination Sequencing" by going to go.hrw.com and typing in the keyword HX8GTCF13.

DNA Sequencing Among the great achievements of modern biology are DNA sequencing methods. **DNA sequencing** is the process of determining the exact order of every nucleotide in a gene. The major modern method is *chain termination sequencing,* as shown in **Figure 13.** This method has been improved over time.

Step 1 Start Copying a Template The gene (DNA segment) of interest is copied (using PCR) and split into single strands. The copies are placed in solution with primers, DNA polymerase, and an assortment of bases. The primers will bond to the "template" strand, and then DNA polymerase will begin to add bases to the "copy" strand, as in normal DNA replication.

Step 2 Randomly Terminate the Copies Some of the bases act as "terminator" bases. When one of these bases is placed in one of the growing copy strands, copying will stop on that strand. Thus, an assortment of randomly "cut-off" sequence copies is produced.

Step 3 Sort the Copies by Size At this point, the sequence of bases can be deduced by sorting the segments by size. When sequencing was first developed, scientists would use four batches of radioactively tagged "terminators" (one for each base type). Then, they would perform electrophoresis in four lanes, side by side, which would reveal the relative order of each end-base. Today, scientists use color-coded fluorescent tags (one color for each base type) and run a single batch through a tiny tube of gel. A machine with a laser can detect the wavelengths of the tags and thus "read" the sequence.

❯ Reading Check *When are primers used in DNA sequencing?*

Figure 13 Chain termination sequencing modifies DNA replication processes in order to deduce a DNA sequence. **❯ Why is this method so important?**

DNA sequencing (SEE kwuhns ing) the process of determining the order of every nucleotide in a gene or genetic fragment

---

Differentiated Instruction

English Learners

Sequencing Have pairs of students make drawings on separate index cards to represent each step in chain termination sequencing. Then, ask partners to use the drawing to explain to each other the steps in the process. **LS Visual**

Demonstration

Recombinant DNA Take a piece of yarn tied to form a ring (representing a plasmid) out of a plastic bag (representing a bacterial cell). Use a longer piece of yarn of a different color to represent human DNA (hDNA) containing a gene of interest. Using scissors smeared with a bit of glue to represent a specific restriction enzyme, make a single cut through the plasmid. Make two cuts through the hDNA to remove a "gene." Remind students that the cuts made by the scissors produced the *same* sticky ends on both pieces of yarn. Using fingertips as ligase, glue the ends of the hDNA piece to the plasmid. Ask what the plasmid represents. (a vector) Ask why the new circle of yarn represents recombinant DNA. (The plasmid now contains foreign DNA.) Ask what is the next step in recombination. (The plasmid is placed into a host cell.) Place the connected yarn into a plastic bag. Tell students that at this point, the plasmid would begin replicating the hDNA gene with its own DNA. **LS Visual**

go.hrw.com
✱ interact online

Students can interact with "Recombinant Cloning" by going to go.hrw.com and typing in the keyword HX8GTCF14.

Figure 14 The earliest gene cloning and recombination methods used the steps shown here. The first GMOs were produced in this way.

go.hrw.com
✱ interact online
Keyword: HX8GTCF14

Recombinant Cloning

Human chromosome

Bacterium

Insulin gene

Plasmid DNA

❶ Two sets of DNA are cut with the same kind of restriction enzyme.

Sticky ends

❷ The sticky ends of the two kinds of DNA bind together. The result is a recombinant plasmid (vector).

❸ The recombinant plasmids are taken up by bacterial cells (hosts).

❹ Each time that the recombinant bacteria divide, the recombinant plasmids are cloned many times.

❺ The plasmid clones also have an antibiotic-resistance gene. When the bacteria are exposed to an antibiotic, only those cells that have the new plasmids will live.

Gene Recombination and Cloning The first attempts at gene recombination and cloning were done by inserting a gene into an organism that replicates easily, as shown in **Figure 14.** Other methods may use similar steps.

Step ❶ Cut DNA Samples Two sets of DNA are cut by the same kind of restriction enzyme so that all fragments have matching sticky ends. One set of DNA is from an organism containing a specific gene (in this case, the human insulin gene). The other DNA is part of a vector, such as a virus or a bacterial plasmid, that can carry or move DNA between cells. The vector will be replicated when placed in a host, such as a bacterial cell.

Step ❷ Splice Pieces Together The DNA fragments from the first organism are combined with the fragments from the vector. Then, an enzyme called *DNA ligase* is added to help bond the sticky ends of all the fragments together.

Step ❸ Place into Host At this point, some plasmids are recombinant with human DNA. When the plasmids are placed in a culture of bacteria, some cells take up the plasmids. The cells are allowed to replicate normally.

Step ❹ Replicate Gene Each time that a bacterial cell divides, its plasmids are copied many times. In a few generations, the cells make millions of clones of the recombinant plasmids.

Step ❺ Screen for Gene At this point, only some of the bacterial cells contain the recombinant plasmids. These cells must be identified in some way. One clever solution is to use vectors that contain another gene that is easy to detect. In this example, the original plasmids contained a gene that makes bacteria resistant to an antibiotic chemical. When the bacteria from step 4 are exposed to that chemical, only the cells that have taken up the vectors will survive.

These steps are just the beginning of genetic-engineering applications. Before PCR, this process of recombination was the main way to clone genes for further research. Another use is simply to produce a protein, such as insulin, from a cloned gene. As you have learned, recombinant organisms are created for many applications, from agriculture to medicine.

❭ **Reading Check** *What is a vector?*

Why It Matters

Molecular Scissors Molecular biologists have determined the structure of more than 3,000 restriction enzymes. Imagine their surprise when one of them actually turned out to resemble a pair of scissors! The enzyme, BglII, recognizes and cleaves the DNA sequence AGACTC. Using X-ray crystallography, scientists found that the enzyme's two subunits swing away from each other in a scissorlike motion. The sliding of the BglII subunits past each other results in cutting of the DNA. After cutting, the enzyme resets itself to an open position. Other restriction enzymes, such as BamHI, grip DNA like a pair of tongs.

Differentiated Instruction

Special Education Students

Modeling Processes After students have observed you model recombinant cloning, provide them with assorted materials so that they can model other processes discussed in this section. Pair or group students with different abilities together and challenge them to ensure that all group members can demonstrate the model in action. **LS Kinesthetic/Visual**

Exploring Genomes

Until recently, the human genome was largely "unexplored." But now, specific genes are being identified and their locations "mapped." These first steps lead to understanding how each gene works. Like geographic maps, maps of genetic data can have different levels of detail or scale. For example, one can view a map of an entire nation or "zoom in" to view a particular state, city, neighborhood, or street. In a similar way, **❯ one can explore and map a genome at many levels, including species, individual, chromosome, gene, or nucleotide.**

Managing Genomic Data Your school library has a system for organizing and keeping track of books, as **Figure 15** shows. Similarly, scientists need systems for managing the vast amounts of data in a genome. Today, they use information technologies. The application of information technologies in biology is **bioinformatics. ❯** Genomic **bioinformatics starts with the mapping and assembly of the many parts of each genome.** The major stages of this work include the following:

- **Mapping and Assembly** Many genes have been "mapped" to reveal their location relative to other genes. In addition, large collections of sequences are being pieced together like a puzzle.

- **Organized Storage** Genomic information is stored in a logical system or database. This way, the information can be sorted and searched, and new information can be added easily.

- **Annotation** Each gene or sequence is named and categorized according to its location, structure, or function in each genome.

- **Analysis** The ultimate goal of genomics is to understand the exact function of each gene or sequence. This analysis includes studying the complex interactions among genes and proteins.

❯ **Reading Check** *What are the first steps of studying genomes?*

Figure 15 Like a library full of books, genomic data must be organized in order to be useful. ❯ **What other actions are needed to manage genomic data?**

bioinformatics the application of information technologies in biology, especially in genetics

READING TOOLBOX

Learning Steps If you have not yet completed your pattern puzzle for **Figure 14,** do so now. Then, close your book, scramble the pieces, and see if you can put them in order.

Teaching Key Ideas

Human Genome Library To help students understand that the application of information from the Human Genome Project has just begun, use the analogy of a book. In this book, there are only four letters—A, T, C, and G—arranged in any order. Most of the book is a just a series of letters; on a few pages letters make "words." (analogous to the amino acids that make up a gene) Most words have not been organized into sentences with meaning. (analogous to gene expression that has not been determined) **LS Visual**

READING TOOLBOX

Learning Steps Student pattern-puzzle steps should be in order. (Cut DNA Samples; Splice Pieces Together; Place into Host; Replicate Gene; Screen for Gene) **LS Logical**

Answers to Caption Questions
Figure 15: mapping, annotation, and analysis

Differentiated Instruction

Advanced Learners/GATE

Computational Biology Perhaps one of the most important tasks in bioinformatics involves computational biology, the analysis of DNA sequence information. Have students research this branch of science and report on how DNA sequences are used to model protein structure. **LS Logical**

Teaching Key ideas

Linkage vs. Physical Mapping Direct students' attention to **Figure 16.** First, ask students to look at the linkage map. Ask what the map shows. (the relative order of genes along a chromosome) Point out that the map identifies the position of the gene, but not its composition. Ask why *Black body* is closer to *Purple eyes* than to *Shriveled wings* on the map. (There is a smaller percent of crossing over in the former, meaning the genes for these two traits are closer together along a chromosome.) Next, have students look at the physical chromosome map. Tell students that because of the prevalence of sex-linked disorders associated with the X chromosome, it became the first human chromosome to be mapped. Ask what this map measures. (physical distance between genes on the chromosome) Point out that relatively little recombination may occur between two genes on the same chromosome, even though they may be very far apart physically with many thousands of base pairs separating them.
LS **Visual**

Answers to Caption Questions

Figure 16: Sex-linked genes are relatively easy to trace through family histories.

genome mapping the process of determining the relative position of genes in a genome

genetic library a collection of genetic sequence clones that represent all of the genes in a given genome

Mapping Methods Genome mapping is the process of determining the relative position of all of the genes on chromosomes in an organism's genome. To make a city map from scratch, you might start with landmarks that are easy to find and recognize. Similarly, genome mapping methods use *genetic markers,* or traits that can be easily detected, to trace the movement and location of genes. Examples are shown in **Figure 16.** Any detectable physical, behavioral, or chemical trait can be used as a marker. As the next step in making a map, you might try to determine the location of each thing relative to other things. Similarly, genome mapping uses several methods.

Linkage Mapping Linkage mapping methods identify the relative order of genes along a chromosome. Recall that the closer together that two genes are, the less frequently they will be separated during chromosome crossover. So, closely linked genes are more often associated, or found together, in the same individual. By comparing how often genes are associated, scientists can deduce their location relative to one another, as **Figure 16** shows.

Physical Mapping Physical mapping methods determine the exact number of base pairs between specific genes. These methods manipulate DNA to deduce exactly how close together genes are.

Human Chromosome Mapping Early attempts to map human genes used historical family records. By studying the patterns of inheritance of specific traits, scientists could infer which genes tend to be inherited together. This method was especially useful for initial mapping of the X chromosome. Such maps have since been filled in with data from physical mapping, as **Figure 16** shows.

Figure 16 Each of these maps shows the relative positions of genes on chromosomes. The physical map is more specific than the linkage map. **>** Why was the X chromosome mapped more easily than other chromosomes?

Basic Genome Mapping

Gene Locations on a Fruit Fly Chromosome Map

0
48.5
54.5
67.0

6% crossover
18.5% crossover
12.5% crossover

Black body
Purple eyes
Shriveled wings

Linkage Map This map shows the frequencies of crossover of specific genes in the *Drosophila* genome.

Human X Chromosome

Duchenne muscular dystrophy
Retinitis pigmentosa 3
Synapsin I
Cleft palate, X-linked
Angiotensin receptor 2
Albinism-deafness syndrome
Ribosomal protein L10

Physical Chromosome Map This map shows the locations of some genes on the human X chromosome.

Differentiated Instruction

English Learners

Mapping Students may be confused by the term *mapping* as it is used in this lesson. Show students a geographical map and ask what it shows. (where things such as cities, mountain, lakes, and roads are located) Tell students **Figure 16** also shows where things are located, but the things that are mapped are not mountains, cities or the like. Ask what is being mapped. (genes) Where are the genes found? (on chromosomes) **LS** **Verbal**

Genome Sequence Assembly As they zoom in on the map of genes, scientists want to record all of the nucleotide sequences in a genome. The process of deducing and recording the exact order of every base and gene in a genome is called *sequence assembly*. The process involves collecting, sorting, and comparing large samples of genetic material.

Genetic Libraries To study an entire genome, scientists break up the genome into small fragments and clone all of the fragments. A collection of clones that represent all of the genes in a given genome is called a **genetic library.** Two kinds of genetic libraries are made. A *genomic library* is made by cloning all of the DNA in a cell. A genomic library includes all functional genes as well as all noncoding DNA. An *expressed sequence tag* (EST) *library* starts with the mRNA that results from transcription. The mRNA is used to make cDNA segments, which are then cloned to make the library.

Using the Libraries Once the clones are assembled, they can be sequenced, sorted, and organized. Early methods involved sorting through libraries one gene at a time by repeated probing and deduction. More recently, a method called *shotgun sequencing* was developed. In this method, an entire genome is cut up randomly into segments of varying size. All resulting segments are cloned and sequenced. Then, by looking for overlapping parts, researchers put together the entire sequence like a puzzle. The resulting genome sequence is stored as data and can be searched for specific genes or sequences of any size.

Automated Sequencing Robotic devices are now used to sequence a genome in a fraction of the time that it took to complete such a project only decades ago. Automated sequencing devices can quickly "read" many tiny sequence gels at one time. In such a device, a laser beam scans each gel tube, and detectors identify each of the four kinds of tags. Finally, a computer compiles the data into a string of letters, as **Figure 17** shows.

❯ **Reading Check** *What are the two kinds of genetic libraries?*

Each column represents a DNA segment.

Each color represents one of the four bases.

Figure 17 This computer screen shows the output of an automated sequencing device. The device "reads" DNA sequences by detecting color-coded, "tagged" bases in tiny gel-electrophoresis tubes. ❯ What advantages do computers provide?

Section 3 Review

❯ **KEY IDEAS**

1. **Identify** the basic tools of genetic manipulation.
2. **Outline** any one of the major processes of modern gene technologies.
3. **Identify** the major stages of the work of genomics, in terms of bioinformatics.

CRITICAL THINKING

4. **Relating Concepts** Differentiate between SNPs and RFLPs.
5. **Predicting Outcomes** If samples of nerve cells and bone cells from the same person were run through the same type of microarray, would the results differ? Explain.
6. **Analyzing Information** Why is *expressed sequence tag library* a fitting name for a collection of clones made from mRNA?

METHODS OF SCIENCE

7. **Choosing Appropriate Tools** Suppose that you are a genetic scientist who has been asked to help stop the illegal killing of some tropical bird species. These birds are being killed so that their feathers can be sold for fashionable hat decorations. Propose some ways that you could use gene technologies to help protect these birds.

Lab

Time Required
Three 30-minute lab periods

Ratings

Teacher Prep   🧪🧪🧪🧪
Concept Level   🧪🧪🧪🧪
Student Setup   🧪🧪🧪
Cleanup   🧪🧪🧪

Safety Caution
Instruct students on the importance of following directions when using electrical equipment. Make sure that the wires from the electrophoresis chamber are inserted into the appropriate port before turning on the power source.

Preparation
For ease of preparation, obtain a forensic DNA fingerprinting kit and simulated suspect DNA samples. A typical kit includes prepared agarose, concentrated TBE buffer, loading dye, and chemical reagents, in addition to a coupon for DNA samples, with enough materials for eight lab stations.

Prepare 2400 mL of 1X TBE buffer. (This is enough buffer to construct and run 8 gels.) Prepare 200 mL 0.8% agarose or place a bottle of prepared agarose in the water bath to melt agarose. (This is enough prepared agarose to pour eight 25 mL gels.) Determine the volume of running buffer that will be needed by each lab group in advance so that accurate volumes of buffer can

be dispensed in graduated cylinders to each group. Pour TBE buffer into the electrophoresis chamber, and establish a 37 °C hot water bath.

Tips and Tricks
Make sure students keep all DNA and reagents on ice throughout the procedure unless otherwise directed, because the enzymes and DNA samples will begin to degrade at room temperature. Also remind them to avoid touching any tube openings, pipette tips, or buffers, because molecules from their skin can degrade the restriction enzymes and DNA samples.

If time permits, have students practice loading sugar-saturated food-coloring dyes into

Objectives
- ▶ Model the forensic analysis of evidence from a crime scene.
- ▶ Use restriction enzymes, PCR, and gel electrophoresis to manipulate DNA samples.
- ▶ Compare DNA fingerprints to match identical DNA samples.

Materials
- lab apron, safety goggles, and disposable gloves
- marker, permanent, waterproof
- microcentrifuge tubes (5)
- micropipettes, sterile, disposable (25)
- DNA samples (5)
- restriction enzyme buffer
- restriction enzyme
- incubator or hot water bath
- ice, crushed
- cup, plastic-foam
- gel, agarose, precast for electrophoresis chamber
- electrophoresis chamber with power supply and wires
- running buffer
- loading dye
- bag, plastic, resealable
- DNA staining solution
- tray for staining gel
- water, distilled
- paper, white, or light table

Safety

DNA Fingerprint Analysis

Each person's DNA is unique. This fact can be used to match crime suspects to DNA samples taken from crime scenes. *DNA fingerprints* can be made by using restriction enzymes and gel electrophoresis to reveal unique patterns in each individual's DNA.

Procedure

Cut DNA with Restriction Enzyme

❶ Read all procedures, and prepare to collect your data. Label each microcentrifuge tube with a code for each DNA sample provided. For example, label one tube "C" for "crime scene sample" and the remaining tubes "S1" to "S4," one for each suspect.

❷ 🔺 ◈ ◈ Wear a lab apron, safety goggles, and gloves during all parts of this lab.

❸ ◈ CAUTION: **Never taste chemicals or allow them to contact your skin.** Using a clean pipette each time, transfer 10 µL of each DNA sample to the microcentrifuge tube that has the matching label.

❹ Using a clean pipette each time, transfer 2 µL of restriction enzyme buffer to each of the tubes.

❺ Using a clean pipette each time, transfer 2 µL of restriction enzyme to each of the tubes. Close all of the tubes. Gently flick the bottom of each tube to mix the DNA and reagents.

❻ ◈ CAUTION: **Use caution when working with heating devices.** Transfer the tubes to the incubator or water bath set at 37 °C. Let the samples incubate for one hour.

❼ Stand the tubes in crushed ice in the plastic-foam cup.

❽ If you need to pause this lab at this point, store the cup at 4 °C.

Separate Fragments by Gel Electrophoresis

❾ Place the precast gel on the level surface of the electrophoresis chamber. The wells in the gel should be closest to the black, or negative, electrode. Keep the gel level and flat at all times.

❿ Fill the chamber with enough buffer to barely cover the gel. Do not pour the buffer directly onto the gel. Sketch a diagram of your gel in your lab notebook, as the sample diagram shows.

⓫ Using a clean pipette each time, transfer 2 µL of loading dye to each of the tubes. Gently flick the tubes to mix the contents.

⓬ Using a clean pipette, load the crime scene DNA into the well for Lane 1 of your gel. Be careful not to overflow or puncture the well.

⓭ Repeat step 12 for the remaining DNA samples and gel lanes. End with the DNA from Suspect 4. Use a clean pipette for each transfer.

agarose wells to improve their loading technique and to reduce their risk of puncturing the wells. This could be done the day before, at which time students could also make their own agarose gels for the experiment.

Draw a large microfuge tube on the board, and show how to dispense the reagents along the inside of the tube to eliminate contamination. Also demonstrate how to gently flick a closed tube, twice on the bottom, to create a mixing vortex.

Have students use the inner wells to load DNA, to prevent an "eddy effect." More advanced students should load *HindIII* in an outer lane, because the fragments from this digest serve as a standard.

⑭ ◆ **CAUTION: Use caution when working with electrical equipment; use only as directed by your teacher.** Make sure that everything outside the chamber is dry before proceeding. Attach the power connectors to the chamber and power supply as directed by your teacher. Set the power supply to the voltage determined by your teacher, and turn on the power supply.

⑮ Allow the gel to run undisturbed for the time directed by your teacher. Observe the gel periodically, and stop the process when the dye front is about 3 cm away from the end of the gel. At that point, turn off the power supply. Then, disconnect the power connectors from the power supply and chamber.

⑯ ◆ **CAUTION: Dispose of all waste materials as directed by your teacher.** Carefully remove the casting tray from the chamber. Pour off the running buffer according to your teacher's instructions.

⑰ If you need to pause this lab at this point, carefully slide the gel into a resealable bag. Add 2 mL running buffer, seal the bag, and store the bag in a refrigerator. Remember to keep the gel flat.

View Separated DNA Fragments

⑱ Gently slide the gel onto the staining tray. Pour enough stain into the tray to barely cover the gel. Do not pour the stain directly onto the gel. Let the gel sit for at least 30 min.

⑲ Carefully pour off the stain as directed by your teacher.

⑳ Gently pour distilled water into the tray to cover the gel. Do not pour the water directly onto the gel. After 5 min, carefully pour off the water as directed by your teacher.

㉑ Repeat step 20 until bands are clearly visible on the gel.

㉒ Gently transfer the gel to a white sheet of paper or to a light table. Sketch and describe your observations in your lab notebook.

㉓ ◆ ◆ Clean up your lab materials according to your teacher's instructions. Wash your hands before leaving the lab.

Analyze and Conclude

1. **SCIENTIFIC METHODS** **Organizing Data** Organize your data into a table. How many different fragment sizes resulted from the treatment of each DNA sample?

2. **Analyzing Data** Identify any bands of fragments that are the same size among any of the samples. Mark these bands on your sketch.

3. **Forming Conclusions** Use this evidence to determine which suspect most likely committed the crime. Explain your answer.

4. **SCIENTIFIC METHODS** **Evaluating Methods** Do these results provide enough evidence to convict the suspect? Explain your answer.

Loading the gel

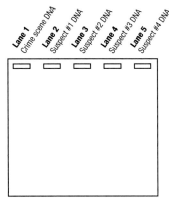

Sample gel diagram

(Lane labels: Lane 1 Crime scene DNA, Lane 2 Suspect #1 DNA, Lane 3 Suspect #2 DNA, Lane 4 Suspect #3 DNA, Lane 5 Suspect #4 DNA)

Extension

5. **Applying Concepts** Some bands appeared in the same position in several lanes. Propose an explanation for this result.

6. **Predicting Results** How might the results have been affected if a different restriction enzyme had been used? Explain your answer.

Answers to Analyze and Conclude

1. Sample data table:

DNA Sample	Number of Fragments
Standard (if used)	6
Crime scene	9
Suspect 1	8
Suspect 2	7
Suspect 3	9
Suspect 4	9

2. Check that students have marked their sketches as directed. Several of the samples will have some matching bands formed by fragments of the same size (thus, in the same horizontal position).

3. Sample answer: Suspect 3 most likely committed the crime. The bands in suspect 3's lane were identical to the bands formed by DNA from the crime scene.

4. No, because this is a single line of evidence and may be the result of a coincidence

Answers to Extensions

5. There is low variability in these regions of human DNA.

6. A different restriction enzyme would produce different-sized fragments, but since it would be used for both the crime scene DNA and suspects' DNA, there would still be bands that match.

Follow the directions provided for your materials for time of incubation. Remove the microfuge tubes and freeze them overnight. Remove them from freezer 30 minutes before class. If time permits for the students to monitor the electrophoresis process, make sure they understand that the band they see migrating is the loading dye, which is used as a marker.

Stain gels for thirty minutes; destain overnight.

For analysis, use a piece of transparency film over the white paper if no light box is available.

Key Resources

 Holt Lab Generator

 Lab Datasheet (Levels A, B, C)

 Holt Science Biology Video Labs

 Virtual Investigations

Chapter 15

Chapter 15 Summary

go.hrw.com
SUPER SUMMARY
Keyword: HX8GTCS

Reteaching Key Ideas

Human Genome Project Have students describe the HGP and give applications for the information provided by this project. Make sure they understand the scope of the project. Ask them to identify some concerns raised and how these are being addressed. **LS** Logical

Cloning and Stem Cells Ask students to explain the difference between cloning and stem cell culture techniques and to identify the purpose and the ethical issues of each technique. Have students provide other examples of how gene technologies are being used with plants. **LS** Verbal

Recombinant Products Ask students to explain how to make a recombinant product, such as insulin. Make sure students understand the use of PCR, Southern blotting, and gene sequencing. **LS** Verbal

Key Ideas	Key Terms
1 The Human Genome › The sequencing of the human genome has advanced the study of human biology yet created new questions › Genomics and gene technologies have many applications in human healthcare and society. › Many important questions about the human genome remain to be investigated or decided.	genomics (345) microarray (346) DNA fingerprint (347)
2 Gene Technologies in Our Lives › Today, gene technologies are widely applied to study organisms in new ways, to alter organisms for human use, and to improve human lives. › Cloning and stem cell techniques are used in research on animal development and have potential for treating certain diseases. › Ethical issues can be raised for every use of gene technologies.	genetic engineering (350) recombinant DNA (350) clone (352) stem cell (353)
3 Gene Technologies in Detail › The basic tools of DNA manipulation rely on the chemical nature of genetic material and are adapted from natural processes discovered in cells. These tools include restriction enzymes, polymorphisms, gel electrophoresis, denaturation, and hybridization. › The major methods for working with genes use some combination of the basic tools of cellular machinery. These methods include PCR, blotting, DNA sequencing, and gene recombination. › One can explore and map a genome at many levels, including species, individual, chromosome, gene, or nucleotide. Genomic bioinformatics starts with the mapping and assembly of the many parts of each genome.	restriction enzyme (355) DNA polymorphisms (356) electrophoresis (356) polymerase chain reaction (PCR) (357) DNA sequencing (359) bioinformatics (361) genome mapping (362) genetic library (363)

Regents Exam Practice

PART A: Answer all questions in this part.

Directions: For each statement or question, write on your separate answer sheet the number of the word or expression that best completes the statement or answers the question.

1 Steps in a preproductive process used to produce a sheep with certain traits are listed below. Which sheep would be most genetically similar to sheep D?

Step 1: The nucleus was removed from an unfertilized egg taken from sheep *A*;

Step 2: The nucleus of a body cell taken from sheep *B* was then inserted into this unfertilized egg from sheep *A*;

Step 3: The resulting cell was then implanted into the uterus of sheep *C*;

Step 4: Sheep *C* gave birth to sheep *D*.

(1) sheep A, only   (3) both sheep A and B
(2) sheep B, only   (4) both sheep A and C

2 Which transplant method would prevent the rejection of tissue after an organ transplant?

(1) using organs cloned from the cells of the patient
(2) using organs produced by genetic engineering to get rid of all proteins in the donated organs
(3) using organs only from pigs or monkeys
(4) using an organ donated by a close relative because the proteins will always be identical to those of the recipient

3 People with cystic fibrosis inherit defective genetic information and cannot produce normal CFTR proteins. Scientists have used gene therapy to insert normal DNA segments that code for the missing CFTR protein into the lung cells of people with cystic fibrosis. Which statement does not describe a result of this therapy?

(1) Altered lung cells can produce the normal CFTR protein.
(2) Altered lung cells can divide to produce other lung cells with the normal CFTR gene.
(3) The normal CFTR gene may be expressed in altered lung cells.
(4) Offspring of someone with altered lung cells will inherit the normal CFTR gene.

4 The diagram below represents a common laboratory technique in molecular genetics. One common use of this technology is the

(1) production of a human embryo to aid women who are unable to have children
(2) change of single-celled organisms to multicellular organisms.
(3) introduction of a toxic substance to kill bacterial cells.
(4) production of hormones or enzymes to replace missing human body chemicals.

5 A product of genetic engineering technology is represented below. Which substance was needed to join the insulin gene to the bacterial DNA as shown?

(1) a specific carbohydrate
(2) a specific enzyme
(3) hormones
(4) antibodies

6 Researchers Cohn and Boyer transferred a gene from an African clawed frog into a bacterium. To accomplish this, these scientists had to use

(1) enzymes to cut out and insert the gene.
(2) hereditary information located in amino acids.
(3) radiation to increase the gene mutation rate of the bacterial cells.
(4) cancer cells to promote rapid cell division.

PART A

1. **(2)** Since the genetic material was removed from the cell of sheep A, it's genetic information is not carried in Sheep D. Sheep C allowed for the development of Sheep D, but it did not contribute genetic information to Sheep D. *(#14, June 2006 Regents Exam)*

2. **(1)** The choice about relatives is incorrect as relatives may share only a percentage of genes with the recipient. The choice about pigs and monkeys is untrue. The choice about genetic engineered organs is not the best choice as the organ may still be rejected due to other incompatibilities. *(#21, January 2006 Regents Exam)*

3. **(4)** People who receive gene therapy to treat cystic fibrosis cannot pass on the normal CFTR gene to offspring, because the normal CFTR gene was inserted into lung cells, not sex cells. *(#12, August 2003 Regents Exam)*

4. **(4)** Recombinant DNA plasmids that carry human genes are not used to make human embryos or to change one organism into another one. They are also not used to kill bacterial cells. *(#08, January 2006 Regents Exam)*

5. **(2)** Antibodies, hormones, and carbohydrates do not allow genes to be fused together. Specific enzymes do cut and seal genes together, though. *(#08, June 2005 Regents Exam)*

6. **(1)** Enzymes are used to remove genes from DNA (not amino acids) and to insert them into the DNA of another organism. Radiation or cancer cells are not used in this process. *(#13, August 2005 Regents Exam)*

Regents Exam Practice Correlations

1.1.1c 14	**4.2.2e** 4, 11, 13, 18
4.2.2b 9, 12	**4.4.1b** 1, 7, 10
4.2.2c 5, 6, 8, 16, 17	**4.5.2g** 2
4.2.2d 3	

7. (2) Cloning an organism involves producing offspring organisms from a parent organism by asexual means. This results in the offspring being genetically identical to the parent. (*#01, June 2004 Regents Exam*)

8. (2) Hormones are not the products of amino acids. Crossing two different species of bacteria would not cause the bacteria to the produce a human hormone. Amino acids are not present on DNA. For a bacteruim to produce a human hormone, the gene for that hormone would first have to be placed into the bacterial genome. (*#12, January 2004 Regents Exam*)

9. (1) DNA sequencing and cloning involve analyzing and manipulating the genome of an organism. Such a process is not described in the question. The tomatoes are not harvested, instead the pollen is transferred by artificial means. This process is known as artificial selection. (*#10, January 2004 Regents Exam*)

10. (3) The question describes the process of artificial selection or selective breeding, not natural selection. Plant hormone therapy would not increase the speed of obtaining additional apple trees, it would instead improve the growth and productivity of existing trees. Propagating the apple trees is the easiest and quickest way to grow additional, identical apple trees. Plant propagation is a form of asexual reproduction. (*#25, August 2004 Regents Exam*)

11. (2) The human DNA first needs to be spliced into the tobacco plant DNA before any other action is taken. The growing of and specific selection of antibody-producing plants are steps that are taken after the human DNA has been placed into the plant DNA. (*#13, August 2004 Regents Exam*)

12. (4) The gene confers resistance to the weedkiller glyphosate, therefore the plants with the resistance gene will express this gene while growing and will not be affected by the weedkiller. (*#12, August 2004 Regents Exam*)

7 Cloning an individual usually produces organisms that

(1) contain dangerous mutations.
(2) contain identical genes.
(3) are identical in appearance and behavior.
(4) produce enzymes different from the parent.

8 The production of certain human hormones by genetically engineered bacteria results from

(1) inserting a specific group of amino acids into the bacteria.
(2) combining a portion of human DNA with bacterial DNA and inserting this into bacteria.
(3) crossing two different species of bacteria.
(4) deleting a specific amino acid from human DNA and inserting it into bacterial DNA.

9 To produce large tomatoes that are resistant to cracking and splitting, some seed companies use the pollen from one variety of tomato plant to fertilize a different variety of tomato plant. This process is an example of

(1) selective breeding.
(2) DNA sequencing.
(3) direct harvesting.
(4) cloning.

10 A variation causes the production of an improved variety of apple. What is the best method to use to obtain additional apple trees of this variety in the shortest period of time?

(1) selective breeding
(2) natural selection
(3) asexual reproduction
(4) hormone therapy

11 A biotechnology firm has produced tobacco plants that synthesize human antibodies that prevent bacterial diseases. One of the first steps in the production of these plants required

(1) using natural selection to increase the survival of antibody-producing tobacco plants.
(2) inserting human DNA segments into the cells of tobacco plants.
(3) using selective breeding to increase the number of antibody genes in tobacco plants.
(4) growing tobacco plants in soil containing a specific fertilizer.

12 A gene that codes for resistance to glyphosate, a biodegradable weedkiller, has been inserted into certain plants. As a result, these plants will be more likely to

(1) produce chemicals that kill weeds growing near them.
(2) die when exposed to glyphosate.
(3) convert glyphosate into fertilizer.
(4) survive when glyphosate is applied to them.

13 Which statement best describes human insulin that is produced by genetically engineered bacteria?

(1) This insulin will not function normally in humans because it is produced by bacteria.
(2) This insulin is produced as a result of human insulin being inserted into bacteria cells.
(3) This insulin is produced as a result of exposing bacteria cells to radiation, which produces a mutation.
(4) This insulin may have fewer side effects than the insulin previously extracted from the pancreas of other animals.

14 A great deal of information can now be obtained about the future health of people by examining the genetic makeup of their cells. There are concerns that this information could be used to deny an individual health insurance or employment. These concerns best illustrate that

(1) scientific explanations depend upon evidence collected from a single source.
(2) scientific inquiry involves the collection of information from a large number of sources.
(3) acquiring too much knowledge in human genetics will discourage future research in that area.
(4) while science provides knowledge, values are essential to making ethical decisions using this knowledge.

15 What do linkage mapping methods identify?

(1) only genes that are inherited together
(2) the exact nucleotide sequence of a chromosome
(3) the relative position of genes along a chromosome
(4) the exact number of base pairs between specific genes

13. (4) To produce insulin, scientists transfer a human insulin gene into genetically engineered bacteria. The insulin created is human insulin, so it is unlikely to be attacked by the immune system as a foreign invader. (*#19, June 2003 Regents Exam*)

14. (4) As scientific knowledge is gathered from many sources, scientists and policymakers work to determine how to ethically apply this knowledge. (*#04, June 2003 Regents Exam*)

15. (3)

16 The diagrams below represent some steps in a procedure used in biotechnology. Letters X and Y represent the

Bacterial DNA

Foreign DNA

(1) hormones that stimulate the replication of bacterial DNA.
(2) biochemical catalysts involved in the insertion of genes into other organisms.
(3) hormones that trigger rapid mutation of genetic information.
(4) gases needed to produce the energy required for gene manipulation.

PART D

17 Gel electrophoresis is used to separate DNA fragments on the basis of their

(1) size.
(2) color.
(3) functions.
(4) chromosomes.

Base your answers to question 18 on the information and diagram below and on your knowledge of biology.

The DNA of three different species of birds was analyzed to help determine if there is an evolutionary relationship between these species. The diagram shows the results of this analysis.

18 Identify the technique normally used to separate the DNA fragments to produce the patterns shown in the diagram.

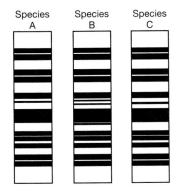

16. (2) Biochemical catalysts, or enzymes, are used to remove genes from one organism and insert it into a different organism. The genetically modified organism is then allowed to reproduce. Hormones or gases are not used in this process. (*#12, January 2003 Regents Exam*)

PART D

17. (1) The larger the molecule of DNA the slower it moves through the polyacrylamide gel matrix when an electric charge is applied to the gel. Thus a large number of fragments of different sizes can be sorted on a gel. (*#63, June 2004 Regents Exam*)

18. Allow 1 credit for identifying the technique normally used to separate the DNA fragments to produce the patterns shown in the diagram. Acceptable responses include but are not limited to: electrophoresis; gel electrophoresis. (*#62, August 2006 Regents Exam*)

UNIT 5 Evolution

16 Evolutionary Theory

17 Population Genetics and Speciation

18 Classification

19 History of Life on Earth

The Living Environment

Standard 1 Students will use mathematical analysis, scientific inquiry, and engineering design, as appropriate, to pose questions, seek answers, and develop solutions.

   Key Idea 1 The central purpose of scientific inquiry is to develop explanations of natural phenomena in a continuing and creative process.

   Key Idea 2 Beyond the use of reasoning and consensus, scientific inquiry involves the testing of proposed explanations involving the use of conventional techniques and procedures and usually requiring considerable ingenuity.

Standard 4 Students will understand and apply scientific concepts, principles, and theories pertaining to the physical setting and living environment and recognize the historical development of ideas in science.

   Key Idea 2 Organisms inherit genetic information in a variety of ways that result in continuity of structure and function between parents and offspring.

   Key Idea 3 Individual organisms and species change over time

   Key Idea 4 The continuity of life is sustained through reproduction and development.

   Key Idea 6 Plants and animals depend on each other and their physical environment.

Kingfisher male with courtship gift

Insect of the newly named order Mantophasmatodea

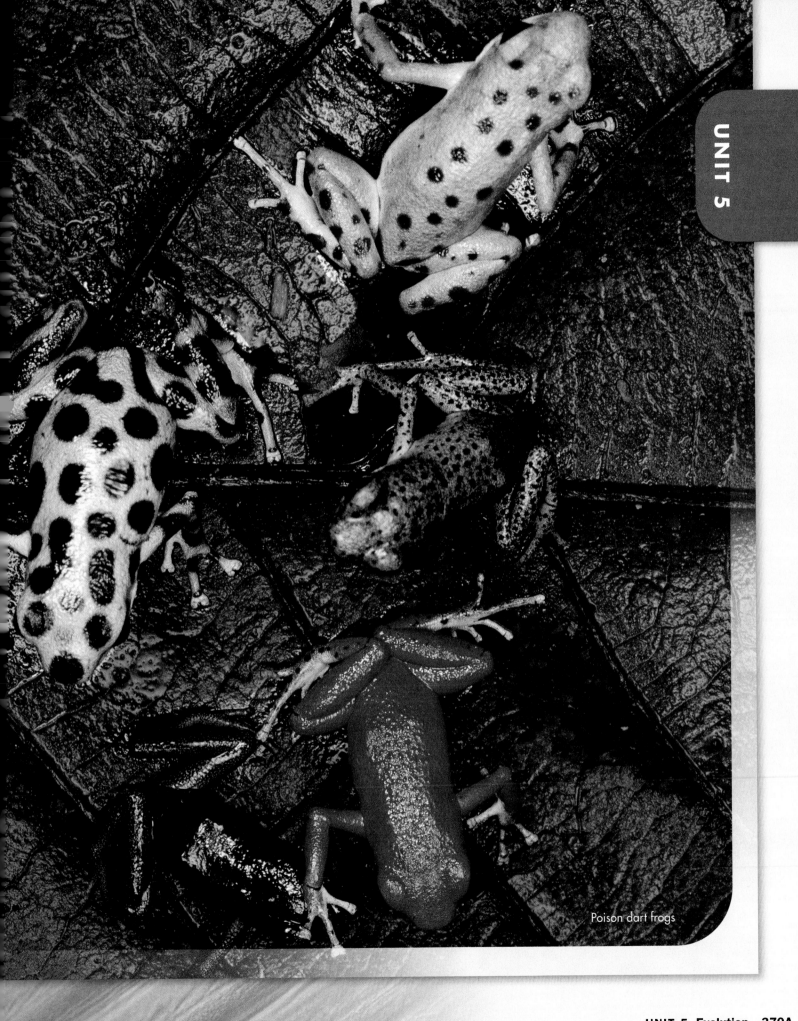

Poison dart frogs

Evolution and Life on Earth

1753

Carolus Linnaeus publishes the first of two volumes containing the classification of all known species. In doing so, Linnaeus establishes a consistent system for naming and classifying species. The system is widely used thereafter.

1859

Charles Darwin suggests that natural selection is the mechanism of evolution. Within months, public debates regarding the truth and significance of his theory ensue.

Galápagos tortoises

1907

In his book, *Plant Breeding,* Hugo de Vries, Dutch botanist, joins Mendel's laws of heredity with the newer theory of mutation. De Vries asserts that inheritable mutations are the mechanism by which species change and new species form.

1960

Mary and Jonathan Leakey discover fossil bones of a human ancestor, *Homo habilis,* in Olduvai Gorge, Tanzania.

Mary Leakey, paleoanthropologist

1974

Donald Johansen discovers a fossilized skeleton of one of the first hominids, *Australopithecus afarensis.* This specimen was nicknamed "Lucy."

Skull of *A. afarensis*

1980

Walter and Luis Alvarez, Frank Asaro, and Helen Michel publish a paper providing evidence that 65 million years ago, an asteroid collided with Earth and caused severe environmental changes. The changes may have led to the extinction of the majority of species that lived during that time.

1994

Reinhardt Kristensen and Peter Funch discover a tiny animal living on the lips of lobsters. They name the new species *Symbion pandora.* This species is so different from other animals that scientists classify it within a new phylum, Cycliophora, within kingdom Animalia.

2006

A team of biologists announces a study of Camiguin Island, the smallest island of the Philippines. They find 54 species of birds and 24 of species of mammals.

As-yet-unnamed parrot species

Beetles—one of the most diverse groups of animals on Earth

BIOLOGY CAREER

Museum Curator
Rob DeSalle

Rob DeSalle is a curator in the Division of Invertebrate Zoology at the American Museum of Natural History in New York City. He is an adjunct professor at Columbia University and City University of New York and is a Distinguished Research Professor at New York University. His current research focuses on molecular evolution in various organisms, including pathogenic bacteria and insects.

DeSalle enjoys being a scientist because he can investigate the diversity of life every day. He also enjoys the opportunity to serve as a mentor to students. Most of all, he enjoys the thrill of discovering something that no one else on the planet has found.

He considers his most significant accomplishment in science to be his work communicating scientific ideas through his writing and museum exhibitions.

Besides his work, DeSalle loves baseball and is a passionate fan of the Chicago Cubs.

Fossil and eggs of dinosaur called *oviraptor*

Evolutionary Theory

	Standards	Teach Key Ideas

CHAPTER OPENER, pp. 372–373   15 min.

The Living Environment

SECTION 1 Developing a Theory, pp. 375–379   30 min.

〉 A Theory to Explain Change over Time
〉 Darwin's Ideas from Experience
〉 Darwin's Ideas from Others

Standards: 1.1.1a, 1.1.4a, 4.2.2a, 4.3.1a

Teach Key Ideas:
- **Bellringer Transparency**
- **Transparencies** D10 Darwin's Finches
- **Visual Concepts** Darwin's Theories • Lamarck's Theory of Evolution • Population

---

SECTION 2 Applying Darwin's Ideas, pp. 380–385   120 min.

〉 Evolution by Natural Selection
〉 What Darwin Explained
〉 Evaluating Darwin's Ideas

Standards: 4.3.1e, 4.3.1f, 4.3.1g, 4.3.1h, 4.3.1I

Teach Key Ideas:
- **Bellringer Transparency**
- **Transparencies** D13 Evidence of Whale Evolution • D14 Forelimbs of Vertebrates • D16 Hemoglobin Comparison
- **Visual Concepts** Natural Selection • Adaption • Biology • Similarities in Macromolecules • Homologous Feature • Similarities in Embryology

---

SECTION 3 Beyond Darwinian Theory, pp. 386–391   30 min.

〉 Darwin's Theory Updated
〉 Studying Evolution at All Scales

Standards: 4.3.1b, 4.3.1f, 4.3.1g, 4.3.1k

Teach Key Ideas:
- **Bellringer Transparency**
- **Visual Concepts** Gradualism • Comparing Punctuated Equilibrium and Gradualism • Reproductive Isolation

See also PowerPoint® Resources

Chapter Review and Assessment Resources

SE Super Summary, p. 392
SE Regents Exam Practice, p. 393
Regents Review Guide
Review Resources
Chapter Tests A and B
Holt Online Assessment
Regents Question Banks on Teacher's One-Stop Planner

CHAPTER
Fast Track   *Thorough instruction will require the times shown.*

Basic Learners

TE Evolution Examples, p. 376
TE Anatomical Comparisons, p. 382
TE Organizing Concepts, p. 383
TE What Can Evolve?, p. 387
Directed Reading Worksheets*
Active Reading Worksheets*
Lab Manuals, Level A*
Study Guide*■
Note-taking Workbook*
Special Needs Activities and Modified Tests*

Advanced Learners

TE Lamarckian Inheritance, p. 378
TE What Would You Say?, p. 381
TE Cytochrome c Evidence, p. 384
Critical Thinking Worksheets*
Concept Mapping Worksheets*
Science Skills Worksheets*
Lab Datasheets, Level C*

All resources listed below are also available on the Teacher's One-Stop Planner.

Why It Matters	Hands-On	Skills Development	Assessment
Build student motivation with resources about high-interest applications.	**SE Inquiry Lab** Scientific Inference, p. 373*■	**TE Reading Toolbox** Assessing Prior Knowledge, p. 372 **SE Reading Toolbox**, p. 374	
TE Demonstration They're All Related, p. 375 **TE How the Tortoise Got Its Name,** p. 376 **SE Breeding,** p. 377	**SE Quick Lab** Two Kinds of Growth, p. 378*■	**SE Reading Toolbox** Key-Term Fold, p. 376 **TE Reading Toolbox** Key-Term Fold, p. 376	**SE Section Review** **TE Formative Assessment** Spanish Assessment*■ ▭ Section Quiz ■
TE Extinct Organisms, p. 382	**SE Skills Practice Lab** Natural Selection Simulation, p. 390*■ ▭ **Quick Lab** Comparing Limb Structure and Function* ▭ **Skills Practice Lab** Melanism in Insects*	**SE Reading Toolbox** Hypothesis or Theory, p. 381 **TE Reading Toolbox** Hypothesis or Theory, p. 381 **TE Reading Toolbox** Visual Literacy, p. 383 **TE Reading Toolbox** Visual Literacy, p. 384	**SE Section Review** **TE Formative Assessment** Spanish Assessment*■ ▭ Section Quiz ■
TE Antibiotic-Resistant Bacteria, p. 386	**SE Quick Lab** Selection Model, p. 387*■	**SE Reading Toolbox** Taking Notes, p. 389 **TE Reading Toolbox** Taking Notes, p. 389	**SE Section Review** **TE Formative Assessment** Spanish Assessment*■ ▭ Section Quiz ■

See also Lab Generator

See also Holt Online Assessment Resources

Resources for Differentiated Instruction

English Learners
TE Steps in Darwin's Theory, p. 380
▭ Directed Reading Worksheets*
▭ Active Reading Worksheets*
▭ Lab Manuals, Level A*
▯ Study Guide*■
▯ Note-taking Workbook*
▯ Multilingual Glossary

Struggling Readers
TE Everyday Words, p. 387
TE Key-Term Fold, p. 388
▭ Directed Reading Worksheets*
▭ Active Reading Worksheets*
▭ Lab Manuals, Level A*
▯ Study Guide*
▯ Note-taking Workbook*
▯ Special Needs Activities and Modified Tests*

Special Education Students
TE Darwin's Theory, p. 381
▭ Directed Reading Worksheets*
▭ Active Reading Worksheets*
▭ Lab Manuals, Level A*
▯ Study Guide*■
▯ Note-taking Workbook*
▯ Special Needs Activities and Modified Tests*

Alternative Assessment
TE Evidence Brochure, p. 384
▭ Science Skills Worksheets*
▭ Section Quizzes*■
▯ Chapter Tests A, B, and C*■

Chapter 16

Evolutionary Theory

Overview

The purpose of this chapter is to introduce scientific ideas about evolution and natural selection. Students will develop an understanding of the basic elements of evolutionary theory and will evaluate supporting evidence from fossils, molecules, anatomy, and embryonic development.

READING TOOLBOX

Assessing Prior Knowledge Students should understand the following concepts:
• cellular nature of life
• basic genetics concepts

Visual Literacy Have students study the photographs of the pygmy seahorse. Ask students to think of the advantages of looking like coral. (Seahorses that look like coral may avoid being eaten by predators.) Ask students to predict what would happen to this seahorse's chances of survival if it were living in an environment it did not closely resemble. (It would not blend in as well and would be more likely to be captured by predators.)

Preview

1 Developing a Theory
A Theory to Explain Change over Time
Darwin's Ideas from Experience
Darwin's Ideas from Others

2 Applying Darwin's Ideas
Evolution by Natural Selection
What Darwin Explained
Evaluating Darwin's Ideas

3 Beyond Darwinian Theory
Darwin's Theory Updated
Studying Evolution at All Scales

Why It Matters

Modern evolutionary theory provides strong and detailed explanations for many aspects of biology, such as anatomy and behavior.

The Living Environment

Standard 1 Students will use mathematical analysis, scientific inquiry, and engineering design, as appropriate, to pose questions, seek answers, and develop solutions.
  Key Idea 1 The central purpose of scientific inquiry is to develop explanations of natural phenomena in a continuing and creative process. *Major Understandings* - 1.1a, 1.4a
  Key Idea 2 Beyond the use of reasoning and consensus, scientific inquiry involves the testing of proposed explanations involving the use of conventional techniques and procedures and usually requiring considerable ingenuity. *Major Understandings* - 2.2a
Standard 4 Students will understand and apply scientific concepts, principles, and theories pertaining to the physical setting and living environment and recognize the historical development of ideas in science.
  Key Idea 3 Individual organisms and species change over time. *Major Understandings* – 3.1a, 3.1b, 3.1e, 3.1f, 3.1g, 3.1h, 3.1k, 3.1l

This pygmy sea horse is smaller than your fingernail. It lives exclusively among certain kinds of coral in coral reefs of the western Pacific Ocean.

The pygmy sea horse looks very similar to the coral among which it lives. This camouflage is an inherited characteristic that may keep other animals from seeing the sea horse.

Several other species of pygmy sea horses live among other kinds of corals. Each species resembles the specific kind of coral among which it lives. Camouflage is a characteristic of many organisms.

Chapter Correlations   The Living Environment

Standard 1

1.1a Scientific explanations are built by combining evidence that can be observed with what people already know about the world.

1.4a Well-accepted theories are ones that are supported by different kinds of scientific investigations often involving the contributions of individuals from different disciplines.

2.2a For thousands of years new varieties of cultivated plants and domestic animals have resulted from selective breeding for particular traits.

Standard 4

3.1a The basic theory of biological evolution states that the Earth's present-day species developed from earlier, distinctly different species.

3.1b New inheritable characteristics can result from new combinations of existing genes or from mutations of genes in reproductive cells.

3.1e Natural selection and its evolutionary consequences provide a scientific explanation for the fossil record of ancient life-forms, as well as for the molecular and structural similarities observed among the diverse species of living organisms.

3.1f Species evolve over time. Evolution is the consequence of the interactions of (1) the potential for a species to increase its numbers, (2) the genetic variability of offspring due to mutation and recombination of genes, (3) a finite supply of the resources required for life, and (4) the ensuing selection by the environment of those offspring better able to survive...

3.1g Some characteristics give individuals an advantage over others in surviving and reproducing...

3.1h The variation of organisms within a species increases the likelihood that at least some members of the species will survive under changed environmental conditions.

Charles Darwin's theory of evolution by natural selection provides an explanation for how characteristics such as camouflage can arise over time. Darwin's theory continues to be supported and expanded by modern scientists.

Teacher's Notes Emphasize that the purpose of this activity is not to guess the exact arrangement of pasta; instead, the purpose is to experience a recurring challenge in science, which is making inferences about things that cannot be directly observed. For example, tell students that we know about the composition of the sun, yet we've never traveled there.

Materials
- petri dish
- flat noodles
- tape
- metric ruler
- ball bearing
- brown paper bag

Safety Caution Review safety rules. Remind students not to eat or taste food items used in the lab and to wash their hands after completing this activity. Food items used in the lab should be treated as potentially pathogenic and should be disposed of as such.

Answers to Analysis

1. Students should describe their inferred arrangement of the pasta and explain how they used clues such as hearing sounds and feeling the weight of the rolling ball.
2. If others replicate the activity and come to the same or similar conclusions, the inference gains support. By forming testable hypotheses, further investigations could be run to determine if the inference is valid.

InquiryLab

⏱ **15 min**

◈ ◈ ◼ 1.1.2a

Scientific Inference

Much of science is based on making inferences. Not all inferences can be supported by direct observation. Instead, many are tested by modeling, prediction, and experimentation. Doing so requires attention to detail and, sometimes, creative thinking.

Procedure

1. Break a piece of flat-noodle pasta into two smaller segments about 8 cm long and 3 cm long.
2. Erect two "walls" in the bottom of a Petri dish by securing the pasta pieces to the dish with tape.
3. Place a ball bearing in the dish.
4. Secure the lid onto the dish with tape. Keeping the dish upright, place it in a brown paper bag.
5. Exchange bags with another student. Without looking inside the bag, try to infer the arrangement of the pasta in the dish.

Analysis

1. **Describe** your inference, and explain how you formed it.
2. **Suggest** how your inference could be supported or confirmed.

3.1k Evolution does not necessitate long-term progress in some set direction. Evolutionary changes appear to be like the growth of a bush: Some branches survive from the beginning with little or no change, many die out altogether, and others branch repeatedly, sometimes giving rise to more complex organisms.

3.1l Extinction of a species occurs when the environment changes and the adaptive characteristics of a species are insufficient to allow its survival. Fossils indicate that many organisms that lived long ago are extinct. Extinction of species is common; most of the species that have lived on Earth no longer exist.

Using Words

Check that students have made their key-term folds correctly. It should include all of the terms on the Summary page of this chapter.

Using Language

1. Sample answers: theory of gravity, cell theory, "big bang" theory, atomic theory, theory of relativity
2. Sample concept map shown below.
3. Evolutionary theory describes the general trends and areas of investigation about how living things have come to change over time.

Taking Notes

1. Natural selection is the idea that the most well-adapted organisms survive and reproduce.
2. Macroevolution is the study of large scale observations representing events that have occurred over a very long time, such as the fossil record or homologous structures.
3. Microevolution is the study of small scale events that happen over a short period of time such as changes in allele frequencies through inheritance.

These reading tools can help you learn the material in this chapter. For more information on how to use these and other tools, see **Appendix: Reading and Study Skills.**

Using Words

Key-Term Fold A key-term fold is useful for studying definitions of key terms in a chapter. Each tab can contain a key term on one side and the term's definition on the other.

Your Turn Prepare a key-term fold for the key terms in this chapter. Fill it in as you read. Use it later to quiz yourself on the definitions.
1. Fold a sheet of lined notebook paper in half from left to right.
2. Using scissors, cut along every third line from the right edge of the paper to the center fold to make tabs.

Using Language

Hypothesis or Theory? In everyday language, there is little difference between a *hypothesis* and a *theory*. But in science, the meanings of these words are more distinct. A *hypothesis* is a specific, testable prediction for a limited set of conditions. A *theory* is a general explanation for a broad range of data. A theory can include hypotheses that have been tested and can also be used to generate new hypotheses. The strongest scientific theories explain the broadest range of data and incorporate many well-tested hypotheses.

Your Turn Use what you have learned about a hypothesis and a theory to answer the following questions.
1. List some scientific theories that you have heard of.
2. Make a simple concept map or Venn diagram to show the relationship between hypotheses and theories.
3. The word *theory* may also be used to describe general trends and areas of active investigation in a scientific field. In this context, what does the term *evolutionary theory* mean?

Taking Notes

Summarizing Ideas Summarizing ideas helps you condense important information. When you summarize, use your own words and keep your sentences short. Focus on key ideas.

Your Turn Prepare to take notes for this chapter. Use this table as an example. As you read, be sure to summarize the following concepts:
1. natural selection
2. macroevolution
3. microevolution

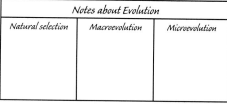

Notes about Evolution		
Natural selection	Macroevolution	Microevolution

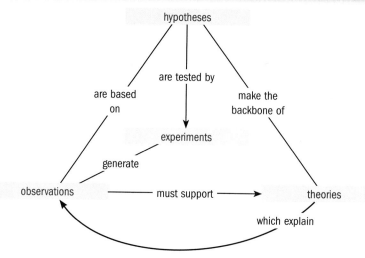

Developing a Theory

Key Ideas	Key Terms	Why It Matters
❯ Why is evolutionary theory associated with Charles Darwin? ❯ How was Darwin influenced by his personal experiences? ❯ How was Darwin influenced by the ideas of others?	evolution artificial selection	Many aspects of biology are best explained by evolutionary theory.

Recall that in biology, **evolution** is the process by which species may change over time. The idea that life evolves is not new. Yet for centuries, scientists lacked clear evidence that evolution happens. They also lacked a strong theory to explain how evolution happens. In 1859, Charles Darwin pulled together these missing pieces. Darwin, shown in **Figure 1,** was an English naturalist who studied the diversity of life and proposed a broad explanation for it.

A Theory to Explain Change over Time

Recall that in science, a *theory* is a broad explanation that has been scientifically tested and supported. ❯ **Modern evolutionary theory began when Darwin presented evidence that evolution happens and offered an explanation of how evolution happens.** Like most scientific theories, evolutionary theory keeps developing and expanding. Many scientists since Darwin have tested and added to his ideas. Most of Darwin's ideas, including his main theory, remain scientifically supported.

❯ **Reading Check** *What does* evolution *mean in biology? (See the Appendix for answers to Reading Checks.)*

 The Living Environment

Standard 1

1.1a Scientific explanations are built by combining evidence that can be observed with what people already know about the world.

1.4a Well-accepted theories are ones that are supported by different kinds of scientific investigations often involving the contributions of individuals from different disciplines.

Standard 4

2.2a For thousands of years new varieties of cultivated plants and domestic animals have resulted from selective breeding for particular traits.

3.1a The basic theory of biological evolution states that the Earth's present-day species developed from earlier, distinctly different species.

evolution the process of change by which new species develop from preexisting species over time

NORTH AMERICA

EUROPE

ATLANTIC OCEAN

PACIFIC OCEAN

Galápagos Islands

AFRICA

SOUTH AMERICA

INDIAN OCEAN

AUSTRALIA

HMS *Beagle*

Figure 1 Charles Darwin took many years to publish his theory of evolution by natural selection. Many of his ideas were first inspired by his 1831 global voyage on a ship called the *Beagle.*

Key Resources

 Transparencies
D10 Darwin's Finches

 Visual Concepts
Darwin's Theories
Lamarck's Theory of Evolution
Population

❯ Focus

This section describes Darwin's experiences as a naturalist, how he concluded that evolution occurs, how he developed an explanation for the mechanism of evolution, and how his theory has been modified by other scientists with regard to formation of new species.

🔊 Bellringer

Use the Bellringer transparency to prepare students for this section.

❯ Teach

[Demonstration]

They're All Related! Bring to class as many of the following food crops as possible: cabbage, brussels sprouts, broccoli, cauliflower, kale, and kohlrabi. Try to get a wild mustard plant or a picture of one. Point out the parts of the plants that are eaten. Tell students that all of these different varieties have been bred from the same species, *Brassica oleracea.* Ask students how these varieties of the same species could look so different. (There is so much variation in the genes of this species.) Do you think is it possible for these varieties to become separate species? (Accept all reasonable responses.) **LS Visual**

Section Correlations	
1.1.1a	4.2.2a
1.1.4a	4.3.1a

Teaching Key Ideas

Finch Adaptation Have students examine **Figure 2** and describe the features of the finches' bills. Have students describe how each finch's bill is adapted to the bird's diet. (For example, the large ground finch's bill is thick and heavy, which enables these birds to crack open large seeds.) **LS** Visual

READING TOOLBOX

Key-Term Fold Check that students have the following terms, with similar definitions, in their key-term folds: **evolution** changes in species over time; **artificial selection** breeding organisms to produce offspring with specific traits **LS** Visual

Answers to Caption Questions

Figure 2: that all of the Galápagos finch species descended from a single South American finch population

READING TOOLBOX

Key-Term Fold On the back half of your key-term fold, under each flap, write your own definition for the key terms in this section.

artificial selection the human practice of breeding animals or plants that have certain desired traits

Figure 2 Darwin eventually learned that all Galápagos finch species were similar to each other and to one particular South American finch. ❯ **What explanation did Darwin propose for this similarity?**

Darwin's Ideas from Experience

In Darwin's time, most people did not think that living things had changed over time. In fact, many doubted that Earth itself had ever changed. But Darwin saw evidence of gradual change. ❯ **Darwin's experiences provided him with evidence of evolution at work.**

The Voyage of the _Beagle_ Darwin's first evidence was gathered during a global voyage on a ship called the _Beagle_. As part of his work as a naturalist, Darwin collected natural objects from each place that he visited. For example, in South America, he collected fossils of giant, extinct armadillos. Darwin noticed that these fossils were similar, but not identical, to the living armadillos in the area.

Darwin also visited the Galápagos Islands in the Pacific Ocean. There, he collected several different species of birds called _finches_. Each of the finches are very similar, but differences can be seen in the size and shape of the bill (or beak), such as those shown in **Figure 2**. Each finch has a bill that seems suited to the finch's usual food.

Darwin noticed that many of the islands' plants and animals were similar, but not identical, to the plants and animals he saw in South America. Later, Darwin proposed that the Galápagos species had descended from species that came from South America. For example, he suggested that all of the finch species descended from one ancestral finch species that migrated from South America. Then, the descendant finches were modified over time as different groups survived by eating different types of food. Darwin called such change _descent with modification_. This idea was a key part of his theory.

Years of Reflection After returning from his voyage at the age of 27, Darwin spent years studying his data. He also continued studying many sciences. As he studied, his confidence grew stronger that evolution must happen. But Darwin did not report his ideas about evolution until much later. Instead, he took time to gather more data and to form a strong explanation for how evolution happens.

Cactus finch
eats insects and cactus

Warbler finch
eats small insects

Large ground finch
eats large seeds

Why It Matters

How the Tortoise Got Its Name Tell students that the Galápagos Islands were named for the large tortoises that inhabit this archipelago. When Spanish explorers arrived, they found so many giant tortoises they called the islands "Galápagos," Spanish for tortoises. Galápagos tortoises metabolize fat stored in their tissues and can survive without food or water for long periods of time. Because of this characteristic, the Spanish sailors collected and stored the tortoises for a convenient source of fresh meat. There were an estimated 250,000 tortoises. Approximately 15,000 remain today. **LS** Interpersonal

Differentiated Instruction

Basic Learners

Evolution Examples Ask students what the word _evolution_ means. (change over time) Ask students to brainstorm examples of groups of animals or plants that have changed over time. (They are likely to mention dinosaurs, birds, or mammals.) Direct them to think about plant evolution examples from agriculture. (trees, as opposed to mosses and ferns; modern hardy or pest-resistant varieties, and hybrid forms) **LS** Verbal

Breeding and Selection Darwin took interest in the practice of breeding, especially the breeding of exotic pigeons. He bred pigeons himself and studied the work of those who bred other kinds of animals and plants, such as dogs, orchids, and food crops. Eventually, Darwin gained a new insight: breeders take advantage of natural variation in traits within a species. If a trait can be inherited, breeders can produce more individuals that have the trait. Breeders simply select individuals that have desireable traits to be the parents of each new generation. Darwin called this process **artificial selection** because the selection is done by humans and not by natural causes.

❯ **Reading Check** *When did Darwin first see evidence of evolution?*

ACADEMIC
VOCABULARY

insight a clear understanding of something

Why It Matters

Breeding

The power of artificial selection can be seen today in the amazing variety of pets, show animals, and agricultural food crops. For example, more than 400 breeds of dogs exist today, from tiny Chihuahuas to Great Danes. All of these breeds, including wolves, are considered part of the same species (*Canis lupus*) because most can interbreed.

Dog Diversity

People have lived with dogs—or the wolf ancestors of dogs—throughout history. Over time, people learned to selectively breed dogs by choosing certain individuals to become parents. People have selected dogs that have various kinds of physical and behavioral traits. So today, each breed of dog is known for its appearance as well as its degree of playfulness, friendliness, watchfulness, or cleverness. Some breeds are also known for certain quirks or problems.

Quick Project Visit a local pet store, and ask which breeds are most popular or most expensive. Ask why.

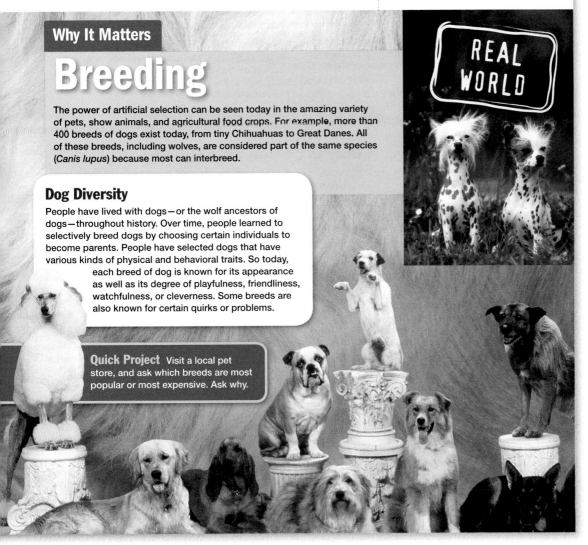

REAL WORLD

Definition of Species Be sure students understand that the ability to mate with each other is what defines a species (in sexually reproducing organisms). Ask why all dogs are the same species, but the finches on the previous page are different species. (Students may erroneously believe that a *breed* is synonymous with a *species*. Even though the finches look very similar, they are different species because they do not interbreed.) Now is a good time to reinforce the definition of population. **LS Visual**

Why It Matters

Teacher's Notes Typically, expensive breeds are rare or have highly controlled and well-documented pedigrees. Some unusual breeds have been extensivly in-bred and consequently have recessive traits that may require special care. Popular breeds generally have this status because they are reliable, friendly, and make good pets, or good guard dogs. Fads can influence the popularity of certain breeds, such as Dalmatians. The selection of a dog should fit well with one's lifestyle and environment.

Answer to Quick Project

Typically, the most expensive breeds are the ones that are rare or have strict, documented pedigrees. Breeds that result from extreme inbreeding tend to have many recessive traits and require special care. Popular breeds are often the reliable, friendly pet or guard dogs, such as Labradors, but sometimes certain breeds become a fad. Many people prefer dogs that fit well into their lifestyle.

Teacher's Notes Review the sample graphs, so students see how the shape of the line indicates linear or exponential growth.

Materials
• rice
• egg carton

Safety Caution Remind students not to taste food items and to wash their hands after this activity. Food items used should be treated as potentially pathogenic and should be disposed of as such.

Answers to Analysis
1. The graph from Step 2 should show linear growth; the graph from Step 4 should show exponential growth. Values should be as follows:
   Graph 1: 1, 2, 3, 4, 5, 6
   Graph 2: 1, 2, 4, 8, 16, 32

2. "Arithmetic" is related to the simple addition of an equal amount each time. "Geometric" is related to the multiplication of amounts each time. The second growth pattern is actually a series of powers of two (2^1, 2^2, 2^3, 2^4, etc.).

Answers to Caption Questions
Figure 3: Darwin's theory of evolution by natural selection assumed the existence of a mechanism for inheritance and variation in traits over time.

Hands-On
QuickLab

⏱ 15 min

Two Kinds of Growth

Can you visualize the difference between linear growth and exponential growth?

Procedure
1. Place **grains of rice** in the cups of an **egg carton** in the following sequence: Place one grain in the first cup. Place two grains in the second cup. Place three grains in the third cup. In each of the remaining cups, place *one more* grain of rice than in the cup before.
2. Use a line graph to graph the results of step 1.
3. Repeat step 1, but use the following sequence: Place one grain in the first cup, two in the second cup, and four in the third cup. In each remaining cup, place twice as many grains as placed in the cup before.
4. Use a line graph to graph the results of step 3.

Linear Growth
(graph: Number of organisms vs. Time — straight line)

Exponential Growth
(graph: Number of organisms vs. Time — curved line)

Analysis
1. **Match** your graphs to the graphs shown.
2. **CRITICAL THINKING** **Analyzing Terminology** Linear growth is also called *arithmetic growth,* and exponential growth is also called *geometric growth.* Propose an explanation for the use of these terms.

Darwin's Ideas from Others

In Darwin's time, most people—including scientists—believed that each species was created once and stayed the same forever. But this view could not explain fossils of organisms that no longer exist, such as dinosaurs. Some scientists tried to explain such observations by saying that species could die out but never change. Others, including Darwin's own grandfather, proposed various mechanisms to explain how species may change over time. ❯ **Darwin was influenced by ideas from the fields of natural history, economics, and geology.** The ideas of Lamarck, Malthus, Cuvier, and Lyell were especially important.

Figure 3 According to Lamarck's idea of inheritance, this baseball player's children would inherit strong arm muscles. ❯ Why was this idea important to Darwin?

Lamarckian Inheritance In 1809, the French scientist Jean Baptiste Lamarck proposed an explanation for how organisms may change over generations. Like Darwin and others, Lamarck noticed that each organism is usually well adapted to its environment. He proposed, as Darwin would later, that organisms change over time as they adapt to changing environments.

However, Lamarck had an incorrect idea about inheritance. He proposed that changes due to use or disuse of a character would be passed on to offspring. For example, he knew that a person's muscles may increase in size because of use or may decrease in size because of disuse, as shown in **Figure 3.** He believed that offspring inherited these kinds of changes. This idea was eventually disproved, but not in Darwin's time. Darwin once accepted this idea because it proposed a role for inheritance in evolution.

Differentiated Instruction

Advanced Learners/GATE

Lamarckian Inheritance Have students design a simple, hypothetical experiment to test Lamarck's theory of evolution and inheritance of acquired characteristics. They should ask questions, formulate a testable hypothesis, and suggest how they would conduct the experiment. **LS** Logical

Population Growth Another key influence on Darwin's thinking about evolution was an essay by Thomas Malthus. In 1798, this English economist observed that human populations were increasing faster than the food supply. Malthus pointed out that food supplies were increasing *linearly*. More food was being produced each year, but the amount by which the food increased was the same each year. In contrast, the number of people was increasing *exponentially*. More people were added each year than were added the year before. Malthus noted that the number of humans could not keep increasing in this way, because many people would probably die from disease, war, or famine.

Darwin simply applied Malthus's idea to all populations. Recall that a *population* is all of the individuals of the same species that live in a specific place. Darwin saw that all kinds of organisms tend to produce more offspring than can survive. So, all populations must be limited by their environments.

Geology and an Ancient Earth In Darwin's time, scientists had become interested in the study of rocks and landforms, and thus began the science of *geology*. In particular, scientists such as Georges Cuvier, James Hutton, and Charles Lyell studied fossils and rock layers, such as those shown in **Figure 4**. Cuvier argued that fossils in rock layers showed differences in species over time and that many species from the past differed from those of the present. But Cuvier did not see species as changing gradually over time. He thought that changes in the past must have occurred suddenly.

Hutton and Lyell, on the other hand, thought that geologic processes—such as those that wear away mountains and form new rocks and fossils—work gradually and constantly. Lyell carefully and thoroughly presented his ideas in a book, which Darwin read. Lyell's ideas fit well with Darwin's observations and showed that Earth's history was long enough for species to have evolved gradually.

> **Reading Check** *What belief did Darwin and Lamarck share?*

Figure 4 Layers of rock contain evidence of changes occurring over millions of years in organisms and environments on Earth. Darwin realized that such evidence supported his ideas about evolution.

www.scilinks.org
Topic: Charles Darwin
Code: HX80262

Teaching Key Ideas

Lamarkian Inheritance Lamarck theorized that when an organism uses a part of its body, that part becomes more developed as a result of its use, as shown in **Figure 3**. He reasoned that the modified part is then passed on to the organism's offspring. Tell students that if Lamarck were correct, the offspring of bodybuilders would be born with enormously developed muscles.

> Close

Formative Assessment

What term best describes the deliberate breeding of drought-resistant crops by humans?
A. adaptation (Incorrect. Adaptation is a result of natural selection.)
B. artificial selection (Correct! Desirable traits are selected by humans for growing the next generation of plants.)
C. speciation (Incorrect. Speciation occurs when a new species evolves.)
D. mutation (Incorrect. A mutation is a change in alleles from one generation to the next.)

Section 1 Review

> KEY IDEAS

1. **Describe** Darwin's relationship to modern evolutionary theory.
2. **Identify** personal experiences that contributed to Darwin's thinking about evolution.
3. **Identify** other scientists that influenced Darwin's thinking.

CRITICAL THINKING

4. **Applying Process Concepts** Darwin observed that artificial selection can produce specific traits. Suppose a farmer has a corn crop in which each ear of corn has some yellow kernels and some white kernels. Describe how the farmer could produce a variety of corn that has all white kernels.

METHODS OF SCIENCE

5. **Scientific Testing** According to Lamarck's idea of inheritance, an individual that developed an improved trait within its lifetime, especially through repeated use, could pass that trait on to its offspring. Propose a way to test the accuracy of this idea.

Answers to Section Review

1. Darwin presented evidence that evolution occurs, along with an explanation for how it occurs.
2. his travels, his years of study and reflection, and his experience and observation of artificial breeding
3. Darwin was influenced by ideas about inheritance from Lamarck, ideas about economics from Malthus, and ideas about geology from Cuvier, Hutton, and Lyell.

4. The farmer would look for ears of corn that had more white kernels than usual. The farmer would breed those plants and any corn plants from the next generation that had even more white kernels would be chosen for breeding. This process would continue until the farmer had plants that produced corn with all white kernels.
5. Test the idea by having individuals change a trait. Then, study the offspring to look for the appearance of the trait. For example, train a batch of mice to run fast and then see if all of their offspring run faster than untrained mice.

›Focus

This section provides examples of population changes that have resulted from natural selection. It also provides the evidence of evolution that scientists use to make inferences from fossil records, molecular similarities, anatomical similarities, and similarities between the developmental patterns of organisms.

Bellringer

Use the Bellringer transparency to prepare students for this section.

›Teach

Teaching Key Ideas

Looks Like a Leaf Have students study **Figure 5** showing *Phyllium pulchrifolium* (the name means "beautiful leaf"). Ask students to describe the advantage of looking like a leaf. (Leaf-dwelling insects that resemble leaves may avoid being eaten by predators.) Ask students to predict what would happen to this insect's chances of survival if it were growing in an environment that had plants only with red leaves. (It would not blend in as well, so it would be more likely to be captured by predators.) **LS Visual**

Answers to Caption Questions

Figure 5: Darwin's theory provided a mechanism (natural selection) by which organisms could become adapted to their environment over time.

Section Correlations	
4.3.1e	4.3.1h
4.3.1f	4.3.1l
4.3.1g	

Key Ideas

› What does Darwin's theory predict?

› Why are Darwin's ideas now widely accepted?

› What were the strengths and weaknesses of Darwin's ideas?

Key Terms

natural selection
adaptation
fossil
homologous structures

Why It Matters

The principles of evolution are used daily in medicine, biology, and other areas of modern life to understand, predict, and develop advancements in each area.

The Living Environment
Standard 4

3.1e Natural selection and its evolutionary consequences provide a scientific explanation for the fossil record of ancient life-forms, as well as for the molecular and structural similarities observed among the diverse species of living organisms.

3.1f Species evolve over time. Evolution is the consequence of the interactions of (1) the potential for a species to increase its numbers, (2) the genetic variability of offspring due to mutation and recombination of genes, (3) a finite supply of the resources required for life, and (4) the ensuing selection by the environment of those offspring better able to survive...

3.1g Some characteristics give individuals an advantage over others in surviving and reproducing...

3.1h The variation of organisms within a species increases the likelihood that at least some members of the species will survive under changed environmental conditions.

3.1l Extinction of a species occurs when the environment changes and the adaptive characteristics of a species are insufficient to allow its survival. Fossils indicate that many organisms that lived long ago are extinct. Extinction of species is common; most of the species that have lived on Earth no longer exist.

Figure 5 This insect is well adapted to its environment. › How does Darwin's theory help explain this observation?

Darwin applied Malthus's idea to all species. Every living thing has the potential to produce many offspring, but not all of those offspring are likely to survive and reproduce.

Evolution by Natural Selection

Darwin formed a key idea: Individuals that have traits that better suit their environment are more likely to survive. For example, the insect in **Figure 5** is less likely to be seen (and eaten) than a brightly colored insect is. Furthermore, individuals that have certain traits tend to produce more offspring than others do. These differences are part of **natural selection.** Darwin proposed that natural selection is a cause of evolution. In this context, *evolution* is a change in the inherited characteristics of a population from one generation to the next.

Steps of Darwin's Theory Darwin's explanation is often called the *theory of evolution by natural selection.* › Darwin's theory predicts that over time, the number of individuals that carry advantageous traits will increase in a population. As shown in **Figure 6,** this theory can be summarized in the following four logical steps:

Step ❶ Overproduction Every population is capable of producing more offspring than can possibly survive.

Step ❷ Variation Variation exists within every population. Much of this variation is in the form of inherited traits.

Step ❸ Selection In a given environment, having a particular trait can make individuals more or less likely to survive and have successful offspring. So, some individuals leave more offspring than others do.

Step ❹ Adaptation Over time, those traits that improve survival and reproduction will become more common.

Key Resources

Transparencies
D13 Evidence of Whale Evolution
D14 Forelimbs of Vertebrates
D16 Hemoglobin Comparison

Visual Concepts
Natural Selection
Adaptation
Biology
Similarities in Macromolecules
Homologous Features
Similarities in Embryology

Differentiated Instruction

English Learners

Steps of Darwin's Theory Help students understand **Figure 6,** by asking the following. How is *overproduction* shown? (There are too many organisms in a small space.) How is *variation* shown? (The animals are of two different sizes and coat colors.) What has happened to show *selection*? (There's a change in the environment. Smaller animals with light-colored coats have died, changing the ratio of light and dark coats in the population.) How is *adaptation* shown? (The population now has a greater number of animals with dark-colored coats.)

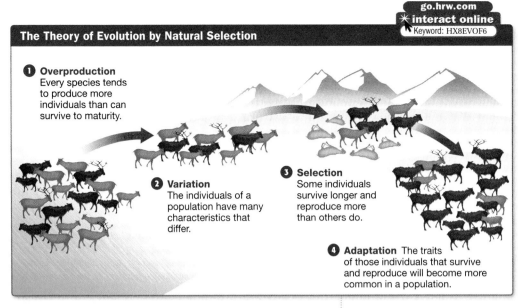

The Theory of Evolution by Natural Selection

go.hrw.com
✳ interact online
Keyword: HX8EVOF6

1 Overproduction Every species tends to produce more individuals than can survive to maturity.

2 Variation The individuals of a population have many characteristics that differ.

3 Selection Some individuals survive longer and reproduce more than others do.

4 Adaptation The traits of those individuals that survive and reproduce will become more common in a population.

Selection and Adaptation Darwin's theory explains why living things vary in form yet seem to match their environment. Each habitat presents unique challenges and opportunities to survive and reproduce. So, each species evolves because of the "selection" of those individuals that survive the challenges or make best use of the opportunities. Put another way, each species becomes *adapted* to its environment as a result of living in it over time. An **adaptation** is an inherited trait that is present in a population because the trait helps individuals survive and reproduce in a given environment.

In sum, Darwin's theory explains evolution as a gradual process of adaptation. Note that Darwin's theory refers to *populations* and *species*—not *individuals*—as the units that evolve. Also, keep in mind that a species is a group of populations that that can interbreed.

Publication of the Theory In 1844, Darwin finally wrote an outline of his ideas about evolution and natural selection. But he showed it only to a few scientists that he knew well. He was afraid that his ideas would be controversial. Then in 1858, he received a letter from another young English naturalist named Alfred Russel Wallace. Wallace asked for Darwin's opinion on a new theory—a theory much like Darwin's! Because of this similarity, Darwin and Wallace jointly presented their ideas to a group of scientists. Darwin was finally motivated to publish a full book of his ideas within the next year.

Darwin's book *On the Origin of Species by Means of Natural Selection* presented evidence that evolution happens and offered a logical explanation of how it happens. Biologists began to accept that evolution occurs and that natural selection helps explain it.

❯ Reading Check *Is natural selection the same thing as evolution?*

Figure 6 Darwin proposed a logical process by which evolution may occur.
❯ Can this process act on individuals?

Hypothesis or Theory? Why isn't Darwin's explanation simply called *the theory of evolution*? Why isn't it called a *hypothesis*?

natural selection the process by which individuals that are better adapted to their environment survive and reproduce more successfully than less well adapted individuals do

adaptation a trait that improves an organism's ability to survive and reproduce; the process of becoming adapted

---

go.hrw.com
✳ interact online

Students can interact with "Evolution by Natural Selection" by going to go.hrw.com and typing in the code HX8EVOF6.

Answers to Caption Questions
Figure 6: No; natural selection acts only to change the traits of populations or species over time.

Teaching Key Ideas
Process of Natural Selection Have students make a labeled diagram showing the process of natural selection using the species of their choice. The chosen species could even be one that the student makes up. In their diagrams, students should include the four important points about natural selection discussed in this section.
(Example: taller trees
Overproduction: too many trees of the same height competing for light
Variation: trees that are slightly taller have an advantage
Selection: taller trees survive longer producing seeds with characters for tallness
Adaptation: taller trees become more common in the population) **LS** Visual

READING TOOLBOX

Hypothesis or Theory? Evolutionary theory today has grown beyond Darwin's original ideas and continues to be modified. Darwin's explanation for evolution is much more than a hypothesis; it explains a broad range of observations and forms the basis of multiple, testable hypotheses.

Differentiated Instruction

Advanced Learners/GATE
What Would You Say? Tell students that while Wallace was in Indonesia, he wrote a paper describing his idea about how evolution occurred and sent it to Darwin. Ask students to write a letter that Darwin could have written to Wallace in response. **LS** Verbal

Special Education Students
Darwin's Theory To help visually impaired students understand **Figure 6**, provide them with sets of plastic farm animals. Each set should feel slightly different from the others to represent variation in the population. Give each student 16 animals to represent the overproduction stage in the figure. Take students through the stages of the theory by telling them how the population would change at each successive step. **LS** Kinesthetic

Teaching Key Ideas

Fossil Evidence Tell students that the first three animals in **Figure 7** are known only from their fossil remains. The fourth animal is a living species. It is rare to find a complete skeleton for any one fossil. As more fossils of a species are found, all of the skeleton bones may eventually be found. Paleontologists estimate what these bones probably looked like. Ask students how the backbones of the fossils in the figure correlate to the ratio of time the animal spent in water. (The backbones became larger.) What is the advantage of this change? (Whales use up-and-down motions of their bodies to swim. A larger backbone better supports the muscles.) **LS Visual**

Teaching Key Ideas

Intermediate Forms Another form of evidence linking whales to other mammals is molecular. Recent genetic phylogenetic analysis of many mammals suggests that whales are most closely related to hippos, meaning that these two orders share a common ancestor more recently than any other two mammal orders. Interestingly enough, manatees and dugongs, which are another branch of marine mammals, seem most closely related to elephants.

---

fossil the trace or remains of an organism that lived long ago, most commonly preserved in sedimentary rock

ACADEMIC VOCABULARY

infer to derive by reasoning

What Darwin Explained

Darwin's book was more than an explanation of his theory. It also included a thorough presentation of the evidence that living species evolved from organisms that lived in the past. Darwin had studied much of the data that was available in his time. ⟩ **Darwin presented a unifying explanation for data from multiple fields of science.** Today, these sciences include geology, geography, ecology, developmental biology, anatomy, genetics, and biochemistry. Scientists continue to draw upon the power of Darwin's explanations.

The Fossil Record Have you ever looked at a series of historical maps of a city? You can <u>infer</u> that buildings and streets have been added, changed, or destroyed over time. Similarly, you can infer past events by looking at **fossils**, traces of organisms that lived in the past. All fossils known to science make up the *fossil record.*

Sometimes, comparing fossils and living beings reveals a pattern of gradual change from the past to the present. Darwin noticed these patterns, but he was aware of many gaps in the patterns. For example, Darwin suggested that whales might have evolved from a mammal that lived on land. But at the time, no known fossils were "in between" a land mammal and a whale.

Figure 7 Darwin once hypothesized that modern whales evolved from ancient, four-legged, land-dwelling, meat-eating mammals. Over the years since, scientists have collected a series of fossil skeletons that support this hypothesis.

Bones of hind legs

Hip bones

❶ *Pakicetus* **(PAK uh SEE tuhs)** Scientists think that whales evolved from land-dwelling mammals such as those in the genus *Pakicetus*. The fossil skeleton of a pakicetid is shown here. These mammals lived about 50 million years ago, walked or ran on four legs, and ate meat.

❷ *Ambulocetus* **(AM byoo loh SEE tuhs)** Mammals of this genus lived in coastal waters about 49 million years ago. These mammals could swim by kicking their legs and using their tail for balance. They could also use their short legs to waddle on land. They breathed air through their mouth.

❸ *Dorudon* **(DOHR oo DAHN)** Mammals of this genus lived in the oceans about 40 million years ago. They resembled giant dolphins in the way that they swam and breathed. They had tiny hind limbs that were of no use in swimming.

❹ Modern Whales All modern whales have forelimbs that are flippers used for swimming. No whales have hind legs, but some toothed whales have tiny hipbones. All modern whales must come to the surface of the water to breathe through a hole at the top of their head.

Why It Matters

Extinct Organisms Tell students that scientists estimate that 99 percent of all animal and plant species that ever existed are now extinct. A large number of extinct species have been discovered by paleontologists. In one small area in Wyoming, early Eocene rocks have yielded fossils of more than 50 species of animals.

Differentiated Instruction

Basic Learners

Anatomical Comparisons Have students look online at museum sites to find photos or artistic skeletal reconstructions for the whale, hippo, manatee, and elephant. Students should compare images of the skulls and leg bones of these mammals. Have them create a poster of their findings. **LS Visual, Kinesthetic**

Rhea (South America)

Ostrich (Africa)

Emu (Australia)

READING TOOLBOX

Visual Literacy Tell students that the three birds illustrated in **Figure 8** may have evolved from the same ancestral species. Early geologic history suggests that the Earth's continents separated, thus separating the original lines of descent into different groups.

Answers to Caption Questions
Figure 8: that environments influence the evolution of new organisms

Darwin predicted that *intermediate forms* between groups of species might be found. And indeed, many new fossils have been found, such as those shown in **Figure 7.** But the conditions that create fossils are rare, so we will never find fossils of every species that ever lived. The fossil record will grow but will never be complete.

Biogeography *Biogeography* is the study of the locations of organisms around the world. When traveling, Darwin and Wallace saw evolution at work when they compared organisms and environments. For example, Darwin saw the similarity of the three species of large birds in **Figure 8.** He found each bird in a similar grassland habitat but on a separate continent. This finding was evidence that similar environments shape the evolution of organisms in similar ways.

Sometimes, geography separates populations. For example, a group of organisms may become separated into two groups living on two different islands. Over time, the two groups may evolve in different patterns. Generally, geologists and biologists have found that the movement of landforms in Earth's past helps to explain patterns in the types and locations of both living and fossil organisms.

Developmental Biology The ancestry of organisms is also evident in the ways that multicellular organisms develop from embryos. The study of such development is called *embryology.* This study is interesting because embryos undergo many physical and genetic changes as they develop into mature forms.

Scientists may compare the embryonic development of species to look for similar patterns and structures. Such similarities most likely derive from an ancestor that the species have in common. For example, at some time during development, all vertebrate embryos have a tail. *Vertebrates* are animals that have backbones.

❯ **Reading Check** *Why is the fossil record incomplete?*

Figure 8 Three unique bird species are shown here. Each of these is similar in size, shape, eating habits, and habitat. However, each species seems to have first appeared on a separate continent. ❯ What does this pattern suggest about evolution?

SC*i*LINKS
www.scilinks.org
Topic: Fossil Record
Code: HX80615

Differentiated Instruction

Basic Learners
Organizing Concepts Have students study samples or pictures of different types of fossils. Students should note any similarities between the fossils and modern organisms. **LS Visual**

MISCONCEPTION ALERT

Selection, Not Induction Selection cannot induce changes. Some people think the environment can induce mutations in organisms, or that organisms can be "forced" to adapt. This is similar to Lamarck's mistaken idea. We now know that natural selection does not induce changes in genes; rather it selects organisms with genes that are most adaptive. The "selected" genes do not always provide an advantage. Adaptation is the net average result of many individual instances of survival and reproduction (or death and extinction) over time.

Teaching Key Ideas

Wing Structure Tell students that, although penguins are not able to fly, the movement of their wings under water resembles the motion of flying. Penguins have much heavier bones than birds that fly. Ask students what adaptive advantage this bone structure gives penguins. (The hefty bone structure of a penguin's wings is an advantage for moving through water, which is far denser than air. Also, heavier bones are not a disadvantage because of the buoyancy provided by water.)

READING TOOLBOX

Visual Literacy Direct students' attention to **Figure 9.** Have students identify the homologous parts of each animal (bones with matching colors). Another example of homologous structures is *vestigial* structures. For example, some bones in some animals are very small and have no apparent function. But similar bones in other, similar animals have a definite function. A hypothesis is that the animals with the "useless" bones evolved from animals with the functional bones. The hind limb bones of whales are vestigial structures.

Answers to Caption Questions

Figure 9: that all vertebrates share a common ancestor

Figure 10: Genes change (by mutation) over time; the genes of populations may diverge over time after once-related populations no longer interbreed.

Figure 9 Although they look very different from one another on the outside, the forelimbs of most tetrapods (vertebrates that have four limbs) include a similar group of bones. ❱ What hypothesis does this observation support?

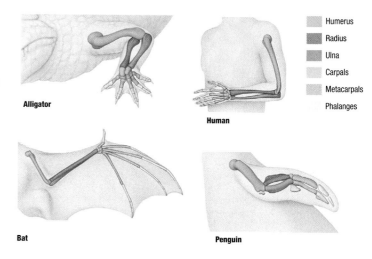

Alligator

Human

Bat

Penguin

Humerus
Radius
Ulna
Carpals
Metacarpals
Phalanges

Hemoglobin Comparison	
Animal with hemoglobin	Amino acids that differ from human hemoglobin
Gorilla	1
Rhesus monkey	8
Mouse	27
Chicken	45
Frog	67
Lamprey	125

Figure 10 Scientists have compared the amino acids that make up hemoglobin proteins in several species. Organisms that have fewer differences are more likely to be closely related. ❱ How does this pattern relate to genetic change?

Anatomy Another place to observe the results of evolution is inside the bodies of living things. The bodily structure, or *anatomy,* of different species can be compared. Many internal similarities are best explained by evolution and are evidence of how things are related.

For example, the hypothesis that all vertebrates descended from a common ancestor is widely accepted. Observations of the anatomy of both fossil and living vertebrates support this hypothesis. When modern vertebrates are compared, the difference in the size, number, and shape of their bones is clear. Yet the basic pattern of bones is similar. In particular, the forelimbs of many vertebrates are composed of the same basic groups of bones, as **Figure 9** shows. This pattern of bones is thought to have originated in a common ancestor. So, the bones are examples of **homologous** structures, characteristics that are similar in two or more species and that have been inherited from a common ancestor of those species.

Biochemistry To explain the patterns of change seen in anatomy, scientists make testable predictions. For example, if species have changed over time, the genes that determine their characteristics should also have changed. Recall that genes can change by mutation and that such change can make new varieties appear. Then, natural selection may "select against" some varieties and so "favor" others.

Scientists have observed that genetic changes occur over time in all natural populations. A comparison of DNA or amino-acid sequences shows that some species are more genetically similar than others. These comparisons, like those in anatomy, are evidence of hereditary relationships among the species. For example, comparing one kind of protein among several species reveals the pattern shown in **Figure 10.** The relative amount of difference is consistent with hypotheses based on fossils and anatomy.

❱ **Reading Check** *What explains similarities in bone structure?*

Differentiated Instruction

Advanced Learners/GATE

Cytochrome c Evidence Have students research studies of Cytochrome c as evidence for common ancestry among organisms. What is Cytochrome c? Have students find out how this substance has changed the way organisms are classified. Interested students could report their findings to the class. **LS Verbal, Logical**

Alternative Assessment

Evidence Brochure Have students create a brochure with the title "Why Are Darwin's Ideas Now Widely Accepted?" The brochure should include examples of the evidence used by the scientific community to support Darwin's ideas. Students should conclude the brochure with some of the unanswered evolution questions that are being explored by scientists. **LS Verbal**

Evaluating Darwin's Ideas

Why was Darwin such an important scientist? **> Darwin's work had three major strengths: evidence of evolution, a mechanism for evolution, and the recognition that variation is important.** Today, Darwin is given credit for starting a revolution in biology.

Strengths Darwin was *not* the first to come up with the idea that evolution happens, but he was the first to gather so much evidence about it. He described his most famous book as "one long argument" that evolution is possible. Before publishing, Darwin collected and organized many notes, observations, and examples, such as the illustration shown in **Figure 11.** So, one strength of Darwin's work is that it is supported by, and helps explain, so much data.

Darwin also presented a logical and testable mechanism that could account for the process of evolution. His theory of natural selection was well thought out and convincing to scientists of his time as well as today. It has since become a foundation of biology.

Finally, Darwin changed the way scientists thought about the diversity of life. Before Darwin, most scientists saw species as stable, unchanging things. They classified species based on average appearances and ignored variation. But Darwin showed that variation was everywhere and could serve as the starting point for evolution.

Weaknesses Darwin's explanations were incomplete in one major way: He knew very little about genetics. **> Inherited variation was crucial to Darwin's theory of natural selection, yet his theory lacked a clear mechanism for inheritance.** At different times, Darwin proposed or accepted several ideas for such a mechanism, but none of them were correct. He thought about this problem for much of his life.

Darwin never knew it, but Gregor Mendel had begun to solve this problem. However, Mendel's findings about heredity were not widely published until 1900. Those findings opened the door to a new age in the study of evolution. Today, an understanding of genetics is essential to understanding evolution.

> Reading Check *What did Darwin do before publishing his ideas?*

Figure 11 This drawing of a rhea was printed in one of Darwin's books. Darwin collected and organized a large amount of data to help explain his ideas. **> How else did Darwin support his main theory?**

homologous (hoh MAHL uh guhs) describes a character that is shared by a group of species because it is inherited from a common ancestor

> Close

Formative Assessment
Darwin's theory of evolution by natural selection explains changes in _____.
- **A.** individuals (Incorrect. Individuals within a population do not evolve.)
- **B.** genetic make up (Incorrect. The genetic make up of an individual refers to traits that are inherited; these can help in survival and reproduction, but are not explained by Darwin's theory.)
- **C.** populations or species (Correct. Only populations or species are the units that can evolve due to natural selection.)
- **D.** the environment (Incorrect. Darwin's theory explains changes in populations as a result of adapting to the environment.)

Section 2 Review

> KEY IDEAS

1. **Outline** Darwin's theory of evolution by natural selection. Be sure to include four logical steps.
2. **List** the kinds of data that Darwin helped explain.
3. **Compare** the strengths and weaknesses of Darwin's ideas.

CRITICAL THINKING

4. **Applying Information** Use the theory of natural selection to explain how the average running speed of a population of zebras might increase over time.
5. **Elaborating on Explanations** Describe how a single pair of seed-eating bird species could have arrived on an island and evolved into an insect-eating species. (Hint: Consider the food available.)

USING SCIENCE GRAPHICS

6. **Process Cartoon** Create your own version of **Figure 6** in the form of a four-panel cartoon. Choose a unique type of organism to represent the population undergoing natural selection. Also, depict a unique set of traits and limiting conditions for the population.

Answers to Section Review

1. Every population has overproduction and variation; only some individuals will be "selected" to survive; over time, the number of individuals that carry advantageous traits will increase in a population (adaptation).

2. data from geology, geography, ecology, developmental biology, anatomy, and biochemistry

3. strengths: his evidence of evolution, his mechanism for evolution, and his recognition that variation was important; weaknesses: lack of a clear mechanism for inheritance to explain inherited variations

4. Sample answer: Some zebras born into a population may be faster than others. These zebras could escape from predators better than slower zebras could. The faster zebras would be more likely to survive and reproduce. Over time, faster zebras would become more common in the population.

5. Sample answer: If the finches could eat and survive to reproduce several times, then finches with bills that were better for catching and eating insects would be more likely to survive and reproduce. Eventually, the insect-eating bill would be the most common trait in the population. Over time, the population would continue to change as it adapted to the island environment. If the population became so different from its ancestral population that it could no longer interbreed, then it would be considered a new species.

6. Students' cartoons will vary, but should describe and demonstrate visually the same four steps of natural selection shown in Figure 6.

Beyond Darwinian Theory

Key Ideas	Key Terms	Why It Matters
❯ How has Darwin's theory been updated? ❯ At what scales can evolution be studied?	speciation	The study of evolution was new in Darwin's day, but it is essential to biology today.

❯Focus

This section describes how discoveries in genetics and ongoing developments in other fields have been used to update Darwin's theory. Students then see how Darwin's updated theory is applied to explain evolution at different levels, or scales.

🔊Bellringer

Use the Bellringer transparency to prepare students for this section.

❯Teach

Why It Matters

Antibiotic-Resistant Bacteria

Antibiotic resistance has become a problem because of the widespread use of antibiotics to treat human diseases, prevent diseases, and to prevent disease in domestic animals used for food. In the presence of antibiotics, a bacterium's DNA with a mutation that allows it to survive in the antibiotic environment, will reproduce and pass on the mutation. Soon, bacteria with these mutations may constitute the majority of disease-causing bacteria.

Answers to Caption Questions

Figure 12: by looking at genetic changes in populations over time, or relating genes to changes in species

The Living Environment

Standard 4

3.1b New inheritable characteristics can result from new combinations of existing genes or from mutations of genes in reproductive cells.

3.1f Species evolve over time. Evolution is the consequence of the interactions of (1) the potential for a species to increase its numbers, (2) the genetic variability of offspring due to mutation and recombination of genes, (3) a finite supply of the resources required for life, and (4) the ensuing selection by the environment of those offspring better able to survive and leave offspring.

3.1g Some characteristics give individuals an advantage over others in surviving and reproducing, and the advantaged offspring, in turn, are more likely than others to survive and reproduce. The proportion of individuals that have advantageous characteristics will increase.

3.1k Evolution does not necessitate long-term progress in some set direction. Evolutionary changes appear to be like the growth of a bush: Some branches survive from the beginning with little or no change, many die out altogether, and others branch repeatedly, sometimes giving rise to more complex organisms.

Figure 12 Modern genetic science and Darwin's theory have been united. ❯ **How could this genetic scientist study evolution?**

Does modern evolutionary theory differ from Darwin's theory? Yes and no. Darwin observed and explained much about the large-scale patterns of biology, but some patterns have yet to be explained. He proposed a logical process (natural selection) for evolution, even though he could not explain evolution at the genetic level. Biology has made great progress since Darwin's time. Modern evolutionary theory relates patterns and processes at many levels.

Darwin's Theory Updated

Since Darwin's work was published, his theory has been thoroughly investigated. ❯ **Discoveries since Darwin's time, especially in genetics, have been added to his theory to explain the evolution of species.** Some parts of Darwin's theory have been modified, and new parts have been added. But mostly, Darwin's theory has been supported.

The first major advance beyond Darwin's ideas was the rediscovery, in 1900, of Mendel's *Laws of Heredity*. These ideas opened the door for a genetic explanation of evolution. By the 1940s, scientists began to weave Darwin's theory together with newer studies of fossils, anatomy, genetics, and more. This unification is called the *modern synthesis* of evolutionary theory.

In particular, biologists have learned that evolution can result from processes other than natural selection. For example, survival and reproduction can be limited by chance or by the way that genes work. In the modern view, any or all of these forces may combine with natural selection (as described by Darwin). This synthesis helps explain some of the patterns of evolution that were unexplained by natural selection alone.

Remaining Questions Some of the most important questions about evolution have been asked only recently. So, many questions are still being investigated, as shown in **Figure 12.** Modern biologists have tentative answers to the following questions:

• **Can an individual evolve?** Darwin correctly inferred that individuals do not evolve. They may respond to outside forces, but individuals do not pass on their responses as heritable traits. Rather, populations evolve when natural selection acts (indirectly) on genes.

Section Correlations

4.3.1b	4.3.1g
4.3.1f	4.3.1k

Key Resources

Visual Concepts

Gradualism

Comparing Punctuated Equilibrium and Gradualism

Reproductive Isolation

QuickLab

🕐 15 min

Selection Model

In this lab, you will model the process of natural selection. Can you predict the outcome?

Procedure

❶ Work with a partner. Spread out a handful of small, colored candies onto a piece of cloth or paper that has a colorful design. One person should act as "predator" of the candies while the other uses a stopwatch to monitor time and then records the results.

❷ The "predator" should use tweezers to try to "capture" as many candies as possible within 10 s.

❸ Record the results, and switch roles. Repeat 10 times.

Analysis

1. **Graph** the total number of each color of candy that was "captured." Use a bar graph.

2. **CRITICAL THINKING** **Evaluating Results** Explain why some colors were "captured" more often than others.

3. **CRITICAL THINKING** **Forming Hypotheses** Predict the outcome if the background is changed to solid red.

• **Is evolution the survival of the fittest?** Natural selection can act only on the heritable variation that exists in a population. Chance variations do not always provide the best adaptation for a given time and place. So, evolution does not always produce the "fittest" forms, just those that "fit" well enough to leave offspring.

• **Is evolution predictable?** Evolution sometimes results in larger or more-complex forms of life, but this result cannot be predicted. Many forms of life are simple yet successful. For example, bacteria have been abundant for billions of years. In contrast, some complex organisms, such as dinosaurs, have appeared, been successful for a time, and then almost completely disappeared. Mostly, scientists cannot predict the exact path that evolution will take.

Studying Evolution at All Scales

❭ Because it affects every aspect of biology, scientists can study evolution at many scales. Generally, these scales range from microevolution to macroevolution, with speciation in between. Informally, *microevolution* refers to evolution as a change in the genes of populations, whereas *macroevolution* refers to the appearance of new species over time.

Speciation The link between microevolution and macroevolution is speciation. **Speciation,** the formation of new species, can be seen as a process of genetic change or as a pattern of change in the form of organisms. Recall that a *species* is a group of organisms that are closely related and that can mate to produce fertile offspring. So, speciation can begin with the separation of populations of the same species. For example, the two kinds of squirrels shown in **Figure 13** seem to be evolving from one species into two because of separation.

❭ **Reading Check** *At what scales can evolution be studied?*

speciation (SPEE shee AY shuhn) the formation of new species as a result of evolution

Figure 13 These squirrels are closely related but are almost different enough to be unique species. Their populations are separated by the Grand Canyon.

Teaching Key Ideas

Visual Literacy Tell students that the moth and orchid in **Figure 14** are examples of coevolution. When Darwin studied this orchid (*Angraecum sesquipedale*), he predicted that there must be a moth with a tongue long enough to reach into the 11-inch nectar tube. When the Madagascan sphinx moth was discovered 40 years later, it was named *Xanthopan morganii praedicta,* to honor Darwin's prediction. Ask students what it means to say that these species have coevolved to the point of being codependent. (Each species relies and benefits from the presence of the other. If either species were eliminated, the other would be less able to reproduce and survive.) **LS Visual**

SCI
LINKS.
www.scilinks.org
Topic: Evolution
Code: HX80546

ACADEMIC VOCABULARY

random without aim or plan; purposeless

Figure 14 This moth species and this orchid species have coevolved in a close relationship. The moth feeds exclusively on the orchid, and the orchid's pollen is spread by the moth.

Processes of Microevolution To study microevolution, we look at the processes by which inherited traits change over time in a population. Five major processes can affect the kinds of genes that will exist in a population from generation to generation. These processes are summarized below. Notice that natural selection is only one of the five. You will learn more about these processes soon.

• **Natural Selection** As you have learned, natural selection can cause an increase or decrease in certain alleles in a population.

• **Migration** *Migration* is the movement of individuals into, out of, or between populations. Migration can change the numbers and types of alleles in a population.

• **Mate Choice** If parents are paired up randomly in a population, a <u>random</u> assortment of traits will be passed on to the next generation. However, if parents are limited or selective in their choice of mates, a limited set of traits will be passed on.

• **Mutation** Mutation can change the numbers and types of alleles from one generation to the next. However, such changes are rare.

• **Genetic Drift** The random effects of everyday life can cause differences in the survival and reproduction of individuals. Because of these differences, some alleles may become more or less common in a population, especially in a small population.

Patterns of Macroevolution To study macroevolution, we look at the patterns in which new species evolve. We may study the direction, diversity, or speed of change. Patterns of change are seen when relationships between living and fossil species are modeled.

• **Convergent Evolution** If evolution is strongly directed by the environment, then species living in similar environments should evolve similar adaptations. Many examples of this pattern were observed by Darwin and can be seen today.

• **Coevolution** Organisms are part of one other's environment, so they can affect one another's evolution. Species that live in close contact often have clear adaptations to one another's existence, as shown in **Figure 14.**

Differentiated Instruction

Struggling Readers

Key-Term Fold Have students create a Key-Term Fold with all of the bulleted paragraph titles on these two pages. Students should then provide an example or explanation of how each term relates to the topic of evolution. Terms to include are: *natural selection, migration, mate choice, mutation, genetic drift, convergent evolution, coevolution, adaptive radiation, extinction, gradualism,* and *punctuated equilibrium.* **LS Verbal, Kinesthetic**

Gradualism

Punctuated equilibrium

Time

Taking Notes Notes should resemble the example shown on the Reading Toolbox page at the beginning of this chapter.

〉Close

Formative Assessment

What term describes patterns in the overall direction, diversity or rate of change of species?

A. speciation (Incorrect. Speciation is the formation of new species.)

B. gradualism (Incorrect. Gradualism is one specific model of the pace of evolution.)

C. microevolution (Incorrect.)

D. macroevolution (Correct.)

- **Adaptive Radiation** Over time, species may split into two or more lines of descendants, or *lineages*. As this splitting repeats, one species can give rise to many new species. The process tends to speed up when a new species enters an environment that contains few other species. In this case, the pattern is called *adaptive radiation*.

- **Extinction** If all members of a lineage die off or simply fail to reproduce, the lineage is said to be *extinct*. The fossil record shows that many lineages have arisen and radiated, but only a few of their descendants survived and evolved into the species present today.

- **Gradualism** In Darwin's day, the idea of slow, gradual change was new to geology as well as biology. Darwin had argued that large-scale changes, such as the formation of new species, must require many small changes to build up gradually over a long period of time. This model is called *gradualism* and is shown in **Figure 15.**

- **Punctuated Equilibrium** Some biologists argue that species do not always evolve gradually. Species may remain stable for long periods until environmental changes create new pressures. Then, many new species may "suddenly" appear. This model is called *punctuated equilibrium* and is shown in **Figure 15.**

Figure 15 Two differing models of the pace of evolution have been proposed. 〉 **Do these models show microevolution or macroevolution?**

READING TOOLBOX

Taking Notes Complete your notes summarizing the major concepts from this chapter. Be sure to include microevolution and macroevolution.

Section 3 Review

〉KEY IDEAS

1. **Describe** how Darwin's ideas have been updated. Be sure to mention the role of natural selection in modern evolutionary theory.

2. **List** the scales at which evolution can be studied, and list the patterns and processes studied.

CRITICAL THINKING

3. **Arguing Logically** A classmate states that because land animals evolved from fishes and then flying things evolved from walking things, we can predict that future life will evolve to travel in outer space. Write a logical argument against this statement. Be sure to support your argument with examples.

ALTERNATIVE ASSESSMENT

4. **Who's Who** Make a brochure or poster entitled "Who's Who of Evolutionary Theory." Use reference sources to find basic facts about major evolutionary scientists that lived during or after Darwin's lifetime.

Answers to Section Review

1. Discoveries since Darwin's time, especially in genetics, have been added to his theory to explain the evolution of species.

2. microevolution, speciation, and macroevolution.

3. The argument assumes that evolution has a direction or destination. However, there are many examples of lineages that evolve "back" to a prior type of adaptation, such as mammals that became adapted to ocean life (whales), or reptiles that evolved to lack limbs (snakes). Evolution is not exactly predictable.

4. possible scientists include: Ronald A. Fisher, J.B.S. Haldane, Sewall Wright, Theodosius Dobzhansky, Ernst Mayr, George Gaylord Simpson, Julian Huxley, Steven J. Gould, and Douglas J. Futuyma

Lab

Time Required
Two 45-minute class periods

Ratings

🧪	🧪🧪	🧪🧪🧪	🧪🧪🧪🧪
EASY			HARD

Teacher Prep 🧪🧪
Student Setup 🧪🧪
Concept Level 🧪🧪🧪
Cleanup 🧪

Safety Caution
Remind students to be careful with scissors and always cut in a direction away from the face and body.

Tips and Tricks
You may wish to review and clarify the principles of selection. Students will simulate the breeding of several generations of birds and observe the effect of changes in phenotype on the evolutionary success of these animals. The random nature of mutations is demonstrated by randomly changing the anterior and posterior wing position and wing circumference of the birds. To save time, have students create their data tables before beginning the lab.

4.3.1e

Objectives
▶ Model natural selection.
▶ Relate favorable mutations to selection and evolution.

Materials
- construction paper
- meterstick or tape measure
- scissors
- cellophane tape
- soda straws
- marker, felt-tip
- penny or other coin
- die, six-sided

Safety

Natural Selection Simulation

In this lab, you will use a paper model of a bird to model the selection of favorable traits in a new generation. This imaginary bird, the Egyptian origami bird (*Avis papyrus*), lives in dry regions of North Africa. Imagine that the birds must fly long distances between water sources in order to live and reproduce successfully.

Procedure

Model Parental Generation

❶ Cut a sheet of paper into two strips that are 2 cm × 20 cm each. Make a loop with one strip of paper. Let the paper overlap by 1 cm, and tape the loop closed. Repeat for the other strip.

❷ Tape one loop 3 cm from one end of the straw and one loop 3 cm from the other end, as pictured. Use a felt-tip marker to mark the front end of the "bird." This bird represents the parental generation.

❸ Test how far your parent bird can fly by releasing it with a gentle overhand pitch. Test the bird twice. Record the bird's average flight distance in a data table like the one shown.

Model First (F₁) Generation

❹ Each origami bird lays a clutch of three eggs. Assume that one of the chicks is identical to the parent. Use the parent data to fill in your data table for the first new chick (Chick 1).

❺ Make two more chicks (Chick 2 and Chick 3). Assume that these chicks have mutations. Follow Steps A through C for each chick to determine the effects of each mutation.

Data for All Generations

Bird	Coin flip (H or T)	Die throw (1-6)	Anterior wing (cm)			Posterior wing (cm)			Average distance flown (m)
			Width	Circum.	Distance from front	Width	Circum.	Distance from back	
Parent	NA	NA	2	19	3	2	19	3	
Generation 1									
Chick 1									
Chick 2									
Chick 3									
Generation 2									
Chick 1									

Step A Flip a coin to find out which end is affected by the mutation.

Heads = Front wing is affected.

Tails = Back wing is affected.

Step B Throw a die to find out how the mutation affects the wing.

⚀ = Wing position moves 1 cm toward the end of the straw.

⚁ = Wing position moves 1 cm toward the middle.

⚂ = Wing circumference increases by 2 cm.

⚃ = Wing circumference decreases by 2 cm.

⚄ = Wing width increases by 1 cm.

⚅ = Wing width decreases by 1 cm.

Step C If a mutation causes a wing to fall off the straw or makes a wing's circumference smaller than the circumference of the straw, the chick cannot "survive." If such a mutation occurs, record it as "lethal," and then produce another chick.

6 For each new chick, record the mutation and the new dimensions of each wing.

7 Test each bird twice by releasing it with a gentle overhand pitch. Release the bird as uniformly as possible. Record the distance that each bird flies. The most successful bird is the one that flies the farthest.

Model Subsequent Generations

8 Assume that the most successful bird in the previous generation is the sole parent of the next generation. Using this bird, repeat steps 4–7.

9 Continue to produce chicks and to test and record data for eight more generations.

Clean Up and Dispose

10 Clean up your work area and all lab equipment. Return lab equipment to its proper place. Dispose of paper scraps in the designated waste container. Wash your hands thoroughly before you leave the lab and after you finish all work.

Analyze and Conclude

1. **Summarizing Results** Describe any patterns in the evolution of the birds in your model.

2. **Evaluating Models** How well does this lab model natural biological processes? What are the limitations of this model?

3. **Analyzing Data** Compare your data with your classmates' data. Identify any similarities and differences. Try to explain any trends that you notice in terms of the theory of natural selection.

Extensions

4. **Design an Experiment** Propose a new hypothesis about natural selection that you could test by observing real organisms. Write a brief proposal describing an experiment that could test this hypothesis. Be sure to give your prediction, explain your methods, identify variables, and plan for control groups.

Answers to Analyze and Conclude

1. Most students should find a pattern of improving flight distance after a few generations.

2. This lab models a simple organism with only a few possible traits to affect success, so the selection and adaptation are quick and obvious, which is much simpler than real life. The process would be much slower and less obvious with real populations. The obvious and rapid results of the model present an advantage over doing an experiment with living populations.

3. Some students may have higher rates of chick mortality and lower rates of adaptation. Some students may reach a maximum flight distance after some generations, corresponding to the best possible combination of traits (within the bird's physical limits) for flight distance. The patterns of variation and gradual adaptation are consistent with the theory of natural selection.

4. Check that students include a prediction, explain methods, identify variables, and plan for control groups.

Key Resources

 Holt Lab Generator

 Lab Datasheet (Levels A, B, C)

 Holt Science Biology Video Labs

 Virtual Investigations

Reteaching Key Ideas

Models Explain that models are abstractions that describe and help us understand the mechanics of evolutionary change. Emphasize that a good scientist tries to make a model fit his or her research results, not the other way around. **LS Visual Crossword Study Tool** Have students use the information in their Key-Term Folds to construct crossword puzzles using the definitions as the clues. Students should trade puzzles and complete them to test their understanding of the definitions. **LS Verbal**

Key Ideas	Key Terms

1 Developing a Theory

> Modern evolutionary theory began when Darwin presented evidence that evolution happens and offered an explanation of how evolution happens.

> Darwin's experiences provided him with evidence of evolution at work.

> Darwin was influenced by ideas from the fields of natural history, economics, and geology.

evolution (375)
artificial selection (377)

2 Applying Darwin's Ideas

> Darwin's theory of evolution by natural selection predicts that over time, the number of individuals that carry advantageous traits will increase in a population.

> Darwin presented a unifying explanation for data from multiple fields of science.

> The strengths of Darwin's work—evidence of evolution, a mechanism for evolution, and the recognition that variation is important—placed Darwin's ideas among the most important of our time. However, Darwin lacked a mechanism for inheritance.

natural selection (380)
adaptation (381)
fossil (382)
homologous structures (384)

3 Beyond Darwinian Theory

> Discoveries since Darwin's time, especially in genetics, have been added to his theory to explain the evolution of species.

> Because it affects every aspect of biology, scientists can study evolution at many scales. Generally, these scales range from microevolution to macroevolution, with speciation in between.

speciation (387)

PART A: Answer all questions in this part.

Directions: For each statement or question, write on your separate answer sheet the number of the word or expression that best completes the statement or answers the question.

1 The illustration below shows an insect resting on some green leaves. The size, shape, and green color of this insect are adaptations that would most likely help the insect to

(1) compete successfully with all birds
(2) make its own food
(3) hide from predators
(4) avoid toxic waste materials

2 Natural selection and its evolutionary consequences provide a scientific explanation for each of the following except
(1) the fossil record
(2) protein and DNA similarities between different organisms
(3) similar structures among different organisms
(4) a stable physical environment

3 Which factor is least likely to contribute to an increase in the rate of evolution?
(1) presence of genetic variations in a population
(2) environmental selection of organisms best adapted to survive
(3) chromosomal recombinations
(4) a long period of environmental stability

4 A new chemical was discovered and introduced into a culture containing one species of bacteria. Within a day, most of the bacteria were dead, but a few remained alive. Which statement best explains why some of the bacteria survived?
(1) They had a genetic variation that gave them resistance to the chemical.
(2) They were exposed to the chemical long enough to develop a resistance to it.
(3) They mutated and became a different species after exposure to the chemical.
(4) They absorbed the chemical and broke it down in their digestive systems.

5 Thousands of years ago, giraffes with short necks were common within giraffe populations. Nearly all giraffe populations today have long necks. This difference could be due to
(1) giraffes stretching their necks to keep their heads out of reach of predators
(2) giraffes stretching their necks so they could reach food higher in the trees
(3) a mutation in genetic material controlling neck size occurring in some skin cells of a giraffe
(4) a mutation in genetic material controlling neck size occurring in the reproductive cells of a giraffe

6 The teeth of carnivores are pointed and are good for puncturing and ripping flesh. The teeth of herbivores are flat and are good for grinding and chewing. Which statement best explains these observations?
(1) Herbivores have evolved from carnivores.
(2) Carnivores have evolved from herbivores.
(3) The two types of teeth most likely evolved as a result of natural selection.
(4) The two types of teeth most likely evolved as a result of the needs of an organism.

7 Which factor contributed most to the extinction of many species?
(1) changes in the environment
(2) lethal mutations
(3) inability to evolve into simple organisms
(4) changes in migration patterns

Regents Exam Practice Correlations

4.3.1e 2	**4.3.1h** 10, 12	
4.3.1f 5	**4.3.1k** 7, 8, 9	
4.3.1g 1, 4, 6, 11	**4.3.1l** 3	

1. **(3)** Insects are not autotrophs so they would not make their own food. Competing with all birds is incorrect as this assumes that all birds compete with this insect. Avoiding wastes is incorrect. The fact that the insect rests on leaves and makes itself vulnerable to predators would make it advantageous for the insect to be camouflaged. *(#10, June 2006 Regents Exam)*

2. **(4)** Natural selection affects organisms and not the environment, although the environment can influence natural selection. *(#10, June 2005 Regents Exam)*

3. **(4)** Species evolve through natural selection when traits that are best adapted to the environment are selected for. Therefore, the presence of many traits (produced through chromosomal recombinations) and a changing environment would contribute to an increase in the rate of evolution. A stable environment would tend to decrease the rate of evolution. *(#12, August 2005 Regents Exam)*

4. **(1)** A chemical would not cause speciation. Resistance is not developed due to or transmitted from a chemical. Rather, resistance is the result of selection for existing genetic variation in some of the bacteria. *(#12, January 2006 Regents Exam)*

5. **(4)** Evolutionary changes in giraffe populations are not acquired by generations of giraffes stretching their necks. In addition, mutations in body cells do not affect the evolution of future generations. *(#10, January 2006 Regents Exam)*

6. **(3)** Herbivores do not necessarily evolve from carnivores, nor do carnivores necessarily evolve from herbivores. Teeth adaptations are a product of evolution by natural selection due to a particular diet, and not due to the need or desire of an organism. *(#13, August 2006 Regents Exam)*

7. **(1)** Lethal mutations rarely get passed on and affect an entire species. Species generally do not evolve into simpler ones. Migration patterns are generally not related to extinction patterns. *(#11, June 2005 Regents Exam)*

PART B

8. **(2)** Species B remained the same from the initial to the final branches of the tree, so it appears to have been most successful in surviving environmental changes. *(#44, June 2003 Regents Exam)*

9. **(4)** Species D occupies one of the lowest branches on the tree and gives rise to no new branches, so it was the first to become extinct. *(#43, June 2003 Regents Exam)*

PART C

10. Allow a maximum of 3 credits for providing a biological explanation for the loss of effectiveness of the insecticides, allocated as follows: Allow 1 credit for identifying the original event that resulted in the evolution of insecticide resistance in some insects. Acceptable responses include, but are not limited to: A mutation (or genetic change) probably occurred that led to the resistance to the insecticide. Note: Do not accept that the insects became "immune" to the insecticide.; Allow 1 credit for explaining why the percentage of resistant insects in the population has increased. Acceptable responses include, but are not limited to: The percentage of resistant insects in the population has increased over the years because they survived when the insecticide was used, and were then able to reproduce and pass on the resistance. Note: Do not allow credit for simply stating that they survived.; Allow 1 credit for describing one alternative form of insect control, other than using a different insecticide, that fruit growers could use to protect their crops from insect attack. Acceptable responses include, but are not limited to: release natural predators of the insects; the release of large numbers of sterile males of insect species that damage fruits provide conditions that help predators of the insects live in the area; genetically engineer insect-resistant plants *(#56, June 2006 Regents Exam)*

PART B

Base your answers to questions 8 and 9 on the diagram below and on your knowledge of biology. Letters *A* through *J* represent different species of organisms. The vertical distances between the dotted lines represent long periods of time in which major environmental changes occurred.

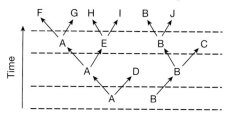

8 Which species appears to have been most successful in surviving changes in the environment over time?

(1) A
(2) B
(3) C
(4) H

9 Which species was the first to become extinct?

(1) E
(2) J
(3) C
(4) D

PART C

10 Growers of fruit trees have always had problems with insects. Insects can cause visible damage to fruits, making them less appealing to consumers. As a result of this damage, much of the fruit cannot be sold. Insecticides have been useful for controlling these insects, but in recent years, some insecticides have been much less effective. In some cases, insecticides do nothing to stop the insect attacks. Provide a biological explanation for this loss of effectiveness of the insecticides. In your answer, be sure to:

- identify the original event that resulted in the evolution of insecticide resistance in some insects
- explain why the percentage of resistant insects in the population has increased
- describe one alternative form of insect control, other than using a different insecticide, that fruit growers could use to protect their crops from insect attack

Base your answers to questions 11 and 12 on the information below and on your knowledge of biology.

A small village was heavily infested with mosquitoes. The village was sprayed weekly with an insecticide for a period of several months. The results of daily counts of the mosquito population are shown in the graph below.

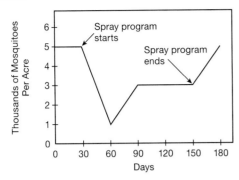

11 Which statement best explains the decreased effectiveness of the insecticide?

(1) The insecticide caused mutations that resulted in immunity in the mosquito.

(2) Mosquitoes resistant to the insecticide lived and produced offspring.

(3) The insecticide reacted chemically with the DNA of the mosquitoes and was destroyed.

(4) All of the mosquitoes produced antibodies that activated the insecticide.

12 Which statement best explains why some mosquitoes survived after the first spraying?

(1) Some mosquitoes were adapted to the climatic change that occurred over the several-month period of spraying.

(2) All of the mosquitoes contained DNA unique to the species.

(3) The spraying of the insecticide represented a change in the environment to which all adult mosquitoes were adapted.

(4) A natural variation existed within the mosquito population.

11. **(2)** The insecticide did not produce mutations or antibodies that caused immunity, and it did not react with DNA. The insecticide became less effective because mosquitoes that were already resistant to the insecticide could survive the sprayings and produce offspring that were also resistant. *(#41, August 2003 Regents Exam)*

12. **(4)** Even though all mosquitoes contained DNA unique to the species, natural variation in the mosquito population allowed some mosquitoes to survive the spraying. Because most mosquitoes died, it is clear that most were not adapted to the chemical. The change in temperatures or rainfall would not explain the survival of some mosquitoes. *(#40, August 2003 Regents Exam)*

Population Genetics and Speciation

	Standards	Teach Key Ideas

CHAPTER OPENER, pp. 396–397 `15 min.`

The Living Environment

SECTION 1 Genetic Variation, pp. 399–403 `45 min.`

> Population Genetics
> Phenotypic Variation
> Measuring Variation and Change
> Sources of Genetic Variation

Standards: 4.2.1h, 4.3.1b, 4.3.1c, 4.3.1d, 4.3.1f

Teach Key Ideas:
- **Bellringer Transparency**
- **Visual Concepts** Population • Population and Gene Movement • Comparing Single Allele, Multiple Allele, and Polygenic Traits • Mutation

---

SECTION 2 Genetic Change, pp. 404–410 `60 min.`

> Equilibrium and Change
> Sexual Reproduction and Evolution
> Population Size and Evolution
> Natural Selection and Evolution
> Patterns of Natural Selection

Standards: 1.3.2, 4.3.1b, 4.3.1c, 4.3.1f, 4.3.1g, 4.3.1i

Teach Key Ideas:
- **Bellringer Transparency**
- **Transparencies** D20 Two Kinds of Selection
- **Visual Concepts** Hardy-Weinberg Genetic Equilibrium Example • Comparing the Effects of Random and Nonrandom Mating • Genetic Drift • Natural Selection • Directional Selection • Stabilizing Selection

---

SECTION 3 Speciation, pp. 411–414 `45 min.`

> Defining Species
> Forming New Species
> Extinction: The End of Species

Standards: 4.3.1l

Teach Key Ideas:
- **Bellringer Transparency**
- **Visual Concepts** Reproductive Isolation • Geographic Isolation

See also PowerPoint® Resources

Chapter Review and Assessment Resources

- **SE** Super Summary, p. 416
- **SE** Regents Exam Practice, p. 417
- Regents Review Guide
- Review Resources
- Chapter Tests A and B
- Holt Online Assessment
- Regents Question Banks on Teacher's One-Stop Planner

CHAPTER

Fast Track

Thorough instruction will require the times shown. Topics in this Chapter support math-related curriculum objectives.

Basic Learners
- **TE** Normal Distribution, p. 401
- **TE** Genetic Mutations, p. 408
- **TE** Reproductive Isolation, p. 413
- Directed Reading Worksheets*
- Active Reading Worksheets*
- Lab Manuals, Level A*
- Study Guide* ■
- Note-taking Workbook*
- Special Needs Activities and Modified Tests*

Advanced Learners
- **TE** Species Divergence, p. 412
- Critical Thinking Worksheets*
- Concept Mapping Worksheets*
- Science Skills Worksheets*
- Lab Datasheets, Level C*

Why It Matters	Hands-On	Skills Development	Assessment
Build student motivation with resources about high-interest applications.	**SE Inquiry Lab** Normal Variation, p. 397* ■	**TE Reading Toolbox** Assessing Prior Knowledge, p. 396 **SE Reading Toolbox**, p. 398	
TE Blood Types, p. 402	**SE Quick Lab** Alleles: The Next Generation, p. 403* ■ 📁 **Quick Lab** Using Random Sampling*	**TE Reading Toolbox** Visual Literacy, p. 400 **SE Reading Toolbox** Everyday Words in Science, p. 401 **TE Reading Toolbox** Everyday Words in Science, p. 401 **TE Math Skills** Mean, Median, and Mode, p. 401 **TE Reading Toolbox** Visual Literacy, p. 402	**SE Section Review** **TE Formative Assessment** Spanish Assessment* ■ 📁 **Section Quiz** ■
TE Genetic Bottleneck, p. 406 **SE Wild Laboratories,** p. 410	**SE Quick Lab** Genetic Risk Assessment, p. 407* ■ **SE Inquiry Lab** Genetic Drift, p. 415* ■ 📁 **Skills Practice Lab** Determining Growth Rate*	**SE Reading Toolbox** Visual Literacy, p. 400 **TE Reading Toolbox** General Statements, p. 408 **TE Reading Toolbox** Visual Literacy, p. 410	**SE Section Review** **TE Formative Assessment** Spanish Assessment* ■ 📁 **Section Quiz** ■
TE Demonstration Recognizing Subtle Differences, p. 411 **TE Demonstration** Forming a New Species, p. 412		**TE Reading Toolbox** Using Words, p. 412 **SE Science Skills** Mating Activity of Frogs, p. 413 **SE Reading Toolbox** Outlining, p. 413 **TE Reading Toolbox** Outlining, p. 413	**SE Section Review** **TE Formative Assessment** Spanish Assessment* ■ 📁 **Section Quiz** ■
	See also Lab Generator		**See also Holt Online Assessment Resources**

Resources for Differentiated Instruction

English Learners

TE Prefixes Micro- and Macro, p. 399
TE Normal Distribution, p. 401
📁 Directed Reading Worksheets*
📁 Active Reading Worksheets*
📁 Lab Manuals, Level A*
📓 Study Guide* ■
📓 Note-taking Workbook*
📓 Multilingual Glossary
💿 Interactive Tutor

Struggling Readers

TE Paired Reading, p. 404
TE Reproductive Isolation, p. 413
📁 Directed Reading Worksheets*
📁 Active Reading Worksheets*
📁 Lab Manuals, Level A*
📓 Study Guide*
📓 Note-taking Workbook*
📓 Special Needs Activities and Modified Tests*
💿 Interactive Tutor

Special Education Students

TE Allele Frequency Model, p. 404
📁 Directed Reading Worksheets*
📁 Active Reading Worksheets*
📁 Lab Manuals, Level A*
📓 Study Guide* ■
📓 Note-taking Workbook*
📓 Special Needs Activities and Modified Tests*

Alternative Assessment

TE Identifying Genotypes and Phenotypes, p. 400
TE How Populations Evolve, p. 405
📁 Science Skills Worksheets*
📁 Section Quizzes* ■
📓 Chapter Tests A, B, and C* ■

Population Genetics and Speciation

Overview

The purpose of this chapter is to explain genetic variation and change in greater detail. Scientists study polygenic phenotypes by measuring each individual in the population and then analyzing the distribution of the measurements. Students will learn that populations are subject to many forces and undergo constant genetic change, and that species that exist at any time are the net result of both speciation and extinction.

READING TOOLBOX

Assessing Prior Knowledge The students should understand the following concepts:
• populations and communities
• genotype and phenotype
• natural selection
• evolution

Visual Literacy Ask students to list some physical shell variations that might effect the survival and reproduction of the species. (examples: color of stripes, brightness of stripes, hardness of shell, size of shell, shape of shell, ability to blend in with the environment)

Chapter 17

Preview

1 Genetic Variation
Population Genetics
Phenotypic Variation
Measuring Variation and Change
Sources of Genetic Variation

2 Genetic Change
Equilibrium and Change
Sexual Reproduction and Evolution
Population Size and Evolution
Natural Selection and Evolution
Patterns of Natural Selection

3 Speciation
Defining Species
Forming New Species
Extinction: The End of Species

Why It Matters

The fields of ecology, genetics, and evolutionary theory are brought together to understand how genetic changes in populations result in changes to species over time.

Every population, such as this group of banded wood snails, contains variation. Some of this variation can be seen, but much is hidden in DNA.

Physical variation in these snails includes variation in shell coloration, number of stripes, shell size, and shell thickness. Each trait affects the survival and reproduction of individual snails.

Banding patterns can give the snails camouflage protection against predators, especially birds. Each pattern may provide better camouflage in some seasons or locations than in others.

 The Living Environment
Standard 4 Students will understand and apply scientific concepts, principles, and theories pertaining to the physical setting and living environment and recognize the historical development of ideas in science.
Key Idea 2 Organisms inherit genetic information in a variety of ways that result in continuity of structure and function between parents and offspring. *Major Understandings* – 2.1h
Key Idea 3 Individual organisms and species change over time. *Major Understandings* – 3.1b, 3.1c, 3.1d, 3.1f, 3.1g, 3.1i, 3.1l

---

Chapter Correlations   *The Living Environment*

Standard 4

2.1h Genes are segments of DNA molecules. Any alteration of the DNA sequence is a mutation. Usually, an altered gene will be passed on to every cell that develops from it.

3.1b New inheritable characteristics can result from new combinations of existing genes or from mutations of genes in reproductive cells.

3.1c Mutation and the sorting and recombining of genes during meiosis and fertilization result in a great variety of possible gene combinations.

3.1d Mutations occur as random chance events. Gene mutations can also be caused by such agents as radiation and chemicals. When they occur in sex cells, the mutations can be passed on to offspring; if they occur in other cells, they can be passed on to other body cells only.

3.1f Species evolve over time. Evolution is the consequence of the interactions of (1) the potential for a species to increase its numbers, (2) the genetic variability of offspring due to mutation and recombination of genes, (3) a finite supply of the resources required for life, and (4) the ensuing selection by the environment of those offspring better able to survive and leave offspring.

3.1g Some characteristics give individuals an advantage over others in surviving and reproducing, and the advantaged offspring, in turn, are more likely than others to survive and reproduce. The proportion of individuals that have advantageous characteristics will increase.

3.1i Behaviors have evolved through natural selection. The broad patterns of behavior exhibited by organisms are those that have resulted in greater reproductive success.

InquiryLab

Normal Variation 4.3.1f

Variation is normal and is evident in all populations. Just look down.

Procedure

1. Read step 2, and prepare a table for the class data.

2. Use a **ruler or tape-measure** to measure the length of one of **your shoes** to the nearest centimeter. Record this number, as well as your shoe size and gender. Share these data with the class.

3. Make a table of the shoe lengths of everyone in your class. In the first column, record the name of each student. In the second column, record each shoe length.

4. Make a tally of the numbers of each shoe size in your class.

Analysis

1. **Compare** the table that you made in step 3 to the tally that you made in step 4.

2. **Describe** how the table you made in step 3 could be converted into a tally like that of step 4.

3. **Propose** additional methods by which these kinds of data could be collected and analyzed.

4. **Predict** how the tally that you made in step 4 would change if the data for males were deleted.

🕐 15 min

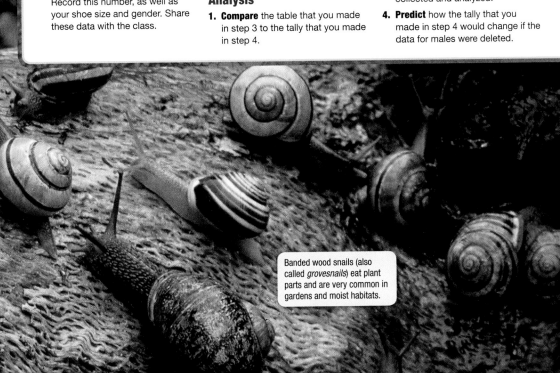

Banded wood snails (also called *grovesnails*) eat plant parts and are very common in gardens and moist habitats.

InquiryLab

Teacher's Notes Tell students to measure the bottom of their shoes from tip to heel.

Materials
• ruler or tape measure

Answers to Analysis

1. Students should note that both methods represent the same data, but the tally represents data shown in a simpler manner (shows sizes instead of lengths), shows data clusters, and makes the patterns in the data more obvious at a glance.

2. Each shoe size could be correlated to a range of shoe lengths (in cm), and then each shoe length would be converted to shoe size and tallied.

3. Students may suggest other ways to survey shoe sizes or to graph the data; some students may suggest making a histogram (a special type of bar graph, used later in this chapter).

4. The average would probably move toward smaller shoe sizes.

Key Resources

💿 Interactive Tutor

3.1l Extinction of a species occurs when the environment changes and the adaptive characteristics of a species are insufficient to allow its survival. Fossils indicate that many organisms that lived long ago are extinct. Extinction of species is common; most of the species that have lived on Earth no longer exist.

READING TOOLBOX

Using Words

1. Sample answers: *normal:* "regular" or "not strange"; *distribution:* "the way something is spread out"; *drift:* "wander"; *fitness:* "good health"
2. Check that students have prepared their table as shown in the example and that they complete their table by the end of the chapter.

Using Language

1. Sample answer: Apples, bananas, tomatoes, and peanuts are fruits.
2. Sample answers: Some baby humans are shorter than some adult monkeys. Most monkey arms are proportionally longer than human arms.

Taking Notes

Check that students have prepared their outline as shown in the example and that they complete their outline by the end of the chapter.

READING TOOLBOX

These reading tools can help you learn the material in this chapter. For more information on how to use these and other tools, see **Appendix: Reading and Study Skills.**

Using Words

Everyday Words in Science Many words that we use every day have special meanings in science. For example, *matter* in everyday use is a topic, issue, or problem. In science, *matter* is the substance of which all things are made.

Your Turn Make a table like the one shown here.
1. Before you read, write in your own words the everyday meaning of the terms in the table.
2. As you read, fill in the scientific meaning for the terms in the table.

Everyday Words in Science		
Word	Everyday Meaning	Science Meaning
normal		
distribution		
drift		
fitness		

Using Language

General Statements A general statement often summarizes the features of a group or describes an average or typical feature of members of the group. But if many features are summarized, some individuals in the group probably do not share all of those features. And if an average feature is described, some members of the group will not match the average. So, general statements may be true most of the time, but not always.

Your Turn Use what you know about general statements to complete the following tasks.
1. Write a general statement about apples, bananas, tomatoes, and peanuts.
2. List exceptions to the statement "Humans are bigger than monkeys."

Taking Notes

Outlining Outlining is a note-taking skill that helps you organize information. An outline can give you an overview of the topics in a chapter and help you understand how the topics are related.

Your Turn Create outlines for each section of this chapter. Start with the example shown here.
1. Copy all of the headings for a section, in order, on a piece of paper.
2. Leave plenty of space between each heading.
3. As you read the material under each heading of a section, write the important facts under that heading on your outline.

> *Population Genetics and Speciation*
> *Genetic Variation*
>   *Population Genetics*
>   *Phenotypic Variation*
>   *Measuring Variation and Change*
>   *Studying Alleles*
>   *Allele Frequencies*
>   *Sources of Genetic Variation*
> *Genetic Change*
>   *Equilibrium and Change*

Key Ideas	Key Terms	Why It Matters
❯ How is microevolution studied? ❯ How is phenotypic variation measured? ❯ How are genetic variation and change measured? ❯ How does genetic variation originate?	population genetics normal distribution	Without variation, evolution cannot occur.

One of Charles Darwin's contributions to biology was his careful study of variation in characteristics, such as the many flower colors shown in **Figure 1.** As you have learned, Darwin knew that heredity influences characteristics, but he did not know about genes. We now know a great deal about genes. We are able to study and predict the relationships between genotypes and phenotypes. We can also study the genetic variation and change that underlie evolution.

Population Genetics

Recall that evolution can be studied at different scales, from that of microevolution to macroevolution. And recall that *microevolution* is evolution at the level of genetic change in populations.
❯ Microevolution can be studied by observing changes in the numbers and types of alleles in populations. The study of microevolution in this sense is **population genetics**. Thus, the studies of genetics and evolution are advancing together. Furthermore, the link from microevolution to macroevolution—*speciation*—can be studied in detail.

❯ **Reading Check** *What do we now know about heredity that Darwin did not know? (See the Appendix for answers to Reading Checks.)*

The Living Environment
Standard 4

2.1h Genes are segments of DNA molecules. Any alteration of the DNA sequence is a mutation. Usually, an altered gene will be passed on to every cell that develops from it.

3.1b New inheritable characteristics can result from new combinations of existing genes or from mutations of genes in reproductive cells.

3.1c Mutation and the sorting and recombining of genes during meiosis and fertilization result in a great variety of possible gene combinations.

3.1d Mutations occur as random chance events. Gene mutations can also be caused by such agents as radiation and chemicals. When they occur in sex cells, the mutations can be passed on to offspring; if they occur in other cells, they can be passed on to other body cells only.

3.1f Species evolve over time. Evolution is the consequence of the interactions of (1) the potential for a species to increase its numbers, (2) the genetic variability of offspring due to mutation and recombination of genes, (3) a finite supply of the resources required for life, and (4) the ensuing selection by the environment of those offspring better able to survive and leave offspring.

population genetics the study of the frequency and interaction of alleles and genes in populations

Figure 1 Genetic variation is found in all living things and forms the basis on which evolution acts. ❯ What kinds of variation can be seen in this photograph?

Key Resources

◉ **Visual Concepts**
Population
Population and Gene Movement
Comparing Single Allele, Multiple Allele, and Polygenic Traits
Mutation

Section Correlations

4.2.1h	4.3.1d
4.3.1b	4.3.1f
4.3.1c	

Teaching Key Ideas

Human Heredity Most students transfer what they learn about Mendelian genetics to the inheritance pattern for all traits, including those in humans. Stress that in humans, very few traits involve only one gene with two alleles. In fact, most human traits are the result of polygenic inheritance. In addition to height, polygenic traits include weight, skin color, and metabolic rate. Explain that the way most genes interact in polygenic traits is not well understood.

READING TOOLBOX

Visual Literacy Have students look at **Figure 3,** and ask them why a normal distribution is often called a "bell-shaped curve." Ask them what grade (in a traditional A–F grading system) most students would get if a teacher grades "on a curve." (C grade) How would the number of A grades compare to the number of F grades? (very similar) **LS** **Visual**

Answers to Caption Questions

Figure 3: The more genes that affect a character, the more variations there can be.

Figure 2 Eye color is a polygenic character. Different genes control different pigments, which combine to produce various shades of blue, green, or brown.

Figure 3 Measurements of characters that have a wide range of variation, such as shoe size, can be arranged into a histogram and are likely to form a bell curve. **>** How do the number of genes for a character relate to its variation?

Phenotypic Variation

Before anyone understood genetics, the only kind of variation that could be observed and measured was phenotypic variation. Gregor Mendel was the first to suspect that some kind of inherited units determined the various phenotypes that he observed. (In Mendel's day, the term *phenotype* was not used.) We now know that the inherited units are alleles. Mendel used his data on phenotypes to mathematically deduce the ratio of alleles in each individual. Today, we call these ratios *genotypes*.

Mendel's work was made simple by the fact that he studied pea plants with only two phenotypes for each character. As you have learned, genetics is rarely so simple. For example, listing every possible phenotype for height in humans would be difficult. If you compare many humans, you find a range of possible heights, with many slight variations.

The variety of phenotypes that exist for a given character depends on how many genes affect that character. Recall that a character that is influenced by several genes is a *polygenic* character. Human height and human eye color, for example, are polygenic. Polygenic characters may exist as a variety of traits, as shown in **Figure 2,** or a range of trait values, as shown in **Figure 3.**

> Biologists study polygenic phenotypes by measuring each individual in the population and then analyzing the distribution of the measurements. A *distribution* is an overview of the relative frequency and range of a set of values. Mathematically, a distribution is a tally or a histogram with a smooth line to show the overall pattern of the values.

Often, some values in a range are more common than others. For example, suppose that you were to collect one shoe from each student in your class. If you ordered and grouped the shoes by size, you would probably form a hill-shaped curve such as the one shown in **Figure 3.** This pattern of distribution is called a **normal distribution** or a *bell curve.* "Normal" in this case simply means a tendency to cluster around an average value (mean, median, or mode).

> **Reading Check** *Why do polygenic characters vary so much?*

Size 6 — Size 7 — Size 8 — Size 9 — Size 10 — Size 11

Differentiated Instruction

Alternative Assessment

Identifying Genotypes and Phenotypes Have students identify all the possible genotypes for a hypothetical character controlled by two genes. Each gene has two alleles: X and x represent the alleles for one gene, and Y and y represent the alleles for a second gene. (*XXYY, XXYy, XXyy, XxYY, XxYy, Xxyy, xxYY, xxYy, xxyy*) Ask how the variety of this character would compare to the variety of a character that is determined by three genes. (The character determined by three genes would have greater variety.) **LS** **Logical**

Suppose that you were to measure the height of every student in your school. You would proably gather a wide range of data. The best way to graph this data would be to use a histogram. A *histogram* is a special kind of bar graph for displaying a range of values. The histogram clearly shows the range of values as well as the values that are most common.

To make a histogram, list the values in order from smallest to largest. Then, determine the *range* from the smallest value to the largest. Draw the *x*-axis of the histogram to cover this range. Then, group the values into convenient intervals. For example, values for height in meters could be grouped into intervals of 0.2 m each, as shown here.

Next, count the number of values that fall within each interval. (Hint: Making a tally of the counts is helpful.) Draw the *y*-axis of the histogram to allow for the highest count in any one interval. Finally, draw bars to show the count for each interval. The bars should touch each other because the graph is showing a continuous range of data.

You can use math software to make a histogram and further analyze these kinds of data. For example, you can "fit a curve" to the data, adding a line through the bars to show the general shape, or *distribution*, of the data. You can group the data into smaller or larger intervals, or add or subtract values, and then see changes in the shape of the curve. Finally, you can find the mean, median, and mode(s) of the data. A *normal distribution* will have similar values for the mean, median, and mode.

Measuring Variation and Change

To study population genetics, we need to study how genes in populations change over time. To measure these changes, we must look at how alleles are passed on from generation to generation as organisms mate and produce offspring. The particular combination of alleles in a population at any one point in time makes up a *gene pool*.

Studying Alleles   To study genetic variation, we need to estimate the number of alleles in a population. For characters with simple Mendelian inheritance, we can estimate by using simple math combined with our knowledge of genetics. For example, we may start by counting the number of individuals in the population and recording the phenotype of each. Then, we can deduce each genotype.

As you have learned, to keep track of alleles, we can represent alleles with letters. For example, a particular gene may have two alleles, *R* and *r*. In addition, we represent genotypes as combinations of alleles. So, if two alleles exist for a particular gene, then there are three genotypes: *RR*, *Rr*, and *rr*. To compare the numbers of alleles or genotypes, we measure or calculate the frequency of each. ❯ Genetic variation and change are measured in terms of the frequency of alleles in the gene pool of a population. A *frequency* is the proportion or ratio of a group that is of one type.

❯ **Reading Check**   *What is the main measure of genetic variation?*

> **normal distribution**   a line graph showing the general trends in a set of data of which most values are near the mean

READING TOOLBOX

Everyday Words in Science   The word *normal* in science and math is often used to describe measurements that fit within a normal distribution. What does a doctor mean when talking about "normal height" for a person of your age?

Answers to Caption Questions

Figure 4: No. Even if an allele is dominant, it may not be the most frequent
allele in a population.

READING TOOLBOX

Visual Literacy Help students relate
Figure 4 to the genotype-frequency
equations. Have them locate the
attached earlobe on the circle graph
and note the percent of genotype
frequencies represented by this
part of the whole. (32%) Ask how
the genotype for this trait is represented. (by *ee*) Next, have students
look at the first equation and find
"frequency of ee". Point out that in
the equation *"frequency of ee"* has
been replaced with the value 0.32,
representing 32%. Note that the
other values have been derived in a
similar manner. Then, ask students
to relate the 1 in the equation to the
graph. (It represents 100% of genotype frequencies). **LS** Visual

Genotype Frequencies Vs. Allele Frequencies

Figure 4 You cannot see alleles, and
you cannot always tell genotype based
on phenotype. You have to use math and
know dominance patterns to calculate
allele frequencies. ❯ Is the dominant
allele always the most frequent?

SCLINKS.

www.scilinks.org
Topic: Genotype/
Phenotype
Code: HX80662

Tracking Frequencies To study genetic
change, biologists want to keep track of the
frequency of each allele in a population over time.
They can keep track in several ways. A direct way
would be to detect and count every allele in every
individual, which is rarely practical. An indirect
way is to use mathematics along with a knowledge of how alleles combine. Recall that alleles
combine to form genotypes that, in turn, produce
recognizable phenotypes.

To understand the basic mathematics of allele
frequencies, consider the simple example shown in
Figure 4. Human ear lobes have two phenotypes:
unattached (free hanging) or attached at the base.
The ear lobe character is thought to be controlled
by a single gene, and the unattached trait is
thought to be dominant. So, the unattached allele
is represented as *E,* and the attached allele is represented as *e.* People
with attached ear lobes are homozygous recessive, or genotype *ee.*
People with unattached ear lobes are either homozygous dominant
(*EE*) or heterozygous (*Ee*).

Genotype Frequencies Notice how genotype frequencies differ
from allele frequencies. Suppose that the population in **Figure 4** consists of 100 people. In this case, 37% of the population, or 37 people,
are genotype *ee*; 32 are *Ee*; and 31 are *EE*. Keep in mind that in ratios
and percentages, all of the parts add up to one whole, or 100%. So, the
sum of genotype frequencies in a population should always be equal
to 1 (or 100%). This fact leads to the following equation:

(frequency of *EE*) + (frequency of *Ee*) + (frequency of *ee*) = 1

Using the numbers in our example, the equation proceeds as follows:

$$0.31 + 0.32 + 0.37 = 1$$

Allele Frequencies Similarly, the sum of allele frequencies for any
gene must equal 1, as in the following equation:

(frequency of *E*) + (frequency of *e*) = 1

or

$$\frac{(\text{count of } E)}{(\text{total})} + \frac{(\text{count of } e)}{(\text{total})} = 1$$

In our example population, there are 94 *E* alleles and 106 *e* alleles,
and the total is 200 alleles. The equation proceeds as follows:

$$\frac{94}{200} + \frac{106}{200} = 0.47 + 0.53 = 1$$

As you can see, the frequency of the *E* allele is 0.47, and the frequency
of the *e* allele is 0.53. Notice that the dominant allele is not necessarily the most frequent! Also keep in mind that you often cannot tell
genotypes by looking at phenotypes. However, you will soon learn
how these equations can be used to track changes in populations.

❯ **Reading Check** *What is the sum of all allele frequencies for any
one gene?*

Why It Matters

Blood Types Tell students that allele frequencies
in humans often differ among populations. The
alleles for the ABO blood groups are an example.
The chart shows genotype frequencies for several
populations. **LS** Visual

Blood Types in Populations Within the United States				
Blood Types (genotypes)	Caucasians	African Americans	Alaskan Eskimos	Navajo
O (*ii*)	45%	49%	38%	73%
A (*I^{A}i*)	40%	27%	44%	27%
B (*I^{B}i*)	11%	20%	13%	0%
AB (*I^{A}I^B*)	4%	4%	5%	0%

⏱ 15 min

Alleles: The Next Generation 🔊 4.3.1b

Model the allele frequencies in a population over time.

Procedure

1. Work in a group, which will represent a population. Obtain **two colors of marbles (one pair) for each member in the group.** Each color will represent a unique allele. Choose one color to be "dominant."

2. Mix the marbles. Each member of the "population" should randomly take two "alleles." Record the resulting genotype and phenotype of each member.

3. Each member should hide one marble in each hand and then randomly exchange one of these "alleles" with another member. Record the resulting genotypes and phenotypes of each member.

4. Repeat the steps to model four more "generations."

Analysis

1. **Determine** the genotype and phenotype ratios for each "generation." Do the ratios change over time?

2. **Propose** a way to change the ratios in your population from one generation to the next. Propose a way that this change could happen in a real population.

Quick Lab

Teacher's Notes If groups have less than five people, students should exchange alleles with the same person more than once.

Materials
• marbles, two different colors

Answers to Analysis

1. The ratios should remain the same for all generations.

2. Marbles could be added or subtracted; alleles could be added or subtracted.

> ## Close

Formative Assessment

The sum of all allele frequencies in a population at any time is called

_____.

A. polygenic (Incorrect. This refers to a character influenced by several genes.)

B. genotype frequency (Incorrect. This refers to the frequency of genotypes in a population at a given time.)

C. a phenotypic variation (Incorrect. This refers to the variations of observable traits among individuals.)

D. a gene pool (Correct! The gene pool consists of all possible alleles present in a population at a given time.)

Sources of Genetic Variation

Evolution cannot proceed if there is no variation. As you have learned, this variation must originate as new alleles. ❯ **The major source of new alleles in natural populations is mutation in germ cells.**

Mutation is important, but it generates new alleles at a slow rate. New alleles first arise in populations as changes to DNA in the sperm and ova (called *germ* cells) of individuals. If a germ cell with a mutation goes on to form offspring, then a new allele is added to the gene pool. Mutations can also occur in nongerm cells (called *somatic* cells), but these mutations are not passed on to offspring.

❯ **Reading Check** *Why is mutation so important?*

ACADEMIC VOCABULARY

generate produce; bring into being; cause to be

Section 1 Review

> ### KEY IDEAS

1. **Describe** the scope of population genetics.

2. **Relate** the number of genes that affect a phenotype to the variation in traits that may exist.

3. **Explain** how genetic variation is measured.

4. **Identify** the major source of genetic variation in a population.

CRITICAL THINKING

5. **Analyzing Concepts** Even in cases of simple Mendelian inheritance within a population, the ratio of phenotypes of a specific character is rarely the same as the ratio of alleles for that character. Explain why these ratios differ.

6. **Applying Logic** Can an individual organism evolve in the Darwinian sense? Explain your answer in terms of genetic variation within populations.

MATH SKILLS

7. **Distribution Curves** Suppose that **Figure 3** represents the distribution of shoe sizes in a class of twelfth graders. How might the distribution change if the shoes of a class of first graders were added to those of the twelfth graders? Explain your answer.

Answers to Section Review

1. Population genetics is the study of microevolution by observing changes in the numbers and types of alleles in populations.

2. Polygenic characters may exist as a variety of traits; the more genes that contribute to the production of the trait, the greater the potential for variation.

3. Genetic variation and change are measured in terms of the frequency of alleles in the gene pool of a population.

4. mutation

5. Ratios differ because of dominance. Phenotypes that are homozygous dominant and heterozygous for a characteristic will appear identical. Only individuals that are homozygous recessive for that characteristic will have a different phenotype.

6. Individual organisms cannot evolve. With more individuals and genetic variation in a population, more opportunities exist for members of that population to survive and reproduce. Evolution of populations is dependent on genetic variation of alleles combined with differences in survival among individuals.

7. The normal distribution would have two "hills"; that is, the shoe sizes would have two different average values (modes): the average height of the younger students on the left side of the graph, and the average values of the older students on the right side of the graph. The mean would lie in between these hills, but few values would fall there.

Genetic Change

Key Ideas

> What does the Hardy-Weinberg principle predict?

> How does sexual reproduction influence evolution?

> Why does population size matter?

> What are the limits of the force of natural selection?

> What patterns can result from natural selection?

Key Terms

genetic equilibrium

Why It Matters

The mathematics of genetics can be used to make predictions about future generations.

> Focus

The purpose of this section is to explain the Hardy-Weinberg principle, the forces that can change allele frequencies how each force can affect populations, and how natural selection can change the distribution of traits in populations.

Bellringer

Use the Bellringer transparency to prepare students for this section.

> Teach

Teaching Key Ideas

Allele Frequencies Tell students that polydactyly (extra fingers) in humans is caused by a dominant allele. Ask students if therefore, they think the frequency of polydactyly should be increasing, decreasing, or staying the same. (Some students may think that it must be increasing since dominant alleles "overpower" recessive alleles.) Explain that the Hardy-Weinberg equation shows that allele frequency will remain the same if no evolutionary forces are acting.

The Living Environment
Standard 4

3.1b New inheritable characteristics can result from new combinations of existing genes or from mutations of genes in reproductive cells.

3.1c Mutation and the sorting and recombining of genes during meiosis and fertilization result in a great variety of possible gene combinations.

3.1f Species evolve over time. Evolution is the consequence of the interactions of (1) the potential for a species to increase its numbers, (2) the genetic variability of offspring due to mutation and recombination of genes, (3) a finite supply of the resources required for life, and (4) the ensuing selection by the environment of those offspring better able to survive and leave offspring.

3.1g Some characteristics give individuals an advantage over others in surviving and reproducing, and the advantaged offspring, in turn, are more likely than others to survive and reproduce. The proportion of individuals that have advantageous characteristics will increase.

3.1i Behaviors have evolved through natural selection. The broad patterns of behavior exhibited by organisms are those that have resulted in greater reproductive success.

Figure 5 Allele frequencies can remain stable while genotype frequencies change.

You might think that a dominant trait would always be the most common trait in a population. When biologists began to study population genetics, they found that this was not always true.

Equilibrium and Change

In 1908, the English mathematician G. H. Hardy and the German physician Wilhelm Weinberg began to model population genetics by using algebra and probabilities. They showed that in theory, the frequency of alleles in a population should not change from one generation to the next. Moreover, the ratio of heterozygous individuals to homozygous individuals (the genotype frequencies) should not change. Such a population, in which no genetic change occurred, would be in a state of **genetic equilibrium.**

Measuring Change Genetic change in a population can be measured as a change in genotype frequency or allele frequency. A change in one does not necessarily mean a change in the other. For example, as shown in **Figure 5,** the genotype frequencies changed between generations, but the allele frequencies did not.

Allele Frequencies in Two Generations

Genotype frequency	Allele frequency	Generation
RR (red) = 0.5 *Rr* (pink) = 0.5 *rr* (white)= 0	R = 0.75 r = 0.25	1 RR RR Rr Rr RR Rr Rr RR
RR (red) = 0.625 *Rr* (pink) = 0.25 *rr* (white)= 0.125	R = 0.75 r = 0.25	2 RR Rr rr RR RR Rr RR RR

Section Correlations

4.3.1b	4.3.1g
4.3.1c	4.3.1i
4.3.1f	

Key Resources

 Transparencies
D20 Two Kinds of Selection

Visual Concepts
Hardy-Weinberg Genetic Equilibrium Example

Comparing the Effects of Random and Nonrandom Mating

Genetic Drift

Natural Selection

Directional Selection

Stabilizing Selection

Differentiated Instruction

Struggling Readers

Paired Reading Assign students to cooperative pairs. Have each student copy the blue and red headings of section onto a piece of paper. Then, have them read each passage silently. As they read, have them indicate parts they understand with a check mark and parts they do not understand with a question mark. After reading each passage, have the partners discuss what they did or did not understand.
LS Verbal

Math Skills — Hardy-Weinberg Equation

The Hardy-Weinberg principle can be expressed as an equation that can be used to predict stable genotype frequencies in a population.

The equation is usually written as follows:

$$p^2 \quad + \quad 2pq \quad + \quad q^2 \quad = \quad 1$$

(frequency of RR individuals)   (frequency of Rr individuals)   (frequency of rr individuals)   (sum of all frequencies)

Recall that the sum of the genotype frequencies in a population must always equal 1.

By convention, the frequency of the more common of the two alleles is referred to as p, and the frequency of the rarer allele is referred to as q.

Individuals that are homozygous for allele R occur at a frequency of p times p, or p^2. Individuals that are homozygous for allele r occur at the frequency of q times q, or q^2.

Heterozygotes have one copy of R and one copy of r, but heterozygotes can occur in two ways—R from the father and r from the mother, or r from the father and R from the mother. Therefore, the frequency of heterozygotes is $2pq$.

Hardy-Weinberg Principle Hardy and Weinberg made a mathematical model of genetic equilibrium. This model is the basis of the *Hardy-Weinberg principle.* ❭ The Hardy-Weinberg principle predicts that the frequencies of alleles and genotypes in a population will not change unless at least one of five forces acts upon the population.

Forces of Genetic Change In reality, populations are subject to many forces and undergo genetic change constantly. ❭ The forces that can act against genetic equilibrium are gene flow, nonrandom mating, genetic drift, mutation, and natural selection.

Gene Flow *Gene flow* occurs when genes are added to or removed from a population. Gene flow can be caused by *migration,* the movement of individuals from one population to another, as shown in **Figure 6.** Each individual carries genes into or out of the population, so genetic frequencies may change as a result.

Nonrandom Mating In sexually reproducing populations, any limits or preferences of mate choice will cause nonrandom mating. If a limited set of genotypes mates to produce offspring, the genotype frequencies of the population may change.

Genetic Drift Chance events can cause rare alleles to be lost from one generation to the next, especially when populations are small. Such random effects on allele frequencies are called *genetic drift*. The allele frequencies are changed directly and genotype frequencies change as a result.

Mutation A mutation can add a new allele to a population. Allele frequencies are changed directly, if only slightly.

Natural Selection Natural selection acts to eliminate individuals with certain traits from a population. As individuals are eliminated, the alleles for those traits may become less frequent in the population. Thus, both allele and genotype frequencies may change.

❭ **Reading Check** *What can cause gene flow?*

> **genetic equilibrium** a state in which the allele frequencies of a population remain in the same ratios from one generation to the next

Figure 6 These caribou are migrating from one place to another. If they meet other groups of caribou and interbreed, gene flow may occur.

Teaching Key Ideas

The Founder Effect Ask students to imagine a population of 100 birds inhabiting a coastal area. Two alleles, *W* and *w*, affect wing color. *W* is the dominant allele that produces red wings; *w* is the recessive allele that produces white wings. In this population, 96 out of 100 birds have red wings (64 *WW* and 32 *Ww*); only 4 have white wings (*ww*). A hurricane blows 10 birds 500 miles out to sea, where they land on a small island. Two of the birds have white wings (*ww*); 8 have red wings (4 *WW*, 4 *Ww*). Have students determine the frequency of the *w* allele in the new population. (Total alleles = 20; *W* = 12/20, or 60%; *w* = 8/20, or 40%.) Point out that the frequency of allele *w* has jumped from 20% to 40%! Tell students that this form of genetic drift is called the "founder effect" and is similar to the effect of inbreeding or population size reduction. **LS** **Logical**

go.hrw.com
✳ interact online

Students can interact with populations by going to go.hrw.com and typing in the keyword HX8POPF8.

Figure 7 Sexual selection favors the development of extreme phenotypic traits in some species. The vibrant red stripe on the blue muzzle of this male mandrill baboon does not appear in females.

Figure 8 Alleles are more likely to be lost from smaller populations. So, variation tends to decrease over time in smaller populations but not in larger populations.

go.hrw.com
✳ interact online
Keyword: HX8POPF8

Sexual Reproduction and Evolution

Recall that sexual reproduction creates chances to recombine alleles and thus increase variation in a population. So, sexual reproduction has an important role in evolution. ❯ **Sexual reproduction creates the possibility that mating patterns or behaviors can influence the gene pool of a population.** For example, in animals, females sometimes select mates based on the male's size, color, ability to gather food, or other characteristics, as shown in **Figure 7.** This kind of behavior is called *sexual selection* and is an example of nonrandom mating.

Another example of nonrandom mating is *inbreeding*, in which individuals either self-fertilize or mate with others like themselves. Inbreeding tends to increase the frequency of homozygotes, because a smaller pool of alleles is recombined. For example, populations of self-fertilizing plants consist mostly of homozygotes. However, inbreeding does not change the overall frequency of alleles. Inbreeding is more likely to occur if a population is small.

Population Size and Evolution

Population size strongly affects the probability of genetic change in a population. ❯ **Allele frequencies are more likely to remain stable in large populations than in small populations.** In a small population, the frequency of an allele can be quickly reduced by a chance event. For example, a fire or drought can reduce a large population to a few survivors. At that point, each allele is carried in a few individuals. The loss of even one individual from the population can severely reduce an allele's frequency. So, a particular allele may disappear in a few generations, as shown in **Figure 8.** This kind of change is called *genetic drift* because allele frequencies drift around randomly. The force of genetic drift is strongest in small populations. In a larger population, alleles may increase or decrease in frequency, but the alleles are not likely to disappear.

❯ **Reading Check** *What is the genetic effect of inbreeding?*

Year 1

A large population usually contains a wide variety of alleles. A smaller sample of this population may contain less variety.

Year 10

The smaller group will tend to lose variation over time.

Year 100

The larger population will tend to maintain its variation.

Why It Matters

Genetic Bottleneck The cheetah is a species whose evolution has been seriously affected by genetic drift. Cheetahs have undergone drastic population declines within the last 5,000 years. As a result, the cheetahs alive today are descendants of only a few individuals, and each cheetah is genetically similar to other cheetahs. This kind of drastic reduction in the variation of a gene pool is called a *genetic bottleneck*. One consequence of the cheetahs' current genetic uniformity is a reduced ability to survive diseases. This lack of genetic diversity makes cheetahs more vulnerable to extinction than the other large cats, perhaps even more than some cats that have smaller populations.

QuickLab

Genetic Risk Assessment 4.2.2e

How can the Hardy-Weinberg equation be used? It can be used to predict the risk of genetic disorders in a population. For example, medical professionals may know how many people have been diagnosed with a genetic disorder. From this information, they can predict how many people are at risk of passing on the disorder.

Procedure

❶ Consider these facts: Cystic fibrosis (CF) is a disorder that occurs in 1 out of every 2,500 Caucasians in North America. CF is caused by a recessive allele.

❷ Use the Hardy-Weinberg equation to predict the percentage of carriers of the allele that causes CF.

🕐 15 min

Lungs of a person with cystic fibrosis

Analysis

1. **Calculate** the frequency of the recessive allele.
2. **Calculate** the frequency of the dominant allele.
3. **Calculate** the frequency of carriers (heterozygotes).
4. **Determine** how many of every 1,000 Caucasian North Americans are likely to carry the cystic fibrosis allele.

Natural Selection and Evolution

Recall that Charles Darwin proposed natural selection as a mechanism that could drive evolution. Scientists have studied many examples of natural selection in action.

How Selection Acts Keep in mind that the process of natural selection is a result of the following facts.

- **All populations have genetic variation.** Any population has an array of individuals that differ slightly from one another in genetic makeup. Although this variation may be obvious in humans, variation also exists in species whose members may appear identical, such as a species of bacteria.

- **Individuals tend to produce more offspring than the environment can support.** Individuals of a population often struggle to survive, whether competing with one another or not.

- **All populations depend upon the reproduction of individuals.** Some biologists have noted that "evolutionary fitness is measured in grandchildren." The statement means that an individual must survive to reproduce, and also produce offspring that can reproduce, to pass its genes on to future generations.

Genetic Results of Selection The result of natural selection is that the frequency of an allele may increase or decrease depending on the allele's effects on survival and reproduction. Natural selection causes <u>deviations</u> from genetic equilibrium by directly changing the frequencies of alleles. Although natural selection is not the only force of evolution, it is a powerful force.

❯ **Reading Check** *How is "fitness" measured in evolutionary terms?*

SC*LINKS*.

www.scilinks.org
Topic: Natural Selection
Code: HX81016

ACADEMIC VOCABULARY

deviate to turn aside; to diverge or differ

QuickLab

Teacher's Notes Hardy-Weinberg proportions seldom, if ever, occur in nature because at least one of the five forces of evolution is always affecting populations.

Answers to Analysis

1. If q^2, the frequency of recessive homozygotes, is 0.0004, then q is the square root of 0.0004, or 0.02.
2. $p + q = 1, p = 1 - q$. So, $p = 1 - 0.02$, or 0.98.
3. $2pq = 2 \times 0.98 \times 0.02 = 0.0392$
4. 39 of every 1,000 Caucasian North Americans would be predicted to carry the cystic fibrosis allele unexpressed (without disease).

Teaching Key Ideas

Changing Allele Frequency Have groups of students come up with scenarios that result in a change in the frequency of a particular allele. Have groups answer the following questions about their scenarios: What change occurred? What genetic variations existed in individuals before and after the change? What characteristics of the new environment contributed to changing the frequency of alleles?
🅛🅢 **Logical**

Answers to Caption Questions

Figure 9: A colorless crayfish that was previously adapted for a dark environment might be found by predators more easily when placed in a well-lit environment.

Teaching Key Ideas

Natural Selection and Phenotypes
Reinforce the concept that natural selection operates on phenotypes and not genotypes. Show students two photographs, one of a canine population in which differences among phenotypes are obvious and one of another species in which phenotypic differences are not very apparent. The latter could be one of penguins, which, also, form large populations of sexually reproducing individuals. Point out that no two penguins are exactly alike and that every penguin is able to recognize its mate, offspring, and nesting-ground neighbors. Ask students what type of variations in the phenotypes might be favored by natural selection. (Answers will vary.) **Visual**

READING TOOLBOX

General Statements Sample answer: some phenotypes may be barely successful yet not be removed; some combinations of phenotypes may succeed better than others.
 Logical

Figure 9 Crayfish species exist in a variety of colorations. In many cases, the coloration helps the crayfish hide from predators or attract mates. But for crayfish species that live in lightless caves, having color gives no fitness advantage. ❯ What might happen to a colorless crayfish placed in a well-lit pond?

READING TOOLBOX

General Statements List possible exceptions to the statement "Natural selection removes unsuccessful phenotypes from a population."

Why Selection Is Limited The key lesson that scientists have learned about evolution by natural selection is that the environment does the selecting. If the environment changes in the future, the set of characteristics that are most adaptive may change. For example, each of the animals shown in **Figure 9** is adapted to a specific environment and may not be able to survive if placed in another environment.

Natural selection is limited by nature. ❯ **Natural selection acts only to change the relative frequency of alleles that exist in a population.** Natural selection cannot direct the creation of new alleles, nor will it necessarily delete every allele that is not adaptive. So, natural selection does not create perfectly adapted organisms.

Indirect Force Natural selection does not act directly on genes. It merely allows individuals who express favorable traits to reproduce and pass those traits on to their offspring. Darwin's idea of natural selection, stated in modern terms, is that ❯ **natural selection acts on genotypes by removing unsuccessful phenotypes from a population.** Biologists say that certain phenotypes are "selected against" and that certain genotypes are thus "favored."

Role of Mutation Think about how natural selection might operate on a new allele that has arisen by mutation. At first, the mutation may make no difference. Even if the mutation results in a nonfunctional protein, the cell may have a functional copy of the original gene as its second allele. However, the new, nonfunctioning version could be passed on as a recessive allele. This kind of mutation is the probable origin of many recessive genetic disorders. Genetic disorders can persist in populations because only those traits that are expressed can be targets of natural selection.

Natural Selection and Behavior Behaviors can evolve in much the same way that physical traits do. Natural selection will favor behaviors that are influenced by genes and that help individuals to survive, reproduce, and pass on their genes. The effects of selection can often be seen in behaviors related to courtship, mating, and caring for offspring and close relatives. Selection will favor any behavior that helps an individual to pass on genes to future generations.

Differentiated Instruction

Basic Learners

Genetic Mutations Have students research different genetic mutations found in nature and explain how the phenotype is either favorable or unfavorable in a given environment for the individual. Have them predict the outcome for the individual with the genetic mutation. Students should share their results with the class. **Verbal**

Patterns of Natural Selection

Recall that many traits, such as human height, have a bell-curve distribution in natural populations. When natural selection acts on polygenic traits, it essentially acts to eliminate some part of the bell curve.

❯ Three major patterns are possible in the way that natural selection affects the distribution of polygenic characters over time. These patterns are directional selection, stabilizing selection, and disruptive selection, as **Figure 10** illustrates.

Directional Selection In *directional selection,* the "peak" of a normal distribution moves in one direction along its range. In this case, selection acts to eliminate one extreme from a range of phenotypes. Thus, the alleles for the extreme phenotype become less common in the population. This pattern of selection is often seen in the evolution of single-gene traits, such as pesticide resistance in insects.

Stabilizing Selection In *stabilizing selection,* the bell-curve shape becomes narrower. In this case, selection eliminates individuals that have alleles for any extreme type. So, the ratio of intermediate phenotypes increases. In other words, this pattern of selection tends to "stabilize" the average by favoring a narrow range of phenotypes. Stabilizing selection is very common in nature.

Disruptive Selection In *disruptive selection,* the bell curve is "disrupted" and pushed apart into two peaks. In this case, selection acts to eliminate individuals with average phenotype values. Each peak is pushed in an opposite direction, away from the average. The result is increasingly distinct or variable phenotypes in the population. Mathematically, the new distribution is said to have two mode values, each of which differs from the mean value.

❯ **Reading Check** *Which form of selection increases the range of variation in a distribution?*

Directional Selection

Number of animals — Tongue length

Stabilizing Selection

Number of animals — Body size

Disruptive Selection

Number of animals — Shell color

Figure 10 Selection can shift a distribution from an original bell curve (green) toward a new shape (purple).

Section 2 Review

❯ KEY IDEAS

1. **Restate** the Hardy-Weinberg principle in your own terms.
2. **Relate** sexual reproduction to evolutionary forces.
3. **Explain** why a small population is subject to genetic drift.
4. **Describe** the limits of the force of natural selection.
5. **List** the patterns that can result from natural selection acting on polygenic traits.

CRITICAL THINKING

6. **Comparing Concepts** In what way is the genetic effect of nonrandom mating similar to the genetic effect of gene flow?
7. **Reasoning Opinions** Are all organisms perfectly adapted for their habitat? Explain.

USING SCIENCE GRAPHICS

8. **Prediction** Redraw each of the graphs in **Figure 10.** Use as examples birds with a range of beak sizes. Describe possible situations that would cause each pattern of selection.

Teaching Key Ideas

Visual Literacy Test students' understanding of **Figure 10.** Ask: How might a shorter tongue affect the anteater's survival? (A shorter tongue reaches a shorter distance, so fewer ants are reached.) Why might a mid-size salamander have an advantage over larger or smaller ones? (A smaller one might be caught easily while a larger one might have difficulty finding enough food.) How can either of two shell colors be advantageous to barnacles? (The environment might contain different colored surfaces.) **LS Logical**

❯ Close

Formative Assessment

Natural selection indirectly affects _____ by removing unsuccessful _____ from a population.
- **A.** phenotypes, genotypes (Incorrect. Natural selection does not act directly on genes.)
- **B.** populations, genotypes (Incorrect. Natural selection acts upon genotypes in a population by removing phenotypes.)
- **C.** genotypes, phenotypes (Correct. The gene pool is indirectly changed by removing individuals with specific phenotypic traits from the population.)
- **D.** individuals, genotypes (Incorrect. Natural selection acts upon genotypes by removing individuals with specific phenotypes.)

Answers to Section Review

1. Neither allele nor genotype frequencies should change unless a force, such as natural selection or genetic drift, acts on a population.
2. Sexual reproduction creates the possibility that mating patterns or behaviors can cause genetic change and thus act as a force of evolution.
3. Allele frequencies are more likely to become unstable in small populations.
4. Natural selection is limited by nature; it can only act to change the relative frequency of commonly expressed alleles that exist in a population.
5. directional selection, stabilizing selection, and disruptive selection
6. Both change genotype frequencies with addition or removal of individuals from the gene pool.
7. No, natural selection cannot direct the creation of new alleles, and it will not necessarily delete every allele that is not adaptive.
8. Student graphs should show all three patterns of selection using a scale of beak sizes from small to large. Situations should include changes that would affect the fitness value of certain sizes of beak. For example, availability of two very different seed types might cause disruptive selection on bill sizes.

Why It Matters
Wild Laboratories

REAL WORLD

What do the finches of the Galápagos Islands, the anole lizards of the Caribbean Islands, and the *Drosophila* flies of the Hawaiian Islands have in common? Each of these groups of related species has been extensively studied by evolutionary biologists. And each group has undergone a similar pattern of evolution on each group of islands.

Roles in the Landscape

Darwin found that each Galápagos finch species ate certain types of food and had a beak that was adapted for that food. Similarly, biologists have found that each Caribbean anole species tends to live in a certain part of the landscape and has body parts adapted for running, climbing, or hiding in that area. On each Caribbean island, a unique set of species fulfills each "specialist" role.

Trunk-Ground Specialist *Anolis lineatopus* specializes in running along tree trunks and the ground.

Trunk-Crown Specialist *Anolis allisoni* specializes in crawling along the tops and trunks of tropical plants.

Twig Specialist *Anolis angusticeps* specializes in clinging to twigs.

Grass-Bush Specialist *Anolis bahorucoensis* specializes in clinging to grass and stems.

Quick Project Find out how many species of anoles have been identified in the Caribbean islands as compared with the total number of anole species worldwide. Likewise, find out the number of species of Hawaiian flies in the family Drosophilidae.

Key Ideas	Key Terms	Why It Matters
❯ How can species be defined? ❯ How do we know when new species have been formed? ❯ Why is studying extinction important to understanding evolution?	reproductive isolation subspecies	How we define species relates to how we study evolution and ecology.

All of the beetles in **Figure 11** belong to the same species, but each looks different. Identifying species or telling species apart is often difficult. Part of the difficulty lies in the very definition of *species*.

Defining Species

Since the days of Darwin, scientists have understood that species are not permanent, stable things. And thanks to Mendel, scientists have learned that genetics underlie the variation and change in species. With this knowledge, they have reconsidered the very definition of *species*. ❯ **Today, scientists may use more than one definition for *species*. The definition used depends on the organisms and field of science being studied.** Increasingly, scientists want to do more than name and describe things—they want to know how things are related.

As you have learned, a *species* is generally defined as a group of natural populations that can interbreed. This definition is based on the *biological species concept*, which adds the requirement that the interbreeding produce healthy, fertile offspring. Applying this concept, any populations that do not share future offspring could be considered separate species.

However, the biological species concept cannot be applied to all organisms. It does not apply to those that reproduce asexually or that are known only from fossils. And any form of reproduction may be difficult to confirm. So, species may instead be defined based on their physical features, their ecological roles, and their genetic relatedness.

❯ **Reading Check** *Why is a species hard to define?*

The Living Environment
Standard 4
3.1I Extinction of a species occurs when the environment changes and the adaptive characteristics of a species are insufficient to allow its survival. Fossils indicate that many organisms that lived long ago are extinct. Extinction of species is common; most of the species that have lived on Earth no longer exist.

Figure 11 How many species of beetles are in this photo? Just one!
❯ What problems arise when defining species based on appearances?

Key Resources

 Visual Concepts
Reproductive Isolation
Geographic Isolation

Answers to Caption Questions

Figure 12: ecological niche, mating behavior, polyploidy, and hybridization

---

Demonstration

Forming a New Species Organize students into small groups. Have each group brainstorm and select an existing species and create a fictitious set of circumstances that would create divergence within the population, resulting in speciation. Each group should draw both the existing species and new species and explain how natural selection acted upon the populations. Post the drawings on the bulletin board and have each group discuss their predictions. **Verbal**

READING TOOLBOX

Using Words Ask students what the word *net* means in everyday usage. (Sample answer: "open-meshed material commonly used to catch something") Point out *net* in the boldfaced sentence in the second paragraph. Ask what *net* means in the sentence. (Sample answer: "overall" or "total") **LS Verbal**

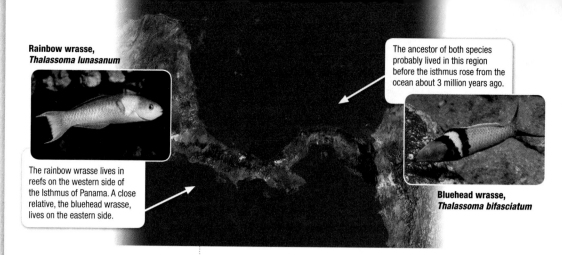

Rainbow wrasse, *Thalassoma lunasanum*

The ancestor of both species probably lived in this region before the isthmus rose from the ocean about 3 million years ago.

The rainbow wrasse lives in reefs on the western side of the Isthmus of Panama. A close relative, the bluehead wrasse, lives on the eastern side.

Bluehead wrasse, *Thalassoma bifasciatum*

Figure 12 These two species probably evolved from a single species that was separated into two groups by geographic change. ❯ What other mechanisms can isolate species?

reproductive isolation a state in which a population can no longer interbreed with other populations to produce future generations

subspecies a taxonomic classification below the level of species; refers to populations that differ from, but can interbreed with, other populations of the same species

Forming New Species

Each population of a single species lives in a different place. In each place, natural selection acts on the population and tends to result in offspring that are better adapted to the environment. If the environments differ, the adaptations may differ. The accumulation of differences between populations is called *divergence* and can lead to the formation of new species.

Recall that *speciation* is the process of forming new species by evolution from preexisting species. Speciation rarely occurs overnight; it usually occurs in stages over generations. ❯ **Speciation has occurred when the net effects of evolutionary forces result in a population that has unique features and is reproductively isolated.**

Reproductive Isolation Recall that the biological species concept defines species as interbreeding groups. Thus, if two groups stop interbreeding, they take a step toward speciation. **Reproductive isolation** is a state in which two populations can no longer interbreed to produce future offspring. From this point on, the groups may be subject to different forces, so they will tend to diverge over time.

Through divergence over time, populations of the same species may differ enough to be considered subspecies. **Subspecies** are simply populations that have taken a step toward speciation by diverging in some detectable way. This definition is imprecise because reproductive isolation is only apparent after the passage of time.

Mechanisms of Isolation Divergence and speciation can happen in many ways. Any of the following mechanisms may contribute to the reproductive isolation of populations.

- **Geography** A physical barrier, such as the one shown in **Figure 12,** may arise between populations. Such a barrier could prevent interbreeding. Over time, if the populations diverge enough, they will probably not interbreed even if the barrier is removed.

Differentiated Instruction

Advanced Learners/GATE

Species Divergence Ask students to research an animal species, such as the black bear, and how a subspecies, such as the Florida black bear, may have diverged. Have them share the results of their research with the class. **LS Verbal**

- **Ecological Niche** Recall that the *niche* of a species is the role that the species has in its environment, including all of its interactions with other species. Divergence can occur when populations use different niches. The divergence of multiple lineages into many new species in a specific area and time is called *adaptive radiation*.

- **Mating Behavior and Timing** Many species that sexually reproduce have specific behaviors for attracting mates, such as a pattern of sounds or actions. Some undergo mating at specific times or in response to environmental events. If two populations develop differences in these behaviors, they may no longer attract each other for mating. This mechanism seems to be responsible for the species divergence shown in **Figure 13.**

- **Polyploidy** Recall that a *polyploid* organism has received a duplicate set of chromosomes by accident. A polyploid individual may be reproductively isolated because it cannot pair gametes with others from the original population. However, it may reproduce by vegetative growth, self-fertilize, or find a polyploid mate. In these cases, a new species can arise rapidly. Polyploidy has been observed in many plant species.

- **Hybridization** In some cases, two closely related species may come back into contact with each other and attempt to mate. The offspring of such a mating are called *hybrids*. In cases in which the two parent species are sufficiently diverged from each other, their offspring may be sterile. For example, a mule is a sterile hybrid of a horse and a donkey. Another possibility is that hybrid offspring may not be well adapted to the environment of either parent. Finally, if the parents have many genetic differences, the offspring may not develop successfully. However, there are also many cases in which hybridization leads to new and successful species.

❯ **Reading Check** *Is hybridization always successful?*

READING TOOLBOX

Outlining Complete your outline for this chapter. Be sure to include each of the headings on this page, such as "Polyploidy" and "Hybridization." When you finish the chapter, review your outline and add notes to any heading whose meaning is unclear to you.

Figure 13 The pickerel frog and the leopard frog are closely related species. Differences in mating times may have caused their reproductive isolation. ❯ What other aspects of mating can push populations to diverge?

Mating Activity of Frogs

Pickerel frog, *Rana palustris*

Leopard frog, *Rana pipiens*

Science Skills

Mating Activity of Frogs Have students refer to **Figure 13.** Ask students to predict how reproductive isolation might result in different mating times of the original species. (The original population may have become geographically isolated, resulting in different mating times due to differences in the microclimate.) **LS** **Logical**

READING TOOLBOX

Outlining Remind students that an outline should summarize information and not repeat it verbatim. **LS** **Verbal**

Answers to Caption Questions
Figure 13: other aspects of behavior, or genetics of sexual reproduction (such as chromosome number)

Differentiated Instruction

Basic Learners/Struggling Readers

Reproductive Isolation Have students create a chart listing the five mechanisms that may contribute to the reproductive isolation of a population. Ask them to research and list an animal or plant that has or could become an example of speciation as a result of each mechanism. (*Geography:* Kaibab and Aberts squirrels becoming separated by the Grand Canyon; *Ecological Niche:* some green anoles now occupying different niches because of competition with brown anoles; *Mating Behavior and Timing:* pickerel and leopard frogs have separate mating times; *Polyploidy:* bananas are triploid crops; *Hybridization:* wolves and dogs produce fertile offspring) **LS** **Verbal**

Teaching Key Ideas

Extinction Rate Tell students that studies of the fossil record estimate that species have disappeared on the average of one to four per year for every million species living except for five periods during the last 600 million years when the rates dramatically increased. However, scientists estimate that the rate is now 100 to 10,000 times Earth's past average.

> **Close**

Formative Assessment

A new species forms when a population _____.

A. diverges in some way from another population (Incorrect. Populations can differ but still belong to the same species.)

B. has unique features and is reproductively isolated (Correct! These two factors together result in speciation.)

C. lives separately from another population (Incorrect. A population living separately becomes a new species only if it develops unique features and is reproductively isolated.)

D. produces no offspring (Incorrect. With no offspring, the population will become extinct.)

Figure 14 The Tasmanian wolf was driven to extinction by ranchers and dogs in Australia in the early 1900s. **>** What is the role of extinction in evolution?

SciLINKS
www.scilinks.org
Topic: Extinction
Code: HX80558

Extinction: The End of Species

Extinction occurs when a species fails to produce any more descendants. The animal in **Figure 14** is extinct. Extinction, like speciation, can be detected only after it is complete. And extinction is as much a part of evolution as speciation is. Scientists estimate that more than 99% of all of the species that have ever lived on Earth have become extinct. **> The species that exist at any time are the net result of both speciation and extinction.** If you think of speciation as a branching of a "family tree," then extinction is like the loss of one of the branches.

As you will learn, many cases of extinction are the result of environmental change. Almost all of the dinosaurs died off because of some combination of meteor impacts, volcanism, and climate change on Earth millions of years ago. Anytime that an environment changes, species that were once well adapted may become poorly adapted. If the environment changes more rapidly than new adaptations arise within a species, the species may be driven to extinction.

> **Reading Check** *When do we know that extinction has happened?*

Section 3 Review

> **KEY IDEAS**

1. **List** features that may be used to define species in biology.
2. **Summarize** a general process by which one species can evolve into two species.
3. **Relate** extinction to changes that occur in the numbers and types of species over time.

CRITICAL THINKING

4. **Making Inferences** Would the biological species concept be useful for classifying bacterial species? Explain your answer.
5. **Relating Concepts** Relate the idea of reproductive isolation to the biological species concept.
6. **Describing Relationships** Describe the relationship between speciation and extinction in terms of a "family tree" of descent.

ALTERNATIVE ASSESSMENT

7. **Speciation-in-Action Poster** Sometimes, the easiest way to explain a concept is to illustrate real-world examples of the concept. Create a poster that illustrates examples of reproductive barriers between species. Show how these barriers relate to the biological species concept. Present your poster to the class.

Answers to Section Review

1. A species can be defined as a group of natural populations that can interbreed and produce fertile offspring or as a group of organisms with specific physical features, ecological roles, and genetic relatedness.

2. Two populations of the same species can become reproductively isolated. From this point on, the groups may be subject to different forces, so they will tend to diverge over time. Eventually, the populations may become different species that can no longer interbreed.

3. Extinctions reduce the number of species and changes the competition for resources.

4. Sample answer: Not always, because many bacteria reproduce asexually.

5. Reproductive isolation occurs when a population is unable to produce fertile offspring with other populations. The biological species concept defines a species as a group of natural populations that can interbreed.

6. Speciation is the beginning of a lineage of a species; extinction is the end of a lineage of a species.

7. Posters should illustrate reproductive barriers such as two species living in different habitats, differing coloration of males of two species, differing chromosomal numbers that would lead to non-viable zygotes, or size differences between members of different species.

Objectives

▶ Investigate the effect of population size on genetic drift.

▶ Analyze the mathematics of the Hardy-Weinberg principle.

Materials

■ buttons, blue (10 to 100)

■ buttons, red (10 to 100)

■ buttons, white (10 to 100)

■ jar or beaker, large, plastic

Genetic Drift

Random chance affects the frequencies of alleles in a population over time. This effect, called *genetic drift*, also depends on population size.

Preparation

1. **SCIENTIFIC METHODS** **State the Problem** How does population size affect allele frequencies? Read the procedure to see how you will test this.

2. **SCIENTIFIC METHODS** **Form a Hypothesis** Form a hypothesis that predicts the results of this procedure for three different population sizes.

Procedure

Possible alleles

Blood type molecules
- 🔺 Molecule A
- 🔺 Molecule B

① Prepare to model the populations. First, assign each color button to one of the alleles (I^A, I^B, or i) of the ABO blood types. Notice how each possible pairing of alleles matches one of the four types (A, B, AB, or O). Then, choose three different population sizes. Also choose one ratio of alleles at which to start all three populations (for example, I^A:I^B:i = 2:2:1). Create tables for your data.

② Represent the first population's alleles by placing the appropriate number of blue, red, and white buttons in a jar.

③ Randomly select two buttons from the jar to represent one person. Record this person's genotype and phenotype. Place the buttons back into the jar.

④ Repeat step 3 until you have modeled the appropriate number of people in the population. Tally the total number of each allele within this generation.

⑤ Empty the jar. Refill it with the number and color of buttons that matches the tallies recorded in step 4.

⑥ Repeat steps 3 through 5 until you have modeled four generations.

⑦ Repeat steps 2 through 6 to model two more populations.

Analyze and Conclude

1. **Analyzing Data** Describe any changes in genotype and phenotype ratios within each population over time.

2. **Explaining Results** Did any population maintain genetic equilibrium? Explain how you can tell.

3. **SCIENTIFIC METHODS** **Analyzing Results** Which population showed the greatest amount of genetic drift? Explain.

Time Required

25 minutes

Ratings

EASY ⟶ HARD

Teacher Prep 🧪

Student Setup 🧪

Concept Level 🧪🧪

Cleanup 🧪

Tips and Tricks

Stop students periodically during this activity, and ask them to predict what will happen next. Because the process is random, predictions are not likely to hold. However, students may begin to see the risk that certain alleles (button colors) will disappear from the population. When students repeat this activity with a different population size, they should begin to see that the effect of drift, loss of alleles, is stronger in smaller populations.

Answers to Analyze and Conclude

1. Answers will vary. Most populations should undergo changes in both ratios.

2. No (most likely). Genetic equilibrium would be indicated by having the same ratios in both genotype and phenotype in each successive generation.

3. The smallest population is most likely to show the greatest amount of drift. (This may not hold true if differences in population sizes are slight.) A single given allele makes up a greater proportion of the gene pool of a smaller population.

Lab Correlations

1.3.2 Apply statistical analysis techniques when appropriate to test if chance alone explains the results.

4.3.1f Species evolve over time. Evolution is the consequence of the interactions of (1) the potential for a species to increase its numbers, (2) the genetic variability of offspring...

Key Resources

 Holt Lab Generator

 Lab Datasheet (Levels A, B, C)

 Holt Science Biology Video Labs

 Virtual Investigations

SUPER SUMMARY

Have students connect the major concepts in this chapter through an interactive Super Summary. Visit **go.hrw.com** and type in the keyword **HX8POPS** to access the Super Summary for this chapter.

Reteaching Key Ideas

Allele Frequency Tell students that a certain population of plants contains only blue red flowers. Blue (B) is dominant to red (b). The population has 16% red-flowered plants. Have students calculate the frequency of the red allele (0.4), of the blue allele (0.6). **LS** Logical

Hardy-Weinberg Principle Tell students that a fictional trait, fuzzy wings, is caused by a dominant allele and prevents birds from flying swiftly. Ask students to explain if Hardy-Weinberg genetic equilibrium is likely in the frequency of this allele. (No. A recessive, fuzzy-wing phenotype makes the bird unable to catch food or flee from predators, so natural selection is likely to act on this phenotype, and reduce the frequency of this allele.) **LS** Logical

| Key Ideas | Key Terms |

1 Genetic Variation

> Microevolution can be studied by observing changes in the numbers and types of alleles in populations.

> Biologists study polygenic phenotypes by measuring each individual in the population and then analyzing the distribution of the measurements.

> Genetic variation and change are measured in terms of the frequency of alleles in the gene pool of a population.

> The major source of new alleles in natural populations is mutation in germ cells.

population genetics (399)
normal distribution (400)

2 Genetic Change

> The Hardy-Weinberg principle predicts that the frequencies of alleles and genotypes in a population will not change unless at least one of five forces acts upon the population. The forces that can act against genetic equilibrium are gene flow, nonrandom mating, genetic drift, mutation, and natural selection.

> Sexual reproduction creates the possibility that mating patterns or behaviors can influence the gene pool of a population.

> Allele frequencies are more likely to remain stable in large populations than in small populations.

> Natural selection acts only to change the relative frequency of alleles that exist in a population. Natural selection acts on genotypes by removing unsuccessful phenotypes from a population.

> Three major patterns are possible in the way that natural selection affects a distribution of polygenic characters over time. These patterns are directional selection, stabilizing selection, and disruptive selection.

genetic equilibrium (404)

3 Speciation

> Today, scientists may use more than one definition for species. The definition used depends on the organisms and field of science being studied.

> Speciation has occurred when the net effects of evolutionary forces result in a population that has unique features and is reproductively isolated.

> The species that exist at any time are the net result of both speciation and extinction.

reproductive isolation (412)
subspecies (412)

PART A: Answer all questions in this part.

Directions: For each statement or question, write on your separate answer sheet the number of the word or expression that best completes the statement or answers the question.

1 Which factor could be the cause of the other three in an animal species?

(1) the inability of the species to adapt to changes
(2) a lack of genetic variability in the species
(3) extinction of the species
(4) a decrease in the survival rate of the species

2 Which statement describing a cause of extinction includes the other three?

(1) Members of the extinct species were unable to compete for food.
(2) Members of the extinct species were unable to conceal their presence by camouflage.
(3) Members of the extinct species lacked adaptations essential for survival.
(4) Members of the extinct species were too slow to escape from predators.

3 Which process is least likely to add to the variety of traits in a population?

(1) deletion of bases from DNA
(2) genetic engineering
(3) accurate replication of DNA
(4) exchange of segments between chromosomes

4 Which of the following is a reason why natural selection is limited in its influence on evolution?

(1) Natural selection cannot direct the creation of new alleles.
(2) All populations depend on the reproduction of individuals.
(3) Natural selection eliminates certain genotypes from populations.
(4) Individuals tend to produce more offspring than the environment can support.

5 The diagram below shows the evolution of some different species of flowers. Which statement about the species is correct?

(1) Species A, B, C, and D came from different ancestors.
(2) Species C evolved from species B.
(3) Species A, B, and C can interbreed successfully.
(4) Species A became extinct.

6 In order for new species to develop, there must be a change in the

(1) temperature of the environment.
(2) migration patterns within a population.
(3) genetic makeup of a population.
(4) rate of succession in the environment.

7 In evolution, extinction describes the end of

(1) an allele.
(2) a single species.
(3) an individual organism.
(4) a population of organisms.

8 Which of the following is an example of nonrandom mating?

(1) Genes are removed from the population when individuals migrate.
(2) A change in a population's allele frequency is due to chance.
(3) An individual chooses a mate that has the brightest coloration.
(4) An individual is eliminated from the gene pool by natural selection.

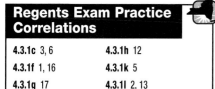

Regents Exam Practice Correlations

4.3.1c	3, 6	4.3.1h	12
4.3.1f	1, 16	4.3.1k	5
4.3.1g	17	4.3.1l	2, 13

PART A

1. **(2)** Only the lack of genetic variability in a species can lead to the inability of a species to adapt, a decrease in survivorship, and possibly even extinction. *(#09, June 2005 Regents Exam)*

2. **(3)** Adaptions essential for survival include the ability to find and eat food, the ability to conceal oneself by camouflage, and the ability to escape predators. *(#12, January 2005 Regents Exam)*

3. **(3)** The accurate replication of DNA will not cause a change in DNA base sequence, nor will it lead to the exchange of segments between chromosomes. Genetic engineering involves the changing of genetic sequences which may lead to a variety of traits in a genetically engineered population. *(#08, January 2005 Regents Exam)*

4. **(1)**

5. **(4)** Species A, B, C, and D all had a common ancestor at one point, indicated by the single "trunk" of the "tree". Species C did not evolve from species B, but they do have a common ancestor. Different species cannot interbreed sucessfully, inability to interbreed sucessfully is one of the factors that defines one species from another. There are no members of species A living at the present time, therefore Species A is extinct. *(#14, June 2004 Regents Exam)*

6. **(3)** A genetic change in a population may lead to such changes as behavioral differences or differences in markings or coloration. If these changes are involved in courtship and mating (such as courtship behaviors or coloration of the sexes) the organisms that differ may no loner interbreed. *(#12, June 2004 Regents Exam)*

7. **(2)**

8. **(2)**

9. (2)
10. (2)
11. (4)
12. (2) Genetic variation in a population increases the likelihood that some individuals will be adapted to a changing environment. Because there is little genetic variation in the Florida panther population, they are less likely to survive environmental changes. *(#19, August 2003 Regents Exam)*
13. (1) Extinction can occur when a species is no longer adapted to its environment. In natural selection, individuals with the most advantageous traits will increase in a population. Genes are recombined during meiosis. A mutation occurs when a DNA sequence becomes altered. *(#16, August 2003 Regents Exam)*
14. (2)
15. (4)

Base your answers to the following questions on the diagram below and on your knowledge of biology.

Flower Color in a Population of Snapdragons

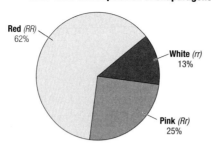

Red *(RR)* 62%
White *(rr)* 13%
Pink *(Rr)* 25%

9 In this population, which genotype has the lowest frequency?
(1) RR
(2) rr
(3) red
(4) white

10 In this population, what is the frequency of heterozygotes?
(1) 13%
(2) 25%
(3) 38%
(4) 62%

11 The diagram represents which form of selection?

Distribution of Body Colors in Bark Beetles

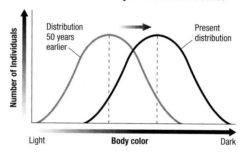

Distribution 50 years earlier
Present distribution
Number of Individuals
Light | Body color | Dark

(1) sexual selection
(2) stabilizing selection
(3) disruptive selection
(4) directional selection

12 The Florida panther, a member of the cat family, has a population of fewer than 100 individuals and has limited genetic variation. Which inference based on this information is valid?
(1) These animals will begin to evolve rapidly.
(2) Over time, these animals will become less likely to survive in a changing environment.
(3) These animals are easily able to adapt to the environment.
(4) Over time, these animals will become more likely to be resistant to disease.

13 Which process is correctly matched with its explanation?

	Process	Explanation
(1)	extinction	adaptive characteristics of a species are not adequate
(2)	natural selection	the most complex organisms survive
(3)	gene recombination	genes are copied as a part of mitosis
(4)	mutation	overproduction of offspring takes place within a certain population

(1) row 1
(2) row 2
(3) row 3
(4) row 4

14 Genetic drift has the greatest impact on
(1) large populations.
(2) small populations.
(3) growing populations.
(4) migrating populations.

15 Population genetics is the study of
(1) how individuals evolve.
(2) how populations interact.
(3) how genes determine traits.
(4) how alleles change within populations.

PART B

Base your answers to the following questions on the information below and on your knowledge of biology.

Variations in Lake Water Levels

Lake Victoria

Lake Tanganyika

Lake Malawi

Past ⟶ Present

    The three great lakes in Africa (Victoria, Tanganyika, and Malawi) contain a greater number of fish species than any other lakes in the world. Lake Malawi alone has 200 species of cichlid fish. The diversity of cichlid species in these African lakes could have been caused by changes in water level over thousands of years.

    According to one hypothesis, at one time the three lakes were connected as one large lake and all the cichlids could interbreed. When the water level fell, groups of cichlids were isolated in smaller lakes as shown in the diagram. Over time, the groups of cichlids developed genetic differences. When the water levels rose again, the isolated populations were brought back into contact. Due to significant genetic differences, these populations were unable to interbreed. Variations in water level over thousands of years resulted in today's diversity of cichlid species.

16 Which discovery would support this explanation of cichlid diversity?

(1) The water level changed little over time.

(2) The local conditions in each of the small lakes were very different.

(3) Differences between cichlid species are small and interbreeding is possible.

(4) Once formed, the lakes remained isolated from each other.

17 As the water level of the lakes changed, many species of cichlids survived while others became extinct. State why some species survived while others became extinct.

PART B

16. **(2)** Decreasing water levels formed smaller lakes. The different conditions within each lake selected for different variations in each cichlid population, so different species evolved. If the water level had not decreased and formed isolated lakes, cichlids could have continued to interbreed and no new species would have developed. According to the diagram, the lakes did not remain isolated, but species remain isolated from each other due to genetic differences. *(#50, August 2005 Regents Exam)*

17. Allow 1 credit for stating why many species of cichlids survived while others became extinct. Acceptable responses include, but are not limited to: some species are better adapted to the environment; some species have a greater ability to compete for food or escape predators or breed; natural selection *(#51, August 2005 Regents Exam)*

Classification

	Standards	Teach Key Ideas
CHAPTER OPENER, pp. 420–421 — 15 min.	🔹 *The Living Environment*	
SECTION 1 The Importance of Classification, pp. 423–426 — 30 min. ❯ The Need for Systems ❯ Scientific Nomenclature ❯ The Linnaean System		📦 **Bellringer Transparency** 📦 **Transparencies** D29 Biological Hierarchy of Classification • D30 Classification of a Bee 💿 **Visual Concepts** Classification • Linnaeus's Levels of Classification • Species Name • Species
SECTION 2 Modern Systematics, pp. 427–432 — 45 min. ❯ Traditional Systematics ❯ Phylogenetics ❯ Cladistics ❯ Inferring Evolutionary Relatedness		📦 **Bellringer Transparency** 📦 **Transparencies** D31 Evolutionary Systematics and Cladistic Taxonomy 💿 **Visual Concepts** Analogous features • Phylogeny • Cladistics • Cladogram • Systematics
SECTION 3 Kingdoms and Domains, pp. 433–439 — 90 min. ❯ Updating Classification Systems ❯ The Three-Domain System	1.1.3b	📦 **Bellringer Transparency** 📦 **Transparencies** D27 Six Kingdoms • D28 Kingdom and Domain Characteristics 💿 **Visual Concepts** Kingdoms of Life • Kingdom Characteristics • Parts of a Cell Wall • Comparing Prokaryotes and Eukaryotes • Comparing Organisms That Are Unicellular and Multicellular • Comparing Autotrophs and Heterotrophs • Origin of Eukaryotic Cells • Bacteria • Characteristics of Bacteria

See also PowerPoint® Resources

Chapter Review and Assessment Resources

- **SE** Super Summary, p. 440
- **SE** Regents Exam Practice, p. 441
- 📘 Regents Review Guide
- 📘 Review Resources
- 📘 Chapter Tests A and B
- 🌐 Holt Online Assessment
- 📀 Regents Question Banks on Teacher's One-Stop Planner

CHAPTER
FastTrack
Thorough instruction will require the times shown.

Basic Learners
- **TE** Making Analogies, p. 424
- 📁 Directed Reading Worksheets*
- 📁 Active Reading Worksheets*
- 📁 Lab Manuals, Level A*
- 📘 Study Guide*■
- 📘 Note-taking Workbook*
- 📘 Special Needs Activities and Modified Tests*

Advanced Learners
- **TE** Analogous Structures, p. 428
- **TE** Classification Characteristics, p. 433
- **TE** Types of Archaebacteria, p. 435
- 📁 Critical Thinking Worksheets*
- 📁 Concept Mapping Worksheets*
- 📁 Science Skills Worksheets*
- 📁 Lab Datasheets, Level C*

Why It Matters	Hands-On	Skills Development	Assessment
Build student motivation with resources about high-interest applications.	SE **Inquiry Lab** What Is Your System?, p. 421*■	TE **Reading Toolbox** Assessing Prior Knowledge, p. 420 SE **Reading Toolbox,** p. 422	
TE **Binomial Nomenclature,** p. 424 TE **Naming Species,** p. 425	📁 **Inquiry Lab** Identifying Unknown Organisms*	SE **Reading Toolbox** Mnemonic Devices, p. 426 TE **Reading Toolbox** Mnemonic Devices, p. 426	SE **Section Review** TE **Formative Assessment** Spanish Assessment*■ 📁 **Section Quiz**■
TE **Demonstration** Using the Linnaean System, p. 427 TE **DNA Analysis,** p. 430 SE **New Species,** p. 432	SE **Quick Lab** Cladogram Construction, p. 430*■	SE **Reading Toolbox** Word Origins, p. 429 TE **Reading Toolbox** Word Origins, p. 429	SE **Section Review** TE **Formative Assessment** Spanish Assessment*■ 📁 **Section Quiz**■
TE **Demonstration** Classification Systems, p. 433 TE **Alternate Classification,** p. 434 TE **Demonstration** Observing Protists, p. 436	SE **Quick Lab** Field Guides, p. 435*■ SE **Skills Practice Lab** Dichotomous Keys, p. 438*■ 📁 **Skills Practice Lab** Analyzing Amino-Acid Sequences*	TE **Math Skills** Average Bacterial Cell, p. 435 SE **Reading Toolbox** Phylogenetic Tree, p. 436 TE **Reading Toolbox** Phylogenetic Tree, p. 436	SE **Section Review** TE **Formative Assessment** Spanish Assessment*■ 📁 **Section Quiz**■

See also Lab Generator

See also Holt Online Assessment Resources

Resources for Differentiated Instruction

English Learners
TE Making Analogies, p. 424
TE Word Origins, p. 434
📁 Directed Reading Worksheets*
📁 Active Reading Worksheets*
📁 Lab Manuals, Level A*
📓 Study Guide*■
📓 Note-taking Workbook*
📓 Multilingual Glossary
💿 Interactive Tutor

Struggling Readers
TE Note-Taking, p. 427
📁 Directed Reading Worksheets*
📁 Active Reading Worksheets*
📁 Lab Manuals, Level A*
📓 Study Guide*
📓 Note-taking Workbook*
📓 Special Needs Activities and Modified Tests*
💿 Interactive Tutor

Special Education Students
TE Common Names, p. 424
📁 Directed Reading Worksheets*
📁 Active Reading Worksheets*
📁 Lab Manuals, Level A*
📓 Study Guide*■
📓 Note-taking Workbook*
📓 Special Needs Activities and Modified Tests*

Alternative Assessment
TE Constructing Cladograms, p. 429
📁 Science Skills Worksheets*
📁 Section Quizzes*■
📓 Chapter Tests A, B, and C*■

Chapter 18

Chapter 18

Classification

Overview

The purpose of this chapter is to explain how living organisms are classified and to identify the traits biologists use to classify them. Students will learn how scientists have developed classification schemes to organize their knowledge of life's diversity and to represent inferences about the evolutionary relationships among organisms.

READING TOOLBOX

Assessing Prior Knowledge Students should understand the following concepts:
- cellular basis of life
- evolutionary theory

Visual Literacy Tell students that these butterflies are part of a collection in the Milan Natural History Museum in Italy and that they show common European examples. Discuss with students whether they think the butterflies are all the same species. (They are not, but accept all reasonable answers.)

Preview

1 The Importance of Classification
The Need for Systems
Scientific Nomenclature
The Linnaean System

2 Modern Systematics
Traditional Systematics
Phylogenetics
Cladistics
Inferring Evolutionary Relatedness

3 Kingdoms and Domains
Updating Classification Systems
The Three-Domain System

Why It Matters

More than one million species on Earth have been given scientific names, but many more species exist that have not been identified.

 The Living Environment
Standard 1 Students will use mathematical analysis, scientific inquiry, and engineering design, as appropriate, to pose questions, seek answers, and develop solutions.
Key Idea 1 The central purpose of scientific inquiry is to develop explanations of natural phenomena in a continuing and creative process. *Major Understandings* - **1.3b**

These butterflies look similar, but does that mean they are related? There is more to that answer than meets the eye.

Sometimes, butterflies that look different are actually members of the same species.

Scientists use systems for naming and grouping species. These butterflies have been classified as belonging to the family Pieridae.

Chapter Correlations   **The Living Environment**

Standard 1

1.3b All scientific explanations are tentative and subject to change or improvement. Each new bit of evidence can create more questions than it answers. This leads to increasingly better understanding of how things work in the living world.

Sometimes, two butterflies that look alike are *not* actually members of the same species.

Teacher's Notes Students are likely to disagree with one another during steps 2 and 3. Tell them that there is no "correct" system, but that they do need to come to agreement.

Materials
10–20 loosely related everyday objects, such as hardware (nuts, bolts, screws) or office supplies (paper clips, rubber bands, binder clips)

Answers to Analysis
1. Students should have several groups with names and definitions; each group should include at least two items from the initial assortment of items.
2. Students may have revised their scheme to incorporate the new object.
3. Students should analyze how easy their scheme is for others to understand and use.

InquiryLab

⏱ 15 min

What Is Your System?

Often, more than one way exists to organize or group things. In this lab, you will work with others to decide on a system.

Procedure
1. Work with a partner. Examine the **assortment of objects** provided by your teacher.
2. Sort your objects into groups of "related" objects. Try to get every object into a group with at least one other object.
3. Choose a name for each group.
4. Choose one object from your collection, and trade it with an object from another pair of students.
5. Try to fit the new object into one of your groups.

Analysis
1. **List** and define each of your group names from step 3.
2. **Describe** how you classified the new object in step 4.
3. **Predict** whether another person would be able to "correctly" classify one of your objects by using your list of groups. Explain your reasoning.

READING
TOOLBOX

Using Words

1. arrange things in order using a system; name an arrangement or order
2. giving names to things in the system

Using Language

1. Answers will vary.
2. Sample answer (JFMAMJJASOND): Jimmy Finds Money And Makes Jane Jump After Sleeping Over Nine Days

Using Science Graphics

1. birds
2. turtles

READING TOOLBOX

These reading tools can help you learn the material in this chapter. For more information on how to use these and other tools, see **Appendix: Reading and Study Skills.**

Using Words

Word Origins Many scientific words derive their parts from Greek or Latin words. Learning the meanings of some Greek and Latin word parts can help you understand the meaning of many scientific words.

Your Turn Answer the following questions.
1. What do taxonomists probably do?
2. What role might nomenclature have in taxonomy?

Word Parts		
Word part	Origin	Meaning
tax	Greek	arrangement, order, movement
nom	Greek; Latin	law, order, system; name
clatur	Latin	calling, naming
clad	Greek	shoot, branch, twig
phyl	Greek	tribe, race, class, clan
gram	Greek	write, a written record
gen	Greek, Latin	birth, descent, origin, creation
morph	Greek	shape, form, appearance

Using Language

Mnemonics Mnemonic devices are tools that help you remember lists or parts in their proper order. Use the first letter of every word that you want to remember as the first letter of a new word in a memorable sentence. You may be more likely to remember the sentence if the sentence is funny.

Your Turn Create mnemonic devices that could help you remember all of the parts of the following groups of items.
1. the names of all of your teachers
2. the 12 months of the year

Using Science Graphics

Phylogenetic Tree A phylogenetic tree shows the relationships of different groups of organisms to each other. The groups that are most closely related appear on branches that lie close together. Branch points represent a point in time where groups became separated and speciation began. Time is represented as moving forward from the bottom (or trunk) toward the top (or branches) of the tree.

Your Turn Use this phylogenetic tree to answer the following questions.
1. Which group is most closely related to extinct dinosaurs?
2. Which group existed before the other groups did?

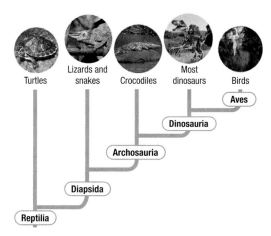

The Importance of Classification

Key Ideas	Key Terms	Why It Matters
❯ Why do biologists have taxonomic systems? ❯ What makes up the scientific name of a species? ❯ What is the structure of the modern Linnaean system of classification?	taxonomy genus binomial nomenclature	In order to study and make use of living things, we need a name for each specific thing.

The number of species that exist in the world is much greater than the number known. About 1.7 million species have been named and described by scientists. But scientists think that millions more are undiscovered. We have little knowledge of Earth's variety of species.

The Need for Systems

In biology, the practice of naming and classifying organisms is called **taxonomy**. Scientists use a logical system of classification to manage large amounts of information. Similarly, a library uses a system for organizing books. ❯ **Biologists use taxonomic systems to organize their knowledge of organisms. These systems attempt to provide consistent ways to name and categorize organisms.**

Common names of organisms are not organized into a system. One species may have many common names, and one common name may be used for more than one species. For example, the bird called a *robin* in Great Britain is a different bird from the bird called a *robin* in North America. To avoid confusion, biologists need a way to name organisms that does not depend on language or location.

Biologists also need a way to organize lists of names. A system that has categories is more efficient than a simple list. So, biologists group organisms into large categories as well as smaller and more specific categories. The general term for any one of these categories is a *taxon* (plural, *taxa*).

❯ **Reading Check** *What is the problem with common names of species? (See the Appendix for answers to Reading Checks.)*

taxonomy (taks AHN uh mee) the science of describing, naming, and classifying organisms

Figure 1 Museums are full of biological specimens, yet only a fraction of Earth's species have been scientifically named.

Key Resources

 Transparencies
D29 Biological Hierarchy of Classification
D30 Classification of a Bee

Visual Concepts
Classification
Linnaeus's Levels of Classification
Species Name
Species

❯ **Focus**

This section describes Linnaeus's role in developing the modern system of biological classification and discusses the eight level scheme used by scientists today.

Bellringer

Use the Bellringer transparency to prepare students for this section.

❯ **Teach**

Teaching Key Ideas

Differentiating Individuals Ask students if they have ever heard of two people who have the same name. Have them consider what kinds of problems could arise from this situation. Ask how two people could differentiate themselves if they had the same name. (possible answers: social security number, address, age, nickname) **LS Interpersonal**

Teaching Key Ideas

Scientific Names Write the following scientific names on the board: *Carnegiea gigantea* (giant saguaro cactus), *Nymphaea odorata* (fragrant water lily), *Canis familiaris* (domestic dog), *Viola tricolor* (pansy with three-colored flowers), and *Peromyscus californicus* (a common California mouse). Have students look for descriptive clues in each name. Have them predict the common name for each before telling them the names. **LS** Verbal

Why It Matters

Binomial Nomenclature Tell students that Linnaeus did not invent binomial nomenclature but popularized its use. Swiss scientist Gaspard Bauhin pioneered the use of two-word names about 200 years before Linnaeus. **LS** Logical

Answers to Caption Questions
Figure 2: *Panthera*

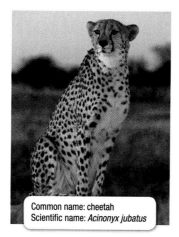

Common name: cheetah
Scientific name: *Acinonyx jubatus*

Common names: leopard, panther
Scientific name: *Panthera pardus*

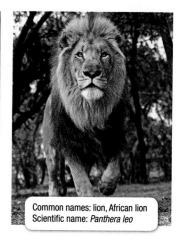

Common names: lion, African lion
Scientific name: *Panthera leo*

Figure 2 Each species may have many common names but only one scientific name. The scientific name is made up of a genus name and a species identifier. Each genus is a group of closely related species. ❯ **To what genus do both lions and leopards belong?**

genus (JEE nuhs) a level of classification that contains similar species

binomial nomenclature (bie NOH mee uhl NOH muhn KLAY chuhr) a system for giving each organism a two-word scientific name that consists of the genus name followed by the species name

SCI*LINKS*.
www.scilinks.org
Topic: Carl Linnaeus
Code: HX80226

Scientific Nomenclature

As biology became established as a science, biologists began to create systems for naming and classifying living things. A major challenge was to give each species a unique name.

Early Scientific Names In the early days of European biology, various naming systems were invented. Some used long, descriptive Latin phrases called *polynomials*. Names for taxa were inconsistent between these systems. The only taxon that was somewhat consistent was the **genus,** which was a taxon used to group similar species.

A simpler and more consistent system was developed by the Swedish biologist Carl Linnaeus in the 1750s. He wanted to catalog all known species. He wrote books in which he used the polynomial system but added a two-word Latin name for each species. His two-word system is called **binomial nomenclature.** For example, his two-part name for the European honeybee was *Apis mellifera*, the genus name followed by a single descriptive word for each species. **Figure 2** shows the binomial names of three other animals.

Naming Rules In the years since Linnaeus created his system, his basic approach has been universally adopted. The unique two-part name for a species is now called a *scientific name*. Scientific names must conform to rules established by an international commission of scientists. No two species can have the same scientific name.

❯ All scientific names for species are made up of two Latin or Latin-like terms. All of the members of a genus share the genus name as the first term. The second term is called the *species identifier* and is often descriptive. For example, in the name *Apis mellifera,* the term *mellifera* derives from the Latin word for "honey." When you write the scientific name, the genus name should be capitalized and the species identifier should be lowercased; both terms should be italicized.

❯ **Reading Check** *Why did Linnaeus devise a new naming system?*

Differentiated Instruction

English Learners/Basic Learners
Making Analogies Explain that a useful classification system should include both broad and specific categories. In geography, categories might be continent, country, region, state, and city. An extension of this scheme could be to add the mail delivery system with zip code, street name, and house number. Work with students to develop a list of other things that are categorized in this way. **LS** Logical

Special Education Students
Common Names Help developmentally delayed students understand how common names can be misleading when describing an organism. Use examples such as the starfish (not a fish), sea horse (not a horse), silverfish (not a fish), horseshoe crab (not a crab), and ringworm (not a worm). Review the characters that usually define a fish, horse, crab, and worm. **LS** Verbal

The Linnaean System

In trying to catalog every known species, Linnaeus devised more than just a naming system. He devised a system to classify all plants and animals that were known during his time. His system formed the basis of taxonomy for centuries. ❯ In the Linnaean system of classification, organisms are grouped at successive levels of a hierarchy based on similarities in their form and structure. Since Linnaeus's time, many new groups and some new levels have been added, as **Figure 3** shows. ❯ The eight basic levels of modern classification are domain, kingdom, phylum, class, order, family, genus, and species.

Domain Eukarya includes a wide diversity of eukaryotes but no prokaryotes.

Domain: Eukarya — leopard, lion, cheetah, wolf, human, shark, sponge, paramecium

Kingdom: Animalia

Phylum: Chordata

Kingdom Animalia includes multicellular organisms but not plants or fungi.

Class: Mammalia

All animals with nerve cords are grouped in Phylum Chordata, but only warm-blooded chordates with hair belong in Class Mammalia.

Order: Carnivora

Family: Felidae

Many kinds of meat-eating mammals belong in Order Carnivora, but only the catlike carnivores belong in Family Felidae.

Genus: *Panthera*

Species: *Panthera pardus*

The leopard is a unique species, but it is closely related to the lion. So, the two species are placed in Genus *Panthera*.

Figure 3 The Linnaean system has been updated and now includes eight levels, from domain to species. ❯ **Which level includes the greatest number of species?**

Why It Matters

Naming Species Some names are given to honor people, and some names are deliberately playful. For example, *Arthurdactylus conandoylensis* is a Brazilian pterosaur named after Arthur Conan Doyle and his novel *The Lost World.* Some names have accidental origins. The 18th century French naturalist Pierre Sonnerat gave the name *Indri indri* to a species of Malagasy lemur because he thought that the natives called it that, but they were just saying "Look! Look!"

Mnemonic Devices sample answer: Dear King Phillip Came Over For Ginger Snaps

> **Close**

Formative Assessment

In the Linnaean system, scientists classify organisms based on _____.

A. external characteristics (Incorrect. Internal characteristics are also important.)

B. similarities in form and structure (Correct! The more similarities in form and structure, the more closely two organisms are probably related.)

C. where organisms live (Incorrect. Organisms located very far apart can be very closely related.)

D. species name (Incorrect. The process of classification results in the species name.)

Example: human

Domains — Domain Eukarya

Kingdoms — Kingdom Animalia

Phyla — Phylum Chordata

Classes — Class Mammalia

Orders — Order Primates

Families — Family Hominidae

Genera — Genus *Homo*

Species — *Homo sapiens*

Figure 4 A species can be classified at each level of the Linnaean system.

Mnemonics To remember the eight levels in their proper order, use a phrase, such as "Do Kindly Pay Cash Or Furnish Good Security," to represent *Domain, Kingdom, Phylum, Class, Order, Family, Genus,* and *Species.*

Levels of the Modern Linnaean System

Each level has its own set of names for taxa at that level. Each taxon is identified based on shared traits. Similar species are grouped into a genus; similar genera are grouped into a family; and so on up to the level of domain. **Figure 4** shows the classification of humans in this system.

- **Domain** Since Linnaeus's time, the category *domain* has been invented in order to recognize the most basic differences among cell types. All living things are now grouped into one of three domains. For example, humans belong to the domain Eukarya.

- **Kingdom** The category *kingdom* encompasses large groups such as plants, animals, or fungi. Six kingdoms fit within the three domains.

- **Phylum** A *phylum* is a subgroup within a kingdom. Many phyla exist within each kingdom. Humans belong to the phylum Chordata.

- **Class** A *class* is a subgroup within a phylum.

- **Order** An *order* is a subgroup within a class.

- **Family** A *family* is a subgroup within an order. Humans belong to the family Hominidae.

- **Genus** A *genus* (plural, *genera*) is a subgroup within a family. Each genus is made up of species with uniquely shared traits, such that the species are thought to be closely related. Humans belong to the genus *Homo*.

- **Species** A *species* is usually defined as a unique group of organisms united by heredity or interbreeding. But in practice, scientists tend to define species based on unique features. For example, *Homo sapiens* is recognized as the only living primate species that walks upright and uses spoken language.

> **Reading Check** *How many kingdoms are in the Linnaean system?*

Section 1 Review

> **KEY IDEAS**

1. **Explain** why biologists have systems for naming and grouping organisms.

2. **Describe** the structure of a scientific name for a species.

3. **List** the categories of the modern Linnaean system of classification in order from general to specific.

CRITICAL THINKING

4. **Logical Reasoning** Describe additional problems that might occur for biologists without a logical taxonomic system.

5. **Anticipating Change** Although the basic structure of the system that Linnaeus invented is still in use, many aspects of this system have changed. Suggest some possible ways that the system may have changed.

ALTERNATIVE ASSESSMENT

6. **Classification Poster** Create a poster that shows the major levels of classification for your favorite organism. Write a description of the general characteristics of the organism at each level. For each level, include a list of other organisms that belong to the same taxon.

Answers to Section Review

1. Biologists use taxonomic systems to name and categorize organisms in consistent ways to prevent confusion.

2. All scientific names for species are made up of two Latin or Latin-like terms; no two species may have the same two-part name.

3. domain, kingdom, phylum, class, order, family, genus, species

4. Biologists might not realize that they are studying the same species; they might not see similarities and relationships between organisms.

5. Scientists might have added more levels or "in between" levels; names of taxa at each level might have changed; taxa might have been "promoted" or "demoted" among levels.

6. Posters should show the classification of an organism at all eight levels, as well as a general description of characteristics and a list of similar organisms in each taxon. Check that students capitalize and italicize taxon names as appropriate.

Key Ideas

> What problems arise when scientists try to group organisms by apparent similarities?

> Is the evolutionary past reflected in modern systematics?

> How is cladistics used to construct evolutionary relationships?

> What evidence do scientists use to analyze these relationships?

Key Terms

phylogeny
cladistics

Why It Matters

Modern systematics unites evolutionary science with traditional studies of anatomy.

Have you ever wondered how scientists tell one species from another? For example, how can you tell a mushroom that is harmless from a mushroom that is poisonous? Identification is not easy, even for experts. The experts often revise their classifications as well as their procedures. This field of expertise is known as *systematics*.

Traditional Systematics

Linnaeus's system was based on his judgment of the importance of various similarities among living things. **> Scientists traditionally have used similarities in appearance and structure to group organisms. However, this approach has proven problematic.** Some groups look similar but turn out to be distantly related. Other groups look different and turn out to be closely related. Often, new data or new analyses suggest relationships between organisms that were not apparent before.

For example, dinosaurs were once seen as a group of reptiles that became extinct millions of years ago. And birds were seen as a separate, modern group that was not related to any reptile group. However, fossil evidence has convinced scientists that birds evolved from one of the many lineages of dinosaurs. Some scientists now classify birds as a subgroup of dinosaurs, as described in **Figure 5.**

> **Reading Check** *What is systematics?*

Figure 5 In a sense, birds are dinosaurs. Scientists think that modern birds are descended from a subgroup of dinosaurs called *theropods.* This inference is based on thorough comparisons of modern birds and fossilized theropods.

Deinonychus This is a model of an extinct theropod dinosaur.

Cassowary This is a modern bird species.

Differentiated Instruction

Struggling Readers

Note-Taking Have students fold a sheet of paper in half vertically, creating four columns. Ask them to list each of the four headings in this section at the top of a column (*Problems with Traditional Classification, Phylogenetics, Cladistics,* and *Analyzing Evolutionary Relatedness*). As they read, have students add pertinent details and note any material that they do not understand. **LS Verbal**

Section 2

> Focus

This section identifies problems with traditional classification and describes the relationship between an organism's classification and its evolutionary history.

Bellringer

Use the Bellringer transparency to prepare students for this section.

> Teach

Demonstration

Using the Linnaean System Tell students that Linnaeus classified all living things into two groups—plants and animals. Show pictures of plants and animals and ask students into which of the two groups they would place each organism. Then show students pictures of unicellular organisms. Ask students to classify them according to Linnaeus' system. Students probably will not be able to classify most of the organisms. Point out that Linnaeus did not include unicellular organisms in his system because he didn't know they existed; the microscope had not yet been invented. Tell students that today scientists use more than obvious similarities to classify organisms. **LS Logical**

Key Resources

Transparencies
D31 Evolutionary Systematics and Cladistic Taxonomy

Visual Concepts
Analogous features
Phylogeny
Cladistics
Cladogram
Systematics

Teaching Key Ideas

Dolphin Evolution Tell students that Aristotle recognized that dolphins and whales differed from fishes in their respiration and reproduction, among other characteristics. This fact was overlooked for over 2,000 years. Today we know that whales show many similarities with early land mammals and probably share ancestry with most hoofed mammals. Emphasize to students that all phylogenies represent hypotheses and are subject to revision any time that new data, such as fossils, embryology, or molecular evidence, does not fit the previously established criteria.

Answers to Caption Questions

Figure 6: The Linnaean system simply puts groups into boxes based on a lists of characters; modern phylogenetics puts successively more-inclusive groups onto a "tree" based on inferences of relatedness.

phylogeny the evolutionary history of a species or taxonomic group

cladistics a phylogenetic classification system that uses shared derived characters and ancestry as the sole criterion for grouping taxa

Figure 6 Traditional systematics grouped birds separately from other reptiles by emphasizing the unique features of birds. However, modern phylogenetics places birds as a subgroup of reptiles on a phylogenetic tree. ❯ How do these two systems differ in structure?

Phylogenetics

Today, scientists who study systematics are interested in **phylogeny,** or the ancestral relationships between species. ❯ Grouping organisms by similarity is often assumed to reflect phylogeny, but inferring phylogeny is complex in practice. Reconstructing a species' phylogeny is like trying to draw a huge family tree that links ancestors and descendants across thousands or millions of generations.

Misleading Similarities Inferring phylogenies from similarities can be misleading. Not all similar characters are inherited from a common ancestor. Consider the wings of a bird and of an insect. Both types of wings enable flight, but the structures of the two kinds of wings differ. Moreover, fossil evidence shows that insects with wings existed long before birds with wings appeared. Through the process called *convergent evolution,* similarities may evolve in groups that are not closely related to one another, often because the groups become adapted to similar habitats or lifestyles. Similarities that arise through convergent evolution are called *analogous* characters.

Judging Relatedness Another problem is that grouping organisms by similarities is subjective. Are all characters equally important, or are some more important than others? Often, different scientists may give different answers to these questions.

For example, systematists historically placed birds in a separate class from reptiles, giving importance to characters such as feathers, as **Figure 6** shows. But more recently, fossil evidence and detailed studies of bird and dinosaur anatomy have changed the view of these groups. **Figure 6** shows that birds are now considered part of the "family tree" of dinosaurs. This family tree, or *phylogenetic tree,* represents a hypothesis of the relationships between several groups.

Linnaean Classification

Classes of Animals	
Class Reptilia	Class Aves
egg-laying, exothermic, scales	egg-laying, endothermic, feathers
lizards, snakes, turtles, crocodiles, and dinosaurs	birds

Modern Phylogeny

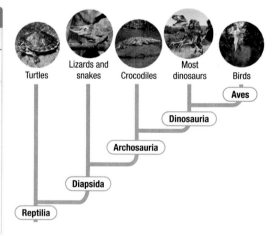

Cladistics

To unite systematics with phylogenetics, scientists need an objective way to sort out relatedness. Today, the preferred method is cladistics. **Cladistics** is a method of analysis that infers phylogenies by careful comparisons of shared characters. ❯ Cladistic analysis is used to select the most likely phylogeny among a given set of organisms.

Comparing Characters Cladistics focuses on finding characters that are *shared* between different groups of organisms because of shared ancestry. With respect to two groups, a shared character is defined as *ancestral* if it is thought to have evolved in a common ancestor of both groups. In contrast, a *derived* character is one that evolved in one group but not in the other group. Cladistics infers relatedness by identifying shared derived and shared ancestral characters among groups while avoiding the use of analogous characters.

For example, consider the relationship between flowering plants and conifers. The production of seeds is a character that is present in all living conifers and flowering plants and in some prehistoric plants. So, it is a shared ancestral character among these groups. The production of flowers, however, is a derived character that is shared only among flowering plants. Flowers evolved in some ancestor of flowering plants but did not evolve in the group that led to conifers.

Constructing Cladograms Cladistics uses a strict comparison of many characters among several groups in order to construct a cladogram. A *cladogram* is a phylogenetic tree that is drawn in a specific way, as **Figure 7** shows. Organisms are grouped together through identification of their shared derived characters. All groups that arise from one point on a cladogram belong to a clade. A *clade* is a set of groups that are related by descent from a single ancestral lineage.

Each clade in a tree is usually compared with an *outgroup,* or group that lacks some of the shared characters. For example, **Figure 7** shows that flowering plants and conifers share a character with each other that they do not share with ferns. So, conifers and flowering plants form a clade, and ferns form the outgroup.

❯ **Reading Check** *What does a cladogram show?*

Characters in Plants			
Type of plants	Vascular tissue	Seeds	Flowers
Mosses	no	no	no
Ferns	yes	no	no
Conifers	yes	yes	no
Flowering plants	yes	yes	yes

Word Origins The word root *clad* means "shoot, branch or twig" and the word root *gram* means "to write or record." Use this information to analyze the meaning of the term *cladogram.*

Figure 7 This cladogram organizes plants by using a strict comparison of the characters shown in the table. Each clade is united by a specific shared derived character. ❯ **Which groups are united by having seeds?**

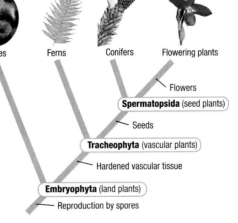

Mosses Ferns Conifers Flowering plants

- Flowers
- **Spermatopsida** (seed plants)
- Seeds
- **Tracheophyta** (vascular plants)
- Hardened vascular tissue
- **Embryophyta** (land plants)
- Reproduction by spores

Teaching Key Ideas

Comparing Tools A key difference between cladistics and Linnaean taxonomy is that cladistics allows for an infinite number of nested levels. Cladograms can be "zoomed in" (or out) almost infinitely, with each node leading to more detailed branches. Also, some branches may have many more sub-branches (evolutionary radiations or diversifications) than others.

READING TOOLBOX

Word Origins a record showing how groups of organisms branch off from one another

Answers to Caption Questions
Figure 7: conifers and flowering plants

Differentiated Instruction

Alternative Assessment

Constructing Cladograms Using the same collection of materials from the Inquiry Lab at the beginning of the chapter, have students construct charts of characteristics and corresponding cladograms to show the relationship among the objects. **LS Logical**

Teacher's Notes Note that after the initial outgroup is chosen, the remaining characters (those not found in the outgroup) are the derived characters of the remaining groups.

Answers to Analysis

1. The first outgroup should be tuna and should appear on the first branch from the base.

2. The most common character among the rest is *Four legs*. This label should appear just above the branch that leads to *Tuna* on the part of the tree that leads to the remaining three groups.

3. The next branch should lead to *Frog*, with *Amniotic egg* leading to the remaining two groups; then a branch to *Lizard*, with *Hair* leading only to *Cat*.

4. amniotic egg

5. four legs

Data

QuickLab

⏱ 10 min

Cladogram Construction

Use this table of shared characters to construct a clado-gram. Use the other cladograms in this section to help you draw your cladogram.

Analysis

1. **Identify** the outgroup. The outgroup is the group that does not share any of the characters in this list. Draw a diagonal line and then a single branch from its base. Write the outgroup at the tip of this first branch.

2. **Identify** the most common character. Just past the "fork" of the first branch, write the most common de-rived character. This character should be present in all of the subsequent groups added to the tree.

Characters in Vertebrates

	Four legs	Amniotic egg	Hair
Tuna	no	no	no
Frog	yes	no	no
Lizard	yes	yes	no
Cat	yes	yes	yes

3. **Complete** the tree. Repeat step 2 for the second most-common character. Repeat until the tree is filled with all of the groups and characters from the table.

4. **CRITICAL THINKING** **Applying Concepts** What is a shared derived character of cats and lizards?

5. **CRITICAL THINKING** **Applying Concepts** What character evolved in the ancestor of frogs but not in that of fish?

SC*LINKS*.
www.scilinks.org
Topic: Phylogenetic Tree
Code: HX81141

Inferring Evolutionary Relatedness

As you have seen, phylogenetics relies heavily on data about charac-ters that are either present or absent in taxa. But other kinds of data are also important. ▶ Biologists compare many kinds of evidence and apply logic carefully in order to infer phylogenies. They constantly revise and add details to their definitions of taxa.

Morphological Evidence *Morphology* refers to the physical structure or anatomy of organisms. Large-scale morphological data are most obvious and have been well studied. For example, the major characters used to define plant groups—vascular tissue, seeds, and flowers—were recognized long ago. But because convergent evolu-tion can lead to analogous characters, scientists must consider many characters and look carefully for similarities and differences. For example, many animals have wings that are merely analagous.

An important part of morphology in multicellular species is the pattern of development from embryo to adult. Organisms that share ancestral genes often show additional similarities during the process of development. For example, in all vertebrate species, the jaw of an adult develops from the same part of an embryo. In many cases, studies of embryos bring new information to phylogenetic debates.

Molecular Evidence In recent decades, scientists have used genetic information to infer phylogenies. Recall that as genes are passed on from generation to generation, mutations occur. Some mutations may be passed on to all species that descend from a com-mon ancestor. So, DNA, RNA, and proteins can be compared in the same manner as morphology is compared to infer phylogenies.

▶ **Reading Check** *What is an example of morphological data?*

MISCONCEPTION ALERT

Teleology Evolution is often mistakenly described in terms of purposefulness; that wings, for example, evolved so an organism could fly. This view of evolution is based on teleology (Greek *telos*, "end"; *logos*, "discourse"), or the doctrine that explains phenomena in terms of ends or final causes. Make sure students understand that the process of natural selection only determines whether a new characteristic is advanta-geous in a given time and place and thus whether it may be passed on to offspring in that context.

Why It Matters

DNA Analysis Point out that DNA analysis is changing some long-held beliefs about evolu-tionary relationships (beliefs that were based on anatomical traits alone). For example, an American cheetah-like cat found in the west is more closely related to pumas than to the African cheetah that it more closely resembles. The genetic data indicates that the similarities in the American and African species are an exam-ple of parallel evolution as a result of similar ecological pressures.

Sequence Data Today, genetic sequence data are widely used for cladistic analysis. First, the sequence of DNA bases in a gene (or of amino acids in a protein) is determined for several species. Then, each letter (or amino acid) at each position in the sequence is compared. Such a comparison can be laid out in a large table, but computers are best able to calculate the relative similarity of many sequences.

Genomic Data At the level of genomes, alleles may be added or lost over time. So, another form of molecular evidence is the presence or absence of specific alleles—or the proteins that result from them. Finally, the relative timing between genetic changes can be inferred.

Evidence of Order and Time Cladistics can determine only the relative order of divergence, or branching, in a phylogenetic tree. To infer the actual time when a group may have begun to "branch off," extra information is needed. Often, this information comes from the fossil record. For example, by using cladistics, scientists have identified lancelets as the closest relative of vertebrates. The oldest known fossils of vertebrates are about 450 million years old, but the oldest lancelet fossils are 535 million years old. So, these two lineages must have diverged more than 535 million years ago.

More recently, scientists have noticed that most DNA mutations occur at relatively constant rates. So, genetic change can be used as an approximate "molecular clock," as **Figure 8** shows. Scientists can measure the genetic differences between taxa and then estimate the time at which the taxa began to diverge.

Inference Using Parsimony Modern systematists use the *principle of parsimony* to construct phylogenetic trees. This principle holds that the simplest explanation for something is the most reasonable, unless strong evidence exists against the simplest explanation. So, given two possible cladograms, the one that implies the fewest character changes between branch points is preferred.

❯ **Reading Check** *What kinds of molecular data inform cladistics?*

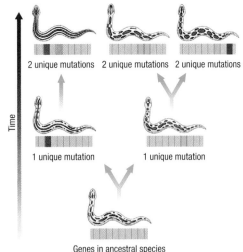

2 unique mutations 2 unique mutations 2 unique mutations

1 unique mutation 1 unique mutation

Time

Genes in ancestral species

Figure 8 Because mutation occurs randomly at any time, an average rate of mutation can be measured and used as a "clock" to estimate the time any two species took to accumulate a number of genetic differences.

❯ **Close**

Formative Assessment

A cladogram shows several four-footed vertebrates: frog, turtle, alligator, kangaroo, armadillo, wolf, and dog. What would the character *presence of fur* tell you about the inferred relationship among these organisms?

A. The armadillo is more closely related to the alligator than the wolf because it does not have very much fur. (Incorrect. The *amount* of fur is not the defining characteristic.)

B. All these animals are related. (Incorrect. The derived character of fur shows that some are more closely related than others.)

C. The kangaroo, wolf, and dog are most closely related because they have the greatest amount of fur. (Incorrect. *Amount* of fur is not the defining characteristic.)

D. The frog, turtle, and alligator are not as closely related as are the other animals that have fur. (Correct! Fur is a derived character that divides this group into two subgroups.)

Section 2 Review

❯ KEY IDEAS

1. **Identify** the kinds of problems that arise when scientists try to group organisms by similarities.
2. **Relate** classification to phylogeny.
3. **Describe** the method of cladistics.
4. **Identify** the kinds of evidence used to infer phylogenies.

CRITICAL THINKING

5. **Justifying Reasoning** Some scientists who study dinosaurs have stated that dinosaurs are not extinct. How could this statement be justified?
6. **Analyzing Relationships** Explain how the outgroup in a cladogram relates to the difference between ancestral and derived characters.

METHODS OF SCIENCE

7. **Taxonomic Challenge** In the past, mammals were identified as animals that have fur and give birth, and reptiles were identified as animals that have scales and lay eggs. Then, an animal was found that has fur and lays eggs. How might this problem have been resolved?

Answers to Section Review

1. Similarities can arise by convergent evolution, especially similarities in basic function or outward appearance.
2. Ideally, classification should reflect phylogeny.
3. Cladistics uses strict and careful comparisons of shared characters to decide between all possible relationships among several groups.
4. morphology, comparisons of biological molecules, fossil record, and parsimony
5. If birds are descendants of dinosaurs, then they are essentially a subgroup of dinosaurs. Using this reasoning, dinosaurs could be considered a living group.
6. Any characters that outgroup organisms have in common with ingroup organisms are ancestral. Characters that are unique to ingroup organisms are the derived characters of that clade only, and must have arisen in a lineage that was separate from the outgroup.
7. Scientists might have revised the list of defining characteristics of mammals or reptiles, or they might have created a new group that includes both mammals and reptiles.

Why It Matters

Teacher's Notes Scientists agree that many undiscovered species remain in all parts of the world. Yet some unidentified specimens are stored in museums, waiting for closer observation or information on their native habitat. Such was the case with specimens of Mantophasmatodea, an insect order only recently established.

READING TOOLBOX

Visual Literacy Have students research information about the animals shown.

- Lemur (in hand): *Microcebus lehilahytsara* or Goodman's mouse lemur. (named after researcher Steve Goodman; thought to be part of the lineage that led to early humans)
- Insect: Genus *Lobophasma,* order Mantophasmatodea (heelwalkers). (carnivores restricted to South Africa; veat other small insects)
- Monkey: *Callicebus bernhardi* or Prince Bernhard's titi monkey. (dark orange sideburns; named in honor of His Royal Highness Prince Bernhard of the Netherlands)
- Frog: *Philautua poppiae* or knuckles leaf-nesting frog. (one of many new frog species discovered in tropical forests)
- Bird: Smoky honeyeater. (about the size of a blue jay; lives only in the Foya Mountains of Indonesia)

Why It Matters

New Species

REAL WORLD

The work of biology is never finished. Indeed, the work of finding, naming, and classifying all living species has barely begun. Scientists have estimated that 1 km² of rain forest may contain hundreds or thousands of species, most of which are currently unknown to science. In fact, new species are "discovered" all of the time, all around the world.

When is a species "new"?

What does discovering a new species mean? Typically, it means collecting a specimen, giving it a name, and classifying it for the first time by using modern taxonomy. Although truly new species may be evolving at any time, most new species are simply new to science.

Mantophasmatodea— a new order of insects

Big, Small, Far, Near
Undiscovered species are everywhere! Even mammals, such as this monkey, are still being discovered. Of course, we may never find all of the tiny bugs and microbes in the world.

Biodiversity Hot Spots
Some parts of the world, such as tropical rain forests, contain an extreme diversity of species. This frog is from a region of Sri Lanka that is home to many amphibian species.

Undiscovered Worlds
In 2005, an expedition went into a "lost world" of rain forest in New Guinea that was previously unexplored by scientists. The expedition quickly found dozens of new species, such as this honeyeater bird.

Lemur from Madagascar

Quick Project Find out if any new species have been discovered in your local area in the last few decades. Try to find the name of the new species, the story behind the name, and a photo of the species.

Answers to Quick Project
Such information is most likely to be found on the Internet from the following sources: a state Department of Natural Resources, a large science or agricultural university or a science news service. The phrase "new species AND [state name]" should help narrow the search.

Kingdoms and Domains

Key Ideas	Key Terms	Why It Matters
> Have biologists always recognized the same kingdoms? > What are the domains and kingdoms of the three-domain system of classification?	bacteria archaea eukaryote	The three-domain system is one of the latest revolutions in biology.

If you read old books or stories, you might read about plants and animals, or "flora and fauna," but probably not "fungi" or "bacteria."

Updating Classification Systems

For many years after Linnaeus created his system, scientists recognized only two kingdoms: Plantae (plants) and Animalia (animals). Relatively few of Earth's species were known, and little was known about them. **> Biologists have added complexity and detail to classification systems as they have learned more.** Throughout history, many new taxa have been proposed and some groups have been reclassified.

For example, **Figure 9** shows sponges, which were first classified as plants. Then, the invention of the microscope allowed scientists to look at cells. Scientists learned that sponges have cells that are much more like animal cells than like plant cells. So today, sponges are classified as animals. The microscope prompted many such changes.

From Two to Five Kingdoms In the 1800s, scientists added Kingdom Protista as a taxon for unicellular organisms. Soon, they noticed the differences between prokaryotic cells and eukaryotic cells. So, scientists created Kingdom Monera for prokaryotes and left single-celled eukaryotes in Kingdom Protista. By the 1950s, five kingdoms were used: Monera, Protista, Fungi, Plantae, and Animalia.

Six Kingdoms In the 1990s, Kingdom Monera came into question. Genetic data suggested two major groups of prokaryotes. So, Kingdom Monera was split into two new kingdoms: Eubacteria and Archaebacteria.

> **Reading Check** *What were the original Linnaean kingdoms?*

Sponge cells with flagella

Figure 9 Early scientists classified sponges as plants because sponges are attached to the sea floor. Further study and microscopic views in particular led to a reclassification of sponges as animals. **> What features of sponges might have led to this reclassification?**

The Living Environment
Standard 1
1.3b All scientific explanations are tentative and subject to change or improvement. Each new bit of evidence can create more questions than it answers. This leads to increasingly better understanding of how things work in the living world.

Differentiated Instruction

Advanced Learners

Classification Characteristics Have students research the basic characteristics that differentiated the two-, three-, five-, and six-kingdom systems of classification. Have them document the discoveries that led to a change in the number of kingdoms. **LS Verbal**

Key Resources

 Transparencies
D27 Six Kingdoms
D28 Kingdom and Domain Characteristics

Visual Concepts
Kingdoms of Life
Kingdom Characteristics
Parts of a Cell Wall
Comparing Prokaryotes and Eukaryotes
Comparing Organisms That Are Unicellular and Multicellular
Comparing Autotrophs and Heterotrophs
Origin of Eukaryotic Cells
Bacteria
Characteristics of Bacteria

> **Focus**

This section describes how classification systems change as scientists learn new information.

Bellringer

Use the Bellringer transparency to prepare students for this section.

> **Teach**

Demonstration

Classification Systems Give groups of students several colored plastic eggs. Place a small object, such as a coin, paper clip, or foil ball, inside each egg. On the inside surface, mark a plus or circle symbol. Challenge students to group the eggs without opening them and to give reasons for their system. Then have students open the eggs and reclassify them based on their internal characteristics. Have students explain how they changed their systems based on new information. Connect their explanations to how scientists revise the classification of organisms based on new information. **LS Logical**

Answers to Caption Questions
Figure 9: having flagella

Section Correlations
1.1.3b

Teaching Key Ideas

Relationships and Characteristics
Work with students to make comparisons between **Figure 10** and **Figure 11** on the next page. Make sure they understand how the presence or absence of the major characteristics are connected to the relationships shown in the tree.
LS Visual

Why It Matters

Alternate Classification An alternate classification system—the PhyloCode—grew out of a Harvard workshop in 1998 and is the work of international scientists. It is designed to be used concurrently with the rank-based codes or (after rules governing species names are added) as the code governing the names of taxa. The intent is not to replace existing names but to provide an alternative system for governing the application of both existing and newly proposed names for clades and species. **LS** Verbal

Answers to Caption Questions
Figure 10: genetics

Characteristics of Domains and Kingdoms

Domain	Bacteria	Archaea	Eukarya			
Kingdom	Eubacteria	Archae-bacteria	Protista	Fungi	Plantae	Animalia
Example	*Streptococcus pneumoniae*	*Staphylo-thermus marinus*	paramecium	spore cap mushroom	Texas paintbrush	white-winged dove
Cell type	prokaryote		eukaryote			
Cell walls	cell walls with peptidoglycan	cell walls with unique lipids	some species with cell walls	cell walls with chitin	cell walls with cellulose	no cell walls
Number of cells	unicellular		unicellular or multicellular	mostly multicellular	mostly multicellular	multicellular
Nutrition	autotroph or heterotroph			heterotroph	autotroph	heterotroph

Figure 10 This table shows the major characteristics used to define the domains and kingdoms of the modern Linnaean system. ❯ **What other kind of characteristic differs between kingdoms?**

The Three-Domain System

As biologists began to see the differences between the two kinds of prokaryotes, they also saw the similarities among all eukaryotes. So, a new system was proposed that divides all organisms into three domains: Bacteria, Archaea, and Eukarya. ❯ Today, most biologists tentatively recognize three domains and six kingdoms. **Figure 10** shows the major characteristics of these taxa.

Major Characteristics Major taxa such as kingdoms are defined by major characteristics. These characteristics include:

- **Cell Type** The cells may be either *prokaryotic* or *eukaryotic*.
- **Cell Walls** The cells may either have a cell wall or lack a cell wall.
- **Body Type** An organism is either *unicellular* or *multicellular*.
- **Nutrition** An organism is either an *autotroph* (makes nutrients from inorganic materials) or a *heterotroph* (gets nutrients from other organisms). Some taxa have unique means of nutrition.
- **Genetics** As you have learned, related groups of organisms will have similar genetic material and systems of gene expression. So, organisms may have a unique system of DNA, RNA, and proteins.

Domain Bacteria ❯ Domain Bacteria is equivalent to Kingdom Eubacteria. The common name for members of this domain is *bacteria*. **Bacteria** are prokaryotes that have a strong exterior cell wall and a unique genetic system. However, bacteria have the same kind of cell membrane lipid as most eukaryotes do.

Differentiated Instruction

English Learners

Word Origins Review with students the prefixes that differentiate among the major characteristics discussed on this page: *pro-* (before), *eu-* (good, well, normal), *uni-* (one), *multi-* (many), *auto-* (by oneself), *hetero-* (other). Ask students to suggest other words that begin with these prefixes. (Sample answers: *pro-*: program, prologue, prohibit; *eu-*: eutropic, eubacteria, euglena; *uni-*: uniform, universe, unify; *multi-*: multiply, multicolor, multivitamin; *auto-*: automobile, automatic, autobiography, *hetero-*: heterogenous, heterozygote) **LS** Verbal

⏱ **20 min**

Field Guides

Have you ever used field guides to identify animals or plants? Do you know how these guides are organized? Take a few guides outside, and take a closer look.

Procedure

1 Gather **several different field guides** for plants or other organisms in your area. Also gather a **magnifying glass** and a **specimen jar.** Take these items with you to a **local natural area.**

2 ⬥ CAUTION: **Do not touch or disturb any organisms without your teacher's permission; leave all natural items as you found them.** Try to find and identify at least two organisms that are listed in your field guides. Make notes to describe each organism.

Analysis

1. **Analyzing Methods** How difficult was identifying your organisms? How certain are you of your identification?

2. **Comparing Systems** How are the field guides organized? What other ways could they be organized?

All bacteria are similar in physical structure, with no internal compartments. Traditionally, bacteria have been classified according to their shape, the nature of their cell wall, their type of metabolism, or the way that they obtain nutrients. Bacteria are the most abundant organisms on Earth and are found in almost every environment.

Domain Archaea ❯ **Domain Archaea is equivalent to Kingdom Archaebacteria.** The common name for members of this domain is *archaea.* **Archaea** have a chemically unique cell wall and membranes and a unique genetic system. The genetic systems of archaea share some similarities with those of eukaryotes that they do not share with those of prokaryotes. Scientists think that archaea began to evolve in a separate lineage from bacteria early in Earth's history and that some archaea eventually gave rise to eukaryotes.

Archaea were first found by scientists in extreme environments, such as salt lakes, the deep ocean, or hot springs that exceed 100°C. These archaea are called *extremophiles.* Other archaea called *methanogens* live in oxygen-free environments. However, some archaea live in the same environments as many bacteria do.

Domain Eukarya ❯ **Domain Eukarya is made up of Kingdoms Protista, Fungi, Plantae, and Animalia.** Members of the domain Eukarya are **eukaryotes,** which are organisms composed of eukaryotic cells. These cells have a complex internal structure. This structure enabled the cells to become larger than the earliest cells and enabled the evolution of multicellular life. While eukaryotes vary in many fundamental respects, they share several key features.

❯ **Reading Check** *Which kingdoms are prokaryotic?*

---

bacteria (bak TIR ee uh) extremely small, single-celled organisms that usually have a cell wall and that usually reproduce by cell division; members of the domain Bacteria

archaea (ahr KEE uh) prokaryotes that are distinguished from other prokaryotes by differences in their genetics and in the makeup of their cell wall; members of the domain Archaea

eukaryote an organism made up of cells that have a nucleus enclosed by a membrane, multiple chromosomes, and a mitotic cycle; members of the domain Eukarya

---

Teaching Key Ideas

Visual Literacy Discuss the evolutionary relationships shown in **Figure 11.** Help students to differentiate among the lineages that lead to each of the six kingdoms. Check that students understand the meaning of the branching. Ask: Are algae more closely related to bacteria or plants? (plants) Are fungi more like animals or plants? (animals) **LS Visual**

Demonstration

Observing Protists Set up microscope stations with various protists for students to observe. Ask students to compare what they see with the characteristics of plants and animals. Make sure that they understand that protists are grouped together because they lack the defining characteristics of fungi, plants, and animals, and that in the future their classification may change. **LS Visual**

Answers to Caption Questions

Figure 11: Because scientists are constantly revising and testing their hypotheses about the phylogenies of various groups. Many parts of the "tree" are rearranged often.

READING TOOLBOX

Phylogenetic Tree There is close relationship between plants and algae with chloroplasts. Birds are closely related to reptiles. Roundworms, arthropods, flatworms, segmented worms, mollusks, and echinoderms have a common cnidarian ancestor. Protista is the group that did not descend from a common single ancestor.

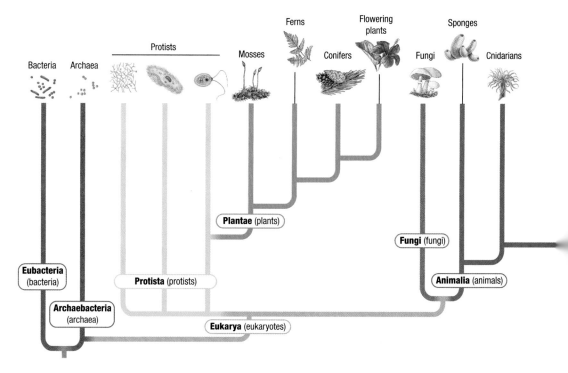

Figure 11 This tree of life shows current hypotheses of the relationships between all major groups of organisms. For updates on phylogenetic information, visit **go.hrw.com** and enter the keyword **HX8 Phylo.** ❯ Why might this type of model be revised?

READING TOOLBOX

Phylogenetic Tree Look carefully at **Figure 11.** Try to identify which groups are most closely related to each other. Which label includes lineages that do not share a unique common ancestor?

Characteristics of Eukaryotes Eukaryotes have highly organized cells. All eukaryotes have cells with a nucleus and other internal compartments. Also, true multicellularity and sexual reproduction occur only in eukaryotes. True multicellularity means that the activities of individual cells are coordinated and the cells themselves are in contact. Sexual reproduction means that genetic material is recombined when parents mate. Sexual reproduction is an important part of the life cycle of most eukaryotes.

Kinds of Eukaryotes The major groups of eukaryotes are defined by number of cells, body organization, and types of nutrition.

- **Plantae** Almost all plants are autotrophs that produce their own food by absorbing energy and raw materials from their environment. This process is *photosynthesis,* which occurs inside chloroplasts. The cell wall is made of a rigid material called *cellulose.* More than 350,000 known species of plants exist.

- **Animalia** Animals are multicellular heterotrophs. Their bodies may be simple collections of cells or highly complex networks of organ systems. Animal cells lack the rigid cell walls that plant cells have. More than 1 million known species of animals exist.

- **Fungi** Fungi are heterotrophs and are mostly multicellular. Their cell wall is made of a rigid material called *chitin.* Fungi are considered to be more closely related to animals than to any other kingdom. More than 70,000 known species of fungi exist.

MISCONCEPTION ALERT

Numbers of Individuals Make sure students understand that animals are not the most numerous organisms even though the animal kingdom takes up most of the branches on the tree. The animal kingdom includes the most known species, but the bacteria domain probably contains the most organisms.

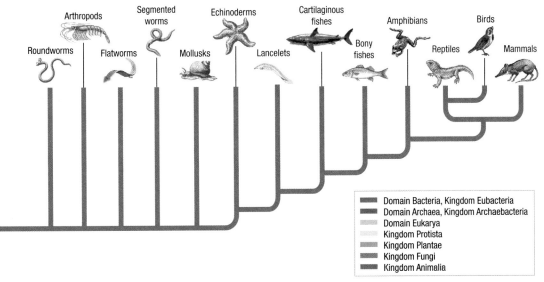

Roundworms Arthropods Flatworms Segmented worms Mollusks Echinoderms Lancelets Cartilaginous fishes Bony fishes Amphibians Reptiles Birds Mammals

Domain Bacteria, Kingdom Eubacteria
Domain Archaea, Kingdom Archaebacteria
Domain Eukarya
Kingdom Protista
Kingdom Plantae
Kingdom Fungi
Kingdom Animalia

go.hrw.com
✶ interact online
Students can interact with the "Tree of Life" by going to go.hrw.com and typing in the keyword HX8CLSF11.

go.hrw.com
✶ interact online
Keyword: HX8CLSF11

> **Close**

Formative Assessment

Which of the following are distinguishing characteristics of fungi?

A. unicellular, heterotrophic (Incorrect. Most fungi are not unicellular.)

B. multicellular, heterotrophic, cell walls containing chitin (Correct! The characteristic of cell walls distinguishes fungi from animals, which are also multicellular heterotrophs.)

C. unicellular or multicellular, some species with cell walls (Incorrect. These are characteristics of Protista.)

D. multicellular, autotrophic, cell walls (Incorrect. Fungi are not autotrophic.)

• **Protista** Kingdom Protista is a diverse group. Unlike the other three Kingdoms of Eukarya, Protista is not a natural group but rather a "leftover" taxon. Any single-celled eukaryote that is *not* a plant, animal, or fungi can be called a *protist*. Protists did not descend from a single common ancestor.

For many years, biolgists recognized four major groups of protists: flagellates, amoebas, algae, and parasitic protists. More recently, biologists have proposed to replace Protista with several new kingdoms. These kingdoms would classify protists that seem to be unrelated to any other groups. However, some protists are being reclassified into other kingdoms. For example, algae that have chloroplasts are thought to be most closely related to plants, as shown in **Figure 11.** Biologists have not yet agreed how to resolve all of these issues.

> **Reading Check** *Which kingdoms are heterotrophic?*

Section 3 Review

> **KEY IDEAS**

1. **Outline** how biologists have changed the major levels of the Linnaean system over time.

2. **List** the three domains, identify the kingdoms that align with each domain, and list the major characteristics of each kingdom.

CRITICAL THINKING

3. **Finding Evidence** The *theory of endosymbiosis* proposes that eukaryotes descended from a primitive combination of both archaea and bacteria. What evidence supports this theory?

4. **Science and Society** Microscopes led scientists to recognize new kingdoms. What other technology has impacted classification?

ALTERNATIVE ASSESSMENT

5. **Tree of Life Poster** Make a poster of the tree of life. At appropriate places on the tree, add images of representative organisms, along with labels. Include all domains and kingdoms as well as at least three major taxa within each kingdom.

Answers to Section Review

1. Answers should show a progression from Linnaeus' two-kingdom system of plants and animals through the later addition of protists, monerans, and fungi. Monerans were eventually split into two kingdoms that became domains Archaea and Bacteria. The remaining kingdoms make up the third domain, Eukarya.

2. **Archaea** Archaebacteria: unicellular, prokaryotic, unique genetic systems, cell walls with unique lipids

   Bacteria Eubacteria: unicellular, prokaryotic, unique genetic systems, cell walls with peptidoglycan

   Eukarya Animalia: multicellular, eukaryotic, heterotrophic; no cell walls

   Plantae: mostly multicellular, eukaryotic, autotrophic; cell walls with cellulose

   Fungi: mostly multicellular, eukaryotic, heterotrophic; cell walls with chitin

   Protista: unicellular or colonial, eukaryotic, autotrophic or heterotrophic, some with cell walls

3. The cell membrane lipid of bacteria and eukaryotes is similar, whereas the genetic systems of archaea and eukaryotes are similar.

4. Genetic analysis has led to understanding fundamental differences among cells, such as those between archaea and bacteria.

5. Student posters should be similar to Figure 10, but should include novel images with labels of organisms representing each group.

Lab

Time Required

One 45-minuted class period

Safety Caution

Review with students the safety cautions represented by the safety symbols before beginning the lab.

Tips and Tricks

Have students design a key for a random collection of objects from the classroom or school. An alternative collection of items could include small pieces of hardware or dry food items, such as noodles, beans, whole grains of wheat, rice, and other seeds.

Emphasize that a dichotomous key includes pairs of descriptions that lead to the identification of an object. Lead students through a discussion of using the process of elimination when working with a dichotomous key.

If students are unsure how to begin, tell them to start with the simplest way to split their collection into two groupings, or to find the "odd one out." Remind them that the groups do not have to be equal in size, just clearly differentiated. Then they simply repeat the splitting process for each remaining subgroup of items, until they have sorted through every item in their collection.

Chapter 18 Lab

Objectives

> Identify objects by using a dichotomous key.

> Design a dichotomous key for a group of objects.

Materials

- objects, common (6 to 10)
- labels, adhesive
- pencil

Safety

Dichotomous Keys

One way to identify an unknown organism is to use an identification key, which contains the major characteristics of groups of organisms. A dichotomous key is an identification key that contains pairs of contrasting descriptions. After each description, a key either directs the user to another pair of descriptions or identifies an object. In this lab, you will design and use a dichotomous key. A dichotomous key can be written for any group of objects.

Procedure

Use a Dichotomous Key

1 Work with a small group. Use the dichotomous key to identify the tree that produced each of the leaves shown here. Identify one leaf at a time. Always start with the first pair of statements (1a and 1b). Follow the direction beside the statement that describes the leaf.

2 Proceed through the key until you get to the name of a tree. Record your answer for each leaf shown.

Key to Forest Trees		
1a	Leaf edge is smooth or barely curved.	go to 2
1b	Leaf edge has teeth, waves, or lobes.	go to 3
2a	Leaf has a sharp bristle at its tip.	shingle oak
2b	Leaf has no bristle at its tip.	go to 4
3a	Leaf edge has small, shallow teeth.	Lombardy poplar
3b	Leaf edge has deep waves or lobes.	go to 5
4a	Leaf is heart shaped.	eastern redbud
4b	Leaf is not heart shaped.	live oak
5a	Leaf edge has less than 20 large lobes.	English oak
5b	Leaf edge has more than 20 waves.	chestnut oak

Design a Dichotomous Key

3 Put on safety goggles, gloves, and a lab apron.Choose 6 to 10 objects from around the classroom or from a collection supplied by your teacher. Before you go to the next step, have your teacher approve the objects your group has chosen.

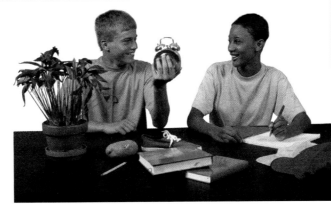

4 Study the structure and organization of the dichotomous key, which includes pairs of contrasting descriptions that form a "tree" of possibilities. Use this key as a model for the next step.

5 Work with the members of your group to design a new dichotomous key for the objects that your group selected. Be sure that each part of the key leads to either a definite identification of an object or another set of possibilities. Be sure that every object is included.

6 Test your key by using each one of the objects in your collection.

Exchange and Test Keys

7 After each group has completed the steps above, exchange your key and your collection of objects with another group. Use the key you receive to identify each of the new objects. If the new key does not work, return it to the group so that corrections can be made.

Cleanup

8 Clean up your work area and return or dispose of materials as directed by your teacher. Wash your hands thoroughly before you leave the lab and after you finish all of your work.

Analyze and Conclude

1. **Summarizing Data** List the identity of the tree for each of the leaves that you analyzed in step 2.

2. **SCIENTIFIC METHODS Critiquing Procedures** What other characteristics might be used to identify leaves by using a dichotomous key?

3. **Analyzing Results** What challenges did your group face while making your dichotomous key?

4. **Evaluating Results** Were you able to use another group's key to identify the group's collection of objects? Describe your experience.

5. **SCIENTIFIC METHODS Analyzing Methods** Does a dichotomous key begin with general descriptions and then proceed to more specific descriptions, or vice versa? Explain your answer by using examples.

6. **SCIENTIFIC METHODS Evaluating Methods** Is a dichotomous key the same as the Linnaean classification system? Explain your answer.

SC**L**INKS®
www.scilinks.org
Topic: Classification
Code: HX80295

Extension

7. **Research** Do research in the library or media center to find out what types of methods, other than dichotomous keys, are used to identify organisms.

Answers to Analysis and Conclusions

1. A: eastern redbud; B: live oak; C: English oak; D: Lombardy poplar; E: shingle oak; F: chestnut oak

2. Other leaf characteristics might include whether the leaf is compound or simple, whether it is needlelike, the arrangement of leaves on the branches, and the leaf's vein pattern.

3. Answers will vary. Accept all reasonable responses.

4. Students might have found that some of the pairs of statements were not contrasting enough, that some of the items were not correctly described, or that the key did not include a sufficient number of descriptions to distinguish all the items from one another.

5. Dichotomous keys proceed from general characteristics to specific characteristics. Examples from keys will vary but should reflect this gradation.

6. No, because a dichotomous key is used primarily to identify individual things, where the Linnaean classification system is used to group things.

Answers to Extension

7. Answers will vary. Some keys, such as field guides, use descriptive paragraphs, diagrams, and/or photos for comparison to identify organisms.

Key Resources

 Holt Lab Generator

 Lab Datasheet (Levels A, B, C)

 Holt Science Biology Video Labs

 Virtual Investigations

Chapter 18 Summary

SUPER SUMMARY

Have students connect the major concepts in this chapter through an interactive Super Summary. Visit **go.hrw.com** and type in the key word **HX8CLSS** to access the Super Summary for this chapter.

Reteaching Key Ideas

Scientific Names Have students determine what is incorrect about each of the following "scientific" names: spotted leopard (common name), *Tabanus b.* (species name missing), *Acer Rubrum* (species name is capitalized). **LS Logical**

Cladograms Have students work with a partner to devise a table and cladogram for the following animals: eagle, frog, goldfish, dog, and mouse. They should compare at lease five different traits. **LS Logical**

Classification Systems Have students prepare a graphic organizer to show the relationships of the following shapes: triangle, hexagon, trapezoid, parallelogram, square, pentagon, rectangle, quadrilateral, and polygon. Ask students to justify the rationale for their graphic organizer. **LS Logical**

Key Ideas	Key Terms

1 The Importance of Classification

❯ Biologists use taxonomic systems to organize their knowledge of organisms. These systems attempt to provide consistent ways to name and categorize organisms.

❯ All scientific names for species are made up of two Latin or Latin-like terms.

❯ In the Linnaean system of classification, organisms are grouped at successive levels of a hierarchy based on similarities in their form and structure. The eight levels of modern classification are domain, kingdom, phylum, class, order, family, genus, and species.

Key Terms
taxonomy (423)
genus (424)
binomial nomenclature (424)

2 Modern Systematics

❯ Scientists traditionally have used similarities in appearance and structure to group organisms. However, this approach has proven problematic.

❯ Grouping organisms by similarity is often assumed to reflect phylogeny, but inferring phylogeny is complex in practice.

❯ Cladistic analysis is used to select the most likely phylogeny among a given set of organisms.

❯ Biologists compare many kinds of evidence and apply logic carefully in order to infer phylogenies.

phylogeny (428)
cladistics (429)

3 Kingdoms and Domains

❯ Biologists have added complexity and detail to classification systems as they have learned more.

❯ Today, most biologists tentatively recognize three domains and six kingdoms. Domain Bacteria is equivalent to Kingdom Eubacteria. Domain Archaea is equivalent to Kingdom Archaebacteria. Domain Eukarya is made up of Kingdoms Protista, Fungi, Plantae, and Animalia.

bacteria (434)
archaea (435)
eukaryote (435)

PART A: Answer all questions in this part.

Directions: For each statement or question, write on your separate answer sheet the number of the word or expression that best completes the statement or answers the question.

1 The evolutionary pathways of ten different species are represented in the diagram below. Which two species are the most closely related?

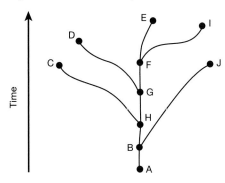

(1) C and D   (3) G and J
(2) E and I   (4) A and F

2 A current proposal in the field of classification divides life into three broad categories called domains. This idea is illustrated below. Which concept is best supported by this diagram?

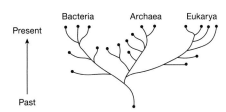

(1) Evolutionary pathways proceed only in one set direction over a short period of time.
(2) All evolutionary pathways will eventually lead to present-day organisms.
(3) All evolutionary pathways are the same length and they all lead to present-day organisms.
(4) Evolutionary pathways can proceed in several directions with only some pathways leading to present-day organisms.

3 The bones in the forelimbs of three mammals are shown below. For these mammals, the number, position, and shape of the bones most likely indicates that they may have

(1) developed in a common environment.
(2) developed from the same earlier species.
(3) identical genetic makeup.
(4) identical methods of obtaining food.

4 The evolutionary pathways of seven living species are shown in the diagram below. Which two species are likely to have the most similar DNA base sequences?

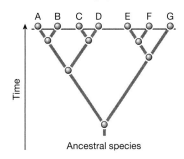

(1) B and G
(2) E and G
(3) B and C
(4) C and D

PART A

1. **(2)** Species E and I are more closely related because they are grouped closer together on a branch than species found in the other choices, as shown in the diagram. Species E and I directly share a common recent ancestor, that is, species F. All choices that do not have organisms descending directly from the same shared ancestor are more distantly related than species E and I. *(#02, June 2006 Regents Exam)*

2. **(4)** According to the diagram, not all branching pathways are the same length, proceed in one direction, or lead to present-day organisms. *(#13, January 2006 Regents Exam)*

3. **(2)** The bones of the organisms' forelimbs are considered homologous structures. They are all very similar in structure. The most likely evolutionary reasoning is that all of these organisms developed from the same earlier species. *(#14, January 2004 Regents Exam)*

4. **(4)** Organisms that branch off from the most recent ancestor are likely to have the most similar DNA. Organisms C and D branch from the most recent ancestor, as do organisms A and B. *(#14, August 2005 Regents Exam)*

Regents Exam Practice Correlations

4.3.1a 1, 3, 6, 7
4.3.1e 4, 9
4.3.1k 2, 5, 8

5. (3) The diagrams demonstrate that some species give rise to other species over time. These new species may persist, evolve into different species, or become extinct. The diagrams show that organisms living today have evolved at different rates. Only organisms at the end of a branch that lines up with the present time are alive today. *(#13, January 2003 Regents Exam)*

PART B

6. (2) Species A is a more distant shared common ancestor of D and F than species B as shown in the diagram. Species C is the common ancestor of only species F and I. Species I does not give rise to other species so it is not an ancestor in the diagram. *(#36, August 2006 Regents Exam)*

7. (1) Species F and I are more closely related because they are grouped closer together on a branch than species found in the other choices as shown in the diagram. Species F and I directly share a common recent ancestor, that is species C. All choices that do not have organisms descending directly from the same shared ancestor are more distantly related than species F and I. *(#35, August 2006 Regents Exam)*

5 According to some scientists, patterns of evolution can be illustrated by the diagrams below. Which statement best explains the patterns seen in these diagrams?

(1) The organisms at the end of each branch can be found in the environment today.

(2) The organisms that are living today have all evolved at the same rate and have undergone the same kinds of changes.

(3) Evolution involves changes that give rise to a variety of organisms, some of which continue to change through time while others die out.

(4) These patterns cannot be used to illustrate the evolution of extinct organisms.

PART B

Base your answers to questions 6 and 7 on the diagram below that shows some evolutionary pathways. Each letter represents a different species.

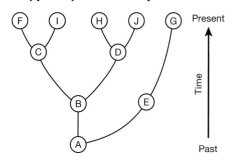

6 The most recent ancestor of organisms D and F is

(1) A   (3) C

(2) B   (4) I

7 Which two organisms are most closely related?

(1) F and I   (3) A and G

(2) F and H   (4) G and J

8 According to the diagram below, which three species lived on Earth during the same time period?

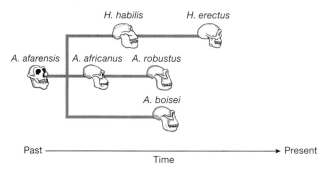

Past ────────────────────→ Present

Time

(1) robustus, africanus, afarensis   (3) habilis, robustus, boisei
(2) habilis, erectus, afarensis   (4) africanus, boisei, erectus

PART D

Base your answers to the questions on the information below and on your knowledge of biology.

Scientists found members of a plant species they did not recognize. They wanted to determine if the unknown species was related to one or more of four known species, A, B, C, and D. The relationship between species can be determined most accurately by comparing the results of gel electrophoresis of the DNA from different species. The chart below represents the results of gel electrophoresis of the DNA from the unknown plant species and the four known species.

Results of Gel Electrophoresis of
DNA from Five Plant Species

Unknown Species	Species A	Species B	Species C	Species D

Key

───── = Band in the gel

9 The unknown species is most closely related to which of the four known species? Support your answer.

---

8. **(3)** All choices that contain afarensis are incorrect as afarensis is the ancestor that gave rise to the other species shown. The choice with erectus is incorrect as erectus existed after the time period of all other species shown. *(#37, June 2005 Regents Exam)*

PART D

9. Allow 1 credit for stating that the unknown plant species is most closely related to species C and supporting that answer. Acceptable responses include, but are not limited to: It is most closely related to species C. The bands from the DNA of species C are the closest match to those of the unknown species. *(#62, January 2006 Regents Exam)*

History of Life on Earth

	Standards	**Teach Key Ideas**
CHAPTER OPENER, pp. 444–445 *15 min.*	*The Living Environment*	
SECTION 1 How Did Life Begin?, pp. 447–449 *45 min.* 〉 The Basic Chemicals of Life 〉 Where Did Life Begin? 〉 The First Cells		🖳 **Bellinger Transparency** 🖳 **Transparencies** D5 Miller-Urey Experiment 💿 **Visual Concepts** Spontaneous Origin
SECTION 2 The Age of Earth, pp. 450–453 *75 min.* 〉 The Fossil Record 〉 Analyzing Fossil Evidence 〉 Describing Geological Time	4.3.1l	🖳 **Bellinger Transparency** 🖳 **Transparencies** D4 Radioactive Decay 💿 **Visual Concepts** Radiometric Dating • Half-Life • Mass Extinction
SECTION 3 Evolution of Life, pp. 454–460 *45 min.* 〉 Precambrian Time 〉 Paleozoic Era 〉 Mesozoic and Cenozoic Eras	4.3.1j, 4.3.1l, 4.6.2a	🖳 **Bellinger Transparency** 🖳 **Transparencies** D7 Ozone Shields the Earth • D8 Evolution of Eukaryotes 💿 **Visual Concepts** Comparing Prokaryotes and Eukaryotes • Origin of Eukaryotic Cells • Endosymbiosis • Comparing Organisms that Are Unicellular and Multicellular • Ozone and Ecosystems • Characteristics of Arthropods • Vertebrates • Characteristics of Fish

See also PowerPoint® Resources

Chapter Review and Assessment Resources

SE Super Summary, p. 462
SE Regents Exam Practice, p. 463
📄 Regents Review Guide
📄 Review Resources
📄 Chapter Tests A and B
💻 Holt Online Assessment
💿 Regents Question Banks on Teacher's One-Stop Planner

CHAPTER
Fast Track
To shorten instruction due to time limitations, eliminate the Skills Practice Lab.

Basic Learners
TE First Cells, p. 448
TE Rate of Decay, p. 452
TE Evolution of Vertebrates, p. 458
TE Pattern Puzzles, p. 458
📁 Directed Reading Worksheets*
📁 Active Reading Worksheets*
📁 Lab Manuals, Level A*
📄 Study Guide* ■
📄 Note-taking Workbook*
📄 Special Needs Activities and
Modified Tests*

Advanced Learners
TE Burgess Shale, p. 451
📁 Critical Thinking Worksheets*
📁 Concept Mapping Worksheets*
📁 Science Skills Worksheets*
📁 Lab Datasheets, Level C*

Why It Matters	Hands-On	Skills Development	Assessment
Build student motivation with resources about high-interest applications.	**SE Inquiry Lab** Logical Order, p. 445* ■	**TE Reading Toolbox** Assessing Prior Knowledge, p. 444 **SE Reading Toolbox**, p. 446	
TE Demonstration First Billion Years, p. 447 **TE Space Science**, p. 448		**SE Reading Toolbox** Process Chart, p. 449 **TE Reading Toolbox** Process Chart, p. 449	**SE Section Review** **TE Formative Assessment** Spanish Assessment* ■ 📁 **Section Quiz** ■
TE Demonstration Fossils, p. 450	**SE Quick Lab** Radioactive Decay, p. 452* ■ **SE Skills Practice Lab** Model of Rock Strata, p. 461* ■ 📁 **Skills Practice Lab** Determining the Age of Artifacts Using C-14*	**SE Reading Toolbox** Word Parts, p. 451 **TE Reading Toolbox** Word Parts, p. 451	**SE Section Review** **TE Formative Assessment** Spanish Assessment* ■ 📁 **Section Quiz** ■
TE Demonstration Earth's Timeline, p. 454 **TE Effects of UV Radiation**, p. 455 **SE Nearing the End**, p. 460	**SE Quick Lab** Timeline of Earth, p. 457* ■ 📁 **Quick Lab** Analyzing Adaptations: Living on Land*	**SE Reading Toolbox** Describing Time, p. 455 **TE Reading Toolbox** Describing Time, p. 455 **TE Reading Toolbox** Visual Literacy, p. 460	**SE Section Review** **TE Formative Assessment** Spanish Assessment* ■ 📁 **Section Quiz** ■
	See also Lab Generator		**See also Holt Online Assessment Resources**

Resources for Differentiated Instruction

English Learners

TE Cellular Specialization, p. 457
📁 Directed Reading Worksheets*
📁 Active Reading Worksheets*
📁 Lab Manuals, Level A*
📋 Study Guide* ■
📋 Note-taking Workbook*
📋 Multilingual Glossary

Struggling Readers

TE Key-Term Fold, p. 450
TE Endosymbiosis and Bacteria, p. 456
TE Pattern Puzzles, p. 458
📁 Directed Reading Worksheets*
📁 Active Reading Worksheets*
📁 Lab Manuals, Level A*
📋 Study Guide*
📋 Note-taking Workbook*
📋 Special Needs Activities and Modified Tests*

Special Education Students

📁 Directed Reading Worksheets*
📁 Active Reading Worksheets*
📁 Lab Manuals, Level A*
📋 Study Guide* ■
📋 Note-taking Workbook*
📋 Special Needs Activities and Modified Tests*

Alternative Assessment

TE Timeline Interpretation, p. 452
📁 Science Skills Worksheets*
📁 Section Quizzes* ■
📋 Chapter Tests A, B, and C* ■

Chapter 19

Chapter 19

History of Life on Earth

Overview

The purpose of this chapter is to explore how life may have begun and how scientists estimate the age of Earth. The chapter also discusses how life increased in complexity from its first forms on Earth.

READING TOOLBOX

Assessing Prior Knowledge Students should understand the following concepts:
• cellular nature of life
• biodiversity
• evolution

Visual Literacy Tell students that the Black Rock Desert is one of the flattest surfaces on Earth. During the Ice Age, the area was covered by a large lake that at its peak was about 150 m deep.

Today, Fly Geyser continuously sprays water onto the desert sand. The plumes can be seen for miles. As the water has spewed from the geyser over the years, mineral deposits left behind when the water evaporates have created the colorful mounds shown in the picture. The bright colors on the mounds and the surrounding area are due to thermophilic prokaryotes, which flourish in the hot, moist environment.

Preview

1 How Did Life Begin?
The Basic Chemicals of Life
Life's Building Blocks
The First Cells

2 The Age of Earth
The Fossil Record
Analyzing Fossil Evidence
Describing Geologic Time

3 Evolution of Life
Precambrian Time
Paleozoic Era
Mesozoic and Cenozoic Eras

Why It Matters

The history of life on Earth is like a puzzle; scientists continue to search for evidence and to put it together into a cohesive theory.

 The Living Environment
Standard 4 Students will understand and apply scientific concepts, principles, and theories pertaining to the physical setting and living environment and recognize the historical development of ideas in science.
Key Idea 3 Individual organisms and species change over time. *Major Understandings* - 3.1j, 3.1l
Key Idea 6 Plants and animals depend on each other and their physical environment. *Major Understandings* - 6.2a

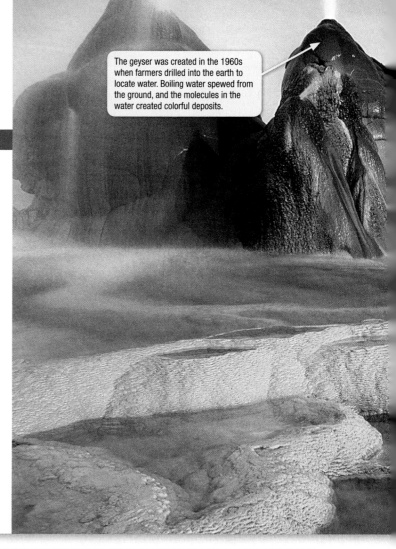

The Fly Geysers of the Black Rock Desert in Nevada are surrounded by a pool of water in which many different types of minerals are dissolved.

The geyser was created in the 1960s when farmers drilled into the earth to locate water. Boiling water spewed from the ground, and the molecules in the water created colorful deposits.

Chapter Correlations **The Living Environment**

Standard 4

3.1j Billions of years ago, life on Earth is thought by many scientists to have begun as simple, single-celled organisms. About a billion years ago, increasingly complex multicellular organisms began to evolve.

3.1l Extinction of a species occurs when the environment changes and the adaptive characteristics of a species are insufficient to allow its survival. Fossils indicate that many organisms that lived long ago are extinct. Extinction of species is common; most of the species that have lived on Earth no longer exist.

6.2a As a result of evolutionary processes, there is a diversity of organisms and roles in ecosystems. This diversity of species increases the chance that at least some will survive in the face of large environmental changes. Biodiversity increases the stability of the ecosystem.

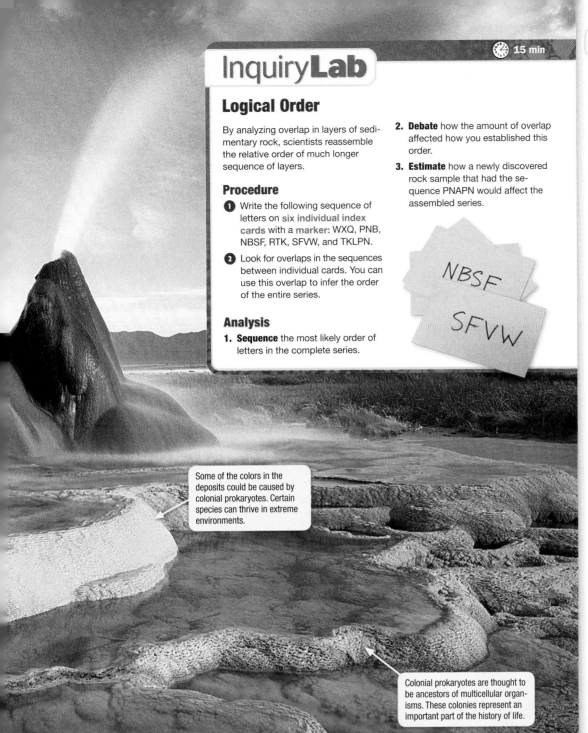

InquiryLab

⏱ 15 min

Logical Order

By analyzing overlap in layers of sedimentary rock, scientists reassemble the relative order of much longer sequence of layers.

Procedure

❶ Write the following sequence of letters on **six individual index cards** with a **marker**: WXQ, PNB, NBSF, RTK, SFVW, and TKLPN.

❷ Look for overlaps in the sequences between individual cards. You can use this overlap to infer the order of the entire series.

Analysis

1. **Sequence** the most likely order of letters in the complete series.

2. **Debate** how the amount of overlap affected how you established this order.

3. **Estimate** how a newly discovered rock sample that had the sequence PNAPN would affect the assembled series.

> Some of the colors in the deposits could be caused by colonial prokaryotes. Certain species can thrive in extreme environments.

> Colonial prokaryotes are thought to be ancestors of multicellular organisms. These colonies represent an important part of the history of life.

InquiryLab

Teacher's Notes Have students work with a partner. Briefly introduce the law of superposition, which states that underlying layers of rock will be older if the rock layers have not been rearranged by tectonic processes. As new sedimentary rock forms atop older rock, it creates a permanent record of the strata's history. Older layers are formed first, and are therefore found deeper in a column of rock than younger layers. The relative age of the rocks and their fossils can be determined by examining the order of the layers. Scientists also compare the order of layers from columns of rock in different geologic locations in order to devise the most logical sequence of strata.

Materials
- index cards (6)
- marker

Answers to Analysis
1. RTKLPNBSFVWXQ
2. The more overlap there is, the more likely that the inferred sequence is correct.
3. The series would most likely be updated to RTKLPNAPNBSFVWXQ.

READING TOOLBOX

Using Words

Answers will vary.
1. A microsphere is a small, ball-shaped object.
2. The lithosphere is a ball of rock or stone.
3. Paleolithic refers to something made of ancient rock.

Using Language

1. 16th, Saturday, two weeks ago
2. 65 million years ago, end of the Cretaceous period

Using Science Graphics

1. RNA nucleotides
2. RNA molecules catalyze protein synthesis.
3. First, inorganic molecules are processed into RNA nucleotides. Then, they form RNA macro-nucleoles that self-replicate. Next, smaller RNA molecules catalyze protein synthesis. Finally, proteins form.

READING TOOLBOX

These reading tools can help you learn the material in this chapter. For more information on how to use these and other tools, see **Appendix: Reading and Study Skills.**

Using Words

Word Parts You can tell a lot about a word by taking it apart and examining its prefix and root.

Your Turn Use the information in the table to write your own definition for the following terms.
1. *microsphere*
2. *lithosphere*
3. *paleolithic*

Word Parts		
Word part	**Type**	**Meaning**
micro-	prefix	small
paleo-	prefix	ancient
lith	root	rock, stone
sphere	root	ball-shaped object

Using Language

Describing Time Certain words and phrases can help you get an idea of when something happened and for how long it happened. These phrases are called *specific time markers*. Specific time markers include phrases such as 1 hour, yesterday, the 20th century, and 30 years later.

Your Turn Read the sentences below, and write the specific time markers.
1. Jennifer celebrated her 16th birthday on Saturday two weeks ago.
2. Dinosaurs became extinct about 65 million years ago, at the end of the Cretaceous Period.

Using Science Graphics

Process Chart Process charts show the steps that a process takes to get from one point to another point. Events in a process happen in a certain order. There are many words that can be used to describe the order in which things happen. Some of these words include *first, next, then,* and *last.*

Your Turn Use the diagram to answer the following questions.
1. Which event happens second?
2. Which event follows RNA self-replication?
3. Describe the process illustrated in this chart in paragraph form. Use sequence words to indicate in what order things happen.

How Did Life Begin?

Key Ideas	Key Terms	Why It Matters
❯ What did the Miller-Urey experiment show about the formation of the basic molecules of life? ❯ What are two theories that propose where the building blocks of life originated on early Earth? ❯ How could molecules have become packaged into cells that contain heritable cellular instructions?	microsphere ribozyme	Studying the origin of life on Earth allows scientists to discover key biological and chemical processes.

Most scientists think that life on Earth evolved through natural processes. The point when life started likely involved simple chemicals.

The Basic Chemicals of Life

In the 1920s, Russian scientist Aleksandr I. Oparin and British scientist John B. S. Haldane suggested that Earth's early oceans contained large amounts of organic molecules. They proposed that these molecules formed spontaneously in chemical reactions that were activated by energy from the sun, volcanic eruptions, and lightning.

Oparin and American scientist Harold Urey, along with other scientists, hypothesized that the early atmosphere was rich in hydrogen gas, H_2, and hydrogen-containing gases, such as water vapor, H_2O, ammonia, NH_3, and methane, CH_4. They thought that if the atmosphere lacked oxygen, a variety of organic compounds made up of the elements found in these gases could form. This hypothesis was tested in the 1950s by Urey and American scientist Stanley Miller.

The Miller-Urey Experiment Miller placed the gases into a device like the one in **Figure 1.** To simulate lightning, he used electrical sparks. After a few days, Miller found organic molecules in his device, which included some of life's basic building blocks: amino acids, fatty acids, and other hydrocarbons (molecules made of carbon and hydrogen). ❯ **The Miller-Urey experiment showed that, under certain conditions, organic compounds could form from inorganic molecules.**

We now know that the molecules used in Miller's experiment could not have existed in abundance on early Earth. Four billion years ago, shortly after Earth formed, it did not have a protective layer of ozone gas. Ultraviolet radiation from the sun would have destroyed any ammonia and methane in the atmosphere when the ozone layer did not exist. When ammonia and methane gases are absent from the Miller-Urey experiment, key biological molecules are not made. However, the Miller-Urey experiment clearly shows that complex biological compounds can form from simple building blocks.

❯ **Reading Check** *What compounds were formed in the Miller-Urey experiment? (See the Appendix for answers to the Reading Checks.)*

CH_4
 H_2
 NH_3

 Spark

 Condenser

 H_2O vapor

 Hot water

 Collecting chamber
 Organic compounds

Figure 1 Miller simulated an atmosphere that Oparin and others incorrectly hypothesized as the atmosphere of early Earth. His experiment produced several organic compounds.

Key Resources

 Transparencies
 D5 Miller-Urey Experiment

 Visual Concepts
 Spontaneous Origin

❯ **Focus**

This section explains models that scientists have developed to explain how life originated on Earth from the chemicals present at the time.

🔊 **Bellringer**

Use the Bellringer transparency to prepare students for this section.

❯ **Teach**

Demonstration

First Billion Years Students may have difficulty understanding the enormity of time represented by Earth's history. To help them visualize the concept of 1 billion, ask if they think they could physically carry 1 million dollars. (Answers will vary.) Then, explain that 1 million dollars would be a stack of $100 bills approximately 1 m in height (10,000 bills). One billion dollars would be a stack of the same bills to a height of the Washington Monument (1 million bills). Now, relate this image to the first billion years of our planet's existence without any form of life. **LS Visual**

Teaching Key Ideas

Pass the Salt Early oceans were probably similar in composition to modern freshwater lakes. The salt concentration in today's oceans is the result of million of years of water running over rocks and picking up mineral salts before flowing to the sea.

Teaching Key Ideas

Cell Structure Before students read the information about the first cells, review with them the parts of a cell and the types of molecules that make up these structures. Ask students why the cell membrane is important to the cell. (It controls what materials enter and leave the cell.) **LS** Logical

Answers to Caption Questions

Figure 2: Scientists study the conditions around hydrothermal vents because these conditions approximate those thought to have existed on Earth. These conditions might provide clues to where the first building blocks of life were formed.

SCILINKS
www.scilinks.org
Topic: Origin of Life
Code: HX81083

ACADEMIC VOCABULARY
impact collision

Figure 2 Scientists have suggested that the basic chemicals of life could have originated in deep-sea vents or from outside our atmosphere. ❯ Why do scientists study the conditions around hydrothermal vents?

Life's Building Blocks

Scientists agree that the building blocks of life formed under special conditions. They research environments that could have made these molecules. ❯ Among the hypotheses that address the origin of life, one states that early biological molecules formed close to hydrothermal vents. Organic molecules may also have arrived on early Earth in meteorites.

Hydrothermal Vents Some scientists think that the chemical reactions that produced the first biological molecules occurred in the oceans of early Earth. The heat from hydrothermal vents, shown in **Figure 2,** could have provided energy for chemical reactions. Within the sea, biological molecules also would have been protected from potentially harmful solar radiation.

Space Some scientists think that organic molecules could have arrived on Earth on meteorites or comets. For example, the meteorite shown in **Figure 2** contains amino acids. Such molecules could have arrived on early Earth from outside of our atmosphere. It is unknown, however, whether meteorites that hit early Earth contained any such chemicals. But we know that such impacts were more frequent in the early history of Earth than they are now.

The First Cells

Research continues that might provide clues to how biological molecules first began to group together and become packaged into cells. For example, how did amino acids link to form proteins? There are major differences between simple organic molecules and the large organic molecules found in living cells. Research has shown that amino acids can form proteins under certain conditions.

Forming a Cell How did molecules become packaged together inside a cell membrane? To answer this question, scientists have studied the behavior of organic molecules in water. Lipids, which make up cell membranes, tend to combine in water. Certain lipids, when combined with other molecules, can form a tiny droplet that has a surface that resembles a cell membrane.

Why It Matters

Space Science Investigators in the fields of biology, chemistry, physics, geology, and astrophysics are all working together to learn more about other planets in the quest to learn more about our own. Indeed, whole new fields of study, such as planetary geology, were unheard of until recently. In fact, the characteristics of a planet have been called into question with the reevaluation of Pluto. Ask students to discuss new fields of study that might arise from exploration of the planets in our solar system. (Answers will vary but might include planetary mining and refining and mass transit between planets.) **LS** Verbal

Differentiated Instruction

Basic Learners

First Cells Have students answer this question: Were the first cells that evolved on Earth prokaryotes or eukaryotes? Have students justify their answers. (The first cells were prokaryotes. At this point in the chapter, students should conclude that, because prokaryotes are single-cell organisms lacking a nucleus, they probably evolved earlier than more complex eukaryotes.) **LS** Visual

Further research has shown that, in water, short chains of amino acids can form tiny spherical structures called **microspheres.** ❯ Many scientists think that the formation of microspheres may have been the first step toward cellular organization. Microspheres could not be considered cells, however, unless they had characteristics of living things, including heredity.

Origin of Heredity How did heredity begin? Recall that our DNA contains instructions for making proteins. DNA is also passed on from one generation to the next. In the laboratory, scientists have not been able to make proteins or DNA form spontaneously in water. However, scientists have been able to form short chains of RNA, the nucleic acid that helps carry out the instructions of DNA, in water. So as life began, did DNA or RNA come first?

Scientists now know that RNA molecules perform many tasks in a cell. There are several types of RNA that accomplish these tasks. Each type of RNA has a unique structure that relates to its function. In the 1980s, American scientists Thomas Cech and Sidney Altman found that a certain type of RNA molecule, called a **ribozyme,** can act like an enzyme. Also, they showed that RNA can form spontaneously in water, without DNA. They hypothesized that RNA was the first self-replicating molecule that stored information and that catalyzed the formation of the first proteins. One idea of how RNA could have been involved in protein synthesis is shown in **Figure 3.** Cech and Altman further hypothesized that RNA could have changed—evolved—from one generation to the next. Scientists hypothesize that DNA and proteins eventually took over these roles in the cell.

❯ **Reading Check** *Explain how RNA could have existed before DNA.*

Figure 3 In this proposed model of protein formation, chemical reactions between inorganic molecules formed RNA nucleotides. The nucleotides assembled into large RNA molecules which were able to replicate and to catalyze the formation of proteins.

Process Chart Use the process chart in **Figure 3** to understand the hypothesis about how proteins were created. What is the significance of the loop at the self-replication step?

---

microsphere (MIE kroh SFIR) a hollow microscopic spherical structure that is usually composed of proteins or a synthetic polymer

ribozyme (RIE buh ZIEM) a type of RNA that can act as an enzyme

Section 1 Review

❯ **KEY IDEAS**

1. **State** what the Miller-Urey experiment demonstrated.

2. **Describe** two theories that address where the building blocks of life evolved.

3. **Explain** a prevailing theory of how cells evolved.

CRITICAL THINKING

4. **Evaluating Hypotheses** How does the Miller-Urey experiment demonstrate the importance of basing experiments on valid assumptions?

5. **Inferring Conclusions** How might the hypothesis about the origin of heredity change if DNA could form spontaneously in water?

USING SCIENCE GRAPHICS

6. **Analyzing Models** Using **Figure 1,** determine what changes to the apparatus used by Miller and Urey would be necessary to model the production of amino acids and other organic compounds near hydrothermal vents.

Teaching Key Ideas

First Hereditary Molecule Some students may not understand how RNA, which in most cases relies on a template provided by DNA, could have developed before DNA. Explain that today certain viruses (called *retroviruses*), including HIV, contain only RNA as their genetic material. Their viral RNA, when released into a host cell, is used as a template to then make DNA. **LS Verbal**

READING TOOLBOX

Process Chart If the RNA copied itself and formed larger molecules, they could hold the code for more complex proteins.

❯ **Close**

Formative Assessment

What do some scientists think provided the energy for chemical reactions that produced the first biological molecules?

A. meteors (Incorrect. Meteors may have carried the first organic molecules to Earth.)

B. heat from hydrothermal vents (Correct!)

C. ribosomes (Incorrect. Ribosomes are a type of RNA molecule that can act like an enzyme.)

D. microspheres (Incorrect. These are tiny spherical structures composed of proteins.)

Answers to Section Review

1. The Miller-Urey experiment showed that under certain conditions organic compounds could form from inorganic molecules.

2. Some scientists think that the chemical reactions that produced the first organic molecules occurred deep in Earth's ocean. Others think that the molecules could have arrived on Earth with meteorites or comets.

3. Scientists think that the formation of microspheres might have been the first step toward cellular organization. Microspheres cannot be considered true cells, however, unless they have the characteristics of living things, including heredity.

4. The Miller-Urey experiment was based on the invalid assumption that ammonia and methane were present in Earth's early atmosphere. When these gases were removed from the experiment, key biological molecules were not made. The experiment shows that invalid assumptions can lead to invalid conclusions.

5. Scientists might hypothesize that DNA was the first self-replicating information-storage molecule. However, RNA could remain part of the hypothesis if DNA was not found to be a necessary catalyst for the assembly of proteins.

6. Instead of gases, the model would use inorganic chemicals dissolved in sea water. Instead of generating a spark, the model would heat the sea water to an extremely high temperature.

Key Ideas	Key Terms	Why It Matters
> How is the fossil record used to chronicle the history of life? > How do paleontologists date fossils? > What evidence was used to make the geologic time scale?	fossil record geologic relative dating time scale radiometric mass dating extinction half-life	The fossil record is used to understand the diversity of life on Earth.

 The Living Environment
Standard 4
3.1l Extinction of a species occurs when the environment changes and the adaptive characteristics of a species are insufficient to allow its survival. Fossils indicate that many organisms that lived long ago are extinct. Extinction of species is common; most of the species that have lived on Earth no longer exist.

Figure 4 Fossils can form in several ways. The most common way is when an organism dies and is buried in sediment. **> What happens when an organism is covered by sediment?**

Scientists think Earth formed more than 4.5 billion years ago. Fossil evidence indicates that for much of that long history, Earth has been the home of living things.

The Fossil Record

The **fossil record** includes all fossil remains of living things on Earth. **> Both the geographical distribution of organisms and when they lived on Earth can be inferred from the fossil record. It chronicles the diversity of life on Earth.** The fossil record also provides evidence of intermediate forms of life and suggests how organisms are related to each other. Although our examination of the fossil record will never be complete, it presents strong evidence that evolution has taken place.

How Fossils Form Most fossils are found in sedimentary rock. These fossils form when organisms and traces of organisms are rapidly buried in fine sediments that are deposited by water, wind, or volcanic eruptions. The formation of one kind of fossil from a marine animal is shown in **Figure 4.** Environments that often cause fossil formation are wet lowlands, slow-moving streams, lakes, shallow seas, and areas near volcanoes that spew volcanic ash. However, many species have lived in environments where fossils do not form. Even if an organism lives in an environment where fossils can form, its dead body might not be buried in sediment before it decays or is eaten.

❶ This trilobite dies and becomes buried under layers of sediment that are deposited by water.

❷ The organism gradually dissolves and leaves a hollow impression, or mold, in the sediment.

❸ Over time, the mold may fill with minerals, which forms a cast of the organism.

Analyzing Fossil Evidence

Earth's surface changes constantly. Rocks are eroding and are laid down as sediment. This sediment forms layers of sedimentary rock called *strata,* shown in **Figure 5.** According to the *law of superposition,* older strata are covered by younger strata. However, geologic events such as earthquakes can affect how the strata are arranged. ❯ In order to analyze fossil evidence, paleontologists use both relative and absolute dating methods to date fossils.

Types of Fossils Mineralized fossils are the most common types of fossils. In some cases, as shown in **Figure 4,** an organism breaks down, leaving a hollow space. This mold may fill with minerals. In other cases, the pores of the organism are filled with minerals, preserving the shape of the organism. An example of a mineralized fossil is shown in **Figure 5.** In rare cases, fossils are preserved in hardened plant sap, or amber. In these fossils, soft parts of the tissue are preserved in detail.

Relative Age A process called **relative dating** is used to estimate ages of fossils found within strata. Relative dating cannot reveal a fossil's age, in years. But it can reveal the order that strata and the fossils within them were laid down over time. Paleontologists organize fossils into a sequence based on the relative age of the strata in which the fossil was found.

Index Fossils An *index fossil* is a fossil of an organism that was common and had widespread geographical distribution during a certain time in Earth's history. Index fossils are used to estimate the age of other strata that contain the same type of fossil. Scientists have compared patterns of strata and the index fossils within them to make the geologic time scale.

❯ **Reading Check** *What is the law of superposition?*

---

fossil record the history of life in the geologic past as indicated by the traces or remains of living things

relative dating a method of determining whether an event or object, such as a fossil, is older or younger than other events or objects

---

READING TOOLBOX

Word Parts The suffix *-ologist* means "one who studies." What do you think a paleontologist does?

Figure 5 Rock strata are easily visible in the Grand Canyon. Gastropod fossils like this one have been found in the region.

Strata on top formed more recently than strata beneath them.

Older strata are underneath younger strata.

Teacher's Notes Have pennies counted and placed in paper or plastic cups. If time allows, multiple trials (two or three) would provide a better set of data. Make sure all pennies are accounted for at the end of the lab.

Materials
• pennies (100)
• box-like container, with lid

Answers to Analysis
1. It represents the amount of radio isotope remaining after some decay has occurred.
2. When only 25 coins remain, two half-lives have passed. Therefore, the age of the sample is 11,460 years.
3. Answers will vary. Accept all reasonable answers that demonstrate knowledge of what the variables represent in the model and that are supported by data.

MISCONCEPTION ////ALERT\\\\

Dating Fossils It is commonly stated that fossils can be dated using radiometric dating techniques. However, radiometric dating indicates the time when the particles in rock were originally formed. Because most fossils are formed from sedimentary rock, dating the particles within them does not indicate when the fossil was formed. So, most fossils are dated indirectly, by inference from surrounding igneous or metamorphic rock that has been directly dated.

Hands-On
QuickLab

🕐 15 min

Radioactive Decay
You can use pennies to model radioactive decay.

Procedure
❶ Work in pairs. Make a data table like the one shown.

❷ Place **100 pennies** into a **box that has a lid**.

❸ Shake the box gently. Remove the pennies showing heads. This process models one half-life. Record the number of coins remaining in the box.

❹ Repeat step 3 until every coin has been removed.

❺ Make a line graph of your data. Label "Half-life" on the x-axis and "Coins remaining" on the y-axis.

Half-life	Number of coins remaining
1	
2	
3	

Analysis
1. **Identify** what "Number of coins remaining" represents.

2. **Calculate** the age of your sample if 25 coins remained. Assume that each half-life equals 5,730 years.

3. CRITICAL THINKING **Evaluating Models** Describe how this model illustrates radioactive decay.

---

radiometric dating a method of determining the absolute age of an object by comparing the relative percentages of a radioactive (parent) isotope and a stable (daughter) isotope

half-life the time required for half of a sample of a radioactive substance to decay

geologic time scale the standard method used to divide Earth's long natural history into manageable parts

mass extinction an episode during which large numbers of species become extinct

Figure 6 This graph shows the rate of decay of a radioactive isotope.

Decay of Radioactive Isotope

All

$\frac{1}{2}$

$\frac{1}{4}$

$\frac{1}{8}$

$\frac{1}{16}$

Portion of isotope remaining

Number of half-lives

Absolute Age Relative dating can show only whether an object is older or younger than another object. A method called **radiometric dating** estimates the age in years of an object by measuring certain radioactive isotopes that the object contains. An *isotope* is a form of an element whose atomic mass differs from that of other atoms of the same element. Radioactive isotopes, or *radioisotopes,* are unstable isotopes that break down and give off energy in the form of charged particles, or radiation. This breakdown is called *radioactive decay*.

When the radioactive isotope, called a "parent," decays, it produces new isotopes—*daughter* isotopes—that are smaller and more stable. The time required for half of a sample of parent radioisotope to decay into a daughter isotope is the isotope's **half-life. Figure 6** shows this concept. Each radioisotope has a specific half-life, and the rate at which a radioisotope decays is not affected by external factors.

Measuring Age As the parent radioisotope decays, the amount of the daughter radioisotope increases. By comparing the amounts of certain radioisotopes and their daughter isotopes, scientists can calculate how many half-lives have passed since a material formed. One radioisotope that is widely used to date organic materials, such as mummified remains, is carbon-14. The half-life of carbon-14 is relatively short—5,730 years. Carbon-14 is used to measure the age of carbon-containing materials that are younger than 75,000 years old. Older materials have too little isotope remaining for scientists to accurately measure the age of the materials. To find the age of the older materials, scientists have to measure other radioisotopes.

Differentiated Instruction

Basic Learners
Rate of Decay Ask students to explain why the graph of the rate of decay shown in **Figure 6** is not a straight line. (The rate of radioactive decay is based on the half-life of a radioactive isotope. The amount of material that decays in one half-life is half of the undecayed portion of the sample present at the beginning of the time period. With each successive half-life, the total amount of remaining radioactive isotope decreases.) **LS** Visual

Alternative Assessment
Timeline Interpretation Ask students the following to determine whether they understand the relationships shown in **Figure 7.** What is the most recent era? (Cenozoic) What was the longest era? (Precambrian) In what period would a 356 million year old fossil have lived? (Carboniferous) Which dinosaurs remains are older, Jurassic or Triassic? (Triassic) Which period was the shortest in history? (Silurian)

Describing Geologic Time

The **geologic time scale** organizes geologic and evolutionary events. ❭ **The geologic time scale is based on evidence in the fossil record and has been shaped by mass extinctions.** A shortened geologic time scale is shown in **Figure 7.**

Divisions of Geologic Time Earth has existed for more than 4 billion years. From the beginning of Earth to about 542 million years ago is often referred to as Precambrian time. From the end of Precambrian time to the present, Earth's history is divided into three *eras*—the Paleozoic Era, the Mesozoic Era, and the Cenozoic Era. These three eras are further divided into periods. Humans appeared during the Quaternary Period.

Mass Extinction Recall that the extinction of a species is the death of all members of that species. When large numbers of species become extinct, the event is called a **mass extinction.** The fossil record indicates that many mass extinctions have occurred during Earth's history. Evidence indicates that worldwide geologic and weather changes are common factors that contribute to mass extinctions. Mass extinctions may have contributed to overall biodiversity on Earth. After a mass extinction, opportunities open for new life-forms to emerge.

Mass extinctions have been used to mark the divisions of geologic time. Large mass extinctions mark the boundaries between eras, as shown on **Figure 7.** For example, mass extinctions occurred at the end of Precambrian time, at the end of the Paleozoic Era, and at the boundary between the Mesozoic Era and Cenozoic Era. Smaller mass extinctions mark the divisions between periods.

❭ **Reading Check** *What evidence shows that mass extinctions occur?*

Geologic Time Scale

Era	Period	Time*
Cenozoic	Quaternary	0.01
	Tertiary	65.5
MASS EXTINCTION		
Mesozoic	Cretaceous	146
	Jurassic	200
	Triassic	251
MASS EXTINCTION		
Paleozoic	Permian	299
	Carboniferous	359
	Devonian	416
	Silurian	444
	Ordovician	488
	Cambrian	542
MASS EXTINCTION		
Precambrian time		>4,500

*indicates how many millions of years ago the period began

Figure 7 The geologic time scale is based on fossil evidence. The time in the scale refers to the number of years ago that the time period started. ❭ **How long did the Permian period last?**

Section 2 Review

❭ **KEY IDEAS**

1. **Describe** how the fossil record chronicles the history of life.
2. **Explain** how dating methods are used to analyze fossil evidence.
3. **State** the evidence that scientists have used to create the geologic time scale.

CRITICAL THINKING

4. **Constructing Explanations** Why might the fossil record give an inaccurate picture of the history of biodiversity? Explain your answer.
5. **Explaining Relationships** How could index fossils in two different rock strata in a series help a paleontologist to estimate the absolute age of fossils in a layer of rock between them? Explain your reasoning.

METHODS OF SCIENCE

6. **Describing Methods** You are a paleontologist who is digging for fossils in a remote area. Describe the methods you would use on the dig to make sure that you could estimate the age of the fossils.

Answers to Section Review

1. Both the geographic and chronologic distribution of organisms can be inferred by examining the fossil record. The fossil record also chronicles the diversity of life on Earth.

2. Paleontologists organize fossils into a sequence based on the relative age of the strata in which the fossil was found. They also use radiometric dating to estimate the age of an object by measuring certain radioisotopes that the object contains.

3. The geologic time scale is based on evidence in the fossil record.

4. Organisms with hard parts have more representation in the fossil record than organisms with soft parts. Organisms that lived in certain places, such as shallow seas, also get more representation.

Therefore, the fossil record would not represent the correct relative abundance or total number of species.

5. The paleontologist could use the age of each index fossil to estimate an age range for the fossils in between. For example, if the index fossil in the higher strata formed around 350 million years ago and the index fossil in the lower strata formed around 420 million years ago, the fossil in between would have formed between 350 and 420 million years ago.

6. Sample answer: I would record the rock layer in which each fossil was found so that I could use relative dating to estimate the age of the fossils.

Answers to Caption Questions
Figure 7: The Permian period lasted approximately 48 million years.

Teaching Key Ideas

Geologic Time Scale Help students understand that the geologic time scale is a scientific model. This organizational scheme has been and will continue to be revised based on new discoveries. Intervals for each era and period can change based on documented discoveries. This is one reason why you can find conflicting dates in reference materials depending on the timeliness of that reference. Be sure students recognize that Precambrian time covers the longest interval on the scale. Periods and Epochs are smaller divisions in more recent history signifying major changes in the fossil record.

❭ **Close**

Formative Assessment

What process is used to estimate the ages of fossils within strata?
A. half-life (Incorrect. This is the time required for half of a radioactive substance to decay.)
B. radioactive decay (Incorrect. This is the breakdown of radioisotopes.)
C. radiometric dating. (Incorrect. This process estimates absolute age.)
D. relative dating (Correct! This process can reveal the sequence in which the fossils and strata were laid.)

Key Ideas	Key Terms	Why It Matters
❯ What major evolutionary developments occurred during Precambrian time? ❯ What dominant organisms evolved during the Paleozoic Era? ❯ What dominant organisms evolved during the Mesozoic Era and the Cenozoic Era?	cyanobacteria endosymbiosis	Knowing the order in which life-forms evolved helps scientists form new hypotheses of how life forms are related.

 The Living Environment
Standard 4

3.1j Billions of years ago, life on Earth is thought by many scientists to have begun as simple, single-celled organisms. About a billion years ago, increasingly complex multicellular organisms began to evolve.

3.1l Extinction of a species occurs when the environment changes and the adaptive characteristics of a species are insufficient to allow its survival. Fossils indicate that many organisms that lived long ago are extinct. Extinction of species is common; most of the species that have lived on Earth no longer exist.

6.2a As a result of evolutionary processes, there is a diversity of organisms and roles in ecosystems. This diversity of species increases the chance that at least some will survive in the face of large environmental changes. Biodiversity increases the stability of the ecosystem.

cyanobacteria
(SIE uh noh bak TIR ee uh) bacteria that carry out photosynthesis; blue-green algae

When did life first evolve on Earth? To find out, scientists study fossils and other evidence of early life, such as "signatures" of certain isotopes in rock. These isotopes are associated with living things.

Precambrian Time

Precambrian time spanned between about 4.5 billion and 542 million years ago. Many critical events occurred during this long period of Earth's history. ❯ Single-celled prokaryotes and later, eukaryotes, evolved and flourished in Precambrian time. The evolution of multicellular organisms set the stage for the evolution of modern organisms. The accumulation of atmospheric oxygen allowed organisms to live on land.

Early Earth was a dangerous place. Meteors bombarded the planet in large numbers. This activity heated Earth's surface repeatedly and made our planet a hostile place for living things. Eventually, fewer meteor impacts occurred, which allowed early cells to evolve.

Prokaryotic Life Recall that organisms on Earth are divided into three groups: archaea, bacteria, and eukaryotes. Archaea and bacteria are typically grouped together as prokaryotes. Living examples from these two groups are shown in **Figure 8**. The ancestors of modern bacteria and archaea diverged and flourished. Scientists think that eukaryotes diverged from archaea later in the Precambrian.

Figure 8 *Sulfolobus* (left) is a living example of archaea. *Escherichia coli* (right) is a living example of bacteria. Both archaea and bacteria are groups of organisms that have existed since ancient times.

Figure 9 Fossilized mats of cyanobacteria, called *stromatolites*, are the most common Precambrian fossils. These modern stromatolites are similar to stromatolites that existed during Precambrian time.

Recall that prokaryotes are single-celled organisms that lack membrane-bound organelles. The oldest known fossils, which are microscopic fossils of prokaryotes, come from rock that is at least 3.5 billion years old. The earliest common fossils are those of marine cyanobacteria. **Cyanobacteria** are photosynthetic prokaryotes. Modern cyanobacteria, clustered in layered structures called *stromatolites* are shown in **Figure 9.**

Formation of Oxygen Scientists think that about 2.5 billion years ago, cyanobacteria began adding oxygen to Earth's atmosphere. Before cyanobacteria appeared, oxygen gas was scarce on Earth. But as ancient cyanobacteria carried out photosynthesis, they released oxygen gas into Earth's oceans. This oxygen eventually escaped into the air. The increase of oxygen in the ocean destroyed many marine prokaryotes. These organisms had evolved to live without oxygen, which was a poison to them.

As oxygen reached Earth's upper atmosphere, the sun's rays caused some of the oxygen gas, O_2, to chemically react and form molecules of ozone, O_3. In the upper atmosphere, the ozone layer blocks some of the ultraviolet radiation of the sun. The sun provides both life-giving light, but overexposure to ultraviolet radiation is dangerous to living things. Organisms on the very early Earth could not survive on land because ultraviolet radiation damaged their DNA. After millions of years however, enough ozone had accumulated to make land a safe place for organisms to live. The first organisms to live on land were prokaryotes.

Eukaryotic Life Later in Precambrian time, the first eukaryotes appeared. A eukaryotic cell is much larger than a prokaryotic cell is. Eukaryotes have a complex system of internal membranes, and their DNA is enclosed within a nucleus. Recall that all eukaryotes have mitochondria. Plants and some protists also have chloroplasts, which carry out photosynthesis. Mitochondria and chloroplasts are the size of prokaryotes, and they contain their own DNA, which is similar to that of prokaryotes.

READING TOOLBOX

Describing Time Scientists describe events in Earth's history in terms of geologic time. Look for references to time in this section, and construct a table of their meanings.

ACADEMIC VOCABULARY

accumulate to collect, especially over a period of time

Teaching Key Ideas

Endosymbiosis The term *endosymbiosis* refers to any symbiotic relationship in which one organism lives inside another. Help students understand the hypothesis for the endosymbiotic origin of mitochondria and chloroplasts by reviewing other examples of endosymbiosis. Examples include wood-digesting bacteria that live within the digestive tracts of termites, bacteria that break down plant cell walls within the digestive tract of cows, and bacteria in the human digestive tract that break down otherwise undigested materials and synthesize vitamin K as a by-product.
LS Verbal

Answers to Caption Questions

Figure 10: Mitochondria and chloroplasts both have DNA that is similar to that found in bacteria, which suggests that they descended from a common bacterial ancestor.

endosymbiosis (EN doh SIM bie OH ses) a mutually beneficial relationship in which one organism lives within another

SCI*LINKS*
www.scilinks.org
Topic: Endosymbiosis
Code: HX80506

Figure 10 The theory of endosymbiosis states that energy-producing organelles that evolved from ancestors of bacteria. ❯ What genetic evidence supports the theory of endosymbiosis?

Origin of Energy-Producing Organelles Mitochondria and chloroplasts likely originated as described by the endosymbiotic theory proposed by Lynn Margulis, which is illustrated in **Figure 10.** **Endosymbiosis** is a mutually beneficial relationship in which one organism lives within another. Endosymbiotic theory proposes that larger bacteria engulfed smaller bacteria, which then began to live inside larger cells. According to this theory, mitochondria are the descendants of symbiotic, aerobic (oxygen-requiring) bacteria. Likewise, scientists think that chloroplasts are thought to be the descendants of symbiotic, photosynthetic bacteria.

The following observations support the theory that mitochondria and chloroplasts descended from bacteria:

- **Size and Structure** Mitochondria are the same size as most bacteria. Chloroplasts are the same size as some cyanobacteria.

- **Genetic Material** Both chloroplasts and mitochondria contain genes that are different from those found in the nucleus of the host cell and that are closely related to bacterial genes.

- **Ribosomes** Mitochondrial and chloroplast ribosomes are similar in size and structure to bacterial ribosomes.

- **Reproduction** Like bacteria, chloroplasts and mitochondria reproduce by simple fission. This replication takes place independently of the cell cycle of the host cell.

Multicellularity The development of multicellular organisms marked an important step in the evolution of life-forms that are familiar to us. Multicellularity first developed in protists in Precambrian time. Scientists think that the first multicellular organisms began as colonies, or clusters of single-celled organisms. *Volvox,* a colonial protist, is shown in **Figure 11.** Eventually these cells took on specialized functions. These colonies were able to carry out many of the functions that we associate with multicellular organisms.

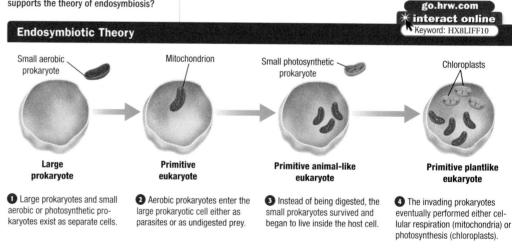

Endosymbiotic Theory

Small aerobic prokaryote — Large prokaryote

Mitochondrion — Primitive eukaryote

Small photosynthetic prokaryote — Primitive animal-like eukaryote

Chloroplasts — Primitive plantlike eukaryote

❶ Large prokaryotes and small aerobic or photosynthetic prokaryotes exist as separate cells.

❷ Aerobic prokaryotes enter the large prokaryotic cell either as parasites or as undigested prey.

❸ Instead of being digested, the small prokaryotes survived and began to live inside the host cell.

❹ The invading prokaryotes eventually performed either cellular respiration (mitochondria) or photosynthesis (chloroplasts).

Differentiated Instruction

Struggling Readers

Endosymbiosis and Bacteria Have students work in small groups to create posters of chloroplasts, mitochondria, and both non-photosynthetic and photosynthetic bacterial cells. Their projects should have clearly labeled internal structures and realistic colors (i.e., green for chloroplasts or photosynthetic bacteria). They should also identify the names of the bacteria used for these models or pictures. **LS** Visual

QuickLab

Timeline of Earth 4.3.1j, 4.3.1l

Using some calculations, you can create your own time-line of Earth's history.

🕐 15 min

Procedure

❶ Copy the table shown onto a piece of paper.

❷ Complete the table by using this scale: 1 cm is equal to 10 million years.

❸ Lay a 5 m strip of adding-machine paper flat on a hard surface. Use a meterstick, a metric ruler, and a pencil to mark off the beginning and end of Precambrian time according to the time scale that you calculated. Do the same for the three eras. Label each division of time, and make each a different color with colored pencils.

Era	Length of time (years)	Scale length
Precambrian	4,058,000,000	
Paleozoic	291,000,000	
Mesozoic	185,500,000	
Cenozoic	65,500,000 (to present)	

❹ Refer to the geologic time scale shown in **Figure 7.** Using the same scale as in step 2, calculate the scale length for each period listed. Mark the boundaries of each period on the paper strip, and label them.

❺ Decorate your strip by adding names or drawings of the organisms that lived in each division of time.

Analysis

1. **Identify** in which period humans appeared.

2. **Calculate** the length from the period in which humans appeared to the present.

3. CRITICAL THINKING **Interpreting Graphics** What percentage of the geologic time scale do these eras combined represent? What percentage of the geologic time scale does Precambrian time represent?

Dominant Life For most of the end of Precambrian time, life probably was limited to prokaryotes and protists, which are eukaryotes. Recent evidence suggests that the oldest known fossils of multicellular eukaryotes have been found in rock that is about 1 billion years old. The first known fossils of true multicellular animals are about 600 million years old. Very early animal fossils are scarce because most animals at that time had soft body parts that did not fossilize well. Fossils of marine animals similar to modern jellyfishes and segmented worms are dated to late Precambrian time.

Mass Extinctions The first known mass extinction in Precambrian time occurred at the time of oxygen build-up and of extreme cold. This mass extinction killed many cyanobacteria as well as other types of bacteria. A second mass extinction, late in Precambrian time, killed off many animals that had recently evolved. This mass extinction opened up new ecological niches, and preceded a burst of diversification in animals. The animals, with their hard exoskeletons and shells, that evolved after this extinction have left a rich fossil record as evidence of evolution.

❯ **Reading Check** *Why is the evolution of colonial organisms an important step in evolution?*

Figure 11 Multicellular protists were the first multicellular organisms. *Volvox* is an example of a multicellular protist.

Teaching Key Ideas

Cambrian Explosion Point out to students that the diversity of multicellular organisms expanded rapidly during the period known as the "Cambrian explosion." Changing geologic and atmospheric conditions during this period are thought to have increased the number of available habitats for animals. Primitive multicellular organisms could then specialize differently, become more complex, and take advantage of the newly available resources. This first explosion of biological diversity was the foundation from which most complex life evolved.

Teaching Key ideas

Hard As a Rock Ask students what kinds of organisms could survive on bare rock. What would it take to be successful? (Students may suggest an association similar to lichen, in which a fungus and a cyanobacterium or alga coexist in a symbiotic relationship.) Remind students that as life emerged from the oceans, living things were confronted with this kind of problem. **LS Logical**

Figure 12 The Devonian Period, which began about 416 million years ago, was dominated by large forests, such as the one shown in this illustration.

Paleozoic Era

The Cambrian Period, the first period in the Paleozoic Era, was a time of great evolutionary expansion. The rapid diversification of animals that appeared in the fossil record is sometimes referred to as the "Cambrian explosion," though it occurred over several million years.

Dominant Life The Paleozoic Era was a time of great evolutionary expansion. > During the Paleozoic Era, marine invertebrates diversified, and marine vertebrates evolved. The first land plants evolved. Some arthropods, and then some vertebrates, left the oceans to colonize land.

Plants and Fungi on Land The first multicellular organisms to live on land may have been fungi living together with plants or algae. Plants and fungi began living together on the surface of the land about 475 million years ago. Eventually, great forests, illustrated in **Figure 12,** covered much of Earth's landscape.

Plant life from the Paleozoic Era still has an impact on our lives. In the great coal swamps of the Carboniferous Period, organic materials were subjected to pressure from overlying earth. Over millions of years this produced fossil fuels—beds of coal and reservoirs of oil. Humans now burn both oil and coal to release stored energy.

Arthropods An arthropod is an animal that has a hard outer skeleton, a segmented body, and paired, jointed limbs. Although many arthropods continued to live in the oceans, the first animals to successfully live on land were also arthropods. An important terrestrial arthropod—the insect—evolved in the late Devonian.

Vertebrates A vertebrate is an animal with a backbone. According to the fossil record, the first vertebrates were small, jawless fishes that evolved in the oceans about 530 million years ago. Fishes that have jaws appeared about 430 million years ago. For hundreds of millions of years, vertebrates lived only in the sea. The first land vertebrates, amphibians, came out of the sea about 370 million years ago. Reptiles evolved from amphibian ancestors about 340 million years ago.

Differentiated Instruction

Basic Learners

Evolution of Vertebrates Have students work in small groups. Distribute soft gelatin-based candy, such as "gummy worms," toothpicks, glue, and tape to each group. Challenge them to create an internal skeleton for some worms and an external skeleton for others. Caution students not to eat the candy. After groups complete their skeletons, ask whether internal or external skeletons require less material and which weigh less. (Internal skeletons should be smaller and lighter.) Help students list other adaptive advantages of internal skeletons. **LS Kinesthetic**

Struggling Readers/Basic Learners

Pattern Puzzles To help students sequence events correctly, have them put each of the following events on index cards: *prokaryotes and protists; plants and fungi on land; arthropods and vertebrates; reptiles and birds; mammals; modern humans; Precambrian; Paleozoic; Mesozoic; Cenozoic.* Then have students match the event to the era and arrange the cards in the correct sequence. **LS Verbal/Visual**

Mass Extinctions The fossil record indicates that mass extinctions occurred both at the end of the Ordovician Period (440 million years ago) and at the end of the Devonian Period (365 million years ago). These events eliminated about 70% of all of the species on Earth. The most devastating of all mass extinctions occurred at the end of the Permian Period, about 245 million years ago. About 96% of all animals species living at the time became extinct.

Mesozoic and Cenozoic Eras

Many of the dominant life-forms on our planet diverged during the Mesozoic and Cenozoic Eras. ❯ **Reptiles, dinosaurs, and birds were the dominant animals during the Mesozoic Era, and mammalian animals dominated the Cenozoic Era.**

Dominant Life During the Mesozoic Era, dinosaurs and other reptiles evolved to be the dominant life-forms. Therapsids, which were reptilelike mammals, gave rise to modern mammals at about the same time that dinosaurs evolved, during the Triassic Period. Scientists think that birds evolved from feathered dinosaurs during the Jurassic Period. Flowering plants evolved during the Cretaceous Period of the Mesozoic Era. The Cenozoic Era is the current era. During this era, mammals, such as the woolly mammoth shown in **Figure 13,** became the dominant life-form. The first hominids (early human ancestors) evolved during the Tertiary Period. Modern humans did not appear until the Quaternary Period.

Mass Extinction A mass extinction 65 million years ago included about two-thirds of all land species, including most of the dinosaurs. This mass extinction is often called the K-T extinction, because it marks the boundary between the Cretaceous Period (K) of the Mesozoic Era and the Tertiary Period (T) of the Cenozoic Era. Scientists think that this mass extinction was caused by a catastrophic event that had widespread effects.

Figure 13 This woolly mammoth is an example of an animal that lived during the middle Cenozoic Era. ❯ **Did woolly mammoths live before or after the K-T extinction?**

Teacher's Notes There are many different theories concerning why the dinosaurs and other organisms became extinct. Most groups agree that a permanent global climatic change occurred around 65 million years ago. Some theorists state that the cause of the K-T extinction was due to forces here on Earth (intrinsic) and that the extinction occurred gradually, over several million years. These theorists cite the most probable causes as huge volcanic eruptions and movement of the continental plates. Others believe that the ultimate cause of the K-T extinction was due to forces created outside Earth (extrinsic) and that the event was fairly sudden and punctuated. These theorists cite the most probable cause as an asteroid colliding with Earth, precipitating global climatic change. Another theory hypothesizes that shock waves from the impact of a large asteroid moved through Earth and triggered intense volcanic eruptions.

READING TOOLBOX

Visual Literacy Have students study the picture in the circle. Ask how the scene compares to what Earth is like today. (Plants look similar to those found today, but animals have changed dramatically.)

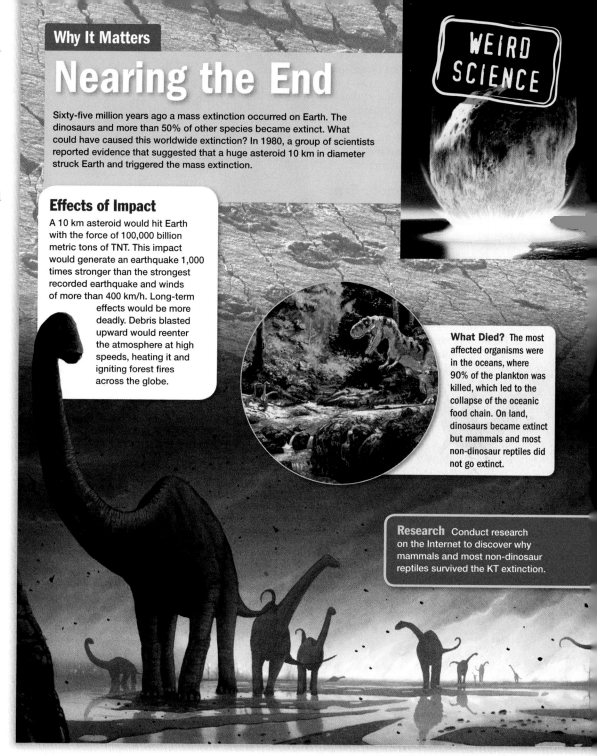

Why It Matters

Nearing the End

Sixty-five million years ago a mass extinction occurred on Earth. The dinosaurs and more than 50% of other species became extinct. What could have caused this worldwide extinction? In 1980, a group of scientists reported evidence that suggested that a huge asteroid 10 km in diameter struck Earth and triggered the mass extinction.

WEIRD SCIENCE

Effects of Impact
A 10 km asteroid would hit Earth with the force of 100,000 billion metric tons of TNT. This impact would generate an earthquake 1,000 times stronger than the strongest recorded earthquake and winds of more than 400 km/h. Long-term effects would be more deadly. Debris blasted upward would reenter the atmosphere at high speeds, heating it and igniting forest fires across the globe.

What Died? The most affected organisms were in the oceans, where 90% of the plankton was killed, which led to the collapse of the oceanic food chain. On land, dinosaurs became extinct but mammals and most non-dinosaur reptiles did not go extinct.

Research Conduct research on the Internet to discover why mammals and most non-dinosaur reptiles survived the KT extinction.

Answer to Research
Accept all reasonable answers. Sample answer: although the answer to this question is largely unknown, scientists have many hypotheses about how mammals and non-dinosaur reptiles survived the K-T extinction. One hypothesis states that the debris sent into the atmosphere by an impact event would have blocked much of the sun's warming rays. Cold-blooded dinosaurs would have been affected by this cold much more than smaller reptiles or warm-blooded mammals. Although not all small reptiles and mammals survived these events, enough survived to allow these species to continue to evolve.

Objectives

❯ Model the formation and analysis of strata.

❯ Apply the criteria used to identify index fossils to the strata model.

❯ Evaluate the effectiveness of the model to illustrate relative fossil age.

Materials

■ graduated cylinder, 100 mL
■ water, tap
■ aquarium gravel, four distinct colors
■ dish, small (8 per group)
■ tablespoon
■ beans, dried (navy, black, pinto)

Safety

Model of Rock Strata

Sedimentary strata are arranged so that, if they remain undisturbed, any layer is older than the strata on top of it but younger than the strata beneath it. One way to study strata and the fossils within them is to take core samples through the earth and compare them to samples taken at different locations. Paleontologists can determine the original order of strata by comparing multiple samples from many locations. In this lab, you will model how strata are formed and how they can be used to construct a record of Earth's geologic and biologic history.

Procedure

❶ Work in groups of three or four. Each student in the group should make a separate model. You will build up a series of layers in a column. You will model eight periods of time using different colors of gravel and different beans. The gravel represents sediment and the beans represent fossils. One tablespoon represents deposition that occurs over a 10,000-year period.

❷ ◈ **CAUTION: Glass items such as graduated cylinders are fragile and may break.** Add 30 mL of tap water to the graduated cylinder.

❸ For the first time period, choose a color. Have each member of the group add 1 Tbsp of that gravel color to their column. Randomly choose one member of the group to omit this layer.

❹ Repeat step 3 using another color of your choice until you have modeled eight periods. At the third time period, insert some navy beans; at the fifth time period, insert pinto beans; at the seventh time period, insert black beans. Record the strata order used by your group. Keep this record as a key to your models.

❺ Exchange the models from your group with those of another group. Try to determine the order of strata used by that group.

❻ ◈ ◆ Clean up your lab materials according to your teacher's instructions. Wash your hands before leaving the lab.

Analyze and Conclude

1. **Recognizing Relationships** Explain how this model relates to how sedimentary strata are formed.

2. **SCIENTIFIC METHODS** **Analyzing Conclusions** Describe your success at inferring the other group's strata order.

3. **SCIENTIFIC METHODS** **Inferring Conclusions** Compare the occurrence of the three types of "fossils" across the models from each group. What is the significance of these fossils? Explain your reasoning.

4. **Analyzing Models** If the same fossils are contained within different kinds of strata, can they be classified as index fossils? Explain.

Time Required

One 30-minute class period

Ratings

🧪	🧪🧪	🧪🧪🧪	🧪🧪🧪🧪
EASY			HARD

Teacher Prep 🧪🧪🧪
Student Setup 🧪🧪
Concept Level 🧪🧪🧪
Cleanup 🧪🧪

Safety Cautions

Remind students to be careful when handling any glass objects.

Tips and Tricks

Substitutions Most of the materials in this activity can be replaced with supplies you have on hand. A large test tube or small plastic beverage container can be substituted for the graduated cylinder. If you use a beverage container, you may need to remove its neck to allow easier introduction of materials. Remember that larger containers will require a larger amount of "sediments." Inexpensive colored gravel is available at craft or pet stores. Colored beads or similar materials maybe substituted for the gravel. You can use any type of bean that will sink. You can substitute other objects, including jewelry beads, game markers, and charms. You can even have students sculpt fossil models from waterproof clay and include them in the mixture.

Answers to Analyze and Conclude

1. When the gravel is poured into the graduated cylinder, it models the formation of sedimentary layers.

2. Answers should include reasons why the inferred order is correct or incorrect.

3. These fossils are in the same layers across all the groups. Therefore, they could be used as index fossils.

4. Index fossils are fossils of organisms that were common and had a widespread geographical distribution during a certain time in Earth's history. Therefore, the type of layer the fossils are found in is less important than when the layer was formed.

Key Resources

 Holt Lab Generator

 Lab Datasheet (Levels A, B, C)

 Holt Science Biology Video Labs

 Virtual Investigations

SUPER SUMMARY

Have students connect the major concepts in this chapter through an interactive Super Summary. Visit **go.hrw.com** and type in the keyword **HX8LIFS** to access the Super Summary for this chapter.

Reteaching Key Ideas

Miller-Urey Apparatus Ask students to draw a diagram of the Miller-Urey apparatus. Have them label all components of the diagram. **LS** Visual
Evolution of Life Draw a table on the board. Across the top of the table, write the following headings: *Time Span, Evolutionary Developments,* and *Mass Extinctions.* Down the left side of the table write these headings: *Precambrian Time, Paleozoic Era, Mesozoic Era,* and *Cenozoic Era.* Have students take turns filling in the information. **LS** Visual

Key Ideas	Key Terms

1 How Did Life Begin?

› The Miller-Urey experiment showed that, under certain conditions, organic compounds could form from inorganic molecules.

› Among the scientific theories that address the origin of life, one suggests that life began close to hydrothermal vents, and another proposes that organic molecules arrived on early Earth from a meteorite.

› The formation of microspheres might have been the first step toward cellular organization.

microsphere (449)
ribozyme (449)

2 The Age of Earth

› Both the geographical distribution of organisms and when organisms lived on Earth can be inferred by examining the fossil record.

› In order to analyze fossil evidence, paleontologists use both relative and absolute dating methods to date fossils.

› The geologic time scale is based on evidence in the fossil record and has been shaped by mass extinctions.

fossil record (450)
relative dating (451)
radiometric dating (452)
half-life (452)
geologic time scale (453)
mass extinction (453)

3 Evolution of Life

› Prokaryotes and later, eukaryotes, evolved in the Precambrian. The evolution of multicellular life preceded the evolution of modern life-forms. Atmospheric oxygen allowed life to survive on land.

› During the Paleozoic Era, marine invertebrates diversified, and marine vertebrates evolved. The first land plants evolved. Some arthropods, and then some vertebrates, colonized the land.

› Reptiles, dinosaurs, and birds were the dominant animals in the Mesozoic Era, and mammalian animals were dominant in the Cenozoic Era.

cyanobacteria (455)
endosymbiosis (456)

The Living Environment
Regents Exam Practice

PART A: Answer all questions in this part.

Directions: For each statement or question, write on your separate answer sheet the number of the word or expression that best completes the statement or answers the question.

1 Organism X appeared on Earth much earlier than organism Y. Many scientists believe organism X appeared between 3 and 4 billion years ago, and organism Y appeared approximately 1 billion years ago. Which row in the chart below most likely describes organisms X and Y?

Row	Organism X	Organism Y
(1)	simple multicellular	unicellular
(2)	complex multicellular	simple multicellular
(3)	unicellular	simple multicellular
(4)	complex multicellular	unicellular

(1) row 1
(2) row 2
(3) row 3
(4) row 4

Base your answer to question 2 on the diagram below that shows some evolutionary pathways. Each letter represents a different species.

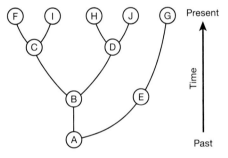

2 If A represents a simple multicellular heterotrophic organism, B would most likely represent

(1) a single-celled photosynthetic organism
(2) an autotrophic mammal
(3) a complex multicellular virus
(4) another type of simple multicellular heterotroph

Base your answer to question 3 on the chart below and on your knowledge of biology.

A	B	C
The diversity of multicellular organisms increases.	Simple, single-celled organisms appear.	Multicellular organisms begin to evolve.

3 According to most scientists, which sequence best represents the order of biological evolution on Earth?

(1) A → B → C
(2) B → C → A
(3) B → A → C
(4) C → A → B

4 The first multicellular organisms to invade land were

(1) reptiles.
(2) mammals.
(3) amphibians.
(4) fungi and plants.

5 Cell specialization came about as a result of

(1) endosymbiosis.
(2) archaebacteria.
(3) the Cambrian period.
(4) multicellularity.

6 Which ancient organisms were most likely responsible for the development of the ozone layer?

(1) protists
(2) sulfur bacteria
(3) cyanobacteria
(4) plantlike eukaryotes

7 In the Miller-Urey experiment, which of the following substances were formed after electricity activated chemical reactions?

(1) ozone
(2) methane
(3) hydrocarbons
(4) inorganic molecules

PART A

1. (3) The oldest organisms on Earth were unicellular. Evolution led to simple multicellular organisms, followed by complex multicellular organisms. *(#17, June 2003 Regents Exam)*

2. (4) The choice that indicates that single-celled organisms evolved directly from multicellular organisms is not true. The choice about autotrophic mammals is incorrect as there are no autotrophic mammals. The choice about viruses is incorrect as viruses are not cellular and not considered to be living organisms. *(#37, August 2006 Regents Exam)*

3. (2) The order of biological evolution: Simple, single-celled organisms were first to appear, then multicellular organisms begin to evolve from the single-celled organisms. The diversity of the multicellular organisms then increased. *(#19, June 2004 Regents Exam)*

4. (4)
5. (4)
6. (3)
7. (3)

Regents Exam Practice Correlations

4.3.1j 1, 2, 3

8. (2)

9. (1)

10. (1)

11. (2) A dry desert is least likely to allow fossil formation. A stream can leave sediment layers over an organism to form a fossil. Fossils can form in wet lowlands because of wet layers of soil. A volcano can cause fossilization by covering an organism in layers of lava.

12. (1) Mitochondria are thought to have evolved from symbiotic, aerobic bacteria. Chloroplasts are descendants of photosynthetic bacteria. Eukaryotes contain mitochondria and other organelles. Anaerobic archaea are prokaryotic, single-celled organisms that evolved early in Precambrian time.

13. (4) Jawless fishes are considered the first vertebrates of the oceans. Reptiles evolved from amphibians. Jawed fishes evolved from the jawless fishes 100 million years later. Amphibians were the first land vertebrates that came out of the sea.

14. (3)

15. (3)

16. (3)

---

8 What is the function of a ribozyme?

(1) to form microspheres
(2) to catalyze protein assembly
(3) to catalyze RNA formation
(4) to store genetic information

Base your answers to question 9 and 10 on the table below and on your knowledge of biology.

9 Which element is found in a greater abundance on Earth than in meteorites?

Estimated Abundance of Elements

Element	Percentage of total mass of Earth	Percentage of total mass of meteorites
Iron	36.0	27.2
Oxygen	28.7	33.2
Magnesium	13.6	17.1
Silicon	14.8	14.3
Sulfur	1.7	1.9

(1) iron
(2) sulfur
(3) oxygen
(4) magnesium

10 If this table is typical of the abundance of all elements on Earth, in meteorites, and on other planets, which statement would be supported?

(1) Earth and meteorites have similar origins.
(2) Earth and meteorites have different origins.
(3) All meteorites formed from parts of Earth.
(4) All elements on Earth come from meteorites.

11 Which of the following environments is least likely to cause fossil formation?

(1) stream
(2) desert plain
(3) wet lowland
(4) area near a volcano

12 Most scientists believe that mitochondria are formed from

(1) aerobic bacteria.
(2) photosynthetic bacteria.
(3) aerobic eukaryotes.
(4) anaerobic archaea.

---

13 What were the first vertebrates?

(1) reptiles
(2) jawed fishes
(3) amphibians
(4) jawless fishes

Base your answers to question 14 on the diagram below and on your knowledge of biology.

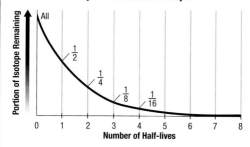

Decay of Radioactive Isotope

14 If the half-life of carbon-14 is 5,730 years, how many years would it take for 7/8 of the original amount of carbon-14 in the sample to decay?

(1) 5,014 years
(2) 11,460 years
(3) 17,190 years
(4) 22,920 years

15 Which gases did Oparin and Urey think were in the atmosphere of early Earth?

(1) water vapor, ammonia, and ozone
(2) oxygen gas, ozone, and water vapor
(3) hydrogen gas, ammonia, and methane
(4) methane, oxygen gas, and hydrogen gas

16 In an area that has not been disturbed, which rock layer is the oldest?

(1) the layer closest to Earth's surface
(2) the layer closest to Earth's crust
(3) the layer deepest within Earth's crust
(4) the layer that contains fossils

PART C

17 If the building blocks for life came to Earth on a meteorite, under what conditions might those building blocks have formed in space?

_____

Base your answers to questions 18 and 19 on the table below and on your knowledge of biology.

Radioactive Isotope Half-Life

Number of half-lives	Parent isotope	Daughter isotope
0	100,000 g	0 g
1	50,000 g	50,000 g
2	25,000 g	75,000 g
3	12,500 g	87,500 g
4	6,250 g	93,750 g
5	3,125 g	96,875 g

18 How many half-lives have passed when there is three times more daughter isotope than parent isotope?

19 How many grams of the parent isotope are left in the sample after three half-lives?

20 Justify the argument that today's organisms would not exist if mass extinction had not occurred.

21 Propose a hypothesis for the appearance of all animal phyla on Earth within a relatively short period during late Precambrian time and the early Cambrian Period.

22 Some forms of air pollution reduce the thickness of Earth's ozone layer. How might this change affect modern life?

---

17. They might have formed in an atmosphere that was rich in hydrogen and that experienced electrical storms.

18. two

19. 12,500

20. Adaptations help ensure the reproductive success of an organism in changing environments. Mass extinctions occurred as a result of environmental change. Without this change, features of today's organisms would likely be quite different.

21. Students may propose that changes in the sea environment might have increased selection pressure and resulted in rapid evolution and diversification.

22. Damage to the ozone would allow more ultraviolet radiation to reach Earth. Ultraviolet radiation can damage the DNA of living things.

UNIT 6 Humans

20 Homeostasis and Body Systems

21 Homeostasis and Human Disease

22 The Body's Defenses

23 Reproduction & Development

The Living Environment

Standard 4 Students will understand and apply scientific concepts, principles, and theories pertaining to the physical setting and living environment and recognize the historical development of ideas in science.

Key Idea 1 Living things are both similar to and different from each other and from nonliving things.

Key Idea 2 Organisms inherit genetic information in a variety of ways that result in continuity of structure and function between parents and offspring.

Key Idea 4 The continuity of life is sustained through reproduction and development.

Key Idea 5 Organisms maintain a dynamic equilibrium that sustains life.

Magnetic resonance imaging (MRI) scan of a human brain

New growth (green) on nerve cells

The human body

Medical Advances

400 BCE

Hippocrates writes the oath taken by physicians—to treat all patients with honesty, understanding, and confidentiality.

Hippocrates

910 CE

A Persian physician and pharmacist, al-Razi, known as Rhazes, publishes his comprehensive medical book, *Kitab-al-hawi*. The book includes the earliest description of smallpox and, once translated into Latin, becomes an influential medical text in Europe.

1552

An anonymous Aztec artist creates *The Badianus Manuscript*, which describes Aztec medical practices. The manuscript includes information about the effective uses of medicinal herbs; the cleaning, suturing, and dressing of wounds; preventive dental hygiene; and the setting of broken bones.

1628

William Harvey, an English physician, describes how blood circulates and how the heart acts as a pump. He challenges the belief that the liver creates blood from food.

Human heart

1846

In Boston, a dentist named W.T.G. Morton performs the first public demonstration of ether anesthesia on a person during a surgical procedure. Ether had been used as an anesthetic as early as 1842.

1895

X rays are discovered by Wilhelm Röntgen. The first "röntgenogram" ever taken was of Röntgen's wife's hand.

X ray

1982

Dr. William DeVries implants an artificial heart into Barney Clark. The heart, a Jarvik-7, is designed by Dr. Robert Jarvik. Barney Clark lives 117 days with the artificial heart.

2005

Claudia Mitchell becomes the first woman to be fitted with a computerized ("bionic") prosthetic arm.

Claudia Mitchell using bionic limb

Thyroid (red) and thyroid hormone (orange)

BIOLOGY CAREER

Administrator
Ellen Mandel

Ellen Mandel is the assistant principal and supervisor for Science at a New York City public high school. She is also a New York Biology Mentor, president of the Science Supervisors' Association of New York City, and executive board member of the Science Council of New York.

Mandel's favorite part of teaching is opening students' minds to science and to the importance of science in people's daily lives.

Mandel loves to cook and enjoys reading, gardening, needlepoint, and shopping.

Teacher
Alan Seidman

Alan Seidman teaches biology, chemistry, and a class on current topics in science at Margaretville Central School in Margaretville, New York. He is also a Fellow of the Science Teachers Association of New York State.

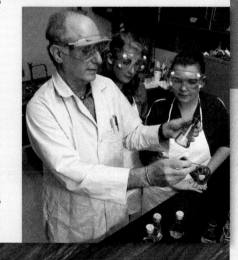

Seideman loves seeing faces light up when students grasp a new idea or discover that they are good scientists. He feels his most significant accomplishment is having inspired students to pursue science careers.

Seidman is an avid gardener, reader, hiker, and biker. He and his wife enjoy raising dairy goats.

		Standards	**Teach Key Ideas**

CHAPTER OPENER, pp. 468–469 *(15 min.)*

The Living Environment

Section 1 Homeostasis, pp. 471–475 *(30 min.)*

> A Changing Environment
> Responses to Change
> Humans and Homeostasis

Standards: 4.1.2c, 4.1.2d, 4.1.2e, 4.1.3a, 4.5.2a, 4.5.3a

Teach Key Ideas:
- Bellringer Transparency
- Transparencies G26 Water Movement in Plants • G32 Control of the Stomatal Opening • J3 Major Organ Systems of the Human Body
- Visual Concepts Stomata • Overview of Organ Systems

SECTION 2 Human Body Systems, pp. 476–483 *(45 min.)*

> Skeletal and Muscular Systems
> Integumentary System
> Nervous and Endocrine Systems
> Digestive and Excretory Systems
> Respiratory and Circulatory Systems

Standards: 4.1.2a, 4.1.2b, 4.1.2c, 4.5.3b

Teach Key Ideas:
- Bellringer Transparency
- Transparencies J3 Major Organ Systems of the Human Body • J17 Opposing Muscles in the Arm • J18 Structure of Skin • J63 Human Brain • J64 Human Spinal Cord • J78 The Endocrine System • J49 Digestive System in the Human Body • J57 Excretory System in the Human Body • J22 Cardiovascular System
- Visual Concepts Overview of Organ Systems • Muscular Movement and Bones • Human Skin • Nervous System Overview • Anatomy of Human Endocrine Glands • Anatomy of the Human Digestive System

---

SECTION 3 Feedback Mechanisms, pp. 484–488 *(45 min.)*

> Mechanisms of Control
> Controlling Breathing Rate
> Controlling Blood-Glucose Level

Standards: 4.1.2c, 4.1.2e, 4.5.3b

Teach Key Ideas:
- Bellringer Transparency
- Transparencies J89 Negative Feedback • J32 O_2 and CO_2 in the Blood • J87 Maintaining a Normal Blood Glucose Level
- Visual Concepts Comparing Positive and Negative Feedback • Hemoglobin and the Transport of Oxygen • Blood and the Transport of Carbon Dioxide

See also PowerPoint® Resources

Chapter Review and Assessment Resources

- **SE** Super Summary, p. 492
- **SE** Regents Exam Practice, p. 493
- Regents Review Guide
- Review Resources
- Chapter Tests A and B
- Holt Online Assessment
- Regents Question Banks on Teacher's One-Stop Planner

CHAPTER Fast Track
Thorough instruction will require the times shown.

Basic Learners
- **TE** Location of Kidneys, p. 481
- **TE** Skin Cancer, p. 477
- Directed Reading Worksheets*
- Active Reading Worksheets*
- Lab Manuals, Level A*
- Study Guide* ■
- Note-taking Workbook*
- Special Needs Activities and Modified Tests*

Advanced Learners
- **TE** Hormone Mimics, p. 485
- **TE** Researching Hypertension, p. 482
- **TE** Sports Drinks, p. 481
- **TE** Homeostasis and Endocrine Disorders, p. 479
- **TE** Researching, p. 474
- Critical Thinking Worksheets*
- Concept Mapping Worksheets*
- Science Skills Worksheets*
- Lab Datasheets, Level C*

Key

SE Student Edition
TE Teacher's Edition

📁 Chapter Resource File
📓 Workbook
🖨 Transparency

💿 CD or CD-ROM
* Datasheet or blackline master available

■ Also available in Spanish

All resources listed below are also available on the Teacher's One-Stop Planner.

Why It Matters	Hands-On	Skills Development	Assessment
Build student motivation with resources about high-interest applications.	**SE Inquiry Lab** Blood Pressure and Homeostasis, p. 469 * ■	**TE Reading Toolbox** Assessing Prior Knowledge, p. 468 **SE Reading Toolbox,** p. 470	
TE Dehydration, p. 473 **TE Qi and the Body,** p. 474	**SE Quick Lab** Investigation of Homeostasis, p. 475 * ■ 📁 **Skills Practice Lab** Modeling Capillaries *	**SE Reading Toolbox** Outlining, p. 475 **TE Reading Toolbox** Outlining, p. 475	**SE Section Review** ■ **TE Formative Assessment** Spanish Assessment * ■ 📁 **Section Quiz** * ■
TE Stress and the Brain, p. 478 **TE Heart Hormones,** p. 479 **TE Digestion and Absorption,** p. 480 **TE A Newborn's First Breath,** p. 482	**SE Quick Lab** Filtration Rate in the Kidneys, p. 481 * ■ **SE Inquiry Lab** Epinephrine and Heart Rate, pp. 490–491 * ■ 📁 **Skills Practice Lab** Leptin and the Endocrine System *	**SE Reading Toolbox** Word Origin, p. 477 **TE Reading Toolbox** Word Origin, p. 477	**SE Section Review** ■ **TE Formative Assessment** Spanish Assessment * ■ 📁 **Section Quiz** * ■
SE Diabetes, p. 489	**SE Quick Lab** Blood pH and Homeostasis, p. 487 * ■ 📁 **Inquiry Lab** Observing the Effect of Thyroxine on Frog Metamorphosis *	**SE Reading Toolbox** Analogies, p. 487 ■ **TE Reading Toolbox** Analogies, p. 487 ■	**SE Section Review** ■ **TE Formative Assessment** Spanish Assessment * ■ 📁 **Section Quiz** * ■
	See also Lab Generator		**See also Holt Online Assessment Resources**

Resources for Differentiated Instruction

English Learners

TE Reading Organizer, p. 478
TE Vocabulary, p. 474
📁 Directed Reading Worksheets*
📁 Active Reading Worksheets*
📁 Lab Manuals, Level A*
📓 Study Guide* ■
📓 Note-taking Workbook*
📓 Multilingual Glossary

Struggling Readers

TE Paired Summarizing, p. 486
TE Paired Reading, p. 471
📁 Directed Reading Worksheets*
📁 Active Reading Worksheets*
📁 Lab Manuals, Level A*
📓 Study Guide*
📓 Note-taking Workbook*
📓 Special Needs Activities and Modified Tests*

Special Education Students

TE Breathing Rate, p. 487
TE Modelling Villi, p. 480
TE Sensing and Responding, p. 472
📁 Directed Reading Worksheets*
📁 Active Reading Worksheets*
📁 Lab Manuals, Level A*
📓 Study Guide* ■
📓 Note-taking Workbook*
📓 Special Needs Activities and Modified Tests*

Alternative Assessment

TE Feedback Loops, p. 485
📁 Science Skills Worksheets*
📁 Section Quizzes* ■
📓 Chapter Tests A, B, and C* ■

Chapter 20

Chapter 20

Homeostasis and Human Body Systems

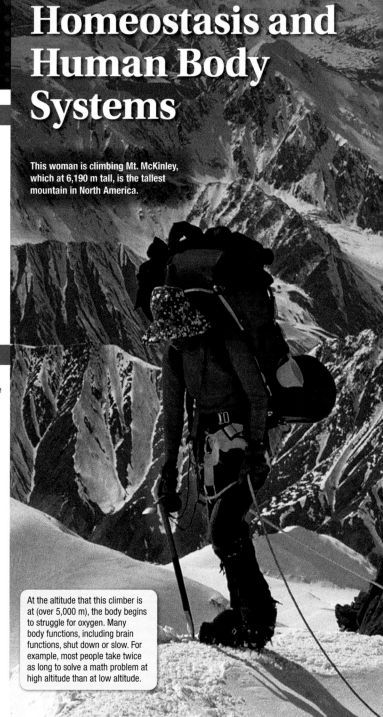

Overview

The purpose of this chapter is to explain the concept of homeostasis and to describe how human body systems work together to maintain a stable internal environment. The role of feedback mechanisms in maintaining homeostasis is also discussed.

READING TOOLBOX

Assessing Prior Knowledge Students should understand the following concepts:
- cellular communication
- body organization
- basic biochemistry

Visual Literacy Ask students to study the picture and to discuss what types of environmental changes the climbers must cope with at high altitude. (low temperatures, low levels of oxygen) Ask students to list body systems that might be affected by these environmental factors. (respiratory system, circulatory system, nervous system)

Preview

1 Homeostasis
A Changing Environment
Responses to Change
Humans and Homeostasis

2 Human Body Systems
Skeletal and Muscular Systems
Integumentary System
Nervous and Endocrine Systems
Digestive and Excretory Systems
Respiratory and Circulatory Systems

3 Feedback Mechanisms
Mechanisms of Control
Controlling Breathing Rate
Controlling Blood-Glucose Level

Why It Matters

Your body is made of a network of organ systems that work together to maintain a stable internal environment, no matter where you go or what you do.

This woman is climbing Mt. McKinley, which at 6,190 m tall, is the tallest mountain in North America.

At the altitude that this climber is at (over 5,000 m), the body begins to struggle for oxygen. Many body functions, including brain functions, shut down or slow. For example, most people take twice as long to solve a math problem at high altitude than at low altitude.

The Living Environment
Standard 4 Students will understand and apply scientific concepts, principles, and theories pertaining to the physical setting and living environment and recognize the historical development of ideas in science.
Key Idea 1 Living things are both similar to and different from each other and from nonliving things. *Major Understandings* - 1.2a, 1.2b, 1.2c, 1.2d, 1.2e
Key Idea 5 Organisms maintain a dynamic equilibrium that sustains life. *Major Understandings* - 5.2a, 5.3a, 5.3b

---

Chapter Correlations The Living Environment

Standard 4

1.2a Important levels of organization for structure and function include organelles, cells, tissues, organs, organ systems, and whole organisms.

1.2b Humans are complex organisms. They require multiple systems for digestion, respiration, reproduction, circulation, excretion, movement, coordination, and immunity. The systems interact to perform the life functions.

1.2c The components of the human body, from organ systems to cell organelles, interact to maintain a balanced internal environment...

1.2d If there is a disruption in any human system, there may be a corresponding imbalance in homeostasis.

1.2e The organs and systems of the body help to provide all the cells with their basic needs. The cells of the body are of different kinds and are grouped in ways that enhance how they function together.

5.2a Homeostasis in an organism is constantly threatened. Failure to respond effectively can result in disease or death.

5.3a Dynamic equilibrium results from detection of and response to stimuli. Organisms detect and respond to change in a variety of ways both at the cellular level and at the organismal level.

5.3b Feedback mechanisms have evolved that maintain homeostasis. Examples include the changes in heart rate or respiratory rate in response to increased activity in muscle cells, the maintenance of blood sugar levels by insulin from the pancreas, and the changes in openings in the leaves of plants by guard cells to regulate water loss and gas exchange.

InquiryLab

Blood Pressure and Homeostasis 4.1.2b, 4.1.2c, 4.5.3a, 4.5.3b

Blood pressure is a measurement of the force that blood applies to artery walls. Many factors can affect blood pressure, so the body must work to maintain homeostasis and keep blood pressure within an acceptable range.

Procedure

❶ Working in a group, familiarize yourself with the operation of a **digital blood-pressure monitor.**

❷ Have each group member lay down for 5 min. Take and record everybody's blood pressure.

❸ Have members stand up, and immediately retake and record each person's blood pressure.

❹ Have members continue standing for 5 min. After the 5 min have passed, retake and record each person's blood pressure.

Analysis

1. **Draw** a line graph that illustrates how the blood pressure of the test subjects changed over the course of the lab. Be sure to plot all of the readings on your graph.

2. **Explain** what you think caused any changes in blood pressure that you observed.

To compensate for the low levels of oxygen at high altitude, the body begins to make more rod blood cells, the heart beats faster, and breathing rate increases.

At Mt. McKinley's peak, the air temperature is usually well below 0°C. Climbers must wear special clothing to deal with the frigid temperatures. Without this special clothing, they could lose body heat so rapidly that death could result in less than an hour.

InquiryLab

Teacher's Notes Make sure that students' use the blood-pressure monitor correctly.

Materials

• digital blood-pressure monitor

Safety Caution Blood-pressure cuffs can restrict blood flow. The cuff should not be used repeatedly on the same subject, and it should not be kept inflated on a subject for an extended period of time.

Answers to Analysis

1. Line graphs may show the blood pressure falling when the person stands up and then returning to normal after five minutes.

2. When standing up from a prone position, blood pressure drops at first as gravity makes it harder for the heart to push blood through the body. After a few minutes, feedback mechanisms engage and return the body's blood pressure to normal.

Using Words

1. remaining or staying the same
2. When internal conditions are the same, the chemical reactions that the body depends on can take place reliably.

Using Language

1. filter
2. glands

Taking Notes

Check students' work for accuracy.

These reading tools can help you learn the material in this chapter. For more information on how to use these and other tools, see **Appendix: Reading and Study Skills.**

Using Words

Word Origins Many common English words derive from Greek or Latin words. Learning the meanings of some Greek or Latin words can help you understand the meaning of many modern English words.

Word Origins		
Word part	**Origin**	**Meaning**
homeo-	Greek	same
-stasis	Greek	standing still

Your Turn Answer the following questions.
1. What do you think *homeostasis* might mean?
2. How might your body benefit from homeostasis?

Using Language

Analogies Analogies compare words that have similar relationships. You can write analogies with words or with colons. For example, the analogy "up is related to down in the same way that top is related to bottom" can be written "up : down :: top : bottom". To answer an analogy problem, you must figure out how the words are related. In the example given, up is above down and top is above bottom.

Your Turn Use information found in the chapter to complete the following analogies.
1. heart : pump :: kidney : _____
2. nervous system: nerves :: endocrine system : _____

Taking Notes

Outlining Outlining is a note-taking skill that helps you organize information. You can create a simple outline of a section in this chapter by copying all of the headings for that section, in order, on a piece of paper. Leave plenty of space between each heading. As you read the material under a heading of the chapter, write the important facts under that heading on your outline.

Your Turn Create outlines for each section of this chapter.

> *Homeostasis and Human Body Systems*
>
> *I. Homeostasis*
>
> *A. A Changing Environment*
>
> *1. The environment around an organism is constantly changing.*
>
> *2. Organisms must respond to these changes in order to survive.*
>
> *B. Responses to Change*

Section

1

Key Ideas	Key Terms	Why It Matters
❯ How does a change in the external environment affect an organism? ❯ How does an organism respond to changes, and what happens if the organism fails to respond to the changes? ❯ What organ systems do humans need in order to survive?	homeostasis	When things don't change, it may not seem as if anything interesting is going on. But failure to maintain a 'steady state' can result in disease or death.

Many people would find the idea of frogs hopping around the Arctic strange, but one type of frog—the wood frog—is able to survive in the Arctic Circle. When temperatures drop, the frog goes into hibernation and about 65% of its body freezes solid. An antifreeze-like chemical that is made by the frog's liver keeps the other 35% of the frog thawed so that the frog's tissues are not frostbitten.

A Changing Environment

A wood frog's ability to keep part of its body from freezing is one of the many adaptations that enable the frog to react to environmental changes. ❯ **The external environment around an organism is constantly changing. These changes threaten the stability of an organism's internal environment.** The maintenance of a relatively stable internal environment is called **homeostasis.** Almost any kind of change in the external environment, such as a change in seasons, light levels, or water availability, can result in a change to an organism's internal environment. In addition, an organism's internal environment can also be a source of change. For example, if waste products build up inside an organism, they can cause an internal chemical imbalance.

Different organisms may respond to similar environmental changes in different ways. For example, when the environment changes by getting colder, the wood frog maintains its homeostasis by hibernating and thus conserving energy. The pine grosbeak shown in **Figure 1,** on the other hand, responds to a colder environment by eating more food, flying to warmer areas, and puffing out its feathers, as the photograph shows. All organisms, including humans, need ways to respond to change.

❯ **Reading Check** *How is homeostasis related to environmental change? (See the Appendix for answers to Reading Checks.)*

The Living Environment
Standard 4

1.2c The components of the human body, from organ systems to cell organelles, interact to maintain a balanced internal environment. To successfully accomplish this, organisms possess a diversity of control mechanisms that detect deviations and make corrective actions.

1.2d If there is a disruption in any human system, there may be a corresponding imbalance in homeostasis.

1.2e The organs and systems of the body help to provide all the cells with their basic needs. The cells of the body are of different kinds and are grouped in ways that enhance how they function together.

1.3a The structures present in some single-celled organisms act in a manner similar to the tissue and systems found in multicellular organisms, thus enabling them to perform all of the life processes needed to maintain homeostasis.

5.2a Homeostasis in an organism is constantly threatened. Failure to respond effectively can result in disease or death.

5.3a Dynamic equilibrium results from detection of and response to stimuli. Organisms detect and respond to change in a variety of ways both at the cellular level and at the organismal level.

homeostasis the maintenance of a constant internal state in a changing environment

These puffed-out feathers trap air and help keep the bird warm.

Figure 1 Feathers insulate this pine grosbeak from cold weather and help it maintain a stable body temperature.

Teaching Key Ideas

Homeothermy Tell students that when a person's body temperature rises above 41°C (106°F), enzymes in the brain begin to denature. The result is brain damage. Have students describe the appearance of a raw egg white. (clear, runny, slimy) Then have them describe the appearance of a cooked egg white. (white, firm) Explain that the egg white changes when it is cooked because its proteins become deformed, or denatured. Enzymes also are proteins, and at high temperatures they no longer function normally. **LS Verbal**

Answers to Caption Questions

Figure 2: The plant is not trying to conserve water. You can tell this because two of the shown stomata are open.

ACADEMIC VOCABULARY

internal located within something

Figure 2 The surface of a leaf has many pores, each of which is surrounded by a pair of guard cells. ❯ Is the plant from which this leaf was taken trying to conserve water? How can you tell?

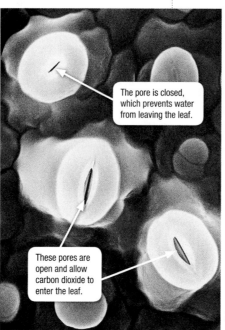

The pore is closed, which prevents water from leaving the leaf.

These pores are open and allow carbon dioxide to enter the leaf.

Responses to Change

Organisms carry out many different chemical reactions to grow, obtain energy, and reproduce. Many organisms also move, breathe, produce heat, and do other tasks. However, none of these activities can happen unless the organism can maintain a relatively stable internal environment. For example, photosynthesis and cellular respiration can take place only inside a cell that is within a certain temperature and pH range. Thus, an organism must be able to detect and respond to changes in both its internal and external environment so that the temperature and the pH stay within a favorable range.

❯ Organisms detect and respond to change in a variety of ways: both at the cellular level and at the organismal level. Failure to respond to change can result in an organism's death.

From Cells to Organ Systems Every organism, even organisms as small as a single-celled bacterium, responds to changes in the environment. The organelles present in some single-celled organisms work in a way that is similar to the way tissues and systems in multicellular organisms work. Thus, single-celled organisms are able to perform all of the life processes needed to maintain homeostasis. For example, suppose you place a member of the genus *Euglena*, a single-celled photosynthetic protist, in a darkened tank of water. You then turn on a light at one end of the tank. The protist's eyespot, which is a light-sensing organelle, will detect the light. In response, the protist's long flagellum will begin to propel the protist toward the light. The chloroplasts inside the protist's cell will then be able to use the light to perform photosynthesis. By moving toward the light, the protist is able to produce enough energy for its cell to maintain homeostasis and stay healthy.

Response in Multicellular Organisms Multicellular organisms also respond to environmental changes at the cellular level. However, multicellular organisms can respond at the tissue, organ system, or organismal levels, too. The way that plants regulate water loss is a good example of how a multicellular organism responds to change. The pores on a plant's leaf help the plant regulate water loss and gas exchange. As **Figure 2** shows, guard cells on either side of a pore enlarge or shrink to open or close pores. During the day, tissues in the leaf perform photosynthesis. The guards cells near the active tissues react by swelling with water. The swollen cells bow apart, which causes the pore to open. Carbon dioxide, a gas necessary for photosynthesis, can then enter the leaf. Likewise, water can exit the leaf. More water is then drawn up to the leaf by the plant's vascular system. At night, when photosynthesis slows, water exits the guard cells. The cells then shrink and the pore closes. This response allows the leaf to prevent excess water loss at night.

❯ **Reading Check** *Give an example of an organism reacting to a change in its environment.*

Differentiated Instruction

Special Education Students

Sensing and Responding Group projects help learners with disabilities participate fully. Have students work in groups of three or four students. Ask each group to create a poster showing examples of the human body sensing and responding to change. If students have trouble coming up with ideas, use some of these starters: You are barefoot and step on something that hurts you, so you ____; your arm itches, so you ____. **LS Logical/Interpersonal**

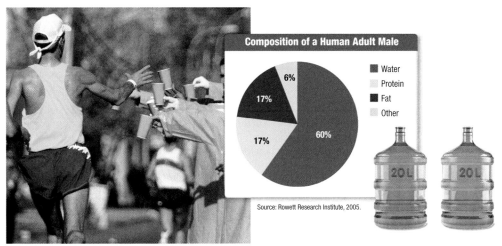

Composition of a Human Adult Male

- Water
- Protein
- Fat
- Other

6%
17%
17%
60%

Source: Rowett Research Institute, 2005.

Figure 3 A healthy adult male's body contains approximately 40 L of water.
❯ If an athlete loses 2 L of water by sweating, how much water does he need to drink to maintain his homeostasis?

Failure to Respond If an organism is not able to respond to changes in its environment, disease or death can result. To understand why homeostasis is so important, consider what would happen to a plant if its guard cells could not slow water loss. When the amount of water in a plant's tissues gets too low, the plant wilts. This loss of cell pressure, or turgor, can lead to a plant cell collapsing in on itself and dying. Unless water is added, more cells will collapse and die, until the entire organism is at risk of dying.

Water Balance in Humans Although very different from plants, humans must also control internal water levels. As **Figure 3** shows, about 2/3 of a human body is made up of water. If a person loses too much water by sweating or urinating, dehydration will occur unless the water is replaced. As in plants, dehydration in humans involves a drop in cell turgor. In addition, dehydration causes blood pressure to significantly decrease until death results.

Water Pressure and Deep-Sea Fish Of course, the correct body composition is just one way that homeostasis is maintained. There are many other factors involved. One example is the coelacanth, a fish that lives in very deep waters off the coast of Africa. At the depth of the fish's usual environment, the water pressure is several hundred times greater than the water pressure at the ocean's surface. If a person tried to swim to this depth without any special equipment, the enormous pressure would crush the person's body. Similarly, if a coelacanth was brought to the surface, the lack of pressure would cause the fish's death. Without the high pressure, dissolved gases would bubble out of the fish's bloodstream. The gas bubbles would join and form larger bubbles, until some were big enough to block blood flow through the fish's heart. Because of this need for high pressure, each coelacanth that has been caught has died shortly after being brought to the surface.

SCI LINKS.

www.scilinks.org
Topic: Homeostasis
Code: HX80753

Teaching Key Ideas

Effects of Air Pressure Point out that air pressure affects respiration in humans. Gases are exchanged between the air in the alveoli and the blood in the capillaries entirely by diffusion. Have students infer why a person breathes deeper and more quickly at higher altitudes, where there is decreased pressure. (At high altitudes, less oxygen is available.) Explain that at 6,000 m (19,685 ft), the oxygen saturation of hemoglobin is only 67 percent compared to 98 percent at sea level. One must become acclimated over time to the low levels of oxygen. Athletes who train at high altitudes tend to perform better at lower altitudes than those who train at low altitudes. **LS Logical**

Answers to Caption Questions
Figure 3: 2 L of water

Why It Matters

Dehydration Dehydration is a lack of the body fluids that are needed to carry out normal functions. This condition can result from vomiting, diarrhea, excessive urine output, excessive sweating, or inadequate water intake. A person who is dehydrated may have sunken eyes, a dry mouth, greatly decreased urine output, low blood pressure, and a rapid heart rate. Providing water orally may be sufficient for the successful treatment of mild dehydration, but intravenous fluids (given in a hospital or clinic) may be necessary for moderate to severe dehydration.

Teaching Key Ideas

Tissue and Organ Transplants Ask students to study the table on this page and think of body parts that have been transplanted in humans. Have them identify whether the part is a tissue or an organ. (Their list may include organs such as the heart, kidney, liver, lung, skin, and pancreas; and tissues such as blood, bone marrow, cornea, and bone.) **LS Visual**

Why It Matters

Qi and the Body Many people, especially those in some Asian countries, believe the body has an energy field, called qi (chee), which moves through the body in channels called meridians. The function of qi is thought to be similar to the functions of the nervous and circulatory systems—moving information and energy within the body. Acupuncture, an ancient treatment for pain and many other ailments, is based on the concept of qi. Many scientists now believe that acupuncture is effective for pain because it activates the body's endogenous opiates.

Answers to Caption Questions

Figure 4: the testes, ovaries, lymph nodes and vessels, and mouth

Humans and Homeostasis

Humans, like all other organisms, are constantly subjected to environmental stresses that threaten to upset the delicate balance that exists within our cells and tissues. **>Humans require multiple systems for digestion, respiration, reproduction, circulation, movement, coordination, and immunity. The systems interact to maintain homeostasis.**

Body Systems The organs and systems of the human body help to provide all of the cells with their basic needs. Each cell needs a constant supply of nutrients and oxygen, removal of waste materials, and protection from disease. With the exception of the reproductive system, each of the human body systems performs a task that helps stabilize the body's internal environment. In the next section, you will learn how many of the body systems work to maintain homeostasis.

Figure 4 The table below lists the major structures and functions of the organ systems of the body. **>** Which organs function in more than one system?

Major Organ Systems of the Body

System	Major structures	Functions
Circulatory system	heart, blood vessels, blood, lymph nodes and vessels, and lymph	to transport nutrients, wastes, hormones, and gases
Digestive system	mouth, throat, esophagus, stomach, liver, pancreas, and small and large intestines	to absorb nutrients from food; to remove wastes; to maintain water and chemical balances
Endocrine system	hypothalamus, pituitary gland, pancreas, testis, ovaries, and many other glands	to regulate body temperature, metabolism, development, and reproduction; to maintain homeostasis; to regulate other organ systems
Urinary system	kidneys, urinary bladder, ureters, and urethra	to remove wastes from blood; to regulate concentration of body fluids
Immune system	white blood cells, lymph nodes and vessels, and skin	to defend against pathogens and disease
Integumentary system	skin, nails, and hair	to protect against injury, infection, and fluid loss; to help regulate body temperature
Muscular system	skeletal, smooth, and cardiac muscle tissues; tendons	to move limbs and trunk; to move substances through the body; to provide structure and support
Nervous system	brain, spinal cord, nerves, and sense organs	to regulate behavior; to maintain homeostasis; to regulate all other organ systems; to control senses and movement
Reproductive system	testes, penis, ovaries, uterus, and breasts	to produce gametes (eggs and sperm) and offspring
Respiratory system	nose, mouth, trachea, bronchi, and lungs	to move air into and out of lungs; to control gas exchange between blood and lungs
Skeletal system	bones, ligaments, and cartilage	to protect and support the body and organs; to work with skeletal muscles; to produce red blood cells, white blood cells, and platelets

Differentiated Instruction

English Learners

Vocabulary Have students work in pairs to prepare index cards listing the name of an organ system on one side and the structures and functions on the other side. Students can quiz each other on organ systems. **LS Verbal**

Advanced Learners/GATE

Researching Have interested students find out about the increasing inclusion of acupuncture into mainstream western medicine. They can access reliable information by visiting the web site of the National Institutes of Health, which includes the National Center for Complementary and Alternative Medicine. Ask students to write a report of their findings. **LS Verbal**

Main Components of Homeostasis

In the human body, the main components of homeostasis are the following:

- the concentration of salts
- the pH of the internal environment
- the concentration of nutrients and waste products
- the concentration of oxygen and carbon dioxide
- the volume and pressure of extracellular fluid, which includes blood and the fluids surrounding body cells

When these five components are adequately controlled, homeostasis is maintained and the body is most likely healthy. No organ system can maintain homeostasis by itself. Organ systems must work together in a synchronized manner. For example, the concentration of oxygen and carbon dioxide is controlled by four different body systems. First, the respiratory system brings oxygen into and carbon dioxide out of the body. The circulatory system distributes the oxygen to all of the body's tissues and picks up carbon dioxide. If the level of carbon dioxide gets too high, the nervous system instructs the muscular system to make the muscles around the rib cage work harder. This action allows the lungs of the respiratory system to breathe faster in order to rid the body of the excess carbon dioxide. Later in this chapter, you will learn more about how the concentration of oxygen and carbon dioxide is maintained by the body systems.

❯ **Reading Check** *List the five main components of homeostasis in the human body.*

Section 2

Human Body Systems

> Focus

This section provides an overview of human body systems and discusses how each system helps the body maintain homeostasis.

Bellringer

Use the Bellringer transparency to prepare students for this section.

> Teach

Teaching Key Ideas

Using Analogies Use a relationship with which students are familiar to help them learn the levels of organization in the body. For example, a house is part of a city, which is part of a county, which is part of a state, which is part of the United States. Ask students to brainstorm other analogies. (Sample answer: Members of a family or students in a school represent cells, and so forth.) **LS Logical**

Section Correlations

4.1.2a
4.1.2b
4.1.2c

Key Ideas	Key Terms	Why It Matters
> How do the skeletal and muscular systems help the body maintain homeostasis? > How does the integumentary system help the body maintain homeostasis? > How do the nervous and endocrine systems help the body maintain homeostasis? > How do the digestive and excretory systems help the body maintain homeostasis? > How do the circulatory and respiratory systems help the body maintain homeostasis?	tendon excretion epidermis alveoli hormone capillary endocrine lymph gland digestion	Like all humans, you are a very complex organism. Your body contains many systems that must work together to maintain a healthy dynamic equilibrium within the body.

The Living Environment
Standard 4

1.2a Important levels of organization for structure and function include organelles, cells, tissues, organs, organ systems, and whole organisms.

1.2b Humans are complex organisms. They require multiple systems for digestion, respiration, reproduction, circulation, excretion, movement, coordination, and immunity. The systems interact to perform the life functions.

1.2c The components of the human body, from organ systems to cell organelles, interact to maintain a balanced internal environment. To successfully accomplish this, organisms possess a diversity of control mechanisms that detect deviations and make corrective actions.

Even when you are sitting still, your body systems constantly react to changes within and around you to maintain homeostasis.

Skeletal and Muscular Systems

> **The skeletal and muscular systems enable movement and provide support and protection for tissues and organs.** Bones and muscles work together to make movement possible. This ability increases the chance of survival by allowing a person to gather food, seek shelter, and escape from danger. As **Figure 5** shows, the skeleton provides an anchor for the muscles that move the body. **Tendons** attach muscles to bones. When muscles contract, tendons pull on bones to cause movement. Other types of muscles, known as involuntary muscle, move material within the body. This type of muscle surrounds some blood vessels' inner walls and makes up organs such as the stomach and heart. A heartbeat occurs when this type of muscle contracts rhythmically.

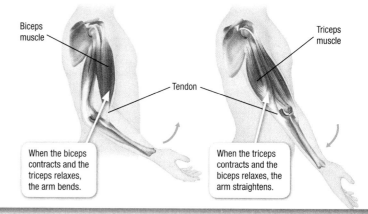

Figure 5 Pairs of opposing muscles work together to move bones at joints. When one muscle in the pair contracts, the other muscle relaxes to produce movement.

Biceps muscle

Triceps muscle

Tendon

When the biceps contracts and the triceps relaxes, the arm bends.

When the triceps contracts and the biceps relaxes, the arm straightens.

Key Resources

Transparencies
J3 Major Organ Systems of the Human Body
J17 Opposing Muscles in the Arm
J18 Structure of Skin
J63 Human Brain
J64 Human Spinal Cord
J78 The Endocrine System
J82 Major Endocrine Glands
J49 Digestive System in the Human Body
J57 Excretory System in the Human Body
J22 Cardiovascular System
J31 The Human Respiratory System

Visual Concepts
Overview of Organ Systems
Muscular Movement and Bones
Human Skin
Nervous System Overview
Anatomy of Human Endocrine Glands
Anatomy of the Human Digestive System
Sources of Water Balance in Humans
Anatomy of the Human Cardiovascular System
Movement of Lymph
Parts of the Human Respiratory System

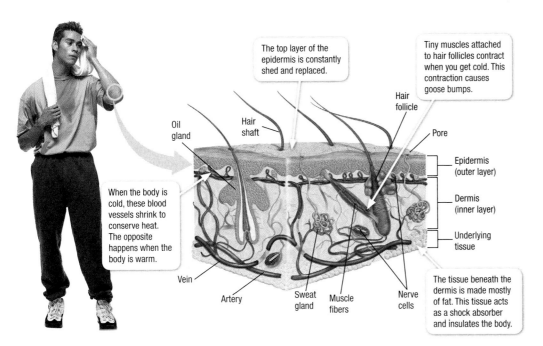

The top layer of the epidermis is constantly shed and replaced.

Tiny muscles attached to hair follicles contract when you get cold. This contraction causes goose bumps.

When the body is cold, these blood vessels shrink to conserve heat. The opposite happens when the body is warm.

Oil gland

Hair shaft

Hair follicle

Pore

Epidermis (outer layer)

Dermis (inner layer)

Underlying tissue

Vein

Artery

Sweat gland

Muscle fibers

Nerve cells

The tissue beneath the dermis is made mostly of fat. This tissue acts as a shock absorber and insulates the body.

Integumentary System

Skin is the largest organ of the human body. It makes up about 7% of your total body weight. The skin, along with the hair and nails, form the integumentary system. ❯ The integumentary system protects the body from injury and UV radiation, defends against disease, helps regulate body temperature, and prevents the body from drying out.

Waterproofing The **epidermis**, shown in **Figure 6,** is the outermost layer of the skin. It is made of flattened, dead cells composed of a protein called *keratin.* This protein is also found in hair and nails. Keratin makes the skin tough and waterproof. Glands in the *dermis,* the layer of skin under the epidermis, secrete oil that lubricates the skin. Without the protection of keratin and oil, our bodies would lose water through evaporation or absorb water from the environment.

Disease Prevention The epidermis forms a tight barrier that keeps bacteria out and protects the body from disease. Damage to large areas of skin allows bacteria to enter the body freely. This lack of protection is one reason why severe burns are so dangerous.

UV Protection The lower layers of the epidermis contain cells that make *melanin,* a pigment that absorbs ultraviolet (UV) radiation. This absorption prevents DNA damage, which can cause skin cancer.

Temperature Regulation A network of blood vessels and nerves in the dermis helps regulate body temperature. Sweat glands also help remove excess body heat through the evaporation of sweat.

❯ **Reading Check** *How does your skin protect you from diseases?*

Figure 6 The epidermis and dermis keep water inside the body and harmful bacteria out. ❯ What is the function of the tissue beneath the dermis?

> **tendon** a tough connective tissue that attaches a muscle to a bone or another body part
>
> **epidermis** the outer surface layer of skin cells

READING TOOLBOX

Word Origin Use a dictionary to find out the origin of the word *epidermis.*

READING TOOLBOX

Word Origins The word *epidermis* comes from the Greek *epi-,* meaning "upon" and *derma,* meaning "skin."

Teaching Key Ideas

Melanin and Tanning Explain that a suntan is actually a defense mechanism of the skin. Additional melanin is produced by the skin when it is exposed to ultraviolet radiation, either from the sun or from tanning beds. We call this additional melanin a tan; the darkened skin protects the dermis somewhat from damaging radiation. Emphasize the importance of using SPF 15 or higher sunscreen to prevent sunburn. Burns early in life increase the chances of skin cancer later.

Answers to Caption Questions

Figure 6: This tissue acts as a shock absorber and insulates the body.

Differentiated Instruction

English Learners

Skin Layers Have students make a graphic organizer to demonstrate the relationship between the skin's two primary layers and the subcutaneous tissue. Below the name of each of the three layers, have students describe its components. **LS Visual**

Basic Learners

Skin Cancer Ask students to use the Internet to research skin cancer. Have them write a paragraph on the risk factors and signs of two relatively common carcinomas: basal cell carcinoma and squamous cell carcinoma. Ask students to identify the primary risk factor for nearly all types of skin cancer. (exposure of the skin to UV light) Have them prepare a poster or brochure that explains how to reduce the risk of skin cancer. **LS Verbal**

Teaching Key Ideas

Nervous System Function Ask students to brainstorm about the functions of the nervous system. Write their responses on the board. Make three columns on the board with the following headings: *Monitoring internal and external environments, Coordinating bodily activities,* and *Functioning of intellect and memory.* Ask students to place their responses in the appropriate categories and explain why they grouped the responses this way.
LS Verbal/Visual

Teaching Key Ideas

Control of Movement Ask students to brainstorm a list of movements that are controlled by the autonomic nervous system and by the somatic nervous system. Point out that "being under our conscious control" is not the same as having to actively think about each movement. When you walk, for example, you can decide whether to walk, but you do not have to actively think about how to carry out this activity. Have students construct a chart that compares the two systems.
LS Visual

Answers to Caption Questions

Figure 7: hypothalamus

SCLINKS.
www.scilinks.org
Topic: The Human Brain
Code: HX80190

Nervous and Endocrine Systems

>The nervous system is composed of signaling cells that collect and respond to information about the body's internal and external environment. There are two main parts of the nervous system—the central nervous system (CNS) and the peripheral nervous system (PNS).

CNS The CNS includes the brain and spinal cord. The spinal cord is a column of nerves that links the brain to most of the PNS. The brain, shown in **Figure 7,** is the body's main processing center. This organ coordinates the body's efforts to maintain homeostasis. Sensory information from all parts of the body converges on the brain's thalamus. The thalamus relays the information to the cerebrum for processing. At the base of the brain is the brainstem, which regulates heart rate, breathing rate, and blood pressure.

PNS The PNS contains sensory and motor nerves. Sensory nerves carry information to the central nervous system from sense organs such as the skin. Motor nerves carry commands from the central nervous system to muscles and other organs, such as glands. These motor nerves are grouped into two independent systems—the autonomic nervous system and the somatic nervous system.

Autonomic Nervous System Motor nerves that are not in our conscious control are part of the autonomic nervous system. Some ways that the autonomic nervous system maintains homeostasis include stimulating digestion after a meal, slowing down the heart rate after exercise, and preparing the body to respond in stressful situations.

Somatic Nervous System The motor nerves under our conscious control, such as the nerves we use to signal our legs to walk, are part of the somatic nervous system. The somatic system also operates without conscious control, as it does to help us maintain balance.

Figure 7 The cerebrum is the largest part of the brain. It controls most sensory and motor processing. >**Which part of the brain regulates body temperature?**

The hypothalamus controls feelings of hunger and thirst, regulates body temperature, and controls the secretion of many hormones.

Thalamus
Hypothalamus
Cerebrum
The cerebellum regulates balance, posture, and movement.
Cerebellum
Brainstem
Spinal cord

Why It Matters

Stress and the Brain Medical scientists think that some psychosomatic illnesses may be mediated by the hypothalamus through its connections to the autonomic nervous system and the endocrine system. Some stress-related illnesses, such as asthma and high blood pressure, are clearly connected to hypothalamic functions.

Differentiated Instruction

English Learners

Reading Organizer Encourage students to keep a vocabulary notebook, a stack of vocabulary cards, or some other way of recording and reviewing unfamiliar vocabulary. Each entry should include the correct spelling of the word and a definition in the student's own words.
LS Verbal

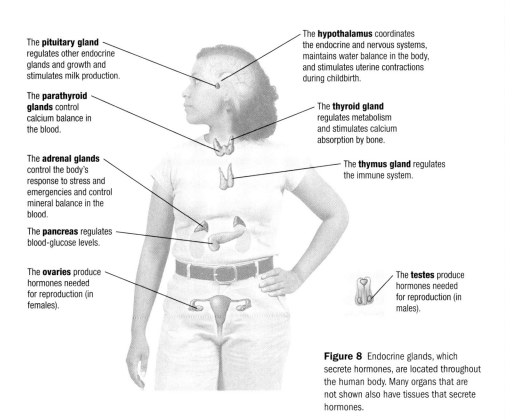

The **pituitary gland** regulates other endocrine glands and growth and stimulates milk production.

The **parathyroid glands** control calcium balance in the blood.

The **adrenal glands** control the body's response to stress and emergencies and control mineral balance in the blood.

The **pancreas** regulates blood-glucose levels.

The **ovaries** produce hormones needed for reproduction (in females).

The **hypothalamus** coordinates the endocrine and nervous systems, maintains water balance in the body, and stimulates uterine contractions during childbirth.

The **thyroid gland** regulates metabolism and stimulates calcium absorption by bone.

The **thymus gland** regulates the immune system.

The **testes** produce hormones needed for reproduction (in males).

Figure 8 Endocrine glands, which secrete hormones, are located throughout the human body. Many organs that are not shown also have tissues that secrete hormones.

Endocrine System Like the nervous system, the endocrine system sends messages to the body's cells. However, endocrine signals act over a longer period of time than nerve signals do. When the body calls for an immediate reaction, those messages are sent along the nervous system. When the body needs to bring about a more long-term change, the endocrine system does the task. ❯ **The endocrine system regulates metabolism; maintains salt, water, and nutrient balance in the blood; controls the body's responses to stress; and regulates growth, development, and reproduction.**

The endocrine system uses chemical messengers called **hormones.** Hormones are made in one part of the body and cause change in another part of the body. Hormones cause cells to change their activities. For example, as people sweat, they lose water and salts. A hormone signals the kidneys to make less urine and conserve water. Another hormone signals the kidneys to reabsorb salt from urine and the sweat glands to decrease the amount of salt in sweat.

Hormones are produced by special cells. Often, these cells are part of an **endocrine gland,** an organ that produces and releases hormones directly into the bloodstream or into the fluid around cells. The major endocrine glands are shown in **Figure 8.**

❯ **Reading Check** *How do hormones help maintain homeostasis?*

hormone a substance that is made in one cell or tissue and that causes a change in another cell or tissue located in a different part of the body

endocrine gland (EN doh KRIN) a ductless gland that secretes hormones into the blood

Teaching Key Ideas
Demonstrating Response to Noise
At the beginning of class while students are settling down, make a loud, startling noise, such as banging a book on your desk. Immediately afterward, ask students to describe their feelings in response to the noise. List responses on the board or overhead. Tell students that the effects they felt were the result of a hormone. At intervals during the class period, ask if anyone still feels jittery.

Teaching Key Ideas
Calcium in Bones Bone tissue is a storage site for calcium. Calcium needed elsewhere in the body (such as for nerve or muscle function) may be released from the bones in a process called reabsorption. Parathyroid glands release a hormone in response to low blood calcium levels that stimulates the release of calcium from bone cells into the blood. Conversely, high blood calcium levels trigger the release of calcitonin from the thyroid gland, which stimulates absorption of calcium into bone cells.

Differentiated Instruction

Advanced Learners/GATE
Homeostasis and Endocrine Disorders Point out to students that the maintenance of homeostasis in a multicellular organism is a difficult and complex process. Communication must be maintained among organ systems, organs, tissues, and even individual cells. Multicellular organisms have elaborate signaling systems that are only now being discovered. Many diseases result from the disruption of homeostasis. Have students select an endocrine disorder and write a short report about it. **LS Verbal**

Why It Matters

Heart Hormones The first hormone produced by the heart was discovered in the early 1990s. This hormone, atrial natriuretic factor, results in lower blood volume and pressure. In 1999, three more heart hormones were discovered: vessel dilator, which removes sodium and lowers blood pressure; long-acting natriuretic peptide, which removes salt from the blood; and kaliuretic peptide, which removes potassium from the blood. Researchers are currently testing whether one or more of these heart hormones can be used to treat congestive heart failure.

Teaching Key Ideas

Nutrients Have students brainstorm nutrients necessary for proper body function and food sources where each nutrient can be found. (Sample answer: Calcium is necessary for healthy teeth and bones; calcium can be found in dairy products.) Have students revisit the list after reading this section. **LS Verbal**

Teaching Key Ideas

Vitamin Overdoses Some people think that if a little is good, a lot is better. Unfortunately, this is not the case with certain vitamins. For example, overdoses of vitamin A can cause liver damage. Overdoses of vitamin D can cause kidney damage and calcification of soft tissues. Although vitamins A and D are both fat soluble, making them more difficult for the body to eliminate, even the water soluble vitamins have some negative effects if overused.

Math Skills

Graphing Provide students with the following average lengths of the digestive organs: esophagus, 25 cm; stomach, 25 cm; small intestine, 6 m; and large intestine, 1.5 m. Then have students prepare a bar graph to compare the average lengths of these organs. **LS Logical**

---

digestion the breaking down of food into chemical substances that can be used for energy

excretion the process of eliminating metabolic wastes

ACADEMIC VOCABULARY

contraction the act of drawing together or shrinking

Figure 9 Villi, as shown in the SEM (137×) and the diagram, expand the surface area of the small intestine to allow greater absorption of nutrients.

Digestive and Excretory Systems

Suppose you have just eaten your favorite meal. What happens to the food? **›The digestive system converts food into nutrients that a body's cells can use.** Some nutrients are used in metabolic reactions. Others are used to build new cells. The excretory system removes the materials in food that cannot be converted into nutrients along with wastes from metabolic reactions, and expels them from the body.

Digestive System Digestion is the breaking down of large food molecules into smaller, more-usable ones. Large food molecules must be broken down both physically and chemically. The physical breakdown of food is called *mechanical digestion*. This form of digestion begins in the mouth, where food is chewed into small pieces that are easy to swallow. As the food is chewed, it mixes with saliva. Saliva moistens the food particles and makes them easier to swallow. It also begins chemical digestion by adding digestive enzymes to the food.

The Esophagus and Stomach When food is swallowed, it enters the esophagus, a muscular tube that pushes the food along with wavelike contractions. Food is pushed into the stomach, where digestion of protein begins. Acid that is produced in the stomach kills most of the bacteria that entered with the food, and it acts as a 'switch' to turn on enzymes that will continue chemical digestion.

The Intestines From the stomach, food is pushed into the small intestine. There, bile from the liver and enzymes made by the small intestine and pancreas complete digestion. The proteins are reduced to amino acids, complex carbohydrates are changed into simple sugars, and lipids are changed to fatty acids and glycerol. The nutrients can then be absorbed into the blood and the lymph. Millions of tiny, fingerlike projections, called *villi,* line the small intestine. The villi, shown in **Figure 9,** increase the small intestine's surface area so that most nutrients are absorbed by the time the food reaches the large intestine. The undigested material enters the large intestine, where water, some vitamins, and minerals are absorbed into the bloodstream. The remaining materials exit the body through the anus.

Capillaries

Villus

Small intestine

Lymphatic vessels

Inner lining of small intestine

Why It Matters

Digestion and Absorption All nutrient absorption into the bloodstream occurs in the small intestine, not the stomach. However, alcohol is absorbed from the stomach directly into the bloodstream, accounting for its fast-acting effects on the body. Absorption is slowed when the stomach contains food.

Differentiated Instruction

Special Education Students

Modeling Villi Have students look at the structure of the small intestine in **Figure 9**. Then, give each student two pieces of yarn. Have them make a circle with a short piece of yarn, and then use a much longer piece of yarn to simulate villi inside of the shorter piece. When they compare the lengths of the yarn, it becomes clear that villi significantly increase surface area. **LS Kinesthetic**

QuickLab

🕐 15 min

4.1.2b, 4.5.2a, 4.5.3a

Filtration Rate in the Kidneys

A human kidney filters fluid from the blood at the rate of about 125 mL/min. However, only a small percentage of this fluid is excreted as urine. Use this information to answer the questions below.

Analysis

1. **Calculate** how many milliliters of fluid the human kidneys filter each hour.

2. **Calculate** how many milliliters of fluid the kidneys filter each day.

3. **CRITICAL THINKING** **Analyzing Data** Convert your answer in item 2 from milliliters to liters.

4. **CRITICAL THINKING** **Predicting Outcomes** What would happen if the kidneys could not return water to the body?

Excretory System The human body must remove wastes that are produced by metabolism in a process known as **excretion.** ❯ By removing wastes and toxic chemicals, excretion enables the body to maintain its osmotic and pH balance. When you sweat, your skin excretes excess water, salts, and some nitrogen wastes. Carbon dioxide and water are excreted as you exhale. The blood also carries other cellular wastes to the kidneys, the primary organs of excretion.

The Kidneys The body uses a two-step process to maintain a healthy level of salts and other substances in the blood. Each kidney, shown in **Figure 10,** is composed of nearly one million microscopic filtration units called *nephrons*. At one end of the nephron is the Bowman's capsule, a cup-shaped structure. As blood flows through capillaries in the capsule, blood pressure forces fluid out of the capillaries into the capsule. This fluid is made of water, salt, glucose, amino acids, urea, and other substances. *Urea* is a nitrogen-containing waste product that is released into the blood by the liver. The fluid passes into a narrow tubule, which is surrounded by capillaries. There, glucose and some other molecules in the fluid reenter the bloodstream, which allows the body to take back useful molecules that were removed during filtration. The remaining fluid then passes out of the nephron through collecting ducts, where much of the water is removed. The remaining solution is now called *urine.*

The Urinary Bladder Urine flows from the kidneys through a ureter to the urinary bladder, where the urine is collected and stored. When the bladder's muscular walls contract, urine exits through the urethra.

❯ **Reading Check** *Summarize how blood is filtered.*

Figure 10 Urine exits the kidneys by way of two ureters that empty into a storage organ called the *urinary bladder.* ❯ What structure does urine flow through to exit the body?

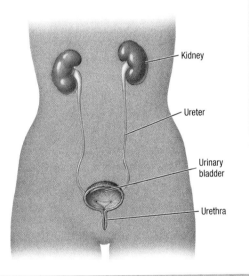

- Kidney
- Ureter
- Urinary bladder
- Urethra

Differentiated Instruction

Advanced Learners/GATE

Sports Drinks Ask students to research the ingredients in sports drinks and why they are thought to improve performance in athletes. (Sports drinks consist of water with about a 6 percent concentration of carbohydrates and electrolytes. The carbohydrates maintain blood glucose levels during exercise, when muscle glycogen levels start to run low. The electrolytes in the sports drink replace those lost through sweat.) **LS** **Verbal**

Basic Learners

Location of Kidneys Some students think the kidneys are lower than they actually are. Ask students to place their hands where they think their kidneys are. (in the middle of the back, near the spine, just under the last ribs) **LS** **Kinesthetic**

Blood Pressure Show students that the farther blood is from the heart, the lower the pressure. You will need two hoses, about 8 cm and 15 cm long. Fill two plastic syringes with water, attach each snugly to the end of each hose, and force out the water. The stream should travel 8 to 15 cm from the end of the longer hose (vein) and 15 to 30 cm from the end of the shorter hose (artery). Be sure to apply equal pressure to the plunger each time so that students recognize that the distance from plunger tip to exit, not pressure on the plunger, causes the change. **LS** **Visual**

Teaching Key Ideas

Nourishing the Heart Point out that the heart cannot get nutrients and oxygen from the blood that is in its own chambers. The heart muscle is too thick for diffusion to be an effective means of distribution. Two coronary arteries supply blood for the heart's needs. They lie in grooves that spiral around the heart.

Answers to Caption Questions

Figure 11: from the alveoli, into the capillary

Figure 11 Concentration gradients allow oxygen and carbon dioxide to diffuse across the alveoli and capillary walls.

> In which direction does an oxygen molecule diffuse in the lungs?

go.hrw.com
* interact online
Keyword: HX8BODF11

alveolus (al VEE uh luhs) any of the tiny air sacs of the lungs where oxygen and carbon dioxide are exchanged

capillary (KAP uh LER ee) a tiny blood vessel that allows an exchange between blood and cells in tissue

lymph (LIMF) the fluid that is collected by the lymphatic vessels and nodes

Figure 12 The exchange of materials across capillary walls is possible because capillary walls are only one cell thick, which allows molecules to easily pass through them.

Respiratory and Circulatory Systems

The respiratory system and circulatory system function together to ensure that oxygen reaches all cells of the body. As you can see in **Figure 11,** the two systems are interwoven within the tissues of the lungs, where the exchange of respiratory gases takes place.

Respiratory System > The respiratory system brings oxygen, O_2, into the body and carries carbon dioxide, CO_2, a waste product of cellular respiration, out of the body. Air enters the respiratory system when you inhale through your nose or mouth. Inhalation occurs when muscles around the chest area contract and expand the rib cage. Inhaled air passes through a series of tubes to reach the lungs. Within each lung, the tubes carrying the air splits into smaller and smaller tubes, called *bronchioles*. The smallest bronchioles end in groups of tiny air sacs called **alveoli** (singular, *alveolus*), which are surrounded by blood vessels. The actual exchange of gases takes place across the thin, moist membranes of the alveoli. Oxygen leaves the alveoli and enters the blood, while CO_2 leaves the blood and enters the alveoli.

Circulatory System > The circulatory system carries nutrients, oxygen, hormones, and wastes through the body and distributes heat to maintain homeostasis. Together, the cardiovascular system and the lymphatic system make up the body's circulatory system.

Cardiovascular System Blood, blood vessels, and the heart—a muscular organ that acts like a pump—make up the cardiovascular system. This system acts like a network of highways that transports materials to and from the body's cells. The network is made up of three kinds of vessels: arteries, capillaries, and veins. *Arteries* have thick, muscular walls to withstand the force of the blood pumped out of the heart. Arteries carry blood to the capillaries. A **capillary,** shown in **Figure 12,** has an extremely thin wall that allows gases and nutrients in the blood to pass across it into the fluid around body cells. From the capillaries, blood enters the *veins,* which return blood to the heart.

Why It Matters

A Newborn's First Breath In addition to using lungs for the first time, a newborn's heart and cardiovascular system change with the first breath. Before birth, an opening, the foramen ovale, lies between the left and right atria. Another structure, the ductus arteriosus, connects the pulmonary artery to the aorta. Upon inspiration for the first time, the lungs are inflated, closing the opening and separating pulmonary circulation from the systemic circulation.

Differentiated Instruction

Advanced Learners/GATE

Researching Hypertension Ask students to use outside sources to research hypertension and prepare a report that explains the causes of this condition, and how it can be prevented and managed. They also should include the incidence of hypertension in the United States compared with that of other countries.

Blood Blood moves through blood vessels and interacts with every body system. It brings the materials a body system needs and carries away the products the system makes. Blood also carries wastes away from a system. About 45% of blood is cells and cell fragments. The remaining 55% is plasma, the liquid portion of blood. Plasma is a solution made of about 90% water and 10% solutes. The solutes include nutrients, wastes, and salts. The salts have many functions, including maintaining osmotic balance with the fluids inside of cells and regulating the pH of the blood.

In addition to carrying materials, blood distributes body heat, which helps the body maintain a steady temperature. When the body is warm, blood vessels in the skin widen. More blood pumps through the skin and allows heat to leave the body. When the body is cold, blood vessels in the skin narrow. This change helps the body conserve heat by diverting more of the blood to deeper tissues so that less heat will escape.

Lymphatic System Every time the heart pumps, some of the fluid in blood is forced out of the capillaries. The escaped fluid collects in spaces around the body's cells. As **Figure 13** shows, this fluid, called **lymph,** is picked up by the lymphatic system and returned to the blood. The lymphatic system is made up of a network of vessels, tiny bean-shaped structures called *lymph nodes,* and lymph tissue. Lymph vessels collect lymph and return it to two large veins in the neck. As lymph moves through lymph vessels, the fluid passes through lymph nodes, where white blood cells collect. The white blood cells destroy any bacteria or other dangerous materials in the lymph. In this way, the lymphatic system helps the body fight infection.

❯ **Reading Check** *What are two functions of the lymphatic system?*

These arrows show the direction that lymph flows.

Figure 13 Skeletal muscles squeeze lymph vessels and thus force the lymph through the lymphatic system. ❯ What might happen if a lymphatic vessel becomes blocked?

Section 2 Review

❯ KEY IDEAS

1. **Explain** how the skeletal and muscular systems work together to produce movement.

2. **List** four functions of the integumentary system.

3. **Summarize** how the brain controls the maintenance of the body's homeostasis.

4. **Describe** how the excretory system helps the body maintain homeostasis.

5. **Relate** the function of the respiratory system with that of the cardiovascular system.

CRITICAL THINKING

6. **Recognizing Relationships** Why is a third-degree burn, which destroys the epidermis and dermis of the skin, a serious injury?

METHODS OF SCIENCE

7. **Formulating Hypotheses** Choose one of the body systems discussed in this section, and write a short paragraph in which you hypothesize how homeostasis would most likely be disrupted if that body system stopped functioning properly.

Answers to Section Review

1. Pairs of opposing muscles work together to move bones at joints. When one muscle in the pair contracts, the other muscle relaxes to produce movement.

2. The integumentary system protects the body from injury and UV radiation, defends against disease, helps regulate body temperature, and prevents the body from drying out.

3. The brain synchronizes the body's efforts to maintain homeostasis. Sensory information is processed by the brain. This information is used to regulate heart rate, breathing rate, blood pressure, the release of hormones, and so on.

4. By removing wastes and toxic chemicals, excretion enables the body to maintain its osmotic and pH balance.

5. The respiratory system and circulatory system function together to ensure that oxygen reaches all cells of the body. The respiratory system takes in oxygen. The cardiovascular system transports the oxygen throughout the body.

6. The epidermis and dermis perform several vital functions, including waterproofing the body, keeping microorganisms out, and regulating body temperature. Loss of the dermis and epidermis removes the barrier between the interior tissues and external environment.

7. Answers will vary depending on which body systems students choose to discuss.

Key Ideas	Key Terms	Why It Matters
❯ How do feedback mechanisms help maintain homeostasis? ❯ How does a feedback mechanism control a person's breathing rate? ❯ How does a feedback mechanism maintain the concentration of glucose in the bloodstream?	feedback mechanism	The human body must be able to detect changes in its internal environment and quickly react to maintain the body's homeostasis.

 The Living Environment
Standard 4

1.2c The components of the human body, from organ systems to cell organelles, interact to maintain a balanced internal environment. To successfully accomplish this, organisms possess a diversity of control mechanisms that detect deviations and make corrective actions.

1.2.e The organs and systems of the body help to provide all the cells with their basic needs. The cells of the body are of different kinds and are grouped in ways that enhance how they function together.

5.3b Feedback mechanisms have evolved that maintain homeostasis. Examples include the changes in heart rate or respiratory rate in response to increased activity in muscle cells, the maintenance of blood sugar levels by insulin from the pancreas, and the changes in openings in the leaves of plants by guard cells to regulate water loss and gas exchange.

Have you ever walked across a balance beam? When you feel yourself falling toward the right, you shift your weight to the left. Your body maintains its internal balance, or homeostasis, in a similar way.

Mechanisms of Control

The word *homeostasis* is derived from Greek words that mean "to stay the same," but this definition can be misleading. A body's internal state does not stay exactly the same. Instead, as **Figure 14** shows, it varies around a certain average value. Homeostasis maintains a dynamic equilibrium. ❯To maintain homeostasis, your body has a diversity of feedback mechanisms that detect deviations in the body's internal environment and make corrective actions. A **feedback mechanism** is a mechanism in which the last step in a series of events controls the first step. A feedback mechanism has three parts. First, a receptor, such as a nerve, detects change in the internal or external environment. Second, a control center, such as the brain, selects a response to the information from the receptor. Third, an effector, such as a muscle or gland, carries out the response, and this effect is detected by the receptor, which starts the process again.

Dynamic Equilibrium in the Human Body

Too high / Average / Too low — Internal condition vs. Time

Feedback mechanism engages — Stress occurs — Return to average — Feedback mechanism engages

Figure 14 Just as acrobats use their sense of balance to keep from falling, feedback mechanisms are used to keep the body functioning within a normal range. ❯What causes the body's internal environment to deviate from its average state?

Negative Feedback

Concentration | Time

Effecting substance

Reacting substance

Positive Feedback

Concentration | Time

Effecting substance

Reacting substance

Figure 15 In negative feedback, an effecting substance causes the body to stop making a reacting substance. In positive feedback, an effecting substance causes the body to make more of the reacting substance. ❯ Summarize how negative feedback differs from positive feedback.

Negative Feedback The two main types of feedback mechanisms, negative feedback and positive feedback, are illustrated in **Figure 15.** Homeostasis is maintained mostly through negative feedback. In negative feedback, the final step in a series of events inhibits the first step in the series. Negative feedback works like a home heating system that is controlled by a thermostat. When the room temperature drops below a set point, the thermostat activates the heater to warm the room. When room temperature reaches the set point, the thermostat shuts off the heater. These actions maintain the temperature within a narrow range.

Positive Feedback In positive feedback, a change in the body causes even more change in the same direction. During positive feedback, the production of a hormone causes the release of another hormone. This process usually progresses until a specific event triggers hormone production to stop. For example, positive feedback occurs in blood clotting, where one clotting factor activates another in a cascade that leads quickly to the formation of a clot. In another example, the hormone that causes a female's ovary to release an egg works through positive feedback. Rising levels of the main female sex hormone, estrogen, cause another hormone to be secreted until an egg is released from one of the two ovaries. You will learn more about this feedback mechanism in Chapter 23.

Antagonistic Hormones Some hormones work in opposing pairs to control levels of important substances. Hormones that work in this way are called *antagonistic hormones* because their actions have opposite effects. The release of each hormone of the pair is regulated by negative feedback. The idea of the thermostat can also apply to antagonistic hormones. Suppose that, instead of just a heater that turns on when the air temperature drops below a certain level, there is also an air conditioner that turns on when the air temperature rises above a certain level. The paired functions of the heater and the air conditioner, each controlled by negative feedback, can maintain a nearly constant air temperature.

❯ **Reading Check** *How does the body use feedback mechanisms to maintain homeostasis?*

> **feedback mechanism** a cycle of events in which information from one step controls or affects a previous step

www.scilinks.org
Topic: Hormones
Code: HX80758

Teaching Key Ideas
Malfunction in Feedback Systems
Have students describe what would happen if a negative feedback system were damaged and began to function as a positive feedback system. (The hormones would be over-secreted.) Use the examples shown in **Figure 8** of functions regulated by endocrine glands to discuss the effects of such malfunctions. **LS** Verbal

Answers to Caption Questions
Figure 15: Negative feedback slows the release of a certain substance, and positive feedback causes more of the substance to be released.

Teaching Key Ideas
Growth Hormone Tell students that growth hormone (GH) promotes the growth and division of many body cells, and that its major targets are bone and muscle cells. GH enables protein synthesis, cellular uptake of amino acids from the blood, and the mobilization of fats in the blood to areas of high energy demand. Point out the connection between the hypothalamus and pituitary gland by telling students that the release of GH is itself controlled by two hypothalamic hormones: growth hormone releasing hormone (GHRH) and growth hormone inhibiting hormone (GHIH). Ask students what they think the relationship is between these two hypothalamic hormones. (As the names imply, they are antagonistic hormones.) **LS** Verbal

Differentiated Instruction

Alternative Assessment
Feedback Loops Have students choose a function of the endocrine system described in this section, such as preventing dehydration. Ask them to write a short explanation of how a negative feedback system would work to regulate the hormones involved in that function. **LS** Verbal

Advanced Learners/GATE
Hormone Mimics Some synthetic chemicals, known as endocrine disrupters or hormone mimics, can disrupt hormones in humans and other animals. Many have structures similar to estrogens, androgens, or thyroid hormones. By binding to hormone receptors, they can disrupt or enhance the message normally sent to a cell. Ask students to research some endocrine disrupters such as DDT, PCBs (polychlorinated biphenyls), and dioxins and to report their effects in humans. **LS** Verbal

Teaching Key Ideas

Respiratory Control Center Tell students that changes in blood gas and pH levels trigger changes in the rate of respiration. Chemoreceptors in the carotid arteries (on either side of the neck) and in the aorta detect CO_2 and O_2 concentration in the blood and blood pH. When CO_2 levels are too high or pH is too low, these receptors send signals to the respiratory control center in the medulla oblongata of the brain. The brain, in turn, sends signals to the muscles involved in breathing to contract more frequently, increasing the respiration rate. The increased respiration rate, in turn, lowers CO_2 levels, raises O_2 levels, and raises blood pH.

Answers to Caption Questions

Figure 16: When people exercise, their muscle cells need more energy. Therefore, the muscle cells perform cellular respiration at a greater rate. CO_2 is a waste product of cellular respiration. When CO_2 enters the bloodstream, it reacts with chemicals in the blood and forms an acid, which decreases the blood's pH.

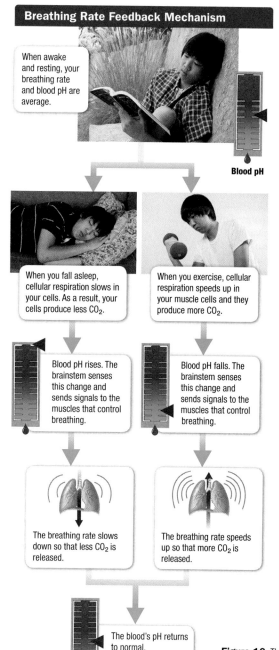

Breathing Rate Feedback Mechanism

When awake and resting, your breathing rate and blood pH are average.

Blood pH

When you fall asleep, cellular respiration slows in your cells. As a result, your cells produce less CO_2.

When you exercise, cellular respiration speeds up in your muscle cells and they produce more CO_2.

Blood pH rises. The brainstem senses this change and sends signals to the muscles that control breathing.

Blood pH falls. The brainstem senses this change and sends signals to the muscles that control breathing.

The breathing rate slows down so that less CO_2 is released.

The breathing rate speeds up so that more CO_2 is released.

The blood's pH returns to normal.

Controlling Breathing Rate

Remember that the concentration of oxygen, O_2, and carbon dioxide, CO_2, and the pH of the internal environment are two components of homeostasis. One way your body keeps these two components within an acceptable range is by adjusting your breathing rate. The brain carefully monitors the blood's pH, which is affected by the concentration of CO_2 in the blood, and adjusts the breathing rate accordingly. This feedback mechanism is illustrated in **Figure 16.**

Blood pH Each breath that you take is initiated by nerve cells in the respiratory control center of the brainstem. **> When the brainstem senses a change in the blood's pH, it adjusts the breathing rate.** But what causes the blood's pH to fluctuate? Suppose a person has a normal blood pH. If that person then begins to exercise, the amount of activity in his or her muscle cells will increase. The muscle cells will need more energy to handle the increased activity. Therefore, the mitochondria in the muscle cells will begin to perform cellular respiration at a faster rate. The waste products of cellular respiration are CO_2 and water. These two molecules will exit the muscle cells and be absorbed through capillary walls into the bloodstream.

When CO_2 enters the bloodstream, a chemical reaction occurs and most of the CO_2 becomes part of a bicarbonate ion molecule, HCO_3^-. These ions form in the presence of an enzyme that catalyzes the reaction of carbon dioxide and water to form carbonic acid, H_2CO_3, as the equation below shows. The carbonic acid breaks up to form a bicarbonate ion and a hydrogen ion, H^+:

$$H_2O + CO_2 \longrightarrow H_2CO_3 \longrightarrow HCO_3^- + H^+$$

(water) (carbon dioxide) (carbonic acid) (bicarbonate ion) (hydrogen ion)

The higher the concentration of the hydrogen ion in the bloodstream, the more acidic the blood becomes. Thus, the reaction that forms the hydrogen ion results in a decrease in the blood's pH.

Figure 16 The amount of CO_2 in your blood directly affects your breathing rate. **> Why does exercise decrease the blood's pH?**

QuickLab

🕐 15 min

Blood pH and Homeostasis 4.1.2d

You can use pH indicator paper, water, and baking soda to model the role of bicarbonate ions in maintaining blood pH levels in the presence of carbon dioxide.

Procedure

1. Label **one beaker** "A," and label **another beaker** "B." Fill each beaker halfway with **distilled water.**

2. Add **1.4 g of baking soda** to beaker B, and stir well.

3. Use **pH indicator paper** to test and record the pH of the contents of each beaker.

4. Gently blow through a **straw** into the water in beaker A. Test and record the pH of the resulting solution.

5. Repeat step 4 for beaker B.

Analysis

1. **Describe** what happened to the pH in the two beakers during the experiment.

2. **State** the chemical name for baking soda.

3. **Propose** the chemical reaction that may have caused a change in pH in beaker A.

4. **Summarize** the effect of the baking soda on the pH of the solution in beaker B after blowing through a straw.

5. CRITICAL THINKING **Analyzing Information** Relate what happened in beaker B to what happens in the bloodstream.

QuickLab

Teacher's Notes Caution students not to suck any solution up through the straw. Disposable plastic drinking cups can be substituted for beakers.

Materials
- baking soda
- beakers (2)
- pH indicator paper
- plastic soda straws
- water

Answers to Analysis
1. A became acidic; B became basic.
2. sodium hydrogen carbonate or sodium bicarbonate, $NaHCO_3$
3. $H_2O + CO_2 \rightarrow H_2CO_3 \rightarrow HCO_3^- + H^+$
4. It buffered the carbonic acid.
5. Most of the CO_2 in the blood travels as bicarbonate ions, HCO_3^-.

READING TOOLBOX

Analogies pancreas

The Brainstem Cells on the surface of the brainstem are sensitive to the acidity of the fluid that bathes the brain. In turn, the acidity of this fluid is strongly affected by the blood's acidity. Through this chain of connections, the brainstem's cells are responding to the acidity of the blood, which is directly related to the concentration of carbon dioxide. When this concentration is high, nerve centers in the brainstem signal muscles that control breathing to contract at a faster rate. As the muscles contract faster, the breathing rate increases. As a result, the lungs are able to exhale more carbon dioxide. Thus, excess CO_2 is removed from the bloodstream. Less CO_2 in the blood (and thus fewer hydrogen ions) results in the rise of the blood's pH level. When the blood's pH returns to normal, the brainstem will signal the muscles that control breathing to slow down.

Oxygen Levels Even though oxygen is essential for every cell's survival, the amount of oxygen in the blood does not affect a person's breathing rate unless oxygen levels fall dangerously low. Receptors in the arteries that connect the heart to the lungs are sensitive to the concentration of oxygen in the blood. If these receptors detect a sharp decrease in oxygen concentration, they send an emergency signal to the brainstem to speed the breathing rate. If a faster breathing rate does not increase the amount of oxygen in the blood quickly enough, then brain cells will begin to die. Because even small decreases in oxygen levels can kill brain cells, the body relies on carbon dioxide levels to control the breathing rate.

❯ **Reading Check** *How does the body control its breathing rate?*

READING TOOLBOX

Analogies After reading this section, complete the following analogy. Breathing rate : brainstem :: blood-glucose level : _____.

Differentiated Instruction

Special Education Students

Breathing Rate Have students determine the average breathing rate for students in their class. Students should record how many breaths (inhale and exhale equals one breath) each student takes for one minute. Have students add each rate and divide by the number of students included in the test to figure the average breathing rate. Additionally, students may recruit adult volunteers and determine their breath rates and compare the results with those taken in class. **LS Interpersonal**

Teaching Key Ideas

Obesity and Diabetes Explain that type 2 diabetes is linked to obesity and physical inactivity. The hormone resistin is released by fat cells and causes other tissues to become resistant to insulin, a hormone that helps move glucose into cells. Insulin-resistance is often the first step to developing type 2 diabetes. Ask students to infer how obesity is linked with diabetes. (Obese people have more fat cells that produce more resistin, which blocks more insulin. This condition can lead to diabetes.)

LS Logical

Answers to Caption Questions

Figure 17: the pancreas and liver

> Close

Formative Assessment

When you fall asleep and cellular respiration slows in your cells, ____.

A. your cells produce more CO_2 (Incorrect. Your cells produce less CO_2.)

B. your blood pH falls (Incorrect. Blood pH rises.)

C. your breathing rate speeds up (Incorrect. Breathing rate slows down.)

D. less CO_2 is released (Correct! When the breathing rate slows down, the lungs exhale less CO_2.)

When the glucose level in the blood is high, the pancreas releases the hormone insulin into the blood.

Insulin signals the liver to take in glucose from the blood, convert the glucose into glycogen, and to store glycogen for future energy needs.

The glucose level in the blood returns to normal.

After you eat, glucose is absorbed into the bloodstream from the small intestine.

When your blood-glucose level is normal, the pancreas stops releasing insulin. If your blood-glucose level is too low, the pancreas releases glucagon.

Glucagon from the pancreas signals the liver to break down glycogen and release the glucose into your blood.

Figure 17 After eating a meal, a person's blood-glucose level increases.
> Which two organs are primarily responsible for maintaining your blood-glucose level?

ACADEMIC VOCABULARY

regulate to control or direct according to a rule

Controlling Blood-Glucose Level

Your body's cells need glucose in order to perform cellular respiration. When you digest a big meal, you introduce a large amount of glucose into your body in a short period of time. What prevents the level of glucose in your blood from quickly rising to a high level? > **Two hormones released by the pancreas, insulin and glucagon, control the level of glucose in a person's bloodstream.** Insulin and glucagon act antagonistically to regulate the blood-glucose level. Insulin lowers blood glucose levels by communicating with the liver to convert glucose into glycogen that can be stored for future use. Between meals, when glucose levels in the blood fall below the normal range, glucagon stimulates the liver to break down glycogen in order to add more glucose to the bloodstream. Thus, the glucose levels in the blood do not stay very high immediately after a meal and do not drop too low between meals. The feedback mechanism that controls the level of glucose in the blood is shown in **Figure 17.**

> **Reading Check** *What are the functions of insulin and glucagon?*

Section 3 Review

> **KEY IDEAS**

1. **Identify** how feedback mechanisms are used to help the body maintain homeostasis.

2. **Explain** why you begin to breathe faster when you are exercising.

3. **Describe** how your body maintains its blood-glucose level after you have eaten a large meal.

CRITICAL THINKING

4. **Recognizing Relationships** How do you think the endocrine system and the nervous system work together to maintain the body's homeostasis?

5. **Making Inferences** Infer how the health of a person would be affected if the person's brainstem became insensitive to the pH of the fluid surrounding the brain.

USING SCIENCE GRAPHICS

6. **Drawing Diagrams** Research a feedback mechanism that is used by the body to maintain homeostasis. For example, you could research the mechanism that controls body temperature. Draw a diagram similar to Figures 16 and 17 to show how the feedback mechanism works.

Answers to Section Review

1. Feedback mechanisms detect deviations in the body's internal environment and make corrective actions to maintain homeostasis.

2. As the carbon dioxide level in the blood increases during exercise, the medulla responds by increasing the rate of breathing until the CO_2 level has returned to normal.

3. Insulin and glucagon, two antagonistic hormones produced in the pancreas, regulate blood glucose levels.

4. Sample answer: The nervous system senses changes in the external and internal environment. Then the nervous system directs endocrine glands to release hormones that will change the actions of some cells. The changed actions help the body recover from the changes in the external or internal environment.

5. Sample answer: The person's brainstem would not be able to effectively control the breathing rate, the tissues may not receive enough oxygen, and the person could suffocate.

6. Diagrams will vary depending on the feedback mechanisms students choose to feature.

Diabetes

Diabetes mellitus is the most common disorder of the endocrine system. Nine out of 10 diabetics have type 2 diabetes, and 90% of those affected are obese. In type 2 diabetes, cells stop responding to insulin. Type 2 diabetes usually begins in adults, but it is possible to develop in childhood.

REAL WORLD

Type 1 or Type 2?

In diabetes, cells are unable to take up enough glucose from the blood, which results in high blood-glucose levels. Symptoms of diabetes include weight loss, increased urination, and thirst. In type 1 diabetes, the immune system destroys insulin-producing cells in the pancreas. In type 2 diabetes, cells stop responding to insulin. Many people are unaware they have the disease. In both types, the kidneys excrete excess glucose and water, which results in large amounts of urine and persistent thirst. Glucose-starved cells use the body's supply of fats and proteins for energy.

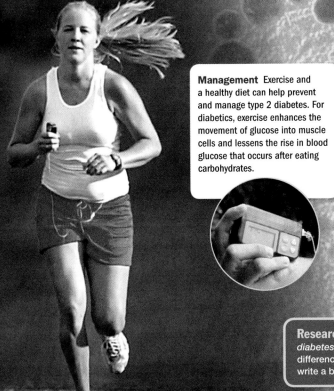

Management Exercise and a healthy diet can help prevent and manage type 2 diabetes. For diabetics, exercise enhances the movement of glucose into muscle cells and lessens the rise in blood glucose that occurs after eating carbohydrates.

Treatment Most diabetics monitor their blood-glucose levels by using small testing devices. Diabetics who cannot make insulin receive it in an injection or from an insulin pump, a device that is worn by the patient and delivers a preset dose of insulin.

Research Research the origin of the names *diabetes mellitus* and *diabetes insipidus*. Find out the difference between these two types of diabetes, and write a brief report about your findings.

Why It Matters

Teacher's Notes Most cases of type 2 diabetes can be prevented with a healthful lifestyle. Obesity is the major risk factor for this disease. The incidence of type 2 diabetes is rising as the rate of obesity is increasing.

READING TOOLBOX

Visual Literacy Ask students why this page features a girl who is exercising. (Exercise helps people manage diabetes.) Draw attention to the blood glucose monitor. Ask students to infer how monitoring blood glucose levels helps to control the disease. (It helps people adjust their diet or medication.) **LS Visual**

Answer to Research

Reports should include the following: *Diabetes* is a Greek word meaning "that which passes through." The Latin *mellitus* means "honey." *Insipidus* is a Latin word meaning "without taste." People with diabetes mellitus excrete a large amount of glucose in their urine. People with diabetes insipidus do not. Diabetes mellitus is a dysfunction of the body's production or use of insulin. Diabetes insipidus is caused by a defect in the pituitary gland or kidney so that too little water is retained.

Lab

Time Required
One 45- to 60-minute lab period

Ratings

EASY ——————— HARD

Teacher Prep 🧪🧪🧪
Student Setup 🧪🧪
Concept Level 🧪🧪🧪
Cleanup 🧪🧪

Safety Cautions
Tell students that epinephrine is toxic and is absorbed through intact skin. Remind students that chemicals used in the lab should not be touched or tasted. Spills should be reported immediately. Instruct students how to disinfect surfaces following a spill. Tell students to wash hands with soap and water after the lab is finished.

Tips and Tricks
Solution Preparation When preparing solutions, mix each solution continuously for 5 minutes, reversing the direction of stirring every 10 to 20 seconds.
Epinephrine Solution To make a 0.0001 percent solution of epinephrine, dilute 10 mL of the 0.001 percent solution with distilled water to make 100 mL. To make a 0.00001 percent solution, dilute 1 mL of 0.001 percent solution with distilled water to make 100 mL. To make 0.000001 percent solution, dilute 0.1 mL of 0.001 percent solution with distilled water to make 100 mL.

Lab Correlations
4.5.3b Dynamic equilibrium results from detection of and response to stimuli. Organisms detect and respond to change in a variety of ways both at the cellular level and at the organismal level.

Objectives
▸ Measure the heart rate of daphnia.
▸ Observe the effect of the hormone epinephrine on heart rate in daphnia.
▸ Determine the threshold concentration for the effects of epinephrine on daphnia.

Materials
- medicine dropper
- daphnia
- daphnia culture water
- depression slide
- petroleum jelly
- coverslip
- compound microscope
- watch or clock with second hand
- paper towels
- beaker, 100 mL
- graduated cylinder, 10 mL
- epinephrine solutions, 0.001%, 0.0001%, 0.00001%, and 0.000001%

Safety

Epinephrine and Heart Rate

Epinephrine is a hormone that increases blood pressure, blood-glucose level, and heart rate (HR). The lowest concentration that stimulates a response is called the *threshold concentration*.

In this lab, you will design an experiment to investigate the threshold concentration of epinephrine that affects heart rate. To do this, you will observe heart rate of the crustacean daphnia under experimental conditions that you determine.

Preparation
1. **SCIENTIFIC METHODS** **State the Problem** What is the threshold concentration of epinephrine that affects the heart rate of daphnia?
2. **SCIENTIFIC METHODS** **Form a Hypothesis** Form a testable hypothesis that explains how epinephrine might affect the heart rate of daphnia. Record your hypothesis.

Procedure
Observe Heart Rate in Daphnia
❶ ◇ ◇ ♠ Put on safety goggles, gloves, and a lab apron.
❷ ◇ **CAUTION: Do not touch your face while handling microorganisms.** Use a clean medicine dropper to transfer one daphnia to the well of a clean depression slide. Place a dab of petroleum jelly in the well. Add a coverslip. Observe the daphnia with a compound microscope under low power.
❸ Count the daphnia's heartbeats for 10 s. Divide this number by 10 to find the HR in beats per second. Record your observations in a data table as Trial 1. Turn off the microscope light, and wait 20 s. Repeat this step two times, and record your observations as Trials 2 and 3.
❹ Calculate the average HR in beats per second. Then, calculate the average heart rate in beats per minute using the following formula:

$$\text{Average HR (beats per minute)} = \text{Average HR (beats per second)} \times 60 \text{ s/min.}$$

Daphnia Heart Rate

Solution	HR (beats per second) Trial 1 (A)	HR (beats per second) Trial 2 (B)	HR (beats per second) Trial 3 (C)	Average HR (beats per second) [(A+B+C)/3]	Average HR (beats per minute)

Disposal Prepare separate containers for the disposal of solutions and broken glass. Collect all wastes containing epinephrine. To the combined liquid, add 5 mL of full-strength chlorine bleach. Stir the mixture, and then heat to boiling. Boil gently for 5 minutes. Let the solution cool and pour it down the drain.
Daphnia Recovery Instruct students to get *Daphnia* from the classroom stock and then return the *Daphnia* to a 100 mL beaker with 50 mL of *Daphnia* culture water to allow the *Daphnia* to recover.

Answers to Preparation
2. Sample hypothesis: Increasing the amount of epinephrine in the water will increase the daphnia's heart rate.

Daphnia

Design an Experiment

5 Design an experiment that tests your hypothesis and that uses the materials listed for this lab. Predict what will happen during your experiment if your hypothesis is supported.

6 ✦ CAUTION: Handle animals carefully and with respect. Write a procedure for your experiment. Identify the dependent variables and the independent variables. Construct any tables that you will need to record your data. Make a list of all of the safety precautions that you will take. Have your teacher approve your procedure and safety precautions before you begin.

Conduct Your Experiment

7 ✦ CAUTION: Glassware such as coverslips and slides are fragile. Notify your teacher of broken glass or cuts. To add a solution to a prepared slide, first place a drop of the solution at the edge of the coverslip. Then, place a piece of paper towel along the opposite edge to draw the solution under the coverslip. Wait 1 min for the solution to take effect.

8 ✦ CAUTION: Epinephrine is toxic and is absorbed through the skin. Wear gloves at all times during this experiment. Notify your teacher of any spills. Perform your experiment. Record your observations in a data table.

9 ✦ ✦ Clean up your lab materials according to your teacher's instructions. Wash your hands before leaving the lab.

Analyze and Conclude

1. **Summarizing Results** Make a graph of your data. Plot "Epinephrine concentration (%)" on the *x*-axis. Plot "Average heart rate (beats per minute)" on the *y*-axis.

2. **SCIENTIFIC METHODS Analyzing Data** Which solutions affected the heart rate of daphnia?

3. **SCIENTIFIC METHODS Interpreting Data** What was the threshold concentration of epinephrine?

4. **Making Predictions** Based on the information that you have and based on your data, predict how epinephrine concentration would affect heart rates in humans.

SCI**LINKS**
www.scilinks.org
Topic: Endocrine
System
Code: HX80504

Extensions

5. **Inferring Relationships** Research anaphylactic shock. Explain why epinephrine is used to treat anaphylactic shock.

6. **Further Inquiry** Write a new question about hormones that could be explored with another investigation.

Answers to Procedure

5. Sample answer: Increasing the amount of epinephrine will cause the daphnia's heart rate to increase.

6. Answers will vary. Look for a step-by-step procedure that includes a control slide of the daphnia in the plain culture water as a comparison with slides that include increasing concentrations of epinephrine.

Answers to Analyze and Conclude

1. Answers will vary.

2. The 0.001 percent and 0.0001 percent solutions should increase heart rate.

3. Answers may vary. It is usually 0.0001 percent.

4. Increased concentration would increase heart rate.

Answers to Extensions

5. Anaphylactic shock is an acute systemic allergic reaction. Symptoms include agitation, flushing, heart palpitations, and difficulty breathing, followed by collapse of the cardiovascular system. Epinephrine raises heart rate and blood pressure, reducing anaphylactic symptoms. It reduces swelling of bronchial tubes and increases smooth muscle tone in the vascular system.

6. Answers will vary. Sample question: How do other hormones affect heart rate in *Daphnia*?

Sample Data Table

Solution	Trial 1	Trial 2	Trial 3	Average HR (beats/min)	Average HR (beats/s)
Control	24	24	25	2.4	146
0.000001%	24	25	25	2.5	148
0.00001%	25	26	25	2.5	152
0.0001%	31	32	33	3.2	192
0.001%	34	37	36	3.6	214

Key Resources

 Holt Lab Generator

 Lab Datasheet (Levels A, B, C)

 Holt Science Biology Video Labs

SUPER SUMMARY

Have students connect the major concepts in this chapter through an interactive Super Summary. Visit **go.hrw.com** and type in the keyword **HX8BODS** to access the Super Summary for this chapter.

Reteaching Key Ideas

Understanding Concepts On the board or overhead projector, list the major concepts in this section. Have the class review the text to identify examples that can be used to illustrate each of these concepts. **Verbal**

Application Ask students to think of a daily activity, such as studying, eating, or playing sports, and then describe which systems of the body are involved in carrying out the activity. **LS Logical/Verbal**

Feedback Mechanisms Have students describe to a partner the difference between positive and negative feedback mechanisms. **LS Interpersonal**

Key Ideas	Key Terms

1 Homeostasis

> The external environment around an organism is constantly changing. These changes threaten the stability of an organism's internal environment.

> Organisms detect and respond to change in a variety of ways: both at the cellular level and at the organismal level. Failure to respond to change can result in an organism's death.

> Humans require multiple systems for digestion, respiration, reproduction, circulation, movement, coordination, and immunity. The systems interact to maintain homeostasis.

homeostasis (471)

2 Human Body Systems

> The skeletal and muscular systems enable movement and provide support and protection for tissues and organs.

> The integumentary system protects the body from injury and UV radiation, defends against disease, helps regulate body temperature, and prevents the body from drying out.

> The nervous system collects and responds to information about the body's internal and external environment. The endocrine system regulates metabolism; maintains salt, water, and nutrient balance in the blood; and regulates growth, development, and reproduction.

> The digestive system converts food into nutrients that a body's cells can use. Excretion enables the body to maintain its osmotic and pH balance.

> The respiratory system brings oxygen, O_2, into the body and carries carbon dioxide, CO_2, out of the body. The circulatory system carries nutrients, oxygen, hormones, and wastes through the body and distributes heat to maintain homeostasis.

tendon (476)
epidermis (477)
hormone (479)
endocrine gland (479)
digestion (480)
excretion (481)
alveoli (482)
capillary (482)
lymph (483)

3 Feedback Mechanisms

> To maintain homeostasis, your body has a diversity of feedback mechanisms that detect deviations in the body's internal environment and make corrective actions.

> When the brainstem senses a change in the blood's pH, it adjusts the breathing rate.

> Two hormones that are released by the pancreas, insulin and glucagon, control the level of glucose in a person's bloodstream.

feedback mechanism (484)

Regents Exam Practice

PART A: Answer all questions in this part.

Directions: For each statement or question, write on your separate answer sheet the number of the word or expression that best completes the statement or answers the question.

1 When a person does strenuous exercise, small blood vessels (capillaries) near the surface of the skin increase in diameter. This change allows the body to be cooled. These statements best illustrate
(1) synthesis
(2) homeostasis
(3) excretion
(4) locomotion

2 Some human body cells are shown in the diagrams below. These groups of cells represent different

Cells from skin   Blood cells

Cells from lining of bladder   Cells from lining of trachea

(1) tissues in which similar cells function together.
(2) organs that help to carry out a specific life activity.
(3) systems that are responsible for a specific life activity.
(4) organelles that carry out different functions.

3 Which statement does *not* describe an example of a feedback mechanism that maintains homeostasis?
(1) The guard cells close the openings in leaves, preventing excess water loss from a plant.
(2) White blood cells increase the production of antigens during an allergic reaction.
(3) Increased physical activity increases heart rate in humans.
(4) The pancreas releases insulin, helping humans to keep blood sugar levels stable.

4 Feedback interactions in the human body are important because they
(1) determine the diversity necessary for evolution to occur
(2) direct the synthesis of altered genes that are passed on to every cell in the body
(3) regulate the shape of molecules involved in cellular communication
(4) keep the internal body environment within its normal range

5 Which situation is *not* an example of the maintenance of a dynamic equilibrium in an organism?
(1) Guard cells contribute to the regulation of water content in a geranium plant.
(2) Water passes into an animal cell causing it to swell
(3) The release of insulin lowers the blood sugar level in a human after eating a big meal.
(4) A runner perspires while running a race on a hot summer day.

6 The most immediate response to a high level of blood sugar in a human is an increase in the
(1) muscle activity in the arms
(2) blood flow to the digestive tract
(3) activity of all cell organelles
(4) release of insulin

7 The pancreas produces one hormone that lowers blood sugar level and another that increases blood sugar level. The interaction of these two hormones most directly helps humans to
(1) maintain a balanced internal environment
(2) digest needed substances for other body organs
(3) dispose of wastes formed in other body organs
(4) increase the rate of cellular communication

8 The central nervous system includes
(1) only the brain.
(2) the brain and the spinal cord.
(3) the brain, the spinal cord, and the cranial nerves.
(4) the brain, the spinal cord, the cranial nerves, and the spinal nerves.

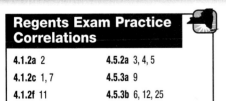

Regents Exam Practice Correlations

4.1.2a 2	**4.5.2a** 3, 4, 5
4.1.2c 1, 7	**4.5.3a** 9
4.1.2f 11	**4.5.3b** 6, 12, 25

PART A

1. **(2)** The body's homeostasis is maintained by thermoregulation, which is accomplished in this case by the loss of heat to the atmosphere. Locomotion causes the body to heat up, which triggers a response from the capillaries. Synthesis and excretion are not described in this example. (*#06, June 2003 Regents Exam*)

2. **(1)** The diagrams illustrate groups of similar cells that carry out similar functions, e.g. blood cells. A group of similar cells that performs a common function is called a tissue. (*#07, January 2005 Regents Exam*)

3. **(2)** White blood cells produce antibodies, not antigens during an allergic reaction. Therefore this statement that refers to antigen production by white blood cells is not an example of a process that maintains homeostasis. (*#19, August 2004 Regents Exam*)

4. **(4)** Feedback interactions help the body to maintain homeostasis. They do not regulate molecule shape or direct mutations in genes. Natural variation, not feedback interactions, determines diversity. (*#22, August 2005 Regents Exam*)

5. **(2)** Water passing into an animal cell which causes it to swell is an example of diffusion, not homeostasis. (*#30, January 2004 Regents Exam*)

6. **(4)** The body releases insulin to lower blood sugar levels and maintain homeostasis. The presence of extra sugars provides energy to the body, which may eventually (not immediately) power muscle activity, organelle activity, and increased activity in the digestive tract. (*#28, June 2003 Regents Exam*)

7. **(1)** Hormones keep blood sugar levels within a certain range in order to maintain homeostasis, or a balanced internal environment. These hormones do not contribute to digestion or waste disposal. They react to cellular communications about blood sugar level, but they do not increase these communications. (*#01, August 2003 Regents Exam*)

8. **(2)**

9. (3) Plants do not have nerve cells. Plants do not usually grow more in response to lack of water. Water is an abiotic factor, not a biotic factor. The plant closes the guard cells as part of a response to the stimulus of low concentrations of water. (*#23, June 2004 Regents Exam*)

10. (2)

11. (3) Carbon dioxide is moving out of and oxygen is moving into the cell across the cell membrane, similar to what happens in the respiratory system. Nitrogenous waste is removed from the cell, similar to what happens in the kidneys. The food particle is being digested in a digestive vacuole, which is akin to the digestive process of the digestive system. (*#05, August 2004 Regents Exam*)

12. (3) Nitrogen does not affect photosynthesis, chloroplasts do not release oxygen when the rate of photosynthesis decreases, and guard cells do not release oxygen at night. (*#21, June 2006 Regents Exam*)

13. In a positive feedback mechanism, a change in the body causes even more change in the same direction. In a negative feedback mechanism, the final step in a series of events inhibits the first step in the series.

14. The nephron is the filtering unit of the kidney.

15. Answers should include three of the following: metabolism; salt, water, and nutrient balance; the body's response to stress; growth, development, and reproduction.

16. The walls of these vessels are relatively thick; gases and nutrients diffuse through them very slowly.

17. Amylase in saliva breaks down starch into simple sugars. Pepsin in gastric juice breaks down proteins into peptide chains.

18. negative feedback, positive feedback, and antagonistic hormones

19. When hormone Y decreases, hormone X is produced. This causes the production of hormone Y, and the level of hormone Y increases.

20. A person would have severe diarrhea and could die from dehydration.

---

9 When a certain plant is without water for an extended period of time, guard cells close openings in the leaves of the plant. This activity conserves water and illustrates

(1) cellular communication involving the action of nerve cells and receptor sites

(2) an increase in rate of growth due to a low concentration of water

(3) maintenance of a dynamic equilibrium through detection and response to stimuli

(4) a response to one biotic factor in the environment

10 What is the function of the lymphatic system?

(1) It opens two-way vessels.

(2) It helps the body fight infections.

(3) It interacts with the respiratory system.

(4) It transports fluids away from the heart.

11 In the diagram of a single-celled organism shown below, the arrows indicate various activities taking place.

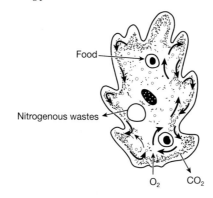

Which systems perform these same activities in humans?

(1) digestive, circulatory, and immune

(2) excretory, respiratory, and reproductive

(3) respiratory, excretory, and digestive

(4) respiratory, nervous, and endocrine

---

12 Which process illustrates a feedback mechanism in plants?

(1) Chloroplasts take in more nitrogen, which increases the rate of photosynthesis.

(2) Chloroplasts release more oxygen in response to a decreased rate of photosynthesis.

(3) Guard cells change the size of leaf openings, regulating the exchange of gases.

(4) Guard cells release oxygen from the leaf at night.

Part B

13 Distinguish between a positive feedback mechanism and a negative feedback mechanism.

14 Describe the relationship between the kidney and the nephron.

15 List three major types of activities in the body that are regulated by the endocrine system.

16 Why does exchange of gases between the blood and body tissues not occur through the walls of arteries?

17 Distinguish between the chemical digestion that occurs in the mouth and in the stomach.

Part C

18 Describe how the endocrine system regulates hormone levels.

19 X and Y are hormones. X stimulates the secretion of Y. Y exerts negative feedback on the cells that secrete X. What happens when the level of Y in the blood decreases?

20 Why is it important that the large intestine reabsorb water and not eliminate it?

21 Relate the similarities in the components and fluids of the cardiovascular and lymphatic systems.

22 Prostaglandins are hormones that cause the body to feel pain when the body is injured. Why might it be important for the body to feel pain after an injury?

23 The liver and pancreas are accessory organs of the digestive tract. In what two ways do the liver and pancreas differ from other digestive organs?

24 One of your classmates states a hypothesis that all organisms must have organ systems. Is your classmate's hypothesis valid? Explain your answer.

Part D

25 A student measures his pulse rate while he is watching television and records it. Next, he walks to a friend's house nearby and when he arrives, measures and records his pulse rate again. He and his friend then decide to run to the mall a few blocks away. On arriving at the mall, the student measures and records his pulse rate once again. Finally, after sitting and talking for a half hour, the student measures and records his pulse rate for the last time.

Which graph below best illustrates the expected changes in his pulse rate according to the activities described above?

---

21. Both have a system of vessels; at least some of these vessels have valves; the vessels contain a watery fluid that has at least some blood cells; and the systems transport fluid toward the heart.

22. Answers may vary but may include that feeling pain signals the presence of an injury so that a person will not continue to cause damage to that area.

23. Food does not pass through them, and they have other roles besides digestion.

24. not valid; unicellular organisms have no tissues, organs, or organ systems

PART D

25. (1) The heart rate increases in relation to the intensity of the physical. The heart rate is at its lowest when at rest. Therefore, the boy's heart rate would be at its lowest while he is sitting down watching TV and talking. His heart rate would be fastest after running to the mall. (*#66, June 2004 Regents Exam*)

	Standards	Teach Key Ideas
CHAPTER OPENER, pp. 496–497 — 15 min.	**The Living Environment**	
Section 1 Disease, pp. 499–501 — 30 min. 〉 The Cause of Disease 〉 The Spread of Pathogens 〉 Avoiding Disease	4.1.2d, 4.5.2a, 4.5.2b, 4.5.2h, 4.5.2j	**Bellringer Transparency** **Visual Concepts** Bacteria • Virus • Pathogen • Types of Animal-like Protists
SECTION 2 Infectious Diseases, pp. 502–508 — 45 min. 〉 Bacteria 〉 Viruses 〉 Fungi 〉 Parasitic Worms 〉 Protists	4.5.2b, 4.5.2j	**Bellringer Transparency** **Transparencies** F4 *Escherichia coli* • F6 Important Bacterial Diseases • F10 Important Viral Diseases • F11 Structure of HIV • F19 Diseases Caused by Protists • F29 Life Cycle of *Plasmodium* • H21 Life Cycle of Schistosoma • H22 Life Cycle of Beef Tapeworm **Visual Concepts** Bacteria and Food • AIDS (Acquired Immune Deficiency Syndrome) • Anatomy of a Tapeworm • Life Cycle of Tapeworms • Life Cycle of Flukes • Malaria • Malaria Life Cycle
SECTION 3 Noninfectious Diseases, pp. 510–515 — 45 min. 〉 Personal Behavior 〉 Inheritance 〉 Organ Malfunction 〉 Poor Nutrition 〉 Toxic Substances	4.2.2e, 4.5.2a, 4.5.2h	**Bellringer Transparency** **Transparencies** J77 Effects of Blood Alcohol Concentration • C28 Pedigree of Cystic Fibrosis • C30 Some Important Genetic Disorders • J44 Nutrition Label • J45 Nutrients in Food • J46 Vitamins **Visual Concepts** Alcoholism • Heart Attack • Stroke • Emphysema • Lung Cancer • Genetic Disorder • Sickle Cell Anemia • Types of Nutrients

See also PowerPoint® Resources

Chapter Review and Assessment Resources

SE Super Summary, p. 518
SE Regents Exam Practice, p. 519
Regents Review Guide
Review Resources
Chapter Tests A and B
Holt Online Assessment
Regents Question Banks on Teacher's One-Stop Planner

CHAPTER
Fast Track
Thorough instruction will require the times shown.

Basic Learners
TE Graphing TB Cases, p. 503
TE *E. coli* in the Intestine, p. 503
TE County Health Department, p. 504
Directed Reading Worksheets*
Active Reading Worksheets*
Lab Manuals, Level A*
Study Guide* ■
Note-taking Workbook*
Special Needs Activities and Modified Tests*

Advanced Learners
TE AIDS Drugs, p. 505
Critical Thinking Worksheets*
Concept Mapping Worksheets*
Science Skills Worksheets*
Lab Datasheets, Level C*

Why It Matters	Hands-On	Skills Development	Assessment
Build student motivation with resources about high-interest applications.	**SE Inquiry Lab** Cigarette Smoke and Disease, p. 497 * ■	**TE Reading Toolbox** Assessing Prior Knowledge, p. 496 **SE Reading Toolbox,** p. 498	
TE Spread of Disease to Isolated Communities, p. 500	📁 **Quick Lab** Calculating Contagion *	**SE Reading Toolbox** Key-Term Fold, p. 500 ■ **TE Reading Toolbox** Key-Term Fold, p. 500	**SE Section Review** ■ **TE Formative Assessment** Spanish Assessment * ■ 📁 **Section Quiz** * ■
TE Food Poisoning, p. 503 **TE Witches and Ergotism,** p. 506 **TE Ascomycota,** p. 506 **TE Tapeworm Infections,** p. 507 **SE Protist Plague,** p. 509	**SE Quick Lab** Emergence of Bird Flu, p. 504 * ■ **SE Skills Practice Lab** Tobacco Mosaic Virus, pp. 516–517 * ■ 📁 **Quick Lab** Preventing Parasites *	**SE Reading Toolbox** Classification, p. 508 **TE Reading Toolbox** Classification, p. 506 **TE Reading Toolbox** Visual Literacy, p. 509	**SE Section Review** ■ **TE Formative Assessment** Spanish Assessment * ■ 📁 **Section Quiz** * ■
TE Deaths from Lung Disease, p. 511 **TE Sickle Cell Anemia,** p. 512 **TE Exercise and Healthy Bones,** p. 513	**SE Quick Lab** The Nutrition Facts Label, p. 514 * ■ 📁 **Quick Lab** Blood Typing: Pregnancy and Hemolytic Disease * 📁 **Inquiry Lab** Testing Simulated Urine Samples *	**SE Reading Toolbox** Two-Column Notes, p. 513 **TE Reading Toolbox** Two-Column Notes, p. 513	**SE Section Review** ■ **TE Formative Assessment** Spanish Assessment * ■ 📁 **Section Quiz** * ■

See also Lab Generator

See also Holt Online Assessment Resources

Resources for Differentiated Instruction

English Learners
TE Vocabulary, p. 500
📁 Directed Reading Worksheets*
📁 Active Reading Worksheets*
📁 Lab Manuals, Level A*
📓 Study Guide* ■
📓 Note-taking Workbook*
📓 Multilingual Glossary

Struggling Readers
TE Vocabulary, p. 500
📁 Directed Reading Worksheets*
📁 Active Reading Worksheets*
📁 Lab Manuals, Level A*
📓 Study Guide*
📓 Note-taking Workbook*
📓 Special Needs Activities and Modified Tests*

Special Education Students
TE Surgeon General's Warning, p. 511
📁 Directed Reading Worksheets*
📁 Active Reading Worksheets*
📁 Lab Manuals, Level A*
📓 Study Guide* ■
📓 Note-taking Workbook*
📓 Special Needs Activities and Modified Tests*

Alternative Assessment
TE World Health Summit, p. 507
TE Understanding Hereditary Diseases, p. 512
TE Analyzing Eating Habits, p. 514
📁 Science Skills Worksheets*
📁 Section Quizzes* ■
📁 Chapter Tests A, B, and C* ■

Chapter 21

Homeostasis and Human Diseases

Overview

The purpose of this chapter is to introduce students to the link between disease and the disruption of homeostasis. The chapter focuses on the causes and prevention of infectious and noninfectious diseases.

READING TOOLBOX

Assessing Prior Knowledge Students should understand the following concepts:
- cells
- homeostasis
- body systems
- inheritance

Visual Literacy Ask students to study the picture and to state how the bone cancer in the photo disrupts homeostasis. (constricts nearby tissues, such as blood vessels and nerves) Ask students which body systems are affected. (skeletal system, circulatory system, nervous system)

Preview

1 Disease
The Cause of Disease
The Spread of Pathogens
Avoiding Disease

2 Infectious Diseases
Bacteria
Viruses
Fungi
Parasitic Worms
Protists

3 Noninfectious Diseases
Personal Behavior
Inheritance
Organ Malfunction
Poor Nutrition
Toxic Substances

Why It Matters

Disease can result when your body's homeostasis is disrupted. Understanding the link between homeostasis and disease can help you stay healthy.

The Living Environment
Standard 4 Students will understand and apply scientific concepts, principles, and theories pertaining to the physical setting and living environment and recognize the historical development of ideas in science.
  Key Idea 1 Living things are both similar to and different from each other and from nonliving things. **Major Understandings - 1.2d**
  Key Idea 2 Organisms inherit genetic information in a variety of ways that result in continuity of structure and function between parents and offspring. **Major Understandings - 2.2e**
  Key Idea 5 Organisms maintain a dynamic equilibrium that sustains life. **Major Understandings - 5.2a, 5.2b, 5.2h, 5.2j**

This X ray of a hand shows a cancerous tumor growing on a metacarpal, one of the bones that form the hand's palm.

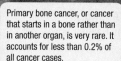

Healthy bone can support more than 5,000 kg of pressure per square inch. Cancerous bone is so weakened that it can break from stress as slight as the pressure of a firm handshake.

Primary bone cancer, or cancer that starts in a bone rather than in another organ, is very rare. It accounts for less than 0.2% of all cancer cases.

Chapter Correlations

 The Living Environment

Standard 4

1.2d If there is a disruption in any human system, there may be a corresponding imbalance in homeostasis.

2.2e Knowledge of genetics is making possible new fields of health care; for example, finding genes which may have mutations that can cause disease will aid in the development of preventive measures to fight disease. Substances, such as hormones and enzymes, from genetically engineered organisms may reduce the cost and side effects of replacing missing body chemicals.

5.2a Homeostasis in an organism is constantly threatened. Failure to respond effectively can result in disease or death.

5.2b Viruses, bacteria, fungi, and other parasites may infect plants and animals and interfere with normal life functions.

5.2h Disease may also be caused by inheritance, toxic substances, poor nutrition, organ malfunction, and some personal behavior. Some effects show up right away; others may not show up for many years.

5.2j Biological research generates knowledge used to design ways of diagnosing, preventing, treating, controlling, or curing diseases of plants and animals.

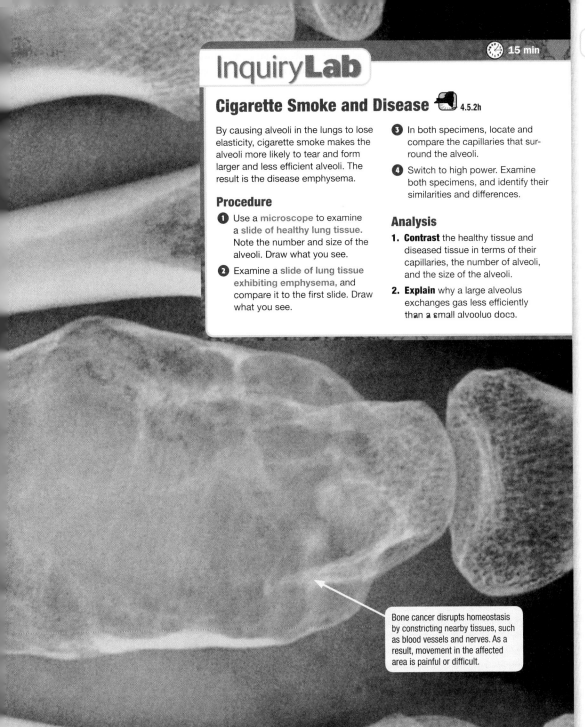

InquiryLab

🕐 15 min

Cigarette Smoke and Disease 4.5.2h

By causing alveoli in the lungs to lose elasticity, cigarette smoke makes the alveoli more likely to tear and form larger and less efficient alveoli. The result is the disease emphysema.

Procedure

❶ Use a microscope to examine a slide of healthy lung tissue. Note the number and size of the alveoli. Draw what you see.

❷ Examine a slide of lung tissue exhibiting emphysema, and compare it to the first slide. Draw what you see.

❸ In both specimens, locate and compare the capillaries that surround the alveoli.

❹ Switch to high power. Examine both specimens, and identify their similarities and differences.

Analysis

1. **Contrast** the healthy tissue and diseased tissue in terms of their capillaries, the number of alveoli, and the size of the alveoli.

2. **Explain** why a large alveolus exchanges gas less efficiently than a small alveolus does.

Bone cancer disrupts homeostasis by constricting nearby tissues, such as blood vessels and nerves. As a result, movement in the affected area is painful or difficult.

InquiryLab

Teacher's Notes Tell students that even if a smoker does not develop emphysema, the smoker will eventually have difficulty breathing because of the buildup of tar in the lungs.

Materials
- Microscope
- Prepared slide of healthy lung tissue
- Prepared slide of lung tissue with emphysema

Safety Caution Remind students that slides and coverslips are fragile and have sharp edges.

Answers to Analysis

1. The healthy lung had a denser structure with more air sacs and capillaries. The diseased tissue had fewer and much larger air sacs and fewer capillaries.

2. The larger sac has less surface area through which the gases can pass.

Using Words
Students should have a tab for each key term in the chapter.

Using Language
1. infectious diseases and noninfectious diseases
2. heart disease, hypertension, emphysema, lung cancer, and cirrhosis

Taking Notes
Check students' work for accuracy.

READING TOOLBOX These reading tools can help you learn the material in this chapter. For more information on how to use these and other tools, see **Appendix: Reading and Study Skills.**

Using Words

Key-Term Fold A key-term fold is a useful tool for studying definitions of key terms in a chapter. Each tab can contain a key term on one side and its definition on the other.

Your Turn Use the key-term fold to quiz yourself on the definitions of the key terms in a chapter. Fold a sheet of lined notebook paper in half from left to right. Using scissors, cut along every third line from the right edge of the paper to the center fold to make tabs.

Using Language

Classification As you read the chapter, identify general words that describe categories of something and specific words that describe individuals within a category. Often, the general category will be named in a large heading, and the smaller headings will describe individuals in the category.

Your Turn Answer the following questions by using information that you read in the chapter.
1. What are two major classifications of disease?
2. What are five diseases that are often caused by personal behavior?

Taking Notes

Two-Column Notes Two-column notes can help you learn the key ideas from each section.

Your Turn Create a two-column notes table for this chapter.
1. Write the key ideas in the left column. The key ideas are listed at the beginning of each section. Include one key idea in each row.
2. As you read the section, add detailed notes and examples in the right column. Be sure to put these details and examples in your own words.

Infectious Diseases	
Key Idea	Supporting Details

Key Ideas	Key Terms	Why It Matters
❯ What causes disease? ❯ How are pathogens spread? ❯ What can you do to help avoid diseases?	noninfectious disease infectious disease pathogen vector	When you're sick, you probably wish you could have prevented your illness. By understanding disease, you may avoid getting sick.

In May 1720, a ship loaded with silk and other fine cloth arrived at the French port city of Marseille. The ship's captain warned city officials that several passengers were violently ill, but the city's merchants were eager for the cloth. So, the ship was unloaded swiftly, and within days, a disease—bubonic plague—was racing through the city. Within two years, more than half of the city's population was dead. **Figure 1** shows a painting in which the citizens of Marseille are burying plague victims in mass graves.

The Cause of Disease

What causes bubonic plague or, for that matter, any other disease? ❯ Disease is caused by a disruption in a human body system that leads to a corresponding disruption in homeostasis. Once homeostasis has been disrupted and a person is ill, the disruption may result in further imbalances in other body systems. If the imbalances continue, the end result may be death.

Diseases fall into two categories. **Noninfectious diseases** are diseases that cannot be transmitted from one organism to another. Examples include genetic disorders, heart disease, and most cancers. Diseases that can be transmitted from one organism to another are known as **infectious diseases.** Bubonic plague, for instance, is an infectious disease. It is caused by a **pathogen,** which is a virus, a microorganism, or other organism that causes illness.

❯ **Reading Check** *What causes infectious diseases? (See the Appendix for answers to Reading Checks.)*

Standard 4

1.2d If there is a disruption in any human system, there may be a corresponding imbalance in homeostasis.

5.2a Homeostasis in an organism is constantly threatened. Failure to respond effectively can result in disease or death.

5.2b Viruses, bacteria, fungi, and other parasites may infect plants and animals and interfere with normal life functions.

5.2h Disease may also be caused by inheritance, toxic substances, poor nutrition, organ malfunction, and some personal behavior. Some effects show up right away; others may not show up for many years.

5.2j Biological research generates knowledge used to design ways of diagnosing, preventing, treating, controlling, or curing diseases of plants and animals.

noninfectious disease a disease that cannot spread from one individual to another

infectious disease a disease that is caused by a pathogen and that can be spread from one individual to another

pathogen a microorganism, another organism, a virus, or a protein that causes disease; an infectious agent

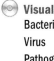

Figure 1 The Great Plague of Marseille in the 1720s was caused by the bacterium *Yersinia pestis.* Fleas spread this bacterium throughout the city.

MISCONCEPTION ALERT

Catching Colds Students may think that going outside during cold or wet weather without a jacket or with wet hair will cause you to catch a cold. Viruses, not bad weather, cause colds. However, research indicates that becoming chilled can stress the body and weaken the immune system. A weakened immune system can make someone more vulnerable to catching a cold.

Key Resources

◉ **Visual Concepts**
  Bacteria
  Virus
  Pathogen
  Types of Animal-like Protists

❯ Focus

This section introduces the causes of disease and relates the disruption in body systems to the disruption of homeostasis. The section also discusses the spread of pathogens and how one can help avoid diseases by avoiding disruptions in homeostasis.

🔊 Bellringer

Use the Bellringer transparency to prepare students for this section.

❯ Teach

Teaching Key Ideas

Pathogens Write the following terms on the board: *Bacteria, Viruses, Fungi, Protists,* and *Parasites.* Name infectious diseases caused by these organisms. Ask for volunteers to write the diseases under the appropriate term on the board. (Answers may vary but may include the following: Bacteria: tuberculosis, tetanus, strep throat, Lyme disease; Viruses: chickenpox, measles, HIV/AIDS, bird flu; Fungi: athlete's foot, ringworm, histoplasmosis; Protists: malaria, giardiasis, toxoplasmosis; Parasites: hookworm infection, schistosomiasis, elephantiasis)
LS Logical

Section Correlations	
4.1.2d	4.5.2h
4.5.2a	4.5.2j
4.5.2b	

Teaching Key Ideas

Spreading Pathogens Divide the class into groups of four. Give each group four pieces of paper. Each group member should write on the pieces of paper one of the following methods by which infectious diseases are spread: through the air, contaminated objects or infected organisms, contaminated food or water, or vectors. Pose each of the following scenarios, and have each group member read out how disease can be spread in that scenario:

• Food isn't stored correctly. (contaminated food or water)
• Your friend gets a tick bite. (vector)
• Two friends shake hands. (contaminated objects or infected organisms)
• A person sitting next to you on the bus sneezes. (through the air)

READING TOOLBOX

Key-Term Fold Make sure that students' lists of key terms are complete.

Answers to Caption Questions

Figure 2: Sample answer: If the syringe is used to inject a medicine, the bacteria could enter the bloodstream.

READING TOOLBOX

Key-Term Fold As you read this section, record all of the highlighted terms, such as the word *vector*, in your key-term fold.

vector an intermediate host that transfers a pathogen or a parasite to another organism

Figure 2 A sneeze can force thousands of pathogens out of your body at up to 160 km/h. These pathogens may land on and contaminate solid surfaces, such as the tip of an unsterilized syringe, shown on the right. ⟩ **How might the bacteria on this syringe be transmitted to your body?**

The Spread of Pathogens

There are many types of pathogens, including bacteria, viruses, protists, fungi, and parasitic worms. ⟩ **Pathogens can be spread through the air, through contact with contaminated objects or an infected organism, through the ingestion of contaminated food or water, or through vectors.**

Air As **Figure 2** shows, when an infected person coughs or sneezes, thousands of pathogen-carrying droplets can be released into the air. These pathogens then can infect a new host through the nose, mouth, or eyes. The common cold, influenza, strep throat, and tuberculosis are spread through the air.

Contaminated Objects or Infected Organisms When an object, such as the syringe needle in **Figure 2,** becomes contaminated with pathogens, the object can transmit the pathogens to a host. Objects that commonly transmit pathogens include eating utensils, hairbrushes, and doorknobs. Pathogens are also transmitted by infected organisms. For example, humans can get rabies from an infected dog or cat. Also, direct person-to-person contact, such as shaking hands, kissing, or sexual intercourse, can spread pathogens.

Contaminated Food or Water Food and water may carry pathogens. For instance, raw chicken can be covered in salmonellae, bacteria that can cause food poisoning. In addition, if a water line breaks or a water treatment plant becomes flooded, pathogens can enter the public water supply and cause diseases such as cholera.

Vectors A **vector** is an intermediate organism that transfers pathogens between humans or from animals to humans. Vectors usually do not get ill from the pathogen. The mosquito is the most common vector for humans. Mosquitoes can transmit malaria and West Nile virus. Fleas, ticks, and rodents are also vectors for pathogens such as the bacteria that cause bubonic plague.

⟩ **Reading Check** *How might you prevent the spread of a pathogen?*

Why It Matters

Spread of Disease to Isolated Communities Spanish conqueror Hernán Cortéz was aided in his conquest of the Aztecs by a smallpox epidemic that struck those Native Americans. Prior to the arrival of the Europeans, smallpox had been unknown in the New World. The disease killed millions of Native Americans. Today, the Yanomamo tribe of Brazil and Venezuela is being decimated because of the onslaught of malaria, influenza, measles, and chickenpox brought by miners in search of gold.

Differentiated Instruction

English Learners/Struggling Readers

Vocabulary Have students begin a vocabulary notebook or vocabulary flash cards. Tell them to include the Key Terms and any other terms that are unfamiliar in each section. Have them use their own words to write definitions for the terms. Suggest that they also include diagrams and pictures when helpful. Allow time for students to share the information in their notebooks or flashcards with a partner who can make suggestions for improvement. **LS Verbal**

Avoiding Disease

Whether infectious or noninfectious, disease results from the same general condition: a disruption of homeostasis. If an individual could avoid the disruption of homeostasis, his or her health would not deteriorate. Therefore, actions that help you maintain your body's homeostasis will also help you maintain your overall health. ❯ You can maintain your homeostasis and can avoid many diseases by practicing good hygiene, avoiding close contact with infected organisms, maintaining a healthy diet, and exercising on a regular basis.

Good Hygiene Pathogens disrupt your homeostasis by damaging cells, tissues, or organs. You can decrease the chance of being infected by a pathogen by practicing good hygiene. Consider all of the ways in which pathogens can be transmitted, and take precautions against these modes of transmission. For example, wash your hands thoroughly and frequently to lower dramatically your risk of being infected by a pathogen. In addition, avoid contact with infected animals or people.

A Healthy Lifestyle To maintain homeostasis, your body needs a regular supply of nutrients, such as protein, vitamins, and minerals. Nutrients are used to power healthy cells, repair damaged cells, and replace dead cells. By eating a balanced diet that supplies all of the nutrients that your body needs, you are supporting the health of all of your tissues and organs. Thus, your body will be better able to resist pathogens and noninfectious diseases. Exercise is also very important for maintaining your body's homeostasis. People who engage in regular physical activity, such as the student shown in **Figure 3,** improve their muscle strength, flexibility, cardiovascular health, and immune system response. People who exercise also strengthen their bones and improve the efficiency of their respiratory system.

❯ **Reading Check** *Explain why a healthy diet is necessary for maintaining the body's homeostasis.*

Figure 3 Exercise increases the health and strength of many of your body systems. ❯ **How does exercise help you avoid disease?**

www.scilinks.org
Topic: Disease
Code: HX80413

Section 1 Review

❯ KEY IDEAS

1. **Describe** what happens when the internal balance of human body systems is disrupted.
2. **Identify** three ways in which pathogens can be transmitted to humans.
3. **List** the actions that people can take to avoid many kinds of diseases.

CRITICAL THINKING

4. **Compare and Contrast** What do infectious diseases and noninfectious diseases have in common? What are their main differences?
5. **Inferring Relationships** Describe the relationship between a person's lifestyle and the ability of the person's body systems to maintain homeostasis.

CONNECTING KEY IDEAS

6. **Relating Concepts** Suppose that you touch an object that is contaminated by a pathogen. Explain how your skin can help your body maintain its homeostasis by providing protection from the pathogen.

Focus

This section focuses on infectious diseases and how they are spread by various pathogens.

 Bellringer

Use the Bellringer transparency to prepare students for this section.

Teach

Teaching Key Ideas

Current Infections Ask students to research current newspapers and magazines for articles that discuss any of the bacterial diseases shown in **Figure 4.** Create a class information center, such as a bulletin board, where students can post the latest information about research, outbreaks, controversies, and other details about the diseases.
LS Verbal/Visual

Answers to Caption Questions
Figure 4: bacterial meningitis

	Key Ideas	Key Terms	Why It Matters
	How do pathogenic bacteria cause disease?	toxin	You may not realize that your body is constantly under attack by other organisms. If they succeed in infecting you, your homeostasis and your health will suffer.
	Why do viruses cause damage to their hosts?		
	How are pathogenic fungi similar to pathogenic bacteria?		
	How do parasitic worms cause disease?		
	What diseases are caused by protists?		

Standard 4
5.2b Viruses, bacteria, fungi, and other parasites may infect plants and animals and interfere with normal life functions.

The term *pathogen* derives from Greek words that mean "the birth of pain." In this section, you will learn why pathogens have received such an ominous name.

Bacteria

Most bacteria are harmless to humans. Many are even helpful. However, a few bacteria can cause diseases that are as minor as acne or as deadly as anthrax. **Pathogenic bacteria cause disease by producing toxins and by destroying body tissues. Toxins** are poisonous chemicals. Most bacterial diseases, including several of the diseases listed in **Figure 4,** are caused when pathogenic bacteria release toxins inside their host. For example, botulism occurs when canned food is not heated enough to kill the bacterium *Clostridium botulinum.* When eaten, the bacteria begin to reproduce and release a toxin that destroys the tips of nerve cells. Paralysis can result.

A second way that bacteria cause disease is by producing enzymes that break down the host's tissues into nutrients that the bacteria can use. Tuberculosis, discussed on the next page, is an example of a disease caused by bacteria that break down tissue for its nutrients.

Figure 4 Many bacterial diseases, such as tooth decay, are very common.
Which bacterial disease listed in the table can lead to hearing loss?

Some Bacterial Diseases	
Disease	**Description**
Bacterial meningitis	infection of the fluid surrounding the brain and spinal cord; results in high fever, headache, and stiff neck and may lead to brain damage or hearing loss
Cholera	infection of the intestine by *Vibrio cholerae;* results in acute diarrhea, vomiting, and leg cramps and may lead to dehydration, shock, and death if not treated
Stomach ulcer	sore in the lining of the stomach; is usually caused by *Helicobacter pylori* and results in burning pain in the abdomen
Tetanus	body rigidity and convulsive spasms of the skeletal muscles caused by *Clostridium tetani*
Tooth decay	a hole (cavity) in the tooth formed by bacteria that live in dental plaque and produce acids that demineralize tooth enamel

Section Correlations
4.5.2b

 Key Resources

Transparencies
F4 *Escherichia coli*
F6 Important Bacterial Diseases
F10 Important Viral Diseases
F11 Structure of HIV
F19 Diseases Caused by Protists
F29 Life Cycle of *Plasmodium*
H21 Life Cycle of Schistosoma
H22 Life Cycle of Beef Tapeworm

Visual Concepts
Bacteria and Food
AIDS (Acquired Immune Deficiency Syndrome)
Anatomy of a Tapeworm
Life Cycle of Tapeworms
Life Cycle of Flukes
Malaria
Malaria Life Cycle

Tuberculosis About 2 million people die from tuberculosis every year. Tuberculosis is a disease caused by the bacterium *Mycobacterium tuberculosis.* This bacterium can attack any organ, but it usually infects the lungs. As the bacteria feed off of nutrients in the lung tissue, they can make a hole in the alveoli. As a result, the lungs' efficiency in gas exchange decreases, and homeostasis is disrupted. The lungs must then work harder to obtain the oxygen needed by the body's cells. Yet because tuberculosis often causes coughing and painful breathing, it is difficult for the lungs to work harder. In the end, the body is not able to get as much oxygen as it needs. The effects of this oxygen shortage are fatigue and, in some cases, a loss in appetite. In turn, other body systems become weakened. The infection may spread to other tissues in the body and may cause damage similar to the damage that the bacteria cause in the lungs. If the infection is not treated, the person eventually may die.

Lyme Disease Lyme disease is the most common insect-borne disease in the United States and is caused by the bacterium *Borrelia burgdorferi.* The main vector of the bacterium is the blacklegged tick, such as the one shown in **Figure 5.** Like the bacterium that causes tuberculosis, the bacterium that causes Lyme disease feeds off of the tissues of its host. The bacterium mostly attacks the nervous system and the blood vessels that supply this system. The results of this untreated infection in the nervous system include concentration problems, loss of memory, muscle weakness or paralysis, tingling and numbness in the arms, headaches, and severe joint pain. None of these symptoms is severe enough to cause death, but the disease does disrupt homeostasis and make physical activity difficult. A lack of physical activity can cause a decline in the health of other body systems, including the muscular and cardiovascular systems.

Acne Acne is not as serious as tuberculosis or Lyme disease, but it is probably a bacterial infection with which you are familiar. Acne results when hair follicles become clogged with oil, dead skin cells, and bacteria. These bacteria produce toxins that attract white blood cells. The white blood cells cause the tissue around the follicle to become inflamed, as **Figure 6** shows. A pimple or cyst can form around the inflamed follicle. When the pimple or cyst bursts, the skin may scar. In addition, if the bursting causes an open wound on the skin, other pathogens may enter the body. Thus, it is important that people with acne avoid deliberately bursting their acne lesions.

❯ **Reading Check** *Compare the causes of, symptoms of, and organs affected by tuberculosis and Lyme disease.*

Figure 5 When this blacklegged tick feeds on the blood of a mouse, a squirrel, or another animal infected with the bacteria that cause Lyme disease, the tick takes the bacteria into its body.

toxin a substance that is produced by one organism and that is poisonous to other organisms

Figure 6 Oil glands are especially active during adolescence. Therefore, teenagers are more likely to suffer from acne than adults are.

Quick Lab

Teacher's Notes You may want to make sure that students understand that each colored band represents the total number of human cases of bird flu in that country. For example, in April, there was only one human case of bird flu in Djibouti, not three.

Answers to Analysis

1. Azerbaijan, Cambodia, China, Egypt, Indonesia
2. ten

Teaching Key Ideas

Influenza Commonly called the flu, influenza has been perhaps the most lethal viral disease in human history. Because the influenza virus is airborne, it is highly contagious. A common flu virus can be lethal to people who have respiratory ailments or compromised immune systems, as well as to elderly people and young children. Tell students that every year in the United States about 5 to 20 percent of the population gets influenza and more than 200,000 people are hospitalized because of it. About 36,000 people die from it. Sometimes a new type of flu virus emerges that is very harmful. For example, in 1918 and 1919, a new type of influenza killed 22 million people—more people than were killed in combat during World War I.

Explain that flu spreads from person to person when those infected with the disease cough or sneeze. Ask students how a person can best prevent contracting the flu. (Get a flu vaccine; avoid contact with infected people; wash hands frequently; and avoid touching eyes, nose, or mouth.) **LS Intrapersonal**

Data

QuickLab

⏱ 15 min

Emergence of Bird Flu 🖐 4.5.2a

Although bird flu infection is rare in humans, the disease has emerged in several countries. This graph identifies the onset of new cases in the first half of 2006.

Analysis

1. **Identify** the countries in which new cases of humans infected with bird flu appeared in March 2006.
2. **Calculate** the total number of new cases that appeared in China between January and April 2006.

Human Cases of Bird Flu

Legend:
- Turkey
- Iraq
- Indonesia
- Egypt
- Djibouti
- China
- Cambodia
- Azerbaijan

X-axis: Number of Cases (0, 5, 10, 15, 20, 25)
Y-axis: January 2006, February 2006, March 2006, April 2006

SC **LINKS**
www.scilinks.org
Topic: Emerging Viruses
Code: HX80499

Viruses

Viruses cause many diseases, such as flu, chickenpox, and viral hepatitis, in humans. Typically, a virus infects a specific organ of the body. For example, flu infects the lungs, and hepatitis viruses infect the liver. Viruses are passed to humans by sneezing or coughing, sexual contact, sharing blood products, or the bite of insect vectors, such as mosquitoes.

Viruses cannot reproduce on their own. ❯ **Instead, viruses must use a living cell to reproduce. This process damages or destroys the living cell.** A viral infection begins when the virus's genetic material enters a host cell. The virus then uses the host's organelles to replicate the virus's genetic material and to make proteins. The proteins are then assembled with the viral DNA to form new complete viruses. The host cell dies and breaks open, and the newly made viruses are released. If the new viruses infect other cells, they may kill the cells and spread the infection. A viral infection disrupts homeostasis if it destroys cells faster than the body can replace them.

HIV In an HIV infection, the destruction of the T cells of the immune system results in the disruption of the body's homeostasis. T cells, a type white blood cells, normally defend the body against pathogens. If enough T cells are destroyed, the body cannot defend itself against infection. The person who has an HIV infection often becomes ill from other infectious diseases until his or her body systems are overwhelmed and cease to function. You can read more about how HIV infects and destroys T cells in the Up Close feature.

Bird Flu Bird flu is an infection caused by avian influenza viruses. These viruses generally infect birds. So far, bird flu does not seem to be spread from one person to another. However, because many viruses mutate easily, this situation could change and result in a global flu epidemic. In 2005, a new form of bird flu appeared in Asia and then spread to other parts of the world. The symptoms of this form of bird flu are similar to those of the common flu but are much more severe. Like the common flu, bird flu infects the respiratory tract. For an unknown reason, though, the bird flu virus sets off a violent immune response. The body's airways become highly inflamed, so breathing becomes very difficult. Without immediate medical attention, the person may suffocate and die.

❯ **Reading Check** *How does viral reproduction damage a host cell?*

Differentiated Instruction

Basic Learners

County Health Department Ask a county public health official to speak to your class about the kind of work the county public health department does to prevent contagious diseases. Be sure to ask the speaker to discuss viral diseases that are of concern in your county (e.g., mosquito-transmitted viral encephalitis, TB, pertussis, influenza, and HIV). Check with your school's guidelines about the kinds of subject areas that are appropriate. Ask the speaker to bring samples of equipment that the county uses for health work. **LS Verbal**

Up Close HIV Reproduction

Human immunodeficiency virus (HIV) is the virus that causes acquired immune deficiency syndrome (AIDS). HIV is considered to be a pandemic, a worldwide epidemic. About 22 million people have died as a result of AIDS. Currently, an estimated 33 million to 46 million people worldwide are living with HIV. Several drugs are effective in slowing HIV, but there is no cure.

HIV

Full name: human immunodeficiency virus
Size: 110 to 128 nm
Habitat: human CD4+ T lymphocyte
Diet: none
Mode of nutrition: none

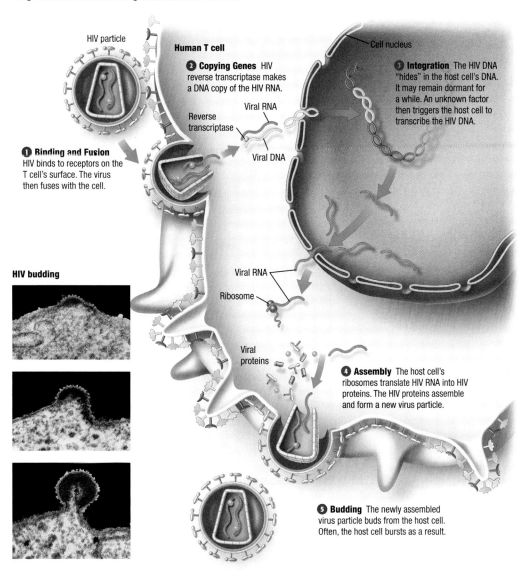

HIV particle

HIV budding

Human T cell

② Copying Genes HIV reverse transcriptase makes a DNA copy of the HIV RNA.

Reverse transcriptase

Viral RNA

Viral DNA

① Binding and Fusion HIV binds to receptors on the T cell's surface. The virus then fuses with the cell.

Cell nucleus

③ Integration The HIV DNA "hides" in the host cell's DNA. It may remain dormant for a while. An unknown factor then triggers the host cell to transcribe the HIV DNA.

Viral RNA

Ribosome

Viral proteins

④ Assembly The host cell's ribosomes translate HIV RNA into HIV proteins. The HIV proteins assemble and form a new virus particle.

⑤ Budding The newly assembled virus particle buds from the host cell. Often, the host cell bursts as a result.

Discussion

Why It Matters

Witches and Ergotism Ergot is the common name of the fungus *Claviceps purpurea,* which infects the seeds of rye, wheat, and other grains. Alkaloids produced by the fungus are derivatives of lysergic acid and, when eaten, may cause gangrene, convulsions, mental disturbances, and perceptual distortions. The symptoms are referred to as *ergotism,* or St. Anthony's fire. Scientists think that the accusers during the 1692 Salem witch trials in Massachusetts may have been suffering from ergotism.

Math Skills

Transmitting an Infection Tell students to imagine they have a fungal infection on their feet. One day in the locker room, they forget to wear their sandals. Five people are exposed to the fungus. The next day, each of those people exposes five more people to the fungus. If this pattern continues for five more days, how many people will be exposed to the fungus? (1st day: 5 people exposed; 2nd day: 25 (5^2) people exposed; 7th day: 78,125 (5^7) people exposed)

READING TOOLBOX

Classification Histoplasmosis is caused by a fungus. Elephantiasis is caused by a parasitic worm.

Figure 7 Ringworm is a fungal infection of the skin. The dried skin that falls off a sore is contaminated with fungal spores. These spores can infect other people or other areas of the body, such as the toenails. **>** Which body system does ringworm infect?

ACADEMIC VOCABULARY

via by way of

READING TOOLBOX

Classification Use the headings on this page to classify histoplasmosis and elephantiasis by the types of pathogens that causes these two diseases.

Fungi

The human body normally hosts a variety of fungi. Some of these organisms are useful to the body. Others are pathogenic and, if they multiply, may disrupt the body's homeostasis and may cause a disease. **>** Like pathogenic bacteria, pathogenic fungi cause disease by absorbing nutrients from the cells of the body and producing toxins. Some common fungal infections are discussed below.

Athlete's Foot and Ringworm Tinea is a fungus that infects the skin and nails and results in ringworm. Athlete's foot is a ringworm infection of the foot. **Figure 7** shows the red, itchy, and ring-shaped patch on the skin that a ringworm infection causes. These patches may blister and ooze. If the nails are infected, they may crumble. Ringworm can be passed <u>via</u> contact with an infected person or contaminated items, such as combs, clothing, towels, or showers.

Yeast Infection A yeast called *Candida albicans* is a normal resident of a healthy human body. This yeast has a mutualistic relationship with humans. It obtains nutrients from the food we eat, and in return, it makes toxins that can kill pathogens. Beneficial bacteria in the body keep the population of yeast in check. However, if these beneficial bacteria are disturbed or killed (for example, by taking antibiotics), the yeast may then grow out of control. The toxins made by a large population of yeast can cause diarrhea, sores on the skin or in the digestive tract, or a vaginal infection.

Histoplasmosis Fungal diseases that affect the internal organs can be very serious. Histoplasmosis is caused by *Histoplasmosis capsolatum,* which is found in soil, especially soil mixed with bat and bird feces. If the spores are inhaled, they cause severe respiratory illness and may infect the liver, heart, and central nervous system, too.

> **Reading Check** *How is homeostasis related to yeast infections?*

Why It Matters

Ascomycota Tell students that ascomycetes cause many plant diseases. However, ascomycetes are also known for an important contribution to human health. The fungus *Penicillium* is an ascomycete that has given us the antibiotic penicillin.

Parasitic Worms

> Flukes, tapeworms, and many species of roundworms are parasitic to humans. These worms cause disease by feeding off of the body and damaging tissues. Several serious diseases, including the three diseases discussed below, are caused by parasitic worms.

Hookworm Infection About 1 billion people are infected with hookworm, an intestinal parasite. Infection occurs when a person walks barefoot on soil that contains the worms' larvae. The larvae can penetrate the soles of the person's feet, enter the blood vessels, and be carried to the lungs. From the lungs, they migrate through tissue to the mouth and are swallowed. After reaching the small intestine, the larvae mature into adults and use sharp, teethlike structures on their mouth, shown in **Figure 8,** to latch onto the wall of the intestine. The worms then get their nourishment by sucking blood from the intestinal lining.

Symptoms of hookworm infection are cramps and mild diarrhea. Diarrhea, a symptom of many digestive tract diseases, is a way in which the body attempts to expel the pathogen and maintain homeostasis. Diarrhea can be dangerous to the body's homeostasis, though, because it causes the body to lose a large amount of water. However, in hookworm infections, the host rarely becomes dangerously dehydrated from diarrhea. It is more common for the host to develop anemia, a decrease in red blood cells that leads to fatigue and stress on body organs. Anemia is caused by blood loss to the worms.

Schistosomiasis *Schistosoma* flukes cause the disease schistosomiasis. This disease is common in tropical regions of Asia, Africa, and South America. Infection occurs when people use or wade in water contaminated by human feces or urine that contains the larvae of the *Schistosoma* flukes. First, the larvae bore through the skin. Then, they migrate via blood vessels to the lungs, intestines, bladder, or liver, where they mature and the females lay eggs. The eggs may block blood vessels in the affected organs. The eggs may also cause irritation, bleeding, and tissue decay in these organs. In rare cases, eggs may be laid in the blood vessels of the brain or spinal cord, and seizures or paralysis could result.

Elephantiasis Elephantiasis, shown in **Figure 9,** is the chronic, extreme swelling of the arms, breasts, legs, or male genitals and the hardening of nearby skin tissues. It is caused by years of repeated infections of the lymphatic system by small parasitic worms, known as *filarial worms*. The filiarial worms that cause elephantiasis are transmitted by the bite of an infected mosquito. The worms' larvae migrate into lymph vessels, where they mature into adults, mate, and produce many eggs. Over time, the lymph vessels become blocked and cannot function properly anymore. Because fluids in the area of the blocked vessels cannot drain, the surrounding tissues swell.

> **Reading Check** *How do* Schistosoma *flukes harm humans?*

These sharp structures are used to cut into the host's intestine.

Figure 8 A hookworm attaches itself to the wall of its host's intestine and feeds on the blood that oozes from the cut.

Figure 9 Elephantiasis is caused by the breakdown of the lymphatic system.
> **How is the breakdown of this woman's lymphatic system related to the swelling of her leg?**

Teaching Key Ideas

Disease Outbreaks Typically, diseases caused by protists occur because of unsafe food or other sanitary conditions. Have students form small groups and research to find examples of recent disease outbreaks. Have them prepare a short report on what they find.
LS Interpersonal

Answers to Caption Questions

Figure 10: Amebic dysentery causes diarrhea, which could lead to dehydration and the loss of large amounts of salt and other nutrients.

Figure 11: You can practice good hygiene, avoid eating undercooked meat, and avoid infected cats.

>Close

Formative Assessment

An example of a disease caused by a parasitic worm is _____.
A. ringworm (Incorrect. Ringworm is caused by a fungus.)
B. schistosomiasis (Correct! Schistosomiasis is caused by *Schistosoma* flukes.)
C. Lyme disease (Incorrect. Lyme disease is caused by a bacterium and transmitted through a vector, such as a tick.)
D. toxoplasmosis (Incorrect. Toxoplasmosis is caused by the protist *Toxoplasma gondii*.)

Figure 10 This table lists three common diseases caused by protists. > How could amebic dysentery disrupt a body's homeostasis?

Figure 11 *Toxoplasma gondii* is commonly found in cat feces. > How can you avoid contracting toxoplasmosis?

Some Diseases Caused by Protists

Disease	Description and cause
Amebic dysentery	bowel infection that is caused by amoebas and that results in diarrhea and intestinal sores
Chagas' disease	infection by *Trypanosoma cruzi*, which leads to heart disease and digestive abnormalities
Cryptosporidiosis	infection of the small intestine that is caused by *Cryptosporidium* sp. and that results in diarrhea

Protists

> Protists cause a number of human diseases, including giardiasis, amebic dysentery, toxoplasmosis, and malaria. Some pathogenic protists cause few or no symptoms. Others can cause diseases such as the ones in **Figure 10,** which can devastate body systems and kill a human host.

Giardiasis Giardiasis is a disease caused by intestinal parasites of the genus *Giardia*. The parasite enters the body when a person consumes contaminated food or water. The parasite then moves through the small intestine toward the large intestine. Symptoms are severe diarrhea and intestinal cramps. Though rarely fatal, the disease can affect one's homeostasis by disrupting one's water and salt balance.

Toxoplasmosis Toxoplasmosis, caused by *Toxoplasma gondii,* is spread by cysts. They can enter a body if one eats undercooked meat infected with cysts, consumes contaminated soil, or has frequent contact with cats. Infected cats, such as the one in **Figure 11,** have spores in their feces. Adults who have healthy immune systems are usually not affected by contact with the spores. In rare cases, flulike symptoms occur, and the nerves, brain, or eyes are damaged. A pregnant woman without symptoms can pass the infection to a fetus. The infant may develop central nervous system disorders, brain or eye damage, mental retardation, or an enlarged spleen and liver.

Section 2 Review

> **KEY IDEAS**
1. **Describe** how pathogenic bacteria can cause disease.
2. **Relate** viral reproduction to the pathogenic nature of viruses.
3. **Summarize** how pathogenic fungi are detrimental to human health.
4. **Describe** the path that a hookworm takes through the body when the worm infects a human.

5. **List** three protist diseases whose symptoms include diarrhea.

CRITICAL THINKING
6. **Integrating Information** Why are people infected with HIV more likely to contract other infectious diseases?
7. **Predicting Outcomes** What would happen to disease transmission if all drinking water were filtered and chlorinated and all people maintained good hygiene, cooked food thoroughly, and wore shoes?

ALTERNATIVE ASSESSMENT

8. **Communicating Information** Research an infectious disease. Then, make a brochure that explains the cause and symptoms of the disease, identifies where the disease commonly occurs, describes how the disease disrupts homeostasis, and lists some preventive measures that people can take to avoid contracting the disease.

Answers to Section Review

1. Pathogenic bacteria produce toxins that interfere with proper functioning of the body systems or manufacture enzymes that break down the host's body tissues. Both result in illness.

2. When a virus is finished reproducing within a host cell, the virus bursts and kills the cell. When this occurs many times, many cells die, disrupting the affected body system and resulting in illness.

3. Fungi steal nutrients from body cells and produce toxins, causing infection and sometimes severe symptoms.

4. When a person walks barefoot on soil contaminated with hookworm larvae, the larvae may penetrate the soles of the feet, enter blood vessels and are carried to the lungs. The larvae migrate to the mouth and are swallowed. They make their way through the digestive system, reaching the small intestine, where the larvae mature into adults and suck blood from the intestinal lining.

5. giardiasis, amebic dysentery, and cryptosporidiosis

6. People with suppressed immune systems cannot fight off disease as well as people with healthy immune systems.

7. Transmission of many of the infectious diseases would stop or be lessened dramatically.

8. Brochures will vary depending on the diseases students choose to feature.

Protist Plague

Malaria was eradicated from the United States in the 1950s. Yet today it is the third most deadly disease in the world. Up to 500 million people are infected. Up to 3 million die every year. A child dies from malaria every 30 seconds.

WEIRD SCIENCE

Malaria

Malaria is caused by several types of sporozoans of the genus *Plasmodium*. It is spread by the bite of the *Anopheles* mosquito. When an infected mosquito bites a human, it injects saliva containing the parasite.

The first stage of the malaria parasite, called a *sporozoite*, infects and destroys the liver's cells as it makes millions of copies of the second stage, called a *merozoite*. Merozoites infect red blood cells, in which they divide to make 8 to 24 more merozoites that burst out and destroy the cell. The new merozoites repeat the cycle of invading and destroying red blood cells every 48 to 72 hours.

The death of red blood cells causes anemia and cycles of fever. If left untreated, malaria can cause rupture of the spleen, kidney failure, coma, brain damage, and death.

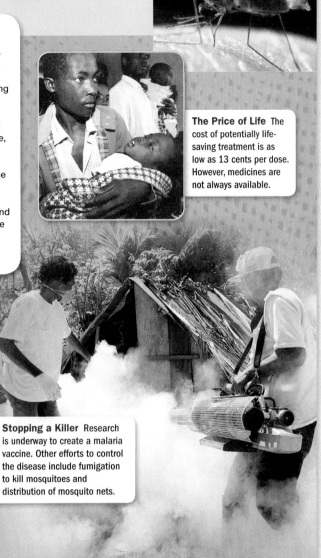

The Price of Life The cost of potentially life-saving treatment is as low as 13 cents per dose. However, medicines are not always available.

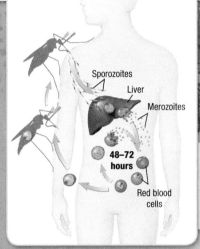

Sporozoites

Liver

Merozoites

48–72 hours

Red blood cells

Stopping a Killer Research is underway to create a malaria vaccine. Other efforts to control the disease include fumigation to kill mosquitoes and distribution of mosquito nets.

Research Use library and Internet sources to find out more about the efforts to eradicate malaria worldwide.

Teacher's Notes Explain that forty-one percent of the world's population live in areas where malaria is transmitted. These areas include Africa, Asia, the Middle East, Central and South America. Several species of *Anopheles* mosquitoes carry and spread the pathogen to humans while feeding on their blood. In tropical Africa, one person can receive more than 300 bites by infected mosquitoes per year. International researchers hope to introduce a pathogen-inhibiting gene into the genomes of these mosquitoes. Releasing transgenic mosquitoes to spread the new gene throughout the *Plasmodium*-carrying mosquito populations could help to combat malaria.

READING TOOLBOX

Visual Literacy Have the students examine the life cycle of *Plasmodium* in the feature. Point out the merozoites and the sporozoites. Be sure that students can differentiate these two stages. **LS Visual**

Answer to Research

Students will find that several strategies are being applied to combat malaria. The development of a malaria vaccine is underway, with several potential candidates. Efforts to prevent malaria by controlling mosquitoes include insecticide treated mosquito nets, indoor spraying of mosquito poison, insecticide to kill mosquito larvae, wearing protective clothing to avoid mosquito bites, and area-wide fogging with insecticide.

Noninfectious Diseases

❯ Focus

This section focuses on noninfectious diseases, including genetic disorders and diseases linked to personal behavior.

📻 Bellringer

Use the Bellringer transparency to prepare students for this section.

❯ Teach

Teaching Key Ideas

Long-Term Effects of Alcohol

Organize the class into four groups. Assign each group one of the following systems: circulatory, nervous, respiratory, and muscular. Have each group research how alcohol affects the assigned system and then present their information to the class. Students should give both an oral and a visual presentation.

LS Verbal/Interpersonal

Answers to Caption Questions

Figure 12: 28%

Key Ideas	Key Terms	Why It Matters
❯ How does personal behavior affect a person's health? ❯ How are genetic disorders transmitted? ❯ Why do some organs malfunction? ❯ What causes a nutritional disease? ❯ Why are toxic substances dangerous?	heart attack stroke	Who wouldn't avoid getting sick if they knew how? Many of the diseases that Americans have are noninfectious and can be avoided or managed by making healthier lifestyle choices.

Standard 4

2.2e Knowledge of genetics is making possible new fields of health care; for example, finding genes which may have mutations that can cause disease will aid in the development of preventive measures to fight disease. Substances, such as hormones and enzymes, from genetically engineered organisms may reduce the cost and side effects of replacing missing body chemicals.

5.2a Homeostasis in an organism is constantly threatened. Failure to respond effectively can result in disease or death.

5.2h Disease may also be caused by inheritance, toxic substances, poor nutrition, organ malfunction, and some personal behavior. Some effects show up right away; others may not show up for many years.

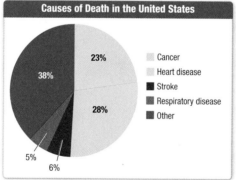

Causes of Death in the United States

23%
38%
28%
5%
6%

- Cancer
- Heart disease
- Stroke
- Respiratory disease
- Other

Source: Centers for Disease Control and Prevention, *National Vital Statistics Report*, 2003.

Take a look at **Figure 12,** which shows the major causes of death in the United States. The top four causes of death—heart disease, cancer, stroke, and respiratory disease—are noninfectious diseases. Personal behavior greatly influences the onset and course of all four of these diseases. Noninfectious diseases can also be caused by genetic diseases, organ malfunction, poor nutrition, or toxic substances in the environment.

Personal Behavior

❯**The majority of Americans die from heart disease, lung cancer, or other noninfectious diseases that are linked to personal behavior.** These diseases can be avoided or minimized by leading a healthy lifestyle. For example, the diet you maintain, the amount of exercise you do, and other personal choices directly affect the state of your health.

Alcoholism One personal choice that every person must face is whether to use drugs. Several drugs are legal for adults to use, but they still pose serious health dangers. Alcohol is one of these drugs. Currently, more than 17 million Americans abuse alcohol or suffer from alcoholism. Alcoholism is a disease in which a person has a strong need to drink despite bad consequences. Alcohol acts on the brain's neurons and thus disrupts cellular function. This disruption in function slows reaction times and decreases one's ability to judge situations. Therefore, it is no surprise that alcohol is a factor in almost half of all U.S. traffic deaths. Alcohol abuse can also cause long-term damage. Heavy drinking can increase the risk for certain cancers and can cause liver cirrhosis, hypertension, dementia, and heart disease.

❯ **Reading Check** *How can drinking alcohol affect the state of your health?*

Figure 12 Heart disease is the leading cause of death in the United States. ❯ What percentage of deaths in the United States are caused by heart disease?

Section Correlations

4.2.2e
4.5.2a
4.5.2h

Key Resources

 Transparencies
J77 Effects of Blood Alcohol Concentration
C28 Pedigree for Cystic Fibrosis
C30 Some Important Genetic Disorders
J44 Nutrition Label
J45 Nutrients in Food
J46 Vitamins

Visual Concepts
Alcoholism
Heart Attack
Stroke
Emphysema
Lung Cancer
Genetic Disorder
Sickle Cell Anemia
Types of Nutrients

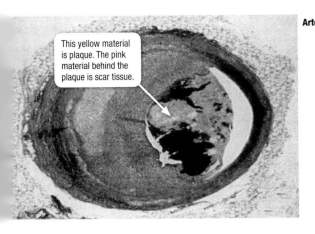

This yellow material is plaque. The pink material behind the plaque is scar tissue.

Artery wall

Human heart

If an artery supplying the heart, such as this one, is blocked, a heart attack will occur.

Figure 13 Heart attacks and most strokes occur when a vessel supplying the heart or brain becomes blocked with plaque.

heart attack the death of heart tissues due to a blockage of their blood supply

stroke a sudden loss of consciousness or paralysis that occurs when the blood flow to the brain is interrupted

Figure 14 This tumor was surgically removed from a lung cancer victim. Only about 15% of lung cancer victims live more than five years after diagnosis.

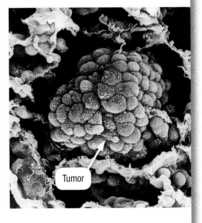

Tumor

Cardiovascular Disease The causes of cardiovascular disease include alcohol and tobacco use, a diet high in fat, and a genetic predisposition. Cardiovascular disease is so deadly because it can result in the blood supply being cut off to part of the heart, an event called a **heart attack,** or to part of the brain, an event called a **stroke.** Unlike many other diseases, which slowly disrupt homeostasis, a heart attack or stroke immediately disables the heart or part of the brain and thus causes a sudden threat to all other systems in the body. Without the heart pumping blood through the body, tissues can suffocate in minutes. Without the brain acting as a control center, feedback mechanisms quickly break down.

Most heart attacks and strokes are the result of high blood pressure and the buildup of plaque (deposits of fats and other materials) on vessel walls. By causing the heart to work harder than it normally does, high blood pressure weakens the heart and damages arteries. As **Figure 13** shows, plaque can narrow artery walls. If a blood clot breaks off from a blood vessel wall, it may get stuck in a narrow blood vessel. The stuck clot may cut off blood flow to part of the body. If a blood clot gets stuck in the vessels of the heart, a heart attack occurs. If a clot blocks blood supply to the brain, a stroke occurs.

Emphysema and Lung Cancer A heart attack kills by depriving cells of oxygen. Most lung diseases kill in the same way—but at a slower rate. One reason that lung diseases are more common today than 100 years ago is that more people smoke now. In fact, smoking causes up to 90% of all cases of emphysema and lung cancer.

In emphysema, the lungs' normally elastic alveoli become brittle and break. Over time, the alveoli become larger and less efficient. The lack of oxygen that results leads to fatigue and breathlessness.

In lung cancer, which causes about 28% of all deaths due to cancer in the United States, lung cells begin to grow at an abnormal rate. The abnormal cell growth causes tumors, which take away resources from the body. A tumor is shown in **Figure 14.**

Teaching Key Ideas

Sickle Cell Anemia Draw students' attention to **Figure 15**. Point out to students the shape of the normal and sickled red blood cells. Tell students that the sickled cells are actually longer than the normal red blood cells. Remind students that the capillaries are barely wide enough for normal red blood cells to move through them. Ask students what they think would happen when sickled cells travel through blood capillaries. (They can become caught in the capillary walls and block blood flow.)

Answers to Caption Questions

Figure 15: The sickle-shaped RBC has pointed tips that could easily get caught in bends of the vessels or at junctions between two or more capillaries.

Why It Matters

Sickle Cell Anemia Sickle cell anemia is the most common inherited blood disorder in the United States, affecting about 72,000 Americans. It is characterized by episodes of pain, chronic anemia, and severe infections. Sickle cell anemia is a recessive disease caused by a single mutation in one of the hemoglobin genes. A *carrier* of the genetic disorder is a person with only one copy of the gene. The normal copy prevents a person from being severely affected by the disease. There is a significantly higher percentage of carriers of sickle cell anemia in zones of high malaria incidence. This occurs because carriers are somewhat protected against malaria.

SCILINKS.
www.scilinks.org
Topic: Genetic Diseases
Code: HX80650

Figure 15 One out of every 500 African Americans has sickle cell disease, which is caused by a gene mutation that produces a defective form of hemoglobin. **>** Why is a sickle-shaped red blood cell more likely to block a capillary than a normal red blood cell is?

This RBC has been stretched out of shape by long chains of abnormal hemoglobin.

Inheritance

As previous chapters have explained, for a person to develop and function normally, the proteins encoded by his or her genes must work correctly. Proteins that do not perform their jobs properly compromise the body's homeostasis. Unfortunately, sometimes genes are damaged or copied incorrectly. These faulty genes may cause a genetic disease. **>** Genetic diseases are passed on through heredity rather than through a pathogen. Two common genetic diseases—cystic fibrosis and sickle cell disease—are discussed below.

Cystic Fibrosis Cystic fibrosis is one of the most common fatal genetic diseases among Caucasians. About 1 in 2,500 Caucasian infants is born with the illness. Cystic fibrosis occurs when a person inherits two copies of a defective gene for a certain protein. One copy comes from the mother; the other, from the father. Ordinarily, this protein moves salt into and out of cells. In people with two copies of the defective gene for this protein, the body's cells make a thick, sticky mucus. The mucus builds up in the pancreas and in breathing passages of the lungs. When mucus clogs the pancreas, the pancreas cannot perform its role in food digestion. Malnutrition, bowel problems, and weight loss may result. When mucus clogs the lungs, the results are respiratory system problems, lung damage, and infections.

Sickle Cell Disease Red blood cells (RBCs) are normally disk shaped. However, in people who have sickle cell disease, the RBCs often become crescent (sickle) shaped. The sickling is caused by a mutation in the gene that produces hemoglobin, a protein that enables RBCs to carry oxygen. The mutated gene produces defective hemoglobin that sticks together inside of a RBC to form long chains of the protein. By stretching out the RBC, the chains cause the RBC to sickle, as **Figure 15** shows. The sickle-shaped cell can get lodged in small vessels and can disrupt blood flow. Without enough blood, tissues in the affected region can become damaged. When blood flow is interrupted repeatedly, damage to many body systems can occur.

The long chains of hemoglobin can cause other problems, as well. When the chains stretch and pull the RBC's cell membrane, they can cause the membrane to weaken and to leak nutrients. This weakening leads to the cell's early death. While normal RBCs live about 120 days, sickle-cell RBCs live only about 16 days. A person who has sickle cell disease develops a severe anemia because too few RBCs are in the bloodstream to meet the oxygen needs of all of the body's cells.

> **Reading Check** *How might sickle cell disease disrupt a body's homeostasis?*

Differentiated Instruction

Alternative Assessment

Understanding Hereditary Diseases Label shoe boxes with the following diseases: Huntington's disease, hemophilia, sickle cell anemia, cystic fibrosis, and Down syndrome. Give students squares of blue paper and squares of red paper. Tell students to place a red square in a box if they know somebody who has that disease and a blue square if they have heard of the disease but don't know anyone with the disease. Afterward, count the number of colored paper squares for each disease. Have students research the disease with the most red squares. **LS** Interpersonal

Organ Malfunction

Homeostasis is dependent upon all of the body or organ systems working together. What affects one system will affect others, which in turn affect still other organ systems. Thus, your organs are very important to homeostasis and your well-being. ❯ Organs malfunction for a variety of reasons, including birth defects, trauma, and aging.

Birth Defects A birth defect is an abnormality of structure, function, or metabolism and is present at birth. Some birth defects are caused by genetic disorders, but birth defects can also be caused by environmental factors, such as drug or alcohol abuse by a pregnant woman. For example, when a pregnant woman drinks alcohol, the development of her baby's body systems may be affected. The baby may develop fetal alcohol syndrome (FAS). FAS is characterized by a cluster of related problems, including abnormal facial features, faulty enamel on teeth, heart defects, bones that are deformed, nearsightedness, and behavioral problems.

Trauma Trauma, such as what happens in an automobile accident or a fall, can damage the body's organs. In a serious motor vehicle accident, injury to the brain and spinal cord are common and can be devastating. Brain damage, coma, paralysis, concussion, and death are possible. The body may also collide with the steering wheel. Such a collision may cause blunt force trauma to internal organs and the skeletal system. Wearing a seat belt and driving a car equipped with air bags help make severe injury less likely.

Aging Machinery, such as a car, becomes less efficient as it ages. So do the organs of the human body. Older people are not as strong and flexible and do not heal as well as younger people. Because of this, aging can lead to many diseases. Osteoporosis, for example, is a disease associated with aging. It is characterized by the thinning and weakening of bones. Osteoporosis increases the risk of bone fractures. The man in **Figure 16** is suffering from osteoporosis.

❯ **Reading Check** *How can trauma affect the body's organs?*

READING TOOLBOX

Two-Column Notes Use the headings on this page to find examples that support the key idea.

Why It Matters

Exercise and Healthy Bones Exercise becomes especially important as people grow older, when bone mass begins to decrease due to hormonal and other physiological changes. Two types of exercises are important for maintaining healthy bones: weight-bearing and resistance exercises. Weight-bearing exercises are exercises in which your bones and muscles bear your body weight and include activities such as jogging, walking, and dancing. Resistance exercises involve using the bones and muscles to work against a force or weight and include activities such as using free weights and weight machines found at gyms and health clubs.

Teacher's Notes Review with students how to interpret a Nutrition Facts label. Ask the following: "What is the serving size?" (2 oz) "How many Calories are in one serving?" (210) "Is this food a good source of vitamin C?" (no) "Does this food contain cholesterol?" (no) "How much of the carbohydrate content is fiber?" (2 g) "What percentage of the Daily Value (DV) of iron does this food provide?" (10%)

Answers to Analysis

1. 10 Cal / 210 Cal × 100 = 4.76% or about 5%
2. 2 g / 30 g × 100 = 6.66% or about 7%

Answers to Caption Questions

Figure 17: All three of these diseases are eating disorders which result in a person not obtaining the correct amount of nutrients needed for the body to stay healthy.

Teaching Key Ideas

Obesity Being obese or overweight have been shown to increase the risk for developing type 2 diabetes, heart disease, some forms of cancer, and other disabling medical conditions. An estimated 65 percent of U.S. adults are overweight or obese. This figure includes over 60 million who are obese. Over 9 million children and teens are considered overweight. The percentage of overweight children and adolescents has more than tripled since 1980. **LS** Logical

---

Data

QuickLab

🕐 15 min

The Nutrition Facts Label

The Nutrition Facts label provides a convenient source of nutritional information about foods and can help you see how a food fits into your daily diet. It lists the number of Calories and quantity of nutrients per serving size. Nutrients are listed by weight and as a percentage of the daily values for a 2,000 Cal diet. Daily values (DVs) are recommended daily amounts of nutrients.

Analysis

1. **Calculate** the percentage of the food's total Calories that come from fat according to the label shown here.

Nutrition Facts	Amount/serving	%DV*	Amount/serving	%DV*
Serv. size 2 oz (56g/ box) Servings per container 8	**Total fat** 1g	1%	**Total carb.** 43g	14%
	Saturated fat 0g	0%	Dietary fiber 2g	8%
	Trans fat 0g		Sugars 3g	
Calories 210 Fat Cal. 10	**Cholesterol** 0mg	0%	**Protein** 6g	
	Sodium 0mg	0%		
Percent Daily Values (DV) are based on a 2,000 Calorie diet.	Vitamin A 0% • Vitamin C 0% • Calcium 2% • Iron 10% Thiamin 30% • Riboflavin 10% • Niacin 15%			

2. **CRITICAL THINKING** **Applying Information** If your diet requires 30 g of fiber, what percentage of the daily value for fiber does one serving of this food provide?

Poor Nutrition

Your body needs a great deal of energy to maintain its temperature, which is an important aspect of homeostasis. Food supplies this energy. Food also supplies the building blocks needed to build your cells and tissues. For you to stay healthy, your body requires specific amounts of certain nutrients. **> If you ingest too few or too many of the necessary nutrients, you could develop a nutritional disease.**

Eating Disorders Eating disorders are extremely common among Americans. The most common eating disorder by far is overeating, which leads to obesity. The extra weight carried by people who are obese, such as the woman in **Figure 17,** increases the risk of heart disease and diabetes. Two other eating disorders are bulimia and anorexia nervosa. In bulimia, a person avoids weight gain by purging the food that he or she eats. Damage to the digestive system results. In anorexia nervosa, a person undereats to maintain a below-average weight. This disorder causes anemia, a weakened immune system, and, in some cases, kidney failure.

Vitamin Deficiencies Vitamins are needed for metabolic reactions. Most vitamins are obtained from food. If your diet lacks the right vitamins, some metabolic reactions will slow or stop. Homeostasis will be disturbed, and you may fall ill. One disease caused by a vitamin deficiency is scurvy. Specifically, scurvy is due to a diet low in vitamin C. Without vitamin C, one's tissues begin to break down. Early symptoms of scurvy include bleeding gums and joint pain.

> Reading Check *Relate eating disorders to a person's personal behavior.*

Figure 17 Currently, one of every three Americans has a body weight that is more than 20% greater than a weight that is considered healthy. **>** How is obesity related to anorexia nervosa and bulimia?

Differentiated Instruction

Alternative Assessment

Analyzing Eating Habits Have students access the Web site MyPyramid.gov, or provide copies of information from this site. Have them analyze their eating habits and propose changes, if needed, to bring their diets in line with the guidelines. **LS** Logical

Toxic Substances

Many common substances, such as the mouthwash shown in **Figure 18,** can be toxic to humans. **>Toxic substances have the ability to damage cells, tissues, organs, or entire body systems.** Most toxins enter the body through the mouth. From the mouth, the toxins travel to the stomach, where they may be absorbed into the bloodstream. In this way, toxins can travel throughout the body and can damage or interfere with every body system. Sometimes, the damage to a body system is so severe that death occurs. Toxic substances can be found everywhere. For instance, toxins are present in many types of household chemicals and even in some kinds of fungi.

Household Chemicals Substances around your house may contain toxic chemicals. For example, many homes have lead-based paints. Exposure to lead can cause high blood pressure, fertility problems, and nervous system disorders. Pesticides and weed killers also contain many toxic ingredients. These chemicals can harm humans by damaging the nervous system, irritating the skin or eyes, affecting the endocrine system, or causing cancer.

Toxic Fungi Many houses have damp areas, such as basements. In these areas, various types of molds can grow. Some of these molds may release spores that are toxic to humans. Asthma, bronchitis, and various other diseases are linked to inhaling toxic mold spores. Molds, mushrooms, and other fungi may also be toxic if they are eaten. For example, many species of the genus *Amanita* resemble edible mushrooms. However, they contain extremely dangerous toxins that quickly destroy a person's liver. Liver failure severely disrupts digestion and causes excessive bleeding because the liver no longer makes essential blood-clotting compounds.

> **Reading Check** *Explain how eating a mushroom of the genus* **Amanita** *can affect a person's homeostasis.*

Figure 18 If swallowed, mouthwash that contains alcohol is toxic to children. Each year, about 250 cases of mouthwash poisoning occur in the United States.

Section 3 Review

> **KEY IDEAS**

1. **List** three behaviors that can affect a person's health.
2. **Describe** the role that genes play in genetic disorders.
3. **Summarize** three ways in which organ malfunction can occur.
4. **Relate** the role of diet to nutritional diseases.

5. **State** the ways in which toxic substances may cause illness.

CRITICAL THINKING

6. **Comparing Effects** Explain how lifestyle choices can be important to the health of a person who has heart disease and to the health of a person who has diabetes.
7. **Relating Concepts** Can alcohol be considered a toxic substance in the same way that pesticides and poisonous mushrooms are? Explain your answer.

WRITING FOR SCIENCE

8. **Oral Report** Research a genetic disorder, such as polycystic kidney disease, familial dysautonomia, Huntington's disease, or hemophilia. Prepare a brief oral report. Discuss the genetic cause, the symptoms, the organ systems affected, and the treatment.

Answers to Section Review

1. Behaviors include diet, exercise, risk-taking behavior (drug use, drinking), hygiene, and smoking.
2. Errors in a gene's coding result in mistakes that affect cells, organs and body systems.
3. trauma, birth defects, or aging
4. Our bodies require the proper array and amount of nutrients in order to function properly. If our diet does not include the proper nutrients (or amounts), disease can occur.
5. Toxic substances are poisonous to cells, organs, and body systems. When these poisons damage parts of the body, illness results. Toxins from different sources affect different cells, organs, and, therefore, body systems.
6. A person with heart disease must make careful choices about diet and exercise so that the damage the disease causes does not progress (or progress as quickly). Proper diet is also important for a person with diabetes, as is good personal hygiene. Both need to have conscientious medical care.
7. Alcohol is toxic to the human body. Alcohol can damage body systems; so can pesticides and poisonous mushrooms.
8. Oral reports will vary depending on the genetic diseases that students choose to feature.

Lab

Time Required

One 45-minute class period and 10 minutes per day for seven consecutive days

Ratings

EASY ———————————→ HARD

Teacher Prep   🧪🧪
Student Setup   🧪🧪
Concept Level   🧪🧪🧪
Cleanup   🧪🧪

Safety Caution

Students must thoroughly wash their hands and all lab equipment that comes into contact with tobacco. Students should conduct this investigation away from gardens and house plants to prevent the spread of TMV. Students should wear disposable gloves, lab aprons, and goggles at all times during this lab. If dibasic sodium potassium phosphate solutions or carborundum powder get into a student's eye, flush immediately and seek medical attention.

Tips and Tricks

Preparation Tomato plants may be substituted for tobacco plants. To prepare 0.1 M dibasic potassium phosphate solution, use 6.8 g KH_2PO_4 and dilute to 500 mL with distilled water. Extract tobacco from cigarettes of various brands before lab. Prepare a mixture of tobacco from the various brands.

Lab Correlations

4.5.2j Biological research generates knowledge used to design ways of diagnosing, preventing, treating, controlling, or curing diseases of plants and animals.

Objectives

❯ Study the effect of cigarette tobacco on leaves of tomato plants.

❯ Observe how a viral infection affects plant tissues.

Materials

- lab apron
- protective gloves
- safety goggles
- tomato plants (2)
- glass-marking pencil
- tobacco from several brands of cigarettes
- mortar and pestle
- dibasic potassium phosphate solution, 0.1 M (10 mL)
- beaker, 100 mL
- cotton swabs
- carborundum powder, 400 grit

Safety

Tobacco Mosaic Virus

The tobacco mosaic virus (TMV) infects tobacco as well as other plants. Plants damaged by wind, low temperatures, injury, or insects are more susceptible to plant viruses than healthy plants are. Plants that are infected with TMV have lesions and yellow patches on their leaves. In this lab, you will study how a tomato plant can be infected with TMV and how the infection affects the plant.

Procedure

Set Up the Experiment

1 🔷 🔶 🔷 Put on a lab apron, gloves, and goggles before beginning this investigation.

2 Obtain two tomato plants that have not been infected with TMV. Label one plant "Control plant" and the other plant "Experimental plant."

3 🔷 🔷 **CAUTION: Use poisonous chemicals with extreme caution.** Keep your hands away from your face when handling plants or chemicals. Place pinches of tobacco from different brands of cigarettes into a mortar. Add 5 mL of dibasic potassium phosphate solution, and grind the mixture with a pestle as shown in the figure.

4 Pour the mixture into a labeled beaker. This mixture can be used to test whether cigarette tobacco can infect plants with TMV.

5 🔷 Wash your hands and all laboratory equipment used in the previous steps with soap and water to avoid the accidental spread of the virus.

Procedure Have students label the control and experimental plant immediately upon receiving them. To prevent contamination of the dibasic potassium phosphate solution, have students pour a small amount of the solution into a small container for their personal use. Alternatively, set out small bottles of the solution at each lab bench from which students can collect the solution. Have students prepare their data tables ahead of time.

Answers to Procedure

6. The carborundum powder abrades the leaf and facilitates infection.

6 Moisten a sterile cotton swab with the mixture, and sprinkle a small amount of carborundum powder onto the moistened swab. Apply the mixture to two leaves on the experimental plant by swabbing the surface of the leaves several times. Why might swabbing the leaves with carborundum powder facilitate infection?

7 Moisten a clean swab with dibasic potassium phosphate solution, and sprinkle a small amount of carborundum powder onto the moistened swab. This swab should *not* come into contact with the mixture of cigarette tobacco. Swab over the surface of two leaves on the control plant several times.

8 Do not allow the control plants to touch the experimental plants. Keep both plants away from other plants that may be in your investigation area, such as houseplants or garden plants. Wash your hands after handling each plant to avoid the accidental spread of TMV.

9 Treat both plants in precisely the same manner. The only difference between the two plants should be the experimental factor—exposure to cigarette tobacco. Both plants should receive the same amount of light and the same amount of water.

10 ◆ ❖ Clean up your materials according to your teacher's instructions, and wash your hands before leaving the lab.

Collect Data

11 In your lab report, create a data table similar to the table shown. Allow plenty of space to record your observations of each plant.

12 Check the control and experimental plants each day for one week. Record your observations of each plant in your lab report. To prevent contaminating your results, wash your hands after handling each plant.

Analyze and Conclude

1. **SCIENTIFIC METHODS** **Making Systematic Observations** What differences, if any, did you detect in the two plants after one week?

2. **Interpreting Observations** Did the plants exposed to cigarette tobacco become infected with the tobacco mosaic virus?

3. **SCIENTIFIC METHODS** **Critiquing Procedures** What are some possible sources of error in the experiment?

4. **Drawing Conclusions** Examine a plant that contracted TMV. How might the virus be affecting the plant's homeostasis?

5. **SCIENTIFIC METHODS** **Using Evidence to Support Arguments** Greenhouse operators generally do not allow smoking in their greenhouses for various reasons, including health and safety reasons. How might your results also support this practice?

Observations of Tomato Plants

Day	Control plant	Experimental plant
1		
2		
3		
4		
5		
6		
7		

*SCI**LINKS**.*

www.scilinks.org
Topic: Pathogens
Code: HX81118

Extensions

6. **Making Inferences** Why was it necessary to use tobacco from different brands of cigarettes?

7. **Designing Experiments** The tobacco mosaic virus is capable of infecting various species of plants. Design an experiment to determine which of several types of plants are susceptible to the tobacco mosaic virus.

Answers to Analyze and Conclude

1. Answers may vary. Sample answer: The experimental plant had blotches on its leaves. The leaves on the control plant were healthy.

2. Sample answer: Yes, the experimental plant became infected.

3. Errors could include insufficient grinding of tobacco to obtain virus, using an inappropriate amount of carborundum, uneven amounts or uneven application of virus mixture, insufficient sampling of each leaf type, and contamination of the control.

4. Sample answer: The TMV seems to cause damage to cells containing chlorophyll. This could lead to a decrease in the rate of photosynthesis that the plant is able to perform, thus causing the plant to not be able to produce enough sugars in order to stay healthy.

5. TMV in cigarettes or cigars may infect greenhouse plants.

Answers to Extensions

6. It increased the chance of obtaining TMV.

7. Designs will vary, but should be similar to this lab's procedures using a variety of other plants.

Key Resources

 Holt Lab Generator

 Lab Datasheet (Levels A, B, C)

 Holt Science Biology Video Labs

go.hrw.com
SUPER SUMMARY
Keyword: HX8DISS

SUPER SUMMARY

Have students connect the major concepts in this chapter through an interactive Super Summary. Visit **go.hrw.com** and type in the keyword **HX8DISS** to access the Super Summary for this chapter.

Reteaching Key Ideas

Graphic Organizer Have students prepare a graphic organizer that shows the main ideas and details presented in this section. Make sure students include the causes of disease, the spread of pathogens, and avoiding disease. **LS Visual**

Bacterial and Viral Diseases Ask students which of the following diseases are caused by bacteria (b) and which are caused by viruses (v): Lyme disease (b), measles (v), stomach ulcers (b), tetanus (b), Avian flu (v), AIDS (v), cervical cancer (v). Ask whether all the diseases can be cured by antibiotics. (no) Have students give their reasoning. (Antibiotics are not usually effective at curing viral infections.) **LS Logical**

Healthful Practices Have students work in pairs to summarize the benefits to the cardiovascular system of a healthful diet, regular exercise, and avoiding tobacco and alcohol. **LS Verbal**

Key Ideas

1 Disease

> Disease is caused by a disruption in a human body system that leads to a corresponding disruption in homeostasis.

> Pathogens can be spread through the air, through contact with contaminated objects or an infected organism, through the ingestion of contaminated food or water, or through vectors.

> You can maintain your homeostasis and can avoid many diseases by practicing good hygiene, avoiding close contact with infected organisms, maintaining a healthy diet, and exercising on a regular basis.

2 Infectious Diseases

> Pathogenic bacteria cause disease by producing toxins and by destroying body tissues.

> Viruses must use a living cell to reproduce. This process damages or destroys the living cell.

> Like pathogenic bacteria, pathogenic fungi cause disease by absorbing nutrients from the cells of the body and producing toxins.

> Flukes, tapeworms, and many species of roundworms are parasitic to humans. These worms cause disease by feeding off of the body and damaging tissues.

> Protists cause a number of human diseases, including giardiasis, amebic dysentery, toxoplasmosis, and malaria.

3 Noninfectious Diseases

> The majority of Americans die from heart disease, lung cancer, or other noninfectious diseases that are linked to personal behavior.

> Genetic diseases are passed on through heredity rather than through a pathogen.

> Organs malfunction for a variety of reasons, including birth defects, trauma, and aging.

> If you ingest too few or too many of the necessary nutrients, you could develop a nutritional disease.

> Toxic substances have the ability to damage cells, tissues, organs, or entire body systems.

Key Terms

noninfectious disease (499)
infectious disease (499)
pathogen (499)
vector (500)

toxin (502)

heart attack (511)
stroke (511)

PART A: Answer all questions in this part.

Directions: For each statement or question, write on your separate answer sheet the number of the word or expression that best completes the statement or answers the question.

1 The presence of parasites in an animal will usually result in
   (1) an increase in meiotic activity within structures of the host
   (2) the inability of the host to maintain homeostasis
   (3) the death of the host organism within twenty-four hours
   (4) an increase in genetic mutation rate in the host organism

2 Blood can be tested to determine the presence of the virus associated with the development of AIDS. This blood test is used directly for
   (1) cure.
   (2) treatment.
   (3) diagnosis.
   (4) prevention.

3 The diagram below represents two single-celled organisms. These organisms carry out the activities needed to maintain homeostasis by using specialized internal

   (1) tissues.
   (2) organelles.
   (3) systems.
   (4) organs.

4 The use of a vaccine to stimulate the immune system to act against a specific pathogen is valuable in maintaining homeostasis because
   (1) once the body produces chemicals to combat one type of virus, it can more easily make antibiotics.
   (2) the body can digest the weakened microbes and use them as food.
   (3) the body will be able to fight invasions by the same type of microbe in the future.
   (4) the more the immune system is challenged, the better it performs.

5 Botulism can cause paralysis because a toxin
   (1) can poison the blood.
   (2) can damage the heart.
   (3) can destroy the tips of nerve cells.
   (4) can stress the body and can enable other infectious agents to grow.

6 Which two fungal infections are caused by the same type of fungus?
   (1) athlete's foot and histoplasmosis
   (2) athlete's foot and hookworm
   (3) athlete's foot and ringworm
   (4) hookworm and ringworm

7 Causes of cardiovascular disease include all of the following *except*
   (1) fungal infection.
   (2) tobacco use.
   (3) genetic predisposition.
   (4) a high-fat diet.

8 Which of the following is *not* a lifestyle choice that can help you maintain your body's homeostasis and avoid many diseases?
   (1) avoiding close contact with infected animals or people
   (2) exercising regularly and maintaining a healthy diet
   (3) practicing good hygiene, such as washing hands often
   (4) drinking alcohol heavily and using tobacco products

PART A

1. **(2)** A parasite generallly does not kill its host quickly, but it does cause the host to lose the ability to maintain homeostasis. A parasite does not affect the rate of meiosis or genetic mutation within a host. *(#25, January 2003 Regents Exam)*

2. **(3)** A blood test to determine the presence of the AIDS virus is a diagnostic tool. If the virus is detected, treatment can begin. Prevention is an action that stops the virus from entering the body. The virus can be isolated in a laboratory so that scientists can work on a cure for AIDS. *(#19, January 2003 Regents Exam)*

3. **(2)** Single-celled organisms do not have tissues, organs, or systems. They have organelles that have similar functions to organs and organ systems. *(#06, January 2004 Regents Exam)*

4. **(3)** The body does not produce antibiotics. The body does not digest weakened microbes and use them as food. Challenging the immune system does not necessarily make it "perform better". Challenging the body with a vaccine causes the body to produce antibodies against the microbial antigens in the vaccine. The body will be ready to fight against an invasion of the same microbes in the future. *(#17, August 2004 Regents Exam)*

5. **(3)**

6. **(3)**

7. **(1)**

8. **(4)**

Regents Exam Practice Correlations

4.1.2d 9, 12		**4.5.2e** 4	
4.1.2e 10		**4.5.2h** 13	
4.1.3a 3		**4.5.2j** 2, 11	
4.5.2a 1			

9. (3) The increase in temperature between points C and D moved the body out of homeostasis, disrupting its dynamic equilibrium. The decrease in temperature between points D and E moved the body back into homeostasis. *(#09, January 2003 Regents Exam)*

PART B

10. (2) The biofilms include tubes that carry in nutrients into the colony and to carry wastes out. These tubes have a similar function to the human circulatory and excretory systems. *(#33, June 2004 Regents Exam)*

PART C

11. Allow a maximum of 3 credits, 1 each for the name of the genetic disorder, the technique used in diagnosis, and one characteristic of the disorder. Acceptable responses include, but are not limited to: sickle cell anemia, microscopic examination of blood, low oxygen supply to the cells; Down syndrome, karyotype analysis, mental retardation; PKU, urine analysis, mental retardation. *(#67, January 2003 Regents Exam)*

12. Allow a maximum of 3 credits, allocated as follows: Allow 1 credit for stating a malfunction associated with the selected system. Acceptable responses include, but are not limited to: digestive - ulcer; circulatory - heart attack; respiratory - emphysema; excretory - kidney stones; nervous - Parkinson's disease. Allow 1 credit for stating a direct or indirect cause of the malfunction identified. Acceptable responses include, but are not limited to: ulcer - excess stomach acid; heart attack - high fat diet; emphysema - smoking; kidney stones - genetic causes; Parkinson's disease - brain stops making a sufficient supply of a critical chemical (dopamine). Allow 1 credit for stating the effect the malfunction has on any other system. Acceptable responses include, but are not limited to: ulcer - causes bleeding; heart attack - reduces oxygen to the brain; emphysema - reduces oxygen in the circulatory system; kidney stones - stimulates nervous system resulting in pain;

9 The data in the graph below show evidence of disease in the human body. A disruption in dynamic equilibrium is indicated by the temperature change between points

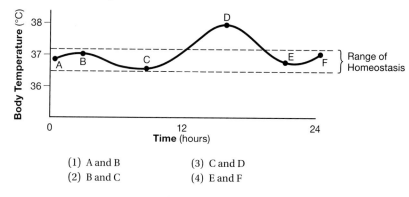

(1) A and B   (3) C and D
(2) B and C   (4) E and F

PART B

Base your answer to question 10 on the passage below and on your knowledge of biology.

. . . Some of the most common and deadly bacteria do their mischief by forming a sticky scum called biofilm. Individually, the microbes are easy to control, but when they organize themselves into biofilms they can become deadly, said Dr. Barbara Iglewski of the University of Rochester. . . .

Biofilms are actually intricately organized colonies of billions of microbes, all working in a coordinated way to defend against attack and to pump out a toxin that can be deadly.

Once they are organized, the bacteria are highly resistant to antibiotics and even strong detergents often cannot wash them away or kill them.

Iglewski and colleagues from Montana State University and the University of Iowa report in *Science* that they discovered how the microbes in the colonies communicate and found that once this conversation is interrupted, the deadly bugs can be easily washed away.

Using *Pseudomonas aeruginosa,* a common bacteria that is a major infection hazard in hospitals and among cystic fibrosis patients, the researchers isolated a gene that the bacteria uses to make a communications molecule. The molecule helps the microbes organize themselves into a biofilm — a complex structure that includes tubes to carry in nutrients and carry out wastes, including deadly toxins.

In their study, the researchers showed that if the gene that makes the communications molecule was blocked, the *Pseudomonas aeruginosa* could form only wimpy [weak], unorganized colonies that could be washed away with just a soap that has no effect on a healthy colony. . . .

Adapted from: Paul Recer, "Researchers find new means to disrupt attack by microbes," *The Daily Gazette,* April 26, 1998.

Parkinson's disease - involuntary muscle contractions. *(#66, January 2003 Regents Exam)*

10 The tubes in biofilms function much like the human

(1) muscular and nervous systems.

(2) circulatory and excretory systems.

(3) digestive and endocrine systems.

(4) reproductive and respiratory systems.

PART C

11 Biological research has generated knowledge used to diagnose genetic disorders in humans. Explain how a specific genetic disorder can be diagnosed. Your answer must include at least:

- the name of a genetic disorder that can be diagnosed
- the name or description of a technique used to diagnose the disorder
- a description of one characteristic of the disorder

12 Select one human body system from the list below.

Body Systems
Digestive
Circulatory
Respiratory
Excretory
Nervous

Describe a malfunction that can occur in the system chosen. Your answer must include at least:

- the name of the system and a malfunction that can occur in this system
- a description of a possible cause of the malfunction identified
- an effect this malfunction may have on any other body system

13 Not all diseases are caused by pathogenic organisms. Other factors, such as inheritance, poor nutrition, and toxic substances, may also cause disease. Describe a disease or disorder that can occur as a result of one of these other factors. Your answer must include at least:

- the name of the disease
- one specific factor that causes this disease
- one major effect of this disease on the body, other than death
- one way this disease can be prevented, treated, or cured

PART D

Base your answers to the following questions on your knowledge of biology.

14 How might the current epidemic of obesity in the United States be related to the increases in portion sizes served at restaurants?

15 The drug AZT works by blocking the enzyme reverse transcriptase. Explain how AZT can help patients infected with HIV.

13. Allow a maximum of 4 credits for describing a disease or disorder that can occur as a result of a factor other than a pathogenic organism, allocated as follows: Allow 1 credit for the name of the disease or disorder; Allow 1 credit for one specific factor that causes this disease or disorder; Allow 1 credit for one major effect of this disease or disorder on the body, other than death; Allow 1 credit for one way this disease or disorder can be prevented, treated, or cured. Examples of 4-credit responses: PKU is a disorder that can result in damage to the brain. It is caused by inheritance of a mutation. Children with PKU will be developmentally delayed. If a specific amino acid is removed from the child's diet, the symptoms will not occur. Or diabetes is a disease that can result from an inability to produce enough insulin. The level of glucose in the blood and urine will be high. This may lead to blindness or kidney problems. Frequent urination and thirst are major symptoms. Insulin injections can be used to regulate blood sugar levels. Note: If a disease caused by a pathogenic organism is chosen, a maximum of 3 credits may be allowed if the other three bullets are addressed correctly for the disease chosen. (#57, August 2006 Regents Exam)

PART D

14. One typical meal may contain a day's worth of calories for females and two-thirds of the daily calories for males.

15. HIV is an RNA virus that relies on its own enzyme, reverse transcriptase, to transcribe the HIV RNA into DNA. If AZT blocks reverse transcriptase, it can prevent the HIV RNA from being transcribed into DNA and embedded in an infected cell's DNA.

The Body's Defenses

		Standards	**Teach Key Ideas**

CHAPTER OPENER, pp. 522–523   `15 min.`

The Living Environment

SECTION 1 Protecting Against Disease,   `45 min.`
         pp. 525–528

〉 Preventing Entry
〉 Nonspecific Immune Responses
〉 Specific Immune Responses

1.2b, 5.2c, 5.2d

- **Bellringer Transparency**
- **Transparencies** J36 Inflammatory Response
- **Visual Concepts** Pathogen • Mucous Membranes • Inflammatory Response • Fever as a Nonspecific Defense • Interferon as a Nonspecific Defense

---

SECTION 2 Eliminating Invaders,   pp. 529–533   `90 min.`

〉 Activating the Immune Response
〉 Destroying Infected Cells
〉 Removing Pathogens at Large
〉 Long-Term Protection

1.2b, 5.1g, 5.2c, 5.2d, 5.2e

- **Bellringer Transparency**
- **Transparencies** J101 Immune Response
- **Visual Concepts** Recognition of Pathogens • Cell Mediated Immune Response • Primary and Secondary Immune Response • Vaccine • Antigen Shifting

---

SECTION 3 Immune System Dysfunctions,   `45 min.`
         pp. 534–539

〉 Allergies
〉 Autoimmune Diseases
〉 Immune Deficiency

5.2f, 5.2g

- **Bellringer Transparency**
- **Transparencies** J40 Number of Helper T Cells Following HIV Infection
- **Visual Concepts** Multiple Sclerosis • AIDS (Acquired Immunodeficiency Syndrome) • Course of an HIV Infection • Spread of AIDS • Allergy

See also PowerPoint® Resources

Chapter Review and Assessment Resources

SE Super Summary, p. 542
SE Regents Exam Practice, p. 543
Regents Review Guide
Review Resources
Chapter Tests A and B
Holt Online Assessment
Regents Question Banks on Teacher's One-Stop Planner

CHAPTER
Fast Track   *To shorten instruction due to time limitations, eliminate the Inquiry Lab and the Quick Labs in Sections 1 and 3. Eliminate Section 3 as well.*

Basic Learners
TE White Blood Cell Quiz, p. 527
TE The White Cell War, p. 529
TE Sequencing, p. 531
TE Health Advice Project, p. 537
Directed Reading Worksheets*
Active Reading Worksheets*
Lab Manuals, Level A*
Study Guide* ■
Note-taking Workbook*
Special Needs Activities and Modified Tests*

Advanced Learners
TE Autoimmune Diseases, p. 537
Critical Thinking Worksheets*
Concept Mapping Worksheets*
Science Skills Worksheets*
Lab Datasheets, Level C*

Why It Matters	Hands-On	Skills Development	Assessment
Build student motivation with resources about high-interest applications.	**SE Inquiry Lab** Barrier Breaking, p. 523* ■	**TE Reading Toolbox** Assessing Prior Knowledge, p. 522 **SE Reading Toolbox** p. 524	
TE Symbiotic Bacteria, p. 527	**SE Quick Lab** Antigen Binding, p. 528* ■ 📁 **Quick Lab** Calculating Contagion*	**SE Reading Toolbox** Word Parts, p. 526 **TE Reading Toolbox** Word Parts, p. 526	**SE Section Review** **TE Formative Assessment** Spanish Assessment* ■ 📁 Section Quiz ■
TE Demonstration Germs Everywhere, p. 530	**SE Quick Lab** The Eradication of Polio, p. 533* ■ **SE Science Skills Lab** Disease Transmission Model, p. 540* ■	**SE Reading Toolbox** Pattern Puzzle, p. 530 **TE Reading Toolbox** Pattern Puzzle, p. 530	**SE Section Review** **TE Formative Assessment** Spanish Assessment* ■ 📁 Section Quiz ■
TE Career Development p. 534 **SE Allergies and Culture** p. 536 **TE SCID,** p. 538	**SE Quick Lab** Constricted Airways, p. 535* ■ 📁 **Skills Practice Lab** Testing for Vitamin C*	**SE Reading Toolbox** Mnemonics, p. 538 **TE Reading Toolbox** Mnemonics, p. 538 **TE Math Skills** Chain Reaction, p. 539	**SE Section Review** **TE Formative Assessment** Spanish Assessment* ■ 📁 Section Quiz ■
	See also Lab Generator		**See also Holt Online Assessment Resources**

Resources for Differentiated Instruction

English Learners

TE Sequencing the Lines of Defense, p. 526
TE White Blood Cell Quiz, p. 527
📁 Directed Reading Worksheets ■
📁 Active Reading Worksheets ■
📁 Lab Manuals, Level A ■
📓 Study Guide ■
📓 Note-taking Workbook ■
📓 Multilingual Glossary ■

Struggling Readers

TE Paired Summaries, p. 530
TE Sequencing, p. 531
TE The "A" List, p. 534
📁 Directed Reading Worksheets*
📁 Active Reading Worksheets*
📁 Lab Manuals, Level A*
📓 Study Guide*
📓 Note-taking Workbook*
📓 Special Needs Activities and Modified Tests*

Special Education Students

TE Sequencing the Lines of Defense, p. 526
TE Following the Immune Response, p. 531
📁 Directed Reading Worksheets*
📁 Active Reading Worksheets*
📁 Lab Manuals, Level A*
📓 Study Guide* ■
📓 Note-taking Workbook*
📓 Special Needs Activities and Modified Tests*

Alternative Assessment

TE Immune Response, p. 532
📁 Science Skills Worksheets*
📁 Section Quizzes* ■
📓 Chapter Tests A, B, and C* ■

The Body's Defenses

Overview

The purpose of this chapter is to explore the way the body protects itself against disease. Students will also learn that the immune system sometimes fails, often with serious consequences.

READING TOOLBOX

Assessing Prior Knowledge Students should understand the following concepts:
• role of receptor proteins in cellular communication
• differences between antibodies and antigens
• relationship between HIV and AIDS

Visual Literacy Ask the students if they knew that there were parasitic organisms living inside their bodies. Tell them that a "war" is being fought every day by white blood cells and their helpers.

Chapter 1

Preview

1 Protecting Against Disease
Preventing Entry
Nonspecific Immune Responses
Specific Immune Responses

2 Eliminating Invaders
Activating the Immune Response
Destroying Infected Cells
Removing Pathogens at Large
Long-Term Protection

3 Immune System Dysfunctions
Allergies
Autoimmune Diseases
Immune Deficiency

Why It Matters

Each day, your body is assaulted by millions of different bacteria, viruses, and other disease-causing agents. Fortunately, your body has ways to defend against these invaders. These defenses prevent you from getting sick and help heal the body if you do get sick.

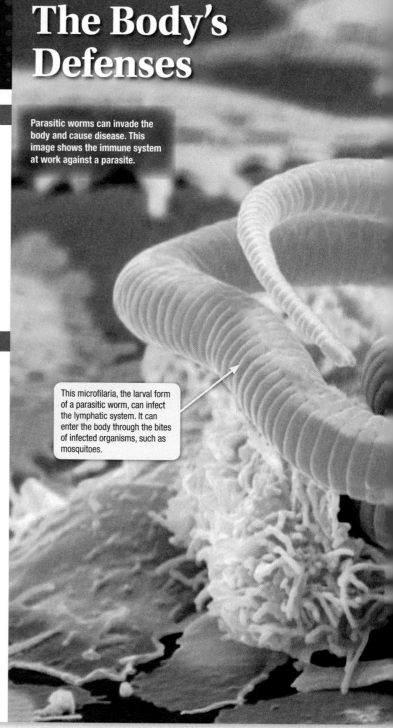

Parasitic worms can invade the body and cause disease. This image shows the immune system at work against a parasite.

This microfilaria, the larval form of a parasitic worm, can infect the lymphatic system. It can enter the body through the bites of infected organisms, such as mosquitoes.

The Living Environment
Standard 4 Students will understand and apply scientific concepts, principles, and theories pertaining to the physical setting and living environment and recognize the historical development of ideas in science.
  Key Idea 1 Living things are both similar to and different from each other and from nonliving things. *Major Understandings - 1.2b*
  Key Idea 5 Organisms maintain a dynamic equilibrium that sustains life. *Major Understandings - 5.1g, 5.2c, 5.2d, 5.2e, 5.2f, 5.2g*

Chapter Correlations   The Living Environment

Standard 4

1.2b Humans are complex organisms. They require multiple systems for digestion, respiration, reproduction, circulation, excretion, movement, coordination, and immunity. The systems interact to perform the life functions.

5.1g Enzymes and other molecules, such as hormones, receptor molecules, and antibodies, have specific shapes that influence both how they function and how they interact with other molecules.

5.2c The immune system protects against antigens associated with pathogenic organisms or foreign substances and some cancer cells.

5.2d Some white blood cells engulf invaders. Others produce antibodies that attack them or mark them for killing. Some specialized white blood cells will remain, able to fight off subsequent invaders of the same kind.

5.2e Vaccinations use weakened microbes (or parts of them) to stimu-late the immune system to react. This reaction prepares the body to fight subsequent invasions by the same microbes.

5.2f Some viral diseases, such as AIDS, damage the immune system, leaving the body unable to deal with multiple infectious agents and cancerous cells.

5.2g Some allergic reactions are caused by the body's immune responses to usually harmless environmental substances. Sometimes the immune system may attack some of the body's own cells or transplanted organs..

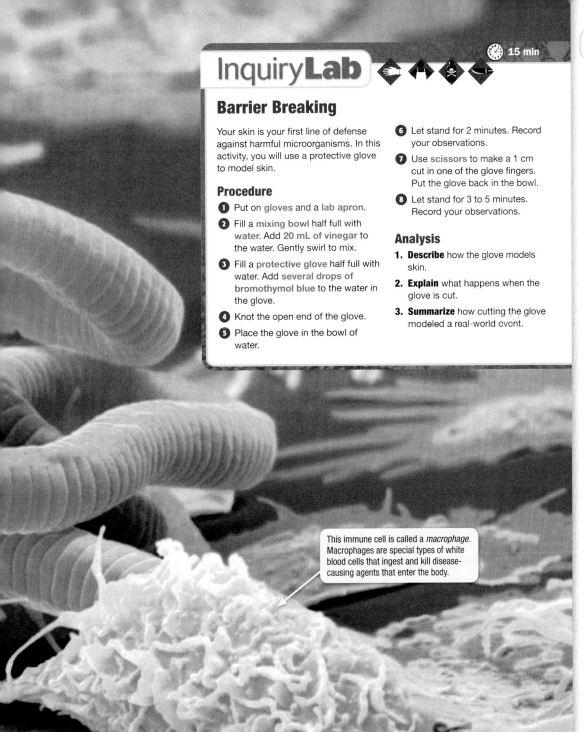

InquiryLab

⏱ 15 min

Barrier Breaking

Your skin is your first line of defense against harmful microorganisms. In this activity, you will use a protective glove to model skin.

Procedure

1. Put on **gloves** and a **lab apron.**
2. Fill a **mixing bowl** half full with **water.** Add **20 mL of vinegar** to the water. Gently swirl to mix.
3. Fill a **protective glove** half full with water. Add **several drops of bromothymol blue** to the water in the glove.
4. Knot the open end of the glove.
5. Place the glove in the bowl of water.
6. Let stand for 2 minutes. Record your observations.
7. Use **scissors** to make a 1 cm cut in one of the glove fingers. Put the glove back in the bowl.
8. Let stand for 3 to 5 minutes. Record your observations.

Analysis

1. **Describe** how the glove models skin.
2. **Explain** what happens when the glove is cut.
3. **Summarize** how cutting the glove modeled a real-world event.

This immune cell is called a *macrophage.* Macrophages are special types of white blood cells that ingest and kill disease-causing agents that enter the body.

InquiryLab

Teacher's Notes Bromothymol blue, also known as bromthymol blue is a common indicator solution that can often be purchased from local tropical fish stores. It is purchased to monitor the pH of aquariums. You might wish to demonstrate the indicator's response to an acid environment by bubbling exhaled air through it. When discussing compromised barriers, remind students that disease such as HIV and hepatitis are often transferred through skin that has been compromised by insertion of infected needles. Have students work together in pairs. If using latex gloves, be sure to ask if any students have latex allergies before they begin the lab. Neoprene gloves can be used instead.

Materials

- protective gloves (3)
- bromothymol blue
- large mixing bowl
- vinegar
- graduated cylinder, 25 mL
- safety goggles

Answers to Analysis

1. It forms a physical barrier to the passage of materials.
2. The cut in the glove releases the indicator, which mixes with the vinegar and produces a color change.
3. When the protective glove is cut, it no longer forms a barrier against its surroundings. This action models a cut or similar injury to the skin.

Using Words

1. **inflammation** to cause burning; accept anything related to the characteristics of burning, redness, or swelling
2. **cytotoxic** poison to a cell

Using Language

Answers will vary. Accept any answer that has the correct first letters of the words listed.

1. Sample response: **R**ead **w**hile **p**ainting **p**ictures.
2. Sample response: **E**ating **n**uts **c**an **m**atter.

Using Graphic Organizers

Using the steps shown in the diagram on the right, the order is as follows:

1. Pathogens enter the body.
2. Cells recognize invaders.
3. Histamine is released.
4. Redness and swelling occur.
5. White blood cells travel to the area.

READING TOOLBOX

These reading tools can help you learn the material in this chapter. For more information on how to use these and other tools, see **Appendix: Reading and Study Skills.**

Using Words

Word Parts Knowing the meanings of word parts can help you figure out the meanings of words that you do not know.

Your Turn Use the table to answer the following questions.

1. Define *inflammation* in your own words.
2. What do you think the word *cytotoxic* means? Use your dictionary to find out if your guess is correct.

Word Parts		
Part	Type	Meaning
in-, en-	prefix	cause, make, enable
flam	root	burn, flame
cyto-	prefix	cell
toxic	root	poison

Using Language

Mnemonics Mnemonic devices are tools that can help you memorize words, steps, concepts that go together. Use the first letter of every word you want to remember as the first letter of a new word, in a sentence that is easy to remember. For example, the trees *maple, dogwood, ash,* and *sycamore* can be remembered by the mnemonic "My Dear Aunt Sally."

Your Turn Create mnemonic devices to help you remember the following groups of words.

1. The four parts of blood: *red cells, white cells, platelets,* and *plasma*
2. The four major tissue types: *epithelial, nervous, connective,* and *muscle*

Using Graphic Organizers

Pattern Puzzles A pattern puzzle is useful for organizing and remembering the steps of a process. Pattern puzzles can help you understand how the steps of a process fit together.

Your Turn Use a pattern puzzle to learn the steps of the inflammatory immune response.

1. Write the steps of the inflammatory immune response in your own words. Write one step per line. Do not number the steps.
2. Cut the sheet of paper so that there is one step per strip of paper.
3. Shuffle the paper strips so that they are out of sequence.
4. Place the strips in their proper sequence.
5. Confirm the order of the process by checking your text or class notes.
6. Use this exercise to model another immune response.

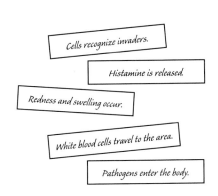

Section 1

Key Ideas

> What physical barriers protect the human body?

> What are three general defense mechanisms that the body uses to fight pathogens?

> How does the body respond to pathogens that have infected a cell?

Key Terms

pathogen
mucous membrane
inflammation
histamine
antigen
macrophage

Why It Matters

To survive, the body must protect itself from infections. The body has both general and specific responses to prevent and fight infections.

> Focus

This section introduces students to the nonspecific defenses of the human body, including skin and mucous membranes. Students will learn that pathogens that make it past the first line of defense face the inflammatory and temperature responses. These responses can be very effective in killing an invader.

> Bellringer

Use the Bellringer transparency to prepare students for this section.

> Teach

Teaching Key Ideas

Mosquito Bites Ask students why mosquito bites turn red, swell, and itch if a mosquito is simply sucking blood. (The mosquito injects a small amount of saliva, which contains an anticoagulant and digestive enzymes. The anticoagulant initiates the inflammatory response, making the bite site swell, turn red, and itch.)
LS Logical

Microorganisms are everywhere! Some are harmless, but others can cause illness by invading your body and infecting your cells. Disease-causing microorganisms and viruses are called **pathogens.** Your body protects against disease by preventing pathogens from entering the body, or by fighting pathogens if they do enter.

Preventing Entry

> Skin and mucous membranes form strong barriers that prevent pathogens from entering the body. Your skin is the first line of defense against pathogens. Oil makes the skin's surface acidic, which inhibits the growth of many pathogens. Sweat also contains enzymes that digest bacterial cell walls and kill the bacteria. Mucous membranes form a second barrier to pathogens. **Mucous membranes** are layers of epithelial tissue that produce a sticky, viscous fluid called *mucus*. They cover many internal body surfaces, including the linings of the digestive, respiratory, and reproductive tracts. Mucus traps pathogens before they can cause infections.

Sometimes pathogens cross one of these two physical barriers. Cuts and abrasions allow pathogens to enter through the skin. Tears in the epithelium allow pathogens to cross mucous membranes. Airborne pathogens, shown in **Figure 1,** can enter the body through the respiratory system. You can ingest pathogens via contaminated food or water. Some pathogens can cross mucous membranes of the reproductive tract during sexual contact. Sometimes, pathogens are injected directly into the bloodstream. This can occur through insect bites or through the use of contaminated needles.

> **Reading Check** *How do physical barriers prevent pathogens from entering the body? (See the Appendix for answers to Reading Checks.)*

The Living Environment
Standard 4
1.2b Humans are complex organisms. They require multiple systems for digestion, respiration, reproduction, circulation, excretion, movement, coordination, and immunity. The systems interact to perform the life functions.
5.2c The immune system protects against antigens associated with pathogenic organisms or foreign substances and some cancer cells.
5.2d Some white blood cells engulf invaders. Others produce antibodies that attack them or mark them for killing. Some specialized white blood cells will remain, able to fight off subsequent invaders of the same kind.

pathogen a microorganism, another organism, a virus, or a protein that causes disease; an infectious agent

mucous membrane (MYOO kuhs) the layer of epithelial tissue that covers internal surfaces of the body and that secretes mucus

Figure 1 The flu virus can be released into the air through a cough or sneeze and can infect another person who inhales the air.

Key Resources

Transparencies
J36 Inflammatory Response

Visual Concepts
Pathogen
Mucous Membranes
Inflammatory Response
Fever as a Nonspecific Defense
Interferon as a Nonspecific Defense

Section Correlations
1.2b
5.2c
5.2d

Teaching Key Ideas

Monitoring the Immune Response
Ask students what happens when they get a wood splinter in their finger and it is not removed within the first day or so. (The area turns red, becomes sore, and may swell.) What happens after several more days, if the splinter isn't removed? (Pus may form around the splinter; years ago, this was called festering.) Ask them why the pus is whitish in color. (White blood cells are converging on the area of the wood splinter, and are digesting bacteria on the splinter.)
LS **Verbal**

go.hrw.com
✴ interact online

Students can interact with "The Steps of the Inflammatory Response" by going to go.hrw.com and typing in the keyword HX8IMNF2.

READING TOOLBOX

Word Parts The study of disease-causing agents (pathogens) is called pathology.

Answers to Caption Questions
Figure 2: White blood cells are activated by the inflammatory response.

READING TOOLBOX

Word Parts The word part _path-_ means "disease." The suffix _-gen_ means "to bring forth." Write a sentence explaining how pathology and pathogens are related.

---

inflammation a protective response of tissues affected by disease or injury

histamine (HIS tuh MEEN) a chemical that stimulates the dilation of capillaries

antigen a substance that stimulates an immune response

macrophage an immune system cell that engulfs pathogens and other materials

---

Figure 2 When pathogens enter your body, an inflammatory response is triggered. ❯ Which cells are activated by the inflammatory response?

Nonspecific Immune Responses

❯ When pathogens break through the body's physical barriers, the body quickly responds with second-line defenses. These defenses are fever, inflammation, and the activation of special proteins that kill or inhibit pathogens. These second-line defenses depend on your body's ability to know its own cells and proteins and to separate these "self" cells and proteins from outside invaders.

Fever The body's temperature, normally 36.5 °C to 37.2 °C (97.8 °F to 99 °F), rises several degrees as the body begins to fight against an invading pathogen. High body temperature, or fever, is a common symptom of sickness. Higher temperatures are harmful to many bacterial pathogens, so fever helps the body fight infection. However, fever can be dangerous. Fever above 39 °C (103 °F) can destroy the body's cellular proteins, and fever above 41 °C (105 °F) can be fatal.

Inflammation An injury or local infection stimulates inflammation, shown in **Figure 2**. During **inflammation,** chemicals and cells that attack and destroy pathogens gather around the area of injury or infection. ❶ When the skin is damaged, pathogens can enter the body. ❷ Infected or injured cells recognize the "nonself" invaders and release chemicals such as histamine. **Histamine** causes local blood vessels to dilate, which increases blood flow to the area and causes swelling and redness. ❸ White blood cells travel to the infection site to attack pathogens. The whitish liquid, or pus, connected with many infections is filled with white blood cells, dead body cells, and dead pathogens. Three types of white blood cells play a role in this response: macrophages, neutrophils, and natural killer cells. These cells are described in **Figure 3**.

go.hrw.com
✴ interact online
Keyword: HX8IMNF2

Inflammation

❶ When skin is damaged, such as from a puncture wound, pathogens enter the body.

❷ Increased blood flow to the area causes swelling and redness.

❸ White blood cells attack and destroy the pathogens.

Pathogens
Capillary

White blood cells

Differentiated Instruction

Special Education Students/ English Learners

Sequencing the Lines of Defense Have students work in groups of three or four. Provide each group with index cards that have the names of the body's first and second lines of defense. The function of each protection should be on the back of the card. Students can also add illustrations to the cards. Have the groups shuffle the cards and then organize them. They should check their answers, then reshuffle the cards, and try again until they get the sequence right several times in a row. Next, students should turn the cards over and do the same thing with the functions of each defense. Finally, they should use the cards to quiz each other on the various components of the first and second lines of defense and how they function.
LS **Kinesthetic**

White Blood Cells Involved in Inflammation		
Macrophage	**Neutrophil**	**Natural Killer Cell**
Target: pathogens, dead cells, and cellular debris	Target: pathogens	Target: cells infected with pathogens and cancer cells
Method of action: ingests and kills pathogens	Method of action: ingests and kills pathogens	Method of action: punctures an infected cell membrane, and causes water to rush in and burst the cell
Location: lymph and fluid between cells, concentrated in the spleen and lungs	Location: blood and fluid between cells and in the walls of capillaries	Location: lymph nodes and other tissues

Figure 3 Different types of white blood cells (each shown in yellow) help defend the body against pathogens.

Protein Activation Some pathogens activate proteins that boost the body's general responses to infection. Complement proteins attack cellular pathogens, such as bacteria, by punching holes in the cell membranes and causing the contents to leak out. Interferons, another group of proteins, are released by cells infected with viruses. These proteins prevent viruses from making proteins and RNA.

Specific Immune Responses

Most pathogens are destroyed by the general, nonspecific defenses that have been looked at so far. But what happens if an invader gets past these responses? The third line of defense is the specific immune response, in which special white blood cells target a particular invader. ❯ **When a pathogen infects a cell, the body produces immune cells that specialize in detecting and destroying that specific pathogen.**

Antigen Display Macrophages are one type of white blood cell that destroys pathogens. Pathogens have unique proteins on their surfaces that help your body identify them as "nonself." These proteins, called **antigens,** identify the cell as foreign and start an immune response. After a macrophage or similar cell swallows up and destroys a pathogen, pieces of the pathogen that contain its antigens move to the surface of the macrophage. This "display" of antigens changes the cell surface markers on the macrophage. The antigen display alerts the immune system to an invader and the immune system cells are put into action.

Every antigen has its own receptor, which is located on the surface of an immune cell. The shape of antigen receptors allows the immune system to be specific to certain antigens. As **Figure 4** shows, antigen receptors bind to antigens that match their shape exactly, in the same way that two pieces of a puzzle fit together. The body produces a great variety of immune cells, each of which has receptors for a different antigen. This variety allows the immune system to respond to millions of different antigens.

❯ **Reading Check** *How does the body recognize "nonself" invaders?*

Complementary shapes bind.

Figure 4 Specific antigens (green) located on foreign cells (yellow) bind to antigen receptors (red) that are located on immune system cells (purple).

Teaching Key Ideas

Frequency of Colds Have students hypothesize why adults and teens tend to get fewer colds than children. (The immune system has learned to recognize and immediately attack many of the viruses that cause colds because of the antigen display/receptor binding.) Ask students to speculate why colds may be more prevalent during the winter months. (People may spend more time indoors in close proximity to each other.)
LS Logical

Differentiated Instruction

Basic Learners/English Learners

White Blood Cell Quiz Ask students to use **Figure 3** and make three flashcards with labeled drawings of each type of white blood cell on one side. On the reverse side, students should list the cell's location and its action. Have them work in pairs to quiz each other. Add these flashcards to the ones made for the lines of defense. **LS Interpersonal**

Why It Matters

Symbiotic Bacteria Some of the body's protection from pathogens comes from symbiotic bacteria. For example, beneficial bacteria in the vagina inhibit the growth of harmful bacteria and fungi. The use of antibiotics to kill pathogens often kills the body's beneficial bacteria as well. This can lead to vaginal and urinary tract infections.

QuickLab

Teacher's Notes Before the lab, review antigens and antibodies.

Materials
- gloves
- safety goggles
- lab apron
- blood typing trays (2)
- simulated blood (types AB and O)
- simulated anti-A and anti-B blood typing serums
- toothpicks (4)

Answers to Analysis
1. AB
2. Antibodies are bound to antigens.
3. Type A would clot only with anti-A serum. Type B would clot only with anti-B serum.

> **Close**

Formative Assessment

What causes blood vessels to dilate in the area of an injury to the skin?

A. fever (Incorrect. Fever is a full body response.)

B. inflammation (Incorrect. This condition is local swelling and burning. Review the definitions of key words.)

C. histamine (Correct! Histamine stimulates local blood vessels to dilate and increase the blood flow to the injury area.)

D. antigens (Incorrect. An antigen labels a pathogen as "foreign" to the body.)

Hands-On

 QuickLab

 30 min

Antigen Binding

In this lab, you will observe what happens when receptors in blood-typing serum bind to the antigens on simulated red blood cells.

Procedure

❶ Put on **safety goggles**, a **lab apron**, and **gloves**.

❷ Use only simulated blood provided by your teacher. Place three or four drops of **type AB simulated blood** into each well of a clean **blood-typing tray**.

❸ Add three drops of **anti-A blood-typing serum** to one well. Stir the mixture with a **toothpick** for 30 s.

❹ Add three drops of **anti-B serum** to the other well. Stir the mixture with a new toothpick. Look for clumps separating from the mixtures.

❺ Using **type O simulated blood**, repeat steps 1–4.

Analysis

1. **Determine** which blood type has antigens that are recognized by the blood-typing serums.

2. **Evaluating Results** What does the clumping of the blood mixtures indicate?

3. **CRITICAL THINKING** **Predicting Outcomes** What would happen if you used type A, type B, and type O simulated blood in the same experiment? Explain your answer.

---

www.scilinks.org
Topic: Immune Systems
Code: HX80786

Two-Part Assault When a displayed antigen binds to its antigen receptor on an immune cell, another response is triggered—more immune cells are produced that have the same antigen receptor. These immune cells carry out two processes at the same time. One process destroys a person's body cells that are no longer normal. These cells may be infected by pathogens or may be other altered body cells, such as cancer cells. The other process removes extracellular pathogens, pathogens that have not entered body cells. Together, these two processes form an integrated response to an infection. These two immune processes will be described in more detail in the next section.

Section 1 **Review**

KEY IDEAS

1. **Summarize** how the skin and mucous membranes help prevent infection by a pathogen.

2. **Identify** the three general defense mechanisms that protect the body from infection.

3. **Describe** how a cell responds to pathogens.

CRITICAL THINKING

4. **Relating Concepts** Identify the process that would occur immediately if you cut your foot on a piece of glass, and describe how it would help keep the cut from getting infected.

5. **Drawing Conclusions** In the disease leukemia, abnormal white blood cells are produced. Why are people who have leukemia at greater risk for infections than other people are?

WRITING FOR SCIENCE

6. **Short Story** Imagine that you are a pathogen trying to get into a human body. Write a short story that describes the challenges that you face as you attempt to get past the body's defenses. Be sure to include at least three different types of immune system defenses.

Answers to Section Review

1. They are physical barriers to pathogens.

2. fever, inflammation, and protein activation

3. Antigens from the pathogen are displayed on the surface of the macrophage. Immune system cells that have matching antigen receptors bind the antigens and stimulate the production of immune cells that destroy the cells infected by pathogens.

4. Bleeding at the site will slow the entry of pathogens. The injured cells release histamine and other chemicals, which causes blood flow to the area to increase. Swelling and redness occur. White blood cells attack and destroy pathogens. Clot formation helps seal the wound preventing further invasion.

5. Abnormal white blood cells do not fight infections as well as normal white blood cells do.

6. Stories may vary but should include oil and sweat on the skin and the protection from mucous membranes.

Key Ideas

> How is the specific immune response activated?

> How does the body eliminate intracellular pathogens?

> How does the body eliminate extracellular pathogens?

> How does the immune system protect the body from repeated infection by the same pathogen?

Key Terms

helper T cell
cytotoxic T cell
B cell
plasma cell
antibody

memory cell
immunity
vaccine

Why It Matters

At the same time that the immune system is fighting an infection, it is creating a reserve army of cells to fight the same pathogen in the future.

The immune system consists of many types of white blood cells, including macrophages, T cells, and B cells. The first time your body meets a particular pathogen, the immune response launches an attack on the invader. The coordinated effort of all of the immune system cells not only destroys invading pathogens but also provides protection against future infection by a similar pathogen.

Activating a Specific Immune Response

As part of the body's general immune response, macrophages engulf and destroy pathogens. The result is the display of antigens on the surface of infected cells. These "altered" cells now become a target of the specific immune response. > A specialized white blood cell called a *helper T cell* activates the immune system. These cells coordinate two responses: destroying cells that have been infected by a pathogen, and cleaning up pathogens at large in the body.

Helper T Cells Helper T cells, shown in **Figure 5,** are white blood cells that regulate the function of other cells in the immune system. Recall that helper T cells have specific antigen receptors on their surfaces that bind to specific antigens that are displayed on the surface of a macrophage. The binding of receptor to the antigen activates the helper T cell, which causes the release of chemical signals.

Activated helper T cells do not directly attack infected body cells or pathogens. Instead, they grow and divide to produce more helper T cells that have identical receptors on their surfaces. The helper T cells activate the two processes of the specific immune response: the destruction of infected cells by cytotoxic T cells and the removal of extracellular pathogens from the body by B cells.

Thymus

Helper
T cell

Cytotoxic
T cell

Figure 5 Some white blood cells, such as helper T cells and cytotoxic T cells, are produced in bone marrow and mature in the thymus.

 The Living Environment
Standard 4

1.2b Humans are complex organisms. They require multiple systems for digestion, respiration, reproduction, circulation, excretion, movement, coordination, and immunity. The systems interact to perform the life functions.

5.1g Enzymes and other molecules, such as hormones, receptor molecules, and antibodies, have specific shapes that influence both how they function and how they interact with other molecules.

5.2c The immune system protects against antigens associated with pathogenic organisms or foreign substances and some cancer cells.

5.2d Some white blood cells engulf invaders. Others produce antibodies that attack them or mark them for killing. Some specialized white blood cells will remain, able to fight off subsequent invaders of the same kind.

5.2e Vaccinations use weakened microbes (or parts of them) to stimulate the immune system to react. This reaction prepares the body to fight subsequent invasions by the same microbes.

> **helper T cell** a white blood cell necessary for B cells to develop normal levels of antibodies

Focus

This section introduces students to the body's third line of defense, the specific immune response. Students will learn that to destroy pathogens, the third line of defense must be able to recognize an invader as "foreign." Students will also learn about immunity and its lasting effects.

Bellringer

Use the Bellringer transparency to prepare students for this section.

Teach

Teaching Key Ideas

Graphic Organizer Have students create a summary table. Along the top of the table, have them list the following categories: *Type of cell, Function,* and *Location in the body.* In the first column, they should list all the types of cells that play a role in the body's defenses. (macrophage, neutrophil, natural killer cell, helper T cell, cytotoxic T cell, B cell, plasma cell, antibodies, and memory cell) Then ask students to complete the information in the second and third columns. **LS Visual**

Differentiated Instruction

Basic Learners

The White Cell War Have students diagram the process used by a white blood cell to eliminate pathogens that invade the body. Tell students to be creative when depicting the war that is occurring inside the body. Judge their work on creativity and accuracy.

Key Resources

Transparencies
J101 Immune Response

Visual Concepts
Recognition of Pathogens
Cell-Mediated Immune Response
Primary and Secondary Immune Response
Vaccine
Antigen Shifting

Section Correlations	
1.2b	5.2d
5.1g	5.2e
5.2c	

Germs Everywhere To show that microorganisms are ubiquitous, gather five sterile Petri dishes filled with sterile nutrient agar. Collect microorganisms from five different areas in the room by sweeping surfaces with sterile swabs moistened with sterile distilled water. Inoculate one dish with one swab, and tape each dish closed with masking tape. Label each dish, and place all five upside down in a warm, dark place or in an incubator kept at room temperature for several days. At the end of this period, show students the colonies of microorganisms that have grown on the agar. Explain that most of the microorganisms in the dishes are probably harmless, but some may be pathogens. Dispose of swabs and Petri dishes after sterilizing them in an autoclave or pressure cooker at 121°C for 15 minutes or soaking them in chlorine bleach for 30 minutes. **LS** **Visual**

READING
TOOLBOX

Pattern Puzzle Students should copy the eight steps shown in **Figure 7** on the next page. The steps are not numbered on the puzzle pieces. The order matches **Figure 7**.

cytotoxic T cell a type of T cell that recognizes and destroys cells infected by viruses

B cell a white blood cell that matures in bones and makes antibodies

plasma cell a type of white blood cell that produces antibodies

antibody a protein that reacts to a specific antigen or that inactivates or destroys toxins

READING
TOOLBOX

Pattern Puzzles Make a pattern puzzle to help you remember the steps of the immune response system.

Figure 6 When a helper T cell (blue) activates a B cell (purple), they come in close contact with each other.

Destroying Infected Cells

Helper T cells produce chemical signals that activate the second kind of T cell, called a *cytotoxic T cell*. **Cytotoxic T cells** are white blood cells that carry pathogen-specific receptors on their surfaces. **> Cytotoxic T cells destroy cells that have been infected by pathogens.** They can also kill cancer cells and attack foreign tissues, such as tissues that are received during an organ transplant. The cytotoxic T cell response is summarized in **Figure 7**.

Activating Cytotoxic T Cells Recall that when a body cell becomes infected by a virus, it displays specific antigens on its surface. These antigens activate matching antigen receptors on helper T cells. The activated helper T cells then turn on the production of cytotoxic T cells that will have the same antigen receptor. As a result, the new cytotoxic T cells will bind to matching antigens on the surface of infected cells. When they bind, the cytotoxic T cells release chemicals that punch holes in the membranes of the infected cells. The infected cells die when water enters them and splits them open.

Removing Pathogens at Large

Helper T cells also activate the second part of the specific immune response, which is carried out by B cells. **B cells** are white blood cells that produce proteins that bind to pathogens outside of body cells. This action tags the pathogens for destruction by macrophages. **> The B cell response removes extracellular pathogens from the body and prevents further infection.** This response is summarized in **Figure 7**.

Activating B Cells The B cell response is triggered when B cells are activated by helper T cells, as shown in **Figure 6**. Like T cells in the T cell response, only B cells that have antigen receptors matching a specific antigen are activated. Activated B cells produce **plasma cells,** which are white blood cells that produce and release antibodies. **Antibodies** are Y-shaped protein molecules that bind to the specific antigen that they match.

Antibody Binding Antibodies are released by plasma cells and circulate in the blood and lymph fluid. When antibodies encounter extracellular pathogens that they match, they attach to the pathogens. This binding is like the specific binding of cytotoxic T cells to matching infected body cells. However, antibodies do not remain attached to the plasma cells that produced them.

Each Y-shaped antibody has two binding sites, which are located at the tips of the Ys. Antibodies can either bind to two antigens on the surface of a single pathogen cell or to single antigens on two pathogen cells. The binding of multiple antibodies to pathogens forms an antigen-antibody complex. These complexes are then destroyed by general defense mechanisms, such as macrophages or defense proteins that puncture the pathogen membranes.

> Reading Check *Which cells produce antibodies?*

MISCONCEPTION
/// ALERT \\\

Immune Response to Cancer Students may think that the immune system only defends the body against pathogens such as bacteria and viruses. Make sure students are aware that the immune system also defends the body against defective body cells as well, such as cancer cells.

Differentiated Instruction

Struggling Readers

Paired Summaries Pair each student with a partner. Have each student read Section 2 silently while making notes on a piece of paper. Have students list or put a question mark next to anything they do not clearly understand. After they finish reading, ask one student to summarize and the second to add anything omitted. Both readers should then help each other with any passages that either (or both) did not understand. Have them create a list of questions to ask. Discuss each group's questions as a class. **LS** **Verbal**

Figure 7 Antigens (small green knobs), such as those from a virus (yellow), activate helper T cells. Helper T cells then activate both the intracellular response (by stimulating T cells) and the extracellular response (by stimulating B cells).

❶ A virus, which displays viral antigens, can infect body cells.

Virus particles in the body

Macrophage

Viral antigen

Virus

❷ Macrophages engulf the virus and display the viral antigens.

❸ Virus-containing macrophages activate helper T cells.

B cell response

T cell response

Helper T cells

❹ Helper T cells start production of B cells that have the specific receptor.

B cell

❼ Helper T cells start production of cytotoxic T cells that have the specific receptor.

Cytotoxic T cell

Plasma cells

❺ B cells form specific plasma cells.

Cytotoxic T cell

❽ If a body cell becomes infected, cytotoxic T cells destroy it.

❻ Plasma cells make and release antibodies that bind to the viral antigens. This action tags the virus for destruction.

Antibodies

Infected body cell

Virus particles

Teaching Key Ideas

Know Your White Cells Once you have discussed **Figure 7,** have students answer the following questions: "Which types of white blood cells are involved in the immune response?" (helper T, cytotoxic T, and B cells) "Which type of cell directly destroys pathogens?" (cytotoxic T cell) "What is the role of helper T cells?" (They regulate the T- and B-cell actions.) **LS Verbal**

Differentiated Instruction

Basic Learners/English Learners

Sequencing Have students make index cards with the T-cell functions from **Figure 7;** Steps 3, 4, 7, and 8). Have students work in pairs. One student shuffles the cards, and the other student puts them in the correct order. Students should then switch roles. These cards should also be added to the growing deck of flashcards for this chapter. **LS Interpersonal**

Special Education Students

Following the Immune Response Have students trace the pathway for the immune response shown in **Figure 7.** As students move through the diagram, they should be describing what is occurring in their own words. Ask them to describe what a cytotoxic T cell does.

Teaching Key Ideas

Antigen Shifting Changes in the surface proteins of viruses, such as cold and influenza, allow these viruses to reinfect individuals many times. Ask students why this reinfection occurs. (The mutations prevent the immune system from recognizing the virus as one that it has encountered before. Without this recognition, the cells are not able to immediately destroy the virus.) Have students create an illustration, model, or computer animation illustrating their answer. Ask them to find out why it may be difficult to create a vaccine for a mutating virus. **LS** **Kinesthetic**

Answers to Caption Questions

Figure 8: Vaccines trigger a response called immunity.

memory cell an immune system B cell or T cell that does not respond the first time that it meets with an antigen or an invading cell but that recognizes and attacks the antigen or invading cell during subsequent infections

immunity the ability to resist or recover from an infectious disease

vaccine a substance prepared from killed or weakened pathogens and introduced into a body to produce immunity

Figure 8 This young person is receiving a vaccination shot. A vaccine is produced from a killed or weakened pathogen.
> Vaccines trigger which type of immune response?

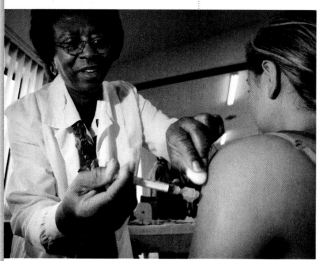

Long-Term Protection

When a pathogen has been destroyed, the specific T cells, plasma cells, and antibodies involved are no longer needed. But if the same pathogen invades the body again, the immune system is prepared.

Activating Memory Cells Recall that when the body first meets a pathogen, B cells make plasma cells that produce antibodies to that pathogen. At the same time, activated B cells also produce another kind of white blood cell called a *memory cell*. Like plasma cells, **memory cells** carry antigen receptors to the target antigen. These cells also continue to patrol the body's tissues, in some cases for the rest of a person's life. If the same pathogen invades the body again, the memory cells rapidly divide and produce a group of immune cells—helper T cells, cytotoxic T cells, and plasma cells. > After an immune response, memory cells continue to protect the body from pathogens the body had already encountered. An individual who recovers from an infectious disease becomes resistant to that particular pathogen.

The secondary immune response that is started by memory cells is called *immunity*. **Immunity** is a long-lasting resistance that is usually effective only against the specific pathogen that triggered the response. This secondary response starts much more quickly than when the body first faced the pathogen. It also produces many more specialized cells. As a result, the invader is stopped before it can cause illness.

Vaccination Infection by a pathogen allows the body to gain immunity to that particular pathogen. However, the body can also become immune through the use of vaccines. A **vaccine** is a solution that contains a dead or weakened form of a pathogen. They are typically injected into the bloodstream so that the pathogens can get past the general defenses of the immune system. Vaccines are available for many serious and deadly diseases.

A vaccine triggers an immune response against a pathogen without causing symptoms. How? Vaccines carry surface antigens from the pathogen that the body recognizes as harmful. This recognition triggers the immune response and forms memory cells against the pathogen. However, the genetic material in a vaccine is weakened or destroyed so that the pathogen cannot cause illness. In this way, immunity is built against the disease without the disease occurring in the body. Future contact with the pathogen will trigger the immune system to respond.

Most vaccines are given as a shot directly into the bloodstream. This method is used so that the vaccine can get past the body's general defenses. Vaccination is shown in **Figure 8.**

QuickLab

The Eradication of Polio 4.5.2e

The graph shows the global incidence of polio, and the percent of the population covered by polio vaccines.

Analysis

1. **Determine** how many cases of polio were reported globally in 1980. In 2000?

2. **Determine** what percent of the population was covered by protective polio vaccine in 1980. In 2000?

3. **Describe** the relationship between the number of polio cases and the coverage by preventative vaccine.

4. **Name** the two-year period over which the greatest drop in cases occurred. Explain this decrease.

⏱ 15 min

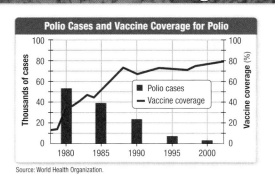

Polio Cases and Vaccine Coverage for Polio

Source: World Health Organization.

5. **CRITICAL THINKING** **Inferring Conclusions** What might cause a sudden yearly increase in the number of polio cases?

How Pathogens Evade Immunity Microorganisms have short life cycles. Several generations can be produced in as little as an hour. Also, changes in the genetic material of a microorganism often occur. These genetic changes may cause *antigen shifting,* an abrupt change in a pathogen's antigens. This process can allow a pathogen to avoid being recognized by the immune system of a person who had already become immune to the pathogen.

Influenza viruses are well known for frequent antigen shifts. New forms of the flu appear rapidly, and people at risk of serious complications from the flu must receive new vaccines annually. Human immunodeficiency virus (HIV) also undergoes antigen shifts. As a result, making a vaccine against HIV is very difficult. Antigen shifting also causes the virus to become resistant to drugs that are used to treat HIV infection.

❯ **Reading Check** *What causes antigen shifting?*

www.scilinks.org
Topic: Vaccines
Code: HX81590

Section 2 Review

❯ **KEY IDEAS**

1. **Describe** the role of helper T cells in fighting an infection.

2. **Explain** how cytotoxic T cells destroy infected body cells.

3. **Sequence** how B cells fight an infection.

4. **Explain** how memory cells ensure immunity to a specific pathogen.

CRITICAL THINKING

5. **Drawing Conclusions** In the first vaccine developed, cowpox virus was used to protect against smallpox. This fact seems to contradict the high specificity that characterizes immune responses. What conclusion can you draw about the cowpox virus in relation to the smallpox virus?

WRITING FOR SCIENCE

6. **Short Essay** Scientists have created an effective vaccine for smallpox but have not been able to do so for HIV. What does this fact suggest about the rate of mutation of the smallpox virus? Write a short essay to explain your reasoning.

QuickLab

Teacher's Notes Polio is a disease caused by a small RNA virus called the poliovirus (PV). The pathogen is known for its devastating effects on the nervous system that can result in paralysis. In the US, the vaccination programs were successful enough to eradicate natural polio infections by 1979.

Answers to Analysis

1. over 50,000 cases, less than 2,000 cases

2. about 30%; almost 80%

3. In general, developing and maintaining a high percentage of vaccine coverage is associated with a significant drop in polio cases.

4. 1981–1983 appears to have the greatest drop in cases. The decline is most likely the direct response to the significant increase in the percentage of vaccine coverage.

5. a drop in vaccine coverage or the introduction of a vaccine-resistant strain of the virus

❯Close

Formative Assessment

Which cells produce antibodies and release them into the blood?

A. cytotoxic T cells (Incorrect. Cytotoxic T cells are white blood cells that attack and kill infected cells.)

B. helper T cells (Incorrect. Helper T cells function to activate both cytotoxic T cells and B cells.)

C. macrophages (Incorrect. Macrophages ingest and kill pathogens.)

D. plasma cells (Correct! Plasma cells release specialized, Y-shaped proteins called antibodies into the blood.)

Answers to Section Review

1. Helper T cells do not directly attack infected body cells or pathogens. They stimulate the production of cytotoxic T cells and the B-cell response.

2. Cytotoxic T cells attack and kill infected body cells.

3. B cells produce plasma cells that make antibodies.

4. Memory cells patrol the body and activate antibody production if they detect the same pathogen in the future.

5. The cowpox virus must have antigens that are similar to the smallpox virus antigens.

6. Answers will vary, but should include that the mutation rate of the smallpox virus must be much slower than that of HIV.

Section 3 Immune System Dysfunctions

Key Ideas	Key Terms	Why It Matters
> What causes allergic reactions? > What are autoimmune diseases? > What happens when your immune system is compromised?	allergy allergen autoimmune disease AIDS HIV	Only when the immune system breaks down do we realize how important it is to our survival.

 The Living Environment
Standard 4
5.2f Some viral diseases, such as AIDS, damage the immune system, leaving the body unable to deal with multiple infectious agents and cancerous cells.
5.2g Some allergic reactions are caused by the body's immune responses to usually harmless environmental substances. Sometimes the immune system may attack some of the body's own cells or transplanted organs.

Figure 9 These allergens cause allergies in some people. > **What causes an allergic response?**

The immune system protects us from a wide variety of diseases. When the immune system malfunctions, the results are usually very serious and often fatal. Allergies, autoimmune disorders, and inherited or acquired immunodeficiency disorders are all examples of what can happen when the immune system does not work properly.

Allergies

If you suffer from hay fever, you experience an immune response to pollen antigens. **Allergies** are immune responses to antigens to which most people do not react. These weak antigens are called **allergens.** > An allergic reaction is the immune system's excessive response to a normally harmless antigen. Common allergens include pollen, dust, fungal spores, the feces of dust mites, and materials found in some foods and drugs. Some allergens are shown in **Figure 9.**

In a sensitive person, exposure to an allergen causes histamine release. This event can cause swelling, redness, high mucus production, a runny or stuffy nose, and itchy eyes. Most allergy medicines contain antihistamines, drugs that prevent the action of histamine. Most allergic reactions are just uncomfortable. However, severe allergic reactions can be life threatening if they are not treated immediately.

Ragweed pollen

House dust

QuickLab

🕐 15 min

Constricted Airways

During an asthma attack, muscles surrounding the airways contract and restrict airflow into the lungs.

Procedure

❶ Get **three clean straws** and **three rubber bands.** Slip one rubber band near one end of a straw. Coil the rubber band around the straw so that it does not change the shape of the straw.

❷ Wrap another rubber band around the end of a second straw so that the straw is slightly crushed.

❸ Wrap the third rubber band around the last straw so that the straw is almost sealed.

❹ Breathe through each of the straws. Only breathe through your own straws. Compare the straws in terms of how easily you can breathe through them.

Analysis

1. **Describe** what the straw and rubber band represent.

2. **State** which straw represented an unrestricted airway.

3. **Describe** how this activity models an asthma attack.

4. **CRITICAL THINKING** **Predicting Outcomes** How might you reduce the prevalence of allergen-induced asthma attacks?

Asthma Asthma is an inflammation of the respiratory tract and is often caused by an allergic reaction to particles in the air. Asthma symptoms include coughing, wheezing, and difficulty in breathing. Asthma affects nearly 20 million Americans and causes more than 4,000 deaths each year.

Other Allergies Some foods that cause allergies are eggs, peanuts, milk, and shellfish. Food allergies may cause vomiting, diarrhea, and hives. They may be so severe that they cause a person to stop breathing and go into shock. Allergies to some detergents, cosmetics, or plants such as poison ivy can cause itchy red rashes and blisters. Some people are allergic to the stings of bees and other insects. Their reaction to a sting may include hives, difficulty in breathing, and loss of consciousness.

❯ **Reading Check** *Why is asthma classified as an allergy?*

allergy a physical response to an antigen, which can be a common substance that produces little or no response in the general population

allergen a substance that causes an allergic reaction

Mold

Dust mite

QuickLab

Teacher's Notes Although the lungs are not muscular organs, surrounding musculature is responsible for breathing and regulating passageway diameter. The intercostals, a series of muscles between the ribs, and the diaphragm muscle are responsible for pressure changes that drive inspiration and exhalation. The smooth muscle that lines air passageways from the trachea to the alveolar sacs maintain the essential muscle tone of these tubes. Paper straws could be used as well. Plastic is suggested because they are easier to obtain.

Materials
plastic straws (3)
rubber bands (3)

Answers to Analysis

1. The straw represents a breathing passageway in the lung. The rubber band represents a muscle that encircles the passageway.

2. The straw whose shape was not changed represents the unrestricted passageway.

3. Like a contracted muscle, the stretched rubber band exerted a force that closed the passageway it surrounded.

4. Reduce the exposure to allergens in the air by using air purifiers to eliminate allergens.

Why It Matters

Teacher's Notes Asthma can be triggered by a wide range of things including cigarette smoke, pollen, and pet dander.

Inner-city residents get asthma three times as often as people who live outside cities. Some scientists think that increased asthma rates in inner-city residents are least partly related to pollution.

Answers to Research

Answers will vary. Answers should incorporate aspects of the cytotoxic T cell response, and demonstrate knowledge of how that response fights infection.

Why It Matters

Allergies & Culture

REAL WORLD

The number of people in the United States suffering from asthma today is 1.75 times higher than in 1980. What is the reason for this trend? One interesting explanation, known as the *hygiene hypothesis,* suggests that improved sanitation conditions can lead to higher rates of asthma, allergies, and autoimmune disorders.

Immune System in Training

As sanitation conditions improve in industrialized nations, children are exposed to far fewer microorganisms. The hygiene hypothesis argues that when a child's immune system is not exposed to common microorganisms, it can become unbalanced and can trigger allergic responses to harmless substances.

The hygiene hypothesis proposes that an imbalance exists between helper T cells and cytotoxic T cells. A newborn child depends primarily on helper T cells to prevent infection. The cytotoxic T cell system grows stronger as a child is exposed to microbes in the environment. The hygiene hypothesis suggests that if a developing child is not exposed to a variety of microbes, the cytotoxic T cell system does not develop properly and helper T cells can become dominant.

How Clean is Too Clean? As a child grows older, the overdeveloped helper T cell system can provoke an aggressive allergic response to harmless substances such as pollen or pet dander or even the body's own cells.

Research Scientists hope that they can develop new treatments to stimulate the cytotoxic T cell system and relieve the suffering of many people with asthma, allergies, and autoimmune disorders. Find out about one such treatment and report on it.

T-cell

Autoimmune Diseases

The ability of the immune system to distinguish between "self" substances, which it ignores, and "nonself" molecules, which it attacks, is crucial to protecting the body from pathogens. Sometimes, the immune system loses its tolerance for "self," attacks certain cells of the body, and thus causes one of many **autoimmune diseases.** ❯ In an autoimmune disease, the body launches an immune response, such that body cells are attacked as if they were pathogens. Autoimmunity causes a wide range of disorders, some of which are shown in **Figure 11.** In all of these diseases, the immune system attacks the very organs that it is programmed to protect.

Common Autoimmune Disorders Diabetes is a disease in which the body does not produce or properly use the hormone insulin. This hormone allows glucose to enter body cells. Type 1 diabetes (or "juvenile" diabetes) is an example of an autoimmune disease. When a person has type 1 diabetes, the body does not produce or properly use insulin, the hormone that allows glucose to enter body cells. His or her immune cells attack the cells of the pancreas that produce insulin. As a result, he or she produces very little insulin, and the body cells starve for glucose while it accumulates in the blood. Type 1 diabetes is treated with insulin through injections or an insulin pump, shown in **Figure 10.**

Multiple sclerosis is an autoimmune disease in which the immune system targets the insulating material that covers nerves. This result is numbness, weakness, paralysis of one or more limbs, poor coordination, and vision impairment.

Autoimmune diseases affect 5% to 7% of the U.S. population and are three times more common in women than men. These diseases are not curable, but they are treatable to some extent. The causes of autoimmune diseases are not well understood but likely involve factors including genetics, environmental factors, or pathogens.

Figure 10 This insulin pump is used to treat type 1 diabetes. ❯ How is the immune system involved in type 1 diabetes?

> **autoimmune disease** a disease in which the immune system attacks the organism's own cells

Examples of Autoimmune Diseases

Disease	Areas affected	Symptoms
Graves' disease	thyroid gland	weakness, irritability, heat intolerance, increased sweating, weight loss, and insomnia
Systemic lupus erythematosus (SLE)	connective tissue, joints, and kidneys	facial skin rash, painful joints, fever, fatigue, kidney problems, and weight loss
Rheumatoid arthritis	joints	severe pain, fatigue, and disabling inflammation of joints
Psoriasis	skin	dry, scaly, red skin patches
Crohn's disease	digestive system	abdominal pain, nausea, vomiting, and weight loss

Figure 11 Autoimmune diseases can affect organs and tissues in various areas of the body.

Teaching Key Ideas

Organ Rejection Drugs such as cyclosporine and corticosteroids, which are immunosuppressants, are given to recipients of organ transplants. Have students hypothesize why this is necessary and what precautions transplant recipients must take. (Immunosuppressive therapy reduces the recipient's immune response to antigens found in the transplanted organ. Precautions against infection are necessary because the patient's immune system is weakened.) Have students explain why transplant patients are more likely than others to develop cancer. (One of the functions of the immune system is to destroy cancer cells before they spread.) **Verbal**

AIDS acquired immune deficiency syndrome, a disease caused by HIV, an infection that results in an ineffective immune system

HIV human immunodeficiency virus, the virus that causes AIDS

READING TOOLBOX

Mnemonics Create a mnemonic device to help you remember the types of immune system dysfunctions described in this section.

Figure 12 Family members like these two sisters are often donors for organ transplants.

Immune Deficiency

A strong immune system works so well and so quietly that we often don't realize how many times it has saved our lives. However, some people have a deficiency in which part of the immune system is missing or does not work properly. ❯ **When the immune system does not function, the body is unable to fight and survive infections by pathogens that do not cause any problems for a robust immune system.** Immune deficiencies can be inherited, acquired through infection, or even produced as an unintended side effect of a drug. They can affect antibodies, T cells, B cells, macrophages, or other substances normally produced by the immune system.

People who have immunodeficiency tend to have one infection after another. The infections are severe, and they last longer than they do in other people. Infections of the skin and the membranes lining the mouth, eyes, and digestive tract are common. The pathogens that cause infection are often ones that do not cause disease when present in the bodies of people who have healthy immune systems. Diseases caused by such agents are called *opportunistic infections*. These infections take advantage of the "opportunity" to infect a person who has a weakened immune system.

Innate Immune Deficiency Some people are born with immune deficiencies. These deficiences are usually inherited but are occasionally caused by problems during pregnancy. B cell and antibody defects are the most common kinds of innate immune deficiency. People who have these conditions are prone not only to infections but also to autoimmune disorders. Often, they do not develop immunity following vaccination. T cell defects are less common but more severe than B cell defects. Individuals fail to grow and develop normally, and they tend to develop overwhelming infections. In rare cases, neither the B cell nor the T cell response works. This condition is called *severe combined immunodeficiency (SCID)*. Babies who have SCID usually develop severe or even life-threatening infections.

Immune Suppression Sometimes, there is a medical reason to suppress the immune response. For example, after having an organ transplant, a person is given drugs that suppress immune function. Because the body does not recognize the transplanted organ as "self," these drugs are needed to keep the immune system from attacking the organ. The organ transplant recipient shown in **Figure 12** will need to take immunosuppressant drugs for life. Some drugs suppress the immune system as a side effect. Chemotherapy often causes supression of the immune system. People who have suppressed immune systems are more susceptible to opportunistic infections than people with healthy immune systems.

Why It Matters

SCID To help students understand our dependence on a functional immune system, show students a picture of David, the "boy in the bubble." David was born with severe combined immune deficiency (SCID), a disease characterized by the inability to produce lymphocytes, B cells, and T cells, which play key roles in the immune system. SCID patients must live in a protected environment because the slightest infection can lead to death. David died at the age of 12 after multiple unsuccessful bone marrow transplants.

AIDS The best-known acquired immune deficiency disease is **AIDS,** or acquired immune deficiency syndrome. In AIDS, a virus infects and kills helper T cells, shown in **Figure 13.** People who have AIDS are very susceptible to infections. Because only a few helper T cells are left in the body, neither the T cell nor the B cell response is triggered.

The virus that causes AIDS is called **HIV,** or human immunodeficiency virus. HIV is most commonly transmitted through human body fluids, such as semen, blood, and breast milk. Although HIV has been found in saliva, tears, and urine, these body fluids usually contain too few HIV particles to cause an infection. HIV is not transmitted through the air, on toilet seats, by kissing or handshaking, or by other forms of casual contact. Mosquitoes and ticks do not transmit HIV.

Once inside helper T cells, HIV is protected from the normal processes that would destroy it. The virus also uses the organelles of the host cell to produce copies of itself. Helper T cells that are loaded with HIV particles burst open, which releases large numbers of viruses into the bloodstream that can infect new cells. Initially, the immune system responds to the viruses. Antibodies to HIV can be detected in the blood. Someone whose blood contains antibodies to HIV is said to be HIV positive. As the infection progresses, the number of helper T cells decreases and the number of HIV particles increases, as shown in **Figure 13.** It takes an average of 10 years for HIV infection to progress to AIDS. AIDS is fatal in nearly every case. Currently, there is no vaccine or cure for HIV. However, some drugs can slow the progression from HIV infection to AIDS.

❯ **Reading Check** *Which immune cells does HIV destroy, and how does the virus destroy them?*

Course of HIV Infection

Figure 13 The graph plots the amount of helper T cells and viral RNA copies in the blood during HIV infection. In the micrograph, small HIV particles (orange) surround a helper T cell (white).

Lab

Time Required
30 minutes

Ratings

EASY ——————→ HARD

Teacher Prep   🧪🧪🧪
Student Setup   🧪🧪🧪
Concept Level   🧪🧪
Cleanup   🧪🧪🧪

Materials and Equipment
Materials for this lab can be ordered from WARD'S.

Safety Cautions
Review all safety symbols with students before beginning the lab. Emphasize that the solutions should not come in contact with their skin or clothes.

Tips and Tricks
Use stock dropper bottles of distilled water for all of the students except one. This one student will model the original disease carrier and should be given a dropper bottle containing 10 percent ascorbic acid. Both solutions will be clear and identical. A 10 percent solution of ascorbic acid is prepared by dissolving 10 g of ascorbic acid in 50 mL of water and diluting the mixture to 100 mL with water.

    Each student should randomly select a dropper bottle of unknown solution. Students will also need a large test tube and indophenol indicator solution. If the procedure is followed precisely, the route of transmission can be traced easily. Warn students not to select a new partner until each round is over and all students have exchanged liquids for that round. If one student makes a mistake, it can be very difficult to trace the transmission route. You will need a working group of at least 10 students to trace the disease transmission route back to the original disease carrier.

Objectives
➤ Model disease transmission.
➤ Organize and analyze data.

Materials
- safety goggles
- lab apron
- disposable gloves
- dropper bottle of unknown solution
- test tube, large
- dropper bottle of idophenol indicator

Safety

Disease Transmission Model

Communicable diseases are caused by pathogens and can be transmitted from one person to another. You can become infected by a pathogen in several ways, including by drinking contaminated water, eating contaminated foods, receiving contaminated blood, and inhaling infectious aerosols (droplets from coughs or sneezes). In this lab, you will model the transmission of a communicable disease. To do this, you will create a simulation of disease transmission. After the simulation, you will try to identify the person who was originally infected in the closed class population.

Procedure
Simulate Disease Transmission
1 Make two data tables similar to the ones shown.

Disease Transmission

Round number	Partner's name

Disease Source

Name of infected person	Names of infected person's partners		
	Round 1	Round 2	Round 3

2 🔶🔺🔷 Put on disposable gloves, a lab apron, and safety goggles.

3 ☠️ ⚗️ **CAUTION: Do not touch or taste any chemicals. Exercise caution when working with glassware such as a test tube.** You will be given a dropper bottle of an unknown solution. When your teacher says to begin, transfer three dropperfuls of your solution to a clean test tube.

4 Select a partner for Round 1. Record the name of this partner in your Disease Transmission table.

Answers to Procedure
3. One student will have an acidic solution but will be unaware that this solution differs from the other solutions.

5. After they share solutions, some students will have acidic mixtures ("infected" + "noninfected" or "infected" + "infected" solutions). Some students will have non-acidic solutions ("noninfected" + "noninfected" solutions).

7. Each repetition of the infection activity will increase the number of "infected" individuals.

8. Some solutions will remain colorless or turn pink. Others will turn blue.

9. All students will need to announce whether they are infected for this step.

10. If the procedure is followed precisely, the route of transmission can be traced easily.

11. A student volunteer should construct a diagram of the route of infection on the board or overhead projector.

5 Together, you and your partner have two test tubes. Pour the contents of one of the test tubes into the other test tube. Then, pour half of the solution back into the first test tube. You and your partner now share any pathogens either of you might have.

6 On your teacher's signal, select a new partner for Round 2. Record this partner's name in your Disease Transmission table. Repeat step 5.

7 On your teacher's signal, select a new partner for Round 3. Record this partner's name in your Disease Transmission table. Repeat step 5.

8 Add one dropperful of indophenol indicator to your test tube. "Infected" solutions will be colorless or will turn light pink. "Uninfected" solutions will turn blue. Record the results of your test.

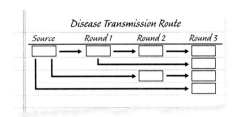

Disease Transmission Route

Trace the Disease Source

9 If you are infected, write your name and the name of your partner in each round on the board or on an overhead projector. Mark your infected partners. Record all of the data for your class in your Disease Source table.

10 To trace the source of the infection, cross out the names of the uninfected partners in Round 1. There should be only two names left. One is the name of the original disease carrier. To find the original disease carrier, place a sample from his or her dropper bottle in a clean test tube, and test it with indophenol indicator.

11 To show the disease transmission route, make a diagram similar to the one labeled "Disease Transmission Route." Show the original disease carrier and the people each disease carrier infected.

12 Clean up your lab materials according to your teacher's instructions. Wash your hands thoroughly before leaving the lab.

SCI LINKS.
www.scilinks.org
Topic: Disease
Code: HX80413

Analyze and Conclude

1. **SCIENTIFIC METHODS** **Interpreting Data** After Round 3, how many people were infected? Express this number as a percentage of your class.

2. **Relating Concepts** What do you think the clear fluids each student started with represent? Explain your response.

3. **Drawing Conclusions** Can someone who does not show any symptoms of a disease transmit that disease? Explain.

4. **SCIENTIFIC METHODS** **Further Inquiry** Write a new question about disease transmission that could be explored with another investigation.

Extensions

5. On the Job Public health officials, such as food inspectors, research and work to prevent the spread of diseases in human populations. Do research to find out how public health officials trace the origin of communicable diseases.

Answers to Analyze and Conclude

1. Answers will vary depending on class size.

2. The clear fluids represent uncontaminated aerosols, food, water, or blood (distilled water) and contaminated aerosols, food, water, or blood (ascorbic acid).

3. Yes, because some pathogens multiply in the body before symptoms appear. During this period of time, pathogens can be transmitted to another person.

4. Answers will vary. Sample questions: How does dividing the class into two or three quarantined groups before repeating the experiment affect the disease transmission rate? Would introducing two original disease carriers instead of one before repeating the experiment affect disease transmission rate?

Answers to Extensions

5. Answers will vary. Students should include information on the products and places public health officials inspect and what an inspection entails. Students should bring in the role of the Centers for Disease Control (CDC).

Key Resources

 Holt Lab Generator

 Lab Datasheet (Levels A, B, C)

 Holt Science Biology Video Labs

Reteaching Key Ideas

Lines of Defense Ask students to list the lines of defense against a pathogen. (1. barriers: skin, mucous membranes, fine hairs or cilia. 2. non-specific immune response: fever inflammation, histamine release, and protein activation 3. specific immune response: antigen detection and response)

Immune Response Review the eight steps of the immune response using **Figure 7.** Ask students to describe the role of each of the following pains in their own words.
- antigen and antibody
- helper T cell and cytotoxic T cell
- intracellular response and extra-cellular response

Key Ideas	Key Terms

1 Protecting Against Disease

❯ Skin and mucous membranes form strong barriers that prevent pathogens from entering the body.

❯ When pathogens break through the body's physical barriers, the body quickly responds with second-line defenses—fever, inflammation, and the activation of special proteins that kill or inhibit pathogens.

❯ When a pathogen infects a cell, the body produces immune cells that specialize in detecing and destroying that specific pathogen.

Key Terms

pathogen (525)
mucous membrane (525)
inflammation (526)
histamine (526)
antigen (526)
macrophage (526)

2 Eliminating Invaders

❯ A specialized white blood cell called a helper T cells activates the specific immune response. These cells coordinate two responses; the destruction of cells that have been infected by a pathogen, and the removal of pathogens at large in the body.

❯ Cytotoxic T cells attack and kill cells that have been infected by pathogens.

❯ The B cell response removes extracellular pathogens from the body and prevents further infection.

❯ After an immune response, memory cells continue to protect the body from previously encountered pathogens.

helper T cell (529)
cytotoxic T cell (530)
B cell (530)
plasma cell (530)
antibody (530)
memory cell (532)
immunity (532)
vaccine (532)

3 Immune System Dysfunctions

❯ An allergic reaction is an excessive immune response to a normally harmless antigen.

❯ In an autoimmune disease, the body launches an immune response so that body cells are attacked as if they were pathogens.

❯ When the immune system does not function, the body is unable to fight and survive infections by pathogens that do not cause problems for a robust immune system.

allergy (535)
allergen (535)
autoimmune disease (537)
AIDS (538)
HIV (538)

PART A: Answer all questions in this part.

Directions: For each statement or question, write on your separate answer sheet the number of the word or expression that best completes the statement or answers the question.

1 The purpose of introducing weakened microbes into the body of an organism is to stimulate the

(1) production of living microbes that will protect the organism from future attacks.

(2) production of antigens that will prevent infections from occurring.

(3) immune system to react and prepare the organism to fight future invasions by these microbes.

(4) replication of genes that direct the synthesis of hormones that regulate the number of microbes.

2 Certain microbes, foreign tissues, and some cancerous cells can cause immune responses in the human body because all three contain

(1) antigens.

(2) enzymes.

(3) fats.

(4) cytoplasm.

3 Which activity would stimulate the human immune system to provide protection against an invasion by a microbe?

(1) receiving antibiotic injections after surgery

(2) choosing a well-balanced diet and following it throughout life

(3) being vaccinated against chicken pox

(4) receiving hormones contained in mother's milk while nursing

4 Many vaccinations stimulate the immune system by exposing it to

(1) antibodies

(2) enzymes

(3) mutated genes

(4) weakened microbes

Base your answer to question 5 on the graph below and on your knowledge of biology.

Incidence of Three Human Diseases in Four Different Years

Key
▨ Diabetes
▨ Measles
▨ Bacterial pneumonia

5 Which statement best explains a change in the incidence of disease in 1970?

(1) Children were vaccinated against measles.

(2) New drugs cured diabetes.

(3) The bacteria that cause pneumonia developed a resistance to drugs.

(4) New technology helped to reduce the incidence of all three diseases.

6 Vaccinations help prepare the body to fight invasions of a specific pathogen by

(1) inhibiting antigen production

(2) stimulating antibody production

(3) inhibiting white blood cell production

(4) stimulating red blood cell production

7 The immune system of humans may respond to chemicals on the surface of an invading organism by

(1) releasing hormones that break down these chemicals

(2) synthesizing antibodies that mark these organisms to be destroyed

(3) secreting antibiotics that attach to these organisms

(4) altering a DNA sequence in these organisms

1. **(3)** Weakened microbes stimulate the immune system to act. This produces antibodies (not antigens) that destroy the invading microbes. The immune system then retains memory cells that will attack the microbes if they enter the body again. Hormones do not regulate microbe numbers. *(#24, August 2005 Regents Exam)*

2. **(1)** The immune system attacks cells that are labeled with antigens. Enzymes, fats, and cytoplasm in cells do not trigger an immune reaction. *(#31, June 2003 Regents Exam)*

3. **(3)** Vaccinations stimulate the immune system by introducing a weakened microbe into the body. Receiving antibodies, not hormones, while nursing can also stimulate the immune system. Eating a well-balanced diet can help a person to remain healthy, but it does not specifically stimulate the immune system. Receiving antibiotic injections can help to kill any dangerous bacteria, but it does stimulate the immune system to fight invading microbes such as viruses. *(#26, June 2003 Regents Exam)*

4. **(4)** When the body is exposed to weaked microbes, the immune system is stimulated to respond. Memory cells remain in the body after the immune response. These cells can recognize and attack the microbe if it invades the body again. Mutated genes and enzymes do not stimulate the immune system. Antibodies are cells within the immune system that attack pathogens. *(#08, January 2003 Regents Exam)*

5. **(1)** The number of people contracting measles dropped significantly, which indicates that children were vaccinated against measles during that year. The number of cases of diabetes increased, so a cure was not found and new technology did not decrease its incidence. The number of cases of pneumonia decreased, so it is unlikely that a resistant strain developed. *(#36, August 2005 Regents Exam)*

6. **(2)** Vaccinations stimulate an immune response, and thus do not inhibit white blood cell production or antigen production. Moreover, red blood cells are not

Regents Exam Practice Correlations

| 4.5.2c | 2, 17 | 4.5.2e | 1, 3, 4, 5, 6, 12 |
| 4.5.2d | 7, 8, 11, 13, 16 | 4.5.2g | 10 |

involved in an immune response. (#23, January 2006 Regents Exam)

7. **(2)** The immune system does not alter the DNA of invading organisms, nor does it secrete antibiotics that attach to pathogens. Also, the immune system does not release hormones, but it does make antibodies that target pathogens. (#18, January 2006 Regents Exam)

8. **(2)** The choice describing mutations is incorrect because white blood cells are immune system cells that locate and destroy, but not mutate, bacteria. The choices describing toxins and DNA insertion are not true. (#21, August 2006 Regents Exam)

9. **(2)**

10. **(3)** The immune system does not produce antibiotics, antigens against antibodies, or enzymes against antibodies. However, antibodies are produced that react with specific antigens to cause allergic reactions. (#49, June 2006 Regents Exam)

11. **(4)** White blood cells are not involved in nerve impulses. Different types of white blood cells can engulf bacteria, produce antibodies against bacteria, and help the body prepare for a future invasion by a particular type of bacteria. (#20, January 2005 Regents Exam)

12. **(2)** Antibodies are not present in a vaccination, they are produced by the body in response to the foreign antigen in the vaccination. Vaccinations are not designed to reduce the body's ability to produce antibodies. A vaccination usually allows the body to build a resistance to one type of disease. It does not confer the ability to resist most types of diseases. (#22, June 2004 Regents Exam)

8 Some human white blood cells help destroy pathogenic bacteria by
(1) causing mutations in the bacteria
(2) engulfing and digesting the bacteria
(3) producing toxins that compete with bacterial toxins
(4) inserting part of their DNA into the bacterial cells

9 How does altering the DNA of a peanut affect the proteins in peanuts that cause allergic reactions?
(1) The altered DNA is used to synthesize changed forms of these proteins.
(2) The altered DNA leaves the nucleus and becomes part of the allergy-producing protein.
(3) The altered DNA is the code for the antibodies against the allergens.
(4) The altered DNA is used as an enzyme to break down the allergens in peanuts.

10 Allergic reactions usually occur when the immune system produces
(1) antibiotics against usually harmless antigens
(2) antigens against usually harmless antibodies
(3) antibodies against usually harmless antigens
(4) enzymes against usually harmless antibodies

11 Which activity is not a function of white blood cells in response to an invasion of the body by bacteria?
(1) engulfing these bacteria
(2) producing antibodies to act against this type of bacteria
(3) preparing for future invasions of this type of bacteria
(4) speeding transmissions of nerve impulses to detect these bacteria

12 Which statement best describes what will most likely happen when an individual receives a vaccination containing a weakened pathogen?
(1) The ability to fight disease will increase due to antibodies received from the pathogen.
(2) The ability to fight the disease caused by the pathogen will increase due to antibody production.
(3) The ability to produce antibodies will decrease after the vaccination.
(4) The ability to resist most types of diseases will increase.

13 A part of the Hepatitis B virus is synthesized in the laboratory. This viral particle can be identified by the immune system as a foreign material but the viral particle is not capable of causing disease. Immediately after this viral particle is injected into a human it
(1) stimulates the production of enzymes that are able to digest the Hepatitis B virus.
(2) triggers the formation of antibodies that protect against the Hepatitis B virus.
(3) synthesizes specific hormones that provide immunity against the Hepatitis B virus.
(4) breaks down key receptor molecules so that the Hepatitis B virus can enter body cells.

Base your answer to question 14 on the graph below and on your knowledge of biology.

14 A diagnosis of AIDS is made when the helper T cell count is less than 200 cells per mL of blood. How many months after infection did the onset of AIDS occur?

(1) 18   (3) 54
(2) 39   (4) 69

15 HIV causes AIDS by attacking and destroying
(1) B cells.   (3) neutrophils.
(2) helper T cells.   (4) natural killer cells.

13. **(2)** Enzymes alone do not digest invading pathogens. Hormones do not offer immunity against pathogens. The breaking down of receptor molecules is not a mechanism of the immune system. The viral particle triggers the immune system to produce antibodies. (#28, January 2004 Regents Exam)

14. **(3)**

15. **(2)**

16 The diagram below represents one possible immune response that can occur in the human body. The structures that are part of the immune system are represented by

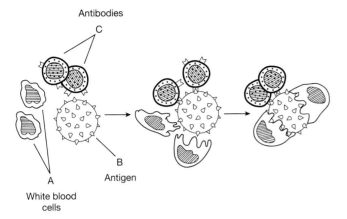

(1) A, only

(2) A and C, only

(3) B and C, only

(4) A, B, and C

17 Many people become infected with the chicken pox virus during childhood. After recovering from chicken pox, these people are usually immune to the disease for the rest of their lives. However, they may still be infected by viruses that cause other diseases, such as measles.

Discuss the immune response to the chicken pox virus. In your answer, be sure to include:

- the role of antigens in the immune response
- the role of white blood cells in the body's response to the virus
- an explanation of why recovery from an infection with the chicken pox virus will not protect a person from getting a different disease, such as measles
- an explanation of why a chicken pox vaccination usually does not cause a person to become ill with chicken pox

18 What is represented by the sequence below?

(1) a feedback mechanism in multicellular organisms

(2) an immune response

(3) differentiation of organic molecules

(4) the disruption of cellular communication

---

antigens are shaped differently.; Allow 1 credit for explaining why a chicken pox vaccination usually does not cause a person to become ill with chicken pox. Acceptable responses include, but are not limited to: A vaccine contains weakened virus.; A vaccine usually consists of a dead or weakened form of the disease organism that stimulates the production of antibodies without causing the disease. (*#56 June 2005»Regents Exam*)

18. Activated B cells are the source of memory cells and plasma cells, which produce antibodies. Without B cells, the body's response to another exposure to that antigen will be impaired.

---

16. (2) Antibodies and white blood cells can locate and destroy a pathogen by recognizing and binding to the antigens on that pathogen. (*#29, August 2003 Regents Exam*)

PART C

17. Allow a maximum of 4 credits for discussing the immune response to the chicken pox virus, allocated as follows: Allow 1 credit for stating the role of antigens in the immune response. Acceptable responses include, but are not limited to: Antigens stimulate the immune response.; Antigens on the chicken pox virus are recognized by the person's immune system and it responds by producing antibodies.; Allow 1 credit for stating the role of white

blood cells in the body's response to the virus. Acceptable responses include, but are not limited to: White blood cells attack and destroy the virus.; White blood cells are able to recognize foreign antigens.; White blood cells make antibodies against the virus.; Allow 1 credit for explaining why recovery from an infection with the chicken pox virus will not protect a person from getting a different disease, such as measles. Acceptable responses include, but are not limited to: These antibodies are specific for the chicken pox virus.; The antibodies the body makes against the chicken pox antigens (or virus) have specific shapes that only work against the antigens on the chicken pox virus, not the measles virus, because their

Reproduction and Development

		Standards	Teach Key Ideas

CHAPTER OPENER, pp. 546–547   `15 min.`

The Living Environment

SECTION 1 The Male Reproductive System, pp. 549–551   `30 min.`

> Sperm Production
> Sperm's Path Through the Body
> Semen
> Sperm Delivery

Standards: 4.4.1e, 4.4.1g

Teach Key Ideas:
- **Bellringer Transparency**
- **Transparencies** J90 Structure of the Testis • J91 Sperm Cell • J92 Male Hormones and Reproduction • J93 Male Reproductive System
- **Visual Concepts** Formation of Sperm • Human Male Reproductive System • Path of Sperm Through the Male Body • Parts of a Human Sperm

---

SECTION 2 The Female Reproductive System, pp. 552–556   `35 min.`

> Egg Production
> Preparation for Pregnancy
> Menstrual Cycle

Standards: 4.4.1e, 4.4.1f

Teach Key Ideas:
- **Bellringer Transparency**
- **Transparencies** J95 Female Reproductive System • J96 Ovarian and Menstrual Cycles
- **Visual Concepts** Formation of an Ovum • Human Female Reproductive System • Path of an Egg Through the Female Body • Menstrual Cycle and Hormones • Menstrual Cycle and Uterine Lining

---

SECTION 3 Human Development, pp. 557–560   `60 min.`

> Fertilization
> First Trimester
> Second and Third Trimesters

Standards: 4.4.1c, 4.4.1d, 4.4.1f, 4.4.1h

Teach Key Ideas:
- **Bellringer Transparency**
- **Transparencies** J97 Early Zygote Development • J100 Structure of the Placenta
- **Visual Concepts** Fertilization • Cleavage and Implantation • Pregnancy Overview • Infertility • Parts of the Placenta • Function of the Placenta • First Trimester • Second Trimester • Third Trimester • Afterbirth

---

SECTION 4 Sexually Transmitted Infections, pp. 561–565   `30 min.`

> STI Transmission and Treatment
> Common STIs

Standards: 4.5.2b, 4.5.2f

Teach Key Ideas:
- **Bellringer Transparency**
- **Transparencies** J35 Sexually Transmitted Diseases • J42 Known Routes of HIV Transmission
- **Visual Concepts** Gonorrhea • Syphilis • Chlamydia • Pelvic Inflammatory Disease • AIDS (Acquired Immunodeficiency Syndrome)

See also PowerPoint® Resources

Chapter Review and Assessment Resources

- **SE** Super Summary, p. 566
- **SE** Regents Exam Practice, p. 567
- Regents Review Guide
- Review Resources
- Chapter Tests A and B
- Holt Online Assessment
- Regents Question Banks on Teacher's One-Stop Planner

CHAPTER Fast Track   *If students will get this material in a health class, you may want to eliminate the labs and cover the 4 sections in 3 days.*

Basic Learners
- **TE** K-W-L Chart, p. 550
- **TE** Harmful Factors, p. 559
- **TE** Making a Chart, p. 562
- Directed Reading Worksheets*
- Active Reading Worksheets*
- Lab Manuals, Level A*
- Study Guide* ■
- Note-taking Workbook*
- Special Needs Activities and Modified Tests*

Advanced Learners
- **TE** PMS, p. 554
- **TE** HPV Vaccine, p. 562
- Critical Thinking Worksheets*
- Concept Mapping Worksheets*
- Science Skills Worksheets*
- Lab Datasheets, Level C*

Why It Matters	Hands-On	Skills Development	Assessment
Build student motivation with resources about high-interest applications.	SE **Inquiry Lab** A Closer Look at Gametes, p. 547*■	TE **Reading Toolbox** Assessing Prior Knowledge, p. 546 SE **Reading Toolbox,** p. 548	
TE **Risk of Disorders in Offspring,** p. 549			SE **Section Review** TE **Formative Assessment** Spanish Assessment*■ 📁 **Section Quiz**■
TE **Sperm and Egg Size,** p. 553 TE **Fertility and Youth,** p. 554 TE **Fat Intake,** p. 555	SE **Quick Lab** Hormone Secretions, p. 556*■ 📁 **Inquiry Lab** Observing the Effect of Thyroxine on Frog Metamorphosis*	SE **Reading Toolbox** Finding Main Ideas, p. 553 TE **Reading Toolbox** Finding Main Ideas, p. 553 TE **Math Skills** Calculating Percent, p. 554	SE **Section Review** TE **Formative Assessment** Spanish Assessment*■ 📁 **Section Quiz**■
TE **Pregnancy Side Effects,** p. 559 TE **Demonstration** Sonogram Video, p. 560	SE **Quick Lab** An Amniotic Shock Absorber, p. 559*■ SE **Inquiry Lab** Sonography, p. 565*■ 📁 **Quick Lab** Blood-Typing: Pregnancy and Hemolytic Disease*	SE **Reading Toolbox** Recognizing Main Ideas, p. 558 TE **Reading Toolbox** Recognizing Main Ideas, p. 558	SE **Section Review** TE **Formative Assessment** Spanish Assessment*■ 📁 **Section Quiz**■
SE **Seeing Double,** p. 564	SE **Quick Lab** STI Rates, p. 562	TE **Reading Toolbox** Visual Literacy, p. 561 TE **Math Skills** Calculating, p. 563 TE **Reading Toolbox** Visual Literacy, p. 564	SE **Section Review** TE **Formative Assessment** Spanish Assessment*■ 📁 **Section Quiz**■

See also Lab Generator

See also Holt Online Assessment Resources

Resources for Differentiated Instruction

English Learners
TE Cause and Effect, p. 555
📁 Directed Reading Worksheets*
📁 Active Reading Worksheets*
📁 Lab Manuals, Level A*
📓 Study Guide*■
📓 Note-taking Workbook*
📓 Multilingual Glossary
💿 Interactive Tutor

Struggling Readers
TE Cause and Effect, p. 555
📁 Directed Reading Worksheets*
📁 Active Reading Worksheets*
📁 Lab Manuals, Level A*
📓 Study Guide*
📓 Note-taking Workbook*
📓 Special Needs Activities and Modified Tests*
💿 Interactive Tutor

Special Education Students
TE Demonstrating Diffusion, p. 558
📁 Directed Reading Worksheets*
📁 Active Reading Worksheets*
📁 Lab Manuals, Level A*
📓 Study Guide*■
📓 Note-taking Workbook*
📓 Special Needs Activities and Modified Tests*

Alternative Assessment
TE Vocabulary, p. 553
📁 Science Skills Worksheets*
📁 Section Quizzes*■
📓 Chapter Tests A, B, and C*■

Chapter 23

Chapter 23

Reproduction and Development

Overview

The purpose of this chapter is to explain human reproduction and development. The male reproductive system produces sperm cells, and the female reproductive system produces egg cells. These cells join during fertilization to form a zygote, which develops into an embryo and then a fetus. The gestation period of humans is about nine months. Diseases of the reproductive tract include sexually transmitted infections.

READING TOOLBOX

Assessing Prior Knowledge Students should understand the following concepts:
- mitosis and meiosis
- negative and positive feedback systems
- etiology and transmission of communicable diseases

Visual Literacy Ask students what they can infer about the development of major organs in a four-month-old fetus that is capable of moving, sleeping, and swallowing. (Its organs are highly developed by this time.)

Preview

1 The Male Reproductive System
Sperm Production
Sperm's Path Through the Body
Semen
Sperm Delivery

2 The Female Reproductive System
Egg Production
Preparation for Pregnancy
Menstrual Cycle

3 Human Development
Fertilization
First Trimester
Second and Third Trimesters

4 Sexually Transmitted Infections
STI Transmission and Treatment
Common STIs

Why It Matters

All people start life as a single fertilized egg. Thus, the story of a fertilized egg's formation and development is the story of how your own life began.

This human fetus has been developing inside its mother for four months.

The Living Environment
Standard 4 Students will understand and apply scientific concepts, principles, and theories pertaining to the physical setting and living environment and recognize the historical development of ideas in science.
Key Idea 4 The continuity of life is sustained through reproduction and development. *Major Understandings* - 4.1c, 4.1d, 4.1e, 4.1f, 4.1g, 4.1h
Key Idea 5 Organisms maintain a dynamic equilibrium that sustains life. *Major Understandings* - 5.2b, 5.2f

This fetus is only a little longer than 10 cm, but it is already able to hear, move, sleep, and swallow.

Chapter Correlations The Living Environment

Standard 4

4.1c The processes of meiosis and fertilization are key to sexual reproduction in a wide variety of organisms. The process of meiosis results in the production of eggs and sperm which each contain half of the genetic information. During fertilization, gametes unite to form a zygote, which contains the complete genetic information for the offspring.

4.1d The zygote may divide by mitosis and differentiate to form the specialized cells, tissues, and organs of multicellular organisms.

4.1e Human reproduction and development are influenced by factors such as gene expression, hormones, and the environment. The reproductive cycle in both males and females is regulated by hormones such as testosterone, estrogen, and progesterone.

4.1f The structures and functions of the human female reproductive system, as in almost all other mammals, are designed to produce gametes in ovaries, allow for internal fertilization, support the internal development of the embryo and fetus in the uterus, and provide essential materials through the placenta, and nutrition through milk for the newborn.

4.1g The structures and functions of the human male reproductive system, as in other mammals, are designed to produce gametes in testes and make possible the delivery of these gametes for fertilization.

4.1h In humans, the embryonic development of essential organs occurs in early stages of pregnancy. The embryo may encounter risks from faults in its genes and from its mother's exposure to environmental factors such as inadequate diet, use of alcohol/drugs/tobacco, other toxins, or infections throughout her pregnancy.

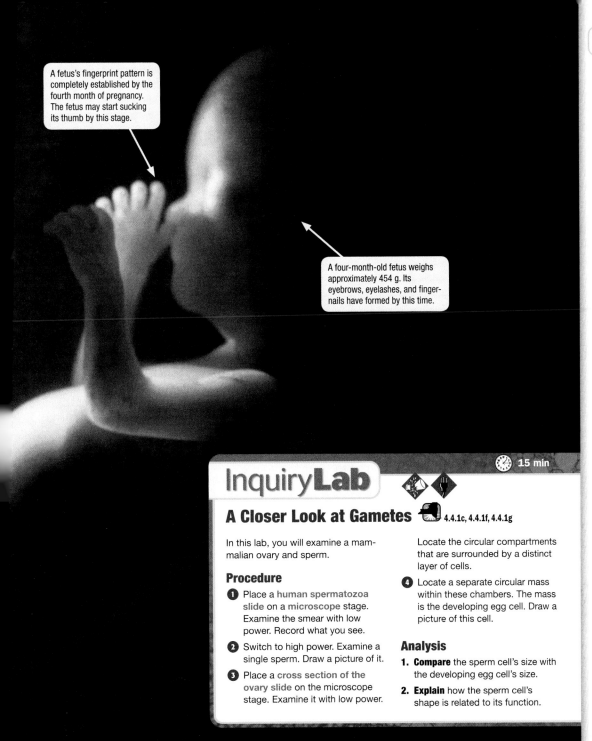

A fetus's fingerprint pattern is completely established by the fourth month of pregnancy. The fetus may start sucking its thumb by this stage.

A four-month-old fetus weighs approximately 454 g. Its eyebrows, eyelashes, and finger-nails have formed by this time.

InquiryLab

Teacher's Notes Explain that although sperm is a male gamete, it may carry either an X chromosome or a smaller Y chromosome. The larger X chromosome has about 1000 genes, while the Y chromosome carries about 80 genes. In humans, sex is determined by the XY or XX outcome of fertilization.

Materials
- microscope
- prepared mammal ovary and sperm slides

Safety Caution Have students review the safety rules for handling sharp objects.

Answers to Analysis
1. The sperm is much smaller than the egg.
2. It has a streamlined body with a tail that can propel the cell.

Key Resources
 Interactive Tutor

⏱ 15 min

InquiryLab

A Closer Look at Gametes 4.4.1c, 4.4.1f, 4.4.1g

In this lab, you will examine a mammalian ovary and sperm.

Procedure

1. Place a **human spermatozoa slide** on a **microscope** stage. Examine the smear with low power. Record what you see.

2. Switch to high power. Examine a single sperm. Draw a picture of it.

3. Place a **cross section of the ovary slide** on the microscope stage. Examine it with low power.

Locate the circular compartments that are surrounded by a distinct layer of cells.

4. Locate a separate circular mass within these chambers. The mass is the developing egg cell. Draw a picture of this cell.

Analysis

1. **Compare** the sperm cell's size with the developing egg cell's size.

2. **Explain** how the sperm cell's shape is related to its function.

5.2b Viruses, bacteria, fungi, and other parasites may infect plants and animals and interfere with normal life functions.

5.2f Some viral diseases, such as AIDS, damage the immune system, leaving the body unable to deal with multiple infectious agents and cancerous cells.

Using Words
1. ovum
2. women

Using Language
Pathogens are transmitted in many ways.

Using FoldNotes
Check students' work for accuracy.

These reading tools can help you learn the material in this chapter. For more information on how to use these and other tools, see **Appendix: Reading and Study Skills.**

Using Words

Word Families Word families are terms that share a root. The meanings of words within a family differ according to the suffixes, prefixes, and other roots which have been added to the roots.

Your Turn Use the information in the table to answer the questions below.

1. What do you think is carried through an oviduct?
2. Who do you think are more likely to get ovarian cancer, men or women?

Word Parts		
Word	Part of speech	Meaning
ovum	noun	egg
ovary	noun	organ that produces eggs
ovulate	verb	to release an egg from the ovary

Using Language

Recognizing Main Ideas A main idea is a sentence that states the main point of a paragraph. The main idea is often, but not always, one of the first few sentences of a paragraph. All the other sentences of the paragraph give support to the main idea.

Your Turn Find the main idea in the paragraph below.

Disease-causing pathogens are transmitted in many ways. Some pathogens can be passed by drinking contaminated water. Other pathogens are present in body fluids such as semen. These pathogens can be passed from one person to another through sexual contact.

Using FoldNotes

Pyramid A pyramid is a unique method for taking notes. The three sides of the pyramid can summarize information in three categories.

Your Turn Create a pyramid to summarize the development of a human fetus during the three trimesters.

1. Start with a square sheet of paper. Fold the paper in half diagonally to form a triangle.
2. Fold the triangle in half to form a smaller triangle.
3. Open the paper. The creases of the two folds will have created an X.
4. Using scissors, cut along one of the creases. Start from any corner, and stop at the center point to create two flaps.
5. Use tape or glue to attach one flap on top of the other flap.

The Male Reproductive System

Key Ideas	Key Terms	Why It Matters
➤ Where are male gametes produced? ➤ What path do sperm take to exit the body? ➤ What occurs as sperm move into the urethra? ➤ What happens to sperm after they exit the body?	testis seminiferous tubules epididymis vas deferens prostate gland semen penis	When humans reproduce, they pass their genes to their children. You have about half of your father's genes and half of your mother's genes.

Humans reproduce sexually by internal fertilization. The roles of the male reproductive system are to produce sperm and to deliver sperm to the female reproductive system.

Sperm Production

➤ **The male reproductive system has two testes (testicles) that produce the male gametes, *sperm*, and the primary male sex hormone, testosterone.** The **testes** are inside the *scrotum,* a sac that hangs from the body. Normal body temperature, 37 °C, is too high for proper sperm development. The temperature in the scrotum is about 3 °C lower than normal body temperature, so it is ideal for sperm production.

Seminiferous Tubules As **Figure 1** shows, testes have hundreds of compartments packed with tightly coiled tubes called **seminiferous tubules.** Sperm cells are produced through meiosis in the seminiferous tubules. Thus, human sperm cells have only 23 chromosomes (the haploid number) instead of the usual 46 chromosomes (the diploid number) found in other body cells. Two hormones released by the pituitary, luteinizing hormone (LH) and follicle-stimulating hormone (FSH), regulate the functioning of the testes. LH causes cells surrounding the seminiferous tubules to secrete testosterone. This hormone, along with FSH, stimulates sperm production. Testosterone also stimulates the growth of facial hair and other male features.

➤ **Reading Check** *Describe how hormones regulate sperm production. (See the Appendix for answers to Reading Checks.)*

The Living Environment
Standard 4

4.1e Human reproduction and development are influenced by factors such as gene expression, hormones, and the environment. The reproductive cycle in both males and females is regulated by hormones such as testosterone, estrogen, and progesterone.

4.1g The structures and functions of the human male reproductive system, as in other mammals, are designed to produce gametes in testes and make possible the delivery of these gametes for fertilization.

> **testis** (TES TEEZ) the primary male reproductive organ, which produces sperm cells and testosterone
>
> **seminiferous tubule** (sem uh NIF uhr uhs) one of the many tubules in the testis where sperm are produced

Epididymis

Seminiferous tubules

Developing sperm cells

Testis

Figure 1 Sperm are produced in the testes' seminiferous tubules. If these tubules were uncoiled, they would extend the length of six football fields!

Key Resources

Transparencies
J90 Structure of the Testis
J91 Sperm Cell
J92 Male Hormones and Reproduction
J93 Male Reproductive System

Visual Concepts
Formation of Sperm
Human Male Reproductive System
Path of the Sperm Through the Male Body
Parts of a Human Sperm

➤ Focus

Overview

This section explains the male reproductive system, focusing on the production of sperm, the path sperm take to exit the body, and what happens to sperm that enter the female reproductive system.

🔔 Bellringer

Use the Bellringer transparency to prepare students for this section.

➤ Teach

Teaching Key Ideas

Identifying Preconceptions Ask students if they think they are at risk for developing cancer. (Students may answer "no" because they think cancer is a disease of older people.) Explain that testicular cancer generally strikes young men between the ages of 15 and 35 years. **LS Verbal**

Why It Matters

Risk of Disorders in Offspring Tell students that researchers have found links between increasing paternal age (>35) and a higher risk of disorders in their offspring, such as autism, heart defects, and schizophrenia. Explain that some researchers propose that the causes of these disorders may stem from mutations that may occur in the cells that make sperm.

Section Correlations
4.4.1e
4.4.1g

Teaching Key Ideas

Vasectomy Explain to students that a vasectomy is a minor operation performed on adult males as a method of birth control. In a vasectomy, both vas deferens are cut to stop sperm from exiting the body. Ask students how a vasectomy might affect secondary sex characteristics. (Not at all; cutting the vas deferens does not affect the production of male hormones, only the release of sperm. Therefore secondary sex characteristics will not be affected.) **LS Verbal/Logical**

Teaching Key Ideas

Using Visuals Have students identify which part of the sperm shown in **Figure 3** must penetrate the egg for fertilization to take place. (the head, which contains paternal DNA) Which parts help sperm move toward and fertilize an egg? (the tail, which propels the sperm, and midpiece, which houses mitochondria that provide energy for movement) **LS Visual**

Answers to Caption Questions

Figure 2: Sperm leave the testes and enter the epididymis. From there, they move through the vas deferens, into the urethra, and from there exit the body.

Figure 3: the sperm's head

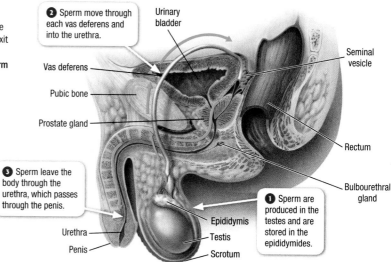

Figure 2 The arrows show the path that sperm take as they exit the body. ❯ After leaving the testes, what structures do sperm move through?

❷ Sperm move through each vas deferens and into the urethra.

❸ Sperm leave the body through the urethra, which passes through the penis.

❶ Sperm are produced in the testes and are stored in the epididymides.

Urinary bladder · Vas deferens · Pubic bone · Prostate gland · Seminal vesicle · Rectum · Bulbourethral gland · Epididymis · Testis · Scrotum · Urethra · Penis

Figure 3 A sperm cell consists of a head, a midpiece, and a tail. ❯ Which part of the sperm cell is able to fertilize an egg?

Enzymes · Mitochondria · Head · Nucleus · Midpiece · Tail

Sperm's Path Through the Body

Sperm production starts during puberty and continues throughout adulthood. A typical adult male produces several hundred million sperm cells each day. The path sperm travel through the male reproductive system is illustrated in **Figure 2.** When sperm first form in the seminiferous tubules, they are not capable of swimming or of fertilizing an egg. The immature sperm travel along tubes to the epididymis. The **epididymis** is a long coiled tube attached to the top of each testis. Within each of these tubes, the sperm mature and are stored for up to two weeks. From the epididymis, sperm move to another long tube, the **vas deferens.** ❯ The vas deferens carries sperm into the urethra. Sperm leave the body by passing through the urethra, the same duct through which urine exits the body. A valve at the bladder-urethra connection prevents urine from entering the urethra when sperm are moving through it.

Structure of Mature Sperm As **Figure 3** shows, a mature sperm cell has a head with very little cytoplasm, a midpiece, and a long tail. Enzymes produced at the tip of the head help the sperm cell to penetrate an egg cell during fertilization. The midpiece contains many mitochondria that supply sperm with the energy they need to propel themselves through the female reproductive system. The tail of a sperm cell is a powerful flagellum that whips back and forth. This whipping motion allows the sperm cell to move. ATP produced within the mitochondria powers the movements of the tail. During fertilization, only the head of a sperm cell enters an egg. As a result, a male's mitochondria are not passed to his offspring.

❯ **Reading Check** *Why does a sperm cell need mitochondria?*

Differentiated Instruction

Basic Learners

K-W-L Chart Before students continue further in this chapter, have each construct a K-W-L chart. Ask them to list what they know about reproduction, development, and STIs (sexually-transmitted infections) in the *K* column. Then have students list things they want to know in the *W* column. Because some students may be embarrassed to talk about this material, provide a box for students to submit their *W* questions anonymously. Have students save their lists and add what they learn to the *L* column. They should correct *K* information if needed as they study the chapter. **LS Verbal**

Semen

> As sperm cells move into the urethra, they mix with fluids secreted by the seminal vesicles, the prostate gland, and the bulbourethral glands. As you can see in **Figure 4,** these fluids nourish the sperm and aid their passage through the female reproductive system. The *seminal vesicles* lie between the bladder and the rectum. These exocrine glands produce a fluid rich in sugars that sperm use for energy. The **prostate gland** is located just below the bladder. This gland secretes an alkaline fluid that helps to balance the acidic pH in the female reproductive system. Fluid from the *bulbourethral glands* neutralizes traces of acidic urine in the urethra and lubricates the path as sperm leave the body. The mixture of these fluids that are secreted with sperm is called **semen.**

Sperm Delivery

The urethra passes through the **penis,** the male organ that deposits sperm into the female reproductive system during sexual intercourse. During arousal, blood flow to the penis increases. The penis contains a high volume of spongy tissue. Small spaces separate the cells of the spongy tissue. Blood collects within these spaces, which causes the penis to become erect. Muscles around each vas deferens contract, moving sperm into the urethra. The ejection of semen out of the penis through the urethra is called *ejaculation.*

> After semen is deposited in the female reproductive system, sperm swim until they encounter an egg cell or until they die. If sperm cells are unable to reach an egg, fertilization does not occur. About 3.5 mL of semen, which contains 300–400 million sperm, are expelled during ejaculation. Many sperm die in the acidic environment of the female reproductive system. In order for even one sperm cell to reach and penetrate an egg, the sperm count (sperm per mL of semen) must be high. Males with fewer than 20 million sperm per mL of semen are generally considered sterile.

> **Reading Check** *Explain why a high sperm count is necessary for fertilization.*

Figure 4 These sperm are swimming in a mixture of fluids that nourish, protect, and lubricate the sperm.

epididymis (ep uh DID i mis) the long, coiled tube that is on the surface of a testis and in which sperm mature

vas deferens (vas DEF uh renz) a duct through which sperm move from the epididymis to the ejaculatory duct at the base of the penis

prostate gland (PRAHS TAYT) a gland in males that contributes to the seminal fluid

semen (SEE muhn) the fluid that contains sperm and various secretions produced by the male reproductive organs

penis the male organ that transfers sperm to a female and that carries urine out of the body

---

Section 1 Review

>KEY IDEAS

1. **Describe** the testes' function.
2. **State** where sperm go after leaving the epididymis.
3. **List** the components of semen.
4. **Explain** what happens to sperm when they enter a female's body.

CRITICAL THINKING

5. **Recognizing Relationships** How do secretions by exocrine glands help the delivery of sperm to the female reproductive system? Explain your reasoning.
6. **Inferring Relationships** If a male's left vas deferens is blocked by scar tissue, how will his sperm count most likey be affected? Explain your answer.

PROBLEM SOLVING

7. **Applying Concepts** Sperm cells contain many more mitochondria than most other types of cells. Why do you think sperm have such a large number of mitochondria?

Answers to Review

1. Testes produce gametes, called sperm, and the sex hormone testosterone.

2. Sperm enter the vas deferens and then exit the body through the urethra.

3. sperm; a sugary fluid produced by the seminal vesicles; and alkaline fluids, produced by the prostate gland and the bulbourethral glands

4. The sperm continue to swim until they reach either an egg or run out of energy.

5. Exocrine secretions provide alkalinity, which decreases the acidity of the male urethra and the female reproductive tract. Exocrine secretions also provide nourishment and a fluid environment in which the sperm can swim.

6. The sperm count is likely reduced by half since mature sperm from the left epididymis will be blocked.

7. Mitochondria produce ATP, which powers most cellular processes. Sperm need a large amount of fuel to be able to swim along a female's reproductive tract and fertilize an egg.

Section **2**

The Female Reproductive System

Key Ideas	Key Terms	Why It Matters
❯ What are the functions of the ovaries? ❯ How does the female body prepare for pregnancy? ❯ What changes occur in the female's body when an ovum is not fertilized?	ovary ovulation ovum menstrual cycle fallopian tube menstruation uterus vagina	Human babies develop inside the female reproductive system.

The Living Environment
Standard 4
4.1e Human reproduction and development are influenced by factors such as gene expression, hormones, and the environment. The reproductive cycle in both males and females is regulated by hormones such as testosterone, estrogen, and progesterone.
4.1f The structures and functions of the human female reproductive system, as in almost all other mammals, are designed to produce gametes in ovaries, allow for internal fertilization, support the internal development of the embryo and fetus in the uterus, and provide essential materials through the placenta, and nutrition through milk for the newborn.

Each month, the female reproductive system prepares for a possible pregnancy by producing a mature egg cell—the female gamete. The mature egg is called an *ovum.* If the ovum is fertilized by a sperm cell, and if the fertilized ovum implants in the uterus, a pregnancy will begin. The fertilized egg will be fed and protected through nine months of development.

Egg Production

Two **ovaries,** shown in **Figure 5,** are found within the female's abdomen. ❯ The ovaries produce egg cells. Ovaries also secrete estrogen and progesterone, the female sex hormones. The ovaries of a newborn female contain about 2 million immature egg cells. Egg cells have 23 chromosomes (the haploid number) because eggs, like sperm, are formed through meiosis. This process begins in the egg cells of a female before she is born, but it becomes stalled in prophase of the first meiotic division. When a female reaches puberty, the levels of sex hormone rises. This event allows meiosis to start again. However, only one egg cell completes development each month inside one of an adult female's ovaries.

Figure 5 The ovaries of the female reproductive system produce egg cells. The uterus nurtures the fetus during pregnancy.

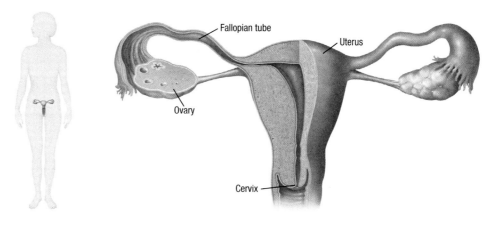

Focus

This section explains the female reproductive system, focusing on the production and maturation of eggs, ovulation, and the menstrual cycle.

Bellringer
Use the Bellringer transparency to prepare students for this section.

Teach

Teaching Key Ideas

Female Fertility Ask students at what age women can no longer become pregnant and give birth. (Some will be familiar with menopause, which occurs at an average age of 51.) Ask students at what age men can no longer father children. (There is no age limit unless disability or disease causes him to be unable to father children.) Ask students to infer why the probability of birth defects increases with maternal age, beginning at about age 35. (A woman is born with all the eggs she will ever have. A woman's eggs age as she ages, increasing the probability of genetic damage.) **LS Verbal**

Section Correlations	
4.4.1e	
4.4.1f	

Key Resources

Transparencies
J95 Female Reproductive System
J96 Ovarian and Menstrual Cycles

Visual Concepts
Formation of an Ovum
Human Female Reproductive System
Path of an Egg Through the Female Body
Menstrual Cycle and Hormones
Menstrual Cycle and Uterine Lining

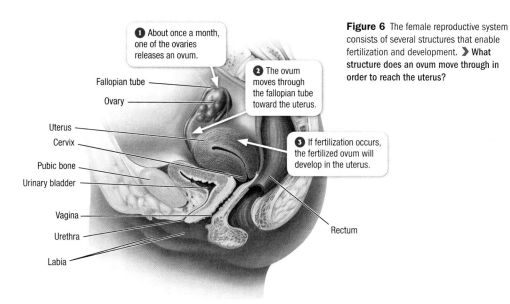

① About once a month, one of the ovaries releases an ovum.

Fallopian tube

Ovary

② The ovum moves through the fallopian tube toward the uterus.

Uterus

Cervix

Pubic bone

Urinary bladder

③ If fertilization occurs, the fertilized ovum will develop in the uterus.

Vagina

Urethra

Rectum

Labia

Figure 6 The female reproductive system consists of several structures that enable fertilization and development. ❯ **What structure does an ovum move through in order to reach the uterus?**

The Egg's Path In contrast to the male reproductive system, which produces millions of gametes each day, the female reproductive system produces about one viable egg each month. Although a female is born with about 2 million eggs in her ovaries, only 300–400 egg cells will mature in her lifetime. When an egg cell matures, it is called an **ovum.** An ovum is about 75,000 times larger than a sperm cell and can be seen with the unaided eye.

After an ovum is released from an ovary, cilia sweep the ovum into a fallopian tube. The **fallopian tube,** shown in **Figures 5 and 6,** is a passageway through which an ovum moves from an ovary to the uterus. Rhythmic contractions of the smooth muscles lining the fallopian tube move the ovum down the tube and toward the uterus. An ovum's journey through a fallopian tube usually takes three or four days to complete. If sperm are present in the fallopian tube during this time, the ovum may become fertilized.

The Vagina and Uterus The external structures of the female reproductive system are collectively called the *vulva.* The vulva includes the *labia,* which are folds of skin and mucous membranes that cover and protect the opening of the vagina. The **vagina** is a muscular tube that leads from the vulva to the entrance to the uterus, the *cervix.* A sphincter muscle in the cervix controls the opening to the uterus. The **uterus** is a muscular, triangle-shaped organ that is about the size of a small fist. During sexual intercourse, sperm are deposited inside the vagina. If fertilization occurs, the ovum develops into a baby inside the uterus. During childbirth, a baby passes through the cervix and leaves the mother's body through the vagina.

❯ **Reading Check** *Where does an ovum become fertilized?*

ovary (OH vuh ree) an organ that produces eggs in the female reproductive system

ovum (OH vuhm) a mature egg cell

fallopian tube (fuh LOH pee uhn) a tube through which eggs move from the ovary to the uterus

vagina (vuh JIE nuh) the female reproductive organ that connects the outside of the body to the uterus and that receives sperm during reproduction

uterus (YOOT uhr uhs) in female mammals, the hollow, muscular organ in which an embryo embeds itself and develops into a fetus

READING TOOLBOX

Finding Main Ideas Read the first paragraph on this page. What is its main idea of that paragraph?

❯❯Teach, continued

Teaching Key Ideas

Location of the Uterus Students are often confused about the location of the uterus. Point out that the uterus sits above the bladder but under the intestine. As the fetus grows, compression of the abdominal and thoracic organs can become a problem late in the pregnancy, causing an expectant mother to experience fatigue, backache, indigestion, circulatory problems, or reduced lung capacity.

Math Skills

Calculating Percent At puberty, females have more than 400,000 immature egg cells in their ovaries. Have students calculate the percent of eggs that will be released, assuming 13 ovarian cycles per year and a reproductive life span of a woman of approximately 40 years.
(40 years × 13 eggs = 520 eggs; 520 eggs/400,000 eggs × 100 = 0.13%)
LS Logical

Answers to Caption Questions

Figure 7: The follicle nourishes the maturing egg.

SCiLINKS.
www.scilinks.org
Topic: Reproductive System
Code: HX81296

---

ovulation (AHV yoo LAY shuhn) the release of an ovum from a follicle of the ovary

---

Figure 7 Ovulation occurs about midway through the 28-day ovarian cycle.
❯ What is the function of the follicle?

Preparation for Pregnancy

The female reproductive organs are structured to prepare a fertilized egg for development into a baby. This process is called *pregnancy.*
❯ Throughout a female's reproductive years, her body undergoes a hormonal cycle that causes periodic changes. These changes prepare the body in the event that an egg is fertilized. Two sets of hormones control the female cycle. Follicle-stimulating hormone (FSH) and luteinizing hormone (LH) are secreted by the pituitary gland. Estrogen and progesterone are secreted by the ovaries. All of these hormones tell the body to prepare for fertilization. Each of these hormones has a role in preparing the body for a pregnancy. If fertilization occurs, some of these hormones continue to be released. This process keeps the body from producing another egg and ovulating while a fertilized egg is developing. If fertilization does not occur, production of progesterone and estrogen slows and eventually stops. Thus, the hormonal cycle is complete for that month. After the uterine lining is shed, the cycle begins again.

The Ovarian Cycle The ovaries prepare and release an ovum in a series of events collectively called the *ovarian cycle.* This cycle has three parts: the follicular phase, ovulation, and the luteal phase. All three phases are regulated by changes in the levels of the female hormones. The release of an ovum from an ovary is called **ovulation.** **Figure 7** illustrates the process of ovulation. After ovulation, the ovum is drawn into the fallopian tube and begins to move toward the uterus. The lining of the uterus becomes enriched with nutrients and liquids. Although the duration of the ovarian cycle varies, the cycle generally lasts about 28 days.

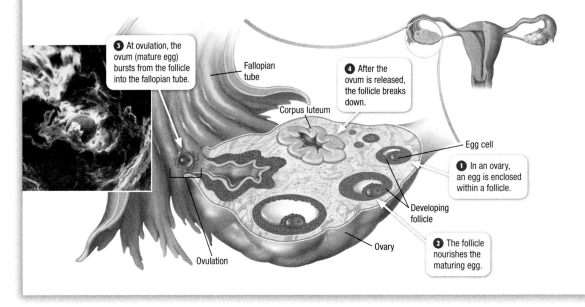

❸ At ovulation, the ovum (mature egg) bursts from the follicle into the fallopian tube.

Fallopian tube

❹ After the ovum is released, the follicle breaks down.

Corpus luteum

Egg cell

❶ In an ovary, an egg is enclosed within a follicle.

Developing follicle

Ovary

❷ The follicle nourishes the maturing egg.

Ovulation

Why It Matters

Fertility and Youth It is a common belief that females cannot become pregnant before they menstruate. However, ovulation precedes a menstrual flow. Therefore, a young female ovulates *before* her first menstrual period. It is therefore possible for a girl to become pregnant before her first period.

Differentiated Instruction

Advanced Learners

PMS Premenstrual syndrome (PMS) refers to symptoms such as mood changes, depression, anxiety, irritability, headaches, and bloating just before menstruation. Ask students to research the cause of these symptoms (hormonal changes) and treatments for PMS. (hormonal contraceptives, antidepressants, nutritional approaches, counseling, and exercise)
LS Verbal

Follicular Phase In an ovary, egg cells mature within follicles. A *follicle* is a cluster of cells that surrounds an immature egg cell and provides the egg with nutrients. The follicular phase, shown in **Figure 8,** marks the beginning of the ovarian cycle. Levels of hormones in the blood control the maturation of the egg. The egg begins to mature when the pituitary releases FSH into the bloodstream. FSH causes the follicle to develop and to produce estrogen. Estrogen does many things during this phase. First, it aids in the growth of the follicle. Second, it stimulates the lining of the uterus to thicken. Finally, it causes the anterior pituitary to secrete more LH. The rise in LH leads to ovulation.

Ovulation Ovulation occurs when a mature egg bursts out of a follicle. At first, a small increase in the level of estrogen slows the release of FSH from the pituitary. This kind of interaction, in which an increase in one hormone results in a decrease in another hormone, is called *negative feedback.* As the follicle nears maturity, it secretes larger and larger amounts of estrogen. The pituitary responds to the rising level of estrogen in the blood by causing the anterior pituitary gland to secrete more LH. This interaction, in which an increase in one hormone results in an increase in another hormone, is called *positive feedback.* The large amount of LH in the bloodstream causes the egg cell to complete its first meiotic division. LH also causes the follicle to burst. Ovulation occurs when the follicle bursts and the ovum is released.

Luteal Phase After ovulation, LH causes the cells of the ruptured follicle to grow and fill the cavity of the follicle. The new structure which forms is called a *corpus luteum.* Therefore, this stage of the ovarian cycle is called the *luteal phase.* The corpus luteum is a mass of follicle cells that acts like an endocrine gland. This mass of cells secretes estrogen and progesterone. These hormones turn on the growth of new blood vessels in the uterus. They also stimulate the storage of fluids and nutrients in the lining of the uterus, which causes the lining to thicken further. In addition, the estrogen and progesterone inhibit the release of more FSH and LH by the pituitary by negative feedback. Levels of FSH and LH in the blood fall, which prevents the formation of new follicles (and a second opportunity for fertilization) within a single ovarian cycle. The luteal phase lasts about 14 days. If an egg does not become embedded in the lining of the uterus during this period, the lining will be shed in a process known as *menstruation.*

❯ **Reading Check** *What event causes the ovarian cycle to enter the luteal phase?*

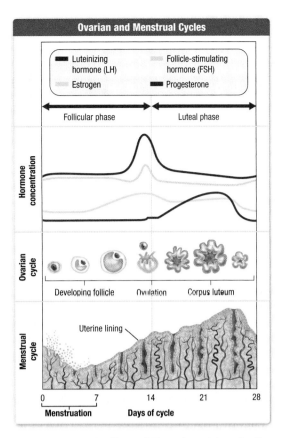

Figure 8 The ovarian cycle is regulated by hormones produced by the hypothalamus and the pituitary gland. The menstrual cycle is regulated by hormones produced by the follicle and the corpus luteum. ❯ **During which stage of the ovarian cycle does the corpus luteum form?**

ACADEMIC
VOCABULARY

mature to reach full growth or development

QuickLab

Teacher's Notes Remind students to use the key to properly assign hormone names to the colored curves.

Answers to Analysis

1. LH, estrogen, and FSH
2. A peak in estrogen production precedes and causes a spike (the LH surge) in LH production.
3. negative feedback; as progesterone increases, LH and FSH decrease.
4. positive feedback; as estrogen increases, LH also increases.

> **Close**

Formative Assessment

Which hormone causes the release of an egg?

A. estrogen (Correct. Estrogen causes the release of an egg during ovulation.)

B. progesterone (Incorrect. Progesterone does not stimulate the release of an egg.)

C. LH (Incorrect. LH causes follicular rupture.)

D. FSH (Incorrect. FSH causes the follicle to develop.)

Data

QuickLab

🕐 15 min

4.4.1e, 4.4.1f

Ovulation

Hormone Secretions

The ovarian and menstrual cycles are regulated by hormones secreted by the hypothalamus, the pituitary, and the ovaries. Feedback mechanisms play a major role in these cycles. Use **Figure 8** and the explanation in the text to answer the following questions.

Analysis

1. **Identify** the hormones that are secreted in large amounts prior to ovulation.

2. **Describe** the effect of estrogen on the secretion of LH.

3. **CRITICAL THINKING** **Analyzing Concepts** What type of feedback mechanism causes a decrease in the secretion of LH and FSH during the luteal phase?

4. **CRITICAL THINKING** **Analyzing Concepts** What type of feedback mechanism causes the surge of LH secretion during the follicular phase?

---

menstrual cycle the female reproductive cycle, characterized by a monthly change of the lining of the uterus and the discharge of blood

menstruation the discharge of blood and discarded tissue from the uterus during the menstrual cycle

---

Menstrual Cycle

The series of changes that prepares the egg for fertilization is the ovarian cycle. The series of changes that prepares the uterus for a possible pregnancy is the **menstrual cycle.** The menstrual cycle lasts about 28 days and is driven by the changing levels of estrogen and progesterone during the ovarian cycle. Before ovulation, increasing levels of estrogen cause the lining of the uterus to thicken with blood vessels. This prepares the uterus for the possible implantation of a fertilized egg. The blood vessels will nourish the egg as it develops into an embryo.

After ovulation, high levels of both estrogen and progesterone cause further development and maintenance of the uterine lining. ❯ **If pregnancy does not occur, the levels of estrogen and progesterone fall. This decrease causes the lining of the uterus to be shed.** The menstrual cycle ends at the same time as the hormonal cycle ends. Both cycles then begin again. Every month, the uterus is preparing for pregnancy.

Menstruation When the lining of the uterus is shed, blood vessels break and bleeding results. A mixture of blood and discarded tissue then leaves the body through the vagina. This process, called **menstruation,** usually begins about 14 days after ovulation and lasts for three to five days. The ovarian and menstrual cycles eventually stop, usually when a woman is between the ages of 45 and 55. The end of menstruation, called *menopause,* marks the end of the child-bearing phase of a woman's life.

❯ **Reading Check** *What causes menstruation to occur?*

Section 2 Review

❯ KEY IDEAS

1. **Identify** the functions of the ovaries.

2. **Summarize** the path of an egg through the female reproductive system.

3. **Compare** the roles of LH and FSH in the ovarian cycle.

4. **Explain** how the menstrual cycle is related to the ovarian cycle.

CRITICAL THINKING

5. **Recognizing Relationships** What causes the lining of the uterus to thicken and then to be shed during the menstrual cycle?

6. **Relating Concepts** How could the maturation of an egg cell in an ovary be halted?

MATH SKILLS

7. **Problem Solving** A woman does not ovulate while she is pregnant. Pregnancy generally lasts nine months. If a woman goes through three pregnancies, how many fewer mature eggs will she release in her lifetime than if she never became pregnant?

Answers to Review

1. to produce eggs and female sex hormones

2. A mature egg is released by the ovary and enters a fallopian tube. From there, it travels to the uterus. If the egg has been fertilized, it implants in the uterus's wall. If it has not been fertilized, it is flushed out of the vagina along with part of the uterine lining during menstruation.

3. LH and FSH both induce the follicle to produce estrogen. Increased secretion of LH causes the follicle to rupture and ovulation to occur. Continued secretion of LH stimulates the growth of the corpus luteum. Estrogen and progesterone secreted by the corpus luteum suppress further release of LH and FSH.

4. Changes in sex hormone levels caused by the ovarian cycle drive the changes that take place in the uterus during the menstrual cycle.

5. Rising estrogen and progesterone levels cause the uterine lining to thicken in preparation for pregnancy. When estrogen and progesterone levels drop, the lining is shed.

6. reduced levels of FSH or LH

7. 27

Section 3

Human Development

Key Ideas	Key Terms	Why It Matters
➤ How does fertilization occur? ➤ What important events occur in the first trimester of pregnancy? ➤ What important event occurs at the end of the third trimester of pregnancy?	embryo implantation fetus	All humans go through the same developmental stages as they change from a single fertilized egg into a complex organism composed of billions of cells.

Development begins with a single diploid cell. Billions of other cells arise from this one cell. During pregnancy, the uterus provides protection and nourishment to the developing human being.

Fertilization

If sperm are present in the female reproductive system within a few days after ovulation, fertilization may occur. To fertilize an ovum, a sperm cell must move up into a fallopian tube. ➤ **During fertilization, a sperm cell penetrates an ovum by releasing enzymes from the tip of its head. These enzymes break down the jellylike outer layers of the ovum. The head of the sperm enters the ovum, and the nuclei of the ovum and sperm fuse together.** This fusion produces a diploid cell called a *zygote*.

Cleavage and Implantation The zygote undergoes a series of mitotic divisions known as cleavage, as **Figure 9** shows. Cleavage produces many smaller cells—first two cells, then four, then eight, and so on. The resulting clump of cells is called an **embryo.** Cleavage continues as the embryo moves toward the uterus. By the time it reaches the uterus, the embryo is a hollow ball of cells called a *blastocyst*. About six days after fertilization, the blastocyst burrows into the lining of the uterus in an event called **implantation.**

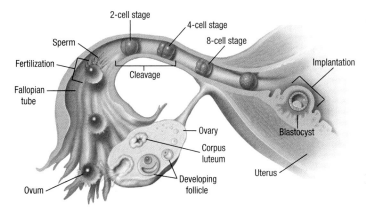

Figure 9 labels: 2-cell stage, 4-cell stage, 8-cell stage, Sperm, Fertilization, Cleavage, Fallopian tube, Implantation, Ovary, Corpus luteum, Blastocyst, Developing follicle, Uterus, Ovum

The Living Environment
Standard 4

4.1c The processes of meiosis and fertilization are key to sexual reproduction in a wide variety of organisms. The process of meiosis results in the production of eggs and sperm which each contain half of the genetic information. During fertilization, gametes unite to form a zygote, which contains the complete genetic information for the offspring.

4.1d The zygote may divide by mitosis and differentiate to form the specialized cells, tissues, and organs of multicellular organisms.

4.1f The structures and functions of the human female reproductive system, as in almost all other mammals, are designed to produce gametes in ovaries, allow for internal fertilization, support the internal development of the embryo and fetus in the uterus, and provide essential materials through the placenta, and nutrition through milk for the newborn.

4.1h In humans, the embryonic development of essential organs occurs in early stages of pregnancy. The embryo may encounter risks from faults in its genes and from its mother's exposure to environmental factors such as inadequate diet, use of alcohol/drugs/tobacco, other toxins, or infections throughout her pregnancy.

embryo (EM bree OH) an organism in an early stage of development; in humans, a developing individual from first cleavage through the next eight weeks

implantation the process by which a blastocyst embeds itself in the lining of the uterus

 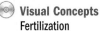

Figure 9 Fertilization, cleavage, and implantation may occur after ovulation.
➤ What has the embryo become by the time it reaches the uterus?

Key Resources

Transparencies
J97 Early Zygote Development
J100 Structure of the Placenta

Visual Concepts
Fertilization
Cleavage and Implantation
Pregnancy Overview
Infertility
Parts of the Placenta
Function of the Placenta
First Trimester
Second Trimester
Third Trimester
Afterbirth

➤ Focus

This section explains fertilization and development of the embryo and fetus, beginning with conception and ending with birth.

🎧 Bellringer

Use the Bellringer transparency to prepare students for this section.

➤ Teach

Teaching Key Ideas

Rates of Development Draw a small dot on the board. Ask students how the size of this dot compares with a newly fertilized egg. (It is larger than a fertilized egg.) Tell students that a fertilized egg is about 0.14 mm (0.005 in.) in diameter. Then, tell students that the average length of a newborn baby is approximately 51 cm (20 in.). Have them calculate a fetus's average rate of growth per month (5.7 cm [2.2 in.] per month) and their own average rate of growth per month since birth. Use 0.6 cm, or 0.23 in. as an average for a 16-year-old. Ask them how the rate of growth during prenatal growth compares with that of postnatal growth. (It is 9.5 times faster; $5.7/0.6 = 9.5$) **LS Logical**

Answers to Caption Questions
Figure 9: a blastocyst

Section Correlations	
4.4.1c	4.4.1f
4.4.1d	4.4.1h

Teaching Key Ideas

Exchange of Materials Ask students to explain what relationship the right side of **Figure 10** has to the left side. (The figure to the right is an enlargement of the area encircled in the figure to the left.) Ask students to describe what the enlargement shows. (how the blood vessels of the fetus and the blood vessels of the mother come into close contact, how maternal blood bathes fetal vessels, and how fetal and maternal blood do not mix) Ask students which structure carries nutrients and oxygen from the placenta to the embryo. (the umbilical cord) **LS Visual**

Recognizing Main Ideas Tell students that sometimes the same words in the text head appear in the topic sentence. (First Trimester: The most important events for development occur in the first trimester; Supportive Membranes: Membranes that will protect and feed the embryo begin to develop very shortly after implantation.) **LS Verbal**

Answers to Caption Questions

Figure 10: Materials diffuse across the walls of the fetus's capillaries inside the placenta. Nutrients diffuse into the capillaries, while wastes diffuse out of the capillaries. The wastes are carried away by the mother's bloodstream.

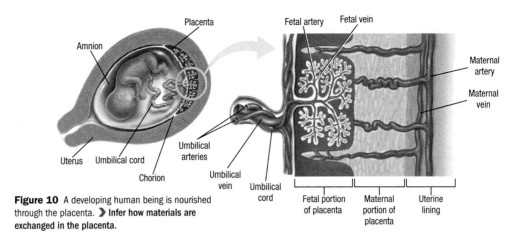

Figure 10 A developing human being is nourished through the placenta. ❯ **Infer how materials are exchanged in the placenta.**

fetus a developing human from the end of the eighth weeks after fertilization until birth

READING TOOLBOX

Recognizing Main ideas How do the text heads on this page relate to the main ideas of the paragraphs following the heads? Which sentence states the main idea for each paragraph?

First Trimester

Human development takes about nine months—a period known as *gestation,* or pregnancy. Pregnancy begins when the embryo implants itself in the wall of the uterus. The nine months of pregnancy are typically divided into three *trimesters,* or three-month periods. The most important events of development occur in the first trimester. ❯ **All of the embryo's organ systems, as well as the supportive membranes that feed and protect the embryo, develop during the first trimester of pregnancy.**

Supportive Membranes Membranes that will protect and feed the embryo begin to develop very shortly after implantation. One membrane, the *amnion,* encloses and protects the embryo. Another membrane, the *chorion,* interacts with the uterus to form the placenta. The umbilical cord connects the amnion with the placenta. The placenta, shown in **Figure 10,** is the structure through which the mother feeds the embryo. The placenta forms by the third week of pregnancy. The mother's blood does not mix with the blood of the embryo. Instead, nutrients in the mother's blood diffuse through the placenta. The nutrients are carried to the embryo through blood vessels in the umbilical cord, which is fully formed by the sixth week of pregnancy. The waste products of the embryo diffuse back through the placenta into the mother's blood.

Other substances, including drugs, can also diffuse through the placenta. Thus, if the mother ingests any harmful substances, the embryo is also affected. Pregnant women who smoke may have premature births and underweight babies. Pregnant women who abuse alcohol, especially during early pregnancy, may have babies that suffer from fetal alcohol syndrome. Fetal alcohol syndrome is a group of birth defects which may include facial deformation and severe mental, behavioral, and physical retardation. All drugs that are inappropriate for infants should be avoided, or used only with a physician's prescription, throughout pregnancy.

Differentiated Instruction

Special Education Students

Demonstrating Diffusion Have students place a few drops of food coloring into a beaker of water and observe the coloring move or diffuse through the water. Explain that the food coloring particles move from an area of greater concentration to an area of lesser concentration. This is how oxygen moves from mother to baby and how carbon dioxide moves from baby to mother. Glucose diffuses from mother to baby with the help of a special protein. **LS Kinesthetic/Visual**

Embryonic Development As the placenta takes shape, the inner cells of the blastocyst form the three primary tissue layers of the embryo—endoderm, mesoderm, and ectoderm. By the end of the third week, blood vessels and the digestive system begin to develop. The embryo is about 2 mm long. In the fourth week, arm and leg buds form. By the end of the fourth week, all of the major organs begin to form, and the heart begins to beat. The embryo has more than doubled its length. During the second month, the final stages of embryonic development take place. The arms and legs take shape. By the end of the second month, the embryo is about 25 mm long and weighs about 1 g.

Fetal Development From the end of eighth week after fertilization until childbirth, the developing human is called a **fetus**. By the end of the first trimester, the sex of the fetus can be distinguished. The fetus has recognizable body features, as **Figure 11** shows. The fetus's major organ systems continue to develop.

> **Reading Check** *During which trimester do the embryo's organs begin to form?*

Hands-On
QuickLab

🕐 15 min

An Amniotic Shock Absorber 4.4.1f

In this lab, you will model how amniotic fluid serves as a shock absorber for a developing fetus.

Procedure

❶ Stand a paper clip upright in a base of clay. Tap the top of the clip to see how much force is needed to topple it.

❷ Fill a sandwich bag with water. Place the clip within its clay base at the center of the water-filled bag, and seal the bag. Gently tap the bag. Does this impact topple the clip?

Analysis

1. **Compare** the parts of this model to an actual amnion.

2. **CRITICAL THINKING** **Analyzing Concepts** Explain how the water-filled bag affected the force needed to topple the paper clip.

QuickLab

Teacher's Note Have students work in pairs.

Materials
- clay
- paper clip
- sandwich bag, plastic
- water

Answers to Analysis

1. sandwich bag: the amnion membrane; water: the amniotic fluid; clip: the developing organism

2. The clip required a great deal of force to be toppled.

Teaching Key Ideas

Nutrition During Pregnancy A mother-to-be must have a sufficient supply of the B vitamin folic acid in her body before and during pregnancy or the fetus may be at risk for neural tube defects. Folic acid is found in some enriched foods and vitamin supplements. Have students access the Web site of the National Institutes of Health for more information on prenatal care.

Answers to Caption Questions

Figure 11: Possible answer: The facial features are more defined, the arms and legs are longer, and the eyelids have formed.

---

8 weeks Major organ systems have begun to form. Limbs are forming.

12 weeks Skin and nails form. Organs are developing.

21 weeks Hair forms on body and head. Facial features are developing.

Figure 11 Near the end of the third trimester, a fetus doubles and then triples in size. > How does the 8-week-old fetus compare with the 12-week-old fetus?

8 months Subcutaneous tissue is forming. Fetal development nears completion.

Differentiated Instruction

Basic Learners

Harmful Factors Ask students to brainstorm environmental factors that could damage the fetus. Write them on the board. (Answers may include alcohol, lead, rubella, drugs, and X-rays.) Some studies show that large quantities of caffeine can cause low birth weight. Other research suggests that small amounts of caffeine are safe. Students may want to research other harmful substances. **LS Verbal**

Why It Matters

Pregnancy Side Effects Early in pregnancy, elevated progesterone and estrogen levels may cause excessive salivation and nausea, or morning sickness. Abdominal pressure may cause stomach acid to wash backward into the esophagus, causing heartburn. Total blood volume rises, and blood pressure and pulse rate increase. The heart pumps 20 to 40 percent more blood, depending on the stage of pregnancy. Pressure by the uterus on pelvic blood vessels may cause varicose veins to result due to the restricted blood flow back from the legs.

Teach, continued

Demonstration

Sonogram Video Obtain a video of a sonogram. Have students identify as many structures as they can. Ask them to explain the uses of ultrasound during pregnancy. (detect pregnancy, determine the size and age of a fetus, and check for fetal health and abnormalities) **LS** Visual

Close

Formative Assessment

Following fertilization, cleavage begins while the zygote is in _____.

A. a fallopian tube (Correct! Fertilization and then cleavage take place when the zygote is in the fallopian tube.)

B. an ovary (Incorrect. Fertilization and cleavage can take place only after ovulation, which is the release of the egg from the ovary.)

C. the uterus (Incorrect. By the time the egg reaches the uterus, it already has undergone cleavage several times.)

D. the placenta (Incorrect. The placenta is the structure through which the mother feeds the embryo.)

Answers to Caption Questions

Figure 12: If the baby was pushed out of the mother feet first or in some other position, it would be easy for a limb to be caught and the baby's passage through the vagina to be stopped.

Placenta — Umbilical cord — Uterus — Vagina

Figure 12 Doctors use ultrasound imaging to monitor a fetus's growth. The fetus shown in this ultrasound (left) is near birth. During childbirth (right), the fetus exits the mother's body through the vagina. **>** Why is it important that the baby exit the mother head first?

www.scilinks.org
Topic: Before Birth
Code: HX80140

Second and Third Trimesters

During the second trimester (4–6 months) the fetus grows to about 15 cm in length. Bone development continues. Toenails and fingernails form. The brain develops and begins to control muscle responses. By the end of the fifth month, the fetus begins to move. It stretches its arms and legs, and may even suck its thumb. The mother may be able to feel these movements. The fetus has a fast heartbeat. Doctors may use ultrasound images, such as the one shown in **Figure 12,** to monitor the fetus's growth.

In the third trimester (7–9 months) the fetus gains about 2.5 kg. The brain and nerves develop. The fetus can hear smell, and see light. The lungs mature. The fetus moves into a head down position during the ninth month, and becomes less active. **> By the end of the third trimester, the fetus is able to live outside the mother's body. The fetus leaves the mother's body in a process called labor, which usually lasts several hours. During labor, the walls of the uterus contract and expel the fetus from the uterus, as shown in Figure 12.** The fetus leaves the mother's body through the vagina. Further contractions of the uterus expel the placenta and the umbilical cord.

> Reading Check *How does the fetus change in the third trimester?*

Section 3 Review

> KEY IDEAS

1. **Summarize** the events in development that occur during fertilization.

2. **Explain** what important events occur in the first trimester of pregnancy.

3. **Describe** the events that occur at the end of the third trimester.

CRITICAL THINKING

4. **Relating Concepts** Why can some drugs be harmful to a fetus if the mother takes them while she is pregnant?

5. **Predicting Outcomes** What might happen if more than one egg were released from the ovaries prior to fertilization?

ALTERNATIVE ASSESSMENT

6. **Sequencing Events** Draw a timeline that illustrates the developmental changes that occur during each of the three trimesters of pregnancy. Use photos, drawings, and/or charts to illustrate your timeline.

Answers to Section Review

1. The zygote undergoes cleavage. The resulting clump is an embryo, which moves toward the uterus. Cleavage continues during this time and the embryo is a blastocyst by the time it reaches the uterus. About six days after fertilization, the blastocyst implants itself in the uterus.

2. All of the embryo's organ systems, as well as the supportive membranes that feed and protect the embryo, develop during the first trimester.

3. The walls of the uterus begin to contract and push the fetus out of the mother's vagina. Once the fetus is born, the placenta and umbilical cord are also expelled.

4. They can cross the placenta from mother to fetus.

5. A multiple birth may occur if all eggs are fertilized.

6. Timelines will vary.

Sexually Transmitted Infections

Key Ideas	Key Terms	Why It Matters
› How can you avoid being infected by an STI? › What are some common STIs in the United States?	genital herpes pelvic inflammatory disease	STIs are some of the most common infectious diseases in the world.

Diseases spread by sexual contact are called sexually transmitted diseases (STIs). Some of the most common STIs in the United States are listed in **Figure 13.**

STI Transmission and Treatment

Disease-causing pathogens are transmitted in many ways. Pathogens present in body fluids, such as semen, can be passed from one person to another through sexual contact. STIs can be caused by both viruses and bacteria. › **Abstinence is the only sure way to protect yourself from contracting an STI.** Early detection and treatment are necessary to prevent serious consequences that can result from infection. Some viral STIs can be treated with antiviral medication. Many bacterial STIs can be treated and cured with antibiotics. However, early symptoms of most bacterial STIs are very mild and often are not detected. Untreated bacterial STIs can cause sterility in both men and women.

› **Reading Check** *How are different kinds of STIs treated?*

The Living Environment
Standard 4
5.2b Viruses, bacteria, fungi, and other parasites may infect plants and animals and interfere with normal life functions.
5.2f Some viral diseases, such as AIDS, damage the immune system, leaving the body unable to deal with multiple infectious agents and cancerous cells.

Figure 13 The table shows the estimated new cases of STIs per year for the entire American population.

Sexually Transmitted Infections		
Infection	New cases per year	Symptoms
Genital HPV	5,500,000	warts on genital or anal region
Trichomoniasis	5,000,000	often no symptoms in males; yellow-green vaginal discharge with strong odor in females
Chlamydia	3,000,000	painful urination and penile discharge in males; abdominal pain and vaginal discharge in females
Genital herpes	1,000,000	painful blisters around the genital region; flulike symptoms
Gonorrhea	650,000	painful urination and penile discharge in males; abdominal pain and vaginal discharge in females
Hepatitis B	120,000	flulike symptoms and yellowing of skin
Syphilis	70,000	sores on penis in males; sores in vagina or on cervix in females; fever and rash; destruction of body tissue
HIV/AIDS	40,000	immune-system failure and susceptibility to infections

Source: Centers for Disease Control and Prevention

Key Resources

Transparencies
J35 Sexually Transmitted Diseases
J42 Known Routes of HIV Transmission

Visual Concepts
Gonorrhea
Syphilis
Chlamydia
Pelvic Inflammatory Disease
AIDS (Acquired Immunodeficiency Syndrome)

› Focus

This section describes the causes, symptoms and treatments of some STIs that are common in the United States.

Bellringer

Use the Bellringer transparency to prepare students for this section.

› Teach

Teaching Key Ideas

STIs Are "Silent" Tell students that one reason STIs are such a health problem is that many people do not realize they are infected. People with STIs have no symptoms 70 to 80 percent of the time. This is one reason that it is very important for a person who has been diagnosed with an STI to communicate with all partners because they are at risk. It should be made clear that a lack of symptoms does not mean that an individual is disease free.

READING TOOLBOX

Visual Literacy Be sure that students realize that **Figure 13** shows infection rates, not the total number of cases for each infection. To help students fully appreciate the incidence of these infections, use the QuickLab on the next page.

Section Correlations	
4.5.2b	
4.5.2f	

QuickLab

Teacher's Notes Remind students to place the number of cases along the *y*-axis and STIs along the *x*-axis.

Answers to Analysis

1. Graphs should match the data given in **Figure 13.**
2. herpes simplex virus and human papilloma virus
3. genital herpes: 66.9 million; genital HPV: 20.1 million; trichomoniasis: 5.1 million; chlamydia: 3.9 million; HIV/AIDS: 1 million: gonorrhea: 750,000; hepatitis B: 750,000; syphilis: 75,000
4. Antibiotic use was becoming widespread in the 1940s. Syphilis can be treated with antibiotics.

Data

QuickLab

⏱ 15 min

STI Rates 4.5.2f

STIs are the most widespread type of infection in the United States. Use **Figure 13** and the explanation in the text to complete the following activities.

Analysis

1. **Draw** a bar graph showing new cases of STIs.
2. **Identify** the type of pathogen that causes the two most common STIs.

3. **CRITICAL THINKING** **Predicting Patterns** Calculate the number of Americans that each of the STIs shown in **Figure 13** will infect within the next five years if the estimated number of new cases per year remains constant.

4. **CRITICAL THINKING** **Analyzing Data** Genital herpes is not the STI with the most new cases per year, but it is the most common STI in the United States. Suggest a possible reason for this.

SCI
LINKS

www.scilinks.org
Topic: Sexually Transmitted Diseases
Code: HX81388

Figure 14 The blisters of genital herpes may appear on or near the genitals.

Common STIs

❯ The most common STIs include genital herpes, genital HPV, trichomoniasis, AIDS, hepatitis B, chlamydia, and gonorrhea. For example, around one in every five Americans has had a genital herpes infection.

Genital Herpes At a rate of 22,300 cases per 100,000 Americans, **genital herpes** is the most common STI in the United States. This STI is caused by herpes simplex virus (HSV). About 70% of genital herpes infections are caused by HSV-2. The rest are caused by HSV-1, which more commonly causes cold sores around and inside the mouth. Symptoms of genital herpes include periodic outbreaks of painful blisters, such as those shown in **Figure 14.** Symptoms may also include flulike aches and fever. Antiviral drugs can temporarily get rid of the blisters caused by genital herpes, but they cannot remove HSV from the body. Although genital herpes is not life threatening, it can have serious consequences. Women who have genital herpes have a greater risk of developing cervical cancer.

Genital HPV Human papilloma virus (HPV) causes genital warts and other symptoms. Current statistics indicate that 50% of all Americans will be infected by genital HPV at some point in their lives. Most people who are infected with HPV show no symptoms and do not know that they are infected. Some people who have HPV infections get genital warts. Some experience cell changes in the cervix, which could lead to cancer. No therapy has been shown to get rid of the virus; the infection often comes back following treatment.

Trichomoniasis Trichomoniasis is the only major STI caused by a protistan parasite rather than by a virus or a bacterium. Some men with this infection have a mild discharge and temporary irritation inside the penis. Most men, though, have no symptoms. Women with trichomoniasis often have vaginal itching and a yellow-green vaginal discharge with a strong odor. Trichomoniasis can usually be cured with medication.

Differentiated Instruction

Basic Learners

Making a Chart Have students construct the outline of a chart that includes all the STIs discussed in this section. The chart should include the cause, symptoms, treatments, long-term health effects to the person, and long-term health effects on a baby born to an infected mother. Encourage students to use the text and access the Web site of the Centers for Disease Control and Prevention, which has fact sheets on each of these STIs. **LS Verbal/Visual**

Advanced Learners/GATE

HPV Vaccine In 2006, a vaccine against HPV for women ages 9–26 was licensed in the United States. Have students research who should be vaccinated and how many cases of cervical cancer the vaccine will prevent. **LS Verbal**

AIDS AIDS is a fatal disease caused by the human immunodeficiency virus (HIV). HIV infection occurs most commonly through sexual contact. HIV attacks the immune system by destroying white blood cells. People who have AIDS usually die from infections that generally affect only people who have weakened immune systems.

Hepatitis B Of the five forms of hepatitis, form B is the most common in the United States. Like HIV, hepatitis B is a viral STI that is transmitted typically through sexual contact or contaminated needles. The virus infects the liver and damages liver cells. Any injury to the liver is a problem, because the liver fights infections and removes poisons from the body. A vaccine is <u>available</u> for hepatitis B, and can give unexposed people immunity to the virus. The vaccine also helps to treat people who have been exposed to the virus. However, the vaccine cannot cure hepatitis B.

Chlamydia and Gonorrhea Chlamydia and gonorrhea are the most common bacterial STIs in the United States. Some people show no symptoms. Some men experience painful urination, and some women experience vaginal discharge. Gonorrhea may cause pus to discharge from the penis. Chlamydia (and less often, gonorrhea) can cause scar tissue to form inside the fallopian tubes.

Pelvic Inflammatory Disease Most cases of **pelvic inflammatory disease** (PID) result from gonorrhea or chlamydia infections. A normal fallopian tube has a highly-folded lining and many spaces through which gametes can pass. The spaces in a fallopian tube of a woman who has PID may become blocked with scar tissue.

Syphilis Syphilis is a serious bacterial STI that has a low incidence level in the United States, but is still common in much of the rest of the world. Syphilis usually begins with the appearance of a small sore on the genitals a few weeks after infection. Fever and rash are also common symptoms. These symptoms disappear without treatment. Years later, however, untreated syphilis begins to destroy body tissues, including bone and skin tissue, as you can see in **Figure 15.**

Figure 15 The sores on this man's face are caused by syphilis. Syphilis also eats away at other body tissues, including skeletal tissue.

ACADEMIC VOCABULARY

available that can be used

genital herpes a sexually transmitted infection that is caused by a herpes simplex virus

pelvic inflammatory disease a sexually transmitted infection of the upper female reproductive system, including the uterus, ovaries, fallopian tubes, and other structures

Math Skills

Calculating Tell students that about 19 million people are newly infected with an STI every year. Half of these cases are people under age 25. Ask students to calculate how many young people every day are infected with an STI. (26,027) **LS Logical**

> **Close**

Formative Assessment

Which STI can be cured with antibiotics?

A. genital herpes (Incorrect. This is a viral infection; antibiotics do not work against viruses.)

B. hepatitis B (Incorrect. This is a viral infection; antibiotics do not work against viruses.)

C. chlamydia (Correct! Chlamydia is a bacterial infection that can be treated with antibiotics.)

D. genital HPV (Incorrect. This is a viral infection; antibiotics do not work against viruses.)

Section 4 Review

> **KEY IDEAS**

1. **State** the best way to avoid becoming infected by an STI.
2. **List** three symptoms of genital herpes.
3. **Identify** which bacterial STIs are the most common in the United States.

CRITICAL THINKING

4. **Making Inferences** Why is a symptomless STI just as dangerous as an STI that exhibits symptoms? Explain your answer.
5. **Applying Information** Do you think that an STI can be transmitted from a mother to her fetus? Explain your answer.

ALTERNATIVE ASSESSMENT

6. **Making Bar Graphs** Research the rate of incidence of STIs among teenagers compared to the rate of incidence in the rest of the population. Use the information you discover to construct a bar graph.

Answers to Section Review

1. abstinence from sexual activity
2. painful genital blisters, flu-like aches, and fever
3. chlamydia and gonorrhea
4. People who are infected with an STI but do not show symptoms can transmit the disease to others without being aware of it. They also do not know to seek treatment for their infection, a practice that could help control the spread of the disease. The infection can damage organs and tissues, even in the absence of symptoms.

5. Yes, STIs could be transmitted across the placenta or through body fluids when the fetus is passing through the vagina during labor.
6. Accept any well-researched answer. Advise students to access the Web site of the Centers for Disease Control and Prevention, which collects surveillance data on STIs.

Teacher's Notes Researchers have studied many aspects of twins, from their cellular development to their behavior as adults. These studies have provided much information about the process of twinning. There does not appear to be any genetic basis for identical twins. Identical twins occur randomly, and their frequency has not increased over the last two decades. If the embryo begins to split but does not completely divide, the result is conjoined twins.

READING TOOLBOX

Visual Literacy Explain that triplets can be identical, a pair of identical twins with a fraternal sibling, or three fraternal siblings. Ask students to infer how the triplets shown here were formed. (a single zygote split into three embryos)

Answer to Research

Students may discover that twin language occurs in about 40 percent of twins. Some researchers are looking into whether this crytophasia is a language or masks a developmental speech disorder. Over half of twins are premature, a condition that is related to delayed speech.

Why It Matters

Seeing Double

REAL WORLD

Multiple births occur when two or more children are carried during the same pregnancy. In humans, the most common type of multiple births occurs when the mother gives birth to two children, which are also known as twins. About 3% of all births in the United States result in twins.

Twins in Your Genes?

There are two types of twins: identical and fraternal. While there does not seem to be any genetic basis for identical twins, fraternal twins are another matter. Women with fraternal twins in their families are more likely to give birth to fraternal twins. Also, the frequency of fraternal twinning has increased over the last 20 years, probably due to the increased use of fertility drugs.

One sperm → One egg → Embryo divides in two

Identical Twins Identical twins form when a single sperm fertilizes a single egg. The developing embryo then divides in two. Identical twins are always the same gender and are genetically identical.

Two sperm → Two eggs

Fraternal Twins Fraternal twins form when two sperm fertilize two separate eggs. Fraternal twins can be the same or different genders and are as different genetically as any ordinary siblings.

Triplets While twinning is the most common type of multiple birth, other multiples do occur. About 0.1% of all births are triplets.

Research It is common for twins to develop their own language. Find out more about this occurence, which is known as cryptophasia or idioglossia.

Chapter 23 Lab

⏱ 15 min

Lab

Time Required
15 minutes

Objectives

▶ Analyze how different materials affect the pattern of water waves.

▶ Form a hypothesis about how a viscous fluid alters the wave.

Materials

- lab apron
- shallow pan
- metric ruler
- water, tap
- corn syrup
- timer
- large spoon
- various objects such as a wooden block, a domino, and paper clips

Safety

Sonography

Sonography is a medical technique that is frequently used to obtain images of a developing fetus. During this process, ultrasonic waves are directed into the uterus. Upon hitting hard surfaces, the waves reflect. These returning waves produce a distinct pattern, which is used to generate an image of the fetus. In this lab, you will explore the reflection and bending of water waves. You will use your data to develop a better understanding of sonography as a tool in prenatal observation.

Preparation

1. **SCIENTIFIC METHODS** **State the Problem** How does a viscous fluid affect the wave's pattern in a model of a sonogram?

2. **SCIENTIFIC METHODS** **Form a Hypothesis** Form a testable hypothesis that explains how corn syrup affects the wave pattern of the model.

Procedure

1. ✥ Put on a lab apron. Place a shallow pan on a flat, level surface. Carefully fill it with water to a depth of about 0.5 cm.

2. Position a spoon at one end of the tray. Keeping the spoon level over the water's surface, gently tap down once on the water. Be sure that your fingertips don't touch the water. What do you observe? Continue tapping to form a regular rhythm.

3. Place a domino or other target with a flat edge midway in the tray. Tap out a regular rhythm. What do you observe?

4. Alter the distance between the target and the spoon. Tap again.

5. Use a variety of targets with different shapes including curved and angular edges. Note how these targets affect the return wave.

6. Place several drops of corn syrup in the center of the tray. Observe how this more dense liquid affects the waves that pass through it.

7. ✥ ✥ Clean up your materials according to your teacher's instructions. Wash your hands before leaving the lab.

Analyze and Conclude

1. **Describing Observations** What happened to the wave when it struck a hard surface? Did the wave vary with the type of object?

2. **SCIENTIFIC METHODS** **Drawing Conclusions** How did the distance to the target affect the wave's return?

3. **Evaluating Models** How does this activity model the use of sonography in prenatal observation?

4. **SCIENTIFIC METHODS** **Analyzing Results** How did traveling though the corn syrup affect the wave? How might this be applied to sonography?

Ratings

🧪	🧪🧪	🧪🧪🧪	🧪🧪🧪🧪
EASY			HARD

Teacher Prep 🧪🧪
Student Setup 🧪🧪
Concept Level 🧪🧪
Cleanup 🧪🧪

Safety Caution

Make sure students clean up any spills during and following this activity. Have paper towels on hand.

Tips and Tricks

Have students work in pairs, one collecting data while the other does the activity. Lunchroom trays and baking pans can be substituted for the cookie trays. During setup, remind students that they need to level out the pan to limit the amount of water needed to cover the entire surface. They can use pieces of folded paper to support the tray where needed. Suggest that students use sponges and small basins to drain off some of the tray's water before disposing of it in the sink.

Answers to Preparation

1. A viscous fluid will make the waves move more slowly.

2. Answers will vary.

Answers to Analyze and Conclude

1. It produced a visible wave that moved back across the surface. The solidity of the object might vary the wave's reflection.

2. Waves that struck closer targets returned sooner than waves that struck more distant targets.

3. The water waves represented sound waves. The dominos and other targets represented the developing fetus. The reflected water waves modeled the reflection of the ultrasonic waves that are used in sonography.

4. Because the corn syrup was more viscous, the wave traveled more slowly. The viscosity of the fluid would affect how quickly a wave was reflected back to the source.

Key Resources

💿 Holt Lab Generator

📄 Lab Datasheet (Levels A, B, C)

📀 Holt Science Biology Video Labs

Chapter **23** Summary

go.hrw.com
SUPER SUMMARY
Keyword: HX8RPRS

Reteaching Key Ideas

Identifying Structures Show an overhead transparency of the male reproductive system. Have students identify the structures and functions of the various parts. **LS Verbal**
Creating Graphics Have students create graphics of the female reproductive system that show the location of the egg during each phase of the ovarian cycle. **LS Visual**
Sequencing Ask students to construct a flowchart that indicates the main stages and events between fertilization and birth. **LS Visual**
Recalling Place students in small groups, and have each member write a question and answer about each STI. Have students take turns quizzing one another. **LS Interpersonal**

Key Ideas	Key Terms

1 The Male Reproductive System

> The male reproductive system has two testes that produce sperm and testosterone.

> The vas deferens carries sperm into the urethra. Sperm leave the body by passing through the urethra.

> As sperm cells move into the urethra, they mix with fluids secreted by three exocrine glands: the seminal vesicles, the prostate gland, and the bulbourethral glands.

> After the semen is deposited in the female reproductive system, sperm swim until they encounter an egg cell or until they die.

testis (549)
seminiferous tubule (549)
epididymis (550)
vas deferens (550)
prostate gland (551)
semen (551)
penis (551)

2 The Female Reproductive System

> The ovaries produce egg cells. Ovaries also secrete estrogen and progesterone.

> During the reproductive years, the female body undergoes a hormonal cycle that causes periodic changes. These changes prepare the body in the event that an egg is fertilized.

> If pregnancy does not occur, levels of estrogen and progesterone fall. The decrease in these two hormones causes the lining of the uterus to be shed during menstruation.

ovary (552)
ovum (553)
fallopian tube (553)
uterus (553)
vagina (553)
ovulation (554)
menstrual cycle (556)
menstruation (556)

3 Human Development

> When a sperm cell encounters an ovum, the sperm cell releases enzymes that break down the outer layers of the ovum. The head of the sperm enters the ovum, and the nuclei of the ovum and sperm fuse. This process, from encounter to fusion, is called fertilization.

> All of the embryo's organ systems, as well as the supportive membranes that feed and protect the embryo, develop during the first trimester of pregnancy.

> By the end of the third trimester, a fetus is able to live outside the mother's body. A baby leaves the mother's body after labor.

embryo (557)
implantation (557)
fetus (559)

4 Sexually Transmitted Infections

> Abstinence is the only sure way to protect yourself from contracting an STI.

> Common STIs include genital herpes, genital HPV, trichomoniasis, AIDS, hepatitis B, chlamydia, and gonorrhea.

genital herpes (562)
pelvic inflammatory disease (563)

Chapter 23

The Living Environment

Regents Exam Practice

PART A: Answer all questions in this part.

Directions: For each statement or question, write on your separate answer sheet the number of the word or expression that best completes the statement or answers the question.

1 Toxins can harm a developing fetus. They usually enter the fetus by the process of
(1) blood flow from the mother to the fetus
(2) active transport from the ovary
(3) diffusion across placental membranes
(4) recombination of genes from the fetus and mother

2 Which substance usually passes in the greatest amount through the placenta from the blood of the fetus to the blood of the mother?
(1) oxygen   (3) amino acids
(2) carbon dioxide (4) glucose

3 Removal of one ovary from a human female would most likely
(1) affect the production of eggs.
(2) make fertilization impossible.
(3) make carrying a fetus impossible.
(4) decrease her ability to provide essential nutrients to an embryo.

4 Which reproductive structure is correctly paired with its function?
(1) uterus—usual site of fertilization
(2) testis—usual location for egg development
(3) ovary—delivers nutrients to the embryo
(4) sperm—transports genetic material

5 The reproductive cycle of a human is usually regulated by
(1) gametes
(2) hormones
(3) natural selection
(4) immune responses

6 Some body structures of a human male are represented in the diagram below. An obstruction in the structures labeled X would directly interfere with the

(1) transfer of sperm to a female.
(2) production of sperm.
(3) production of urine.
(4) transfer of urine to the external environment.

7 One function of the placenta in a human is to
(1) surround the embryo and protect it from shock.
(2) allow for mixing of maternal blood with fetal blood.
(3) act as the heart of the fetus, pumping blood until the fetus is born.
(4) permit passage of nutrients and oxygen from the mother to the fetus.

8 The characteristics of a developing fetus are most influenced by
(1) gene combinations and their expression in the embryo.
(2) hormone production by the father.
(3) circulating levels of white blood cells in the placenta.
(4) milk production in the mother.

Regents Exam Practice Correlations

4.4.1d 10	**4.4.1g** 4, 6, 11
4.4.1e 5, 8, 12	**4.4.1h** 1, 14
4.4.1f 2, 3, 7, 9, 13	

PART A

1. **(3)** Toxins, as well as nutrients and oxygen, enter the fetus through diffusion across placental membranes. The placenta prevents the direct flow of blood between the mother and fetus. No materials move from the ovary to the fetus. Toxins are not delivered to the fetus during genetic recombination. (*#18, August 2005 Regents Exam*)

2. **(2)** Oxygen is abundant in maternal blood and thus it readily passes from maternal blood to the fetus, whereas carbon dioxide is abundant in the fetus and thus passes into maternal circulation. Amino acids and glucose are transported from maternal to fetal blood. (*#17, August 2006 Regents Exam*)

3. **(1)** The choices about fertilization and development are inaccurate because fertilization mostly occurs in the fallopian tubes and fetal development and nutrition occurs in the uterus. Egg production occurs inside the two ovaries. (*#16, August 2006 Regents Exam*)

4. **(4)** Sperm transports genetic material to the female reproductive system. The fallopian tube is the usual site of fertilization. The ovary is the site of egg development. The placenta delivers nutrients to the developing embryo in the uterus. (*#17, August 2005 Regents Exam*)

5. **(2)** The hormones estrogen and progesterone regulate the female reproductive cycle. Testosterone and other hormones regulate sperm production in males. The gametes themselves are part of reproductive cycles but do not regulate them. Natural selection is a mechanism for evolution. Immune responses are stimulated by pathogens. (*#16, August 2005 Regents Exam*)

6. **(1)** The structures labeled X are the vas deferens, which are the routes that sperm take from each epididymis to the urethra and out of the body. Therefore, blocking the vas deferns would interfere with the passage of sperm into the female body. (*#17, June 2004 Regents Exam*)

7. (4) Amniotic fluid surrounds and cushions the embryo. Maternal and fetal blood do not mix. The fetus' blood is pumped by its own heart. The placenta allows passage of nutrients and oxygen to the fetus, and allows the removal of waste such as carbon dioxide from the fetus. *(#16, June 2004 Regents Exam)*

8. (1) Hormone levels in the father, white blood cell levels in the placenta, and the mother's milk production do not influence the characteristics of a developing embryo or fetus. The combination of genes and their expression has the most direct affect on the developing human. *(#28, August 2004 Regents Exam)*

9. (2) Label A points to the fallopian tube which does not release estrogen and progesterone. Label C points to uterus, which is not the usual site of fertilization. Label D points to the vagina which does not nourish the developing embryo. The correct choice is label B which points to the ovary. The ovaries produce and release eggs into the fallopian tubes. *(#16, August 2004 Regents Exam)*

PART B

10. (4) The zygote produced when a male gamete fertilizes a female gamete divides within the female reproductive system. *(#49, June 2003 Regents Exam)*

11. (1) Both the male and female reproductive systems are involved in internal fertilization. *(#48, June 2003 Regents Exam)*

9 A diagram of human female reproductive structures is shown below. Which structure is correctly paired with its function?

(1) A — releases estrogen and progesterone
(2) B — produces and releases the egg
(3) C — provides the usual site for fertilization
(4) D — nourishes a developing embryo

PART B

The diagrams below represent organs of two individuals. The diagrams are followed by a list of sentences. For each phrase in questions 10 through 11, select the sentence from the list below that best applies to that phrase. Then record the number in the space provided.

Individual A   Individual B

Sentences

1. The phrase is correct for both Individual *A* and Individual *B*.

2. The phrase is not correct for either Individual *A* or Individual *B*.

3. The phrase is correct for Individual *A*, only.

4. The phrase is correct for Individual *B*, only.

10 Contains a structure in which a zygote divides by mitosis

11 Contains organs involved in internal fertilization

12 Part of embryonic development in a species is illustrated in the diagram below. Which set of factors plays the most direct role in controlling the events shown in the diagram?

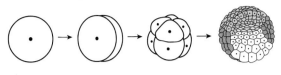

Fertilized egg   Embryo

(1) genes, hormones, and cell location
(2) antibodies, insulin, and starch
(3) ATP, amino acids, and inorganic compounds
(4) abiotic resources, homeostasis, and selective breeding

PART C
Base your answers to questions 13 and 14 on the statement and diagram below and on your knowledge of biology.

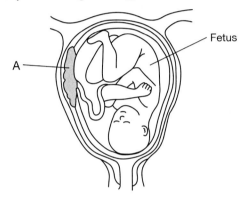

Fetus

A

Women are advised to avoid consuming alcoholic beverages during pregnancy.

13 Identify the structure labeled A and explain how the functioning of structure A is essential for the normal development of the fetus.

14 Explain why consumption of alcoholic beverages by a pregnant woman is likely to be more harmful to her fetus than to herself.

12. (**1**) The process illustrated is called cleavage. The cells of the blastocyst are specializing. This process is controlled by genes within the blastocyst cells and the location of the cells within the blastocyst. The mother's hormones help maintain the lining of the uterus into which the blastocyst implants. (*#27, January 2005 Regents Exam*)

PART C

13. Allow a maximum of 2 credits, allocated as follows: Allow 1 credit for identifying the structure labeled A as the placenta.; Allow 1 credit for explaining how the functioning of structure A is essential for the normal development of the fetus. Acceptable responses include, but are not limited to: exchange surface for nutrients or wastes or O_2 between mother and fetus. (*#58, June 2006 Regents Exam*)

14. Allow 1 credit for explaining why the consumption of alcoholic beverages by a pregnant woman is likely to be more harmful to her fetus than to herself. Acceptable responses include, but are not limited to: When the alcohol from the mother's bloodstream enters the fetus, the relative amount is much greater due to the smaller size of the fetus; The fetus is still developing. (*#59, June 2006 Regents Exam*)

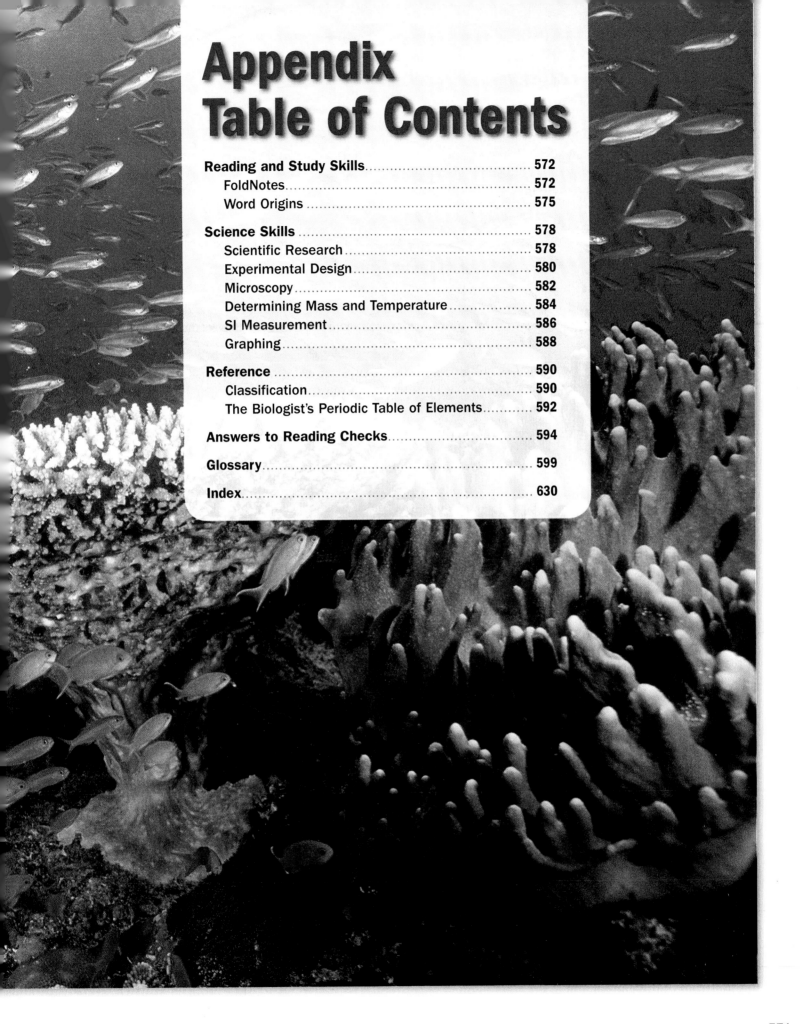

Appendix
Table of Contents

Reading and Study Skills......................................572
    FoldNotes..572
    Word Origins 575

Science Skills 578
    Scientific Research..................................578
    Experimental Design..............................580
    Microscopy..582
    Determining Mass and Temperature.......584
    SI Measurement.....................................586
    Graphing..588

Reference 590
    Classification...590
    The Biologist's Periodic Table of Elements...........592

Answers to Reading Checks...............................594

Glossary..599

Index..630

FoldNotes

FoldNotes are a useful study tool that you can use to organize concepts. One FoldNote focuses on a few main concepts. By using a FoldNote, you can learn how concepts fit together. FoldNotes are designed to make studying concepts easier, so you can remember the ideas for tests.

Key-Term Fold

A key-term fold is useful for studying definitions of key terms in a chapter. Each tab can contain a key term on one side and its definition on the other. Use the key-term fold to quiz yourself on the definitions of the key terms in a chapter.

❶ Fold a **sheet of lined notebook paper** in half from left to right.

❷ Using **scissors**, cut along every third line from the right edge of the paper to the center fold to make tabs.

Double-Door Fold

A double-door fold is useful when you want to compare the characteristics of two topics. The double-door fold can organize characteristics of the two topics side by side under the flaps. Similarities and differences between the two topics can then be easily identified.

❶ Fold a **sheet of paper** in half from the top to the bottom. Then, unfold the paper.

❷ Fold the top and bottom edges of the paper to the center crease.

Four-Corner Fold

A four-corner fold is useful when you want to compare the characteristics of four topics. The four-corner fold can organize the characteristics of the four topics side by side under the flaps. Similarities and differences between the four topics can then be easily identified.

❶ Fold a **sheet of paper** in half from top to bottom. Then, unfold the paper.

❷ Fold the top and bottom of the paper to the crease in the center of the paper.

❸ Fold the paper in half from side to side. Then, unfold the paper.

❹ Using **scissors**, cut the top flap creases made in step 3 to form four flaps.

Booklet

A booklet is a useful tool for taking notes as you read a chapter. Each page of the booklet can contain a main topic from the chapter. Write details of each main topic on the appropriate page to create an outline of the chapter.

1. Fold a **sheet of paper** in half from top to bottom.

2. Fold the sheet of paper in half again from left to right.

3. Fold the sheet of paper one more time from top to bottom.

4. Completely unfold the paper.

5. Refold the paper from top to bottom. Using **scissors**, cut a slit along the vertical crease of the sheet from the folded edge to the horizontal crease in the middle of the folded paper. Do not cut the entire sheet in half. Unfold the paper.

6. Fold the sheet of paper in half from left to right. While holding the bottom and top edges of the paper, push the bottom and top edges together so that the center collapses at the center slit. Fold the four flaps to form a four-page book.

Layered Book

A layered book is a useful tool for taking notes as you read a chapter. The four flaps of the layered book can summarize information into four categories. Write details of each category on the appropriate flap to create a summary of the chapter.

1. Lay one **sheet of paper** on top of **another sheet**. Slide the top sheet up so that 2 cm of the bottom sheet is showing.

2. Holding the two sheets together, fold down the top of the two sheets so that you see four 2 cm tabs along the bottom.

3. Using a stapler, staple the top of the FoldNote.

Pyramid

A pyramid provides a unique way for taking notes. The three sides of the pyramid can summarize information into three categories. Use the pyramid as a tool for studying information in a chapter.

1. Place a **sheet of paper** in front of you. Fold the lower left-hand corner of the paper diagonally to the opposite edge of the paper.

2. Cut off the tab of paper created by the fold (at the top).

3. Open the paper so that it is a square. Fold the lower right-hand corner of the paper diagonally to the opposite corner to form a triangle.

4. Open the paper. The creases of the two folds will have created an X.

5. Using **scissors**, cut along one of the creases. Start from any corner, and stop at the center point to create two flaps. Use **tape** or **glue** to attach one of the flaps on top of the other flap.

Table Fold

A table fold is a useful tool for comparing the characteristics of two or three topics. In a table fold, all topics are described in terms of the same characteristics so that you can easily make a thorough comparison.

❶ Fold a **piece of paper** in half from the top to the bottom. Then, fold the paper in half again.

❷ Fold the paper in thirds from side to side.

❸ Unfold the paper completely. Carefully trace the fold lines by using a pen or pencil.

Tri-Fold

A tri-fold is a useful tool that helps you track your progress. By organizing the chapter topic into what you know, what you want to know, and what you learn, you can see how much you have learned after reading a chapter.

❶ Fold a piece a paper in thirds from the top to the bottom.

❷ Unfold the paper so that you can see the three sections. Then, turn the paper sideways so that the three sections form vertical columns.

❸ Trace the fold lines by using a **pen** or **pencil**. Label the columns "Know," "Want," and "Learn."

Three-Panel Flip Chart

A three-panel flip chart is useful when you want to compare the characteristics of three topics. The three-panel flip chart can organize the characteristics of the three topics side by side under the flaps. Similarities and differences between the three topics can then be easily identified.

❶ Fold a **piece of paper** in half from the top to the bottom.

❷ Fold the paper in thirds from side to side. Then, unfold the paper so that you can see the three sections.

❸ From the top of the paper, cut along each of the vertical fold lines to the fold in the middle of the paper. You will now have three flaps.

Two-Panel Flip Chart

A two-panel flip chart is useful when you want to compare the characteristics of two topics. The two-panel flip chart can organize the characteristics of the two topics side by side under the flaps. Similarities and differences between the two topics can then be easily identified.

❶ Fold a **piece of paper** in half from the top to the bottom.

❷ Fold the paper in half from side to side. Then, unfold the paper so that you can see the two sections.

❸ From the top of the paper, cut along the vertical fold line to the fold in the middle of the paper. You will now have two flaps.

Word Origins

Determining the Meanings of Words

The challenge of understanding a new word can often be simplified by carefully examining the word. Many words can be divided into three parts: a prefix, root, and suffix. The prefix consists of one or more syllables placed in front of a root. The root is the main part of the word. The suffix consists of one or more syllables at the end of a root. Prefixes and suffixes modify or add to the meaning of the root. A knowledge of common prefixes, roots, and suffixes can give you clues to the meaning of unfamiliar words and can help make learning new words easier. For example, each of the word parts in **Table 1** can be combined with the root *derm* to form a word.

Table 2 lists prefixes and suffixes commonly used in biology. Each word part is followed by its common meaning, an example of a word in which the word part is used, and a definition of that word. Examine the word meaning and the example. Decide whether each word part in the first column is a prefix or suffix, depending on how the word part is used in the example.

Use **Table 1** to form five words using the root *derm*.

Table 1 Word Parts

Prefix	Root	Suffix
hypo-	derm	-ic
pachy-	derm	
	derm	-atology
	derm	-atologist
	derm	-atitis

Then, use the list of word parts and their meanings to write what you think each word that you formed means. An example is shown below.

Example: **dermatologist**
derm (root): skin
-logy (suffix): the study of
-ist (suffix): someone who practices or deals with something
dermatologist: someone who studies or deals with skin

Table 2 Word Prefixes and Suffixes

Prefix or suffix	Meaning	Example
a-	not, without	asymmetrical: not symmetrical
ab-	away, apart	abduct: move away from the middle
-able	able	viable: able to live
ad-	to, toward	adduct: move toward the middle
amphi-	both	amphibian: type of vertebrate that lives both on land and in water
ante-	before	anterior: front of an organism
anti-	against	antibiotic: substance, such as penicillin, capable of killing bacteria
arche-	ancient	Archaeopteryx: a fossilized bird
arthro-	joint	arthropod: jointed-limbed organism belonging to the phylum Arthropoda
auto-	self, same	autotrophic: able to make its own food
bi-	two	bivalve: mollusk with two shells
bio-	life	biology: the study of life
blast-	embryo	blastula: hollow ball stage in the development of an embryo
carcin-	cancer	carcinogenic: cancer-causing
cereb-	brain	cerebrum: part of the vertebrate brain
chloro-	green	chlorophyll: green pigment in plants that is needed for photosynthesis

Table 2 Word Prefixes and Suffixes, con't.

Word part	Meaning	Example
chromo-	color	chromosome: structure found in eukaryotic cells that contains DNA
chondro-	cartilage	Chondrichthyes: cartilaginous fish
circ-	around	circulatory: system for moving fluids through the body
-cide	kill	insecticide: a substance that kills insects
co-, con-	with, together	conjoined twins: identical twins physically joined by a shared portion of anatomy at birth
-cycle	circle	pericycle: layer of plant cells
cyt-	cell	cytology: the study of cells
de-	remove	dehydration: removal of water
derm-	skin	dermatology: study of the skin
di-	two	diploid: full set of chromosomes
dia-	through	dialysis: separating molecules by passing them through a membrane
ecol-	dwelling, house	ecology: the study of living things and their environments
ecto-	outer, outside	ectoderm: outer germ layer of developing embryo
-ectomy	removal	appendectomy: removal of the appendix
endo-	inner, inside	endoplasm: cytoplasm within the cell membrane
epi-	upon, over	epiphyte: plant growing upon another plant
ex-, exo-	outside of	exobiology: the search for life elsewhere in the universe
gastro-	stomach	gastropod: type of mollusk
-gen	type	genotype: genes in an organism
-gram	write or record	climatogram: report depicting the annual precipitation and temperature for an area
hemi-	half	hemisphere: half of a sphere
hetero-	different	heterozygous: different alleles inherited from parents
hist-	tissue	histology: the study of tissues
homeo-	the same	homeostasis: the maintenance of a constant condition
hydro-	water	hydroponics: growing plants in water instead of soil
hyper-	above, over	hypertension: blood pressure that is higher than normal
hypo-	below, under	hypothalamus: part of the brain located below the thalamus
-ic	of or pertaining to	hypodermic: pertaining to under the skin
inter-	between, among	interbreed: breed within a family or strain
intra-	within	intracellular: inside a cell
iso-	equal	isogenic: having the same genotype
-ist	practices or deals	biologist: someone who studies life
-logy	study of	biology: the study of life
macro-	large	macromolecule: large molecule, such as DNA or proteins
mal-	bad	malnourishment: poor nutrition

Table 2 Word Prefixes and Suffixes, con't.

Word part	Meaning	Example
mega-	large	megaspore: larger of two types of spores produced by some ferns and flowering plants
meso-	in the middle	mesoglea: jellylike material found between outer and inner layers of coelenterates
meta-	change	metamorphosis: change in form
micro-	small	microscopic: too small to be seen with unaided eye
mono-	one, single	monoploid: one set of alleles
morph-	form	morphology: study of the form of organisms
neo-	new	neonatal: newborn
nephr-	kidney	nephron: functional unit of the kidneys
neur-	neuron	neurotransmitter: chemical released by a neuron
oo-	egg	oogenesis: gamete formation in female diploid organisms
org-	living	organism: living thing
-oma	swelling	carcinoma: cancerous tumor
orth-	straight	orthodontics: the practice of straightening teeth
pachy-	thick	pachyderm: thick-skinned animal, such as an elephant
para-	near, on	parasite: organism that lives on and gets nutrients from another organism
path-	disease	pathogen: disease-causing agent
peri-	around	pericardium: membrane around the heart
photo-	light	phototropism: bending of plants toward light
phyto-	plants	phytoplankton: plankton that consists of plants
poly-	many	polypeptide: sequence of many amino acids joined together to form a protein
-pod	foot	pseudopod: false foot that projects from the main part of an amoeboid cell
pre-	before	prediction: a forecast of events before they take place
-scope	instrument used	microscope: instrument used to see very small objects
semi-	partially	semipermeable: allowing some particles to move through
-some	body	chromosome: structure found in eukaryotic cells that contains DNA
sub-	under	substrate: molecule on which an enzyme acts
super-, supra-	above	superficial: on or near the surface of a tissue or organ
syn-	with	synapse: junction of a neuron with another cell
-tomy	to cut	appendectomy: operation in which the appendix is removed
trans-	across	transformation: the transfer of genetic material from one organism to another
ur-	referring to urine	urology: study of the urinary tract
visc-	organ	viscera: internal organs of the body

Scientific Research

The Process of Science

The word *research* is derived from the French word *recherché,* which means "to investigate thoroughly." Nearly all of us have done some kind of research, but scientific research has special characteristics. At its core is systematic observation and objective recording of these observations. The goals of scientific research are the understanding of the natural world and the application of this understanding to benefit people and the world in which we live.

Science is a process of gaining knowledge about the world around us. The state of scientific knowledge is always changing. Any conclusion drawn from scientific research is subject to change if further research uncovers new information or new insights.

Scientific research is also a collaborative process. It relies on open communcation and cooperation between scientists. The results of one scientist's research are supported only when other scientists reproduce the studies and obtain the same results.

A scientist works in a greenhouse lab.

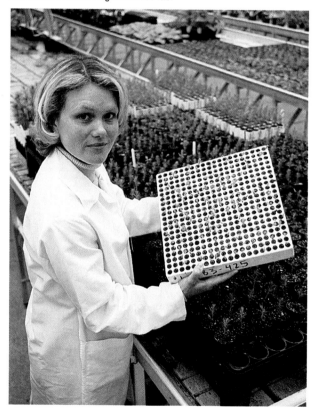

Preparation for Scientific Research

Before beginning a scientific study, it is important to learn about research that has already been conducted on the subject. Scientists learn about the latest discoveries in their fields by reading the "primary" literature on the subject. Primary literature consists of articles that are published in scientific journals and that have been reviewed by other scientists in the same field. (By comparison, textbooks, encyclopedias, and similar types of publications are referred to as "secondary" literature.) Today, many scientific journals publish online versions of their articles.

Types of Scientific Research

Scientific research typically involves asking very specific questions and then designing studies to collect answers to these questions. There are two broad styles of scientific research: experimental and observational.

In an experiment, some aspect of an organism, an object, or part of the environment is deliberately changed. The researcher then observes the effects of this change. For example, a scientist might study the effects of adding different amounts of nitrogen fertilizer to the soil in which a crop is grown.

Sometimes, it is not possible or desirable to perform an experiment. Observational research uses the senses, such as sight and hearing, to take in information. Scientific observation may also make use of instruments such as microscopes that allow us to see small things and balances that weigh objects. During scientific observation, a scientist observes but usually does not disturb or change his or her subject. For example, for a study of bird song, a scientist might quietly observe birds by recording their songs to be analyzed later in a laboratory.

The application of science for a specific purpose is referred to as *technology.* Pure scientific inquiry and research related to technology have different purposes. Scientific inquiry is conducted to advance our knowledge about the natural world. In contrast, research related to technology may be founded on prior scientific inquiry and is generally aimed at solving problems and meeting the needs of society. Scientific inquiry on the structure and function of DNA, for example, paved the way for technology that is aimed at preventing or curing diseases and improving crops.

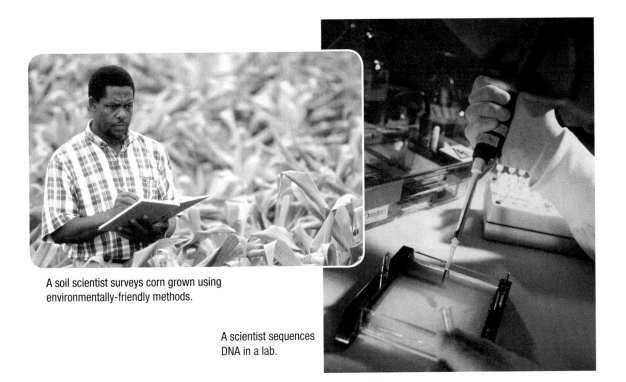

A soil scientist surveys corn grown using environmentally-friendly methods.

A scientist sequences DNA in a lab.

Conclusions of Scientific Research

Scientific research relies upon the evaluation of hypotheses, which are testable explanations for observations. If a hypothesis cannot be tested, then it cannot be studied using the tools of science.

Scientific investigation cannot prove that a hypothesis is correct. Rather, it can provide evidence that supports a hypothesis or it can disprove the hypothesis. Hypotheses can be supported but are never proven because scientists cannot be sure that there is not another hypothesis that could better explain their results.

An example of a testable hypothesis is that poinsettia plants flower when the day length is less than 12 hours. This hypothesis about flowering was accepted until scientists discovered that poinsettias would not bloom if they were exposed to day lengths shorter than 12 hours and nights that were interrupted with a period of light. The currently accepted hypothesis is that poinsettias will flower when the length of the night is at least 12 hours.

Scientists are human. They are disappointed if a hypothesis that they favored is disproved or replaced. But scientists are bound by ethics and service to the truth. They must be truthful about their methods and results. They must open their work to the scrutiny of their peers, and they must share their work with the scientific community for the common good.

Science, Technology and Society

Science is part of society. You have read how science and technology can affect society. In a similar way, society can directly affect progress in science and in technology through laws and by giving or withholding government or private funding for research. Certain healthcare issues, such as the use of human embryonic stem cells, are subject to public debate and to governmental control. The progress made in understanding and curing certain diseases can partly depend upon funding for research.

Pure scientific inquiry often drives technological developments. Technology, in turn, enables scientists to conduct experiments that could not otherwise be done. One large difference between the two is that scientific knowledge is made freely available to the scientific community by publication in peer-reviewed scientific journals. Technology, on the other hand, is often funded by private companies. Technological advances may be closely guarded secrets, which may be patented or sold.

The use of science and technology for the benefit of society is subject to political, economic, and ethical concerns. It is the responsibility of all citizens to remain aware of these issues in order to make informed, sound decisions about science, technology, and society.

Experimental Design

Before Experiments

Scientists conduct experiments in order to explore and better understand the world around us. A key element of scientific experiments is that they address very specific questions. Scientists first ask the questions, then propose answers, and then test these possible answers using objective methods that can be repeated by other scientists.

This scientific method, as it is called, is often thought to consist of a rigid set of steps and related rules. In fact, the ways that experiments are carried out do not always fit this mold. Nevertheless, experiments must be done and explained in such a way that other scientists can repeat the procedures and obtain the same results. Producing consistent results between trials of the same experiment allows scientists to verify their conclusions.

Making Observations

An experiment always starts with an observation—something that has made someone wonder. When scientists, or any of us, wonder about something, we ask questions. How do bats catch their prey in the dark? Why do all nests from a single species of bird look the same? Why do I feel cold when I have a fever?

The questions, like these questions, are rather broad at first. But they become very focused as the investigator prepares to systematically study the subject. At this stage, scientists also typically collect and study other information on the subject, such as articles published in scientific journals.

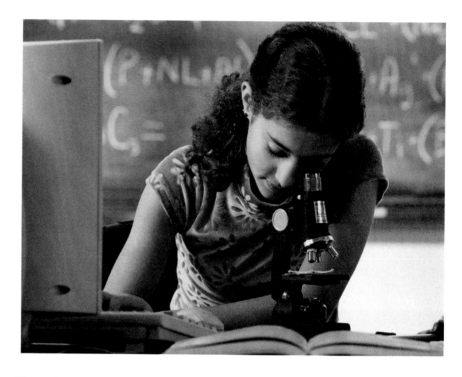

Forming a Hypothesis

The first step a scientist takes in answering a question is to develop a possible explanation for what he or she has observed. This explanation is essentially an educated guess that is based on the evidence that the scientist has collected. The critical feature of this educated guess is that it can be tested. These educated guesses are **hypotheses.**

For example, a plant biologist (a botanist) observes that healthy plants often grow in nitrogen-rich soil. The botanist might hypothesize that nitrogen is important for plant growth. Hypotheses allow scientists to develop **predictions,** or specific expectations about what should occur if a hypothesis is true. Although it might not be worded exactly as such, a prediction takes the form of an if-then statement. The botanist might predict that if most soils do not contain a lot of nitrogen, then adding nitrogen to soil will enhance plant growth.

In addition to being testable, a scientific hypothesis must also be falsifiable. That is, an experiment is designed so that it will show the hypothesis to be false, if indeed it is. Scientists often have several alternative hypotheses that they consider when they conduct an experiment or a series of experiments.

Designing an Experiment

Next, the scientist carefully designs an experiment to test the hypothesis. He or she might grow plants in soils that contain different amounts of nitrogen. In a scientific experiment, only one factor, or *variable,* is changed. This factor that changes is the **independent variable.** The independent variable in this experiment would be the nitrogen level in the soil.

Types of Variables

Other factors must be kept constant in the experiment. These factors are **controlled variables.** Some of the variables that could affect plant growth are air temperature and the amount of rainfall and sunlight.

The factor that changes in response to a change in the independent, or tested, variable is the **dependent variable.** In the soil-nitrogen experiment, the size of plants is the dependent variable.

An experiment that has controlled variables is called a *controlled experiment.* Controlled experiments such as this one allow researchers to conclude that changes in the dependent variable are due only to changes in the independent variable.

Performing the Experiment

Once a reliable experimental design is in place, performing the experiment is often easy. It is important that researchers carefully collect data and record all of their measurements and other observations.

Analyzing Data

When an experiment has been completed, the scientist analyzes the data collected. He or she makes computations, creates tables, draws graphs, and often does statistical analyses. The primary goal of the analysis is to organize and interpret the data so that conclusions can be drawn from them. The scientist also evaluates the procedures and results for possible sources of error— human mistakes, problems with equipment, or unexpected interferences, such as bad weather.

Drawing Conclusions

The final task in an experiment is to determine whether or not the results support the tested hypothesis. If the hypothesis is supported by the findings, the researcher details the supporting evidence and notes any inconsistencies. If the hypothesis is not supported, the researcher offers possible explanations. In either case, the researcher might also discuss alternative hypotheses. These hypotheses might include new ones that have occurred to the scientist during the course of the experiments. One or more hypotheses may be falsified by the experiments, and one or more may be supported. Usually, a single hypothesis emerges that is best supported by the experimental evidence. The scientist also generally compares his or her results to those obtained by other researchers conducting related experiments.

Follow-up Experiments

Scientists usually repeat their experiments, even multiple times, to verify their findings. They also distribute their findings to other scientists, often in the form of articles published in scientific journals. The scientists may also conduct related experiments to test other hypotheses.

Microscopy

Parts of the Compound Light Microscope

- The **eyepiece** magnifies the image, usually 10x.

- The **low-power objective** further magnifies the image, up to 4x.

- The **high-power objectives** further magnify the image, from 10x to 43x.

- The **nosepiece** holds the objectives and can be turned to change from one objective to another.

- The **body tube** maintains the correct distance between the eyepiece and the objectives. This distance is usually about 25 cm, the normal distance for reading and viewing objects with the unaided eye.

- The **coarse adjustment** moves the stage up and down in large increments to allow gross positioning and focusing of the objective lens.

- The **fine adjustment** moves the stage slightly to bring the image into sharp focus.

- The **stage** supports a slide that contains the viewed specimen.

- The **stage clips** secure the slide in position for viewing.

- The **diaphragm** (not labeled), located under the stage, controls the amount of light allowed to pass through the object being viewed.

- The **light source** provides light for viewing the image. It can be either a light reflected with a mirror or an incandescent light from a small lamp. Never use reflected direct sunlight as a light source.

- The **arm** supports the body tube.

- The **base** supports the microscope.

Proper Handling and Use of the Compound Light Microscope

1. Carry the microscope to your lab table using both hands, one supporting the base and the other holding the arm of the microscope. Hold the microscope close to your body.

2. Place the microscope on the lab table at least 5 cm from the edge of the table.

3. Check to see what type of light source the microscope has. If the microscope has a lamp, plug it in, making sure that the cord is out of the way. If the microscope has a mirror, adjust it to reflect light through the hole in the stage.

   CAUTION: If your microscope has a mirror, do not use direct sunlight as a light source. Using direct sunlight can damage your eyes.

4. Adjust the revolving nosepiece so that the low-power objective is aligned with the body tube.

5. Place a prepared slide over the hole in the stage, and secure the slide with the stage clips.

6. Look through the eyepiece, and move the diaphragm to adjust the amount of light that passes through the specimen.

7. Now look at the stage at eye level. Slowly turn the coarse adjustment to raise the stage until the objective almost touches the slide. Do not allow the objective to touch the slide.

8. While looking through the eyepiece, turn the coarse adjustment to lower the stage until the image is in focus. Never focus objectives downward. Use the fine adjustment to achieve a sharply focused image. Keep both eyes open while viewing a slide.

9. Make sure that the image is exactly in the center of your field of vision. Then switch to the high-power objective. Focus the image with the fine adjustment. Never use the coarse adjustment at high power.

10. When you are finished using the microscope, remove the slide. Clean the eyepiece and objectives with lens paper, and return the microscope to its storage area.

Procedure for Making a Wet Mount

1. Use lens paper to clean a glass slide and coverslip.

   CAUTION: Glass slides and coverslips break easily. Handle them carefully. Notify your teacher if you break a slide or coverslip.

2. Place the specimen that you wish to observe in the center of the slide.

3. Using a medicine dropper, place one drop of water on the specimen.

4. Position the coverslip so that it is at the edge of the drop of water and at a 45° angle to the slide. Make sure that the water runs along the edge of the coverslip.

5. Lower the coverslip slowly to avoid trapping air bubbles.

6. If a stain or solution will be added to a wet mount, place a drop of the staining solution on the microscope slide along one side of the coverslip. Place a small piece of paper towel on the opposite side of the coverslip to draw the stain under the coverslip.

7. As the water evaporates from the slide, add another drop of water by placing the tip of the medicine dropper next to the edge of the coverslip, just as you would when adding stains or solutions to a wet mount. If the slide is too wet, remove the excess water by using the corner of a paper towel as a blotter. Do not lift the coverslip to add or remove water.

Determining Mass and Temperature

Reading a Balance

A **single-pan balance,** such as the one shown at right, has one pan and three or four beams. The scale of measure for each beam depends on the model of the balance. When an object is placed on the pan, the riders are moved along the beams until the mass on the beams equals the mass of the object in the pan.

0–500 g
0–100 g
0–10 g

Measuring Mass When determining the mass of a chemical or powder, use weighing or filter paper. Determine the mass of the paper, and subtract that mass from the total mass of the paper and the sample. Use the following procedure for determining an object's mass:

1. Make sure the balance is on a level surface and the pan is allowed to move freely. Position all riders at zero. If the pointer does not come to rest in the middle of the scale, calibrate the balance by using the adjustment knob (usually located under and to the left of the pan).

   CAUTION: **Never place a hot object or chemical directly on a balance pan.**

2. Place the object on the pan.

3. Move the largest rider along the beam to the right until it is at the last notch that does not move the pointer below the zero point in the middle of the scale.

4. Follow the same procedure with the next rider.

5. Move the smallest rider until the pointer rests at zero in the middle of the scale.

6. Add up the readings on all of the beams to determine the mass of the object.

Your Turn Complete the following exercises.

1. Determine the mass of each of the following items by using a single-pan balance:
   a. an empty 250 mL beaker
   b. 250 mL beaker filled with 100 mL of water
   c. 250 mL beaker filled with 100 mL of vegetable oil
   d. a house key
   e. a small book
   f. a paper clip or small safety pin

2. Determine the mass of each object represented by the balance readings shown.

a.

b.

c.

Answers to Your Turn
1. Student answers will vary.
2. a. 47.51 g
   b. 273.16 g
   c. 14.71 g

Reading a Thermometer

Many laboratory thermometers are the bulb-type shown below. The sensing bulb of the thermometer is filled with a colored liquid (alcohol) that expands when heated. When the liquid expands, it moves up the stem of the thermometer through the capillary tube. Thermometers usually measure temperature in degrees Celsius (°C).

Measuring Temperature Use the following procedure when measuring the temperature of a substance.

1. Carefully lower the bulb of the thermometer into the substance. The stem of the thermometer may rest against the side of the container, but the bulb should never rest on the bottom, where heat is being applied. If the thermometer has an adjustable clip for the side of the container, the thermometer can be suspended in the liquid.

   CAUTION: Do not hold a thermometer in your hand while measuring the temperature of a heated substance.

2. Gently rotate the thermometer in the clip. Watch the rising colored liquid in the capillary tube. When the liquid in the capillary tube stops rising, note the whole-degree increment nearest the top of the liquid column. If your thermometer is marked in whole degrees, report temperature to the nearest half degree. For example, if the top of the colored liquid column is closest to the 52 °C mark but somewhat above it, as shown at right, what is the accurate temperature reading? Because the top of the column is slightly but not halfway above the 52 °C mark, the temperature is read as 52 °C.

Your Turn Use the thermometer shown above to answer the following questions:

1. Identify the scale used for this thermometer.
2. Determine whether this thermometer is marked only in whole degrees or in tenths of degrees.
3. Estimate the temperature reading shown on this thermometer.

4. **Interpreting Variables** What would be the temperature reading if the top of the column were resting at each of the following points?
   a. A   d. D
   b. B   e. E
   c. C   f. F

Answers to Your Turn

1. Celcius scale
2. in whole degrees
3. 52 °C
4. a. 85 °C
   b. 73 °C
   c. 66 °C
   d. 39 °C
   e. 8 °C
   f. −11 °C

SI Measurement

SI Units

Scientists throughout the world use the metric system. The metric system is now officially known as the Système International d'Unités, or the International System of Units. It is usually referred to simply as the SI. Most measurements in this book are expressed in SI units. You will always use SI units when you take measurements in the lab.

SI Prefixes The SI is a decimal system; that is, all relationships between SI units are based on powers of 10. Most units have a prefix that indicates the relationship of a particular unit to a base unit. For example, the SI base unit for length is the meter. A meter equals 100 centimeters (cm), or 1,000 millimeters (mm). A meter also equals 0.001 kilometer (km). **Table 1** summarizes the prefixes used in SI units.

Conversion Factors Conversion between SI units requires a conversion factor. For example, to convert from meters to centimeters, you need to know the relationship between meters and centimeters.

$$1 \text{ cm} = 0.01 \text{ m} \text{ and } 1 \text{ m} = 100 \text{ cm}$$

Table 1	SI Prefixes	
Prefix	**Symbol**	**Factor of base unit**
giga-	G	1,000,000,000
mega-	M	1,000,000
kilo-	k	1,000
hecto-	h	100
deka-	da	10
deci-	d	0.1
centi-	c	0.01
milli-	m	0.001
micro-	μ	0.000001
nano-	n	0.000000001
pico-	p	0.000000000001

If you need to convert 15.5 cm to meters, you could do either of the following:

$$15.5 \text{ cm} \times \frac{1 \text{ m}}{100 \text{ cm}} = 0.155 \text{ m}$$

or

$$15.5 \text{ cm} \times \frac{0.01 \text{ m}}{1 \text{ cm}} = 0.155 \text{ m}$$

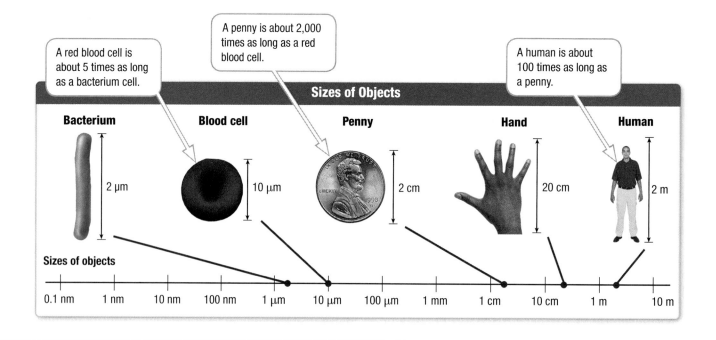

A red blood cell is about 5 times as long as a bacterium cell.

A penny is about 2,000 times as long as a red blood cell.

A human is about 100 times as long as a penny.

Sizes of Objects

Bacterium	Blood cell	Penny	Hand	Human
2 μm	10 μm	2 cm	20 cm	2 m

Sizes of objects

0.1 nm | 1 nm | 10 nm | 100 nm | 1 μm | 10 μm | 100 μm | 1 mm | 1 cm | 10 cm | 1 m | 10 m

Base Units In this book, you will see three fundamental quantities represented by base units in SI: mass, length, and time. The base units of these quantities are the kilogram (kg), the meter (m), and the second (s). These quantities, their base units and symbols, and some unit conversions are listed in **Table 2.**

Derived Units Other quantities, such as area and liquid volume, are expressed in derived units. A derived unit is a combination of one or more base units. Like base units, derived units can be expressed by using SI prefixes. Some SI-derived units, including their symbols and common unit conversions, are listed in **Table 3.**

Table 2 Conversions for SI Base Units
Mass: unit = kilogram (kg)
1 kilogram (kg) = 1,000 g
1 gram (g) = 0.001 kg
1 milligram (mg) = 0.001 g
1 microgram (µg) = 0.000001 g
Length: unit = meter (m)
1 kilometer (km) = 1,000 m
1 meter (m) = 100 cm
1 centimeter (cm) = 0.01 m
1 millimeter (mm) = 0.001 m
1 micrometer (µm) = 0.000001 m
Time: unit = second (s)
1 minute (min) = 60 s
1 hour (h) = 3,600 s = 60 min
1 day (d) = 24 h

Table 3 Conversions for SI-Derived Units
Area: unit = square meter (m^2)
1 square kilometer (km^2) = 100 ha
1 hectare (ha) = 10,000 m^2
1 square meter (m^2) = 10,000 cm^2
1 square centimeter (cm^2) = 100 mm^2
Liquid volume: unit = cubic meter (m^3)
1 cubic meter (m^3) = 1 kL
1 kiloliter (kL) = 1,000 L
1 liter (L) = 1,000 mL
1 milliliter (mL) = 0.001 L
1 cubic centimeter (cm^3) = 1 mL
Mass density: unit = kilograms per cubic meter (kg/m^3)
Temperature: unit = degrees Celsius (°C)
Velocity: unit = meters per second (m/s)

Temperature

Though not part of the SI, the Celsius scale is commonly used to express temperature. In the Celsius scale, 0 °C is the freezing point of water, and 100 °C is the boiling point of water. You can use the temperature scale shown below to convert between the Celsius scale and the Fahrenheit scale, which is commonly used in the United States. You can also use the following equation to convert between degrees Celsius (T_C) and degrees Fahrenheit (T_F):

$$T_F = \frac{9}{5}T_C + 32$$

For example, to convert 0 °C to degrees Fahrenheit, perform the following calculation:

$$T_F = \frac{9}{5}(0\ °C) + 32\ °F = 0 + 32\ °F = 32\ °F$$

F (Fahrenheit)
0 10 20 30 40 50 60 70 80 90 100 110 120 130 140 150 160 170 180 190 200 210 220 230

−20 −10 0 10 20 30 40 50 60 70 80 90 100 110
C (Celsius)
▲ Freezing point of water
▲ Boiling point of water

Graphing

Constructing Graphs

After finishing an experiment, scientists often illustrate experimental data in graphs. There are three main types of graphs: line graphs, bar graphs, and pie graphs. Organizing data visually helps us identify relationships between variables—factors that change.

The data table shows data collected by a researcher who has hypothesized that increased salt intake will cause an increase in blood pressure. In this experiment, the independent variable was daily salt intake. Recall that the **independent variable** is the one that is changed by the researcher. You can see in the data table that the researcher varied daily salt intake between 0 and 30 g.

Recall that the **dependent variable** is the one that is observed to determine if it is affected by changes in the independent variable. The dependent variable in this experiment was systolic pressure. You can see that in this case, an increase in salt intake corresponds to an increase in systolic pressure. These data support the hypothesis that increases in salt intake cause a rise in blood pressure.

Data Table

Systolic pressure (mm Hg)	Daily salt intake (g)
110	0
120	10
140	20
165	30

The dependent variable is graphed on the vertical (y) axis.

This last data pair is plotted here on the graph.

Salt Intake and Blood Pressure

The independent variable is graphed on the horizontal (x) axis.

Line Graphs

Line graphs, such as the one shown above, are most often used to compare or relate one or more sets of data that show continuous change. Each set of data—the independent variable and its corresponding dependent variables—is called a *data pair*.

To make a line graph, draw the horizontal (x) and vertical (y) axes of your graph. Label the y-axis with the independent variable and the x-axis with the dependent variable. (Refer to your data table to determine the scale and appropriate units for each axis). Plot each data pair, and then connect the data points to make a line, or

curve. Finally, give the graph a title that clearly indicates the relationship between the data shown by the graph.

Sometimes, line graphs can be more complex than the one shown. When a line graph has more than one line, each extra line illustrates another dependent variable. A key must accompany the graph so that the data plotted on the two or more lines are clear. Line graphs can also have data presented on two y-axes, which may have different units. In these graphs, the effect of the independent variable can be observed on two dependent variables.

Bar Graphs

Sometimes, it is not appropriate to use a line graph to represent data. A bar graph can clearly display data that are not continuous. A bar graph is a good indicator of trends if the data are taken over a sufficiently long period of time. For example, studying color variations in moths requires that data be collected over a long period of time. Even after years of study, predictions can still be difficult to make with certainty. Notice that a bar graph is also useful in comparing multiple sets of data, such as those for the light and dark moths found in the woods near Birmingham and Dorset.

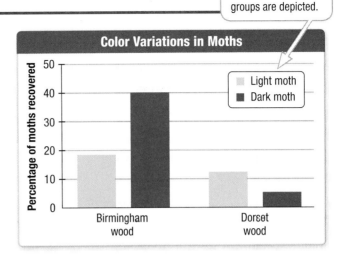

The key shows which groups are depicted.

Color Variations in Moths

Pie Graphs

Pie graphs are an easy way to visualize the composition of a whole. Frequently, pie graphs are made from percentage data. For example, you could create a pie graph showing the percentage of known insect species that various insect groups represent. To create a pie graph from data in a table, begin by drawing a circle to represent the whole, or total. Then, imagine dividing the circle into 100 equal sections to represent 100%. Shade in the number of consecutive sections that are represented by each group, and label the slice with the name of that group.

A source line identifies the source of the data.

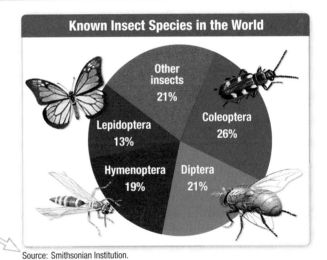

Known Insect Species in the World

Source: Smithsonian Institution.

Using Graphs to Make Predictions

Graphs show trends in data that allow us to make predictions. For example, how might taking in 40 g of salt per day affect blood pressure? Referring to the graph of blood pressure and salt intake, you might estimate that systolic pressure could be 190 mm Hg or more. Using a trend in a range of data to estimate values beyond that range is called **extrapolation.**

Likewise, we can use graphs to estimate values that are untested but that lie *within* the range of our data. How might taking in 15 g of salt per day affect blood pressure? You might use the graph to estimate that blood

pressure would be about 130 mm Hg. Using a trend in a range of data to estimate values missing from that range is called **interpolation.**

Some data, such as the values for salt intake and blood pressure, interact in an expected way and seem to indicate a causal relationship. But beware of hastily drawing conclusions based on a graph of two variables that change together. In September, the number of school buses on the road and the number of trees turning fall colors rise. But school buses do not make leaves change color! Both are affected by the time of year.

Classification

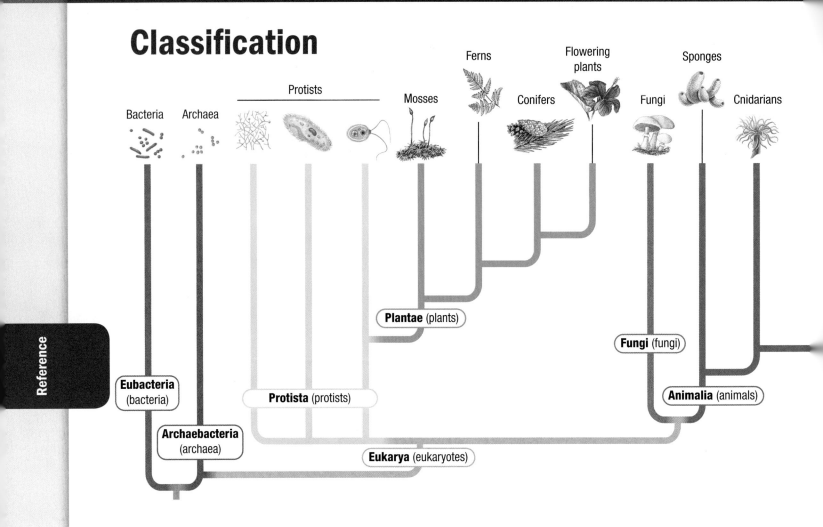

Ferns

Flowering plants

Sponges

Protists

Mosses

Conifers

Fungi

Cnidarians

Bacteria   Archaea

Plantae (plants)

Fungi (fungi)

Eubacteria (bacteria)

Protista (protists)

Animalia (animals)

Archaebacteria (archaea)

Eukarya (eukaryotes)

How Organisms Are Classified Like many areas of science, the classification of organisms is an active and ever-changing endeavor. Throughout history, many new taxa have been proposed, and some taxa have been reclassified. Biologists have added complexity and detail to their classification systems as they have learned more about organisms. Scientists are unlikely to discover and name all species, much less to agree on the exact relationships between all species.

Today, most biologists use and recognize the Linnaean system, shown here, which consists of three domains and six kingdoms. Also, there is general agreement on the relationships between most of the groups shown in this phylogenetic tree. However, many groupings remain the subject of strong debate and active investigation.

In particular, the relationships between protists are poorly understood, and many scientists are beginning to agree that "Protista" should no longer be considered a single, related taxon. The relationships between invertebrates, such as worms, arthropods, and mollusks, are also strongly debated. For these reasons, this phylogenetic tree does not indicate any particular relationships between these groups.

Any part of a phylogenetic tree—and any taxonomic name—may be revised when scientists gather enough evidence and agree upon revisions. In fact, the entire Linnaean system may someday be replaced with another system that is based on phylogenetic trees rather than lists and tables.

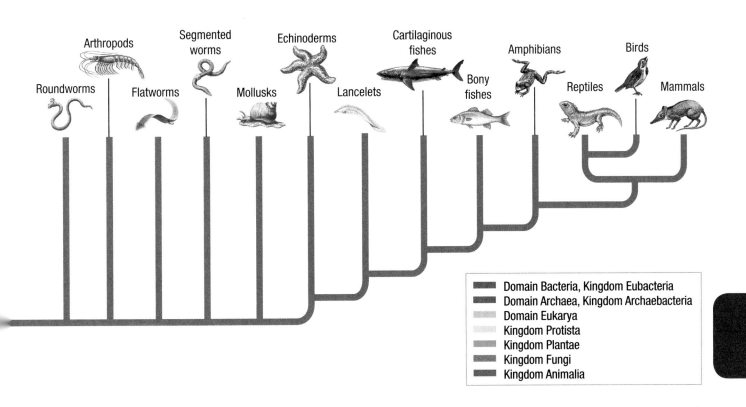

Characteristics of Domains and Kingdoms

Domain	Bacteria	Archaea	Eukarya			
Kingdom	Eubacteria	Archae-bacteria	Protista	Fungi	Plantae	Animalia
Example	*Streptococcus pneumoniae*	*Staphylo-thermus marinus*	paramecium	spore cap mushroom	Texas paintbrush	white-winged dove
Cell type	prokaryotic		eukaryotic			
Cell walls	cell walls with peptidoglycan	cell walls with unique lipids	cell walls in some species	cell walls with chitin	cell walls with cellulose	no cell walls
Number of cells	unicellular		unicellular or multicellular	mostly multicellular	mostly multicellular	multicellular
Nutrition	autotroph or heterotroph			heterotroph	autotroph	heterotroph

The Biologist's Periodic Table of Elements

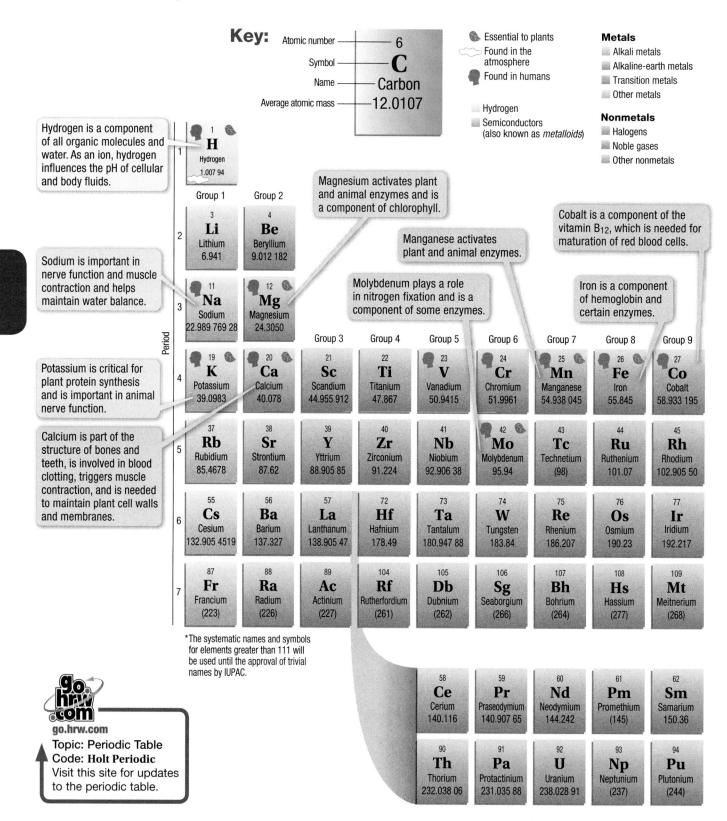

Key:

Atomic number — 6
Symbol — **C**
Name — Carbon
Average atomic mass — 12.0107

Essential to plants
Found in the atmosphere
Found in humans

Hydrogen
Semiconductors (also known as *metalloids*)

Metals
Alkali metals
Alkaline-earth metals
Transition metals
Other metals

Nonmetals
Halogens
Noble gases
Other nonmetals

Hydrogen is a component of all organic molecules and water. As an ion, hydrogen influences the pH of cellular and body fluids.

Magnesium activates plant and animal enzymes and is a component of chlorophyll.

Manganese activates plant and animal enzymes.

Cobalt is a component of the vitamin B_{12}, which is needed for maturation of red blood cells.

Sodium is important in nerve function and muscle contraction and helps maintain water balance.

Molybdenum plays a role in nitrogen fixation and is a component of some enzymes.

Iron is a component of hemoglobin and certain enzymes.

Potassium is critical for plant protein synthesis and is important in animal nerve function.

Calcium is part of the structure of bones and teeth, is involved in blood clotting, triggers muscle contraction, and is needed to maintain plant cell walls and membranes.

		Group 1	Group 2

1	H Hydrogen 1.007 94

Period

2	3 Li Lithium 6.941	4 Be Beryllium 9.012 182

3	11 Na Sodium 22.989 769 28	12 Mg Magnesium 24.3050

Group 3 · Group 4 · Group 5 · Group 6 · Group 7 · Group 8 · Group 9

4	19 K Potassium 39.0983	20 Ca Calcium 40.078	21 Sc Scandium 44.955 912	22 Ti Titanium 47.867	23 V Vanadium 50.9415	24 Cr Chromium 51.9961	25 Mn Manganese 54.938 045	26 Fe Iron 55.845	27 Co Cobalt 58.933 195

5	37 Rb Rubidium 85.4678	38 Sr Strontium 87.62	39 Y Yttrium 88.905 85	40 Zr Zirconium 91.224	41 Nb Niobium 92.906 38	42 Mo Molybdenum 95.94	43 Tc Technetium (98)	44 Ru Ruthenium 101.07	45 Rh Rhodium 102.905 50

6	55 Cs Cesium 132.905 4519	56 Ba Barium 137.327	57 La Lanthanum 138.905 47	72 Hf Hafnium 178.49	73 Ta Tantalum 180.947 88	74 W Tungsten 183.84	75 Re Rhenium 186.207	76 Os Osmium 190.23	77 Ir Iridium 192.217

7	87 Fr Francium (223)	88 Ra Radium (226)	89 Ac Actinium (227)	104 Rf Rutherfordium (261)	105 Db Dubnium (262)	106 Sg Seaborgium (266)	107 Bh Bohrium (264)	108 Hs Hassium (277)	109 Mt Meitnerium (268)

*The systematic names and symbols for elements greater than 111 will be used until the approval of trivial names by IUPAC.

58 Ce Cerium 140.116	59 Pr Praseodymium 140.907 65	60 Nd Neodymium 144.242	61 Pm Promethium (145)	62 Sm Samarium 150.36
90 Th Thorium 232.038 06	91 Pa Protactinium 231.035 88	92 U Uranium 238.028 91	93 Np Neptunium (237)	94 Pu Plutonium (244)

go.hrw.com

go.hrw.com
Topic: Periodic Table
Code: **Holt Periodic**
Visit this site for updates to the periodic table.

Boron is used by plants during photosynthesis.

Zinc is required by plants to make chlorophyll and by humans to maintain a healthy digestive system.

Nitrogen is a component of amino acids, hormones, and coenzymes.

Carbon forms the backbone of all organic molecules.

Oxygen is needed for aerobic respiration and is a component of all organic compounds.

Fluorine maintains bone structure.

Copper is needed to metabolize iron.

Nickel is an important cofactor for plants to help them metabolize nitrogenous foods.

Phosphorus is a component of nucleic acids, phospholipids, ATP, and coenzymes.

Chlorine is found as a negative ion and helps the human body maintain a balanced pH.

Sulfur is a component of some amino acids.

Iodine is used to make thyroid hormones.

Group 18

2
He
Helium
4.002 602

Group 13 | Group 14 | Group 15 | Group 16 | Group 17

5 **B** Boron 10.811
6 **C** Carbon 12.0107
7 **N** Nitrogen 14.0067
8 **O** Oxygen 15.9994
9 **F** Fluorine 18.998 4032
10 **Ne** Neon 20.1797

13 **Al** Aluminum 26.981 5836
14 **Si** Silicon 28.0855
15 **P** Phosphorus 30.973 762
16 **S** Sulfur 32.065
17 **Cl** Chlorine 35.453
18 **Ar** Argon 39.948

Group 10 | Group 11 | Group 12

28 **Ni** Nickel 58.6934
29 **Cu** Copper 63.546
30 **Zn** Zinc 65.409
31 **Ga** Gallium 69.723
32 **Ge** Germanium 72.64
33 **As** Arsenic 74.921 60
34 **Se** Selenium 78.96
35 **Br** Bromine 79.904
36 **Kr** Krypton 83.798

46 **Pd** Palladium 106.42
47 **Ag** Silver 107.8682
48 **Cd** Cadmium 112.411
49 **In** Indium 114.818
50 **Sn** Tin 118.710
51 **Sb** Antimony 121.760
52 **Te** Tellurium 127.60
53 **I** Iodine 126.904 47
54 **Xe** Xenon 131.293

78 **Pt** Platinum 195.084
79 **Au** Gold 196.966 569
80 **Hg** Mercury 200.59
81 **Tl** Thallium 204.3833
82 **Pb** Lead 207.2
83 **Bi** Bismuth 208.980 40
84 **Po** Polonium (209)
85 **At** Astatine (210)
86 **Rn** Radon (222)

110 **Ds** Darmstadtium (271)
111 **Rg** Roentgenium (272)
112 **Uub*** Ununbium (285)
114 **Uuq*** Ununquadium (289)
116 **Uuh*** Ununhexium (292)

The discovery of elements 112, 114, and 116 has been reported but not confirmed.

63 **Eu** Europium 151.964
64 **Gd** Gadolinium 157.25
65 **Tb** Terbium 158.925 35
66 **Dy** Dysprosium 162.500
67 **Ho** Holmium 164.930 32
68 **Er** Erbium 167.259
69 **Tm** Thulium 168.934 21
70 **Yb** Ytterbium 173.04
71 **Lu** Lutetium 174.967

95 **Am** Americium (243)
96 **Cm** Curium (247)
97 **Bk** Berkelium (247)
98 **Cf** Californium (251)
99 **Es** Einsteinium (252)
100 **Fm** Fermium (257)
101 **Md** Mendelevium (258)
102 **No** Nobelium (259)
103 **Lr** Lawrencium (262)

The atomic masses listed in this table reflect the precision of current measurements. (Each value listed in parentheses is the mass number of that radioactive element's most stable or most common isotope.)

Chapter 1 Biology and You

Section 1, p. 8 Sample answer: If a scientist falsely claims to have found a cure for a disease, people who have that disease may try to use the false cure and may be harmed.

Section 2, p. 13 Sample answer: In science, the word *theory* describes a well-tested, generally accepted principle. In general use, the word *theory* describes a good guess.

Section 3, p. 14 Most SI units have a prefix that indicates the relationship of that unit to a base unit.

Section 3, p. 15 Sterile technique is used in a lab when one is trying to avoid contaminating a specimen or is trying to grow only a certain type of microorganism.

Section 3, p. 16 Sample answer: Listen to your teacher, and follow all instructions. Read your lab procedure before beginning the lab. Always wear any needed safety equipment when working in the lab. Measure chemicals precisely. Do not use damaged or defective equipment.

Section 4, p. 19 Sample answer: Evolution is the change in inherited characteristics in a population over generations.

Chapter 2 Applications of Biology

Section 1, p. 29 It causes disease.

Section 1, p. 30 Warm water causes the copepod host to mature more quickly. As a result, the cholera bacteria also increase in number.

Section 1, p. 31 Vaccines allow one's immune system to develop resistance to a pathogen without contracting it.

Section 1, p. 32 a bionic limb

Section 2, p. 35 Relative to the eyes of other animals, lobster eyes focus light waves in a unique way. The lobster eye telescope incorporated this technology to focus X-rays, something that other telescopes cannot do.

Section 2, p. 36 DNA fingerprinting is an identification technique based on a pattern of DNA that represents the total of an organism's genetic material. It uses DNA material, such as skin cells, to identify someone.

Section 2, p. 37 Some people are concerned that eating genetically modified food may be harmful to their health.

Section 3, p. 39 A GIS allows researchers to access data from many different studies so that they can work together.

Section 3, p. 40 to help students understand the natural world through hands-on activities

Chapter 3 Chemistry of Life

Section 1, p. 51 a positively charged particle that is part of the nucleus of an atom

Section 1, p. 52 the attractive force that holds atoms or ions together

Section 1, p. 54 The partial positive charge of the H atoms in water molecules attracts the negatively charged chloride ions in salt crystals. The partial negative charge of the O atom of water molecules attracts the positively charged sodium ions in salt crystals.

Section 2, p. 59 carbon

Section 2, p. 60 a sugar

Section 2, p. 62 the order of amino acids

Section 3, p. 64 a change that occurs when the identity of the substance changes

Section 3, p. 65 their negatively charged electron clouds

Section 3, p. 67 because the shape of the active site determines which reactant will bind to the active site

Chapter 4 Ecosystems

Section 1, p. 80 Sample answer: water, sunlight, and oxygen

Section 1, p. 81 Pioneer species change the habitat so that other species can live in that habitat.

Section 1, p. 83 low latitudes

Section 1, p. 84 marine communities and estuaries

Section 2, p. 86 Consumers get their energy by eating producers or other consumers. Ultimately, all living organisms get their energy from the sun.

Section 2, p. 88 Ninety percent of the energy in a predator's prey is lost to the environment as heat as the predator burns the energy to do work, such as breathing and running.

Section 3, p. 91 Respiration is part of the carbon cycle because it is a process in which oxygen and carbon are exchanged between living organisms and their environment.

Section 3, p. 92 Bacteria breaks down N_2 into a form that other organisms can use.

Section 3, p. 93 Phosphorus is absorbed by the roots of plants.

Chapter 5 Populations and Communities

Section 1, p. 103 A zebra population consists of a group of zebras that live together and interbreed. A different zebra population lives separately from the other zebra population and does not interbreed with that population.

Section 1, p. 104 Sample answer: A population that grows exponentially grows slowly when it is small but grows quickly as it gets larger. An exponential growth curve is J shaped.

Section 1, p. 106 Biotic factors are living factors that affect a population's growth. Abiotic factors are nonliving factors that affect a population's growth.

Section 1, p. 107 by improving sanitation, controlling disease, and allowing for efficient production of food

Section 2, p. 110 Sample answer: Plants develop chemical compounds that make the plants taste terrible to the herbivores. The herbivores develop defenses against the toxic compounds so that they may eat the plants.

Section 2, p. 111 Mutualism is a relationship in which both species benefit. Commensalism is a relationship in which one species benefits and the other species is not harmed.

Section 3, p. 112 A niche is the function of a species in a community. A habitat is the place where the species lives.

Section 3, p. 113 because they usually have to compete with other species for limited resources

Section 3, p. 114 by feeding in slightly different ways or slightly different areas

Section 3, p. 115 Sample answer: Competition between species and high biodiversity contribute to the stability of an ecosystem.

Chapter 6 The Environment

Section 1, p. 125 Humans and other organisms are part of the environment and depend on resources from the environment to survive. In turn, the environment is affected by the actions of humans and other organisms.

Section 1, p. 126 It takes millions of years for natural gas to form.

Section 2, p. 129 The burning of fossil fuels releases CO_2 into the atmosphere. An increase in CO_2 in the atmosphere due to the burning of fossil fuels may be responsible for an increase in global temperatures.

Section 2, p. 130 Sample answer: runoff from roads, leaking underground septic tanks, and pesticides that run off from farms

Section 2, p. 131 Erosion causes soil to be washed away. Without soil, crops cannot be grown.

Section 2, p. 133 The zebra mussel clogs treatment facilities and causes millions of dollars in damage.

Section 3, p. 134 Restoration involves cleaning up and restoring a damaged ecosystem. Conservation involves protecting an existing ecosystem.

Section 3, p. 135 Sample answer: I can reduce resource use by using recycled materials, low-flow toilets, and low-flow shower heads.

Section 3, p. 136 by releasing less pollution into the atmosphere than the average car does

Section 3, p. 137 by having people become more aware of the problems and by motivating people to help solve the problems

Section 3, p. 138 because we can avoid damage to the environment

Chapter 7 Cell Structure

Section 1, p. 151 Hooke's microscope could magnify objects to 30 times their normal size.

Section 1, p. 153 Smaller cells can exchange substances more efficiently than larger cells of the same shape can.

Section 1, p. 154 a cellular structure on which proteins are made

Section 2, p. 157 proteins that remain in the cell, such as proteins that build new organelles or enzymes to speed chemical reactions

Section 2, p. 161 Nearly all eukaryotic cells, including plant cells, contain mitochondria.

Section 3, p. 163 long, threadlike structures that rotate quickly to move an organism through its environment

Section 3, p. 166 the process by which cells of a multicellular organism develop specialized forms and functions

Chapter 8 Cells and Their Environment

Section 1, p. 175 The cell membrane provides structural support to the cytoplasm, recognizes foreign material, communicates with other cells, and helps transport substances.

Section 1, p. 176 Small, nonpolar molecules, ions, and most polar molecules are repelled by the nonpolar interior of the lipid bilayer.

Section 2, p. 179 because its concentration is higher outside the cell than it is inside the cell

Section 2, p. 183 lipid bilayer

Section 3, p. 184 Both signals have long-distance targets. Hormones are distributed widely but affect only certain cells; nerve cells' signals are not widely distributed and instead affect cells in certain locations.

Section 3, p. 186 Transport proteins open or close in response to signals.

Chapter 9 Cellular Respiration and Photosynthesis

Section 1, p. 197 in order to maintain homeostasis

Section 1, p. 198 Solar energy powers part of the carbon cycle by providing the energy needed for autotrophs to convert carbon dioxide into glucose.

Section 1, p. 200 ATP is used as an energy source for cellular processes. When the cell needs to perform an activity, ATP can be broken down in order to release energy.

Section 2, p. 202 A chloroplast has an outer membrane and an inner membrane. The space inside the inner membrane is the stroma. Within the stroma lies the thylakoid membrane, which contains stacks of thylakoids.

Section 2, p. 205 Pigment molecules in the thylakoids of chloroplasts absorb light energy. Electrons in the pigments are excited by light and move through electron transport chains in thylakoid membranes. These chains generate both ATP and NADPH for the final stage of photosynthesis. Enzymes remove electrons from water to form O_2. These electrons replace the excited electrons that passed through the electron transport chains.

Section 2, p. 207 Temperatures that are too high or too low could inactivate enzymes that are used to perform photosynthesis, which would slow or stop the process.

Section 3, p. 209 pyruvate, ATP, and NADH

Section 3, p. 211 Glycolysis breaks down glucose into pyruvate, which is small enough to diffuse across mitochondrial membranes into the mitochondria, where the Krebs cycle takes place.

Section 3, p. 212 Electrons carried by NADH are transferred to pyruvate produced during glycolysis.

Chapter 10 Cell Growth and Division

Section 1, p. 225 A chromatid is a strand of a duplicated and condensed chromosome and is made of a single, long molecule of DNA.

Section 1, p. 226 between the two DNA copies, where a new cell membrane forms

Section 2, p. 229 G_1, S, and G_2

Section 2, p. 231 a network of several spindle fibers (microtubules)

Section 2, p. 232 a large, membrane-bound cell wall that forms across the middle of a dividing plant cell (and other cells that have cell walls)

Section 3, p. 233 protein signals within the cell; signals from other cells; environmental signals/conditions

Section 3, p. 234 The cell checks for and corrects any mistakes in the copied DNA. Proteins check that the cell is large enough to divide.

Section 3, p. 235 damage to a cell's DNA, especially genes that control the cell cycle

Chapter 11 Meiosis and Sexual Reproduction

Section 1, p. 247 Fragmentation is a kind of reproduction in which the body breaks into several pieces.

Section 1, p. 248 Germ cells produce gametes, which are reproductive cells.

Section 2, p. 251 in prophase 1

Section 2, p. 252 Meiosis produces haploid cells that contain only one set of chromosomes. Mitosis produces diploid cells that contain two sets of chromosomes.

Section 2, p. 253 Crossing-over increases genetic variation because pieces of two chromatids exchange material during meiosis.

Section 3, p. 257 One gamete is formed from one female germ cell.

Chapter 12 Mendel and Heredity

Section 1, p. 267 Mendel crossed different types of pea plants and recorded the number of each type of offspring.

Section 1, p. 268 A character is a physical feature that is inherited. A trait is one of several possible forms of a character.

Section 1, p. 269 a cross that is done to study one pair of contrasting traits

Section 1, p. 270 In the F_1 generation, all of the plants expressed the same trait for a given character. In the F_2 generation, the missing trait reappeared.

Section 2, p. 272 The blending hypothesis states that traits of offspring are always a blend of the traits from parents.

Section 2, p. 275 A dihybrid cross is a cross involving two characters.

Section 3, p. 277 Each box inside a Punnett square shows a possible genotype from a given cross.

Section 3, p. 279 1/4

Section 3, p. 280 Traits that are not expressed equally in both sexes are commonly sex-linked traits.

Section 4, p. 283 Codominance is a condition in which both alleles for the same gene are fully expressed. Incomplete dominance occurs when a phenotype that is intermediate between the two traits is expressed.

Section 4, p. 284 linked

Chapter 13 DNA, RNA, and Proteins

Section 1, p. 293 DNA

Section 1, p. 297 by weak hydrogen bonds

Section 1, p. 299 X-ray diffraction studies suggested that DNA's structure resembled a tightly coiled helix.

Section 2, p. 301 It reduces the number of replication errors.

Section 2, p. 303 Two distinct replication forks form at each start site, and replication occurs in opposite directions.

Section 3, p. 305 RNA is composed of one strand of nucleotides instead of two, and it has a ribose backbone rather than a deoxyribose backbone. In RNA, adenine pairs with uracil rather than thymine.

Section 3, p. 306 The promoter is the "start" site on a sequence of DNA.

Section 3, p. 309 Codons are the three-nucleotide sequence of mRNA that is created during transcription. An anticodon is the complementary three-nucleotide sequence that is assembled during translation.

Chapter 14 Genes in Action

Section 1, p. 319 from mutations of existing genes

Section 1, p. 321 A point mutation is often silent because the genetic code is redundant; a single nucleotide letter in a codon can change without changing the amino acid that is coded for.

Section 1, p. 323 Cancer is the uncontrolled growth of tumors, which may be caused by mutations in somatic cells.

Section 1, p. 324 When the sister chromatids in one of the parent gametes fail to separate, the gamete passes on both copies instead of one.

Section 2, p. 325 no; The expression of many genes may be turned on or off.

Section 2, p. 327 almost all parts (before and after transcription and after translation)

Section 2, p. 329 the sequence of amino acids that forms the protein

Section 3, p. 331 plants

Section 3, p. 332 Both consist of DNA or RNA, carry a small set of genes, and move around within and between genomes.

Section 3, p. 333 a DNA sequence that codes for a DNA-binding domain of a regulatory protein

Section 3, p. 334 CDK and cyclin act as the engine and gears of the protein cycle.

Chapter 15 Gene Technologies and Human Applications

Section 1, p. 345 3.2 billion base pairs (although much of human DNA is noncoding!)

Section 1, p. 346 when they are considering having children

Section 1, p. 347 because insulin is not produced by the person's body (because a gene is defective)

Section 1, p. 348 It seems to be affected by many genes as well as by the environment; we are not likely to find a simple cure

Section 2, p. 350 a genetically modified organism, or an organism that had recombinant genes

Section 2, p. 351 to cause a plant to produce an insecticide

Section 2, p. 353 adult and embryonic

Section 2, p. 354 issues of who should get the information and what decisions should be made based on the information

Section 3, p. 355 restriction enzymes and plasmids

Section 3, p. 356 It is semisolid, so molecules can travel through it.

Section 3, p. 358 transferring genetic samples from one surface or medium to another

Section 3, p. 359 in the first step, to start copying the template sequence

Section 3, p. 360 a structure such as a virus or plasmid that can carry and transfer DNA between cells

Section 3, p. 361 identifying specific genes and mapping their locations

Section 3, p. 363 genomic and EST

Chapter 16 Evolutionary Theory

Section 1, p. 375 the development of new species over time

Section 1, p. 377 when he visited the Galápagos Islands during his voyage on the *Beagle*

Section 1, p. 379 that traits acquired during a lifetime could be passed on to offspring

Section 1, p. 381 No, natural selection is a mechanism that can cause evolution.

Section 2, p. 383 because not all organisms leave fossils and not all fossils are found

Section 2, p. 384 descent from a common ancestor

Section 2, p. 385 carefully collect and consider a great deal of data

Section 3, p. 387 small-scale genetic changes in populations (microevolution) to large-scale changes in species (macroevolution)

Chapter 17 Population Genetics and Speciation

Section 1, p. 399 We know about genetics, such as how genotype relates to phenotype.

Section 1, p. 400 because many unique combinations of alleles are possible

Section 1, p. 401 frequency of alleles

Section 1, p. 402 1 (or 100%)

Section 1, p. 403 because it is the source of variation in populations

Section 2, p. 405 migration

Section 2, p. 406 increased homozygosity

Section 2, p. 407 success in leaving future generations of offspring

Section 2, p. 408 by remaining unexpressed, recessive alleles can be inherited and yet not acted upon by selection

Section 2, p. 409 disruptive selection

Section 3, p. 411 because not all species reproduce the same way and the definition of *species* depends on why the species are being studied

Section 3, p. 413 no; It sometimes results in sterile, unhealthy, or poorly adapted offspring.

Section 3, p. 414 when it's over!

Chapter 18 Classification

Section 1, p. 423 Common names have no system.

Section 1, p. 424 He wanted to catalog all known species.

Section 1, p. 426 six

Section 2, p. 427 the field of classifying species and revising systems of classification

Section 2, p. 429 It shows relatedness and shared characters between groups of organisms.

Section 2, p. 430 Sample answer: embryonic development pattern

Section 2, p. 431 comparisons between DNA, RNA, and proteins

Section 3, p. 433 Plantae (plants) and Animalia (animals)

Section 3, p. 435 Archaebacteria and Eubacteria

Section 3, p. 437 Animalia and Fungi

Chapter 19 History of Life on Earth

Section 1, p. 447 simple organic compounds, such as amino acids, fatty acids, and other hydrocarbons

Section 1, p. 449 RNA can form spontaneously in water, and DNA cannot. RNA can also perform many functions that DNA performs in cells.

Section 2, p. 451 As layers of sedimentary rock form, layers that are older form beneath layers that are younger.

Section 2, p. 453 fossil evidence

Section 3, p. 457 Colonial organisms developed the first example of separate functions being performed by different parts in a larger unit.

Chapter 20 Homeostasis and Human Body Systems

Section 1, p. 471 Homeostasis is the tendency of an organism to attempt to maintain a stable internal environment as the environment around the organism changes.

Section 1, p. 472 Sample answer: A plant's cells react to an increase in light in the plant's environment by performing photosynthesis.

Section 1, p. 475 (1) concentration of oxygen and carbon dioxide, (2) pH of the internal environment, (3) concentration of nutrients and waste products, (4) Concentration of salts, and (5) volume and pressure of extracellular fluid

Section 2, p. 477 The epidermis forms a tight barrier that keeps bacteria out.

Section 2, p. 479 Hormones are used to regulate metabolism; maintain salt, water, and nutrient balance in the blood; control the body's responses to stress; and regulate growth and development.

Section 2, p. 481 As blood flows through capillaries in the Bowman's capsule, fluid is forced out of the blood into the capsule. This fluid is composed of water, salt, glucose, amino acids, and urea. The fluid passes into a tubule, where glucose and some other molecules in the fluid reenter the bloodstream.

Section 2, p. 483 to return fluids to the bloodstream and to help the body fight infections

Section 3, p. 485 Feedback mechanisms are designed to detect changes in the body's internal environment and bring about corrective actions so that the body returns to its normal state.

Section 3, p. 487 The brainstem detects changes in the amount of carbon dioxide in the bloodstream and signals the muscles that control breathing to speed up or slow down in order to return the carbon dioxide levels to normal.

Section 3, p. 488 Insulin is the hormone that lowers the blood glucose level by telling the liver to take in glucose and convert it into glycogen. Glucagon is the hormone that raises the blood glucose level between meals by signaling the liver to break down glycogen into glucose to be released into the bloodstream.

Chapter 21 Homeostasis and Human Diseases

Section 1, p. 499 pathogens

Section 1, p. 500 Sample answer: by covering my mouth when I sneeze, washing my hands before eating, washing and cooking food thoroughly, and avoiding contact with infected organisms

Section 1, p. 501 A healthy diet ensures that your body has the building blocks needed to power healthy cells, repair damaged cells, and replace dead cells.

Section 2, p. 503 Both diseases are caused by bacteria that cause disease by feeding off of tissues. Fatigue is a symptom of both diseases. The diseases differ in the areas of the body that they typically infect. The bacteria that case tuberculosis typically infect the lungs, while the bacteria that cause Lyme disease typically infect the nervous system and related tissues.

Section 2, p. 504 Viruses use their host cell to reproduce. When they exit the cell, they often cause the host cell to burst, which results in its death.

Section 2, p. 506 Yeast infection can occur when the homeostasis of other microorganisms in the body, such as bacteria, is disrupted.

Section 2, p. 507 The flukes lay eggs in the blood vessels lining the walls of organs. The eggs block the vessels and cause the organs to be damaged.

Section 3, p. 510 Drinking alcohol can lead to dangerous behavior and can cause serious diseases, such as liver cirrhosis.

Section 3, p. 512 The disease causes tissue damage through oxygen deprivation and blood clotting. The damaged tissue cannot perform its job as well, which leads to an imbalance in homeostasis.

Section 3, p. 513 Trauma can damage large parts of an organ. As a result, the organ may be unable to function efficiently or may stop functioning altogether.

Section 3, p. 514 People choose what they eat and how much they eat. If they make unhealthy choices, an eating disorder may develop.

Section 3, p. 515 Eating an amanita mushroom can cause liver failure, which will decrease the ability of the blood to clot. As a result, a person could bleed to death. In addition, liver failure severely disrupts digestion and thus leads to an overall weakening of every cell in the body due to malnutrition.

Chapter 22 The Body's Defenses

Section 1, p. 525 Skin prevents many pathogens from invading the body (unless there is a tear in the skin).

Section 1, p. 9527 Viruses display antigens on their cell surfaces, which tells the body that the viral cells are different from "self" cells.

Section 2, p. 530 plasma cells

Section 2, p. 533 Antigen shifting is caused by the mutation of viral cells.

Section 3, p. 535 because the body is launching a strong immune response against harmless airborne particles

Section 3, p. 539 HIV destroys helper T cells by infecting them and causing them to burst open.

Chapter 23 Reproduction and Development

Section 1, p. 549 The anterior pituitary releases LH, which stimulates the production of testosterone. Testosterone, along with FSH, stimulates sperm production.

Section 1, p. 550 The mitochondria supply sperm with the energy that the sperm need to propel themselves through the female reproductive system.

Section 1, p. 551 Many sperm die in the acidic environment of the female reproductive system.

Section 2, p. 553 The ovum is fertilized in a fallopian tube.

Section 2, p. 555 Elevated levels of LH cause the corpus luteum to secrete estrogen and progesterone, sex hormones.

Section 2, p. 556 If a fertilized egg does not implant on the wall of the uterus, the levels of estrogen and progesterone will fall. The thick uterine lining will no longer be maintained and will be shed.

Section 3, p. 559 by the end of the fourth week of pregnancy

Section 3, p. 560 The fetus gains a great deal of weight, and all of its organ systems become developed enough such that it can live outside of the mother.

Section 4, p. 561 Some viral STDs can be treated with antiviral medication. Many bacterial STDs can be treated and cured with antibiotics.

abiotic (AY bie AHT ik) describes the nonliving part of the environment, including water, rocks, light, and temperature (80)

abiótico término que describe la parte sin vida del ambiente, incluyendo el agua, las rocas, la luz y la temperatura (80)

abiotic factor (AY bie AHT ik FAK tuhr) an environmental factor that is not associated with the activities of living organisms (106)

factor abiótic un factor ambiental que no está asociado con las actividades de los seres vivos (106)

acid any compound that increases the number of hydronium ions when dissolved in water; acids turn blue litmus paper red and react with bases and some metals to form salts (56)

ácido cualquier compuesto que aumenta el número de iones de hidrógeno cuando se disuelve en agua; los ácidos cambian el color del papel tornasol a rojo y forman sales al reaccionar con bases y con algunos metales (56)

acid rain precipitation that has a pH below normal and has an unusually high concentration of sulfuric or nitric acids, often as a result of chemical pollution of the air from sources such as automobile exhausts and the burning of fossil fuels (128)

lluvia ácida precipitación con un pH inferior al normal, que tiene una concentración inusualmente alta de ácido sulfúrico y ácido nítrico como resultado de la contaminación química del aire por fuentes tales como los escapes de los automóviles y la quema de combustibles fósiles (128)

activation energy the minimum amount of energy required to start a chemical reaction (65)

energía de activación la cantidad mínima de energía que se requiere para iniciar una reacción química (65)

active site on an enzyme, the site that attaches to a substrate (66)

sitio activo el sitio en una enzima que se une al sustrato (66)

active transport the movement of chemical substances, usually across the cell membrane, against a concentration gradient; requires cells to use energy (178)

transporte activo el movimiento de sustancias químicas, normalmente a través de la membrana celular, en contra de un gradiente de concentración; requiere que la célula gaste energía (178)

adaptation (AD uhp TAY shuhn) the process of becoming adapted to an environment; an anatomical, physiological, or behavioral change that improves a population's ability to survive (381)

adaptación el proceso de adaptarse a un ambiente; un cambio anatómico, fisiológico o en la conducta que mejora la capacidad de supervivencia de una población (381)

adaptive radiation (uh DAP tiv RAY dee AY shuhn) an evolutionary pattern in which many species evolve from a single ancestral species (389, 413)

radiación adaptativa un patrón evolucionista en el cual muchas especies evolucionan a partir de una sola especie ancestral (389, 413)

adenine (AD uh NEEN) one of the four bases that combine with sugar and phosphate to form a nucleotide subunit of DNA; adenine pairs with thymine (297)

adenina una de las cuatro bases que se combinan con un azúcar y un fosfato para formar una de las subunidades de nucleótidos del ADN; la adenina se une a la timina (297)

adhesion (ad HEE zhuhn) the attractive force between two bodies of different substances that are in contact with each other (55)

adhesión la fuerza de atracción entre dos cuerpos de diferentes sustancias que están en contacto (55)

aerobic (er OH bik) describes a process that requires oxygen (209)

aeróbico término que describe un proceso que requiere oxígeno (209)

AIDS (AYDZ) acquired immune deficiency syndrome, a disease caused by HIV, an infection that results in an ineffective immune system (539)

SIDA síndrome de inmunodeficiencia adquirida, enfermedad causada por una infección de VIH, la cual resulta en un sistema inmunológico ineficiente (539)

alcoholic fermentation (FUHR muhn TAY shuhn) the anaerobic process by which yeasts and other microorganisms break down sugars to form carbon dioxide and ethanol (212)

fermentación alcohólica el proceso anaeróbico por medio del cual las levaduras y otros microorganismos descomponen los azúcares para formar dióxido de carbono y alcohol etílico (212)

allele (uh LEEL) one of the alternative forms of a gene that governs a characteristic, such as hair color (272)

alelo una de las formas alternativas de un gene que rige un carácter, como por ejemplo, el color del cabello (272)

allergen (AL uhr juhn) a substance that causes an allergic reaction (534)

alergeno una sustancia que causa una reacción alérgica (534)

allergy (AL uhr jee) a physical response to an antigen, which can be a common substance that produces little or no response in the general population (534)

alergia una reacción física a un antígeno, el cual puede ser una sustancia común que produce una reacción ligera o que no produce ninguna reacción en la población general (534)

alveolus (al VEE uh luhs) any of the tiny air sacs of the lungs where oxygen and carbon dioxide are exchanged (482)

alveolo cualquiera de las diminutas bolsas de aire de los pulmones, en donde ocurre el intercambio de oxígeno y dióxido de carbono (482)

amino acid (uh MEE noh) a compound of a class of simple organic compounds that contain a carboxyl group and an amino group and that combine to form proteins (62)

aminoácido un compuesto de una clase de compuestos orgánicos simples que contienen un grupo carboxilo y un grupo amino y que al combinarse forman proteínas (62)

ammonification (uh MAHN i fi KAY shuhn) the formation of ammonia compounds in the soil by the action of bacteria on decaying matter (92)

amonificación la formación compuestos de amoniaco en el suelo debido a la acción de las bacterias en la materia en descomposición (92)

amnion (AM nee uhn) the membrane that contains a developing embryo and its surrounding fluid (558)

membrana amniótica la membrana que contiene al embrión en desarrollo y el líquido que lo rodea (558)

anaerobic (AN uhr OH bik) describes a process that does not require oxygen (209)

anaeróbico término que describe un proceso que no requiere oxígeno (209)

analogous (uh NAL uh guhs) in comparisons of different organisms, describes features that are similar in function and appearance but not in structure or origin (428)

análogo en comparaciones de diferentes organismos, término que describe características que son similares en función y apariencia, pero no en estructura u origen (428)

anatomy (uh NAT uh mee) the bodily structure of an organism (384)

anatomía la estructura corporal de un organismo (384)

antibody (AN ti BAHD ee) a protein that reacts to a specific antigen or that inactivates or destroys toxins (530)

anticuerpo una proteína que reacciona ante un antígeno específico o que inactiva o destruye toxinas (530)

anticodon (ANT ie KOH DAHN) a region of a tRNA molecule that consists of a sequence of three bases that is complementary to an mRNA codon (308)

anticodón una región de una molécula de ARNt formada por una secuencia de tres bases que complementan el codón del ARNm (308)

antigen (AN tuh juhn) a substance that stimulates an immune response (527)

antígeno una sustancia que estimula una respuesta inmunológica (527)

antigen shifting the production of new antigens by a virus as it mutates over time (533)

cambio antigénico la producción de antígenos nuevos por un virus cuando éste muta con el paso del tiempo (533)

apoptosis (AP uhp TOH sis) in multicellular organisms, a genetically controlled process that leads to the death of a cell; programmed cell death (334)

apoptosis en los organismos pluricelulares, un proceso controlado genéticamente que lleva a la muerte de una célula; la muerte programada de una célula (334)

archaea (ahr KEE uh) prokaryotes (most of which are known to live in extreme environments) that are distinguished from other prokaryotes by differences in their genetics and in the makeup of their cell wall; members of the domain Archaea (singular, *archaeon*) (435)

arqueas procariotes (la mayoría de los cuales viven en ambientes extremos) que se distinguen de otros procariotes por diferencias genéticas y por la diferente composición de su pared celular; miembros del dominio Archaea (435)

artery (AHRT uhr ee) a blood vessel that carries blood away from the heart to the body's organs (482)

arteria un vaso sanguíneo que transporta sangre del corazón a los órganos del cuerpo (482)

artificial selection the human practice of breeding animals or plants that have certain desired traits (377)

selección artificial la práctica humana de criar animales o cultivar plantas que tienen ciertos caracteres deseados (377)

asexual reproduction (ay SEK shoo uhl) reproduction that does not involve the union of gametes and in which a single parent produces offspring that are genetically identical to the parent (247)

reproducción asexual reproducción que no involucra la unión de gametos, en la que un solo progenitor produce descendencia que es genéticamente igual al progenitor (247)

atom the smallest unit of an element that maintains the chemical properties of that element (51)

átomo la unidad más pequeña de un elemento que conserva las propiedades químicas de ese elemento (51)

ATP adenosine triphosphate, an organic molecule that acts as the main energy source for cell processes; composed of a nitrogenous base, a sugar, and three phosphate groups (63, 198)

ATP adenosín trifosfato; molécula orgánica que funciona como la fuente principal de energía para los procesos celulares; formada por una base nitrogenada, un azúcar y tres grupos fosfato (63, 198)

ATP synthase (SIN THAYZ) an enzyme that catalyzes the synthesis of ATP (201)

ATP sintetasa una enzima que cataliza la síntesis del ATP (201)

autoimmune disease (AWT oh i MYOON) a disease in which the immune system attacks the organism's own cells (537)

enfermedad autoinmune una enfermedad en la que el sistema inmunológico ataca las células del propio organismo (537)

autosome (AWT uh SOHM) any chromosome that is not a sex chromosome (249)

autosoma cualquier cromosoma que no es un cromosoma sexual (249)

autotroph (AWT oh TRAHF) an organism that produces its own nutrients from inorganic substances or from the environment instead of consuming other organisms (197, 434, 437)

autótrofo un organismo que produce sus propios nutrientes a partir de sustancias inorgánicas o del ambiente, en lugar de consumir otros organismos (197, 434, 437)

bacteria (bak TIR ee uh) extremely small, single-celled organisms that usually have a cell wall and that usually reproduce by cell division (singular, *bacterium*) (435)

bacterias organismos extremadamente pequeños, unicelulares, que normalmente tienen pared celular y se reproducen por división celular (435)

base any compound that increases the number of hydroxide ions when dissolved in water; bases turn red litmus paper blue and react with acids to form salts (56)

base cualquier compuesto que aumenta el número de iones de hidróxido cuando se disuelve en agua; las bases cambian el color del papel tornasol a azul y forman sales al reaccionar con ácidos (56)

base pairing rules the rules stating that in DNA cytosine pairs with guanine and adenine pairs with thymine and that in RNA cytosine pairs with guanine and adenine pairs with uracil (297)

regla de apareamiento de las bases las reglas que establecen que en el ADN, la citosina se une a la guanina y la adenina se une a la timina, y que en el ARN, la citosina se une a la guanina y la adenina se une al uracilo (297)

B cell a white blood cell that matures in bones and makes antibodies (530)

célula B un glóbulo blanco de la sangre que madura en los huesos y fabrica anticuerpos (530)

bell curve a symmetrical frequency curve (400)

curva de campana una curva simétrica de frecuencia (400)

benign tumor (bi NIEN TOO muhr) an abnormal but noncancerous cell mass or growth (235)

tumor benigno un bulto o masa de células anormal, pero que no es cancerosa (235)

binary fission (BIE nuh ree FISH uhn) a form of asexual reproduction in single-celled organisms by which one cell divides into two cells of the same size (247)

fisión binaria una forma de reproducción asexual de los organismos unicelulares, por medio de la cual la célula se divide en dos células del mismo tamaño (247)

binomial nomenclature (bie NOH mee uhl NOH muhn KLAY chuhr) a system for giving each organism a two-word scientific name that consists of the genus name followed by the species name (424)

nomenclatura binomial un sistema para darle a cada organismo un nombre científico de dos palabras, el cual está formando por el género seguido de la especie (424)

biodiversity (BIE oh duh VUHR suh tee) the variety of organisms in a given area, the genetic variation within a population, the variety of species in a community, or the variety of communities in an ecosystem (80, 132)

biodiversidad la variedad de organismos que se encuentran en un área determinada, la variación genética dentro de una población, la variedad de especies en una comunidad o la variedad de comunidades en un ecosistema (80, 132)

biogeography (BIE oh jee AH gruh fee) the study of the geographical distribution of living organisms and fossils on Earth (383)

biogeografía el estudio de la distribución geográfica de los seres vivos y los fósiles en la Tierra (383)

bioinformatics (BIE oh in fuhr MA tiks) the application of information technologies in biology, especially in genetics (361)

bioinformática la aplicación de las tecnologías de la información en la biología, especialmente la genética (361)

biological species concept the principle that defines a species as a group of organisms whose members can interbreed to produce offspring (411)

concepto de especie biológica el principio que define a una especie como un grupo de organismos que pueden producir descendencia al cruzarse entre ellos (411)

biology the scientific study of living organisms and their interactions with the environment (17)

biología el estudio científico de los seres vivos y sus interacciones con el medio ambiente (17)

biome (BIE OHM) a large region characterized by a specific type of climate and certain types of plant and animal communities (82)

bioma una región extensa caracterizada por un tipo de clima específico y ciertos tipos de comunidades de plantas y animales (82)

biometrics (BIE oh ME triks) the statistical analysis of biological data; especially the measurement and analysis of unique physical or behavioral characteristics to verify the identity of a person (36)

biométrica el análisis estadístico de datos biológicos, especialmente la medición y el análisis de características físicas o características de conducta únicas para verificar la identidad de una persona (36)

bioremediation (BIE oh ri MEE dee AY shuhn) the biological treatment of hazardous waste by natural or genetically engineered microorganisms (349)

bioremediación el tratamiento biológico de desechos peligrosos por medio de microorganismos naturales o modificados genéticamente (349)

biotic (bie AHT ik) describes living factors in the environment (79)

biótico término que describe los factores vivientes del ambiente (79)

biotic factor an environmental factor that is associated with or results from the activities of living organisms (106)

factor biótico un factor ambiental que está asociado con las actividades de los seres vivos o que resulta de ellas (106)

blastocyst (BLAS toh SIST) in placental mammals, a developing embryo that consists of a hollow ball of cells surrounding an inner cell mass (557)

blastoquistela en los mamíferos placentarios, un embrión en desarrollo que consiste en una bola hueca de células que rodean una masa de células interna (557)

budding asexual reproduction in which a part of the parent organism pinches off and forms a new organism (247)

yemación reproducción asexual en la que una parte del organismo progenitor se separa y forma un nuevo organismo (247)

buffer (BUHF uhr) a solution made from a weak acid and its conjugate base that neutralizes small amounts of acids or bases added to it (57)

búfer una solución que contiene un ácido débil y su base conjugada y que neutraliza pequeñas cantidades de ácidos y bases que se le añaden (57)

bulbourethral gland (BUHL boh yoo REE thruhl) one of the two glands in the male reproductive system that add fluid to the semen during ejaculation (551)

glándula bulbouretral una de las dos glándulas del aparato reproductor masculino que añaden líquido al semen durante la eyaculación (551)

Calvin cycle (KAL vin) a biochemical pathway of photosynthesis in which carbon dioxide is converted into glucose using ATP (206)

ciclo de Calvin una vía bioquímica de la fotosíntesis en la que el dióxido de carbono se convierte en glucosa usando ATP (206)

cancer a type of disorder of cell growth that results in invasion and destruction of surrounding healthy tissue by abnormal cells (235, 323)

cáncer un tipo de trastorno del crecimiento celular en el que células anormales invaden y destruyen los tejidos sanos que las rodean (235, 323)

capillary (KAP uh LER ee) a tiny blood vessel that allows an exchange between blood and cells in tissue (482)

capilar diminuto vaso sanguíneo que permite el intercambio entre la sangre y las células de los tejidos (482)

capsule in mosses, the part that contains spores; in bacteria, a protective layer of polysaccharides around the cell wall (154)

cápsula en los musgos, la parte que contiene las esporas; en las bacterias, una capa protectora de polisacáridos que se encuentra alrededor de la pared celular (154)

carbohydrate (KAHR boh HIE drayt) a class of molecules that includes sugars, starches, and fiber; contains carbon, hydrogen, and oxygen (60)

carbohidrato una clase de moléculas entre las que se incluyen azúcares, almidones y fibra; contiene carbono, hidrógeno y oxígeno (60)

carbon cycle the movement of carbon from the nonliving environment into living things and back (91)

ciclo del carbono el movimiento del carbono del ambiente sin vida a los seres vivos y de los seres vivos al ambiente (91)

carnivore (KAHR nuh VAWR) an organism that eats animals (87)

carnívoro un organismo que se alimenta de animales (87)

carrier in biology, an individual who has one copy of a recessive autosomal allele that causes disease in the homozygous condition (323)

portador en biología, un individuo que tiene una copia de un alelo recesivo autosómico, el cual causa enfermedades en la condición homocigótica (323)

carrier protein a protein that transports substances across a cell membrane (179)

proteína transportadora una proteína que transporta sustancias a través de la membrana celular (179)

carrying capacity (kuh PAS i tee) the largest population that an environment can support at any given time (104)

capacidad de carga la población más grande que un ambiente puede sostener en cualquier momento dado (104)

cell in biology, the smallest unit that can perform all life processes; cells are covered by a membrane and contain DNA and cytoplasm (18, 151)

célula en biología, la unidad más pequeña que puede realizar todos los procesos vitales; las células están cubiertas por una membrana y tienen ADN y citoplasma (18, 151)

cell cycle the life cycle of a cell; in eukaryotes, it consists of a cell-growth period in which DNA is synthesized and a cell-division period in which mitosis takes place (228, 334)

ciclo celular el ciclo de vida de una célula; en los eucariotes, consiste de un período de crecimiento celular en el que el ADN se sintetiza, y un período de división celular en el que ocurre la mitosis (228, 334)

cell differentiation (DIF uhr EN shee AY shuhn) the process by which a cell becomes specialized for a specific structure or function during multicellular development (333)

diferenciación celular el proceso por medio del cual una célula se especializa en una estructura o función específica durante el desarrollo pluricelular (333)

cell membrane (MEM BRAYN) a phospholipid layer that covers a cell's surface and acts as a barrier between the inside of a cell and the cell's environment (154)

membrana celular una capa de fosfolípidos que cubre la superficie de la célula y funciona como una barrera entre el interior de la célula y el ambiente de la célula (154)

cell theory the theory that states that all living things are made up of cells, that cells are the basic units of organisms, that each cell in a multicellular organism has a specific job, and that cells come only from existing cells (152)

teoría celular la teoría que establece que todos los seres vivos están formados por células, que las células son las unidades fundamentales de los organismos y que las células provienen únicamente de células existentes (152)

cellular respiration (SEL yoo luhr RES puh RAY shuhn) the process by which cells produce energy from carbohydrates; atmospheric oxygen combines with glucose to form water and carbon dioxide (198)

respiración celular el proceso por medio del cual las células producen energía a partir de los carbohidratos; el oxígeno atmosférico se combina con la glucosa para formar agua y dióxido de carbono (198)

cellulose (SEL yoo LOHS) a carbohydrate that consists of linked glucose units and that adds rigidity to the cell walls in plants, many algae, and some fungi; it is a component of dietary fiber (60, 437)

celulosa un carbohidrato compuesto por unidades de glucosa ligadas que agrega rigidez a las paredes celulares de las plantas, de muchas algas y de algunos hongos; es un componente de la fibra dietaria (60, 437)

central vacuole (VAK yoo OHL) a large cavity or sac that is found in plant cells or protozoans and that contains air or partially digested food (160)

vacuola central una cavidad o bolsa grande que se encuentra en las células vegetales o en los protozoarios y que contiene aire o alimentos parcialmente digeridos (160)

centromere (SEN troh MIR) the region of the chromosome that holds the two sister chromatids together during mitosis (225)

centrómero la región de un cromosoma que mantiene unidas las dos cromátidas hermanas durante la mitosis (225)

centrosome (SEN truh SOHM) an organelle that contains the centrioles and is the center of dynamic activity in mitosis (230)

centrosoma un organelo que contiene los centríolos y es el centro de actividad dinámica en la mitosis (230)

cervix (SUHR VIKS) the inferior portion of the uterus (553)

cuello del útero la porción inferior del útero (553)

character (KAR uhk tuhr) a recognizable inherited feature or characteristic of an organism; in Mendelian heredity, a feature that exists in one of two or more possible variations called *traits* (268)

carácter un elemento o característica heredada reconocible de un organismo; en la herencia mendeliana, una característica que existe en una de dos o más variaciones posibles llamadas *rasgos* (268)

chemical bond the attractive force that holds atoms or ions together (52)

enlace químico la fuerza de atracción que mantiene unidos a los átomos o iones (52)

chitin (KIE tin) a carbohydrate that forms part of the cell walls of fungi and part of the exoskeleton of arthropods, such as insects and crustaceans (60, 437)

quitina un carbohidrato que forma parte de la pared celular de los hongos y del exoesqueleto de los artrópodos, como por ejemplo los insectos y los crustáceos (60, 437)

chlorofluorocarbons (KLAWR oh FLUR uh KAWR buhnz) hydrocarbons in which some or all of the hydrogen atoms are replaced by chlorine and fluorine; used in coolants for refrigerators and air conditioners and in cleaning solvents; their use is restricted because they destroy ozone molecules in the stratosphere (abbreviation, CFCs) (128)

clorofluorocarbonos hidrocarburos en los que algunos o todos los átomos de hidrógeno son reemplazados por cloro y flúor; se usan en líquidos refrigerantes para refrigeradores y aires acondicionados y en solventes para limpieza; su uso está restringido porque destruyen las moléculas de ozono de la estratosfera (abreviatura: CFC) (128)

chlorophyll (KLAWR uh FIL) a green pigment that is present in most plant and algae cells and some bacteria, that gives plants their characteristic green color, and that absorbs light to provide energy for photosynthesis (203)

clorofila un pigmento verde presente en la mayoría de las células de las plantas y las algas y en algunas bacterias, que les da a las plantas su color verde característico y que absorbe luz para brindar energía para la fotosíntesis (203)

chloroplast (KLAWR uh PLAST) an organelle found in plant and algae cells where photosynthesis occurs (161)

cloroplasto un organelo que se encuentra en las células vegetales y en las células de las algas, en el cual se lleva a cabo la fotosíntesis (161)

chorion (KAWR ee AHN) the outer membrane that surrounds an embryo (558)

membrana coriónica la membrana exterior que rodea al embrión (558)

chromatid (KROH muh TID) one of the two strands of a chromosome that become visible during meiosis or mitosis (225)

cromátida una de las dos hebras de un cromosoma que se vuelve visible durante la meiosis o mitosis (225)

chromatin (KROH muh TIN) the substance that composes eukaryotic chromosomes; it consists of specific proteins, DNA, and small amounts of RNA (224)

cromatina la sustancia que compone los cromosomas eucarióticos; contiene proteínas específicas, ADN y pequeñas cantidades de ARN (224)

chromosome (KROH muh SOHM) in a eukaryotic cell, one of the structures in the nucleus that are made up of DNA and protein; in a prokaryotic cell, the main ring of DNA (224, 249, 251, 302)

cromosoma en una célula eucariótica, una de las estructuras del núcleo que está hecha de ADN y proteína; en una célula procariótica, el anillo principal de ADN (224, 249, 251, 302)

clade a group of organisms that includes all of the evolutionary descendants of a common ancestral lineage (429)

clado un grupo de organismos que incluye a todos los descendientes evolutivos de un linaje ancestral en común (429)

cladistics (kluh DIS tiks) a phylogenetic classification system that uses shared derived characters and ancestry as the sole criterion for grouping taxa (428)

cladística un sistema de clasificación filogénica en el que los únicos criterios de agrupación de los taxa son los caracteres comunes derivados y la ascendencia (428)

cladogram (KLAD uh GRAM) a diagram that is based on patterns of shared, derived traits and that shows the evolutionary relationships between groups of organisms (429)

cladograma un diagrama basado en modelos de caracteres comunes derivados, que muestra las relaciones evolutivas entre grupos de organismos (429)

class a taxonomic category containing orders with common characteristics (426)

clase una categoría taxonómica que contiene órdenes con características comunes (426)

climate the average weather conditions in an area over a long period of time (82)

clima las condiciones promedio del tiempo en un área durante un largo período de tiempo (82)

clone an organism, cell, or piece of genetic material that is genetically identical to one from which it was derived; to make a genetic duplicate (352)

clon un organismo, una célula o una muestra de material genético que es genéticamente idéntico a aquél del cual deriva; hacer un duplicado genético (352)

codominance (koh DAHM uh nuhns) a condition in which both alleles for a gene are fully expressed (283)

codominancia una condición en la que los dos alelos de un gene están totalmente expresados (283)

codon (KOH DAHN) in DNA and mRNA, a three-nucleotide sequence that encodes an amino acid or signifies a start signal or a stop signal (307)

codón en el ADN y el ARN, una secuencia de tres nucleótidos que codifica un aminoácido o indica una señal de inicio o una señal de terminación (307)

coevolution (KOH ev uh LOO shuhn) the evolution of two or more species that is due to mutual influence, often in a way that makes the relationship more mutually beneficial (109)

coevolución la evolución de dos o más especies que se debe a su influencia mutua, a menudo de un modo que hace que la relación sea más mutuamente beneficiosa (109)

cohesion (coh HEE zhuhn) the force that holds molecules of a single material together (55)

cohesión la fuerza que mantiene unidas a las moléculas de un solo material (55)

colonial organism (kuh LOH nee uhl) a collection of genetically identical cells that are permanently associated but in which little or no integration of cell activities occurs (165)

organismo colonial un conjunto de células genéticamente idénticas que están asociadas permanentemente, pero en el que no se da una gran integración de las actividades celulares (165)

combustion (kuhm BUHS chuhn) the burning of a substance (91)

combustión fenómeno que ocurre cuando una sustancia se quema (91)

commensalism (kuh MEN suhl IZ uhm) a relationship between two organisms in which one organism benefits and the other is unaffected (110)

comensalismo una relación entre dos organismos en la que uno se beneficia y el otro no es afectado (110)

community a group of various species that live in the same habitat and interact with each other (79)

comunidad un grupo de varias especies que viven en el mismo hábitat e interactúan unas con otras (79)

competitive exclusion (eks KLOO zhuhn) the exclusion of one species by another due to competition (114)

exclusión competitiva la exclusión de una especie por otra debido a la competencia (114)

compound a substance made up of atoms of two or more different elements joined by chemical bonds (52)

compuesto una sustancia formada por átomos de dos o más elementos diferentes unidos por enlaces químicos (52)

concentration (KAHN suhn TRAY shuhn) the amount of a particular substance in a given quantity of a mixture, solution, or ore (178)

concentración la cantidad de una cierta sustancia en una cantidad determinada de mezcla, solución o mena (178)

concentration gradient a difference in the concentration of a substance across a distance (178)

gradiente de concentración una diferencia en la concentración de una sustancia a través de una distancia (178)

condensation (KAHN duhn SAY shuhn) the change of state from a gas to a liquid (90)

condensación el cambio de estado de gas a líquido (90)

consumer an organism that eats other organisms or organic matter instead of producing its own nutrients or obtaining nutrients from inorganic sources (86)

consumidor un organismo que se alimenta de otros organismos o de materia orgánica, en lugar de producir sus propios nutrientes o de obtenerlos de fuentes inorgánicas (86)

contractile vacuole (kunh TRAK til VAK yoo OHL) in protozoans, an organelle that accumulates water and then releases it periodically to maintain osmotic pressure (181)

vacuola contráctil en los protozoarios, un organelo que acumula agua y luego la libera periódicamente para mantener la presión osmótica (181)

control group in an experiment, a group that serves as a standard of comparison with another group to which the control group is identical except for one factor (11)

grupo de control en un experimento, un grupo que sirve como estándar de comparación con otro grupo, al cual el grupo de control es idéntico excepto por un factor (11)

convergent evolution (kuhn VUHR juhnt) the process by which unrelated species become more similar as they adapt to the same kind of environment (428)

evolución convergente el proceso por medio del cual especies no relacionadas se vuelven más parecidas a medida que se adaptan al mismo tipo de ambiente (428)

corpus luteum (KAWR puhs LOOT ee uhm) the structure that forms from the ruptured follicle in the ovary after ovulation; it releases hormones (555)

cuerpo lúteo la estructura que se forma a partir de los folículos rotos del ovario después de la ovulación; libera hormonas (555)

covalent bond (koh VAY luhnt) a bond formed when atoms share one or more pairs of electrons (52)

enlace covalente un enlace formado cuando los átomos comparten uno o más pares de electrones (52)

crossing-over the exchange of genetic material between homologous chromosomes during meiosis; can result in genetic recombination (251)

recombinación el intercambio de material genético entre cromosomas homólogos durante la meiosis; puede resultar en la recombinación genética (251)

cross-pollination (PAHL uh NAY shuhn) a reproductive process in which pollen from one plant is transferred to the stigma of another plant (268)

polinización cruzada un proceso reproductor en el que el polen de una planta es transferido al estigma de otra (268)

cyanobacterium (SIE uh noh bak TIR ee uhm) a bacterium that carries out photosynthesis; a blue-green alga (455)

cianobacteria una bacteria que efectúa la fotosíntesis; un alga verdiazul (455)

cytokinesis (SIET oh ki NEE sis) the division of the cytoplasm of a cell; cytokinesis follows the division of the cell's nucleus by mitosis or meiosis (229)

citoquinesis la división del citoplasma de una célula; la citoquinesis ocurre después de que el núcleo de la célula se divide por mitosis o meiosis (229)

cytoplasm (SIET oh PLAZ uhm) the region of the cell within the membrane that includes the fluid, the cytoskeleton, and all of the organelles except the nucleus (154)

citoplasma la región de la célula dentro de la membrana, que incluye el líquido, el citoesqueleto y los organelos, pero no el núcleo (154)

cytosine (SIET oh SEEN) one of the four bases found in DNA and RNA; cytosine pairs with guanine (297)

citosina una de las cuatro bases que se encuentran en el ADN y ARN; la citosina se une con la guanina (297)

cytoskeleton (SIET oh SKEL uh tuhn) the cytoplasmic network of protein filaments that plays an essential role in cell movement, shape, and division (156)

citoesqueleto la red citoplásmica de filamentos de proteínas que juega un papel esencial en el movimiento, forma y división de la célula (156)

cytosol (SIE tuh SAWL) the soluble portion of the cytoplasm, which includes molecules and small particles, such as ribosomes, but not the organelles covered with membranes (154)

citosol la porción soluble del citoplasma, que incluye moléculas y partículas pequeñas, tales como los ribosomas, pero no los organelos que están cubiertos por membranas (154)

cytotoxic T cell (SIE tuh TAHK sik) a type of T cell that recognizes and destroys cells infected by virus (530)

célula T citotóxica un tipo de célula T que reconoce y destruye las células infectadas por un virus (530)

decomposer (DEE kuhm POH zuhr) an organism that feeds by breaking down organic matter from dead organisms; examples include bacteria and fungi (86)

descomponedor un organismo que desintegra la materia orgánica de organismos muertos y se alimenta de ella; entre los ejemplos se encuentran las bacterias y los hongos (86)

deforestation (dee FAWR i STAY shuhn) the process of clearing forests (132)

deforestación el proceso de talar bosques (132)

denitrification (dee NIE truh fi KAY shuhn) the liberation of nitrogen from nitrogen-containing compounds by bacteria in the soil (92)

desnitrificación ocurre cuando las bacterias liberan nitrógeno contenido en compuestos que se encuentran en el suelo (92)

density-dependent factor a variable affected by the number of organisms present in a given area (105)

factor dependiente de la densidad una variable afectada por el número de organismos presentes en un área determinada (105)

density-independent factor a variable that affects a population regardless of the population density, such as climate (105)

factor independiente de la densidad una variable que afecta a una población independientemente de la densidad de la población, por ejemplo, el clima (105)

deoxyribose (dee AHKS ee RIE bohs) a five-carbon sugar that is a component of DNA nucleotides (296)

desoxirribosa azúcar de cinco carbonos que es un componente de los nucleótidos de ADN (296)

dermis (DUHR mis) the layer of skin below the epidermis (477)

dermis la capa de piel que está debajo de la epidermis (477)

diffusion (di FYOO zhuhn) the movement of particles from regions of higher density to regions of lower density (178)

difusión el movimiento de partículas de regiones de mayor densidad a regiones de menor densidad (178)

digestion (die JES chuhn) the breaking down of food into chemical substances that can be used for energy (480)

digestión la descomposición de la comida en sustancias químicas que se usan para generar energía (480)

dihybrid cross (die HIE brid) a cross between individuals that have different alleles for the same gene (275)

cruza dihíbrida un cruzamiento entre individuos que tienen diferentes alelos para el mismo gene (275)

diploid (DIP LOYD) a cell that contains two haploid sets of chromosomes (249)

diploide una célula que contiene dos juegos de cromosomas haploides (249)

directional selection a natural selection process in which one genetic variation is selected and that causes a change in the overall genetic composition of the population (409)

selección direccional un proceso de selección natural en el cual se selecciona una variación genética que origina un cambio en la composición genética global de la población (409)

disaccharide (die SAK uh RIED) a sugar formed from two monosaccharides (60)

disacárido un azúcar formada a partir de dos monosacáridos (60)

disruptive selection a type of natural selection in which two extreme forms of a trait are selected (409)

selección disruptiva un tipo de selección natural en el cual se seleccionan dos formas extremas de un carácter (409)

distribution (DIS tri BYOO shuhn) the relative arrangement of the members of a statistical population; usually shown in a graph (400)

distribución la organización relativa de los miembros de una población estadística; normalmente se muestra en una gráfica (400)

DNA deoxyribonucleic acid, the material that contains the information that determines inherited characteristics (63, 293)

ADN ácido desoxirribonucleico, el material que contiene la información que determina las características que se heredan (63, 293)

DNA fingerprint a pattern of DNA characteristics that is unique, or nearly so, to an individual organism (347, 358)

huella de ADN un patrón de características del ADN que pertenece exclusivamente, o casi exclusivamente, a un organismo individual (347, 358)

DNA helicase (HEEL uh KAYS) an enzyme that unwinds the DNA double helix during DNA replication (301)

helicasa AND una enzima que separa las hebras de la doble hélice del ADN durante la replicación del ADN (301)

DNA polymerase (puh LIM uhr AYS) an enzyme that catalyzes the formation of the DNA molecule (301)

polimerasa AND una enzima que actúa como catalizadora en la formación de la molécula de ADN (301)

DNA polymorphisms (PAHL ee MAWR FIZ uhmz) variations in DNA sequences; can be used as a basis for comparing genomes (356)

polimorfismos de ADN variaciones en las secuencias de ADN; puede usarse como base para comparar genomas (356)

DNA replication (REP luh KAY shuhn) the process of making a copy of DNA (300)

replicación del AND el proceso de hacer una copia del ADN (300)

DNA sequencing (SEE kwuhns ing) the process of determining the order of every nucleotide in a gene or genetic fragment; also referred to as *gene sequencing* (345, 359)

secuenciación de ADN el proceso de determinar el orden de cada nucleótido de un gene o un fragmento genético; también conocido como *secuenciación de genes* (345, 359)

domain in a taxonomic system based on rRNA analysis, one of the three broad groups that all living things fall into; in a protein, a functional unit that has a distinctive pattern of structural folding (329, 426)

dominio en el sistema taxonómico basado en el análisis de ARNr, uno de los tres amplios grupos al que pertenecen todos los seres vivos; en una proteína, una unidad funcional que tiene un patrón distintivo de plegamiento estructural (329, 426)

dominant (DAHM uh nuhnt) in genetics, describes an allele that is fully expressed whenever the allele is present in an individual (273)

dominante en la genética, término que describe a un alelo que se expresa por completo siempre que el alelo está presente en un individuo (273)

double helix (HEE LIKS) the spiral-staircase structure characteristic of the DNA molecule (296)

doble hélice la estructura en forma de escalera en espiral característica de la molécula del ADN (296)

Down syndrome (SIN DROHM) a disorder caused by an extra 21st chromosome and characterized by a number of physical and mental abnormalities; also called *trisomy-21* (324)

síndrome de Down un trastorno producido por un cromosoma 21 adicional y caracterizado por una variedad de anormalidades físicas y mentales; también se llama *trisomía-21* (324)

ecology (ee KAHL uh jee) the study of the interactions of living organisms with one another and with their environment (38)

ecología el estudio de las interacciones de los seres vivos entre sí mismos y entre sí mismos y su ambiente (38)

ecosystem (EE koh SIS tuhm) a community of organisms and their abiotic environment (79)

ecosistema una comunidad de organismos y su ambiente abiótico (79)

ecotourism (EK oh TUR IZ uhm) a form of tourism that supports the conservation and sustainable development of ecologically unique areas (137)

ecoturismo una forma de turismo que apoya la conservación y desarrollo sustentable de áreas ecológicamente únicas (137)

ejaculation (ee JAK yoo LAY shuhn) the expulsion of seminal fluids from the urethra of the penis during sexual intercourse (551)

eyaculación la expulsión de fluidos seminales de la uretra del pene durante las relaciones sexuales (551)

electron (ee LEK TRAHN) a subatomic particle that has a negative charge (51)

electrón una partícula subatómica que tiene carga negativa (51)

electron cloud a region around the nucleus of an atom where electrons are likely to be found (51)

nube de electrones una región que rodea al núcleo de un átomo en la cual es probable encontrar a los electrones (51)

electron transport chain a series of molecules, found in the inner membranes of mitochondria and chloroplasts, through which electrons pass in a process that causes protons to build up on one side of the membrane (201)

cadena de transporte de electrones una serie de moléculas que se encuentran en las membranas internas de las mitocondrias y cloroplastos y a través de las cuales pasan los electrones en un proceso que hace que los protones se acumulen en un lado de la membrana (201)

electrophoresis (ee LEK troh fuh REE sis) the process by which electrically charged particles suspended in a liquid move through the liquid because of the influence of an electric field (356)

electroforesis el proceso por medio del cual las partículas con carga eléctrica que están suspendidas en un líquido se mueven por todo el líquido debido a la influencia de un campo eléctrico (356)

element a substance that cannot be separated or broken down into simpler substances by chemical means; all atoms of an element have the same atomic number (51)

elemento una sustancia que no se puede separar o descomponer en sustancias más simples por medio de métodos químicos; todos los átomos de un elemento tienen el mismo número atómico (51)

embryo (EM bree OH) in plants and animals, one of the early stages of development of an organism (557)

embrión en las plantas y los animales, un organismo en una de las primeras etapas del desarrollo (557)

embryology (EM bree AHL uh jee) the study of the development of an animal from the fertilized egg to the new adult organism; sometimes limited to the period between fertilization of the egg and hatching or birth (383)

embriología el estudio del desarrollo de un animal desde el óvulo fecundado hasta el nuevo organismo adulto; a veces se limita al período entre la fecundación del óvulo y la salida del cascarón o el nacimiento (383)

emigration (EM i GRAY shuhn) the movement of an individual or group out of its native area (104)

emigración la salida de un individuo o grupo de la región de la que es originario (104)

endocrine gland (EN doh KRIN) a ductless gland that secretes hormones into the blood (479)

glándula endocrina una glándula sin conductos que secreta hormonas a la sangre (479)

endocytosis (EN doh sie TOH sis) the process by which a cell membrane surrounds a particle and encloses the particle in a vesicle to bring the particle into the cell (183)

endocitosis el proceso por medio del cual la membrana celular rodea una partícula y la encierra en una vesícula para llevarla al interior de la célula (183)

endoplasmic reticulum (EN doh PLAZ mik ri TIK yuh luhm) a system of membranes that is found in a cell's cytoplasm and that assists in the production, processing, and transport of proteins and in the production of lipids (158)

retículo endoplásmico un sistema de membranas que se encuentra en el citoplasma de la célula y que tiene una función en la producción, procesamiento y transporte de proteínas y en la producción de lípidos (158)

endosymbiosis (EN doh SIM bie OH ses) a mutually beneficial relationship in which one organism lives within another (456)

endosimbiosis una relación mutuamente beneficiosa en la que un organismo vive dentro de otro (456)

endosymbiotic theory a theory that some cell organelles (mainly mitochondria and chloroplasts) are descended from prokaryotic cells that came to live within other cells during early evolutionary history (331)

teoría endosimbiótica una teoría según la cual los organelos celulares (principalmente las mitocondrias y los cloroplastos) descienden de células procarióticas que comenzaron a vivir dentro de otras células al comienzo de la historia evolutiva (331)

energy the capacity to do work (64)

energía la capacidad de realizar un trabajo (64)

energy pyramid a triangular diagram that shows an ecosystem's loss of energy, which results as energy passes through the ecosystem's food chain; each row in the pyramid represents a trophic (feeding) level in an ecosystem, and the area of a row represents the energy stored in that trophic level (89)

pirámide de energía un diagrama con forma de triángulo que muestra la pérdida de energía que ocurre en un ecosistema a medida que la energía pasa a través de la cadena alimenticia del ecosistema; cada hilera de la pirámide representa un nivel trófico (de alimentación) en el ecosistema, y el área de la hilera representa la energía almacenada en ese nivel trófico (89)

environmental science (en VIE ruhn MENT'l) the study of the air, water, and land surrounding an organism or a community, which ranges from a small area to Earth's entire biosphere; it includes the study of the impact of humans on the environment (38, 125)

ciencias ambientales el estudio del aire, agua y tierra circundantes en relación con un organismo o comunidad, desde un área pequeña de la Tierra hasta la biosfera completa; incluye el estudio del impacto que los seres humanos tienen en el ambiente (38, 125)

enzyme (EN ziem) a molecule, either protein or RNA, that acts as a catalyst in biochemical reactions (66)

enzima una molécula, ya sea una proteína o ARN, que actúa como catalizador en las reacciones bioquímicas (66)

epidemiology (EP uh DEE mee AHL uh jee) the study of the distribution of diseases in populations and the study of factors that influence the occurrence and spread of disease (31)

epidemiología el estudio de la distribución de las enfermedades en poblaciones y el estudio de los factores que influyen en la incidencia y propagación de las enfermedades (31)

epidermis (EP uh DUHR mis) the outer surface layer of cells of a plant or animal (477)

epidermis la superficie externa de las células de una planta o animal (477)

epididymis (EP uh DID i mis) the long, coiled tube that is on the surface of a testis and in which sperm mature (550)

epidídimo el conducto largo y enrollado que se encuentra en la superficie de los testículos, en el que los espermatozoides maduran (550)

equilibrium (EE kwi LIB ree uhm) in biology, a state that exists when the concentration of a substance is the same throughout a space (178)

equilibrio en biología, un estado que existe cuando la concentración de una sustancia es la misma en un espacio dado (178)

era a unit of geologic time that includes two or more periods (453)

era una unidad de tiempo geológico que incluye dos o más períodos (453)

erosion (ee ROH zhuhn) a process in which the materials of Earth's surface are loosened, dissolved, or worn away and transported from one place to another by a natural agent, such as wind, water, ice, or gravity (131)

erosión un proceso por medio del cual los materiales de la superficie de la Tierra se aflojan, disuelven o desgastan y son transportados de un lugar a otro por un agente natural, como el viento, el agua, el hielo o la gravedad (131)

estrogen (ES truh juhn) a hormone that regulates the sexual development and reproductive function of females (554)

estrógeno una hormona que regula el desarrollo sexual y la función reproductiva en las hembras (554)

estuary (ES tyoo er ee) an area where fresh water from rivers mixes with salt water from the ocean; the part of a river where the tides meet the river current (84)

estuario un área donde el agua dulce de los ríos se mezcla con el agua salada del océano; la parte de un río donde las mareas se encuentran con la corriente del río (84)

eukaryote (yoo KAR ee OHT) an organism made up of cells that have a nucleus enclosed by a membrane, multiple chromosomes, and a mitotic cycle; eukaryotes include protists, animals, plants, and fungi but not archaea or bacteria (155, 436)

eucariote un organismo cuyas células tienen un núcleo contenido en una membrana, varios cromosomas y un ciclo mitótico; entre los eucariotes se encuentran protistas, animales, plantas y hongos, pero no arqueas ni bacterias (155, 436)

evaporation (ee VAP uh RAY shuhn) the change of state from a liquid to a gas (90)

evaporación el cambio de estado de líquido a gas (90)

evolution (EV uh LOO shuhn) generally, in biology, the process of change by which new species develop from preexisting species over time; at the genetic level, the process in which inherited characteristics within populations change over time; the process defined by Darwin as "descent with modification" (19, 375)

evolución generalmente, en biología, el proceso de cambio por el cual se desarrollan nuevas especies a partir de especies preexistentes a lo largo del tiempo; a nivel genético, el proceso por el cual las características heredadas dentro de las poblaciones cambian con el tiempo; el proceso que Darwin llamó "descendencia con modificación" (19, 375)

excretion (eks KREE shuhn) the process of eliminating metabolic wastes (481)

excreción el proceso de eliminar desechos metabólicos (481)

exocytosis (EK soh sie TOH sis) the process by which a substance is released from the cell through a vesicle that transports the substance to the cell surface and then fuses with the membrane to let the substance out (183)

exocitosis el proceso por medio del cual una sustancia se libera de la célula a través de una vesícula que la transporta a la superficie de la célula en donde se fusiona con la membrana para dejar salir a la sustancia (183)

exon (EK sahn) one of several nonadjacent nucleotide sequences that are part of one gene and that are transcribed, joined together, and then translated (329)

exón una de las varias secuencias de nucleótidos no adyacentes que forman parte de un gene y que se transcriben, se unen y luego se traducen (329)

experiment (ek SPER uh muhnt) a procedure that is carried out under controlled conditions to discover, demonstrate, or test a fact, theory, or general truth (11)

experimento un procedimiento que se lleva a cabo bajo condiciones controladas para descubrir, demostrar o probar un hecho, teoría o verdad general (11)

exponential growth (EKS poh NEN shuhl) logarithmic growth, or growth in which numbers increase by a certain factor in each successive time period (104, 379)

crecimiento exponencial crecimiento logarítmico o crecimiento en el que los números aumentan en función de un cierto factor en cada período de tiempo sucesivo (104, 379)

extinct (ek STINGKT) describes a species that has died out completely (389)

extinto término que describe a una especie que ha desaparecido por completo (389)

extinction (ek STINGK shuhn) the death of every member of a species (133, 389, 414)

extinción la muerte de todos los miembros de una especie (133, 389, 414)

F₁ generation the first generation of offspring obtained from an experimental cross of two organisms (269)

generación F₁ la primera generación de descendencia que se obtiene de la cruza experimental de dos organismos (269)

F₂ generation the second generation of offspring, obtained from an experimental cross of two organisms; the offspring of the F₁ generation (269)

generación F₂ la segunda generación de descendencia que se obtiene de la cruza experimental de dos organismos de una generación F₁ (269)

facilitated diffusion (fuh SIL uh TAYT id di FYOO zhuhn) the transport of substances through a cell membrane along a concentration gradient with the aid of carrier proteins (179)

difusión facilitada el transporte de sustancias a través de la membrana celular de una región de mayor concentración a una de menor concentración con la ayuda de proteínas transportadoras (179)

fallopian tube (fuh LOH pee uhn) a tube through which eggs move from the ovary to the uterus (553)

trompa de Falopio un conducto a través del cual se mueven los óvulos del ovario al útero (553)

family the taxonomic category below the order and above the genus (426)

familia la categoría taxonómica debajo del orden y arriba del género (426)

Glossary · Glosario

feedback mechanism (MEK uh NIZ uhm) a cycle of events in which information from one step controls or affects a previous step (484)

mecanismo de retroalimentación un ciclo de sucesos en el que la información de una etapa controla o afecta a una etapa anterior (484)

fermentation the breakdown of carbohydrates by enzymes, bacteria, yeasts, or mold in the absence of oxygen (212)

fermentación la descomposición de carbohidratos por enzimas, bacterias, levaduras o mohos, en ausencia de oxígeno (212)

fertilization (FUHR'tl i ZAY shuhn) the union of a male and female gamete to form a zygote (248)

fecundación la unión de un gameto masculino y femenino para formar un cigoto (248)

fetus (feetus) a developing human from the end of the eighth weeks after fertilization until birth (559)

feto un ser humano en desarrollo, desde el final de la octava semana después de la fecundación hasta el nacimiento (559)

flagellum (fluh JEL uhm) a long, hairlike structure that grows out of a cell and enables the cell to move (162)

flagelo una estructura larga parecida a una cola, que crece hacia el exterior de una célula y le permite moverse (162)

follicle (FAHL i kuhl) a small, narrow cavity or sac in an organ or tissue, such as the ones on the skin that contain hair roots or the ones in the ovaries that contain the developing eggs (555)

folículo una bolsa o cavidad angosta y pequeña en un órgano o tejido, como las que se encuentran en la piel y contienen las raíces de los pelos, o las que se encuentran en los ovarios y contienen los óvulos en desarrollo (555)

food chain the pathway of energy transfer through various stages as a result of the feeding patterns of a series of organisms (87)

cadena alimenticia la vía de transferencia de energía través de varias etapas, que ocurre como resultado de los patrones de alimentación de una serie de organismos (87)

food web a diagram that shows the feeding relationships between organisms in an ecosystem (87)

red alimenticia un diagrama que muestra las relaciones de alimentación entre los organismos de un ecosistema (87)

fossil (FAHS uhl) the trace or remains of an organism that lived long ago, most commonly preserved in sedimentary rock (382)

fósil los indicios o los restos de un organismo que vivió hace mucho tiempo, comúnmente preservados en las rocas sedimentarias (382)

fossil fuel a nonrenewable energy resource formed from the remains of organisms that lived long ago; examples include oil, coal, and natural gas (126)

combustible fósil un recurso energético no renovable formado a partir de los restos de organismos que vivieron hace mucho tiempo; algunos ejemplos incluyen el petróleo, el carbón y el gas natural (126)

fossil record the history of life in the geologic past as indicated by the traces or remains of living things (382, 450)

registro fósil la historia de la vida en el pasado geológico según la indican los rastros o restos de seres vivos (382, 450)

frameshift mutation a mutation, such as the insertion or deletion of a nucleotide in a coding sequence, that results in the misreading of the code during translation because of a change in the reading frame (320)

mutación de desplazamiento del marco una mutación, tal como la inserción o supresión de un nucleoide en una secuencia de codificación, que tiene como resultado una lectura equivocada del código durante la traducción debido a un cambio en el marco de lectura (320)

frequency (FREE kwuhn see) the number of cycles or vibrations per unit of time; *also* the number of waves produced in a given amount of time (401)

frecuencia el número de ciclos o vibraciones por unidad de tiempo; *también,* el número de ondas producidas en una cantidad de tiempo determinada (401)

fundamental niche (FUHN duh MENT'l NICH) the largest ecological niche where an organism or species can live without competition (113)

nicho fundamental el nicho ecológico más grande en el que un organismo o especie vive sin experimentar competencia (113)

gamete (GAM eet) a haploid reproductive cell that unites with another haploid reproductive cell to form a zygote (248)

gameto una célula reproductiva haploide que se une con otra célula reproductiva haploide para formar un cigoto (248)

gametophyte (guh MEET uh FIET) in alternation of generations, the phase in which gametes are formed; a haploid individual that produces gametes (258)

gametofito en generaciones alternadas, la fase en la que los gametos se forman; un individuo haploide que produce gametos (258)

gene (JEEN) the most basic physical unit of heredity; a segment of nucleic acids that codes for a functional unit of RNA and/or a protein (224, 293)

gene la unidad física más básica de la herencia; un segmento de ácidos nucleicos que codifica una unidad funcional de ARN y/o una proteína (224, 293)

gene expression (eks PRESH uhn) the manifestation of the genetic material of an organism in the form of specific traits (304)

expresión de los genes la manifestación del material genético de un organismo en forma de caracteres específicos (304)

gene flow the movement of genes into or out of a population due to interbreeding (405)

flujo de genes el movimiento de genes a una población o fuera de ella debido al entrecruzamiento (405)

gene pool the total set of genes, including all alleles, that are present in a population at any one point in time (401)

fondo común de genes el conjunto total de genes, incluyendo todos los alelos, que están presentes en una población en un momento determinado (401)

generation (JEN uhr AY shuhn) the entire group of offspring produced by a given group of parents (269)

generación el grupo completo de descendientes producido por un grupo determinado de progenitores (269)

gene technology any of a wide range of procedures that analyze, decipher, or manipulate the genetic material of organisms (350)

tecnología genética cualquiera de una gran variedad de procedimientos para analizar, descifrar o manipular el material genético de los organismos (350)

gene therapy a technique that places a gene into a cell to correct a hereditary disease or to improve the genome (347)

terapia genética una técnica que coloca un gene en una célula para corregir una enfermedad hereditaria o para mejorar el genoma (347)

genetically modified organism an organism containing genetic material that has been artificially altered so as to produce a desired characteristic (abbreviation, GMO) (350)

organismo modificado genéticamente un organismo que contiene material genético que ha sido alterado en forma artificial para producir una característica deseada (abreviatura: OMG) (350)

genetic code the rule that describes how a sequence of nucleotides, read in groups of three consecutive nucleotides (triplets) that correspond to specific amino acids, specifies the amino acid sequence of a protein (63, 307)

código genético la regla que describe la forma en que una secuencia de nucleótidos, leídos en grupos de tres nucleótidos consecutivos (triplete) que corresponden a aminoácidos específicos, especifica la secuencia de aminoácidos de una proteína (63, 307)

genetic counseling the process of testing and informing potential parents about their genetic makeup and the likelihood that they will have offspring with genetic defects or hereditary diseases (346)

orientación genética el proceso de hacer pruebas e informar a una pareja de padres potenciales acerca de su constitución genética y acerca de la posibilidad de que tengan hijos con defectos genéticos o enfermedades hereditarias (346)

genetic disorder an inherited disease or disorder that is caused by a mutation in a gene or by a chromosomal defect (280, 323)

trastorno genético una enfermedad o trastorno hereditario que es causado por una mutación en un gene o por un defecto cromosómico (280, 323)

genetic drift the random change in allele frequency in a population (405)

desviación genética el cambio aleatorio en la frecuencia de los alelos de una población (405)

genetic engineering a technology in which the genome of a living cell is modified for medical or industrial use (33, 346, 350)

ingeniería genética una tecnología en la que el genoma de una célula viva se modifica con fines médicos o industriales (33, 346, 350)

genetic equilibrium (EE kwi LIB ree uhm) a state in which the allele frequencies of a population remain in the same ratios from one generation to the next (404)

equilibrio genético un estado en el que las frecuencias de los alelos de una población permanecen en la misma proporción de generación en generación (404)

genetic library a collection of genetic sequence clones that represent all of the genes in a given genome (363)

biblioteca genética un grupo de clones de secuencia genética que representan a todos los genes de un genoma determinado (363)

genetic marker a gene whose phenotype is easily identified (362)

marcador genético un gene cuyo fenotipo se identifica fácilmente (362)

genetics (juh NET iks) the science of heredity and of the mechanisms by which traits are passed from parents to offspring (31)

genética la ciencia de la herencia y de los mecanismos por los cuales los caracteres son transmitidos de padres a hijos (31)

genital herpes (JEN i tuhl HUHR PEEZ) a sexually transmitted infection that is caused by a herpes simplex virus (562)

herpes genital una infección de transmisión sexual causada por el virus herpes simplex (562)

genome (JEE NOHM) the complete genetic material contained in an individual or species (31, 330)

genoma el material genético completo contenido en un individuo o especie (31, 330)

genome mapping the process of determining the relative position of genes in a genome (362)

mapeo genómico el proceso de determinar la posición relativa de los genes en un genoma (362)

genomics (juh NOH miks) the study of entire genomes, especially by using technology to compare genes within and between species (345)

genómica el estudio de genomas completos, en especial mediante el uso de tecnología para comparar genes dentro de las especies y entre ellas (345)

genotype (JEE nuh TIEP) the entire genetic makeup of an organism; *also* the combination of genes for one or more specific traits (274, 400)

genotipo la constitución genética completa de un organismo; *también,* la combinación de genes para uno o más caracteres específicos (274, 400)

genus (JEE nuhs) the level of classification that comes after family and that contains similar species (424)

género el nivel de clasificación que viene después de la familia y que contiene especies similares (424)

geologic time scale the standard method used to divide Earth's long natural history into manageable parts (453)

escala de tiempo geológico el método estándar que se usa para dividir la larga historia natural de la Tierra en partes razonables (453)

geology (jee AHL uh jee) the scientific study of the origin, history, and structure of Earth and the processes that shape Earth (379)

geología el estudio científico del origen, la historia y la estructura del planeta Tierra y los procesos que le dan forma (379)

germ cell in a multicellular organism, any reproductive cell (as opposed to a somatic cell) (248, 322, 403)

célula germinal en un organismo pluricelular, cualquier célula reproductiva (en contraposición a una célula somática) (248, 322, 403)

gestation (jes TAY shuhn) in mammals, the process of carrying young from fertilization to birth (558)

gestación en los mamíferos, el proceso de llevar a las crías de la fecundación al nacimiento (558)

global warming a gradual increase in average global temperature (128)

calentamiento global un aumento gradual de la temperatura global promedio (128)

glycolysis (glie KAHL i sis) the anaerobic breakdown of glucose to pyruvic acid, which makes a small amount of energy available to cells in the form of ATP (209)

glicólisis la descomposición anaeróbica de glucosa en ácido pirúvico, la cual hace que una pequeña cantidad de energía en forma de ATP esté disponible para las células (209)

glycoprotein (GLIE koh PROH TEEN) a protein to which carbohydrate molecules are attached (177)

glicoproteína una proteína que tienen unidas moléculas de carbohidratos (177)

Golgi apparatus (GOHL jee AP uh RAT uhs) a cell organelle that helps make and package materials to be transported out of the cell (158)

aparato de Golgi un organelo celular que ayuda a hacer y a empacar los materiales que serán transportados al exterior de la célula (158)

gradualism (GRA joo uhl IZ uhm) a model of evolution in which gradual change over a long period of time leads to biological diversity (389)

gradualismo un modelo de evolución en el que un cambio gradual a través de un largo período de tiempo conlleva a la diversidad biológica (389)

greenhouse effect the warming of the surface and lower atmosphere of Earth that occurs when carbon dioxide, water vapor, and other gases in the air absorb and reradiate infrared radiation (129)

efecto invernadero el calentamiento de la superficie terrestre y de la parte más baja de la atmósfera, el cual se produce cuando el dióxido de carbono, el vapor de agua y otros gases del aire absorben radiación infrarroja y la vuelven a irradiar (129)

guanine (GWAH NEEN) one of the four bases that combine with sugar and phosphate to form a nucleotide subunit of DNA; guanine pairs with cytosine (297)

guanina una de las cuatro bases que se combinan con el azúcar y fosfato para formar una subunidad de nucleótidos del ADN; la guanina se une con la citosina (297)

habitat the place where an organism usually lives (80, 112)

hábitat el lugar donde un organismo vive normalmente (80, 112)

half-life the time required for half of a sample of a radioactive isotope to break down by radioactive decay to form a daughter isotope (452)

vida media el tiempo que se requiere para que la mitad de una muestra de un isótopo radiactivo se descomponga por desintegración radiactiva y forme un isótopo hijo (452)

haploid (HAP LOYD) describes a cell, nucleus, or organism that has only one set of unpaired chromosomes (249)

haploide término que describe a una célula, núcleo u organismo que tiene sólo un juego de cromosomas que no están asociados en pares (249)

Hardy-Weinberg principle (HAHR dee WIEN BUHRG) the principle that states that the frequency of alleles in a population does not change unless evolutionary forces act on the population (405)

principio de Hardy-Weinberg el principio que establece que la frecuencia de alelos en una población no cambia a menos que fuerzas evolutivas actúen en la población (405)

heart attack the death of heart tissues due to a blockage of their blood supply (511)

ataque cardíaco la muerte de los tejidos del corazón debido a una obstrucción de su suministro sanguíneo (511)

helper T cell a white blood cell necessary for B cells to develop normal levels of antibodies (529)

célula T auxiliar un glóbulo blanco de la sangre necesario para que las células B desarrollen niveles normales de un anticuerpo (529)

heredity (huh RED i tee) the passing of genetic traits from parent to offspring (19)

herencia la transmisión de caracteres genéticos de padres a hijos (19)

heterotroph (HET uhr uh TROHF) an organism that obtains organic food molecules by eating other organisms or their byproducts and that cannot synthesize organic compounds from inorganic materials (434)

heterótrofo un organismo que obtiene moléculas de alimento al comer otros organismos o sus productos secundarios y que no puede sintetizar compuestos orgánicos a partir de materiales inorgánicos (434)

heterozygous (HET uhr OH ZIE guhs) describes an individual that carries two different alleles of a gene (275)

heterocigoto término que describe un individuo que tiene dos alelos diferentes para un gen (275)

histamine (HIS tuh MEEN) a chemical that stimulates the autonomous nervous system, secretion of gastric juices, and dilation of capillaries (526)

histamina una sustancia química que estimula el sistema nervioso autónomo, la secreción de jugos gástricos y la dilatación de capilares (526)

histone (HIS TOHN) a type of protein molecule found in the chromosomes of eukaryotic cells but not prokaryotic cells (224, 302)

histona un tipo de molécula de proteína que se encuentra en los cromosomas de las células eucarióticas, pero nunca en las procarióticas (224, 302)

HIV human immunodeficiency virus, the virus that causes AIDS (539)

VIH virus de inmunodeficiencia humana; el virus que causa el SIDA (539)

homeobox (HOH mee uh BAHKS) a DNA sequence within a homeotic gene that regulates development in animals (333)

homeocaja una secuencia de ADN dentro de un gene homeótico que regula los patrones de desarrollo en los animales (333)

homeostasis (HOH mee OH STAY sis) the maintenance of a constant internal state in a changing environment; a constant internal state that is maintained in a changing environment by continually making adjustments to the internal and external environment (19, 471)

homeostasis la capacidad de mantener un estado interno constante en un ambiente en cambio; un estado interno constante que se mantiene en un ambiente en cambio al hacer ajustes continuos al ambiente interno y externo (19, 471)

homeotic gene (HOH mee AHD ik) a gene that controls the development of a specific adult structure (333)

gene homeótico un gene que controla el desarrollo de una estructura específica de la etapa adulta (333)

homologous (hoh MAHL uh guhs) describes a character that is shared by a group of species because it is inherited from a common ancestor (384)

homólogo término que describe un carácter compartido por un grupo de especies porque es heredado de un ancestro en común (384)

homologous chromosomes chromosomes that have the same sequence of genes, that have the same structure, and that pair during meiosis (249)

cromosomas homólogos cromosomas con la misma secuencia de genes, que tienen la misma estructura y que se acoplan durante la meiosis (249)

homozygous (HOH moh ZIE guhs) describes an individual that has identical alleles for a trait on both homologous chromosomes (274)

homocigoto término que describe a un individuo que tiene alelos idénticos para un carácter en los dos cromosomas homólogos (274)

hormone (HAWR MOHN) a substance that is made in one cell or tissue and that causes a change in another cell or tissue located in a different part of the body (479)

hormona una sustancia que es producida en una célula o tejido, la cual causa un cambio en otra célula o tejido ubicado en una parte diferente del cuerpo (479)

host an organism from which a parasite takes food or shelter (110)

huésped el organismo del cual un parásito obtiene alimento y rcfugio (110)

Human Genome Project a research effort to sequence and locate the entire collection of genes in human cells (345)

Proyecto del Genoma Humano un esfuerzo de investigación para determinar la secuencia y ubicación de todo el conjunto de genes de las células humanas (345)

hybrid (HIE brid) in biology, the offspring of a cross between parents that have differing traits; a cross between individuals of different species, subspecies, or varieties (268, 413)

híbrido en biología, la descendencia de una cruza entre padres que tienen características diferentes; una cruza entre individuos de especies, subespecies o variedades diferentes (268, 413)

hydrogen bond (HIE druh juhn) the intermolecular force occurring when a hydrogen atom that is bonded to a highly electronegative atom of one molecule is attracted to two unshared electrons of another molecule (54)

enlace de hidrógeno la fuerza intermolecular producida por un átomo de hidrógeno que está unido a un átomo muy electronegativo de una molécula y que experimenta atracción a dos electrones no compartidos de otra molécula (54)

hypertonic (HIE puhr TAHN ik) describes a solution whose solute concentration is higher than the solute concentration inside a cell (180)

hipertónico término que describe una solución cuya concentración de soluto es más alta que la concentración del soluto en el interior de la célula (180)

hypothesis (hie PAHTH uh sis) a testable idea or explanation that leads to scientific investigation (10)

hipótesis una idea o explicación que conlleva a la investigación científica y que se puede probar (10)

hypotonic (HIE poh TAHN ik) describes a solution whose solute concentration is lower than the solute concentration inside a cell (180)

hipotónico término que describe una solución cuya concentración de soluto es más baja que la concentración del soluto en el interior de la célula (180)

immigration (IM uh GRAY shuhn) the movement of an individual or a group to a new community or region (104)

inmigración la llegada de un individuo o grupo a una nueva comunidad o región (104)

immunity (im MYOON i tee) the ability to resist or recover from an infectious disease (532)

inmunidad la capacidad de resistir una enfermedad infecciosa o recuperarse de ella (532)

implantation (IM plan TAY shuhn) the process by which a blastocyst embeds itself in the lining of the uterus; occurs about six days after fertilization (557)

implantación el proceso por medio del cual la blastoquistela se incrusta en la cubierta interior del útero; ocurre unos seis días después de la fecundación (557)

inbreeding (IN BREED ing) the crossing or mating of plants or animals with close relatives (406)

endogamia el cruzamiento de plantas o animales con parientes cercanos (406)

incomplete dominance a condition in which a trait in an individual is intermediate between the phenotype of the individual's two parents because the dominant allele is unable to express itself fully (282)

dominancia incompleta una condición en la que un carácter de un individuo es intermedio entre el fenotipo de los dos padres del individuo porque el alelo dominante no puede expresarse por completo (282)

independent assortment the random distribution of the pairs of genes on different chromosomes to the gametes (253)

distribución independiente la distribución al azar de pares de genes de diferentes cromosomas a los gametos (253)

index fossil a fossil that is used to establish the age of a rock layer because the fossil is distinct, abundant, and widespread and the species that formed that fossil existed for only a short span of geologic time (451)

fósil guía un fósil que se usa para establecer la edad de una capa de roca debido a que puede diferenciarse bien de otros, es abundante y está extendido; la especie que formó ese fósil existió sólo por un corto período de tiempo geológico (451)

Infectious disease a disease that is caused by a pathogen and that can be transmitted from one individual to another(499)

enfermedad infecciosa una enfermedad que es causada por un patógeno y que puede transmitirse de un individuo a otro (499)

inflammation (IN fluh MAY shuhn) a protective response of tissues affected by disease or injury; characterized by pain, swelling, redness, and heat (526)

inflamación una reacción de protección de los tejidos afectados por una enfermedad o lesión (526)

interphase (IN tuhr FAYZ) the period of the cell cycle during which activities such as cell growth and protein synthesis occur without visible signs of cell division (228)

interfase el período del ciclo celular durante el cual las actividades como el crecimiento celular y la síntesis de proteínas existen sin signos visibles de división celular (228)

intron (IN trahn) a nucleotide sequence that is part of a gene and that is transcribed from DNA into mRNA but not translated into amino acids (328)

intrón una secuencia de nucleótidos que es parte de un gene y que se transcribe del ADN al ARNm pero no se traduce en aminoácidos (328)

ion (IE AHN) an atom, radical, or molecule that has gained or lost one or more electrons and has a negative or positive charge (53)

ion un átomo, radical o molécula que ha ganado o perdido uno o más electrones y que tiene una carga negativa o positiva (53)

ionic bond (ie AHN ik) the attractive force between oppositely charged ions, which form when electrons are transferred from one atom to another (53)

enlace iónico la fuerza de atracción entre iones con cargas opuestas, que se forman cuando se transfieren electrones de un átomo a otro (53)

isotonic solution (IE soh TAHN ik) a solution whose solute concentration is equal to the solute concentration inside a cell (180)

solución isotónica una solución cuya concentración de soluto es igual a la concentración de soluto en el interior de la célula (180)

isotope (IE suh TOHP) an atom that has the same number of protons (or the same atomic number) as other atoms of the same element do but that has a different number of neutrons (and thus a different atomic mass) (51, 452)

isótopo un átomo que tiene el mismo número de protones (o el mismo número atómico) que otros átomos del mismo elemento, pero que tiene un número diferente de neutrones (y, por lo tanto, otra masa atómica) (51, 452)

keystone species a species that is critical to the functioning of the ecosystem in which it lives because it affects the survival and abundance of many other species in its community (114)

especie clave una especie que es crítica para el funcionamiento del ecosistema en el que vive porque afecta la supervivencia y abundancia de muchas otras especies en su comunidad (114)

kingdom the highest taxonomic category, which contains a group of similar phyla (426)

reino la categoría taxonómica más alta, que contiene un grupo de phyla similares (426)

Krebs cycle a series of biochemical reactions that convert pyruvic acid into carbon dioxide and water; it is the major pathway of oxidation in animal, bacterial, and plant cells, and it releases energy (210)

ciclo de Krebs una serie de reacciones bioquímicas que convierten el ácido pirúvico en dióxido de carbono y agua; es la vía principal de oxidación en las células animales, bacterianas y vegetales, y libera energía (210)

labia (LAY bee uh) liplike structures, usually referring to fleshy folds located on a female's pubis and at the opening of the vagina (553)

labia estructuras parecidas a labios, que normalmente se refieren a los pliegues carnosos que se encuentran en el pubis de una hembra a la entrada de la vagina (553)

lactic acid fermentation (FUHR muhn TAY shuhn) the chemical breakdown of carbohydrates that produces lactic acid as the main end product (212)

fermentación del ácido láctico la descomposición química de los carbohidratos que produce ácido láctico como producto final principal (212)

law of conservation of energy the law that states that energy cannot be created or destroyed but can be changed from one form to another (64)

ley de la conservación de la energía la ley que establece que la energía ni se crea ni se destruye, sólo se transforma de una forma a otra (64)

law of conservation of mass the law that states that mass cannot be created or destroyed in ordinary chemical and physical changes (64)

ley de la conservación de la masa la ley que establece que la masa no se crea ni se destruye por cambios químicos o físicos comunes (64)

law of independent assortment the law that states that genes separate independently of one another in meiosis (284)

ley de la distribución independiente la ley que establece que los genes se separan de manera independiente durante la meiosis (284)

life cycle all of the events in the growth and development of an organism until the organism reaches sexual maturity (256)

ciclo de vida todos los sucesos en el crecimiento y desarrollo de un organismo hasta que el organismo llega a su madurez sexual (256)

linked in genetics, describes two or more genes that tend to be inherited together (275, 284)

ligado en genética, término que describe dos o más genes que tienden a heredarse juntos (275, 284)

lipid (LIP id) a fat molecule or a molecule that has similar properties; examples include oils, waxes, and steroids (61)

lípido una molécula de grasa o una molécula que tiene propiedades similares; algunos ejemplos son los aceites, las ceras y los esteroides (61)

lipid bilayer (BIE LAY uhr) the basic structure of a biological membrane, composed of two layers of phospholipids (176)

bicapa de lípidos la estructura básica de la membrana biológica, formada por dos capas de fosfolípidos (176)

logistic growth (loh JIS tik) population growth that starts with a minimum number of individuals and reaches a maximum depending on the carrying capacity of the region; described by an S-shaped curve (104)

crecimiento logístico crecimiento de la población que comienza con un número mínimo de individuos y llega al máximo dependiendo de la capacidad de carga de la región; se describe por medio de una curva en forma de S (104)

lung the central organ of the respiratory system in which oxygen from the air is exchanged with carbon dioxide from the blood (482)

pulmón el órgano central del aparato respiratorio en el que el oxígeno del aire se intercambia con el dióxido de carbono de la sangre (482)

luteal phase (LOOT ee uhl) the menstrual stage in which the corpus luteum develops (555)

fase luteal la etapa de la menstruación en la que se desarrolla el corpus luteum (555)

lymph (LIMF) the fluid that is collected by the lymphatic vessels and nodes (483)

linfa el fluido que es recolectado por los vasos y nodos linfáticos (483)

lymph node an organ that filters lymph and that is found along the lymphatic vessels (483)

nodo linfático un órgano que filtra la linfa y que se encuentra a lo largo de los vasos linfáticos (483)

macrophage (MAK roh FAYJ) an immune system cell that engulfs pathogens and other materials (527)

macrófago una célula del sistema inmunológico que envuelve a los patógenos y otros materiales (527)

malignant tumor (muh LIG nuhnt) a cancerous mass of cells (235)

tumor maligno una masa cancerosa de células (235)

marine ecosystem (muh REEN) an ecosystem in the sea (84)

ecosistema marino un ecosistema en el mar (84)

mass extinction (ek STINGK shuhn) an episode during which large numbers of species become extinct (453)

extinción masiva un episodio durante el cual grandes cantidades de especies se extinguen (453)

meiosis (mie OH sis) a process in cell division during which the number of chromosomes decreases to half the original number by two divisions of the nucleus, which results in the production of sex cells (gametes or spores) (250)

meiosis un proceso de división celular durante el cual el número de cromosomas disminuye a la mitad del número original por medio de dos divisiones del núcleo, lo cual resulta en la producción de células sexuales (gametos o esporas) (250)

melanin (MEL uh nin) a pigment that helps determine the color of skin, hair, eyes, fur, feathers, and scales (477)

melanina un pigmento que ayuda a determinar el color de la piel, el cabello, los ojos, el pelaje, las plumas y las escamas (477)

memory cell an immune system B cell or T cell that does not respond the first time that it meets with an antigen or an invading cell but that recognizes and attacks the antigen or invading cell during subsequent infections (532)

célula de memoria un célula B o una célula T del sistema inmunológico que no responde la primera vez que se encuentra con un antígeno o célula invasora, pero que reconoce y ataca al antígeno o célula invasora durante infecciones posteriores (532)

menopause (MEN uh PAWZ) the termination of the menstrual cycle; occurs between the ages of 45 and 55 (556)

menopausia la terminación del ciclo menstrual; ocurre entre los 45 y 55 años de edad (556)

menstrual cycle the female reproductive cycle, characterized by a monthly change of the lining of the uterus and the discharge of blood (556)

ciclo menstrual el ciclo reproductor femenino, caracterizado por un cambio mensual en el revestimiento del útero y una descarga de sangre (556)

menstruation (MEN STRAY shuhn) the discharge of blood and discarded tissue from the uterus during the menstrual cycle (556)

menstruación la descarga de sangre y tejido de desecho del útero durante el ciclo menstrual (556)

metabolism (muh TAB uh LIZ uhm) the sum of all chemical processes that occur in an organism (19)

metabolismo la suma de todos los procesos químicos que ocurren en un organismo (19)

methanogen (muh THAN uh JEN) a microorganism that produces methane gas (435)

metanógeno un microorganismo que produce gas metano (435)

microarray (MIE kroh uh RAY) a device that contains, in microscopic scale, an orderly arrangement of biomolecules; a device that is used to rapidly test for the presence of a range of similar substances, such as specific DNA sequences (346, 358)

chip de ADN un aparato que contiene, a escala microscópica, una organización ordenada de biomoléculas; un aparato que se usa para probar rápidamente la presencia de una variedad de sustancias similares, como secuencias específicas de ADN (346, 358)

microfilament (MIE kroh FIL uh muhnt) a fiber found inside eukaryotic cells that is composed mainly of the protein actin and that has a role in cell structure and movement (156)

microfilamento una fibra que se encuentra dentro de las células eucarióticas, compuesta principalmente por la proteína actina, y que está relacionada con la estructura y movimiento de la célula (156)

microsphere (MIE kroh SFIR) a hollow microscopic spherical structure that is usually composed of proteins or a synthetic polymer (449)

microesfera una estructura microscópica esférica y hueca compuesta generalmente por proteínas o por un polímero sintético (449)

microtubule (MIE kroh TOO BYOOL) one of the small, tubular fibers composed of the protein tubulin that are found in the cytoplasm of eukaryotic cells, that compose the cytoskeleton, and that play a role in cell structure and movement (156)

microtúbulo una de las fibras pequeñas y tubulares compuestas de la proteína tubulina, las cuales se encuentran en el citoplasma de las células eucarióticas, forman el citoesqueleto y están involucradas en el movimiento y estructura de la célula (156)

migration (mie GRAY shuhn) in general, any movement of individuals or populations from one location to another; specifically, a periodic group movement that is characteristic of a given population or species (388, 405)

migración en general, cualquier movimiento de individuos o poblaciones de un lugar a otro; específicamente, un movimiento periódico en grupo que es característico de una población o especie determinada (388, 405)

missense mutation a type of point mutation that converts one codon to another such that the codon specifies a different amino acid (320)

mutación de sentido erróneo un tipo de mutación puntual que convierte a un codón en otro de manera que el codón especifica un aminoácido diferente (320)

mitochondrion (MIET oh KAHN dree uhn) in eukaryotic cells, the cell organelle that is surrounded by two membranes and that is the site of cellular respiration, which produces ATP (161)

mitocondria en las células eucarióticas, el organelo celular rodeado por dos membranas que es el lugar donde se lleva a cabo la respiración celular, la cual produce ATP (161)

mitosis (mie TOH sis) in eukaryotic cells, a process of cell division that forms two new nuclei, each of which has the same number of chromosomes (229)

mitosis en las células eucarióticas, un proceso de división celular que forma dos núcleos nuevos, cada uno de los cuales posee el mismo número de cromosomas (229)

mobile genetic element a genetic sequence that is sometimes removed or copied from one place and inserted into another within chromosomes or genomes; includes plasmids, transposons, and other elements (abbreviation, MGE) (332)

elemento genético móvil una secuencia genética que a veces se elimina o se copia de un lugar y se inserta en otro dentro de los cromosomas o genomas; incluye a los plásmidos, los transposones y otros elementos (abreviatura: EGM) (332)

molecule (MAHL i KYOOL) a group of atoms that are held together by chemical forces; a molecule is the smallest unit of matter that can exist by itself and retain all of a substance's chemical properties (52)

molécula un conjunto de átomos que se mantienen unidos por acción de las fuerzas químicas; una molécula es la unidad más pequeña de la materia capaz de existir en forma independiente y conservar todas las propiedades químicas de una sustancia (52)

monohybrid cross (MAHN oh HIE brid) a cross between individuals that involves one pair of contrasting traits (269)

cruza monohíbrida una cruza entre individuos que involucra un par de caracteres contrastantes (269)

monosaccharide (MAHN oh SAK uh RIED) a simple sugar that is the basic subunit of a carbohydrate (60)

monosacárido un azúcar simple que es una subunidad fundamental de los carbohidratos (60)

morphology (mawr FAHL uh jee) the study of the structure and form of an organism (430)

morfología el estudio de la estructura y forma de un organismo (430)

mRNA messenger RNA, a single-stranded RNA molecule that encodes the information to make a protein (305)

ARNm ARNm mensajero; una molécula de ARN de una sola hebra que codifica la información para hacer una proteína (305)

mucous membrane (MYOO kuhs) the layer of epithelial tissue that covers internal surfaces of the body and that secretes mucus (525)

membrana mucosa la capa de tejido epitelial que cubre las superficies internas del cuerpo y que secreta moco (525)

multicellular (muhl ti SEL yoo luhr) describes a tissue, organ, or organism that is made of many cells (434)

pluricelular término que describe a un tejido, órgano u organismo constituido por muchas células (434)

multiple alleles (uh LEELZ) more than two alleles (versions of the gene) for a genetic trait (283)

alelos múltiples más de dos alelos (versiones del gene) para un carácter genético (283)

mutation (myoo TAY shuhn) a change in the structure or amount of the genetic material of an organism (319)

mutación un cambio en la estructura o cantidad del material genético de un organismo (319)

mutualism (MYOO choo uhl ɪz uhm) a relationship between two species in which both species benefit (110)

mutualismo una relación entre dos especies en la que ambas se benefician (110)

natural selection the process by which individuals that are better adapted to their environment survive and reproduce more successfully than less well adapted individuals do; a theory to explain the mechanism of evolution (380)

selección natural el proceso por medio del cual los individuos que están mejor adaptados a su ambiente sobreviven y se reproducen con más éxito que los individuos menos adaptados; una teoría que explica el mecanismo de la evolución (380)

negative feedback a change in one direction of a feedback mechanism that stops further change in that direction (555)

retroalimentación negativa un cambio en una dirección o un mecanismo de retroalimentación que detiene otros cambios en esa dirección (555)

nephron (NEF RAHN) the functional unit of the kidney (481)

nefrona la unidad funcional del riñón (481)

neutron (NOO TRAHN) a subatomic particle that has no charge and that is located in the nucleus of an atom (51)

neutrón una partícula subatómica que no tiene carga y que está ubicada en el núcleo de un átomo (51)

niche (NICH) the unique position occupied by a species, both in terms of its physical use of its habitat and its function within an ecological community (113, 413)

nicho la posición única que ocupa una especie, tanto en lo que se refiere al uso de su hábitat como en cuanto a su función dentro de una comunidad ecológica (113, 413)

nitrification (NIE truh fi KAY shuhn) the process by which nitrites and nitrates are produced by bacteria in the soil (92)

nitrificación el proceso por medio del cual las bacterias del suelo producen nitritos y nitratos (92)

nitrogen cycle (NIE truh juhn) the cycling of nitrogen between organisms, soil, water, and the atmosphere (91)

ciclo del nitrógeno el ciclado del nitrógeno entre los organismos, el suelo, el agua y la atmósfera (91)

nitrogen fixation (NIE truh juhn fiks AY shuhn) the process by which gaseous nitrogen is converted into ammonia, a compound that organisms can use to make amino acids and other nitrogen-containing organic molecules (92)

fijación de nitrógeno el proceso por medio del cual el nitrógeno gaseoso se transforma en amoniaco, un compuesto que los organismos utilizan para elaborar aminoácidos y otras moléculas orgánicas que contienen nitrógeno (92)

nondisjunction (NAHN dis JUHNK shuhn) the failure of homologous chromosomes to separate during meiosis I or the failure of sister chromatids to separate during mitosis or meiosis II (324)

no-disyunción fenómeno que se produce cuando los cromosomas homólogos no se separan durante la meiosis I o cuando las cromátidas hermanas no se separan durante la meiosis II (324)

noninfectious disease (NAHN in FEK shuhs di ZEEZ) a disease that cannot spread from one individual to another (499)

enfermedad no infecciosa una enfermedad que no se contagia de una persona a otra (499)

nonsense mutation a mutation that alters a gene so that a nonsense (or noncoding) codon is inserted; a mutation that usually results in the abnormal termination of an amino-acid chain during translation (321)

mutación sin sentido una mutación que altera un gene de modo que se inserta un codón sin sentido (o que no codifica); una mutación que suele tener como resultado la interrupción anormal de una cadena de aminoácidos (321)

normal distribution a distribution of numerical data whose graph forms a bell-shaped curve that is symmetrical about the mean (400)

distribución normal una distribución de datos numéricos cuya gráfica forma una curva en forma de campana que es simétrica respecto a la media (400)

nuclear envelope (NOO klee uhr) the double membrane that surrounds the nucleus of a eukaryotic cell (157)

envoltura nuclear la doble membrana que rodea el núcleo de una célula eucariótica (157)

nucleic acid (noo KLAY ik) an organic compound, either RNA or DNA, whose molecules are made up of one or two chains of nucleotides and carry genetic information (63)

ácido nucleico un compuesto orgánico, ya sea ARN o ADN, cuyas moléculas están formadas por una o más cadenas de nucleótidos y que contiene información genética (63)

nucleolus (noo KLEE uh luhs) the part of the eukaryotic nucleus where ribosomal RNA is synthesized (157)

nucleolo la parte del núcleo eucariótico donde se sintetiza el ARN ribosomal (157)

nucleosome (NOO klee uh SOHM) a eukaryotic structural unit of chromatin that consists of DNA wound around a core of histone proteins (224)

nucleosoma una unidad estructural eucariótica de cromatina formada por ADN que rodea un núcleo de proteínas de histona (224)

nucleotide (NOO klee oh TIED) an organic compound that consists of a sugar, a phosphate, and a nitrogenous base; the basic building block of a nucleic-acid chain (63, 296)

nucleótido un compuesto orgánico formado por un azúcar, un fosfato y una base nitrogenada; el componente básico de una cadena de ácidos nucleicos (63, 296)

nucleus (NOO klee uhs) in a eukaryotic cell, a membrane-bound organelle that contains the cell's DNA and that has a role in processes such as growth, metabolism, and reproduction (155)

núcleo en una célula eucariótica, un organelo cubierto por una membrana, el cual contiene el ADN de la célula y participa en procesos tales como el crecimiento, metabolismo y reproducción (155)

observation (AHB zuhr VAY shuhn) the process of obtaining information by using the senses; the information obtained by using the senses (10)

observación el proceso de obtener información por medio de los sentidos; la información que se obtiene al usar los sentidos (10)

omnivore (AHM ni VAWR) an organism that eats both plants and animals (87)

omnívoro un organismo que come tanto plantas como animales (87)

operator (AHP uh RAY tuhr) a short sequence of viral or bacterial DNA to which a repressor binds to prevent transcription (mRNA synthesis) of the adjacent gene in an operon (326)

operador una secuencia corta de ADN viral o bacteriano a la que se une un represor para impedir la transcripción (síntesis de ARNm) del gene adyacente en un operón (326)

operon (AHP uhr AHN) a unit of adjacent genes that consists of functionally related structural genes and their associated regulatory genes; common in prokaryotes and phages (326)

operón una unidad de genes adyacentes formada por genes estructurales de función relacionada y sus genes reguladores asociados; es común en los procariotes y los fagos (326)

order the taxonomic category below the class and above the family (426)

orden la categoría taxonómica que se encuentra debajo de la clase y arriba de la familia (426)

organ a collection of tissues that carry out a specialized function of the body (164)

órgano un conjunto de tejidos que desempeñan una función especializada en el cuerpo (164)

organelle (AWR guh NEL) one of the small bodies that are found in the cytoplasm of a cell and that are specialized to perform a specific function (155)

organelo uno de los cuerpos pequeños que se encuentran en el citoplasma de una célula y que están especializados para llevar a cabo una función específica (155)

organism (AWR guh NIZ uhm) a living thing; anything that can carry out life processes independently (17)

organismo un ser vivo; cualquier cosa que pueda llevar a cabo procesos vitales independientemente (17)

organ system a group of organs that work together to perform body functions (165)

aparato (o sistema) de órganos un grupo de órganos que trabajan en conjunto para desempeñar funciones corporales (165)

osmosis (ahs MOH sis) the diffusion of water or another solvent from a more dilute solution (of a solute) to a more concentrated solution (of the solute) through a membrane that is permeable to the solvent (180)

ósmosis la difusión de agua u otro solvente de una solución más diluida (de un soluto) a una solución más concentrada (del soluto) a través de una membrana que es permeable al solvente (180)

ovarian cycle (oh VAHR ee uhn) a series of hormone-induced changes in which the ovaries prepare and release a mature ovum each month (554)

ciclo ovárico una serie de cambios inducidos por hormonas en los cuales los ovarios preparan y liberan un óvulo maduro todos los meses (554)

ovary (OH vuh ree) in flowering plants, the lower part of a pistil that produces eggs in ovules (552)

ovario en las plantas con flores, la parte inferior del pistilo que produce óvulos (552)

ovulation (AHV yoo LAY shuhn) the release of an ovum from a follicle of the ovary (554)

ovulación la liberación de un óvulo de un folículo del ovario (554)

ovule (AHV YOOL) a structure in the ovary of a seed plant that contains an embryo sac and that develops into a seed after fertilization (554)

óvulo una estructura del ovario de una planta con semillas que contiene un saco embrionario y se desarrolla para convertirse en una semilla después de la fecundación (554)

ovum (OH vuhm) a mature egg cell (553)

óvulo una célula sexual madura (553)

parasitism (PAR uh SIET IZ uhm) a relationship between two species in which one species, the parasite, benefits from the other species, the host, which is harmed (110)

parasitismo una relación entre dos especies en la que una, el parásito, se beneficia de la otra, el huésped, que resulta perjudicada (110)

parthenogenesis (PAHR thuh NOH JEN uh sis) reproduction in which a female gamete grows into a new individual without being fertilized by a male (247)

partenogénesis reproducción en la cual un gameto femenino se convierte en un nuevo individuo sin ser fecundado por un macho (247)

passive transport the movement of substances across a cell membrane without the use of energy by the cell (178)

transporte pasivo el movimiento de sustancias a través de una membrana celular sin que la célula tenga que usar energía (178)

pathogen (PATH uh juhn) a microorganism, another organism, a virus, or a protein that causes disease; an infectious agent (499, 525)

patógeno un microorganismo, otro organismo, un virus o una proteína que causa enfermedades; un agente infeccioso (499, 525)

pedigree (PED i GREE) a diagram that shows the occurrence of a genetic trait in several generations of a family (280)

pedigrí un diagrama que muestra la incidencia de un carácter genético en varias generaciones de una familia (280)

pelvic inflammatory disease (in FLAM uh TAWR ee) a sexually transmitted infection of the upper female reproductive system, including the uterus, ovaries, and fallopian tubes (563)

enfermedad pélvica inflamatoria una infección de transmisión sexual del aparato reproductor femenino superior, que incluye el útero, los ovarios y las trompas de Falopio (563)

penis (PEE nis) the male organ that transfers sperm to a female and that carries urine out of the body (551)

pene el órgano masculino que transfiere espermatozoides a una hembra y que lleva la orina hacia el exterior del cuerpo (551)

peptide bond (PEP TIED) the chemical bond that forms between the carboxyl group of one amino acid and the amino group of another amino acid (62)

enlace peptídico el enlace químico que se forma entre el grupo carboxilo de un aminoácido y el grupo amino de otro aminoácido (62)

period a unit of geologic time that is longer than an epoch but shorter than an era (453)

período una unidad de tiempo geológico que es más larga que una época pero más corta que una era (453)

P generation parental generation, the first two individuals that mate in a genetic cross (269)

generación P generación parental; los primeros dos individuos que se aparean en una cruza genética (269)

pH (PEE AYCH) a value that is used to express the acidity or alkalinity (basicity) of a system; each whole number on the scale indicates a tenfold change in acidity; a pH of 7 is neutral, a pH of less than 7 is acidic, and a pH of greater than 7 is basic (57)

pH un valor que expresa la acidez o la alcalinidad (basicidad) de un sistema; cada número entero de la escala indica un cambio de 10 veces en la acidez; un pH de 7 es neutro, un pH de menos de 7 es ácido y un pH de más de 7 es básico (57)

phenotype (FEE noh TIEP) an organism's appearance or other detectable characteristic that results from the organism's genotype and the environment (274, 400)

fenotipo la apariencia de un organismo u otra característica perceptible que resulta debido al genotipo del organismo y a su ambiente (274, 400)

phospholipid (FAHS foh LIP id) a lipid that contains phosphorus and that is a structural component in cell membranes (176)

fosfolípido un lípido que contiene fósforo y que es un componente estructural de la membrana celular (176)

phosphorus cycle (FAHS fuh ruhs) the cyclic movement of phosphorus in different chemical forms from the environment to organisms and then back to the environment (93)
ciclo del fósforo el movimiento cíclico del fósforo en diferentes formas químicas del ambiente a los organismos y de regreso al ambiente (93)

photosynthesis (FOHT oh SIN thuh sis) the process by which plants, algae, and some bacteria use sunlight, carbon dioxide, and water to produce carbohydrates and oxygen (197)
fotosíntesis el proceso por medio del cual las plantas, algas y algunas bacterias utilizan la luz solar, dióxido de carbono y agua para producir carbohidratos y oxígeno (197)

phylogenetic tree (FIE loh juh NET ik) a branching diagram that shows how organisms are related through evolution (428)
árbol filogenético un diagrama ramificado que muestra cómo se relacionan los organismos a través de la evolución (428)

phylogeny (fie LAHJ uh nee) the evolutionary history of a species or taxonomic group (428)
filogenia la historia evolutiva de una especie o grupo taxonómico (428)

phylum (FIE luhm) the taxonomic group below kingdom and above class (426)
phylum el grupo taxonómico que se ubica debajo del reino y arriba de la clase (426)

pigment (PIG muhnt) a substance that gives another substance or a mixture its color (203)
pigmento una sustancia que le da color a otra sustancia o mezcla (203)

pioneer species a species that colonizes an uninhabited area and that starts an ecological cycle in which many other species become established (81)
especie pionera una especie que coloniza un área deshabitada y empieza un ciclo ecológico en el cual se establecen muchas otras especies (81)

placenta (pluh SEN tuh) the structure that attaches a developing fetus to the uterus and that enables the exchange of nutrients, wastes, and gases between the mother and the fetus (558)
placenta la estructura que une al feto en desarrollo con el útero y que permite el intercambio de nutrientes, desechos y gases entre la madre y el feto (558)

plasma cell a type of white blood cell that produces antibodies (530)
célula plasmática un tipo de glóbulo blanco que produce anticuerpos (530)

plasmid (PLAZ mid) a genetic structure that can replicate independently of the main chromosome(s) of a cell; usually, a circular DNA molecule in bacteria (prokaryotes) (331)
plásmido una estructura genética que puede duplicarse en forma independiente del cromosoma principal o los cromosomas principales de una célula; generalmente, una molécula de ADN circular de las bacterias (procariotes) (331)

point mutation a mutation in which only one nucleotide or nitrogenous base in a gene is changed (320)
mutación puntual una mutación en la que sólo cambia un nucleótido o una base nitrogenada en un gene (320)

polar (POH luhr) describes a molecule in which the positive and negative charges are separated (54)
polar término que describe una molécula en la que las cargas positivas y negativas están separadas (54)

polar body one of the small cells that separate from an oocyte during meiosis, that have little cytoplasm, and that are ultimately discarded (255)
cuerpo polar una de las células pequeñas que se separan de un oocito durante la meiosis, que tienen poco citoplasma y que finalmente se descartan (255)

polygenic character (PAHL uh JEN ik) a character that is influenced by more than one gene (282, 400)
carácter poligénico un carácter que es influenciado por más de un gene (282, 400)

polymerase chain reaction (PAHL i muhr AYZ) a technique that is used to make many copies of selected segments of DNA (abbreviation, PCR) (357)
reacción en cadena de la polimerasa una técnica que se usa para hacer muchas réplicas de segmentos seleccionados de ADN (abreviatura: PCR, por sus siglas en inglés) (357)

polyploidy (PAH lee PLOY dee) an abnormal condition of having more than two sets of chromosomes (324)
poliploidia la condición anormal de tener más de dos conjuntos de cromosomas (324)

polysaccharide (PAHL i SAK uh RIED) one of the carbohydrates made up of long chains of simple sugars; polysaccharides include starch, cellulose, and glycogen (60)
polisacárido uno de los carbohidratos formados por cadenas largas de azúcares simples; algunos ejemplos de polisacáridos incluyen al almidón, celulosa y glucógeno (60)

population (PAHP yoo LAY shuhn) a group of organisms of the same species that live in a specific geographical area (103, 379)

población un grupo de organismos de la misma especie que viven en un área geográfica específica (103, 379)

population genetics the study of the frequency and interaction of alleles and genes in populations (399)

genética de poblaciones el estudio de la frecuencia e interacción de los alelos y genes en las poblaciones (399)

positive feedback in a system, the mechanism by which a cycle of events establishes conditions that favor repetition of the cycle (555)

retroalimentación positiva en un sistema, el mecanismo por el cual un ciclo de sucesos establece condiciones que favorecen la repetición del ciclo (555)

precipitation (pree SIP uh TAY shuhn) any form of water that falls to Earth's surface from the clouds; includes rain, snow, sleet, and hail (90)

precipitación cualquier forma de agua que cae de las nubes a la superficie de la Tierra; incluye a la lluvia, nieve, aguanieve y granizo (90)

predation (pree DAY shuhn) an interaction between two organisms in which one organism, the predator, kills and feeds on the other organism, the prey (109)

depredación la interacción entre dos organismos en la que un organismo, el depredador, mata a otro organismo, la presa, y se alimenta de él (109)

pregnancy (PREG nuhn see) in developmental biology, the period of time in which a woman carries a developing human from fertilization until the birth of the baby (about 266 days, or 38 weeks); in medical practice, this period of time is measured from the first day of a woman's last menstrual period to the delivery of her baby (about 280 days, or 40 weeks) (558)

embarazo en biología del desarrollo, el período de tiempo durante el cual una mujer lleva en su interior a un ser humano en desarrollo desde la fecundación hasta el nacimiento del bebé (aproximadamente 266 días, o 38 semanas); en medicina, este período se mide desde el primer día del último período menstrual de una mujer hasta el nacimiento del bebé (aproximadamente 280 días, o 40 semanas) (558)

primer (PRIEM uhr) a short, single-stranded fragment of DNA or RNA that is required for the initiation of DNA replication (357)

cebador un fragmento corto de una sola hebra de ADN o ARN que se requiere para iniciar la replicación del ADN (357)

probability (PRAHB uh BIL uh tee) the likelihood that a possible future event will occur in any given instance of the event; the mathematical ratio of the number of times one outcome of any event is likely to occur to the number of possible outcomes of the event (278)

probabilidad término que describe qué tan probable es que ocurra un posible evento futuro en un caso dado del evento; la proporción matemática del número de veces que es posible que ocurra un resultado de cualquier evento respecto al número de resultados posibles del evento (278)

producer (proh DOOS uhr) an organism that can make organic molecules from inorganic molecules; a photosynthetic or chemosynthetic autotroph that serves as the basic food source in an ecosystem (86)

productor un organismo que elabora moléculas orgánicas a partir de moléculas inorgánicas; un autótrofo fotosintético o quimiosintético que funciona como la fuente fundamental de alimento en un ecosistema (86)

product a substance that forms in a chemical reaction (65)

producto una sustancia que se forma en una reacción química (65)

progesterone (proh JES tuhr OHN) a steroid hormone that is secreted by the corpus luteum of the ovary, that stimulates changes in the uterus to prepare for the implantation of a fertilized egg, and that is produced by the placenta during pregnancy (554)

progesterona una hormona esteroide que es secretada por el corpus luteum del ovario, la cual estimula cambios en el útero con el fin de prepararlo para la implantación del óvulo fecundado, y que es producida por la placenta durante el embarazo (554)

prokaryote (proh KAR ee OHT) a single-celled organism that does not have a nucleus or membrane-bound organelles; examples are archaea and bacteria (154)

procariote un organismo unicelular que no tiene núcleo ni organelos cubiertos por una membrana, por ejemplo, las arqueas y las bacterias (154)

promoter (proh MOHT uhr) a nucleotide sequence on a DNA molecule to which an RNA polymerase molecule binds, which initiates the transcription of a specific gene (306, 326)

promotor una secuencia de nucleótidos en una molécula de ADN a la cual se une una molécula de ARN polimerasa, lo cual inicia la transcripción de un gene específico (306, 326)

prostate gland (PRAHS TAYT) a gland in males that contributes to the seminal fluid (551)

glándula próstata una glándula que contribuye al fluido seminal en los machos (551)

protein (PROH TEEN) an organic compound that is made of one or more chains of amino acids and that is a principal component of all cells (62)

proteína un compuesto orgánico que está hecho de una o más cadenas de aminoácidos y que es el principal componente de todas las células (62)

protist (PROH tist) an organism that belongs to the kingdom Protista (436)

protista un organismo que pertenece al reino Protista (436)

proton (PROH TAHN) a subatomic particle that has a positive charge and that is located in the nucleus of an atom; the number of protons in the nucleus is the atomic number, which determines the identity of an element (51)

protón una partícula subatómica que tiene una carga positiva y que está ubicada en el núcleo de un átomo; el número de protones que hay en el núcleo es el número atómico, y éste determina la identidad del elemento (51)

punctuated equilibrium (PUHNGK choo AYT id EE kwi LIB ree uhm) a model of evolution in which short periods of drastic change in species, including mass extinctions and rapid speciation, are separated by long periods of little or no change (389)

equilibrio puntuado un modelo de evolución en el que períodos cortos en los que ocurren cambios drásticos en una especie (incluyendo extinciones masivas y especiación rápida) están separados por períodos largos en los que ocurren muy pocos cambios o en los que no ocurre ningún cambio (389)

Punnett square (PUH nuht) a graphic used to predict the results of a genetic cross (276)

cuadro de Punnett una gráfica que se usa para predecir los resultados de una cruza genética (276)

purine (PYOOR EEN) a nitrogenous base that has a double-ring structure; one of the two general categories of nitrogenous bases found in DNA and RNA; either adenine or guanine (297)

purina una base nitrogenada que tiene una estructura de anillo doble; una de las dos categorías generales de bases nitrogenadas que se encuentran en el ADN y ARN; ya sea la adenina o la guanina (297)

pyrimidine (pi RIM uh DEEN) a nitrogenous base that has a single-ring structure; one of the two general categories of nitrogenous bases found in DNA and RNA; thymine, cytosine, or uracil (297)

pirimidina una base nitrogenada que tiene una estructura de anillo sencillo; una de las dos categorías generales de bases nitrogenadas que se encuentran en el ADN y ARN; timina, citosina o uracilo (297)

radiometric dating (RAY dee oh MET rik) a method of determining the absolute age of an object by comparing the relative percentages of a radioactive (parent) isotope and a stable (daughter) isotope (452)

datación radiométrica un método para determinar la edad absoluta de un objeto comparando los porcentajes relativos de un isótopo radiactivo (precursor) y un isótopo estable (hijo) (452)

reactant (ree AK tuhnt) a substance or molecule that participates in a chemical reaction (65)

reactivo una sustancia o molécula que participa en una reacción química (65)

realized niche (REE uh LIEZD NICH) the range of resources that a species uses, the conditions that the species can tolerate, and the functional roles that the species plays as a result of competition in the species' fundamental niche (113)

nicho realizado la gama de recursos que una especie usa, las condiciones que la especie tolera y los papeles funcionales que la especie juega como resultado de la competencia en su nicho fundamental (113)

receptor protein (ri SEP tuhr) a protein that binds specific signal molecules, which causes the cell to respond (185)

proteína receptora una proteína que liga moléculas señal específicas, lo cual hace que la célula responda (185)

recessive (ri SES iv) in genetics, describes an allele that is expressed only when no dominant allele is present in an individual (273)

recesivo en genética, término que describe un alelo que se expresa sólo cuando no hay un alelo dominante presente en el individuo (273)

recombinant DNA (ree KAHM buh nuhnt) DNA molecules that are artificially created by combining DNA from different sources (350)

ADN recombinante moléculas de ADN que son creadas artificialmente al combinar ADN de diferentes fuentes (350)

recycling (ree SIE kling) the process of recovering valuable or useful materials from waste or scrap; the process of reusing some items (135)

reciclar el proceso de recuperar materiales valiosos o útiles de los desechos o de la basura; el proceso de reutilizar algunas cosas (135)

relative dating a method of determining whether an event or object, such as a fossil, is older or younger than other events or objects without referring to the object's age in years (451)

datación relativa un método para determinar si un acontecimiento u objeto, tal como un fósil, es más viejo o más joven que otros acontecimientos u objetos sin referirse a la edad del objeto en años (451)

replication fork (REP luh KAY shuhn) a Y-shaped point that results when the two strands of a DNA double helix separate so that the DNA molecule can be replicated (300)

bifurcación de replicación un punto que tiene forma de Y, el cual se produce cuando las dos hebras de una doble hélice de ADN se separan de modo que la molécula de ADN pueda duplicarse (300)

reproduction (REE pruh DUHK shuhn) the process of producing offspring (19, 247)

reproducción el proceso de producir descendencia (19, 247)

reproductive isolation (REE pruh DUHK tiv IE suh LAY shuhn) a state in which a particular set of populations can no longer interbreed to produce future generations of offspring (412)

aislamiento reproductivo un estado en el cual un conjunto particular de poblaciones ya no puede reproducirse entre sí para crear generaciones futuras de descendientes (412)

respiration (RES puh RAY shuhn) in biology, the exchange of oxygen and carbon dioxide between living cells and their environment; includes breathing and cellular respiration (91)

respiración en biología, el intercambio de oxígeno y dióxido de carbono entre células vivas y su ambiente; incluye la respiración y la respiración celular (91)

restriction enzyme (ri STRIK shuhn EN ziem) an enzyme that cuts double-stranded DNA into fragments by recognizing specific nucleotide sequences and cutting the DNA at those sequences (355)

enzima de restricción una enzima que corta en fragmentos las moléculas de doble hebra del ADN reconociendo secuencias de nucleótidos específicas y cortando el ADN en esas secuencias (355)

retrovirus (RE troh VIE ruhs) a virus that contains single-stranded RNA and produces a reverse transcriptase, which converts RNA to DNA (332)

retrovirus un virus que contiene ARN de una sola hebra y que produce transcriptasa inversa, la cual convierte el ARN en ADN (332)

ribose (RIE BOHS) a five-carbon sugar present in RNA (305)

ribosa un azúcar de cinco carbonos presente en el ARN (305)

ribosome (RIE buh SOHM) a cell organelle composed of RNA and protein; the site of protein synthesis (154, 305)

ribosoma un organelo celular compuesto de ARN y proteína; el sitio donde ocurre la síntesis de proteínas (154, 305)

ribozyme (RIE buh ZIEM) a type of RNA that can act as an enzyme (449)

ribozima un tipo de ARN que puede funcionar como una enzima (449)

RNA ribonucleic acid, a natural polymer that is present in all living cells and that plays a role in protein synthesis (63, 304)

ARN ácido ribonucleico; un polímero natural que se encuentra en todas las células vivas y que juega un papel en la síntesis de proteínas (63, 304)

RNA polymerase (puh LIM uhr AYS) an enzyme that starts (catalyzes) the formation of RNA by using a strand of a DNA molecule as a template (306)

ARN polimerasa una enzima que comienza (cataliza) la formación de ARN usando una hebra de una molécula de ADN como plantilla (306)

rough endoplasmic reticulum (EN doh PLAZ mik ri TIK yuh luhm) the portion of the endoplasmic reticulum to which ribosomes are attached (158)

retículo endoplásmico rugoso la porción del retículo endoplásmico a la que se unen los ribosomas (158)

rRNA ribosomal RNA, an organelle that contains most of the RNA in the cell and that is responsible for ribosome function (305)

ARNr ARN ribosomal; un organelo que contiene la mayor parte del ARN en la célula y que es responsable del funcionamiento de los ribosomas (305)

savanna (suh VAN uh) a plain full of grasses and scattered trees and shrubs; found in tropical and subtropical habitats and mainly in regions with a dry climate, such as East Africa (83)

sabana una planicie llena de pastizales y árboles y arbustos dispersos; se encuentra en los hábitats tropicales y subtropicales y, sobre todo, en regiones con un clima seco, como en el este de África (83)

scrotum (SKROHT uhm) the sac that contains the testes in most male mammals (549)

escroto la bolsa que contiene los testículos en la mayoría de los mamíferos machos (549)

second messenger a molecule that is generated when a specific substance attaches to a receptor on the outside of a cell membrane, which produces a change in cellular function (186)

mensajero secundario una molécula que se genera cuando una sustancia específica se une a un receptor en el exterior de la membrana celular, lo cual produce un cambio en la función celular (186)

semen (SEE muhn) the fluid that contains sperm and various secretions produced by the male reproductive organs (551)

semen el fluido que contiene espermatozoides y varias secreciones producidas por los órganos reproductores masculinos (551)

seminal vesicle (SEM uh nuhl VES i kuhl) one of two glandular structures in male vertebrates that hold and secrete seminal fluid (551)

vesícula seminal una de las dos estructuras glandulares en los vertebrados macho, las cuales acumulan y secretan fluido seminal (551)

seminiferous tubule (sem uh NIF uhr uhs) one of the many tubules in the testis where sperm are produced (549)

túbulo seminífero uno de los muchos túbulos que hay en los testículos, en donde se producen los espermatozoides (549)

sex chromosome one of the pair of chromosomes that determine the sex of an individual (249)

cromosoma sexual uno de los dos cromosomas que determinan el sexo de un individuo (249)

sexual reproduction reproduction in which gametes from two parents unite (248)

reproducción sexual reproducción en la que se unen los gametos de los dos progenitores (248)

sexual selection an evolutionary mechanism by which traits that increase the ability of individuals to attract or acquire mates appear with increasing frequency in a population; selection in which a mate is chosen on the basis of a particular trait or traits (406)

selección sexual un mecanismo evolutivo por medio del cual los caracteres que aumentan la capacidad de los individuos de atraer o adquirir una pareja aparecen con más frecuencia en una población; selección en la que se elige una pareja con base en un carácter o caracteres particulares (406)

SI (ES IE) Le Système International d'Unités, or the International System of Units, which is the measurement system that is accepted worldwide (15)

SI Le Système International d'Unités, o el Sistema Internacional de Unidades, que es el sistema de medición que se acepta en todo el mundo (15)

signal anything that serves to direct, guide, or warn (184)

señal cualquier cosa que sirve para dirigir, guiar o advertir (184)

silent mutation an alteration of genetic information that has no apparent effect on the phenotype of an organism (320)

mutación silenciosa una alteración de la información genética que no tiene un efecto aparente en el fenotipo de un organismo (320)

skepticism (SKEP ti sIZ uhm) a habit of mind in which a person questions the validity of accepted ideas (7)

escepticismo un hábito de la mente que hace que la persona cuestione la validez de las ideas aceptadas (7)

smooth endoplasmic reticulum (EN doh PLAZ mik ri TIK yuh luhm) the portion of the endoplasmic reticulum that lacks attached ribosomes (158)

retículo endoplásmico liso la porción del retículo endoplásmico que no tiene ribosomas adjuntos (158)

sodium-potassium pump (SOH dee uhm poh TAS ee uhm) a carrier protein that uses ATP to actively transport sodium ions out of a cell and potassium ions into the cell (182)

bomba de sodio-potasio una proteína transportadora que utiliza el ATP para efectuar el transporte activo de iones de sodio hacia el exterior de la célula y de iones de potasio hacia el interior de la célula (182)

solution (suh LOO shuhn) a homogeneous mixture throughout which two or more substances are uniformly dispersed (56)

solución una mezcla homogénea en la cual dos o más sustancias se dispersan de manera uniforme (56)

somatic cell (soh MAT ik) a cell other than a gamete or germ cell; a body cell (248, 322, 403)

célula somática una célula que no es un gameto o una célula germinal; una célula del cuerpo (248, 322, 403)

speciation (SPEE shee AY shuhn) the formation of new species as a result of evolution (387, 412)

especiación la formación de especies nuevas como resultado de la evolución (387, 412)

species (SPEE seez) a group of organisms that are closely related and can mate to produce fertile offspring; *also* the level of classification below genus and above subspecies (19, 387, 411, 426)

especie un grupo de organismos que tienen un parentesco cercano y que pueden aparearse para producir descendencia fértil; *también,* el nivel de clasificación debajo de género y arriba de subespecie (19, 387, 411, 426)

sperm (SPUHRM) the male gamete (sex cell) (549)

espermatozoide el gameto masculino (célula sexual) (549)

spindle (SPIN duhl) a network of microtubules that forms during mitosis and moves chromatids to the poles (230)

huso mitótico una red de microtúbulos que se forma durante la mitosis y que mueve cromátidas a los polos (230)

sporophyte (SPOH ruh FIET) in plants and algae that have alternation of generations, the diploid individual or generation that produces haploid spores (258)

esporofito en las plantas y algas que tienen generaciones alternas, el individuo o generación diploide que produce esporas haploides (258)

stabilizing selection (STAY buh LIEZ ing) a type of natural selection in which the average form of a trait is favored and becomes more common (409)

selección de estabilización un tipo de selección natural en la que se favorece la forma promedio de un carácter, el cual se vuelve más común (409)

stem cell a cell that can divide repeatedly and can differentiate into specialized cell types (353)

célula madre una célula que puede dividirse repetidamente y puede diferenciarse y formar tipos de células especializados (353)

sticky end a single-stranded end of a double-stranded DNA molecule; can base-pair with a complementary sticky end (355)

extremo cohesivo el extremo de una hebra de la molécula de ADN de doble hebra; puede formar pares de bases con un extremo cohesivo complementario (355)

stroke a sudden loss of consciousness or paralysis that occurs when the blood flow to the brain is interrupted (511)

ataque de apoplejía una pérdida súbita de la conciencia o parálisis que ocurre cuando se interrumpe el flujo sanguíneo al cerebro (511)

subspecies (SUHB SPEE sheez) a taxonomic classification below species that groups organisms that live in different geographical areas, differ morphologically from other populations of the species, but can interbreed with other populations of the species (412)

subespecie una clasificación taxonómica que se ubica debajo de la especie y agrupa a organismos que viven en áreas geográficas diferentes y difieren en forma morfológica de otras poblaciones de la especie, pero tienen la capacidad de cruzarse con otras poblaciones de la especie (412)

substrate (SUHB STRAYT) a part, substance, or element that lies beneath and supports another part, substance, or element; the reactant in reactions catalyzed by enzymes (66)

sustrato una parte, sustancia o elemento que se encuentra debajo de otra parte, sustancia o elemento y lo sostiene; el reactivo en reacciones que son catalizadas por enzimas (66)

succession (suhk SESH uhn) the replacement of one type of community by another at a single location over a period of time (81)

sucesión el reemplazo de un tipo de comunidad por otro en un mismo lugar a lo largo de un período de tiempo (81)

symbiosis (SIM bie OH sis) a relationship in which two different organisms live in close association with each other (110, 331)

simbiosis una relación en la que dos organismos diferentes viven estrechamente asociados uno con el otro (110, 331)

systematics (SIS tuh MAT iks) the classification of living organisms in terms of their natural relationships; it includes describing, naming, and classifying the organisms (427)

sistemática la clasificación de los seres vivos en función de sus relaciones naturales; involucra describir, nombrar y clasificar a los organismos (427)

taiga (TIE guh) a region of evergreen, coniferous forest below the arctic and subarctic tundra regions (83)

taiga una región de bosques siempreverdes de coníferas, ubicado debajo de las regiones árticas y subárticas de tundra (83)

target cell a specific cell to which a hormone is directed to produce a specific effect (184)

célula blanco una célula específica a la que se dirige una hormona para producir un efecto específico (184)

taxon (TAKS AHN) any named taxonomic group of any rank in the hierarchical classification of organisms; for example, family, genus, or species (423)

taxón cualquier grupo taxonómico nombrado de cualquier rango en la clasificación jerárquica de los organismos; por ejemplo: familia, género o especie (423)

taxonomy (taks AHN uh mee) the science of describing, naming, and classifying organisms (423)

taxonomía la ciencia de describir, nombrar y clasificar organismos (423)

telomere (TEL uh MIR) the region at the tip of a chromosome; a region of repeating DNA sequences that forms one of the end points of the DNA segment that makes up a chromosome (334)

telómero la región de la punta de un cromosoma; una región de secuencias de ADN repetidas que forma uno de los extremos del segmento de ADN que compone un cromosoma (334)

temperate grassland a community (or biome) that is dominated by grasses, has few trees, and is characterized by cold winters and rainfall that is intermediate between that of a forest and a desert (83)

  pradera templada una comunidad (o bioma) que está dominada por pastos, tiene pocos árboles y se caracteriza por inviernos fríos y precipitación pluvial que es intermedia entre la de un bosque y la de un desierto (83)

tendon (TEN duhn) a tough connective tissue that attaches a muscle to a bone or to another body part (476)

  tendón un tejido conectivo duro que une un músculo con un hueso o con otra parte del cuerpo (476)

testes (TES TEEZ) the primary male reproductive organs, which produce sperm cells and testosterone (singular, *testis*) (549)

  testículos los principales órganos reproductores masculinos, los cuales producen espermatozoides y testosterona (549)

tetrad (TE TRAD) the four chromatids in a pair of homologous chromosomes that come together as a result of synapsis during meiosis (252)

  tétrada las cuatro cromátidas que se encuentran en un par de cromosomas homólogos, las cuales vienen juntas como resultado de la sinapsis durante la meiosis (252)

theory (THEE uh ree) a system of ideas that explains many related observations and is supported by a large body of evidence acquired through scientific investigation (13, 375)

  teoría un sistema de ideas que explica muchas observaciones relacionadas y que está respaldado por una gran cantidad de pruebas obtenidas mediante la investigación científica (13, 375)

thylakoid (THIE luh KOYD) a membrane system found within chloroplasts that contains the components for photosynthesis (202)

  tilacoide un sistema de membranas que se encuentra dentro de los cloroplastos y que contiene los componentes para que se lleve a cabo la fotosíntesis (202)

thymine (THIE MEEN) one of the four bases that combine with sugar and phosphate to form a nucleotide subunit of DNA; thymine pairs with adenine (297)

  timina una de las cuatro bases que se combinan con un azúcar y un fosfato para formar una subunidad de nucleótido de ADN; la timina se une a la adenina (297)

tissue (TISH oo) a group of similar cells that perform a common function (164)

  tejido un grupo de células similares que llevan a cabo una función común (164)

toxin a substance that is produced by one organism and that is poisonous to other organisms (502)

  toxina una sustancia que un organismo produce y que es venenosa para otros organismos (502)

trait (TRAYT) a genetically determined characteristic (268)

  carácter una característica determinada genéticamente (268)

transcription (tran SKRIP shuhn) the process of forming a nucleic acid by using another molecule as a template; particularly the process of synthesizing RNA by using one strand of a DNA molecule as a template (305)

  transcripción el proceso de formar un ácido nucleico usando otra molécula como plantilla; en particular, el proceso de sintetizar ARN usando una de las hebras de la molécula de ADN como plantilla (305)

transcription factor an enzyme that is needed to begin and/or continue genetic transcription (327)

  factor de transcripción una enzima que se necesita para comenzar y/o continuar la transcripción genética (327)

transfer RNA an RNA molecule that transfers amino acids to the growing end of a polypeptide chain during translation (305)

  ARN de transferencia una molécula de ARN que transfiere aminoácidos al extremo en crecimiento de una cadena de polipéptidos durante la traducción (305)

transformation (TRANS fuhr MAY shuhn) the transfer of genetic material in the form of DNA fragments from one cell to another or from one organism to another (294)

  transformación la transferencia de material genético en forma de fragmentos de ADN de una célula a otra o de un organismo a otro (294)

transgenic organism (trans JE nik) an organism that has been transformed by the introduction of novel DNA into its genome (350)

  organismo transgénico un organismo que ha sido transformado por la introducción de ADN nuevo a su genoma (350)

translation (trans LAY shuhn) the portion of protein synthesis that takes place at ribosomes and that uses the codons in mRNA molecules to specify the sequence of amino acids in polypeptide chains (305)

  traducción la porción de la síntesis de proteínas que tiene lugar en los ribosomas y que usa los codones de las moléculas de ARNm para especificar la secuencia de aminoácidos en las cadenas de polipéptidos (305)

transpiration (TRAN spuh RAY shuhn) the process by which plants release water vapor into the air through stomata; *also* the release of water vapor into the air by other organisms (90)

  transpiración el proceso por medio del cual las plantas liberan vapor de agua al aire por medio de los estomas; *también,* la liberación de vapor de agua al aire por otros organismos (90)

transposon (trans POH ZAHN) a genetic sequence that is randomly moved, in a functional unit, to new places in a genome (332)

transposón una secuencia genética que se mueve al azar, en una unidad funcional, a lugares nuevos dentro de un genoma (332)

trophic level (TRAHF ik) one of the steps in a food chain or food pyramid; examples include producers and primary, secondary, and tertiary consumers (86)

nivel trófico uno de los pasos de la cadena alimenticia o de la pirámide alimenticia; entre los ejemplos se encuentran los productores y los consumidores primarios, secundarios y terciarios (86)

tropical rain forest (TRAHP i kuhl) a forest or jungle near the equator that is characterized by large amounts of rain and little variation in temperature and that contains the greatest known diversity of organisms on Earth (83)

selva tropical un bosque o jungla que se encuentra cerca del ecuador y se caracteriza por una gran cantidad de lluvia y poca variación en la temperatura, y que contiene la mayor diversidad de organismos que se conoce en la Tierra (83)

true-breeding describes organisms or genotypes that are homozygous for a specific trait and thus always produce offspring that have the same phenotype for that trait (269)

variedad pura término que describe organismos o genotipos que son homocigotos para un carácter específico y, por lo tanto, producen descendencia que tiene el mismo fenotipo para ese carácter (269)

tumor (TOO muhr) a growth that arises from normal tissue but that grows abnormally in rate and structure and lacks a function (235, 323)

tumor un bulto que surge en un tejido normal, pero que crece anormalmente en tasa y estructura, y carece de función (235, 323)

tundra (TUHN druh) a treeless plain that is located in the Arctic or Antarctic and that is characterized by very low winter temperatures; short, cool summers; and vegetation that consists of grasses, lichens, and perennial herbs (83)

tundra una llanura sin árboles situada en la región ártica o antártica y se caracteriza por temperaturas muy bajas en el invierno, veranos cortos y frescos y vegetación que consiste en pasto, líquenes y hierbas perennes (83)

unicellular (YOON uh SEL yoo luhr) describes an organism that consists of a single cell (434)

unicelular término que describe a un organismo que está formado por una sola célula (434)

uracil (YOOR uh SIL) one of the four bases that combine with sugar and phosphate to form a nucleotide subunit of RNA; uracil pairs with adenine (305)

uracilo una de las cuatro bases que se combinan con un azúcar y un fosfato para formar una subunidad de nucleótido de ADN; el uracilo se une a la adenina (305)

urea (yoo REE uh) the principal nitrogenous product of the metabolism of proteins that forms in the liver from amino acids and from compounds of ammonia and that is found in urine and other body fluids (481)

urea el principal producto nitrogenado que se obtiene del metabolismo de las proteínas, se forma en el hígado a partir de aminoácidos y compuestos de amoníaco y se encuentra en la orina y otros fluidos del cuerpo (481)

urine (YUR in) the liquid excreted by the kidneys, stored in the bladder, and passed through the urethra to the outside of the body (481)

orina el líquido que excretan los riñones, se almacena en la vejiga y pasa a través de la uretra hacia el exterior del cuerpo (481)

uterus (YOOT uhr uhs) in female placental mammals, the hollow, muscular organ in which an embryo embeds itself and develops into a fetus (553)

útero en los mamíferos placentarios hembras, el órgano hueco y muscular en el que el embrión se incrusta y se desarrolla hasta convertirse en feto (553)

vaccination (VAK suh NAY shuhn) the administration of treated microorganisms into humans or animals to induce an immune response (31)

vacunación la administración a seres humanos o animales de organismos que han sido tratados para inducir una respuesta inmunológica (31)

vaccine (vak SEEN) a substance prepared from killed or weakened pathogens and introduced into a body to produce immunity (532)

vacuna una sustancia que se prepara a partir de organismos patógenos muertos o debilitados y se introduce al cuerpo para producir inmunidad (532)

vacuole (VAK yoo OHL) a fluid-filled vesicle found in the cytoplasm of plant cells or protozoans (160)

vacuola una vesícula llena de líquido que se encuentra en el citoplasma de las células vegetales o de los protozoarios (160)

vagina (vuh JIE nuh) the female reproductive organ that connects the outside of the body to the uterus and that receives sperm during reproduction (553)

vagina el canal de las hembras que se extiende de la vulva al cuello del útero y que recibe al pene durante el coito (553)

valence electron (VAY luhns) an electron that is found in the outermost shell of an atom and that determines the atom's chemical properties (52)

electrón de valencia un electrón que se encuentra en la capa más externa de un átomo y que determina las propiedades químicas del átomo (52)

vas deferens (vas DEF uh renz) a duct through which sperm move from the epididymis to the ejaculatory duct at the base of the penis (550)

conducto deferente un conducto a través del cual los espermatozoides se mueven del epidídimo al conducto eyaculatorio que está en la base del pene (550)

vector (VEK tuhr) in biology, any agent, such as a plasmid or a virus, that can incorporate foreign DNA and transfer that DNA from one organism to another; an intermediate host that transfers a pathogen or a parasite to another organism (360, 500)

vector en biología, cualquier agente, como por ejemplo un plásmido o un virus, que tiene la capacidad de incorporar ADN extraño y de transferir ese ADN de un organismo a otro; un huésped intermediario que transfiere un organismo patógeno o un parásito a otro organismo (360, 500)

vein (VAYN) in biology, a vessel that carries blood to the heart (482)

vena en biología, un vaso que lleva sangre al corazón (482)

vertebrate (VUHR tuh brit) an animal that has a backbone; includes mammals, birds, reptiles, amphibians, and fish (383)

vertebrado un animal que tiene columna vertebral; incluye a los mamíferos, aves, reptiles, anfibios y peces (383)

vesicle (VES i kuhl) a small cavity or sac that contains materials in a eukaryotic cell; forms when part of the cell membrane surrounds the materials to be taken into the cell or transported within the cell (158)

vesícula una cavidad o bolsa pequeña que contiene materiales en una célula eucariótica; se forma cuando parte de la membrana celular rodea los materiales que van a ser llevados al interior la célula o transportados dentro de ella (158)

virus (VIE ruhs) a nonliving, infectious particle composed of a nucleic acid and a protein coat; it can invade and destroy a cell (332)

virus una partícula infecciosa sin vida formada por un ácido nucleico y una cubierta de proteína; puede invadir una célula y destruirla (332)

vulva (VUHL vuh) the external part of the female reproductive organs (553)

vulva la parte externa de los órganos reproductores femeninos (553)

water cycle the continuous movement of water between the atmosphere, the land, and the oceans (90)

ciclo del agua el movimiento continuo del agua entre la atmósfera, la tierra y los océanos (90)

zygote (ZIE GOHT) the cell that results from the fusion of gametes; a fertilized egg (248, 557)

cigoto la célula que resulta debido a la fusión de los gametos; el óvulo fecundado (248, 557)

Note: Page references followed by *f* refer to illustrative material, such as figures and tables.

abiotic factors, 80, 106
ABO blood groups, 283, 283*f*
abstinence, 561
accidents, procedures for, 16
acid rain, 128, 140–141
acids and bases, 56–57, 56*f. See also* **pH**
acne, 503, 503*f*
acquired immune deficiency syndrome
   (AIDS), 539, 539*f*, 561*f*, 563. *See also* **HIV**
actin, 156
activation energy, 65, 65*f*, 66, 66*f*
activators, 327, 327*f*
active sites, 66, 67*f*
active transport, 182–183, 182*f*, 183*f*
adaptation, 380–381, 381*f*
adaptive radiation, 389
adenine, 296*f*, 297, 298
adenosine diphosphate (ADP), 200–201,
   200*f*, 201*f*, 206*f*
adenosine triphosphate (ATP)
   in active transport, 182, 182*f*
   in aerobic respiration, 210–211, 210*f*, 211*f*,
      213*f*
   from cellular respiration, 198, 199*f*
   energy transfer through, 200–201, 200*f*,
      201*f*
   in mitochondria, 161, 161*f*
   in photosynthesis, 160, 204–207, 204*f*, 206*f*
   in sperm, 550
   structure of, 63, 63*f*
adhesion, 55, 55*f*
ADP (adenosine diphosphate), 200–201,
   200*f*, 201*f*, 206*f*
adrenal glands, 479*f*
aerobic respiration, 210–211, 210*f*, 211*f*,
   213*f*
African Americans, sickle cell anemia in,
   319, 319*f*
aging, 333–334, 333*f*, 334*f*, 513
agriculture
   genetic engineering in, 33, 350–351, 350*f*,
      351*f*, 354
   soil damage in, 131
AIDS (acquired immune deficiency syndrome), 539, 539*f*, 561*f*, 563. *See also* **HIV**
air pollution, 127, 128, 128*f*
albinism, 280, 280*f*, 285
alcohol
   alcoholism, 510
   alcohol resistance, 34
   birth defects from, 513, 558
alcoholic fermentation, 212, 212*f*
alcoholism, 510
algae, 165, 457*f*
algal blooms, 130
alleles
   in *Drosophila*, 271
   frequencies, 401–402, 401*f*, 402*f*
   heredity and, 272, 272*f*
   independent assortment of, 275, 275*f*, 284

   multiple, 283, 283*f*
   new, from mutations, 323
   random segregation of, 273
allergens, 534, 534*f*, 535*f*
allergies, 534–536, 534*f*–535*f*, 536*f*
alternation of generations, 258
altitude, body adjustments to, 468*f*–469*f*
Altman, Sidney, 449
alveoli (singular, *alveolus*), 482, 482*f*
Amanita, 515
amber, 451
amebic dysentery, 508*f*
amino acids
   codons for, 307, 307*f*
   evolution and, 384, 384*f*
   in meteorites, 448
   in mutations, 320–321, 320*f*, 321*f*
   in protein synthesis, 308–309, 308*f*–309*f*
   structure of, 62, 62*f*
ammonia, 56, 92, 92*f*
ammonification, 92, 92*f*
amnion, 558
amniotic eggs, 430*f*
amniotic fluid, 560
amoebas, 165, 247
amphibians, 458
anaerobic respiration, 209, 211–212, 211*f*,
   212*f*
analogous characteristics, 428
anaphase, 231, 231*f*, 250*f*–251*f*, 251
anatomy, evolutionary theory and, 384,
   384*f. See also* **human body**
ancestral characters, 429, 431*f*
anemia, in hookworm infections, 507
angiosperms, 429*f*
animal cells, 163*f*, 232, 232*f. See also* **eukaryotic cells**
"animalcules," 151
Animalia (kingdom), 425*f*, 434*f*, 436, 436*f*–
   437*f. See also* **animals**
animals
   classification of, 434*f*, 436, 436*f*–437*f*
   as multicellular organisms, 166
anoles, 227, 227*f*, 410, 410*f*
Anolis spp. (anoles), 410, 410*f*
Anopheles **mosquito,** 509, 509*f*
anorexia nervosa, 514
antagonistic hormones, 485
antibiotic resistance, 332, 332*f*
antibiotics, yeast infections and, 506
antibodies, 530, 531*f*
anticodons, 308–309, 308*f*–309*f*
antigens
   antibody binding of, 528, 530, 531*f*
   macrophages and, 527–528, 527*f*
   T cells and, 530, 531*f*
   in vaccines, 532
antigen shifting, 533
antihistamines, 534
Apis mellifera (European honey bee), 424
apomixis, 255
apoptosis, 334, 334*f*
aquatic ecosystems, 84, 84*f*
archaea, 434*f*, 435, 436*f*–437*f*, 454
Archaea (domain), 434, 434*f*, 435, 436*f*–437*f*
Archaebacteria (kingdom), 433, 434*f*, 435,
   436*f*–437*f*

arithmetic growth, 378, 378*f*, 379
arteries, 482, 511, 511*f*
arthropods, 458
artificial intelligence, 41, 41*f*
artificial selection, 377, 377*f*
asexual reproduction
   apomixis, 255
   binary fission, 247
   budding, 247, 247*f*, 505*f*
   cloning as, 352, 352*f*
   fragmentation, 247
   parthenogenesis, 247, 255, 255*f*
   in plants, 255
assimilation, 92, 92*f*
assistive technologies, 32, 32*f*
asteroids, 448, 448*f*, 460, 460*f*
asthma, 535
athlete's foot, 506
atoms, 51–54, 51*f*
ATP (adenosine triphosphate)
   in active transport, 182, 182*f*
   in aerobic respiration, 210–211, 210*f*, 211*f*,
      213*f*
   from cellular respiration, 198, 199*f*
   energy transfer through, 200–201, 200*f*,
      201*f*
   in mitochondria, 161, 161*f*
   in photosynthesis, 160, 204–207, 204*f*, 206*f*
   in sperm, 550
   structure of, 63, 63*f*
ATP synthase, 200*f*, 201, 204*f*, 205
autoimmune diseases, 537, 537*f*, 538
automated sequencing devices, 363, 363*f*
autonomic nervous system, 478
autosomes, 249
autotrophs, 197, 437
Avery, Oswald, 294
avian influenza H5N1, 504, 504*f*

Bacillus thuringiensis (Bt), 33, 33*f*, 351,
   354, 354*f*
bacteria, 434–435
   antibiotic resistance in, 332, 332*f*
   beneficial roles of, 351, 354
   cells in, 154, 154*f*, 162, 162*f*, 165
   classification of, 433, 434*f*, 435, 436*f*
   disease from, 502–503, 502*f*, 503*f*
   exponential population growth in, 104
   gene regulation by operons in, 326, 326*f*
   growth conditions for, 42–43
   nitrogen fixation by, 92, 92*f*
   origin of mitochondria and chloroplasts
      from, 456, 456*f*
   plasmids in, 331, 331*f*
Bacteria (domain), 434*f*, 435, 436*f*–437*f. See
   also* **bacteria**
bacterial meningitis, 502*f*
bacteriophages, 295*f*
barnacles, 114
base pairs
   base-pairing rules, 296*f*, 297–298, 298*f*,
      306
   complementary, 298, 298*f*
   in DNA replication, 300–301, 301*f*, 306

numbers of, 331
in RNA, 305, 305*f*
structure of, 290*f*–291*f*, 296, 296*f*
bases and acids, 56–57, 56*f*
battlefield medicine, 32, 32*f*
B cells, 292, 530, 530*f*, 531*f*, 538
"beads on a string," 224, 225*f*
HMS *Beagle*, 375–376, 375*f*, 376*f*
bees, 424
bee sting allergies, 535
bell curves, 400, 400*f*
benign tumors, 235
"bergy bits," 58
bias, in investigations, 12
bicarbonate ions, 57, 486
binary fission, 247
binomial nomenclature, 424
biochemistry, evolutionary theory and,
384, 384*f*. *See also* **acids and bases;**
atoms; water
biodiversity, 80, 115, 132, 132*f*
biogeography, 383, 383*f*
bioinformatics, 361
biological reactions, 66–67, 66*f*, 67*f*
biological species concept, 411
biological weapons, 37
biology, study of, 17–19, 18*f*
biomes, 82–83, 82*f*, 83*f*
biometric identification, 36, 36*f*, 37
biomimetics, 35
biomolecules, 59–63
bionics, 41, 41*f*
bioremediation, 349, 349*f*
bioterrorism, 37
biotic factors, 79, 106
bird flu, 504, 504*f*
birds, 459, 471, 471*f*
birth, human, 560, 560*f*
birth defects, 513, 558
blacklegged ticks, 503, 503*f*
blastocysts, 557, 557*f*
blending hypothesis, 272
blood. *See also* **white blood cells**
in the circulatory system, 482–483, 482*f*,
483*f*
clotting, 32, 485, 511
glucose levels in, 488, 488*f*, 537
high blood pressure, 511
pH of, 57, 486–487, 486*f*
plasma, 483, 530, 531*f*
red blood cells, 319, 509, 509*f*, 512, 512*f*,
528
types, 283, 283*f*, 528
blood-glucose level, 488, 488*f*, 537
blood pressure, 469, 473, 511
blotting processes, 358, 358*f*
blue-green algae, 455
body fat, 61, 61*f*, 208
body temperature
blood circulation and, 483
homeostasis in, 55, 180
hypothalamus and, 478*f*
in immune response, 526
skin and, 477
bone cancer, 496*f*–497*f*
bone marrow, adult stem cells from, 353,
353*f*

Borrelia burgdorferi, 503
Boston Harbor, 134, 134*f*
botulism, 502
bound ribosomes, 157, 158, 159*f*
Bowman's capsule, 481
brain, 478, 478*f*
brainstem, 478, 478*f*, 487
breathing
at high altitudes, 469*f*–469*f*
regulation of rate, 486–487, 486*f*
breeding, as artificial selection, 377, 377*f*
bronchioles, 482
brown paper test, 61
Bt corn, 33, 33*f*, 351, 354, 354*f*
bubonic plague, 499, 499*f*, 500
budding, 247, 247*f*, 505*f*
buffers, pH, 57
bulbourethral glands, 550*f*, 551
bulimia, 514
butterflies, 325*f*

caffeine, 187
calories, 514, 514*f*
Calvin cycle, 206–207, 206*f*
Cambrian explosion, 458
cancer. *See also names of specific cancers*
cell production in, 235, 235*f*
definition of, 235
microarray identification of, 358
from mutations, 322*f*, 323
treatment for, 235
Candida albicans, 506
capillaries, 482, 482*f*
capsules, in prokaryotes, 154
carbohydrates, 60, 60*f*, 160–161, 161*f*
carbon, 51, 51*f*, 52, 59–63, 452
carbon cycle, 91–92, 91*f*, 198, 199*f*
carbon dioxide
in aerobic respiration, 210, 210*f*
in the carbon cycle, 91, 91*f*
diffusion through cell membranes, 179
fixation of, 206–207, 206*f*
as greenhouse gas, 129, 129*f*
in human respiratory system, 482, 482*f*,
486–487, 486*f*
in photosynthesis, 206–207, 206*f*
carbonic acid, 486
Carboniferous period, 453*f*, 458
cardiovascular disease, 511, 511*f*
cardiovascular system, 482, 482*f*
caries, 502*f*
Carnivora (order), 425*f*
carnivores, 87, 89, 89*f*
carotenoids, 203, 203*f*
carrier proteins, 179, 179*f*
carrying capacity, 105, 105*f*, 182
Carson, Rachel, *Silent Spring,* 137
cassowary, 427*f*
cats, 425*f*
CAT scans, 35, 35*f*
Caucasians, cystic fibrosis in, 512
CDK protein, 334
cDNA (complementary DNA), 357
Cech, Thomas, 449

cell communication, 184–186, 185*f*, 186*f*
cell cycle, 228–229, 228*f*, 233, 233*f*
cell differentiation, 166, 333, 333*f*
cell digestion, 158
cell division. *See also* **cell reproduction**
cytokinesis in, 228*f*, 229, 232, 232*f*
meiosis, 250–254, 250*f*–251*f*
mitosis, 230–231, 230*f*–231*f*
cell membranes
active transport through, 182–183, 182*f*,
183*f*, 204*f*, 205
cell communication and, 184–186, 185*f*,
186*f*
homeostasis and, 175
lipid bilayer in, 61, 176, 176*f*
location of, 154, 154*f*
origin of, 448
osmosis through, 180–181, 180*f*, 181*f*
passive transport through, 178–179, 179*f*
in protein processing, 158, 159*f*
transport proteins in, 176–177, 177*f*, 179,
179*f*
cell plates, 232, 232*f*
cell recognition, 60, 177
cell reproduction, 223–226
checkpoints in, 234, 234*f*
chromosomes, 224–225, 225*f*
controls on, 233, 233*f*
cytokinesis, 228*f*, 229, 232, 232*f*
definition of, 223
eukaryotic cell cycle, 228–229, 228*f*
meiosis, 250–251, 250*f*–251*f*
mitosis, 228*f*, 229, 230–231, 230*f*–231*f*
preparation for, 226, 226*f*
cell respiration
aerobic, 210–211, 210*f*, 211*f*, 213*f*
anaerobic, 209, 211–212, 211*f*, 212*f*
in the carbon cycle, 198, 199*f*
efficiency of, 213, 213*f*
electron transport chain in, 211, 211*f*
by fermentation, 211–212, 211*f*, 212*f*
glycolysis in, 208–209, 209*f*, 213*f*
Krebs cycle in, 210–211, 210*f*, 213*f*
lab on, 215
cells. *See also* **cell structure; eukaryotic**
cells; prokaryotic cells
carbohydrates in, 60, 60*f*
carbon compounds in, 59
cell cycle, 228–229, 228*f*, 233, 233*f*, 334
as characteristic of life, 18
in colonial organisms, 165
discovery of, 151–152
endosymbiotic theory, 331
energy production in, 160–161, 161*f*
examples of, 152, 152*f*
germ, 248, 322, 403
levels of organization of, 164–165, 164*f*
lipids in, 61, 61*f*
cells
multicellularity, 165–166
nerve, 152, 152*f*
nucleic acids in, 63, 63*f*
number in the human body, 153
origin of first, 448–449, 449*f*
plant, 160, 160*f*, 163*f*, 232, 232*f*
protein processing in, 158, 159*f*
proteins in, 62, 62*f*

cells (*continued*)
  recognition of neighbors, 60, 177
  somatic, 322
  storage in, 158, 160, 160*f*
  surface area-to-volume ratio in, 152-153
cell size, 152-153, 223
cell structure, 148-166
  chloroplasts, 160, 160*f*
  cytoskeleton, 156, 156*f*
  endoplasmic reticulum, 158, 159*f*
  in eukaryotic cells, 155, 155*f*, 163*f*
  Golgi apparatus, 158, 159*f*
  lysosomes, 158
  mitochondria, 161, 161*f*
  modeling, 160
  nucleus structure, 157, 157*f*
  in prokaryotic cells, 154, 154*f*, 163*f*
  ribosome function, 157
  vacuoles, 160, 181
  vesicles, 158-160, 159*f*, 160*f*
cell-surface markers, 177, 177*f*
cell theory, 152
cell transport, 178-183
  active, 182-183, 182*f*, 183*f*
  by osmosis, 180-181, 180*f*, 181*f*
  passive, 178-179, 179*f*
  transport proteins, 177, 177*f*, 179, 179*f*
cellulose, 60, 437
cell walls
  during cell division, 226, 226*f*, 232, 232*f*
  cellulose in, 437
  chitin in, 60, 437
  in prokaryotes, 154, 154*f*
Cenozoic era, 453, 453*f*, 459, 459*f*
central nervous system (CNS), 478, 478*f*
central vacuoles, 160, 160*f*
centrioles, 230, 230*f*
centromeres, 225, 225*f*, 250*f*-251*f*, 251
centrosomes, 230, 230*f*
cerebellum, 478*f*
cerebrospinal fluid, 487
cerebrum, 478*f*
cervical cancer, 562
cervix, 553, 553*f*
CFCs (chlorofluorocarbons), 128, 136
Chagas' disease, 508*f*
chain termination sequencing, 359, 359*f*
channel proteins, 179-180, 179*f*
characters, 268
Chargaff, Erwin, 298, 299*f*
Chase, Martha, 294-295, 295*f*
cheetahs (*Acinomyx jubatus*), classification
  of, 424*f*, 425*f*
chemical bonds
  breaking and forming, 65
  carbon, 59
  covalent, 52, 52*f*
  hydrogen, 54, 55*f*, 269*f*, 296, 297
  ionic, 53, 53*f*
  peptide, 62, 62*f*, 308-309, 308*f*-309*f*
chemical digestion, 480
chemical energy, 60, 197
chemical reactions, 65-67, 65*f*, 66*f*, 67*f*
chemical signals, 184
chemotherapy, 235
chickens, genome of, 330*f*-331*f*
childbirth, 560, 560*f*

chitin, 60, 437
chlamydia, 561*f*, 563
chlorofluorocarbons (CFCs), 128, 136
chlorophyll, 203, 203*f*
chloroplasts
  DNA in, 331
  in endosymbiotic theory, 331, 456
  energy production in, 160, 160*f*, 161
  origin of, 455-456, 456*f*
  photosynthesis in, 202-203, 202*f*-203*f*
  structure of, 202, 202*f*-203*f*
cholera
  on copepods, 29-30, 29*f*, 30*f*
  symptoms and cause of, 500, 502*f*
  water pollution and, 127
cholesterol, 177*f*
Chordata (phylum), 425*f*
chorion, 558
chromatids
  in chromosome structure, 225, 225*f*
  in meiosis, 250*f*-251*f*, 251, 253
  in mitosis, 230-231, 230*f*-231*f*
chromatin, 224, 225*f*
chromosome number, 248-249, 249*f*
chromosomes
  30 nm fiber, 225, 225*f*
  aging and, 334
  autosomes, 249
  definition of, 224, 302
  eukaryotic, 224-225, 225*f*
  genes in, 224
  homologous, 249
  in meiosis, 250-254, 250*f*-251*f*, 252*f*, 254*f*
  in mitosis, 230-231, 230*f*-231*f*
  mobile genetic elements in, 332
  mutations in, 321, 321*f*
  nondisjunction, 324, 324*f*
  polyploidy in, 324, 324*f*
  prokaryotic, 224
  replication of, 302-303, 302*f*, 334, 334*f*
  sex chromosomes, 249
cigarettes
  emphysema from, 497
  lung cancer from, 235, 511, 511*f*
  during pregnancy, 558
circulatory system, 474*f*, 475, 482-483, 482*f*,
  483*f*
cladistics, 428*f*, 429, 429*f*, 431
cladograms, 429-430, 429*f*
classes, 425*f*, 426, 426*f*
classification, 420-439, 590-591
  characteristics used in, 434
  cladistics, 428*f*, 429, 429*f*
  dichotomous keys, 438-439, 438*f*
  discovering new species, 432, 432*f*
  evolutionary relatedness in, 430-431, 431*f*
  Linnaean system levels, 425-426, 425*f*,
    426*f*
  mnemonic device for, 426
  need for systems of, 423
  phylogenetics, 428, 428*f*
  scientific nomenclature, 424, 424*f*
  systematics, 427, 427*f*
  three-domain system, 434-437, 434*f*,
    436*f*-437*f*
  updating number of kingdoms in, 433,
    433*f*, 436*f*-437*f*

cleavage, 557, 557*f*
climate
  definition of, 82
  global warming, 128, 129, 129*f*
  impact on population size, 106, 106*f*
cloning, 352, 352*f*, 357, 360
Clostridium botulinum, 502
clotting, blood, 32, 485, 511
CNS (central nervous system), 478, 478*f*
coal, 126, 458
codominance, 283
codons, 307-309, 307*f*, 308*f*-309*f*, 321
coelacanths, 473
coevolution, 109, 388, 388*f*
cohesion, 55
coin toss predictions, 265, 278-279, 279*f*
colonial organisms, 165
colonial prokaryotes, 444*f*-445*f*, 456
colorblindness, 280
combustion, 91, 91*f*
commensalism, 111, 111*f*
common cold, 500
communities. *See also* **biomes; ecosys-
    tems; populations**
  commensalism in, 111, 111*f*
  competition for resources in, 113-114,
    113*f*, 114*f*
  definition of, 79, 79*f*
  herbivore-plant interactions in, 110, 110*f*
  mutualism in, 111, 111*f*
  niches in, 112-113, 112*f*
  parasitism in, 110
  predator-prey interactions in, 109-110
  stability of, 115, 115*f*
compensatory hypertrophy, 227
competition, 113-115, 113*f*, 114*f*
competitive exclusion, 114
complementary bases, 298, 298*f*
complementary DNA (cDNA), 357
compounds, 52
concentration gradients, 178
condensation, 90, 90*f*
conifers, 429*f*
conservation, environmental, 134
conservation of energy, 64
conservation of mass, 64
consumers, 9, 86, 86*f*, 88
contour plowing, 131
contractile vacuoles, 160, 181
control groups, 11
convergent evolution, 388, 428
copepods, 29-31, 29*f*
coral reefs, 84, 84*f*
corn
  genetically modified, 33, 33*f*, 351, 354,
    354*f*
  Indian, 332
corpus luteum, 555, 555*f*
covalent bonds, 52, 52*f*
crabs, 100*f*-101*f*
crayfish, 408*f*
Crick, Francis, 296, 298-299, 299*f*
Crohn's disease, 537*f*
crop rotation, 131
crossing over, 250*f*, 251, 253, 321, 324
cross-pollination, 267-268, 267*f*, 269*f*
cryptosporidiosis, 508*f*

Cryptosporidium sp., 508*f*
cubes, surface area-to-volume in, 153
Cuvier, Georges, 379
cyanobacteria, 455
cycles. *See also* **life cycles**
    Calvin, 206–207, 206*f*
    carbon, 91, 91*f*, 92, 198, 199*f*
    Krebs, 210–211, 210*f*, 213*f*
    nitrogen, 92, 92*f*
    oxygen, 91, 91*f*
    phosphorus, 93
    water, 77, 90, 90*f*
cyclin, 334
cystic fibrosis, 323*f*, 407*f*, 512
cytokinesis, 228*f*, 229, 232, 232*f*
cytoplasm, 154, 154*f*, 156, 232
cytosine, 296*f*, 297, 298
cytoskeleton, 156, 156*f*
cytosol, 154
cytotoxic T cells, 529*f*, 530, 531*f*

daily values (DVs), 514, 514*f*
Daphnia, 491–492, 491*f*
Darwin, Charles
    on breeding and artificial selection, 377, 377*f*
    influence of Cuvier, Hutton, and Lyell on, 379, 379*f*
    influence of Lamarck on, 378, 378*f*
    influence of Malthus on, 379
    influence of rate of geologic change on, 379, 379*f*
    on natural selection, 380–381, 381*f*
    publication of *Origin of Species*, 381
    strengths and weaknesses of ideas of, 385
    voyage of HMS *Beagle,* 375–376, 375*f*, 376*f*
dating methods, 451–452, 451*f*, 452*f*, 461–462
daughter cells, 232, 232*f*
daughter isotopes, 452
DDT restrictions, 130, 137
death, causes of, 510, 510*f*
decomposers, 86, 86*f*
deep sea vents, 448, 448*f*
deforestation, 132, 132*f*
Deinonychus, 427*f*
deletion mutations, 320–321, 321*f*
denaturation, 357
denitrification, 92, 92*f*
density-dependent factors, 105
dental caries, 502*f*
deoxyribonucleic acid (DNA). *See also* **genes**
    Avery's experiments, 294
    base pairing in, 297–298, 298*f*
    categories of, 331
    in cell cycle, 228*f*, 229
    Chargaff's observations, 298, 299*f*
    cloning, 357, 357*f*
    complementary, 357
    denaturation of, 357
    deoxyribose in, 63, 296, 296*f*, 305, 305*f*
    errors in replication of, 301, 324
    in eukaryotic cells, 155, 155*f*, 157, 157*f*

evolution and, 384, 384*f*, 430–431, 431*f*
extraction from wheat germ, 311
fingerprinting, 36, 347, 347*f*, 358, 364–365
forensic analysis of, 347, 347*f*
in forensic genealogy, 335, 335*f*
function of, 154, 223, 224, 293
Griffith's discovery of transformation, 294, 294*f*
Hershey-Chase experiments, 295, 295*f*
hybridization of, 357
kinds of mutations in, 320–321, 320*f*, 321*f*
mobile genetic elements in, 332
non-coding, 328, 331, 345
nucleotides in, 63, 63*f*
origin of, 449
packaging during cell division, 224–225, 225*f*
polymorphisms, 343, 356
in prokaryotic cells, 154, 154*f*
recombinant, 350, 359*f*, 360, 360*f*
repeating sequences in, 343
replication of, 223, 226, 228–229, 228*f*, 300–303, 300*f*, 301*f*, 302*f*, 307
RNA compared with, 305, 305*f*
sequencing of, 359
size of, 303
structure of, 63, 290*f*–291*f*, 296–297, 296*f*
transcription of, 304–305, 306–307, 306*f*
transcription factors and, 327, 327*f*
Watson and Crick's model, 299, 299*f*
X-ray diffraction of, 298–299, 299*f*
deoxyribose, 63, 296, 296*f*, 305, 305*f*
dependent variables, 11
derived characters, 429
dermis, 477, 477*f*
descent with modification, 375
Devonian period, 453*f*, 458*f*, 459
diabetes mellitus, 489, 489*f*, 537
diarrhea, 507
dichotomous keys, 438–439, 438*f*
diet, disease prevention and, 501
differentiation, 166, 333, 333*f*
diffusion, 178–179, 179*f*, 188–189
digestion, definition of, 480
digestive system
    in bacteria, 326, 326*f*
    in humans, 474*f*, 480, 480*f*
dihybrid crosses, 275, 275*f*
dinosaurs, 459, 460, 460*f*
diploid cell, 249
diploid life cycle, 256–257, 256*f*, 257*f*
diploid phases, 249, 256–257, 256*f*, 257*f*
directional selection, 409, 409*f*
disaccharides, 60
disease, 496–515. *See also names of specific diseases*
    avoiding, 501
    from bacteria, 502–503, 502*f*, 503*f*
    cause of, 499
    from fungi, 506, 506*f*
    inheritance and, 512
    nutrition and, 501, 514
    organ malfunction and, 513, 513*f*
    from parasitic worms, 507, 507*f*
    personal behavior and, 510–511
    from protists, 508–509, 508*f*, 509*f*
    from toxic substances, 515

transmission of, 500, 500*f*, 540–541
from viruses, 504–505, 504*f*, 505*f*
disjunction, 324, 324*f*
disruptive selection, 409, 409*f*
distributions, 400–401, 400*f*, 401*f*
DNA (deoxyribonucleic acid). *See also* **genes**
    Avery's experiments, 294
    base pairing in, 297–298, 298*f*
    categories of, 331
    in cell cycle, 228*f*, 229
    Chargaff's observations, 298, 299*f*
    cloning, 357, 357*f*
    complementary, 357
    denaturation of, 357
    deoxyribose in, 63, 293, 296, 296*f*, 305, 305*f*
    errors in replication of, 301, 324
    in eukaryotic cells, 155, 155*f*, 157, 157*f*
    evolution and, 384, 384*f*
    evolutionary relatedness and, 430–431, 431*f*
    extraction from wheat germ, 311
    fingerprinting, 36, 347, 347*f*, 358, 364–365
    forensic analysis of, 347, 347*f*
    in forensic genealogy, 335, 335*f*
    function of, 154, 223, 224, 293
    Griffith's discovery of transformation, 294, 294*f*
    Hershey-Chase experiments, 295, 295*f*
    HIV, 505*f*
    hybridization of, 357
    kinds of mutations in, 320–321, 320*f*, 321*f*
    mobile genetic elements in, 332
    non-coding, 328, 331, 345
    nucleotides in, 63, 63*f*, 296, 296*f*
    origin of, 449
    packaging during cell division, 224–225, 225*f*
    polymorphisms, 343, 356
    in prokaryotic cells, 154, 154*f*
    recombinant, 350, 359*f*, 360, 360*f*
    repeating sequences in, 343
    replication of, 223, 226, 228–229, 228*f*, 300–303, 300*f*, 301*f*, 302*f*, 307
    RNA compared with, 305, 305*f*
    sequencing of, 359
    size of, 303
    structure of, 63, 290*f*–291*f*, 296–297, 296*f*
    transcription of, 304–305, 306–307, 306*f*
    transcription factors and, 327, 327*f*
    Watson and Crick's model, 299, 299*f*
    X-ray diffraction of, 298–299, 299*f*
DNA barcodes, 358
DNA fingerprints, 36, 347, 347*f*, 358, 364–365
DNA helicases, 301, 301*f*
DNA ligase, 360, 360*f*
DNA polymerase, 301, 301*f*
DNA sequencing, 359, 359*f*, 363, 363*f*
dogs, 330*f*–331*f*, 377, 377*f*
domains
    as classification level, 425*f*, 426, 426*f*
    three-domain system, 434–437, 434*f*, 436*f*–437*f*
domains, protein, 329, 329*f*
dominant alleles, 273, 281, 282
double helix shape, 296, 296*f*
dove, white wing, 434*f*

Down syndrome, 324, 324*f*
Drosophila melanogaster
   evolution of, 410
   genome of, 330*f*–331*f*
   genome mapping, 362, 362*f*
   studies of mutations in, 271, 271*f*
drug use and abuse
   alcoholism, 510
   during pregnancy, 558
ducks, 61, 61*f*
duplication mutations, 321, 321*f*
DVs (daily values), 514, 514*f*

eating disorders, 514
E. coli (*Escherichia coli*)
   as ancient organism, 454*f*
   gene regulation by operons in, 326, 326*f*
   genome compared with that of *Salmo-
      nella,* 332
   structure of, 162*f*
ecosystems, 76–93
   abiotic factors in, 80, 82
   aquatic, 84, 84*f*
   biodiversity in, 80, 115
   carbon and oxygen cycles in, 91, 91*f*
   closed, 94–95
   coevolution in, 109, 388, 388*f*
   communities, 79, 79*f*
   definition of, 79
   disruption of, 132–133, 132*f*, 133*f*
   energy pyramid in, 88–89, 88*f*, 89*f*
   fires and, 85*f*
   nitrogen cycle in, 92, 92*f*
   phosphorus cycle in, 93
   population growth models in, 104–105,
      104*f*, 105*f*
   populations in, 103
   stability of, 115, 115*f*
   succession in, 81, 81*f*
   terrestrial biomes, 82–83, 82*f*, 83*f*
   trophic levels in, 86–87, 86*f*, 87*f*
   water cycle in, 90, 90*f*
ecotourism, 137, 137*f*
ectoderm, 559
eggs, human, 552–555, 552*f*, 553*f*, 554*f*
ejaculation, 551
electromagnetic radiation, 203, 203*f*
electron carriers, 63, 201*f*, 203, 210
electron clouds, 51, 51*f*, 52*f*
electrons, 51–52, 51*f*, 203
electron transport chain
   in aerobic respiration, 211, 211*f*
   in cellular respiration, 201, 201*f*
   in photosynthesis, 204–205, 204*f*
electrophoresis, 336–337, 356, 356*f*, 358*f*
elements, 51
elephantiasis, 507, 507*f*
embryology, 383
embryonic stem cells, 353
embryonic structures, 383
embryos, 557, 557*f*
emigration, 104
emphysema, 497, 511
endangered species, 39

endocrine glands, 479, 479*f*
endocrine system, 474*f*, 479, 479*f*. *See also*
   hormones
endocytosis, 183, 183*f*
endoderm, 559
endoplasmic reticulum (ER), 158, 159*f*
endosymbiosis, 456, 456*f*
endosymbiotic theory, 331
energy
   activation, 65–66, 65*f*, 66*f*
   from aerobic respiration, 210–211, 210*f*,
      211*f*, 213*f*
   from anaerobic respiration, 212–213, 212*f*,
      213*f*
   from carbohydrates, 60
   carriers, 63
   chemical, 60, 64–65, 197
   conservation of, 64
   flow of, in ecosystems, 86–89, 86*f*, 87*f*, 88*f*,
      89*f*
   from glycolysis, 208–209, 209*f*, 213*f*
   from lipids, 61
   from metabolism of food, 67
   from photosynthesis, 197, 202–205, 202*f*–
      203*f*, 204*f*
   production in cells, 160–161, 161*f*
   transferring, 63, 200–201, 200*f*, 201*f*
   usable, 64
energy pyramid, 88–89, 88*f*, 89*f*
enhancers, 327, 327*f*
environment, 122–139. *See also* **ecosystems**
   air pollution, 127, 128, 128*f*
   cars of the future, 139, 139*f*
   conservation and restoration of, 134, 134*f*
   ecosystem disruption, 132–133, 132*f*, 133*f*
   environmental awareness, 137, 137*f*
   gene regulation in prokaryotes and, 326
   genetically engineered bioremediation
      microbes, 349, 349*f*
   global warming, 128, 129, 129*f*
   health and, 127
   humans and, 125
   planning for the future, 138, 138*f*
   resources in, 126, 126*f*, 135
   soil damage, 131
   technological innovation, 39, 136, 136*f*
   water pollution, 130, 130*f*
environmental clubs, 40, 40*f*
enzymes. *See also names of specific enzymes*
   action of, 66, 67*f*
   in cell membranes, 177, 177*f*, 186
   in detergents, 68–69
   in lysosomes, 158, 160
   in protein processing, 158
   restriction, 355–356, 355*f*, 360, 360*f*
   RNA as, 449
   second messenger activation of, 186, 186*f*
   in transcription and translation, 329
epidemiology, 31
epidermis, 477, 477*f*
epididymis, 549*f*, 550, 550*f*
epinephrine, 490–491
equilibrium, 81, 178
ER (endoplasmic reticulum), 158
erosion, 131
Escherichia coli (*E. coli*)
   as ancient organism, 454*f*

   gene regulation by operons in, 326, 326*f*
   genome compared with that of *Salmo-
      nella,* 332
   structure of, 162*f*
esophagus, 480
EST (expressed sequence tag) library, 363
estrogen, 552, 555–556, 555*f*
estuaries, 84
ethanol cars, 139, 139*f*
ethical issues
   in biometric identification, 37
   in cloning, 37, 352
   in diagnosing genetic disorders, 354
   in experimentation, 8, 11
   in human genome research, 348
   safety of GMOs, 37, 354, 354*f*
   in stem cell research, 353
Ethical, Legal and Social Implications
   (ELSI), 348
Eubacteria (kingdom), 433, 434*f*, 435,
   436*f*–437*f*
Euglena, 472
Eukarya (domain), 434*f*, 436–437, 436*f*–437*f*
eukaryotes. *See also* **eukaryotic cells**
   characteristics of, 434*f*, 436
   major groups of, 434*f*, 436–437, 436*f*–437*f*
   structure of, 155, 155*f*
eukaryotic cells
   aging and, 333–334
   animal cell structure, 163*f*
   cell cycle in, 228–229, 228*f*
   chloroplasts in, 160, 160*f*, 455
   cytoskeleton in, 156, 156*f*
   diversity in, 163, 163*f*
   DNA replication in, 302–303, 302*f*
   gene regulation in, 327–329, 327*f*, 328*f*
   mitochondria in, 161, 161*f*, 455
   non-coding DNA in, 328, 331, 345
   nucleus in, 157, 157*f*
   plant cell structure, 163*f*
   preparation for cell division in, 226
   protein processing in, 158, 159*f*
   reproduction controls, 233–234, 233*f*, 234*f*
   ribosomes in, 157
   storage in, 158, 160, 160*f*
   structure of, 155, 155*f*, 163*f*
evaporation, 90, 90*f*
evolution. *See also* **evolutionary theory**
   analyzing relatedness in, 430–431, 431*f*
   of birds, 459
   as characteristic of life, 19
   coevolution, 109, 388, 388*f*
   convergent, 388, 428
   definition of, 375
   extinction and, 414
   gradualism in, 389, 389*f*
   of herbivores, 110, 110*f*
   macroevolution, 388–389, 389*f*
   microevolution, 388
   of mitochondria and chloroplasts, 456,
      456*f*
   natural selection and, 407–408, 408*f*
   in the Paleozoic era, 458–459, 458*f*
   of populations, not individuals, 380–381,
      381*f*, 386
   in Precambrian time, 454–457, 454*f*, 455*f*,
      456*f*

punctuated equilibrium in, 389, 389*f*
sexual selection and, 406, 406*f*
speciation and, 387, 387*f*
unpredictability of, 387
evolutionary theory, 373–389
anatomy and, 384, 384*f*
biochemistry and, 384
biogeography and, 383, 383*f*
breeding and artificial selection, 377, 377*f*
embryonic structures and, 383
fossil record and, 382–383, 382*f*
influence of Lamarck on, 378, 378*f*
influence of population growth patterns on, 379
modern synthesis of, 386
natural selection in, 380–381, 380*f*, 381*f*, 387, 390–391
population growth pattern in, 378, 378*f*, 379
publication of, 381
rate of geologic change and, 379, 379*f*
speciation, 387, 387*f*
strengths and weaknesses of Darwin's, 385
updates to, 386–387
voyage of HMS *Beagle* and, 375–376, 375*f*, 376*f*
excretion, definition of, 481
excretory system, 474*f*, 481, 481*f*
exercise, disease prevention and, 501
exocytosis, 183, 183*f*
exons, 328, 328*f*
experimental design, 578–579
experiments, 11
exponential growth, 104, 104*f*, 378, 378*f*, 379
expressed sequence tag (EST) library, 363
extinction, 133, 389, 414, 414*f. See also*
    mass extinction
extremophiles, 435
eye color, 400*f*

F₁ generation, 269
F₂ generation, 269
facilitated diffusion, 179–180, 179*f*
FADH₂, 210–211, 210*f*, 211*f*, 213
fallopian tubes, 552*f*, 553, 553*f*, 563
family, 425*f*, 426, 426*f*
FAS (fetal alcohol syndrome), 513, 558
fats, 61, 61*f*, 208
feathers, 429
feedback mechanisms, 234, 484–488
antagonistic hormones, 485
in blood-glucose level, 488, 488*f*
in breathing rate regulation, 486–487, 486*f*
in dynamic equilibrium, 484, 484*f*
negative vs. positive, 485, 485*f*
Felidae (family), 425*f*
female reproductive system, 552–556
cleavage and implantation in, 557, 557*f*
egg production in, 485, 552–553, 552*f*
menstrual cycle in, 556
ovarian cycle in, 554–555, 554*f*, 555*f*
structure of, 474*f*, 553, 553*f*
fermentation, 211–213, 211*f*, 213*f*

ferns, 429*f*
fertilization
gametes in, 248, 248*f*
genetic variation from, 253–254, 254*f*
in humans, 551, 557, 557*f*
fetal alcohol syndrome (FAS), 513, 558
fetus, 546*f*–547*f*, 559–560, 559*f*
fevers, 526
field guides, using, 435
filial (F) generation, 269, 269*f*
finches, Galápagos, 375, 375*f*, 410
fingerprints, DNA, 36, 347, 347*f*, 358, 364–365
fires, ecosystems and, 85*f*
first gap phase (G1), 228*f*, 229
fishes
jawless, 458
in the Paleozoic era, 458
water pressure and, 473
flagella (singular, *flagellum*)
in bacteria, 220*f*
in prokaryotes, 162, 162*f*
in sperm, 550, 550*f*
flukes, 507
flu viruses, 533
FoldNotes, 572–574
follicles, 555, 555*f*
follicle-stimulating hormone (FSH), 549, 554–555, 555*f*
follicular phase, 555, 555*f*
food allergies, 535
food chains, 87
food vacuoles, 160
food webs, 87, 87*f*, 94–95
forensic genealogy, 335, 335*f*
forensic science, DNA analysis in, 36, 347, 347*f*
forests, 83, 83*f*, 458*f*
fossil fuels
air pollution from, 128, 128*f*
carbon dioxide from, 91
as nonrenewable resource, 126, 126*f*
origin of, 458
fossil record, 379, 379*f*, 382–383, 382*f*, 450
fossils
definition of, 382, 382*f*
formation of, 450, 450*f*
index, 451
oldest known, 455, 456
types of, 451
fragmentation, 247
frameshift mutations, 320
frameshifts, 320
Franklin, Rosalind, 298–299, 299*f*
fraternal twins, 564, 564*f*
freshwater ecosystems, 84, 84*f*
frogs
in cold temperatures, 471
mutations in, 316*f*–317*f*
speciation in, 413, 413*f*
tadpoles, 334
fruit flies
evolution of, 410
genome of, 330*f*–331*f*
genome mapping, 362, 362*f*
hox genes in, 333*f*
studies of mutations in, 271, 271*f*

FSH (follicle-stimulating hormone), 549, 554–555, 555*f*
fuel cell cars, 139, 139*f*
fundamental niche, 113
fungi
characteristics of, 436
classification of, 434*f*, 436, 436*f*–437*f*
diseases from, 506, 506*f*
haploid life cycle in, 258, 258*f*
multicellular, 166*f*
in mycorrhizae, 458
in the Paleozoic era, 458
toxic, 515
Fungi (kingdom), 434*f*, 436*f*, 437

G1/G2 checkpoints, 234, 234*f*
Galápagos island finches, 375, 375*f*
gametes, 248, 248*f*, 272*f*, 273
gametophytes, 258, 258*f*
gases, 129, 129*f*, 482
gastropods, 451*f*
geckos, 227, 227*f*
gel electrophoresis, 336–337, 356, 356*f*, 358*f*
gels, 336
genealogy, 335, 335*f*
gene expression
codons in, 307, 307*f*
complexities of, 310
factors regulating, 325, 325*f*
gene technologies in, 351, 351*f*
overview of, 304–305, 304*f*
RNA types in, 305
RNA vs. DNA, 305, 305*f*
transcription, 304–305, 306–307, 306*f*
translation, 304–305, 304*f*, 308–309, 308*f*–309*f*
gene flow, 405
gene pool, 401
generations, 269
gene rearrangements, 321
gene regulation
cell differentiation and, 333, 333*f*
definition of, 325
gene regulation
in eukaryotes, 327–329, 327*f*, 328*f*
factors in, 325, 325*f*
in prokaryotes, 326, 326*f*
by regulatory proteins, 329
by transcription factors, 327, 327*f*
genes. *See also* **alleles**
associated, 362
definition of, 224, 293
DNA in, 293
in HIV reproduction, 505*f*
homeotic, 333, 333*f*
independent assortment of, 275, 275*f*, 284
jumping, 332
linked, 275, 284
multiple alleles, 283, 283*f*
mutation types in, 320–321, 320*f*
number in human genome, 345
processing RNA after transcription, 328, 328*f*
promoters, 306

genes (*continued*)
  sequencing, 345, 363, 363*f*
  sex-linked, 280
  in sexual reproduction, 248
gene technologies
  in bioremediation, 349, 349*f*
  blotting processes, 358, 358*f*
  cloning, 352, 352*f*
  data management in, 361, 363
  definition of, 350
  denaturation, 357
  in disease diagnosis and treatment, 346–347, 346*f*
  DNA polymorphisms, 356
  DNA sequencing, 359, 359*f*, 363, 363*f*
  ethical issues in, 37, 348, 350, 352–354, 354*f*
  future work in, 39, 348
  gene cloning and recombination, 360, 360*f*
  genetically modified organisms, 33, 350–351, 350*f*, 354
  genome mapping, 362, 362*f*
  genome sequence assembly, 363
  hybridization, 357
  manipulating cell interactions in, 351, 351*f*
  polymerase chain reaction, 357, 357*f*
  property laws and, 354
  restriction enzymes in, 355, 355*f*
  tissue culture in, 351, 351*f*
  using stem cells, 353, 353*f*
gene therapy, 347, 351
genetically modified organisms (GMOs), 33, 350–351, 350*f*, 354
genetic code, 63, 307, 307*f*, 330. *See also* **genomes**
genetic counseling, 346
genetic diseases and disorders
  albinism, 280–281, 280*f*, 281*f*
  cystic fibrosis, 323*f*, 407*f*, 512
  diagnosing and preventing, 346, 354
  Down syndrome, 324, 324*f*
  examples of, 323, 323*f*
  gene therapy, 347, 351
  natural selection and, 408
  pedigree analysis of, 280–281, 280*f*, 281*f*
  recessive, 323
  risk assessment of, 407
  sickle cell anemia, 319, 319*f*, 323*f*, 512, 512*f*
genetic drift, 388, 405, 406, 406*f*, 415
genetic engineering. *See also* **gene technologies**
  in bioremediation, 349, 349*f*
  of Bt corn, 33, 33*f*, 351, 354, 354*f*
  definition of, 346, 350
  ethical issues in, 37, 350, 354, 354*f*
  and GMOs, 350, 351
  of human proteins, 351, 360
  of vaccines, 346
genetic equilibrium, 404–405, 404*f*
genetic libraries, 363
genetic markers, 362, 362*f*
genetics. *See also* **heredity**
  Avery's experiments in, 294
  chromosome sorting errors, 324, 324*f*

  definition of, 31, 267
  Griffith's discovery of transformation, 294, 294*f*
  Hershey-Chase experiments in, 295, 295*f*
  phenotypic variation, 400, 400*f*
  role of genes in, 293
genetic switches, 325, 329, 334*f*
genetic variation
  allele frequency, 401–402, 401*f*, 402*f*
  gene pools, 401
  genetic equilibrium, 404–405, 404*f*
  meiosis and, 253–254, 254*f*
  natural selection and, 407–408, 408*f*
  phenotypic variation, 400, 400*f*
  population genetics, 399
  population size and, 406, 406*f*
  sources of, 403
genital herpes, 561*f*, 562, 562*f*
genital HPV, 561*f*, 562
genital warts, 562
genomes. *See also* **human genome**
  of cell organelles, 331
  data management of, 361, 363
  definition of, 31, 330
  mapping of, 362, 362*f*
  rearrangement of materials in, 332
  sequence assembly, 363
  sizes of, 331
  universal code of, 330, 330*f*–331*f*
genomic imprinting, 352
genomic libraries, 363
genomics, 345–348
  disease and, 346, 347
  future work in, 348
  individual identification through, 347
  pharmacogenomics, 347
genotypes, 274, 274*f*, 402, 402*f*, 408
genus (plural, *genera*), 424, 425*f*, 426, 426*f*
geographic information systems (GIS), 39
geologic time scale, 453, 453*f*
geology, influence on Darwin, 379, 379*f*
geometric growth, 378, 378*f*, 379
germ cells, 248, 322, 403
gestation, 557–560, 557*f*, 558*f*, 559*f*, 560*f*
Giardia, 508
giardiasis, 508
GIS (geographic information systems), 39
glaciers, 58, 81, 81*f*
global positioning system (GPS), 15
global warming, 128, 129, 129*f*
"glow" gene, 342*f*–343*f*, 350*f*, 351
glucagon, 488, 488*f*
glucose
  blood-level regulation, 488, 488*f*
  cell transport of, 182
  chemical structure of, 60, 60*f*
  energy from, 67
  glycolysis of, 208–209, 209*f*, 213*f*
glycogen, 60, 488, 488*f*
glycolysis, 208–209, 209*f*, 213*f*
glycoproteins, 177, 177*f*
GMOs (genetically modified organisms), 33, 350–351, 350*f*, 354
Golgi apparatus, 158, 159*f*
gonorrhea, 561*f*, 563
goose bumps, 477*f*
GPS (global positioning system), 15

gradualism, 389, 389*f*
grandchildren, as sign of evolutionary fitness, 407
graphing, 588–589
grasslands, 83, 83*f*
Grave's disease, 537*f*
greenhouse effect, 123, 129, 129*f*
Griffith, Frederick, 294, 294*f*
guanine, 296*f*, 297, 298
guard cells, 472, 472*f*

habitat, 112, 127, 132, 132*f*, 133*f*
Haldane, John B. S., 447
half-life, 452, 452*f*
handwashing, disease prevention and, 501
haploid cell, 249
haploid life cycle, 258, 258*f*
haploid phases, 249, 250*f*–251*f*, 251–252, 252*f*
Hardy, G. H., 404
Hardy-Weinberg principle, 404–405, 404*f*
healing, 223, 223*f*, 233, 233*f*
health
  assistive technologies, 32, 32*f*
  battlefield medicine, 32, 32*f*
  cholera research and, 29–30, 29*f*, 30*f*
  eradication of specific diseases, 31
  future challenges in, 29
  Human Genome Project and, 31, 345
heart attacks, 511, 511*f*
heart rate, epinephrine and, 490–491
height, factors in, 284
helicases, 301, 301*f*
Helicobacter pylori, 7, 502*f*
helper T cells
  HIV and, 539, 539*f*
  in immune response, 529–530, 529*f*, 530*f*, 531*f*
hemoglobin
  evolution and, 384, 384*f*
  in sickle cell anemia, 319, 512, 512*f*
hemophilia, 323*f*, 351
hepatitis B, 561*f*, 563
herbivores, 87, 89, 89*f*, 110
heredity, 267–284. *See also* **genetics**
  characters and traits in, 268, 268*f*
  codominance, 283
  definition of, 19
  dominant and recessive alleles, 273
  environmental conditions and, 284
  genotype and phenotype, 274, 274*f*
  homozygous vs. heterozygous, 274*f*, 275
  incomplete dominance, 282–283
  Lamarckian inheritance, 378, 378*f*
  Mendelian theory of, 272–275, 272*f*, 274*f*, 275*f*
  Mendel's pea plant experiments, 267–270, 267*f*, 268*f*, 269*f*
  multiple alleles, 283, 283*f*
  of mutations, 322
  origin of, 449
  pedigrees, 280–281, 281*f*
  phenotypic variation, 400, 400*f*
  polygenic, 282

probability in, 278–279, 278*f*, 279*f*
Punnett squares in, 276–277, 276*f*
random segregation of alleles, 273
herpes, 561*f*, 562, 562*f*
herpes simplex virus (HSV), 562
Hershey, Alfred, 294–295, 295*f*
Hershey-Chase experiments, 295, 295*f*
heterotrophs, 437
heterozygous crosses, 276*f*, 277
heterozygous individuals, 274*f*, 275
HGP (Human Genome Project), 31, 345
high blood pressure, 511
high-latitude biomes, 83
histamine, 526, 534
histograms, 401, 401*f*
histones, 224, 225*f*, 302
histoplasmosis, 506, 538
Histoplasmosis capsolatum, 506
history of life
dating methods in, 451–452, 451*f*, 452*f*
eukaryotic life, 455
first cells, 448–449, 449*f*
first organic molecules, 447, 447*f*
formation of oxygen, 455
fossil record and, 450, 450*f*
geologic time scale, 453, 453*f*
location of first life, 448, 448*f*
multicellular organisms, 455, 455*f*
origin of mitochondria and chloroplasts,
456, 456*f*
Paleozoic era, 453, 453*f*, 458–459, 458*f*
in Precambrian time, 454–457, 454*f*, 455*f*,
456*f*
prokaryotic life, 454–455, 454*f*
HIV (human immunodeficiency virus)
antigenic shifting in, 533
course of infection, 539*f*
prevalence of, 505, 561*f*
symptoms of, 561*f*, 563
T cell destruction by, 504
transmission of, 525, 539
viral reproduction, 505, 505*f*
homeobox genes, 333, 333*f*
homeostasis, 471–475. *See also* **disease**
altitude adjustments, 468*f*–469*f*
cell membranes and, 175
as characteristic of life, 19
definition of, 471
disease caused from disruption of, 499
energy for, 197
environmental changes and, 471, 471*f*
enzymes in, 66
feedback mechanisms in, 484–488, 484*f*,
485*f*, 486*f*, 488*f*
in human organ systems, 474–475, 474*f*
labs on, 475, 487, 516–517
main components of, 475
responses to change, 472–473, 472*f*
vesicles in, 158
homeotic genes, 333, 333*f*
homologous chromosomes, 249, 250*f*–251*f*,
251, 253
homologous structures, 383, 384, 384*f*
Homo sapiens, 425*f*, 426*f*
homozygous crosses, 276*f*, 277
homozygous individuals, 274*f*, 275
Hooke, Robert, 151

hookworm infection, 507, 507*f*
hormones. *See also names of specific hormones*
antagonistic, 485
diffusion through the cell membrane, 179
from endocrine system, 479, 479*f*
heart rate and, 490–491
pituitary, 479*f*, 549, 554
as signal molecules, 184
target cells, 184
hosts
in gene recombination, 360, 360*f*
in parasitism, 110
household chemicals, 515, 515*f*
hox **sequence,** 333, 333*f*
HPV (human papilloma virus), 561*f*, 562
H. pylori, 7, 502*f*
HSV (herpes simplex virus), 562
human body
chromosome number in, 248, 249*f*
circulatory system, 474*f*, 482–483, 482*f*,
483*f*
composition of, 473, 473*f*
digestive system, 474*f*, 480, 480*f*
endocrine system, 474*f*, 479, 479*f*
female reproductive system, 552–556,
552*f*, 553*f*, 554*f*, 555*f*
immune system, 474*f*
integumentary system, 474*f*, 477, 477*f*
male reproductive system, 549–551, 549*f*,
550*f*, 551*f*
muscular system, 474*f*, 476, 476*f*
nervous system, 474*f*, 478, 478*f*
during pregnancy, 557–560, 557*f*, 558*f*,
559*f*, 560*f*
respiratory system, 474*f*, 482, 482*f*
skeletal system, 474*f*, 476
systems overview, 474*f*
urinary system, 474*f*, 481, 481*f*
water balance in, 473, 473*f*
human genome
ethical issues in research, 348
future work in, 348
Human Genome Project, 31, 345
mapping of, 362, 362*f*
non-coding genes in, 345
number of genes in, 345
similarity to other genomes, 330, 330*f*–
331*f*, 345
Human Genome Project (HGP), 31, 345
human immunodeficiency virus (HIV)
antigenic shifting in, 533
course of infection, 539*f*
prevalence of, 561*f*
symptoms of, 561*f*, 563
T cell destruction by, 504
transmission of, 525, 539
viral reproduction, 505, 505*f*
human papilloma virus (HPV), 561*f*, 562
human population growth, 107–108, 107*f*,
108*f*, 125
humans, classification of, 425*f*, 426*f*. *See
also* **human body**
Huntington disease, 323*f*
Hutton, James, 379
hybrid cars, 136, 139, 139*f*
hybridization, 268, 357, 413
hydras, 247*f*

hydrochloric acid, 56
hydrogen bonds, 54–55, 54*f*, 296, 296*f*, 297
hydrogen ion pumps, 201, 201*f*, 204*f*, 205,
211
hydrogen ions. *See also* **pH**
in acids and bases, 56–57, 56*f*
in aerobic respiration, 210–211, 210*f*, 211*f*
in ATP energy transfer, 200–201, 200*f*, 201*f*
hydrothermal vents, 448, 448*f*
hypertonic solutions, 180, 180*f*
hypothalamus, 478*f*, 479*f*
hypotheses (singular, *hypothesis*), 6, 10
hypotonic solutions, 180–181, 180*f*, 181*f*

icebergs, 58, 58*f*
identical twins, 564, 564*f*
immigration, 104
immune deficiency, 538–539, 538*f*, 539*f*
immune system, 525–539
activation of, 529
allergies and, 534–536, 534*f*, 535*f*, 536*f*
autoimmune diseases, 537, 537*f*
destroying infected cells, 530, 531*f*
immune deficiency, 538–539, 538*f*, 539*f*
long-term protection by, 532–533
non-specific responses, 526–527, 526*f*,
527*f*
physical barriers in, 525
removing pathogens, 530, 531*f*
skin in, 477, 525
specific responses, 527–528, 527*f*
immunity, 532
immunosuppression, 538
impacts, asteroid, 448, 460, 460*f*
implantation, 557, 557*f*
inbreeding, 406
incomplete dominance, 282–283
independent assortment, 254, 254*f*, 275,
275*f*, 284
independent variables, 11
index fossils, 451
Indian corn, 332
infectious diseases, 502–509
from bacteria, 502–503, 502*f*, 503*f*
definition of, 499
from fungi, 506, 506*f*
from parasitic worms, 507, 507*f*
from protists, 508–509, 508*f*, 509*f*
spread of, 127, 540–541
from viruses, 504–505, 504*f*, 505*f*
inferences, scientific, 373, 382
infertility, from STIs, 563
inflammation, 526, 526*f*, 527*f*, 535
influenza viruses, 504, 504*f*, 533
insects, 458
insect sting allergies, 535
insertion mutations, 320
insight, 377
insulin
in blood-glucose regulation, 488, 488*f*
diabetes and, 489, 489*f*, 537
produced by genetically engineered organisms, 34, 347, 360, 360*f*

integumentary system, 474f, 477, 477f. See also skin
intellectual property (IP), 354
interdependence, 19
intermediate fibers, 156
intermediate forms, 382f, 383
International System of Units (SI), 14, 14f, 20–21
interphase, 228–229, 228f
intestines, 480, 480f
introns, 328, 328f, 331
invasive species, 133, 133f
inversion mutations, 321, 321f
involuntary muscle, 476
ionic bonds, 53, 53f
ions, 56, 56f
iris scans, 36, 36f
isotonic solutions, 180, 180f
isotopes, 51, 452, 452f

jawless fishes, 458
jumping genes, 332
Jurassic period, 453f

kangaroos, 106
Katrina, Hurricane, 335
kelp, 115
keratin, 310, 477
keystone species, 115, 115f
kidneys, 481, 481f
kingdoms, 425f, 426, 426f, 433, 434f
kleptoparasitism, 113
Krebs cycle, 210–211, 210f, 213f
Krebs, Hans, 210
K-T extinction, 459, 460, 460f

labia, 553, 553f
labor, 560
lab safety, 16
lac operon, 326, 326f
lactic acid, 212, 212f
lactose, 60, 60f, 326, 326f
ladders, in electrophoresis, 356
Lamarckian inheritance, 378, 378f
Lamarck, Jean Baptiste, 378
land plants, evolution of, 429f
large intestine, 480
latitude, ecosystems and, 82–83
law of conservation of energy, 64
law of conservation of mass, 64
law of independent assortment, 275, 275f, 284
law of segregation, 273, 279
law of superposition, 451, 451f
laws of heredity, 386
laws, scientific, 8

lead, 515
Leeuwenhoek, Anton van, 151
leopards (Panthera pardus), classification of, 424f, 425f
LH (luteinizing hormone), 549, 554–555, 555f
life, characteristics of, 18–19, 149
life cycles
    definition of, 256
    diploid, 256–257, 256f, 257f
    haploid, 258, 258f
light energy, 202–205, 203f, 204f, 207
lineages, 389
linear growth, 378, 378f, 379
linkage mapping, 362, 362f
linked genes, 275, 284
Linnaean system, 426
Linnaeus, Carl, 424–425, 425f
lions (Panthera leo), 424f
lipid bilayer, 176, 176f, 177f
lipids, 61, 448. See also fats
liver, 480, 509, 509f, 515, 563
lizards, 101f, 227, 227f
lobster eye telescope, 35
lock-and-key enzyme action, 66, 67f
logistic growth, 105, 105f
looped domains, 225, 225f
lung cancer, 235, 511, 511f
lungs, 482, 482f
lupus, 537f
luteal phase, 555, 555f
luteinizing hormone (LH), 549, 554–555, 555f
Lyell, Charles, 379
Lyme disease, 503, 503f
lymph, 483, 483f
lymphatic system, 483, 483f
lymph nodes, 483
lysosomes, 158, 160

macroevolution, 388–389, 389f
macrophages, 522f–523f, 526–527, 527f
malaria, 509, 509f
male reproductive system, 474f, 549–551, 549f, 550f, 551f
malignant tumors, 235
Malthus, Thomas, 379
Mantophasmatodea, 432f
mapping, genome, 362, 362f
marine ecosystems, 84, 84f
mass
    conservation of, 64
    determining, 584
mass extinction
    definition of, 453
    during the Devonian period, 459
    at the end of the Ordovician period, 459
    at the end of the Permian period, 457
    geologic time scale and, 453, 453f
    K-T extinction, 459, 460, 460f
    in the Paleozoic era, 459
    in Precambrian times, 457
mate selection, 388, 406, 406f
matter, 51–54, 51f, 52f, 53f, 54f, 64

measurement systems, 14, 14f, 20–21
mechanical digestion, 480
meiosis, 250–254
    alleles in, 272f, 273
    diploid life cycle, 256–257, 256f, 257f
    genetic variation in, 253–254, 254f
    haploid life cycle, 258, 258f
    in humans, 552
    independent assortment in, 254, 254f
    mitosis compared with, 252, 252f
    mutations during, 321
    stages of, 250–251, 250f–251f
melanin, 477
melanomas, 322, 322f
membrane pumps, 182, 182f, 204f, 205
memory cells, 532
Mendel, Gregor Johann
    first pea plant experiments, 267–270, 267f, 268f, 269f
    heredity theory of, 272–275, 272f, 274f, 275f
    laws of heredity, 386
    life of, 267
    ratios in results of, 270
    second pea plant experiments, 275, 275f
menopause, 556
menstrual cycle, 555f, 556
menstruation, 555f, 556
meristems, 236
merozoites, 509, 509f
mesoderm, 559
Mesozoic era, 453, 453f, 459
messenger RNA (mRNA), 305–307, 306f, 307f
metabolism
    as characteristic of life, 19
    chemical reactions in, 67
    photosynthesis and respiration, 198, 199f
metaphase
    in meiosis, 250f–251f, 251
    in mitosis, 230f, 231, 234, 234f
metastasis, 235
methanogens, 435
metric system, 14, 14f, 20–21
mice (Mus musculus), hox genes in, 333f
microarrays, 346, 346f, 358
microevolution, 388, 399
microfilaments, 156
microscopes, 15, 151, 582–583
microspheres, 449
microtubules, 156, 229, 230, 230f
migration, 388, 405
Miller, Stanley, 447
Miller-Urey experiment, 447, 447f
mineralized fossils, 451, 451f. See also fossils
missense mutations, 320
mites, 535f
mitochondria
    ATP energy reactions in, 201, 201f
    DNA in, 331, 335
    in endosymbiotic theory, 331
    origin of, 455–456, 456f
    in sperm, 550, 550f
    structure of, 161, 161f
mitosis
    checkpoint, 234, 234f

in eukaryotic cell cycles, 228*f*, 229
  meiosis compared with, 252, 252*f*
  stages of, 230–231, 230*f*–231*f*, 236
mobile genetic elements, 332
modern synthesis of evolutionary theory,
  386. *See also* **evolutionary theory**
molds, 515, 535*f*
"molecular clocks," 431, 431*f*
molecular evidence, 430–431
molecules, 52
Molina, Mario, 136
monarch butterflies, 354, 354*f*
monohybrid crosses, 269, 276*f*, 277
monosaccharides, 60
morphological evidence, 430
mosses, 429*f*
motor nerves, 478
mouse-ear cress, genome of, 330*f*–331*f*
mouthwash poisoning, 515, 515*f*
mRNA (messenger RNA), 305–307, 306*f*,
  307*f*
mucous membranes, 525
mucus, 525
multicellular organisms
  aging and, 333–334, 333*f*, 334*f*
  eukaryotes as, 436
  interdependence of cells in, 165–166, 166*f*
  levels of organization in, 164–165, 164*f*
  responses to change, 472, 472*f*
  stromatolites, 455, 455*f*
multiple alleles, 283, 283*f*
multiple sclerosis (MS), 537
multipotent cells, 353
muscle cells, 163
muscles, contraction of, 476, 476*f*
muscular system, 474*f*, 475, 476, 476*f*
mushrooms, toxic, 515
Mus musculus (house mouse), *hox* genes
  in, 333*f*
mussels, 114, 115
mutants, 319. *See also* **mutations**
mutations, 319–324
  cancer from, 322*f*, 323
  chromosomal, 321
  effects of, 319–321, 320*f*
  in frogs, 316*f*–317*f*
  in fruit flies, 271, 271*f*
  genetic disorders from, 323, 323*f*
  genetic variation from, 403, 405
  inheritance of, 322
  microevolution and, 388
  modeling, 321
  as "molecular clock," 431, 431*f*
  nonsense, 321
  single nucleotide polymorphisms, 356
  types of, 320–321, 320*f*, 321*f*
mutualism, 100*f*–101*f*, 111, 111*f*
Mycobacterium tuberculosis, 503
mycorrhizae, 458

NAD⁺ (nicotinamide adenine dinucleo-
  tide), 201, 201*f*
NADH, 210–213, 210*f*, 211*f*, 212*f*
NADPH, 204*f*, 205–206, 205*f*

nanotechnology, 34, 34*f*
natural gas, 126
natural killer cells, 526, 527*f*
natural selection. *See also* **evolutionary**
    theory
  chance variations and, 387
  genetic change from, 405
  limitations of, 408
  modeling exercise, 387, 390–391
  patterns of, 409, 409*f*
  role in evolution, 407
  steps in, 380–381, 380*f*, 381*f*
negative feedback, 485, 485*f*
nematodes, genome of, 330*f*–331*f*
nephrons, 481
nerve cells, 152, 152*f*, 228
nervous system, 474*f*, 475, 478, 478*f*
neutrons, 51
neutrophils, 526, 527*f*
Neversink Pit (Alabama), 122*f*–123*f*
New Guinea, "lost world" in, 38, 38*f*
niches, 112–113, 112*f*, 413
nicotinamide adenine dinucleotide
    (NAD+), 201, 201*f*
nitric acid, 128
nitrification, 92, 92*f*
nitrogen, 92, 92*f*
nitrogen cycle, 92, 92*f*
nitrogen fixation, 92, 92*f*
nitrogenous bases
  base-pairing rules, 296*f*, 297–298, 298*f*, 306
  complementary, 298, 298*f*
  in DNA replication, 300–301, 301*f*, 306
  numbers of, 331
  in RNA, 305, 305*f*
  structure of, 290*f*–291*f*, 296, 296*f*
non-coding sequences, 328, 331, 345
nondisjunction, 324
noninfectious diseases, 510–515
  definition of, 499
  inheritance and, 512
  nutrition and, 501, 514
  organ malfunction, 513, 513*f*
  personal behavior and, 510–511
  toxic substances and, 515, 515*f*
nonrandom mating, 406
nonrenewable resources, 126, 126*f*
nonsense mutations, 321
normal distribution, 400, 400*f*
northern blot process, 358
nuclear envelope, 157, 157*f*
nuclear pores, 157, 157*f*
nuclear waste dumps, 349, 349*f*
nucleic acids, 63, 294. *See also* **DNA; RNA**
nucleolus, 157, 157*f*
nucleosomes, 224–225, 225*f*
nucleotides, 63, 63*f*, 296, 296*f*
nucleus, atomic, 51, 51*f*
nucleus, cell, 155, 155*f*, 157, 157*f*
nutrition, disease prevention and, 501, 514
Nutrition Facts label, 514, 514*f*

obesity, 514
observations, 10

oil, 61, 126, 458
oil spills, 349, 349*f*
omnivores, 87
On the Origin of Species (Darwin), 381
Oparin, Aleksandr I., 447
operator sites, 326, 326*f*
operons, 326, 326*f*
opportunistic infections, 538
orders, 425*f*, 426, 426*f*
Ordovician period, 453*f*, 459
organelles, 155, 155*f*, 331
organic compounds, 59–63, 447, 447*f*
organ malfunction, 513, 513*f*
organs, 164, 164*f*. *See also under specific*
    organs
organ systems, 164*f*, 165. *See also under*
    specific systems
organ transplants, 538
osmosis, 180–181, 180*f*, 181*f*
osteoporosis, 513, 513*f*
outgroups, 429
ovarian cycle, 554–555, 554*f*, 555*f*
ovaries
  in endocrine system, 479*f*
  in reproductive system, 552, 552*f*, 553*f*,
    554–555, 554*f*
overeating, 514
overproduction, 380, 381*f*
ovulation, 554–555, 554*f*, 555*f*
ovum (plural, *ova*), 256, 553, 554, 554*f*
oxygen
  in aerobic respiration, 211, 211*f*
  in carbon and oxygen cycles, 91, 91*f*
  combustion and, 91
  from cyanobacteria, 455
oxygen
  diffusion through the cell membrane, 179,
    179*f*
  formation of atmospheric, 455
  in human respiratory system, 482, 482*f*,
    487
  mass extinction from rise of, 457
  oxygen cycle, 91
ozone layer, 128, 136, 447, 455

Paine, Charles, 10
paint brush, Texas, 434*f*
Paleozoic era, 453, 453*f*, 458–459, 458*f*
pancreas, 479*f*, 480, 488, 488*f*, 489
Panthera pardus (leopard), 424*f*, 425*f*
Panthera spp. (leopards and lions), clas-
    sification of, 424*f*, 425*f*
paramecium, 425*f*, 434*f*
parasites
  diseases from parasitic worms, 507, 507*f*
  trichomoniasis from, 562
parasitism, 110, 113
parathyroid glands, 479*f*
parental (P) generation, 269, 269*f*
parent isotopes, 452
parsimony, principle of, 431
parthenogenesis, 247, 255, 255*f*
passive transport, 178–180, 179*f*
patents, 354

pathogens
  antigen shifting in, 533
  bacteria as, 29, 502–503, 502f, 503f
  definition of, 499, 525
  fungi as, 506, 506f
  immune response to, 529–530, 531f
  immunity to, 532
  spread of, 500, 500f, 540–541
  viruses as, 504–505, 504f, 505f
PCR (polymerase chain reaction), 357, 357f
pea plants, 267–270, 267f, 268f, 269f
pedigrees, 280–281, 281f
pelvic inflammatory disease (PID), 563
penguins, 106
penis, 550f, 551
peptide bonds, 62, 62f, 308–309, 308f–309f
percentage calculations, 237
percolation, 90, 90f
periodic table of the elements, 592–593f
peripheral nervous system (PNS), 478
permeability, 176, 176f, 186
Permian extinction, 459
pet breeding, 377, 377f
P generation, 269
pH
  of blood, 57, 486–487, 486f
  buffers, 57
  of cerebrospinal fluid, 487
  enzymes and, 66, 68–69
  pH scale, 56f, 57
phages, 295f
pharmaceuticals, 133
pharmacogenomics, 347
phenotypes, 274, 274f, 400, 400f, 408
phosphates
  in ATP energy transfer, 182, 182f, 200–201
  in DNA, 290f–291f, 296, 296f
  in phosphorus cycle, 93
phospholipids, 61, 176, 176f
phosphorus cycle, 93. See also **phosphates**
photosynthesis, 197, 202–207
  in carbon and oxygen cycles, 91, 91f
  chemical equation for, 199f
  electron transport chains in, 204–205, 204f
  factors affecting, 202
  light energy and, 202–203, 202f–203f
  origin of atmospheric oxygen from, 455
  respiration and, 198, 199f
  sugar production in, 206–207, 206f
  water loss and gas exchange in, 472, 472f
phyla (singular, *phylum*), 425f, 426, 426f
phylogenetics, 411, 428, 428f
phylogenetic species concept, 411
phylogenetic trees, 422, 428–429, 428f, 429f
phylogeny, 428, 428f
physical mapping, 362, 362f
phytoplankton, 88f
PID (pelvic inflammatory disease), 563
pigments, 202f–203f, 203
pili, 162, 162f
pimples, 503, 503f
pine grosbeak, 471
pioneer species, 81, 81f
pituitary gland, 479f, 549, 554
placenta, 558, 558f, 560f
plague, 499, 499f, 500
plankton, 460

Plantae (kingdom), 434f, 436f, 437
plant cells, 160, 160f, 163f, 232, 232f
plants
  albinism in, 285
  alternation of generations, 258
  cells in, 160, 160f, 163f, 232, 232f
  cladogram of, 429f
  homeostasis in, 472–473, 472f
  microscope exercise on, 167
  as multicellular organisms, 166
  in the Paleozoic era, 458, 458f
  signaling in, 184
  viruses, 516–517
  wilting of, 181f, 473
plaque, 511, 511f
plasma, blood, 483, 530, 531f
plasmids, 331–332, 331f, 360, 360f
Plasmodium, 509, 509f
pluripotent cells, 353
PNS (peripheral nervous system), 478, 478f
point mutations, 320
poisoning, 515, 515f
polar biomes, 82–83, 82f, 83f
polar body, 257, 257f
polarity, 54, 54f, 176, 176f
polio, 533
pollen, 245, 534f
pollution
  air, 127, 128, 128f
  health effects of, 127
  ozone layer damage from, 128, 136
  water, 127, 130, 130f
polygenic characters, 282, 400, 400f
polymerase chain reaction (PCR), 357, 357f
polymerases
  DNA, 301, 301f
  RNA, 306, 306f, 327f, 329
polymorphisms, 356
polynomials, in classification, 424
polypeptides, from RNA translation, 308–309, 308f–309f
polyploidy, 324, 324f, 413
polysaccharides, 60
population genetics
  definition of, 399
  divergence in, 412
  forces of genetic change, 405
  genetic drift, 388, 405–406, 415
  genetic equilibrium, 404–405, 404f
  genetic variation and change, 401–402, 402f
  phenotypic variation, 400–401, 400f, 401f
  population size and, 406, 406f
  role of natural selection in, 407–409, 408f, 409f
  sources of genetic variation, 403
population growth
  evolution and, 378, 378f, 379
  exponential, 104, 104f, 378, 378f, 379
  of humans, 125
  logistic, 105, 105f
populations, 103–108. See also **population growth**
  definition of, 103
  factors in size of, 106, 106f
  genetic drift in, 388, 405, 415
  human, 107–108, 107f, 108f, 125, 125f

  lab on, 116–117
  microevolution in, 388
  migration and, 104
  natural selection in, 380–381, 381f, 387, 390–391
  separation of, 376, 387, 387f
positive feedback, 485, 485f
Precambrian time, 453–457, 453f, 454f, 456f, 457f
precipitation, 90, 90f
predation, definition of, 109
predators
  in communities, 79, 79f, 109
  ecosystem stability and, 115
  impact on population sizes, 106
prefixes, in units, 14, 14f
pregnancy
  cleavage and implantation in, 557, 557f
  first trimester, 558–559, 558f, 559f
  preparation for, 554–555, 554f, 555f
  second trimester, 560
  third trimester, 560, 560f
prey, 79, 79f, 109
primary structure of proteins, 62, 329, 329f
Primates (order), 426f
primers, 357
probability, 278–279, 278f, 279f
probes, 357
producers, 86, 86f, 88–89, 89f
products, reaction, 64–65
progesterone, 552, 555–556, 555f
prokaryotes, 154, 433, 456. See also **prokaryotic cells**
prokaryotic cells
  DNA replication in, 302, 302f
  gene regulation in, 326, 326f
  origin of mitochondria and chloroplasts from, 456, 456f
  plasmids in, 331, 331f
  in Precambrian time, 454–455
  preparation for cell division in, 226, 226f
  structure of, 154, 154f, 162, 162f
promoters, 306, 306f, 326–327, 326f, 327f
prophase, 230, 231f, 250f–251f, 251
prostate gland, 550f, 551
proteases, 68
protein activation, 527
protein fibers, in cells, 156, 156f, 230
proteins
  active domains on, 329, 329f
  amino acids in, 62, 62f
  carrier, 179, 179f
  in the cell cycle, 334
  cell maintenance by, 223
  in cell membranes, 176–177, 177f
  in cell transport, 179, 179f
  constructed from RNA translation, 304–305, 304f, 308–309, 308f–309f
  Cro, 329f
  in the cytoskeleton, 156, 156f
  detection of, 317, 336–337
  DNA helicases, 301, 301f
  domains on, 329, 329f
  in the endoplasmic reticulum, 158, 159f
  folding and structure of, 329, 329f
  in gene expression, 329, 329f
  genes, 293

histones, 302
in immune response, 527
in mutations, 320–321, 320*f*, 321*f*
origin of first, 448–449, 449*f*
production in cells, 157, 158, 159*f*
regulatory, 329
roles in cells, 156, 158, 176, 179, 223, 329, 334, 527
separation by electrophoresis, 336–337
size of, 329
sorting, after translation, 328–329
structure of, 62, 329, 329*f*
in vesicles, 158, 159*f*
protein sorting, 328–329
protein test strips, 317
proteomics, 351
Protista (kingdom), 434*f*, 436, 436*f*
protists
alternation of generations, 258
characteristics of, 434, 437
classification of, 433, 434*f*, 436, 436*f*, 437*f*
contractile vacuoles in, 160
diseases from, 508–509, 508*f*, 509*f*
multicellular, 166, 166*f*, 456–457
protons, 51
psoriasis, 537*f*
pumps, membrane, 182, 182*f*, 204*f*
punctuated equilibrium, 389, 389*f*
Punnett squares, 276–277, 276*f*
purines, 296*f*, 297
pyridines, 296*f*, 297
pyruvate, 209, 209*f*, 210, 210*f*

qualitative experiments, 11
quantitative experiments, 11
Quaternary period, 453, 453*f*
quaternary structure of proteins, 62

rabbits, in Australia, 103
radiation pattern of divergence, 410, 413
radioactive decay, 452, 452*f*
radioactive waste, 349, 349*f*
radioisotopes, 452, 452*f*
radiometric dating, 452, 452*f*
rain forests, 83, 83*f*
Rana **spp.** (frogs), evolution in, 413
randomness, 254, 273
Raptor Rehabilitation Center (Kentucky), 40, 40*f*
RBCs (red blood cells)
blood typing and, 528
malaria in, 509, 509*f*
in sickle cell disease, 319, 319*f*, 323*f*, 512, 512*f*
reactants, 64–65
reading frames, 320–321
realized niche, 113, 113*f*
receptor proteins, 177, 177*f*, 185–186, 185*f*, 186*f*
recessive alleles, 273, 281

recombinant DNA, 350, 350*f*, 360, 360*f*
recombination, 324
recycling resources, 108, 108*f*, 135
red blood cells (RBCs)
blood typing and, 528
malaria in, 509, 509*f*
in sickle cell disease, 319, 319*f*, 323*f*, 512, 512*f*
regeneration, 227, 227*f*
regulatory proteins, 329
relative dating, 451, 451*f*, 461–462
remote data collection, 15
renewable resources, 126, 126*f*
replication bubbles, 302*f*, 303
replication forks, 300–302, 300*f*, 301*f*, 302*f*
replication of DNA, 300–303, 300*f*, 301*f*, 302*f*, 307
repressors, 327, 327*f*
reproduction, 244–258. *See also* **asexual reproduction; reproduction, human; sexual reproduction**
as characteristic of life, 19
haploid life cycle, 258, 258*f*
mate selection, 388, 406, 406*f*
nonrandom mating, 405–406
reproduction, human, 549–560
birth, 560, 560*f*
cleavage and implantation in, 557, 557*f*
female reproductive system, 552–556, 552*f*, 553*f*, 554*f*, 555*f*
fertilization, 551, 557, 557*f*
first trimester, 558–559, 558*f*, 559*f*
male reproductive system, 549–551, 549*f*, 550*f*, 551*f*
second trimester, 560
third trimester, 560, 560*f*
reproductive isolation, 412–413, 412*f*, 413*f*
reptiles, 459
resources
competition for, 113–114, 113*f*, 114*f*
recycling, 108, 108*f*, 135
use of, 126, 126*f*, 135
respiration. *See also* **cell respiration**
aerobic, 210–211, 210*f*, 211*f*, 213*f*
anaerobic, 209, 211–212, 211*f*, 212*f*
in carbon and oxygen cycles, 91, 91*f*
respiratory system, 474*f*, 475, 482, 482*f*
restoration, environmental, 134, 134*f*
restriction enzymes, 355–356, 355*f*, 360, 360*f*
restriction fragment length polymorphisms (RFLPs), 356
restriction sites, 355–356
retroviruses, 332
reuse of resources, 135
RFLPs (restriction fragment length polymorphisms), 356
rheumatoid arthritis, 537*f*
ribonucleic acid (RNA)
codons in, 307, 307*f*
DNA compared with, 305, 305*f*
in DNA transcription, 304–307, 306*f*
origin of, 449, 449*f*
processing after transcription, 328, 328*f*
ribose in, 63, 305, 305*f*
splicing of, 328, 328*f*

translation of, 304–305, 304*f*, 308–309, 308*f*–309*f*
types of, 305
ribose, 63, 305, 305*f*
ribosomal RNA (rRNA), 305, 331
ribosomes
formation of, 157
free vs. bound, 157
function of, 157, 158, 159*f*
location of, 154, 154*f*, 155*f*
protein synthesis in, 308–309, 308*f*–309*f*
RNA in, 305
ribozymes, 449
ringworm, 506, 506*f*
RNA (ribonucleic acid)
codons in, 307, 307*f*
DNA compared with, 305, 305*f*
in DNA transcription, 304–307, 306*f*
HIV, 505*f*
origin of, 449, 449*f*
processing after transcription, 328, 328*f*
ribose in, 63, 305, 305*f*
splicing of, 328, 328*f*
translation of, 304–305, 304*f*, 308–309, 308*f*–309*f*
types of, 305
RNA polymerase, 306, 306*f*, 327*f*, 329
RNA splicing, 328, 328*f*
robots, 41, 41*f*
rough endoplasmic reticulum, 158, 159*f*
rRNA (ribosomal RNA), 305, 331

safety precautions, 16
salamanders, acid rain and, 140
Salmonella, 332, 500
salts, 53–54, 53*f*, 54*f*
satellite data, 15, 30*f*
satellite tagging, 39, 39*f*
savannas, 83
Schistosoma, 507
schistosomiasis, 507
Schleiden, Matthias, 152
Schwann, Theodor, 152
SCID (severe combined immunodeficiency), 538
science
ethics and, 8 (*See also* **ethical issues**)
human population size and, 107
reasons for studying, 9
scientific investigations, 10–13, 13*f*
scientific thought, 7
universal laws in, 8
scientific claims, 9
scientific names, 424, 424*f*
scientific nomenclature, 424, 424*f*
scientific research, 580–581
scientific theories, 13, 375
SCNT (somatic-cell nuclear transfer), 352–353
scrotum, 549
scrubbers, 136
scurvy, 514
sea otters, 115, 115*f*
sea stars, 227, 227*f*, 247

seat belts, 513
seaweed, 115, 160, 160*f*
secondary structure of proteins, 62
second gap phase (G2), 228*f*, 229
second messengers, 186, 186*f*
seed plants, 429, 429*f*
seeds, effects of acid rain on, 140–141
segregation, law of, 273, 279
self-pollination, 268, 269*f*
semen, 551, 551*f*
seminal vesicles, 551
seminiferous tubules, 549, 549*f*
sequence assembly, 363
severe combined immunodeficiency
    (SCID), 538
sex chromosomes, 249
sex determination, 249, 335
sex-linked genes, 280
sexually transmitted infections (STIs),
    561–563, 561*f*, 562*f*, 563*f*. *See also names*
    of specific infections
sexual reproduction
    advantages of, 248, 253
    chromosome number and, 248–249, 249*f*
    diploid life cycle, 256–257, 256*f*, 257*f*
    evolution and, 406
    meiosis in, 250–254, 250*f*–251*f*, 252*f*, 254*f*
    overview of, 248, 248*f*
sexual selection
    evolution and, 406, 406*f*
    microevolution and, 388
shared characters, 429
shark skin, 27
shotgun sequencing method, 363
SI (International System of Units), 14, 14*f*,
    20–21, 586–587
sickle cell anemia, 319, 319*f*, 323*f*, 512, 512*f*
signal molecules, 184–186, 185*f*, 186*f*
silent mutations, 320
Silent Spring (Carson), 137
simple carbohydrates, 60
simple diffusion, 179, 179*f*
single nucleotide polymorphisms (SNPs), 356
sister chromatids, 230–231, 230*f*–231*f*
skeletal system, 474*f*, 476
skepticism, 7
skin
    acne, 503, 503*f*
    immune function of, 525
    skin cells, 152*f*
    structure of, 477, 477*f*
skin cancer, 477
SLE (systemic lupus erythematosus), 537*f*
slime molds, 165, 330*f*–331*f*
small intestine, 480, 480*f*
smallpox, 31
smears, in electrophoresis, 356
smoking
    emphysema from, 497
    lung cancer from, 235, 511, 511*f*
    during pregnancy, 558
smooth endoplasmic reticulum, 158
snails, 396*f*–397*f*
snakes, 255
sneezing, 500, 500*f*
SNPs (single nucleotide polymorphisms),
    356

sodium, 53, 53*f*, 54*f*, 179, 179*f*
sodium chloride, 53–54, 53*f*, 54*f*
sodium hydroxide, 56
sodium-potassium pump, 182, 182*f*
soil, 131
solar panels, 136, 136*f*
solar-powered cars, 139, 139*f*
solubility, 54, 54*f*
solutions, 56
somatic-cell nuclear transfer (SCNT),
    352–353
somatic cells, 248, 322–323, 322*f*, 403
somatic nervous system, 478
sonography, 560, 560*f*, 565
sorting signals, 329
Southern blot process, 358, 358*f*
speciation, 399, 412
species
    biological concept, 411
    chromosome number in, 248–249, 249*f*
    in classification system, 425*f*, 426, 426*f*
    definition of, 19, 387, 411
    discovering new, 432, 432*f*
    extinction of, 414, 414*f*
    formation of new, 412–413, 412*f*, 413*f*
    invasive, 133, 133*f*
    natural selection in, 380–381, 381*f*
    pioneer, 81, 81*f*
sperm
    definition of, 256
    delivery of, 551
    fertilization by, 557
    path through the body, 550, 550*f*
    production of, 549, 549*f*
    semen and, 551, 551*f*
    structure of, 550, 550*f*
spiders
    effect of caffeine on, 187, 187*f*
    reproduction in, 244*f*–245*f*
    web-building behavior in, 187, 187*f*
spinal cord, 478, 478*f*
spindles, 230, 230*f*–231*f*, 250*f*–251*f*, 251
sponges, 425*f*, 433, 433*f*
spores, in amoebas, 165
sporophytes, 258, 258*f*
sporozoites, 509, 509*f*
stabilizing selection, 409, 409*f*
Staphylococcus aureus, 332*f*
Staphylothermus marinus, 434*f*
starch, dietary, 60
starfish (sea stars), 227, 227*f*, 247
stem cells, 37, 353, 353*f*
sterile technique, 15, 42
sterility, from STIs, 561
steroid hormones, 61
sticky ends, 355, 355*f*, 360*f*
STIs (sexually transmitted infections),
    561–563, 561*f*, 562*f*, 563*f*. *See also names*
    of specific STIs
stomach, 480
stomach ulcers, 7, 502*f*
stop codons, 308–309, 308*f*–309*f*
strata, sediment, 451, 451*f*, 461
strep throat, 500
Streptococcus pneumoniae, 434*f*
stroke, 511
stromatolites, 455, 455*f*

submarine engineering, 34
subspecies, 412
substrates, enzyme, 66, 67*f*
subunits, of proteins, 329
succession, 81, 81*f*
sucrose, 60
sugars. *See also names of specific sugars*
    in cell membranes, 177
    chemical structure of, 60, 60*f*
    in DNA, 290*f*–291*f*, 296, 296*f*
    in foods, 60, 60*f*
    production of, 206–207, 206*f*
sulfuric acid, 128
sunburn, 334, 334*f*
superposition, law of, 451, 451*f*
surface area–to-volume ratio, 152–153,
    188–189, 223
sweat, 481, 525
swim bladders, 34
symbiosis, 111, 111*f*, 331
synthesis phase, 228*f*, 229
syphilis, 561*f*, 563, 563*f*
systematics, 427, 427*f*, 430
systemic lupus erythematosus (SLE), 537*f*

taiga, 83, 83*f*
target cells, 184–185, 185*f*
taxon (plural, *taxa*), 423
taxonomy, definition of, 423. *See also*
    classification
Tay-Sachs disease, 323*f*
T cells
    in AIDS, 539, 539*f*
    cytotoxic, 529*f*, 530, 531*f*
    defects in, 538
    helper, 529–530, 529*f*, 530*f*, 531*f*
telomeres, 334
telophase, 231, 231*f*, 250*f*–251*f*, 251
temperate biomes, 82–83, 83*f*
temperature. *See also* **body temperature**
    cholera and, 30, 30*f*
    enzymes and, 66
    microbial growth and, 42–43
    phenotype and, 284, 284*f*
    photosynthesis and, 207
tendons, 476, 476*f*
ten percent rule, 88, 88*f*
terracing, 131
terrestrial biomes, 82–83, 82*f*, 83*f*
Tertiary period, 453*f*
tertiary structure of proteins, 62
testcrosses, 277
testes, 479*f*, 549, 549*f*
testosterone, 549
tetanus, 502*f*
tetrads, 252
Texas paint brush, 434*f*
thalamus, 478, 478*f*
***Thalassoma* spp.** (wrasses), 412*f*
theories, scientific, 6, 13, 375
therapsids, 459
thermometers, reading, 585
thermostats, 485. *See also* **feedback**
    mechanisms

Index

theropods, 427*f*
threshold concentration, 490
thylakoid membrane, 204, 204*f*
thylakoids, 202–203, 202*f*–203*f*
thymine, 296*f*, 297, 298
thymus gland, 479*f*, 529*f*
thyroid gland, 479*f*
ticks, Lyme disease from, 503, 503*f*
tissue culture, 351, 351*f*
tissues, 164, 164*f*
tobacco mosaic virus (TMV), 516–517
tobacco smoking
  emphysema from, 497
  lung cancer from, 235, 511, 511*f*
  during pregnancy, 558
tooth decay, 502*f*
totipotent cells, 353
toxic substances, 515, 515*f*
toxins, 502
Toxoplasma gondii, 508, 508*f*
toxoplasmosis, 508
traits, 268, 280–282, 281*f*
transcription
  gene expression and, 304–305
  gene regulation of, 327, 327*f*
  replication compared to, 307
  RNA processing after, 328, 328*f*
  steps in, 306, 306*f*
transcription factors, 327, 327*f*
transfer RNA (tRNA), 305, 308–309, 308*f*–309*f*, 331
transformation, of genotype, 294
transgenic organisms, 350, 350*f*
translation, 304–305, 304*f*, 308–309, 308*f*–309*f*
translocation mutations, 321, 321*f*
transpiration, 90, 90*f*
transplants, organ, 538
transport, cell, 178–183
  active, 182–183, 182*f*, 183*f*
  by osmosis, 180–181, 180*f*, 181*f*
  passive, 178–179, 179*f*
transport proteins, 177, 177*f*, 179, 179*f*
transposons, 332
trauma, organ malfunction from, 513
trichomoniasis, 561*f*, 562
tRNA (transfer RNA), 305, 308–309, 308*f*–309*f*, 331
trophic levels, 86–87, 86*f*, 87*f*
tropical biomes, 82–83, 83*f*
true-breeding plants, 269, 269*f*
Trypanosoma cruzi, 508*f*
tuberculosis, 500, 503
tubulin, 156
tumors, 235, 235*f*, 323
tundra, 83
turgor, 473
twins, 564, 564*f*
type 1 diabetes, 489, 489*f*
type 2 diabetes, 489, 489*f*

ulcers, 7, 502*f*
ultrasound imaging, 560, 560*f*, 565

ultraviolet radiation (UV radiation), 234–235, 477
umbilical cord, 558, 560*f*
unicellular organisms, 165
units, 14, 14*f*, 20–21
universal laws, 8
uracil, 305, 305*f*, 306
urea, 481
urethra, 481, 481*f*
Urey, Harold, 447
urinary bladder, 481, 481*f*
urinary system, 474*f*, 481, 481*f*
urine, 481
uterus, 553, 553*f*, 556, 560*f*
UV radiation, 234–235

vaccines, 31, 346, 532–533
vacuoles, 160, 160*f*, 181
vagina, 553, 553*f*
valence electrons, 52
vascular plants, 429, 429*f*
vas deferens, 550, 550*f*, 551
vectors, 360, 360*f*, 500
veins, 482, 483
vertebrates
  embryology of, 383
  evolution of, 383, 384, 384*f*
  general characteristics of, 383
  homologous structures in, 384, 384*f*
  in the Paleozoic era, 458
vesicles
  in cell transport, 183, 183*f*
  in protein processing, 158, 159*f*
  seminal, 551
  in storage and maintenance, 158, 160, 160*f*
Vibrio cholerae, 502*f*
villi, 480, 480*f*
Virchow, Rudolph, 152
viruses
  bacteriophages, 295, 295*f*
  diseases from, 504–505, 504*f*, 505*f*
  plant, 516–517
  rearrangement of genetic material by, 332
  reproduction of, 504
vitamin C, 514
vitamin deficiencies, 514
vulva, 553, 553*f*

Wallace, Alfred Russel, 381
warblers, 114, 114*f*
waste recycling, 108, 108*f*, 135
water, 55–58. *See also* **water transport**
  acids and bases in, 56–57, 56*f*
  adhesion in, 55, 55*f*
  balance in human body, 473, 473*f*
  cell transport of, 180–181, 180*f*, 181*f*
  cohesion in, 55, 55*f*
  contamination of, 127
  cycle, 77, 90, 90*f*

  disease transmission through, 500
  drinking, 30
  floating ice, 55, 55*f*
  as greenhouse gas, 129, 129*f*
  hydrogen bonds in, 54, 54*f*, 55
  molecular structure of, 52, 52*f*
  in photosynthesis reaction, 204, 204*f*
  in plants, 55, 55*f*, 472, 472*f*
  polarity of, 54, 54*f*
  properties of, 55, 55*f*
water cycle, 77, 90, 90*f*
water pollution, 130, 130*f*
water pressure, in deep-sea fish, 473
water transport, in cells, 180–181, 180*f*, 181*f*
Watson, James, 296, 299, 299*f*
waxes, 61, 61*f*
Weinberg, Wilhelm, 404
wetlands, 84, 84*f*
whales, 382*f*
wheat germ extraction, 311
white blood cells
  B cells, 530, 530*f*, 531*f*
  cytotoxic T cells, 529*f*, 530, 531*f*
white blood cells
  helper T cells, 529, 529*f*, 530*f*
  in inflammation, 526, 526*f*, 527*f*
  in lymphatic system, 483
  macrophages, 522*f*–523*f*, 526–527, 527*f*
  natural killer cells, 526, 527*f*
  neutrophils, 526, 527*f*
  shapes of, 152
white wing dove, 431*f*
Wilkins, Maurice, 298–299
wood frog, 471
word origins, 575–577
worms, parasitic, 507, 507*f*
wrasses, evolution in, 412*f*

X chromosome, 249, 362, 362*f*

Y chromosome, 249, 335
yeast infections, 506
yeasts, 116–117, 506
Yersinia pestis, 499*f*

zebra fish, genome of, 330*f*–331*f*
zebra mussels, 133, 133*f*
zygotes, 248, 248*f*, 557

Credits

Photography

Abbreviations used: (t) top, (b), bottom, (c) center, (l) left, (r) right, (bkgd) background

LABS (bkgd) Brand X/SuperStock; **UNIT OPENERS** (bkgd), (border) Royalty-Free/Getty Images; **UNIT 1** (section borders) Michael Melford/Royalty-Free/Getty Images; **UNITS 2–4** (section borders) Royalty-Free/Creatas Images; **UNITS 5–6** (section borders) PhotoDisc/Veer

COVER AND TITLE © Frank Lane/Parfitt/Getty Images; iii (tl, bl) Andy Christiansen/HRW; (tr, br) Patrick Greene/National Geographic Image Collection; iv (Gaul) Sam Dudgeon/HRW; (Govind) Andy Christiansen/ HRW; (Lumsden) Paul Draper/HRW; (Mandel) Andy Christiansen/HRW; (Seidman) Andy Christiansen/HRW; (Zavaleta) Robert Houser; vii (b) Barbara Strnadova/Photo Researchers, Inc.; viii (bl) Stephen Alvarez/National Geographic Image Collection; (tl) James M. Bell/Photo Researchers, Inc.; ix (b) ABPL/Daryl Balfour/Animals Animals/Earth Scenes; x (cl) Dr. Linda Stannard, UCT/ Photo Researchers, Inc.; xi (tr) Joe Outland/Alamy; (bl) Dr. Paul Andrews, University of Dundee/Photo Researchers, Inc.; xii (tl) Andrew Leonard/Photo Researchers, Inc.; xiii (cr) Toni Angermayer/Photo Researchers, Inc.; xiv (tl) Sam Dudgeon/HRW; (b) Anatomical Travelogue/Photo Researchers, Inc.; xv (b) Derek Berwin/Getty Images; xvi (t) AP Photo/Katsumi Kasahara; xviii (t) Sam Dudgeon/ HRW; xix (b) Sam Dudgon/HRW; 2 (bl) Bill Curtsinger/ National Geographic Image Collection; (br) Katherine Feng/Globio/Minden Pictures; (tl) Royalty-Free/Corbis; 2A Bill Hatcher/National Geographic Image Collection; 2B (bl) Meul/ARCO/Nature Picture Library; (tr) (cl) Bettmann/ Corbis; (cr) Time & Life Pictures/Getty Images; 3 (tl) (cr) Sam Dudgeon/HRW; (cl) Age Fotostock/SuperStock

CHAPTER 1: 4–5 Frans Lanting/Minden Pictures; 7 (br) Deep Light Productions/Photo Researchers, Inc.; (bc) P. Hawtin/University of Southhampton/Photo Researchers, Inc.; 8 (tr) National Optical Astronomy Observatories/ Photo Researchers, Inc.; (tl) David Tipling/Nature Picture Library; 9 (tr) Victoria Smith/HRW; 10 (bl) Georgette Douwma/Nature Picture Library; 11 (tr) Sam Dudgeon/ HRW; 12 (bl) Millard H. Sharp/Photo Researchers, Inc.; (br) AP Photo/Marcio Jose Sanchez; 13 (tr) Royalty-Free/ Corbis; 14 (r) Sam Dudgeon/HRW; (cl) PhotoDisc/Getty Images; (cr), 15 (tr) Victoria Smith/HRW; 16 (tl) Carsten Peter/National Geographic Image Collection; 17 (bl) Phil Schermeister/National Geographic Image Collection; 18 (bl) Stephen Alvarez/National Geographic Image Collection; (tr) Paul Nicklen/National Geographic Image Collection; (c) Douglas Faulkner/Photo Researchers, Inc.; (bkgd) Michael Martin/Photo Researchers, Inc.; 19 (tr) Gabe Palmer/Alamy; 21 Victoria Smith/HRW; 22 (t) Stephen Alvarez/National Geographic Image Collection; (t) P. Hawtin/University of Southhampton/ Photo Researchers, Inc.; (tc) Sam Dudgeon/HRW; (bc) PhotoDisc/Getty Images

CHAPTER 2: 26–27 Roger Harris/Photo Researchers, Inc.; 29 (b) James M. Bell/Photo Researchers, Inc.; 30 (b) Jeremy Horner/Corbis; (cl) Amit Dave/NewsCom; 31 (tr) Victoria Smith/HRW; 32 (tl) epa/Corbis; (tr) Vo Trung Dung/Corbis Sygma; 33 (bl) Taxi/Getty Images; (br) Don Farrall/Photographer's Choice RF/Getty Images; 34 (bl) Peter Menzel/Photo Researchers, Inc.; 35 (b) ORNL/Photo Researchers, Inc.; 36 (br) Eric Miller/Getty Images; (bl) Mark Maio/King-Holmes/Photo Researchers, Inc.; 37 (tr) Getty Images; 38 (cl), (br), (cr) David Brabyn/Sipa Photos/ NewsCom; 39 (t) Mike Johnson. All rights reserved.; 40 (tl) Courtesy of Dr. Rita Colwell; (t) Andrew Dunn; 41 (tr) Yuriko Nakao/NewsCom; (bl) Jim Sulley/NewsCom; (c) Volker Steger/Photo Researchers, Inc.; (bkgd) Royalty-Free/Corbis; 43 (tr) Sam Dudgeon/HRW; 44 (t) Amit Dave/NewsCom; (c) David Brabyn/NewsCom; (b) Don Farrall/Photographer's Choice RF/Getty Images; 46 (tc) AP Photo/Katsumi Kasahara

CHAPTER 3: 48–49 Daniel Boschung/zefa/Corbis; 51 (bl) Victoria Smith/HRW; 52 (tc) blickwinkel/Alamy; 53 (br) Sergio Purtell/Foca/HRW; 55 (bl) Botanica/The Garden Picture Library; 56 (b-all) Sam Dudgeon/HRW; 57 (t) Victoria Smith/HRW; 58 (tr) O.S.F./Animals Animals/ Earth Scenes; (cl) Bernard, George/Animals Animals/Earth Scenes; (t-bkgd) PhotoDisc/Getty Images; (cr) Layne Kennedy/Corbis; (b-bkgd) Bernhard Edmaier/SPL/Photo Researchers, Inc.; 59 (br) Andrew Holt/Alamy; (bl) Andy Christiansen/HRW; 60 (bc) Sam Dudgeon/HRW; 61 (t) Sam Dudgeon/HRW; (bl) Suzanne Danegger/NHPA; (br) Tony Hamblin; Frank Lane Picture Agency/Corbis; 62 (br) SuperStock; 64 (b) Victor Ruiz Caballero/AP/Wide World Photos; 68 Sam Dudgeon/HRW; 70 (t) Victoria Smith/HRW; (b) Botanica/The Garden Picture Library; (b) Victor Ruiz Caballero/AP/Wide World Photos; 74 (br) A ROOM WITH VIEWS/Alamy; (bl) FRANS LANTING/Minden Pictures; 74A Doug Perrine/Nature Picture Library; 74B (bl) Mark Moffett/Minden Pictures; (tl) Brand X Pictures; (tr) Royalty-Free/Corbis; (cl) Erich Hartmann/Magnum Photos; (cr) Iain Masterton/Alamy; 75 (tl, cr) Robert Houser; (cl) Heidi & Hans-Jurgen Koch/Minden Pictures

CHAPTER 4: 76–77 Ingo Arndt/Nature Picture Library; 79 (b) Kim Taylor/Nature Picture Library; 80 (t) Randal Alhadeff/HRW Photo; 81 (l) Ken M. Johns, The National Audubon Society Collection/Photo Researchers; (c) Glenn M. Oliver/Visuals Unlimited; (r) ER Degginger/Color-Pic, Inc.; 82–83 (t) Michael DeYoung/Corbis; 83 (tc) Brenda Tharp/Photo Researchers, Inc.; (tr) ER Degginger/Color-Pic, Inc.; 84 (tl) Tamara Dormier/Seapics; (tr) Mark Conlin/Seapics; 85 (b-bkgd) Jan Baks/Alamy; (tr) Paul Chesley/National Geographic/Getty Images; (t-bkgd) Victoria Smith/HRW; (c) Roger W. Archibald/Animals Animals/Earth Scenes; 86 (l) blickwinkel/Alamy; (cl) B.A.E. Inc./Alamy; (cr) James Carmichael, Jr./NHPA; (r) Tom Vezo/VIREO; 88 (t) Michael Keller/Corbis; 89 (t) Brian Wheeler/VIREO; (c) D. Robert & Lorri Franz/Corbis; (b) Jason Brindel Photography/Alamy Photos; 93, 94, 95 Sam Dudgeon/HRW; 96 (t) Kim Taylor/Nature Picture Library; (b) Michael Keller/Corbis

CHAPTER 5: 100–101 Tui De Roy/Minden Pictures; 103 (b) ABPL/Balfour, Daryl/Animals Animals/Earth Scenes; 104 (t) Terry Andrewartha/Nature Picture Library; 105 (b) Frans Lanting/Minden Pictures; 106 (b) Fritz Polking/Peter Arnold, Inc.; 107 (t-bkgd) Janine Wiedel Photolibrary/Alamy; 108 (cl) Yoshikazu Tsuno/AFP/Getty Images; (b-bkgd) SETBOUN/Corbis; (tr) Iain Masterton/ Alamy; (t-bkgd) Corbis/PunchStock; 109 (b) Mitsuaki Iwago/Minden Pictures; 110 (tc) Patti Murray/Animals Animals/Earth Scenes; 111 (tl) Doug Perrine/Nature Picture Library; (tr) Clay Perry/Corbis; 112 (b) Ilene MacDonald/Alamy; 114 (tl) Robert Royse/VIREO; (tcl) John Dunning/VIREO; (tc) Bob Steele/VIREO; (tcr) Rob & Ann Simpson/VIREO; (tr) Arthur Morris/VIREO; 115 (t) James D. Watt/Seapics; 117 (tl) Victoria Smith/HRW; (tr) Dr. David B. Fankhouser; 118 (t) Frans Lanting/Minden Pictures; (c) Doug Perrine/Nature Picture Library; (b) James D. Watt/Seapics

CHAPTER 6: 122–123 George Steinmetz/Corbis; 123 (br) Victoria Smith/HRW; 125 (br) Cameron Davidson/ Getty Images; 126 (br) George Steinmetz/Corbis; (bl) Lester Lefkowitz/Corbis; 127 (tr) Victoria Smith/HRW; 128 (b) China Photos/Getty Images; 131 (tr) Victoria Smith/ HRW; 132 (b) Peter Oxford/Nature Picture Library; 133 (tl) Will Meinderts/Foto Natura/Minden Pictures; (tr) Shin Yoshino/Minden Pictures; 134 (b) Royalty-free/Robert Harding; 135 (tr) Victoria Smith/HRW; 136 (bl) Courtesy Cliff Lerner/HRW; (br) Richard Price/Getty Images; 137 (t) Stuart Westmorland/Corbis; 138 (tr) Image entitled "Fresh Kills Future Parkland" used with permission of the New York City Department of City Planning. All rights reserved; (tl) Louie Psihoyos/Corbis; 139 (cr) Handout-Obvio!/Reuters/Corbis; (tr) Reuters/Corbis; (b) Issei Kato/Reuters/Corbis; (bkgd) Royalty-Free/Corbis; 141 (tr) Sam Dudgeon/HRW; 142 (br) Royalty-free/Robert Harding; (c) Shin Yoshino/Minden Pictures; (tr) Lester Lefkowitz/Corbis; 146 (bl) PHOTOTAKE Inc./Alamy; (br) Andrew Syred/Photo Researchers, Inc.; 146A James Cavallini/Photo Researchers, Inc.; 146B (bl) Jennifer C. Waters/Photo Researchers, Inc.; (tl) Kevin Collins/Visuals Unlimited; (tr) PhotoDisc/Getty Images; (cl) Gary D. Gaugler/Photo Researchers, Inc.; (cr) Paula Lerner/ Aurora; 147 (tl, cr) Andy Christiansen/HRW; (cl) Don W. Fawcett/Photo Researchers, Inc.

CHAPTER 7: 148–149 Volker Steger/Christian Bardele/Photo Researchers, Inc.;149 (tr) Victoria Smith/HRW;151 (bc) Michael Newman/Photo Edit; (br) Michael Abbey/Visuals Unlimited;152 (tr) Andrew Syred/Photo Researchers, Inc.; (c) Laude Nuridsany & Marie Perennou/Photo Researchers, Inc.; (tr) Thomas Deerinck/Visuals Unlimited; (bl), (bkgd) Francois Paquet-Durand/Photo Researchers, Inc.;154 (tr) CNRI/Photo Researchers, Inc.;155 (tl) Dr. Donald Fawcett/Visuals Unlimited;157 (tr) Don Fawcett/Visuals Unlimited;159 (tr), (cr) R. Boldender/D. Fawcett/Visuals Unlimited; (tr) Professor Birgit H. Satir;160 (br) Dr. Jeremy Burgess/ Photo Researchers, Inc.; 161 (tr) Dr. Don Fawcett/Visuals Unlimited; 162 (bl) Dr. Linda Stannard, UCT/Photo Researchers, Inc.; 164 (cl) Dr. George Chapman/Visuals Unlimited; (c) Clouds Hill Imaging Ltd./Corbis; (cr) Gentl & Hyers/Botanica/Jupiter Images; (bl) Photo Insolite Realite/SPL/Photo Researchers, Inc.; 166 (tl) Lawrence Naylor/Photo Researchers, Inc.; (cl) Eddy Marissen/Foto Natura/Minden Pictures; (tr) Age FotoStock/SuperStock; (br) IT Stock International/Jupiter Images; 167 (tr) E.R. Degginger/Color-Pic, Inc.; 168 (br) Eddy Marissen/Foto Natura/Minden Pictures; (tr) Michael Newman/Photo Edit

CHAPTER 8: 172–173 CNRI/Photo Researchers, Inc.; 173 (cr) Runk/Schoenberger/Grant Heilman Photography; 175 (b) Marc Chamberlain/Seapics; 178 (b) Keith Levit/ Alamy; 180 (all) Dr. David M. Phillips/Visuals Unlimited; 181 (t) Sam Dudgeon/HRW; (b) Nigel Cattlin/Photo Researchers, Inc.; 184 (b) Bob Daemmrich/PhotoEdit, Inc.; 185 (t) Kevin Schafer/Corbis; 187 (cl, cr) NASA/SPL/ Photo Researchers, Inc.; (tr) Meul/ARCO/Nature Picture Library; (tl) PhotoDisc/Getty Images; (bkgd) Dr. Jeremy Burgess/SPL/Photo Researchers, Inc.; (br) Lourens Smak/Alamy; 188 (bl) WARD'S Natural Science; (br) Sam Dudgeon/HRW; 190 (t) Marc Chamberlain/Seapics; (c) Keith Levit/Alamy; (b) Bob Daemmrich/PhotoEdit, Inc.

CHAPTER 9: 194–195 Frans Lanting/Minden Pictures; 195 (tr) Victoria Smith/HRW; 197 (b) Terry W. Eggers/ Corbis; 198 (tr) Victoria Smith/HRW; 199 (cr) Michael Newman/PhotoEdit; (cl) Royalty-Free/Corbis; 200 (br) Troy and Mary Parlee/Alamy; 202 (bl) Copyright Dorling Kindersley; 207 (tl) Richard Cummins/Corbis; (tr) Wolfgang Kaehler/Corbis; 208 John Henley/Corbis; 213 (tl) Mike Powell/Allsport Concepts/Getty Images; (tc) David Madison/Getty Images; 214 (bkgd), (tr), (cr) Roger Ressmeyer/Corbis; (b) James Marshall/Corbis; 215 (bl) Victoria Smith/HRW; 216 (t) Richard Cummins/Corbis; (b) David Madison/Getty Images; (t) Troy and Mary Parlee/Alamy

CHAPTER 10: 220–221 Dr. Linda Stannard, UCT/Photo Researchers, Inc.; 221 (tr) Carolina Biological Supply/ Visuals Unlimited; 223 (b) Pixoi Ltd./Alamy; 224 (t) Victoria Smith/HRW; 225 (br) David M. Philips/Visuals Unlimited; 226 (tl) Visuals Unlimited/Corbis; 227 (c) R. Andrew Odum/Peter Arnold, Inc.; (t-bkgd) Robert Yin/Corbis; (b-bkgd) Doug Perrine/Seapics; (tr) Dwight R. Kuhn; (cl, cr) R. Andrew Odum/Peter Arnold, Inc.; 230–231 (b-all) Dr. Conly L. Rieder and Dr. Alexey

Khodjakov/Visuals Unlimited; 232 (tr) R. Calentine/Visuals Unlimited; (tl) RMF/Visuals Unlimited; 233 (bl) Antonia Reeve/Science Photo Library/Photo Researchers, Inc.; 235 (cr) Steve Gschmeissner/Science Photo Library/Photo Researchers, Inc.; (tr) Jose Luis Pelaez, Inc./Corbis; 237 (tr) Victoria Smith/HRW; (tl) Dr. John D. Cunningham/Visuals Unlimited; 238 (t) Visuals Unlimited/Corbis; (c) Dr. Conly L. Rieder and Dr. Alexey Khodjakov/Visuals Unlimited; (b) Jose Luis Pelaez, Inc./Corbis; 239 (br) David M. Philips/Visuals Unlimited; 242 (br) Steve Paddock, Jim Langeland, Sean Carroll/Visuals Unlimited; (bl) Christian Ziegler/Danita Delimont; 242A Frans Lanting/Minden Pictures; 242B (bl) Ted Horowitz/Corbis; (tl) James King-Holmes/Science Photo Library; (tr) MBL/WHOI Library; (cr) David Parker/Photo Researchers, Inc.; 243 (r), (cr) Andy Christiansen/HRW Photo; 243 (bl) Dynamic Graphics Value/SuperStock

CHAPTER 11: 244–245 Heidi Hans-Jurgen Koch/Minden Pictures; 245 (br) Martin Gabriel/Nature Picture Library; 247 (br) BPA/SS/Photo Researchers, Inc.; 248 (bl) David M. Phillips/Photo Researchers, Inc.; 249 (cr) Frans Lanting/Minden Pictures; (tr) Eye of Science/Photo Researchers, Inc.; 255 (cr) Konrad Wothe/Minden Pictures; (bl) George Bernard/Photo Researchers, Inc.; (br) Tom Brakefield/Corbis; (bkgd) Frank Lukasseck/zefa/Corbis; (tr) Francesco Tomasinelli/Natural Visions; 256 (br) David M. Phillips/Visuals Unlimited; (cl) (c) Image 1999 PhotoDisc, Inc./HRW; (bc) Yorgos Nikas/Tony Stone/Getty Images; (bl) Jason Burns/Ace/Phototake; (cr), (b) Image 1999 PhotoDisc, Inc./HRW; 259 Sam Dudgeon/HRW; 260 (t) David M. Phillips/Photo Researchers, Inc.

CHAPTER 12: 263–264 Leszczynski, Zigmund/Animals Animals-Earth Scenes; 265 (tl), (tr) Sam Dudgeon/HRW; 271 (bkgd) Manfred Kage/Peter Arnold, Inc.; (bl) Eye of Science/Photo Researchers, Inc.; (tr) David M. Phillips/Photo Researchers, Inc.; 273 (tl) Picture Press/Corbis; (tr) Royalty-Free/Alamy Images; (tl) Picture Press/Corbis; 274 (c), (bc) Christian Grzimek/Okapia/Photo Researchers, Inc.; (cr), (br) Barry Runk/Grant Heilman Photography; 277 (t), (b) Lynn M. Stone/DRK Photo; 278 Irving J. Buchbinder/Community Health Services; 279 (tl), (tr) Ken Lax/HRW Photo; 280 Joe Outland/Alamy; 281 Ben Klaffke; 282 Arthur Tilley/FPG International; 284 (t) Dan Guravich/Photo Researchers, Inc.; (b) Tom Walker/Tony Stone Images; 285 Victoria Smith/HRW; 286 (br) Arthur Tilley/FPG International

CHAPTER 13: 290–291 Alfred Pasieka/Photo Researchers, Inc.; 293 (b) Rick Gomez/Corbis; 297 (tr) Sam Dudgeon/HRW; 299 (cr) SPL/Photo Researchers, Inc.; (tr) A. Barrington Brown/Photo Researchers, Inc.; 300 (bl) Dr. Gopal Murti/SPL/Photo Researchers, Inc.; 303 (tr) Dr Paul Andrews, University Of Dundee/Photo Researchers, Inc.; 309 (br) Alfred Pasieka/Photo Researchers, Inc.; 310 (tr) Dr. Dennis Kunkel/Visuals Unlimited; (tc) John Langford/HRW; 311 (bl) Victoria Smith/HRW; 312 (tr) Rick Gomez/Corbis; (br) Alfred Pasieka/Photo Researchers, Inc; (c) Dr. Gopal Murti/SPL/Photo Researchers, Inc.

CHAPTER 14: 316–317 Frans Lanting/Minden Pictures; 317 (tr) Sheila Terry/Photo Researchers, Inc.; 319 Dr. Stanley Flegler/Visuals Unlimited; 321 (tr) Sam Dudgeon/HRW; 322 (bl) Lauren Shear/Photo Researchers, Inc.; (tc) Dr. P. Marazzi/Photo Researchers, Inc.; (br) Biophoto Associates/Science Source/Photo Researchers, Inc.; 323 (b) Custom Medical Stock Photo; (t) Dr. Stanley Flegler/Visuals Unlimited; (c) Simon Fraser/Photo Researchers, Inc.; (bc) Robert Caughey/Visuals Unlimited; (tc) Dr. S. Walkley/Peter Arnold, Inc.; 324 (tr) L. Willatt, East Anglian Regional Genetics Service/Photo Researchers, Inc.; (br) L. Willatt, East Anglian Regional Genetics Service/Photo Researchers, Inc.; (tl) Stockbyte/SuperStock; 325 (bl) Westend61/Royalty-Free/Getty Images; (br) Leslie J. Borg/Photo Researchers, Inc.; 326 (tl) Dr. Dennis Kunkel/

Visuals Unlimited; 328 (t) Victoria Smith/HRW; 329 (tr) Corbis; 330 (l) Phototake, Inc./Alamy; (cl) Wally Eberhart/Visuals Unlimited; (cr) Nathalie Pujol/Visuals Unlimited; (r) Hermann Eisenbeiss/Photo Researchers, Inc.; 331 (r) Rubberball/Jupiter Images; (l) Mark Smith/Photo Researchers, Inc.; (cl) Digital Vision Ltd./SuperStock; (cr) PhotoDisc Blue/Royalty-Free/Getty Images; Martha Powell/Visuals Unlimited; 332 (tl) Alix/Photo Researchers, Inc.; (cl) Dr. Dennis Kunkel/Visuals Unlimited; 334 Peter Skinner/Photo Researchers, Inc.; 335 (b) Chris Graythen/Getty Images; (bkgd) Matthias Kulka/zefa/Corbis; (tr) AP Photo/Cristina Quicler; 337 (t) Ward's Natural Science; 338 (b) PhotoDisc Blue/Royalty-Free/Getty Images; (c) Corbis; (t) Lauren Shear/Photo Researchers, Inc.

CHAPTER 15: 342–343 Simon Lin/AP Wide World Photos; 345 (br) Roy Morsch/zefa/Corbis; 346 Science VU/Visuals Unlimited; 347 (tr) Courtesy of Cellmark Diagnostics, Inc., Germantown, Maryland; 348 Photo by Russ Morris, The Tech Museum of Innovation; 349 (b) Bettmann/Corbis; (tr), (cr) Reuters/Corbis; (bkgd) Royalty-Free/Corbis; 350 (bl) AFP/Getty Images; 351 (br) Jim Richardson/Corbis; 353 (tl) Andrew Leonard/Photo Researchers, Inc.; (tr) CC Studio/Photo Researchers, Inc.; (tc) Mauro Fermariello/Photo Researchers, Inc.; 354 Wolfgang Flamisch/zefa/Corbis; 356 (tr) Sam Dudgeon/HRW; (bl) Louise Lockley/CSIRO/Photo Researchers, Inc.; 361 (b) Royalty-Free/Corbis; 362 (br) Lisa Peardon/Taxi/Getty Images; 363 (tr) David Parker/Photo Researchers, Inc.; 365 (tr) Tek Image/Photo Researchers, Inc.; 366 (t) Roy Morsch/zefa/Corbis; (c) Jim Richardson/Corbis; (b) Louise Lockley/CSIRO/Photo Researchers, Inc.; 370 (br) Photo by Simon van Noort, courtesy Iziko Museums of Cape Town; (bl) Rob Reijnen/Foto Natura/Minden Pictures; 370A Mark Moffett/Minden Pictures; 370B (tl) Jeff Greenberg/Lonely Planet Images; (tr) John Reader/Photo Researchers, Inc.; (cl) Index Stock Imagery/Newscom; (cr) STR/AFP/Getty Images; 371 (tl), (cr) Andy Christiansen/HRW Photo; (bl) Louie Psihoyos/Corbis; (bl) Edwin L. Wisherd/National Geographic Image Collection/Getty Images

CHAPTER 16: 372–373 Paul Osmond/Deep Sea Images; 373 (cr) Victoria Smith/HRW; 375 (c) Bridgeman Art Library, London/New York; 376 (bc) Images & Stories/Alamy; (br) Adrienne Gibson/Animals Animals/Earth Scenes; (b) Reinhard Dirscheri/Peter Arnold, Inc.; (bl) David Hosking/Alamy; 377 (cr) Toni Angermayer/Photo Researchers, Inc.; (b) Carol Kaelson/Animals Animals/Earth Scenes; (bkgd) Sam Dudgeon/HRW; 378 (bl) Markus Boesch/Getty Images; 379 (tr) Russell Wood; 380 (bl) Robert & Linda Mitchell; 382 (br) Bruce Coleman, Inc./Alamy; t Courtesy of Research Casting International and Dr. J. G. M. Thewissen; tc Courtesy of Research Casting International and Dr. J. G. M. Thewissen; 382 bc 1998 Philip Gingerich/Courtesy of the Museum of Paleontology, The University of Michigan; 382 cl 1998 Philip Gingerich/Courtesy of the Museum of Paleontology, The University of Michigan; 382 b Courtesy of Betsy Webb, Pratt Museum, Homer, Alaska; 382 (bl) Courtesy of Betsy Webb, Pratt Museum, Homer, Alaska; 383 (tr) Martin Harvey/Alamy; (tl) Tui De Roy/Minden Pictures; (tc) Gavriel Jecan/Getty Images; 385 (tr) The Natural History Museum, London; 386 (bl) Eurelios/Phototake; 387 (br) Tom & Pat Leeson/DRK Photo; (cr) Tom & Pat Leeson/DRK Photo; (tr) Victoria Smith/HRW; 388 (bl) Robert Clark Photography; (br) Robert Clark Photography; 391 (tr) Tim Fuller/HRW; 392 (tr) Images & Stories/Alamy; (cr) Robert & Linda Mitchell; (br) Eurelios/Phototake

CHAPTER 17: 396–397 Wil Meinderts/Foto Natura/Nature Picture Library; 397 (tr) Victoria Smith/HRW; 399 Royalty-Free/Corbis; 400 (b) Victoria Smith/HRW; (tl), (tr), (c), (bl), (br), Sam Dudgeon/HRW; 402 (tl), (tr), (b) Victoria Smith/HRW; 403 Victoria Smith/HRW; 405 (br) Michio Hoshino/Minden Pictures; 406 (tl) Art Wolfe/Getty Images; 407 (tr) ISM/Phototake-All rights reserved; 408 (tl) Barry

Mansell/Nature Picture Library; (cl) Mark Smith/Photo Researchers, Inc.; (tr) Gerard Lacz/Animals Animals-Earth Scenes; 410 (bkgd) David Lawrence/Corbis; (tc), (c), (bl), (bc) Jonathan Losos; (tr) NASA/Photo Researchers, Inc.; 411 Barbara Strnadova/Photo Researchers, Inc.; 412 (tl) Norbert Wu; (tc) WorldSat; (tr) Doug Perrine/SeaPics; 413 (b) Gary Mezaros/Visuals Unlimited; (tr) Zig Leszczynski/Animals Animals-Earth Scenes; 414 (tr) Tom McHugh/Photo Researchers, Inc.; (tl) Photo Researchers, Inc.; 416 (c) Art Wolfe/Getty Images; (b) Gary Mezaros/Visuals Unlimited; (t) HRW

CHAPTER 18: 420–421 Mauro Fermariello/Photo Researchers, Inc.; 421 (br) Sam Dudgeon/HRW; 422 (l) ROBINSON, JAMES/Animals Animals/Earth Scenes; (cl) WATT, JAMES/Animals Animals/Earth Scenes; (c) ERLACH, JOHN/Animals Animals/Earth Scenes; (cr) Roger Harris/Photo Researchers, Inc.; (r) Michael & Patricia Fogden/Minden Pictures; 423 (b) Frans Lanting/Corbis; 424 (tl) Winfried Wisniewski/Foto Natura/Minden Pictures; (tc) Angela Scott/Nature Picture Library; (tr) Martin Harvey/NHPA; 425 (sponge) Doug Perrine/Seapics; (shark) Masa Ushioda/Seapics; (teen) Simon Marcus/Corbis; (wolf) Pryor, Maresa/Animals Animals/Earth Scenes; (cheetah) Winfried Wisniewski/Foto Natura/Minden Pictures; (leopard) Angela Scott/Nature Picture Library; (lion) Martin Harvey/NHPA; (paramecium) Dr. Dennis Kunkel/Visuals Unlimited; 426 (tl) Don Couch/HRW Photo; 427 (br) Michael & Patricia Fogden/Minden Pictures; (bl) Roger Harris/Photo Researchers, Inc.; 428 (turtle) Robinson, James/Animals Animals/Earth Scenes; (chameleon) Watt, James/Animals Animals/Earth Scenes; (crocodile) Erlach, John/Animals Animals/Earth Scenes; (bird-cassoway) Michael & Patricia Fogden/Minden Pictures; (dinosaur) Roger Harris/Photo Researchers, Inc.; (bird-warbler) Robert Royse/VIREO; 429 (bl) H. Taylor/OSF/Animals Animals/Earth Scenes; 429 (bcl) Dani/Jeske/Animals Animals/Earth Scenes; (bcr. br) age fotostock/SuperStock; 432 (c) AP Photo/Courtesy Wild Life Heritage Trust, HO; (bl) Robert Zingg; (tr) Dr. Mike Picker; (ct) AP Photo/Conservation International; (cb) Stephen Richards, Conservation International; (bkgd) COMSTOCK, Inc.; 433 (br) Doug Perrine/Seapics; (bl) Louis De Vos - Free University of Brussels; 434 (Eubacteria) Gary D. Gaugler/Photo Researchers, Inc.; (archaebacteria) Wolfgang Baumeister/Science Photo Library/Photo Researchers, Inc.; (protista) Dr. Dennis Kunkel/PhotoTake; (fungi) Rod Planck/Photo Researchers Inc.; (plantae) Adam Jones/Photo Researchers Inc.; (animalia) Myron Jay Dorf/Corbis; 435 (t) Victoria Smith/HRW; 438 (E) John Gilmore; (C, D) BIOS (Klein/Hubert)/Peter Arnold, Inc.; (A) Runk/Schoenberger/Grant Heilman Photography; (B) Robert & Linda Mitchell; (F) Barry Runk/Grant Heilman Photography; 439 (t) Sam Dudgeon/HRW; 440 (t) Don Couch/HRW Photo; (c) Roger Harris/Photo Researchers, Inc.; (b) Doug Perrine/Seapics

CHAPTER 19: 444–445 Jack Dykinga/Stone/Getty Images; 445 (tr) Victoria Smith/HRW; 448 (br) B. Murton/Southhampton Oceanography Centre/Photo Researchers, Inc.; (bl) Breck P. Kent/Animals Animals-Earth Scenes; 450 (br) James L. Amos/Corbis; 451 Theo Allofs/Corbis; (cr) Tom Bean/Corbis; 454 (bl) Eye of Science/Photo Researchers, Inc.; (br) Dr. Dennis Kunkel/Visuals Unlimited; 455 John Reader/SPL/Photo Researchers, Inc.; 457 (tr) John Morrison/Morrison Photography; (br) Spike Walker/Getty Images; 458 Chase Studio/Photo Researchers, Inc.; 459 Jonathan Blair/Corbis; 460 (tr) Reuters/Corbis; (c) Chris Butler/Photo Researchers, Inc.; (bkgd) Robert Harding Picture Library Ltd./Alamy; (b) Mark Garlick/Photo Researchers, Inc.; 461 Victoria Smith/HRW; 462 (t) Breck P. Kent/Animals Animals-Earth Scenes; (c) Theo Allofs/Corbis; (b) Jonathan Blair/Corbis; 466 (bl) FLIP NICKLIN/Minden Pictures; (br) Scimat/Photo Researchers, Inc.; 466A Steve Gschmeissner/Photo Researchers, Inc.; 466B (bl) Steve Axford; (tr)

POPPERFOTO/Alamy; (cl) Bettmann/Corbis; (cr) Photo by Erskine Palmer/Time Magazine/Time & Life Pictures/Getty Images; 467 (all) Andy Christiansen/HRW

CHAPTER 20: 468–469 Galen Rowell/CORBIS; 471 (bl) Stephen J. Krasemann/Photo Researchers; 472 (l) Dr. Jeremy Burgess/Science Photo Library/Photo Researchers; 473 (tl) Mario Tama/Getty Images; 474 (cr) Anatomical Travelogue/Photo Researchers; 475 (cr) Stockbyte/Getty Images; 477 (tl) Sergio Purtell/Foca/HRW; 479 (t) Sam Dudgeon/HRW; 480 (br) P. MOTTA/Department of Anatomy/University La Sapienza, Rome/Photo Researchers; 481 (tr) Sergio Purtell/Foca/HRW; 482 (bl) Ed Reschke/Peter Arnold; 484 (br) Larry Lilac/Alamy; 486 (all) Sam Dudgeon/HRW; 487 (tr) Sam Dudgeon/HRW; 488 (t) Royalty-Free/CORBIS; 489 (bkgd) CNRI/Photo Researchers; (bc, bl) Justin Hayworth/Duluth News Tribune/AP/Wide World Photos; (cr) BSIP/Phototake; (tr) Volker Steger/Science Photo Library/Photo Researchers; 490 (t) M.I. Walker/ Photo Researchers

CHAPTER 21: 496–497 CNRI/Photo Researchers; 499 (b) The Bridgeman Art Library/Getty Images; 500 (br) Dr. Tony Brain/Photo Researchers; (bl) Kent Wood/Photo Researchers; 501 (tr) Scott Markewitz/Getty Images; 503 (br) Dr. P. Marazzi/Photo Researchers; (tr) David M. Phillips/Photo Researchers; 505 (bl) Eye of Science/Photo Researchers; 506 (bl) Mediscan/Visuals Unlimited; (tl) Science Photo Library/Photo Researchers; 507 (br) John Greim/Photo Researchers; (tr) Peter Arnold/Peter Arnold; 508 (cl) Tetsu Yamazaki/International Stock Photography; (inset) VEM/Photo Researchers; 509 (bkgd) iStockphoto.com/Luba Nel; (br) AP Photo/Eugene Hoshiko; (cr) REUTERS/Corinne Dufka; (tr) Jack Clark /Animals Animals/Earth Scenes; 511 (br) Moredun Scientific/Photo Reseachers; (tl) GJLP/Photo Researchers; (tr) Morris Huberland/Photo Researchers; 512 (bl) Meckes/Ottawa/Photo Researchers; 513 (br) SPL/Photo Researchers; (tr) Michael Donne/Photo Researchers; 514 (bl) Dr. Arthur Tucker/Photo Researchers; 515 (tr) Sam Dudgeon/HRW; 516 (bl) Norm Thomas/Photo Researchers; (br) Jeff Smith/fotosmith

CHAPTER 22: 522–523 Eye of Science/Photo Researchers, Inc.; 525 (bc) A. Davidhazy/Custom Medical Stock Photo; (br) Gopal Murti/Phototake, Inc./Alamy; 527 (tl), (tc) Dr. Dennis Kunkel/Phototake; (tr) Meckes/Ottawa/Photo Researchers, Inc.; 528 (tr) Sam Dudgeon/HRW; 529 (br) Victoria Smith/HRW; 530 (bl) Dennis Kunkel/Phototake; 532 (bl) David McNew/Getty Images; 534 (bl) Sam Dudgeon/HRW; (br) Peter Arnold, Inc./Alamy; (bc) SciMAT/Photo Researchers, Inc.; 535 (br) Derek Berwin/Getty Images; (bl) Dennis Kunkel/Phototake; (tr) Victoria Smith/HRW; 536 (cr) Science Pictures Ltd/Photo Researchers, Inc.; (bl) Steve Jems/Photo Researchers, Inc.; (tr) Brand X Pictures; (bkgd) Luca DiCecco/Alamy; 537 (tr) Animas Corp; 538 (bl) AP Photo/Damian Dovarganes; 539 (cr) NIBSC/Photo Researchers, Inc.; 540 (cl) Tim Fuller/HRW; 542 (tc) A. Davidhazy/Custom Medical Stock Photo; (bc) SciMAT/Photo Researchers, Inc.

CHAPTER 23: 546–547 OSF/Derek Bromhall/Animals Animals-Earth Scenes; 549 (br) CNRI/Photo Researchers, Inc.; 551 (tr) Professor P. Motta, Dept. of Anatomy, Rome University/Photo Researchers, Inc.; 554 (bl) Professors P.M. Motta & J. Van Blerkom/Photo Researchers, Inc.; 556 (t) C. Edelmann/La Villette/SS/Photo Researchers, Inc.; 559 (tl), (bl) Lennart Nilsson/Albert Bonniers Förlag; (tr) D. Bromhall/OSF/Animals Animals-Earth Scenes; (br) Petit Format/Nestle/Photo Researchers, Inc.; 560 (tr) Zephyr/Photo Researchers, Inc.; 562 (bl) SPL/Custom Medical Stock Photo; 563 (t) NMSB/Custom Medical Stock Photo; 564 (cl) Big Cheese Photo/Royalty-Free/Getty Images; (b) Robert W. Ginn/Photo Edit; (cr) Tony Freeman/Photo Edit; (tr) Dr. Najeeb Layyous/Photo Researchers, Inc.; (bkgd) P. Motta/G. Macchiarelli/S. Nottola/Photo Researchers, Inc.; 566 (tr) Professor

P. Motta, Dept. of Anatomy, Rome University/Photo Researchers, Inc.; (tr) D. Bromhall/OSF/Animals Animals-Earth Scenes

Appendix: 570–571 Mark Conlin/Seapics; 578 (bl) Rob Melnychuk/gettyimages; 579 (tl) Scott Bauer/Agricultural Research Service, USDA; (tr) Tek Image/Photo Researchers, Inc. 580 (t) LWA-Dann Tardif/Corbis; 581 (b) Victoria Smith/HRW; 582 (b) Sergio Purtell/Foca/HRW; 583 (bc), (br) Sergio Purtell/Foca/HRW; 584 (all) Sergio Purtell/Foca/HRW; 586 (cl) Dr. Dennis Kunkel/Phototake; (c), (cr), (br) Sam Dudgeon/HRW; 591 (animalia) Myron Jay Dorf/Corbis; (Eubacteria) © Gary D. Gaugler/Photo Researchers, Inc.; (archaebacteria) Wolfgang Baumeister/Science Photo Library/Photo Researchers, Inc.; (protista) Dr. Dennis Kunkel/PhotoTake; (fungi) Rod Planck/Photo Researchers Inc.; (plantae) Adam Jones/Photo Researchers Inc.